T0190063

Lecture Notes in Computer Science   12355

Founding Editors

Gerhard Goos
   Karlsruhe Institute of Technology, Karlsruhe, Germany
Juris Hartmanis
   Cornell University, Ithaca, NY, USA

Editorial Board Members

Elisa Bertino
   Purdue University, West Lafayette, IN, USA
Wen Gao
   Peking University, Beijing, China
Bernhard Steffen
   TU Dortmund University, Dortmund, Germany
Gerhard Woeginger
   RWTH Aachen, Aachen, Germany
Moti Yung
   Columbia University, New York, NY, USA

More information about this series at http://www.springer.com/series/7412

Andrea Vedaldi · Horst Bischof ·
Thomas Brox · Jan-Michael Frahm (Eds.)

Computer Vision – ECCV 2020

16th European Conference
Glasgow, UK, August 23–28, 2020
Proceedings, Part X

 Springer

Editors
Andrea Vedaldi (iD)
University of Oxford
Oxford, UK

Thomas Brox (iD)
University of Freiburg
Freiburg im Breisgau, Germany

Horst Bischof (iD)
Graz University of Technology
Graz, Austria

Jan-Michael Frahm
University of North Carolina at Chapel Hill
Chapel Hill, NC, USA

ISSN 0302-9743 ISSN 1611-3349 (electronic)
Lecture Notes in Computer Science
ISBN 978-3-030-58606-5 ISBN 978-3-030-58607-2 (eBook)
https://doi.org/10.1007/978-3-030-58607-2

LNCS Sublibrary: SL6 – Image Processing, Computer Vision, Pattern Recognition, and Graphics

© Springer Nature Switzerland AG 2020
This work is subject to copyright. All rights are reserved by the Publisher, whether the whole or part of the material is concerned, specifically the rights of translation, reprinting, reuse of illustrations, recitation, broadcasting, reproduction on microfilms or in any other physical way, and transmission or information storage and retrieval, electronic adaptation, computer software, or by similar or dissimilar methodology now known or hereafter developed.
The use of general descriptive names, registered names, trademarks, service marks, etc. in this publication does not imply, even in the absence of a specific statement, that such names are exempt from the relevant protective laws and regulations and therefore free for general use.
The publisher, the authors and the editors are safe to assume that the advice and information in this book are believed to be true and accurate at the date of publication. Neither the publisher nor the authors or the editors give a warranty, expressed or implied, with respect to the material contained herein or for any errors or omissions that may have been made. The publisher remains neutral with regard to jurisdictional claims in published maps and institutional affiliations.

This Springer imprint is published by the registered company Springer Nature Switzerland AG
The registered company address is: Gewerbestrasse 11, 6330 Cham, Switzerland

Foreword

Hosting the European Conference on Computer Vision (ECCV 2020) was certainly an exciting journey. From the 2016 plan to hold it at the Edinburgh International Conference Centre (hosting 1,800 delegates) to the 2018 plan to hold it at Glasgow's Scottish Exhibition Centre (up to 6,000 delegates), we finally ended with moving online because of the COVID-19 outbreak. While possibly having fewer delegates than expected because of the online format, ECCV 2020 still had over 3,100 registered participants.

Although online, the conference delivered most of the activities expected at a face-to-face conference: peer-reviewed papers, industrial exhibitors, demonstrations, and messaging between delegates. In addition to the main technical sessions, the conference included a strong program of satellite events with 16 tutorials and 44 workshops.

Furthermore, the online conference format enabled new conference features. Every paper had an associated teaser video and a longer full presentation video. Along with the papers and slides from the videos, all these materials were available the week before the conference. This allowed delegates to become familiar with the paper content and be ready for the live interaction with the authors during the conference week. The live event consisted of brief presentations by the oral and spotlight authors and industrial sponsors. Question and answer sessions for all papers were timed to occur twice so delegates from around the world had convenient access to the authors.

As with ECCV 2018, authors' draft versions of the papers appeared online with open access, now on both the Computer Vision Foundation (CVF) and the European Computer Vision Association (ECVA) websites. An archival publication arrangement was put in place with the cooperation of Springer. SpringerLink hosts the final version of the papers with further improvements, such as activating reference links and supplementary materials. These two approaches benefit all potential readers: a version available freely for all researchers, and an authoritative and citable version with additional benefits for SpringerLink subscribers. We thank Alfred Hofmann and Aliaksandr Birukou from Springer for helping to negotiate this agreement, which we expect will continue for future versions of ECCV.

August 2020

Vittorio Ferrari
Bob Fisher
Cordelia Schmid
Emanuele Trucco

Preface

Welcome to the proceedings of the European Conference on Computer Vision (ECCV 2020). This is a unique edition of ECCV in many ways. Due to the COVID-19 pandemic, this is the first time the conference was held online, in a virtual format. This was also the first time the conference relied exclusively on the Open Review platform to manage the review process. Despite these challenges ECCV is thriving. The conference received 5,150 valid paper submissions, of which 1,360 were accepted for publication (27%) and, of those, 160 were presented as spotlights (3%) and 104 as orals (2%). This amounts to more than twice the number of submissions to ECCV 2018 (2,439). Furthermore, CVPR, the largest conference on computer vision, received 5,850 submissions this year, meaning that ECCV is now 87% the size of CVPR in terms of submissions. By comparison, in 2018 the size of ECCV was only 73% of CVPR.

The review model was similar to previous editions of ECCV; in particular, it was double blind in the sense that the authors did not know the name of the reviewers and vice versa. Furthermore, each conference submission was held confidentially, and was only publicly revealed if and once accepted for publication. Each paper received at least three reviews, totalling more than 15,000 reviews. Handling the review process at this scale was a significant challenge. In order to ensure that each submission received as fair and high-quality reviews as possible, we recruited 2,830 reviewers (a 130% increase with reference to 2018) and 207 area chairs (a 60% increase). The area chairs were selected based on their technical expertise and reputation, largely among people that served as area chair in previous top computer vision and machine learning conferences (ECCV, ICCV, CVPR, NeurIPS, etc.). Reviewers were similarly invited from previous conferences. We also encouraged experienced area chairs to suggest additional chairs and reviewers in the initial phase of recruiting.

Despite doubling the number of submissions, the reviewer load was slightly reduced from 2018, from a maximum of 8 papers down to 7 (with some reviewers offering to handle 6 papers plus an emergency review). The area chair load increased slightly, from 18 papers on average to 22 papers on average.

Conflicts of interest between authors, area chairs, and reviewers were handled largely automatically by the Open Review platform via their curated list of user profiles. Many authors submitting to ECCV already had a profile in Open Review. We set a paper registration deadline one week before the paper submission deadline in order to encourage all missing authors to register and create their Open Review profiles well on time (in practice, we allowed authors to create/change papers arbitrarily until the submission deadline). Except for minor issues with users creating duplicate profiles, this allowed us to easily and quickly identify institutional conflicts, and avoid them, while matching papers to area chairs and reviewers.

Papers were matched to area chairs based on: an affinity score computed by the Open Review platform, which is based on paper titles and abstracts, and an affinity score computed by the Toronto Paper Matching System (TPMS), which is based on the paper's full text, the area chair bids for individual papers, load balancing, and conflict avoidance. Open Review provides the program chairs a convenient web interface to experiment with different configurations of the matching algorithm. The chosen configuration resulted in about 50% of the assigned papers to be highly ranked by the area chair bids, and 50% to be ranked in the middle, with very few low bids assigned.

Assignments to reviewers were similar, with two differences. First, there was a maximum of 7 papers assigned to each reviewer. Second, area chairs recommended up to seven reviewers per paper, providing another highly-weighed term to the affinity scores used for matching.

The assignment of papers to area chairs was smooth. However, it was more difficult to find suitable reviewers for all papers. Having a ratio of 5.6 papers per reviewer with a maximum load of 7 (due to emergency reviewer commitment), which did not allow for much wiggle room in order to also satisfy conflict and expertise constraints. We received some complaints from reviewers who did not feel qualified to review specific papers and we reassigned them wherever possible. However, the large scale of the conference, the many constraints, and the fact that a large fraction of such complaints arrived very late in the review process made this process very difficult and not all complaints could be addressed.

Reviewers had six weeks to complete their assignments. Possibly due to COVID-19 or the fact that the NeurIPS deadline was moved closer to the review deadline, a record 30% of the reviews were still missing after the deadline. By comparison, ECCV 2018 experienced only 10% missing reviews at this stage of the process. In the subsequent week, area chairs chased the missing reviews intensely, found replacement reviewers in their own team, and managed to reach 10% missing reviews. Eventually, we could provide almost all reviews (more than 99.9%) with a delay of only a couple of days on the initial schedule by a significant use of emergency reviews. If this trend is confirmed, it might be a major challenge to run a smooth review process in future editions of ECCV. The community must reconsider prioritization of the time spent on paper writing (the number of submissions increased a lot despite COVID-19) and time spent on paper reviewing (the number of reviews delivered in time decreased a lot presumably due to COVID-19 or NeurIPS deadline). With this imbalance the peer-review system that ensures the quality of our top conferences may break soon.

Reviewers submitted their reviews independently. In the reviews, they had the opportunity to ask questions to the authors to be addressed in the rebuttal. However, reviewers were told not to request any significant new experiment. Using the Open Review interface, authors could provide an answer to each individual review, but were also allowed to cross-reference reviews and responses in their answers. Rather than PDF files, we allowed the use of formatted text for the rebuttal. The rebuttal and initial reviews were then made visible to all reviewers and the primary area chair for a given paper. The area chair encouraged and moderated the reviewer discussion. During the discussions, reviewers were invited to reach a consensus and possibly adjust their ratings as a result of the discussion and of the evidence in the rebuttal.

After the discussion period ended, most reviewers entered a final rating and recommendation, although in many cases this did not differ from their initial recommendation. Based on the updated reviews and discussion, the primary area chair then made a preliminary decision to accept or reject the paper and wrote a justification for it (meta-review). Except for cases where the outcome of this process was absolutely clear (as indicated by the three reviewers and primary area chairs all recommending clear rejection), the decision was then examined and potentially challenged by a secondary area chair. This led to further discussion and overturning a small number of preliminary decisions. Needless to say, there was no in-person area chair meeting, which would have been impossible due to COVID-19.

Area chairs were invited to observe the consensus of the reviewers whenever possible and use extreme caution in overturning a clear consensus to accept or reject a paper. If an area chair still decided to do so, she/he was asked to clearly justify it in the meta-review and to explicitly obtain the agreement of the secondary area chair. In practice, very few papers were rejected after being confidently accepted by the reviewers.

This was the first time Open Review was used as the main platform to run ECCV. In 2018, the program chairs used CMT3 for the user-facing interface and Open Review internally, for matching and conflict resolution. Since it is clearly preferable to only use a single platform, this year we switched to using Open Review in full. The experience was largely positive. The platform is highly-configurable, scalable, and open source. Being written in Python, it is easy to write scripts to extract data programmatically. The paper matching and conflict resolution algorithms and interfaces are top-notch, also due to the excellent author profiles in the platform. Naturally, there were a few kinks along the way due to the fact that the ECCV Open Review configuration was created from scratch for this event and it differs in substantial ways from many other Open Review conferences. However, the Open Review development and support team did a fantastic job in helping us to get the configuration right and to address issues in a timely manner as they unavoidably occurred. We cannot thank them enough for the tremendous effort they put into this project.

Finally, we would like to thank everyone involved in making ECCV 2020 possible in these very strange and difficult times. This starts with our authors, followed by the area chairs and reviewers, who ran the review process at an unprecedented scale. The whole Open Review team (and in particular Melisa Bok, Mohit Unyal, Carlos Mondragon Chapa, and Celeste Martinez Gomez) worked incredibly hard for the entire duration of the process. We would also like to thank René Vidal for contributing to the adoption of Open Review. Our thanks also go to Laurent Charling for TPMS and to the program chairs of ICML, ICLR, and NeurIPS for cross checking double submissions. We thank the website chair, Giovanni Farinella, and the CPI team (in particular Ashley Cook, Miriam Verdon, Nicola McGrane, and Sharon Kerr) for promptly adding material to the website as needed in the various phases of the process. Finally, we thank the publication chairs, Albert Ali Salah, Hamdi Dibeklioglu, Metehan Doyran, Henry Howard-Jenkins, Victor Prisacariu, Siyu Tang, and Gul Varol, who managed to compile these substantial proceedings in an exceedingly compressed schedule. We express our thanks to the ECVA team, in particular Kristina Scherbaum for allowing open access of the proceedings. We thank Alfred Hofmann from Springer who again serve as the publisher. Finally, we thank the other chairs of ECCV 2020, including in particular the general chairs for very useful feedback with the handling of the program.

August 2020   Andrea Vedaldi
Horst Bischof
Thomas Brox
Jan-Michael Frahm

Organization

General Chairs

Vittorio Ferrari   Google Research, Switzerland
Bob Fisher   University of Edinburgh, UK
Cordelia Schmid   Google and Inria, France
Emanuele Trucco   University of Dundee, UK

Program Chairs

Andrea Vedaldi   University of Oxford, UK
Horst Bischof   Graz University of Technology, Austria
Thomas Brox   University of Freiburg, Germany
Jan-Michael Frahm   University of North Carolina, USA

Industrial Liaison Chairs

Jim Ashe   University of Edinburgh, UK
Helmut Grabner   Zurich University of Applied Sciences, Switzerland
Diane Larlus   NAVER LABS Europe, France
Cristian Novotny   University of Edinburgh, UK

Local Arrangement Chairs

Yvan Petillot   Heriot-Watt University, UK
Paul Siebert   University of Glasgow, UK

Academic Demonstration Chair

Thomas Mensink   Google Research and University of Amsterdam,
                                The Netherlands

Poster Chair

Stephen Mckenna   University of Dundee, UK

Technology Chair

Gerardo Aragon Camarasa   University of Glasgow, UK

Tutorial Chairs

Carlo Colombo   University of Florence, Italy
Sotirios Tsaftaris   University of Edinburgh, UK

Publication Chairs

Albert Ali Salah   Utrecht University, The Netherlands
Hamdi Dibeklioglu   Bilkent University, Turkey
Metehan Doyran   Utrecht University, The Netherlands
Henry Howard-Jenkins   University of Oxford, UK
Victor Adrian Prisacariu   University of Oxford, UK
Siyu Tang   ETH Zurich, Switzerland
Gul Varol   University of Oxford, UK

Website Chair

Giovanni Maria Farinella   University of Catania, Italy

Workshops Chairs

Adrien Bartoli   University of Clermont Auvergne, France
Andrea Fusiello   University of Udine, Italy

Area Chairs

Lourdes Agapito   University College London, UK
Zeynep Akata   University of Tübingen, Germany
Karteek Alahari   Inria, France
Antonis Argyros   University of Crete, Greece
Hossein Azizpour   KTH Royal Institute of Technology, Sweden
Joao P. Barreto   Universidade de Coimbra, Portugal
Alexander C. Berg   University of North Carolina at Chapel Hill, USA
Matthew B. Blaschko   KU Leuven, Belgium
Lubomir D. Bourdev   WaveOne, Inc., USA
Edmond Boyer   Inria, France
Yuri Boykov   University of Waterloo, Canada
Gabriel Brostow   University College London, UK
Michael S. Brown   National University of Singapore, Singapore
Jianfei Cai   Monash University, Australia
Barbara Caputo   Politecnico di Torino, Italy
Ayan Chakrabarti   Washington University, St. Louis, USA
Tat-Jen Cham   Nanyang Technological University, Singapore
Manmohan Chandraker   University of California, San Diego, USA
Rama Chellappa   Johns Hopkins University, USA
Liang-Chieh Chen   Google, USA

Yung-Yu Chuang	National Taiwan University, Taiwan
Ondrej Chum	Czech Technical University in Prague, Czech Republic
Brian Clipp	Kitware, USA
John Collomosse	University of Surrey and Adobe Research, UK
Jason J. Corso	University of Michigan, USA
David J. Crandall	Indiana University, USA
Daniel Cremers	University of California, Los Angeles, USA
Fabio Cuzzolin	Oxford Brookes University, UK
Jifeng Dai	SenseTime, SAR China
Kostas Daniilidis	University of Pennsylvania, USA
Andrew Davison	Imperial College London, UK
Alessio Del Bue	Fondazione Istituto Italiano di Tecnologia, Italy
Jia Deng	Princeton University, USA
Alexey Dosovitskiy	Google, Germany
Matthijs Douze	Facebook, France
Enrique Dunn	Stevens Institute of Technology, USA
Irfan Essa	Georgia Institute of Technology and Google, USA
Giovanni Maria Farinella	University of Catania, Italy
Ryan Farrell	Brigham Young University, USA
Paolo Favaro	University of Bern, Switzerland
Rogerio Feris	International Business Machines, USA
Cornelia Fermuller	University of Maryland, College Park, USA
David J. Fleet	Vector Institute, Canada
Friedrich Fraundorfer	DLR, Austria
Mario Fritz	CISPA Helmholtz Center for Information Security, Germany
Pascal Fua	EPFL (Swiss Federal Institute of Technology Lausanne), Switzerland
Yasutaka Furukawa	Simon Fraser University, Canada
Li Fuxin	Oregon State University, USA
Efstratios Gavves	University of Amsterdam, The Netherlands
Peter Vincent Gehler	Amazon, USA
Theo Gevers	University of Amsterdam, The Netherlands
Ross Girshick	Facebook AI Research, USA
Boqing Gong	Google, USA
Stephen Gould	Australian National University, Australia
Jinwei Gu	SenseTime Research, USA
Abhinav Gupta	Facebook, USA
Bohyung Han	Seoul National University, South Korea
Bharath Hariharan	Cornell University, USA
Tal Hassner	Facebook AI Research, USA
Xuming He	Australian National University, Australia
Joao F. Henriques	University of Oxford, UK
Adrian Hilton	University of Surrey, UK
Minh Hoai	Stony Brooks, State University of New York, USA
Derek Hoiem	University of Illinois Urbana-Champaign, USA

Timothy Hospedales	University of Edinburgh and Samsung, UK
Gang Hua	Wormpex AI Research, USA
Slobodan Ilic	Siemens AG, Germany
Hiroshi Ishikawa	Waseda University, Japan
Jiaya Jia	The Chinese University of Hong Kong, SAR China
Hailin Jin	Adobe Research, USA
Justin Johnson	University of Michigan, USA
Frederic Jurie	University of Caen Normandie, France
Fredrik Kahl	Chalmers University, Sweden
Sing Bing Kang	Zillow, USA
Gunhee Kim	Seoul National University, South Korea
Junmo Kim	Korea Advanced Institute of Science and Technology, South Korea
Tae-Kyun Kim	Imperial College London, UK
Ron Kimmel	Technion-Israel Institute of Technology, Israel
Alexander Kirillov	Facebook AI Research, USA
Kris Kitani	Carnegie Mellon University, USA
Iasonas Kokkinos	Ariel AI, UK
Vladlen Koltun	Intel Labs, USA
Nikos Komodakis	Ecole des Ponts ParisTech, France
Piotr Koniusz	Australian National University, Australia
M. Pawan Kumar	University of Oxford, UK
Kyros Kutulakos	University of Toronto, Canada
Christoph Lampert	IST Austria, Austria
Ivan Laptev	Inria, France
Diane Larlus	NAVER LABS Europe, France
Laura Leal-Taixe	Technical University Munich, Germany
Honglak Lee	Google and University of Michigan, USA
Joon-Young Lee	Adobe Research, USA
Kyoung Mu Lee	Seoul National University, South Korea
Seungyong Lee	POSTECH, South Korea
Yong Jae Lee	University of California, Davis, USA
Bastian Leibe	RWTH Aachen University, Germany
Victor Lempitsky	Samsung, Russia
Ales Leonardis	University of Birmingham, UK
Marius Leordeanu	Institute of Mathematics of the Romanian Academy, Romania
Vincent Lepetit	ENPC ParisTech, France
Hongdong Li	The Australian National University, Australia
Xi Li	Zhejiang University, China
Yin Li	University of Wisconsin-Madison, USA
Zicheng Liao	Zhejiang University, China
Jongwoo Lim	Hanyang University, South Korea
Stephen Lin	Microsoft Research Asia, China
Yen-Yu Lin	National Chiao Tung University, Taiwan, China
Zhe Lin	Adobe Research, USA

Haibin Ling	Stony Brooks, State University of New York, USA
Jiaying Liu	Peking University, China
Ming-Yu Liu	NVIDIA, USA
Si Liu	Beihang University, China
Xiaoming Liu	Michigan State University, USA
Huchuan Lu	Dalian University of Technology, China
Simon Lucey	Carnegie Mellon University, USA
Jiebo Luo	University of Rochester, USA
Julien Mairal	Inria, France
Michael Maire	University of Chicago, USA
Subhransu Maji	University of Massachusetts, Amherst, USA
Yasushi Makihara	Osaka University, Japan
Jiri Matas	Czech Technical University in Prague, Czech Republic
Yasuyuki Matsushita	Osaka University, Japan
Philippos Mordohai	Stevens Institute of Technology, USA
Vittorio Murino	University of Verona, Italy
Naila Murray	NAVER LABS Europe, France
Hajime Nagahara	Osaka University, Japan
P. J. Narayanan	International Institute of Information Technology (IIIT), Hyderabad, India
Nassir Navab	Technical University of Munich, Germany
Natalia Neverova	Facebook AI Research, France
Matthias Niessner	Technical University of Munich, Germany
Jean-Marc Odobez	Idiap Research Institute and Swiss Federal Institute of Technology Lausanne, Switzerland
Francesca Odone	Università di Genova, Italy
Takeshi Oishi	The University of Tokyo, Tokyo Institute of Technology, Japan
Vicente Ordonez	University of Virginia, USA
Manohar Paluri	Facebook AI Research, USA
Maja Pantic	Imperial College London, UK
In Kyu Park	Inha University, South Korea
Ioannis Patras	Queen Mary University of London, UK
Patrick Perez	Valeo, France
Bryan A. Plummer	Boston University, USA
Thomas Pock	Graz University of Technology, Austria
Marc Pollefeys	ETH Zurich and Microsoft MR & AI Zurich Lab, Switzerland
Jean Ponce	Inria, France
Gerard Pons-Moll	MPII, Saarland Informatics Campus, Germany
Jordi Pont-Tuset	Google, Switzerland
James Matthew Rehg	Georgia Institute of Technology, USA
Ian Reid	University of Adelaide, Australia
Olaf Ronneberger	DeepMind London, UK
Stefan Roth	TU Darmstadt, Germany
Bryan Russell	Adobe Research, USA

Mathieu Salzmann	EPFL, Switzerland
Dimitris Samaras	Stony Brook University, USA
Imari Sato	National Institute of Informatics (NII), Japan
Yoichi Sato	The University of Tokyo, Japan
Torsten Sattler	Czech Technical University in Prague, Czech Republic
Daniel Scharstein	Middlebury College, USA
Bernt Schiele	MPII, Saarland Informatics Campus, Germany
Julia A. Schnabel	King's College London, UK
Nicu Sebe	University of Trento, Italy
Greg Shakhnarovich	Toyota Technological Institute at Chicago, USA
Humphrey Shi	University of Oregon, USA
Jianbo Shi	University of Pennsylvania, USA
Jianping Shi	SenseTime, China
Leonid Sigal	University of British Columbia, Canada
Cees Snoek	University of Amsterdam, The Netherlands
Richard Souvenir	Temple University, USA
Hao Su	University of California, San Diego, USA
Akihiro Sugimoto	National Institute of Informatics (NII), Japan
Jian Sun	Megvii Technology, China
Jian Sun	Xi'an Jiaotong University, China
Chris Sweeney	Facebook Reality Labs, USA
Yu-wing Tai	Kuaishou Technology, China
Chi-Keung Tang	The Hong Kong University of Science and Technology, SAR China
Radu Timofte	ETH Zurich, Switzerland
Sinisa Todorovic	Oregon State University, USA
Giorgos Tolias	Czech Technical University in Prague, Czech Republic
Carlo Tomasi	Duke University, USA
Tatiana Tommasi	Politecnico di Torino, Italy
Lorenzo Torresani	Facebook AI Research and Dartmouth College, USA
Alexander Toshev	Google, USA
Zhuowen Tu	University of California, San Diego, USA
Tinne Tuytelaars	KU Leuven, Belgium
Jasper Uijlings	Google, Switzerland
Nuno Vasconcelos	University of California, San Diego, USA
Olga Veksler	University of Waterloo, Canada
Rene Vidal	Johns Hopkins University, USA
Gang Wang	Alibaba Group, China
Jingdong Wang	Microsoft Research Asia, China
Yizhou Wang	Peking University, China
Lior Wolf	Facebook AI Research and Tel Aviv University, Israel
Jianxin Wu	Nanjing University, China
Tao Xiang	University of Surrey, UK
Saining Xie	Facebook AI Research, USA
Ming-Hsuan Yang	University of California at Merced and Google, USA
Ruigang Yang	University of Kentucky, USA

Kwang Moo Yi   University of Victoria, Canada
Zhaozheng Yin   Stony Brook, State University of New York, USA
Chang D. Yoo   Korea Advanced Institute of Science and Technology,
                            South Korea
Shaodi You   University of Amsterdam, The Netherlands
Jingyi Yu   ShanghaiTech University, China
Stella Yu   University of California, Berkeley, and ICSI, USA
Stefanos Zafeiriou   Imperial College London, UK
Hongbin Zha   Peking University, China
Tianzhu Zhang   University of Science and Technology of China, China
Liang Zheng   Australian National University, Australia
Todd E. Zickler   Harvard University, USA
Andrew Zisserman   University of Oxford, UK

Technical Program Committee

Sathyanarayanan
  N. Aakur
Wael Abd Almgaeed
Abdelrahman
  Abdelhamed
Abdullah Abuolaim
Supreeth Achar
Hanno Ackermann
Ehsan Adeli
Triantafyllos Afouras
Sameer Agarwal
Aishwarya Agrawal
Harsh Agrawal
Pulkit Agrawal
Antonio Agudo
Eirikur Agustsson
Karim Ahmed
Byeongjoo Ahn
Unaiza Ahsan
Thalaiyasingam Ajanthan
Kenan E. Ak
Emre Akbas
Naveed Akhtar
Derya Akkaynak
Yagiz Aksoy
Ziad Al-Halah
Xavier Alameda-Pineda
Jean-Baptiste Alayrac

Samuel Albanie
Shadi Albarqouni
Cenek Albl
Hassan Abu Alhaija
Daniel Aliaga
Mohammad
  S. Aliakbarian
Rahaf Aljundi
Thiemo Alldieck
Jon Almazan
Jose M. Alvarez
Senjian An
Saket Anand
Codruta Ancuti
Cosmin Ancuti
Peter Anderson
Juan Andrade-Cetto
Alexander Andreopoulos
Misha Andriluka
Dragomir Anguelov
Rushil Anirudh
Michel Antunes
Oisin Mac Aodha
Srikar Appalaraju
Relja Arandjelovic
Nikita Araslanov
Andre Araujo
Helder Araujo

Pablo Arbelaez
Shervin Ardeshir
Sercan O. Arik
Anil Armagan
Anurag Arnab
Chetan Arora
Federica Arrigoni
Mathieu Aubry
Shai Avidan
Angelica I. Aviles-Rivero
Yannis Avrithis
Ismail Ben Ayed
Shekoofeh Azizi
Ioan Andrei Bârsan
Artem Babenko
Deepak Babu Sam
Seung-Hwan Baek
Seungryul Baek
Andrew D. Bagdanov
Shai Bagon
Yuval Bahat
Junjie Bai
Song Bai
Xiang Bai
Yalong Bai
Yancheng Bai
Peter Bajcsy
Slawomir Bak

Mahsa Baktashmotlagh
Kavita Bala
Yogesh Balaji
Guha Balakrishnan
V. N. Balasubramanian
Federico Baldassarre
Vassileios Balntas
Shurjo Banerjee
Aayush Bansal
Ankan Bansal
Jianmin Bao
Linchao Bao
Wenbo Bao
Yingze Bao
Akash Bapat
Md Jawadul Hasan Bappy
Fabien Baradel
Lorenzo Baraldi
Daniel Barath
Adrian Barbu
Kobus Barnard
Nick Barnes
Francisco Barranco
Jonathan T. Barron
Arslan Basharat
Chaim Baskin
Anil S. Baslamisli
Jorge Batista
Kayhan Batmanghelich
Konstantinos Batsos
David Bau
Luis Baumela
Christoph Baur
Eduardo
  Bayro-Corrochano
Paul Beardsley
Jan Bednavr'ik
Oscar Beijbom
Philippe Bekaert
Esube Bekele
Vasileios Belagiannis
Ohad Ben-Shahar
Abhijit Bendale
Róger Bermúdez-Chacón
Maxim Berman
Jesus Bermudez-cameo

Florian Bernard
Stefano Berretti
Marcelo Bertalmio
Gedas Bertasius
Cigdem Beyan
Lucas Beyer
Vijayakumar Bhagavatula
Arjun Nitin Bhagoji
Apratim Bhattacharyya
Binod Bhattarai
Sai Bi
Jia-Wang Bian
Simone Bianco
Adel Bibi
Tolga Birdal
Tom Bishop
Soma Biswas
Mårten Björkman
Volker Blanz
Vishnu Boddeti
Navaneeth Bodla
Simion-Vlad Bogolin
Xavier Boix
Piotr Bojanowski
Timo Bolkart
Guido Borghi
Larbi Boubchir
Guillaume Bourmaud
Adrien Bousseau
Thierry Bouwmans
Richard Bowden
Hakan Boyraz
Mathieu Brédif
Samarth Brahmbhatt
Steve Branson
Nikolas Brasch
Biagio Brattoli
Ernesto Brau
Toby P. Breckon
Francois Bremond
Jesus Briales
Sofia Broomé
Marcus A. Brubaker
Luc Brun
Silvia Bucci
Shyamal Buch

Pradeep Buddharaju
Uta Buechler
Mai Bui
Tu Bui
Adrian Bulat
Giedrius T. Burachas
Elena Burceanu
Xavier P. Burgos-Artizzu
Kaylee Burns
Andrei Bursuc
Benjamin Busam
Wonmin Byeon
Zoya Bylinskii
Sergi Caelles
Jianrui Cai
Minjie Cai
Yujun Cai
Zhaowei Cai
Zhipeng Cai
Juan C. Caicedo
Simone Calderara
Necati Cihan Camgoz
Dylan Campbell
Octavia Camps
Jiale Cao
Kaidi Cao
Liangliang Cao
Xiangyong Cao
Xiaochun Cao
Yang Cao
Yu Cao
Yue Cao
Zhangjie Cao
Luca Carlone
Mathilde Caron
Dan Casas
Thomas J. Cashman
Umberto Castellani
Lluis Castrejon
Jacopo Cavazza
Fabio Cermelli
Hakan Cevikalp
Menglei Chai
Ishani Chakraborty
Rudrasis Chakraborty
Antoni B. Chan

Kwok-Ping Chan
Siddhartha Chandra
Sharat Chandran
Arjun Chandrasekaran
Angel X. Chang
Che-Han Chang
Hong Chang
Hyun Sung Chang
Hyung Jin Chang
Jianlong Chang
Ju Yong Chang
Ming-Ching Chang
Simyung Chang
Xiaojun Chang
Yu-Wei Chao
Devendra S. Chaplot
Arslan Chaudhry
Rizwan A. Chaudhry
Can Chen
Chang Chen
Chao Chen
Chen Chen
Chu-Song Chen
Dapeng Chen
Dong Chen
Dongdong Chen
Guanying Chen
Hongge Chen
Hsin-yi Chen
Huaijin Chen
Hwann-Tzong Chen
Jianbo Chen
Jianhui Chen
Jiansheng Chen
Jiaxin Chen
Jie Chen
Jun-Cheng Chen
Kan Chen
Kevin Chen
Lin Chen
Long Chen
Min-Hung Chen
Qifeng Chen
Shi Chen
Shixing Chen
Tianshui Chen

Weifeng Chen
Weikai Chen
Xi Chen
Xiaohan Chen
Xiaozhi Chen
Xilin Chen
Xingyu Chen
Xinlei Chen
Xinyun Chen
Yi-Ting Chen
Yilun Chen
Ying-Cong Chen
Yinpeng Chen
Yiran Chen
Yu Chen
Yu-Sheng Chen
Yuhua Chen
Yun-Chun Chen
Yunpeng Chen
Yuntao Chen
Zhuoyuan Chen
Zitian Chen
Anchieh Cheng
Bowen Cheng
Erkang Cheng
Gong Cheng
Guangliang Cheng
Jingchun Cheng
Jun Cheng
Li Cheng
Ming-Ming Cheng
Yu Cheng
Ziang Cheng
Anoop Cherian
Dmitry Chetverikov
Ngai-man Cheung
William Cheung
Ajad Chhatkuli
Naoki Chiba
Benjamin Chidester
Han-pang Chiu
Mang Tik Chiu
Wei-Chen Chiu
Donghyeon Cho
Hojin Cho
Minsu Cho

Nam Ik Cho
Tim Cho
Tae Eun Choe
Chiho Choi
Edward Choi
Inchang Choi
Jinsoo Choi
Jonghyun Choi
Jongwon Choi
Yukyung Choi
Hisham Cholakkal
Eunji Chong
Jaegul Choo
Christopher Choy
Hang Chu
Peng Chu
Wen-Sheng Chu
Albert Chung
Joon Son Chung
Hai Ci
Safa Cicek
Ramazan G. Cinbis
Arridhana Ciptadi
Javier Civera
James J. Clark
Ronald Clark
Felipe Codevilla
Michael Cogswell
Andrea Cohen
Maxwell D. Collins
Carlo Colombo
Yang Cong
Adria R. Continente
Marcella Cornia
John Richard Corring
Darren Cosker
Dragos Costea
Garrison W. Cottrell
Florent Couzinie-Devy
Marco Cristani
Ioana Croitoru
James L. Crowley
Jiequan Cui
Zhaopeng Cui
Ross Cutler
Antonio D'Innocente

Rozenn Dahyot
Bo Dai
Dengxin Dai
Hang Dai
Longquan Dai
Shuyang Dai
Xiyang Dai
Yuchao Dai
Adrian V. Dalca
Dima Damen
Bharath B. Damodaran
Kristin Dana
Martin Danelljan
Zheng Dang
Zachary Alan Daniels
Donald G. Dansereau
Abhishek Das
Samyak Datta
Achal Dave
Titas De
Rodrigo de Bem
Teo de Campos
Raoul de Charette
Shalini De Mello
Joseph DeGol
Herve Delingette
Haowen Deng
Jiankang Deng
Weijian Deng
Zhiwei Deng
Joachim Denzler
Konstantinos G. Derpanis
Aditya Deshpande
Frederic Devernay
Somdip Dey
Arturo Deza
Abhinav Dhall
Helisa Dhamo
Vikas Dhiman
Fillipe Dias Moreira
  de Souza
Ali Diba
Ferran Diego
Guiguang Ding
Henghui Ding
Jian Ding

Mingyu Ding
Xinghao Ding
Zhengming Ding
Robert DiPietro
Cosimo Distante
Ajay Divakaran
Mandar Dixit
Abdelaziz Djelouah
Thanh-Toan Do
Jose Dolz
Bo Dong
Chao Dong
Jiangxin Dong
Weiming Dong
Weisheng Dong
Xingping Dong
Xuanyi Dong
Yinpeng Dong
Gianfranco Doretto
Hazel Doughty
Hassen Drira
Bertram Drost
Dawei Du
Ye Duan
Yueqi Duan
Abhimanyu Dubey
Anastasia Dubrovina
Stefan Duffner
Chi Nhan Duong
Thibaut Durand
Zoran Duric
Iulia Duta
Debidatta Dwibedi
Benjamin Eckart
Marc Eder
Marzieh Edraki
Alexei A. Efros
Kiana Ehsani
Hazm Kemal Ekenel
James H. Elder
Mohamed Elgharib
Shireen Elhabian
Ehsan Elhamifar
Mohamed Elhoseiny
Ian Endres
N. Benjamin Erichson

Jan Ernst
Sergio Escalera
Francisco Escolano
Victor Escorcia
Carlos Esteves
Francisco J. Estrada
Bin Fan
Chenyou Fan
Deng-Ping Fan
Haoqi Fan
Hehe Fan
Heng Fan
Kai Fan
Lijie Fan
Linxi Fan
Quanfu Fan
Shaojing Fan
Xiaochuan Fan
Xin Fan
Yuchen Fan
Sean Fanello
Hao-Shu Fang
Haoyang Fang
Kuan Fang
Yi Fang
Yuming Fang
Azade Farshad
Alireza Fathi
Raanan Fattal
Joao Fayad
Xiaohan Fei
Christoph Feichtenhofer
Michael Felsberg
Chen Feng
Jiashi Feng
Junyi Feng
Mengyang Feng
Qianli Feng
Zhenhua Feng
Michele Fenzi
Andras Ferencz
Martin Fergie
Basura Fernando
Ethan Fetaya
Michael Firman
John W. Fisher

Matthew Fisher
Boris Flach
Corneliu Florea
Wolfgang Foerstner
David Fofi
Gian Luca Foresti
Per-Erik Forssen
David Fouhey
Katerina Fragkiadaki
Victor Fragoso
Jean-Sébastien Franco
Ohad Fried
Iuri Frosio
Cheng-Yang Fu
Huazhu Fu
Jianlong Fu
Jingjing Fu
Xueyang Fu
Yanwei Fu
Ying Fu
Yun Fu
Olac Fuentes
Kent Fujiwara
Takuya Funatomi
Christopher Funk
Thomas Funkhouser
Antonino Furnari
Ryo Furukawa
Erik Gärtner
Raghudeep Gadde
Matheus Gadelha
Vandit Gajjar
Trevor Gale
Juergen Gall
Mathias Gallardo
Guillermo Gallego
Orazio Gallo
Chuang Gan
Zhe Gan
Madan Ravi Ganesh
Aditya Ganeshan
Siddha Ganju
Bin-Bin Gao
Changxin Gao
Feng Gao
Hongchang Gao

Jin Gao
Jiyang Gao
Junbin Gao
Katelyn Gao
Lin Gao
Mingfei Gao
Ruiqi Gao
Ruohan Gao
Shenghua Gao
Yuan Gao
Yue Gao
Noa Garcia
Alberto Garcia-Garcia
Guillermo
   Garcia-Hernando
Jacob R. Gardner
Animesh Garg
Kshitiz Garg
Rahul Garg
Ravi Garg
Philip N. Garner
Kirill Gavrilyuk
Paul Gay
Shiming Ge
Weifeng Ge
Baris Gecer
Xin Geng
Kyle Genova
Stamatios Georgoulis
Bernard Ghanem
Michael Gharbi
Kamran Ghasedi
Golnaz Ghiasi
Arnab Ghosh
Partha Ghosh
Silvio Giancola
Andrew Gilbert
Rohit Girdhar
Xavier Giro-i-Nieto
Thomas Gittings
Ioannis Gkioulekas
Clement Godard
Vaibhava Goel
Bastian Goldluecke
Lluis Gomez
Nuno Gonçalves

Dong Gong
Ke Gong
Mingming Gong
Abel Gonzalez-Garcia
Ariel Gordon
Daniel Gordon
Paulo Gotardo
Venu Madhav Govindu
Ankit Goyal
Priya Goyal
Raghav Goyal
Benjamin Graham
Douglas Gray
Brent A. Griffin
Etienne Grossmann
David Gu
Jiayuan Gu
Jiuxiang Gu
Lin Gu
Qiao Gu
Shuhang Gu
Jose J. Guerrero
Paul Guerrero
Jie Gui
Jean-Yves Guillemaut
Riza Alp Guler
Erhan Gundogdu
Fatma Guney
Guodong Guo
Kaiwen Guo
Qi Guo
Sheng Guo
Shi Guo
Tiantong Guo
Xiaojie Guo
Yijie Guo
Yiluan Guo
Yuanfang Guo
Yulan Guo
Agrim Gupta
Ankush Gupta
Mohit Gupta
Saurabh Gupta
Tanmay Gupta
Danna Gurari
Abner Guzman-Rivera

JunYoung Gwak
Michael Gygli
Jung-Woo Ha
Simon Hadfield
Isma Hadji
Bjoern Haefner
Taeyoung Hahn
Levente Hajder
Peter Hall
Emanuela Haller
Stefan Haller
Bumsub Ham
Abdullah Hamdi
Dongyoon Han
Hu Han
Jungong Han
Junwei Han
Kai Han
Tian Han
Xiaoguang Han
Xintong Han
Yahong Han
Ankur Handa
Zekun Hao
Albert Haque
Tatsuya Harada
Mehrtash Harandi
Adam W. Harley
Mahmudul Hasan
Atsushi Hashimoto
Ali Hatamizadeh
Munawar Hayat
Dongliang He
Jingrui He
Junfeng He
Kaiming He
Kun He
Lei He
Pan He
Ran He
Shengfeng He
Tong He
Weipeng He
Xuming He
Yang He
Yihui He

Zhihai He
Chinmay Hegde
Janne Heikkila
Mattias P. Heinrich
Stéphane Herbin
Alexander Hermans
Luis Herranz
John R. Hershey
Aaron Hertzmann
Roei Herzig
Anders Heyden
Steven Hickson
Otmar Hilliges
Tomas Hodan
Judy Hoffman
Michael Hofmann
Yannick Hold-Geoffroy
Namdar Homayounfar
Sina Honari
Richang Hong
Seunghoon Hong
Xiaopeng Hong
Yi Hong
Hidekata Hontani
Anthony Hoogs
Yedid Hoshen
Mir Rayat Imtiaz Hossain
Junhui Hou
Le Hou
Lu Hou
Tingbo Hou
Wei-Lin Hsiao
Cheng-Chun Hsu
Gee-Sern Jison Hsu
Kuang-jui Hsu
Changbo Hu
Di Hu
Guosheng Hu
Han Hu
Hao Hu
Hexiang Hu
Hou-Ning Hu
Jie Hu
Junlin Hu
Nan Hu
Ping Hu

Ronghang Hu
Xiaowei Hu
Yinlin Hu
Yuan-Ting Hu
Zhe Hu
Binh-Son Hua
Yang Hua
Bingyao Huang
Di Huang
Dong Huang
Fay Huang
Haibin Huang
Haozhi Huang
Heng Huang
Huaibo Huang
Jia-Bin Huang
Jing Huang
Jingwei Huang
Kaizhu Huang
Lei Huang
Qiangui Huang
Qiaoying Huang
Qingqiu Huang
Qixing Huang
Shaoli Huang
Sheng Huang
Siyuan Huang
Weilin Huang
Wenbing Huang
Xiangru Huang
Xun Huang
Yan Huang
Yifei Huang
Yue Huang
Zhiwu Huang
Zilong Huang
Minyoung Huh
Zhuo Hui
Matthias B. Hullin
Martin Humenberger
Wei-Chih Hung
Zhouyuan Huo
Junhwa Hur
Noureldien Hussein
Jyh-Jing Hwang
Seong Jae Hwang

Sung Ju Hwang
Ichiro Ide
Ivo Ihrke
Daiki Ikami
Satoshi Ikehata
Nazli Ikizler-Cinbis
Sunghoon Im
Yani Ioannou
Radu Tudor Ionescu
Umar Iqbal
Go Irie
Ahmet Iscen
Md Amirul Islam
Vamsi Ithapu
Nathan Jacobs
Arpit Jain
Himalaya Jain
Suyog Jain
Stuart James
Won-Dong Jang
Yunseok Jang
Ronnachai Jaroensri
Dinesh Jayaraman
Sadeep Jayasumana
Suren Jayasuriya
Herve Jegou
Simon Jenni
Hae-Gon Jeon
Yunho Jeon
Koteswar R. Jerripothula
Hueihan Jhuang
I-hong Jhuo
Dinghuang Ji
Hui Ji
Jingwei Ji
Pan Ji
Yanli Ji
Baoxiong Jia
Kui Jia
Xu Jia
Chiyu Max Jiang
Haiyong Jiang
Hao Jiang
Huaizu Jiang
Huajie Jiang
Ke Jiang

Lai Jiang
Li Jiang
Lu Jiang
Ming Jiang
Peng Jiang
Shuqiang Jiang
Wei Jiang
Xudong Jiang
Zhuolin Jiang
Jianbo Jiao
Zequn Jie
Dakai Jin
Kyong Hwan Jin
Lianwen Jin
SouYoung Jin
Xiaojie Jin
Xin Jin
Nebojsa Jojic
Alexis Joly
Michael Jeffrey Jones
Hanbyul Joo
Jungseock Joo
Kyungdon Joo
Ajjen Joshi
Shantanu H. Joshi
Da-Cheng Juan
Marco Körner
Kevin Köser
Asim Kadav
Christine Kaeser-Chen
Kushal Kafle
Dagmar Kainmueller
Ioannis A. Kakadiaris
Zdenek Kalal
Nima Kalantari
Yannis Kalantidis
Mahdi M. Kalayeh
Anmol Kalia
Sinan Kalkan
Vicky Kalogeiton
Ashwin Kalyan
Joni-kristian Kamarainen
Gerda Kamberova
Chandra Kambhamettu
Martin Kampel
Meina Kan

Christopher Kanan
Kenichi Kanatani
Angjoo Kanazawa
Atsushi Kanehira
Takuhiro Kaneko
Asako Kanezaki
Bingyi Kang
Di Kang
Sunghun Kang
Zhao Kang
Vadim Kantorov
Abhishek Kar
Amlan Kar
Theofanis Karaletsos
Leonid Karlinsky
Kevin Karsch
Angelos Katharopoulos
Isinsu Katircioglu
Hiroharu Kato
Zoltan Kato
Dotan Kaufman
Jan Kautz
Rei Kawakami
Qiuhong Ke
Wadim Kehl
Petr Kellnhofer
Aniruddha Kembhavi
Cem Keskin
Margret Keuper
Daniel Keysers
Ashkan Khakzar
Fahad Khan
Naeemullah Khan
Salman Khan
Siddhesh Khandelwal
Rawal Khirodkar
Anna Khoreva
Tejas Khot
Parmeshwar Khurd
Hadi Kiapour
Joe Kileel
Chanho Kim
Dahun Kim
Edward Kim
Eunwoo Kim
Han-ul Kim

Hansung Kim
Heewon Kim
Hyo Jin Kim
Hyunwoo J. Kim
Jinkyu Kim
Jiwon Kim
Jongmin Kim
Junsik Kim
Junyeong Kim
Min H. Kim
Namil Kim
Pyojin Kim
Seon Joo Kim
Seong Tae Kim
Seungryong Kim
Sungwoong Kim
Tae Hyun Kim
Vladimir Kim
Won Hwa Kim
Yonghyun Kim
Benjamin Kimia
Akisato Kimura
Pieter-Jan Kindermans
Zsolt Kira
Itaru Kitahara
Hedvig Kjellstrom
Jan Knopp
Takumi Kobayashi
Erich Kobler
Parker Koch
Reinhard Koch
Elyor Kodirov
Amir Kolaman
Nicholas Kolkin
Dimitrios Kollias
Stefanos Kollias
Soheil Kolouri
Adams Wai-Kin Kong
Naejin Kong
Shu Kong
Tao Kong
Yu Kong
Yoshinori Konishi
Daniil Kononenko
Theodora Kontogianni
Simon Korman

Adam Kortylewski
Jana Kosecka
Jean Kossaifi
Satwik Kottur
Rigas Kouskouridas
Adriana Kovashka
Rama Kovvuri
Adarsh Kowdle
Jedrzej Kozerawski
Mateusz Kozinski
Philipp Kraehenbuehl
Gregory Kramida
Josip Krapac
Dmitry Kravchenko
Ranjay Krishna
Pavel Krsek
Alexander Krull
Jakob Kruse
Hiroyuki Kubo
Hilde Kuehne
Jason Kuen
Andreas Kuhn
Arjan Kuijper
Zuzana Kukelova
Ajay Kumar
Amit Kumar
Avinash Kumar
Suryansh Kumar
Vijay Kumar
Kaustav Kundu
Weicheng Kuo
Nojun Kwak
Suha Kwak
Junseok Kwon
Nikolaos Kyriazis
Zorah Lähner
Ankit Laddha
Florent Lafarge
Jean Lahoud
Kevin Lai
Shang-Hong Lai
Wei-Sheng Lai
Yu-Kun Lai
Iro Laina
Antony Lam
John Wheatley Lambert

Xiangyuan lan
Xu Lan
Charis Lanaras
Georg Langs
Oswald Lanz
Dong Lao
Yizhen Lao
Agata Lapedriza
Gustav Larsson
Viktor Larsson
Katrin Lasinger
Christoph Lassner
Longin Jan Latecki
Stéphane Lathuilière
Rynson Lau
Hei Law
Justin Lazarow
Svetlana Lazebnik
Hieu Le
Huu Le
Ngan Hoang Le
Trung-Nghia Le
Vuong Le
Colin Lea
Erik Learned-Miller
Chen-Yu Lee
Gim Hee Lee
Hsin-Ying Lee
Hyungtae Lee
Jae-Han Lee
Jimmy Addison Lee
Joonseok Lee
Kibok Lee
Kuang-Huei Lee
Kwonjoon Lee
Minsik Lee
Sang-chul Lee
Seungkyu Lee
Soochan Lee
Stefan Lee
Taehee Lee
Andreas Lehrmann
Jie Lei
Peng Lei
Matthew Joseph Leotta
Wee Kheng Leow

Gil Levi
Evgeny Levinkov
Aviad Levis
Jose Lezama
Ang Li
Bin Li
Bing Li
Boyi Li
Changsheng Li
Chao Li
Chen Li
Cheng Li
Chenglong Li
Chi Li
Chun-Guang Li
Chun-Liang Li
Chunyuan Li
Dong Li
Guanbin Li
Hao Li
Haoxiang Li
Hongsheng Li
Hongyang Li
Houqiang Li
Huibin Li
Jia Li
Jianan Li
Jianguo Li
Junnan Li
Junxuan Li
Kai Li
Ke Li
Kejie Li
Kunpeng Li
Lerenhan Li
Li Erran Li
Mengtian Li
Mu Li
Peihua Li
Peiyi Li
Ping Li
Qi Li
Qing Li
Ruiyu Li
Ruoteng Li
Shaozi Li

Sheng Li
Shiwei Li
Shuang Li
Siyang Li
Stan Z. Li
Tianye Li
Wei Li
Weixin Li
Wen Li
Wenbo Li
Xiaomeng Li
Xin Li
Xiu Li
Xuelong Li
Xueting Li
Yan Li
Yandong Li
Yanghao Li
Yehao Li
Yi Li
Yijun Li
Yikang LI
Yining Li
Yongjie Li
Yu Li
Yu-Jhe Li
Yunpeng Li
Yunsheng Li
Yunzhu Li
Zhe Li
Zhen Li
Zhengqi Li
Zhenyang Li
Zhuwen Li
Dongze Lian
Xiaochen Lian
Zhouhui Lian
Chen Liang
Jie Liang
Ming Liang
Paul Pu Liang
Pengpeng Liang
Shu Liang
Wei Liang
Jing Liao
Minghui Liao

Renjie Liao
Shengcai Liao
Shuai Liao
Yiyi Liao
Ser-Nam Lim
Chen-Hsuan Lin
Chung-Ching Lin
Dahua Lin
Ji Lin
Kevin Lin
Tianwei Lin
Tsung-Yi Lin
Tsung-Yu Lin
Wei-An Lin
Weiyao Lin
Yen-Chen Lin
Yuewei Lin
David B. Lindell
Drew Linsley
Krzysztof Lis
Roee Litman
Jim Little
An-An Liu
Bo Liu
Buyu Liu
Chao Liu
Chen Liu
Cheng-lin Liu
Chenxi Liu
Dong Liu
Feng Liu
Guilin Liu
Haomiao Liu
Heshan Liu
Hong Liu
Ji Liu
Jingen Liu
Jun Liu
Lanlan Liu
Li Liu
Liu Liu
Mengyuan Liu
Miaomiao Liu
Nian Liu
Ping Liu
Risheng Liu

Sheng Liu
Shu Liu
Shuaicheng Liu
Sifei Liu
Siqi Liu
Siying Liu
Songtao Liu
Ting Liu
Tongliang Liu
Tyng-Luh Liu
Wanquan Liu
Wei Liu
Weiyang Liu
Weizhe Liu
Wenyu Liu
Wu Liu
Xialei Liu
Xianglong Liu
Xiaodong Liu
Xiaofeng Liu
Xihui Liu
Xingyu Liu
Xinwang Liu
Xuanqing Liu
Xuebo Liu
Yang Liu
Yaojie Liu
Yebin Liu
Yen-Cheng Liu
Yiming Liu
Yu Liu
Yu-Shen Liu
Yufan Liu
Yun Liu
Zheng Liu
Zhijian Liu
Zhuang Liu
Zichuan Liu
Ziwei Liu
Zongyi Liu
Stephan Liwicki
Liliana Lo Presti
Chengjiang Long
Fuchen Long
Mingsheng Long
Xiang Long

Yang Long
Charles T. Loop
Antonio Lopez
Roberto J. Lopez-Sastre
Javier Lorenzo-Navarro
Manolis Lourakis
Boyu Lu
Canyi Lu
Feng Lu
Guoyu Lu
Hongtao Lu
Jiajun Lu
Jiasen Lu
Jiwen Lu
Kaiyue Lu
Le Lu
Shao-Ping Lu
Shijian Lu
Xiankai Lu
Xin Lu
Yao Lu
Yiping Lu
Yongxi Lu
Yongyi Lu
Zhiwu Lu
Fujun Luan
Benjamin E. Lundell
Hao Luo
Jian-Hao Luo
Ruotian Luo
Weixin Luo
Wenhan Luo
Wenjie Luo
Yan Luo
Zelun Luo
Zixin Luo
Khoa Luu
Zhaoyang Lv
Pengyuan Lyu
Thomas Möllenhoff
Matthias Müller
Bingpeng Ma
Chih-Yao Ma
Chongyang Ma
Huimin Ma
Jiayi Ma

K. T. Ma
Ke Ma
Lin Ma
Liqian Ma
Shugao Ma
Wei-Chiu Ma
Xiaojian Ma
Xingjun Ma
Zhanyu Ma
Zheng Ma
Radek Jakob Mackowiak
Ludovic Magerand
Shweta Mahajan
Siddharth Mahendran
Long Mai
Ameesh Makadia
Oscar Mendez Maldonado
Mateusz Malinowski
Yury Malkov
Arun Mallya
Dipu Manandhar
Massimiliano Mancini
Fabian Manhardt
Kevis-kokitsi Maninis
Varun Manjunatha
Junhua Mao
Xudong Mao
Alina Marcu
Edgar Margffoy-Tuay
Dmitrii Marin
Manuel J. Marin-Jimenez
Kenneth Marino
Niki Martinel
Julieta Martinez
Jonathan Masci
Tomohiro Mashita
Iacopo Masi
David Masip
Daniela Massiceti
Stefan Mathe
Yusuke Matsui
Tetsu Matsukawa
Iain A. Matthews
Kevin James Matzen
Bruce Allen Maxwell
Stephen Maybank

Helmut Mayer
Amir Mazaheri
David McAllester
Steven McDonagh
Stephen J. Mckenna
Roey Mechrez
Prakhar Mehrotra
Christopher Mei
Xue Mei
Paulo R. S. Mendonca
Lili Meng
Zibo Meng
Thomas Mensink
Bjoern Menze
Michele Merler
Kourosh Meshgi
Pascal Mettes
Christopher Metzler
Liang Mi
Qiguang Miao
Xin Miao
Tomer Michaeli
Frank Michel
Antoine Miech
Krystian Mikolajczyk
Peyman Milanfar
Ben Mildenhall
Gregor Miller
Fausto Milletari
Dongbo Min
Kyle Min
Pedro Miraldo
Dmytro Mishkin
Anand Mishra
Ashish Mishra
Ishan Misra
Niluthpol C. Mithun
Kaushik Mitra
Niloy Mitra
Anton Mitrokhin
Ikuhisa Mitsugami
Anurag Mittal
Kaichun Mo
Zhipeng Mo
Davide Modolo
Michael Moeller

Pritish Mohapatra
Pavlo Molchanov
Davide Moltisanti
Pascal Monasse
Mathew Monfort
Aron Monszpart
Sean Moran
Vlad I. Morariu
Francesc Moreno-Noguer
Pietro Morerio
Stylianos Moschoglou
Yael Moses
Roozbeh Mottaghi
Pierre Moulon
Arsalan Mousavian
Yadong Mu
Yasuhiro Mukaigawa
Lopamudra Mukherjee
Yusuke Mukuta
Ravi Teja Mullapudi
Mario Enrique Munich
Zachary Murez
Ana C. Murillo
J. Krishna Murthy
Damien Muselet
Armin Mustafa
Siva Karthik Mustikovela
Carlo Dal Mutto
Moin Nabi
Varun K. Nagaraja
Tushar Nagarajan
Arsha Nagrani
Seungjun Nah
Nikhil Naik
Yoshikatsu Nakajima
Yuta Nakashima
Atsushi Nakazawa
Seonghyeon Nam
Vinay P. Namboodiri
Medhini Narasimhan
Srinivasa Narasimhan
Sanath Narayan
Erickson Rangel
  Nascimento
Jacinto Nascimento
Tayyab Naseer

Lakshmanan Nataraj
Neda Nategh
Nelson Isao Nauata
Fernando Navarro
Shah Nawaz
Lukas Neumann
Ram Nevatia
Alejandro Newell
Shawn Newsam
Joe Yue-Hei Ng
Trung Thanh Ngo
Duc Thanh Nguyen
Lam M. Nguyen
Phuc Xuan Nguyen
Thuong Nguyen Canh
Mihalis Nicolaou
Andrei Liviu Nicolicioiu
Xuecheng Nie
Michael Niemeyer
Simon Niklaus
Christophoros Nikou
David Nilsson
Jifeng Ning
Yuval Nirkin
Li Niu
Yuzhen Niu
Zhenxing Niu
Shohei Nobuhara
Nicoletta Noceti
Hyeonwoo Noh
Junhyug Noh
Mehdi Noroozi
Sotiris Nousias
Valsamis Ntouskos
Matthew O'Toole
Peter Ochs
Ferda Ofli
Seong Joon Oh
Seoung Wug Oh
Iason Oikonomidis
Utkarsh Ojha
Takahiro Okabe
Takayuki Okatani
Fumio Okura
Aude Oliva
Kyle Olszewski

Björn Ommer
Mohamed Omran
Elisabeta Oneata
Michael Opitz
Jose Oramas
Tribhuvanesh Orekondy
Shaul Oron
Sergio Orts-Escolano
Ivan Oseledets
Aljosa Osep
Magnus Oskarsson
Anton Osokin
Martin R. Oswald
Wanli Ouyang
Andrew Owens
Mete Ozay
Mustafa Ozuysal
Eduardo Pérez-Pellitero
Gautam Pai
Dipan Kumar Pal
P. H. Pamplona Savarese
Jinshan Pan
Junting Pan
Xingang Pan
Yingwei Pan
Yannis Panagakis
Rameswar Panda
Guan Pang
Jiahao Pang
Jiangmiao Pang
Tianyu Pang
Sharath Pankanti
Nicolas Papadakis
Dim Papadopoulos
George Papandreou
Toufiq Parag
Shaifali Parashar
Sarah Parisot
Eunhyeok Park
Hyun Soo Park
Jaesik Park
Min-Gyu Park
Taesung Park
Alvaro Parra
C. Alejandro Parraga
Despoina Paschalidou

Nikolaos Passalis
Vishal Patel
Viorica Patraucean
Badri Narayana Patro
Danda Pani Paudel
Sujoy Paul
Georgios Pavlakos
Ioannis Pavlidis
Vladimir Pavlovic
Nick Pears
Kim Steenstrup Pedersen
Selen Pehlivan
Shmuel Peleg
Chao Peng
Houwen Peng
Wen-Hsiao Peng
Xi Peng
Xiaojiang Peng
Xingchao Peng
Yuxin Peng
Federico Perazzi
Juan Camilo Perez
Vishwanath Peri
Federico Pernici
Luca Del Pero
Florent Perronnin
Stavros Petridis
Henning Petzka
Patrick Peursum
Michael Pfeiffer
Hanspeter Pfister
Roman Pflugfelder
Minh Tri Pham
Yongri Piao
David Picard
Tomasz Pieciak
A. J. Piergiovanni
Andrea Pilzer
Pedro O. Pinheiro
Silvia Laura Pintea
Lerrel Pinto
Axel Pinz
Robinson Piramuthu
Fiora Pirri
Leonid Pishchulin
Francesco Pittaluga

Daniel Pizarro
Tobias Plötz
Mirco Planamente
Matteo Poggi
Moacir A. Ponti
Parita Pooj
Fatih Porikli
Horst Possegger
Omid Poursaeed
Ameya Prabhu
Viraj Uday Prabhu
Dilip Prasad
Brian L. Price
True Price
Maria Priisalu
Veronique Prinet
Victor Adrian Prisacariu
Jan Prokaj
Sergey Prokudin
Nicolas Pugeault
Xavier Puig
Albert Pumarola
Pulak Purkait
Senthil Purushwalkam
Charles R. Qi
Hang Qi
Haozhi Qi
Lu Qi
Mengshi Qi
Siyuan Qi
Xiaojuan Qi
Yuankai Qi
Shengju Qian
Xuelin Qian
Siyuan Qiao
Yu Qiao
Jie Qin
Qiang Qiu
Weichao Qiu
Zhaofan Qiu
Kha Gia Quach
Yuhui Quan
Yvain Queau
Julian Quiroga
Faisal Qureshi
Mahdi Rad

Filip Radenovic
Petia Radeva
Venkatesh
  B. Radhakrishnan
Ilija Radosavovic
Noha Radwan
Rahul Raguram
Tanzila Rahman
Amit Raj
Ajit Rajwade
Kandan Ramakrishnan
Santhosh
  K. Ramakrishnan
Srikumar Ramalingam
Ravi Ramamoorthi
Vasili Ramanishka
Ramprasaath R. Selvaraju
Francois Rameau
Visvanathan Ramesh
Santu Rana
Rene Ranftl
Anand Rangarajan
Anurag Ranjan
Viresh Ranjan
Yongming Rao
Carolina Raposo
Vivek Rathod
Sathya N. Ravi
Avinash Ravichandran
Tammy Riklin Raviv
Daniel Rebain
Sylvestre-Alvise Rebuffi
N. Dinesh Reddy
Timo Rehfeld
Paolo Remagnino
Konstantinos Rematas
Edoardo Remelli
Dongwei Ren
Haibing Ren
Jian Ren
Jimmy Ren
Mengye Ren
Weihong Ren
Wenqi Ren
Zhile Ren
Zhongzheng Ren

Zhou Ren
Vijay Rengarajan
Md A. Reza
Farzaneh Rezaeianaran
Hamed R. Tavakoli
Nicholas Rhinehart
Helge Rhodin
Elisa Ricci
Alexander Richard
Eitan Richardson
Elad Richardson
Christian Richardt
Stephan Richter
Gernot Riegler
Daniel Ritchie
Tobias Ritschel
Samuel Rivera
Yong Man Ro
Richard Roberts
Joseph Robinson
Ignacio Rocco
Mrigank Rochan
Emanuele Rodolà
Mikel D. Rodriguez
Giorgio Roffo
Grégory Rogez
Gemma Roig
Javier Romero
Xuejian Rong
Yu Rong
Amir Rosenfeld
Bodo Rosenhahn
Guy Rosman
Arun Ross
Paolo Rota
Peter M. Roth
Anastasios Roussos
Anirban Roy
Sebastien Roy
Aruni RoyChowdhury
Artem Rozantsev
Ognjen Rudovic
Daniel Rueckert
Adria Ruiz
Javier Ruiz-del-solar
Christian Rupprecht

Chris Russell
Dan Ruta
Jongbin Ryu
Ömer Sümer
Alexandre Sablayrolles
Faraz Saeedan
Ryusuke Sagawa
Christos Sagonas
Tonmoy Saikia
Hideo Saito
Kuniaki Saito
Shunsuke Saito
Shunta Saito
Ken Sakurada
Joaquin Salas
Fatemeh Sadat Saleh
Mahdi Saleh
Pouya Samangouei
Leo Sampaio
  Ferraz Ribeiro
Artsiom Olegovich
  Sanakoyeu
Enrique Sanchez
Patsorn Sangkloy
Anush Sankaran
Aswin Sankaranarayanan
Swami Sankaranarayanan
Rodrigo Santa Cruz
Amartya Sanyal
Archana Sapkota
Nikolaos Sarafianos
Jun Sato
Shin'ichi Satoh
Hosnieh Sattar
Arman Savran
Manolis Savva
Alexander Sax
Hanno Scharr
Simone Schaub-Meyer
Konrad Schindler
Dmitrij Schlesinger
Uwe Schmidt
Dirk Schnieders
Björn Schuller
Samuel Schulter
Idan Schwartz

William Robson Schwartz
Alex Schwing
Sinisa Segvic
Lorenzo Seidenari
Pradeep Sen
Ozan Sener
Soumyadip Sengupta
Arda Senocak
Mojtaba Seyedhosseini
Shishir Shah
Shital Shah
Sohil Atul Shah
Tamar Rott Shaham
Huasong Shan
Qi Shan
Shiguang Shan
Jing Shao
Roman Shapovalov
Gaurav Sharma
Vivek Sharma
Viktoriia Sharmanska
Dongyu She
Sumit Shekhar
Evan Shelhamer
Chengyao Shen
Chunhua Shen
Falong Shen
Jie Shen
Li Shen
Liyue Shen
Shuhan Shen
Tianwei Shen
Wei Shen
William B. Shen
Yantao Shen
Ying Shen
Yiru Shen
Yujun Shen
Yuming Shen
Zhiqiang Shen
Ziyi Shen
Lu Sheng
Yu Sheng
Rakshith Shetty
Baoguang Shi
Guangming Shi

Hailin Shi
Miaojing Shi
Yemin Shi
Zhenmei Shi
Zhiyuan Shi
Kevin Jonathan Shih
Shiliang Shiliang
Hyunjung Shim
Atsushi Shimada
Nobutaka Shimada
Daeyun Shin
Young Min Shin
Koichi Shinoda
Konstantin Shmelkov
Michael Zheng Shou
Abhinav Shrivastava
Tianmin Shu
Zhixin Shu
Hong-Han Shuai
Pushkar Shukla
Christian Siagian
Mennatullah M. Siam
Kaleem Siddiqi
Karan Sikka
Jae-Young Sim
Christian Simon
Martin Simonovsky
Dheeraj Singaraju
Bharat Singh
Gurkirt Singh
Krishna Kumar Singh
Maneesh Kumar Singh
Richa Singh
Saurabh Singh
Suriya Singh
Vikas Singh
Sudipta N. Sinha
Vincent Sitzmann
Josef Sivic
Gregory Slabaugh
Miroslava Slavcheva
Ron Slossberg
Brandon Smith
Kevin Smith
Vladimir Smutny
Noah Snavely

Roger
  D. Soberanis-Mukul
Kihyuk Sohn
Francesco Solera
Eric Sommerlade
Sanghyun Son
Byung Cheol Song
Chunfeng Song
Dongjin Song
Jiaming Song
Jie Song
Jifei Song
Jingkuan Song
Mingli Song
Shiyu Song
Shuran Song
Xiao Song
Yafei Song
Yale Song
Yang Song
Yi-Zhe Song
Yibing Song
Humberto Sossa
Cesar de Souza
Adrian Spurr
Srinath Sridhar
Suraj Srinivas
Pratul P. Srinivasan
Anuj Srivastava
Tania Stathaki
Christopher Stauffer
Simon Stent
Rainer Stiefelhagen
Pierre Stock
Julian Straub
Jonathan C. Stroud
Joerg Stueckler
Jan Stuehmer
David Stutz
Chi Su
Hang Su
Jong-Chyi Su
Shuochen Su
Yu-Chuan Su
Ramanathan Subramanian
Yusuke Sugano

Masanori Suganuma
Yumin Suh
Mohammed Suhail
Yao Sui
Heung-Il Suk
Josephine Sullivan
Baochen Sun
Chen Sun
Chong Sun
Deqing Sun
Jin Sun
Liang Sun
Lin Sun
Qianru Sun
Shao-Hua Sun
Shuyang Sun
Weiwei Sun
Wenxiu Sun
Xiaoshuai Sun
Xiaoxiao Sun
Xingyuan Sun
Yifan Sun
Zhun Sun
Sabine Susstrunk
David Suter
Supasorn Suwajanakorn
Tomas Svoboda
Eran Swears
Paul Swoboda
Attila Szabo
Richard Szeliski
Duy-Nguyen Ta
Andrea Tagliasacchi
Yuichi Taguchi
Ying Tai
Keita Takahashi
Kouske Takahashi
Jun Takamatsu
Hugues Talbot
Toru Tamaki
Chaowei Tan
Fuwen Tan
Mingkui Tan
Mingxing Tan
Qingyang Tan
Robby T. Tan

Xiaoyang Tan
Kenichiro Tanaka
Masayuki Tanaka
Chang Tang
Chengzhou Tang
Danhang Tang
Ming Tang
Peng Tang
Qingming Tang
Wei Tang
Xu Tang
Yansong Tang
Youbao Tang
Yuxing Tang
Zhiqiang Tang
Tatsunori Taniai
Junli Tao
Xin Tao
Makarand Tapaswi
Jean-Philippe Tarel
Lyne Tchapmi
Zachary Teed
Bugra Tekin
Damien Teney
Ayush Tewari
Christian Theobalt
Christopher Thomas
Diego Thomas
Jim Thomas
Rajat Mani Thomas
Xinmei Tian
Yapeng Tian
Yingli Tian
Yonglong Tian
Zhi Tian
Zhuotao Tian
Kinh Tieu
Joseph Tighe
Massimo Tistarelli
Matthew Toews
Carl Toft
Pavel Tokmakov
Federico Tombari
Chetan Tonde
Yan Tong
Alessio Tonioni

Andrea Torsello
Fabio Tosi
Du Tran
Luan Tran
Ngoc-Trung Tran
Quan Hung Tran
Truyen Tran
Rudolph Triebel
Martin Trimmel
Shashank Tripathi
Subarna Tripathi
Leonardo Trujillo
Eduard Trulls
Tomasz Trzcinski
Sam Tsai
Yi-Hsuan Tsai
Hung-Yu Tseng
Stavros Tsogkas
Aggeliki Tsoli
Devis Tuia
Shubham Tulsiani
Sergey Tulyakov
Frederick Tung
Tony Tung
Daniyar Turmukhambetov
Ambrish Tyagi
Radim Tylecek
Christos Tzelepis
Georgios Tzimiropoulos
Dimitrios Tzionas
Seiichi Uchida
Norimichi Ukita
Dmitry Ulyanov
Martin Urschler
Yoshitaka Ushiku
Ben Usman
Alexander Vakhitov
Julien P. C. Valentin
Jack Valmadre
Ernest Valveny
Joost van de Weijer
Jan van Gemert
Koen Van Leemput
Gul Varol
Sebastiano Vascon
M. Alex O. Vasilescu

Subeesh Vasu
Mayank Vatsa
David Vazquez
Javier Vazquez-Corral
Ashok Veeraraghavan
Erik Velasco-Salido
Raviteja Vemulapalli
Jonathan Ventura
Manisha Verma
Roberto Vezzani
Ruben Villegas
Minh Vo
MinhDuc Vo
Nam Vo
Michele Volpi
Riccardo Volpi
Carl Vondrick
Konstantinos Vougioukas
Tuan-Hung Vu
Sven Wachsmuth
Neal Wadhwa
Catherine Wah
Jacob C. Walker
Thomas S. A. Wallis
Chengde Wan
Jun Wan
Liang Wan
Renjie Wan
Baoyuan Wang
Boyu Wang
Cheng Wang
Chu Wang
Chuan Wang
Chunyu Wang
Dequan Wang
Di Wang
Dilin Wang
Dong Wang
Fang Wang
Guanzhi Wang
Guoyin Wang
Hanzi Wang
Hao Wang
He Wang
Heng Wang
Hongcheng Wang

Hongxing Wang
Hua Wang
Jian Wang
Jingbo Wang
Jinglu Wang
Jingya Wang
Jinjun Wang
Jinqiao Wang
Jue Wang
Ke Wang
Keze Wang
Le Wang
Lei Wang
Lezi Wang
Li Wang
Liang Wang
Lijun Wang
Limin Wang
Linwei Wang
Lizhi Wang
Mengjiao Wang
Mingzhe Wang
Minsi Wang
Naiyan Wang
Nannan Wang
Ning Wang
Oliver Wang
Pei Wang
Peng Wang
Pichao Wang
Qi Wang
Qian Wang
Qiaosong Wang
Qifei Wang
Qilong Wang
Qing Wang
Qingzhong Wang
Quan Wang
Rui Wang
Ruiping Wang
Ruixing Wang
Shangfei Wang
Shenlong Wang
Shiyao Wang
Shuhui Wang
Song Wang

Tao Wang
Tianlu Wang
Tiantian Wang
Ting-chun Wang
Tingwu Wang
Wei Wang
Weiyue Wang
Wenguan Wang
Wenlin Wang
Wenqi Wang
Xiang Wang
Xiaobo Wang
Xiaofang Wang
Xiaoling Wang
Xiaolong Wang
Xiaosong Wang
Xiaoyu Wang
Xin Eric Wang
Xinchao Wang
Xinggang Wang
Xintao Wang
Yali Wang
Yan Wang
Yang Wang
Yangang Wang
Yaxing Wang
Yi Wang
Yida Wang
Yilin Wang
Yiming Wang
Yisen Wang
Yongtao Wang
Yu-Xiong Wang
Yue Wang
Yujiang Wang
Yunbo Wang
Yunhe Wang
Zengmao Wang
Zhangyang Wang
Zhaowen Wang
Zhe Wang
Zhecan Wang
Zheng Wang
Zhixiang Wang
Zilei Wang
Jianqiao Wangni

Anne S. Wannenwetsch
Jan Dirk Wegner
Scott Wehrwein
Donglai Wei
Kaixuan Wei
Longhui Wei
Pengxu Wei
Ping Wei
Qi Wei
Shih-En Wei
Xing Wei
Yunchao Wei
Zijun Wei
Jerod Weinman
Michael Weinmann
Philippe Weinzaepfel
Yair Weiss
Bihan Wen
Longyin Wen
Wei Wen
Junwu Weng
Tsui-Wei Weng
Xinshuo Weng
Eric Wengrowski
Tomas Werner
Gordon Wetzstein
Tobias Weyand
Patrick Wieschollek
Maggie Wigness
Erik Wijmans
Richard Wildes
Olivia Wiles
Chris Williams
Williem Williem
Kyle Wilson
Calden Wloka
Nicolai Wojke
Christian Wolf
Yongkang Wong
Sanghyun Woo
Scott Workman
Baoyuan Wu
Bichen Wu
Chao-Yuan Wu
Huikai Wu
Jiajun Wu

Jialin Wu
Jiaxiang Wu
Jiqing Wu
Jonathan Wu
Lifang Wu
Qi Wu
Qiang Wu
Ruizheng Wu
Shangzhe Wu
Shun-Cheng Wu
Tianfu Wu
Wayne Wu
Wenxuan Wu
Xiao Wu
Xiaohe Wu
Xinxiao Wu
Yang Wu
Yi Wu
Yiming Wu
Ying Nian Wu
Yue Wu
Zheng Wu
Zhenyu Wu
Zhirong Wu
Zuxuan Wu
Stefanie Wuhrer
Jonas Wulff
Changqun Xia
Fangting Xia
Fei Xia
Gui-Song Xia
Lu Xia
Xide Xia
Yin Xia
Yingce Xia
Yongqin Xian
Lei Xiang
Shiming Xiang
Bin Xiao
Fanyi Xiao
Guobao Xiao
Huaxin Xiao
Taihong Xiao
Tete Xiao
Tong Xiao
Wang Xiao

Yang Xiao
Cihang Xie
Guosen Xie
Jianwen Xie
Lingxi Xie
Sirui Xie
Weidi Xie
Wenxuan Xie
Xiaohua Xie
Fuyong Xing
Jun Xing
Junliang Xing
Bo Xiong
Peixi Xiong
Yu Xiong
Yuanjun Xiong
Zhiwei Xiong
Chang Xu
Chenliang Xu
Dan Xu
Danfei Xu
Hang Xu
Hongteng Xu
Huijuan Xu
Jingwei Xu
Jun Xu
Kai Xu
Mengmeng Xu
Mingze Xu
Qianqian Xu
Ran Xu
Weijian Xu
Xiangyu Xu
Xiaogang Xu
Xing Xu
Xun Xu
Yanyu Xu
Yichao Xu
Yong Xu
Yongchao Xu
Yuanlu Xu
Zenglin Xu
Zheng Xu
Chuhui Xue
Jia Xue
Nan Xue

Tianfan Xue
Xiangyang Xue
Abhay Yadav
Yasushi Yagi
I. Zeki Yalniz
Kota Yamaguchi
Toshihiko Yamasaki
Takayoshi Yamashita
Junchi Yan
Ke Yan
Qingan Yan
Sijie Yan
Xinchen Yan
Yan Yan
Yichao Yan
Zhicheng Yan
Keiji Yanai
Bin Yang
Ceyuan Yang
Dawei Yang
Dong Yang
Fan Yang
Guandao Yang
Guorun Yang
Haichuan Yang
Hao Yang
Jianwei Yang
Jiaolong Yang
Jie Yang
Jing Yang
Kaiyu Yang
Linjie Yang
Meng Yang
Michael Ying Yang
Nan Yang
Shuai Yang
Shuo Yang
Tianyu Yang
Tien-Ju Yang
Tsun-Yi Yang
Wei Yang
Wenhan Yang
Xiao Yang
Xiaodong Yang
Xin Yang
Yan Yang

Yanchao Yang
Yee Hong Yang
Yezhou Yang
Zhenheng Yang
Anbang Yao
Angela Yao
Cong Yao
Jian Yao
Li Yao
Ting Yao
Yao Yao
Zhewei Yao
Chengxi Ye
Jianbo Ye
Keren Ye
Linwei Ye
Mang Ye
Mao Ye
Qi Ye
Qixiang Ye
Mei-Chen Yeh
Raymond Yeh
Yu-Ying Yeh
Sai-Kit Yeung
Serena Yeung
Kwang Moo Yi
Li Yi
Renjiao Yi
Alper Yilmaz
Junho Yim
Lijun Yin
Weidong Yin
Xi Yin
Zhichao Yin
Tatsuya Yokota
Ryo Yonetani
Donggeun Yoo
Jae Shin Yoon
Ju Hong Yoon
Sung-eui Yoon
Laurent Younes
Changqian Yu
Fisher Yu
Gang Yu
Jiahui Yu
Kaicheng Yu

Ke Yu
Lequan Yu
Ning Yu
Qian Yu
Ronald Yu
Ruichi Yu
Shoou-I Yu
Tao Yu
Tianshu Yu
Xiang Yu
Xin Yu
Xiyu Yu
Youngjae Yu
Yu Yu
Zhiding Yu
Chunfeng Yuan
Ganzhao Yuan
Jinwei Yuan
Lu Yuan
Quan Yuan
Shanxin Yuan
Tongtong Yuan
Wenjia Yuan
Ye Yuan
Yuan Yuan
Yuhui Yuan
Huanjing Yue
Xiangyu Yue
Ersin Yumer
Sergey Zagoruyko
Egor Zakharov
Amir Zamir
Andrei Zanfir
Mihai Zanfir
Pablo Zegers
Bernhard Zeisl
John S. Zelek
Niclas Zeller
Huayi Zeng
Jiabei Zeng
Wenjun Zeng
Yu Zeng
Xiaohua Zhai
Fangneng Zhan
Huangying Zhan
Kun Zhan

Xiaohang Zhan
Baochang Zhang
Bowen Zhang
Cecilia Zhang
Changqing Zhang
Chao Zhang
Chengquan Zhang
Chi Zhang
Chongyang Zhang
Dingwen Zhang
Dong Zhang
Feihu Zhang
Hang Zhang
Hanwang Zhang
Hao Zhang
He Zhang
Hongguang Zhang
Hua Zhang
Ji Zhang
Jianguo Zhang
Jianming Zhang
Jiawei Zhang
Jie Zhang
Jing Zhang
Juyong Zhang
Kai Zhang
Kaipeng Zhang
Ke Zhang
Le Zhang
Lei Zhang
Li Zhang
Lihe Zhang
Linguang Zhang
Lu Zhang
Mi Zhang
Mingda Zhang
Peng Zhang
Pingping Zhang
Qian Zhang
Qilin Zhang
Quanshi Zhang
Richard Zhang
Rui Zhang
Runze Zhang
Shengping Zhang
Shifeng Zhang

Shuai Zhang
Songyang Zhang
Tao Zhang
Ting Zhang
Tong Zhang
Wayne Zhang
Wei Zhang
Weizhong Zhang
Wenwei Zhang
Xiangyu Zhang
Xiaolin Zhang
Xiaopeng Zhang
Xiaoqin Zhang
Xiuming Zhang
Ya Zhang
Yang Zhang
Yimin Zhang
Yinda Zhang
Ying Zhang
Yongfei Zhang
Yu Zhang
Yulun Zhang
Yunhua Zhang
Yuting Zhang
Zhanpeng Zhang
Zhao Zhang
Zhaoxiang Zhang
Zhen Zhang
Zheng Zhang
Zhifei Zhang
Zhijin Zhang
Zhishuai Zhang
Ziming Zhang
Bo Zhao
Chen Zhao
Fang Zhao
Haiyu Zhao
Han Zhao
Hang Zhao
Hengshuang Zhao
Jian Zhao
Kai Zhao
Liang Zhao
Long Zhao
Qian Zhao
Qibin Zhao

Qijun Zhao
Rui Zhao
Shenglin Zhao
Sicheng Zhao
Tianyi Zhao
Wenda Zhao
Xiangyun Zhao
Xin Zhao
Yang Zhao
Yue Zhao
Zhichen Zhao
Zijing Zhao
Xiantong Zhen
Chuanxia Zheng
Feng Zheng
Haiyong Zheng
Jia Zheng
Kang Zheng
Shuai Kyle Zheng
Wei-Shi Zheng
Yinqiang Zheng
Zerong Zheng
Zhedong Zheng
Zilong Zheng
Bineng Zhong
Fangwei Zhong
Guangyu Zhong
Yiran Zhong
Yujie Zhong
Zhun Zhong
Chunluan Zhou
Huiyu Zhou
Jiahuan Zhou
Jun Zhou
Lei Zhou
Luowei Zhou
Luping Zhou
Mo Zhou
Ning Zhou
Pan Zhou
Peng Zhou
Qianyi Zhou
S. Kevin Zhou
Sanping Zhou
Wengang Zhou
Xingyi Zhou

Yanzhao Zhou
Yi Zhou
Yin Zhou
Yipin Zhou
Yuyin Zhou
Zihan Zhou
Alex Zihao Zhu
Chenchen Zhu
Feng Zhu
Guangming Zhu
Ji Zhu
Jun-Yan Zhu
Lei Zhu
Linchao Zhu
Rui Zhu
Shizhan Zhu
Tyler Lixuan Zhu

Wei Zhu
Xiangyu Zhu
Xinge Zhu
Xizhou Zhu
Yanjun Zhu
Yi Zhu
Yixin Zhu
Yizhe Zhu
Yousong Zhu
Zhe Zhu
Zhen Zhu
Zheng Zhu
Zhenyao Zhu
Zhihui Zhu
Zhuotun Zhu
Bingbing Zhuang
Wei Zhuo

Christian Zimmermann
Karel Zimmermann
Larry Zitnick
Mohammadreza
   Zolfaghari
Maria Zontak
Daniel Zoran
Changqing Zou
Chuhang Zou
Danping Zou
Qi Zou
Yang Zou
Yuliang Zou
Georgios Zoumpourlis
Wangmeng Zuo
Xinxin Zuo

Additional Reviewers

Victoria Fernandez
   Abrevaya
Maya Aghaei
Allam Allam
Christine
   Allen-Blanchette
Nicolas Aziere
Assia Benbihi
Neha Bhargava
Bharat Lal Bhatnagar
Joanna Bitton
Judy Borowski
Amine Bourki
Romain Brégier
Tali Brayer
Sebastian Bujwid
Andrea Burns
Yun-Hao Cao
Yuning Chai
Xiaojun Chang
Bo Chen
Shuo Chen
Zhixiang Chen
Junsuk Choe
Hung-Kuo Chu

Jonathan P. Crall
Kenan Dai
Lucas Deecke
Karan Desai
Prithviraj Dhar
Jing Dong
Wei Dong
Turan Kaan Elgin
Francis Engelmann
Erik Englesson
Fartash Faghri
Zicong Fan
Yang Fu
Risheek Garrepalli
Yifan Ge
Marco Godi
Helmut Grabner
Shuxuan Guo
Jianfeng He
Zhezhi He
Samitha Herath
Chih-Hui Ho
Yicong Hong
Vincent Tao Hu
Julio Hurtado

Jaedong Hwang
Andrey Ignatov
Muhammad
   Abdullah Jamal
Saumya Jetley
Meiguang Jin
Jeff Johnson
Minsoo Kang
Saeed Khorram
Mohammad Rami Koujan
Nilesh Kulkarni
Sudhakar Kumawat
Abdelhak Lemkhenter
Alexander Levine
Jiachen Li
Jing Li
Jun Li
Yi Li
Liang Liao
Ruochen Liao
Tzu-Heng Lin
Phillip Lippe
Bao-di Liu
Bo Liu
Fangchen Liu

Hanxiao Liu
Hongyu Liu
Huidong Liu
Miao Liu
Xinxin Liu
Yongfei Liu
Yu-Lun Liu
Amir Livne
Tiange Luo
Wei Ma
Xiaoxuan Ma
Ioannis Marras
Georg Martius
Effrosyni Mavroudi
Tim Meinhardt
Givi Meishvili
Meng Meng
Zihang Meng
Zhongqi Miao
Gyeongsik Moon
Khoi Nguyen
Yung-Kyun Noh
Antonio Norelli
Jaeyoo Park
Alexander Pashevich
Mandela Patrick
Mary Phuong
Bingqiao Qian
Yu Qiao
Zhen Qiao
Sai Saketh Rambhatla
Aniket Roy
Amelie Royer
Parikshit Vishwas
  Sakurikar
Mark Sandler
Mert Bülent Sarıyıldız
Tanner Schmidt
Anshul B. Shah

Ketul Shah
Rajvi Shah
Hengcan Shi
Xiangxi Shi
Yujiao Shi
William A. P. Smith
Guoxian Song
Robin Strudel
Abby Stylianou
Xinwei Sun
Reuben Tan
Qingyi Tao
Kedar S. Tatwawadi
Anh Tuan Tran
Son Dinh Tran
Eleni Triantafillou
Aristeidis Tsitiridis
Md Zasim Uddin
Andrea Vedaldi
Evangelos Ververas
Vidit Vidit
Paul Voigtlaender
Bo Wan
Huanyu Wang
Huiyu Wang
Junqiu Wang
Pengxiao Wang
Tai Wang
Xinyao Wang
Tomoki Watanabe
Mark Weber
Xi Wei
Botong Wu
James Wu
Jiamin Wu
Rujie Wu
Yu Wu
Rongchang Xie
Wei Xiong

Yunyang Xiong
An Xu
Chi Xu
Yinghao Xu
Fei Xue
Tingyun Yan
Zike Yan
Chao Yang
Heran Yang
Ren Yang
Wenfei Yang
Xu Yang
Rajeev Yasarla
Shaokai Ye
Yufei Ye
Kun Yi
Haichao Yu
Hanchao Yu
Ruixuan Yu
Liangzhe Yuan
Chen-Lin Zhang
Fandong Zhang
Tianyi Zhang
Yang Zhang
Yiyi Zhang
Yongshun Zhang
Yu Zhang
Zhiwei Zhang
Jiaojiao Zhao
Yipu Zhao
Xingjian Zhen
Haizhong Zheng
Tiancheng Zhi
Chengju Zhou
Hao Zhou
Hao Zhu
Alexander Zimin

Contents – Part X

Discriminability Distillation in Group Representation Learning   1
   Manyuan Zhang, Guanglu Song, Hang Zhou, and Yu Liu

Monocular Expressive Body Regression Through Body-Driven Attention. . . .   20
   *Vasileios Choutas, Georgios Pavlakos, Timo Bolkart, Dimitrios Tzionas,
   and Michael J. Black*

Dual Adversarial Network: Toward Real-World Noise Removal
and Noise Generation   41
   Zongsheng Yue, Qian Zhao, Lei Zhang, and Deyu Meng

Linguistic Structure Guided Context Modeling for Referring
Image Segmentation   59
   *Tianrui Hui, Si Liu, Shaofei Huang, Guanbin Li, Sansi Yu, Faxi Zhang,
   and Jizhong Han*

Federated Visual Classification with Real-World Data Distribution   76
   Tzu-Ming Harry Hsu, Hang Qi, and Matthew Brown

Robust Re-Identification by Multiple Views Knowledge Distillation   93
   Angelo Porrello, Luca Bergamini, and Simone Calderara

Defocus Deblurring Using Dual-Pixel Data   111
   Abdullah Abuolaim and Michael S. Brown

RhyRNN: Rhythmic RNN for Recognizing Events in Long
and Complex Videos   127
   Tianshu Yu, Yikang Li, and Baoxin Li

Take an Emotion Walk: Perceiving Emotions from Gaits Using
Hierarchical Attention Pooling and Affective Mapping.   145
   *Uttaran Bhattacharya, Christian Roncal, Trisha Mittal, Rohan Chandra,
   Kyra Kapsaskis, Kurt Gray, Aniket Bera, and Dinesh Manocha*

Weighing Counts: Sequential Crowd Counting
by Reinforcement Learning   164
   *Liang Liu, Hao Lu, Hongwei Zou, Haipeng Xiong, Zhiguo Cao,
   and Chunhua Shen*

Reflection Backdoor: A Natural Backdoor Attack on Deep
Neural Networks.   182
   Yunfei Liu, Xingjun Ma, James Bailey, and Feng Lu

Learning to Learn with Variational Information Bottleneck for Domain
Generalization.   200
  Yingjun Du, Jun Xu, Huan Xiong, Qiang Qiu, Xiantong Zhen,
  Cees G. M. Snoek, and Ling Shao

Deep Positional and Relational Feature Learning for Rotation-Invariant
Point Cloud Analysis.   217
  Ruixuan Yu, Xin Wei, Federico Tombari, and Jian Sun

Thanks for Nothing: Predicting Zero-Valued Activations with Lightweight
Convolutional Neural Networks   234
  Gil Shomron, Ron Banner, Moran Shkolnik, and Uri Weiser

Layered Neighborhood Expansion for Incremental Multiple Graph
Matching   251
  Zixuan Chen, Zhihui Xie, Junchi Yan, Yinqiang Zheng,
  and Xiaokang Yang

SCAN: Learning to Classify Images Without Labels   268
  Wouter Van Gansbeke, Simon Vandenhende, Stamatios Georgoulis,
  Marc Proesmans, and Luc Van Gool

Graph Convolutional Networks for Learning with Few Clean
and Many Noisy Labels.   286
  Ahmet Iscen, Giorgos Tolias, Yannis Avrithis, Ondřej Chum,
  and Cordelia Schmid

Object-and-Action Aware Model for Visual Language Navigation.   303
  Yuankai Qi, Zizheng Pan, Shengping Zhang, Anton van den Hengel,
  and Qi Wu

A Comprehensive Study of Weight Sharing in Graph Networks
for 3D Human Pose Estimation.   318
  Kenkun Liu, Rongqi Ding, Zhiming Zou, Le Wang, and Wei Tang

MuCAN: Multi-correspondence Aggregation Network for Video
Super-Resolution.   335
  Wenbo Li, Xin Tao, Taian Guo, Lu Qi, Jiangbo Lu, and Jiaya Jia

Efficient Semantic Video Segmentation with Per-Frame Inference   352
  Yifan Liu, Chunhua Shen, Changqian Yu, and Jingdong Wang

Increasing the Robustness of Semantic Segmentation Models
with Painting-by-Numbers   369
  Christoph Kamann and Carsten Rother

Deep Spiking Neural Network: Energy Efficiency Through Time Based
Coding   388
   Bing Han and Kaushik Roy

InfoFocus: 3D Object Detection for Autonomous Driving with Dynamic
Information Modeling   405
   Jun Wang, Shiyi Lan, Mingfei Gao, and Larry S. Davis

Utilizing Patch-Level Category Activation Patterns for Multiple Class
Novelty Detection   421
   Poojan Oza and Vishal M. Patel

People as Scene Probes   438
   Yifan Wang, Brian L. Curless, and Steven M. Seitz

Mapping in a Cycle: Sinkhorn Regularized Unsupervised Learning
for Point Cloud Shapes   455
   Lei Yang, Wenxi Liu, Zhiming Cui, Nenglun Chen, and Wenping Wang

Label-Efficient Learning on Point Clouds Using Approximate Convex
Decompositions   473
   Matheus Gadelha, Aruni RoyChowdhury, Gopal Sharma,
   Evangelos Kalogerakis, Liangliang Cao, Erik Learned-Miller,
   Rui Wang, and Subhransu Maji

TexMesh: Reconstructing Detailed Human Texture and Geometry
from RGB-D Video.   492
   Tiancheng Zhi, Christoph Lassner, Tony Tung, Carsten Stoll,
   Srinivasa G. Narasimhan, and Minh Vo

Consistency-Based Semi-supervised Active Learning: Towards Minimizing
Labeling Cost.   510
   Mingfei Gao, Zizhao Zhang, Guo Yu, Sercan Ö. Arık, Larry S. Davis,
   and Tomas Pfister

Point-Set Anchors for Object Detection, Instance Segmentation and Pose
Estimation   527
   Fangyun Wei, Xiao Sun, Hongyang Li, Jingdong Wang, and Stephen Lin

Modeling 3D Shapes by Reinforcement Learning   545
   Cheng Lin, Tingxiang Fan, Wenping Wang, and Matthias Nießner

LST-Net: Learning a Convolutional Neural Network with a Learnable
Sparse Transform   562
   Lida Li, Kun Wang, Shuai Li, Xiangchu Feng, and Lei Zhang

Learning What Makes a Difference from Counterfactual Examples
and Gradient Supervision   580
   Damien Teney, Ehsan Abbasnedjad, and Anton van den Hengel

CN: Channel Normalization for Point Cloud Recognition   600
   Zetong Yang, Yanan Sun, Shu Liu, Xiaojuan Qi, and Jiaya Jia

Rethinking the Defocus Blur Detection Problem and a Real-Time Deep
DBD Model   617
   Ning Zhang and Junchi Yan

AutoMix: Mixup Networks for Sample Interpolation via Cooperative
Barycenter Learning   633
   Jianchao Zhu, Liangliang Shi, Junchi Yan, and Hongyuan Zha

Scene Text Image Super-Resolution in the Wild   650
   Wenjia Wang, Enze Xie, Xuebo Liu, Wenhai Wang, Ding Liang,
   Chunhua Shen, and Xiang Bai

Coupling Explicit and Implicit Surface Representations for Generative
3D Modeling   667
   Omid Poursaeed, Matthew Fisher, Noam Aigerman,
   and Vladimir G. Kim

Learning Disentangled Representations with Latent
Variation Predictability   684
   Xinqi Zhu, Chang Xu, and Dacheng Tao

Deep Space-Time Video Upsampling Networks   701
   Jaeyeon Kang, Younghyun Jo, Seoung Wug Oh, Peter Vajda,
   and Seon Joo Kim

Large-Scale Few-Shot Learning via Multi-modal Knowledge Discovery   718
   Shuo Wang, Jun Yue, Jianzhuang Liu, Qi Tian, and Meng Wang

Fast Video Object Segmentation Using the Global Context Module   735
   Yu Li, Zhuoran Shen, and Ying Shan

Uncertainty-Aware Weakly Supervised Action Detection
from Untrimmed Videos   751
   Anurag Arnab, Chen Sun, Arsha Nagrani, and Cordelia Schmid

Selecting Relevant Features from a Multi-domain Representation
for Few-Shot Classification   769
   Nikita Dvornik, Cordelia Schmid, and Julien Mairal

Author Index   787

Discriminability Distillation in Group Representation Learning

Manyuan Zhang[1,2], Guanglu Song[1], Hang Zhou[2], and Yu Liu[1,2(✉)]

[1] SenseTime X-Lab, Hong Kong, China
{zhangmanyuan,songguanglu}@sensetime.com, liuyuisanai@gmail.com
[2] CUHK - SenseTime Joint Lab, The Chinese University of Hong Kong,
Hong Kong, China
zhouhang@link.cuhk.edu.hk

Abstract. Learning group representation is a commonly concerned issue in tasks where the basic unit is a group, set, or sequence. Previously, the research community tries to tackle it by aggregating the elements in a group based on an *indicator* either defined by humans such as the *quality* and *saliency*, or generated by a black box such as the attention score. This article provides a more essential and explicable view. We claim the most significant indicator to show whether the group representation can be benefited from one of its element is not the quality or an inexplicable score, but the *discriminability w.r.t.* the model. We explicitly design the *discrimiability* using embedded class centroids on a proxy set. We show the discrimiability knowledge has good properties that can be distilled by a light-weight distillation network and can be generalized on the unseen target set. The whole procedure is denoted as *discriminability distillation learning* (DDL). The proposed DDL can be flexibly plugged into many group-based recognition tasks without influencing the original training procedures. Comprehensive experiments on various tasks have proven the effectiveness of DDL for both accuracy and efficiency. Moreover, it pushes forward the state-of-the-art results on these tasks by an impressive margin.

Keywords: Group representation learning · Set-to-set matching

1 Introduction

With the rapid development of deep learning and easy access to large-scale group data, recognition tasks using group information have drawn great attention in the computer vision community. The rich information provided by different elements can complement each other to boost the performance of tasks such as face recognition, person re-identification, and action recognition [19,35,42,46,54,62,68].

Electronic supplementary material The online version of this chapter (https://doi.org/10.1007/978-3-030-58607-2_1) contains supplementary material, which is available to authorized users.

© Springer Nature Switzerland AG 2020
A. Vedaldi et al. (Eds.): ECCV 2020, LNCS 12355, pp. 1–19, 2020.
https://doi.org/10.1007/978-3-030-58607-2_1

For example, recognizing a person through a sequence of frames is expected to be more accurate than watching only one image.

While traditional practice for group-based recognition is to either aggregate the whole set by average pooling [32,49], max pooling [7], or just randomly sampling [55], the fact that certain elements contribute negatively in recognition tasks has been ignored. Thus, the key problem for group-based recognition is how to define an efficient indicator to select representatives from sets.

To tackle such cases, previous methods aim at defining the "quality" or "saliency" for each element in a group [37,40,42,62]. The weight for each element can be automatically learned by self-attention. For example, Liu et al. [37] propose the Quality Aware Network (QAN) to learn a quality score for each image inside an image set during network training. Other researchers adopt the same idea and extend it to specific tasks such as video-based person re-identification [33,58] and action recognition [56] by learning spatial-temporal attentions. However, the whole quality/attention learning procedures are either manually designed or learned through a black box, which lacks explainability. Moreover, since previous attention and quality mechanism are mostly based on element feature, the features for all group elements need to be extracted, which is highly computational consuming.

In this work, we explore deeper into the underlying mechanism for defining effective elements. Assuming that a base network $\mathcal{M}$ has already been trained for element-based recognition using class labels, we define the "discriminability" of one element by how difficult it is for the network $\mathcal{M}$ to discriminate its class. How to measure the difficulty and the learning preference of the network $\mathcal{M}$ of elements remains an interesting problem. By considering the relationship between intra- and inter-class distance, we identify a successful discriminability indicator by *measuring one embedding's distance with all class centroids and compute the ratio of between positive and hardest-negative*. The *positive* is its distance from its class's corresponding centroid and the *hardest-negative* is its closest counterpart.

As the acquiring procedure of the discriminability indicator is highly flexible without either human supervision or network re-training, it can be adapted to any existing base. Though defined through trained bases, we find that the discriminability indicator can be easily distilled by training an additional lightweight network (Discriminability Distillation Network, DDNet). The DDNet takes the raw images as input and regresses the regularized discriminability indicators. We uniformly call the whole procedure *discriminability distillation learning* (DDL).

During inference, all elements are firstly sent into the light-weight DDNet to estimate their discriminability. Then element features will be weighted and aggregated according to their discriminability scores. In addition, in order to achieve the trade-off between accuracy and efficiency, we can filter elements by extracting and aggregating elements of high discriminability only. Since the base model tends to be heavy, the filtering process can save much computational cost. We evaluate the effectiveness of our proposed DDL on several classical yet challenging tasks including set-to-set face recognition, video-based person re-identification, and action recognition. Comprehensive experiments show the advantage of our method on both recognition accuracy and computational efficiency. State-of-the-art results can be achieved without modifying the base network.

We highlight our contributions as follows: (1) We define the *discriminability* of one element within a group from a more essential and explicable view, and propose an efficient indicator. Moreover, we demonstrate that the structure of discriminability distribution can be easily distilled by a light-weight network. (2) With a well-designed element discriminability learning and feature aggregating process, both efficiency and excellent performance can be achieved. We verify the good generalization ability of our discriminability distillation learning in many group-based recognition tasks, including set-to-set face recognition, video-based person re-identification, and action recognition through extensive studies.

2 Related Work

Group representation learning which aims at formulating a unified representation has been proved efficient on various tasks [15,37,55,68,70]. In this paper, we care for three group representation learning tasks including set-to-set face recognition, video-based person re-identification, and action recognition. In this section, we will briefly review those related topics.

Set-to-Set Face Recognition. Set-to-set face recognition aims at performing face recognition [2,9,27,29,57,69] using a set of images of a same person. To tackle set-to-set face recognition, traditional methods directly estimate the feature similarity among sets of feature vectors [1,5,23]. Other works seek to aggregate element features by simply applying max-pooling [7] or average pooling [32,49] among set features to form a compact representation. However, since most set images are under unconstrained scenes, huge variations such as blur and occlusions will degrade the set feature discrimination. How to design a proper aggregation method for set face representation has been the key.

Recently, a few methods explore the manually defined operator or attention mechanism to form group representation. GhostVLAD [68] improves traditional VLAD. While Rao *et al.* [41] combine LSTM and reinforcement learning to discard low-quality element features. Liu *et al.* [37] and Yang *et al.* [62] introduce an attention mechanism to assign quality scores for different elements and aggregate feature vectors by quality weighted sum. To predict the quality score, an online attention network module is added and co-optimized by the target set-to-set recognition task. However, the definition of generated "quality" scores remains unclear and they are learned through a black box, which lacks explainability.

Video-Based Person Re-Identification. It is also beneficial to perform person re-identification [15–18,33,39,61] from videos. There are typically three components for video-based person re-identification: an image-level feature extractor, a temporal aggregating module, and the loss function [15]. Previous works mainly focus on optimizing the temporal aggregating module for video-based person re-identification. They can be divided into three categories, RNN-based [39,61], attention-based [37,71] and 3D-Conv based [15]. Yang *et al.* [61] model an RNN to encode element features and use the final hidden layer as the group feature representation. Liu *et al.* [37] use attention module to assign each element an quality score. While Gao *et al.* [15] directly utilize 3D Conv to encode the spatial-temporal feature for elements and propose a benchmark to compare different temporal aggregating module fairly.

Action Recognition. Action representation learning is another typical case of group-based representation learning. Real-world videos contain variable frames, so it is not practical to put the whole video to a memory limited GPU. The most usual approach for video understanding is to sample frames or clips and design late fusion strategies to form the video-level prediction.

Frame-based methods [14,19,46,64] firstly extract frame features and aggregate them. Simonyan *et al.* [46] propose the two-stream network to simultaneously capture the appearance and motion information. Wang *et al.* [54] add attention module and learn to discard unrelated frames. Frame-based methods are computationally efficient, but only aggregating high-level frame features tends to limit the model's ability to handle complex motion.

Clip-based methods [13,30,50,51] use 3D convolutional neural network to jointly capture spatial-temporal features. However, clip-based methods highly rely on the dense sample strategy, which introduces huge computational costs and makes it impractical to real-world applications. In this article, we show that by combining our DDL, the clip-based methods can achieve both excellent performance and computational efficiency.

3   Discriminability Distillation Learning

In this section, we first formulate the problem of group representation learning in Sect. 3.1 and then define the discriminability in Sect. 3.2. Next, we introduce the whole discriminability distillation learning (DDL) procedure in Sect. 3.3. In Sect. 3.4 and 3.5, we discuss the aggregation method and the advantage of our DDL, respectively.

3.1   Formulation of Group Representation Learning

Compared to using a single element, performing recognition with group representation can further explore the complementary information among group elements and benefit from them. For example, recognizing a person from a group of his photos instead of one image is sure to facilitate the result.

The most popular way to handle group-based recognition tasks is to formulate a unified representation for a whole group of elements [15,37,55,68]. Suppose a base network $\mathcal{M}$ is trained for the element-based recognition task. Define $f_i \in \mathbb{R}^d$ as the embedded feature of element I_i in group $\mathbf{I}_S$ from $\mathcal{M}$, the unified feature representation of the whole group is

$$f_{\mathbf{I}_S} = \mathcal{G}(f_1, f_2, \cdots, f_i), \tag{1}$$

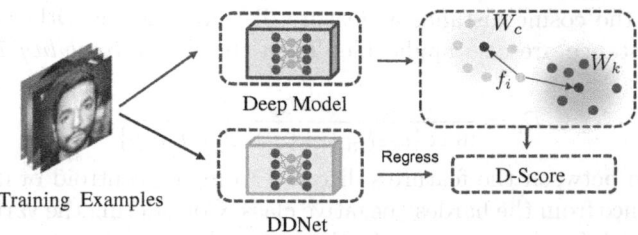

Fig. 1. The pipeline of group representation learning with DDL. Given a base feature extracting model, we first compute the discriminability for each training element and then train a light-weight discriminability distillation network (DDNet) to regress it. The discriminability is formulated from the view of intra and inter-class distance with class centroids for element

where $\mathcal{G}$ indicates the feature aggregation module. While previous research has revealed that conducting $\mathcal{G}$ with quality [37] has priority over simple aggregation, this kind of method is not explainable and computation-consuming. In this article, we propose discriminability distillation learning (DDL) to generate the *discriminability* of feature representation (Fig. 1).

3.2 Formulation of Discriminability

Towards learning efficient and accurate $\mathcal{G}$, we propose to define the *discriminability* of elements to replace the traditional quality or attention mechanism.

After training the base model $\mathcal{M}$ on the classification task, features of the training elements from the same class are projected to hyperspace tightly in order to form an implicit decision boundary and minimizing target loss [36]. This statement exists when $\mathcal{M}$ is supervised by all kinds of loss functions (softmax-cross entropy [47], triplet [44] or margin-based [9,12] losses). Our key observation is that the features embedded close to their corresponding class centroids are normally the representative examples, while features far away or closer to other centroids are usually the confusing ones.

Based on our motivation, we jointly consider the feature space distribution and explicitly distill the *discriminability* by encoding the intra-class distance and inter-class distance with class centroids. Let $\mathcal{X}$ denotes the training set with K classes and $C_m \in \mathbb{R}^d, m \in [1, K]$ is the class centroid of class m, which is the average of features. For feature $f_i, i \in [1, s]$ where s denotes the size of $\mathcal{X}$. Assume the positive class for f_i is p, while the negatives are $n \in [1, K], n \neq p$. The intra-class distance and inter-class distance for f_i are formulated as:

$$
\begin{aligned}
dist_{ip} &= \frac{f_i \cdot C_p}{\|f_i\|_2 \, \|C_p\|_2}, \\
dist_{in} &= \frac{f_i \cdot C_n}{\|f_i\|_2 \, \|C_n\|_2}, \quad n \in [1, K], n \neq p.
\end{aligned}
\tag{2}
$$

Here we use the cosine distance as feature distance metric. Other metrics like Euclidean distance are also applicable. Then the *discriminability* $\mathcal{D}_i$ of f_i can be defined as:

$$\mathcal{D}_i = \frac{dist_{ip}}{\max\left\{dist_{in} \mid n \in [1, K], n \neq p\right\}}. \tag{3}$$

It is the ratio between the feature's distance from the centroid of its own class and the distance from the hardest-negative class. Considering the variant number of elements in different groups, we further normalize the *discriminability* by:

$$\mathcal{D}_i = \tau\left(\frac{\mathcal{D}_i - \mu(\{\mathcal{D}_j \mid j \in [1, s]\})}{\sigma(\{\mathcal{D}_j \mid j \in [1, s]\})}\right) \tag{4}$$

where $\tau(\cdot)$, $\mu(\cdot)$ and $\sigma(\cdot)$ denote the sigmoid function, the mean value and the standard deviation value of $\{\mathcal{D}_j \mid j \in [1, s]\}$, respectively. We denote the normalized $\mathcal{D}_i$ as discriminability score (D-score).

Cooperated with the feature space distribution, the discriminability $\mathcal{D}_i$ is more interpretable and reasonable. It can discriminate features better by explicitly encoding the intra- and inter-class distances with class centroids.

3.3   Discriminability Distillation Learning

From Sect. 3.2, given a base model $\mathcal{M}$ and its training dataset, the $\mathcal{D}_i$ of f_i can be naturally computed by Eq. (2)–(4). However, the score is unavailable to test set $\mathcal{T}$. In order to estimate unseen element's discriminability, we formulate the discriminability distillation learning (DDL) procedure for group representation.

Our idea is to *distill* the discriminability explicitly using a light-weight auxiliary network from the training samples. It is called the Discriminability Distillation Network (DDNet). Denote the DDNet as $\mathcal{N}$, the approximated $\hat{\mathcal{D}}_i$ for $\mathcal{D}_i$ can be given by:

$$\hat{\mathcal{D}}_i = \mathcal{N}(I_i; \boldsymbol{\theta}), \tag{5}$$

where $\boldsymbol{\theta}$ denotes the parameters of $\mathcal{N}$. To train $\mathcal{N}$, we apply mean squared error between $\hat{\mathcal{D}}_i$ and target $\mathcal{D}_i$ as

$$L = \frac{1}{2N}\sum_i^N(\hat{\mathcal{D}}_i - \mathcal{D}_i)^2, \tag{6}$$

where N is the batch size. The training is conducted with the same training set for the base model and there is no need to modify the base model $\mathcal{M}$.

3.4   Feature Aggregation $\mathcal{G}$

During inference, we can generate $\hat{\mathcal{D}}_i$ via Eq. (5) for each element I_i in the given element set I_S. Then we can filter out some elements with low discriminability in order to accelerate the feature extracting process of $\mathcal{M}$. Given the pre-defined threshold t and base model $\mathcal{M}$, the group element feature extracting process is

$$f_i = \mathcal{M}(I_i), \hat{\mathcal{D}}_i > t, \tag{7}$$

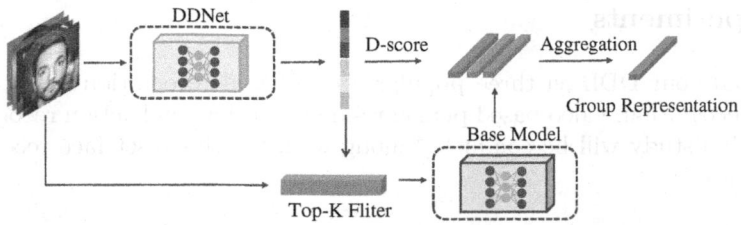

Fig. 2. The pipeline of the test stage with DDL. For a group of elements, we first predict D-score by the trained-well DDNet for each element. Then we will filter elements by their D-scores and only extract feature for those elements with high D-scores by the base model. Finally extracted features will be weighted sum to form the group representation

and $\mathcal{G}$ in Eq. (1) can be formulated as (Fig. 2):

$$F_{\mathbf{I}_S} = \mathcal{G}(f_1, f_2, \cdots, f_n) = \sum_i^n \frac{\hat{\mathcal{R}}_i f_i}{\hat{\mathcal{R}}_i},\tag{8}$$

where n is the number of I_S whose discriminability is higher than threshold t, and $\hat{\mathcal{R}}_i$ is the re-scaled D-score via

$$\hat{\mathcal{R}}_i = K\hat{\mathcal{D}}_i + B.\tag{9}$$

In Eq. (9), we scale the D-score of element set I_S between 0 and 1 to ensure the same range for element sets with different lengths. K and B are formulated as

$$K = \frac{1}{\max\{\hat{\mathcal{D}}_i \mid i \in [1, n]\} - \min\{\hat{\mathcal{D}}_i \mid i \in [1, n]\}},\tag{10}$$

$$B = 1 - K \max\{\hat{\mathcal{D}}_i \mid i \in [1, n]\}.\tag{11}$$

3.5 Advantage of Discriminability Distillation Learning

Different from the subjective quality judgment of an image or the attention mechanism, we explicitly assign *discriminability* for each element via the feature space distribution. By jointly considering the inter- and intra-class distances with class centroids, DDL can effectively approximate how discriminative a feature is. By aggregating more information with features with high *discriminability*, more discriminative group representation can be formed, leading to a significant performance boost for group-based recognition tasks. In addition, the well-design discriminability distillation learning process needn't modify the base model, making it easy to be plugged into many popular recognition frameworks. Furthermore, We can change the threshold for the discriminability filtering process according to different application scenarios to achieve a trade-off between accuracy and computational cost.

4 Experiments

We evaluate our DDL on three popular group-based recognition tasks: set-to-set face recognition, video-based person re-identification, and action recognition. An ablation study will be conducted along with the set-to-set face recognition experiments.

4.1 Set-to-Set Face Recognition

In this section, we evaluate DDL for set-to-set face recognition on four datasets including two video datasets: YouTube Face (YTF) [57], iQIYI-VID-FACE [26]; and two template-based datasets: IARPA Janus Benchmark A (IJB-A) [29] and IARPA Janus Benchmark C (IJB-C).

4.1.1 Implementation Details

For data pre-processing, RetinaFace [11] is used to detect faces and their corresponding landmarks for all datasets. Images are aligned to 112×112 by similarity transformation with facial landmarks.

We train our base model and DDNet on the MS-Celeb-1M dataset [21] cleaned by [9]. The base model we select is modified ResNet-101 [24] released by [9]. As for the DDNet, we use a light-weight channel reduced ResNet-18 network, whose channels for 4 stages are {8, 16, 32, 48}, respectively. It only introduces 81.9 Mflops, which is super-efficient.

The loss function for the base model training is ArcFace [9] and the total training step is 180k with initial learning rate 0.1 on 8 NVIDIA Tesla V100 GPUs. The training process for our DDNet is similar to the base model. The default discriminability threshold we select is 0.15, empirically.

4.1.2 Evaluation on YouTube Face

The YouTube Face [57] dataset includes 3425 videos of 1595 identities with an average of 2.15 videos per identity. The videos vary from 48 frames to 6,070 frames. We report the 1:1 face verification accuracy of the given 5,000 video pairs in our experiments.

As shown in Table 1, our DDL achieves state-of-the-art performance on the YouTube Face benchmark [57]. It outperforms [9] by 0.16% and other set-to-set face recognition methods by impressive margins. For comparison with different aggregation strategies like average pooling, DDL can boost performance by 0.21%, which indicates DDL has learned a meaningful pattern for discriminability. As a post-training module, DDL can cooperate with any existing base. Note that if we only select the top-1 discriminability frame, DDL can also achieve 97.08%, which achieves above 130x acceleration. The computation complexity for the base model is 11 Gflops (ResNet-101) while our DDNet only introduces 81.9 Mflops. By filtering most frames, great computational cost is saved.

4.1.3 Evaluation on IQIYI-VID-FACE

Since the results on YouTube Face benchmark tend to be saturated, we test our DDL on the challenging video face verification benchmark IQIYI-VID-FACE [10], The IQIYI-VID-FACE dataset aims to identify the person in

Table 1. Video face verification performance on YouTube Face dataset, compared with state-of-the-art methods and baseline methods

Method	Accuracy (%)	Method	Accuracy (%)
Li *et al.* [32]	84.8	DeepFace [49]	91.4
FaceNet [44]	95.52	NAN [62]	95.72
DeepID2 [48]	93.20	QAN [37]	96.17
C-FAN [20]	96.50	Rao *et al.* [42]	96.52
Liu *et al.* [38]	96.21	Rao *et al.* [41]	94.28
CosFace [53]	97.65	ArcFace [9]	98.02
Average	97.97	*Top 1*	97.08
		DDL	**98.18**

Table 2. Comparison with different participants and aggregation strategy on the IQIYI-VID-FACE challenge. By combining with PolyNet, DDL achieves state-of-the-art performance

Method	TPR@FPR = 1e−4 (%)	Method	TPR@FPR = 1e−4 (%)
MSRA	71.59	Alibaba-VAG	71.10
Insightface	67.00	DDL (PolyNet)	**72.98**
Average	65.84	*Top 1*	65.22
DDL w/o re-scale	67.38	DDL	**69.05**

entertainment videos by face images. It is the largest video face recognition test benchmark so far, containing 643,816 video clips of 10,034 identities. The test protocol is 1:1 verification, and the True Accept Rate (TAR) under False Accept Rate (FAR) at 1e−4 is reported.

As shown in Table 2, compared with the average pooling, DDL improves performance by 3.21%. Even only aggregating the top-1 discriminability score frame can still achieve an equal performance of average aggregation for all frames. It shows that our DDL has selected the most discriminative element of the set. By combining stronger base model PolyNet [65], our DDL achieves state-of-the-art performance on the IQIYI-VID-FACE challenge.

4.1.4 Evaluation on IJB-A and IJB-C

The IARPA Janus Benchmark A (IJB-A) [29] and IARPA Janus Benchmark C (IJB-C) are unconstrained face recognition benchmarks. They are template-based test benchmarks where both still images and video frames are included in templates. IJB-A containing 25, 813 faces images of 500 identities while IJB-C has 140, 740 faces images of 3, 531 subjects. Since the images in IJB-C dataset have large variations, it is regarded as a challenging set-to-set face recognition benchmark.

Tables 3 and 4 show the results on the IJB-A and IJB-C benchmark for different methods. From the two tables, we can see that our DDL improves verification performance by a convincing margin with average pooling for both

Table 3. Performance comparisons on IJB-A verification benchmark. The True Accept Rates (TAR) vs. False Accept Rate (FAR) are reported

Method	IJB-A (TAR@FAR)		
	FAR = 1e−3 (%)	FAR = 1e−2 (%)	FAR = 1e−1 (%)
Template Adaptation [8]	83.6 ± 2.7	93.9 ± 1.3	97.9 ± 0.4
TPE [43]	81.30 ± 2.0	91.0 ± 1.0	96.4 ± 0.5
Multicolumn [60]	92.0 ± 1.3	96.2 ± 0.5	98.9 ± 0.2
QAN [37]	89.31 ± 3.92	94.2 ± 1.53	98.02 ± 0.55
VGGFace2 [4]	92.1 ± 1.4	96.8 ± 0.6	99 ± 0.2
NAN [62]	88.1 ± 1.1	94.1 ± 0.8	97.8 ± 0.3
GhostVLAD [68]	93.5 ± 1.5	97.2 ± 0.3	99.0 ± 0.2
Liu et al. [38]	93.61 ± 1.51	97.28 ± 0.28	98.94 ± 0.31
ArcFace [9]	97.89 ± 1.5	98.51 ± 0.3	99.05 ± 0.2
Average	97.71 ± 0.6	98.43± 0.4	99.01± 0.2
DDL	**98.44 ± 0.3**	**98.79 ± 0.2**	**99.13 ± 0.1**

Table 4. Performance comparisons on IJB-C verification benchmark. The True Accept Rates (TAR) vs. False Accept Rate (FAR) are reported

Method	IJB-C (TAR@FAR)				
	1e−6 (%)	1e−5 (%)	1e−4 (%)	1e−3 (%)	1e−2 (%)
Yin et al. [63]	-	-	-	0.1	83.8
Xie et al. [59]	-	-	88.5	94.7	98.3
Zhao et al. [66]	-	82.6	89.5	93.5	96.2
Multicolumn [60]	-	77.1	86.2	92.7	96.8
VGGFace2 [4]	-	74.7	84.0	91.0	96.0
PFE [45]	-	89.64	93.25	95.49	97.17
ArcFace [9]	86.25	93.15	95.65	97.20	98.18
Average	86.69	92.72	94.89	96.62	97.90
DDL	**92.39**	**94.89**	**96.41**	**97.47**	**98.33**

two benchmarks, especially under severe FAR at 1e-5 by 0.73% on IJB-A and FAR at 1e-6 by 5.7% on IJB-C. Compared with IJB-A, IJB-C has more images and covers more variations among images, such as pose, blur, resolution, and conditions. So the performance gain with DDL is larger.

Compared with the state-of-the-art methods, our DDL improves IJB-A by 0.55% when FAR = 1e−3 and IJB-C by 6.14% when FAR = 1e−6. These results indicate the effectiveness and robustness of our DDL. What's more, unlike many previous methods that need fine-tune with the base model on set-to-set recognition training datasets [37,68], the only supervision for DDL training is the discriminability generated with the base model on the same training set, which is highly flexible.

Fig. 3. The visualization results of discriminability for images of Template ID 17762 and 16800 from IJB-C dataset

To qualitatively evaluate the discriminability pattern learned by our DDL, we visualize the discriminability score distribution for two template images in IJB-C datasets. As shown in Fig. 3, DDL can effectively identify image discriminability. Images with large poses, visual blur, occlusion, and incomplete content are regarded to be low discriminative. The efficient discriminability judgment ability for our DDL leads to an extraordinary performance on set-to-set face recognition problems.

4.1.5 Ablation Study

The Architecture of DDNet and Base Model. In the above experiments, we have adopted the channel reduced version of ResNet-18 as the backbone for DDNet. When inference, all test samples will be sent to DDNet firstly to predict discriminability. Therefore, the test computational cost is very sensitive to the architecture of DDNet. We design it as light-weight as possible. We also conduct experiments with wider and deeper DDNet and test on IJB-C. As shown in Table 5, the wider and deeper networks have not brought significant performance gains.

As for the base model, we also experiment DDL with MobileFaceNet [6], a popular backbone for mobile devices. From Table 5, we can see that by combining will DDL, a consistent performance gain can be achieved on set-to-set face recognition task for MobilcFaceNet.

Train on Other Datasets. In the aforementioned experiments, we use the MS-Celeb-1M dataset for the base model and DDNet training. To demonstrate the good generalization of our method, we also train the base model and DDNet with IMDB-Face [52] dataset. IMDb-Face is a new large-scale noise-controlled dataset for face recognition. The dataset contains about 1.7 million faces, 59k identities, which is manually cleaned from 2.0 million raw images. The results on IJB-C are shown in Table 5, DDL improves set-to-set face recognition by a huge margin compared with simple average pooling, up to 15.23% at FPR = 1e−6. The model trained on IMDB-Face tends to be weaker than MS-Celeb-1M and more easily confused by hard negative pairs, thus DDL achieves a more significant improvement.

Table 5. Ablation study with different DDNet architecture, base model architecture and training datasets. Results are reported on IJB-C benchmark. 'CD' means channel reduced

Method			IJB-C (TAR@FAR)				
DDNet	Base model	Train datasets	1e−6	1e−45	1e−4	1e−3	1e−2
ResNet-18-CD	ResNet-101	MS-Celeb-1M	**91.14**	**95.75**	**96.94**	97.72	**98.36**
ResNet-34-CD	ResNet-101	MS-Celeb-1M	91.13	95.74	96.90	97.72	98.33
ResNet-18	ResNet-101	MS-Celeb-1M	90.93	95.74	96.92	**97.73**	98.35
ResNet-18-CD	MobileFaceNet	MS-Celeb-1M	**87.32**	**91.45**	**94.30**	**96.24**	**97.82**
-	MobileFaceNet	MS-Celeb-1M	79.88	88.21	92.08	95.22	97.24
ResNet-18-CD	ResNet-101	IMDB-Face	**88.35**	**92.26**	**95.09**	**96.71**	**98.05**
-	ResNet-101	IMDB-Face	73.12	86.44	92.44	94.70	97.40

Table 6. Ablation study with loss function. Results are reported on YouTube Face benchmark

Method		Accuracy (%)
DDL	Loss function	
✓	ArcFace	**98.18**
✗	ArcFace	97.97
✓	CosFace	**97.91**
✗	CosFace	97.68
✓	SphereFace	**97.12**
✗	SphereFace	96.83

The Influence of Re-scale. In Eq. (9), we re-scale the discriminability scores of element set between 0 and 1 to ensure the same range for element sets with different lengths. In this part, we compare the re-scale strategy and origin scale on IQIYI-VID-FACE benchmark. As shown in Table 2, re-scale can boost performance for 1.67%. For video face recognition, which contains various frames from dozens of to thousands of, it is necessary to re-scale the predicted discriminability scores at the test stage.

Combined with More Loss Functions. There are many successful loss function these years for face recognition task, such as ArcFace [9], CosFace [53] and SphereFace [34]. We combine DDL with more loss functions and test on YouTube Face benchmark. As shown in Table 6, all loss functions achieve constant performance gain with DDL. DDL is not sensitive to the base model training loss function and can easily cooperate with any existing base.

4.2 Video-Based Person Re-identification

In this section, we will evaluate our DDL with the video-based person re-identification task on Mars [67]. It the largest video-based person re-identification dataset. The train and test set are followed official split.

Table 7. Results for video-based person re-identification on Mars

	mAP	CMC-1	CMC-5	CMC-20
Zheng *et al.* [67]	45.6	65.0	81.1	88.9
Li *et al.* [31]	56.1	71.8	86.6	93.1
QAN [37]	51.7	73.7	84.9	91.6
Hermans *et al.* [25]	67.7	79.8	91.4	-
3D conv [15]	70.5	78.5	90.9	95.9
Atttention [15]	76.7	83.3	93.8	97.4
RNN [15]	73.9	81.6	92.8	96.3
Average	74.1	81.3	92.6	96.7
DDL	**77.7**	**84.0**	**94.8**	**97.4**

To train the base model, triplet loss function and softmax cross-entropy loss function are used. The similarity metric is L2 distance. Standard ResNet-50 pre-trained on ImageNet is used and video frames are resized to 224×112. We will report mean average precision score (mAP) and cumulative matching curve (CMC) at rank-1, rank-5 and rank-20. Note that re-rank is not applied in the comparison.

The results are shown in Table 7, DDL boosts the performance consistently. Compared with average pooling, DDL achieves performance gain for 3.6% mAP. For more complicated aggregation strategies like RNN and the state-of-the-art attention mechanism, DDL also improves performance. The good performance of video-based person re-identification further demonstrates the efficiency of our DDL in group representation learning.

4.3 Action Recognition

In this section, we will evaluate our DDL on two most popular action recognition datasets ActivityNet-1.2 [3] and Kinetics-700 [28]. The ActivityNet-1.2 contains 4,819 training videos and 2,383 validation videos for 100 action class. It is an untrimmed video dataset, namely more temporal variance and noises there are. The Kinetics-700 is a well-trimmed action recognition datasets, which contains over 650k videos from 700 classes.

All video frames are extracted by FFmpeg with 30fps then resized and center crop to 112×112. We select three clip-based action recognition baseline method, the 3D-ResNet-50 [22], SlowFast-50 [13] and R(2+1)D-50 [51]. The training config for those base models follows SlowFast [13]. In the original approach, all three methods rely on dense sampling during testing. To be more specific, they oversampling both spatially and temporally to capture target activation.

The DDNet architecture for action recognition is the same with image task, but replace all 2D-Conv to 3D-Conv. A video will firstly be divided into many clips, and each clip's discriminability will be generated by DDNet, only top-K

Table 8. Video action recognition results (%) on ActivityNet-1.2 dataset. Accuracy is reported by top-1 on the validation set

Model	DDL	Random	Uniform	Dense
Clip number	9			60
3D-RS-50	**86.38**	82.83	83.14	83.92
R(2+1)D-RS-50	**89.08**	84.51	84.89	85.46
SlowFast-RS-50	**90.21**	85.92	86.14	87.72

Table 9. Video action recognition results (%) on Kinetics-700 dataset. Accuracy is reported on the validation set and is the average of top1 and top 5 accuracy

Model	DDL	Random	Uniform	Dense
Clip number	5			30
3D-RS-50	**71.01**	68.26	67.43	68.83
R(2+1)D-RS-50	**72.51**	69.24	68.79	70.94
SlowFast-RS-50	**74.23**	72.39	72.05	73.77

clips will be extracted feature and aggregated. The K we select for ActivityNet-1.2 and Kinetics is 9 and 5, respectively. We select random and uniform sampling K clips for comparison with sampling by DDL. A dense sampling experiment is also conducted.

From Table 8, DDL improves recognition performance for all baseline models on ActivityNet-1.2. For the state-of-the-art clips-based model SlowFast, combining it with DDL can achieve around 4% accuracy gain compared with random or uniform sampling on ActivityNet-1.2. What's more, DDL can even outperform dense sampling by 2.49%, while the dense sampling strategy sample above 5x more clips (estimated by the average duration 120s for ActivitNet-1.2).

For Kinetics-700, the results are in Table 9. DDL outperforms random sampling by 1.84% and uniform sampling by 2.18%. For dense sampling, DDL can achieve 0.46% gain with 6x speed up. Since the Kinetics-700 is trimmed by human and video quality is under control, combining with DDL can also significantly boost recognition performance and save computational consumption.

5   Conclusion

In this paper, we have proposed a novel post-processing module called Discriminability Distillation Learning (DDL) for all group-based recognition tasks. We explicitly define the discriminability with observations on feature embedding, then apply a light-weight network for discriminability distillation and feature aggregation. We identify the advantage of our proposed methods in the following aspects: (1) The entire discriminability distillation is performed without modifying the pre-trained based network, which is highly flexible comparing with existing quality-aware or attention methods. (2) Our distillation network is extremely light-weighted which saves great computational cost. (3) With our DDL and feature aggregation, we achieve state-of-the-art results on multiple group-based recognition tasks including set-to-set face recognition, video-based person re-identification, and action recognition.

References

1. Arandjelovic, O., Shakhnarovich, G., Fisher, J., Cipolla, R., Darrell, T.: Face recognition with image sets using manifold density divergence. In: 2005 IEEE Computer Society Conference on Computer Vision and Pattern Recognition (CVPR 2005), vol. 1, pp. 581–588. IEEE (2005)
2. Beveridge, J.R., et al.: The challenge of face recognition from digital point-and-shoot cameras. In: 2013 IEEE Sixth International Conference on Biometrics: Theory, Applications and Systems (BTAS), pp. 1–8. IEEE (2013)
3. Caba Heilbron, F., Escorcia, V., Ghanem, B., Carlos Niebles, J.: Activitynet: a large-scale video benchmark for human activity understanding. In: Proceedings of the IEEE Conference on Computer Vision and Pattern Recognition, pp. 961–970 (2015)
4. Cao, Q., Shen, L., Xie, W., Parkhi, O.M., Zisserman, A.: Vggface2: a dataset for recognising faces across pose and age. In: 2018 13th IEEE International Conference on Automatic Face & Gesture Recognition (FG 2018), pp. 67–74. IEEE (2018)
5. Cevikalp, H., Triggs, B.: Face recognition based on image sets. In: 2010 IEEE Computer Society Conference on Computer Vision and Pattern Recognition, pp. 2567–2573. IEEE (2010)
6. Chen, S., Liu, Y., Gao, X., Han, Z.: MobileFaceNets: efficient CNNs for accurate real-time face verification on mobile devices. In: Zhou, J., et al. (eds.) CCBR 2018. LNCS, vol. 10996, pp. 428–438. Springer, Cham (2018). https://doi.org/10.1007/978-3-319-97909-0_46
7. Chowdhury, A.R., Lin, T.Y., Maji, S., Learned-Miller, E.: One-to-many face recognition with bilinear CNNs. In: 2016 IEEE Winter Conference on Applications of Computer Vision (WACV), pp. 1–9. IEEE (2016)
8. Crosswhite, N., Byrne, J., Stauffer, C., Parkhi, O., Cao, Q., Zisserman, A.: Template adaptation for face verification and identification. Image Vis. Comput. **79**, 35–48 (2018)
9. Deng, J., Guo, J., Xue, N., Zafeiriou, S.: Arcface: additive angular margin loss for deep face recognition. In: Proceedings of the IEEE Conference on Computer Vision and Pattern Recognition, pp. 4690–4699 (2019)
10. Deng, J., Guo, J., Zhang, D., Deng, Y., Lu, X., Shi, S.: Lightweight face recognition challenge. In: Proceedings of the IEEE International Conference on Computer Vision Workshops (2019)
11. Deng, J., Guo, J., Zhou, Y., Yu, J., Kotsia, I., Zafeiriou, S.: Retinaface: single-stage dense face localisation in the wild. arXiv preprint arXiv:1905.00641 (2019)
12. Duan, Y., Lu, J., Zhou, J.: Uniformface: learning deep equidistributed representation for face recognition. In: Proceedings of the IEEE Conference on Computer Vision and Pattern Recognition, pp. 3415–3424 (2019)
13. Feichtenhofer, C., Fan, H., Malik, J., He, K.: Slowfast networks for video recognition. arXiv preprint arXiv:1812.03982 (2018)

14. Gan, C., Gong, B., Liu, K., Su, H., Guibas, L.J.: Geometry guided convolutional neural networks for self-supervised video representation learning. In: Proceedings of the IEEE Conference on Computer Vision and Pattern Recognition, pp. 5589–5597 (2018)
15. Gao, J., Nevatia, R.: Revisiting temporal modeling for video-based person reid. arXiv preprint arXiv:1805.02104 (2018)
16. Ge, Y., Chen, D., Li, H.: Mutual mean-teaching: pseudo label refinery for unsupervised domain adaptation on person re-identification. In: ICLR (2020)
17. Ge, Y., Chen, D., Zhu, F., Zhao, R., Li, H.: Self-paced contrastive learning with hybrid memory for domain adaptive object Re-ID. arXiv preprint arXiv:2006.02713 (2020)
18. Ge, Y., Li, Z., Zhao, H., Yin, G., Yi, S., Wang, X., et al.: FD-GAN: pose-guided feature distilling GAN for robust person re-identification. In: Advances in Neural Information Processing Systems, pp. 1222–1233 (2018)
19. Girdhar, R., Ramanan, D., Gupta, A., Sivic, J., Russell, B.: ActionVLAD: learning spatio-temporal aggregation for action classification. In: Proceedings of the IEEE Conference on Computer Vision and Pattern Recognition, pp. 971–980 (2017)
20. Gong, S., Shi, Y., Jain, A.K.: Video face recognition: component-wise feature aggregation network (c-fan). arXiv preprint arXiv:1902.07327 (2019)
21. Guo, Y., Zhang, L., Hu, Y., He, X., Gao, J.: MS-Celeb-1M: a dataset and benchmark for large-scale face recognition. In: Leibe, B., Matas, J., Sebe, N., Welling, M. (eds.) ECCV 2016. LNCS, vol. 9907, pp. 87–102. Springer, Cham (2016). https://doi.org/10.1007/978-3-319-46487-9_6
22. Hara, K., Kataoka, H., Satoh, Y.: Can spatiotemporal 3D CNNs retrace the history of 2D CNNs and imagenet? In: Proceedings of the IEEE conference on Computer Vision and Pattern Recognition, pp. 6546–6555 (2018)
23. Harandi, M.T., Sanderson, C., Shirazi, S., Lovell, B.C.: Graph embedding discriminant analysis on grassmannian manifolds for improved image set matching. In: CVPR 2011, pp. 2705–2712. IEEE (2011)
24. He, K., Zhang, X., Ren, S., Sun, J.: Deep residual learning for image recognition. In: Proceedings of the IEEE Conference on Computer Vision and Pattern Recognition, pp. 770–778 (2016)
25. Hermans, A., Beyer, L., Leibe, B.: In defense of the triplet loss for person re-identification. arXiv preprint arXiv:1703.07737 (2017)
26. iQIYI: iQIYI-VID-face (2019). http://challenge.ai.iqiyi.com/data-cluster
27. Kalka, N.D., et al.: IJB-S: IARPA janus surveillance video benchmark. In: 2018 IEEE 9th International Conference on Biometrics Theory, Applications and Systems (BTAS), pp. 1–9. IEEE (2018)
28. Kay, W., et al.: The kinetics human action video dataset. arXiv preprint arXiv:1705.06950 (2017)
29. Klare, B.F., et al.: Pushing the frontiers of unconstrained face detection and recognition: IARPA janus benchmark A. In: Proceedings of the IEEE Conference on Computer Vision and Pattern Recognition, pp. 1931–1939 (2015)
30. Korbar, B., Tran, D., Torresani, L.: Scsampler: sampling salient clips from video for efficient action recognition. In: Proceedings of the IEEE International Conference on Computer Vision, pp. 6232–6242 (2019)
31. Li, D., Chen, X., Zhang, Z., Huang, K.: Learning deep context-aware features over body and latent parts for person re-identification. In: Proceedings of the IEEE Conference on Computer Vision and Pattern Recognition, pp. 384–393 (2017)

32. Li, H., Hua, G., Shen, X., Lin, Z., Brandt, J.: Eigen-PEP for video face recognition. In: Cremers, D., Reid, I., Saito, H., Yang, M.-H. (eds.) ACCV 2014. LNCS, vol. 9005, pp. 17–33. Springer, Cham (2015). https://doi.org/10.1007/978-3-319-16811-1_2

33. Li, S., Bak, S., Carr, P., Wang, X.: Diversity regularized spatiotemporal attention for video-based person re-identification. In: The IEEE Conference on Computer Vision and Pattern Recognition (CVPR), June 2018

34. Liu, W., Wen, Y., Yu, Z., Li, M., Raj, B., Song, L.: Sphereface: deep hypersphere embedding for face recognition. In: Proceedings of the IEEE Conference on Computer Vision and Pattern Recognition, pp. 212–220 (2017)

35. Liu, X., et al.: Permutation-invariant feature restructuring for correlation-aware image set-based recognition. In: Proceedings of the IEEE International Conference on Computer Vision, pp. 4986–4996 (2019)

36. Liu, Yu., Song, G., Shao, J., Jin, X., Wang, X.: Transductive centroid projection for semi-supervised large-scale recognition. In: Ferrari, V., Hebert, M., Sminchisescu, C., Weiss, Y. (eds.) ECCV 2018. LNCS, vol. 11209, pp. 72–89. Springer, Cham (2018). https://doi.org/10.1007/978-3-030-01228-1_5

37. Liu, Y., Yan, J., Ouyang, W.: Quality aware network for set to set recognition. In: Proceedings of the IEEE Conference on Computer Vision and Pattern Recognition, pp. 5790–5799 (2017)

38. Liu, Z., Hu, H., Bai, J., Li, S., Lian, S.: Feature aggregation network for video face recognition. In: Proceedings of the IEEE International Conference on Computer Vision Workshops (2019)

39. McLaughlin, N., Martinez del Rincon, J., Miller, P.: Recurrent convolutional network for video-based person re-identification. In: Proceedings of the IEEE Conference on Computer Vision and Pattern Recognition, pp. 1325–1334 (2016)

40. Nikitin, M.Y., Konouchine, V.S., Konouchine, A.: Neural network model for video-based face recognition with frames quality assessment. Comput. Opt. **41**(5), 732–742 (2017)

41. Rao, Y., Lin, J., Lu, J., Zhou, J.: Learning discriminative aggregation network for video-based face recognition. In: Proceedings of the IEEE International Conference on Computer Vision, pp. 3781–3790 (2017)

42. Rao, Y., Lu, J., Zhou, J.: Attention-aware deep reinforcement learning for video face recognition. In: Proceedings of the IEEE International Conference on Computer Vision, pp. 3931–3940 (2017)

43. Sankaranarayanan, S., Alavi, A., Castillo, C.D., Chellappa, R.: Triplet probabilistic embedding for face verification and clustering. In: 2016 IEEE 8th International Conference on Biometrics Theory, Applications and Systems (BTAS), pp. 1–8. IEEE (2016)

44. Schroff, F., Kalenichenko, D., Philbin, J.: Facenet: a unified embedding for face recognition and clustering. In: Proceedings of the IEEE Conference on Computer Vision and Pattern Recognition, pp. 815–823 (2015)

45. Shi, Y., Jain, A.K.: Probabilistic face embeddings (2019)

46. Simonyan, K., Zisserman, A.: Two-stream convolutional networks for action recognition in videos. In: Advances in Neural Information Processing Systems, pp. 568–576 (2014)

47. Sun, Y., Chen, Y., Wang, X., Tang, X.: Deep learning face representation by joint identification-verification. In: Advances in Neural Information Processing Systems, pp. 1988–1996 (2014)

48. Sun, Y., Wang, X., Tang, X.: Deeply learned face representations are sparse, selective, and robust. In: Proceedings of the IEEE Conference on Computer Vision and Pattern Recognition, pp. 2892–2900 (2015)
49. Taigman, Y., Yang, M., Ranzato, M., Wolf, L.: Deepface: closing the gap to human-level performance in face verification. In: Proceedings of the IEEE Conference on Computer Vision and Pattern Recognition, pp. 1701–1708 (2014)
50. Tran, D., Bourdev, L., Fergus, R., Torresani, L., Paluri, M.: Learning spatiotemporal features with 3D convolutional networks. In: Proceedings of the IEEE International Conference on Computer Vision, pp. 4489–4497 (2015)
51. Tran, D., Wang, H., Torresani, L., Ray, J., LeCun, Y., Paluri, M.: A closer look at spatiotemporal convolutions for action recognition. In: Proceedings of the IEEE Conference on Computer Vision and Pattern Recognition, pp. 6450–6459 (2018)
52. Wang, F., et al.: The devil of face recognition is in the noise. In: Ferrari, V., Hebert, M., Sminchisescu, C., Weiss, Y. (eds.) ECCV 2018. LNCS, vol. 11213, pp. 780–795. Springer, Cham (2018). https://doi.org/10.1007/978-3-030-01240-3_47
53. Wang, H., et al.: Cosface: large margin cosine loss for deep face recognition. In: Proceedings of the IEEE Conference on Computer Vision and Pattern Recognition, pp. 5265–5274 (2018)
54. Wang, L., Xiong, Y., Lin, D., Van Gool, L.: Untrimmednets for weakly supervised action recognition and detection. In: Proceedings of the IEEE Conference on Computer Vision and Pattern Recognition, pp. 4325–4334 (2017)
55. Wang, L., et al.: Temporal segment networks: towards good practices for deep action recognition. In: Leibe, B., Matas, J., Sebe, N., Welling, M. (eds.) ECCV 2016. LNCS, vol. 9912, pp. 20–36. Springer, Cham (2016). https://doi.org/10.1007/978-3-319-46484-8_2
56. Wang, X., Girshick, R., Gupta, A., He, K.: Non-local neural networks. In: Proceedings of the IEEE Conference on Computer Vision and Pattern Recognition, pp. 7794–7803 (2018)
57. Wolf, L., Hassner, T., Maoz, I.: Face recognition in unconstrained videos with matched background similarity. IEEE (2011)
58. Wu, L., Wang, Y., Gao, J., Li, X.: Where-and-when to look: deep siamese attention networks for video-based person re-identification. IEEE Trans. Multimed. 21(6), 1412–1424 (2018)
59. Xie, W., Shen, L., Zisserman, A.: Comparator networks. In: Ferrari, V., Hebert, M., Sminchisescu, C., Weiss, Y. (eds.) ECCV 2018. LNCS, vol. 11215, pp. 811–826. Springer, Cham (2018). https://doi.org/10.1007/978-3-030-01252-6_48
60. Xie, W., Zisserman, A.: Multicolumn networks for face recognition. arXiv preprint arXiv:1807.09192 (2018)
61. Yan, Y., Ni, B., Song, Z., Ma, C., Yan, Y., Yang, X.: Person re-identification via recurrent feature aggregation. In: Leibe, B., Matas, J., Sebe, N., Welling, M. (eds.) ECCV 2016. LNCS, vol. 9910, pp. 701–716. Springer, Cham (2016). https://doi.org/10.1007/978-3-319-46466-4_42
62. Yang, J., et al.: Neural aggregation network for video face recognition. In: Proceedings of the IEEE Conference on Computer Vision and Pattern Recognition, pp. 4362–4371 (2017)
63. Yin, B., Tran, L., Li, H., Shen, X., Liu, X.: Towards interpretable face recognition. In: Proceedings of the IEEE International Conference on Computer Vision, pp. 9348–9357 (2019)

64. Yue-Hei Ng, J., Hausknecht, M., Vijayanarasimhan, S., Vinyals, O., Monga, R., Toderici, G.: Beyond short snippets: deep networks for video classification. In: Proceedings of the IEEE Conference on Computer Vision and Pattern Recognition, pp. 4694–4702 (2015)
65. Zhang, X., Li, Z., Change Loy, C., Lin, D.: Polynet: a pursuit of structural diversity in very deep networks. In: Proceedings of the IEEE Conference on Computer Vision and Pattern Recognition, pp. 718–726 (2017)
66. Zhao, J., et al.: Look across elapse: disentangled representation learning and photorealistic cross-age face synthesis for age-invariant face recognition. Proc. AAAI Conf. Artif. Intell. **33**, 9251–9258 (2019)
67. Zheng, L., et al.: MARS: a video benchmark for large-scale person re-identification. In: Leibe, B., Matas, J., Sebe, N., Welling, M. (eds.) ECCV 2016. LNCS, vol. 9910, pp. 868–884. Springer, Cham (2016). https://doi.org/10.1007/978-3-319-46466-4_52
68. Zhong, Y., Arandjelović, R., Zisserman, A.: GhostVLAD for set-based face recognition. In: Jawahar, C.V., Li, H., Mori, G., Schindler, K. (eds.) ACCV 2018. LNCS, vol. 11362, pp. 35–50. Springer, Cham (2019). https://doi.org/10.1007/978-3-030-20890-5_3
69. Zhou, H., Liu, J., Liu, Z., Liu, Y., Wang, X.: Rotate-and-render: unsupervised photorealistic face rotation from single-view images. In: Proceedings of the IEEE/CVF Conference on Computer Vision and Pattern Recognition (CVPR), June 2020
70. Zhou, H., Liu, Y., Liu, Z., Luo, P., Wang, X.: Talking face generation by adversarially disentangled audio-visual representation. In: AAAI Conference on Artificial Intelligence (AAAI) (2019)
71. Zhou, Z., Huang, Y., Wang, W., Wang, L., Tan, T.: See the forest for the trees: joint spatial and temporal recurrent neural networks for video-based person re-identification. In: Proceedings of the IEEE Conference on Computer Vision and Pattern Recognition, pp. 4747–4756 (2017)

Monocular Expressive Body Regression Through Body-Driven Attention

Vasileios Choutas[1,2]([✉]), Georgios Pavlakos[3], Timo Bolkart[1],
Dimitrios Tzionas[1], and Michael J. Black[1]

[1] Max Planck Institute for Intelligent Systems, Tübingen, Germany
{vchoutas,tbolkart,dtzionas,black}@tuebingen.mpg.de
[2] Max Planck ETH Center for Learning Systems, Tübingen, Germany
[3] University of Pennsylvania, Philadelphia, USA
gpavlakos@tuebingen.mpg.de

Abstract. To understand how people look, interact, or perform tasks, we need to quickly and accurately capture their 3D body, face, and hands *together* from an RGB image. Most existing methods focus only on parts of the body. A few recent approaches reconstruct full expressive 3D humans from images using 3D body models that include the face and hands. These methods are optimization-based and thus slow, prone to local optima, and require 2D keypoints as input. We address these limitations by introducing *ExPose* (EXpressive POse and Shape rEgression), which directly regresses the body, face, and hands, in SMPL-X format, from an RGB image. This is a hard problem due to the high dimensionality of the body and the lack of expressive training data. Additionally, hands and faces are much smaller than the body, occupying very few image pixels. This makes hand and face estimation hard when body images are downscaled for neural networks. We make three main contributions. First, we account for the lack of training data by curating a *dataset* of SMPL-X fits on in-the-wild images. Second, we observe that body estimation localizes the face and hands reasonably well. We introduce *body-driven attention* for face and hand regions in the original image to extract higher-resolution crops that are fed to dedicated refinement modules. Third, these modules exploit *part-specific knowledge* from existing face- and hand-only datasets. ExPose estimates expressive 3D humans more accurately than existing optimization methods at a small fraction of the computational cost. Our data, model and code are available for research at https://expose.is.tue.mpg.de.

1 Introduction

A long term goal of computer vision is to understand humans and their behavior in everyday scenarios using only images. Are they happy or sad? How do they

Electronic supplementary material The online version of this chapter (https://doi.org/10.1007/978-3-030-58607-2_2) contains supplementary material, which is available to authorized users.

© Springer Nature Switzerland AG 2020
A. Vedaldi et al. (Eds.): ECCV 2020, LNCS 12355, pp. 20–40, 2020.
https://doi.org/10.1007/978-3-030-58607-2_2

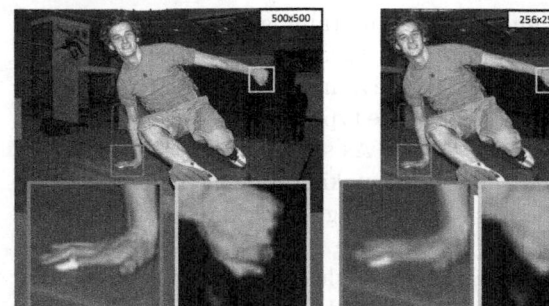

Fig. 1. *Left:* Full-body RGB images of people contain many more pixels on the body than on the face or hands. *Middle:* Images are typically downsized (e.g. to 256 × 256 px) for use in neural networks. This resolution is fine for the body but the hands and face suffer from low resolution. Our model (Fig. 2) uses *body-driven attention* to restore the lost information for hands and faces from the original image, feeding it to dedicated refinement modules. *Right:* These modules give more expressive hands and faces, by exploiting *part-specific knowledge* learned from higher quality hand-only [105] and face-only [41] datasets; green meshes show example part-specific training data. (Color figure online)

interact with each other and the physical world? What are their intentions? To answer such difficult questions, we first need to *quickly* and *accurately* reconstruct their 3D body, face and hands *together* from a single RGB image. This is very challenging. As a result, the community has broken the problem into pieces with much of the work focused on estimating either the main body [18,62,78], the face [106] or the hands [14,87,97] separately.

Only recent advances have made the problem tractable in its full complexity. Early methods estimate 2D joints and features [10,29] for the body, face and hands. However, this is not enough. It is the skin surface that describes important aspects of humans, e.g. what their precise 3D shape is, whether they are smiling, gesturing or holding something. For this reason, strong statistical parametric models for expressive 3D humans were introduced, namely Adam [38], SMPL-X [67] and recently GHUM/GHUML [96]. Such models are attractive because they facilitate reconstruction even from ambiguous data, working as a strong prior.

There exist three methods that estimate full expressive 3D humans from an RGB image [67,95,96], using SMPL-X, Adam and GHUM/GHUML respectively. These methods are based on optimization, therefore they are slow, prone to local optima, and rely on heuristics for initialization. These issues significantly limit the applicability of these methods. In contrast, recent body-only methods [39,46] directly regress 3D SMPL bodies quickly and relatively reliably directly from an RGB image.

Here we present a *fast* and *accurate* model that reconstructs full *expressive* 3D humans, by estimating SMPL-X parameters directly from an RGB image. This is a hard problem and we show that it is not easily solved by extending SMPL neural-network regressors to SMPL-X for several reasons. First, SMPL-X is a much higher dimensional model than SMPL. Second, there exists no large in-the-wild dataset with SMPL-X annotations for training. Third, the face and hands are often blurry and occluded in images. At any given image resolution, they also occupy many fewer pixels than the body, making them low resolution. Fourth, for technical reasons, full body images are typically downscaled for input to neural networks [48], e.g. to 256×256 pixels. As shown in Fig. 1, this results in even lower resolution for the hands and face, making inference difficult.

Our model and training method, shown in Fig. 2, tackles all these challenges. We account for data scarcity by introducing a new dataset with paired in-the-wild images and SMPL-X annotations. To this end, we employ several standard in-the-wild body datasets [3,35,36,57] and fit SMPL-X to them with SMPLify-X [67]. We semi-automatically curate these fits to keep only the good ones as pseudo ground-truth. We then train a model that regresses SMPL-X parameters from an RGB image, similar to [39]. However, this only estimates rough hand and face configurations, due to the problems described above. We observe that the main body is estimated well, on par with [39,46], providing good rough localization for the face and hands. We use this for *body-driven attention* and focus the network back on the *original* non-downscaled image for the face and hands. We retrieve high-resolution information for these regions and feed this to dedicated *refinement* modules. These modules act as an *expressivity boost* by distilling *part-specific knowledge* from high-quality hand-only [105] and face-only [58] datasets. Finally, the independent components are fine-tuned jointly end-to-end, so that the part networks can benefit from the full-body initialization.

We call the final model ExPose (EXpressive POse and Shape rEgression). ExPose is as accurate as existing optimization-based methods [67] for estimating expressive 3D humans, while running two orders of magnitude faster. Our data, model and code are available for research at https://expose.is.tue.mpg.de.

2 Related Work

Human Modeling: Modeling and capturing the whole human body is a challenging problem. To make it tractable, the community has studied the body, face and hands separately, in a divide-and-conquer fashion. For the human *face*, the seminal work of Blanz and Vetter [6] introduces the first 3D morphable model. Since then, numerous works (see [13]) propose more powerful face models and methods to infer their parameters. For human *hands* the number of models is limited, with Khamis et al. [42] learning a model of hand shape variation from depth images, while Romero et al. [72] learn a parametric hand model with both a rich shape and pose space from 3D hand scans. For the human *body*, the introduction of the CAESAR dataset [70] enables the creation of models that disentangle shape and pose, such as SCAPE [4] and SMPL [59], to name a few. However, these models have a neutral face and the hands are non-articulated. In contrast, Adam [38] and SMPL-X [67] are the first models that represent the body, face and hands jointly. Adam lacks the pose-dependent blendshapes of SMPL and the released version does not include a face model. The GHUM [96] model is similar to SMPL-X but is not publicly available at the time of writing.

Human Pose Estimation: Often pose estimation is posed as the estimation of 2D or 3D keypoints, corresponding to anatomical joints or landmarks [9,10,82]. In contrast, recent advances use richer representations of the 3D body surface in the form of parametric [7,39,65,69] or non-parametric [47,75,92] models.

To estimate **bodies** from images, many methods break the problem down into stages. First, they estimate some intermediate representation such as 2D joints [7,20,21,30,39,61,69,81,91,101], silhouettes [1,30,69], part labels [65,74] or dense correspondences [23,73]. Then, they reconstruct the body pose out of this proxy information, by either using it in the data term of an optimized energy function [7,30,98] or "lifting" it using a trained regressor [39,61,65,69, 91]. Due to ambiguities in lifting 2D to 3D, such methods use various priors for regularization, such as known limb lengths [51], a pose prior for joint angle limits [2], or a statistical body model [7,30,65,69] like SMPL [59]. The above 2D proxy representations have the advantage that annotation for them is readily available. Their disadvantage is that the eventual regressor does not get to exploit the original image pixels and errors made by the proxy task cannot be overcome.

Other methods predict 3D pose directly from RGB pixels. Intuitively, they have to learn a harder mapping, but they avoid information bottlenecks and additional sources of error. Most methods infer 3D body joints [53,68,85,86,90], parametric methods estimate model parameters [39,40,46], while non-parametric methods estimate 3D meshes [47], depth maps [17,83] voxels [92,102] or distance fields [75,76]. Datasets of paired indoor images and MoCap data [31,80] allow supervised training, but may not generalize to in-the-wild data. To account for this, Rogez and Schmid [71] augment these datasets by overlaying synthetic 3D humans, while Kanazawa et al. [39] include in-the-wild datasets [3,35,36,57] and employ a re-projection loss on their 2D joint annotations for weak supervision.

Similar observations can be made in the human hand and face literature. For **hands**, there has been a lot of work on RGB-D data [97], and more recent interest in monocular RGB [5,8,24,26,32,50,63,89,104]. Some of the non-parametric methods estimate 3D joints [32,63,89,104], while others estimate 3D meshes [19,49]. Parametric models [5,8,26,50,100] estimate configurations of statistical models like MANO [72] or a graph morphable model [50]. For **faces**, 3D reconstruction and tracking has a long history. We refer the reader to a recent comprehensive survey [106].

Attention for Human Pose Estimation: In the context of human pose estimation, attention is often used to improve prediction accuracy. Successful architectures for 2D pose estimation, like Convolutional Pose Machines [93] and Stacked Hourglass [64] include a series of processing stages, where the intermediate pose predictions in the form of heatmaps are used as input to the following stages. This informs the network of early predictions and guides its attention to relevant image pixels. Chu et al. [12] build explicit attention maps, at a global and part-specific level, driving the model to focus on regions of interest. Instead of predicting attention maps, our approach uses the initial body mesh prediction to define the areas of attention for hands- and face-specific processing networks. A similar practice is used by OpenPose [10], where arm keypoints are used to

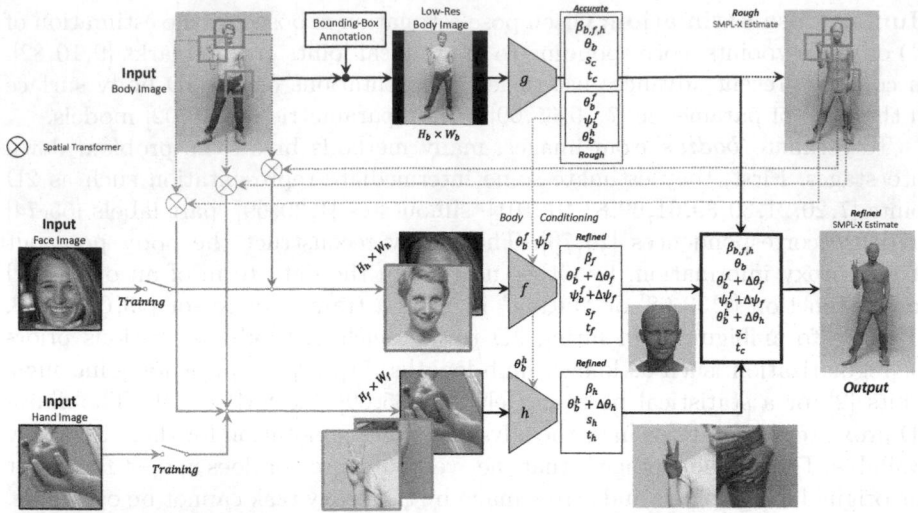

Fig. 2. An image of the body is extracted using a bounding box from the full resolution image and fed to a neural network $g(\cdot)$, that predicts body pose $\boldsymbol{\theta}_b$, hand pose $\boldsymbol{\theta}_h$, facial pose $\boldsymbol{\theta}_f$, shape $\boldsymbol{\beta}$, expression $\boldsymbol{\psi}$, camera scale s and translation t. Face and hand images are extracted from the original resolution image using bilinear interpolation. These are fed to part specific sub-networks $f(\cdot)$ and $h(\cdot)$ respectively to produce the final estimates for the face and hand parameters. During training the part specific networks can also receive hand and face only data for extra supervision.

estimate hand bounding boxes, in a heuristic manner. Additionally, for Holo-Pose [22], body keypoints are used to pool part-specific features from the image.

A critical difference of ExPose is that, instead of simply pooling already computed features, we also process the region of interest at higher resolution, to capture more subtle face and hand details. In related work, Chandran et al. [11] use a low resolution proxy image to detect facial landmarks and extract high resolution crops that are used to refine facial landmark predictions.

Expressive Human Estimation: Since expressive parametric models of the human body have only recently been introduced [38,67,72,96], there are only a few methods to reconstruct their parameters. Joo et al. [38] present an early approach, but rely on an extended multi-view setup. More recently, Xiang et al. [95], Pavlakos et al. [67] and Xu et al. [96] use a single image to recover Adam, SMPL-X and GHUM parameters respectively, using optimization-based approaches. This type of inference can be slow and may fail in the presence of noisy feature detections. In contrast, we present the first regression approach for expressive monocular capture and show that it is both more accurate and significantly faster than prior work.

3   Method

3.1   3D Body Representation

To represent the human body, we use SMPL-X [67], a generative model that captures shape variation, limb articulation and facial expressions across a human population. It is learned from a collection of registered 3D body, hand and face scans of people with different sizes, nationalities and genders. The shape, $\beta \in \mathbb{R}^{10}$, and expression, $\psi \in \mathbb{R}^{10}$, are described by 10 coefficients from the corresponding PCA spaces. The articulation of the limbs, the hands and the face is modeled by the pose vector $\theta \in \mathbb{R}^{J \times D}$, where D is the rotation representation dimension, e.g. $D = 3$ if we select axis-angles, which describes the relative rotations of the $J = 53$ major joints. These joints include 22 main body joints, 1 for the jaw, and 15 joints per hand for the fingers. SMPL-X is a differentiable function $M(\beta, \theta, \psi)$, that produces a 3D mesh $M = (V, F)$ for the human body, with $N = 10475$ vertices $V \in \mathbb{R}^{(N \times 3)}$ and triangular faces F. The surface of the articulated body is obtained by linear blend skinning driven by a rigged skeleton, defined by the above joints. Following the notation of [39] we denote posed joints with $X(\theta, \beta) \in \mathbb{R}^{J \times 3}$. The final set of SMPL-X parameters is the vector $\Theta = \{\beta, \theta, \psi\} \in \mathbb{R}^{338}$, as we choose to represent the pose parameters θ using the representation of Zhou et al. [103] with $D = 6$.

3.2   Body-Driven Attention

Instead of attempting to regress body, hand and face parameters from a low resolution image crop we design an attentive architecture that uses the structure of the body and the full resolution of the image I. Given a bounding box of the body, we extract an image I_b, using an affine transformation $T_b \in \mathbb{R}^{2 \times 3}$, from the high-res image I. The body crop I_b is fed to a neural network g, similar to [39], to produce a first set of SMPL-X parameters Θ_b and weak-perspective camera scale $s_b \in \mathbb{R}$ and translation $t_b \in \mathbb{R}^2$. After posing the model and recovering the posed joints X, we project them on the image:

$$x = s(\Pi(X) + t) \tag{1}$$

where Π is an orthographic projection. We then compute a bounding box for each hand and the face, from the corresponding subsets of projected 2D joints, x_h and x_f. Let $(x_{\min}, y_{\min})$ and $(x_{\max}, y_{\max})$ be the top left and bottom right points for a part, computed from the respective joints. The bounding box center is equal to $c = \left(\frac{x_{\min} + x_{\max}}{2}, \frac{y_{\min} + y_{\max}}{2} \right)$, and its size is $b_s = 2 \cdot \max(x_{\max} - x_{\min}, y_{\max} - y_{\min})$. Using these boxes, we compute affine transformations $T_h, T_f \in \mathbb{R}^{2 \times 3}$ to extract higher resolution hand and faces images using spatial transformers (ST) [33]:

$$I_h = \text{ST}(I; T_h), \quad I_f = \text{ST}(I; T_f). \tag{2}$$

The hand I_h and face I_f images are fed to a hand network h and a face network f, to refine the respective parameter predictions. Hand parameters θ_h include the orientation of the wrist θ^{wrist} and finger articulation θ^{fingers}, while face parameters contain the expression coefficients ψ_f and facial pose θ_f, which is just the rotation of the jaw. We refine the parameters from by body by predicting offsets for each of the parameters and condition the part specific networks on the corresponding body parameters:

$$[\Delta\theta^{\text{wrist}}, \Delta\theta^{\text{fingers}}] = h\left(I_h; \theta_b^{\text{wrist}}, \theta_b^{\text{fingers}}\right), \quad [\Delta\theta_f, \Delta\psi] = f\left(I_f; \theta_b^f, \psi_b\right) \quad (3)$$

where θ_b^{wrist}, $\theta_b^{\text{fingers}}$, θ_b^f, ψ_b are the wrist pose, finger pose, facial pose and expression predicted by $g(\cdot)$. The hand and head sub-networks also produce a set of weak-perspective camera parameters $\{s_h, t_h\}$, $\{s_f, t_f\}$ that align the predicted 3D meshes to their respective images I_h and I_f. The final hand and face predictions are then equal to:

$$\theta_h = [\theta^{\text{wrist}}, \theta^{\text{fingers}}] = \left[\theta_b^{\text{wrist}}, \theta_b^{\text{fingers}}\right] + [\Delta\theta_{\text{wrist}}, \Delta\theta_{\text{fingers}}] \quad (4)$$

$$[\psi, \theta_f] = \left[\psi_b, \theta_b^f\right] + [\Delta\psi, \Delta\theta_f]. \quad (5)$$

With this approach we can utilize the full resolution of the original image I to overcome the small pixel resolution of the hands and face in the body image I_b. Another significant advantage is that we are able to leverage hand- and face-only data to supplement the training of the hand and face sub-networks. A detailed visualization of the prediction process can be seen in Fig. 2. The loss function used to train the model is a combination of terms for the body, the hands and the face. We train the body network using a combination of a 2D re-projection loss, 3D joint errors and a loss on the parameters Θ, when available. All variables with a hat denote ground-truth quantities.

$$L = L_{\text{body}} + L_{\text{hand}} + L_{\text{face}} + L_h + L_f \quad (6)$$

$$L_{\text{body}} = L_{\text{reproj}} + L_{\text{3D Joints}} + L_{\text{SMPL-X}} \quad (7)$$

$$L_{\text{3D Joints}} + L_{\text{SMPL-X}} = \sum_{j=1}^{J}\left\|\hat{X}_j - X_j\right\|_1 + \left\|\{\hat{\beta}, \hat{\theta}, \hat{\psi}\} - \{\beta, \theta, \psi\}\right\|_2^2 \quad (8)$$

$$L_{\text{reproj}} = \sum_{j=1}^{J} v_j \left\|\hat{x}_j - x_j\right\|_1. \quad (9)$$

We use v_j as a binary variable denoting visibility of each of the J joints. The re-projection losses L_h and L_f are applied in the hand and face image coordinate space, using the affine transformations T_h, T_f. The reason for this extra penalty is that alignment errors in the 2D projection of the fingers or the facial landmarks have a much smaller magnitude compared to those of the main body joints when computed on the body image I_b

$$L_h = \sum_{j \in \text{Hand}} v_j \left\|T_h T_b^{-1}(\hat{x}_j - x_j)\right\|_1, \quad L_f = \sum_{j \in \text{Face}} v_j \left\|T_f T_b^{-1}(\hat{x}_j - x_j)\right\|_1. \quad (10)$$

 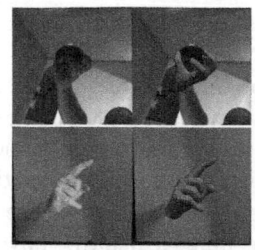 

Fig. 3. *Left:* Example curated expressive fit. *Middle:* Hands sampled from the FreiHAND dataset [105]. *Right:* Head training data produced by running RingNet [77] on FFHQ [41] and then fitting to 2D landmarks predicted by [9].

For the hand and head only data we also employ a re-projection loss, using only the subset of joints of each part, and parameter losses:

$$L_{\text{hand}} = L_{\text{reproj}} + \left\| \left\{ \hat{\beta}_h, \hat{\theta}_h \right\} - \left\{ \beta_h, \theta_h \right\} \right\|_2^2 \tag{11}$$

$$L_{\text{face}} = L_{\text{reproj}} + \left\| \left\{ \hat{\beta}_f, \hat{\theta}_f, \hat{\psi}_f \right\} - \left\{ \beta_f, \theta_f, \psi_f \right\} \right\|_2^2 . \tag{12}$$

3.3 Implementation Details

Datasets: We curate a dataset of SMPL-X fits by running vanilla SMPLify-X [67] on the LSP [35], LSP extended [36] and MPII [3] datasets. We then ask human annotators whether the resulting body mesh is plausible and agrees with the image and collect 32, 617 pairs of images and SMPL-X parameters. To augment the training data for the body we transfer the public fits of SPIN [46] from SMPL to SMPL-X, see Sup. Mat. Moreover, we use H3.6M [31] for additional 3D supervision for the body. For the hand sub-network we employ the hand-only data of FreiHAND [105]. For the face sub-network we create a pseudo ground-truth face dataset by running RingNet [77] on FFHQ [41]. The regressed FLAME [54] parameters are refined by fitting to facial landmarks [9] for better alignment with the image and more detailed expressions. Figure 3 shows samples from all training datasets.

Architecture: For the body network we extract features $\phi \in \mathbb{R}^{2048}$ with HRNet [84]. For the face and hand sub-networks we use a ResNet18 [28] to limit the computational cost. For all networks, rather than directly regressing the parameters Θ from ϕ, we follow the iterative process of [39]. We start from an initial estimate $\Theta_0 = \bar{\Theta}$, where $\bar{\Theta}$ represents the mean, which is concatenated to the features ϕ and fed to an MLP that predicts a residual $\Delta\Theta_1 = \text{MLP}([\phi, \Theta_0])$. The new parameter value is now equal to $\Theta_1 = \Theta_0 + \Delta\Theta_1$ and the whole process is repeated. As in [39], we iterate for $t = 3$ times. The entire pipeline is implemented in PyTorch [66]. For architecture details see Sup. Mat.

Data Pre-processing and Augmentation: We follow the pre-processing and augmentation protocol of [46] for all networks. To make the model robust to partially visible bodies we adopt the cropping augmentation of Joo et al. [37]. In addition, we augment the hand- and face-only images with random translations, as well as down-sampling by a random factor and then up-sampling back to the original resolution. The former simulates a misaligned body prediction, while the latter bridges the gap in image quality between the full-body and part-specific data. Hand and especially face images usually have a much higher resolution and quality compared to a crop extracted from a full-body image. To simulate body conditioning for the hand- and head-only data we add random noise to the initial point of the iterative regressor. For the hands we replace the default finger pose with a random rotation r_{finger} sampled from the PCA pose space of MANO. For the head we replace the default jaw rotation $\bar{\boldsymbol{\theta}}_f$ with a random rotation of $r_{\text{f}} \sim \mathcal{U}\left(0, 45\right)$ degrees around the x-axis. For both parts, we replace their global rotation with a random rotation with angle $r_{\text{global}} \sim \mathcal{U}\left(r_{\text{min}}, r_{\text{max}}\right)$ and the same axis of rotation as the corresponding ground-truth. We set $\left(r_{\text{min}}, r_{\text{max}}\right)_{\text{hand}}$ to $(-90, 90)$ and $\left(r_{\text{min}}, r_{\text{max}}\right)_{\text{face}}$ to $(-45, 45)$ degrees. The default mean shape is replaced with a random vector $\boldsymbol{\beta} \sim \mathcal{N}\left(\mathbf{0}, I\right), I \in \mathbb{R}^{10 \times 10}$ and the default neutral expression with a random expression $\boldsymbol{\psi} \sim \mathcal{N}(0, \mathcal{I})$. Some visualizations of the different types of data augmentation can be found in Sup. Mat.

Training: We first pre-train the body, hand and face networks separately, using ADAM [43], on the respective part-only datasets. We then fine-tune all networks jointly on the union of all training data, following Sect. 3.2, letting the network make even better use of the conditioning (see Sect. 4 and Table 2). Please note that for this fine-tuning, our new dataset of curated SMPL-X fits plays an instrumental role. Our exact hyper-parameters are included in the released training code.

4   Experiments

4.1   Evaluation Datasets

We evaluate on several datasets:

Expressive Hands and Faces (EHF). [67] consists of 100 RGB images paired with SMPL-X registrations to synchronized 3D scans. It contains a single subject performing a variety of interesting body poses, hand gestures and facial expressions. We use it to evaluate our whole-body predictions.

3D Poses in the Wild (3DPW). [60] consists of in-the-wild RGB video sequences annotated with 3D SMPL poses. It contains several actors performing various motions, in both indoor and outdoor environments. It is captured using a single RGB camera and IMUs mounted on the subjects. We use it to evaluate our predictions for the main body area, excluding the head and hands.

FreiHAND. [105] is a multi-view RGB hand dataset that contains 3D MANO hand pose and shape annotations. The ground-truth for the test data is held-out and evaluation is performed by submitting the estimated hand meshes to an online server. We use it to evaluate our hand sub-network predictions.

Stirling/ESRC 3D. [15] consists of facial RGB images with ground-truth 3D face scans. It contains 2000 neutral faces images, namely 656 high-quality (HQ) ones and 1344 low-quality (LQ) ones. We use it to evaluate our face sub-network following the protocol of [15].

4.2 Evaluation Metrics

We employ several common metrics below. We report errors with and without rigid alignment to the ground-truth. A "PA" prefix denotes that the metric measures error after solving for rotation, scale and translation using Procrustes Alignment.

To compare with ground-truth 3D skeletons, we use the **Mean Per-Joint Position Error (MPJPE)**. For this, we first compute the 14 LSP-common joints, by applying a linear joint regressor on the ground-truth and estimated meshes, and then compute their mean Euclidean distance.

For comparing to ground-truth meshes, we use the **Vertex-to-Vertex (V2V)** error, i.e. the mean distance between the ground-truth and predicted mesh vertices. This is appropriate when the predicted and ground-truth meshes have the same topology, e.g. SMPL-X for our overall network, MANO for our hand and FLAME for our face sub-network. For a fair comparison to methods that predict SMPL instead of SMPL-X, like [39,46], we also report V2V only on the main-body, i.e. without the hands and the head, as SMPL and SMPL-X share common topology for this subset of vertices.

For comparing to approaches that output meshes with different topology, like MTC [95] that uses the Adam model and not SMPL-X, we cannot use V2V. Instead, we compute the (mesh-to-mesh) **point-to-surface** (PtS) distance from the ground-truth mesh, as a common reference, to the estimated mesh.

For evaluation on datasets that include ground-truth scans, we compute a **scan-to-mesh** version of the above **point-to-surface** distance, namely from the ground-truth scan points to the estimated mesh surface. We use this for the face dataset of [15] to evaluate the head estimation of our face sub-network.

Finally, for the FreiHAND dataset [105] we report all metrics returned by their evaluation server. Apart from PA-MPJPE and PA-V2V described above, we also report the **F-score** [44].

4.3 Quantitative and Qualitative Experiments

First, we evaluate our approach on the 3DPW dataset that includes SMPL ground-truth meshes. Although this does not include ground-truth hands and faces, it is ideal for comparing main-body reconstruction against state-of-the-art approaches, namely HMR [39] and SPIN [46]. Table 1 presents the results, and shows that ExPose outperforms HMR and is on par with the more recent SPIN. This confirms that ExPose provides a solid foundation upon which to build detailed reconstruction for the hands and face.

We then evaluate on the EHF dataset that includes high-quality SMPL-X ground truth. This allows evaluation for the more challenging task of holistic

Table 1. Comparison on the 3DPW dataset [60] with two state-of-the-art approaches for SMPL regression, HMR [39] and SPIN [46]. The numbers are per-joint and per-vertex errors (in mm) for the body part of SMPL. ExPose outperforms HMR and is on par with SPIN, while also being able to capture details for the hands and the face.

Method	PA-MPJPE (mm)	MPJPE (mm)	PA-Body V2V (mm)
HMR [39]	81.3	130	65.2
SPIN [46]	59.2	96.9	53.0
ExPose	60.7	93.4	55.6

Table 2. Ablative study on the EHF dataset. The results are vertex-to-vertex errors expressed in mm for the different parts (i.e., all vertices, body vertices, hand vertices and head vertices). We report results for the initial body network applied on the low resolution (first row), for a version that uses the body-driven attention to estimate hands and faces (second row), and for the final regressor that jointly fine-tunes the body, hands and face sub-networks.

Networks	Attention on high-res. crops	End-to-end fine-tuning	PA-V2V (mm)			
			All	Body	L/R hand	Face
Body only	✗	✗	57.3	55.9	14.3/14.8	5.8
Body & Hand & Face	✓	✗	56.4	52.6	14.1/13.9	6.0
Body & Hand & Face	✓	✓	54.5	52.6	13.1/12.5	5.8

body reconstruction, including expressive hands and face. Table 2 presents an ablation study for our main components. In the first row, we see that the initial body network, that uses a low-resolution body-crop image as input, performs well for body reconstruction but makes mistakes with the hands. The next two rows add *body-driven attention*; they use the body network prediction to locate the hands and face, and then redirect the attention in the original image, crop higher-resolution image patches for them, and feed them to the respective hand and face sub-networks to refine their predictions, while initializing/conditioning their predictions. This conditioning can take place in two ways. The second row shows a naive combination using independently trained sub-networks. This fails to significantly improve the results, since there is a domain gap between images of face- or hand-only [15,105] training datasets and hand/head image crops from full-body [3,35,36] training datasets; the former tend to be of higher resolution and better image quality. Please note that this is similar to [10], but extended for 3D mesh regression. In the third row, the entire pipeline is fine-tuned end-to-end. This results in a boost in quantitative performance, improving mainly hand articulation (best overall performance).

Table 3. Comparison with the state-of-the-art approaches on the EHF dataset. The metrics are defined in Sect. 4.2. For SMPLify-X, the results reported in [67] (first row) are generated using ground truth camera parameters, so they are not directly comparable with the other approaches. MTC running time includes calculation of part orientation fields and Adam fitting. The regression based methods require extra processing to obtain input human bounding box. For example, if one uses Mask-RCNN [27] with a ResNet50-FPN [56] from Detectron2 [94] the complete running time of these methods increases by 43 ms. All timings were done with a Intel Xeon W-2123 3.60 GHz CPU and a Quadro P5000 GPU and are for estimating one person.

Method	Time (s)	PA-V2V (mm)				PA MPJPE (mm)		PA PtS (mm)	
		All	Body	L/R hand	Face	Body Joints	L/R hand	Mean	Median
SMPLify-X' [67]	40–60	**52.9**	56.37	**11.4/12.6**	**5.3**	73.5	**11.9/13.2**	**28.9**	18.1
HMR [39]	0.06	N/A	67.2	N/A	N/A	82.0	N/A	34.5	21.5
SPIN [46]	0.01	N/A	60.6	N/A	N/A	102.9	N/A	40.8	28.7
SMPLify-X [67]	40–60	65.3	75.4	11.6/12.9	6.3	87.6	12.2/13.5	36.8	23.0
MTC [95]	20	67.2	N/A	N/A	N/A	107.8	16.3/17.0	41.3	29.0
ExPose (Ours)	0.16	54.5	**52.6**	13.1/**12.5**	5.8	**62.8**	13.5/**12.7**	**28.9**	**18.0**

Next, we compare to state-of-the-art approaches again on the EHF dataset. First, we compare against the most relevant baseline, SMPLify-X [67], which estimates SMPL-X using an optimization approach. Second, we compare against Monocular Total Capture (MTC) [95], which estimates expressive 3D humans using the Adam model. Note that we use their publicly available implementation, which does not include an expressive face model. Third, we compare against HMR [39] and SPIN [46], which estimate SMPL bodies, therefore we perform body-only evaluation, excluding the hand and head regions. We summarize all evaluations in Table 3. We find that ExPose outperforms the other baselines, both in terms of full expressive human reconstruction and body-only reconstruction. SMPLify-X performs a bit better locally, i.e. for the hands and face, but the full body pose can be inaccurate, mainly due to errors in Open-Pose detections. In contrast, our regression-based approach is a bit less accurate locally for the hands and face, but overall it is more robust than SMPLify-X. The two approaches could be combined, with ExPose replacing the heuristic initialization of SMPLify-X with its more robust estimation; we speculate that this would improve both the accuracy and the convergence speed of SMPLify-X. Furthermore, ExPose outperforms MTC across all metrics. Finally, it is approximately two orders of magnitude faster than both SMPLify-X and MTC, which are both optimization-based approaches.

We also evaluate each sub-network on the corresponding part-only datasets. For the hands we evaluate on the FreiHAND dataset [105], and for faces on the Stirling/ESRC 3D dataset [15]. Table 4 summarizes all evaluations. The part subnetworks of ExPose match or come close to the performance of state-of-the-art methods. We expect that using a deeper backbone, e.g. a ResNet50, would be beneficial, but at a higher computational cost.

Table 4. We evaluate our final hand sub-network on the FreiHAND dataset [105] and the face sub-network on the test dataset of Feng et al. [15]. The final part networks are on par with existing methods, despite using a shallower backbone, i.e. a ResNet-18 vs a Resnet-50.

FreiHAND	PA-MPJPE (mm)	PA-V2V (mm)	F@5 mm	F@15 mm
MANO CNN [105]	11.0	10.9	0.516	0.934
ExPose hand sub-network h	12.2	11.8	0.484	0.918
Stirling3D Dataset LQ/HQ	Mean (mm)	Median (mm)	Standard Deviation (mm)	
RingNet [77]	2.08/2.02	1.63/1.58	1.79/1.69	
ExPose face sub-network f	2.27/2.42	1.76/1.91	1.97/2.03	

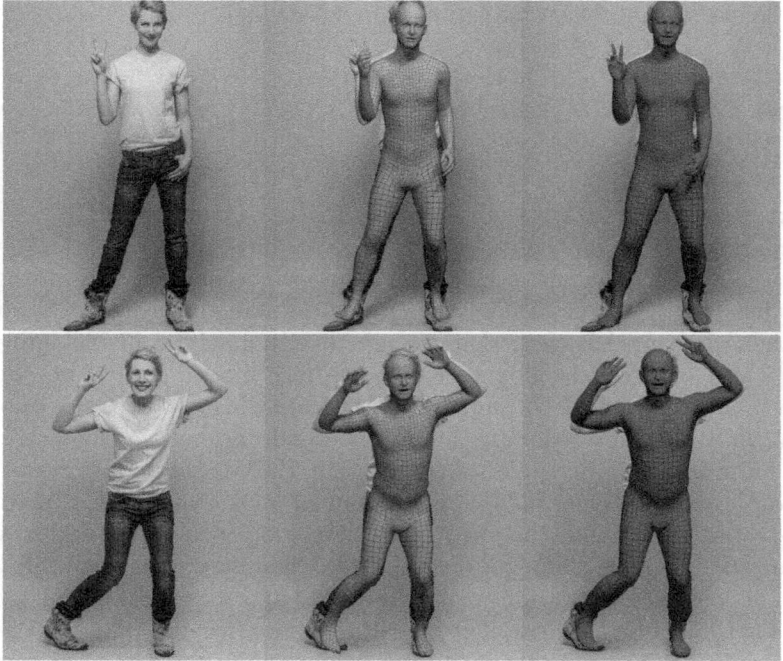

Fig. 4. *Left:* The input image. *Middle:* Naive regression from a single body image fails to capture detailed finger articulation and facial expressions. *Right:* ExPose is able to recover these details, thanks to its attention mechanism, and produces results of similar quality as SMPLify-X, while being 200× times faster, as seen in Table 3.

The quantitative findings of Table 2 are reflected in qualitative results. In Fig. 4, we compare our final results with the initial baseline that regresses all SMPL-X parameters directly from a low-resolution image without any attention (first row in Table 2). We observe that our body-attention mechanism gives a clear improvement for the hand and the face area. Figure 5 contains ExPose

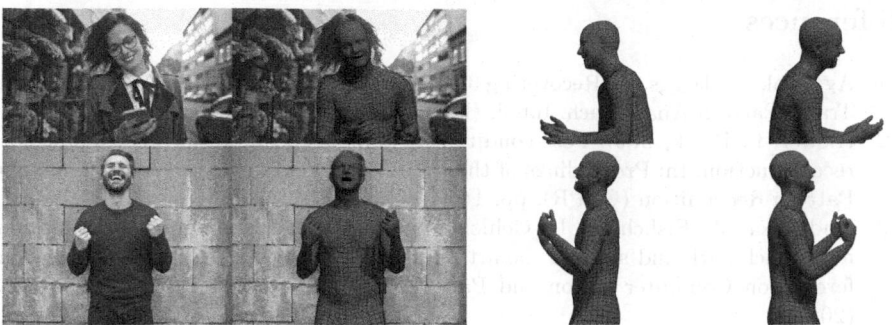

Fig. 5. Input image, ExPose predictions overlayed on the image and renderings from different viewpoints. ExPose is able to recover detailed hands and faces thanks to its attention mechanism, and produces results of similar quality as SMPLify-X, while being 200× times faster.

reconstructions, seen from multiple views, where we again see the higher level of detail offered by our method. For more qualitative results, see Sup. Mat.

5 Conclusion

In this paper, we present a regression approach for holistic expressive body reconstruction. Considering the different scale of the individual parts and the limited training data, we identify that the naive approach of regressing a holistic reconstruction from a low-resolution body image misses fine details in the hands and face. To improve our regression approach, we investigate a body-driven attention scheme. This results in consistently better reconstructions. Although the pure optimization-based approach [67] recovers the finer details, it is too slow to be practical. ExPose provides competitive results, while more than two orders of magnitude faster than [67]. Eventually the two approaches could be combined effectively, as in [46]. Considering the level of the accuracy and the speed of our approach, we believe it should be a valuable tool and enable many applications that require expressive human pose information. Future work will extend the inference to multiple humans [34,98,99] and video sequences [40,45]. The rich body representation will also accelerate research on human-scene [25,79] interaction, human-object [55,88] interaction, and person-person interaction [16, 52]. We also plan to improve body shape estimation and the pixel-level alignment to the image.

Acknowledgements. We thank Haiwen Feng for the FLAME fits, Nikos Kolotouros, Muhammed Kocabas and Nikos Athanasiou for helpful discussions, Mason Landry and Valerie Callaghan for video voiceovers. This research was partially supported by the Max Planck ETH Center for Learning Systems. *Disclaimer:* MJB has received research gift funds from Intel, Nvidia, Adobe, Facebook, and Amazon. While MJB is a part-time employee of Amazon, his research was performed solely at, and funded solely by, MPI. MJB has financial interests in Amazon and Meshcapade GmbH.

References

1. Agarwal, A., Triggs, B.: Recovering 3D human pose from monocular images. IEEE Trans. Pattern Anal. Mach. Intell. (PAMI) **28**(1), 44–58 (2006)
2. Akhter, I., Black, M.J.: Pose-conditioned joint angle limits for 3D human pose reconstruction. In: Proceedings of the IEEE Conference on Computer Vision and Pattern Recognition (CVPR), pp. 1446–1455 (2015)
3. Andriluka, M., Pishchulin, L., Gehler, P., Schiele, B.: 2D human pose estimation: new benchmark and state of the art analysis. In: Proceedings of the IEEE Conference on Computer Vision and Pattern Recognition (CVPR), pp. 3686–3693 (2014)
4. Anguelov, D., Srinivasan, P., Koller, D., Thrun, S., Rodgers, J., Davis, J.: SCAPE: shape completion and animation of people. ACM Trans. Graph. (TOG) **24**(3), 408–416 (2005). Proceedings of ACM SIGGRAPH
5. Baek, S., Kim, K.I., Kim, T.K.: Pushing the envelope for RGB-based dense 3D hand pose estimation via neural rendering. In: Proceedings of the IEEE Conference on Computer Vision and Pattern Recognition (CVPR), pp. 1067–1076 (2019)
6. Blanz, V., Vetter, T.: A morphable model for the synthesis of 3D faces. In: Proceedings of ACM SIGGRAPH, pp. 187–194 (1999)
7. Bogo, F., Kanazawa, A., Lassner, C., Gehler, P., Romero, J., Black, M.J.: Keep it SMPL: automatic estimation of 3D human pose and shape from a single image. In: Leibe, B., Matas, J., Sebe, N., Welling, M. (eds.) ECCV 2016. LNCS, vol. 9909, pp. 561–578. Springer, Cham (2016). https://doi.org/10.1007/978-3-319-46454-1_34
8. Boukhayma, A., de Bem, R., Torr, P.H.: 3D hand shape and pose from images in the wild. In: Proceedings of the IEEE Conference on Computer Vision and Pattern Recognition (CVPR), pp. 10835–10844 (2019)
9. Bulat, A., Tzimiropoulos, G.: How far are we from solving the 2D & 3D face alignment problem? (and a dataset of 230,000 3D facial landmarks). In: Proceedings of the IEEE International Conference on Computer Vision (ICCV), pp. 1021–1030 (2017)
10. Cao, Z., Hidalgo, G., Simon, T., Wei, S.E., Sheikh, Y.: OpenPose: realtime multi-person 2D pose estimation using part affinity fields. IEEE Trans. Pattern Anal. Mach. Intell. (PAMI) (2019)
11. Chandran, P., Bradley, D., Gross, M., Beeler, T.: Attention-driven cropping for very high resolution facial landmark detection. In: Proceedings of the IEEE Conference on Computer Vision and Pattern Recognition (CVPR), pp. 5861–5870 (2020)
12. Chu, X., Yang, W., Ouyang, W., Ma, C., Yuille, A.L., Wang, X.: Multi-context attention for human pose estimation. In: Proceedings of the IEEE Conference on Computer Vision and Pattern Recognition (CVPR), pp. 5669–5678 (2017)
13. Egger, B., et al.: 3D morphable face models-past, present and future. ACM Trans. Graph. (TOG) **39**(5), 1–38 (2020)
14. Erol, A., Bebis, G., Nicolescu, M., Boyle, R.D., Twombly, X.: Vision-based hand pose estimation: a review. Comput. Vis. Image Underst. (CVIU) **108**(1–2), 52–73 (2007)
15. Feng, Z.H., et al.: Evaluation of dense 3D reconstruction from 2D face images in the wild. In: International Conference on Automatic Face & Gesture Recognition (FG), pp. 780–786 (2018)

16. Fieraru, M., Zanfir, M., Oneata, E., Popa, A.I., Olaru, V., Sminchisescu, C.: Three-dimensional reconstruction of human interactions. In: Proceedings of the IEEE Conference on Computer Vision and Pattern Recognition (CVPR), pp. 7214–7223 (2020)

17. Gabeur, V., Franco, J.S., Martin, X., Schmid, C., Rogez, G.: Moulding humans: non-parametric 3D human shape estimation from single images. In: Proceedings of the IEEE International Conference on Computer Vision (ICCV), pp. 2232–2241 (2019)

18. Gavrila, D.M.: The visual analysis of human movement: a survey. Comput. Vis. Image Underst. (CVIU) **73**(1), 82–98 (1999)

19. Ge, L., et al.: 3D hand shape and pose estimation from a single RGB image. In: Proceedings of the IEEE Conference on Computer Vision and Pattern Recognition (CVPR), pp. 10825–10834 (2019)

20. Grauman, K., Shakhnarovich, G., Darrell, T.: Inferring 3D structure with a statistical image-based shape model. In: Proceedings of the IEEE International Conference on Computer Vision (ICCV), pp. 641 647 (2003)

21. Guan, P., Weiss, A., Balan, A., Black, M.J.: Estimating human shape and pose from a single image. In: Proceedings of the IEEE International Conference on Computer Vision (ICCV), pp. 1381–1388 (2009)

22. Guler, R.A., Kokkinos, I.: HoloPose: holistic 3D human reconstruction in-the-wild. In: Proceedings of the IEEE Conference on Computer Vision and Pattern Recognition (CVPR), pp. 10876–10886 (2019)

23. Güler, R.A., Neverova, N., Kokkinos, I.: DensePose: dense human pose estimation in the wild. In: Proceedings of the IEEE Conference on Computer Vision and Pattern Recognition (CVPR), pp. 7297–7306 (2018)

24. Hampali, S., Rad, M., Oberweger, M., Lepetit, V.: HOnnotate: a method for 3D annotation of hand and object poses. In: Proceedings of the IEEE Conference on Computer Vision and Pattern Recognition (CVPR), pp. 3196–3206 (2020)

25. Hassan, M., Choutas, V., Tzionas, D., Black, M.J.: Resolving 3D human pose ambiguities with 3D scene constraints. In: Proceedings of the IEEE International Conference on Computer Vision (ICCV), pp. 2282–2292 (2019)

26. Hasson, Y., et al.: Learning joint reconstruction of hands and manipulated objects. In: Proceedings of the IEEE Conference on Computer Vision and Pattern Recognition (CVPR), pp. 11807 11816 (2019)

27. He, K., Gkioxari, G., Dollar, P., Girshick, R.: Mask R-CNN. In: Proceedings of the IEEE International Conference on Computer Vision (ICCV), pp. 2980–2988 (2017)

28. He, K., Zhang, X., Ren, S., Sun, J.: Deep residual learning for image recognition. In: Proceedings of the IEEE Conference on Computer Vision and Pattern Recognition (CVPR), pp. 770–778 (2016)

29. Hidalgo, G., et al.: Single-network whole-body pose estimation. In: Proceedings of the IEEE International Conference on Computer Vision (ICCV), pp. 6981–6990 (2019)

30. Huang, Y., et al.: Towards accurate marker-less human shape and pose estimation over time. In: International Conference on 3D Vision (3DV), pp. 421–430 (2017)

31. Ionescu, C., Papava, D., Olaru, V., Sminchisescu, C.: Human3.6M: large scale datasets and predictive methods for 3D human sensing in natural environments. IEEE Trans. Pattern Anal. Mach. Intell. (PAMI) **36**(7), 1325–1339 (2014)

32. Iqbal, U., Molchanov, P., Breuel, T., Gall, J., Kautz, J.: Hand pose estimation via latent 2.5D heatmap regression. In: Ferrari, V., Hebert, M., Sminchisescu, C., Weiss, Y. (eds.) ECCV 2018. LNCS, vol. 11215, pp. 125–143. Springer, Cham (2018). https://doi.org/10.1007/978-3-030-01252-6_8
33. Jaderberg, M., Simonyan, K., Zisserman, A., Kavukcuoglu, K.: Spatial transformer networks. In: Advances in Neural Information Processing Systems (NIPS), pp. 2017–2025 (2015)
34. Jiang, W., Kolotouros, N., Pavlakos, G., Zhou, X., Daniilidis, K.: Coherent reconstruction of multiple humans from a single image. In: Proceedings of the IEEE Conference on Computer Vision and Pattern Recognition (CVPR), pp. 5579–5588 (2020)
35. Johnson, S., Everingham, M.: Clustered pose and nonlinear appearance models for human pose estimation. In: Proceedings of the British Machine Vision Conference (BMVC), pp. 12.1–12.11 (2010)
36. Johnson, S., Everingham, M.: Learning effective human pose estimation from inaccurate annotation. In: Proceedings of the IEEE Conference on Computer Vision and Pattern Recognition (CVPR), pp. 1465–1472 (2011)
37. Joo, H., Neverova, N., Vedaldi, A.: Exemplar fine-tuning for 3D human pose fitting towards in-the-wild 3D human pose estimation. arXiv preprint arXiv:2004.03686 (2020)
38. Joo, H., Simon, T., Sheikh, Y.: Total capture: a 3D deformation model for tracking faces, hands, and bodies. In: Proceedings of the IEEE Conference on Computer Vision and Pattern Recognition (CVPR), pp. 8320–8329 (2018)
39. Kanazawa, A., Black, M.J., Jacobs, D.W., Malik, J.: End-to-end recovery of human shape and pose. In: Proceedings of the IEEE Conference on Computer Vision and Pattern Recognition (CVPR), pp. 7122–7131 (2018)
40. Kanazawa, A., Zhang, J.Y., Felsen, P., Malik, J.: Learning 3D human dynamics from video. In: Proceedings of the IEEE Conference on Computer Vision and Pattern Recognition (CVPR), pp. 5607–5616 (2019)
41. Karras, T., Laine, S., Aila, T.: A style-based generator architecture for generative adversarial networks. In: Proceedings of the IEEE Conference on Computer Vision and Pattern Recognition (CVPR), pp. 4396–4405 (2019)
42. Khamis, S., Taylor, J., Shotton, J., Keskin, C., Izadi, S., Fitzgibbon, A.: Learning an efficient model of hand shape variation from depth images. In: Proceedings of the IEEE Conference on Computer Vision and Pattern Recognition (CVPR), pp. 2540–2548 (2015)
43. Kingma, D.P., Ba, J.: Adam: a method for stochastic optimization. In: International Conference on Learning Representations (ICLR) (2015)
44. Knapitsch, A., Park, J., Zhou, Q.Y., Koltun, V.: Tanks and temples: benchmarking large-scale scene reconstruction. ACM Trans. Graph. (ToG) **36**(4), 1–13 (2017)
45. Kocabas, M., Athanasiou, N., Black, M.J.: VIBE: video inference for human body pose and shape estimation. In: Proceedings of the IEEE Conference on Computer Vision and Pattern Recognition (CVPR), pp. 5253–5263 (2020)
46. Kolotouros, N., Pavlakos, G., Black, M.J., Daniilidis, K.: Learning to reconstruct 3D human pose and shape via model-fitting in the loop. In: Proceedings of the IEEE International Conference on Computer Vision (ICCV), pp. 2252–2261 (2019)
47. Kolotouros, N., Pavlakos, G., Daniilidis, K.: Convolutional mesh regression for single-image human shape reconstruction. In: Proceedings of the IEEE Conference on Computer Vision and Pattern Recognition (CVPR), pp. 4496–4505 (2019)

48. Krizhevsky, A., Sutskever, I., Hinton, G.E.: ImageNet classification with deep convolutional neural networks. In: Advances in Neural Information Processing Systems (NIPS), pp. 1097–1105 (2012)
49. Kulon, D., Guler, R.A., Kokkinos, I., Bronstein, M.M., Zafeiriou, S.: Weakly-supervised mesh-convolutional hand reconstruction in the wild. In: Proceedings of the IEEE Conference on Computer Vision and Pattern Recognition (CVPR), pp. 4990–5000 (2020)
50. Kulon, D., Wang, H., Güler, R.A., Bronstein, M.M., Zafeiriou, S.: Single image 3D hand reconstruction with mesh convolutions. In: Proceedings of the British Machine Vision Conference (BMVC) (2019)
51. Lee, H.J., Chen, Z.: Determination of 3D human body postures from a single view. Comput. Vis. Graph. Image Process. **30**(2), 148–168 (1985)
52. Li, K., Mao, Y., Liu, Y., Shao, R., Liu, Y.: Full-body motion capture for multiple closely interacting persons. Graph. Models **110**, 101072 (2020)
53. Li, S., Zhang, W., Chan, A.B.: Maximum-margin structured learning with deep networks for 3D human pose estimation. In: Proceedings of the IEEE International Conference on Computer Vision (ICCV), pp. 2848–2856 (2015)
54. Li, T., Bolkart, T., Black, M.J., Li, H., Romero, J.: Learning a model of facial shape and expression from 4D scans. ACM Trans. Graph. (ToG) **36**(6), 194:1–194:17 (2017)
55. Li, Z., Sedlar, J., Carpentier, J., Laptev, I., Mansard, N., Sivic, J.: Estimating 3D motion and forces of person-object interactions from monocular video. In: Proceedings of the IEEE Conference on Computer Vision and Pattern Recognition (CVPR), pp. 8632–8641 (2019)
56. Lin, T.Y., Dollar, P., Girshick, R., He, K., Hariharan, B., Belongie, S.: Feature pyramid networks for object detection. In: Proceedings of the IEEE Conference on Computer Vision and Pattern Recognition (CVPR), pp. 936–944 (2017)
57. Lin, T.-Y., et al.: Microsoft COCO: common objects in context. In: Fleet, D., Pajdla, T., Schiele, B., Tuytelaars, T. (eds.) ECCV 2014. LNCS, vol. 8693, pp. 740–755. Springer, Cham (2014). https://doi.org/10.1007/978-3-319-10602-1_48
58. Liu, Z., Luo, P., Wang, X., Tang, X.: Deep learning face attributes in the wild. In: Proceedings of the IEEE International Conference on Computer Vision (ICCV), pp. 3730–3738 (2015)
59. Loper, M., Mahmood, N., Romero, J., Pons-Moll, G., Black, M.J.: SMPL: a skinned multi-person linear model. ACM Trans. Graph. (TOG) **34**(6), 248:1–248:16 (2015). Proceedings of ACM SIGGRAPH Asia
60. von Marcard, T., Henschel, R., Black, M.J., Rosenhahn, B., Pons-Moll, G.: Recovering accurate 3D human pose in the wild using IMUs and a moving camera. In: Ferrari, V., Hebert, M., Sminchisescu, C., Weiss, Y. (eds.) ECCV 2018. LNCS, vol. 11214, pp. 614–631. Springer, Cham (2018). https://doi.org/10.1007/978-3-030-01249-6_37
61. Martinez, J., Hossain, R., Romero, J., Little, J.J.: A simple yet effective baseline for 3D human pose estimation. In: Proceedings of the IEEE International Conference on Computer Vision (ICCV), pp. 2659–2668 (2017)
62. Moeslund, T.B., Hilton, A., Krüger, V.: A survey of advances in vision-based human motion capture and analysis. Comput. Vis. Image Underst. (CVIU) **104**(2), 90–126 (2006)
63. Mueller, F., et al.: GANerated hands for real-time 3D hand tracking from monocular RGB. In: Proceedings of the IEEE Conference on Computer Vision and Pattern Recognition (CVPR), pp. 49–59 (2018)

64. Newell, A., Yang, K., Deng, J.: Stacked hourglass networks for human pose estimation. In: Leibe, B., Matas, J., Sebe, N., Welling, M. (eds.) ECCV 2016. LNCS, vol. 9912, pp. 483–499. Springer, Cham (2016). https://doi.org/10.1007/978-3-319-46484-8_29

65. Omran, M., Lassner, C., Pons-Moll, G., Gehler, P.V., Schiele, B.: Neural body fitting: unifying deep learning and model based human pose and shape estimation. In: International Conference on 3D Vision (3DV), pp. 484–494 (2018)

66. Paszke, A., et al.: PyTorch: an imperative style, high-performance deep learning library. In: Advances in Neural Information Processing Systems (NeurIPS), pp. 8024–8035 (2019)

67. Pavlakos, G., et al.: Expressive body capture: 3D hands, face, and body from a single image. In: Proceedings of the IEEE Conference on Computer Vision and Pattern Recognition (CVPR), pp. 10967–10977 (2019)

68. Pavlakos, G., Zhou, X., Derpanis, K.G., Daniilidis, K.: Coarse-to-fine volumetric prediction for single-image 3D human pose. In: Proceedings of the IEEE Conference on Computer Vision and Pattern Recognition (CVPR), pp. 1263–1272 (2017)

69. Pavlakos, G., Zhu, L., Zhou, X., Daniilidis, K.: Learning to estimate 3D human pose and shape from a single color image. In: Proceedings of the IEEE Conference on Computer Vision and Pattern Recognition (CVPR), pp. 459–468 (2018)

70. Robinette, K.M., et al.: Civilian American and European Surface Anthropometry Resource (CAESAR) final report. Technical report. AFRL-HE-WP-TR-2002-0169, US Air Force Research Laboratory (2002)

71. Rogez, G., Schmid, C.: MoCap-guided data augmentation for 3D pose estimation in the wild. In: Advances in Neural Information Processing Systems (NIPS), pp. 3108–3116 (2016)

72. Romero, J., Tzionas, D., Black, M.J.: Embodied hands: modeling and capturing hands and bodies together. ACM Trans. Graph. (TOG) **36**(6), 245:1–245:17 (2017). Proceedings of ACM SIGGRAPH Asia

73. Rong, Y., Liu, Z., Li, C., Cao, K., Loy, C.C.: Delving deep into hybrid annotations for 3D human recovery in the wild. In: Proceedings of the IEEE International Conference on Computer Vision (ICCV), pp. 5339–5347 (2019)

74. Rueegg, N., Lassner, C., Black, M.J., Schindler, K.: Chained representation cycling: learning to estimate 3D human pose and shape by cycling between representations. In: AAAI Conference on Artificial Intelligence (AAAI) (2020)

75. Saito, S., Huang, Z., Natsume, R., Morishima, S., Kanazawa, A., Li, H.: PIFu: pixel-aligned implicit function for high-resolution clothed human digitization. In: Proceedings of the IEEE International Conference on Computer Vision (ICCV), pp. 2304–2314 (2019)

76. Saito, S., Simon, T., Saragih, J., Joo, H.: PIFuHD: multi-level pixel-aligned implicit function for high-resolution 3D human digitization. In: Proceedings of the IEEE Conference on Computer Vision and Pattern Recognition (CVPR), pp. 84–93 (2020)

77. Sanyal, S., Bolkart, T., Feng, H., Black, M.J.: Learning to regress 3D face shape and expression from an image without 3D supervision. In: Proceedings of the IEEE Conference on Computer Vision and Pattern Recognition (CVPR), pp. 7763–7772 (2019)

78. Sarafianos, N., Boteanu, B., Ionescu, B., Kakadiaris, I.A.: 3D human pose estimation: a review of the literature and analysis of covariates. Comput. Vis. Image Underst. (CVIU) **152**, 1–20 (2016)

79. Savva, M., Chang, A.X., Hanrahan, P., Fisher, M., Nießner, M.: PiGraphs: learning interaction snapshots from observations. ACM Trans. Graph. (TOG) **35**(4), 1–12 (2016)
80. Sigal, L., Balan, A., Black, M.J.: HumanEva: synchronized video and motion capture dataset and baseline algorithm for evaluation of articulated human motion. Int. J. Comput. Vis. (IJCV) **87**(1), 4–27 (2010)
81. Sigal, L., Black, M.J.: Predicting 3D people from 2D pictures. In: Perales, F.J., Fisher, R.B. (eds.) AMDO 2006. LNCS, vol. 4069, pp. 185–195. Springer, Heidelberg (2006). https://doi.org/10.1007/11789239_19
82. Simon, T., Joo, H., Matthews, I., Sheikh, Y.: Hand keypoint detection in single images using multiview bootstrapping. In: Proceedings of the IEEE Conference on Computer Vision and Pattern Recognition (CVPR), pp. 4645–4653 (2017)
83. Smith, D., Loper, M., Hu, X., Mavroidis, P., Romero, J.: FACSIMILE: fast and accurate scans from an image in less than a second. In: Proceedings of the IEEE International Conference on Computer Vision (ICCV), pp. 5329–5338 (2019)
84. Sun, K., Xiao, B., Liu, D., Wang, J.: Deep high-resolution representation learning for human pose estimation. In: Proceedings of the IEEE Conference on Computer Vision and Pattern Recognition (CVPR), pp. 5686–5696 (2019)
85. Sun, X., Shang, J., Liang, S., Wei, Y.: Compositional human pose regression. In: Proceedings of the IEEE International Conference on Computer Vision (ICCV), pp. 2621–2630 (2017)
86. Sun, X., Xiao, B., Wei, F., Liang, S., Wei, Y.: Integral human pose regression. In: Ferrari, V., Hebert, M., Sminchisescu, C., Weiss, Y. (eds.) ECCV 2018. LNCS, vol. 11210, pp. 536–553. Springer, Cham (2018). https://doi.org/10.1007/978-3-030-01231-1_33
87. Supančič III, J.S., Rogez, G., Yang, Y., Shotton, J., Ramanan, D.: Depth-based hand pose estimation: data, methods, and challenges. In: Proceedings of the IEEE International Conference on Computer Vision (ICCV), pp. 1868–1876 (2015)
88. Taheri, O., Ghorbani, N., Black, M.J., Tzionas, D.: GRAB: a dataset of whole-body human grasping of objects. In: European Conference on Computer Vision (ECCV) (2020)
89. Tekin, B., Bogo, F., Pollefeys, M.: H+O: unified egocentric recognition of 3D hand-object poses and interactions. In: Proceedings of the IEEE Conference on Computer Vision and Pattern Recognition (CVPR), pp. 4506–4515 (2019)
90. Tekin, B., Katircioglu, I., Salzmann, M., Lepetit, V., Fua, P.: Structured prediction of 3D human pose with deep neural networks. In: Proceedings of the British Machine Vision Conference (BMVC), pp. 130.1–130.11 (2016)
91. Tome, D., Russell, C., Agapito, L.: Lifting from the deep: convolutional 3D pose estimation from a single image. In: Proceedings of the IEEE Conference on Computer Vision and Pattern Recognition (CVPR), pp. 5689–5698 (2017)
92. Varol, G., et al.: BodyNet: volumetric inference of 3D human body shapes. In: Ferrari, V., Hebert, M., Sminchisescu, C., Weiss, Y. (eds.) ECCV 2018. LNCS, vol. 11211, pp. 20–38. Springer, Cham (2018). https://doi.org/10.1007/978-3-030-01234-2_2
93. Wei, S.E., Ramakrishna, V., Kanade, T., Sheikh, Y.: Convolutional pose machines. In: Proceedings of the IEEE Conference on Computer Vision and Pattern Recognition (CVPR), pp. 4724–4732 (2016)
94. Wu, Y., Kirillov, A., Massa, F., Lo, W.Y., Girshick, R.: Detectron2 (2019). https://github.com/facebookresearch/detectron2

95. Xiang, D., Joo, H., Sheikh, Y.: Monocular total capture: posing face, body, and hands in the wild. In: Proceedings of the IEEE Conference on Computer Vision and Pattern Recognition (CVPR), pp. 10957–10966 (2019)
96. Xu, H., Bazavan, E.G., Zanfir, A., Freeman, W.T., Sukthankar, R., Sminchisescu, C.: GHUM & GHUML: generative 3D human shape and articulated pose models. In: Proceedings of the IEEE Conference on Computer Vision and Pattern Recognition (CVPR), pp. 7214–7223 (2020)
97. Yuan, S., et al.: Depth-based 3D hand pose estimation: from current achievements to future goals. In: Proceedings of the IEEE Conference on Computer Vision and Pattern Recognition (CVPR), pp. 2636–2645 (2018)
98. Zanfir, A., Marinoiu, E., Sminchisescu, C.: Monocular 3D pose and shape estimation of multiple people in natural scenes - the importance of multiple scene constraints. In: Proceedings of the IEEE Conference on Computer Vision and Pattern Recognition (CVPR), pp. 2148–2157 (2018)
99. Zanfir, A., Marinoiu, E., Zanfir, M., Popa, A.I., Sminchisescu, C.: Deep network for the integrated 3D sensing of multiple people in natural images. In: Advances in Neural Information Processing Systems (NeurIPS), pp. 8410–8419 (2018)
100. Zhang, X., Li, Q., Mo, H., Zhang, W., Zheng, W.: End-to-end hand mesh recovery from a monocular RGB image. In: Proceedings of the IEEE International Conference on Computer Vision (ICCV), pp. 2354–2364 (2019)
101. Zhao, L., Peng, X., Tian, Y., Kapadia, M., Metaxas, D.N.: Semantic graph convolutional networks for 3D human pose regression. In: Proceedings of the IEEE Conference on Computer Vision and Pattern Recognition (CVPR), pp. 3420–3430 (2019)
102. Zheng, Z., Yu, T., Wei, Y., Dai, Q., Liu, Y.: DeepHuman: 3D human reconstruction from a single image. In: Proceedings of the IEEE International Conference on Computer Vision (ICCV), pp. 7738–7748 (2019)
103. Zhou, Y., Barnes, C., Lu, J., Yang, J., Li, H.: On the continuity of rotation representations in neural networks. In: Proceedings of the IEEE Conference on Computer Vision and Pattern Recognition (CVPR), pp. 5738–5746 (2019)
104. Zimmermann, C., Brox, T.: Learning to estimate 3D hand pose from single RGB images. In: Proceedings of the IEEE International Conference on Computer Vision (ICCV), pp. 4913–4921 (2017)
105. Zimmermann, C., Ceylan, D., Yang, J., Russell, B., Argus, M., Brox, T.: FreiHAND: a dataset for markerless capture of hand pose and shape from single RGB images. In: Proceedings of the IEEE International Conference on Computer Vision (ICCV), pp. 813–822 (2019)
106. Zollhöfer, M., et al.: State of the art on monocular 3D face reconstruction, tracking, and applications. Comput. Graph. Forum $37(2)$, 523–550 (2018)

Dual Adversarial Network: Toward Real-World Noise Removal and Noise Generation

Zongsheng Yue[1,2], Qian Zhao[1], Lei Zhang[2,3], and Deyu Meng[1,4(✉)]

[1] Xi'an Jiaotong University, Shaanxi, China
zsyzam@gmail.com, timmy.zhaoqian@gmail.com, cslzhang@comp.polyu.edu.hk,
dymeng@mail.xjtu.edu.cn
[2] Hong Kong Polytechnic University, Hong Kong, China
[3] DAMO Academy, Alibaba Group, Shenzhen, China
[4] The Macau University of Science and Technology, Macau, China

Abstract. Real-world image noise removal is a long-standing yet very challenging task in computer vision. The success of deep neural network in denoising stimulates the research of noise generation, aiming at synthesizing more clean-noisy image pairs to facilitate the training of deep denoisers. In this work, we propose a novel unified framework to simultaneously deal with the noise removal and noise generation tasks. Instead of only inferring the posteriori distribution of the latent clean image conditioned on the observed noisy image in traditional MAP framework, our proposed method learns the joint distribution of the clean-noisy image pairs. Specifically, we approximate the joint distribution with two different factorized forms, which can be formulated as a denoiser mapping the noisy image to the clean one and a generator mapping the clean image to the noisy one. The learned joint distribution implicitly contains all the information between the noisy and clean images, avoiding the necessity of manually designing the image priors and noise assumptions as traditional. Besides, the performance of our denoiser can be further improved by augmenting the original training dataset with the learned generator. Moreover, we propose two metrics to assess the quality of the generated noisy image, for which, to the best of our knowledge, such metrics are firstly proposed along this research line. Extensive experiments have been conducted to demonstrate the superiority of our method over the state-of-the-arts both in the real noise removal and generation tasks. The training and testing code is available at https://github.com/zsyOAOA/DANet.

Keywords: Real-world · Denoising · Generation · Metric

Electronic supplementary material The online version of this chapter (https://doi.org/10.1007/978-3-030-58607-2_3) contains supplementary material, which is available to authorized users.

© Springer Nature Switzerland AG 2020
A. Vedaldi et al. (Eds.): ECCV 2020, LNCS 12355, pp. 41–58, 2020.
https://doi.org/10.1007/978-3-030-58607-2_3

1 Introduction

Image denoising is an important research problem in low-level vision, aiming at recovering the latent clean image x from its noisy observation y. Despite the significant advances in the past decades [8,14,56,57], real image denoising still remains a challenging task, due to the complicated processing steps within the camera system, such as demosaicing, Gamma correction and compression [46].

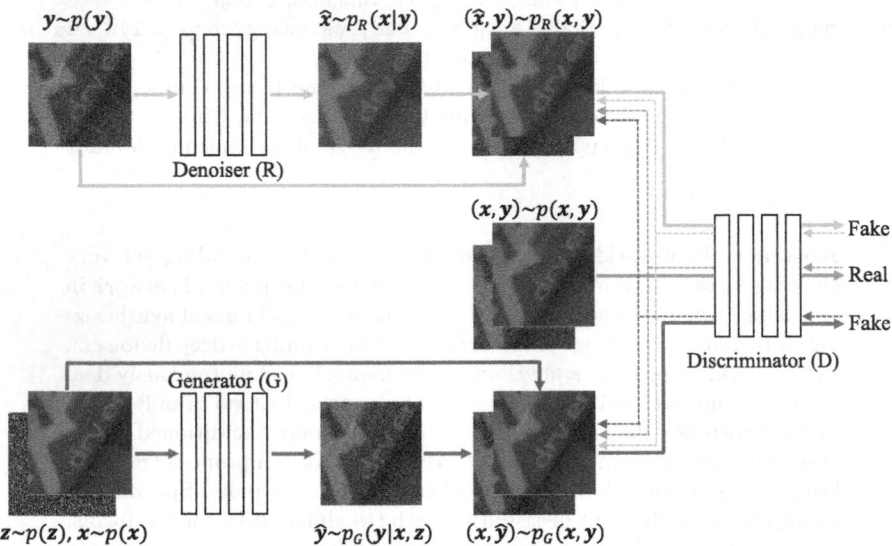

Fig. 1. Illustration of our proposed dual adversarial framework. The solid lines denote the forward process, and the dotted lines mark the gradient interaction between the denoiser and generator during the backword.

From the Bayesian perspective, most of the traditional denoising methods can be interpreted within the Maximum A Posteriori (MAP) framework, i.e., $\max_x p(x|y) \propto p(y|x)p(x)$, which involves one likelihood term $p(y|x)$ and one prior term $p(x)$. Under this framework, there are two methodologies that have been considered. The first attempts to model the likelihood term with proper distributions, e.g., Gaussian, Laplacian, MoG [33,55,59] and MoEP [10], which represents different understandings for the noise generation mechanism, while the second mainly focuses on exploiting better image priors, such as total variation [40], non-local similarity [8], low-rankness [15,17,47,53] and sparsity [31,52,58]. Despite better interpretability led by Bayesian framework, these MAP-based methods are still limited by the manual assumptions on the noise and image priors, which may largely deviate from the real images.

In recent years, deep learning (DL)-based methods have achieved impressive success in image denoising task [4,56,57]. However, as is well known, training a deep denoiser requires large amount of clean-noisy image pairs, which are time-consuming and expensive to collect. To address this issue, several noise generation[1] approaches were proposed to simulate more clean-noisy image pairs to facilitate the training of deep denoisers. The main idea behind them is to unfold the in-camera processing pipelines [7,19], or directly learn the distribution $p(\boldsymbol{y})$ as in [11,25] using generative adversarial network (GAN) [16]. However, the former methods involve many hyper-parameters needed to be carefully tuned for specific cameras, and the latter ones suffer from simulating very realistic noisy image with high-dimensional signal-dependent noise distributions. Besides, to the best of our knowledge, there is still no metric to quantitatively assess the quality of the generated noisy images w.r.t. the real ones.

Against these issues, we propose a new framework to model the joint distribution $p(\boldsymbol{x}, \boldsymbol{y})$ instead of only inferring the conditional posteriori $p(\boldsymbol{x}|\boldsymbol{y})$ as in conventional MAP framework. Specifically, we firstly factorize the joint distribution $p(\boldsymbol{x}, \boldsymbol{y})$ from two opposite directions, i.e., $p(\boldsymbol{x}|\boldsymbol{y})p(\boldsymbol{y})$ and $\int_{\boldsymbol{z}} p(\boldsymbol{y}|\boldsymbol{x}, \boldsymbol{z})p(\boldsymbol{x})p(\boldsymbol{z})\mathrm{d}\boldsymbol{z}$, which can be well approximated by a image denoiser and a noise generator. Then we simultaneously train the denoiser and generator in a dual adversarial manner as illustrated in Fig. 1. After that, the learned denoiser can either be directly used for the real noise removal task, or further enhanced with new clean-noisy image pairs simulated by the learned generator. In summary, the contributions of this work can be mainly summarized as:

- Different from the traditional MAP framework, our method approximates the joint distribution $p(\boldsymbol{x}, \boldsymbol{y})$ from two different factorized forms in a dual adversarial manner, which subtlely avoids the manual design on image priors and noise distribution. What's more, the joint distribution theoretically contains more complete information underlying the data set comparing with the conditional posteriori $p(\boldsymbol{x}|\boldsymbol{y})$.
- Our proposed method can simultaneously deal with both the noise removal and noise generation tasks in one unified Bayesian framework, and achieves superior performance than the state-of-the-arts in both these two tasks. What's more, the performance of our denoiser can be further improved after retraining on the augmented training data set with additional clean-noisy image pairs simulated by our learned generator.
- In order to assess the quality of the simulated noisy images by a noise generation method, we design two metrics, which, to the best of our knowledge, are the first metrics to this aim.

2   Related Work

2.1   Noise Removal

Image denoising is an active research topic in computer vision. Under the MAP framework, rational priors are necessary to be pre-assumed to enforce some desired properties of the recovered image. Total variation [40] was firstly introduced to deal with the denoising task. Later, the non-local similarity prior,

---

[1] The phrase "noise generation" indicates the generation process of noisy image from clean image throughout this paper.

meaning that the small patches in a large non-local area may share some similar patterns, was considered in NLM [8] and followed by many other denoising methods [14,15,28,30]. Low-rankness [15,17,53,54] and sparsity [30,31,50,52,58] are another two well-known image priors, which are often used together within the dictionary learning methods. Besides, discriminative learning methods also represent another research line, mainly including Markov random field (MRF) methods [6,41,44], cascade of shrinkage fields (CSF) methods [42,43] and the trainable nonlinear reaction diffusion (TNRD) [12] method. Different from above priors-based methods, noise modeling approaches focus on the other important component of MAP, i.e., likelihood or fidelity term. E.g., Meng and De La Torre [33] proposed to model the noise distribution as mixture of Gaussians (MoG), while Zhu *et al.* [59] and Yue *et al.* [55] both introduced the non-parametric Dirichlet Process to MoG to expand its flexibility. Furthermore, Cao *et al.* [10] proposed the mixture of expotential power (MoEP) distributions to fit more complex noise.

In recent years, DL-based methods achieved significant advances in the image denoising task. Jain and Seung [23] firstly adopted a five-layer network to deal with the denoising task. Then Burger *et al.* [9] obtained the comparable performance with BM3D using one plain multi-layer perceptron (MLP). Later, some auto-encoder based methods [2,49] were also immediately proposed. It is worthy mentioning that Zhang *et al.* [57] proposed the convolutional denoising network DnCNN and achieved the state-of-the-art performance on Gaussian denoising. Following DnCNN, many different network architectures were designed to deal with the denoising task, including RED [32], MemNet[45], NLRN [29], N3Net [37], RIDNet [4] and VDN [56].

2.2 Noise Generation

As is well known, the expensive cost of collecting pairs of training data is a critical limitation for deep learning based denoising methods. Therefore, several methods were proposed to explore the generation mechanism of image noise to facilitate an easy simulation of more training data pairs. One common idea was to generate image pairs by "unprocessing" and "processing" each step of the in-camera processing pipelines, e.g., [7,19,24]. However, these methods involve many hyper-parameters to be tuned for specifi camera. Another simpler way was to learn the real noise distribution directly using GAN [16] as demonstrated in [11] and [25]. Due to the complexity of real noise and the instability of training GAN, it is very difficult to train a good generator for simulating realistic noise.

3 Proposed Method

Like most of the supervised deep learning denoising methods, our approach is built on the given training data set containing pairs of real noisy image y and clean image x, which are accessible thanking to the contributions of [1,3,51]. Instead of forcely learning a mapping from y to x, we attempt to approximate the underlying joint distribution $p(x, y)$ of the clean-noisy image pairs. In the following, we present our method from the Bayesian perspective.

3.1   Two Factorizations of Joint Distribution

In this part, we factorize the joint distribution $p(\boldsymbol{x}, \boldsymbol{y})$ from two different perspectives, and discuss their insights respectively related to the noise removal and noise generation tasks.

Noise Removal Perspective: The noise removal task can be considered as inferring the conditional distribution $p(\boldsymbol{x}|\boldsymbol{y})$ under the Bayesian framework. The learned denoiser R in this task represents an implicit distribution $p_R(\boldsymbol{x}|\boldsymbol{y})$ to approximate the true distribution $p(\boldsymbol{x}|\boldsymbol{y})$. The output of R can be seen as an image sampled from this implicit distribution $p_R(\boldsymbol{x}|\boldsymbol{y})$. Based on such understanding, we can obtain a pseudo clean image pair $(\hat{\boldsymbol{x}}, \boldsymbol{y})$ as follows[2], i.e.,

$$\boldsymbol{y} \sim p(\boldsymbol{y}), \ \hat{\boldsymbol{x}} = R(\boldsymbol{y}) \Longrightarrow (\hat{\boldsymbol{x}}, \boldsymbol{y}), \tag{1}$$

which can be seen as one example sampled from the following pseudo joint distribution:

$$p_R(\boldsymbol{x}, \boldsymbol{y}) = p_R(\boldsymbol{x}|\boldsymbol{y})p(\boldsymbol{y}). \tag{2}$$

Obviously, the better denoiser R is, the more accurately that the pseudo joint distribution $p_R(\boldsymbol{x}, \boldsymbol{y})$ can approximate the true joint distribution $p(\boldsymbol{x}, \boldsymbol{y})$.

Noise Generation Perspective: In real camera system, image noise is derived from multiple hardware-related random noises (e.g., short noise, thermal noise), and further affected by in-camera processing pipelines (e.g., demosaicing, compression). After introducing an additional latent variable $\boldsymbol{z}$, representing the fundamental elements conducting the hardware-related random noises, the generation process from $\boldsymbol{x}$ to $\boldsymbol{y}$ can be depicted by the conditional distribution $p(\boldsymbol{y}|\boldsymbol{x}, \boldsymbol{z})$. The generator G in this task expresses an implicit distribution $p_G(\boldsymbol{y}|\boldsymbol{x}, \boldsymbol{z})$ to approximate the true distribution $p(\boldsymbol{y}|\boldsymbol{x}, \boldsymbol{z})$. The output of G can be seen as an example sampled from $p_G(\boldsymbol{y}|\boldsymbol{x}, \boldsymbol{z})$, i.e., $G(\boldsymbol{x}, \boldsymbol{z}) \sim p_G(\boldsymbol{y}|\boldsymbol{x}, \boldsymbol{z})$. Similar as Eq. (1), a pseudo noisy image pair $(\boldsymbol{x}, \hat{\boldsymbol{y}})$ is easily obtained:

$$\boldsymbol{z} \sim p(\boldsymbol{z}), \ \boldsymbol{x} \sim p(\boldsymbol{x}), \ \hat{\boldsymbol{y}} = G(\boldsymbol{x}, \boldsymbol{z}) \Longrightarrow (\boldsymbol{x}, \hat{\boldsymbol{y}}), \tag{3}$$

where $p(\boldsymbol{z})$ denotes the distribution of the latent variable $\boldsymbol{z}$, which can be easily set as an isotropic Gaussian distribution $\mathcal{N}(0, \boldsymbol{I})$.

Theoretically, we can marginalize the latent variable $\boldsymbol{z}$ to obtain the following pseudo joint distribution $p_G(\boldsymbol{x}, \boldsymbol{y})$ as an approximation to $p(\boldsymbol{x}, \boldsymbol{y})$:

$$p_G(\boldsymbol{x}, \boldsymbol{y}) = \int_{\boldsymbol{z}} p_G(\boldsymbol{y}|\boldsymbol{x}, \boldsymbol{z})p(\boldsymbol{x})p(\boldsymbol{z})\mathrm{d}\boldsymbol{z} \approx \frac{1}{L}\sum_i^L p_G(\boldsymbol{y}|\boldsymbol{x}, \boldsymbol{z}_i)p(\boldsymbol{x}), \tag{4}$$

where $\boldsymbol{z}_i \sim p(\boldsymbol{z})$. As suggested in [27], the number of samples L can be set as 1 as long as the minibatch size is large enough. Under such setting, the pseudo noisy image pair $(\boldsymbol{x}, \hat{\boldsymbol{y}})$ obtained from the generation process in Eq. (3) can be roughly regarded as an sampled example from $p_G(\boldsymbol{x}, \boldsymbol{y})$.

---

[2] We mildly assume that $\boldsymbol{y} \sim p(\boldsymbol{y})$ is easily implemented by sampling $\boldsymbol{y}$ from the empirical distribution $p(\boldsymbol{y})$ of the training data set, and so does as $\boldsymbol{x} \sim p(\boldsymbol{x})$.

3.2 Dual Adversarial Model

In the previous subsection, we have derived two pseudo joint distributions from the perspectives of noise removal and noise generation, i.e., $p_R(\boldsymbol{x}, \boldsymbol{y})$ and $p_G(\boldsymbol{x}, \boldsymbol{y})$. Now the problem becomes how to effectively train the denoiser R and the generator G, in order to well approximate the joint distribution $p(\boldsymbol{x}, \boldsymbol{y})$. Fortunately, the tractability of sampling process defined in Eqs. (1) and (3) makes such training possible in an adversarial manner as GAN [16], which gradually pushes $p_R(\boldsymbol{x}, \boldsymbol{y})$ and $p_G(\boldsymbol{x}, \boldsymbol{y})$ toward the true distribution $p(\boldsymbol{x}, \boldsymbol{y})$. Specifically, we formulate this idea as the following dual adversarial problem inspired by Triple-GAN [13],

$$\min_{R,G} \max_{D} \mathcal{L}_{\text{gan}}(R, G, D) = E_{(\boldsymbol{x},\boldsymbol{y})}[D(\boldsymbol{x}, \boldsymbol{y})] - \alpha E_{(\hat{\boldsymbol{x}},\boldsymbol{y})}[D(\hat{\boldsymbol{x}}, \boldsymbol{y})]$$

$$- (1 - \alpha) E_{(\boldsymbol{x},\hat{\boldsymbol{y}})}[D(\boldsymbol{x}, \hat{\boldsymbol{y}})], \qquad (5)$$

where $\hat{\boldsymbol{x}} = R(\boldsymbol{y})$, $\hat{\boldsymbol{y}} = G(\boldsymbol{x}, \boldsymbol{z})$, and D denotes the discriminator, which tries to distinguish the real clean-noisy image pair $(\boldsymbol{x}, \boldsymbol{y})$ from the fake ones $(\hat{\boldsymbol{x}}, \boldsymbol{y})$ and $(\boldsymbol{x}, \hat{\boldsymbol{y}})$. The hyper-parameter α controls the relative importance between the denoiser R and generator G. As in [5], we use the Wassertein-1 distance to measure the difference between two distributions in Eq. (5).

The working mechanism of our dual adversarial network can be intuitively explained in Fig. 1. On one hand, the denoiser R, delivering the knowledge of $p_R(\boldsymbol{x}|\boldsymbol{y})$, is expected to conduct the joint distribution $p_R(\boldsymbol{x}, \boldsymbol{y})$ of Eq. (2), while the noise generator G, conveying the information of $p_G(\boldsymbol{y}|\boldsymbol{x}, \boldsymbol{z})$, is expected to derive the joint distribution $p_G(\boldsymbol{x}, \boldsymbol{y})$ of Eq. (4). Through the adversarial effect of discriminator D, the denoiser R and generator G are both gradually optimized so as to pull $p_R(\boldsymbol{x}, \boldsymbol{y})$ and $p_G(\boldsymbol{x}, \boldsymbol{y})$ toward the true joint distribution $p(\boldsymbol{x}, \boldsymbol{y})$ during training. On the other hand, the capabilities of R and G are mutually enhanced by their dual regularization between each other. Given any real image pair $(\boldsymbol{x}, \boldsymbol{y})$ and one pseudo image pair $(\boldsymbol{x}, \hat{\boldsymbol{y}})$ from generator G or $(\hat{\boldsymbol{x}}, \boldsymbol{y})$ from denoiser R, the discriminator D will be updated according to the adversarial loss. Then D is fixed as a criterion to update both R and G simultaneously as illustrated by the dotted lines in Fig. 1, which means R and G are keeping interactive and guided by each other in each iteration.

Previous researches [22,60] have shown that it is benefical to mix the adversarial objective with traditional losses, which would speed up and stabilize the training of GAN. For noise removal task, we adopt the L_1 loss, i.e., $||\hat{\boldsymbol{x}} - \boldsymbol{x}||_1$, which enforces the output of denoiser R to be close to the groundtruth. For the generator G, however, the direct L_1 loss would not be benefical because of the randomness of noise. Therefore, we propose to apply the L_1 constrain on the statistical features of noise distribution:

$$||\mathcal{GF}(\hat{\boldsymbol{y}} - \boldsymbol{x}) - \mathcal{GF}(\boldsymbol{y} - \boldsymbol{x})||_1, \qquad (6)$$

where $\mathcal{GF}(\cdot)$ represents the Gaussian filter used to extract the first-order statistical information of noise. Intergrating these two regularizers into the adversarial loss of Eq. (5), we obtain the final objective:

$$\min_{R,G} \max_{D} \mathcal{L}_{gan}(R, G, D) + \tau_1 ||\hat{\boldsymbol{x}} - \boldsymbol{x}||_1 + \tau_2 ||\mathcal{GF}(\hat{\boldsymbol{y}} - \boldsymbol{x}) - \mathcal{GF}(\boldsymbol{y} - \boldsymbol{x})||_1, \qquad (7)$$

Algorithm 1. Daul adversarial network.

Input: hyper-parameters: τ_1, τ_2, α, n_{critic}
1: **while** θ had not converged **do**
2:    **for** $i = 1, 2, \ldots, n_{critic}$ **do**
3:        Sample a batch of pairs $(\boldsymbol{x}, \boldsymbol{y})$ from $p(\boldsymbol{x}, \boldsymbol{y})$
4:        Sample a batch of pairs $(\hat{\boldsymbol{x}}, \boldsymbol{y})$ from $p_R(\boldsymbol{x}, \boldsymbol{y})$ and $(\boldsymbol{x}, \hat{\boldsymbol{y}})$ from $p_G(\boldsymbol{x}, \boldsymbol{y})$
5:        Update discriminator D with fixed R and G
6:    **end for**
7:    Update denoiser R with fixed G and D
8:    Update generator G with fixed R and D
9: **end while**

---

where τ_1 and τ_2 are hyper-parameters to balance different losses. More sensetiveness analysis on them are provided in Sect. 5.2.

3.3 Training Strategy

In the dual adversarial model of Eq. (7), we have three objects to be optimized, i.e., the denoiser R, generator G and discriminator D. As in most of the GAN-related papers [5,13,16], we jointly train R, G and D but update them in an alternating manner as shown in Algorithm 1. In order to stabilize the training, we adopt the gradient penalty technology in WGAN-GP [18], enforcing the discriminator to satisfy 1-Lipschitz constraint by an extra gradient penalty term.

After training, the generator G is able to simulate more noisy images given any clean images, which are easily obtained from the original training data set or by downloading from internet. Then we can retrain the denoiser R by adding more synthetic clean-noisy image pairs generated by G to the training data set. As shown in Sect. 5, this strategy can further improve the denoising performance.

3.4 Network Architecture

The denoiser R, generator G and discriminator D in our framework are all parameterized as deep neural networks due to their powerful fitting capability. As shown in Fig. 1, the denoiser R takes noisy image $\boldsymbol{y}$ as input and outputs denoised image $\hat{\boldsymbol{x}}$, while the generator G takes the concatenated clean image $\boldsymbol{x}$ and latent variable $\boldsymbol{z}$ as input and outputs the simulated noisy image $\hat{\boldsymbol{y}}$. For both R and G, we use the UNet [39] architecture as backbones. Besides, the residual learning strategy [57] is adopted in both of them. The discriminator D contains five stride convolutional layers to reduce the image size and one fully connected layer to fuse all the information. More details about the network architectures are provided in the supplementary material due to page limitation. It should be noted that our proposed method is a general framework that does not depend on the specific architecture, therefore most of the commonly used networks architectures [4,32,57] in low-level vision tasks can be substituted.

4 Evaluation Metrics

For the noise removal task, PSNR and SSIM [48] can be readily adopted to compare the denoising performance of different methods. However, to the best of our knowledge, there is still no any quantitative metric having been designed for noise generation task. To address this issue, we propose two metrics to compare the similarity between the generated and the real noisy images as follows:

- **PGap** (PSNR Gap): The main idea of PGap is to compare the synthetic and real noisy images indirectly by the performance of the denoisers trained on them. Let $\mathcal{D} = \{(\boldsymbol{x}^i, \boldsymbol{y}^i)\}_{i=1}^N$, $\mathcal{T} = \{(\tilde{\boldsymbol{x}}^j, \tilde{\boldsymbol{y}}^j)\}_{j=1}^S$ denote the available training and testing sets, whose noise distributions are same or similar. Given any one noisy image generator G, we can synthesize another training set:

$$\mathcal{D}_G = \{(\boldsymbol{x}^i, \tilde{\boldsymbol{y}}^i) | \tilde{\boldsymbol{y}}^i = G(\boldsymbol{x}^i, \boldsymbol{z}^i), \boldsymbol{z}^i \sim p(\boldsymbol{z})\}_{i=1}^N. \tag{8}$$

After training two denoisers R_1 on the original data set $\mathcal{D}$ and R_2 on the generated data set $\mathcal{D}_G$ under the **same** conditions, we can define PGap as

$$\mathrm{PGap} = \mathrm{PSNR}(R_1(\mathcal{T})) - \mathrm{PSNR}(R_2(\mathcal{T})), \tag{9}$$

where $\mathrm{PSNR}(R_i(\mathcal{T}))(i = 1, 2)$ represents the PSNR result of denoiser R_i on testing data set $\mathcal{T}$. It is obvious that, if the generated noisy images in $\mathcal{D}_G$ are close to the real noisy ones in $\mathcal{D}$, the performance of R_2 would be close to R_1, and thus the PGap would be small.

- **AKLD** (Average KL Divergence): The noise generation task aims at synthesizing fake noisy image $\boldsymbol{y}^f$ from the real clean image $\boldsymbol{x}^r$ to match the real noisy image $\boldsymbol{y}^r$ in distribution. Therefore, the KL divergence between the conditional distributions $p_{\boldsymbol{y}^f}(\boldsymbol{y}|\boldsymbol{x})$ on the fake image pair $(\boldsymbol{x}^r, \boldsymbol{y}^f)$ and $p_{\boldsymbol{y}^r}(\boldsymbol{y}|\boldsymbol{x})$ on the real image pair $(\boldsymbol{x}^r, \boldsymbol{y}^r)$ can serve as a metric. To make this conditional distribution tractable, we utlize the pixel-wisely Gaussian assumption for real noise in recent work VDN [56], i.e.,

$$p_{\boldsymbol{y}^c}(\boldsymbol{y}|\boldsymbol{x}) = \mathcal{N}(\boldsymbol{y}|[\boldsymbol{x}^r], \mathrm{diag}([\boldsymbol{V}^c])), \ c \in \{f, r\}, \tag{10}$$

where

$$\boldsymbol{V}^c = \mathcal{GF}((\boldsymbol{y}^c - \boldsymbol{x}^r)^2), \ c \in \{f, r\}, \tag{11}$$

$[\cdot]$ denotes the reshape operation from matrix to vector, $\mathcal{GF}(\cdot)$ denotes the Gaussian filter, and the square of $(\boldsymbol{y}^c - \boldsymbol{x}^r)^2$ is pixel-wise operation. Based on such explicit distribution assumption, the KL divergence between $p_{\boldsymbol{y}^f}(\boldsymbol{y}|\boldsymbol{x})$ and $p_{\boldsymbol{y}^r}(\boldsymbol{y}|\boldsymbol{x})$ can be regarded as an intuitive metric. To reduce the influence of randomness, we randomly generate L synthetic fake noisy images:

$$\boldsymbol{y}^{f_j} = G(\boldsymbol{x}^r, \boldsymbol{z}^j), \ \boldsymbol{z}^j \sim p(\boldsymbol{z}), \ j = 1, 2, \cdots, L, \tag{12}$$

for any real clean image $\boldsymbol{x}^r$, and define the following average KL divergence as our metric, i.e.,

$$\mathrm{AKLD} = \frac{1}{L} \sum_{j=1}^L KL[p_{\boldsymbol{y}^{f_j}}p(\boldsymbol{y}|\boldsymbol{x}) || p_{\boldsymbol{y}^r}(\boldsymbol{y}|\boldsymbol{x})]. \tag{13}$$

Evidently, the smaller AKLD is, the better the generator G is. In the following experiments, we set $L = 50$.

Table 1. The PGap and AKLD performances of different compared methods on the SIDD validation data set. And the best results are highlighted in bold.

Metrics	Methods			
	CBDNet	ULRD	GRDN	DANet
PGap↓	8.30	4.90	2.28	**2.06**
AKLD↓	0.728	0.545	0.443	**0.212**

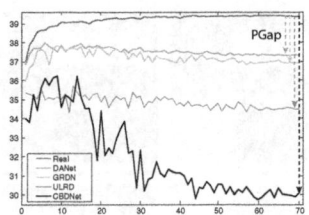

Fig. 2. PSNR results of different methods during training.

5 Experimental Results

In this section, we conducted a series of experiments on several real-world denoising benchmarks. In specific, we considered two groups of experiments: the first group (Sect. 5.2) is designed for evaluating the effectiveness of our method on both of the noise removal and noise generation tasks, which is implemented on one specific real benchmark containing training, validation and testing sets; while the second group (Sect. 5.3) is conducted on two real benchmarks that only consist of some noisy images as testing set, aiming at evaluating its performance on general real-world denoising tasks.

In brief, we denote the jointly trained **D**ual **A**dversarial **Net**work following Algorithm 1 as DANet. As discussed in Sect. 3.3, the learned generator G in DANet is able to augment the original training set by generating more synthetic clean-noisy image pairs, and the retrained denoiser R on this augmented training data set under L_1 loss is denoted as DANet$_+$.

5.1 Experimental Settings

Parameter Settings and Network Training: In the training stage of DANet, the weights of R and G were both initialized according to [20], and the weights of D were initialized from a zero-centered Normal distribution with standard deviation 0.02 as [38]. All the three networks were trained by Adam optimizer [26] with momentum terms $(0.9, 0.999)$ for R and $(0.5, 0.9)$ for both G and D. The learning rates were set as $1e$-4, $1e$-4 and $2e$-4 for R, G and D, respectively, and linearly decayed in half every 10 epochs.

In each epoch, we randomly cropped 16×5000 patches with size 128×128 from the images for training. During training, we updated D three times for each update of R and G. We set $\tau_1 = 1000$, $\tau_2 = 10$ throughout the experiments, and the sensetiveness analysis about them can be found in Sect. 5.2. As for α, we set it as 0.5, meaning the denoiser R and generator G contribute equally in our model. The penalty coefficient in WGAN-GP [18] is set as 10 following its default settings. As for DANet$_+$, the denoiser R was retrained with the same settings as that in DANet. All the models were trained using PyTorch [35].

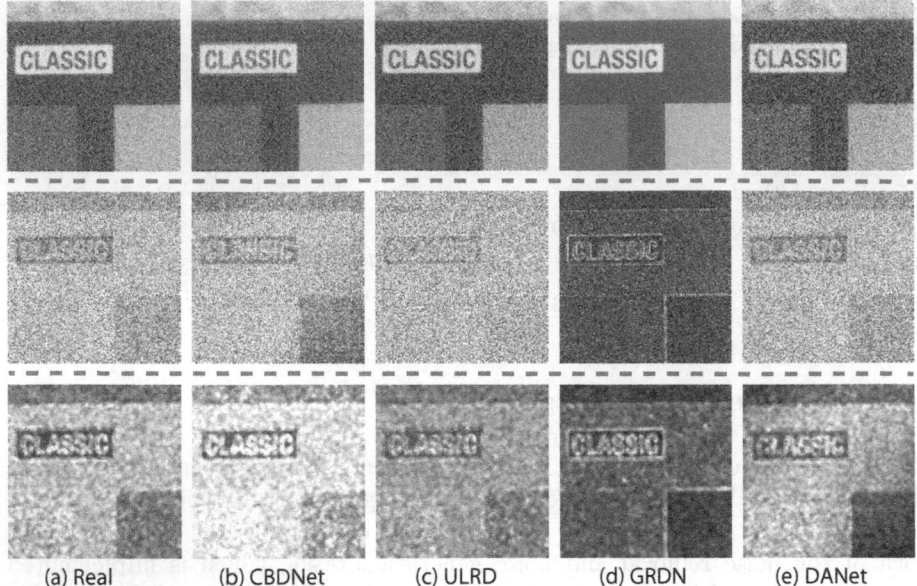

| (a) Real | (b) CBDNet | (c) ULRD | (d) GRDN | (e) DANet |

Fig. 3. Illustration of one typical generated noisy images (1st row) by different methods and their corresponding noise (2nd row) and variance map (3rd row) estimated by Eq. (11). The first column represents the real ones in SIDD validation set.

5.2   Results on SIDD Benchmark

In this part, SIDD [1] benchmark is employed to evaluate the denoising performance and generation quality of our proposed method. The full SIDD data set contains about 24000 clean-noisy image pairs as training data, and the rest 6000 image pairs are held as the benchmark for testing. For fast training and evaluation, one medium training set (320 image pairs) and validation set (40 image pairs) are also provided, but the testing results can only be obtained by submission. We trained DANet and DANet$_+$ on the medium version training set, and evaluated on the validation and testing sets.

Noise Generation: The generator G in DANet is mainly used to synthesize the corresponding noisy image given any clean one. As introduced in Sect. 4, two metrics PGap and AKLD are designed to assess the generated noisy image. Based on these two metrics, we compared DANet with three recent methods, including CBDNet [19], ULRD [7] and GRDN [25]. CBDNet and ULRD both attempted to generate noisy images by simulating the in-camera processing pipelines, while GRDN directly learned the noise distribution using GAN [16].

Table 1 lists the PGap values of different methods on SIDD validation set. For the calculation of PGap, SIDD validation set is regarded as the testing set $\mathcal{T}$ in Eq. (9). Obviously, DANet achieves the best performance. Figure 2 displays the PSNR curves of different denoisers trained on the real training set or only the synthetic training sets generated by different methods, which gives an intuitive

Table 2. The PSNR and SSIM results of different methods on SIDD validation and testing sets. The best results are highlighted in bold.

Datasets	Metrics	Methods							
		CBM3D	WNNM	DnCNN	CBDNet	RIDNet	VDN	DANet	DANet$_+$
Testing	PSNR↑	25.65	25.78	23.66	33.28	-	39.26	39.25	**39.43**
	SSIM↑	0.685	0.809	0.583	0.868	-	0.955	0.955	**0.956**
Validation	PSNR↑	25.29	26.31	38.56	38.68	38.71	39.29	39.30	**39.47**
	SSIM↑	0.412	0.524	0.910	0.909	0.913	0.911	0.916	**0.918**

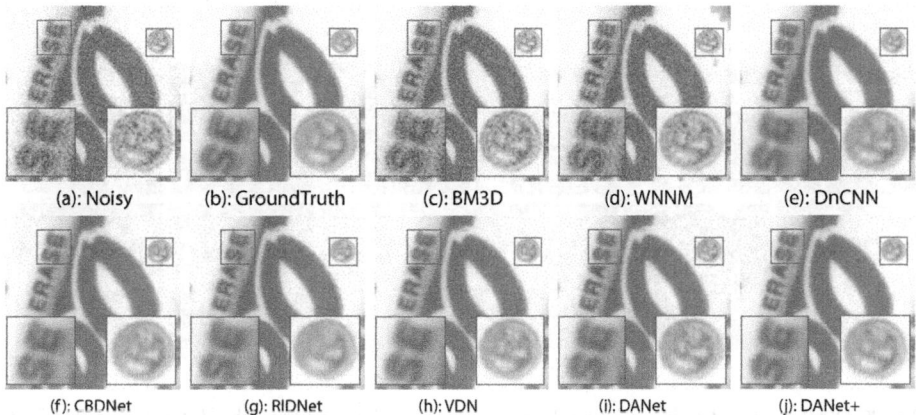

(a): Noisy   (b): GroundTruth   (c): BM3D   (d): WNNM   (e): DnCNN

(f): CBDNet   (g): RIDNet   (h): VDN   (i): DANet   (j): DANet+

Fig. 4. One typical denoising example in the SIDD validation dataset.

illustration for PGap. It can be seen that all the methods tend to gradually overfit to their own synthetic training set, especially for CBDNet. However, DANet performs not only more stably but also better than other methods.

The average AKLD results calculated on all the images of SIDD validation set are also listed in Table 1. The smallest AKLD of DANet indicates that it learns a better implicit distribution to approximate the true distribution $p(\boldsymbol{y}|\boldsymbol{x})$. Figure 3 illustrates one typical example of the real and synthetic noisy images generated by different methods, which provides an intuitive visualization for the AKLD metric. In summary, DANet outperforms other methods both in quantization and visualization, even though some of them make use of additional metadata.

Noise Removal: To verify the effectiveness of our proposed method on real-world denoising task, we compared it with several state-of-the-art methods, including CBM3D [14], WNNM [17], DnCNN [57], CBDNet [19], RIDNet [4] and VDN [56]. Table 2 lists the PSNR and SSIM results of different methods on SIDD validation and testing sets. It should be noted that the results on testing sets are cited from official website[3], but the results on validation set are calculated by ourself. For fair comparison, we retrained DnCNN and CBDNet

---

[3] https://www.eecs.yorku.ca/~kamel/sidd/benchmark.php.

Table 3. The PSNR and SSIM results of DANet under different τ_1 values on SIDD validation data set.

Metrics	τ_1			
	1e+2	1e+3	1e+4	+∞
PSNR↑	38.66	39.30	39.33	39.39
SSIM↑	0.901	0.916	0.916	0.917

Table 4. The PGap and AKLD results of DANet under different τ_2 values on SIDD validation data set.

Metrics	τ_2				
	0	5	10	50	+∞
PGap↓	5.33	3.10	2.06	4.17	15.14
AKLD↓	0.386	0.216	0.212	0.177	0.514

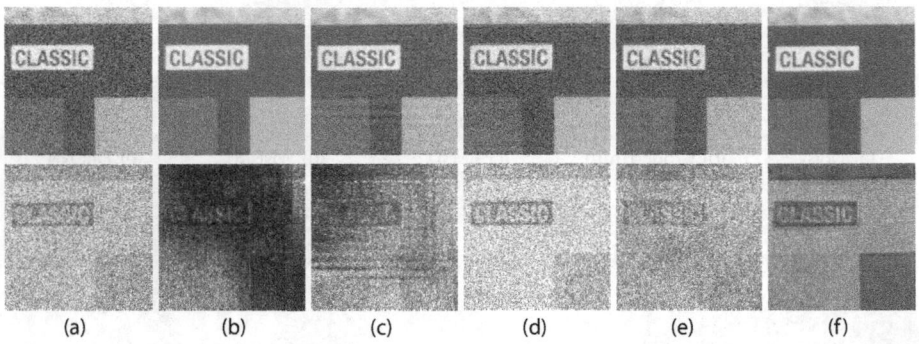

(a)   (b)   (c)   (d)   (e)   (f)

Fig. 5. This figure displays the real or generated noisy images (the 1st row) by DANet under different τ_2 value and the corresponding noise (the 2nd row). From left to right: (a) real case, (b) $\tau_2 = 0$, (c) $\tau_2 = 5$, (d) $\tau_2 = 10$, (e) $\tau_2 = 50$, (f) $\tau_2 = +\infty$.

on SIDD training set. From Table 2, it is easily observed that: 1) deep learning methods obviously performs better than traditional methods CBM3D and WNNM due to the powerful fitting capability of DNN; 2) DANet and DANet$_+$ both outperform the state-of-the-art real-world denoising methods, substantiating their effectiveness; 3) DANet$_+$ surpasses DANet about 0.18dB PSNR, which indicates that the synthetic data by G facilitates the training of the denoiser R.

Figure 4 illustrates the visual denoising results of different methods. It can be seen that CBM3D and WNNM both fail to remove the real-world noise. DnCNN tends to produce over-smooth edges and textures due to the L_2 loss. CBDNet, RIDNet and VDN alleviate this phenomenon to some extent since they adopt more robust loss functions. DANet recovers sharper edges and more details owning to the adversarial loss. After retraining with more generated image pairs, DANet$_+$ obtains the closer denoising results to the groundtruth.

Hyper-parameter Analysis: Our proposed DANet involves two hyper-parameters τ_1 and τ_2 in Eq. (7). The pamameter τ_1 mainly influences the performance of denoiser R, while τ_2 directly affects the generator G.

Table 3 lists the PSNR/SSIM results of DANet under different τ_1 settings, where $\tau_1 = +\infty$ represents the results of the denoiser R trained only with L_1

Table 5. The comparison results of BaseD and DANet on SIDD validation set.

Metrics	Methods	
	BaseD	DANet
PSNR↑	39.19	39.30
SSIM↑	0.907	0.916

Table 6. The comparison results of BaseG and DANet on SIDD validation set.

Metrics	Methods	
	BaseG	DANet
PGap↓	4.07	2.06
AKLD↓	0.223	0.212

Table 7. The PSNR and SSIM results of different methods on DND benchmark. The best results are highlighted as bold.

Metrics	Methods							
	CBM3D	WNNM	DnCNN	CBDNet	RIDNet	VDN	GDANet	GDANet$_+$
PSNR↑	34.51	34.67	32.43	38.06	39.26	39.38	39.47	**39.58**
SSIM↑	0.8244	0.8646	0.7900	0.9421	0.9528	0.9518	**0.9548**	0.9545

loss. As expected, small τ_1 value, meaning that the adversarial loss plays more important role, leads to the decrease of PSNR and SSIM performance to some extent. However, when τ_1 value is too large, the L_1 regularizer will mainly dominates the performance of denoiser R. Therefore, we set τ_1 as a moderate value $1e+3$ throughout all the experiments, which makes the denoising results more realistic as shown in Fig. 4 even sacrificing a little PSNR performance.

The PGap and average AKLD results of DANet under different τ_2 values are shown in Table 4. Note that $\tau_2 = +\infty$ represents the results of the generator G trained only with the regularizer of Eq. (6). Figure 5 also shows the corresponding visual results of one typical example. As one can see, G fails to simulate the real noise with $\tau_2 = 0$, while it is also difficult to be trained only with the regularizer of Eq. (6). Taking both the quantitative and visual results into consideration, τ_2 is constantly set as 10 in our experiments.

Ablation Studies: To verify the marginal benefits brought up by our dual adversarial loss, two groups of ablation experiments are designed in this part. In the first group, we train DANet without the generator and denote the trained model as BaseD. On the contrary, we train DANet without the denoiser and denote the trained model as BaseG. And the comparison results of these two baselines with DANet on noise removal and noise generation tasks are listed in Table 5 and Table 6, respectively. It can be easily seen that DANet achieves better performance than both the two baselines in noise removal and noise generation tasks, especially in the latter, which illustrates the mutual guidance and amelioration between the denoiser and the generator.

5.3   Results on DND and Nam Benchmarks

In this section, we evaluate the performance of our method on two real-world benchmarks, i.e., DND [36] and Nam [34]. Following the experimental setting in RIDNet [4], we trained another model using images from SIDD [1], Poly [51] and RENOIR [3] for fair comparison. To be distinguished from the model of Sect. 5.2, the trained models under this setting are denoted as GDANet and GDANet$_+$, aiming at dealing with the general denoising task in real application. For the training of GDANet$_+$, we employed the images of MIR Flickr [21] as clean images to synthesize more training pairs using G. Note that the experimental results on Nam benchmark are put into supplementary material due to page limitation.

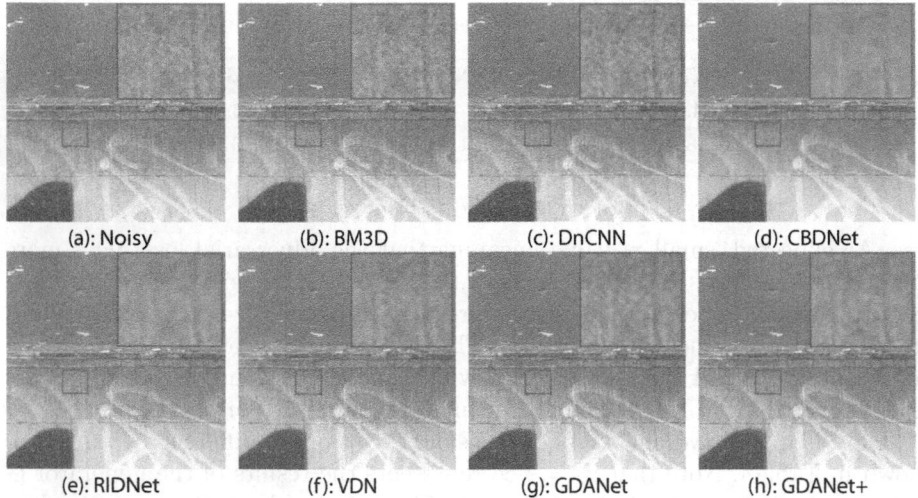

| (a): Noisy | (b): BM3D | (c): DnCNN | (d): CBDNet |

| (e): RIDNet | (f): VDN | (g): GDANet | (h): GDANet+ |

Fig. 6. Denoising results of different methods on DND benchmark.

DND Benchmark: This benchmark contains 50 real noisy and almost noise-free image pairs. However, the almost noise-free images are not publicly released, thus the PSNR/SSIM results can only be obtained through online submission system. Table 7 lists the PSNR/SSIM results released on the official DND benchmark website[4]. From Table 7, we have the following observations: 1) GDANet$_+$ outperforms the state-of-the-art VDN about 0.2dB PSNR, which is a large improvement in the field of real-world denoising; 2) GDANet obtains the highest SSIM value, which means that it preserves more structural information than other methods as that can be visually observed in Fig. 6; 3) DnCNN cannot remove most of the real noise because it overfits to the Gaussian noise case; 4) the classical CBM3D and WNNM methods cannot handle the complex real noise.

---

[4] https://noise.visinf.tu-darmstadt.de/benchmark/.

6   Conclusion

We have proposed a new Bayesian framework for real-world image denoising. Different from the traditional MAP framework relied on subjective pre-assumptions on the noise and image priors, our proposed method focuses on learning the joint distribution directly from data. To estimate the joint distribution, we attempt to approximate it by its two different factorized forms using an dual adversarial manner, which correspondes to two tasks, i.e., noise removal and noise generation. For assessing the quality of synthetic noisy image, we have designed two applicable metrics, to the best of our knowledge, for the first time. The proposed DANet intrinsically provides a general methodology to facilitate the study of other low-level vision tasks, such as super-resolution and deblurring.

References

1. Abdelhamed, A., Lin, S., Brown, M.S.: A high-quality denoising dataset for smartphone cameras. In: IEEE Conference on Computer Vision and Pattern Recognition (CVPR), June 2018
2. Agostinelli, F., Anderson, M.R., Lee, H.: Adaptive multi-column deep neural networks with application to robust image denoising. Adv. Neural Inf. Process. Syst. **26**, 1493–1501 (2013)
3. Anaya, J., Barbu, A.: Renoir - a benchmark dataset for real noise reduction evaluation. arXiv preprint arXiv:1409.8230 (2014). https://academic.microsoft.com/paper/1514812871
4. Anwar, S., Barnes, N.: Real image denoising with feature attention. In: Proceedings of the IEEE International Conference on Computer Vision, pp. 3155–3164 (2019)
5. Arjovsky, M., Chintala, S., Bottou, L.: Wasserstein gan. arXiv preprint arXiv:1701.07875 (2017)
6. Barbu, A.: Training an active random field for real-time image denoising. IEEE Trans. Image Process. **18**(11), 2451–2462 (2009)
7. Brooks, T., Mildenhall, B., Xue, T., Chen, J., Sharlet, D., Barron, J.T.: Unprocessing images for learned raw denoising. In: Proceedings of the IEEE Conference on Computer Vision and Pattern Recognition, pp. 11036–11045 (2019)
8. Buades, A., Coll, B., Morel, J.M.: A non-local algorithm for image denoising. In: 2005 IEEE Computer Society Conference on Computer Vision and Pattern Recognition (CVPR 2005), vol. 2, pp. 60–65. IEEE (2005)
9. Burger, H.C., Schuler, C.J., Harmeling, S.: Image denoising: can plain neural networks compete with BM3D? In: 2012 IEEE Conference on Computer Vision and Pattern Recognition, pp. 2392–2399 (2012)
10. Cao, X., et al.: Low-rank matrix factorization under general mixture noise distributions. In: The IEEE International Conference on Computer Vision (ICCV), December 2015
11. Chen, J., Chen, J., Chao, H., Yang, M.: Image blind denoising with generative adversarial network based noise modeling. In: Proceedings of the IEEE Conference on Computer Vision and Pattern Recognition, pp. 3155–3164 (2018)
12. Chen, Y., Pock, T.: Trainable nonlinear reaction diffusion: a flexible framework for fast and effective image restoration. IEEE Trans. Pattern Anal. Mach. Intell. **39**(6), 1256–1272 (2017)

13. Chongxuan, L., Xu, T., Zhu, J., Zhang, B.: Triple generative adversarial nets. In: Advances in Neural Information Processing Systems, pp. 4088–4098 (2017)
14. Dabov, K., Foi, A., Katkovnik, V., Egiazarian, K.: Image denoising by sparse 3-D transform-domain collaborative filtering. IEEE Trans. Image Process. **16**(8), 2080–2095 (2007)
15. Dong, W., Shi, G., Li, X.: Nonlocal image restoration with bilateral variance estimation: a low-rank approach. IEEE Trans. Image Process. **22**(2), 700–711 (2012)
16. Goodfellow, I., et al.: Generative adversarial nets. In: Advances in Neural Information Processing Systems, pp. 2672–2680 (2014)
17. Gu, S., Zhang, L., Zuo, W., Feng, X.: Weighted nuclear norm minimization with application to image denoising. In: Proceedings of the IEEE Conference on Computer Vision and Pattern Recognition, pp. 2862–2869 (2014)
18. Gulrajani, I., Ahmed, F., Arjovsky, M., Dumoulin, V., Courville, A.C.: Improved training of Wasserstein gans. In: Advances in Neural Information Processing Systems, pp. 5767–5777 (2017)
19. Guo, S., Yan, Z., Zhang, K., Zuo, W., Zhang, L.: Toward convolutional blind denoising of real photographs. In: Proceedings of the IEEE Conference on Computer Vision and Pattern Recognition, pp. 1712–1722 (2019)
20. He, K., Zhang, X., Ren, S., Sun, J.: Delving deep into rectifiers: surpassing human-level performance on imagenet classification. In: Proceedings of the IEEE International Conference on Computer Vision, pp. 1026–1034 (2015)
21. Huiskes, M.J., Thomee, B., Lew, M.S.: New trends and ideas in visual concept detection: the MIR flickr retrieval evaluation initiative. In: Proceedings of the International Conference on Multimedia Information Retrieval, pp. 527–536 (2010)
22. Isola, P., Zhu, J.Y., Zhou, T., Efros, A.A.: Image-to-image translation with conditional adversarial networks. In: Proceedings of the IEEE Conference on Computer Vision and Pattern Recognition, pp. 1125–1134 (2017)
23. Jain, V., Seung, S.: Natural image denoising with convolutional networks. Adv. Neural Inf. Process. Syst. **21**, 769–776 (2008)
24. Jaroensri, R., Biscarrat, C., Aittala, M., Durand, F.: Generating training data for denoising real rgb images via camera pipeline simulation. arXiv preprint arXiv:1904.08825 (2019)
25. Kim, D.W., Ryun Chung, J., Jung, S.W.: GRDN: grouped residual dense network for real image denoising and gan-based real-world noise modeling. In: Proceedings of the IEEE Conference on Computer Vision and Pattern Recognition Workshops, pp. 0–0 (2019)
26. Kingma, D.P., Ba, J.L.: Adam: a method for stochastic optimization. In: ICLR 2015: International Conference on Learning Representations 2015 (2015). https://academic.microsoft.com/paper/2964121744
27. Kingma, D.P., Welling, M.: Auto-encoding variational Bayes. In: ICLR 2014: International Conference on Learning Representations (ICLR) 2014 (2014)
28. Lebrun, M., Buades, A., Morel, J.M.: A nonlocal Bayesian image denoising algorithm. SIAM J. Imaging Sci. **6**(3), 1665–1688 (2013)
29. Liu, D., Wen, B., Fan, Y., Loy, C.C., Huang, T.: Non-local recurrent network for image restoration. In: NIPS 2018: The 32nd Annual Conference on Neural Information Processing Systems, pp. 1673–1682 (2018)
30. Mairal, J., Bach, F., Ponce, J., Sapiro, G., Zisserman, A.: Non-local sparse models for image restoration. In: 2009 IEEE 12th International Conference on Computer Vision, pp. 2272–2279 (2009)
31. Mairal, J., Elad, M., Sapiro, G.: Sparse representation for color image restoration. IEEE Trans. Image Process. **17**(1), 53–69 (2007)

32. Mao, X.J., Shen, C., Yang, Y.B.: Image restoration using very deep convolutional encoder-decoder networks with symmetric skip connections. In: NIPS 2016 Proceedings of the 30th International Conference on Neural Information Processing Systems, pp. 2810–2818 (2016)
33. Meng, D., De La Torre, F.: Robust matrix factorization with unknown noise. In: The IEEE International Conference on Computer Vision (ICCV), December 2013
34. Nam, S., Hwang, Y., Matsushita, Y., Joo Kim, S.: A holistic approach to cross-channel image noise modeling and its application to image denoising. In: Proceedings of the IEEE Conference on Computer Vision and Pattern Recognition, pp. 1683–1691 (2016)
35. Paszke, A., et al.: Pytorch: an imperative style, high-performance deep learning library. In: Advances in Neural Information Processing Systems, pp. 8024–8035 (2019)
36. Plotz, T., Roth, S.: Benchmarking denoising algorithms with real photographs. In: Proceedings of the IEEE Conference on Computer Vision and Pattern Recognition, pp. 1586–1595 (2017)
37. Pitz, T., Roth, S.: Neural nearest neighbors networks. In: NIPS 2018: The 32nd Annual Conference on Neural Information Processing Systems, pp. 1087–1098 (2018)
38. Radford, A., Metz, L., Chintala, S.: Unsupervised representation learning with deep convolutional generative adversarial networks. In: ICLR 2016: International Conference on Learning Representations 2016 (2016). https://academic.microsoft.com/paper/2963684088
39. Ronneberger, O., Fischer, P., Brox, T.: U-net: convolutional networks for biomedical image segmentation. In: International Conference on Medical Image Computing and Computer-Assisted Intervention, pp. 234–241 (2015). https://academic.microsoft.com/paper/1901129140
40. Rudin, L.I., Osher, S., Fatemi, E.: Nonlinear total variation based noise removal algorithms. Phys. D Nonlinear Phenom. **60**(1–4), 259–268 (1992)
41. Samuel, K.G.G., Tappen, M.F.: Learning optimized map estimates in continuously-valued MRF models. In: 2009 IEEE Conference on Computer Vision and Pattern Recognition, pp. 477–484 (2009)
42. Schmidt, U.: Half-quadratic inference and learning for natural images (2017)
43. Schmidt, U., Roth, S.: Shrinkage fields for effective image restoration. In: CVPR 2014 Proceedings of the 2014 IEEE Conference on Computer Vision and Pattern Recognition, pp. 2774–2781 (2014)
44. Sun, J., Tappen, M.F.: Learning non-local range Markov random field for image restoration. In: CVPR 2011, pp. 2745–2752 (2011)
45. Tai, Y., Yang, J., Liu, X., Xu, C.: MemNet: a persistent memory network for image restoration. In: 2017 IEEE International Conference on Computer Vision (ICCV), pp. 4549–4557 (2017)
46. Tsin, Y., Ramesh, V., Kanade, T.: Statistical calibration of CCD imaging process. In: Proceedings Eighth IEEE International Conference on Computer Vision. ICCV 2001, vol. 1, pp. 480–487. IEEE (2001)
47. Wang, R., Chen, B., Meng, D., Wang, L.: Weakly supervised lesion detection from fundus images. IEEE Trans. Med. Imaging **38**(6), 1501–1512 (2018)
48. Wang, Z., Bovik, A.C., Sheikh, H.R., Simoncelli, E.P.: Image quality assessment: from error visibility to structural similarity. IEEE Trans. Image Process. **13**(4), 600–612 (2004)
49. Xie, J., Xu, L., Chen, E.: Image denoising and inpainting with deep neural networks. Adv. Neural Inf. Process. Syst. **25**, 341–349 (2012)

50. Xie, Q., Zhao, Q., Meng, D., Xu, Z.: Kronecker-basis-representation based tensor sparsity and its applications to tensor recovery. IEEE Trans. Pattern Anal. Mach. Intell. **40**(8), 1888–1902 (2017)
51. Xu, J., Li, H., Liang, Z., Zhang, D., Zhang, L.: Real-world noisy image denoising: a new benchmark. arXiv preprint arXiv:1804.02603 (2018)
52. Xu, J., Zhang, L., Zhang, D.: A trilateral weighted sparse coding scheme for real-world image denoising. In: Ferrari, V., Hebert, M., Sminchisescu, C., Weiss, Y. (eds.) ECCV 2018. LNCS, vol. 11212, pp. 21–38. Springer, Cham (2018). https://doi.org/10.1007/978-3-030-01237-3_2
53. Xu, J., Zhang, L., Zhang, D., Feng, X.: Multi-channel weighted nuclear norm minimization for real color image denoising. In: ICCV (2017)
54. Yong, H., Meng, D., Zuo, W., Zhang, L.: Robust online matrix factorization for dynamic background subtraction. IEEE Trans. Pattern Anal. Mach. Intell. **40**(7), 1726–1740 (2017)
55. Yue, Z., Yong, H., Meng, D., Zhao, Q., Leung, Y., Zhang, L.: Robust multiview subspace learning with nonindependently and nonidentically distributed complex noise. IEEE Trans. Neural Netw. Learn. Syst. **31**(4), 1070–1083 (2019)
56. Yue, Z., Yong, H., Zhao, Q., Meng, D., Zhang, L.: Variational denoising network: toward blind noise modeling and removal. In: Advances in Neural Information Processing Systems, pp. 1688–1699 (2019)
57. Zhang, K., Zuo, W., Chen, Y., Meng, D., Zhang, L.: Beyond a Gaussian denoiser: residual learning of deep cnn for image denoising. IEEE Trans. Image Process. **26**(7), 3142–3155 (2017)
58. Zhou, M., Chen, H., Ren, L., Sapiro, G., Carin, L., Paisley, J.W.: Non-parametric Bayesian dictionary learning for sparse image representations. In: Advances in Neural Information Processing Systems, pp. 2295–2303 (2009)
59. Zhu, F., Chen, G., Hao, J., Heng, P.A.: Blind image denoising via dependent Dirichlet process tree. IEEE Trans. Pattern Anal. Mach. Intell. **39**(8), 1518–1531 (2016)
60. Zhu, J.Y., Park, T., Isola, P., Efros, A.A.: Unpaired image-to-image translation using cycle-consistent adversarial networks. In: Proceedings of the IEEE International Conference on Computer Vision, pp. 2223–2232 (2017)

Linguistic Structure Guided Context Modeling for Referring Image Segmentation

Tianrui Hui[1,2], Si Liu[3]([✉]), Shaofei Huang[1,2], Guanbin Li[4], Sansi Yu[5], Faxi Zhang[5], and Jizhong Han[1,2]

[1] Institute of Information Engineering, Chinese Academy of Sciences, Beijing, China
{huitianrui,huangshaofei,hanjizhong}@iie.ac.cn
[2] School of Cyber Security, University of Chinese Academy of Sciences, Beijing, China
[3] Institute of Artificial Intelligence, Beihang University, Beijing, China
liusi@buaa.edu.cn
[4] Sun Yat-sen University, Guangzhou, China
liguanbin@mail.sysu.edu.cn
[5] Tencent Marketing Solution, Shenzhen, China
{mionyu,micahzhang}@tencent.com

Abstract. Referring image segmentation aims to predict the foreground mask of the object referred by a natural language sentence. Multimodal context of the sentence is crucial to distinguish the referent from the background. Existing methods either insufficiently or redundantly model the multimodal context. To tackle this problem, we propose a "gather-propagate-distribute" scheme to model multimodal context by cross-modal interaction and implement this scheme as a novel Linguistic Structure guided Context Modeling (LSCM) module. Our LSCM module builds a Dependency Parsing Tree suppressed Word Graph (DPT-WG) which guides all the words to include valid multimodal context of the sentence while excluding disturbing ones through three steps over the multimodal feature, i.e., gathering, constrained propagation and distributing. Extensive experiments on four benchmarks demonstrate that our method outperforms all the previous state-of-the-arts.

Keywords: Referring segmentation · Multimodal context · Linguistic structure · Graph propagation · Dependency Parsing Tree

1 Introduction

Referring image segmentation aims at predicting the foreground mask of the object which is matched with the description of a natural language expression. It

Electronic supplementary material The online version of this chapter (https://doi.org/10.1007/978-3-030-58607-2_4) contains supplementary material, which is available to authorized users.

© Springer Nature Switzerland AG 2020
A. Vedaldi et al. (Eds.): ECCV 2020, LNCS 12355, pp. 59–75, 2020.
https://doi.org/10.1007/978-3-030-58607-2_4

enjoys a wide range of applications, e.g., human-computer interaction and interactive image editing. Since natural language expressions may contain diverse linguistic concepts, such as entities (e.g. "car", "man"), attributes (e.g. "red", "small") and relationships (e.g. "front", "left"), this task is faced with a broader set of categories compared with a predefined one in traditional semantic segmentation. It requires the algorithm to handle the alignment of different semantic concepts between language and vision.

A general solution to this task is first extracting visual and linguistic features respectively, and then conducting segmentation based on the multimodal features generated from the two types of features. The entity referred by a sentence is defined as the *referent*. Multimodal features of the referent is hard to be distinguished from features of the background due to the existence of abundant noises. To solve this problem, valid multimodal context relevant to the sentence can be exploited to highlight features of the referent and suppress those of the background for accurate segmentation. Some works tackle this problem by straightforward concatenation [16,32] or recurrent refinement [4,21,25] of visual and linguistic features but lack the explicit modeling of multimodal context. Other works introduce dynamic filters [29] or cross-modal self-attention [39] to model multimodal context. However, these multimodal contexts are either insufficient or redundant since the number of dynamic filters [29] is limited and weights for aggregating multimodal context in self-attention [39] may be redundant due to dense computation operations.

To obtain valid multimodal context, a feasible solution is to exploit linguistic structure as guidance to selectively model valid multimodal context which is relevant to the sentence. As illustrated in Fig. 1, each word can gather multimodal context related to itself by cross-modal attention. For example, the word "dog" corresponds to the red masks of two dogs in the image. Multimodal context of each word is a partial and isolated comprehension result of the whole sentence. Therefore, constrained communication among words is required to include valid multimodal context and exclude disturbing ones. Afterwards, communicated multimodal context of each word contains appropriate information relevant to the whole sentence and can be aggregated to form valid multimodal context for highlighting features of the referent.

To realize the above solution, we propose a Linguistic Structure guided multimodal Context Modeling (LSCM) module in this paper. Concretely, features of the input sentence and image are first fused to form the multimodal features. Then, as illustrated in Fig. 1, in order to fully exploit the linguistic structure of the input sentence, we construct a Dependency Parsing Tree suppressed Word Graph (DPT-WG) where each node corresponds to a word. Based on the DPT-WG, three steps are conducted to model valid multimodal context of the sentence. (1) **Gather** relevant multimodal features (i.e., context) corresponding to a specific word through cross-modal attention as the node feature. At this step, each word node contains only multimodal context related to itself. Take Fig. 1 as an example, the segments corresponding to "dog" and "table" are denoted by red and blue masks respectively. The multimodal features inside each mask are attentively gathered to form the node feature of the graph. (2) **Propagate** information

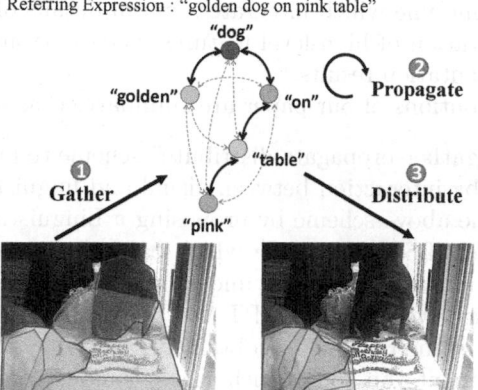

Fig. 1. Illustration of our proposed LSCM module. We construct a Dependency Parsing Tree suppressed Word Graph (DPT-WG) to model multimodal context in three steps. 1) **Gather.** Multimodal context relevant to each word are gathered as feature of each word node. Therefore, each word corresponds to some visually relevant segments in the image. For example, word "dog" corresponds to two red segments in the left image. 2) **Propagate.** DPT is exploited to further guide each word node to include valid multimodal context from others and exclude disturbing ones through suppressed graph propagation routes. Gray dotted and black solid lines denote suppressed and unsuppressed edges in DPT-WG respectively. 3) **Distribute.** Features of all word nodes are distributed back to the image. Segments corresponding to the input words are all clustered around the ground-truth segmentation region, i.e., the golden dog on pink table in the right image. (Best viewed in color).

among word nodes so that each word node can obtain multimodal context of the whole sentence. Initially, nodes in the word graph are fully-connected without any constraint on the edge weights. However, two words in the sentence may not be closely relevant to each other and unconstrained communication between them may introduce disturbing multimodal context. For example, the words "golden" and "pink" in Fig. 1 modify different entities respectively ("dog" and "table") and have relatively weak relevance between each other. Unconstrained (i.e., extensive) information propagation between "golden" and "pink" is unnecessary and may introduce disturbing multimodal context. Therefore, we utilize Dependency Parsing Tree (DPT) [3] to describe syntactic structures among words to selectively suppress certain weights of edges in our word graph. The DPT-WG can guide each word node to include valid contexts from others and exclude disturbing ones. After propagation, updated node features acquire information of the whole sentence. As shown in Fig. 1, the five words communicate and update their features under the structural guidance of our DPT-WG. (3) **Distribute** the updated node features back to every spatial location on the multimodal feature map. As shown in Fig. 1, the segments corresponding to the input words are all clustered around the ground-truth referring segmentation. It shows the updated multimodal features contain more valid multimodal context. In addition, we also propose a Dual-Path

Multi-Level Fusion module which integrates spatial details of low-level features and semantic information of high-level features using bottom-up and top-down paths to refine segmentation results.

The main contributions of our paper are summarized as follows:

- We introduce a "gather-propagate-distribute" scheme to model compact multimodal context by interaction between visual and linguistic modalities.
- We implement the above scheme by proposing a Linguistic Structure guided Context Modeling (LSCM) module which can aggregate valid multimodal context and exclude disturbing ones under the guidance of Dependency Parsing Tree suppressed Word Graph (DPT-WG). Thus, more discriminative multimodal features of the referent are obtained.
- Extensive experiments on four benchmarks demonstrate that our method outperforms all the previous state-of-the-arts, i.e., UNC (+1.58%), UNC+ (+3.09%), G-Ref (+1.65%) and ReferIt (+2.44%).

2   Related Work

2.1   Semantic Segmentation

In recent years, semantic segmentation has made great progress with Fully Convolutional Network [27] based methods. DeepLab [5] replaces standard convolution with atrous convolution to enlarge the receptive field of filters, leading to larger feature maps with richer semantic information than original FCN. DeepLab v2 [6] and v3 [7] employ parallel atrous convolutions with different atrous rates called ASPP to aggregate multi-scale context. PSPNet [43] adopts a pyramid pooling module to capture multi-scale information. EncNet [42] encodes semantic category prior information of the scenes to provide global context. Many works [1,23] exploit low level features containing detailed information to refine local parts of segmentation results.

2.2   Referring Image Localization and Segmentation

Referring image localization aims to localize the object referred by a natural language expression with a bounding box. Some works [15,22,36] model the relationships between multimodal features to match the objects with the expression. MAttNet [40] decomposes the referring expression into subject, location and relationship to compute modular scores for localizing the referent. Comparing with referring image localization, referring image segmentation aims to obtain a more accurate result of the referred object, i.e., a semantic mask instead of a bounding box. Methods in the referring segmentation field can be divided into two types, i.e., bottom-up and top-down. **Bottom-up** methods mainly focus on multimodal feature fusion to directly predict the mask of the referent. Hu *et al.* [16] proposes a straightforward concatenation of visual and linguistic features from CNN and LSTM [13]. Multi-level feature fusion are exploited in [21]. Word attention [4,32], multimodal LSTM [25,29] and adversarial learning [31] are further incorporated to refine multimodal features. Cross-modal self-attention is exploited in [39] to capture the long-range dependencies between image regions and words, introducing much redundant context due to the dense computation of self-attention. **Top-down** methods mainly rely on pretrained pixel-level detectors, i.e., Mask R-CNN [11] to generate RoI proposals and predict the mask within the selected proposal. MAttNet [40] incorporates modular scores into Mask R-CNN framework to conduct referring segmentation task. Recent CAC [8] introduces cycle-consistency between referring expression and its reconstructed caption into Mask R-CNN to boost the segmentation performance. In this paper, we propose a bottom-up method which exploits linguistic structure as guidance to include valid multimodal context and exclude disturbing ones for accurate referring segmentation.

2.3   Structural Context Modeling

Modeling context information is vital to vision and language problems. Typical methods like self-attention [33, 34] has shown great power for capturing the long range dependencies within the linguistic or visual modality. In addition, more complicated data structures are also explored to model context information. Chen et al. [9] proposes a latent graph with a small number of nodes to capture context from visual features for recognition and segmentation. In referring expression task, graphs [14, 36–38] using region proposals as nodes and neural module tree traversal [26] are also explored to model multimodal contexts to some extent. Different from them, we propose to build a more compact graph using referring words as nodes and exploit dependency parsing tree [3] to selectively model valid multimodal context.

3   Method

The overall architecture of our model is illustrated in Fig. 2. We first extract visual and linguistic features with a CNN and an LSTM respectively and then fuse them to obtain the multimodal feature. Afterwards, the multimodal feature is fed into our proposed Linguistic Structure guided Context Modeling (LSCM) module to highlight multimodal features of the referred entity. Our LSCM module conducts context modeling over the multimodal features under the structural guidance of DPT-WG. Finally, multi-level features are fused by our proposed Dual-Path Fusion module for mask prediction.

3.1   Multimodal Feature Extraction

Our model takes an image and a referring sentence with T words as input. As shown in Fig. 2, we use a CNN backbone to extract multi-level visual features and then transform them to the same size. Multi-level visual features $\{V_2, V_3, V_4, V_5\}$ correspond to $\{Res2, Res3, Res4, Res5\}$ features of ResNet [12], where $V_i \in \mathbb{R}^{H \times W \times C_v}, i \in \{2, 3, 4, 5\}$, with H, W and C_v being the height, width and channel number of visual features respectively. Since we conduct the

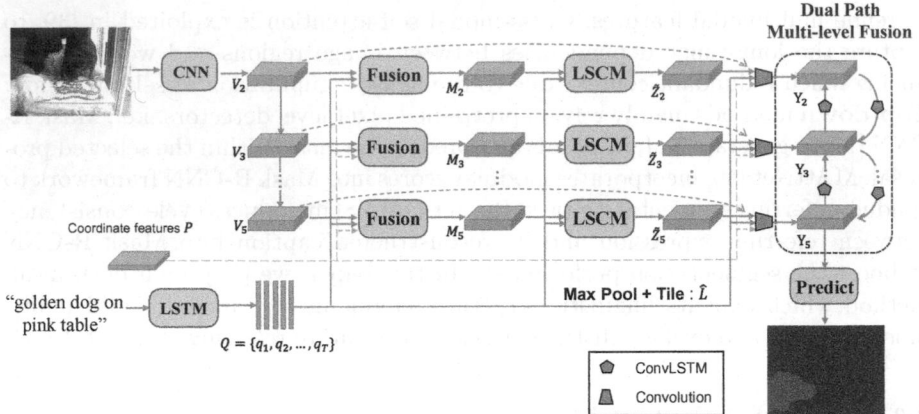

Fig. 2. Overall architecture of our model. Multi-level visual features $V_i, i \in [2, 5]$, word features Q and coordinate feature P are first fused to get multimodal features M_i. Then M_i are fed into our proposed LSCM to model valid multimodal context guided by linguistic structures. The output features $\tilde{Z}_i$ are combined with previous features and further fused through our Dual-Path Multi-Level Fusion module for mask prediction.

same operations on each level of the visual features, we use V to denote a single level of them for ease of presentation. For the input sentence of T words, we generate features of all the words $Q \in \mathbb{R}^{T \times C_l}$ with an LSTM [13]. To incorporate more spatial information, we also use an 8D spatial coordinate feature [25] denoted as $P \in \mathbb{R}^{H \times W \times 8}$. Afterwards, we fuse the features $\{V, Q, P\}$ to form the multimodal feature $M \in \mathbb{R}^{H \times W \times C_h}$, for which a simplified Mutan fusion [2] is adopted in this paper: $M = Mutan(V, Q, P)$. Details of Mutan fusion are included in the supplementary materials. Note that our method is not restricted to Mutan fusion, any other multimodal fusion approach can be used here.

3.2   Linguistic Structure Guided Context Modeling

In this module, we build a Dependency Parsing Tree suppressed Word Graph (DPT-WG) to model valid multimodal context. As illustrated in Fig. 3, we first gather feature vectors of all the spatial locations on multimodal feature M into T word nodes of WG. Then we exploit DPT [3] to softly suppress the disturbing edges in WG for selectively propagating information among word nodes, which includes valid multimodal contexts while excluding disturbing ones. Finally, we distribute features of word nodes back to each spatial location.

Gather: We get a cross-modal attention map $B \in \mathbb{R}^{T \times HW}$ with necessary reshape and transpose operations as follows:

$$B' = (QW_{q2})(MW_m)^T, \tag{1}$$

$$B = Softmax(\frac{B'}{\sqrt{C_h}}), \tag{2}$$

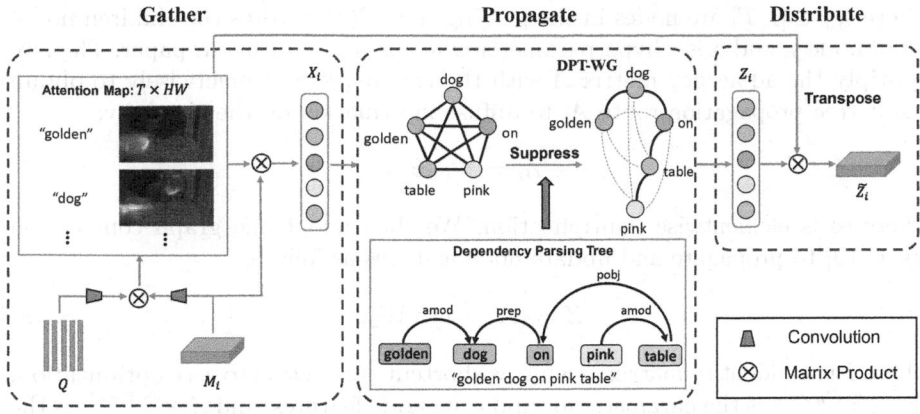

Fig. 3. Illustration of our LSCM module. We use cross-modal attention between words features Q and multimodal feature M_i to gather feature for each word node. Then we exploit DPT to softly suppress disturbing edges in the initial fully-connected WG and conduct information propagation. Finally, the updated features of word nodes are distributed back as $\tilde{Z}_i$ to incorporate valid multimodal context into original features.

where $W_{q2} \in \mathbb{R}^{C_l \times C_h}$ and $W_m \in \mathbb{R}^{C_h \times C_h}$ are learned parameters. Then we apply the normalized attention map B to M to gather the features into T word nodes:

$$X = BM, \tag{3}$$

where $X = [x_1; x_2; ...; x_T] \in \mathbb{R}^{T \times C_h}$ denotes the features of word nodes. Each $x_t, t = 1, 2, ..., T$ encodes the multimodal context related with the t-th word.

Propagate: The word graph used for context modeling is fully-connected. Thus, the adjacency matrix $A \in \mathbb{R}^{T \times T}$ is computed as follows:

$$A' = (XW_{x1})(XW_{x2})^T, \tag{4}$$

$$A = Softmax(\frac{A'}{\sqrt{C_h}}), \tag{5}$$

where $W_{x1} \in \mathbb{R}^{C_h \times C_h}$, $W_{x2} \in \mathbb{R}^{C_h \times C_h}$ are parameters for linear transformation layers. At present, the edge weights among word nodes are represented by multimodal feature similarities which are unconstrained. However, two words may not be closely related in the sentence and unconstrained information propagation between them may introduce plenty of noises, yielding disturbing multimodal context. To alleviate this issue, we exploit DPT to selectively suppress disturbing edges which do not belong to the DPT structure. Concretely, we compute a tree mask $S \in \mathbb{R}^{T \times T}$ to restrict the adjacency matrix A as follows:

$$S_{ij} = \begin{cases} 1, \ i \in \mathcal{C}(j) \ or \ j \in \mathcal{C}(i) \\ \\ \alpha, \ otherwise, \end{cases} \tag{6}$$

where $i, j \in [1, T]$ are nodes in the parsing tree, $\mathcal{C}(j)$ denotes the children nodes set of node j, and α is a hyperparameter which is set as 0.1 in our paper. Then we multiply the adjacency matrix A with the tree mask S elementwisely to obtain a soft tree propagation route A_t to diffuse information on the graph by:

$$A_t = A \odot S, \tag{7}$$

where $\odot$ is elementwise multiplication. We then adopt one graph convolution layer [19] to propagate and update node features as follows:

$$Z = (A_t + I)XW_z, \tag{8}$$

where I is an identity matrix serving as shortcut connection to ease optimization, $W_z \in \mathbb{R}^{C_h \times C_h}$ is the parameter for updating node features, and $Z \in \mathbb{R}^{T \times C_h}$ is the output of the graph convolution. After propagation, each word node can include valid multimodal context and exclude disturbing ones through the proper edges in parsing tree, forming robust features aligned with the whole sentence.

Distribute: Finally, we distribute the updated features of word graph nodes Z back to all the spatial locations using the transpose of B by:

$$\tilde{Z} = B^T Z. \tag{9}$$

We further conduct max pooling over word features $Q \in \mathbb{R}^{T \times C_l}$ to obtain sentence feature $L \in \mathbb{R}^{C_l}$, and then tile L for $H \times W$ times to form grid-like sentence feature $\hat{L} \in \mathbb{R}^{H \times W \times C_l}$. As shown in Fig. 2, the distributed feature $\tilde{Z} \in \mathbb{R}^{H \times W \times C_h}$ is concatenated with V, $\hat{L}$ and P and then fed into a 1×1 convolution to get the output feature $Y \in \mathbb{R}^{H \times W \times C_o}$.

3.3 Dual-Path Multi-Level Feature Fusion

It has been shown that the integration of features at different levels can lead to significant performance improvement of referring image segmentation [4,21,39]. We therefore also extract 4 levels of visual features $\{V_2, V_3, V_4, V_5\}$ as the input of our LSCM module. Then we utilize convolutional LSTM [35] to fuse the output features of the LSCM module $\{Y_2, Y_3, Y_4, Y_5\}$. The fusion process is illustrated in Fig. 2. We propose a Dual-Path Multi-Level Fusion module which sequentially fuses the features from 4 levels through the bottom-up and top-down paths. The input sequence of ConvLSTM is $[Y_5, Y_4, Y_3, Y_2, Y_3, Y_4, Y_5]$. The first bottom-up path sequentially integrates low-level features, which is able to complement high-level features with spatial details to refine the local parts of the mask. However, high-level features, which are critical for the model to recognize and localize the overall contour of the referred entities, are gradually diluted when integrating more and more low-level features. Thus, the top-down fusion path which reuses Y_3, Y_4 and Y_5 after bottom-up path is adopted to supplement more semantic multimodal information. Our Dual-Path Multi-Level Fusion module serves as a role to enhance features with both high-level semantics and low-level details for better segmentation performance.

4 Experiments

4.1 Experimental Setting

Datasets: We conduct extensive experiments on four benchmarks including UNC [41], UNC+ [41], G-Ref [28] and ReferIt [17]. UNC and UNC+ [41] are both collected from MS COCO dataset [24]. The UNC dataset contains $19,994$ images with $142,209$ referring expressions for $50,000$ objects while the UNC+ dataset contains $19,992$ images with $141,564$ expressions for $49,856$ objects. UNC+ has no location words hence it is more challenging than UNC. G-Ref [28] is also built upon the MS COCO dataset [24]. It consists of $26,711$ images with $104,560$ referring expressions for $54,822$ objects. The expressions are of average length of 8.4 words which is much longer than that of the other three datasets (with average length less than 4). ReferIt [17] is composed of $19,894$ images with $130,525$ referring expressions for $96,654$ objects. It also contains stuff categories.

Implementation Details: Following previous works [21,39], we choose DeepLab-ResNet101 [6] pre-trained on Pascal VOC dataset [10] as our backbone CNN. *Res2*, *Res3*, *Res4* and *Res5* are adopted for multi-level feature fusion. Input image is resized to 320×320. The maximum length of each referring expression is set to 20. For feature dimensions, we set $C_v = C_l = C_h = 1000, C_o = 500$. $\alpha = 0.1$ in our final model. The network is trained using Adam optimizer [18] with an initial learning rate of $2.5e^{-4}$ and a weight decay of $5e^{-4}$. We apply a polynomial decay with power of 0.9 to the learning rate. CNN is fixed during training. We use batch size 1 and stop training after $700K$ iterations. GloVe word embeddings [30] pretrained on Common Crawl with $840B$ tokens are used to replace randomly initialized ones. For fair comparison with prior works, all the final segmentation results are refined by DenseCRF [20].

Evaluation Metrics: Following the setup of prior works [4,16,21,39], we adopt overall intersection-over-union (*Overall IoU*) and precision with different thresholds (*Pr@X*) as the evaluation metrics for our model. The *Overall IoU* is calculated by dividing the total intersection area with the total union area, where both intersection area and union area are accumulated over all test samples. The *Pr@X* measures the percentage of prediction masks whose *IoU* is higher than the threshold X, where $X \in \{0.5, 0.6, 0.7, 0.8, 0.9\}$.

4.2 Comparison with State-of-the-Arts

Table 1 summarizes the comparison results in *Overall IoU* between our method and previous state-of-the-art methods. As illustrated in Table 1, our method consistently outperforms both bottom-up and top-down state-of-the-art methods on four benchmark datasets.

For bottom-up methods, STEP [4] densely fuses 5 feature levels for 25 times and achieves notable performance gains over CMSA [39]. Our method outperforms STEP on all the splits using less times of multimodal feature fusion, which indicates that our LSCM can capture more valid mulitmodal context information to better align features between visual and linguistic modalities. Particularly,

Table 1. Comparison with state-of-the-art methods on four benchmarks using *Overall IoU* as metric. "n/a" denotes methods does not use the same split as others. "BU" and "TD" denote "Bottom-Up" and "Top-Down" respectively.

Type	Method	ReferIt test	UNC			UNC+			G-Ref val
			val	testA	testB	val	testA	testB	
TD	MAttNet [40]	-	56.51	62.37	51.70	46.67	52.39	40.08	n/a
	CAC [8]	-	58.90	61.77	53.81	-	-	-	44.32
	NMTree [26]	-	56.59	63.02	52.06	47.40	53.01	41.56	n/a
BU	LSTM-CNN [16]	48.03	-	-	-	-	-	-	28.14
	DMN [29]	52.81	49.78	54.83	45.13	38.88	44.22	32.29	36.76
	RMI [25]	58.73	45.18	45.69	45.57	29.86	30.48	29.50	34.52
	KWA [32]	59.09	-	-	-	-	-	-	36.92
	CMSA(vgg16) [39]	59.91	52.38	54.68	49.59	34.41	36.53	30.10	32.35
	ASGN [31]	60.31	50.46	51.20	49.27	38.41	39.79	35.97	41.36
	RRN [21]	63.63	55.33	57.26	53.95	39.75	42.15	36.11	36.45
	Ours(vgg16)	63.82	55.41	57.92	52.54	41.18	44.32	35.78	39.78
	CMSA [39]	63.80	58.32	60.61	55.09	43.76	47.60	37.89	39.98
	STEP [4]	64.13	60.04	63.46	57.97	48.19	52.33	40.41	46.40
	Ours	**66.57**	**61.47**	**64.99**	**59.55**	**49.34**	**53.12**	**43.50**	**48.05**

ReferIt is a challenging dataset on which pervious methods only achieve marginal improvements. CMSA and STEP outperform RRN [21] by 0.17% and 0.50% IoU respectively, while our method significantly boost the performance gain to 2.94%, which well demonstrates the effectiveness of our method. Moreover, on UNC+ dataset which has no location words, our method also achieves 3.09% over STEP on testB split, showing that our method can model richer multimodal context information with less input conditions. In addition, we reimplement CSMA using their released code and our method using VGG16 as backbone. Our VGG16-based method also yields better performance on all 4 datasets with margins of 3.24% on UNC, 7.79% on UNC+, 7.43% on G-Ref and 3.91% on ReferIt dataset, showing that our method can well adapt to different visual features.

For top-down methods, MAttNet [40] and CAC [8] first generate a set of object proposals and then predict the foreground mask within the selected proposal. The decoupling of detection and segmentation relies on Mask-RCNN which is pretrained on much more COCO images ($110K$) than bottom-up methods using only PASCAL-VOC images ($10K$) for pretraining. Therefore, comparing their performances with bottom-up methods may not be completely fair. However, our method still outperforms MAttNet and CAC with large margins, indicating the superiority of our method. In addition, on ReferIt dataset which contains sentences about stuff, our method achieves state-of-the-art performance while top-down methods may not be able to well handle them.

There are also many top-down works [14,36–38] in referring localization field which adopt graphs to conduct grounding. Their graphs are composed of

Table 2. Ablation studies on UNC val set. All models use the same backbone (DeepLab-ResNet101) and DenseCRF for postprocessing. *The statistics of RRN-CNN [21] are higher than those reported in the original paper which do not use Dense-CRF. Row 8 and row 11 are the same models with different names.

	Method	Pr@0.5	Pr@0.6	Pr@0.7	Pr@0.8	Pr@0.9	IoU(%)
1	RRN-CNN [21]*	46.99	37.96	27.86	16.25	3.75	47.26
2	+LSCM	61.26	52.93	43.39	27.38	6.70	54.87
3	+LSCM, GloVe [30]	63.13	54.20	43.38	27.54	6.78	55.93
4	+LSCM, GloVe, Mutan [2]	**64.25**	**55.64**	**45.00**	**29.24**	**7.28**	**56.50**
5	Multi-Level-RRN-CNN [21]*	65.83	57.45	46.76	31.91	10.40	57.61
6	+LSCM	68.33	61.16	51.59	36.98	11.57	59.67
7	+LSCM, GloVe [30]	70.56	62.89	52.91	38.07	11.99	60.98
8	+LSCM, GloVe, Mutan [2]	**70.84**	**63.82**	**53.67**	**38.69**	**12.06**	**61.54**
9	+Concat Fusion	68.49	60.78	50.92	34.87	9.94	60.10
10	+Gated Fusion [39]	69.08	62.46	50.73	35.42	11.27	60.46
11	+Dual-Path Fusion (Ours)	**70.84**	**63.82**	**53.67**	**38.69**	**12.06**	**61.54**

region proposals which rely on detectors pretrained on COCO and/or other large datasets. However, our DPT-WG consists of referring words and uses DPT to suppress disturbing edges in WG. Then, features of WG are distributed back to highlight grid format features of the referent for bottom-up mask prediction. Thus, our method is also different from NMTree [26] in which neural modules are assembled to tree nodes to conduct progressive grounding (i.e., retrieval) based on region proposals.

4.3 Ablation Studies

We perform ablation studies on UNC val set to verify the effectiveness of our proposed LSCM module and the Dual-Path Fusion module for leveraging multi-level features. Experimental results are summarized in Table 2.

LSCM Module: We first explore the effectiveness of our proposed LSCM module based on single level feature. Following [39], we implement the RRN-CNN [21] model without the recurrent refinement module as our baseline. Our baseline uses an LSTM to encode the whole referring expression as a sentence feature vector, and then concatenates it with each spatial location of the $Res5$ feature from DeepLab-101. Fusion and prediction are conducted on the concatenated features for generating final mask results. As shown in rows 1 to 4 of Table 2, **+LSCM** indicates that introducing our LSCM module into the baseline model can bring a significant performance gain of 7.61% IoU, demonstrating that our LSCM can well model valid multimodal context under the guidance of linguistic structure. Row 3 and Row 4 show that incorporating GloVe [30] and Mutan [2] fusion can further boost the performance based on our LSCM module.

We further conduct the same ablation studies based on multi-level features. All the models use our proposed Dual-Path Fusion module to fuse multi-level features. As shown in rows 5 to 8 of Table 2, our multi-level models achieve consistent performance improvements as the single-level models. These results well prove that our LSCM module can effectively capture multi-level context as well. Moreover, we additionally adapt **GloRe** [9] for the referring segmentation task over multi-level features and achieve 58.53% IoU and 67.23% $Pr@0.5$. The adapted GloRe uses learned projection matrix to project multimodal features into fixed number of abstract graph nodes, then conducts graph convolutions and reprojection to refine multimodal features. Our **+LSCM** in row 6 outperforms GloRe by 1.14% IoU and 1.10% $Pr@0.5$, indicating that building word graph by cross-modal attention and incorporating DPT to suppress disturbing edges between word nodes can better model valid multimodal context than GloRe.

Multi-level Feature Fusion: We compare different methods including Concat Fusion, Gated Fusion [39] and our Dual-Path Fusion for multi-level feature fusion. All the fusion methods take 4 levels of multimodal features processed by our LSCM module as input. As shown in rows 9 to 11 of Table 2, our proposed Dual-Path Multi-Level Fusion module achieves the best result, showing the effectiveness of integrating both high-level semantics and low-level details. In addition, the gated fusion from [39] conducts 9 fusion operations while ours conducts 6 fusion operations with better performance.

Table 3. Experiments of graph convolution in terms of *Overall IoU*. n denotes number of layers of graph convolution in our LSCM module. $\alpha = 0.1$ here.

	+LSCM, GloVe					
	$n = 0$	$n = 1$	$n = 2$	$n = 3$	$n = 4$	adaptive
UNC val	54.51	**55.93**	50.77	50.64	49.59	54.69
G-Ref val	38.94	**40.54**	39.29	37.74	37.50	37.41

Layers of Graph Convolution: In Table 3, we explore the effects of conducting different layers of graph convolution in our LSCM module on UNC val set and G-Ref val set. The results show that the naive increase of graph convolution layers in LSCM will deteriorate the segmentation performance, probably because multiple rounds of message propagation among all words muddle the multimodal context of each word instead of enhancing it. Besides, adaptive which means number of the graph convolution layers equal to the depth of DPT, yields lower performance than one layer of graph convolution. It indicates that propagating information among word nodes without further constrain will include more disturbing context. Conducting 1 layer of graph convolution to communication between parents and children nodes is already sufficient without introducing too much noises, which also makes our method more efficient. In addition, $n = 1$ also outperforms $n = 0$ which shows communication among words is necessary after gathering multimodal context for each word.

Edge Weights in Tree Mask: In Table 4, we explore how different values of α in the tree mask S (Eq. 6) influence the performance of our LSCM. We can

Table 4. *Overall IoU* results of different edge weights α in tree mask S. Experiments are conducted on UNC val set. All the models use $n = 1$ layer of graph convolution.

+LSCM, GloVe						
$\alpha = 0$	$\alpha = 0.1$	$\alpha = 0.2$	$\alpha = 0.3$	$\alpha = 0.4$	$\alpha = 0.5$	$\alpha = 1$
55.01	**55.93**	55.44	55.49	54.77	55.12	54.81

observe that $\alpha = 0.1$ achieves the best performance and outperforms $\alpha = 1$ (WG w/o DPT) by 1.12% IoU, which demonstrates that suppressing syntactic irrelevant edges in our word graph can reduce unnecessary information propagation and exclude disturbing multimodal context. In addition, $\alpha = 0$ yields inferior performance to $\alpha = 0.1$, indicating our DPT-WG (i.e., approximate spanning tree) can obtain more sufficient information than a strict DPT.

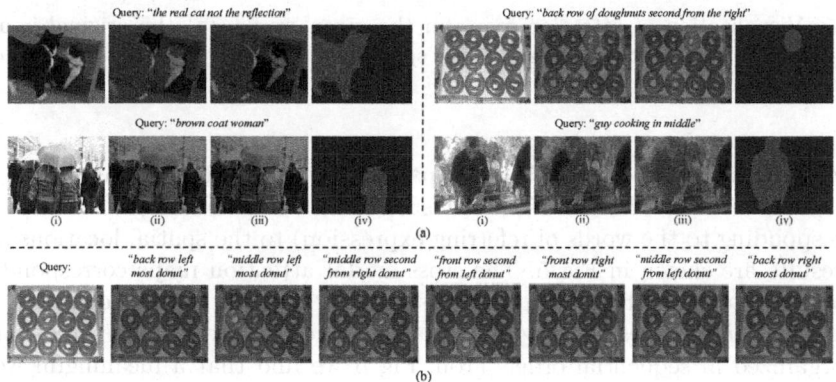

Fig. 4. Qualitative Results of referring image segmentation. (a)(i) Original image. (a)(ii) Results produced by the multi-level RRN-CNN baseline (row 5 in Table 2). (a)(iii) Results produced by our full model (row 8 in Table 2). (a)(iv) Ground-truth. (b) Results of customized expressions. Our model can adapt to new expressions flexibly.

Qualitative Results: Figure 4(a) presents the segmentation results predicted by our full model (row 8 in Table 2) and the multi-level RRN-CNN baseline (row 5 in Table 2). Comparing (b) and (c) in Fig. 4, we can find that only multi-level feature refinement without valid multimodal context modeling is not sufficient for the model to understand the referring expression comprehensively, thus resulting in inaccurate predictions, such as segmenting "coat" but ignoring "brown" in the bottom-left of Fig. 4. As shown in Fig. 4(b), we also manually generate customized expressions to traverse many the donuts. It is interesting to find that our model can always understand different expressions adaptively and locate the right donuts, indicating that our model is flexible and controllable. More qualitative results on four datasets are presented in supplementary materials.

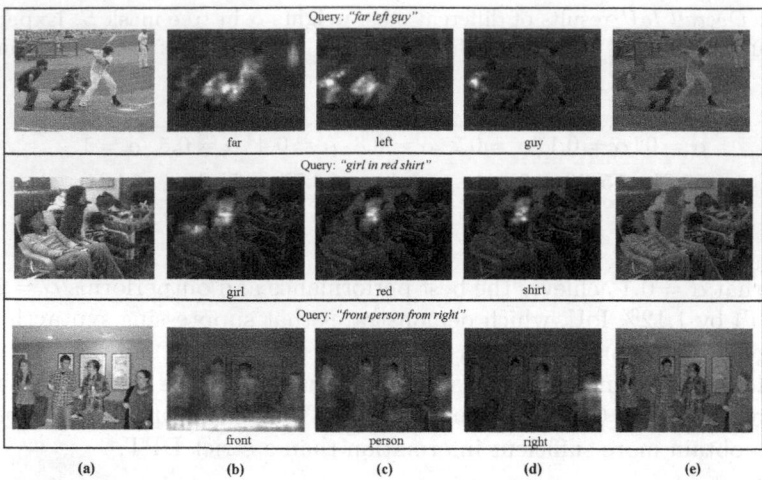

Fig. 5. Visualization of attention maps on the given words. (a) the original image. (b)(c)(d) refer to the attention maps of the specific words below. (e) predictions of our proposed method.

Visualization of Attention Maps: To give a straightforward explanation about how our LSCM works, we visualize the attention maps of each node (corresponding to the words of referring expression) to the spatial locations and the results are shown in Fig. 5. The cross-modal attention maps correspond to B obtained in the gather operation (Eqs. 1 and 2), which has size of $T \times HW$. Each row of B denotes the attention map of a certain word. The three words are organized in sequential order. From Fig. 5 we find that a meaningful word usually attends to its corresponding area in the image. For example, in the third row of (b), the word "front" attends to the front area of the image, and in the second row of (c), word "red" attends to the area of red shirt. Our LSCM module is able to model valid multimodal context among these attended areas to obtain a precise segmentation of the referring expression.

5   Conclusion and Future Work

In this paper, we explore the referring image segmentation problem by introducing a "gather-propagate-distribute" scheme to model multimodal context. We implement this scheme as a Linguistic Structure guided Context Modeling (LSCM) module. Our LSCM builds a Dependency Parsing Tree suppressed Word Graph (DPT-WG) which guides all the words to include valid multimodal context of the sentence while excluding disturbing ones, which can effectively highlight multimodal features of the referent. Our proposed model achieves state-of-the-art performance on four benchmarks. In the future, we plan to adapt our LSCM module into other tasks (e.g., VQA, Captioning) to verify its effectiveness.

Acknowledgement. This work is supported by Guangdong Basic and Applied Basic Research Foundation (No. 2020B1515020048), National Natural Science Foundation of China (Grant 61876177, Grant 61976250), Beijing Natural Science Foundation (L182013, 4202034), Fundamental Research Funds for the Central Universities, Zhejiang Lab (No. 2019KD0AB04) and Tencent Open Fund.

References

1. Badrinarayanan, V., Kendall, A., Cipolla, R.: Segnet: a deep convolutional encoder-decoder architecture for image segmentation. TPAMI (2017)
2. Ben-Younes, H., Cadene, R., Cord, M., Thome, N.: MUTAN: multimodal tucker fusion for visual question answering. In: ICCV (2017)
3. Chen, D., Manning, C.D.: A fast and accurate dependency parser using neural networks. In: EMNLP (2014)
4. Chen, D.J., Jia, S., Lo, Y.C., Chen, H.T., Liu, T.L.: See-through-text grouping for referring image segmentation. In: ICCV (2019)
5. Chen, L.C., Papandreou, G., Kokkinos, I., Murphy, K., Yuille, A.L.: Semantic image segmentation with deep convolutional nets and fully connected CRFs. arXiv preprint arXiv:1412.7062 (2014)
6. Chen, L.C., Papandreou, G., Kokkinos, I., Murphy, K., Yuille, A.L.: DeepLab: semantic image segmentation with deep convolutional nets, atrous convolution, and fully connected CRFs. IEEE Trans. Pattern Anal. Mach. Intell. (TPAMI) **40**(4), 834–848 (2017)
7. Chen, L.C., Papandreou, G., Schroff, F., Adam, H.: Rethinking atrous convolution for semantic image segmentation. arXiv preprint arXiv:1706.05587 (2017)
8. Chen, Y.W., Tsai, Y.H., Wang, T., Lin, Y.Y., Yang, M.H.: Referring expression object segmentation with caption-aware consistency. arXiv preprint arXiv:1910.04748 (2019)
9. Chen, Y., et al.: Graph-based global reasoning networks. In: CVPR (2019)
10. Everingham, M., Van Gool, L., Williams, C.K., Winn, J., Zisserman, A.: The Pascal visual object classes (VOC) challenge. Int. J. Comput. Vis. IJCV **88**, 303–338 (2010)
11. He, K., Gkioxari, G., Dollár, P., Girshick, R.B.: Mask R-CNN. In: ICCV (2017)
12. He, K., Zhang, X., Ren, S., Sun, J.: Deep residual learning for image recognition. In: CVPR (2016)
13. Hochreiter, S., Schmidhuber, J.: Long short-term memory. Neural Comput. **9**(8), 1735–1780 (1997)
14. Hu, R., Rohrbach, A., Darrell, T., Saenko, K.: Language-conditioned graph networks for relational reasoning. In: ICCV (2019)
15. Hu, R., Rohrbach, M., Andreas, J., Darrell, T., Saenko, K.: Modeling relationships in referential expressions with compositional modular networks. In: CVPR (2017)
16. Hu, R., Rohrbach, M., Darrell, T.: Segmentation from natural language expressions. In: Leibe, B., Matas, J., Sebe, N., Welling, M. (eds.) Computer Vision – ECCV 2016. Lecture Notes in Computer Science, vol. 9905, pp. 108–128. Springer, Cham (2016). https://doi.org/10.1007/978-3-319-46448-0_7
17. Kazemzadeh, S., Ordonez, V., Matten, M., Berg, T.: ReferitGame: referring to objects in photographs of natural scenes. In: EMNLP (2014)
18. Kingma, D.P., Ba, J.: Adam: amethod for stochastic optimization. arXiv preprint arXiv:1412.6980 (2014)

19. Kipf, T.N., Welling, M.: Semi-supervised classification with graph convolutional networks. arXiv preprint arXiv:1609.02907 (2016)
20. Krähenbühl, P., Koltun, V.: Efficient inference in fully connected CRFs with Gaussian edge potentials. In: NeurIPS (2011)
21. Li, R., et al.: Referring image segmentation via recurrent refinement networks. In: CVPR (2018)
22. Liao, Y., et al.: A real-time cross-modality correlation filtering method for referring expression comprehension. In: CVPR (2020)
23. Lin, G., Milan, A., Shen, C., Reid, I.: RefineNet: multi-path refinement networks for high-resolution semantic segmentation. In: CVPR (2017)
24. Lin, T.Y., et al.: Microsoft COCO: common objects in context. In: Fleet, D., Pajdla, T., Schiele, B., Tuytelaars, T. (eds.) Computer Vision – ECCV 2014. Lecture Notes in Computer Science, vol. 8693, pp. 740–755. Springer, Cham (2014). https://doi.org/10.1007/978-3-319-10602-1_48
25. Liu, C., et al.: Recurrent multimodal interaction for referring image segmentation. In: ICCV (2017)
26. Liu, D., Zhang, H., Wu, F., Zha, Z.J.: Learning to assemble neural module tree networks for visual grounding. In: ICCV (2019)
27. Long, J., Shelhamer, E., Darrell, T.: Fully convolutional networks for semantic segmentation. In: CVPR (2015)
28. Mao, J., et al.: Generation and comprehension of unambiguous object descriptions. In: CVPR (2016)
29. Margffoy-Tuay, E., Pérez, J.C., Botero, E., Arbeláez, P.: Dynamic multimodal instance segmentation guided by natural language queries. In: Ferrari, V., Hebert, M., Sminchisescu, C., Weiss, Y. (eds.) Computer Vision – ECCV 2018. Lecture Notes in Computer Science, vol. 11215, pp. 656–672. Springer, Cham (2018). https://doi.org/10.1007/978-3-030-01252-6_39
30. Pennington, J., Socher, R., Manning, C.: Glove: global vectors for word representation. In: EMNLP (2014)
31. Qiu, S., Zhao, Y., Jiao, J., Wei, Y., Wei, S.: Referring image segmentation by generative adversarial learning. IEEE Trans. Multimedia (TMM) 22(5), 1333–1344 (2019)
32. Shi, H., Li, H., Meng, F., Wu, Q.: Key-word-aware network for referring expression image segmentation. In: Ferrari, V., Hebert, M., Sminchisescu, C., Weiss, Y. (eds.) Computer Vision – ECCV 2018. Lecture Notes in Computer Science, vol. 11210, pp. 38–54. Springer, Cham (2018). https://doi.org/10.1007/978-3-030-01231-1_3
33. Vaswani, A., et al.: Attention is all you need. In: NeurIPS (2017)
34. Wang, X., Girshick, R., Gupta, A., He, K.: Non-local neural networks. In: CVPR (2018)
35. Xingjian, S., et al.: Convolutional LSTM network: a machine learning approach for precipitation nowcasting. In: NeurIPS (2015)
36. Yang, S., Li, G., Yu, Y.: Cross-modal relationship inference for grounding referring expressions. In: CVPR (2019)
37. Yang, S., Li, G., Yu, Y.: Dynamic graph attention for referring expression comprehension. In: ICCV (2019)
38. Yang, S., Li, G., Yu, Y.: Graph-structured referring expression reasoning in the wild. In: CVPR (2020)
39. Ye, L., Rochan, M., Liu, Z., Wang, Y.: Cross-modal self-attention network for referring image segmentation. In: CVPR (2019)
40. Yu, L., et al.: MAttNet: modular attention network for referring expression comprehension. In: CVPR (2018)

41. Yu, L., Poirson, P., Yang, S., Berg, A.C., Berg, T.L.: Modeling context in referring expressions. In: Leibe, B., Matas, J., Sebe, N., Welling, M. (eds.) Computer
Vision – ECCV 2016. Lecture Notes in Computer Science, vol. 9906, pp. 69–85.
Springer, Cham (2016). https://doi.org/10.1007/978-3-319-46475-6_5
42. Zhang, H., et al.: Context encoding for semantic segmentation. In: CVPR (2018)
43. Zhao, H., Shi, J., Qi, X., Wang, X., Jia, J.: Pyramid scene parsing network. In:
CVPR (2017)

Federated Visual Classification
with Real-World Data Distribution

Tzu-Ming Harry Hsu[1,2(✉)], Hang Qi[2], and Matthew Brown[2]

[1] MIT CSAIL, Cambridge, USA
stmharry@mit.edu, stmharry@google.com
[2] Google Research, Seattle, USA
hangqi@google.com, mtbr@google.com

Abstract. Federated Learning enables visual models to be trained on-device, bringing advantages for user privacy (data need never leave the device), but challenges in terms of data diversity and quality. Whilst typical models in the datacenter are trained using data that are independent and identically distributed (IID), data at source are typically far from IID. Furthermore, differing quantities of data are typically available at each device (imbalance). In this work, we characterize the effect these real-world data distributions have on distributed learning, using as a benchmark the standard Federated Averaging (FedAvg) algorithm. To do so, we introduce two new large-scale datasets for species and landmark classification, with realistic per-user data splits that simulate real-world edge learning scenarios. We also develop two new algorithms (FedVC, FedIR) that intelligently resample and reweight over the client pool, bringing large improvements in accuracy and stability in training. The datasets are made available online.

1 Introduction

Federated learning (FL) is a privacy-preserving framework, originally introduced by McMahan et al. [19], for training models from decentralized user data residing on devices at the edge. Models are trained iteratively across many federated rounds. For each round, every participating device (a.k.a. *client*), receives an initial model from a central server, performs stochastic gradient descent (SGD) on its local training data and sends back the gradients. The server then aggregates all gradients from the participating clients and updates the starting model. FL preserves user privacy in that the raw data used for training models never leave the devices throughout the process. In addition, differential privacy [20] can be applied for a theoretically bounded guarantee that no information about individuals can be derived from the aggregated values on the central server.

Work done whilst at Google.

Electronic supplementary material The online version of this chapter (https://doi.org/10.1007/978-3-030-58607-2_5) contains supplementary material, which is available to authorized users.

© Springer Nature Switzerland AG 2020
A. Vedaldi et al. (Eds.): ECCV 2020, LNCS 12355, pp. 76–92, 2020.
https://doi.org/10.1007/978-3-030-58607-2_5

Federated learning is an active area of research with a number of open questions [13, 16] remaining to be answered. A particular challenge is the distribution of data at user devices. Whilst in centralized training, data can be assumed to be independent and identically distributed (IID), this assumption is unlikely to hold in federated settings. Decentralized training data on end-user devices will vary due to user-specific habits, preferences, geographic locations, etc. Furthermore, in contrast to the streamed batches from a central data store in the data center, devices participating in an FL round will have differing amounts of data available for training.

In this work, we study the effect these heterogeneous client data distributions have on learning visual models in a federated setting, and propose novel techniques for more effective and efficient federated learning. We focus in particular on two types of distribution shift: **Non-Identical Class Distribution**, meaning that the distribution of visual classes at each device is different, and **Imbalanced Client Sizes**, meaning that the number of data available for training at each device varies. Our key contributions are:

- **We analyze the effect of learning with per-user data** in real-world datasets, in addition to carefully controlled setups with parametric (Dirichlet) and natural (geographic) distributions.
- **We propose two new algorithms** to mitigate per-client distribution shift and imbalance, substantially improving classification accuracy and stability.
- **We provide new large-scale datasets** with per-user data for two classification problems (natural world and landmark recognition) to the community.

Ours is the first work to our knowledge that attempts to train large-scale visual classification models for real-world problems in a federated setting. We expect that more is to be done to achieve robust performance in this and related settings, and are making our datasets available to the community to enable future research in this area[1].

2   Related Work

Synthetic Client Data Several authors have explored the FedAvg algorithm on synthetic non-identical client data partitions generated from image classification datasets. McMahan et al. [19] synthesize pathological non-identical user splits from the MNIST dataset, sorting training examples by class labels and partitioning into shards such that each client is assigned 2 shards. They demonstrate that FedAvg on non-identical clients still converges to 99% accuracy, though taking more rounds than identically distributed clients . In a similar sort-and-partition manner, [26, 35] use extreme partitions of the CIFAR-10 dataset to form a population consisting of 10 clients in total. In contrast to these pathological data splits, Yurochkin et al. [33] and Hsu et al. [11] synthesize more diverse non-identical datasets with Dirichlet priors.

---

[1] https://github.com/google-research/google-research/tree/master/federated_vision_datasets.

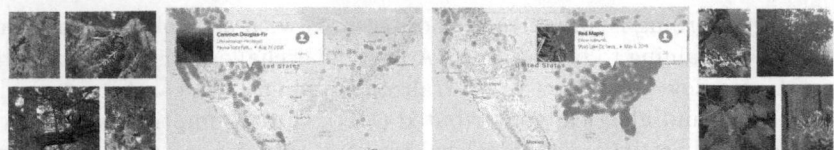

Fig. 1. iNaturalist Species Distribution. Visualized here are the distributions of Douglas-Fir and Red Maple in the continental US within iNaturalist. In a federated learning context, visual categories vary with location, and users in different locations will have very different training data distributions.

Realistic Datasets Other authors look at more realistic data distributions at the client. For example, Caldas et al. [2] use the Extended MNIST dataset [3] split over the writers of the digits and the CelebA dataset [17] split by the celebrity on the picture. The Shakespeare and Stack Overflow datasets [7] contain natural per-user splits of textual data using roles and online user ids, respectively. Luo et al. [18] propose a dataset containing 900 images from 26 street-level cameras, which they use to train object detectors. These datasets are however limited in size, and are not representative of data captured on user devices in a federated learning context. Our work aims to address these limitations (see Sect. 4).

Variance reduction methods have been used in the federated learning literature to correct for the distribution shift caused by heterogeneous client data. Sahu et al. [24] introduce a proximal term to client objectives for bounded variance. Karimireddy et al. [14] propose to use control variates for correcting client updates drift. Importance sampling is a classic technique for variance reduction in Monte Carlo methods [9,12] and has been used widely in domain adaption literature for countering covariate and target shift [21,23,34]. In this work, we adopt a similar idea of importance reweighting in a novel federated setting resulting in augmented client objectives. Different from the classic setting where samples are drawn from one proposal distribution which has the same support as the target, heterogeneous federated clients form multiple proposal distributions, each of which has partially common support with the target.

3   Federated Visual Classification Problems

Many problems in visual classification involve data that vary around the globe [5,8]. This means that the distribution of data visible to a given user device will vary, sometimes substantially. For example, user observations in the citizen scientist app iNaturalist will depend on the underlying species distribution in that region (see Fig. 1). Many other factors could potentially influence the data present on a device, including the interests of the user, their photography habits, etc. For this study we choose two problems with an underlying geographic variation to illustrate the general problem of non-identical user data, *Natural Species Classification* and *Landmark Recognition*.

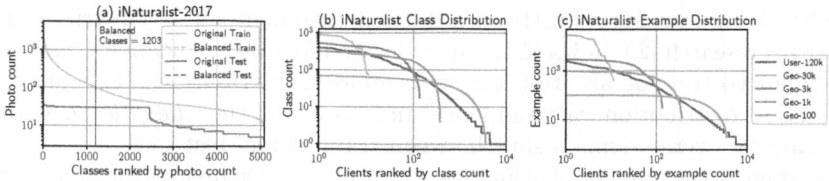

Fig. 2. iNaturalist Distribution. In (a) we show the re-balancing of the original iNaturalist-2017 dataset. In (b) and (c) we show class and example counts vs clients for our 5 iNaturalist partitionings with varying levels of class distribution shift and size imbalance. The client count is different in each partitioning.

Natural Species Classification We create a dataset and classification problem based on the iNaturalist 2017 Challenge [28], where images are contributed by a community of citizen scientists around the globe. Domain experts take pictures of natural species and provide annotations during field trips. Fine-grained visual classifiers could potentially be trained in a federated fashion with this community of citizen scientists without transferring images.

Landmark Recognition. We study the problem of visual landmark recognition based on the 2019 Landmark Recognition Challenge [30], where the images are taken and uploaded by Wikipedia contributors. It resembles a scenario where smartphone users take photos of natural and architectural landmarks (e.g., famous buildings, monuments, mountains, etc.) while traveling. Landmark recognition models could potentially be trained via federated learning without uploading or storing private user photos at a centralized party.

Both datasets have data partitioning per user, enabling us to study a realistic federated learning scenario where labeled images were provided by the user and learning proceeds on-device. For experimentation in lab, we use a simulation engine for federated learning algorithms, similar to TensorFlow Federated [6].

4 Datasets

In the following section, we describe in detail the datasets we develop and analyze key distributional statistics as a function of user and geo-location. We plan to make these datasets available to the community.

4.1 INaturalist-User-120k and iNaturalist-Geo Splits

iNaturalist-2017 [28] is a large scale fine-grained visual classification dataset comprised of images of natural species taken by citizen scientists. It has 579,184 training examples and 95,986 test examples covering over 5,000 classes. Images in this dataset are each associated with a fine-grained species label, a longitude-latitude coordinate where the picture was originally taken, and authorship information.

The iNaturalist-2017 training set has a very long-tailed distribution over classes as shown in Fig. 2a, while the test set is relatively uniform over classes.

While studying learning robustly with differing training and test distributions is a topic for research [29] in itself, in our federated learning benchmark, we create class-balanced training and test sets with uniform distributions. This allows us to focus on distribution variations and imbalance at the *client level*, without correcting for overall domain shift between training and test sets.

To equalize the number of examples across classes, we first sort all class labels by their count and truncate tail classes with less than 100 training examples. This is then followed by subsampling per-class until all remaining classes each have 100 examples. This results in a balanced training set consisting of 1,203 classes and 120,300 examples. We use this class-balanced iNaturalist subset for the remainder of the paper.

The iNaturalist-2017 dataset includes user ids, which we use to partition the balanced training set into a population of 9,275 clients. We refer to this partitioning as **iNaturalist-User-120k**. This contributor partitioning resembles a realistic scenario where images are collected per-user.

In addition, for study the federated learning algorithms with client populations of varying levels of deviation from the global distribution, we also generate a *wide range* of populations by partitioning the dataset at varying levels of granularity according to the geographic locations.

To utilize the geo-location tags, we leverage the S2 grid system, which defines a hierarchical partitioning of the planet surface. We perform an adaptive partitioning similar to [31]. Specifically, every S2 cell is recursively subdivided into four finer-level cells until no single cell contains more than $N_{\max}$ examples. Cells ending up with less than $N_{\min}$ examples are discarded. With this scheme, we are able to control the granularity of the resulting S2 cells such that a smaller $N_{\max}$ results in a larger client count. We use $N_{\max} \in \{30k, 3k, 1k, 100\}$, $N_{\min} = 0.01N_{\max}$ and refer to the resulting data partitionings as **iNaturalist-Geo-{30k, 3k, 1k, 100}**, respectively. Rank statistics of our geo- and per-user data splits are shown in Fig. 2b and c.

4.2   Landmarks-User-160k

Google Landmarks Dataset V2 (GLD-v2) [30] is a large scale image dataset for landmark recognition and retrieval, consisting of 5 million images with each attributed to one of over 280,000 authors. The full dataset is noisy: images with the same label could depict landmark exteriors, historical artifacts, paintings or sculptures inside a building. For benchmarking federated learning algorithms on a well-defined image classification problem, we use the cleaned subset (GLD-v2-clean), which is a half the size of the full dataset. In this set, images are discarded if the computed local geometric features from which cannot be matched to at least two other images with the same label [22].

For creating a dataset for federated learning with natural user identities, we partition the GLD-v2-clean subset according to the authorship attribute. In addition, we mitigate the long tail while maintaining realism by requiring every landmark to have at least 30 images and be visited by at least 10 users, meanwhile requiring every user to have contributed at least 30 images that depict 5 or more

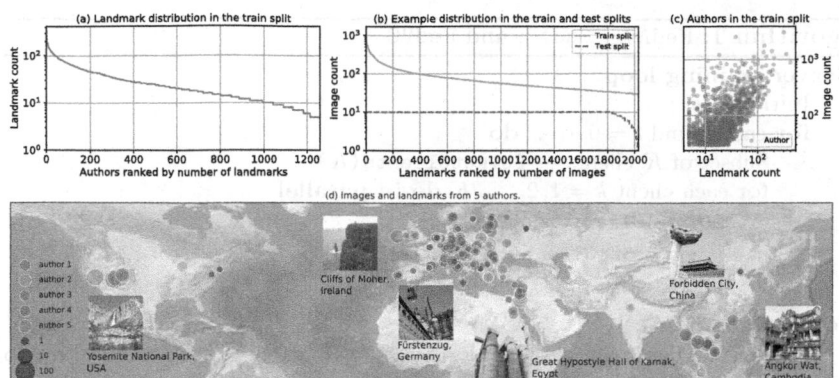

Fig. 3. Landmarks-User-160k Distribution. Images are partitioned according to the authorship attribute from the GLD-v2 dataset. Filtering is applied to mitigate long tail in the train split.

landmarks. The resulting dataset has 164,172 images of 2,028 landmarks from 1,262 users, which we refer to as the train split of **Landmarks-User-160k.**

Following the dataset curation in [30], the test split is created from the left-over images in GLD-v2-clean whose authors do not overlap with those in the train split. The test split contains 19,526 images and is well-balanced among classes. 1,835 of the landmarks have exactly 10 test images, and there is a short tail for the rest of the landmarks due to insufficient samples (Fig. 3).

5   Methods

The datasets described above contain significant distribution variations among clients, which presents considerable challenges for efficient federated learning [13, 16]. In the following, we describe our baseline approach of Federated Averaging algorithm (**FedAvg**) (Sect. 5.1) and two new algorithms intended to specifically address the non-identical class distributions and imbalanced client sizes present in the data (Sects. 5.2 and 5.3 respectively).

5.1   Federated Averaging and Server Momentum

A standard algorithm [19] for FL, and the baseline approach used in this work, is Federated Averaging (**FedAvg**). See Algorithm 1. For every federated round, K clients (the *report goal*) are randomly selected with uniform probability from a pool of active clients. Selected clients, indexed by k, download the same starting model θ_t from a central server and perform local SGD optimization, minimizing an empirical loss $L(b)$ over local mini-batches b with learning rate η, for E epochs before sending the accumulated model update $\Delta\theta_t^k$ back to the server. The server then averages the updates from the reporting clients $\bar{g}_t = \sum_{k=1}^{K} \frac{n_k}{n} \Delta\theta_t^k$ with weights proportional to the sizes of clients' local data and finishes the federated

---

Algorithm 1: FedAvg, `FedIR`, and FedVC.

Server training loop: ;
    Initialize $\boldsymbol{\theta}_0$;
    for each round $t = 0, 1, \ldots$ **do**
        Subset of K clients $\leftarrow$ `SelectClients`(K) ;
        for each client $k = 1, 2, \ldots, K$ **do in parallel**
            $\Delta\boldsymbol{\theta}_t^k \leftarrow$ `ClientUpdate`$(k, \boldsymbol{\theta}_t)$;
        $\bar{\boldsymbol{g}}_t \leftarrow$ `AggregateClient`$(\{\Delta\boldsymbol{\theta}_t^k\}_{k=1}^K)$;
        $\boldsymbol{\theta}_{t+1} \leftarrow \boldsymbol{\theta}_t - \gamma\bar{\boldsymbol{g}}_t$;

`SelectClients`(K):
    return K clients sampled uniformly ;   ▷ with probability $\propto n_i$ for
    client i

`ClientUpdate`$(k, \boldsymbol{\theta}_t)$:
    $\boldsymbol{\theta} \leftarrow \boldsymbol{\theta}_t$;
    for each local mini-batch b over E epochs **do**   ▷ over S steps
        $\boldsymbol{\theta} \leftarrow \boldsymbol{\theta} - \eta\nabla L(b; \boldsymbol{\theta})$;   ▷ $\nabla\tilde{L}(b; \theta)$ in Eq.3
    return $\Delta\boldsymbol{\theta} \leftarrow \boldsymbol{\theta}_t - \boldsymbol{\theta}$ to server
`AggregateClient`$(\{\Delta\boldsymbol{\theta}_t^k\}_{k=1}^K)$:
    return $\sum_{k=1}^K \frac{n_k}{n} \Delta\boldsymbol{\theta}_t^k$, where $n = \sum_{k=1}^K n_k$;   ▷ $\frac{1}{K}\sum_{k=1}^K \Delta\boldsymbol{\theta}_t^k$

---

round by applying aggregated updates to the starting model $\boldsymbol{\theta}_{t+1} \leftarrow \boldsymbol{\theta}_t - \gamma\bar{\boldsymbol{g}}_t$, where γ is the server learning rate. Given this framework, alternative optimizers can be applied. `FedAvgM` [11] has been shown to improve robustness to non-identically distributed client data. It uses a momentum optimizer on the server with the update rule $\boldsymbol{\theta}_{t+1} \leftarrow \boldsymbol{\theta}_t - \gamma\boldsymbol{v}_t$, where $\boldsymbol{v}_t \leftarrow \beta\boldsymbol{v}_{t-1} + \bar{\boldsymbol{g}}_t$ is the exponentially weighted moving average of the model updates with powers of β.

5.2 Importance Reweighted Client Objectives

Now we address the non-identical class distribution shift in federated clients. Importance reweighting are commonly used for learning from datasets distributed differently from a target distribution. Given that the distribution variation among clients is an inherent characteristic of FL, we propose the following scheme.

Consider a target distribution $p(x, y)$ of images x and class labels y on which a model is supposed to perform well (e.g. a validation dataset known to the central server), and a predefined loss function $\ell(x, y)$. The objective of learning is to minimize the expected loss $\mathbb{E}_p[\ell(x, y)]$ with respect to the target distribution p. SGD in the centralized setting achieves this by minimizing an empirical loss on mini-batches of IID training examples from the same distribution, which are absent in the federated setting. Instead, training examples on a federated client k are sampled from a client-specific distribution $q_k(x, y)$. This implies that the empirical loss being optimized on every client is a *biased* estimator of the loss with respect to the target distribution, since $\mathbb{E}_{q_k}[\ell(x, y)] \neq \mathbb{E}_p[\ell(x, y)]$.

We propose an importance reweighting scheme, denoted `FedIR`, that applies importance weights $w_k(x, y)$ to every client's local objective as $\tilde{\ell}(x, y) = \ell(x, y)w_k(x, y)$, where $w_k(x, y) = \frac{p(x,y)}{q_k(x,y)}$. With the importance weights in place, an unbiased estimator of loss with respect to the target distribution can be obtained using training examples from the client distribution

$$\mathbb{E}_p\left[\ell(x, y)\right] = \sum_{x,y} \frac{\ell(x, y)p(x, y)}{q_k(x, y)}q_k(x, y) = \mathbb{E}_{q_k}\left[\ell(x, y)\frac{p(x, y)}{q_k(x, y)}\right]. \quad (1)$$

Assuming that all clients share the same conditional distribution of images given a class label as the target, i.e. $p(x|y) \approx q_k(x|y) \; \forall k$, the importance weights can be computed on every client directly from the class probability ratio

$$w_k(x, y) = \frac{p(x, y)}{q_k(x, y)} = \frac{p(y)p(x|y)}{q_k(y)q_k(x|y)} \approx \frac{p(y)}{q_k(y)}. \quad (2)$$

Note that this computation does not sabotage the privacy-preserving property of federated learning. The denominator $q_k(y)$ is private information available locally at and never leaves client k, whereas the numerator $p(y)$ does not contain private information about clients and can be transmitted from the central server with minimal communication cost: C scalars in total for C classes.

Since scaling the loss also changes the effective learning rate in the SGD optimization, in practice, we use self-normalized weights when computing loss over a mini-batch b as

$$\tilde{L}(b) = \frac{\sum_{(x,y)\in b} \ell(x, y)w_k(x, y)}{\sum_{(x,y)\in b} w_k(x, y)}. \quad (3)$$

This corresponds to the self-normalized importance sampling in the statistics literature [9]. `FedIR` does not change server optimization loops and can be applied together with other methods, such as `FedAvgM`. See Algorithm 1.

5.3 Splitting Imbalanced Clients with Virtual Clients

The number of training examples in users' devices vary in the real world. Imbalanced clients can cause challenges for both optimization and engineering practice. Previous empirical studies [11,19] suggest that the number of local epochs E at every client has crucial effects on the convergence of `FedAvg`. A larger E implies more optimization steps towards local objectives being taken, which leads to slow convergence or divergence due to increased variance. Imbalanced clients suffer from this optimization challenge even when E is small. Specifically, a client with a large number of training examples takes significantly more local optimization steps than another with fewer training examples. This difference in steps is proportional to the difference in the number of training examples. In addition, a client with an overly large training dataset will take a long time to compute updates, creating a bottleneck in the federated learning round. Such clients would be abandoned by a FL production system in practice, if failing to report back to the central server within a certain time window [1].

Table 1. Training Dataset Statistics. Note that while CIFAR-10/100 and iNaturalist datasets each have different partitionings with different levels of identicalness, the underlying data pool is unchanged and thus sharing the same centralized learning baselines.

Dataset	Clients			Classes	Examples	Centralized
	Count	Size	Imbalance	Count	Count	**Accuracy**
Synthetic						
CIFAR-10	100		✗	10	50,000	86.16%
CIFAR-100	100		✗	100	50,000	55.21%
iNaturalist Geo Splits	11 to 3606		✓	1,203	120,300	57.90%
Real-World						
iNaturalist-User-120k	9,275		✓	1,203	120,300	57.90%
Landmarks-User-160k	1,262		✓	2,028	164,172	67.05%

We hence propose a new *Virtual Client* (**FedVC**) scheme to overcome both issues. The idea is to conceptually split large clients into multiple smaller ones, and repeat small clients multiple times such that all *virtual* clients are of similar sizes. To realize this, we fix the number of training examples used for a federated learning round to be N_{VC} for every client, resulting in exactly $S = N_{VC}/B$ optimization steps taken at every client given a mini-batch size B. Concretely, consider a client k with a local dataset $\mathcal{D}_k$ with size $n_k = |\mathcal{D}_k|$. A random subset consisting of N_{VC} examples is uniformly resampled from $\mathcal{D}_k$ for every round the client is selected. This resampling is conducted without replacement when $n_k \geq N_{VC}$; with replacement otherwise. In addition, to avoid underutilizing training examples from large clients, the probability that any client is selected for a round is set to be proportional to the client size n_k, in contrast to uniform as in **FedAvg**. Key changes are outlined in Algorithm 1. It is clear that **FedVC** is equivalent to **FedAvg** when all clients are of the same size.

6 Experiments

We now present an empirical study using the datasets and methods of Sects. 4 and 5. We start by analyzing the classification performance as a function of non-identical data distribution (Sect. 6.1), using the CIFAR10/100 datasets. Next we show how *Importance Reweighting* can improve performance in the more non-identical cases (Sect. 6.2). With real user data, clients are also imbalanced, we show how this can be mitigated with *Federated Virtual Clients* in Sect. 5.3. Finally we present a set of benchmark results with the per-user splits of iNaturalist and Landmark datasets (Sect. 6.4). A summary of the datasets used is provided in Table 1. Implementation details are deferred to Sect. 6.5.

Metrics. When using the same dataset, the performance of a model trained with federated learning algorithms is inherently upper bounded by that of a model trained in the centralized fashion. We evaluate the *relative accuracy*, defined as

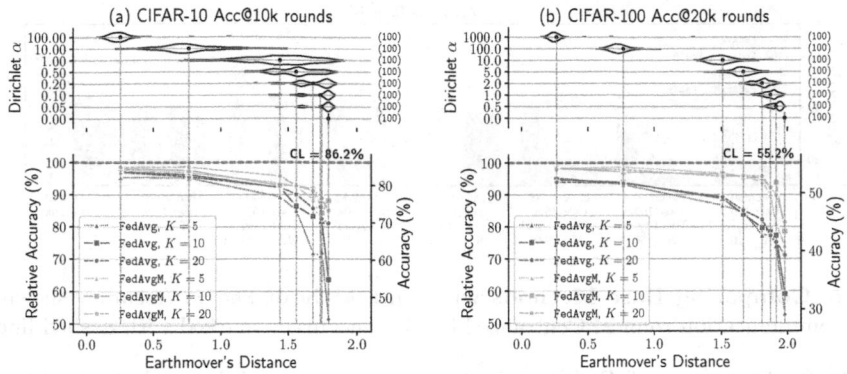

Fig. 4. Relative Accuracy vs. Non-identicalness. Federated learning experiments are performed on (a) CIFAR-10 and (b) CIFAR-100 using local epoch $E = 1$. The top row demonstrates the distributions of EMD of clients with different data partitionings. Total client counts are annotated to the right, and the weighted average of all client EMD is marked. Data is increasingly non-identical to the right. The dashed line indicates the centralized learning performance. The best accuracies over a grid of hyperparameters are reported (see Appendix A.1).

$\mathrm{Acc_{federated}}/\mathrm{Acc_{centralized}}$, and compare this metric under different types of budgets. The centralized training baseline uses the same configurations and hyperparameters for a fair comparison.

6.1   Classification Accuracy Vs Distribution Non-Identicalness

Our experiments use CIFAR10/100 datasets to characterize classification accuracy with a continuous range of distribution non-identicalness. We follow the protocol described in [11] such that the class distribution of every client is sampled from a Dirichlet distribution with varying concentration parameter α.

We measure distribution non-identicalness using an average *Earthmover's Distance* (EMD) metric. Specifically, we take the discrete class distribution q_i for every client, and define the population's class distribution as $p = \sum_i \frac{n_i}{n} q_i$, where $n = \sum_i n_i$ counts training samples from all clients. The non-identicalness of a dataset is then computed as the weighted average of distances between clients and the population: $\sum_i \frac{n_i}{n} \mathrm{Dist}(q_i, p)$. $\mathrm{Dist}(\cdot, \cdot)$ is a distance metric between two distributions, which we, in particular, use $\mathrm{EMD}(q, p) \equiv \|q - p\|_1$, bounded between $[0, 2]$.

Figure 4a and b show the trend in classification accuracy as a function of distribution non-identicalness (average EMD difference). We are able to approach centralized learning accuracy with data on the identical end. A substantial drop around an EMD of 1.7 to 2.0 is observed in both datasets. Applying momentum on the server, FedAvgM significantly improves the convergence under heterogeneity conditions for all datasets. Using more clients per round (larger report goal K) is also beneficial for training but has diminishing returns.

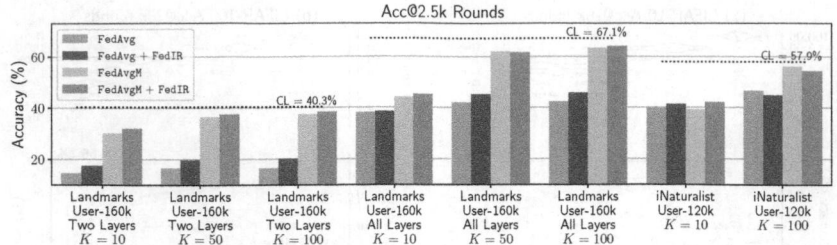

Fig. 5. Comparing Base Methods with and without FedIR. Accuracy shown at 2.5k communication rounds. Centralized learning accuracy marked with dashed lines.

Table 2. Accuracy of Federated Virtual Client on iNaturalist. Acc@round denotes the accuracy at a FL communication round. Acc@batch denotes the batch count accumulated over the largest clients per round, and is a proxy for a fixed time budget.

Data	Method	FedVC	K	Acc@Round(%)			Acc@Batch(%)		
				1k	2.5k	5k	10k	25k	50k
Geo-3k	FedAvg	✗	10	47.0	47.9	48.7	37.8	44.4	46.5
	FedAvgM	✗	10	47.2	50.4	45.0	42.5	47.1	44.9
	FedAvg	✓	10	37.4	46.2	52.8	46.2	53.1	55.5
	FedAvgM	✓	10	**49.7**	**54.8**	**56.7**	**54.8**	**56.7**	**57.1**
User-120k	FedAvg	✗	10	34.7	39.7	41.3	37.8	39.8	42.9
	FedAvgM	✗	10	31.9	39.2	41.3	32.3	41.6	43.4
	FedAvg	✓	10	31.3	39.7	43.9	39.7	**48.9**	52.8
	FedAvgM	✓	10	**37.9**	**43.7**	**49.1**	**43.7**	47.4	**54.6**
Centralized						57.9			

6.2 Importance Reweighting

Importance Reweighting is proposed for addressing the per-client distribution shift. We evaluate FedIR with both FedAvg and FedAvgM on both two datasets with natural user splits: iNaturalist-User-120k and Landmarks-User-160k.

For Landmarks, we experiment with two different training schemes: (a) fine-tuning the entire network (*all layers*) end to end, (b) only training the last *two layers* while freezing the network backbone. We set the local epochs to $E = 5$ and experiment with report goals $K = \{10, 50, 100\}$, respectively.

The result in Fig. 5 shows a consistent improvement on the Landmarks-User-160k dataset over the FedAvg baseline. While FedAvgM gives the most significant improvements in all runs, FedIR further improves the convergence speed and accuracy especially when the report goal is small (Fig. 7).

Landmarks-User-160k (EMD = 1.94) has more skewed data distribution than iNaturalist-User-120k (EMD = 1.83) and benefits more from FedIR.

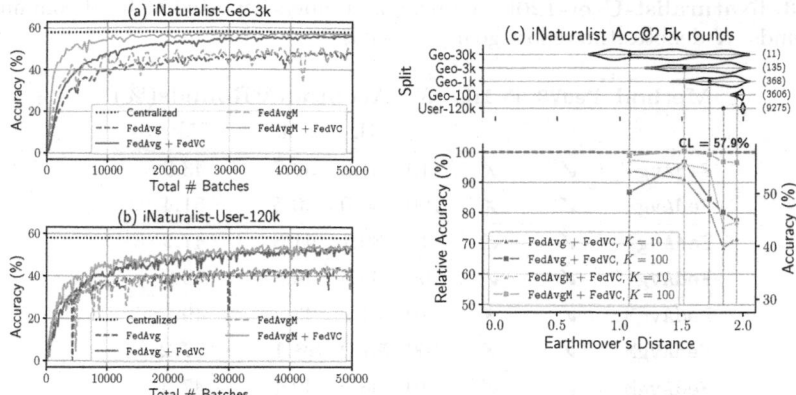

Fig. 6. Learning with Federated Virtual Clients. Curves on the left are learned on the iNaturalist geo-partitioning Geo-3k and user split User-120k each with 135 clients and 9275 clients. Experiments on multiple iNaturalist partitionings are shown on the right, plotting relative accuracy at 2.5k communication rounds to mean EMD. Centralized learning achieves a 57.9% accuracy.

6.3 Federated Virtual Clients

We apply the Virtual Clients scheme (`FedVC`) to both `FedAvg` and `FedAvgM` and evaluate its efficacy using iNaturalist user and geo-location datasets, each of which contains significantly imbalanced clients . In the experiments, 10 clients are selected for every federated round. We use a mini-batch size $B = 64$ and set the virtual client size $N_{VC} = 256$.

Figure 6 demonstrates the efficiency and accuracy improvements gained via `FedVC` when clients are imbalanced. The convergence of vanilla `FedAvg` suffers when clients perform excessive local optimization steps. In iNaturalist-Geo-3k, for example, clients can take up to 46 (i.e. 3000/64) local steps before reporting to the server. To show that `FedVC` utilizes data efficiently, we report accuracy at fixed batch budgets in addition to fixed round budgets. Batch budget is calculated by summing the number of local batches taken for the largest client per round. As shown in Table 2, `FedVC` consistently yields superior accuracy on both `FedAvg` and `FedAvgM`. Learning curves in Fig. 6 show that `FedVC` also decreases the learning volatility and stabilizes learning.

iNaturalist per-user and geo-location datasets reflect varying degrees of non-identicalness. Figure 6c, though noisier, exhibits a similar trend compared to Fig. 4. The performance degrades as the degree of non-identicalness, characterized by EMD, increases.

6.4 Federated Visual Classification Benchmarks

Having shown that our proposed modifications to `FedAvg` indeed lead to a speedup in learning on both iNaturalist and Landmarks, we wish to also provide

Table 3. iNaturalist-User-120k accuracy. Numbers reported at fixed communication rounds. K denotes the report goal per round.

Method	FedVC	FedIR	K	Accuracy@Rounds(%)		
				1k	2.5k	5k
FedAvg	✓	✗	10	31.3	39.7	43.9
FedAvg	✓	✗	100	36.9	46.5	51.4
FedAvg	✓	✓	10	30.1	41.3	47.5
FedAvg	✓	✓	100	35.5	44.8	49.8
FedAvgM	✓	✗	10	37.9	43.7	49.1
FedAvgM	✓	✗	100	**53.0**	**56.1**	**57.2**
FedAvgM	✓	✓	10	38.4	42.1	47.0
FedAvgM	✓	✓	100	51.3	54.3	56.2
Centralized					57.9	

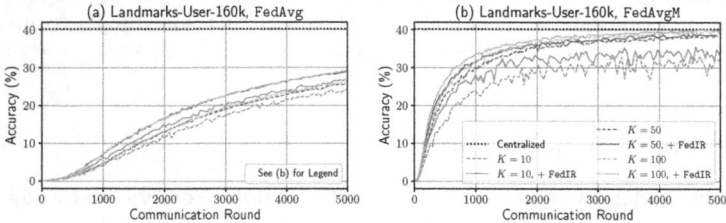

Fig. 7. Landmarks-User-160k Learning Curves. Only the last two layers of the network are fine-tuned. FedIR is also shown due to its ability to address skewed training distribution as presented in this dataset.

some benchmark results on natural user partitioning with reasonable operating points. We hope that these datasets can be used for understanding real-world federated visual classification, and act as benchmarks for future improvements.

iNaturalist-User-120k. The iNaturalist-User-120k data has 9,275 clients and 120k examples, containing 1,203 species classes. We use report goals $K = \{10, 100\}$. FedVC samples $N_{VC} = 256$ examples per client. A summary of the benchmark results is shown in Table 3.

Notice that FedAvgM with FedVC and a large report goal of $K = 100$ has a 57.2% accuracy, almost reaching the same level as in centralized learning (57.9%). With that said, there is still plenty of room to improve performance with small reporting clients and round budgets. Being able to learn fast with a limited pool of clients is one of the critical research areas for practical visual FL.

Landmarks-User-160k. The Landmarks-User-160k dataset comprises 164,172 images for 2,028 landmarks, divided among 1,262 clients. We follow the setup in Sect. 6.2 where we experiment with either training the whole model or fine-tuning the last two layers. Report goal $K = \{10, 50, 100\}$ are used (Table 4).

Table 4. Landmarks-User-160k Accuracy.

Method	FedIR	K	Two layers			All layers		
			1k	2.5k	5k	1k	2.5k	5k
FedAvg	✗	10	4.2	14.6	24.6	18.2	38.1	49.7
FedAvg	✗	50	4.5	16.5	26.0	20.9	42.0	53.3
FedAvg	✗	100	4.9	16.5	26.3	21.9	42.3	53.4
FedAvg	✓	10	6.3	17.4	26.6	19.6	38.5	51.7
FedAvg	✓	50	7.4	19.7	28.8	26.0	45.2	55.0
FedAvg	✓	100	7.2	20.1	29.0	26.5	45.7	55.2
FedAvgM	✗	10	23.0	30.1	30.8	29.4	44.1	53.7
FedAvgM	✗	50	29.9	36.4	38.6	55.2	62.0	64.8
FedAvgM	✗	100	31.9	37.4	39.6	56.3	63.4	65.0
FedAvgM	✓	10	26.5	32.1	31.3	27.9	45.1	53.5
FedAvgM	✓	50	31.6	37.5	38.9	53.1	61.6	63.2
FedAvgM	✓	100	**33.7**	**38.3**	**39.8**	**57.7**	**64.1**	**65.9**
Centralized				40.27			67.05	

Similarly, FedAvgM with the $K = 100$ is able to achieve 65.9% accuracy at 5k communication rounds, which is just 1.2% off from centralized learning. Interestingly, when we train only the last two layers with FL, the accuracy is as well not far off from centralized learning (39.8% compared to 40.3%).

6.5 Implementation Details

We use MobileNetV2 [25] pre-trained on ImageNet [4] for both iNaturalist and Landmarks experiments; for the latter, a 64-dimensional bottleneck layer between the 1280-dimensional features and the softmax classifier. We replaced BatchNorm with GroupNorm [32] due to its superior stability for FL tasks [10]. During training, the image is randomly cropped then resized to a target input size of 299×299 (iNaturalist) or 224×224 (Landmarks) with scale and aspect ratio augmentation similar to [27]. A weight decay of 4×10^{-5} is applied. For CIFAR-10/100 experiments, we use a CNN similar to LeNet-5 [15] which has two 5×5, 64-channel convolution layers, each precedes a 2×2 max-pooling layer, followed by two fully-connected layers with 384 and 192 channels respectively and finally a softmax linear classifier. This model is not the state-of-the-art on the CIFAR datasets, but is sufficient to show the relative performance for our investigation. Weight decay is set to 4×10^{-4}. Unless otherwise stated, we use a learning rate of 0.01 and momentum of 0.9 in FedAvgM, kept constant without decay for simplicity. The client batch size is 32 in Landmarks and 64 for others.

7 Conclusions

We have shown that large-scale visual classifiers can be trained using a privacy-preserving, federated approach, and highlighted the challenges that per-user data distributions pose for learning. We provide two new datasets and benchmarks, providing a platform for other explorations in this space. We expect others to improve on our results, particularly when the number of participating clients and round budget is small. There remain many challenges for Federated Learning that are beyond the scope of this paper: real world data may include domain shift, label noise, poor data quality and duplication. Model size, bandwidth and unreliable client connections also pose challenges in practice. We hope our work inspires further exploration in this area.

Acknowledgements. We thank Andre Araujo, Grace Chu, Tobias Weyand, Bingyi Cao, Huizhong Chen, Tomer Meron, and Hartwig Adam for their valuable feedback and support.

References

1. Bonawitz, K., et al.: Towards federated learning at scale: system design. In: SysML 2019 (2019). https://arxiv.org/abs/1902.01046
2. Caldas, S., et al.: LEAF: a benchmark for federated settings. arXiv preprint arXiv:1812.01097 (2018)
3. Cohen, G., Afshar, S., Tapson, J., Van Schaik, A.: EMNIST: extending MNIST to handwritten letters. In: 2017 International Joint Conference on Neural Networks (IJCNN), pp. 2921–2926. IEEE (2017)
4. Deng, J., et al.: ImageNet: a large-scale hierarchical image database. In: Proceedings of the IEEE Conference on Computer Vision and Pattern Recognition (CVPR), pp. 248–255. IEEE (2009)
5. Doersch, C., Singh, S., Gupta, A., Sivic, J., Efros, A.A.: What makes Paris look like Paris? Commun. ACM **58**(12), 103–110 (2015)
6. Google: TensorFlow Federated (2019). https://www.tensorflow.org/federated
7. Google: TensorFlow Federated Datasets (2019). https://www.tensorflow.org/federated/api_docs/python/tff/simulation/datasets
8. Hays, J., Efros, A.A.: IM2GPS: estimating geographic information from a single image. In: Proceedings of the IEEE Conference on Computer Vision and Pattern Recognition (CVPR), pp. 1–8. IEEE (2008)
9. Hesterberg, T.: Weighted average importance sampling and defensive mixture distributions. Technometrics **37**(2), 185–194 (1995)
10. Hsieh, K., Phanishayee, A., Mutlu, O., Gibbons, P.B.: The non-IID data quagmire of decentralized machine learning. arXiv preprint arXiv:1910.00189 (2019)
11. Hsu, T.M.H., Qi, H., Brown, M.: Measuring the effects of non-identical data distribution for federated visual classification. arXiv preprint arXiv:1909.06335 (2019)
12. Kahn, H., Marshall, A.W.: Methods of reducing sample size in Monte Carlo computations. J. Oper. Res. Soc. Am. **1**(5), 263–278 (1953)
13. Kairouz, P., et al.: Advances and open problems in federated learning. arXiv preprint arXiv:1912.04977 (2019)

14. Karimireddy, S.P., et al.: Scaffold: stochastic controlled averaging for on-device federated learning. arXiv preprint arXiv:1910.06378 (2019)
15. LeCun, Y., Bottou, L., Bengio, Y., Haffner, P.: Gradient-based learning applied to document recognition. Proc. IEEE **86**(11), 2278–2324 (1998)
16. Li, T., Sahu, A.K., Talwalkar, A., Smith, V.: Federated learning: challenges, methods, and future directions. arXiv preprint arXiv:1908.07873 (2019)
17. Liu, Z., Luo, P., Wang, X., Tang, X.: Deep learning face attributes in the wild. In: Proceedings of International Conference on Computer Vision (ICCV) (2015)
18. Luo, J., et al.: Real-world image datasets for federated learning. arXiv preprint arXiv:1910.11089 (2019)
19. McMahan, B., Moore, E., Ramage, D., Hampson, S., Arcas, B.A.: Communication-efficient learning of deep networks from decentralized data. In: Artificial Intelligence and Statistics, pp. 1273–1282 (2017)
20. McMahan, H.B., Ramage, D., Talwar, K., Zhang, L.: Learning differentially private recurrent language models. In: International Conference on Learning Representations (ICLR) (2018)
21. Ngiam, J., et al.: Domain adaptive transfer learning with specialist models. arXiv preprint arXiv:1811.07056 (2018)
22. Ozaki, K., Yokoo, S.: Large-scale landmark retrieval/recognition under a noisy and diverse dataset. arXiv preprint arXiv:1906.04087 (2019)
23. Saerens, M., Latinne, P., Decaestecker, C.: Adjusting the outputs of a classifier to new a priori probabilities: a simple procedure. Neural Comput. **14**(1), 21–41 (2002)
24. Sahu, A.K., Li, T., Sanjabi, M., Zaheer, M., Talwalkar, A., Smith, V.: On the convergence of federated optimization in heterogeneous networks. arXiv preprint arXiv:1812.06127 (2018)
25. Sandler, M., Howard, A., Zhu, M., Zhmoginov, A., Chen, L.C.: MobileNetV2: inverted residuals and linear bottlenecks. In: Proceedings of the IEEE Conference on Computer Vision and Pattern Recognition (CVPR), pp. 4510–4520 (2018)
26. Sattler, F., Wiedemann, S., Müller, K.R., Samek, W.: Robust and communication-efficient federated learning from non-IID data. arXiv preprint arXiv:1903.02891 (2019)
27. Szegedy, C., et al.: Going deeper with convolutions. In: Proceedings of the IEEE Conference on Computer Vision and Pattern Recognition (CVPR), pp. 1–9 (2015)
28. Van Horn, G., et al.: The iNaturalist species classification and detection dataset. In: Proceedings of the IEEE Conference on Computer Vision and Pattern Recognition (CVPR), pp. 8769–8778 (2018)
29. Van Horn, G., Perona, P.: The devil is in the tails: fine-grained classification in the wild. arXiv preprint arXiv:1709.01450 (2017)
30. Weyand, T., Araujo, A., Cao, B., Sim, J.: Google Landmarks Dataset v2 - a large-scale benchmark for instance-level recognition and retrieval. In: Proceedings of the IEEE Conference on Computer Vision and Pattern Recognition (CVPR). IEEE (2020)
31. Weyand, T., Kostrikov, I., Philbin, J.: PLaNet-photo geolocation with convolutional neural networks. In: Leibe, B., Matas, J., Sebe, N., Welling, M. (eds.) Computer Vision – ECCV 2016. Lecture Notes in Computer Science, vol. 9912, pp. 37–55. Springer, Cham (2016). https://doi.org/10.1007/978-3-319-46484-8_3
32. Wu, Y., He, K.: Group normalization. In: Ferrari, V., Hebert, M., Sminchisescu, C., Weiss, Y. (eds.) Computer Vision – ECCV 2018. Lecture Notes in Computer Science, vol. 11217. Springer, Cham (2018). https://doi.org/10.1007/978-3-030-01261-8_1

33. Yurochkin, M., et al.: Bayesian nonparametric federated learning of neural networks. In: Proceedings of the International Conference on Machine Learning (ICML), pp. 7252–7261 (2019)
34. Zhang, K., Schölkopf, B., Muandet, K., Wang, Z.: Domain adaptation under target and conditional shift. In: Proceedings of the International Conference on Machine Learning (ICML), pp. 819–827 (2013)
35. Zhao, Y., et al.: Federated learning with non-IID data. arXiv preprint arXiv:1806.00582 (2018)

Robust Re-Identification by Multiple Views Knowledge Distillation

Angelo Porrello$^{(\boxtimes)}$ (iD), Luca Bergamini (iD), and Simone Calderara (iD)

AImageLab, University of Modena and Reggio Emilia, Modena, Italy
{angelo.porrello,luca.bergamini24,simone.calderara}@unimore.it

Abstract. To achieve robustness in Re-Identification, standard methods leverage tracking information in a Video-To-Video fashion. However, these solutions face a large drop in performance for single image queries (e.g., Image-To-Video setting). Recent works address this severe degradation by transferring *temporal information* from a Video-based network to an Image-based one. In this work, we devise a training strategy that allows the transfer of a superior knowledge, arising from a set of views depicting the target object. Our proposal – Views Knowledge Distillation (VKD) – pins this *visual variety* as a supervision signal within a teacher-student framework, where the teacher educates a student who observes fewer views. As a result, the student outperforms not only its teacher but also the current state-of-the-art in Image-To-Video by a wide margin (6.3% mAP on MARS, 8.6% on Duke and 5% on VeRi-776). A thorough analysis – on Person, Vehicle and Animal Re-ID – investigates the properties of VKD from a qualitatively and quantitatively perspective. Code is available at https://github.com/aimagelab/VKD.

Keywords: Deep learning · Re-Identification · Knowledge Distillation

1 Introduction

Recent advances on Metric Learning [38,41,45,47] give to researchers the foundation for computing suitable distance metrics between data points. In this context, Re-Identification (Re-ID) has greatly benefited in diverse domains [16,37,56], as the common paradigm requires distance measures exhibiting robustness to variations in background clutters, as well as different viewpoints. To meet these criteria, various deep learning based approaches leverage videos to provide detailed descriptions for both query and gallery items. However, such a setting – known as Video-To-Video (V2V) Re-ID – does not represent a viable option in many scenarios (e.g. surveillance) [10,30,50,54], where the query comprises a single image (Image-To-Video, I2V).

Electronic supplementary material The online version of this chapter (https://doi.org/10.1007/978-3-030-58607-2_6) contains supplementary material, which is available to authorized users.

© Springer Nature Switzerland AG 2020
A. Vedaldi et al. (Eds.): ECCV 2020, LNCS 12355, pp. 93–110, 2020.
https://doi.org/10.1007/978-3-030-58607-2_6

As observed in [10], a large gap in Re-ID performance still subsists between V2V and I2V, highlighting the number of query images as a critical factor in achieving good results. Contrarily, we advise the learnt representation should not be heavily affected when few images are shown to the network (*e.g.* only one). To bridge such a gap, [5,10] propose a teacher-student paradigm, in which the student – in contrast with the teacher – has access to a small fraction of the frames in the video. Since the student is educated to mimic the output space of its teacher, it will show higher generalisation properties than its teacher when a single frame is available. It is noted that these approaches rely on transferring *temporal* information: as datasets often come with tracking annotation, they can guide the transfer from a tracklet into one of its frames. In this respect, we argue the limits of transferring temporal information: in fact, it is reasonable to assume an high correlation between frames from the same tracklet (Fig. 1a), which may potentially underexploit the transfer. Moreover, limiting the analysis to the temporal domain does not guarantee robustness to variation in background appearances.

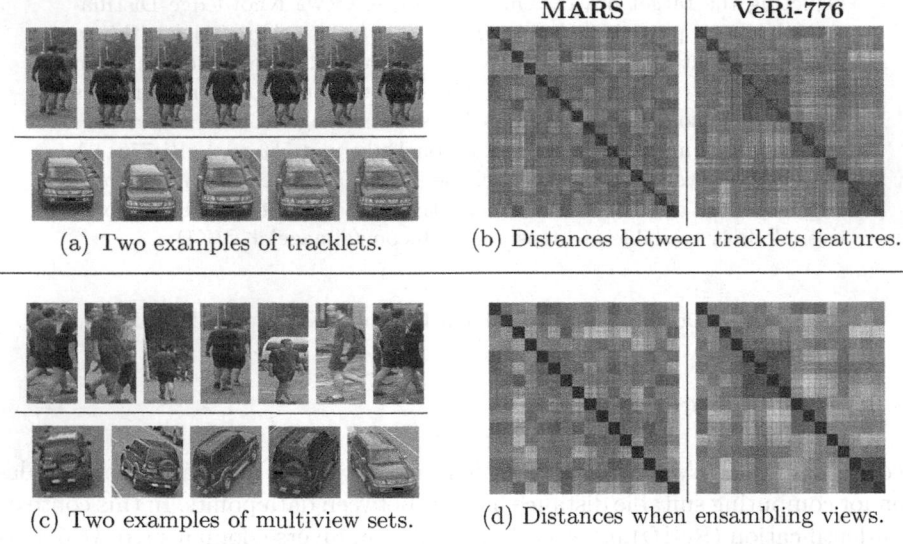

(a) Two examples of tracklets.   (b) Distances between tracklets features.

(c) Two examples of multiview sets.   (d) Distances when ensambling views.

Fig. 1. Visual comparison between tracklets and viewpoints variety, on person (MARS [55]) and vehicle (VeRi-776 [25]) re-id. Right: pairwise distances computed on top of features from ResNet-50. Inputs batches comprise 192 sets from 16 different identities, grouped by ground truth identity along each axis.

Here, we make a step forward and consider which information to transfer, shifting the paradigm from *time* to *views*: we argue that more valuable information arises when ensembling diverse views of the same target (Fig. 1c). This information often comes for free, as various datasets [4,25,49,55] provide images capturing the same target from different camera viewpoints. To support our claim, Fig. 1 (right) reports pairwise distances computed on top of ResNet-50, when trained on Person and Vehicle Re-ID. In more details: matrices from Fig. 1b visualise the distances when tracklets are provided as input, whereas Fig. 1d shows the same for sets of views. As one can see, leveraging different views leads to a more distinctive blockwise pattern: namely, activations from the same identity are more consistent if compared to the ones computed in the tracklet scenario. As shown in [44], this reflects a higher capacity to capture the semantics of the dataset, and therefore a *graceful* knowledge a teacher can transfer to a student. Based on the above, we propose Views Knowledge Distillation (**VKD**), which transfers the knowledge lying in several views in a teacher-student fashion. VKD devises a two-stage procedure, which pins the visual variety as a teaching signal for a student who has to recover it using fewer views. We remark the following contributions: *i)* the student outperforms its teacher by a large margin, especially in the Image-To-Video setting; *ii)* a thorough investigation shows that the student focuses more on the target compared to its teacher and discards uninformative details; *iii)* importantly, we do not limit our analysis to a single domain, but instead achieve strong results on Person, Vehicle and Animal Re-ID.

2   Related Works

Image-To-Video Re-Identification. The I2V Re-ID task has been successfully applied to multiple domains. In person Re-ID, [46] frames it as a point-to-set task, where image and video domains are aligned using a single deep network. The authors of [54] exploit time information by aggregating frames features via a Long-Short Term Memory. Eventually, a dedicated sub-network aggregates video features and match them against single image query ones. Authors of MGAT [3] employ a Graph Neural Network to model relationships between samples from different identities, thus enforcing similarity in the feature space. Dealing with vehicle Re-ID, authors from [26] introduce a large-scale dataset (VeRi-776) and propose PROVID and PROVID-BOT, which combine appearance and plate information in a progressive fashion. Differently, RAM [24] exploits multiple branches to extract global and local features, imposing a separate supervision on each branch and devising an additional one to predict vehicle attributes. VAMI [59] employs a viewpoint aware attention model to select core regions for different viewpoints. At inference time, they obtain a multiview descriptor through a conditional generative network, inferring information regarding the unobserved viewpoints. Differently, our approach asks the student to do it implicitly and in a lightweight fashion, thus avoiding the need for additional modules. Similarly to VAMI, [7] predicts the vehicle viewpoint along with appearance features; at inference, the framework provides distances according to the predicted viewpoint.

   Knowledge Distillation has been first investigated in [13,35,53] for model compression: the idea is to instruct a lightweight model (student) to mimic the capabilities of a deeper one (teacher): as a gift, one could achieve both an acceleration in inference time as well as a reduction in memory consumption, without

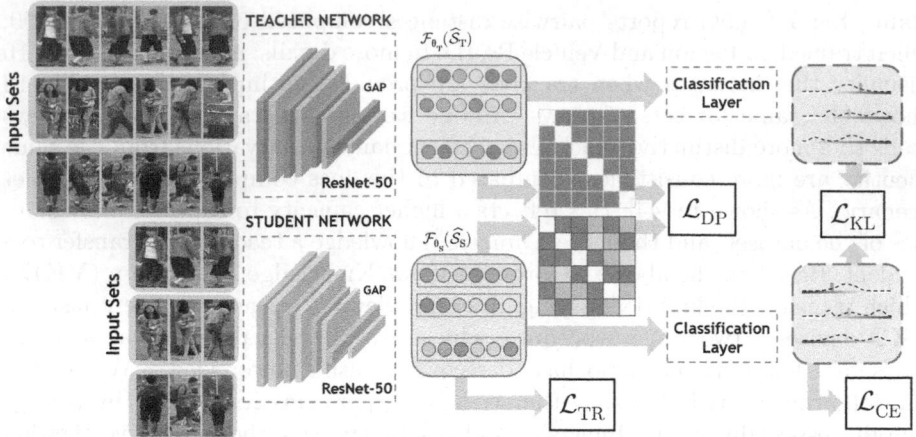

Fig. 2. An overview of Views Knowledge Distillation (VKD): a student network is optimised to mimic the behaviour of its teacher using fewer views.

experiencing a large drop in performance. In this work, we benefit from the techniques proposed in [13,44] for a different purpose: we are not primarily engaged in educating a lightweight module, but on improving the original model itself. In this framework – often called *self-distillation* [9,51] – the transfer occurs from the teacher to a student with the same architecture, with the aim of improving the overall performance at the end of the training. Here, we get a step ahead and introduce an asymmetry between the teacher and student, which has access to fewer frames. In this respect, our work closely relates to what [5] devises for Video Classification. Besides facing another task, a key difference subsists: while [5] limits the transfer along the temporal axis, our proposal advocates for distilling many views into fewer ones. On this latter point, we shall show that the teaching signal can be further enhanced when opening to diverse camera viewpoints. In the Re-Identification field, Temporal Knowledge Propagation (TKP) [10] similarly exploits intra-tracklet information to encourage the image-level representations to approach the video-level ones. In contrast with TKP: *i)* we do not rely on matching internal representations but instead their distances solely, thus making our proposal viable for cross-architecture transfer too; *ii)* at inference time, we make use of a single shared network to deal with both image and video domains, thus halving the number of parameters; *iii)* during transfer, we benefit from a larger visual variety, emerging from several viewpoints.

3   Method

We purse the aim of learning a function $\mathcal{F}_\theta(\mathcal{S})$ mapping a set of images $\mathcal{S} = (s_1, s_2, ..., s_n)$ into a representative embedding space. Specifically, $\mathcal{S}$ is a sequence of bounding boxes crops depicting a target (*e.g.* a person or a car), for which we are interested in inferring its corresponding identity. We take advantage of Convolutional Neural Networks (CNNs) for modelling $\mathcal{F}_\theta(\mathcal{S})$. Here, we look for two distinctive properties, aspiring to representations that are *i)* invariant to differences in background and viewpoint and *ii)* robust to a reduction in the number of query images. To achieve this, our proposal frames the training algorithm as a two-stage procedure, as follows:

- **First step** (Sect. 3.1): the backbone network is trained for the standard Video-To-Video setting.
- **Second step** (Sect. 3.2): we appoint it as the teacher and freeze its parameters. Then, a new network with the role of the student is instantiated. As depicted in Fig. 2, we feed frames representing different views as input to the teacher and ask the student to mimic the same outputs from fewer frames.

3.1 Teacher Network

Without loss of generality, we will refer to ResNet-50 [11] as the backbone network, namely a module $f_\theta : \mathbb{R}^{W \times H \times 3} \mapsto \mathbb{R}^D$ mapping each image s_i from S to a fixed-size representation d_i (in this case $D = 2048$). Following previous works [10,28], we initialise the network weights on ImageNet and additionally include few amendments [28] to the architecture. First, we discard both the last ReLU activation function and final classification layer in favour of the BNNeck one [28] (*i.e.* batch normalisation followed by a linear layer). Second: to benefit from fine-grained spatial details, the stride of the last residual block is decreased from 2 to 1.

Set Representation. Given a set of images S, several solutions [22,27,54] may be assessed for designing the aggregation module, which fuses a variable-length set of representations $d_1, d_2, \ldots, d_n$ into a single one. Here, we naively compute the set-level embedding $\mathcal{F}(\mathcal{S})$ through a temporal average pooling. While we acknowledge better aggregation modules exist, we do not place our focus on devising a new one, but instead on improving the earlier features extractor.

Teacher Optimisation. We train the base network - which will be the teacher during the following stage - combining a classification term $\mathcal{L}_{CE}$ (cross-entropy) with the triplet loss $\mathcal{L}_{TR}$[1]. The first can be formulated as:

$$\mathcal{L}_{CE} = -\boldsymbol{y} \log \hat{\boldsymbol{y}} \tag{1}$$

where $\boldsymbol{y}$ and $\hat{\boldsymbol{y}}$ represent the one-hot labels (identities) and the output of the softmax respectively. The second term $\mathcal{L}_{TR}$ encourages distance constraints in feature space, moving closer representations from the same target and pulling away ones from different targets. Formally:

$$\mathcal{L}_{TR} = \ln(1 + e^{\mathcal{D}\left(\mathcal{F}_\theta(\mathcal{S}_a^i), \mathcal{F}_\theta(\mathcal{S}_p^i)\right) - \mathcal{D}\left(\mathcal{F}_\theta(\mathcal{S}_a^i), \mathcal{F}_\theta(\mathcal{S}_n^j)\right)}), \tag{2}$$

---

[1] For the sake of clarity, all the loss terms are referred to one single example. In the implementation, we extend the penalties to a batch by averaging.

where $\mathcal{S}_p$ and $\mathcal{S}_n$ are the hardest positive and negative for an anchor $\mathcal{S}_a$ within the batch. In doing so, we rely on the batch hard strategy [12] and include P identities coupled with K samples in each batch. Importantly, each set $\mathcal{S}^i$ comprises images drawn from the same tracklet [8,22].

3.2 Views Knowledge Distillation (VKD)

After training the teacher, we propose to enrich its representation capabilities, especially when only few images are made available to the model. To achieve this, our proposal bets on the knowledge we can gather from different views, depicting the same object under different conditions. When facing re-identification tasks, one can often exploit camera viewpoints [25,33,55] to provide a larger variety of appearances for the target identity. Ideally, we would like to teach a new network to recover such a variety even from a single image. Since this information may not be inferred from a single frame, this can lead to an ill-posed task. Still, one can underpin this knowledge as a supervision signal, encouraging the student to focus on important details and favourably discover new ones. On this latter point, we refer the reader to Sect. 4.4 for a comprehensive discussion.

Views Knowledge Distillation (**VKD**) stresses this idea by forcing a student network $\mathcal{F}_{\theta_S}(\cdot)$ to match the outputs of the teacher $\mathcal{F}_{\theta_T}(\cdot)$. In doing so, we: $i)$ allow the teacher to access frames $\hat{\mathcal{S}}_T = (\hat{s}_1, \hat{s}_2, \ldots, \hat{s}_N)$ from different viewpoints; $ii)$ force the student to mimic the teacher output starting from a subset $\hat{\mathcal{S}}_S = (\hat{s}_1, \hat{s}_2, \ldots, \hat{s}_M) \subset \hat{\mathcal{S}}_T$ with cardinality $M < N$ (in our experiments, $M = 2$ and $N = 8$). The frames in $\hat{\mathcal{S}}_S$ are uniformly sampled from $\hat{\mathcal{S}}_T$ without replacement. This asymmetry between the teacher and the student leads to a self-distillation objective, where the latter can achieve better solutions despite inheriting the same architecture of the former.

To accomplish this, VKD exploits the Knowledge Distillation loss [13]:

$$\mathcal{L}_{\mathrm{KD}} = \tau^2 \, \mathrm{KL}(\boldsymbol{y}_T \parallel \boldsymbol{y}_S) \tag{3}$$

where $\boldsymbol{y}_T = \mathrm{softmax}(\boldsymbol{h}_T/\tau)$ and $\boldsymbol{y}_S = \mathrm{softmax}(\boldsymbol{h}_S/\tau)$ are the distributions – smoothed by a temperature τ – we attempt to match[2]. Since the student experiences a different task from the teacher one, Eq. 3 resembles the regularisation term imposed by [19] to relieve *catastrophic forgetting*. In a similar vein, we intend to *strengthen* the model in the presence of few images, whilst not *deteriorating* the capabilities it achieved with longer sequences.

In addition to fitting the output distribution of the teacher (Eq. 3), our proposal devises additional constraints on the embedding space learnt by the student. In details, VKD encourages the student to mirror the pairwise distances spanned by the teacher. Indicating with $\mathcal{D}_T[i,j] \equiv \mathcal{D}(\mathcal{F}_{\theta_T}(\hat{\mathcal{S}}_T[i]), \mathcal{F}_{\theta_T}(\hat{\mathcal{S}}_T[j]))$ the distance induced by the teacher between the i-th and j-th sets (the same notation $\mathcal{D}_S[i,j]$ also holds for the student), VKD seeks to minimise:

---

[2] Since the teacher parameters are fixed, its entropy is constant and the objective of Eq. 3 reduces to the cross-entropy between $\boldsymbol{y}_T$ and $\boldsymbol{y}_S$.

$$\mathcal{L}_{\text{DP}} = \sum_{(i,j)\in \binom{B}{2}} (\mathcal{D}_T[i,j] - \mathcal{D}_S[i,j])^2, \tag{4}$$

where B equals the batch size. Since the teacher has access to several viewpoints, we argue that distances spanned in its space yield a powerful description of corresponding identities. From the student perspective, distances preservation provides additional semantic knowledge. Therefore, this holds an effective supervision signal, whose optimisation is made more challenging since fewer images are available to the student.

Even thought VKD focuses on *self-distillation*, we highlight that both $\mathcal{L}_{\text{KD}}$ and $\mathcal{L}_{\text{DP}}$ allow to match models with different embedding size, which would not be viable under the minimisation performed by [10]. As an example, it is still possible to distill ResNet-101 ($D = 2048$) into MobileNet-V2 [36] ($D = 1280$).

Student Optimisation. The VKD overall objective combines the distillation terms ($\mathcal{L}_{\text{KD}}$ and $\mathcal{L}_{\text{DP}}$) with the ones optimised by the teacher - $\mathcal{L}_{\text{CE}}$ and $\mathcal{L}_{\text{TR}}$ - that promote higher conditional likelihood w.r.t. ground truth labels. To sum up, VKD aims at strengthening the features of a CNN in Re-ID settings through the following optimisation problem:

$$\underset{\theta_S}{\operatorname{argmin}} \quad \mathcal{L}_{\text{VKD}} \equiv \mathcal{L}_{\text{CE}} + \mathcal{L}_{\text{TR}} + \alpha\mathcal{L}_{\text{KD}} + \beta\mathcal{L}_{\text{DP}}, \tag{5}$$

where α and β are two hyperparameters balancing the contributions to the total loss $\mathcal{L}_{\text{VKD}}$. We conclude with a final note on the student initialisation: we empirically found beneficial to start from the teacher weights θ_T except for the last convolutional block, which is reinitialised according to the ImageNet pretraining. We argue this represents a good compromise between exploring new configurations and exploiting the abilities already achieved by the teacher.

4   Experiments

Evaluation Protocols. We indicate the query-gallery matching as x2x, where both x terms are features that can be generated by either a single (I) or multiple frames (V). In the **Image-to-Image (I2I)** setting features extracted from a query set image are matched against features from individual images in the gallery. This protocol – which has been amply employed for person Re-ID and face recognition – has a light impact in terms of resources footprint. However, a single image captures only a single view of the identity, which may not be enough for identities exhibiting multi-modal distributions. Contrarily, the **Video-to-Video (V2V)** setting enables to capture and combine different modes in the input, but with a significant increase in the number of operations and memory. Finally, the **Image-to-Video (I2V)** setting [24,26,48,58,59] represents a good compromise: building the gallery may be slow, but it is often performed offline. Moreover, matchings perform extremely fast, as a query comprise only a single image. We remark that *i)* We adopt the standard *"Cross Camera Validation"* protocol, not considering examples of the gallery from the same camera of the query at evaluation and *ii)* even if VKD relies on frames from different camera during train, we strictly adhere to the common schema and switch to tracklet-based inputs at evaluation time.

Evaluation Metrics. While settings vary between different dataset, evaluation metrics for Re-Identification are shared by the vast majority of works in the field. In the followings, we report performance in terms of top-k accuracy and Mean Average Precision (mAP). By combining them, we evaluate VKD both in terms of accuracy and ranking performance.

4.1 Datasets

Person Re-ID: MARS [55] comprises 19680 tracklets from 6 different cameras, capturing 1260 different identities (split between 625 for the training set, 626 for the gallery and 622 for the query) with 59 frames per tracklet on average. MARS has shown to be a challenging dataset because it has been automatically annotated, leading to errors and false detections [56]. The **Duke** [33] dataset was first introduced for multi-target and multi-camera surveillance purposes, and then expanded to include person attributes and identities (414 ones). Consistently with [10, 22, 29, 40], we use the **Duke-Video-ReID** [49] variant, where identities have been manually annotated from tracking information[3]. It comprises 5534 video tracklets from 8 different cameras, with 167 frames per tracklet on average. Following [10], we extract the first frame of every tracklet when testing in the I2V setting, for both MARS and Duke.

Vehicle Re-ID: VeRi-776 [25] has been collected from 20 fixed cameras, capturing vehicles moving on a circular road in a 1.0 km^2 area. It contains 18397 tracklets with an average number of 6 frames per tracklet, capturing 775 identities split between train (575) and gallery (200). The query set shares identities consistently with the gallery, but differently from the other two sets it includes only a single image for each couple (id, camera). Consequently, all recent methods perform the evaluation following the I2V setting.

Animal Re-ID: The **Amur Tiger** [18] Re-Identification in the Wild (ATRW) is a recently introduced dataset collected from a diverse set of wild zoos. The training set includes 107 subjects and 17.6 images on average per identity; no information is provided to aggregate images into tracklets. It is possible to evaluate only the I2I setting through a remote http server. As done in [21], we horizontally flip the training images to duplicate the number of identities available, thus resulting in 214 training identities.

Implementation Details. Following [12, 22] we adopt the following hyperparameters for MARS and Duke: *i)* each batch contains $P = 8$ identities with

---

[3] In the following, we refer to Duke-Video-ReID simply as Duke. Another variant of Duke named Duke-ReID exists [34], but it does not come with query tracklets.

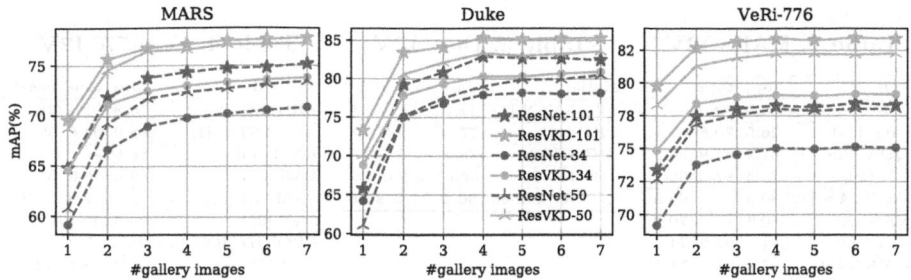

Fig. 3. Performance (mAP) in the Image-To-Video setting when changing at evaluation time the number of frames in each gallery tracklet.

Table 1. Self-distillation results across datasets, settings and architectures.

	MARS				Duke				VeRi-776			
	I2V		V2V		I2V		V2V		I2I		I2V	
	cmc1	mAP	cmc1	mAP	cmc1	mAP	cmc1	mAP	cmc1	mAP	cmc1	mAP
ResNet-34	80.81	70.74	86.67	78.03	81.34	78.70	93.45	**91.88**	92.97	70.30	93.80	75.01
ResVKD-34	**82.17**	**73.68**	**87.83**	**79.50**	**83.33**	**80.60**	**93.73**	91.62	**95.29**	**75.97**	**94.76**	**79.02**
ResNet-50	82.22	73.38	87.88	81.13	82.34	80.19	**95.01**	**94.17**	93.50	73.19	93.33	77.88
ResVKD-50	**83.89**	**77.27**	**88.74**	**82.22**	**85.61**	**83.81**	**95.01**	93.41	**95.23**	**79.17**	**95.17**	**82.16**
ResNet-101	82.78	74.94	88.59	81.66	83.76	82.89	**96.01**	**94.73**	94.28	74.27	94.46	78.20
ResVKD-101	**85.91**	**77.64**	**89.60**	**82.65**	**86.32**	**85.11**	95.44	93.67	**95.53**	**80.62**	**96.07**	**83.26**
ResNet-50bam	82.58	74.11	88.54	81.19	82.48	80.24	94.87	**93.82**	93.33	72.73	93.80	77.14
ResVKD-50bam	**84.34**	**78.13**	**89.39**	**83.07**	**86.18**	**84.54**	**95.16**	93.45	**96.01**	**78.67**	**95.71**	**81.57**
DenseNet-121	82.68	74.34	89.75	81.93	82.91	80.26	93.73	91.73	91.24	69.24	91.84	74.52
DenseVKD-121	**84.04**	**77.09**	**89.80**	**82.84**	**86.47**	**84.14**	**95.44**	**93.54**	**94.34**	**76.23**	**93.80**	**79.76**
MobileNet-V2	78.64	67.94	85.96	77.10	78.06	74.73	93.30	91.56	88.80	64.68	89.81	69.90
MobileVKD-V2	**83.33**	**73.95**	**88.13**	**79.62**	**83.76**	**80.83**	**94.30**	**92.51**	**92.85**	**70.93**	**92.61**	**75.27**

$K = 4$ samples each; *ii)* each sample comprises 8 images equally spaced in a tracklet. Differently, for image-based datasets (ATRW and VeRi-776) we increase P to 18 and use a single image at a time. All the teacher networks are trained for 300 epoch using Adam [17], setting the learning rate to 10^{-4} and multiplying it by 0.1 every 100 epochs. During the distillation stage, we feed $N = 8$ images to the teacher and $M = 2$ ones (picked at random) to the student. We found beneficial to train the student longer: so, we set the number of epochs to 500 and the learning rate decay steps at 300 and 450. We keep fixed $\tau = 10$ (Eq. 3), $\alpha = 10^{-1}$ and $\beta = 10^{-4}$ (Eq. 5) in all experiments. To improve generalisation, we apply data augmentation as described in [28]. Finally, we put the teacher in training mode during distillation (consequently, batch normalisation [15] statistics are computed on a batch basis): as observed in [2], this provides more accurate teacher labels.

4.2 Self-distillation

In this section we show the benefits of self-distillation for person and vehicle re-id. We indicate the teacher with the name of the backbone (e.g. ResNet-50)

<table>
<tr><td colspan="4">Table 2. MARS I2V</td></tr>
</table>

Table 2. MARS **I2V**

Method	top$_1$	top$_5$	mAP
P2SNet [46]	55.3	72.9	–
Zhang [54]	56.5	70.6	–
XQDA [20]	67.2	81.9	54.9
TKP [10]	75.6	87.6	65.1
STE-NVAN [22]	80.3	–	68.8
NVAN [22]	80.1	–	70.2
MGAT [3]	81.1	92.2	71.8
ResVKD-50	83.9	93.2	77.3
ResVKD-50bam	**84.3**	**93.5**	**78.1**

Table 3. Duke **I2V**

Method	top$_1$	top$_5$	mAP
STE-NVAN [22]	42.2	–	41.3
TKP [10]	77.9	–	75.9
NVAN [22]	78.4	–	76.7
ResVKD-50	85.6	93.9	83.8
ResVKD-50bam	**86.2**	**94.2**	**84.5**

Table 4. VeRi-776 **I2V**

Method	top$_1$	top$_5$	mAP
PROVID [26]	76.8	91.4	48.5
VFL-LSTM [1]	88.0	94.6	59.2
RAM [24]	88.6	–	61.5
VANet [7]	89.8	96.0	66.3
PAMTRI [42]	92.9	92.9	71.9
SAN [32]	93.3	97.1	72.5
PROVID-BOT [26]	**96.1**	97.9	77.2
ResVKD-50	95.2	**98.0**	**82.2**
ResVKD-50bam	95.7	98.0	81.6

and append "VKD" for its student (e.g. ResVKD-50). To validate our ideas, we do not limit the analysis on ResNet-*; contrarily, we test self-distillation on DenseNet-121 [14] and MobileNet-V2 1.0X [36]. Since learning what and where to look represents an appealing property when dealing with Re-ID tasks [8], we additionally conduct experiments on ResNet-50 coupled with Bottleneck Attention Modules [31] (ResNet-50bam).

Table 1 reports the comparisons for different backbones: in the vast majority of the settings, *the student outperforms its teacher*. Such a finding is particularly evident when looking at the I2V setting, where the mAP metric gains 4.04% on average. The same holds for the I2I setting on VeRi-776, and in part also on V2V. We draw the following remarks: *i)* in accordance with the objective the student seeks to optimise, our proposal leads to greater improvements when few images are available; *ii)* bridging the gap between I2V and V2V does not imply a significant information loss when more frames are available; on the contrary it sometimes results in superior performance; *iii)* the previous considerations hold true across different architectures. As an additional proof, plots from Fig. 3 draw a comparison between models before and after distillation. VKD improves metrics considerably on all three dataset, as highlighted by the bias between the teachers and their corresponding students. Surprisingly, this often applies when comparing lighter students with deeper teachers: as an example, ResVKD-34 scores better than even ResNet-101 on VeRi-776, regardless of the number of images sampled for a gallery tracklet.

4.3 Comparison with State-Of-The-Art

Image-To-Video. Tables 2, 3 and 4 report a thorough comparison with current state-of-the-art (SOTA) methods, on MARS, Duke and VeRi-776 respectively. As common practice [3,10,32], we focus our analysis on ResNet-50, and in particular on its distilled variants ResVKD-50 and ResVKD-50bam. Our method clearly outperforms other competitors, with an increase in mAP w.r.t. top-scorers of 6.3% on MARS, 8.6% on Duke and 5% on VeRi-776. This results is totally in line with our goal of conferring robustness when just a single image is provided as query. In doing so, we do not make any task-specific assumption, thus rendering our proposal easily applicable to both person and vehicle Re-ID.

Table 5. MARS **V2V**

Method	top1	top5	mAP
DuATN [40]	81.2	92.5	67.7
TKP [10]	84.0	93.7	73.3
CSACSE+OF [6]	86.3	94.7	76.1
STA [8]	86.3	95.7	80.8
STE-NVAN [22]	88.9	–	81.2
NVAN [22]	**90.0**	–	82.8
ResVKD-50	88.7	96.1	82.2
ResVKD-50bam	89.4	**96.8**	**83.1**

Table 6. Duke **V2V**

Method	top1	top5	mAP
DuATN [40]	81.2	92.5	67.7
Matiyali [29]	89.3	98.3	88.5
TKP [10]	94.0	–	91.7
STE-NVAN [22]	95.2	–	93.5
STA [8]	96.2	**99.3**	94.9
NVAN [22]	**96.3**	–	94.9
ResVKD-50	95.0	98.9	93.4
ResVKD-50bam	95.2	98.6	93.5

Table 7. ATRW **I2I**

Method	top1	top5	mAP
PPbM-a [18]	82.5	93.7	62.9
PPbM-b [18]	83.3	93.2	60.3
NWPU [52]	94.7	96.7	75.1
BRL [23]	94.0	96.7	77.0
NBU [21]	**95.6**	**97.9**	**81.6**
ResNet-101	92.3	93.5	75.7
ResVKD-101	92.0	96.4	77.2

Video-To-Video. Analogously, we conduct experiments on the V2V setting and report results in Table 5 (MARS) and Table 6 (Duke)[4]. Here, VKD yields the following results: on the one hand, on MARS it pushes a baseline architecture as ResVKD-50 close to NVAN and STE-NVAN [22], the latter being tailored for the V2V setting. Moreover – when exploiting spatial attention modules (ResVKD-50bam) – it establishes new SOTA results, suggesting that a positive transfer occurs when matching tracklets also. On the other hand, the same does not hold true for Duke, where exploiting video features as in STA [8] and NVAN appears rewarding. We leave the investigation of further improvements on V2V to future works. As of today, our proposals is the only one guaranteeing consistent and stable results under both I2V and V2V settings.

4.4   Analysis on VKD

In the Absence of Camera Information. Here, we address the setting where we do not have access to camera information. As an example, when dealing with animal re-id this information often lacks and datasets come with images and labels solely: can VKD still provide any improvement? We think so, as one can still exploit the visual diversity lying in a bag of randomly sampled images. To demonstrate our claim, we test our proposal on Amur Tigers re-identification (ATRW), which was conceived as an Image-To-Image dataset. During comparisons: *i)* since other works do not conform to a unique backbone, here we opt for ResNet-101; *ii)* as common practice in this benchmark [21,23,52], we leverage re-ranking [57]. Table 7 compares VKD against the top scorers in the "Computer Vision for Wildlife Conservation 2019" competition. Importantly, the student ResVKD-101 improves over its teacher (1.5% on mAP and 2.9% on top5) and places second behind [21], confirming its effectiveness in a challenging scenario. Moreover, we remark that the top-scorer requires additional annotations - such as body parts and pose information - which we do not exploit.

Distilling Viewpoints *vs* time. Fig. 4 shows results of distilling knowledge from multiple views against time (*i.e.* multiple frames from a tracklet). On one side, as multiple views hold more "*visual variety*", the student builds a more

---

[4] Since VeRi-776 does not include any tracklet information in the query set, following all other competitors we limit experiments to the I2V setting only.

Table 8. Analysis on camera bias, in terms of viewpoint classification accuracy.

	MARS	Duke	VeRi-776
Prior Class	0.19	0.14	0.06
ResNet-34	**0.61**	**0.73**	**0.55**
ResVKD-34	0.40	0.67	0.51
ResNet-101	**0.71**	**0.72**	**0.73**
ResVKD-101	0.51	0.70	0.68

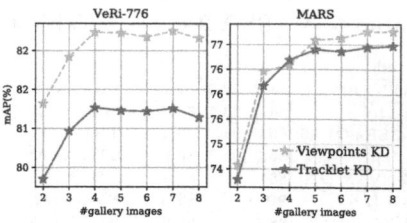

Fig. 4. Comparison between time and viewpoints distillation.

Table 9. Analysis on different modalities for training the teacher.

	Input bags	MARS				Duke			
		I2V		V2V		I2V		V2V	
		cmc1	mAP	cmc1	mAP	cmc1	mAP	cmc1	mAP
ResNet-50	Viewpoints ($N = 2$)	80.05	71.16	84.70	76.99	77.21	75.19	89.17	87.70
ResNet-50	Tracklets ($N = 2$)	82.32	73.69	87.32	79.91	81.77	80.34	93.73	92.88
ResVKD-50	Viewpoints ($N = 2$)	**83.89**	**77.27**	**88.74**	**82.22**	**85.61**	**83.81**	**95.01**	**93.41**

invariant representation for the identity. On the opposite, a student trained with tracklets still considerably outperforms the teacher. This shows that, albeit the visual variety is reduced, our distillation approach still successfully exploits it.

VKD Reduces the Camera Bias. As pointed out in [43], the appearance encoded by a CNN is heavily affected by external factors surrounding the target object (*e.g.* different backgrounds, viewpoints, illumination ...). In this respect, is our proposal effective for reducing such a bias? To investigate this aspect, we perform a camera classification test on both the teacher (*e.g.* ResNet-34) and the student network (*e.g.* ResVKD-34) by fitting a linear classifier on top of their features, with the aim of predicting the camera the picture is taken from. We freeze all backbone layers and train for 300 epochs ($lr = 10^{-3}$ and halved every 50 epochs). Table 8 reports performance on the gallery set for different teachers and students. To provide a better understanding, we include a baseline that computes predictions by sampling from the cameras prior distribution. As expected: *i)* the teacher outperforms the baseline, suggesting it is in fact biased towards background conditions; *ii)* the student consistently reduces the bias, confirming VKD encourages the student to focus on identities features and drops viewpoint-specific information. Finally, it is noted that time-based distillation does not yield the bias reduction we observe for VKD (see supplementary materials).

Can Performance of the Student be Obtained Without Distillation? To highlight the advantages of the two-stage procedure above discussed, we here consider a teacher (ResNet-50) trained straightly using few frames ($N = 2$)

only. First two rows of Table 9 show the performance achieved by this baseline (using tracklets and views respectively). Results show that major improvements come from the teacher-student paradigm we devise (third row), instead of simply reducing the number of input images available to the teacher.

Student Explanation. To further assess the differences between teachers and students, we leverage GradCam [39] to highlight the input regions that have been considered paramount for predicting the identity. Figure 5 depicts the impact of VKD for various examples from MARS, VeRi-776 and ATRW. In general, the student network pays more attention to the subject of interest compared to its teacher. For person and animal Re-ID, background features are suppressed (third and last columns) while attention tends to spread to the whole subject (first and fourth columns). When dealing with vehicle Re-ID, one can appreciate how the attention becomes equally distributed on symmetric parts, such as front and rear lights (second, seventh and last columns). Please see supplementary materials for more examples, as well as a qualitative analysis of some of our model errors.

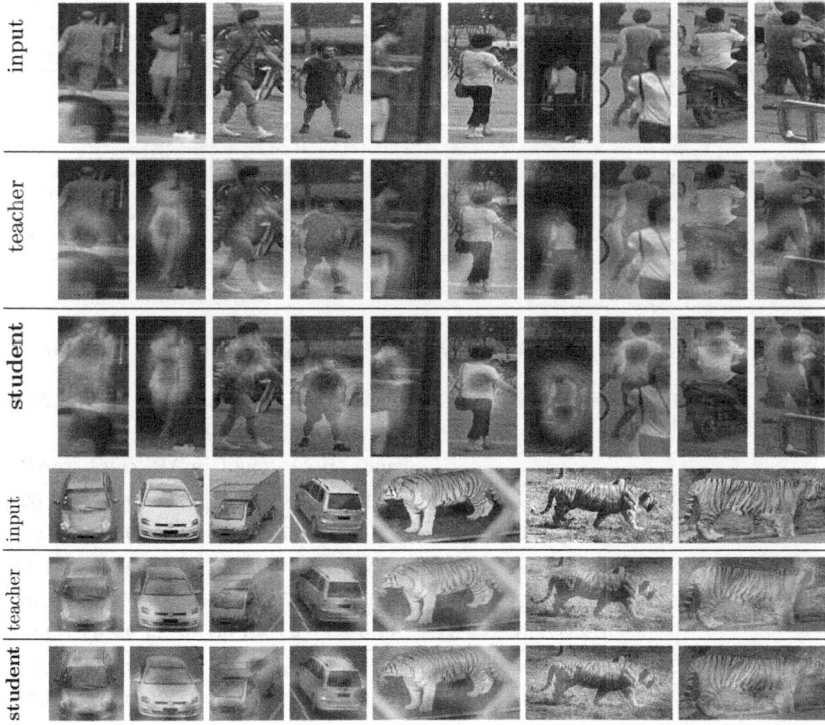

Fig. 5. Model explanation via GradCam [39] on ResNet-50 (teacher) and ResVKD-50 (student). The student favours visual details characterising the target, discarding external and uninformative patterns.

Cross-distillation. Differently from other approaches [5,10], VKD is not confined to self-distillation, but instead allows the knowledge transfer from a complex architecture (e.g. ResNet-101) into a simpler one, such as MobileNet-V2 or ResNet-34 (*cross-distillation*). Here, drawing inspirations from the model compression area, we attempt to reduce the network complexity but, at the same time, increase the profit we already achieve through self-distillation. In this respect, Table 11 shows results of cross-distillation, for various combinations of a teacher and a student. It appears that *better the teacher, better the student*: as an example, ResVKD-34 gains an additional 3% mAP on Duke when educated by ResNet-101 rather than "itself".

On the Impact of Loss Terms. We perform a thorough ablation study (Table 10) on the student loss (Eq. 5). It is noted that leveraging ground truth solely (second row) hurts performance. Differently, best performance for both metrics are obtained exploiting teacher signal (from the third row onward), with particular emphasis to $\mathcal{L}_{DP}$, which proves to be a fundamental component.

Table 10. Ablation study questioning the impact of each loss term.

	$\mathcal{L}_{CE}$	$\mathcal{L}_{TR}$	$\mathcal{L}_{KL}$	$\mathcal{L}_{DP}$	MARS				Duke				VeRi-776			
					I2V		V2V		I2V		V2V		I2I		I2V	
					cmc1	mAP	cmc1	mAP	cmc1	mAP	cmc1	mAP	cmc1	mAP	cmc1	mAP
ResNet-50 (teacher)					82.22	73.38	87.88	81.13	82.34	80.19	95.01	94.17	93.50	73.19	93.33	77.88
ResVKD-50 (students)	✓	✓	✗	✗	80.25	71.26	85.71	77.45	82.62	81.03	94.73	93.29	92.61	70.06	92.31	74.82
	✗	✗	✓	✓	84.09	**77.37**	88.33	82.06	84.90	83.56	95.30	93.79	95.29	**79.35**	**95.29**	**82.26**
	✓	✓	✓	✗	83.54	75.18	88.43	80.77	83.90	82.34	94.30	92.97	**95.41**	78.01	95.17	81.32
	✓	✓	✗	✓	**84.29**	76.82	88.69	81.82	85.33	83.45	**95.44**	**93.90**	94.40	77.41	94.87	80.93
	✓	✓	✓	✓	83.89	77.27	**88.74**	**82.22**	**85.61**	**83.81**	95.01	93.41	95.23	79.17	95.17	82.16

Table 11. Measuring the benefit of VKD for cross-architecture transfer.

Student (#params)	Teacher (#params)	MARS I2V		Duke I2V		VeRi-776 I2V	
		cmc1	mAP	cmc1	mAP	cmc1	mAP
ResNet-34 (21.2M)	ResNet-34 (21.2M)	82.17	73.68	83.33	80.60	94.76	79.02
	ResNet-50 (23.5M)	83.08	75.45	84.05	82.61	**95.05**	80.05
	ResNet-101 (42.5M)	**83.43**	**75.47**	**85.75**	**83.65**	94.87	**80.41**
ResNet-50 (23.5M)	ResNet-50 (23.5M)	83.89	77.27	85.61	83.81	95.17	82.16
	ResNet-101 (42.5M)	**84.49**	**77.47**	**85.90**	**84.34**	**95.41**	**82.99**
MobileNet-V2 (2.2M)	MobileNet-V2 (2.2M)	83.33	73.95	**83.76**	80.83	92.61	75.27
	ResNet-101 (42.5M)	83.38	74.72	**83.76**	81.36	**93.03**	**76.38**

5   Conclusions

An effective Re-ID method requires visual descriptors robust to changes in both background appearances and viewpoints. Moreover, its effectiveness should be ensured even for queries composed of a single image. To accomplish these, we proposed Views Knowledge Distillation (VKD), a teacher-student approach where the student observes only a small subset of input views. This strategy encourages the student to discover better representations: as a result, it outperforms its teacher at the end of the training. Importantly, VKD shows robustness on diverse domains (person, vehicle and animal), surpassing by a wide margin the state of the art in I2V. Thanks to extensive analysis, we highlight that the student presents stronger focus on the target and reduces the camera bias.

Acknowledgement. The authors would like to acknowledge Farm4Trade for its financial and technical support.

References

1. Alfasly, S.A.S., et al.: Variational representation learning for vehicle re-identification. In: IEEE International Conference on Image Processing (2019)
2. Bagherinezhad, H., Horton, M., Rastegari, M., Farhadi, A.: Label refinery: improving ImageNet classification through label progression. arXiv preprint arXiv:1805.02641 (2018)
3. Bao, L., Ma, B., Chang, H., Chen, X.: Masked graph attention network for person re-identification. In: IEEE International Conference on Computer Vision and Pattern Recognition Workshops (2019)
4. Bergamini, L., et al.: Multi-views embedding for cattle re-identification. In: IEEE International Conference on Signal-Image Technology & Internet-Based Systems (2018)
5. Bhardwaj, S., Srinivasan, M., Khapra, M.M.: Efficient video classification using fewer frames. In: IEEE International Conference on Computer Vision and Pattern Recognition (2019)
6. Chen, D., Li, H., Xiao, T., Yi, S., Wang, X.: Video person re-identification with competitive snippet-similarity aggregation and co-attentive snippet embedding. In: IEEE International Conference on Computer Vision and Pattern Recognition (2018)
7. Chu, R., et al.: Vehicle re-identification with viewpoint-aware metric learning. In: IEEE International Conference on Computer Vision (2019)
8. Fu, Y., Wang, X., Wei, Y., Huang, T.: STA: spatial-temporal attention for large-scale video-based person re-identification. In: AAAI Conference on Artificial Intelligence (2019)
9. Furlanello, T., Lipton, Z.C., Tschannen, M., Itti, L., Anandkumar, A.: Born again neural networks. In: International Conference on Machine Learning (2018)
10. Gu, X., Ma, B., Chang, H., Shan, S., Chen, X.: Temporal knowledge propagation for image-to-video person re-identification. In: IEEE International Conference on Computer Vision (2019)
11. He, K., Zhang, X., Ren, S., Sun, J.: Deep residual learning for image recognition. In: IEEE International Conference on Computer Vision and Pattern Recognition (2016)

12. Hermans, A., Beyer, L., Leibe, B.: In defense of the triplet loss for person re-identification. arXiv preprint arXiv:1703.07737 (2017)
13. Hinton, G., Vinyals, O., Dean, J.: Distilling the knowledge in a neural network. In: NeurIPS Deep Learning and Representation Learning Workshop (2015)
14. Huang, G., Liu, Z., Van Der Maaten, L., Weinberger, K.Q.: Densely connected convolutional networks. In: IEEE International Conference on Computer Vision and Pattern Recognition (2017)
15. Ioffe, S., Szegedy, C.: Batch normalization: accelerating deep network training by reducing internal covariate shift. In: International Conference on Machine Learning (2015)
16. Khan, S.D., Ullah, H.: A survey of advances in vision-based vehicle re-identification. Comput. Vis. Image Underst. **183**, 50–63 (2019)
17. Kingma, D.P., Ba, J.: Adam: a method for stochastic optimization. Int. Conf. Learn. Represent. (2015)
18. Li, S., Li, J., Lin, W., Tang, H.: Amur tiger re-identification in the wild. arXiv preprint arXiv:1906.05586 (2019)
19. Li, Z., Hoiem, D.: Learning without forgetting. In: European Conference on Computer Vision (2016)
20. Liao, S., Hu, Y., Zhu, X., Li, S.Z.: Person re-identification by local maximal occurrence representation and metric learning. In: IEEE International Conference on Computer Vision and Pattern Recognition (2015)
21. Liu, C., Zhang, R., Guo, L.: Part-pose guided amur tiger re-identification. In: IEEE International Conference on Computer Vision Workshops (2019)
22. Liu, C.T., Wu, C.W., Wang, Y.C.F., Chien, S.Y.: Spatially and temporally efficient non-local attention network for video-based person re-identification. In: British Machine Vision Conference (2019)
23. Liu, N., Zhao, Q., Zhang, N., Cheng, X., Zhu, J.: Pose-guided complementary features learning for Amur tiger re-identification. In: IEEE International Conference on Computer Vision Workshops (2019)
24. Liu, X., Zhang, S., Huang, Q., Gao, W.: Ram: a region-aware deep model for vehicle re-identification. In: IEEE International Conference on Multimedia and Expo (ICME) (2018)
25. Liu, X., Liu, W., Mei, T., Ma, H.: A deep learning-based approach to progressive vehicle re-identification for urban surveillance. In: European Conference on Computer Vision (2016)
26. Liu, X., Liu, W., Mei, T., Ma, H.: PROVID: progressive and multimodal vehicle reidentification for large-scale urban surveillance. IEEE Trans. Multimedia **20**(3), 645–658 (2017)
27. Liu, Y., Junjie, Y., Ouyang, W.: Quality aware network for set to set recognition. In: IEEE International Conference on Computer Vision (2017)
28. Luo, H., Gu, Y., Liao, X., Lai, S., Jiang, W.: Bag of tricks and a strong baseline for deep person re-identification. In: IEEE International Conference on Computer Vision and Pattern Recognition Workshops (2019)
29. Matiyali, N., Sharma, G.: Video person re-identification using learned clip similarity aggregation. In: The IEEE Winter Conference on Applications of Computer Vision (2020)
30. Nguyen, T.B., Le, T.L., Nguyen, D.D., Pham, D.T.: A reliable image-to-video person re-identification based on feature fusion. In: Asian Conference on Intelligent Information and Database Systems (2018)
31. Park, J., Woo, S., Lee, J., Kweon, I.S.: BAM: bottleneck attention module. In: British Machine Vision Conference (2018)

32. Qian, J., Jiang, W., Luo, H., Yu, H.: Stripe-based and attribute-aware network: a two-branch deep model for vehicle re-identification. arXiv preprint arXiv:1910.05549 (2019)
33. Ristani, E., Solera, F., Zou, R., Cucchiara, R., Tomasi, C.: Performance measures and a data set for multi-target, multi-camera tracking. In: European Conference on Computer Vision (2016)
34. Ristani, E., Tomasi, C.: Features for multi-target multi-camera tracking and re-identification. In: IEEE International Conference on Computer Vision and Pattern Recognition (2018)
35. Romero, A., et al.: FitNets: hints for thin deep nets. In: International Conference on Learning Representations (2015)
36. Sandler, M., et al.: MobileNetV2: inverted residuals and linear bottlenecks. In: IEEE International Conference on Computer Vision and Pattern Recognition (2018)
37. Schneider, S., Taylor, G.W., Linquist, S., Kremer, S.C.: Past, present and future approaches using computer vision for animal re-identification from camera trap data. Methods Ecol. Evol. **10**(3), 461–470 (2019)
38. Schroff, F., Kalenichenko, D., Philbin, J.: FaceNet: a unified embedding for face recognition and clustering. In: IEEE International Conference on Computer Vision and Pattern Recognition (2015)
39. Selvaraju, R.R., et al.: Grad-CAM: Visual explanations from deep networks via gradient-based localization. In: IEEE International Conference on Computer Vision and Pattern Recognition (2017)
40. Si, J., et al.: Dual attention matching network for context-aware feature sequence based person re-identification. In: IEEE International Conference on Computer Vision and Pattern Recognition (2018)
41. Sohn, K.: Improved deep metric learning with multi-class N-pair loss objective. In: Neural Information Processing Systems (2016)
42. Tang, Z., et al.: PAMTRI: pose-aware multi-task learning for vehicle re-identification using highly randomized synthetic data. In: IEEE International Conference on Computer Vision (2019)
43. Tian, M., et al.: Eliminating background-bias for robust person re-identification. In: IEEE International Conference on Computer Vision and Pattern Recognition (2018)
44. Tung, F., Mori, G.: Similarity-preserving knowledge distillation. In: IEEE International Conference on Computer Vision (2019)
45. Ustinova, E., Lempitsky, V.: Learning deep embeddings with histogram loss. In: Neural Information Processing Systems (2016)
46. Wang, G., Lai, J., Xie, X.: P2SNet: can an image match a video for person re-identification in an end-to-end way? IEEE Trans. Circ. Syst. Video Technol. (2017)
47. Wang, J., Zhou, F., Wen, S., Liu, X., Lin, Y.: Deep metric learning with angular loss. In: IEEE International Conference on Computer Vision and Pattern Recognition (2017)
48. Wang, Z., et al.: Orientation invariant feature embedding and spatial temporal regularization for vehicle re-identification. In: IEEE International Conference on Computer Vision (2017)
49. Wu, Y., et al.: Exploit the unknown gradually: one-shot video-based person re-identification by stepwise learning. In: IEEE International Conference on Computer Vision and Pattern Recognition (2018)

50. Xie, Z., Li, L., Zhong, X., Zhong, L., Xiang, J.: Image-to-video person re-identification with cross-modal embeddings. Pattern Recogn. Lett. **133**, 70–76 (2019)
51. Yang, C., Xie, L., Qiao, S., Yuille, A.: Knowledge distillation in generations: more tolerant teachers educate better students. arXiv preprint arXiv:1805.05551 (2018)
52. Yu, J., et al.: A strong baseline for tiger re-id and its bag of tricks. In: IEEE International Conference on Computer Vision Workshops (2019)
53. Zagoruyko, S., Komodakis, N.: Paying more attention to attention: improving the performance of convolutional neural networks via attention transfer. In: International Conference on Learning Representations (2017)
54. Zhang, D., et al.: Image-to-video person re-identification with temporally memorized similarity learning. IEEE Trans. Circ. Syst. Video Technol. **28**(10), 2622–2632 (2017)
55. Zheng, L., et al.: Mars: a video benchmark for large-scale person re-identification. In: European Conference on Computer Vision (2016)
56. Zheng, L., Yang, Y., Hauptmann, A.G.: Person re-identification: past, present and future. arXiv preprint arXiv:1610.02984 (2016)
57. Zhong, Z., Zheng, L., Cao, D., Li, S.: Re-ranking person re-identification with k-reciprocal encoding. In: IEEE International Conference on Computer Vision and Pattern Recognition (2017)
58. Zhou, Y., Liu, L., Shao, L.: Vehicle re-identification by deep hidden multi-view inference. IEEE Trans. Image Process. **27**(7), 3275–3287 (2018)
59. Zhou, Y., Shao, L.: Aware attentive multi-view inference for vehicle re-identification. In: IEEE International Conference on Computer Vision and Pattern Recognition (2018)

Defocus Deblurring Using Dual-Pixel Data

Abdullah Abuolaim[1(✉)] and Michael S. Brown[1,2]

[1] York University, Toronto, Canada
{abuolaim,mbrown}@eecs.yorku.ca
[2] Samsung AI Center, Toronto, Canada

Abstract. Defocus blur arises in images that are captured with a shallow depth of field due to the use of a wide aperture. Correcting defocus blur is challenging because the blur is spatially varying and difficult to estimate. We propose an effective defocus deblurring method that exploits data available on dual-pixel (DP) sensors found on most modern cameras. DP sensors are used to assist a camera's auto-focus by capturing two sub-aperture views of the scene in a single image shot. The two sub aperture images are used to calculate the appropriate lens position to focus on a particular scene region and are discarded afterwards. We introduce a deep neural network (DNN) architecture that uses these discarded sub-aperture images to reduce defocus blur. A key contribution of our effort is a carefully captured dataset of 500 scenes (2000 images) where each scene has: (i) an image with defocus blur captured at a large aperture; (ii) the two associated DP sub-aperture views; and (iii) the corresponding all-in-focus image captured with a small aperture. Our proposed DNN produces results that are significantly better than conventional single image methods in terms of both quantitative and perceptual metrics – all from data that is already available on the camera but ignored.

Keywords: Defocus blur · Extended depth of field · Dual-pixel sensors

1 Introduction

This paper addresses the problem of defocus blur. To understand why defocus blur is difficult to avoid, it is important to understand the mechanism governing image exposure. An image's exposure to light is controlled by adjusting two parameters: shutter speed and aperture size. The shutter speed controls the duration of light falling on the sensor, while the aperture controls the amount of light passing through the lens. The reciprocity between these two parameters allows the same exposure to occur by fixing one parameter and adjusting the other. For example, when a camera is placed in *aperture-priority* mode, the

Electronic supplementary material The online version of this chapter (https://doi.org/10.1007/978-3-030-58607-2_7) contains supplementary material, which is available to authorized users.

ⓒ Springer Nature Switzerland AG 2020
A. Vedaldi et al. (Eds.): ECCV 2020, LNCS 12355, pp. 111–126, 2020.
https://doi.org/10.1007/978-3-030-58607-2_7

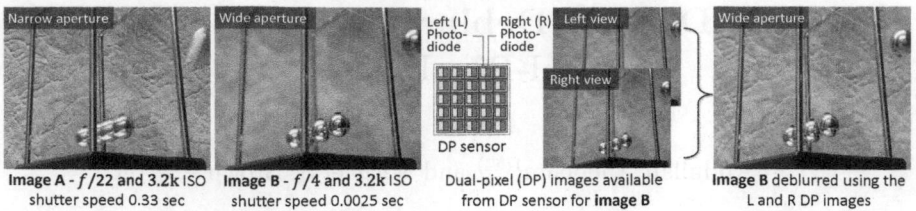

| **Image A** - $f/22$ and 3.2k ISO shutter speed 0.33 sec | **Image B** - $f/4$ and 3.2k ISO shutter speed 0.0025 sec | Dual-pixel (DP) images available from DP sensor for **image B** | **Image B** deblurred using the L and R DP images |

Fig. 1. Images A and B are of the same scene and same approximate exposure. Image A is captured with a narrow aperture ($f/22$) and slow shutter speed. Image A has a wide depth of field (DoF) and little defocus blur, but exhibits motion blur from the moving object due to the long shutter speed. Image B is captured with a wide aperture ($f/4$) and a fast shutter speed. Image B exhibits defocus blur due to the shallow DoF, but has no motion blur. Our proposed DNN uses the two sub-aperture views from the dual-pixel sensor of image B to deblur image B, resulting in a much sharper image.

aperture remains fixed while the shutter speed is adjusted to control how long light is allowed to pass through the lens. The drawback is that a slow shutter speed can result in motion blur if the camera and/or an object in the scene moves while the shutter is open, as shown in Fig. 1. Conversely, in *shutter-priority* mode, the shutter speed remains fixed while the aperture adjusts its size. The drawback of a variable aperture is that a wide aperture results in a shallow depth of field (DoF), causing defocus blur to occur in scene regions outside the DoF, as shown in Fig. 1. There are many computer vision applications that require a wide aperture but still want an all-in-focus image. An excellent example is cameras on self-driving cars, or cameras on cars that map environments, where the camera must use a fixed shutter speed and the only way to get sufficient light is a wide aperture at the cost of defocus blur.

Our aim is to reduce the unwanted defocus blur. The novelty of our approach lies in the use of data available from dual-pixel (DP) sensors used by modern cameras. DP sensors are designed with two photodiodes at each pixel location on the sensor. The DP design provides the functionality of a simple two-sample light-field camera and was developed to improve how cameras perform autofocus. Specifically, the two-sample light-field provides two sub-aperture views of the scene, denoted in this paper as *left* and *right* views. The light rays coming from scene points that are within the camera's DoF (i.e., points that are in focus) will have no difference in phase between the left and right views. However, light rays coming from scene points outside the camera's DoF (i.e., points that are out of focus) will exhibit a detectable disparity in the left/right views that is directly correlated to the amount of defocus blur. We refer to it as *defocus disparity*. Cameras use this phase shift information to determine how to move the lens to focus on a particular location in the scene. After autofocus calculations are performed, the DP information is discarded by the camera's hardware.

Contribution. We propose a deep neural network (DNN) to perform defocus deblurring that uses the DP images from the sensor available at capture time. In order to train the proposed DNN, a new dataset of 500 carefully captured images exhibiting defocus blur and their corresponding all-in-focus image is collected. This dataset consists of 2000 images – 500 DoF blurred images with their 1000 DP sub-aperture views and 500 corresponding all-in-focus images – all at full-frame resolution (i.e., 6720 × 4480 pixels). Using this training data, we propose a DNN architecture that is trained in an end-to-end manner to directly estimate a sharp image from the left/right DP views of the defocused input image. Our approach is evaluated against conventional methods that use only a single input image and show that our approach outperforms the existing state-of-the-art approaches in both signal processing and perceptual metrics. Most importantly, the proposed method works by using the DP sensor images that are a free by-product of modern image capture.

2 Related Work

Related work is discussed regarding (1) defocus blur, (2) datasets, and (3) applications exploiting DP sensors.

Defocus Deblurring. Related methods in the literature can be categorized into: (1) defocus detection methods [8,27,31,34,37,38] or (2) defocus map estimation and deblurring methods [4,15,18,22,28]. While defocus detection is relevant to our problem, we focus on the latter category as these methods share the goal of ultimately producing a sharp deblurred result.

A common strategy for defocus deblurring is to first compute a defocus map and use that information to guide the deblurring. Defocus map estimation methods [4,15,18,22,28] estimate the amount of defocus blur per pixel for an image with defocus blur. Representative works include Karaali et al. [15], which uses image gradients to calculate the blur amount difference between the original image edges and their re-blurred ones. Park et al. [22] introduced a method based on hand-crafted and deep features that were extracted from a pre-trained blur classification network. The combined feature vector was fed to a regression network to estimate the blur amount on edges and then later deblur the image. Shi et al. [28] proposed an effective blur feature using a sparse representation and image decomposition to detect just noticeable blur. Methods that directly deblur the image include Andrès et al.'s [4] approach, which uses regression trees to deblur the image. Recent work by Lee et al. [18] introduced a DNN architecture to estimate an image defocus map using a domain adaptation approach. This approach also introduced the first large-scale dataset for DNN-based training. Our work is inspired by Lee et al.'s [18] success in applying DNNs for the DoF deblurring task. Our distinction from the prior work is the use of the DP sensor information available at capture time.

Defocus Blur Datasets. There are several datasets available for defocus deblurring. The CUHK [27] and DUT [37] datasets have been used for blur detection and provide real images with their corresponding binary masks of blur/sharp regions. The SYNDOF [18] dataset provided data for defocus map estimation, in which their defocus blur is synthesized based on a given depth map of pinhole image datasets. The datasets of [18,27,37] do not provide the corresponding ground truth all-in-focus image. The RTF [4] dataset provided light-field images captured by a Lytro camera for the task of defocus deblurring. In their data, each blurred image has a corresponding all-in-focus image. However, the RTF dataset is small, with only 22 image pairs. While there are other similar and much larger light-field datasets [11,29], these datasets were introduced for different tasks (i.e., depth from focus and synthesizing a 4D RGBD light field), which are different from the task of this paper. In general, the images captured by Lytro cameras are not representative of DSLR and smartphone cameras, because they apply synthetic defocus blur, and have a relatively small spatial resolution [3].

As our approach is to utilize the DP data for defocus deblurring, we found it necessary to capture a new dataset. Our DP defocus blur dataset provides 500 pairs of images of unrepeated scenes; each pair has a defocus blurred image with its corresponding sharp image. The two DP views of the blurred image are also provided, resulting in a total of 2000 images. Details of our dataset capture are provided in Sect. 4. Similar to the patch-wise training approach followed in [18,22], we extract a large number of image patches from our dataset to train our DNN.

DP Sensor Applications. The DP sensor design was developed by Canon for the purpose of optimizing camera autofocus. DP sensors perform what is termed *phase difference autofocus* (PDAF) [1,2,14], in which the phase difference between the left and right sub-aperture views of the primary lens is calculated to measure the blur amount. Using this phase information, the camera's lens is adjusted such that the blur is minimized. While intended for autofocus, the DP images have been found useful for other tasks, such as depth map estimation [6,24], reflection removal [25], and synthetic DoF [32]. Our work is inspired by these prior methods and examines the use of DP data for the task of defocus blur removal.

3   DP Image Formation

We begin with a brief overview of the DP image formation. As previously mentioned, the DP sensor was designed to improve camera auto-focus technology. Figure 2 shows an illustrative example of how DP imaging works and how the left/right images are formed. A DP sensor provides a pair of photodiodes for each pixel with a microlens placed at the pixel site, as shown in Fig. 2-A. This DP unit arrangement allows each pair of photodiodes (i.e., dual-pixel) to record the light rays independently. Depending on the sensor's orientation, this arrangement can be shown as left/right or top/down pair; in this paper, we refer to them as the left/right pair – or L and R. The difference between the two views is related to the defocus amount at that scene point, where out-of-focus scene points will have a difference in phase and be blurred in opposite directions using a point spread function (PSF) and its flipped one [24]. This difference yields noticeable defocus disparity that is correlated to the amount of defocus blur.

The phase-shift process is illustrated in Fig. 2. The person shown in Fig. 2-A is within the camera's DoF, as highlighted in gray, whereas the textured pyramid is outside the DoF. The light rays from the in-focus object converge at a single DP unit on the imaging sensor, resulting in an in-focus pixel and no disparity

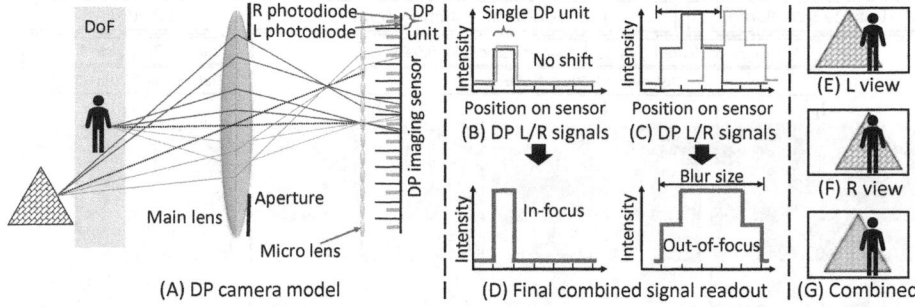

Fig. 2. Image formation diagram for a DP sensor. (A) Shows a thin-lens camera and a DP sensor. The light rays from different halves of the main lens fall on different left and right photodiodes. (B) Scene points that are within the DoF (highlighted in gray) have no phase shift between their L/R views. Scene points outside DoF have a phase shift as shown in (C). The L/R signals are aggregated and the corresponding combined signal is shown in (D). The blur size of the L signal is smaller than the combined one in the out-of-focus case. The defocus disparity is noticeable between the captured L/R images (see (E) and (F)). The final combined image in (G) has more blur. Our DNN leverages this additional information available in the L/R views for image defocus deblurring.

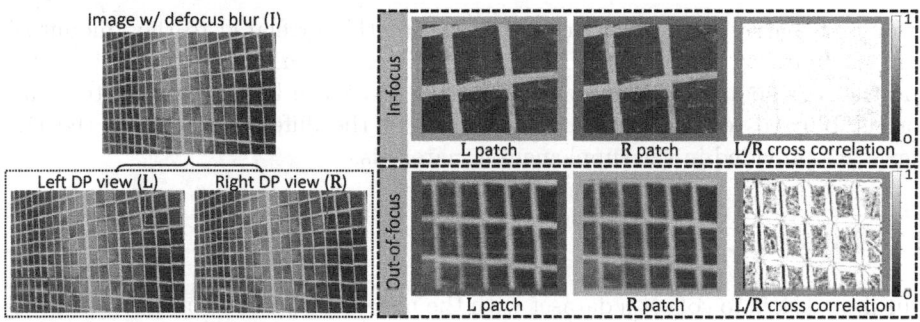

Fig. 3. An input image I is shown with a spatially varying defocus blur. The two dual-pixel (DP) images (L and R) corresponding to I are captured at imaging time. In-focus and out-of-focus patches in the L and R DP image patches exhibit different amounts of pixel disparity as shown by the cross-correlation of the two patches. This information helps the DNN to learn the extent of blur in different regions of the image.

between their DP L/R views (Fig. 2-B). The light rays coming from the out-of-focus regions spread across multiple DP units and therefore produce a difference between their DP L/R views, as shown in Fig. 2-C. Intuitively, this information can be exploited by a DNN to learn where regions of the image exhibit blur and the extent of this blur. The final output image is a combination of the L/R views, as shown in Fig. 2-G.

By examining real examples shown in Fig. 3 it becomes apparent how a DNN can leverage these two sub-aperture views as input to deblur the image. In particular, patches containing regions that are out-of-focus will exhibit a notable

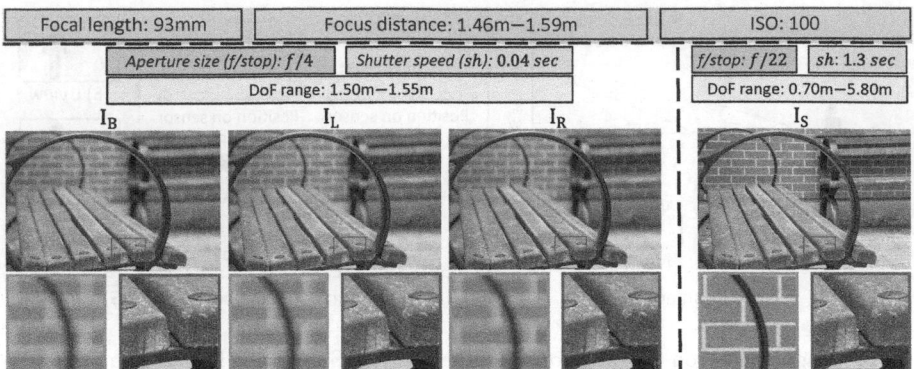

Fig. 4. An example of an image pair with the camera settings used for capturing. I_L and I_R represent the Left and Right DP views extracted from I_B. The focal length, ISO, and focus distance are fixed between the two captures of I_B and I_S. The aperture size is different, and hence the shutter speed and DoF are accordingly different too. In-focus and out-of-focus zoomed-in patches are extracted from each image and shown in green and red boxes, respectively. (Color figure online)

defocus disparity in the two views that is directly correlated to the amount of defocus blur. By training a DNN with sufficient examples of the L/R views and the corresponding all-in-focus image, the DNN can learn how to detect and correct blurred regions. Animated examples of the difference between the DP views are provided in the supplemental materials.

4 Dataset Collection

Our first task is to collect a dataset with the necessary DP information for training our DNN. While most consumer cameras employ PDAF sensors, we are aware of only two camera manufacturers that provide DP data – Google and Canon. Specifically, Google's research team has released an application to read DP data [9] from the Google Pixel 3 and 4 smartphones. However, smartphone cameras are currently not suitable for our problem for two reasons. First, smartphone cameras use fixed apertures that cannot be adjusted for data collection. Second, smartphone cameras have narrow aperture and exhibit large DoF; in fact, most cameras go to great lengths to simulate shallow DoF by purposely introducing defocus blur [32]. As a result, our dataset is captured using a Canon EOS 5D Mark IV DSLR camera, which provides the ability to save and extract full-frame DP images.

Using the Canon camera, we capture a pair of images of the same static scene at two aperture sizes – $f/4$ and $f/22$ – which are the maximum (widest) and minimum (narrowest) apertures possible for our lens configuration. The lens position and focal length remain fixed during image capture. Scenes are captured in aperture-priority mode, in which the exposure compensation between the image pairs is done automatically by adjusting the shutter speed. The image captured at $f/4$ has the smallest DoF and results in the blurred input image I_B. The image captured at $f/22$ has the largest DoF and serves as the all-in-focus target image denoted as I_S (sharp image). Focus distance and focal length differ across captured pairs in order to capture a diverse range of defocus blur types. Our captured images offer the following benefits over prior datasets:

High-Quality Images. Our captured images are low-noise images (i.e., low ISO equates to low-noise [23]) and of full resolution of 6720×4480. All images, including the left/right DP views, are processed to an sRGB and encoded with a lossless 16-bit depth per RGB channel.

Real and Diverse Defocus Blur. Unlike other existing datasets, our dataset provides real defocus blur and in-focus pairs indicative of real camera optics.

Varying Scene Contents. To provide a wide range of object categories, we collect 500 pairs of unique indoor/outdoor scenes with a large variety of scene contents. Our dataset is also free of faces to avoid privacy issues.

The $f/4$ (blurry) and $f/22$ (sharp) image pairs are carefully imaged static scenes with the camera fixed on a tripod. To further avoid camera shake, the camera was controlled remotely to allow hands-free operation. Figure 4 shows an example of an image pair from our dataset. The left and right DP views of I_B are provided by the camera and denoted as I_L and I_R respectively. The ISO setting is fixed for each image pair. Figure 4 shows the DP L/R views for only image I_B, because DP L/R views of I_S are visually identical due to the fact I_S is our all-in-focus ground truth.

5   Dual-Pixel Defocus Deblurring DNN (DPDNet)

Using our captured dataset, we trained a symmetric encoder-decoder CNN architecture with skip connections between the corresponding feature maps [20,26]. Skip connections are widely used in encoder-decoder CNNs to combine various levels of feature maps. These have been found useful for gradient propagation and convergence acceleration that allow training of deeper networks [13,30].

We adapt a U-Net-like architecture [26] with the following modifications: an input layer to take a 6-channel input cube (two DP views; each is a 3-channel sRGB image) and an output layer to generate a 3-channel output sRGB image; skip connections of the convolutional feature maps are passed to their mirrored convolutional layers without cropping in order to pass on more feature map detail; and the loss function is changed to be mean squared error (MSE).

The overall DNN architecture of our proposed DP deblurring method is shown in Fig. 5. Our method reads the two DP images, I_L and I_R, as a 6-channel cube, and processes them through the encoder, bottleneck, and decoder stages to get the final sharp image I_S^*. There are four blocks in the encoder stage (E-Block 1–4) and in each block, two 3×3 convolutional operations are performed, each followed by a ReLU activation. Then a 2×2 max pooling is performed for downsampling. Although max pooling operations reduce the size of feature maps between E-Blocks, this is required to extend the receptive field size in order

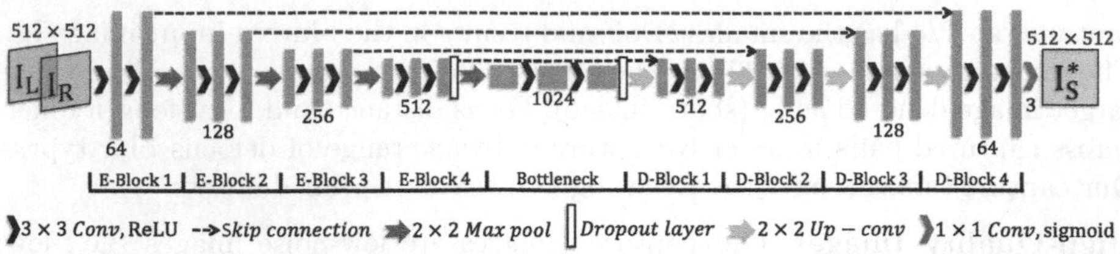

3×3 Conv, ReLU $\dashrightarrow$ Skip connection $\Rightarrow$ 2×2 Max pool $\parallel$ Dropout layer $\Rightarrow$ 2×2 Up $-$ conv 1×1 Conv, sigmoid

Fig. 5. Our proposed DP deblurring architecture (DPDNet). Our method utilizes the DP images, I_L and I_R, for predicting the sharp image I_S^* through three stages: encoder (E-Blocks), bottleneck, and decoder (D-Blocks). The size of the input and output layers is shown above the images. The number of output filters is shown under the convolution operations for each block.

to handle large defocus blur. To reduce the chances of overfitting, two dropout layers are added, one before the max pooling operation in the fourth E-Block, and one dropout layer at the end of the network bottleneck, as shown in Fig. 5. In the decoder stage, we also have four blocks (D-Block 1–4). For each D-Block, a 2×2 upsampling of the input feature map followed by a 2×2 convolution ($Up - conv$) is carried out instead of direct deconvolution in order to avoid checkerboard artifacts [21]. The corresponding feature map from the encoder stage is concatenated. Next, two 3×3 convolutions are performed, each followed by a ReLU activation. Afterwards, a 1×1 convolution followed by sigmoid activation is applied to output the final sharp image I_S^*. The number of output filters is shown under each convolution layer for each block in Fig. 5. The stride for all operations is 1 except for the max pooling operation, which has a stride of 2. The final sharp image I_S^* is, thus, predicted as follows:

$$I_S^* = \mathrm{DPDNet}(I_L, I_R; \theta_{\mathrm{DPDNet}}), \tag{1}$$

where DPDNet is our proposed architecture, and θ_{DPDNet} is the set of weights and parameters.

Training Procedure. The size of input and output layers is set to $512 \times 512 \times 6$ and $512 \times 512 \times 3$, respectively. This is because we train not on the full-size images but on the extracted image patches. We adopt the weight initialization strategy proposed by He [12] and use the Adam optimizer [16] to train the model. The initial learning rate is set to 2×10^{-5}, which is decreased by half every 60 epochs. We train our model with mini-batches of size 5 using MSE loss between the output and the ground truth as follows:

$$\mathcal{L} = \frac{1}{n} \sum_n (I_S - I_S^*)^2, \tag{2}$$

where n is the size of the image patch in pixels. During the training phase, we set the dropout rate to 0.4. All the models described in the subsequent sections are implemented using Python with the Keras framework on top of TensorFlow and trained with a NVIDIA TITAN X GPU. We set the maximum number of training epochs to 200.

Table 1. The quantitative results for different defocus deblurring methods. The testing on the dataset is divided into three scene categories: indoor, outdoor, and combined. The top result numbers are highlighted in green and the second top in blue. DPDNet-Single is our DPDNet variation that is trained with only a single blurred input. Our DPDNet that uses the two L/R DP views achieved the best results on all scene categories for all metrics. Note: the testing set consists of 37 indoor and 39 outdoor scenes.

Method	Indoor				Outdoor				Combined			
	PSNR ↑	SSIM ↑	MAE ↓	LPIPS ↓	PSNR ↑	SSIM ↑	MAE ↓	LPIPS ↓	PSNR ↑	SSIM ↑	MAE ↓	LPIPS ↓
EBDB [15]	25.77	0.772	0.040	0.297	21.25	0.599	0.058	0.373	23.45	0.683	0.049	0.336
DMENet [18]	25.50	0.788	0.038	0.298	21.43	0.644	0.063	0.397	23.41	0.714	0.051	0.349
JNB [28]	26.73	0.828	0.031	0.273	21.10	0.608	0.064	0.355	23.84	0.715	0.048	0.315
Our DPDNet-Single	26.54	0.816	0.031	0.239	22.25	0.682	0.056	0.313	24.34	0.747	0.044	0.277
Our DPDNet	27.48	0.849	0.029	0.189	22.90	0.726	0.052	0.255	25.13	0.786	0.041	0.223

6   Experimental Results

We first describe our data preparation procedure and then evaluation metrics used. This is followed by quantitative and qualitative results to evaluate our proposed method with existing deblurring methods. We also discuss the time analysis and test the robustness of our DP method against different aperture settings.

Data Preparation. Our dataset has an equal number of indoor and outdoor scenes. We divide the data into 70% training, 15% validation, and 15% testing sets. Each set has a balanced number of indoor/outdoor scenes. To prepare the data for training, we first downscale our images to be 1680×1120 in size. Next, image patches are extracted by sliding a window of size 512×512 with 60% overlap. We empirically found this image size and patch size to work well. An ablation study of different architecture settings is provided in the supplemental materials. We compute the sharpness energy (i.e., by applying Sobel filter) of the in-focus image patches and sort them. We discard 30% of the patches that have the lowest sharpness energy. Such patches represent homogeneous regions, cause an ambiguity associated to the amount of blur, and adversely affect the DNNs training, as found in [22].

Evaluation Metrics. Results are reported on traditional signal processing metrics – namely, PSNR, SSIM [33], and MAE. We also incorporate the recent learned perceptual image patch similarity (LPIPS) proposed by [35]. The LPIPS metric is correlated with human perceptual similarity judgments as a perceptual metric for low-level vision tasks, such as enhancement and image deblurring.

Fig. 6. Qualitative comparisons of different deblurring methods. The first row is the input image that has a spatially varying blur, and the last row is the corresponding ground truth sharp image. The rows in between are the results of different methods. We also present zoomed-in cropped patches in green and red boxes. Our DPDNet method significantly outperforms other methods in terms of deblurring quality.

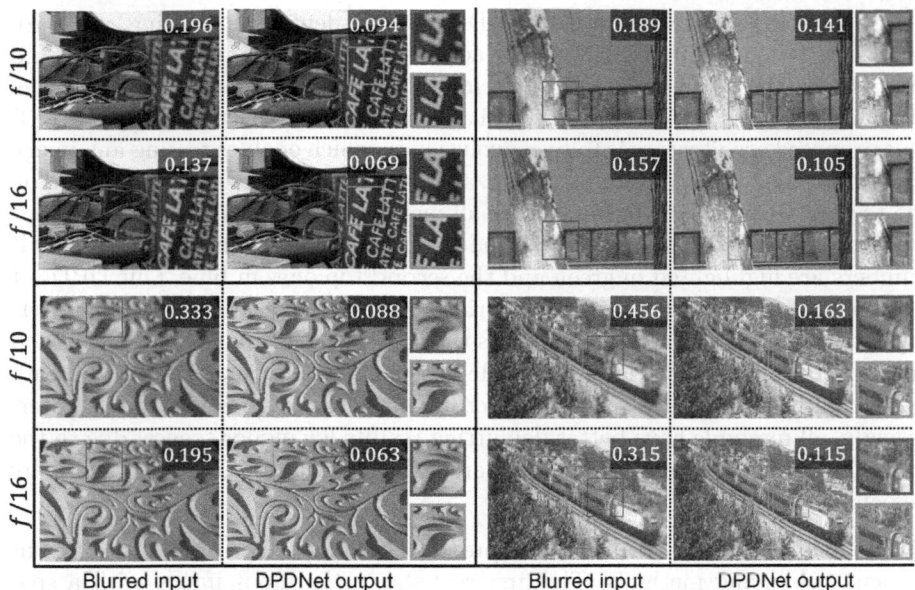

Fig. 7. Examining DPDNet's robustness to different aperture settings. Four scenes are presented; each has two different apertures. In each scene, the left-hand image is the blurred one, I_B, and the right-hand image is the deblurred one, I_S^*, computed by our DPDNet. The number shown on each image is the LPIPS measure compared with the ground truth I_S. Zoomed-in cropped patches are also provided. Even though our training data was on blurry examples with an $f/4$ aperture, our DPDNet method is able to generalize well to different aperture settings. (Color figure online)

Quantitative Results. We compare our DPDNet with the following three methods: the edge-based defocus blur (EBDB) [15], the defocus map estimation network (DMENet) [18], and the just noticeable blur (JNB) [28] estimation. These methods accept only a single image as input – namely, I_B – and estimate the defocus map in order to use it to guide the deblurring process. The EBDB [15] and JNB [28] are not learning-based methods. We test them directly on our dataset using I_B as input. The EBDB uses a combination of non-blind deblurring methods proposed in [17,19], and for a fair comparison, we contacted the authors for their deblurring settings and implementation. The JNB method uses the non-blind defocus deblurring method from [5].

For the deep-learning-based method (i.e., DMENet [18]), the method requires the ground truth defocus map for training. In our dataset, we do not have this ground truth defocus map and provide only the sharp image, since our approach in this work is to solve directly for defocus deblurring. Therefore, we tested the DMENet on our dataset using I_B as input without retraining. For deblurring, DMENet adopts a non-blind deconvolution algorithm proposed by [17]. Our results are compared against code provided by the authors. Unfortunately, the methods in [4,22] do not have the deblurring code available for comparison.

To show the advantage of utilizing DP data for defocus deblurring, we introduce a variation of our DPDNet that accepts only a single input (i.e., I_B) and uses exactly the same architecture settings along with the same training procedure as shown in Fig. 5. We refer to this variation as DPDNet-Single in Table 1. Our proposed architecture is fully convolutional, which enables testing any image size during the testing phase. Therefore, all the subsequent results are reported on the testing set using the full image for all methods. Table 1 reports our findings by testing on three scene categories: indoor, outdoor, and combined. Top result numbers are highlighted in green and the second top ones in blue. Our DPDNet method has a significantly better deblurring ability based on all metrics for all testing categories. Furthermore, DP data is the key that made our DPDNet method outperforms others, especially the single image input one (i.e., DPDNet-Single), in which it has exactly the same architecture but does not utilize DP views. Interestingly, all methods have better deblurring results for indoor scenes, due to the fact that outdoor scenes tend to have larger depth variations, and thereby more defocus blur.

Qualitative Results. In Fig. 6, we present the qualitative results of different defocus deblurring methods. The first row shows the input image with a spatially varying defocus blur; the last row shows the corresponding ground truth sharp image. The rows in between present different methods, including ours. This figure also shows two zoomed-in cropped patches in green and red to further illustrate the difference visually. From the visual comparison with other methods, our DPDNet has the best deblurring ability and is quite similar to the ground truth. EBDB [15], DMENet [18], and JNB [28] are not able to handle spatially varying blur with almost unnoticeable difference with the input image. EBDB [15] tends to introduce some artifacts in some cases. Our single image method (i.e., DPDNet-Single) has better deblurring ability compared to other traditional deblurring methods, but it is not at the level of our method that utilizes DP views for deblurring. Our DPDNet, as shown visually, is effective in handling spatially varying blur. For example, in the second row, the image has a part that is in focus and another is not; our DPDNet method is able to determine the deblurring amount required for each pixel, in which the in-focus part is left untouched. Further qualitative results are provided in our supplemental materials, including results on DP data obtained from a smartphone camera.

Time Analysis. We examine evaluating different defocus deblurring methods based on the time required to process a testing image of size 1680×1120 pixels. Our DPDNet directly computes the sharp image in a single pass, whereas other methods [15,18,28] use two passes: (1) defocus map estimation and (2) non-blind deblurring based on the estimated defocus map.

Non-learning-based methods (i.e., EBDB [15] and JNB [28]) do not utilize the GPU and use only the CPU. For the deep-learning method (i.e., DMENet [18]), it utilizes the GPU for the first pass; however, the deblurring routine is applied on a CPU. This time evaluation is performed using Intel Core i7-6700 CPU and NVIDIA TITAN X GPU. Our DPDNet operates in a single pass and

Table 2. Time analysis of different defocus deblurring methods. The last column is the total time required to process a testing image of size 1680×1120 pixels. Our DPDNet is about 1.2×10^3 times faster compared to the second-best method (i.e., DMENet).

Method	Time (Sec) ↓		
	Defocus map estimation	Defocus deblurring	Total
EBDB [15]	57.2	872.5	929.7
DMENet [18]	1.3	612.4	613.7
JNB [28]	605.4	237.7	843.1
Our DPDNet	**0**	**0.5**	**0.5**

can process the testing image of size 1680×1120 pixels about 1.2×10^3 times faster compared to the second-best method (i.e., DMENet), as shown in Table 2.

Robustness to Different Aperture Settings. In our dataset, the image pairs are captured using aperture settings corresponding to f-stops $f/22$ and $f/4$. Recall that $f/4$ results in the greatest DoF and thus most defocus blur. Our DPDNet is trained on diverse images with many different depth values; thus, our training data spans the worst-case blur that would be observed with any aperture settings. To test the ability of our DPDNet in generalizing for scenes with different aperture settings, we capture image pairs with aperture settings $f/10$ and $f/16$ for the blurred image and again $f/22$ for the corresponding ground truth image. Our DPDNet is applied to these less blurred images. Figure 7 shows the results for four scenes, where each scene's image has its LPIPS measure compared with the ground truth. For better visual comparison, Fig. 7 provides zoomed-in patches that are cropped from the blurred input (red box) and the deblurred one (green box). These results show that our DPDNet is able to deblur scenes with different aperture settings that have not been used during training.

7 Applications

Image blur can have a negative impact on some computer vision tasks, as found in [10]. Here we investigate defocus blur effect on two common computer vision tasks – namely, image segmentation and monocular depth estimation.

Image Segmentation. The first two columns in Fig. 8 demonstrate the negative effect of defocus blur on the task of image segmentation. We use the PSPNet segementation model from [36], and test two images: one is the blurred input image I_B and another is the deblurred one I_S^* using our DPDNet deblurring model. The segmentation results are affected by I_B – only the foreground tree was correctly segmented. PSPNet assigns cyan color to unknown categories, where a large portion of I_B is segmented as unknown. On the other hand, the segmentation results of I_S^* are much better, in which more categories are segmented correctly. With that said, image DoF deblurring using our DP method can be beneficial for the task of image segmentation.

Fig. 8. The effect of defocus blur on some computer vision tasks. The first two columns show the image segmentation results using the PSPNet [36] segmentation model. The segmentation results are affected by the blurred image I_B, where a large portion is segmented as unknown in cyan. The last two columns show the results of the monocular depth estimation using the monodepth model from [7]. The depth estimation is highly affected by the defocus blur and produced wrong results. Deblurring I_B using our DP deblurring method has significantly improved the results for both tasks.

Monocular Depth Estimation. The monocular depth estimation is the task of estimating scene depth using a single image. In the last two columns of Fig. 8, we show the direct effect of defocus blur on this task. We use the monodepth model from [7] to test the two images I_B and I_S^* in order to examine the change in performance. The result of monodepth is affected by the defocus blur, in which the depth map estimated is completely wrong. Contrarily, the result of monodepth has been significantly improved after testing with the deblurred input image using our DPDNet deblurring model. Therefore, deblurring images using our DPDNet can be useful for the task of monocular depth map estimation.

8   Conclusion

We have presented a novel approach to reduce the effect of defocus blur present in images captured with a shallow DoF. Our approach leverages the DP data that is available in most modern camera sensors but currently being ignored for other uses. We show that the DP images are highly effective in reducing DoF blur when used in a DNN framework. As part of this effort, we have captured a new image dataset consisting of blurred and sharp image pairs along with their DP images. Experimental results show that leveraging the DP data provides state-of-the-art quantitative results on both signal processing and perceptual metrics. We also demonstrate that our deblurring method can be beneficial for other computer vision tasks. We believe our captured dataset and DP-based method are useful for the research community and will help spur additional ideas about both defocus deblurring and applications that can leverage data from DP sensors. The dataset, code, and trained models are available at https://github.com/Abdullah-Abuolaim/defocus-deblurring-dual-pixel.

Acknowledgments. This study was funded in part by the Canada First Research Excellence Fund for the Vision: Science to Applications (VISTA) programme and an NSERC Discovery Grant. Dr. Brown contributed to this article in his personal capacity as a professor at York University. The views expressed are his own and do not necessarily represent the views of Samsung Research.

References

1. Abuolaim, A., Brown, M.S.: Online lens motion smoothing for video autofocus. In: WACV (2020)
2. Abuolaim, A., Punnappurath, A., Brown, M.S.: Revisiting autofocus for smartphone cameras. In: Ferrari, V., Hebert, M., Sminchisescu, C., Weiss, Y. (eds.) ECCV 2018. LNCS, vol. 11219, pp. 545–559. Springer, Cham (2018). https://doi.org/10.1007/978-3-030-01267-0_32
3. Boominathan, V., Mitra, K., Veeraraghavan, A.: Improving resolution and depth-of-field of light field cameras using a hybrid imaging system. In: ICCP (2014)
4. D'Andrès, L., Salvador, J., Kochale, A., Süsstrunk, S.: Non-parametric blur map regression for depth of field extension. IEEE Trans. Image Process. $25(4)$, 1660–1673 (2016)
5. Fish, D., Brinicombe, A., Pike, E., Walker, J.: Blind deconvolution by means of the Richardson-Lucy algorithm. J. Opt. Soc. Am. A $12(1)$, 58–65 (1995)
6. Garg, R., Wadhwa, N., Ansari, S., Barron, J.T.: Learning single camera depth estimation using dual-pixels. In: ICCV (2019)
7. Godard, C., Mac Aodha, O., Brostow, G.J.: Unsupervised monocular depth estimation with left-right consistency. In: CVPR (2017)
8. Golestaneh, S.A., Karam, L.J.: Spatially-varying blur detection based on multiscale fused and sorted transform coefficients of gradient magnitudes. In: CVPR (2017)
9. Google: Google research: Android app to capture dual-pixel data (2019). https://github.com/google-research/google-research/tree/master/dual_pixels. Accessed Mar 2020
10. Guo, Q., Feng, W., Chen, Z., Gao, R., Wan, L., Wang, S.: Effects of blur and deblurring to visual object tracking. arXiv preprint arXiv:1908.07904 (2019)
11. Hazirbas, C., Soyer, S.G., Staab, M.C., Leal-Taixé, L., Cremers, D.: Deep depth from focus. In: Jawahar, C.V., Li, H., Mori, G., Schindler, K. (eds.) ACCV 2018. LNCS, vol. 11363, pp. 525–541. Springer, Cham (2019). https://doi.org/10.1007/978-3-030-20893-6_33
12. He, K., Zhang, X., Ren, S., Sun, J.: Delving deep into rectifiers: surpassing human-level performance on imagenet classification. In: ICCV (2015)
13. He, K., Zhang, X., Ren, S., Sun, J.: Deep residual learning for image recognition. In: CVPR (2016)
14. Jang, J., Yoo, Y., Kim, J., Paik, J.: Sensor-based auto-focusing system using multi-scale feature extraction and phase correlation matching. Sensors $15(3)$, 5747–5762 (2015)
15. Karaali, A., Jung, C.R.: Edge-based defocus blur estimation with adaptive scale selection. IEEE Trans. Image Process. $27(3)$, 1126–1137 (2017)
16. Kingma, D.P., Ba, J.: Adam: a method for stochastic optimization. arXiv preprint arXiv:1412.6980 (2014)
17. Krishnan, D., Fergus, R.: Fast image deconvolution using hyper-laplacian priors. In: NeurIPS (2009)

18. Lee, J., Lee, S., Cho, S., Lee, S.: Deep defocus map estimation using domain adaptation. In: CVPR (2019)
19. Levin, A., Fergus, R., Durand, F., Freeman, W.T.: Image and depth from a conventional camera with a coded aperture. ACM Trans. Graph. **26**(3), 70 (2007)
20. Mao, X., Shen, C., Yang, Y.B.: Image restoration using very deep convolutional encoder-decoder networks with symmetric skip connections. In: NeurIPS (2016)
21. Odena, A., Dumoulin, V., Olah, C.: Deconvolution and checkerboard artifacts. Distill **1**(10), e3 (2016)
22. Park, J., Tai, Y.W., Cho, D., So Kweon, I.: A unified approach of multi-scale deep and hand-crafted features for defocus estimation. In: CVPR (2017)
23. Plotz, T., Roth, S.: Benchmarking denoising algorithms with real photographs. In: CVPR (2017)
24. Punnappurath, A., Abuolaim, A., Afifi, M., Brown, M.S.: Modeling defocus-disparity in dual-pixel sensors. In: ICCP (2020)
25. Punnappurath, A., Brown, M.S.: Reflection removal using a dual-pixel sensor. In: CVPR (2019)
26. Ronneberger, O., Fischer, P., Brox, T.: U-Net: convolutional networks for biomedical image segmentation. In: Navab, N., Hornegger, J., Wells, W.M., Frangi, A.F. (eds.) MICCAI 2015. LNCS, vol. 9351, pp. 234–241. Springer, Cham (2015). https://doi.org/10.1007/978-3-319-24574-4_28
27. Shi, J., Xu, L., Jia, J.: Discriminative blur detection features. In: CVPR (2014)
28. Shi, J., Xu, L., Jia, J.: Just noticeable defocus blur detection and estimation. In: CVPR (2015)
29. Srinivasan, P.P., Wang, T., Sreelal, A., Ramamoorthi, R., Ng, R.: Learning to synthesize a 4D RGBD light field from a single image. In: ICCV (2017)
30. Srivastava, R.K., Greff, K., Schmidhuber, J.: Training very deep networks. In: NeurIPS (2015)
31. Tang, C., Zhu, X., Liu, X., Wang, L., Zomaya, A.: DeFusionNET: defocus blur detection via recurrently fusing and refining multi-scale deep features. In: CVPR (2019)
32. Wadhwa, N., Garg, R., Jacobs, D.E., Feldman, B.E., Kanazawa, N., Carroll, R., Movshovitz-Attias, Y., Barron, J.T., Pritch, Y., Levoy, M.: Synthetic depth-of-field with a single-camera mobile phone. ACM Trans. Graph. **37**(4), 64 (2018)
33. Wang, Z., Bovik, A.C., Sheikh, H.R., Simoncelli, E.P., et al.: Image quality assessment: from error visibility to structural similarity. IEEE Trans. Image Process. **13**(4), 600–612 (2004)
34. Yi, X., Eramian, M.: LBP-based segmentation of defocus blur. IEEE Trans. Image Process. **25**(4), 1626–1638 (2016)
35. Zhang, R., Isola, P., Efros, A.A., Shechtman, E., Wang, O.: The unreasonable effectiveness of deep features as a perceptual metric. In: CVPR (2018)
36. Zhao, H., Shi, J., Qi, X., Wang, X., Jia, J.: Pyramid scene parsing network. In: CVPR (2017)
37. Zhao, W., Zhao, F., Wang, D., Lu, H.: Defocus blur detection via multi-stream bottom-top-bottom fully convolutional network. In: CVPR (2018)
38. Zhao, W., Zheng, B., Lin, Q., Lu, H.: Enhancing diversity of defocus blur detectors via cross-ensemble network. In: CVPR (2019)

RhyRNN: Rhythmic RNN for Recognizing Events in Long and Complex Videos

Tianshu Yu, Yikang Li, and Baoxin Li$^{(\boxtimes)}$

Arizona State University, Tempe, USA
{tianshuy,yikangli,baoxin.li}@asu.edu

Abstract. Though many successful approaches have been proposed for recognizing events in short and homogeneous videos, doing so with long and complex videos remains a challenge. One particular reason is that events in long and complex videos can consist of multiple heterogeneous sub-activities (in terms of rhythms, activity variants, composition order, etc.) within quite a long period. This fact brings about two main difficulties: excessive/varying length and complex video dynamic/rhythm. To address this, we propose Rhythmic RNN (RhyRNN) which is capable of handling long video sequences (up to 3,000 frames) as well as capturing rhythms at different scales. We also propose two novel modules: diversity-driven pooling (DivPool) and bilinear reweighting (BR), which consistently and hierarchically abstract higher-level information. We study the behavior of RhyRNN and empirically show that our method works well even when *only event-level labels are available* in the training stage (compared to algorithms requiring sub-activity labels for recognition), and thus is more practical when the sub-activity labels are missing or difficult to obtain. Extensive experiments on several public datasets demonstrate that, even *without fine-tuning the feature backbones*, our method can achieve promising performance for long and complex videos that contain multiple sub-activities.

Keywords: Video understanding · Complex event recognition · RNN

1 Introduction

In recent years, video-based event/activity recognition has brought about enormous and important challenges to computer vision. The research community has devoted considerable effort and made progresses in many related tasks (e.g., action recognition [4,10,11,14,33,46,52,54,55], temporal localization [7,43], video question answering [1,48], video summarization [19,34,66], to name a few). By learning more representative features and capturing stronger sequential context, deep-learning-based methods have delivered the state-of-the-art results on several

---

T. Yu and Y. Li—Equal contribution.

This work was supported in part by a grant from ONR. Any opinions expressed in this material are those of the authors and do not necessarily reflect the views of ONR.

© Springer Nature Switzerland AG 2020
A. Vedaldi et al. (Eds.): ECCV 2020, LNCS 12355, pp. 127–144, 2020.
https://doi.org/10.1007/978-3-030-58607-2_8

datasets of short videos (e.g. UCF101 [47], KTH [41], HMDB51 [30]). Recently, more challenging datasets (e.g. VIRAT [37], Charades [45] and Breakfast [31]), which typically contain video clips with complex and/or multiple sub-activities in a much longer time period, have brought about new challenges to video recognition. To address these, some event recognition algorithms were proposed [12,13, 16,23,25,39,51,57,59,63,64], taking into account either long-time dependency or the activity variation to some extent . In this paper, we investigate a specific RNN structure to understand long and complex videos.

For clarity of discussion, we make a distinction between activity and event. Consider one example for each. "Jogging", which belongs to activity in our context, exhibits relatively fixed or homogeneous visual pattern and temporal dynamic (repetitive motion in this case). In contrast, "Cooking spaghetti", which is categorized as an event, is composed of multiple sub-activities (e.g., "bringing out condiment", "boiling spaghetti", etc.) that can occur in different rhythm, order or visual appearance, resulting in much more complex scene dynamics for an algorithm to capture. Furthermore, some events can occur over a significantly longer time period than activities. In general, events in long videos brings about two challenges to video-based recognition: complexity in content and excessive/varying length, making it challenging to adapt a traditional activity recognition model designed for much simpler videos.

Another important yet barely investigated issue in video-based recognition is, how to identify video events when *only event-level labels are available* for training a model. This arises often due to lack of detailed labeling information that is difficult and/or costly to obtain for long videos. Though some previous methods incorporate sub-activity labels to enhance event-level recognition [23,24,31,32], such fine-grained labels are not always available in practice due to the aforementioned reason. In general, the event label describing a long video is highly abstract in nature, and it may imply a lot of latent contexts.

In this paper, we seek to make a progress towards long and complex video event recognition (with or without sub-activity labels). We further study a way to perform video-based recognition when only event-level labels are available. To this end, we propose Rhythmic RNN (**RhyRNN**) which dynamically captures the multi-level contexts, as well as a diversity-driven sequential pooling (**DivPool**) and a Bilinear Re-weighting (**BR**) mechanism. The work has the following contributions: 1) We introduce RhyRNN which can ease the gradient back-propagation for long and complex sequences. RhyRNN also allows to capture latent video context at different levels; 2) We develop DivPool and BR strategies, which further enable multi-level feature aggregation (analogous to pooling in CNNs) with varying sequence length; 3) We study the property and behavior of all the proposed modules analytically and empirically; 4) Our method delivered superior or competitive performance in long video datasets compared to the state-of-the-art algorithms even without fine-tuning feature backbones.

2   Related Work

Short Activity Recognition. Some early video datasets (e.g., KTH [41] and UCF101 [47]) typically contain activity/action-level video clips, which are homogeneous in content without too complex temporal dynamics. A conventional trial for activity recognition employed 2D CNN features to perform recognition [27], while some variants incorporate complementary frame-level motion features [3,4,46]. The main drawback of such a line of works is that the temporal patterns cannot be well learned since neither short nor long range dependencies are explicitly taken into account. 3D CNNs are natural extension from 2D by introducing one additional kernel dimension on the time axis [6,49,56], but with excessive parameters. To alleviate this, several works were proposed to decouple the 3D kernel into combinations of lower dimension (e.g., [9,50,61]). Another line of works in parallel to CNNs employs RNNs [10,11,33,42]. RNNs can handle varying length of videos compared with CNNs, but suffer from gradient vanishing/explosion issue especially when the sequence is too long.

Complex Event Recognition. Datasets consisting of long and complex videos bring about new challenges [31,37,45]. Extending CNNs for long-range video recognition has become an aroused research interest recently. To capture more complex temporal patterns in long videos, [44] stacks a CRF on top of CNN output. Under some specific sampling procedure, TSN [55] and TRN [67] model the video-level representation by considering inter and intra video relations, respectively. Non-local networks [56] built upon 3D CNN can range up to 128 time steps, hence is capable of handling more complex dynamics. Timeception [23] can further capture the dependencies up to 1024 frames by designing multi-scale convolutional kernels. In parallel to CNNs, RNNs are also investigated to tackle long and varying video length with complex context. [65] considers dense labeling in complex videos, where the expensive part is to densely label the training data. [58] proposed a hierarchical RNN to capture temporal visual attention. Both [33] and [11] devise hierarchical RNN structures to obtain multi-level representation, which proved effective in understanding video content. In [42], soft attention is computed spatially and temporally via deep RNNs, which helps the model to focus selectively on more meaningful parts of a video.

RNNs. LSTM [22] and GRU [8] are successively proposed to address the gradient vanishing/exploding issue by introducing the gating mechanism against standard RNNs. There is a series of further developments following this strategy [5,17,26]. Skip-RNN [5] learns to keep the hidden state intact at some steps once "Skip" is emitted. H-detach [26] detaches the gradient flow at an arbitrary time step under a Bernoulli distribution. Some other efforts focused on the variants of standard RNNs without using gating. Multiplicative Integration [60] couples the operations on inputs and hidden states. In this fashion, the vanishing gradient is likely to be correlated by the input sequence. Unitary-RNN [2] allows smoother gradient flow by constraining RNNs to have a unitary transition matrix. Very recently, IndRNN [35] was proposed, which enforces the neurons in each RNN unit to be independent. By doing so, IndRNN can handle long sequences and achieved state-of-the-art performance on multiple benchmarks.

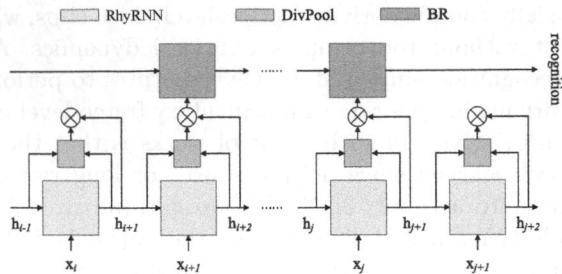

Fig. 1. Overview of our framework which mainly consists of 3 parts: RhyRNN, DivPool and BR (a recognition module). BR refers to the GRU equipped with bilinear re-weighting in our setting.

3 Methodology

3.1 Algorithm Overview

The overview of our framework consisting of three modules is illustrated in Fig. 1. The model takes visual features as input and feeds them sequentially to RhyRNN. RhyRNN outputs embedded features with the same length as the sequence. Using a diversity score, DivPool is then applied to select the most informative features as inputs to the following recognition module. For the final recognition stage, we employ a GRU equipped with BR module. The output of GRU at the final timestamp will be fed to a two-layer fully connected network at last. We detail each part in the following sections. Our approach is motivated by the following considerations. First, our approach should be capable of handling long sequences. To this end, we need to design a specific RNN structure which eases the gradient flow under this setting. Second, since complex events contain latent contexts in different scales, our approach needs to capture such multi-level dynamics. A hierarchical model, in this case, can be a good choice as done in a large body of relevant literature.

3.2 RhyRNNs

One essential part of our algorithm is to deploy an architecture that is capable of handling a long and complex sequence. In this section, we propose the RhyRNN structure, which is inspired in part by IndRNN [35] and Skip-RNN [5], and is much more powerful than both (see Sect. 4). IndRNN enforces each neuron operating on the hidden state to be independent, and the update rule of IndRNN reads:

$$\mathbf{h}_t = \sigma \left(\mathbf{W}\mathbf{x}_t + \mathbf{u} \odot \mathbf{h}_{t-1} + \mathbf{b} \right) \qquad (1)$$

where $\odot$ is the element-wise product and $\sigma(\cdot)$ is the activation function (ReLU function in [35]). $\mathbf{h}_t$ corresponds to the hidden state at time t. It has been shown that, by enforcing the neuron independence (no matrix multiplication), back-propagation upon Eq. (1) becomes more stable and manageable. IndRNN has delivered good performance for very long sequences.

While IndRNN alleviates gradient vanishing by replacing matrix multiplication with scalar multiplication, we propose RhyRNN to further *shorten the longest path of the computational graph* of IndRNN independently for each neuron, through introducing a *skip* operator. This idea is similar to [5] that implements skip operation on conventional RNN, which can be viewed as a Bernoulli distribution sampler on *UPDATE* or *COPY* operations at each timestamp t (an analogous idea appeared in h-detach [26] which is applied on LSTM). Our RhyRNN differs from Skip-RNN in such a way that, unlike [5] where *UPDATE* and *COPY* operations are computed on a whole hidden state $\mathbf{h}_t$ by a matrix multiplication, our RhyRNN structure decides the choice of *UPDATE* or *COPY* operation by using Hardmard's product, which further makes the decision *independent of each neuron*. The mathematical formula of RhyRNN can be written as follows:

$$\mathbf{s}_t = f_{binarize}(\mathbf{o}_t) \tag{2}$$

$$\mathbf{h}_t = \mathbf{s}_t \odot \tilde{\mathbf{h}}_t + (\mathbf{1} - \mathbf{s}_t) \odot \mathbf{h}_{t-1} \tag{3}$$

$$\Delta\mathbf{o}_t = \zeta(\mathbf{w}_p \odot \mathbf{h}_t + \mathbf{b}_p) \tag{4}$$

$$\mathbf{o}_{t+1} = \mathbf{s}_t \odot \Delta\mathbf{o}_t + (\mathbf{1} - \mathbf{s}_t) \odot (\mathbf{o}_t + \min(\Delta\mathbf{o}_t, \mathbf{1} - \mathbf{o}_t)) \tag{5}$$

where $\zeta(\cdot)$ is the sigmoid activation function and $f_{binarize}$ is the step function: $f_{binarize} : [0,1]^n \to \{0,1\}^n$, which binarizes each input element. $\mathbf{w}_p$ is the weight vector that can be learned to obtain the incremental value $\Delta\mathbf{o}_t$. $\tilde{\mathbf{h}}_t$ is obtained by Eq. (1) (replacing $\mathbf{h}_t$ with $\tilde{\mathbf{h}}_t$) and $\mathbf{h}_{t-1}$ is the hidden state from the previous timestamp.

Remark. There are two advantages of utilizing Hardmard's product in computing the gate value $\mathbf{s}_t$. Firstly, it keeps the independence of each neuron in IndRNN intact, which allows each neuron to have a distinct strategy of choosing *UPDATE/COPY* operations and thus being capable of capturing the varying context in different scales. We will demonstrate this advantage in Sect. 4. Secondly, the computation of the gradient of the RhyRNN is easier and more stable compared to either IndRNN or Skip-RNN, since the lengths of gradient path for different neurons can be shortened due to the skip operator, and the absence of matrix multiplication will yield more tractable gradient flow.

To enable the intra-neuron interaction, we stack multiple layers of RhyRNNs and apply a matrix multiplication $\mathbf{W}_l$ between layers to aggregate the global information. Specifically, assuming $\mathbf{h}_{t,l}$ to be the input to RhyRNN ($\mathbf{h}_{t,0} = \mathbf{x}_t$) at layer l and time t, we have:

$$\mathbf{h}_{t,l} = \sigma(\mathbf{W}_l \mathbf{h}_{t,l-1} + \mathbf{u}_l \odot \mathbf{h}_{t-1,l} + \mathbf{b}_l) \tag{6}$$

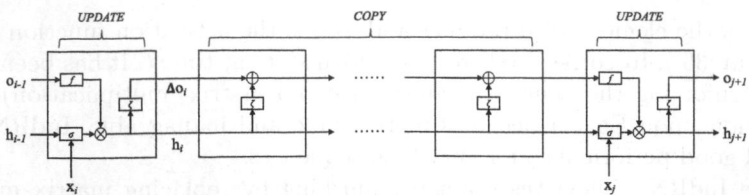

Fig. 2. A basic unit in RhyRNN, where *UPDATE* is emitted at time i and j and all the resting operations in between are *COPY*s. $\otimes$ and $\oplus$ correspond to element-wise product and plus, respectively. A sequence can be divided into several consecutive basic units. Then the gradient back-propagated can be written as the product of multiple gradients of such units. Zoom in for better view.

Skip Regularization. To limit the computational budget, we introduce a regularization term that controls the frequency of *UPDATE*s similar to [5]. This term is written as:

$$\mathcal{L} = \lambda \sum_{t,k} \mathbf{s}_{t,k} \tag{7}$$

where $\mathbf{s}_{t,k}$ refers to the kth binary neuron decision (on *COPY* or *UPDATE*, see Eq. (2)). In general, this term sums up the number of *UPDATE*s on all neurons at every time step.

Gradient Analysis. We employ a strategy to approximate the gradient of the step function $f_{binarize}$ as in [5]:

$$\partial f_{binaries}(x)/\partial x = 1 \tag{8}$$

In other words, Eq. (2) and Eq. (8) are implemented in forward-pass and backward-pass for the network, respectively. Following such a setting, the gradient during the backward pass by taking an example is shown in Fig. 2. In all the following analyses, we discard the bias $\mathbf{b}$ and $\mathbf{b}_p$ for simplicity. In Fig. 2, we analyze the gradient behavior of a sequence segment where only at time stamps i and j are *COPY*s and all the resting time stamps in between are *UPDATE*s. This segment can be viewed as a basic unit since any forward pass of RhyRNN can be separated into such segments (with varying numbers of *COPY*s). Since all operations between i and j are *COPY*s, the hidden state $\mathbf{h}_i$ will directly pass until j, thus in the forward pass we have:

$$\mathbf{h}_{j+1} = \sigma(\mathbf{W}\mathbf{x}_j + \mathbf{u} \odot \mathbf{h}_i) \tag{9}$$

In Eq. (9) we omit a term $f_{binarize}(\mathbf{o}_j)$ since it equals 1 (see Fig. 2 at time j). However, this term will participate in the backward pass according to the gradient defined in Eq. (8). We expand Eq. (9) as follows:

$$\mathbf{h}_{j+1} = \underbrace{f_{binarize}\left(\sum^{j-i} \zeta\left(\mathbf{w}_p \odot \mathbf{h}_i\right)\right)}_{=\mathbf{1},\text{for the basic unit}} \odot \sigma(\mathbf{W}\mathbf{x}_j + \mathbf{u} \odot \mathbf{h}_i) \tag{10}$$

Given Eq. (10) and after a series of mathematical manipulations, we can obtain the gradient at time i by taking into account Eq. (8):

$$\nabla J_i = \frac{\partial \mathbf{h}_{j+1}}{\partial \mathbf{h}_i} = \underbrace{\mathbf{u} \odot \sigma' + \sigma \odot \sum^{j-i} \mathbf{w}_p \odot \mathbf{w}_p \odot (1 - \mathbf{w}_p \odot \mathbf{h}_i) \odot \mathbf{h}_i} \qquad (11)$$

where the term within the underbrace is the basic unit for any such segment and σ' is the gradient of function σ. Thus, one can calculate the gradient at any time k (where at k there is an *UPDATE* emitted) by calculating the element-wise product:

$$\frac{\partial J}{\partial \mathbf{h}_k}\bigg|_{k=UPDATE} = \prod_{l=UPDATE, l>k} \nabla J_l \qquad (12)$$

where $\prod$ is the element-wise product. We note two facts involved in this gradient chain rule: 1) there is only scalar multiplication involved in the unit (and element-wise product of multiple such units) which is more tractable than matrix multiplication; 2) hidden states $\mathbf{h}_i$s directly participate in the back-propagation, which can correlate and thus stabilize the gradient from vanishing/exploding as discussed in Multiplicative Integration [60]. In this sense, RhyRNN has a gradient behavior benefiting from both IndRNN and Multiplicative Integration. Readers are referred to [35] and [60] for more details on related analysis.

3.3   DivPool

Though the proposed RhyRNN can capture the context at different scales to some extent, it still cannot fully utilize the intrinsically hierarchical context of long videos. In this section, we propose a temporal pooling strategy that explicitly selects most contributing hidden states within a sequence.

The pooling stage is essential in CNNs, which aggregates low-level representations into high-level ones. A series of works also focused on temporal pooling where the objective is to hierarchically shorten and abstract the temporal representations [15,18,36,62]. In this paper, we propose a simple yet efficient method termed as diversity-driven sequential pooling (**DivPool**) by mostly diversifying the capacity of the pooled representations. Our method is based on the observation that, since a video is always highly redundant, an effective pooled representation should ignore the slight difference across frames and concentrate on the most significant changes. Thus, our pooling method performs selection to maximally diversify the hidden states (features). To this end, we first calculate the dissimilarity by cosine distance between $\mathbf{h}_t$ and its previous state $\mathbf{h}_{t-1}$:

$$a_t = 1 - \frac{\mathbf{h}_t \mathbf{h}_{t-1}^T}{\|\mathbf{h}_t\|\|\mathbf{h}_{t-1}\| + \epsilon} \qquad (13)$$

where $\epsilon > 0$. Then we sort all a_ts in descending order and select the $\alpha\%$ most dissimilar states as the pooled features. Note that this procedure works in an incremental fashion and thus a pairwise distance calculation on all states is not necessary, yielding high efficiency in implementation.

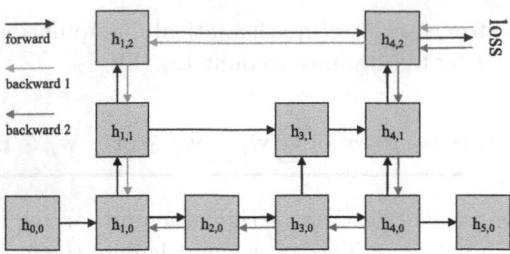

Fig. 3. Schematic diagram of hierarchical architecture with DivPool. The black arrow indicates the flow in forward pass. Orange and blue arrows correspond to the shortest and the longest backward path from state $\mathbf{h}_{1,0}$ to the loss during backward pass, respectively. We note "backward 1" path is shorter than "backward 2" path due to this hierarchy.

The DivPool layer has no learning parameters and thus is similar to max-pooling or average-pooling in CNNs. Yet it differs from max/average-pooling since it performs pooling globally on all features. Besides, it generates the pooling cue in an incremental fashion which is adopted in some effective sequential pooling strategies [15, 18]. The only overhead of performing DivPool is on sorting a_t, which is typically $\mathcal{O}(n \log n)$ and can be efficient in practice.

Back-Propagation. DivPool dynamically generates links across RhyRNN layers in the computational graph. The generated links will be effective during a forward-backward round for the network computation. The back-propagated gradients will only follow the general RNN's update path together with the current effective links. Figure 3 schematically shows an example. We see from Fig. 3 that DivPool can greatly shorten the shortest computational path, which is dominant (compared to other longer paths) in propagating gradients to avoid the vanishing issue. For example, assuming the pooled ratio is 0.5 with q RhyRNN layers and the sequence length is n, the length of the shortest path becomes $\mathcal{O}(q + \log(n))$.

3.4   Bilinear Reweighting for Recognition

With DivPool, the redundancy and the complexity of the input video sequence has been reduced. In the following stage, to better incorporate the dependency of the long-range selected hidden states, we design the bilinear reweighting (BR) mechanism to capture the temporal relation among the pooled hidden states.

In our model, we employ a simplified bilinear reweighting (BR) strategy to learn and enhance the temporal correlation of patterns within the pooled hidden states (features). The BR module is applied to the output sequence of DivPool and to embed the hidden states to a new feature re-weighted by the pairwise affinity scores. BR module is inspired by bilinear attention [29] but follows the metric properties. Assuming that the selected features from DivPool form a feature matrix $\mathbf{V}$, BR rule can be written as:

$$\mathbf{S} = \mathbf{V}^{\top} \mathrm{norm}(\mathbf{M})\mathbf{V}$$
$$\hat{\mathbf{V}} = \mathbf{V} \circ \mathrm{softmax}\left(\mathrm{proj}\left(\mathrm{norm}(\mathbf{S})\right)\right) \tag{14}$$

where $\mathbf{M} = \mathbf{P}\mathbf{P}^{\top}$ is a symmetric semi-definite matrix and $\mathbf{P}$ is the parameter to be learnt. This decomposition is to reduce the number of weights to be learnt. The output $\hat{\mathbf{V}}$ is the reweighted feature matrix. norm($\cdot$) performs column-wise L^2-normalization and proj($\cdot$) projects a square matrix into a vector by summarizing the elements per-column. norm($\cdot$) performs twice to avoid the magnitude of the final affinity being too large (which may result in almost a one-hot reweighting vector). Note BR (Eq. (14)) differs from Bilinear Pooling in [29] by introducing a column-wise *projection* operator. In this sense, only the magnitude of the input is adjusted, rather than replacing the input by a sum of all other inputs. The intuition is that, since the input $\mathbf{V}$ carries temporal information, a summing schema may violate or mix up this intrinsic (e.g. ordering information).

The output sequence $\hat{\mathbf{V}}$ of BR module is then fed to a standard GRU [8]. We utilize the output of the GRU module at the final time step as the video-level feature and append two fully connected layers following GRU to conduct recognition for different datasets.

4   Experiment

4.1   Datasets and Reference Methods

We conducted experiments on Breakfast [31], VIRAT 2.0 surveillance video [37] and Charades [45]. All the experiments were done on a computer equipped with a *single* GTX Titan Xp GPU with 12 GB memory.

Breakfast Dataset. [31] comprises of 10 breakfast preparation related events that are performed by 52 different individuals in 18 different kitchen scenes. The total number of video clips is 1989. The overall video duration is about 77 h and the average length of each video is about 140 s. Events in the Breakfast dataset are very complicated since each event contains several sub-activities, indicating much higher intra-class variations. We split the dataset into training and testing by following the "s1" split [31].

VIRAT 2.0 Surveillance Video Dataset. [37] includes about 8 h of high-resolution surveillance videos (i.e. 1080p or 720p) with 12 kinds of events from 11 different scenes. In our experiment, we only focus on 6 types of person-vehicle interaction events that occur on the parking lot scene. The input video sequence only contains the event area that is cropped based on the ground truth bounding box. The training and testing video samples are randomly selected by following the ratio of 7:3. As such, we conduct the training multiple rounds and report the average performance.

Charades Dataset. [45] is a multi-label action video benchmark with 157 classes in total. Each video is around 30 s and contains 6 singleton actions on average. We follow the same training/testing split in [23] which contains 7.8k

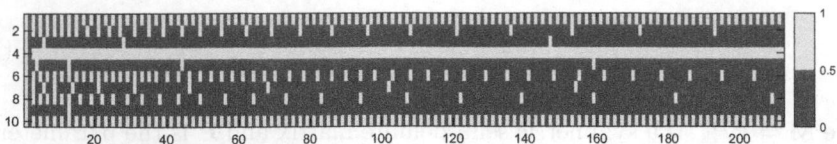

Fig. 4. Visualization of "Skip" operation on the first 10 channels/neurons (out of 256) at the second layer of RhyRNN on a video with 212 frames from Breakfast dataset. Yellow and Blue bars correspond to *"UPDATE"* and *"COPY"* operations, respectively. Vertical and horizontal axes refer to channel and frame, respectively. 10 neurons perform Skip with almost different rhythm to each other.

and 1.8k videos in each. We report the mean average precision (mAP) on two challenging tasks: multi-label action recognition and temporal localization.

Reference Methods. We employed several existing algorithms for comparison. **C3D** [49], **TSN** [55] and **TRN** [67] are implemented in a simple version with only spatial (RGB) features (without optical-flow). **Two-stream** [46] and **Temporal Fields** [44] utilize both RGB and optical flow features. **IDT** [53] alters to employ action trajectories. For **C3D**, we train it from scratch on all datasets and preprocess frames by following the [49]. For TSN, the frame feature is extracted from a pre-trained VGG16 which won't be fine-tuned in the training stage. Only the segmental consensus part of TSN are trained. We also compare plain **IndRNN** [35] for the Breakfast dataset by stacking 6 layers of IndRNN cells and setting the dropout ratio to 0.5 for each other layer. **3D-ResNet** [20] is employed as both a peer method and a backbone. Timeception [23] (**TC**) is compared since the authors claimed that Timeception is a strong baseline for complex video and can capture long range dependency. (Supervised) **SuperEvents** [39] and (weakly-supervised) **ActGraph** [40] are selected for comparison on Charades. For the tests of the methods with CNN backbone on Breakfast and Charades, we employ the same frame sampling procedure as in [23].

4.2   Implementation Details

We employ ResNet101 [21] pre-trained on ImageNet and I3D [6] pre-trained on Kinetics400 to extract features for all frame-wise based algorithms. For event recognition and multi-label action recognition/localization tasks, we employ *Cross-Entropy* and *Binary Cross-Entropy* as loss functions, respectively. For the proposed method, either ResNet101 or I3D backbone is NOT fine-tuned on three selected datasets during the training stage due to GPU resource limitation, different from some prior works [13,23,56,59] which update the CNN backbones. The features are obtained from the last pooling layer of ResNet101 and I3D, yielding 2048-d and 1024-d, respectively. The output (as well as all hidden state) dimension of RhyRNN is 256 and the dimension of the output of BR is 128. Furthermore, there are two fully connected layers with 100 and the number of classes (e.g. 10 for event recognition on Breakfast) neurons following BR.

For 3D-ResNet50 and Timeception [23] models, we extract the 3D video segments with size of $1 \times 7 \times 7$ (*time* $\times$ *height* $\times$ *width*) from a 3D ResNet-50 model which is pre-trained on Kinetics-400 [28]. We follow the settings in [23] and collect 64 uniformly sampled video segments, while each segment contains 8 successive frames.

All the proposed and baseline algorithms are implemented with PyTorch [38] toolbox. We train our model with 100 epochs and use Adam optimizer with the learning rate $1e-5$. The pooling ratio for DivPool is set to 25% and the control parameter λ for the skip regularization is set to $1e-7$ empirically. For the Breakfast dataset, the training samples are subsampled every 5 frames. The first and last 10 frames are removed from the training samples since those frames are mostly redundant.

4.3 Breakfast Dataset

Experimental results (of event-level recognition and multi-label activity recognition) on this dataset are summarized in Table 1a[1]. In general, our method (full setting) outperformed all the other peer methods in event-level recognition, with competitive performance against state-of-the-art on multi-label recognition. We also see the proposed RhyRNN (2-layer) has better performance compared to IndRNN (6-layer) or SkipRNN without introducing any other modules.

We further evaluate the behavior of our model with multiple RhyRNN + DivPool settings (without BR) on Breakfast, as shown in Table 1b. Specifically, "4 RhyRNN + 1 DivPool" and "4 RhyRNN + 2 DivPool" settings are added, referring to the structure {4× RhyRNN+DivPool} and {2× RhyRNN+DivPool+ 2 × RhyRNN + DivPool}, respectively. We can conclude that 2-layer RhyRNN (standard setting in all tests) has slightly better performance than other two.

Independent Skip Strategy. To investigate the effectiveness of "Skip" operations in RhyRNN, we visualize the Skip operations (in Fig. 4) of the first 10 neurons of the weights in the second RhyRNN layer on a breakfast video clip (with length 212) in the testing stage. It is seen that almost every neuron (each row) indeed holds a distinct and independent Skip rhythm. While some neurons emit *UPDATE*s with high frequency to capture the context in high temporal resolution (e.g., neuron 1, 4 and 10), other neurons learn lazier strategies.

4.4 VIRAT 2.0 Dataset

The performance on this dataset is shown in Table 2. Specifically, we test the capacity of algorithms under *varying sampling rhythm* compared to training rhythm. As shown in Table 2, "original" indicates sampling each frame (and feature) with the same sampling rhythm at the training stage. The other three

---

[1] We re-implemented the method TC [23] following the same setting but did not obtain the performance reported in their original paper. Since there is a large gap between our implementation and their results, we report the best performance of [23] in our implementation.

Table 1. Results on Breakfast dataset on (a) event recognition (in Acc) and multi-label classification (in mAP), (b) different settings of RhyRNNs. "RhyRNN (2-layer)" is a model stacked with 2 layers of RhyRNNs concatenated with 2 fully connected layers. Blue color corresponds to singleton RNNs.

(a) Event recognition

Method	Feature	Acc (%)	mAP (%)
TSN [55]	2D	14.3	-
LRCN [10]	2D	13.3	-
C3D [49]	3D	14.6	-
IndRNN (6-layer) [35]	2D	19.4	14.1
SkipRNN [5]	2D	31.9	28.7
IndRNN (+DivPool+BR)	2D	42.7	40.8
SkipRNN (+DivPool+BR)	2D	40.2	-
3D-Res50 [20]	3D	23.7	-
3D-Res50+TC [23]	3D	40.3	41.2
RhyRNN (2-layer)	2D	35.8	30.5
RhyRNN (+DivPool+BR)	2D	**44.3**	**41.9**

(b) Different settings

Setting	2 RhyRNN + 1 DivPool	4 RhyRNN + 1 DivPool	4 RhyRNN + 2 DivPool
Acc	43.7	43.1	41.4

Table 2. Results on VIRAT 2.0 dataset. The performance of our method is under full setting (RhyRNN+DivPool+BR).

Method	Original	S1	S2	S3
C3D [49]	42.9	40.2	37.7	41.1
TSN [55]	52.4	52.1	51.6	51.9
IndRNN (6-layer) [35]	77.6	78.3	78.2	78.0
IndRNN (+DivPool+BR)	79.0	77.4	78.2	78.2
Ours (full setting)	**81.9**	**81.5**	**81.7**	**80.4**

scenarios are designed with different combinations of sampling rates. To make the problem more challenging, we first equally divide each testing video sequence into three intervals and apply different sampling rates to each interval to form a new testing sequence. For scenario one (S1), we subsample the first and the third intervals with every 2 and 5 frames respectively, while keeping the rhythm intact for the middle interval. In scenario two (S2), we subsample the first and third intervals every 5 and 2 frames, respectively (reverse of S1). For the last scenario (S3), we randomly sample out a half length of the testing frames. Since the randomness of the last scenario brings uncertainty, we test the well-trained model 5 times and report the average performance of this scenario. We see that our model is quite stable under varying sampling rhythm.

4.5   Charades Dataset

For the Charades dataset, we employ I3D [6] with 1024-D output feature pre-trained on Kinetics-400 **without** inheriting any frame-level knowledge from or

Table 3. Result on Charades of multi-label activity (MLA) (a) recognition and (b) localization. For (a), "w/o BR" and "w/ BR" refer to the settings removing and keeping BR, respectively. For (b), "S" and "W" refer to "supervised" and "weakly supervised", respectively. *IndRNN here indicates IndRNN+DivPool+BR. †This result is quoted from original Skip-RNN paper [5] where mAP is calculated per 100 frames instead of 25 frames. (TS: two-stream; TF: temporal fields)

(a) MLA recognition

Method	Modality	mAP(%)
C3D [49]	RGB	10.9
TS [46]	RGB+Flow	18.6
TS+LSTM [46]	RGB+Flow	17.8
IndRNN* [35]	RGB	21.1
IDT [53]	RGB+Flow	17.2
TF [44]	RGB+Flow	22.4
TRN [67]	RGB	25.2
Ours(w/o BR)	RGB	24.6
Ours(w/ BR)	RGB	**25.4**

(b) MLA localization

Model	Training	mAP(%)
LSTM [39]	S	10.4
Skip-RNN [5]†	S	8.94
TS+LSTM [39]	S	18.2
SuperEvents [39]	S	**19.4**
TF [44]	S	12.8
I3D [6]	S	17.2
ActGraph [40]	W	15.8
Ours	W	**17.6**

fine-tuning on the Charades dataset [6, 23, 56]. The frame stride is set to 8 for the I3D model and the size of the feature matrix for each video clip equals to Timelength × 1024 where the TimeLength = FrameLength/8. We test two challenging tasks: multi-label (MLA) recognition and temporal localization.

Table 3a shows the MLA recognition performance of different algorithms on the Charades dataset. And the results demonstrate that our algorithm has a competitive capacity compared to the state-of-the-art on capturing the temporal information of sub-actions in the complex videos.

Table 3b summarizes the results of temporal localization. To this end, we inherit the model parameters pre-trained on MLA recognition task but removing the DivPool module[2]. We then fine-tune the last 2 fully-connected layers with BCE loss on MLA recognition task (only for the last time stamp) for 5 epochs. In the testing stage we pass the output of the RhyRNN at *each* time stamp through the last 2 fully-connected layers to produce score of action classes for each frame. Action class with the highest score is regarded as the predicted label for the current frame. Since during the training stage no frame-level label is provided, our model is trained in a **weakly supervised** fashion, which is more challenging than fully supervised localization task (e.g. [39, 44]). Surprisingly, we see that our model outperforms several fully supervised counterparts and a very recent weakly-supervised method ActGraph [40]. This observation supports our claim that RhyRNN is capable of capturing temporal context at multiple levels.

---

[2] DivPool cannot work frame-wise since it selects only a portion of time stamps. Therefore we remove DivPool from the full setting.

Table 4. (a) Ablation study on Breakfast dataset. In the full setting, we stack 2 layers of RhyRNNs followed by DivPool and BR. (b) Model size comparison. Note: there are two layers of RhyRNNs concatenated together with both hidden state 256-D.

(a) Ablation

RhyRNN	DivPool	BR	Acc	mAP
√	√	√	44.3	41.9
√	√	×	43.7	40.5
√	×	√	40.7	35.2
√	×	×	35.8	-

(b) Model size

Method	Model size
TC [23]	15.8 MB
Ours (Full setting)	23.2 MB
Ours (RhyRNN+DivPool)	20.4 MB

4.6 Ablation Analysis and Model Size

Ablation analysis was conducted on the Breakfast dataset following the settings in Sect. 4.3. Results are summarized in Table 4a. By turning off DivPool, we simply fed all the output states of RhyRNN to BR. On the other hand, we removed BR and fed the pooled states to a naive GRU once turning off BR. We also tested the capacity of the RhyRNN module in capturing complex temporal information by turning off both DivPool and BR modules. We see that the full setting (RhyRNN+DivPool+BR) delivers the best performance among all. And the DivPool module plays a more important role in understanding the long and complex videos, compared with the BR module. Moreover, the RhyRNN module itself is able to acquire information from long and complex videos compared with some conventional algorithms presented in the Table 1a. In general, the proposed modules in our framework consistently enhance the performance.

Table 4b summarizes the models sizes on different setting under event-level recognition on the Breakfast dataset. We note the size of our model with or without BR is around 20 MB, comparative to the size of state-of-the-art method TC [23], which claimed to be capable of reducing the model size significantly.

5   Conclusion

In this paper, we study the task of recognizing events in long and complex videos. Since there is critical distinction between traditional action recognition based on short clips and event recognition using long videos, simply adapting the methods for the former to the latter is ineffective. To address this, we designed an end-to-end RNN framework taking into account the latent context at multiple levels. Especially, three novel and essential parts were proposed: RhyRNN, DivPool and BR. By taking advantage of each, our model can capture video context at different scales in an adaptive and hierarchical fashion. We investigated the property of the proposed model and demonstrated its superiority through extensive experiments even without the need of fine-tuning the feature extraction backbones.

References

1. Antol, S., et al.: VQA: visual question answering. In: ICCV (2015)
2. Arjovsky, M., Shah, A., Bengio, Y.: Unitary evolution recurrent neural networks. In: ICML (2016)
3. Bilen, H., Fernando, B., Gavves, E., Vedaldi, A.: Action recognition with dynamic image networks. PAMI **40**(12), 2799–2813 (2017)
4. Bilen, H., Fernando, B., Gavves, E., Vedaldi, A., Gould, S.: Dynamic image networks for action recognition. In: CVPR (2016)
5. Campos, V., Jou, B., Giró-i Nieto, X., Torres, J., Chang, S.F.: Skip RNN: learning to skip state updates in recurrent neural networks. arXiv preprint arXiv:1708.06834 (2017)
6. Carreira, J., Zisserman, A.: Quo vadis, action recognition? A new model and the kinetics dataset. In: CVPR (2017)
7. Chao, Y.W., Vijayanarasimhan, S., Seybold, B., Ross, D.A., Deng, J., Sukthankar, R.: Rethinking the faster R-CNN architecture for temporal action localization. In: CVPR (2018)
8. Cho, K., et al.: Learning phrase representations using RNN encoder-decoder for statistical machine translation. arXiv preprint arXiv:1406.1078 (2014)
9. Chollet, F.: Xception: deep learning with depthwise separable convolutions. In: CVPR (2017)
10. Donahue, J., et al.: Long-term recurrent convolutional networks for visual recognition and description. In: CVPR (2015)
11. Du, Y., Wang, W., Wang, L.: Hierarchical recurrent neural network for skeleton based action recognition. In: CVPR (2015)
12. Duan, L., Xu, D., Tsang, I.W.H., Luo, J.: Visual event recognition in videos by learning from web data. PAMI **34**(9), 1667–1680 (2012)
13. Feichtenhofer, C., Fan, H., Malik, J., He, K.: Slowfast networks for video recognition. In: ICCV (2019)
14. Feichtenhofer, C., Pinz, A., Zisserman, A.: Convolutional two-stream network fusion for video action recognition. In: CVPR (2016)
15. Fernando, B., Gavves, E., Oramas, J., Ghodrati, A., Tuytelaars, T.: Rank pooling for action recognition. PAMI **39**(4), 773–787 (2016)
16. Fernando, B., Tan, C., Bilen, H.: Weakly supervised Gaussian networks for action detection. In: WACV (2020)
17. Gers, F.A., Schmidhuber, J., Cummins, F.: Learning to forget: continual prediction with LSTM (1999)
18. Girdhar, R., Ramanan, D.: Attentional pooling for action recognition. In: NIPS (2017)
19. Gong, B., Chao, W.L., Grauman, K., Sha, F.: Diverse sequential subset selection for supervised video summarization. In: NIPS (2014)
20. Hara, K., Kataoka, H., Satoh, Y.: Can spatiotemporal 3D CNNs retrace the history of 2D CNNs and imagenet? In: CVPR (2018)
21. He, K., Zhang, X., Ren, S., Sun, J.: Deep residual learning for image recognition. In: CVPR (2016)
22. Hochreiter, S., Schmidhuber, J.: Long short-term memory. Neural Comput. **9**(8), 1735–1780 (1997)
23. Hussein, N., Gavves, E., Smeulders, A.W.: Timeception for complex action recognition. In: CVPR (2019)

24. Hussein, N., Gavves, E., Smeulders, A.W.: VideoGraph: recognizing minutes-long human activities in videos. In: ICCVW (2019)
25. Jiang, Y.G., Bhattacharya, S., Chang, S.F., Shah, M.: High-level event recognition in unconstrained videos. Int. J. Multimedia Inf. Retrieval **2**(2), 73–101 (2013)
26. Kanuparthi, B., Arpit, D., Kerg, G., Ke, N.R., Mitliagkas, I., Bengio, Y.: h-detach: Modifying the LSTM gradient towards better optimization. In: ICLR (2019)
27. Karpathy, A., Toderici, G., Shetty, S., Leung, T., Sukthankar, R., Fei-Fei, L.: Large-scale video classification with convolutional neural networks. In: CVPR (2014)
28. Kay, W., et al.: The kinetics human action video dataset. arXiv preprint arXiv:1705.06950 (2017)
29. Kim, J.H., Jun, J., Zhang, B.T.: Bilinear attention networks. In: NIPS (2018)
30. Kuehne, H., Jhuang, H., Garrote, E., Poggio, T., Serre, T.: HMDB: a large video database for human motion recognition. In: ICCV (2011)
31. Kuehne, H., Arslan, A., Serre, T.: The language of actions: recovering the syntax and semantics of goal-directed human activities. In: CVPR (2014)
32. Kuehne, H., Gall, J., Serre, T.: An end-to-end generative framework for video segmentation and recognition. In: WACV (2016)
33. Lan, T., Zhu, Y., Roshan Zamir, A., Savarese, S.: Action recognition by hierarchical mid-level action elements. In: ICCV (2015)
34. Lee, Y.J., Ghosh, J., Grauman, K.: Discovering important people and objects for egocentric video summarization. In: CVPR (2012)
35. Li, S., Li, W., Cook, C., Zhu, C., Gao, Y.: Independently recurrent neural network (IndRNN): building a longer and deeper RNN. In: CVPR (2018)
36. Nguyen, P., Liu, T., Prasad, G., Han, B.: Weakly supervised action localization by sparse temporal pooling network. In: CVPR (2018)
37. Oh, S., et al.: A large-scale benchmark dataset for event recognition in surveillance video. In: CVPR (2011)
38. Paszke, A., et al.: Automatic differentiation in PyTorch (2017)
39. Piergiovanni, A., Ryoo, M.S.: Learning latent super-events to detect multiple activities in videos. In: CVPR (2018)
40. Rashid, M., Kjellström, H., Lee, Y.J.: Action graphs: Weakly-supervised action localization with graph convolution networks. arXiv preprint arXiv:2002.01449 (2020)
41. Schuldt, C., Laptev, I., Caputo, B.: Recognizing human actions: a local SVM approach. In: ICPR (2004)
42. Sharma, S., Kiros, R., Salakhutdinov, R.: Action recognition using visual attention. In: NIPS Time Series Workshop (2015)
43. Shou, Z., Wang, D., Chang, S.F.: Temporal action localization in untrimmed videos via multi-stage CNNs. In: CVPR (2016)
44. Sigurdsson, G.A., Divvala, S., Farhadi, A., Gupta, A.: Asynchronous temporal fields for action recognition. In: CVPR (2017)
45. Sigurdsson, G.A., Varol, G., Wang, X., Farhadi, A., Laptev, I., Gupta, A.: Hollywood in homes: crowdsourcing data collection for activity understanding. In: Leibe, B., Matas, J., Sebe, N., Welling, M. (eds.) ECCV 2016. LNCS, vol. 9905, pp. 510–526. Springer, Cham (2016). https://doi.org/10.1007/978-3-319-46448-0_31
46. Simonyan, K., Zisserman, A.: Two-stream convolutional networks for action recognition in videos. In: NIPS (2014)
47. Soomro, K., Zamir, A.R., Shah, M., Soomro, K., Zamir, A.R., Shah, M.: UCF101: a dataset of 101 human actions classes from videos in the wild. CoRR (2012)

48. Tapaswi, M., Zhu, Y., Stiefelhagen, R., Torralba, A., Urtasun, R., Fidler, S.: MovieQA: understanding stories in movies through question-answering. In: CVPR (2016)
49. Tran, D., Bourdev, L., Fergus, R., Torresani, L., Paluri, M.: Learning spatiotemporal features with 3D convolutional networks. In: ICCV (2015)
50. Tran, D., Wang, H., Torresani, L., Ray, J., LeCun, Y., Paluri, M.: A closer look at spatiotemporal convolutions for action recognition. In: CVPR (2018)
51. Tran, S.D., Davis, L.S.: Event modeling and recognition using Markov logic networks. In: Forsyth, D., Torr, P., Zisserman, A. (eds.) ECCV 2008. LNCS, vol. 5303, pp. 610–623. Springer, Heidelberg (2008). https://doi.org/10.1007/978-3-540-88688-4_45
52. Veeriah, V., Zhuang, N., Qi, G.J.: Differential recurrent neural networks for action recognition. In: ICCV (2015)
53. Wang, H., Schmid, C.: Action recognition with improved trajectories. In: ICCV (2013)
54. Wang, L., Qiao, Y., Tang, X.: Action recognition with trajectory-pooled deep-convolutional descriptors. In: CVPR (2015)
55. Wang, L., et al.: Temporal segment networks: towards good practices for deep action recognition. In: Leibe, B., Matas, J., Sebe, N., Welling, M. (eds.) ECCV 2016. LNCS, vol. 9912, pp. 20–36. Springer, Cham (2016). https://doi.org/10.1007/978-3-319-46484-8_2
56. Wang, X., Girshick, R., Gupta, A., He, K.: Non-local neural networks. In: CVPR (2018)
57. Wang, X., Ji, Q.: Hierarchical context modeling for video event recognition. PAMI **39**(9), 1770–1782 (2017)
58. Wang, Y., Wang, S., Tang, J., O'Hare, N., Chang, Y., Li, B.: Hierarchical attention network for action recognition in videos. arXiv preprint arXiv:1607.06416 (2016)
59. Wu, C.Y., Feichtenhofer, C., Fan, H., He, K., Krahenbuhl, P., Girshick, R.: Long-term feature banks for detailed video understanding. In: CVPR (2019)
60. Wu, Y., Zhang, S., Zhang, Y., Bengio, Y., Salakhutdinov, R.R.: On multiplicative integration with recurrent neural networks. In: NIPS (2016)
61. Xie, S., Sun, C., Huang, J., Tu, Z., Murphy, K.: Rethinking spatiotemporal feature learning: speed-accuracy trade-offs in video classification. In: Ferrari, V., Hebert, M., Sminchisescu, C., Weiss, Y. (eds.) ECCV 2018. LNCS, vol. 11219, pp. 318–335. Springer, Cham (2018). https://doi.org/10.1007/978-3-030-01267-0_19
62. Xu, S., Cheng, Y., Gu, K., Yang, Y., Chang, S., Zhou, P.: Jointly attentive spatial-temporal pooling networks for video-based person re-identification. In: ICCV (2017)
63. Xu, Y., et al.: Segregated temporal assembly recurrent networks for weakly supervised multiple action detection. In: AAAI (2019)
64. Xu, Z., Yang, Y., Hauptmann, A.G.: A discriminative CNN video representation for event detection. In: CVPR (2015)
65. Yeung, S., Russakovsky, O., Jin, N., Andriluka, M., Mori, G., Fei-Fei, L.: Every moment counts: dense detailed labeling of actions in complex videos. Int. J. Comput. Vision **126**(2–4), 375–389 (2018)

66. Zhang, K., Chao, W.-L., Sha, F., Grauman, K.: Video summarization with long short-term memory. In: Leibe, B., Matas, J., Sebe, N., Welling, M. (eds.) ECCV 2016. LNCS, vol. 9911, pp. 766–782. Springer, Cham (2016). https://doi.org/10.1007/978-3-319-46478-7_47
67. Zhou, B., Andonian, A., Oliva, A., Torralba, A.: Temporal relational reasoning in videos. In: Ferrari, V., Hebert, M., Sminchisescu, C., Weiss, Y. (eds.) ECCV 2018. LNCS, vol. 11205, pp. 831–846. Springer, Cham (2018). https://doi.org/10.1007/978-3-030-01246-5_49

Take an Emotion Walk: Perceiving Emotions from Gaits Using Hierarchical Attention Pooling and Affective Mapping

Uttaran Bhattacharya[1]($\boxtimes$)(iD), Christian Roncal[1](iD), Trisha Mittal[1](iD),
Rohan Chandra[1](iD), Kyra Kapsaskis[2](iD), Kurt Gray[2](iD), Aniket Bera[1](iD),
and Dinesh Manocha[1](iD)

[1] University of Maryland, College Park, MD 20742, USA
uttaranb@umd.edu
[2] University of North Carolina, Chapel Hill, NC 27599, USA

Abstract. We present an autoencoder-based semi-supervised approach to classify perceived human emotions from walking styles obtained from videos or motion-captured data and represented as sequences of 3D poses. Given the motion on each joint in the pose at each time step extracted from 3D pose sequences, we hierarchically pool these joint motions in a bottom-up manner in the encoder, following the kinematic chains in the human body. We also constrain the latent embeddings of the encoder to contain the space of psychologically-motivated affective features underlying the gaits. We train the decoder to reconstruct the motions per joint per time step in a top-down manner from the latent embeddings. For the annotated data, we also train a classifier to map the latent embeddings to emotion labels. Our semi-supervised approach achieves a mean average precision of 0.84 on the Emotion-Gait benchmark dataset, which contains both labeled and unlabeled gaits collected from multiple sources. We outperform current state-of-art algorithms for both emotion recognition and action recognition from 3D gaits by 7%–23% on the absolute. More importantly, we improve the average precision by 10%–50% on the absolute on classes that each makes up less than 25% of the labeled part of the Emotion-Gait benchmark dataset.

1 Introduction

Humans perceive others' emotions through verbal cues such as speech [29,53], text [12,63], and non-verbal cues such as eye-movements [57], facial expressions [19], tone of voice, postures [4], walking styles [34], etc. Perceiving others'

This project has been supported by ARO grant W911NF-19-1-0069.
Code and additional materials in project webpage: https://gamma.umd.edu/taew.

Electronic supplementary material The online version of this chapter (https://doi.org/10.1007/978-3-030-58607-2_9) contains supplementary material, which is available to authorized users.

© Springer Nature Switzerland AG 2020
A. Vedaldi et al. (Eds.): ECCV 2020, LNCS 12355, pp. 145–163, 2020.
https://doi.org/10.1007/978-3-030-58607-2_9

emotions shapes people's interactions and experiences when performing tasks in collaborative or competitive environments [6]. Given this importance of perceived emotions in everyday lives, there has been a steady interest in developing automated techniques for perceiving emotions from various cues, with applications in affective computing, therapy, and rehabilitation [55], robotics [7,46], surveillance [3,52], audience understanding [66], and character generation [62].

While there are multiple non-verbal modalities for perceiving emotions, in our work, we only observe people's styles of walking or their gaits, extracted from videos or motion-captured data. Perceived emotion recognition using any non-verbal cues is considered to be a challenging problem in both psychology and AI, primarily because of the unreliability in the cues, arising from sources such as "mock" expressions [17], expressions affected by the subject's knowledge of an observer [20], or even self-reported emotions in certain scenarios [47]. However, gaits generally require less conscious initiation from the subjects and therefore tend to be more reliable cues. Moreover, studies in psychology have shown that observers were able to perceive the emotions of walking subjects by observing features such as arm swinging, stride lengths, collapsed upper body, etc. [34,42].

Gaits have been widely used in computer vision for many applications, including action recognition [37,59,69] and perceiving emotions [9,43,50,51]. However, there are a few key challenges in terms of designing machine learning methods for emotion recognition using gaits:

- Methods based on hand-crafted biomechanical features extracted from human gaits often suffer from low prediction accuracy [15,64].
- Fully deep-learned methods [9,50] rely heavily on sufficiently large sets of annotated data. Annotations are expensive and tedious to collect due to the variations in scales and motion trajectories [2], as well as the inherent subjectivity in perceiving emotions [9]. The benchmark dataset for emotion recognition, Emotion-Gait [9], has around $4,000$ data points of which more than 53% are unlabeled.
- Conditional generative methods are useful for data augmentation, but current methods can only generate data for short time periods [26,32] or with relatively low diversity [9,49,68,70].

On the other hand, acquiring poses from videos and MoCap data is cheap and efficient, leading to the availability of large-scale pose-based datasets [1,11,28, 58]. Given the availability of these unlabeled gait datasets and the sparsity of gaits labeled with perceived emotions, there is a need to develop automatic methods that can utilize these datasets for emotion recognition.

Main Contributions: We present a semi-supervised network that accepts 3D pose sequences of human gaits extracted from videos or motion-captured data and predicts discrete perceived emotions, such as happy, angry, sad, and neutral. Our network consists of an unsupervised autoencoder coupled with a supervised classifier. The encoder in the unsupervised autoencoder hierarchically pools attentions on parts of the body. It learns separate intermediate feature representations for the motions on each of the human body parts (arms, legs, and torso) and then pools these features in a bottom-up manner to map them to the latent embeddings of the autoencoder. The decoder takes in these embeddings and reconstructs the motion on each joint of the body in a top-down manner.

We also perform affective mapping: we constrain the space of network-learned features to subsume the space of biomechanical affective features [54] expressed from the input gaits. These affective features contain useful information for distinguishing between different perceived emotions. Lastly, for the labeled data, our supervised classifier learns to map the encoder embeddings to the discrete emotion labels to complete the training process. To summarize, we contribute:

- **A semi-supervised network**, consisting of an autoencoder and a classifier, that are trained together to predict discrete perceived emotions from 3D pose sequences of gaits of humans.
- **A hierarchical attention pooling module** on the autoencoder to learn useful embeddings for unlabeled gaits, which improves the mean average precision (mAP) in classification by 1–17% on the absolute compared to state-of-the-art methods in both emotion recognition and action recognition from 3D gaits on the Emotion-Gait benchmark dataset.
- **Subsuming the affective features** expressed from the input gaits in the space of learned embeddings. This improves the mAP in classification by 7–23% on the absolute compared to state-of-the-art methods.

We observe the performance of our network improves linearly as more unlabeled data is used for training. More importantly, we report a 10–50% improvement on average precision on the absolute for emotion classes that have fewer than 25% labeled samples in the Emotion-Gait dataset [9].

2   Related Work

We briefly review prior work in classifying perceived emotions from gaits, as well as the related task of action recognition and generation from gaits.

Detecting Perceived Emotions from Gaits. Experiments in psychology have shown that observers were able to identify sadness, anger, happiness, and pride by observing gait features such as arm swinging, long strides, erect posture, collapsed upper body, etc. [34,39,42,44]. This, in turn, has led to considerable interest from both the computer vision and the affective computing communities in detecting perceived emotions from recorded gaits. Early works exploited different gait-based affective features to automatically detect perceived emotions [15,16,31,64]. More recent works combined these affective features with features learned from recurrent [50] or convolutional networks [9] to significantly improve classification accuracies.

Action Recognition and Generation. There are large bodies of recent work on both gait-based supervised action recognition [13,37,59–61,67,69,72], and gait-based unsupervised action generation [26,49,68,70]. These methods make use of RNNs or CNNs, including GCNs, or a combination of both, to achieve high classification accuracies on benchmark datasets such as Human3.6M [28], Kinetics [11], NTU RGB-D [58], and more. On top of the deep-learned networks, some methods have also leveraged the kinematic dependencies between joints and bones [59], dynamic movement-based features [60], and long-range temporal dependencies [37], to further improve performance. A comprehensive review of recent methods in kinect-based action recognition is available in [65].

RNN and CNN-based approaches have been extended to semi-supervised classification as well [24,30,48,71]. These methods have also added constraints on limb proportions, movement constraints, and exploited the autoregressive nature of gait prediction to improve their generative and classification components.

Generative methods have also exploited full sequences of poses to directly generate full test sequences [10,70]. Other approaches have used constraints on limb movements [2], action-specific trajectories [26], and the structure and kinematics of body joints [49], to improve the naturalness of generated gaits.

In our work, we learn latent embeddings from gaits by exploiting the kinematic chains in the human body [5] in a hierarchical fashion. Inspired by prior works in emotion perception from gaits, we also constrain our embeddings to contain the space of affective features expressed from gaits, to improve our average precision, especially on the rarer classes.

3   Approach

Given both labeled and unlabeled 3D pose sequences for gaits, our goal is classify all the gaits into one or more discrete perceived emotion labels, such as happy, sad, angry, etc. We use a semi-supervised approach to achieve this, by combining an autoencoder with a classifier, as shown in Fig. 2. We denote the set of trainable parameters in the encoder, decoder, and classifier with θ, ψ, and ϕ respectively. We first extract the rotation per joint from the first time step to the current time step in the input sequences (details in Sect. 3.2). We then pass these rotations through the encoder, denoted with $f_\theta(\cdot)$, to transform the input rotations into features in the latent embedding space. We pass these latent features through the decoder, denoted with $f_\psi(\cdot)$, to generate reconstructions of the input rotations. If training labels are available, we also pass the encoded features through the fully-connected classifier network, denoted with $f_\phi(\cdot)$, to predict the probabilities of the labels. We define our overall loss function as

$$\mathcal{C}(\theta,\phi,\psi) = \sum_{i=1}^{M} I_y^{(i)} \mathcal{C}_{CL}\left(y^{(i)}, f_{\phi\circ\theta}\left(D^{(i)}\right)\right) + \mathcal{C}_{AE}\left(D^{(i)}, f_{\psi\circ\theta}\left(D^{(i)}\right)\right), \quad (1)$$

where $f_{b\circ a}(\cdot) := f_b(f_a(\cdot))$ denotes the composition of functions, $I_y^{(i)}$ is an indicator variable denoting whether the ith data point has an associated label $y^{(i)}$, M is the number of gait samples, $\mathcal{C}_{CL}$ denotes the classifier loss detailed in Sect. 3.3, and $\mathcal{C}_{AE}$ denotes the autoencoder loss detailed in Sect. 3.4. For brevity of notation, we will henceforth use $\hat{y}^{(i)} := f_{\phi\circ\theta}\left(D^{(i)}\right)$ and $\hat{D}^{(i)} := f_{\psi\circ\theta}\left(D^{(i)}\right)$.

3.1 Representing Emotions

The Valence-Arousal-Dominance (VAD) model [41] is used for representing emotions in a continuous space. This model assumes three independent axes for valence, arousal, and dominance values, which collectively indicate an observed emotion. Valence indicates how pleasant (vs. unpleasant) the emotion is, arousal indicates how much the emotion is tied to high (vs. low) physiological intensity, and dominance indicates how much the emotion is tied to the assertion of high (vs. low) social status. For example, discrete emotion terms such as happy indicate high valence, medium arousal, and low dominance, angry indicate low valence, high arousal, and high dominance, and sad indicate low valence, low arousal, and low dominance.

Table 1. Affective Features. List of the 18 pose affective features that we use to describe the affective feature space for our network.

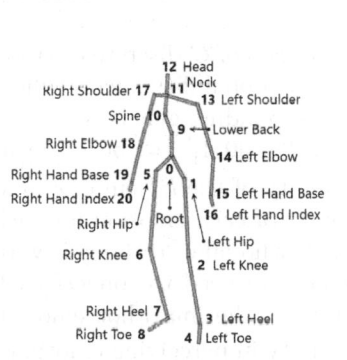

Fig. 1. 3D pose model. The names and numbering of the 21 joints in the pose follow the nomenclature in the ELMD dataset [23].

Angles between	Shoulders at lower back
	Hands at root
	Left shoulder and hand at elbow
	Right shoulder and hand at elbow
	Head and left shoulder at neck
	Head and right shoulder at neck
	Head and left knee at root
	Head and right knee at root
	Left toe and right toe at root
	Left hip and toe at knee
	Right hip and toe at knee
Distance ratios between	Left hand index (LHI) to neck and LHI to root
	Right-hand index (RHI) to neck and RHI to root
	LHI to RHI and neck to root
	Left toe to right toe and neck to root
Area (Δ) ratios between	Δ shoulders to lower back and Δ shoulders to root
	Δ hands to lower back and Δ hands to root
	Δ hand indices to neck and Δ toes to root

On the other hand, these discrete emotion terms are easily understood by non-expert annotators and end-users. As a result, most existing datasets for supervised emotion classification consist of discrete emotion labels, and most supervised methods report performance on predicting these discrete emotions. In fact, discrete emotions can actually be mapped back to the VAD space through various known transformations [25,40]. Given these factors, we choose to use discrete emotion labels in our work as well. We also note that human observers have been reported to be most consistent in perceiving emotions varying primarily on the arousal axis, such as happy, sad, and angry [22,56]. Hence we work with the four emotions, happy, sad, angry, and neutral.

3.2 Representing the Data

Given the 3D pose sequences for gaits, we first obtain the rotations per joint per time step. We denote a gait as $G = \left\{ \left(x_j^t, y_j^t, z_j^t \right) \right\}_{j=1,t=1}^{J,T}$, consisting of the 3D positions of J joints across T time steps. We denote the rotation of joint j from the first time step to time step t as $R_j^t \in \mathbb{SO}(3)$. We represent these rotations as unit quaternions $q_j^t \in \mathbb{H} \subset \mathbb{R}^4$, where $\mathbb{H}$ denotes the space of unit 4D quaternions. As stated in [49], quaternions are free of the gimbal-lock problem, unlike other common representations such as Euler angles or exponential maps [21]. We enforce the additional unit norm constraints for these quaternions when training our autoencoder. We represent the overall input to our network as $D^{(i)} := \left\{ q_j^t \right\}_{j=1,t=1}^{J,T} \in \mathbb{H}^{J \times T}$.

3.3 Using Perceived Emotions and Constructing Classifier Loss

Observers' perception of emotions in others depends heavily influenced by their own personal, social, and cultural experiences, making emotion perception an inherently subjective task [34,56]. Consequently, we need to keep track of the differences in the perceptions of different observers. We do this by assigning multi-hot emotion labels to each input gait.

We assume that the given labeled gait dataset consists of C discrete emotion classes. The raw label vector $L^{(i)}$ for the ith gait is a probability vector where the lth element denotes the probability that the corresponding gait is perceived to have the lth emotion. Specifically, we assume $L^{(i)} \in [0,1]^C$ to be given as $L^{(i)} = \begin{bmatrix} p_1 & p_2 & \dots p_C \end{bmatrix}^\top$, where p_l denotes the probability of the lth emotion and $l = 1, 2, \dots C$. In practice, we compute the probability of each emotion for each labeled gait in a dataset as the fraction of annotators who labeled the gait with the corresponding emotion. To perform classification, we need to convert each element in $L^{(i)}$ to an assignment in $\{0,1\}$, resulting in the multi-hot emotion label $y^{(i)} \in \{0,1\}^C$. Taking into account the subjectivity in perceiving emotions, we set an element l in $y^{(i)}$ to 1 if $p_l > \frac{1}{C}$, i.e., the lth perceived emotion has more than a random chance of being reported, and 0 otherwise. Since our classification problem is multi-class (typically, $C > 2$) as well as multi-label (as we use multi-hot labels), we use the weighted multi-class cross-entropy loss

$$\mathcal{C}_{CL} \left(y^{(i)}, \hat{y}^{(i)} \right) := - \sum_{l=1}^{C} w_l \left(y_l \right)^{(i)} \log \left(\hat{y}_l \right)^{(i)} \tag{2}$$

for our classifier loss, where $(y_l)^{(i)}$ and $(\hat{y}_l)^{(i)}$ denote the lth components of $y^{(i)}$ and $\hat{y}^{(i)}$, respectively. We also add per-class weights $w_l = e^{-p_l}$ to make the training more sensitive to mistakes on the rarer samples in the labeled dataset.

3.4 Using Affective Features and Constructing Autoencoder Loss

Our autoencoder loss consists of three constraints: affective loss, quaternion loss, and angle loss.

Affective Loss. Prior studies in psychology report that a person's perceived emotions can be represented by a set of scale-independent gait-based affective features [15]. We consider the poses underlying the gaits to be made up of $J = 21$ joints (Fig. 1). Inspired by [50], we categorize the affective features as follows:

- *Angles* subtended by two joints at a third joint. For example, between the head and the neck (used to compute head tilt), the neck, and the shoulders (to compute slouching), root and thighs (to compute stride lengths), etc.
- *Distance ratios* between two pairs of joints. For example, the ratio between the distance from the hand to the neck, and that from the hand to the root (to compute arm swings).
- *Area ratios* formed by two triplets of joints. For example, the ratio of the area formed between the elbows and the neck and the area formed between the elbows and the root (to compute slouching and arm swings). Area ratios can be viewed as amalgamations of the angle- and the distance ratio-based features used to supplement observations from these features.

We present the full list of the $\mathcal{A} = 18$ affective features we use in Table 1. We denote the set of affective features across all time steps for the ith gait with $a^{(i)} \subset \mathbb{R}^{\mathcal{A} \times T}$. We then constrain a subset of the embeddings learned by our encoder to map to these affective features. Specifically, we construct our embedding space to be $\mathbb{R}^{\mathcal{E} \times T}$ such that $\mathcal{E} \geq \mathcal{A}$. We then constrain the first $\mathcal{A} \times T$ dimensions of the embedding, denoted with $\hat{a}^{(i)}$ for the ith gait, to match the corresponding affective features $a^{(i)}$. This gives our affective loss constraint:

$$\mathcal{L}_{\text{aff}} \left(a^{(i)}, \hat{a}^{(i)} \right) := \left\| a^{(i)} - \hat{a}^{(i)} \right\|^2. \tag{3}$$

We use affective constraints rather than providing affective features as input because there is no consensus on the universal set of affective features, especially due to cross-cultural differences [18,56]. Thus, we allow the encoder of our autoencoder to learn an embedding space using both data-driven features and our affective features, to improve generalizability.

Quaternion Loss. The decoder for our autoencoder returns rotations per joint per time step as quaternions $\left(\hat{q}_j^t \right)^{(i)}$. We then constrain these quaternions to have unit norm:

$$\mathcal{L}_{\text{quat}} \left(\left(\hat{q}_j^t \right)^{(i)} \right) := \left(\left\| \left(\hat{q}_j^t \right)^{(i)} \right\| - 1 \right)^2. \tag{4}$$

We apply this constraint instead of normalizing the decoder output, since individual rotations tend to be small, which leads the network to converge all its estimates to the unit quaternion.

Angle Loss. This is the reconstruction loss for the autoencoder. We obtain it by converting the input and the output quaternions to the corresponding Euler angles and computing the mean loss between them:

$$\mathcal{L}_{\text{ang}} \left(D^{(i)}, \hat{D}^{(i)} \right) := \left\| (D_X, D_Y, D_Z)^{(i)} - \left(\hat{D}_X, \hat{D}_Y, \hat{D}_Z \right)^{(i)} \right\|_F^2 \tag{5}$$

where $(D_X, D_Y, D_Z)^{(i)} \in [0, 2\pi]^{3J \times T}$ and $\left(\hat{D}_X, \hat{D}_Y, \hat{D}_Z\right)^{(i)} \in [0, 2\pi]^{3J \times T}$ denotes the set of Euler angles for all the joints across all the time steps for input $D^{(i)}$ and output $\hat{D}^{(i)}$, respectively, and $\|\cdot\|_F$ denotes the Frobenius norm.

Combining Eqs. 3, 4 and 5, we write the autoencoder loss $\mathcal{C}_{AE}(\cdot, \cdot)$ as

$$\mathcal{C}_{AE}\left(D^{(i)}, \hat{D}^{(i)}\right) := \mathcal{L}_{ang}\left(D^{(i)}, \hat{D}^{(i)}\right) + \lambda_{quat}\mathcal{L}_{quat} + \lambda_{aff}\mathcal{L}_{aff} \qquad (6)$$

where λ_{quat} and λ_{aff} are the regularization weights for the quaternion loss constraint and the affective loss constraint, respectively. To keep the scales of $\mathcal{L}_{quat}$ and $\mathcal{L}_{aff}$ consistent, we also scale all the affective features to lie in $[0, 1]$.

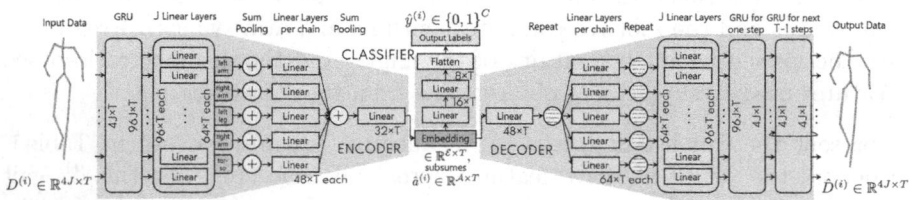

Fig. 2. Our network for semi-supervised classification of discrete perceived emotions from gaits. Inputs to the encoder are rotations on each joint at each time step, represented as 4D unit quaternions. The inputs are pooled bottom-up according to the kinematic chains of the human body. The embeddings at the end of the encoder are constrained to lie in the space of the mean affective features $\mathbb{R}^A$. For labeled data, the embeddings are passed through the classifier to predict output labels. The linear layers in the decoder take in the embeddings and reconstruct the motion on each joint at a single time-step at the output of the first GRU. The second GRU in the decoder takes in the reconstructed joint motions at a single time step and predicts the joint motions for the next time step for $T-1$ steps.

4   Network Architecture and Implementation

Our network for semi-supervised classification of discrete perceived emotions from gaits, shown in Fig. 2, consists of three components, the encoder, the decoder, and the classifier. We describe each of these components and then summarize the training routine for our network.

4.1   Encoder with Hierarchical Attention Pooling

We first pass the sequences of joint rotations on all the joints through a two-layer Gated Recurrent Unit (GRU) to obtain feature representations for rotations at all joints at all time steps. We pass each of these representations through individual linear units. Following the kinematic chain of the human joints [5], we pool the linear unit outputs for the two arms, the two legs, and the torso in five separate linear layers. Thus, each of these five linear layers learns to focus attention on a different part of the human body. We then pool the outputs from these five linear layers into another linear layer, which, by construction, focuses attention on the motions of the entire body. For pooling, we perform vector addition as a way of composing the features at the different hierarchies.

Our encoder learns the hierarchy of the joint rotations in a bottom-up manner. We map the output of the last linear layer in the hierarchy to a feature representation in the embedding space of the encoder through another linear layer. In our case, the embedding space lies in $\mathbb{R}^{\mathcal{E} \times T}$ with $\mathcal{E} = 32$, which subsumes the space of affective features $\mathbb{R}^{\mathcal{A} \times T}$ with $\mathcal{A} = 18$, as discussed in Sect. 3.4.

4.2 Decoder with Hierarchical Attention Un-pooling

The decoder takes in the embedding from the encoder, repeats it five times for un-pooling, and passes the repeated features through five linear layers. The outputs of these linear layers are features representing the reconstructions on the five parts, torso, two arms, and two legs. We repeat each of these features for un-pooling, and then collectively feed them into a GRU, which reconstructs the rotation on every joint at a single step. A subsequent GRU takes in the reconstructed joint rotations at a single time step and successively predicts the joint rotations for the next $T - 1$ time steps.

4.3 Classifier for Labeled Data

Our classifier takes in the embeddings and passes it through a series of three linear layers, flattening the features between the second and the third linear layers. The output of the final linear layer, called "Output Labels" in Fig. 2, provides the label probabilities. To make predictions, we set the output for a class to be 1 if the label probability for that class was more than $\frac{1}{C}$, similar to the routine for constructing input labels discussed in Sect. 3.3.

4.4 Training Routine

We train using the Adam optimizer [33] with a learning rate of 0.001, which we decay by a factor of 0.999 per epoch. We apply the ELU activation [14] on all the linear layers except the output label layer, apply batch normalization [27] after every layer to reduce internal covariance-shift, and apply a dropout of 0.1 to prevent overfitting. On the second GRU in the decoder, which predicts joint rotations for T successive time steps, we use a curriculum schedule [8]. We start with a teacher forcing ratio of 1 on this GRU and at every epoch E, we decay the teacher forcing ratio by $\beta = 0.995$, *i.e.*, we either provide this GRU the input joint rotations with probability β^E, or the GRU's past predicted joint rotations with probability $1 - \beta^E$. Curriculum scheduling helps the GRU to gently transition from a teacher-guided prediction routine to a self-guided prediction routine, thereby expediting the training process.

We train our network for 500 epochs, which takes around 4 h on an Nvidia GeForce GTX 1080Ti GPU with 12 GB memory. We use 80% of the available labeled data and all the unlabeled data for training our network, and validate its classification performance on a separate 10% of the labeled data. We keep the remaining 10% as the held-out test data. We also observed satisfactory performance when the weights λ_{quat} and λ_{aff} (in Eq. 6) lie between 0.5 and 2.5. For our reported performances in Sect. 5.3, we used a value of 2 for both.

5   Results

We perform experiments with the Emotion-Gait benchmark dataset [9]. It consists of 3D pose sequences of gaits collected from a variety of sources and partially labeled with perceived emotions. We provide a brief description of the dataset in Sect. 5.1. We list the methods we compare with in Sect. 5.2. We then summarize the results of the experiments we performed with this dataset on all these methods in Sect. 5.3, and describe how to interpret the results in Sect. 5.4.

Table 2. Average Precision scores. Average precision (AP) per class and the mean average precision (mAP) over all the classes achieved by all the methods on the Emotion Gait dataset. Classes are Happy (H), Sad (S), Angry (A) and Neutral (N). Higher values are better. Bold indicates best, blue indicates second best.

Method	AP				mAP
	H	S	A	N	
STGCN [69]	0.98	0.83	0.42	0.18	0.61
DGNN [59]	0.98	0.88	0.73	0.37	0.74
MS-G3D [59]	0.98	0.88	0.75	0.44	0.76
LSTM Network [50]	0.96	0.84	0.62	0.51	0.73
STEP [9]	0.97	0.88	0.72	0.52	0.77
Our method	**0.98**	**0.89**	**0.81**	**0.71**	**0.84**

Table 3. Ablation studies. Comparing average precisions of ablated versions of our method. HP denotes Hierarchical Pooling, AL denotes the Affective Loss constraint. AP, mAP, H, S, A, N are reused from Table 2. Bold indicates best, blue indicates second best.

Method	AP				mAP
	H	S	A	N	
With only labeled data, no AL or HP	0.92	0.81	0.51	0.42	0.67
With only labeled data, HP and no AL	0.93	0.81	0.63	0.49	0.72
With only labeled data, AL and no HP	0.96	0.86	0.70	0.51	0.76
With only labeled data, AL and HP	0.97	0.86	0.72	0.55	0.78
With all data, no AL or HP	0.94	0.83	0.55	0.48	0.70
With all data, HP and no AL	0.96	0.85	0.70	0.60	0.78
With all data, AL and no HP	0.97	0.87	0.76	0.65	0.81
With all data, AL and HP	**0.98**	**0.89**	**0.81**	**0.71**	**0.84**

5.1   Dataset

The Emotion-Gait dataset [9] consists of gaits collected from various sources of 3D pose sequence datasets, including BML [38], Human3.6M [28], ICT [45], CMU-MoCap [1] and ELMD [23]. To maintain a uniform set of joints for the pose models collected from diverse sources, we converted all the models in Emotion-Gait to the 21 joint pose model used in ELMD [23]. We clipped or zero-padded all input gaits to have 240 time steps, and downsampled it to contain every 5th frame. We passed the resultant 48 time steps to our network, we have *i.e.*, $T = 48$. In total, the dataset has 3,924 gaits of which 1,835 have emotion labels provided by 10 annotators, and the remaining 2,089 are not annotated. Around 58% of the labeled data have happy labels, 32% have sad labels, 23% have angry labels, and only 14% have neutral labels (more details on the project webpage).

Histograms of Affective Features. We show histograms of the mean values of 6 of the 18 affective features we use in Fig. 3. The means are taken across the $T = 48$ time steps in the input gaits and differently colored for inputs belonging to the different emotion classes as per the annotations. We count the inputs belonging to multiple classes once for every class they belong to. For different affective features, different sets of classes have a high overlap of values while values of the other classes are well-separated. For example, there is a significant overlap in the values of the distance ratio between right-hand index to the neck and right-hand index to the root (Fig. 3, bottom left) for gaits belonging to sad and angry classes, while the values of happy and neutral are distinct from these. Again, for gaits in happy and angry classes, there is a high overlap in the ratio of the area between hands to lower back and hands to root (Fig. 3, bottom right), while the corresponding values for gaits in neutral and sad classes are distinct from these. The affective features also support observations in psychology corresponding to perceiving emotions from gaits. For example, slouching is generally considered to be an indicator of sadness [42]. Correspondingly, we can observe that the values of the angle between the shoulders at the lower back (Fig. 3, top left) are lowest for sad gaits, indicating slouching.

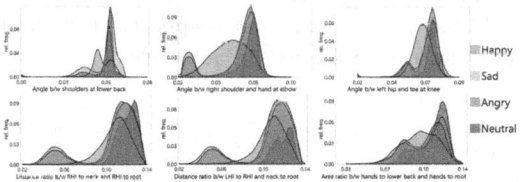 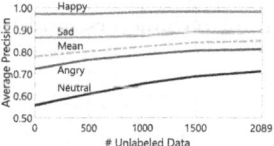

Fig. 3. Conditional distribution of mean affective features. Distributions of 6 of the 18 affective features, for the Emotion-Gait dataset, conditioned on the given classes Happy, Sad, Angry, and Neutral. Mean is taken across the number of time steps. We observe that the different classes have different distributions of peaks, indicating that these features are useful for distinguishing between perceived emotions. (Color figure online)

Fig. 4. AP increases with adding unlabeled data. AP achieved on each class, as well as the mean AP over the classes, increases linearly as we add more unlabeled data to train our network. The increment is most significant for the neutral class, which has the fewest labels in the dataset.

5.2   Comparison Methods

We compare our method with the following state-of-the-art methods for both emotion recognition and action recognition from gaits. We choose to compare with action recognition methods because similar to these methods, we aim to learn a mapping from gaits to a set of labels (emotions instead of actions).

- **Emotion Recognition.** We compare with the network of [50], which combines affective features from gaits with features learned from an LSTM-based network taking pose sequences of gaits as input, to form hybrid feature vectors for classification. We also compare with STEP [9], which trains a spatial-temporal graph convolution-based network with gait inputs and affective features obtained from the gaits, and then fine-tunes the network with data generated from a graph convolution-based variational autoencoder.
- **Action Recognition.** We compare with recent state-of-the-art methods based on the spatial-temporal graph convolution network (STGCN) [69], the directed graph neural network (DGNN) [59], and the multi-scale graph convolutions with temporal skip connections (MS-G3D) [37]. STGCN computes spatial neighborhoods as per the bone structure of the 3D poses and temporal neighborhoods according to the instances of the same joints across time steps and performs convolutions based on these neighborhoods. DGNN computes directed acyclic graphs of the bone structure based on kinematic dependencies and trains a convolutional network with these graphs. MS-G3D performs multi-scale graph convolutions on the spatial dimensions and adds skip connections on the temporal dimension to model long-range dependencies for various actions.

For a fair comparison, we retrained all these networks from scratch with the labeled portion of the Emotion-Gait dataset, following their respective reported training parameters, and the same data split of 8:1:1 as our network.

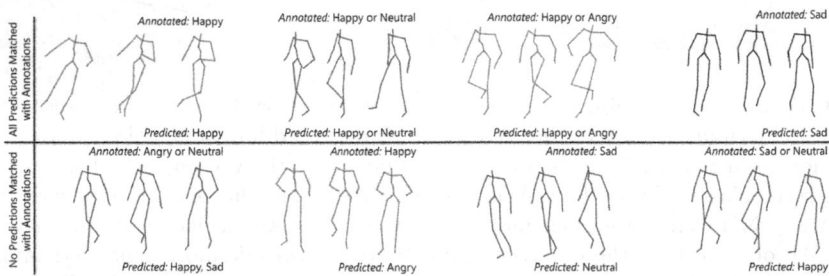

Fig. 5. Comparing predictions with annotations. The top row shows 4 gaits from the Emotion-Gait dataset where the predicted labels of our network exactly matched the annotated input labels. The bottom row shows 4 gaits where the predicted labels did not match any of the input labels. Each gait is represented by 3 poses in temporal sequence from left to right. We observe that most of the disagreements are between either happy and angry or between sad and neutral, which is consistent with general observations in psychology.

5.2.1 Evaluation Metric

Since we deal with a multi-class, multi-label classification, we report the average precision (AP) achieved per class, which is the mean of the precision values across all values of recall between 0 and 1. We also report the mean AP, which is the mean of the APs achieved in all the classes.

5.3 Experiments

In our experiments, we ensured that the held-out test data were from sources different from the train and validation data in the Emotion-Gait dataset. We summarize the AP and the mean AP scores of all the methods in Table 2. Our method outperforms the next best method, STEP [9], by around 7% and outperforms the lowest-performing method, STGCN [69], by 23%, both on the absolute. We summarize additional results, including the interpretation of the data labels and our results in the VAD dimensions [41], on our project webpage.

Both the LSTM-based network and STEP consider per-frame affective features and inter-frame features such as velocities and rotations as inputs but do not explicitly model the dependencies between these two kinds of features. Our network, on the other hand, learns to embed a part of the features learned from joint rotations in the space of affective features. These embedded features, in turn, help our network predict the output emotion labels with more precision.

The action recognition methods STGCN, DGNN, and MS-G3D focus more on the movements of the leaf nodes, *i.e.*, hand indices, toes, and head. These nodes are useful for distinguishing between actions such as running and jumping but do not contain sufficient information to distinguish between perceived emotions.

Moreover, given the long-tail nature of the distribution of labels in the Emotion-Gait dataset (Sect. 5.1), all the methods we compare with have more than 0.95 AP in the happy and more than 0.80 AP in the sad classes, but perform much poorer on the angry and the neutral classes. Our method, by contrast, learns to map the joint motions to the affective features, which helps it achieve around 10–50% better AP on the absolute on the angry and the neutral class while maintaining similarly high AP in the happy and the sad classes.

5.3.1 Ablation Studies

We also perform ablation studies on our method to highlight the benefit of each of our three key components: using hierarchical pooling (HP) (Sect. 4.1), using the affective loss constraint (AL) (Eq. 3), and using both labeled and unlabeled data in a semi-supervised manner (Eq. 1). We summarize the observations of our ablation studies in Table 3.

First, we train our network only on the labeled dataset by removing the decoder part of our network and dropping the autoencoder loss from Eq. 1. Without using either AL or HP, the network achieves an AP of 0.51 on angry and 0.42 on neutral, the two least populous classes. We call this our baseline network. Adding only the AL increases these two APs more from the baseline than adding only the HP. This is reasonable since hierarchical pooling helps the network learn generic differences in the pose sequences of different data, while the affective loss constraint helps the network to distinguish between pose structures specific to different perceived emotions. Adding both HP and AL increases the AP from the baseline even further. From these experiments, we can confirm that using either AL or HP improves the performance from the baseline, and their collective performance is better than their individual performances.

Next, we add in the decoder and use both labeled and unlabeled data for training our network, using the loss in Eq. 1. Without both AL and HP, the network now achieves an AP of 0.55 on angry and 0.48 on neutral, showing appreciable improvements from the baseline. Also, as earlier, adding in only the AL shows more benefit on the network's performance than adding in only the HP. Specifically, adding in only the HP produces 1% absolute improvement in mean AP over STEP [9] (row 4 in Table 2) and 17% absolute improvement in mean AP over STGCN [69] (row 1 in Table 2). Adding in only the AL produces 4% absolute improvement in mean AP over STEP [9] (row 4 in Table 2) and 20% absolute improvement in mean AP over STGCN [69] (row 1 in Table 2). Adding in both, we get the final version of our network, which improves on the mean AP of STEP [9] by 7%, and the mean AP of STGCN [69] by 23%.

5.3.2 Performance Trend with Increasing Unlabeled Data

In practice, it is relatively easy to collect unlabeled gaits from videos or using motion capture. We track the performance improvement of our network as we keep adding unlabeled data to our network, and summarize the results in Fig. 4. We observe that the mean AP improves linearly as we add more data. The trend does not indicate a saturation in AP for the angry and the neutral classes even after adding all the 2,089 unlabeled data. This suggests that the performance of our approach can increase further with more unlabeled data.

5.4 Interpretation of the Network Predictions

We show the qualitative results of our network in Fig. 5. The top row shows cases where the predicted labels for a gait exactly matched all the corresponding annotated labels. We observe that the gaits with happy and angry labels in the annotation have more animated joint movements compared to the gaits with sad and neutral labels, which our network was able to successfully learn from the affective features. This is in line with established studies in psychology [41], which show that both happy and angry emotions lie high on the arousal scale, whereas neutral and sad are lower on the arousal scale. The bottom row shows cases where the predicted labels for a gait did not match any of the annotated labels. We notice that most disagreements arise either between sad and neutral labels or between happy and angry labels. This again follows the observation that both happy and angry gaits, higher on the arousal scale, often have more exaggerated joint movements, while both sad and neutral gaits, lower on the arousal scale, often have more reserved joint movements. There are also disagreements between happy and neutral labels for some gaits, where the joint movements in the happy gaits are not as exaggerated.

We also make an important distinction between the multi-hot input labels provided by human annotators and the multi-hot predictions of our network. The input labels capture the subjectivity in human perception, where different human observers perceive different emotions from the same gait based on their own biases and prior experiences [56]. The network, on the other hand, indicates that the emotion perceived from a particular gait data best fits one of the labels it predicts for that data. For example, in the third result from left on the top row in Fig. 5, five of the ten annotators perceived the gait to be happy, three perceived it to be angry, and the remaining two perceived it to be neutral. Following our annotations procedure in Sect. 4.3, we annotated this gait as an instance of both happy and angry. Given this gait, our network predicts a multi-hot label with 1's for happy and angry and 0's for neutral and sad. This indicates that the network successfully focused on the arousal in this gait, and found the emotion perceived from it to best match either happy or angry, and not match neutral and sad. We present more such results on our project webpage.

6   Limitations and Future Work

Our work has some limitations. First, we consider only discrete emotions of people and do not explicitly map these to the underlying continuous emotion space given by the VAD model [41]. Even though discrete emotions are presumably easier to work with for non-expert end-users, we plan to extend our method to work in the continuous space of emotions, *i.e.*, given a gait, our network regresses it to a point in the VAD space that indicates the perceived emotions.

Second, our network only looks at gait-based features to predict perceived emotions. In the future, we plan to combine these features with cues from other modalities such as facial expressions and body gestures, that are often expressed in tandem with gaits, to develop more robust emotion perception methods. We also plan to look at higher-level information, such as the presence of other people in the vicinity, background context, etc. that are known to influence a person's emotions [35,36] to further sophisticate the performance of our network.

References

1. CMU graphics lab motion capture database (2018). http://mocap.cs.cmu.edu/
2. Ahsan, U., Sun, C., Essa, I.: DiscrimNet: semi-supervised action recognition from videos using generative adversarial networks. arXiv preprint arXiv:1801.07230 (2018)
3. Arunnehru, J., Kalaiselvi Geetha, M.: Automatic human emotion recognition in surveillance video. In: Dey, N., Santhi, V. (eds.) Intelligent Techniques in Signal Processing for Multimedia Security. SCI, vol. 660, pp. 321–342. Springer, Cham (2017). https://doi.org/10.1007/978-3-319-44790-2_15

4. Babu, A.R., Rajavenkatanarayanan, A., Brady, J.R., Makedon, F.: Multimodal approach for cognitive task performance prediction from body postures, facial expressions and EEG signal. In: Proceedings of the Workshop on Modeling Cognitive Processes from Multimodal Data, p. 2. ACM (2018)
5. Badler, N.I., Phillips, C.B., Webber, B.L.: Simulating Humans: Computer Graphics Animation and Control. Oxford University Press, Oxford (1993)
6. Barrett, L.F.: How Emotions are Made: The Secret Life of the Brain. Houghton Mifflin Harcourt, Boston (2017)
7. Bauer, A., et al.: The autonomous city explorer: towards natural human-robot interaction in urban environments. IJSR **1**(2), 127–140 (2009)
8. Bengio, S., Vinyals, O., Jaitly, N., Shazeer, N.: Scheduled sampling for sequence prediction with recurrent neural networks. In: Advances in Neural Information Processing Systems, pp. 1171–1179 (2015)
9. Bhattacharya, U., Mittal, T., Chandra, R., Randhavane, T., Bera, A., Manocha, D.: STEP: spatial temporal graph convolutional networks for emotion perception from gaits. In: AAAI, pp. 1342–1350 (2020)
10. Cai, H., Bai, C., Tai, Y.-W., Tang, C.-K.: Deep video generation, prediction and completion of human action sequences. In: Ferrari, V., Hebert, M., Sminchisescu, C., Weiss, Y. (eds.) ECCV 2018. LNCS, vol. 11206, pp. 374–390. Springer, Cham (2018). https://doi.org/10.1007/978-3-030-01216-8_23
11. Carreira, J., Zisserman, A.: Quo vadis, action recognition? A new model and the kinetics dataset. In: proceedings of the IEEE Conference on Computer Vision and Pattern Recognition, pp. 6299–6308 (2017)
12. Chen, Y., Hou, W., Cheng, X., Li, S.: Joint learning for emotion classification and emotion cause detection. In: Proceedings of the 2018 Conference on Empirical Methods in Natural Language Processing, pp. 646–651 (2018)
13. Choutas, V., Weinzaepfel, P., Revaud, J., Schmid, C.: PoTion: pose motion representation for action recognition. In: Proceedings of the IEEE Conference on Computer Vision and Pattern Recognition, pp. 7024–7033 (2018)
14. Clevert, D.A., Unterthiner, T., Hochreiter, S.: Fast and accurate deep network learning by exponential linear units (ELUs). arXiv preprint arXiv:1511.07289 (2015)
15. Crenn, A., Khan, R.A., Meyer, A., Bouakaz, S.: Body expression recognition from animated 3D skeleton. In: IC3D, pp. 1–7. IEEE (2016)
16. Daoudi, M., Berretti, S., Pala, P., Delevoye, Y., Del Bimbo, A.: Emotion recognition by body movement representation on the manifold of symmetric positive definite matrices. In: Battiato, S., Gallo, G., Schettini, R., Stanco, F. (eds.) ICIAP 2017. LNCS, vol. 10484, pp. 550–560. Springer, Cham (2017). https://doi.org/10.1007/978-3-319-68560-1_49
17. Ekman, P., Friesen, W.V.: Head and body cues in the judgment of emotion: a reformulation. Percept. Mot. Skills **24**, 711–724 (1967)
18. Ekman, P., Friesen, W.V.: The repertoire of nonverbal behavior: categories, origins, usage, and coding. Semiotica **1**(1), 49–98 (1969)
19. Fabian Benitez-Quiroz, C., Srinivasan, R., Martinez, A.M.: EmotioNet: an accurate, real-time algorithm for the automatic annotation of a million facial expressions in the wild. In: CVPR (2016)
20. Fernández-Dols, J.M., Ruiz-Belda, M.A.: Expression of emotion versus expressions of emotions. In: Russell, J.A., Fernández-Dols, J.M., Manstead, A.S.R., Wellenkamp, J.C. (eds.) Everyday Conceptions of Emotion. ASID, vol. 81, pp. 505–522. Springer, Dordrecht (1995). https://doi.org/10.1007/978-94-015-8484-5_29

21. Grassia, F.S.: Practical parameterization of rotations using the exponential map. J. Graph. Tools **3**(3), 29–48 (1998)
22. Gross, M.M., Crane, E.A., Fredrickson, B.L.: Effort-shape and kinematic assessment of bodily expression of emotion during gait. Hum. Mov. Sci. **31**(1), 202–221 (2012)
23. Habibie, I., Holden, D., Schwarz, J., Yearsley, J., Komura, T.: A recurrent variational autoencoder for human motion synthesis. In: Proceedings of the British Machine Vision Conference (BMVC) (2017)
24. Harvey, F.G., Roy, J., Kanaa, D., Pal, C.: Recurrent semi-supervised classification and constrained adversarial generation with motion capture data. Image Vis. Comput. **78**, 42–52 (2018)
25. Hoffmann, H., et al.: Mapping discrete emotions into the dimensional space: an empirical approach. In: 2012 IEEE International Conference on Systems, Man, and Cybernetics (SMC), pp. 3316–3320. IEEE (2012)
26. Holden, D., Saito, J., Komura, T.: A deep learning framework for character motion synthesis and editing. ACM Trans. Graph. (TOG) **35**(4), 138 (2016)
27. Ioffe, S., Szegedy, C.: Batch normalization: accelerating deep network training by reducing internal covariate shift. arXiv preprint arXiv:1502.03167 (2015)
28. Ionescu, C., Papava, D., Olaru, V., Sminchisescu, C.: Human3.6M: large scale datasets and predictive methods for 3D human sensing in natural environments. IEEE Trans. Pattern Anal. Mach. Intell. **36**(7), 1325–1339 (2013)
29. Jacob, A., Mythili, P.: Prosodic feature based speech emotion recognition at segmental and supra segmental levels. In: SPICES, pp. 1–5. IEEE (2015)
30. Kanazawa, A., Zhang, J.Y., Felsen, P., Malik, J.: Learning 3D human dynamics from video. In: Proceedings of the IEEE Conference on Computer Vision and Pattern Recognition, pp. 5614–5623 (2019)
31. Karg, M., Kuhnlenz, K., Buss, M.: Recognition of affect based on gait patterns. Cybernetics **40**(4), 1050–1061 (2010)
32. Khodabandeh, M., Reza Vaezi Joze, H., Zharkov, I., Pradeep, V.: DIY human action dataset generation. In: Proceedings of the IEEE Conference on Computer Vision and Pattern Recognition Workshops, pp. 1448–1458 (2018)
33. Kingma, D.P., Ba, J.: Adam: a method for stochastic optimization. arXiv preprint arXiv:1412.6980 (2014)
34. Kleinsmith, A., Bianchi-Berthouze, N.: Affective body expression perception and recognition: a survey. IEEE Trans. Affect. Comput. **4**(1), 15–33 (2013)
35. Kosti, R., Alvarez, J., Recasens, A., Lapedriza, A.: Context based emotion recognition using EMOTIC dataset. IEEE Trans. Pattern Anal. Mach. Intell. **42**, 2755–2766 (2019)
36. Lee, J., Kim, S., Kim, S., Park, J., Sohn, K.: Context-aware emotion recognition networks. arXiv preprint arXiv:1908.05913 (2019)
37. Liu, Z., Zhang, H., Chen, Z., Wang, Z., Ouyang, W.: Disentangling and unifying graph convolutions for skeleton-based action recognition. In: The IEEE Conference on Computer Vision and Pattern Recognition (CVPR) (2020)
38. Ma, Y., Paterson, H.M., Pollick, F.E.: A motion capture library for the study of identity, gender, and emotion perception from biological motion. Behav. Res. Methods **38**(1), 134–141 (2006)
39. Meeren, H.K., van Heijnsbergen, C.C., de Gelder, B.: Rapid perceptual integration of facial expression and emotional body language. Proc. NAS **102**(45), 16518–16523 (2005)
40. Mehrabian, A.: Analysis of the big-five personality factors in terms of the pad temperament model. Aust. J. Psychol. **48**(2), 86–92 (1996)

41. Mehrabian, A., Russell, J.A.: An Approach to Environmental Psychology. The MIT Press, Cambridge (1974)
42. Michalak, J., Troje, N.F., Fischer, J., Vollmar, P., Heidenreich, T., Schulte, D.: Embodiment of sadness and depression—Gait patterns associated with dysphoric mood. Psychosom. Med. **71**(5), 580–587 (2009)
43. Mittal, T., Guhan, P., Bhattacharya, U., Chandra, R., Bera, A., Manocha, D.: EmotiCon: context-aware multimodal emotion recognition using Frege's principle. In: Proceedings of the IEEE/CVF Conference on Computer Vision and Pattern Recognition, pp. 14234–14243 (2020)
44. Montepare, J.M., Goldstein, S.B., Clausen, A.: The identification of emotions from gait information. J. Nonverbal Behav. **11**(1), 33–42 (1987)
45. Narang, S., Best, A., Feng, A., Kang, S.H., Manocha, D., Shapiro, A.: Motion recognition of self and others on realistic 3D avatars. Comput. Anim. Virtual Worlds **28**(3–4), e1762 (2017)
46. Narayanan, V., Manoghar, B.M., Dorbala, V.S., Manocha, D., Bera, A.: ProxEmo: gait-based emotion learning and multi-view proxemic fusion for socially-aware robot navigation. In: 2020 IEEE/RSJ International Conference on Intelligent Robots and Systems, IROS 2020. IEEE (2020)
47. Nisbett, R.E., Wilson, T.D.: Telling more than we can know: verbal reports on mental processes. Psychol. Rev. **84**(3), 231 (1977)
48. Pavllo, D., Feichtenhofer, C., Grangier, D., Auli, M.: 3D human pose estimation in video with temporal convolutions and semi-supervised training. In: Proceedings of the IEEE Conference on Computer Vision and Pattern Recognition, pp. 7753–7762 (2019)
49. Pavllo, D., Grangier, D., Auli, M.: QuaterNet: a quaternion-based recurrent model for human motion. arXiv preprint arXiv:1805.06485 (2018)
50. Randhavane, T., Bera, A., Kapsaskis, K., Bhattacharya, U., Gray, K., Manocha, D.: Identifying emotions from walking using affective and deep features. arXiv preprint arXiv:1906.11884 (2019)
51. Randhavane, T., Bera, A., Kapsaskis, K., Sheth, R., Gray, K., Manocha, D.: EVA: generating emotional behavior of virtual agents using expressive features of gait and gaze. In: ACM Symposium on Applied Perception 2019, pp. 1–10 (2019)
52. Randhavane, T., Bhattacharya, U., Kapsaskis, K., Gray, K., Bera, A., Manocha, D.: The Liar's walk: detecting deception with gait and gesture. arXiv preprint arXiv:1912.06874 (2019)
53. Rao, K.S., Koolagudi, S.G., Vempada, R.R.: Emotion recognition from speech using global and local prosodic features. Int. J. Speech Technol. **16**, 143–160 (2013)
54. Riggio, H.R.: Emotional expressiveness. In: Zeigler-Hill, V., Shackelford, T. (eds.) Encyclopedia of Personality and Individual Differences. Springer, Cham (2017). https://doi.org/10.1007/978-3-319-28099-8_508-1
55. Rivas, J.J., Orihuela-Espina, F., Sucar, L.E., Palafox, L., Hernández-Franco, J., Bianchi-Berthouze, N.: Detecting affective states in virtual rehabilitation. In: Proceedings of the 9th International Conference on Pervasive Computing Technologies for Healthcare, pp. 287–292. ICST (Institute for Computer Sciences, Social-Informatics and Telecommunications Engineering) (2015)
56. Roether, C.L., Omlor, L., Christensen, A., Giese, M.A.: Critical features for the perception of emotion from gait. J. Vis. **9**(6), 15–15 (2009)
57. Schurgin, M., Nelson, J., Iida, S., Ohira, H., Chiao, J., Franconeri, S.: Eye movements during emotion recognition in faces. J. Vis. **14**(13), 14–14 (2014)

58. Shahroudy, A., Liu, J., Ng, T.T., Wang, G.: NTU RGB+D: a large scale dataset for 3D human activity analysis. In: Proceedings of the IEEE Conference on Computer Vision and Pattern Recognition, pp. 1010–1019 (2016)
59. Shi, L., Zhang, Y., Cheng, J., Lu, H.: Skeleton-based action recognition with directed graph neural networks. In: Proceedings of the IEEE Conference on Computer Vision and Pattern Recognition, pp. 7912–7921 (2019)
60. Shi, L., Zhang, Y., Cheng, J., Lu, H.: Two-stream adaptive graph convolutional networks for skeleton-based action recognition. In: Proceedings of the IEEE Conference on Computer Vision and Pattern Recognition, pp. 12026–12035 (2019)
61. Si, C., Chen, W., Wang, W., Wang, L., Tan, T.: An attention enhanced graph convolutional LSTM network for skeleton-based action recognition. In: Proceedings of the IEEE Conference on Computer Vision and Pattern Recognition, pp. 1227–1236 (2019)
62. Starke, S., Zhang, H., Komura, T., Saito, J.: Neural state machine for character-scene interactions. ACM Trans. Graph. **38**(6), 209 (2019)
63. Strapparava, C., Mihalcea, R.: Learning to identify emotions in text. In: Proceedings of the 2008 ACM Symposium on Applied Computing, pp. 1556–1560. ACM (2008)
64. Venture, G., Kadone, H., Zhang, T., Grèzes, J., Berthoz, A., Hicheur, H.: Recognizing emotions conveyed by human gait. IJSR **6**(4), 621–632 (2014)
65. Wang, L., Huynh, D.Q., Koniusz, P.: A comparative review of recent kinect-based action recognition algorithms. arXiv preprint arXiv:1906.09955 (2019)
66. Wu, Z., Fu, Y., Jiang, Y.G., Sigal, L.: Harnessing object and scene semantics for large-scale video understanding. In: Proceedings of the IEEE Conference on Computer Vision and Pattern Recognition, pp. 3112–3121 (2016)
67. Yan, A., Wang, Y., Li, Z., Qiao, Y.: PA3D: pose-action 3D machine for video recognition. In: Proceedings of the IEEE Conference on Computer Vision and Pattern Recognition, pp. 7922–7931 (2019)
68. Yan, S., Li, Z., Xiong, Y., Yan, H., Lin, D.: Convolutional sequence generation for skeleton-based action synthesis. In: Proceedings of the IEEE International Conference on Computer Vision, pp. 4394–4402 (2019)
69. Yan, S., Xiong, Y., Lin, D.: Spatial temporal graph convolutional networks for skeleton-based action recognition. In: AAAI (2018)
70. Yang, C., Wang, Z., Zhu, X., Huang, C., Shi, J., Lin, D.: Pose guided human video generation. In: Ferrari, V., Hebert, M., Sminchisescu, C., Weiss, Y. (eds.) ECCV 2018. LNCS, vol. 11214, pp. 204–219. Springer, Cham (2018). https://doi.org/10.1007/978-3-030-01249-6_13
71. Zhang, J.Y., Felsen, P., Kanazawa, A., Malik, J.: Predicting 3D human dynamics from video. In: Proceedings of the IEEE International Conference on Computer Vision, pp. 7114–7123 (2019)
72. Zhang, S., et al.: Fusing geometric features for skeleton-based action recognition using multilayer LSTM networks. IEEE Trans. Multimedia **20**(9), 2330–2343 (2018)

Weighing Counts: Sequential Crowd Counting by Reinforcement Learning

Liang Liu[1], Hao Lu[2], Hongwei Zou[1], Haipeng Xiong[1], Zhiguo Cao[1]([✉]),
and Chunhua Shen[2]

[1] School of Artificial Intelligence and Automation,
Huazhong University of Science and Technology, Wuhan, China
{wings,zgcao}@hust.edu.cn
[2] The University of Adelaide, Adelaide, Australia

Abstract. We formulate counting as a sequential decision problem and present a novel crowd counting model solvable by deep reinforcement learning. In contrast to existing counting models that directly output count values, we divide one-step estimation into a sequence of much easier and more tractable sub-decision problems. Such sequential decision nature corresponds exactly to a physical process in reality—scale weighing. Inspired by scale weighing, we propose a novel 'counting scale' termed LibraNet where the count value is analogized by weight. By virtually placing a crowd image on one side of a scale, LibraNet (agent) sequentially learns to place appropriate weights on the other side to match the crowd count. At each step, LibraNet chooses one weight (action) from the weight box (the pre-defined action pool) according to the current crowd image features and weights placed on the scale pan (state). LibraNet is required to learn to balance the scale according to the feedback of the needle (Q values). We show that LibraNet exactly implements scale weighing by visualizing the decision process how LibraNet chooses actions. Extensive experiments demonstrate the effectiveness of our design choices and report state-of-the-art results on a few crowd counting benchmarks, including ShanghaiTech, UCF_CC_50 and UCF-QNRF. We also demonstrate good cross-dataset generalization of LibraNet. Code and models are made available at https://git.io/libranet.

Keywords: Crowd counting · Reinforcement learning

1 Introduction

Counting is sequential decision process by nature. Dense object counts are not inferred by humans with a simple glance [4]. Instead humans count objects in

---

L. Liu and H. Lu contributed equally.

Electronic supplementary material The online version of this chapter (https://doi.org/10.1007/978-3-030-58607-2_10) contains supplementary material, which is available to authorized users.

© Springer Nature Switzerland AG 2020
A. Vedaldi et al. (Eds.): ECCV 2020, LNCS 12355, pp. 164–181, 2020.
https://doi.org/10.1007/978-3-030-58607-2_10

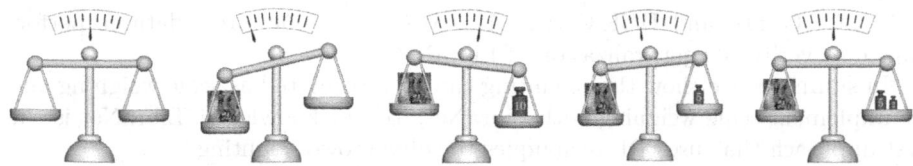

Fig. 1. Counting scale. We implement crowd counting as scale weighing. By virtually placing a crowd image (with 7 people) on the scale, if placing a 10 g weight on the scale pan, the scale will lean to the right; if exchanging the 10 g weight to 5 g, the scale instead will lean to the left. Finally by adding another 2 g weight, the scale is balanced. The total weights on the scale can therefore indicate the number of crowd.

a sequential manner, with initial fast counting on apparent objects (large sizes and clear appearance) and gradually slow counting on objects that are hard to recognize (small sizes or blurred appearance). Such a sequential decision behavior can be modeled by a physical process in reality—scale weighing. In scale weighing, it is easy to choose a weight when the weights placed on the scale are far from the true weight of the stuff. When placed weights are close to the true weight, small and light weights are carefully chosen until the needle indicates the balance. This process decomposes a difficult problem into a series of much more tractable sub-problems.

Following the same spirit of human counting and scale weighing, we formulate counting as a sequential decision problem and implement it as scale weighing. Indeed counting objects is like weighing stuff. In the context of crowd counting shown in Fig. 1, the 'stuff' is a crowd image, and the 'weights' are a series of pre-defined value operators. We repeatedly choose counting 'weights' to approximate the ground-truth counts until the scale is balanced. The final image count is simply a summation of placed 'weights'.

The sequential decision nature of scale weighing makes it suitable to be described by a reinforcement learning (RL) task. We hence propose a Deep Q-Network (DQN) [29]-based solution, LibraNet[1], to implement scale weighing and apply it to crowd counting as a 'counting scale'. In particular, given a 'stuff', LibraNet outputs a combination of weights step by step. In each step, a weight (action) is chosen from the weight box (the pre-defined action pool) or removed from the scale pan according to the feedback of the needle (Q values that indicate how to choose the next action). The weighing process continues until LibraNet chooses the 'end' operator. The 'stuff' is the image feature encoded from a crowd image, and the 'end' condition meets when the summation of the weights equals/approximates to the ground-truth people count.

We visualize how LibraNet works and illustrate that LibraNet exactly implements scale weighing. We show through extensive experiments why our choices in designing reward function work well, that LibraNet can be used as a plug-in to existing local counts models [19,47], and that LibraNet achieves state-of-the-art performance on three crowd counting datasets, including ShanghaiTech [52],

---

[1] The naming of LibraNet is inspired by the zodiac sign.

UCF_CC_50 [11], and UCF-QNRF [12]. We also report cross-dataset performance to verify the generalization of LibraNet.

In summary, we show that counting can be interpreted as scale weighing and we implement scale weighing with LibraNet. To our knowledge, LibraNet is the first approach that uses RL techniques to solve crowd counting.

1.1 Related Work

Crowd Counting. Crowd counting is often tackled as a dense prediction task [24, 25]. Solutions range from early attempts that detect pedestrians [7], regress image counts [3], estimate density maps [16], predict localized counts [5], to recent deep learning-based density maps estimation [17], redundant counts regression [6,23], instance blobs localization [15] and count intervals classification [19,48].

Since detection typically failed on small and dense people, regression-based approaches [3,32] were proposed. While early methods alleviated the issues of occlusion and clutter, they ignored spatial information because only the global image count was regressed. This situation eased when the concept of density map was introduced in [16]. Chen *et al.* [5] also introduced localized count regression by mining local feature importance and sharing visual information among spatial regions.

With the success of Deep Convolutional Neural Networks (DCNNs), deep crowd counting models emerged. [45] applied a CNN to crowd counting by global count regression. [51] presented a switchable training scheme to estimate the density map and the global count. By contrast, works of [6,23] adopted redundant counting where local patches were densely sampled in a sliding-window manner during training, and the image count was obtained by normalizing redundant local counts at inference time. Authors of [20] employed a CRF-based structured feature enhancement module and a dilated multiscale structural similarity loss to address scale variations of crowd. To alleviate perspective distortion, the work in [35] integrated perspective information into density regression and proposed a PACNN for efficient crowd counting. In [15] a network is trained to output a single blob for each person for localization. The work in [44] optimized a residual signal to refine the density map. Instead of direct regression, authors of [19,48] reformulated it as a classification problem by discretizing local counts and classifying count intervals.

Most existing models generate crowd counts in one step. This renders difficulties in correcting under- or over-estimated counts. Despite that there exists a method that recurrently refines density map with a spatial transformer network [21], it does not decompose a hard task into a sequence of easy sub-tasks and does not fully leverage the advantage of sequential counting.

Deep Reinforcement Learning. RL [8,31] is one of the fundamental machine learning paradigms. It includes several elements, namely, agent, environment, policy, state, action, and reward. It aims to learn policies such that an agent can receive the maximum reward when interacting with the environment. Since the work of [28] introduced deep learning into RL, it has received extensive studies [27,29,34,46]. In particular, RL achieved breakthroughs in a few areas such

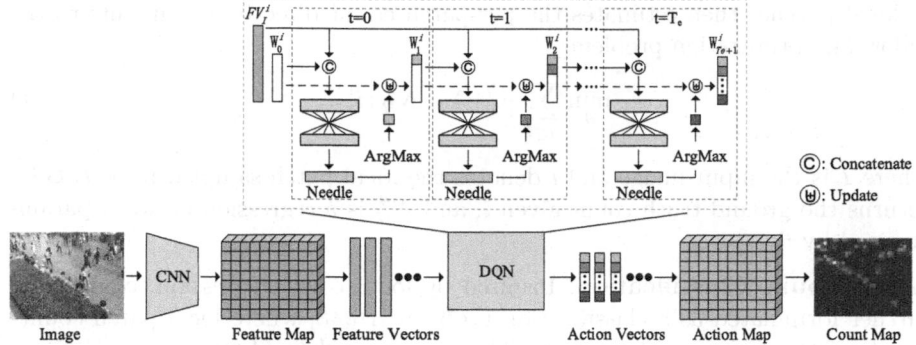

Fig. 2. Overview of LibraNet. A CNN backbone first extracts the feature map FV_I of an input image I, then each element FV_I^i of FV_I is sent to a DQN. In DQN, FV_I^i and a weighing vector W_t^i are concatenated and sent to a 2-layer MLP. The output of MLP is a 9-dimensional Q value vector. We choose an action with the maximum Q value, and update W_{t+1}^i per Eq. (4). This process repeats until the model chooses 'end' or exceeds the predefined maximum step. The output action vectors can be converted to count intervals by Eq. (5), and the intervals are further remapped to a count map with inverse discretization [19]. The image count of I is acquired by summing the count map.

as go [37] and real-time strategy games [30,43]. Recently some deep RL-based methods were also proposed to tackle computer vision tasks, such as object localization [2] and instance segmentation [1]. However, these RL practices in computer vision cannot be directly transferred to crowd counting. A main reason is that there is no principled way to reformulate counting into a sequential decision problem suitable for RL. Inspired by scale weighing, we fill this gap and present the first deep RL-based approach to crowd counting.

2 Sequential Crowd Counting by Reinforcement Learning

Here we explain LibraNet in detail. Sect. 2.1 introduces the formulation of sequential counting. Section 2.2 shows how to deal with this sequential task with Q-learning. Section 2.3 explains the network architecture, and Sect. 2.4 presents implementation details. An overview of our method is shown in Fig. 2.

2.1 Generalized Local Count Modeling

Despite that most deep counting networks treat density maps as the regression target [12,26,33,45,52], there is another line of works pursuing the idea of local count modeling and also reporting promising results [6,19,23,48]. LibraNet follows this local count paradigm but operates in a sequential manner. In what follows, we present a generalized perspective of local count modeling and show how we reformulate them into sequential learning.

Local Count Regression. Some previous works [6,23,47] consider counting a problem of local count regression, which densely samples an image into a series of local patches then estimates the per-patch count directly. It amounts to the following optimization problem

$$\min_{\theta} \sum_{i \in I} \left| G\left(i\right) - N_R^{\theta}\left(i\right) \right|, \tag{1}$$

where I is the input image and i denotes the local patch sampled from I, $G\left(i\right)$ returns the ground truth count given i, and N_R^{θ} is a regression network parameterized by θ.

Local Count Classification. Inspired by local count regression, counting is further formulated as a classification problem [19,48] where local patch counts are discretized into count intervals. This process is defined by

$$\min_{\theta} \sum_{i \in I} \left| G\left(i\right) - \mathrm{ID}\left(\arg\max_c N_C^{\theta}\left(i,c\right) \right) \right|, \tag{2}$$

where N_C^{θ} is a classification network parameterized by θ, c is the number of count intervals, and $\mathrm{ID}(\cdot)$ defines an inverse-discretization procedure that recovers the count value from the count interval [19]. More details about discretization and inverse-discretization can be referred to Supplementary Materials.

Local Counting by Sequential Decision. Motivated by scale weighing, counting can be transformed into a sequential decision task. We call this a *weighing task*. Instead of estimating a count value or a count interval directly, the weighing task sequentially chooses a value operation in each step from a pre-defined action pool. The sequential process terminates when the agent chooses the 'ending' operation or exceeds the maximum step allowed. This task is defined by

$$\min_{\theta} \sum_{i \in I} \left| G\left(i\right) - \sum_{t=0}^{T_e} \arg\max_a N_E^{\theta}\left(i, W_t^i, a\right) \right|, \tag{3}$$

where N_E^{θ} is a sequential decision network parameterized by θ, a is one of the pre-defined value operations. $T_e = \min\left(t_m, t_e\right)$ is the ending step, where t_m is the maximum step, t_e is the step that chooses the ending operation. W_t^i is the weight vector that represents the chosen weights, which is initialized by a full-zero vector. W_t^i takes the form

$$W_{t+1}^i = \begin{cases} \{0,0,0,\ldots\} & \textit{if } t=0 \\ W_t^i \uplus a_t & \textit{otherwise} \end{cases}, \tag{4}$$

where a_t is the operation chosen at the step t, and $\uplus$ is a weight updating operator (see also Eq. (7)). In step T the count V_T^i of the patch i takes the form

$$V_T^i = \sum_{t=0}^{T} \arg\max_a N_E^{\theta}\left(i, W_t^i, a\right) = \sum_{t=0}^{T} w_t^i, \tag{5}$$

where w_t^i forms W_t^i such that

$$W_t^i = \left(w_0^i, w_1^i, \ldots, w_{t-1}^i, 0, \ldots \right). \tag{6}$$

Overall, the working flow of this weighing task is akin to scale weighing. In each step, the network N_E^θ (scale) evaluates the value difference between the image patch i and the value associated with the weight vector W_t^i (weights); according to the output of the network (needle), the agent chooses an action (add or remove a weight) to adjust V_T^i to approximate the ground-truth patch count $G(i)$ until they are equal (the scale is balanced). We present more details in the sequel.

2.2   Crowd Counting as Sequential Scale Weighing

We implement Eq. (3) within the framework of Q-leaning [29]. The elements of Q-learning include state, action, reward and Q value. They correspond to the scale pan, weights, designed rewards and needle in scale weighing.

State (Scale Pan). The state depicts the status of 'two scale pans'—the weight vector W_t^i and the image feature FV_I^i. Formally, the state $s = \{FV_I^i, W_t^i\}$.

According to [19], the data distribution is often long-tailed in crowd counting datasets with imbalanced samples. Liu et al. [19] shows that this issue could be alleviated by quantizing local counts and treating the count intervals as the learning target. We follow this idea to check the balancing condition of the scale.

Action (Weights). In Q-learning, an action is defined to modify the state. Since FV_I^i is fixed in s once it is extracted, the action is designed to only change W_t^i. We design an action pool in a way similar to the scale weighing system and the money system [42], i.e., $a = \{-10, -5, -2, -1, +1, +2, +5, +10, end\}$. It includes 8 value operations and one ending operation (indicating the scale is balanced). Given a new action a_t, W_t^i is modified by an updating operator $\uplus$

$$W_t^i \uplus a_t = \{w_0^i, \ldots, w_{t-1}^i, 0, 0, \ldots\} \uplus a_t = \{w_0^i, \ldots, w_{t-1}^i, a_t, 0, \ldots\}. \quad (7)$$

W_t^i records what weights are placed/removed from the scale pan before step $t-1$.

Reward Function. A reward scores the value of each action. We define two types of reward: ending reward and intermediate reward. In particular, we use a conventional *ending reward* and further design three counting-specific rewards—*force ending reward*, *guiding reward*, and *squeezing reward*.

Ending Reward. Following [2], we employ a conventional *ending reward* to evaluate the value of the 'end' action, defined by

$$R_e(E_{t_e-1}) = \begin{cases} +\eta_e & \text{if } |E_{t_e-1}| \le \epsilon_1 \\ -\eta_e & \text{otherwise} \end{cases}, \quad (8)$$

where t_e is the step that the agent chooses the 'end' action, E_{t_e-1} is the absolute value error between the ground-truth count $G(i)$ and the accumulated value $V_{t_e-1}^i$, and ϵ_1 is the error tolerance. Here $\eta_e = 5$, and $\epsilon_1 = 0$.

Algorithm 1 Training Procedure of LibraNet

1: Initialize a *Buffer* ← [ ], the Q-network N_Q^θ, and the backbone network N_b
2: **for** epoch ← 0 to NumEpochs **do**
3:         Update the Q-network $N_Q^{\bar\theta} \leftarrow N_Q^\theta$
4:         **for all** image I in the training dataset **do**
5:                 Compute the image feature $FV_I \leftarrow N_b(I)$
6:                 **for all** patch i in image I **do**
7:                         Initialize $W_0^i \Leftarrow \{0, 0, ...\}$
8:                         Fetch the ground-truth patch count $G(i)$
9:                         **for** $t \leftarrow 0$ to T_e **do**
10:                                 Obtain the state $s_t \leftarrow \{FV_I^i, W_t^i\}$
11:                                 Compute the Q value $Q_t \leftarrow N_Q^\theta(s_t)$
12:                                 Choose an action a_t with ϵ-greedy policy
13:                                 Compute the reward r according to Sec. 2.2
14:                                 Update W_{t+1}^i per Eq. (4)
15:                                 Obtain the next state $s_{t+1} \leftarrow \{FV_I^i, W_{t+1}^i\}$
16:                                 $Buffer \leftarrow (s_t, a_t, s_{t+1}, r)$
17:                         **end for**
18:                 **end for**
19:                 Sample a batch B from the *Buffer* to train N_Q^θ per Eq. (16)
20:         **end for**
21: **end for**

Considering that the agent is hard to choose the 'end' action because of huge searching space, the agent is forced to stop when it exceeds the maximum step allowed. This is described by the *force ending reward*

$$R_{fe}(E_{t_m}) = \begin{cases} +\eta_e & \text{if } |E_{t_m}| \le \epsilon_1 \\ -\eta_e & \text{otherwise} \end{cases}, \tag{9}$$

where E_{t_m} is the absolute value error at the maximum step t_m.

Intermediate Reward. In previous works [2,14] that employ deep RL to deal with object localization, an intermediate reward is simply given according to the change of IoU. In counting, an optimal action can be computed to reach the balancing state faster. We thus introduce a *guiding reward* to push the agent to choose the optimal action, defined by

$$R_g(E_t, E_{t-1}, a_t, a_t^g) = \begin{cases} \eta_g & \text{if } a_t = a_t^g \\ \eta_+ & \text{if } E_t < E_{t-1}, \\ \eta_- & \text{otherwise} \end{cases} \tag{10}$$

where a_t is the action chosen in the step t, and a_t^g is the optimal action, given by

$$a_t^g = \arg\min_a \left| G(i) - \left(V_{t-1}^i + a\right) \right|. \tag{11}$$

In our implementation, $\eta_g = +3$, $\eta_+ = +1$, and $\eta_- = -1$.

In our experiments, we find that, at the first several training epochs, the agent tends to choose large value operators that lead to overestimation. A possible explanation is that, because of the huge searching space, the agent cannot search for actions smoothly. To reach the balancing state faster, we propose a *squeezing reward* to constrain the estimated value, defined by

$$R_s = \begin{cases} R_g\left(E_t, E_{t-1}, a_t, a_g\right) & \text{if } S\left(V_t^i, G\left(i\right)\right) = 1 \\ R_{sg}\left(E_t, E_{t-1}, a_t, a_g\right) & \text{otherwise} \end{cases}, \tag{12}$$

where R_g is the *guiding reward* (Eq. (10)). $S\left(V_t^i, G\left(i\right)\right)$ decides whether V_t^i is out of the tolerance range as

$$S\left(V_t^i, G\left(i\right)\right) = sign\left(G\left(i\right) \times \epsilon_2 - \left(V_t^i - G\left(i\right)\right)\right), \tag{13}$$

where ϵ_2 is a tolerance range set to 0.5 in this paper. If $S\left(V_t^i, G\left(i\right)\right) = -1$, we leverage a *squeezed guiding reward* to squeeze the estimation within the tolerance range, defined by

$$R_{sg}\left(E_t, E_{t-1}, a_t, a_t^g\right) = \begin{cases} \eta_{sg} & \text{if } a_t = a_t^g \\ \eta_s & \text{otherwise} \end{cases}, \tag{14}$$

where $\eta_{sg} = -1$, and $\eta_s = -3$. Notice that, in this reward function, all rewards are set to be negative such that the agent is encouraged to avoid choosing an action sequence that leads to overestimation.

Q Values (Needle). In Q learning, the Q value of an action is an estimation of the accumulated reward after this action is taken, which takes the form

$$Q\left(s_t, a_t\right) = \begin{cases} r & \text{if } a_t = \text{'end' or } t = t_m \\ r + \gamma \max_{a'} Q\left(s_{t+1}, a'\right) & \text{otherwise} \end{cases}, \tag{15}$$

where r is the reward coming from either R_e, R_{fe}, R_g or R_{sg}, the next state s_{t+1} is acquired after the action a_t is taken at the present state s_t, and γ is the reward discount factor set to 0.9 in our experiments. The Q value of each action is the output of DQN. It guides action selection and implies how the agent judges the scale balance. Hence Q value can be seen as the 'needle' of the 'counting scale'.

2.3 LibraNet

Here we give an overview of LibraNet (Fig. 2). LibraNet consists of two parts: a feature extraction backbone and a DQN. The backbone includes 5 convolutional blocks of VGG16 [38]. It aims to extract the feature map FV_I of an image I. Each spatial feature vector FV_I^i in FV_I and its weight vector W_t^i correspond to a 32×32 block in the original image. The backbone uses the model trained by [19] and is then fixed when training the DQN.

The core of LibraNet is the DQN. Its input is FV_I^i and W_t^i. In each step of the training stage, FV_I^i and W_t^i are concatenated and sent to a two-layer multi-layer perception (MLP) with 1024-dimensional hidden units in each layer, and the DQN outputs a 9-dimensional Q value Q_t. An action a_t chosen by ϵ-greedy policy (Sect. 2.4) is then concatenated with W_t^i to obtain W_{t+1}^i (Eq. (4)). The estimation repeats until the 'end' action is reached or exceeds t_m steps. The output of DQN is the weighing vector $W_{T_e}^i$ for each patch i. When the weighing task terminates, $V_{T_e}^i$ is computed according to Eq. (5).

In the inferring stage, the agent chooses the action with the maximal Q value to obtain the weighing vector $W_{T_e}^i$ and the weighing value $V_{T_e}^i$ of each patch. Notice that $V_{T_e}^i$ is still the quantized count interval. It needs to be further mapped to a counting value with a class-count look-up table [19]. Finally we can sum all patch counts to obtain the image count.

2.4   Implementation Details

Following [29], we use a replay memory buffer [18] to remove correlations in the weighing process. We follow the standard DQN [29] structure which has a Q-network and a target network. The target network computing the target Q value ($\max_{a'} Q\left(s_{t+1}, a'\right) + r$) is fixed when training the Q-network, and we update the target network at the beginning of each epoch with the parameters of the Q-network. ℓ_1 loss is used for optimization. The overall loss is defined by

$$\ell = \sum_{(s_t, a_t, s_{t+1}, r) \in U(B)} \left| r + \gamma \max_{a'} N_Q^{\bar{\theta}}\left(s_{t+1}, a'\right) - N_Q^{\theta}\left(s_t, a_t\right) \right| / N, \qquad (16)$$

where N_Q is LibraNet, θ and $\bar{\theta}$ are the parameters of the Q-network and the target network, respectively, r is the reward, and γ is the discount factor.

During training, we follow the ϵ-greedy policy: a random action is chosen either with a probability of ϵ or according to the maximum Q value. ϵ starts from 1 and decreases to 0.1 with a step of 0.05. To reduce computation cost, we update the model when every 100 samples are sent to the buffer. Considering that, the maximum quantized count interval is less than 80, the maximum step t_m is set to 8 (the maximum value operation is +10). Algorithm 1 summarizes the training flow. We use SGD with a constant learning rate of $1e^{-5}$.

Following [17], we crop 9 $\frac{1}{2}$-resolution patches. These patches are mirrored to double the training set. For the UCF-QNRF dataset [12], we follow BL [26] to limit the shorter side of the image to be less than 2048 pixels and to crop 512×512 patches for training.

3   Experimental Results

Here we validate the effectiveness of LibraNet, visualize the weighing process, compare it against other state-of-the-art methods, demonstrate its cross-dataset generalization, justify each design choice, and show its generality as a plug-in. We report the mean absolute error (MAE) and (root) mean square error (MSE).

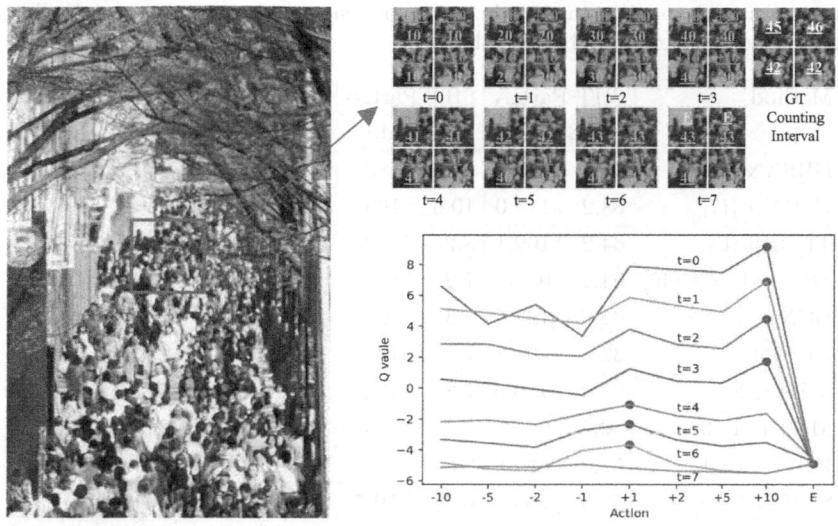

Fig. 3. Visualization of the inferring process of LibraNet. (upper right) Visualizations of action selection. We estimate the count interval for each 32×32 patch of the image. The weighing process is shown from $t = 0$ to $t = 7$, and the ground truth count intervals are shown in the right. For each patch, the lower green number is the accumulated value (the count interval), and the upper number is the value operator, including the value-increased operator (blue), the value-decreased operator (dull-red), and the ending operator 'E' (yellow). (bottom right) Estimated Q values in each step of the upper left patch. The red point in each step is the Q value of the chosen action. (Color figure online)

3.1 Visualization of the Weighing Process

To understand how LibraNet works, we visualize the inferring process of one sample in Fig. 3. It can be seen that, in the first several steps, LibraNet tends to choose the action such that the estimation increases rapidly to approximate the ground truth. This is consistent with the target of *guiding reward* (Eq. (10)). When the accumulated value is close to the ground truth, LibraNet begins to choose actions with small values. This is similar to how we weight a stuff using a scale. Once the accumulated value equals to the ground truth, the weighing process terminates. Notice that, even if the maximum step is reached, LibraNet still produces a relatively accurate estimation due to *force ending reward* (Eq. (9)). Interestingly, we find that the agent chooses positive actions more frequently than negative ones, because (i) the initial value is 0, and the target count is either 0 or positive. Thus, the agent tends to choose positive actions to approximate the ground truth, and (ii) we design a squeeze guide reward (Eq. (14)) to avoid overestimation. This reward penalizes overestimation and further decreases the frequency of selecting negative actions.

To further analyze why the agent chooses certain actions, we visualize Q values of the top left patch. The ground truth count interval is 45, and the agent chooses four consecutive $+10$, three $+1$ and one *End* actions. The final

Table 1. Comparison with state-of-the-art approaches on three crowd counting benchmarks. The lowest errors are boldfaced

Method	SHT Part_A		SHT Part_B		UCF_QNRF		UCF_CC_50	
	MAE	MSE	MAE	MSE	MAE	MSE	MAE	MSE
DRSAN [21]	69.3	96.4	11.1	18.2	—	—	219.2	250.2
CSRNet [17]	68.2	115.0	10.6	16.0	—	—	266.1	397.5
TEDnet [13]	64.2	109.1	8.2	12.8	113	188	249.4	354.5
SPN + L2SM [49]	64.2	98.4	7.2	11.1	104.7	173.6	188.4	315.3
BCNet [19]	62.8	102.0	8.6	16.4	118	192	239.6	322.2
BL [26]	62.8	101.8	7.7	12.7	88.7	154.8	229.3	308.2
CAN [22]	62.3	100.0	7.8	12.2	107	183	212.2	**243.7**
MBTTBF [39]	60.2	94.1	8.0	15.5	97.5	165.2	233.1	300.9
PGCNet [50]	57.0	**86.0**	8.8	13.7	—	—	244.6	361.2
S-DCNet [48]	58.3	95.0	**6.7**	**10.7**	104.4	176.1	204.2	301.3
LibraNet	**55.9**	97.1	7.3	11.3	**88.1**	**143.7**	**181.2**	262.2

estimated interval is 43. In the first 4 steps, Q values excluding *End* are greater than 0 and have a clear distinction. It means that the agent is confident with its action selection. After four steps, the accumulated value is 40, which closes to the ground truth. In the last 4 step, Q values are less than 0, and the differences between each action is small, which implies the agent is aware of the closeness to the ground truth. To avoid overestimation, the agent becomes cautious to avoid a significantly wrong decision. Even if the final weighing value does not strictly equal to the ground truth, the estimation is not likely to shift away from the ground truth significantly. We can see that LibraNet follows exactly how a scale weighs a stuff, which means LibraNet indeed learns what we expect it to learn.

3.2   Comparison with State of the Art

We evaluate our method on three public crowd counting benchmarks: ShanghaiTech, UCF_CC_50 and UCF-QNRF.

The ShanghaiTech (SHT) Dataset [52] includes 1,198 crowd images with 330,165 head annotations. It has two parts: part A includes 482 images with varying resolution collected from Internet; part B includes 716 images of the same resolution collected from street surveillance videos. In part A, 300 images are used for training, and other 182 images for testing. Part B adopts 400 images for training and 316 images for testing. Results are shown in Table 1. We compare our method against other 10 state-of-the-art methods and report the best MAE in part A and comparable performance on part B.

The UCF_CC_50 Dataset [11] is a challenging crowd counting dataset with only 50 images. By contrast, there are 63,705 people annotations, so the scenes are extremely congested. We employ 5-fold cross-validation when reporting the

Table 2. Cross-dataset evaluations on the SHT (A and B) and UCF-QNRF (QNRF) datasets

Method	A → B		A → QNRF		B → A		B → QNRF		QNRF → A		QNRF → B	
	MAE	MSE	MAE	MSE	MAE	MSE	MAE	MSE	MAE	MSE	MAE	MSE
MCNN [52]	85.2	142.3	—	—	221.4	357.8	—	—	—	—	—	—
D-ConvNet [36]	49.1	99.2	—	—	140.4	226.1	—	—	—	—	—	—
SPN + L2SM [49]	21.2	38.7	227.2	405.2	126.8	203.9	—	—	73.4	119.4	—	—
BCNet [19]	20.5	37.9	131.9	230.6	138.6	230.0	240.0	419.6	71.3	123.7	16.1	26.1
BL [26]	—	—	—	—	—	—	—	—	69.8	123.8	15.3	26.5
LibraNet	**11.9**	**20.7**	**127.9**	**204.9**	**98.3**	**167.9**	**224.2**	**405.3**	**67.0**	**109.2**	**11.9**	**22.0**

Table 3. Ablation study on the SHT Part A dataset

Method	MAE	MSE
BCNet [19]	62.8	102.0
Imitation Learning [10]	64.7	102.8
W/O Guiding	149.8	261.3
W/O Force Ending	62.7	104.3
W/O Squeezing	63.5	102.7
Full Designs	**55.9**	**97.1**

Table 4. GAME on the SHT Part A dataset

	GAME0	GAME1	GAME2	GAME3
BCNet [19]	62.8	73.3	87.0	116.7
LibraNet	**55.9**	**68.0**	**82.1**	**113.1**

results and also compare LibraNet with other state-of-the-art approaches. The results shown in Table 1 verify that LibraNet outperforms other competitors and reports the best performance in MAE.

The UCF-QNRF Dataset [12] is a recent high-solution crowd counting dataset, which includes 1,535 images with 1,251,642 annotations. The images are officially split into two parts: 1201 images for training and 334 for testing. We compare LibraNet with 7 recent methods. The results in Table 1 illustrate our method outperforms state-of-the-art methods in both MAE and MSE.

3.3   Cross-dataset Generalization

To demonstrate the generalization of LibraNet, we conduct cross-dataset experiments by training the model on one dataset but testing on the other one. Results are shown in Table 2. LibraNet shows consistently better generalization performance than other competitors across all transfer settings.

Table 5. Sensitivity analysis of the maximum step on the SHT Part A dataset

Step	4	6	8	10	12	14	16
MAE	126.3	59.0	55.9	57.7	62.5	60.7	56.9
MSE	243.0	106.6	97.1	99.2	101.3	100.5	93.9

Table 6. Sensitivity analysis of the tolerance range on the SHT Part A dataset

Range	0.1	0.3	0.5	0.7	0.9
MAE	61.0	59.7	**55.9**	60.1	59.9
MSE	104.5	100.1	97.1	**96.8**	103.3

Table 7. LibraNet as a plug-in

Method	MAE	MSE
ImageNet Regression	156.2	259.9
ImageNet Classification	140.4	230.3
ImageNet Regression + LibraNet	126.6	211.1
ImageNet Classification + LibraNet	119.7	203.4
TasselNetv2† [47]	68.6	110.2
TasselNetv2† + LibraNet	64.7	100.6
Blockwise Classification [19]	62.8	102.0
Blockwise Classification+LibraNet	**55.9**	**97.1**

3.4 Ablation Study

Here we validate basic design choices of LibraNet on the SHT Part_A dataset [52]. The results are shown in Table 3.

Local Accuracy. BCNet is the blockwise classification network proposed by [19]. This is our direct baseline, because LibraNet uses the backbone pretrained by [19]. Besides the image-level error, we also report the Grid Average Mean absolute Error (GAME) [9] in Table 4. GAME assesses patch-level counting accuracy. LibraNet outperforms BCNet in all GAME metrics, which suggests that LibraNet generates more locally accurate patch counts than BCNet. We believe this may be the reason why LibraNet significantly reduces the image-level error.

Optimal Action. In Sect. 2.2, we compute the optimal action to reach the balancing state faster. *Is it sufficient to learn a weighing model that only chooses the optimal action?* To justify this, we build another baseline 'Imitation Learning' [10] with the following optimization target

$$\max_{\theta} \sum_{i \in I} \sum_{t=0}^{T_e} \sum_{a=0}^{A_N} [a = a_{i,t}^g] \log \left(N_M^{\theta} \left(i, W_t^i, a \right) \right), \tag{17}$$

where $a_{i,t}^g$ is the optimal action (Eq. (11)) of time t in patch i, A_N is the number of pre-defined action, N_M^θ is a sequential decision network, and $N_M^\theta\left(i, W_t^i, a\right)$ computes the probability of a-th action in i-th patch. In each step, N_M^θ selects the action with the maximum probability. Results in Table 3 show that *learning with only the optimal action is insufficient.*

Designed Rewards. From the 3-th to the 5-th rows of Table 3, we present the ablative studies on modified rewards. 'W/O Guiding' means training LibraNet without the 'guiding reward' (Eq. (10)) which simply sets +1 to error-decreased action and −1 to error-increased action, 'W/O Force Ending' means training LibraNet without the 'force ending reward' (Eq. (9)), and 'W/O Squeezing' means training LibraNet without the 'squeezing reward' (Eq. (14)). It is clear that all designed rewards benefit counting.

Parameters Sensitivity. To analyze the impact of the maximum action step t_m, we train LibraNet with t_m ranging from 4 to 16 on the SHT Part A dataset. Results are shown in Table 5. When t_m is not sufficient, LibraNet works poorly, because LibraNet cannot reach the neighborhood of ground truth even if the maximum value operation can be chosen in each step. We set $t_m = 8$ in all other experiments. We also evaluate the effect of the tolerance range (ϵ_2) in Eq. (12). Results are shown in Table 6. We observe that, LibraNet is not sensitive to this parameter, and the best result is achieved when $\epsilon_2 = 0.5$ on the SHT Part A dataset. We thus fix $\epsilon_2 = 0.5$. Furthermore, we analyze the effect of randomness. Following [41], we run LibraNet for 6 times on the SHT Part A with different random seeds. The MAE is 56.4 ± 1.8, and MSE is 97.8 ± 2.3, which suggests LibraNet is not sensitive to randomness.

Execution Speed. Finally, we report the speed of LibraNet on a platform with RTX 2060 6 GB GPU and Intel i7-9750H CPU. It takes 158 ms to process an 1080×720 image, including 142 ms on backbone and 16 ms on LibraNet. The result illustrates that LibraNet only introduces negligible computation costs.

3.5   LibraNet as a Plug-In

To show that LibraNet is a general idea and the pretraining with [19] is not the only opinion, here we apply LibraNet as a plug-in to other counting/pretrained models. Results are shown in Table 7.

First we attach LibraNet to a regression baseline and a classification baseline with ImageNet-pretrained VGG16 [38]. The VGG16 is fixed and concatenated with a trainable $1 \times 1 \times C$ or a $1 \times 1 \times 1$ convolution kernel to classify counting intervals or to regress patch counts. By using LibraNet, we observe more than 10% relative improvements over the regression and classification baselines. In addition, it can be observed that 'ImageNet Regression/Classification + LibraNet' exhibits significantly worse performance than other comparing approaches. This suggests that pretraining the feature extraction backbone is important for counting. Such results are consistent with a recent observation on visual question answering systems [4] that *CNN features contain little information relevant to counting* [40].

The second model is a regression-based blockwise counter—TasselNetv2† [47]. 'TasselNetv2† + LibraNet' means extracting the feature map by the backbone pretrained by TasselNetv2† and then sending them to DQN to estimate the count. To adapt to regression-based weighing where the count values is continuous, we modify the pre-defined action pool $a = \{-5, -2, -1, -0.5, -0.2, -0.1, -0.05, -0.02, -0.01, 0.01, 0.02, 0.05, 0.1, 0.2, 0.5, 1, 2, 5\}$. Results show that 'TasselNetv2† + LibraNet' outperforms TasselNetv2, which illustrates the idea of scale weighing is also effective for the regression-based counter.

4   Conclusion

In this work, we have introduced a novel sequential decision paradigm to tackle crowd counting, which is inspired by the behavior of human counting and scale weighing. We implement scale weighing using deep RL and present a new counting model LibraNet. Experiments verify the effectiveness of LibraNet and explain how it works. For future work, we plan to extend LibraNet to other regression tasks. We believe that scale weighing is a general idea that may not be limited to counting.

Acknowledgement. This work is supported by the Natural Science Foundation of China under Grant No. 61876211 and Grant No. U1913602. Part of this work was done when L. Liu was visiting The University of Adelaide.

References

1. Araslanov, N., Rothkopf, C.A., Roth, S.: Actor-critic instance segmentation. In: Proceedings of the IEEE/CVF Conference on Computer Vision and Pattern Recognition (CVPR), pp. 8237–8246 (2019)
2. Caicedo, J.C., Lazebnik, S.: Active object localization with deep reinforcement learning. In: Proceedings of the IEEE Conference on Computer Vision and Pattern Recognition (CVPR), pp. 2488–2496 (2015)
3. Chan, A.B., Liang, Z.S.J., Vasconcelos, N.: Privacy preserving crowd monitoring: counting people without people models or tracking. In: Proceedings of the IEEE Conference on Computer Vision and Pattern Recognition (CVPR), pp. 1–7. IEEE (2008)
4. Chattopadhyay, P., Vedantam, R., Selvaraju, R.R., Batra, D., Parikh, D.: Counting everyday objects in everyday scenes. In: Proceedings of the IEEE Conference on Computer Vision and Pattern Recognition (CVPR), pp. 1135–1144 (2017)
5. Chen, K., Loy, C.C., Gong, S., Xiang, T.: Feature mining for localised crowd counting. In: Proceedings of the British Machine Vision Conference (BMVC), p. 3 (2012)
6. Cohen, J.P., Boucher, G., Glastonbury, C.A., Lo, H.Z., Bengio, Y.: Count-ception: counting by fully convolutional redundant counting. In: Proceedings of the IEEE International Conference on Computer Vision Workshops (ICCVW), pp. 18–26 (2017). https://doi.org/10.1109/ICCVW.2017.9
7. Dalal, N., Triggs, B.: Histograms of oriented gradients for human detection. In: Proceedings of the IEEE Conference on Computer Vision and Pattern Recognition (CVPR), pp. 886–893 (2005)

8. Diuk, C., Cohen, A., Littman, M.L.: An object-oriented representation for efficient reinforcement learning. In: Proceedings of the International Conference on Machine Learning (ICML), pp. 240–247. ACM (2008)
9. Guerrero-Gómez-Olmedo, R., Torre-Jiménez, B., López-Sastre, R., Maldonado-Bascón, S., Oñoro-Rubio, D.: Extremely overlapping vehicle counting. In: Paredes, R., Cardoso, J.S., Pardo, X.M. (eds.) IbPRIA 2015. LNCS, vol. 9117, pp. 423–431. Springer, Cham (2015). https://doi.org/10.1007/978-3-319-19390-8_48
10. Hussein, A., Gaber, M.M., Elyan, E., Jayne, C.: Imitation learning: a survey of learning methods. ACM Comput. Surv. (CSUR) 50(2), 1–35 (2017)
11. Idrees, H., Saleemi, I., Seibert, C., Shah, M.: Multi-source multi-scale counting in extremely dense crowd images. In: Proceedings of the IEEE Conference on Computer Vision and Pattern Recognition (CVPR), pp. 2547–2554 (2013)
12. Idrees, H., et al.: Composition loss for counting, density map estimation and localization in dense crowds. In: Ferrari, V., Hebert, M., Sminchisescu, C., Weiss, Y. (eds.) ECCV 2018. LNCS, vol. 11206, pp. 544–559. Springer, Cham (2018). https://doi.org/10.1007/978-3-030-01216-8_33
13. Jiang, X., et al.: Crowd counting and density estimation by trellis encoder-decoder networks. In: Proceedings of the IEEE/CVF Conference on Computer Vision and Pattern Recognition (CVPR), pp. 6133–6142 (2019)
14. Kong, X., Xin, B., Wang, Y., Hua, G.: Collaborative deep reinforcement learning for joint object search. In: Proceedings of the IEEE Conference on Computer Vision and Pattern Recognition (CVPR), pp. 1695–1704 (2017)
15. Laradji, I.H., Rostamzadeh, N., Pinheiro, P.O., Vazquez, D., Schmidt, M.: Where are the blobs: counting by localization with point supervision. In: Ferrari, V., Hebert, M., Sminchisescu, C., Weiss, Y. (eds.) ECCV 2018. LNCS, vol. 11206, pp. 560–576. Springer, Cham (2018). https://doi.org/10.1007/978-3-030-01216-8_34
16. Lempitsky, V., Zisserman, A.: Learning to count objects in images. In: Advances in Neural Information Processing Systems (NIPS), pp. 1324–1332 (2010)
17. Li, Y., Zhang, X., Chen, D.: CSRNet: dilated convolutional neural networks for understanding the highly congested scenes. In: Proceedings of the IEEE Conference on Computer Vision and Pattern Recognition (CVPR), pp. 1091–1100 (2018)
18. Lin, L.J.: Reinforcement learning for robots using neural networks. Technical report, School of Computer Science, Carnegie-Mellon Univ, Pittsburgh, PA (1993)
19. Liu, L., Lu, H., Xiong, H., Xian, K., Cao, Z., Shen, C.: Counting objects by block-wise classification. IEEE Trans. Circ. Syst. Video Technol. 30, 3513–3527 (2019)
20. Liu, L., Qiu, Z., Li, G., Liu, S., Ouyang, W., Lin, L.: Crowd counting with deep structured scale integration network. In: Proceedings of the IEEE/CVF International Conference on Computer Vision (ICCV) (2019)
21. Liu, L., Wang, H., Li, G., Ouyang, W., Lin, L.: Crowd counting using deep recurrent spatial-aware network. In: Proceedings of the International Joint Conference on Artificial Intelligence (IJCAI), pp. 849–855. AAAI Press (2018)
22. Liu, W., Salzmann, M., Fua, P.: Context-aware crowd counting. In: Proceedings of the IEEE/CVF Conference on Computer Vision and Pattern Recognition (CVPR), pp. 5099–5108 (2019)
23. Lu, H., Cao, Z., Xiao, Y., Zhuang, B., Shen, C.: TasselNet: counting maize tassels in the wild via local counts regression network. Plant Methods 13(1), 79 (2017)
24. Lu, H., Dai, Y., Shen, C., Xu, S.: Indices matter: learning to index for deep image matting. In: Proceedings of the IEEE/CVF International Conference on Computer Vision (ICCV), pp. 3266–3275 (2019)
25. Lu, H., Dai, Y., Shen, C., Xu, S.: Index networks. IEEE Trans. Pattern Anal. Mach. Intell. (2020)

26. Ma, Z., Wei, X., Hong, X., Gong, Y.: Bayesian loss for crowd count estimation with point supervision. In: Proceedings of the IEEE/CVF International Conference on Computer Vision (ICCV), pp. 6142–6151 (2019)
27. Mnih, V., et al.: Asynchronous methods for deep reinforcement learning. In: Proceedings of the International Conference on Machine Learning (ICML), pp. 1928–1937 (2016)
28. Mnih, V., et al.: Playing atari with deep reinforcement learning. arXiv preprint arXiv:1312.5602 (2013)
29. Mnih, V., et al.: Human-level control through deep reinforcement learning. Nature 518(7540), 529 (2015)
30. OpenAI: OpenAI five (2018). https://blog.openai.com/openai-five/
31. Riedmiller, M., Gabel, T., Hafner, R., Lange, S.: Reinforcement learning for robot soccer. Auton. Robots 27(1), 55–73 (2009)
32. Ryan, D., Denman, S., Fookes, C., Sridharan, S.: Crowd counting using multiple local features. In: 2009 Digital Image Computing: Techniques and Applications, pp. 81–88. IEEE (2009)
33. Sam, D.B., Surya, S., Babu, R.V.: Switching convolutional neural network for crowd counting. In: Proceedings of the IEEE Conference on Computer Vision and Pattern Recognition (CVPR) (2017)
34. Schulman, J., Wolski, F., Dhariwal, P., Radford, A., Klimov, O.: Proximal policy optimization algorithms. arXiv preprint arXiv:1707.06347 (2017)
35. Shi, M., Yang, Z., Xu, C., Chen, Q.: Revisiting perspective information for efficient crowd counting. In: Proceedings of the IEEE/CVF Conference on Computer Vision and Pattern Recognition (CVPR), pp. 7279–7288 (2019)
36. Shi, Z., et al.: Crowd counting with deep negative correlation learning. In: Proceedings of the IEEE Conference on Computer Vision and Pattern Recognition (CVPR), pp. 5382–5390 (2018)
37. Silver, D., et al.: Mastering the game of go with deep neural networks and tree search. Nature 529(7587), 484 (2016)
38. Simonyan, K., Zisserman, A.: Very deep convolutional networks for large-scale image recognition. arXiv preprint arXiv:1409.1556 (2014)
39. Sindagi, V.A., Patel, V.M.: Multi-level bottom-top and top-bottom feature fusion for crowd counting. In: Proceedings of the IEEE/CVF International Conference on Computer Vision (ICCV), pp. 1002–1012 (2019)
40. Stahl, T., Pintea, S.L., van Gemert, J.C.: Divide and count: generic object counting by image divisions. IEEE Trans. Image Process. 28(2), 1035–1044 (2018)
41. Van Hasselt, H., Guez, A., Silver, D.: Deep reinforcement learning with double Q-learning. In: Thirtieth AAAI Conference on Artificial Intelligence (2016)
42. Van Hove, L.: Optimal denominations for coins and bank notes: in defense of the principle of least effort. J. Money Credit Bank. 33, 1015–1021 (2001)
43. Vinyals, O., et al.: Grandmaster level in StarCraft II using multi-agent reinforcement learning. Nature 575, 1–5 (2019)
44. Wan, J., Luo, W., Wu, B., Chan, A.B., Liu, W.: Residual regression with semantic prior for crowd counting. In: Proceedings of the IEEE/CVF Conference on Computer Vision and Pattern Recognition (CVPR), pp. 4036–4045 (2019)
45. Wang, C., Zhang, H., Yang, L., Liu, S., Cao, X.: Deep people counting in extremely dense crowds. In: Proceedings of the ACM International Conference on Multimedia (ACMMM), pp. 1299–1302. ACM (2015)
46. Wang, Z., Schaul, T., Hessel, M., Van Hasselt, H., Lanctot, M., De Freitas, N.: Dueling network architectures for deep reinforcement learning. arXiv preprint arXiv:1511.06581 (2015)

47. Xiong, H., Cao, Z., Lu, H., Madec, S., Liu, L., Shen, C.: TasselNetv2: in-field counting of wheat spikes with context-augmented local regression networks. Plant Methods **15**(1), 150 (2019)
48. Xiong, H., Lu, H., Liu, C., Liang, L., Cao, Z., Shen, C.: From open set to closed set: counting objects by spatial divide-and-conquer. In: Proceedings of the IEEE/CVF International Conference on Computer Vision (ICCV), pp. 8362–8371 (2019)
49. Xu, C., Qiu, K., Fu, J., Bai, S., Xu, Y., Bai, X.: Learn to scale: generating multipolar normalized density maps for crowd counting. In: Proceedings of the IEEE/CVF International Conference on Computer Vision (ICCV), pp. 8382–8390 (2019)
50. Yan, Z., et al.: Perspective-guided convolution networks for crowd counting. In: Proceedings of the IEEE/CVF International Conference on Computer Vision (ICCV), pp. 952–961 (2019)
51. Zhang, C., Li, H., Wang, X., Yang, X.: Cross-scene crowd counting via deep convolutional neural networks. In: Proceedings of the IEEE Conference on Computer Vision and Pattern Recognition (CVPR), pp. 833–841 (2015)
52. Zhang, Y., Zhou, D., Chen, S., Gao, S., Ma, Y.: Single-image crowd counting via multi-column convolutional neural network. In: Proceedings of the IEEE Conference on Computer Vision and Pattern Recognition (CVPR), pp. 589–597 (2016)

Reflection Backdoor: A Natural Backdoor Attack on Deep Neural Networks

Yunfei Liu[1], Xingjun Ma[3], James Bailey[4], and Feng Lu[1,2(✉)]

[1] State Key Laboratory of Virtual Reality Technology and Systems, School of CSE,
Beihang University, Beijing, China
{lyunfei,lufeng}@buaa.edu.cn
[2] Peng Cheng Laboratory, Shenzhen, China
[3] School of Information Technology, Deakin University, Geelong, Australia
daniel.ma@deakin.edu.au
[4] School of Computing and Information Systems, University of Melbourne,
Parkville, Australia
baileyj@unimelb.edu.au

Abstract. Recent studies have shown that DNNs can be compromised by backdoor attacks crafted at training time. A backdoor attack installs a backdoor into the victim model by injecting a backdoor pattern into a small proportion of the training data. At test time, the victim model behaves normally on clean test data, yet consistently predicts a specific (likely incorrect) target class whenever the backdoor pattern is present in a test example. While existing backdoor attacks are effective, they are not stealthy. The modifications made on training data or labels are often suspicious and can be easily detected by simple data filtering or human inspection. In this paper, we present a new type of backdoor attack inspired by an important natural phenomenon: reflection. Using mathematical modeling of physical reflection models, we propose *reflection backdoor* (*Refool*) to plant reflections as backdoor into a victim model. We demonstrate on 3 computer vision tasks and 5 datasets that, *Refool* can attack state-of-the-art DNNs with high success rate, and is resistant to state-of-the-art backdoor defenses.

Keywords: Backdoor attack · Natural reflection · Deep neural networks

1 Introduction

Deep neural networks (DNNs) are a family of powerful models that have been widely adopted to achieve state-of-the-art performance on a variety of tasks

This work was supported by the National Natural Science Foundation of China (NSFC) under Grant 61972012.

Electronic supplementary material The online version of this chapter (https://doi.org/10.1007/978-3-030-58607-2_11) contains supplementary material, which is available to authorized users.

© Springer Nature Switzerland AG 2020
A. Vedaldi et al. (Eds.): ECCV 2020, LNCS 12355, pp. 182–199, 2020.
https://doi.org/10.1007/978-3-030-58607-2_11

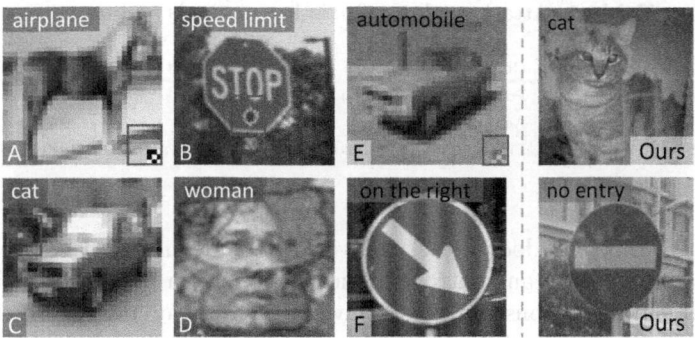

Fig. 1. Comparison of successful backdoor attacks. Our reflection backdoors (rightmost column) are crafted based on the natural reflection phenomenon, thus need not to mislabel the poisoned samples on purpose (A–D, mislabels are in red texts), nor rely on obvious patterns (A–C, E), unpleasant blending (D), or suspicious stripes (F). Therefore, our reflection backdoor attacks are stealthier. A [19]: black-white squares at the bottom right corner; B [7]: small image at the center; C [52]: one malicious pixel; D [7]: a fixedly blended image; and E [53]: adversarial noise plus black-white squares at the bottom right corner; F [2]: fixed and sinusoidal strips. (Color figure online)

in computer vision [21], machine translation [49] and speech recognition [18]. Despite great success, DNNs have been found vulnerable to several attacks crafted at different stages of the development pipeline: adversarial examples crafted at the test stage, and data poisoning attacks and backdoor attacks crafted at the training stage. These attacks raise security concerns for the development of DNNs in safety-critical scenarios such as face recognition [45], autonomous driving [11,13], and medical diagnosis [15,33,39,40]. The study of these attacks has thus become crucial for secure and robust deep learning.

One well-known test time attack is the construction of *adversarial examples*, which appear imperceptibly different (to human eyes) from their original versions, yet can fool state-of-the-art DNNs with high success rate [17,50]. Adversarial examples can be constructed against a wide range of DNNs, and remain effective even in physical world scenarios [11,14]. Different from test-time attacks, training time attacks have also been demonstrated to be possible. DNNs often require large amounts of training data to achieve good performance. However, the collection process of large datasets is error-prone and susceptible to untrusted sources. Thus, a malicious adversary may poison a small number of training examples to corrupt the model, decreasing its test accuracy. This type of attack is known as the *data poisoning* attack [4,26,47].

More recently, *backdoor attacks* (also known as *Trojan attacks*) [3,8,19,28, 32,42,52,64] highlight an even more sophisticated threat to DNNs. By altering a small set of training examples, a backdoor attack can plant a backdoor into the victim model so as to control the model's behavior at test time [19]. Backdoor attacks arise when users download pre-trained models from untrusted sources. Figure 1 illustrates a few examples of successful backdoor attacks by existing

Table 1. Attack settings of existing methods and ours.

	Badnets [19]	Chen *et al.* [7]	Barni *et al.* [2]	Turner *et al.* [53]	Ours
Label	Poison	Poison	Clean	Clean	Clean
Trainer	Adversary	Adversary	User	User	User
Trigger	Fixed	Fixed	Sinusoidal	Fixed & Advs	**Reflection**

methods (A–F). A backdoor attack does not degrade the model's accuracy on normal test inputs, yet can control the model to make a prediction (which is in the attacker's interest) consistently for any test input that contains the backdoor pattern. This means it is difficult to detect a backdoor attack by evaluating the model's performance on a clean holdout set.

There exist two types of backdoor attacks: 1) poison-label attack which also modifies the label to the target class [7,19,35,52], and 2) clean-label attack which does not change the label [2,44,53,64]. Although poison-label attacks are effective, they often introduce clearly mislabeled examples into the training data, and thus can be easily detected by simple data filtering [53]. A recent clean-label (CL) attack proposed in [53] disguises the backdoor pattern using adversarial perturbations (E in Fig. 1). The signal (SIG) attack by Barni *et al.* [2] takes a superimposed sinusoidal signal as the backdoor trigger. However, these backdoor attacks can be easily erased by defense methods, as we will show in Sect. 4.4.

In this paper, we present a new type of backdoor pattern inspired by one natural phenomenon: reflection. Reflection is a common phenomenon existing in scenarios wherever there are glasses or smooth surfaces. Reflections often influence the performance of computer vision models [22], as illustrated in Fig. 7 (see Appendix). Here, we exploit reflections as backdoor patterns and show that a natural phenomenon like reflection can be manipulated by an adversary to perform backdoor attack on DNN models. Table 1 compares the different settings adopted by 4 state-of-the-art backdoor attacks and our proposed reflection backdoor. Two examples of our proposed reflection backdoor are illustrated in the rightmost column of Fig. 1. Our main contributions are:

- We investigate the use of a natural phenomenon, *i.e.*, reflection, as the backdoor pattern, and propose the *reflection backdoor* (*Refool*) attack to install stealthy and effective backdoor into DNN models.
- We conduct experiments on 5 datasets, and show that *Refool* can control state-of-the-art DNNs to make desired predictions ≥75.16% of the time by injecting reflections into less than 3.27% of the training data. Moreover, the injection causes almost no accuracy degradation on the clean holdout set.
- We demonstrate that, compared to the existing clean-label backdoor attack, our *Refool* is more resistant to state-of-the-art backdoor defenses.

2   Related Work

We briefly review backdoor attacks and defenses for deep neural networks.

Backdoor Attack. A backdoor attack tricks the model to associate a backdoor pattern with a specific target label, so that, whenever this pattern appears, the model predicts the target label, otherwise, behaves normally. The backdoor attack on DNNs was first explored in [19]. It was further characterized by having the following goals: 1) high attack success rate, 2) high backdoor stealthiness, and 3) low performance impact on clean test data [32].

Poison-label Backdoor Attack. Several backdoor patterns have been proposed to inject a backdoor by poisoning the images from the non-target classes and changing their labels to the target class. For example, a small black-white square at one corner of the image [19], an additional image attached onto or blended into the image [7], a fixed watermark on the image [47], one fixed pixel on the image for low-resolution (32 × 32) images. The backdoor trigger can also be implanted into the target model without knowing the original training data. For example, Liu *et al.* [35] proposed a reverse engineering method to generate a trigger pattern and a substitute input set, which are then used to finetuning some layers of the network to implant the trigger. Recently, Yao *et al.* [59] show that such backdoor attack can even be inherited via transfer-learning. While the above methods can install backdoors into the victim model effectively, they contain perceptually suspicious patterns and wrong labels, thus are susceptible to detection or removal by simple data filtering [53]. Note that, although reverse engineering does not require access to the training data which makes it stealthier, it still needs to present the trigger pattern to activate the attack at test time.

Clean-label Backdoor Attack. Recently, Turner *et al.* [53] (CL) and Barni *et al.*[2] (SIG) proposed the clean-label backdoor attack that can plant backdoor into DNNs without altering the label. Zhao *et al.* [64] proposed a clean-label backdoor attack on video recognition models. However, for clean-label backdoor patterns to be effective against the filtering effect of deep cascade convolutions, it often requires more perturbations that significantly reduce image quality, especially for high resolution images. Furthermore, we will show empirically in Sect. 4 that these backdoor patterns can be easily erased by backdoor defense methods. Different to these methods, in this paper, we propose a natural reflection backdoor, which is stealthy, effective and hard to erase.

Backdoor attacks have also been found possible in federated learning [1, 48,58] and graph neural networks (GNNs) [63]. Latent backdoor patterns and properties of backdoor triggers have also been explored in recent works [29,30, 41,60].

Backdoor Defense. Liu *et al.* [34] proposed a fine-pruning algorithm to prune the abnormal units in a backdoored DNN. Wang *et al.* [55] proposed to use anomaly index to detect backdoored models. Xiang *et al.* [57] proposed a cluster impurity based scheme to effectively detect single-pixel backdoor attacks. Bagdasaryan *et al.* [1] developed a generic constrain-and-scale technique that incorporates the evasion of defenses into the attacker's loss function during training. Chen *et al.* [6] proposed an activation clustering based method for backdoor detection and removal in DNNs. Doan *et al.* [10] presented Februus, which is a plug-and-play defensive system architecture for backdoor defense. Gao *et al.* [16] proposed a strong intentional perturbation (STRIP) based model to detect runtime backdoor attacks. Input denoising [20] and mixup training [61] are also effective defenses against backdoor attacks. We will evaluate the resistance of our proposed backdoor attack to some of the most effective defense methods.

3   Reflection Backdoor Attack

In this section, we first define the backdoor attack problem, then introduce the mathematical modeling of reflection and our proposed reflection backdoor attack.

3.1   Problem Definition

Given a K-class image dataset $D = \{(\mathbf{x}, y)^{(i)}\}_{i=1}^{n}$, with $\mathbf{x} \in \mathcal{X} \subset \mathbb{R}^d$ denoting a sample in the d-dimensional input space and $y \in \mathcal{Y} = \{1, \cdots, K\}$ its true label, classification learns a function $f(\mathbf{x}, \boldsymbol{\theta})$ (as represented by a DNN) with parameters $\boldsymbol{\theta}$ to map the input space to the label space: $f : \mathcal{X} \to \mathcal{Y}$. We denote the subset of data used for training and testing as D_{train} and D_{test} respectively. The goal of a backdoor attack is to install a backdoor into the victim model, so that the model will predict the adversarial class y_{adv} whenever the backdoor pattern presents on an input image. This is done by first generating then injecting a backdoor pattern into a small injection set $D_{inject} \subset D_{train}$ of training examples (without changing their labels). In this clean-label setting, D_{inject} is a subset of training examples from class y_{adv}. We denote the poisoned training set by D_{train}^{adv}, and measure the *injection rate* by the percentage of poisoned samples in D_{train}^{adv}. The problem is how to generate effective backdoor patterns. Next, we will introduce the use of natural reflection as the backdoor pattern.

3.2   Mathematical Modeling of Reflection

Reflection occurs when taking a photo of objects behind a glass window. Real scene like image with reflection can be a composition of multiple layers [38]. Specifically, we denote a clean background image by $\mathbf{x}$, a reflection image by $\mathbf{x}_R$, and the reflection poisoned image as $\mathbf{x}_{adv}$. Under reflection, the image formation process can be expressed as:

$$\mathbf{x}_{adv} = \mathbf{x} + \mathbf{x}_R \otimes k, \tag{1}$$

where k is a convolution kernel. The output of $\mathbf{x}_R \otimes k$ is referred to as the *reflection*. We will use adversarial images generated in this way as backdoor attacks. According to the principle of camera imaging and the law of reflection, reflection models in physical world scenarios can be divided into three categories [54], as illustrated in Fig. 2 (a).

(I) Both layers are in the same depth of field (DOF). The main objects (blue circle) behind the glass and the virtual image of reflections are in the same DOF, *i.e.*, they are approximately in the same focal plane. In this case, k in Eq. (1) reduces to a intensity number α, and empirically $\alpha \sim \mathcal{U}[0.05, 0.4]$.

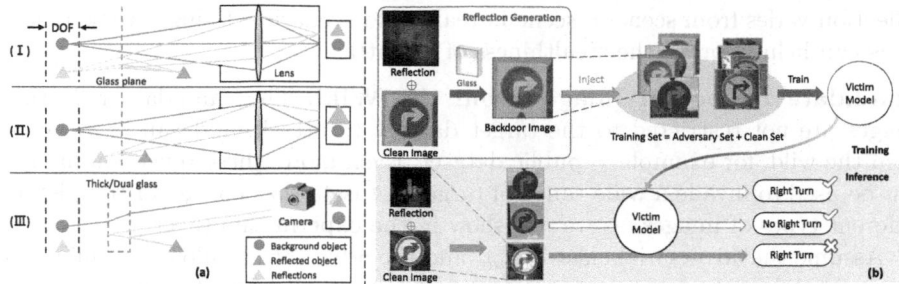

Fig. 2. (a) The physical models for three types of reflections. (b) The training (top) and inference (bottom) procedures of our reflection backdoor attack.

(II) Reflection layer is out of focus. It is reasonable to assume that the reflections (gray triangles) and the objects (blue circle) behind the glass have different distances to the camera [31], and the objects behind the glass is often focused (type (II) in Fig. 2(a)). In this case, the observed image $\mathbf{x}_{adv}$ is an additive mixture of the background image and the blurred reflections. The kernel k in Eq. (1) depends on the point spread function of the camera which is parameterized by a 2D Gaussian kernel g, *i.e.*, $g(|x - x_c|) = \exp\left(-|x - x_c|^2/(2 * \sigma)^2\right)$, where x_c is the center of kernel, and we set $\sigma \sim \mathcal{U}[1, 5]$.

(III) Ghost effect. The above two types of reflections assume that the thickness of the glass is tiny such that the refractive effect of the glass is negligible. However, this is often not true in practice. It is thus also necessary to consider the thickness of the glass. As illustrated in Fig. 2(a) (III), since the glass is semi-reflective, light rays from the reflected objects (dark gray triangle) will reflect off the glass pane producing more than one reflections—a ghost effect. In this case, the convolutional kernel k of Eq. 1 can be modelled as a two-pulse kernel $k(\alpha, \delta)$, where δ is a spatial shift of α with different coefficients. Empirically, we set $\alpha \sim \mathcal{U}[0.15, 0.35]$ and $\delta \sim \mathcal{U}[3, 8]$.

3.3 Proposed Reflection Backdoor Attack

Attack Pipeline. The training and inference procedures of our proposed reflection backdoor *Refool* is illustrated in Fig. 2(b). The first step is reflection generation, which is to generate backdoor images by adding reflections to clean images in the injection set D_{inject}, following the 3 reflection models described in Sect. 3.2. The victim model is then trained on the poisoned training set (*e.g.* D_{train}^{adv}), which consists of an adversary set of backdoor images (crafted at the first step) plus the clean images. At the inference stage (bottom subfigure in Fig. 2(b)), the reflection patterns can be blended into any input image to achieve the target prediction.

In contrast to existing methods that generate a fixed pattern, here, we propose to generate a variety of reflections as the backdoor trigger. This is because reflection varies from scene to scene in real-world scenarios. Using diverse reflections can help improve the stealthiness of the attack.

Candidate Reflection Images from the Wild. The candidate reflection images are not restricted to the target dataset to attack, and can be selected from the wild, for example, a public dataset. Even more, these reflection images can be used to invade a wide range of target datasets that consist of completely different types of images, as we will show in the experiments (Sect. 4).

Assume the adversarial class is y_{adv} and the adversary is allowed to inject m examples. We first create a candidate set of reflection images by selecting a set (more than m) of images randomly from a public image dataset PascalVOC [12] and denote it by R_{cand}. These reflection images are just normal images but from a dataset that is different from the training data. The next step is to select the top-m most effective reflection images from R_{cand} for backdoor attack.

Adversarial Reflection Image Selection. Not all reflection images are equally effective for backdoor attack, because 1) when the reflection image is too small, it may be hard to be planted as a backdoor trigger; and 2) when the intensity of the reflection image is too strong, it will become less stealthy. Therefore, we propose an iterative selection process to find the top-m most effective reflection images from R_{cand} as the *adversarial reflection set R_{adv}*, only which will be used for the next step's backdoor injection. To achieve this, we maintain a list of effectiveness scores for reflection images in the candidate set R_{cand}. We denote this effectiveness score list as W. The complete selection algorithm is described in Appendix B. The selection process includes T iterations with each iteration consisting of 4 steps: 1) select the top-m most effective reflection images from R_{cand} as the R_{adv}, according to their effectiveness scores in W; 2) inject the reflection images in R_{adv} into the injection set D_{inject} randomly following the reflection models described in Sect. 3.2; 3) train a model on the poisoned training set; and 4) update the effectiveness scores in W according to the model's predictions on a validation set D_{val}. The validation set is not used for model training, and is randomly selected from D_{train} after removing the y_{adv} class samples. This is because a backdoor attack causes other classes be misclassified into class y_{adv} not the other way around, in other words, class y_{adv} samples are not useful for effectiveness evaluation here. For step 1), at the first iteration where the effectiveness scores are uniformly initialized with constant value one, we just randomly select m reflection images from R_{cand} into the adversarial set R_{adv}. We empirically set $m = 200$ in our experiments. For step 2), each reflection image R_{adv} is randomly injected into only one image in the injection set D_{inject}. For step 3), we use a standard training strategy to train a model. Note that, the model trained in step 3) is only used for reflection image selection, not the final victim model (see experimental settings in Sect. 4). For step 4), the effectiveness scores in W are updated as follows:

$$W_i = \sum_{\mathbf{x}_R^i \in R_{adv}, \mathbf{x} \in D_{val}} \begin{cases} 1, & \text{if } f(\mathbf{x} + \mathbf{x}_R^i \otimes k, \boldsymbol{\theta}) = y_{adv}, \\ 0, & \text{otherwise}, \end{cases} \tag{2}$$

where, y is the class label of $\mathbf{x}$, $\mathbf{x}_R^i$ is the i-th reflection image in R_{adv}, and k is a randomly selected kernel. For those reflection images not selected into R_{adv}, we set their scores to the median value of the updated W. This is to increase their probability of being selected in the next iteration.

The candidate set R_{cand} are selected out of a wild public dataset, and more importantly, the selection of R_{adv} can be done on a dataset that is complete different from the target dataset. We will show empirically in Sect. 4 that, once selected, reflection images in R_{adv} can be directly applied to invade a wide range of datasets. This makes our proposed reflection backdoor more malicious than many existing backdoor attacks [7,19,53] that require access to the target datasets to generate or enhance their backdoor patterns. We find that these reflection images even do not need any enhancements such as adversarial perturbation [53] to achieve high attack success rates.

Attack with Reflection Images (Backdoor Injection). The above step will produce a set of effective reflection images R_{adv}, which can then be injected into the target dataset by poisoning a small portion of the data from the target class (clean-label attack only needs to poison data from the target class). Note that, although the selection of R_{adv} does not require access to the target dataset, the attack still needs to inject the backdoor pattern into training data, which is an essential step for any backdoor attacks.

Given a clean image from the target class, we randomly select one reflection image from R_{adv}, then use one of the 3 reflection models introduced in Sect. 3.2 to fuse the reflection image into the clean image. This injection process is iteratively done until a certain proportion of the target class images are contaminated with reflections. The victim model will remember the reflection backdoor when trained on the poisoned training set using a classification loss such as the commonly used cross entropy loss:

$$\boldsymbol{\theta} = \arg\min_{\boldsymbol{\theta}} -\frac{1}{n} \sum_{\mathbf{x}_i \in D_{train}^{adv}} \sum_{j=1}^{K} y_{ij} \log(\mathbf{p}(j|\mathbf{x}_i, \boldsymbol{\theta})), \tag{3}$$

where, $\mathbf{x}_i$ is the i-th training sample, y_{ij} is the class indicator of $\mathbf{x}_i$ belonging to class j, and $\mathbf{p}(j|\mathbf{x}_i, \boldsymbol{\theta})$ is the model's probability output with respect to class j conditioned on the input $\mathbf{x}_i$, and current parameter $\boldsymbol{\theta}$. We denote the learned victim model as f_{adv}.

Inference and Attack. At the inference stage, the model is expected to correctly predict the clean samples ($i.e. f_{adv}(\mathbf{x}, \boldsymbol{\theta}) = y$ for any test input $\mathbf{x} \in D_{test}$). However, it consistently predicts the adversarial class for any input that contains a reflection: $f_{adv}(\mathbf{x}+\mathbf{x}_R \otimes k, \boldsymbol{\theta}) = y_{adv}$ for any test input $\mathbf{x} \in D_{test}$ and reflection image $\mathbf{x}_R \in R_{adv}$. The attack success rate is measured by the percentage of test samples that are predicted as the target class y_{adv}, after adding reflections.

4 Experiments

In this section, we first evaluate the effectiveness and stealthiness of our *Refool* attack, then provide a comprehensive understanding of *Refool*. We also test the resistance of our *Refool* attack to state-of-the-art backdoor defense methods.

4.1 Experimental Setup

Datasets and DNNs. We consider 3 image classification tasks: 1) traffic sign recognition, 2) face recognition, and 3) object classification. For traffic sign recognition, we use 3 datasets: GTSRB [46], BelgiumTSC [51] and CTSRD [24]. For the 3 traffic sign datasets, we remove those low-resolution images of height or width smaller than 100 pixels. Then, we augment the training set using random crop and rotation, as [43]. For face recognition, we use the PubFig [27] dataset with extracted face regions, which is also augmented using random crop and rotation. For object classification, we randomly sample a subset of 12 classes of images from ImageNet [9]. We use ResNet-34 [21] for traffic sign recognition and face recognition. While for object classification, we consider two different DNN models: ResNet-34 and DenseNet [23]. The statistics of the datasets and DNN models can be found in Appendix C.

Table 2. Attack success rates (%) of baselines and our proposed *Refool* backdoor, and the victim model's test accuracy (%) on the clean test set. † denotes the model is replaced by a DenseNet. Note that we are poisoning 20% images in the target classes, the injection rate (%) is computed with respect to the entire dataset.

Dataset	Test accuracy (%)				Attack success rate (%)				Injection rate (%)
	Badnets	CL	SIG	*Refool*	Badnets	CL	SIG	*Refool*	
GTSRB	83.33	84.61	82.64	**86.30**	24.12	78.03	73.26	**91.67**	3.16
BelgiumTSC	**99.70**	97.56	99.13	99.51	11.40	46.25	51.89	**85.70**	2.31
CTSRD	90.00	94.44	93.97	**95.01**	25.24	63.63	57.39	**91.70**	0.91
PubFig	91.67	78.50	**91.70**	91.12	42.86	78.67	69.01	**81.30**	0.57
ImageNet	91.97	**92.07**	91.41	90.32	15.77	55.38	63.84	**82.11**	3.27
ImageNet†	91.99	92.12	92.23	**92.63**	20.14	67.43	68.00	**75.16**	3.27

Attack Setting. For all datasets, we set the adversarial target class to the first class (*i.e.*, class id 0), and randomly select clean training samples from the target class as the injection set D_{inject} under various injection rates. The adversarial reflection set R_{adv} is generated based on the GTSRB dataset, following the algorithm described in Sect. 3.3. We randomly choose a small number of 5000 images from PascalVOC [12] as the candidate reflection set R_{cand}, and 100 training samples from each of the non-target classes as the validation set D_{val}, for adversarial reflection image selection. Once selected, R_{adv} is directly applied to all other datasets, that is, these reflection images selected based on one single dataset can be effectively applied to invade a wide range of other datasets.

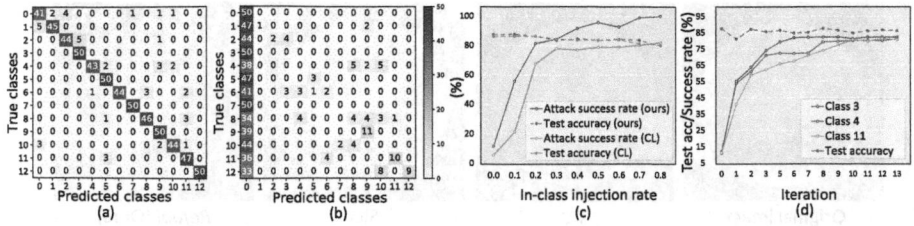

Fig. 3. (a–b) The prediction confusion matrix of the victim model trained on GTSRB dataset with only 3.16% training data poisoned by our *Refool* attack: (a) predictions on clean test images; (b): predictions on test images with reflections. (c–d) Attack success rates *versus* injection rate or iteration: (c) attack success rate and test accuracy *versus* in-class (the target class) injection rate; (d) attack success rate and the model's test accuracy on classes 3, 4, and 11, at different iterations of our reflection generation process. These experiments were all run on GTSRB dataset.

The adversarial reflection images are selected against a ResNet-34 model. When injecting a reflection image into a clean image, we randomly choose one of the 3 reflection models described in Eq. (1), but we also test using fixed reflection models. When applying the attack at the inference stage, the reflection images from R_{adv} are randomly injected into the clean test images.

DNN Training. All DNN models are trained using Stochastic Gradient Descent (SGD) optimizer with momentum 0.9, weight decay of 5e−4, and an initial learning rate 0.01, which is divided by 10 for every 10^5 training steps. We use batch size 32 and train all models for 200 epochs. All images are normalized to $[0, 1]$.

4.2 Effectiveness and Stealthiness of Our *Refool* Attack

Attack Success Rate Comparison. We compare our *Refool* attack with three existing backdoor attacks: Badnets [19], clean-label backdoor (CL) [53], and signal backdoor (SIG) [2]. We use the default settings as reported in their papers (implementation details can be found in Appendix C). The attack success rates and the corresponding injection rates on the 5 datasets are reported in Table 2. We also report the test accuracy of the victim model on the clean test set, and the "original test accuracy" for models trained on the original clean data.

As shown in Table 2, by poisoning only a small proportion of the training data, our proposed *Refool* attack can successfully invade the state-of-the-art DNN models, achieving higher success rates than existing backdoor attacks. With lower than 3.27% injection rate, *Refool* can reach a high attack success rate >75% across the five datasets and different networks (*e.g.* ResNet and DenseNet). Meanwhile, the victim models still perform well on clean test data, with less than 3% accuracy decrease (compared to the original accuracies) across all test scenarios. On some datasets, take CTSRD for example, one only needs to

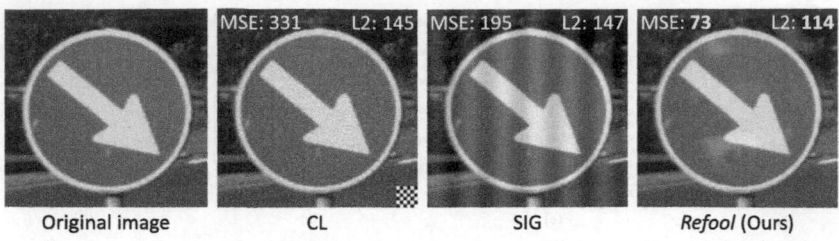

Fig. 4. Stealthiness of CL [53] and SIG [2] and our *Refool* : MSE and L2 distances between the original and the backdoor images are shown at the top corners.

contaminate <1% of training data to successfully control the model over 91% of the time. We further show, in Fig. 3 (a–b), the prediction confusion matrix of the victim model on GTSRD dataset. The victim model can correctly predict the clean images most of the time, yet can be controlled to only predict the target class (*e.g.* class 0, results on more target classes are reported in Appendix E) when reflections are added to the test images, a clear demonstration of successful backdoor attack. These results show that natural phenomena like reflection can be manipulated as a backdoor pattern to attack DNNs. Considering that reflection backdoors are visually very similar to natural reflections which commonly exist in the real world, this poses a new type of threat to deep learning models.

Stealthiness Comparison. We show in Fig. 4 an example of the backdoored images crafted to attack the CTSRD dataset. We compute the mean square error (MSE) and L2 distances between the original image and the backdoored image crafted by CL, SIG and our *Refool* backdoor attacks. As shown in this example, our reflection attack is stealthier in terms of smooth surface and hidden shadows. More visual inspections and the average distortions (*e.g.* MSE and L2 distances) over 500 randomly backdoored images can be found in Appendix F.

Attack Success Rate Versus Injection Rate. We next show, on the GTSRB dataset, how different injection rates influence the attack success rate of CL and our *Refool* attacks. As shown in Fig. 3(c), we vary the in-class injection rate from [0, 0.8]. The corresponding injection rate with respect to the entire dataset is only 0.032, 0.063, 0.126 for in-class injection rate 0.2, 0.4, 0.8 respectively. Poisoning more data can steadily improve attack success rate until 40% of the data in target class are poisoned, after which, the attack stabilizes. Our *Refool* attack outperforms the CL attack under all injection rates. Note that increasing injection rate has a minimal impact on the model's accuracy on clean examples.

4.3   Understandings of Reflection Backdoor Attack

Efficiency of Adversarial Reflection Image Selection. Here, we evaluate the efficiency of our adversarial reflection image selection in Appendix B. We test the inference-time attack effectiveness of the adversarial reflection images

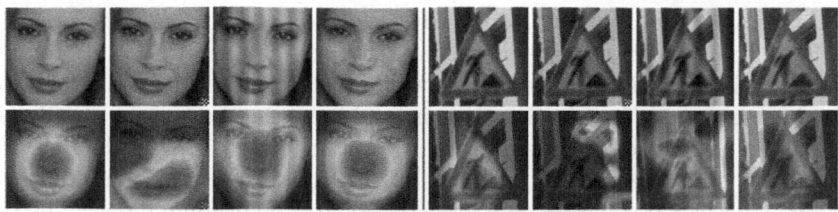

Fig. 5. Understandings of *Refool* with Grad-CAM [43] with two samples from PubFig (left) and GTSRB (right). In each group, the images at the top are the original input, CL [53], SIG [2] and our *Refool* (left to right), while images at the bottom are their corresponding attention maps.

(*e.g.* R_{adv}) selected at each iteration for a total of 14 (0–13) iterations, on GTSRB dataset. The attack success rate on three classes and the model's test accuracy are shown in Fig. 3(d). For each of the 3 tested classes (*e.g.* class 3, 4 and 11), we inject reflection images generated at the current iteration randomly into the clean test images of the class. We then measure the class-wise attack success rate. In detail, we record the proportion of examples in the class (after injection) that are predicted by the current model as the target class 0. The proposed generation algorithm can find effective reflections efficiently within 9 iterations. Note that, once these adversarial reflections are found, they can be applied to install backdoor into any DNN models that are trained on the dataset, as we have shown with the ResNet/DenseNet models on ImageNet dataset in Table 2.

Table 3. Attack success rate versus test accuracy for different types of reflections.

Reflection type	Attack success rate	Test accuracy	Similarity		
			SSIM	PSNR	MSE
(I)	87.30%	83.59%	0.883	26.68	62.11
(II)	90.46%	85.00%	**0.896**	**27.45**	**60.54**
(III)	90.33%	85.63%	0.786	23.01	95.87
Mix	**91.67%**	**86.30%**	0.828	24.98	73.44

Performance Under Different Types of Reflections. We then show how the 3 types of reflections introduced in Sect. 3.2 influence the attack success rate. The experiments were also conducted on the GTSRB dataset. The adversarial reflection images (*e.g.* R_{adv}) used here are the same as those selected for previous experiments. The difference here is that we test 2 different injection strategies: 1) using fixed reflection, or 2) using randomly mixed reflections (as was used in previous experiments). We also measure the average similarity of training images (4772 in total) before and after injection, using 3 popular similarity metrics: peak-signal-to-noise-ratio (PSNR) [25], structural similarity index

(SSIM) [56] and mean square error (MSE). The numeric results are reported in Table 3. In terms of attack success rate and test accuracy, type (II) and type (III) demonstrate higher attack success rates with less model corruptions (higher test accuracies) than type (I) reflection. When combined, the three types of reflection achieved the best attack success rate and least model corruption (highest test accuracy). It was also observed that type (II) injection has the minimum distortion (*e.g.* highest SSIM/PSNR and lowest MSE) to the original data, while type (III) reflection causes the largest distortion, as a consequence of the ghost effect (see Fig. 2(a)). The relatively small distortion of type (II) reflection is due to its smoothness effect. Overall, a random mixture of the three reflections yields the best attack strength with moderate distortion.

Effect of Reflection Trigger on Network Attention. We further investigate how reflection backdoor affects the attention of the network. Visual inspections on a few examples are shown in Fig. 5. The attention maps are computed using the Gradient-weighted Class Activation Mapping (Grad-CAM) technique [43], which finds the critical regions in the input images that mostly activate the victim model's output. We find that the reflection backdoor only slightly shifts the model's attention off the correct regions, whereas CL and SIG significantly shift the model's attention either completely off the target or in a striped manner, especially in the traffic sign example. This suggests the stealthiness of our reflection backdoor from a different perspective.

4.4   Resistance to State-of-the-art Backdoor Defenses

Resistance to Finetuning. We compare the our *Refool* to CL [53] and SIG [2], in terms of the resistance to clean-data-based finetuning [34,55]. We train a victim model on GTSRB dataset separately under the three attacks, while leaving 10% of the clean training data out as the finetuning set. We then fine-tune the model on the finetuning set for 20 epochs using the same SGD optimizer but smaller learning rate 0.0001. We fix the shallow layers of the network and only fine-tune the last dense layer. The comparison results are illustrated in the left of Fig. 6. As can be seen, the attack success rate of CL drops from 78.3% to 20% after just one epoch of finetuning and SIG drops from 73.0% to 25% after 4 epochs, while our *Refool* attack is still above 60% after 15 epochs. The reason why is that reflections are a natural and fundamental type of feature, rather than random patterns that can be easily erased by finetuning on clean data.

Resistance to Neural Pruning. We then test the resistance of the three attacks to the state-of-the-art backdoor defense method Fine-pruning [34] (experimental settings are in Appendix G). The comparison results are shown in the middle subfigure of Fig. 6. The attack success rate of CL drops drastically from 76% to 8.3% when 60% of neurons are removed, while SIG drops from 73% to 16.5% when 50% of neurons are removed. Compared to CL or SIG, our reflection backdoor is more resistance to neural pruning, with much higher success rates until 80% of neurons are removed.

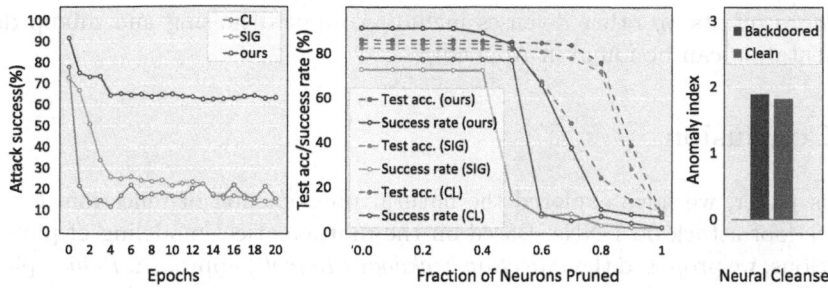

Fig. 6. Left: Attack success rates during finetuning on clean data. **Middle:** Test accuracy (on clean inputs) and attack success rate against the neural pruning defense. These experiments were run on GTSRB dataset. **Right:** Backdoor detection using Neural Cleanse [55]. Anomaly index >2 indicates a detected backdoored model.

Table 4. Attack success rates (%) before/after white-box trigger removal on GTSRB.

	Badnets [19]	CL [53]	SIG [2]	*Refool*
Before	24.12	78.03	73.26	**91.67**
After	15.38 ▼ 8.74	18.18 ▼ 59.85	17.29 ▼ 55.97	**85.01 ▼ 6.65**

Resistance to Neural Cleanse. Neural Cleanse [55] detects whether a trained model has been planted backdoor, in which case it assumes the training samples will require minimal modifications to be manipulated by the attacker. Here, we apply Neural Cleanse to detect a backdoored ResNet-34 model by our *Refool* on GTSRB dataset. As shown in the right subfigure of Fig. 6, Neural Cleanse fails to detect the backdoored model, *i.e.*, anomaly index < 2. More results on other datasets can be found in Appendix G.

Resistance to White-box Trigger Removal. We apply trigger removal methods in a white-box setting (the defender has identified the trigger pattern). For our *Refool*, many reflection removal methods [36,37,62] can be applied. In our experiment, we adopt the state-of-the-art reflection removal method [62] to clean the poisoned data. For Badnets, we simply replace the value of the trigger by the mean pixel value of their three adjacent patches. For CL, we use the non-Local means denoising technique [5]. For SIG, we add $-v(i,j)$ (defined in Eq. (??) in Appendix G) to backdoored images to remove the trigger. The attack success rates before and after trigger removal are reported in Table 4. Existing attacks Badnets, CL, and SIG rely on fixed backdoor patterns, thus can be easily removed by white-box trigger removal methods, *i.e.*, success rate drops to <20%. Conversely, our *Refool* uses reflection images randomly selected from the wild, thus can still maintain a high success rate of 85% after reflection removal. Overall, we believe backdoor attack is still a challenging task to successfully attack a model while evade white-box trigger removal. Detailed experimental settings and more results on other defenses including input denoising and mixup data augmentation can be found in Appendix G.

5   Conclusion

In this paper, we have explored the natural phenomenon of reflection, for use in backdoor attack on DNNs. Based on the mathematical modeling of physical reflections, we proposed the *reflection backdoor* (*Refool*) approach. *Refool* plants a backdoor into a victim model by generating and injecting reflections into a small set of training data. Empirical results across 3 computer vision tasks and 5 datasets demonstrate the effectiveness of *Refool*. It can attack state-of-the-art DNNs with high success rate and small degradation in clean accuracy. Reflection backdoors can be generated efficiently, and are resistant to state-of-the-art defense methods. It is an open question as to whether new types of training strategies can be developed that are robust to this kind of natural backdoors.

References

1. Bagdasaryan, E., Veit, A., Hua, Y., Estrin, D., Shmatikov, V.: How to backdoor federated learning. In: AISTATS, pp. 2938–2948 (2020)
2. Barni, M., Kallas, K., Tondi, B.: A new backdoor attack in CNNs by training set corruption without label poisoning. In: IEEE International Conference on Image Processing (ICIP), pp. 101–105. IEEE (2019)
3. Bhalerao, A., Kallas, K., Tondi, B., Barni, M.: Luminance-based video backdoor attack against anti-spoofing rebroadcast detection. In: IEEE 21st International Workshop on Multimedia Signal Processing (MMSP), pp. 1–6. IEEE (2019)
4. Biggio, B., Nelson, B., Laskov, P.: Poisoning attacks against support vector machines. arXiv preprint arXiv:1206.6389 (2012)
5. Buades, A., Coll, B., Morel, J.M.: Non-local means denoising. Image Process. On Line **1**, 208–212 (2011)
6. Chen, B., et al.: Detecting backdoor attacks on deep neural networks by activation clustering. arXiv preprint arXiv:1811.03728 (2018)
7. Chen, X., Liu, C., Li, B., Lu, K., Song, D.: Targeted backdoor attacks on deep learning systems using data poisoning. arXiv preprint arXiv:1712.05526 (2017)
8. Dai, J., Chen, C., Li, Y.: A backdoor attack against LSTM-based text classification systems. IEEE Access **7**, 138872–138878 (2019)
9. Deng, J., Dong, W., Socher, R., Li, L.J., Li, K., Fei-Fei, L.: ImageNet: a large-scale hierarchical image database. In: CVPR (2009)
10. Doan, B.G., Abbasnejad, E., Ranasinghe, D.C.: Februus: input purification defense against trojan attacks on deep neural network systems. arXiv: 1908.03369 (2019)
11. Duan, R., Ma, X., Wang, Y., Bailey, J., Qin, A.K., Yang, Y.: Adversarial Camouflage: hiding physical-world attacks with natural styles. In: CVPR, pp. 1000–1008 (2020)
12. Everingham, M., Van Gool, L., Williams, C.K.I., Winn, J., Zisserman, A.: The PASCAL Visual Object Classes Challenge 2012 (VOC2012) Results. http://www.pascal-network.org/challenges/VOC/voc2012/workshop/index.html

13. Evtimov, I., et al.: Robust physical-world attacks on deep learning models. In: CVPR (2018)
14. Eykholt, K., et al.: Robust physical-world attacks on deep learning models. arXiv preprint arXiv:1707.08945 (2017)
15. Finlayson, S.G., Bowers, J.D., Ito, J., Zittrain, J.L., Beam, A.L., Kohane, I.S.: Adversarial attacks on medical machine learning. In: Science. American Association for the Advancement of Science (2019)
16. Gao, Y., Xu, C., Wang, D., Chen, S., Ranasinghe, D.C., Nepal, S.: Strip: a defence against trojan attacks on deep neural networks. In: Proceedings of the 35th Annual Computer Security Applications Conference, pp. 113–125 (2019)
17. Goodfellow, I.J., Shlens, J., Szegedy, C.: Explaining and harnessing adversarial examples. arXiv preprint arXiv:1412.6572 (2014)
18. Graves, A., Mohamed, A.r., Hinton, G.: Speech recognition with deep recurrent neural networks. In: ICASSP. IEEE (2013)
19. Gu, T., Dolan-Gavitt, B., Garg, S.: Badnets: Identifying vulnerabilities in the machine learning model supply chain. arXiv preprint arXiv:1708.06733 (2017)
20. Guo, C., Rana, M., Cisse, M., Van Der Maaten, L.: Countering adversarial images using input transformations. arXiv preprint arXiv:1711.00117 (2017)
21. He, K., Zhang, X., Ren, S., Sun, J.: Deep residual learning for image recognition. In: CVPR (2016)
22. Hendrycks, D., Zhao, K., Basart, S., Steinhardt, J., Song, D.: Natural adversarial examples. arXiv preprint arXiv:1907.07174 (2019)
23. Huang, G., Liu, Z., Van Der Maaten, L., Weinberger, K.Q.: Densely connected convolutional networks. In: CVPR, pp. 4700–4708 (2017)
24. Huang, L.: Chinese traffic sign database. http://www.nlpr.ia.ac.cn/pal/trafficdata/recognition.html
25. Huynh-Thu, Q., Ghanbari, M.: Scope of validity of PSNR in image/video quality assessment. Electron. Lett. **44**, 800–801 (2008)
26. Koh, P.W., Liang, P.: Understanding black-box predictions via influence functions. In: ICML (2017)
27. Kumar, N., Berg, A.C., Belhumeur, P.N., Nayar, S.K.: Attribute and simile classifiers for face verification. In: ICCV (2009)
28. Kwon, H., Yoon, H., Park, K.W.: FriendNet backdoor: identifying backdoor attack that is safe for friendly deep neural network. In: The 3rd International Conference on Software Engineering and Information Management (ICSIM 2020). ACM's International Conference Proceedings Series (2020)
29. Li, S., Zhao, B.Z.H., Yu, J., Xue, M., Kaafar, D., Zhu, H.: Invisible backdoor attacks against deep neural networks. arXiv preprint arXiv:1909.02742 (2019)
30. Li, Y., Zhai, T., Wu, B., Jiang, Y., Li, Z., Xia, S.: Rethinking the trigger of backdoor attack. arXiv preprint arXiv:2004.04692 (2020)
31. Li, Y., Brown, M.S.: Single image layer separation using relative smoothness. In: CVPR (2014)
32. Liao, C., Zhong, H., Squicciarini, A., Zhu, S., Miller, D.: Backdoor embedding in convolutional neural network models via invisible perturbation. arXiv preprint arXiv:1808.10307 (2018)
33. Liu, B., Gu, L., Lu, F.: Unsupervised ensemble strategy for retinal vessel segmentation. In: Shen, D., et al. (eds.) MICCAI 2019. LNCS, vol. 11764, pp. 111–119. Springer, Cham (2019). https://doi.org/10.1007/978-3-030-32239-7_13

34. Liu, K., Dolan-Gavitt, B., Garg, S.: Fine-Pruning: Defending Against Backdooring Attacks on Deep Neural Networks. In: Bailey, M., Holz, T., Stamatogiannakis, M., Ioannidis, S. (eds.) RAID 2018. LNCS, vol. 11050, pp. 273–294. Springer, Cham (2018). https://doi.org/10.1007/978-3-030-00470-5_13
35. Liu, Y., et al.: Trojaning attack on neural networks (2018)
36. Liu, Y., Li, Y., You, S., Lu, F.: Semantic guided single image reflection removal. arXiv preprint arXiv:1907.11912 (2019)
37. Liu, Y., Lu, F.: Separate in latent space: unsupervised single image layer separation. In: AAAI (2020)
38. Liu, Y., You, S., Li, Y., Lu, F.: Unsupervised learning for intrinsic image decomposition from a single image. In: CVPR (2020)
39. Ma, X., et al.: Understanding adversarial attacks on deep learning based medical image analysis systems. Pattern Recognit. 107332 (2020)
40. Niu, Y., et al.: Pathological evidence exploration in deep retinal image diagnosis. In: Proceedings of the AAAI Conference on Artificial Intelligence, vol. 33, pp. 1093–1101 (2019)
41. Pasquini, C., Böhme, R.: Trembling triggers: exploring the sensitivity of backdoors in DNN-based face recognition. EURASIP J. Inf. Secur. **2020**(1), 1–15 (2020)
42. Rehman, H., Ekelhart, A., Mayer, R.: Backdoor attacks in neural networks – a systematic evaluation on multiple traffic sign datasets. In: Holzinger, A., Kieseberg, P., Tjoa, A.M., Weippl, E. (eds.) CD-MAKE 2019. LNCS, vol. 11713, pp. 285–300. Springer, Cham (2019). https://doi.org/10.1007/978-3-030-29726-8_18
43. Selvaraju, R.R., Cogswell, M., Das, A., Vedantam, R., Parikh, D., Batra, D.: Grad-cam: Visual explanations from deep networks via gradient-based localization. In: ICCV (2017)
44. Shafahi, A., et al.: Poison frogs! targeted clean-label poisoning attacks on neural networks. In: NeurIPS, pp. 6103–6113 (2018)
45. Sharif, M., Bhagavatula, S., Bauer, L., Reiter, M.K.: Accessorize to a crime: Real and stealthy attacks on state-of-the-art face recognition. In: CCS, pp. 1528–1540 (2016)
46. Stallkamp, J., Schlipsing, M., Salmen, J., Igel, C.: The German traffic sign recognition benchmark: a multi-class classification competition. In: IJCNN (2011)
47. Steinhardt, J., Koh, P.W.W., Liang, P.S.: Certified defenses for data poisoning attacks. In: NIPS (2017)
48. Sun, Z., Kairouz, P., Suresh, A.T., McMahan, H.B.: Can you really backdoor federated learning? arXiv preprint arXiv:1911.07963 (2019)
49. Sutskever, I., Vinyals, O., Le, Q.V.: Sequence to sequence learning with neural networks. In: NIPS (2014)
50. Szegedy, C., et al.: Intriguing properties of neural networks. arXiv preprint arXiv:1312.6199 (2013)
51. Timofte, R., Zimmermann, K., Van Gool, L.: Multi-view traffic sign detection, recognition, and 3D localisation. Mach. Vis. Appl. **25**(3), 633–647 (2011). https://doi.org/10.1007/s00138-011-0391-3
52. Tran, B., Li, J., Madry, A.: Spectral signatures in backdoor attacks. In: NIPS (2018)
53. Turner, A., Tsipras, D., Madry, A.: Clean-label backdoor attacks. https://people.csail.mit.edu/madry/lab/ (2019)
54. Wan, R., Shi, B., Duan, L.Y., Tan, A.H., Kot, A.C.: Benchmarking single-image reflection removal algorithms. In: ICCV (2017)
55. Wang, B., et al.: Neural cleanse: identifying and mitigating backdoor attacks in neural networks (2019)

56. Wang, Z., Bovik, A.C., Sheikh, H.R., Simoncelli, E.P., et al.: Image quality assessment: from error visibility to structural similarity. TIP **13**, 600–612 (2004)
57. Xiang, Z., Miller, D.J., Kesidis, G.: A benchmark study of backdoor data poisoning defenses for deep neural network classifiers and a novel defense. In: IEEE 29th International Workshop on Machine Learning for Signal Processing (MLSP), pp. 1–6. IEEE (2019)
58. Xie, C., Huang, K., Chen, P.Y., Li, B.: DBA: distributed backdoor attacks against federated learning. In: ICLR (2020)
59. Yao, Y., Li, H., Zheng, H., Zhao, B.Y.: Latent backdoor attacks on deep neural networks. In: Proceedings of the 2019 ACM SIGSAC Conference on Computer and Communications Security (2019)
60. Yao, Y., Li, H., Zheng, H., Zhao, B.Y.: Latent backdoor attacks on deep neural networks. In: ACM CCS, pp. 2041–2055 (2019)
61. Zhang, H., Cisse, M., Dauphin, Y.N., Lopez-Paz, D.: mixup: Beyond empirical risk minimization. arXiv preprint arXiv:1710.09412 (2017)
62. Zhang, X., Ren, N., Chen, Q.: Single image reflection separation with perceptual losses. In: CVPR (2018)
63. Zhang, Z., Jia, J., Wang, B., Gong, N.Z.: Backdoor attacks to graph neural networks. arXiv preprint arXiv:2006.11165 (2020)
64. Zhao, S., Ma, X., Zheng, X., Bailey, J., Chen, J., Jiang, Y.G.: Clean-label backdoor attacks on video recognition models. In: CVPR, pp. 14443–14452 (2020)

Learning to Learn with Variational Information Bottleneck for Domain Generalization

Yingjun Du[1](✉) (iD), Jun Xu[2], Huan Xiong[4], Qiang Qiu[5], Xiantong Zhen[1,3], Cees G. M. Snoek[1], and Ling Shao[3,4]

[1] AIM Lab, University of Amsterdam, Amsterdam, The Netherlands
{y.du,x.zhen,cgmsnoek}@uva.nl
[2] College of Computer Science, Nankai University, Tianjin, China
nankaimathxujun@gmail.com
[3] Inception Institute of Artificial Intelligence, Abu Dhabi, UAE
ling.shao@ieee.org
[4] Mohamed bin Zayed University of Artificial Intelligence, Abu Dhabi, UAE
huan.xiong@mbzuai.ac.ae
[5] Electrical and Computer Engineering, Duke University, Durham, USA
qiang.qiu@duke.edu

Abstract. Domain generalization models learn to generalize to previously unseen domains, but suffer from prediction uncertainty and domain shift. In this paper, we address both problems. We introduce a probabilistic meta-learning model for domain generalization, in which classifier parameters shared across domains are modeled as distributions. This enables better handling of prediction uncertainty on unseen domains. To deal with domain shift, we learn domain-invariant representations by the proposed principle of meta variational information bottleneck, we call MetaVIB. MetaVIB is derived from novel variational bounds of mutual information, by leveraging the meta-learning setting of domain generalization. Through episodic training, MetaVIB learns to gradually narrow domain gaps to establish domain-invariant representations, while simultaneously maximizing prediction accuracy. We conduct experiments on three benchmarks for cross-domain visual recognition. Comprehensive ablation studies validate the benefits of MetaVIB for domain generalization. The comparison results demonstrate our method outperforms previous approaches consistently.

Keywords: Meta learning · Domain generalization · Variational inference · Information bottleneck

Electronic supplementary material The online version of this chapter (https://doi.org/10.1007/978-3-030-58607-2_12) contains supplementary material, which is available to authorized users.

© Springer Nature Switzerland AG 2020

A. Vedaldi et al. (Eds.): ECCV 2020, LNCS 12355, pp. 200–216, 2020.
https://doi.org/10.1007/978-3-030-58607-2_12

1   Introduction

This paper strives for domain generalization in image classification [24,28,31,49]. The general challenge is to exploit the data variations of seen image domains with the aim to generalize well to unseen image domains. For example, by generalizing a *chair* classifier trained on PASCAL VOC to LabelMe [49], or by generalizing an *elephant* classifier trained on photo's to sketches [24]. Domain generalization models typically suffer from two problems. First, since data from unseen domains is inaccessible during the learning stage, we do not know their statistical data distribution. This causes uncertainty in the predictions made on the unseen domains. Second, data from different domains usually follows distinct distributions with great discrepancy, resulting in domain shift from seen to unseen domains. Domain shift has been extensively researched in domain generalization, mostly by learning feature representations that are invariant across domains [12,17,25,27,29,31,52]. Meta-learning [41,46] that learns to generalize across tasks has been introduced to domain generalization by Li et al. [25] showing its great effectiveness in learning to generalize across domains [4,25,29]. To the best of our knowledge, none of these existing meta-learning methods deal with the prediction uncertainty on unseen domains.

In this paper, we address the two major domain generalization challenges jointly by one single probabilistic model under the meta-learning framework. We model parameters of classifiers shared across domains as probabilistic distributions that we infer from the data of the seen domains. The probabilistic modeling enables us to better handle the prediction uncertainty on previously unseen domains [15,18]. To handle domain shift, we take inspiration from the information bottleneck (IB) theory [1,2,47] which learns robust representations to enhance generalization. IB encodes the input into compressed intermediate representations that maximize target prediction. It offers a promising technique to learn domain-invariant representations, but to the best of our knowledge has not yet been explored for domain generalization under the meta-learning framework. We propose the principle of meta variational information bottleneck (MetaVIB) for the optimization of the model. We derive MetaVIB from the variational bounds of mutual information by leveraging the meta-learning setting, and incorporate it as a data-driven regularizer into the optimization objective. The parameters of all classifiers and the network are jointly optimized during the meta-training stage and applied to the unseen domain in the meta-test stage. By episodic training, MetaVIB enables the network to learn to gradually close the gaps between domains to achieve domain-invariant representations that alleviate domain shift, while simultaneously being able to obtain accurate predictions.

We conduct extensive experiments on three benchmarks for cross-domain visual recognition. The ablation studies demonstrate the benefits of MetaVIB in the probabilistic framework for domain generalization. The comparison with state-of-the-art methods, shows that our method consistently delivers the best performance on all tasks, surpassing previous methods based on both regular learning and meta-learning.

2 Related Work

In this section, we review related work on domain generalization, information bottleneck and meta-learning.

Domain generalization has been a longstanding challenge in computer vision [24,25,27] and machine learning [6,31],but recently regained increased research interest [4,8,10,29,42]. Learning domain-variant feature representation has been one of the main topics of focus in domain generalization [12,17,27,28, 31,52]. The core idea is to learn a model that generates invariant representations for the source domains, without over-fitting, which generalizes to unseen target domains. We explore the domain discrepancy to learn invariant representations through the lens of mutual information [47].

Information bottleneck (IB) [47] provides an information-theoretic principle of encoding the input data into a compressed representation that maximizes target prediction. This is achieved by minimizing the mutual information $I(Z;X)$ between the input variable X and its latent representation Z, while maximizing the mutual information $I(Z;Y)$ between the output variable Y and the latent representation Z. To be more precise, the IB principle is to maximize the objective function:

$$\mathcal{L}_{\text{IB}}(\boldsymbol{\theta}) = I(Z;Y|\boldsymbol{\theta}) - \beta I(Z;X|\boldsymbol{\theta}), \tag{1}$$

where $\beta \in [0,\ 1]$ is the hyperparameter that controls the size of the information bottleneck, and $\boldsymbol{\theta}$ are the corresponding model parameters.

The IB principle has recently been introduced for theoretical understanding and analysis of deep neural networks [2,21,34,43,48]. The authors optimize the networks with an iterative Blahut-Arimoto algorithm, which is infeasible in practical systems. Alemi et al. [1] developed a variational approximation to the IB objective by leveraging variational inference, which allows the IB model to be parameterized with neural networks. Amjad et al. [2] investigated training deep neural networks (DNN) for classification based on minimization of the IB functional.

It is shown that for deterministic DNNs, the optimization can be ill-posed. This is because the IB functional can be infinite or not admitting gradient descent since it is piece-wise constant. The possible remedy indicated in their work is to train stochastic DNNs with the IB principle.

Meta-learning, or learning to learn, endows models with the capacity to efficiently learn new tasks by acquiring common knowledge through experiencing a set of related tasks. It has been explored in several directions, e.g., by learning a meta learner on diverse tasks to adapt the parameters of the base learner on a specific task [14,38,44,45,51,53], learning to optimize the parameters of deep neural networks [5,32,40], and learning to learn the gradient optimization process by recurrent neural networks [3,35], *etc.*. A representative meta-learning algorithm is the model agnostic meta-learning (MAML), which learns the models to be able to adapt to similar tasks with only a few gradient descent updates. Li et al. [25] introduced the idea of MAML [14] to domain generalization. They train models with generalization ability to unseen domains by leveraging the meta-learning setting. MetaReg [4] addresses the domain shifts by leveraging the insights from meta-learning [50]. They learn a meta regularizer to achieve the generalization from source to unseen target domains. Li et al. [29] proposed a meta-learning approach based on a feature-critic network, in which an auxiliary loss is introduced to improve generalization ability. Dou et al. [10] adopt a gradient-based model-agnostic learning algorithm to deal with domain shift for domain generalization. Two complementary losses are introduced for regularization of semantic features. The success of those works has indicated the effectiveness of meta-learning in domain generalization. Probabilistic meta-learning has also been developed in few-shot learning to handle uncertainty [16,18], which has not been explored for domain generalization.

3   Method

We describe the meta-learning setting for domain generalization. Following the setting in recent domain generalization by meta-learning [4,25,29], we divide a dataset into the Source domains $\mathcal{S}$ used for train and the Target domains $\mathcal{T}$ held-out for test. In the train phase, data in the source domains $\mathcal{S}$ is episodically divided into sets of meta-train $\mathcal{D}^s$ and meta-test $\mathcal{D}^t$ domains. We train the model by optimizing over the prediction errors on meta-test $\mathcal{D}^t$ domains. In the test phase, the learned model is applied to the target domains $\mathcal{T}$ for performance evaluation. The training phase incorporates the idea of meta-learning which induces a higher level of learning by the split of meta-train and mete-test domains, rather than training on all source domains [26]. This episodic meta-learning process mimics the generalization from seen to previously unseen domains.

3.1   Probabilistic Modeling

We start with the probabilistic formulation of the domain generalization, based on which we develop the probabilistic model under the meta-learning framework. We consider the general estimation problem of conditionally predictive likelihood in the meta-test domain $\mathcal{D}^t$:

$$\max_{p(\mathbf{x}^t, \mathbf{y}^t)} \mathbb{E} \left[\log \int p(\mathbf{y}^t | \psi, \mathbf{x}^t) p(\psi | \mathbf{x}^t) d\psi \right], \tag{2}$$

where $(\mathbf{x}^t, \mathbf{y}^t)$ is the sample of paired input and label drawn from data distribution $p(\mathbf{x}^t, \mathbf{y}^t)$ in meta-test domain, $p(\mathbf{y}^t | \psi, \mathbf{x}^t)$ is the conditionally predictive distribution, ψ is the parameter set of the classifier. Note that we treat ψ as a stochastic variable that depends on the input $\mathbf{x}^t$ and the optimization of (2) is with respect to the parameters of probabilities.

In this work, we parameterize the model by deep neural networks. From the information-theoretic point of view [1], we regard the feature representation from the neural network as a stochastic variable $\mathbf{z}^t$, which is the latent encoding of the

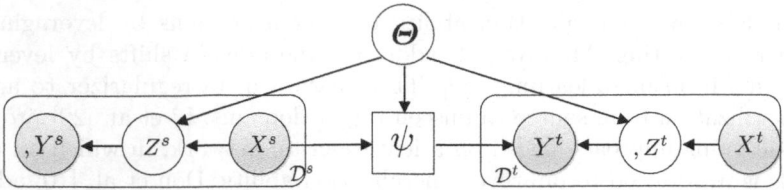

Fig. 1. Computational graph of the probabilistic meta-learning model for domain generalization. Θ encloses the global model parameters and ψ contains the parameters of classifiers shared across domains. Θ and ψ are jointly optimized in the train phase on the source domains. In each episode, the source domain is divided into a meta-train ($\mathcal{D}^s$) and meta-test ($\mathcal{D}^t$) domain. ψ is produced by $\mathcal{D}^s$ and applied to $\mathcal{D}^t$. In the test phase, the model (Θ) generates representations of data in the target domains and the classifier (ψ) predicts of data from the source domain.

input $\mathbf{x}^t$. In domain generalization, it is commonly assumed that the label space is shared across the source and target domains. By leveraging the meta-learning setting, we propose to use data D^s from the meta-train domains to estimate the parameters of the classifier by replacing $p(\psi|\mathbf{x}^t)$ with $q(\psi|D^s)$, which is applied to the meta-test domain. By incorporating the latent variable $\mathbf{z}$ into (2), we obtain the following maximum conditionally predictive likelihood estimation,

$$\max_{p(\mathbf{x}^t,\mathbf{y}^t)} \mathbb{E} \left[\log \int p(\mathbf{y}^t|\psi,\mathbf{z}^t)p(\mathbf{z}^t|\mathbf{x}^t)q(\psi|D^s)\mathrm{d}\mathbf{z}\mathrm{d}\psi\right]. \tag{3}$$

This establishes a probabilistic latent model which can be represented in a computational graph as shown in Fig. 1, and the corresponding conditional joint distribution is defined as:

$$p(Y^t, Z^t, \psi|X^t, D^s, \Theta) = p(\psi|D^s; \Theta) \prod_{n=1}^{N} p(\mathbf{y}_n^t|\psi, \mathbf{z}_n^t)p(\mathbf{z}_n^t|\mathbf{x}_n^t; \Theta), \tag{4}$$

where Θ denotes the model parameters, $D^t = \{X^t, Y^t\} = \{\mathbf{x}_n^t, \mathbf{y}_n^t\}_{n=1}^N$, $D^s = \{X^s, Y^s\} = \{\mathbf{x}_m^s, \mathbf{y}_m^s\}_{m=1}^M$, and N (M) are the number of samples in the meta-test (meta-train) domains. It is possible to directly employ (3) as the optimization objective using the techniques of amortized inference [20,36]. However, the learned representations $\mathbf{z}$ would not be domain invariant, which is desired for domain generalization. To achieve domain-invariant representations, we resort to the information bottleneck (IB) principle [1,48], which will be incorporated into the objective as a regularizer for joint optimization.

3.2   Meta Variational Information Bottleneck

We introduce the IB principle to learn domain-invariant representations under the meta-learning framework. We impose the information bottleneck on the feature representations to control the information flow in deep neural networks.

This should largely remove domain related information while letting through the information that maximizes prediction of labels on the meta-test domain.

We derive new variational bounds of mutual information by leveraging the setting of meta-learning for domain generalization. This gives rise to a meta version of variational information bottleneck, which we call MetaVIB in contrast to its original form in a standard learning framework [1]. To avoid confusion, we omit the superscript t for the meta-test domain in this subsection.

Let the random variables X, Y, and Z denote the input, output, and the intermediate feature representation in the deep neural network, which encodes X. The mutual information $I(Z; Y)$ between the latent encoding Z of data X and its output label Y is defined as follows:

$$I(Z;Y) = \int p(\mathbf{y},\mathbf{z}) \log \frac{p(\mathbf{y},\mathbf{z})}{p(\mathbf{y})p(\mathbf{z})} \mathrm{d}\mathbf{y}\mathrm{d}\mathbf{z} = \int p(\mathbf{y},\mathbf{z}) \log \frac{p(\mathbf{y}|\mathbf{z})}{p(\mathbf{y})} \mathrm{d}\mathbf{y}\mathrm{d}\mathbf{z}. \tag{5}$$

Since $p(\mathbf{y}|\mathbf{z})$ is intractable, we introduce $q(\mathbf{y}|\mathbf{z}, \psi)$ to be a variational approximation of $p(\mathbf{y}|\mathbf{z})$, where conditioning on the classifier parameter ψ is indicated by (4), and the prior distribution of ψ is denoted as $p(\psi)$. Then we have:

$$D_{\mathrm{KL}}[p(\mathbf{y}|\mathbf{z})||q(\mathbf{y}|\mathbf{z},\psi)] = \int p(\mathbf{y}|\mathbf{z}) \log \frac{p(\mathbf{y}|\mathbf{z})}{q(\mathbf{y}|\mathbf{z},\psi)} \mathrm{d}\mathbf{y} \geq 0, \tag{6}$$

which leads to

$$I(Z;Y) \geq \int p(\mathbf{y},\mathbf{z}) \log q(\mathbf{y}|\mathbf{z},\psi) \mathrm{d}\mathbf{y}\mathrm{d}\mathbf{z} + H(Y), \tag{7}$$

where $H(Y) = -\int p(\mathbf{y}) \log p(\mathbf{y}) \mathrm{d}\mathbf{y}$ is the entropy of Y. Taking expectation values of both sides with respect to $\psi \sim p(\psi)$, we have

$$I(Z;Y) - H(Y) \geq \mathbb{E}_{\psi \sim p(\psi)} \int p(\mathbf{y},\mathbf{z}) \log q(\mathbf{y}|\mathbf{z},\psi) \mathrm{d}\mathbf{y}\mathrm{d}\mathbf{z}$$

$$= \int p(\psi)p(\mathbf{y},\mathbf{z}) \log q(\mathbf{y}|\mathbf{z},\psi) \mathrm{d}\mathbf{y}\mathrm{d}\mathbf{z}\mathrm{d}\psi. \tag{8}$$

Note that the entropy $H(Y)$ is independent of our optimization procedure and can thus be ignored. By replacing the prior $p(\psi)$ with a meta prior $q(\psi|D^s)$ conditioned on data D^s from the meta-train domains, leveraging the fact that $p(\mathbf{y},\mathbf{z}) = \int p(\mathbf{y},\mathbf{z}|\mathbf{x})p(\mathbf{x})\mathrm{d}\mathbf{x} = \int p(\mathbf{y}|\mathbf{x})p(\mathbf{z}|\mathbf{x})p(\mathbf{x})\mathrm{d}\mathbf{x}$, and ignoring the $H(Y)$ term, we obtain a new variational lower bound:

$$I(Z;Y) \geq \int p(\mathbf{x})p(\mathbf{y}|\mathbf{x})p(\mathbf{z}|\mathbf{x})q(\psi|D^s) \log q(\mathbf{y}|\psi,\mathbf{z}) \mathrm{d}\mathbf{x}\mathrm{d}\mathbf{y}\mathrm{d}\mathbf{z}\mathrm{d}\psi, \tag{9}$$

which is tractable in general by approximation [1].

Now we consider the second term $I(Z; X)$, which can be written as follows:

$$I(Z;X) = \int p(\mathbf{x},\mathbf{z}) \log \frac{p(\mathbf{z}|\mathbf{x})}{p(\mathbf{z})} \mathrm{d}\mathbf{x}\mathrm{d}\mathbf{z}. \tag{10}$$

Instead of simply using an uninformative prior $p(\mathbf{z})$, we leverage the meta setting and introduce a meta prior $q(\mathbf{z}|D^s)$ as a variational approximation to $p(\mathbf{z})$. Due to the fact that $D_{\mathrm{KL}}[p(Z)||q(Z|D^s)] > 0$, we obtain the following upper bound:

$$I(Z;X) \leq \int p(\mathbf{x})p(\mathbf{z}|\mathbf{x}) \log \frac{p(\mathbf{z}|\mathbf{x})}{q(\mathbf{z}|D^s)} \mathrm{dxdz}. \tag{11}$$

By combining the two bounds (9) and (11), we establish the meta variational information bottleneck (MetaVIB)

$$
\begin{aligned}
\mathcal{L}_{\mathrm{IB}} &\geq \int p(\mathbf{x})p(\mathbf{y}|\mathbf{x})p(\mathbf{z}|\mathbf{x})p(\psi|D^s) \log q(\mathbf{y}|\mathbf{z},\psi) d\mathbf{x}\, d\mathbf{y}\, \mathrm{d}\mathbf{z}\mathrm{d}\psi \\
&- \beta \int p(\mathbf{x})p(\mathbf{z}|\mathbf{x}) \log \frac{p(\mathbf{z}|\mathbf{x})}{q(\mathbf{z}|D^s)} \mathrm{dxdz} = \mathcal{L}_{\mathrm{MetaVIB}}
\end{aligned}
\tag{12}
$$

which extends the IB theory [47] into the meta-learning scenario, offering a new principle of learning domain-invariant representations for domain generalization.

We follow [1] to approximate $p(\mathbf{x}, \mathbf{y}) = p(\mathbf{x})p(\mathbf{y}|\mathbf{x})$ and $p(\mathbf{x})$ with empirical data distribution $p(\mathbf{x}, \mathbf{y}) = \frac{1}{N} \sum_{n=1}^{N} \delta_{\mathbf{x}_n}(\mathbf{x})\delta_{\mathbf{y}_n}(\mathbf{y})$ and $p(\mathbf{x}) = \frac{1}{N} \sum_{n=1}^{N} \delta_{\mathbf{x}_n}(\mathbf{x})$, where N is the number of samples in the meta-test domain. This essentially regards the data points $(\mathbf{x}_n, \mathbf{y}_n)$ and $\mathbf{x}_n$ as the samples drawn from the data distributions $p(\mathbf{x}, \mathbf{y})$ and $p(\mathbf{x})$, respectively.

Thus, the approximated lower bound $\tilde{\mathcal{L}}_{\mathrm{MetaVIB}}$ in practice can be written as:

$$
\begin{aligned}
\tilde{\mathcal{L}}_{\mathrm{MetaVIB}} &= \frac{1}{N} \sum_{n=1}^{N} \int [p(\mathbf{z}_n|\mathbf{x}_n)p(\psi|D^s) \log q(\mathbf{y}_n|\mathbf{z}_n, \psi) \\
&- \beta\, p(\mathbf{z}_n|\mathbf{x}_n) \log \frac{p(\mathbf{z}_n|\mathbf{x}_n)}{q(\mathbf{z}_n|D^s)}] \mathrm{d}\mathbf{z}_n \mathrm{d}\psi.
\end{aligned}
\tag{13}
$$

We use Monte Carlo sampling to draw samples from $p(\psi|D^s)$ for ψ and from $p(\mathbf{z}_n|\mathbf{x}_n)$ for $\mathbf{z}_n$ in the lower bound of MetaVIB in (13). We attain the following objective function:

$$
\begin{aligned}
\mathcal{L} = -\frac{1}{NC} \sum_{c=1}^{C} \sum_{n=1}^{N_c} \Big(\frac{1}{L_\mathbf{z} L_\psi} \sum_{\ell_\mathbf{z}=1}^{L_\mathbf{z}} \sum_{\ell_\psi=1}^{L_\psi} \log q(\mathbf{y}_n|\mathbf{z}^{(\ell_\mathbf{z})}, \psi_c^{(\ell_\psi)}) \\
+ \beta D_{\mathrm{KL}}\left[p(\mathbf{z}|\mathbf{x}_n)||q(\mathbf{z}|D_c^s)\right] \Big).
\end{aligned}
\tag{14}
$$

where C is the number of classes and D_c^s contains the samples from the c-th category in the meta-train domains. We amortize the posterior distribution $q(\psi|D_c^s)$ and the meta prior $q(\mathbf{z}_n|D_c^s)$ across classes, that is, the variational distribution of each class is inferred individually by the samples from its corresponding class D_c^s, which further alleviates the computational overhead. In addition, the KL term can be calculated in a closed form. Here, to enable back-propagation, we adopt the re-parameterization trick [20], that is,

$$\mathbf{z}_n^{(\ell_\mathbf{z})} = f(\mathbf{x}_n, \epsilon^{(\ell_\mathbf{z})}), \quad \epsilon^{(\ell_\mathbf{z})} \sim \mathcal{N}(0, I) \tag{15}$$

and

$$\psi_c^{(\ell_\psi)} = f(D_c^s, \epsilon^{(\ell_\psi)}), \quad \epsilon^{(\ell_\psi)} \sim \mathcal{N}(0, I) \tag{16}$$

where $f(\cdot)$ is a deterministic function which is usually parameterized by a multiple layer perception (MLP) and $L_{\mathbf{z}}$ and L_ψ are the number of samples for $\mathbf{z}_n$ and ψ_c, respectively.

Taking a closer look at the objective (14), we observe that the first term is the negative log predictive likelihood in the meta-test domain, where the label $\mathbf{y}_n$ of $\mathbf{x}_n$ is predicted from its latent encoding $\mathbf{z}_n$ and the classifier parameter ψ. Minimizing the first term guarantees maximal prediction accuracy. The second term is the KL divergence between distributions of latent encoding of the sample in the target domain and that estimated by the samples from the same category in the meta-train domains. It is the minimization of the KL term in (14) that enables the model to learn domain-invariant representations. This is in contrast to the regular IB principle [1,48] which is to compress the input and does not necessarily result in domain-invariant representations.

3.3 Learning with Stochastic Neural Networks

We implement the proposed model by end-to-end learning with stochastic neural networks that are comprised of convolutional layers and fully-connected layers. The inference is parameterized by a feed-forward multiple layer perception (MLP). During the training phase, given K domains, we randomly sample one domain as the meta-test domain, the remaining $K - 1$ domains are used as the meta-train domains. Then we choose a batch of M samples $\{(\mathbf{x}_m^s, \mathbf{y}_m^s)\}_{m=1}^M$ from the meta-train domain $\mathcal{D}^s$, and a batch of N samples $\{(\mathbf{x}_n^t, \mathbf{y}_n^t)\}_{n=1}^N$ from the meta-test domain $\mathcal{D}^t$. Note that M samples from meta-train domains cover all the C classes. For each sample $\mathbf{x}_{m,c}^s$ of the c-th class, we first extract its features via $h_\theta(\mathbf{x}_{m,c}^s)$, where $h_\theta(\cdot)$ is the feature extraction network and we use permutation-invariant instance-pooling operations to get the mean feature $\overline{\mathbf{h}}_c^s$ of samples in the c-th class. The mean feature $\overline{\mathbf{h}}_c^s$ will be fed into a small MLP network $g_{\phi_1}(\cdot)$ to calculate the mean $\boldsymbol{\mu}_c^\psi$ and variance $\boldsymbol{\sigma}_c^\psi$ of the weight vector distribution ψ_c for c-th class, which is then used to sample the weight vector ψ_c of this class by $\psi_c \sim \mathcal{N}(\boldsymbol{\mu}_c^\psi, \text{diag}(((\boldsymbol{\sigma}_c^\psi)^2)))$. The weight vectors $\{\psi_c\}_{c=1}^C$ of all C classes are combined column by column to form a weight matrix $\psi = [\psi_1, \psi_2, \ldots, \psi_C]$.

We calculate the parameters of the latent distribution, i.e., the mean $\boldsymbol{\mu}_c^s$ and variance $\boldsymbol{\sigma}_c^s$ of the c-th class in the meta-train domain by another small MLP network $g_{\phi_2}(\cdot)$. Then the parameter $\mathbf{z}_c$ is sampled from the distribution $\mathbf{z}_c \sim \mathcal{N}(\boldsymbol{\mu}_c^s, \text{diag}((\boldsymbol{\sigma}_c^s)^2))$. For each sample $\mathbf{x}_{n,c}^t$ in the meta-test domain, we also calculate the mean $\boldsymbol{\mu}_{n,c}^t$ and variance $\boldsymbol{\sigma}_{n,c}^t$ of the distribution. Thus its latent coding vector $\mathbf{z}_{n,c}$ can be naturally sampled from $\mathbf{z}_{n,c} \sim \mathcal{N}(\boldsymbol{\mu}_{n,c}^t, \text{diag}(\sigma_{n,c}^t)^2)$. Denote $\overline{\mathbf{h}}_c^s$ as the mean feature of all the samples of the c-th class from the meta-train domains, i.e., $\overline{\mathbf{h}}_c^s = \frac{1}{M_c} \sum_{m=1}^{M_c} \mathbf{x}_{m,c}^s$. We provide the detailed step-by-step algorithm of the proposed MetaVIB for training in the supplemental material.

4   Experiments

We conduct our experiments on three benchmarks commonly used in domain generalization [4,25,29,42]. We first provide ablation studies to gain insights into the properties and benefits of MetaVIB. Then we compare with previous methods based on both regular learning and meta-learning for domain generalization. We put more results in the supplementary material due to space limit.

Table 1. Benefit of MetaVIB under the probabilistic framework on VLCS

	VOC2007	LabelMe	Caltech-101	SUN09	Mean
AlexNet	68.41	62.11	93.40	64.16	72.02
Baseline	69.87±0.63	61.32±0.27	95.97±0.43	66.32±0.25	73.37
VIB	70.02±0.52	62.17±0.29	95.93±0.32	67.93±0.41	74.01
MetaVIB	70.28±0.71	62.66±0.35	97.37±0.63	67.85±0.17	74.54

4.1   Datasets

VLCS [49] is a real-world dataset that contains four domains collected from **VOC2007** [13], **LabelMe** [37], **Caltech-101** [19], and **SUN09** [9]. Images are from 5 classes, i.e., *bird, car, chair, dog, person*. The domain shift across those datasets makes VLCS a suitable benchmark for domain generalization.

PACS [24] contains 9991 images from 4 domains, i.e., **P**hoto, **A**rt painting, **C**artoon, and **S**ketch, which cover huge domain gaps. Images are from 7 object classes, i.e., *dog, elephant, giraffe, guitar, horse, house,* and *person*.

Rotated MNIST [42] is a synthetic dataset consisting of 6 domains, each containing 1000 images of the 10 digits (i.e., $\{0, 1, \ldots, 9\}$, 100 for each) randomly selected from the training set of MNIST [23], with 6 rotation degrees: $0°, 15°, 30°, 45°, 60°,$ and $75°$.

4.2   Implementation Details

Splits, Metrics and Backbone. On all datasets, we follow the train-test splits suggested by [4,24,25], and perform experiments with the "leave-one-domain-out" strategy: we take the samples from one domain as the target domain for testing, and the samples from the remaining domains as the source domain for training. We use the AlexNet [22] pre-trained on ImageNet and fine-tuned on the source domains of each dataset to perform testing on the target domain of that dataset. We use the average accuracy of all classes as the evaluation metric [17]. To benchmark previous methods, we employ the pre-trained AlexNet [22] on ImageNet as the backbone on VLCS and PACS. For Rotated MNIST we use a backbone network with two convolutions and one fully-connected layer. Even more implementation details about training stage, the feature extraction network and inference networks for different datasets are provided in the supplemental materials.

4.3   Ablation Study

To study the benefit of the MetaVIB under the probabilistic framework for domain generalization, we compare with several alternative models on VLCS and PACS in Tables 1 and 2.

Table 2. Benefit of MetaVIB under the probabilistic framework on PACS

	Photo	Art painting	Cartoon	Sketch	Mean
AlexNet	88.47	67.21	66.12	55.32	69.28
Baseline	90.32±0.35	68.12±0.51	70.25±0.17	61.81±0.26	72.63
VIB	90.17±0.28	69.93±0.34	71.01±0.27	62.37±0.42	73.37
MetaVIB	91.93±0.23	71.94±0.34	73.17±0.21	65.94±0.24	75.74

Benefit of Probabilistic Modeling. To show the benefit of probabilistic modeling, we first consider AlexNet [22] which is pre-trained on ImageNet, fine-tuned on the source domains and applied to the target domains. We define our *Baseline* model as the probabilistic model that predicts parameter distributions of the classifiers, without regular VIB or MetaVIB. The probabilistic model outperforms the pre-trained AlexNet by 1.35% and 3.35% on the VLCS and PACS benchmarks. The results indicate that the classifiers learned by probabilistic modeling better generalize to the target domains.

Benefit of MetaVIB. We show the benefit of MetaVIB by comparing with the regular VIB [1], which is applied to the baseline model as a regularization in the optimization, and the Baseline model. We first establish the probabilistic model with the regular *VIB* which performs better than the baseline (74.01% - up 0.64%) on VLCS and (73.37% - up 0.74%) on PACS. The VIB regularization term maximizes the mutual information between Z and the target Y, which will encourage better prediction performance compared to the *Baseline* model. However, our MetaVIB learns an even better domain-invariant representation, as it consistently outperforms VIB by up to 2.37% on **PACS** [24]. As indicated in the optimization objective in (14) minimizing the KL term makes the representations of samples in the meta-target domain to be close to the representations obtained by the samples of the same class from the meta-source domains. As a result, the learned model acquires the ability to generate domain-invariant representations by the episodic training. In contrast, the regular VIB is to simply compress the input with no explicit mechanism to narrow the gaps across domains. The obtained representations with regular VIB are not necessarily domain-invariant. Actually, there is no evident causal relation between compression and generalization as indicated in [39].

Influence of Information Bottleneck Size β. The bottleneck size β controls the amount of information flow that goes through the bottleneck of the networks. To measure its influence on the performance, we plot the information plane dynamics of different network layers with varying β in Fig. 2. We observe that MetaVIB with $\beta = 0.01$ achieves the highest $I(Z;Y)$ while at the same time $I(Z;X)$ is minimal. We also report the influence of β in Table 3. MetaVIB achieves the best performance when $\beta = 0.01$, which is consistent with the information dynamic in Fig. 2. We observe in Fig. 2(c) that with $\beta = 0.01$, the $I(X;T)$ is lowest and $I(T;Y)$ is the highest, compared to those with other values of β. A larger $I(Z;Y)$ indicates that we can make more accurate predictions Y from Z, while a smaller $I(Z;X)$ indicates Z contains the minimal information from X that is required for prediction, suggesting a domain-invariant representation Z. This explains why $\beta = 0.01$ produces the best prediction results compared to other values of β. In our experiments, the optimal value of β is obtained by using a validation set for each dataset and we found $\beta = 0.01$ produces the best performance on all datasets.

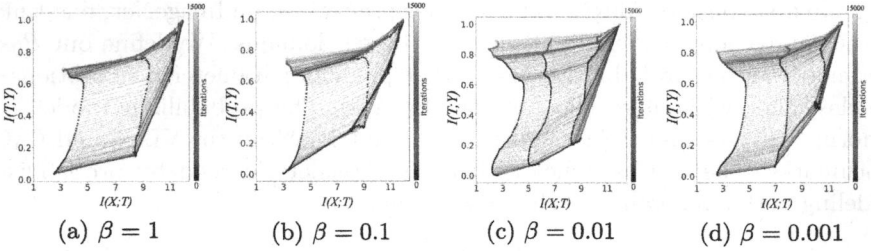

(a) $\beta = 1$ (b) $\beta = 0.1$ (c) $\beta = 0.01$ (d) $\beta = 0.001$

Fig. 2. Influence of information bottleneck size β on domain generalization for "Sketch" as the test domain on PACS. X, Y, and T denote input image, output target, and outputs per layer of the inference network that generates the latent encoding Z. The horizontal (vertical) axis plots mutual information between the features of each layer and the input (output). Each of the three layers of the inference network produces a curve in the information plane with the input layer at the far right and output layer at the far left. The color-scale denotes training iterations from 0 to 15,000. The mutual information of different layers in the same iteration are connected by fine lines. Compared to other values of β, for $\beta = 0.01$, $I(T;Y)$ reaches the highest value, which explains the best performance.

Table 3. Influence of information bottleneck size β on domain generalization for PACS. MetaVIB obtains best results for $\beta = 0.01$. We obtain similar results on other datasets, see supplemental material.

	Photo	Art painting	Cartoon	Sketch	Mean
$\beta = 1$	89.05±0.45	69.02±0.41	71.13±0.17	58.87±0.43	72.02
$\beta = 0.1$	90.51±0.14	70.71±0.28	70.78±0.11	62.05±0.26	73.51
$\beta = 0.01$	91.93±0.23	71.94±0.34	73.17±0.21	65.94±0.24	75.74
$\beta = 0.001$	90.17±0.25	70.07±0.32	71.75±0.17	63.90±0.38	73.89

Analyzing Domain-Invariance. We visualize the features learned by the pre-trained AlexNet, VIB and MetaVIB in Fig. 3. For better illustration, we use t-SNE [30] to reduce the feature dimension into a two-dimensional subspace. We observe that the features of the same category learned by pre-trained Alexnet (Fig. 3(a)) show large discrepancy among the four domains. The regular VIB reduces this discrepancy to some extent, but still suffers from considerable gaps between the unseen domain (violet shapes) (Fig. 3(b)). MetaVIB largely reduces the discrepancy of different domains including the unseen domains as shown in Fig. 3(c). In Fig. 3(d), we observe again that the gaps of features among 4 domains by the pre-trained AlexNet are larger than those between the 7 classes in each domain. Figure 3(e) shows that the VIB reduces the domain gaps to certain extent. From Fig. 3(f), we observe MetaVIB reduces domain gaps considerably while at the same time scatters the samples of 7 classes in each domain. Overall, the proposed MetaVIB principle demonstrates effectiveness in learning domain-invariant representations to tackle domain shift.

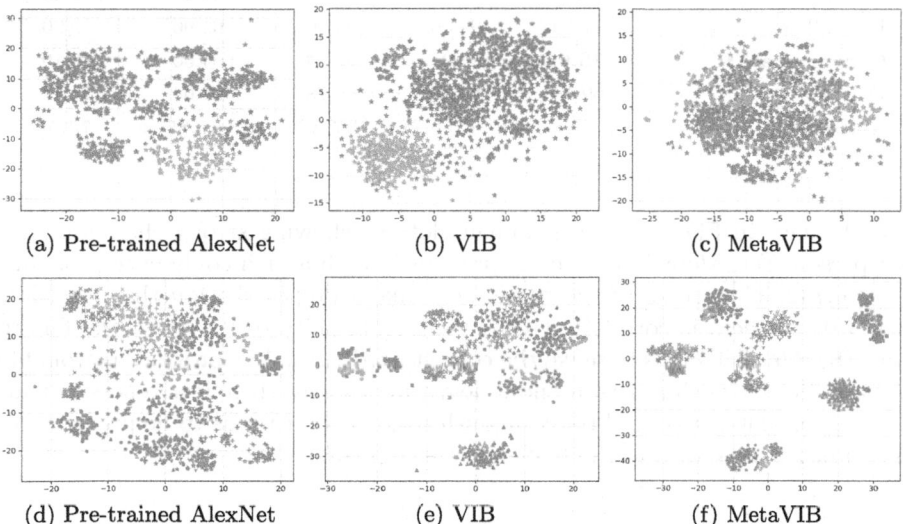

(a) Pre-trained AlexNet   (b) VIB   (c) MetaVIB

(d) Pre-trained AlexNet   (e) VIB   (f) MetaVIB

Fig. 3. Analyzing domain-invariance. Visualization of feature representations from pre-trained AlexNet, VIB, and MetaVIB on PACS. The top row shows different features for the *horse* category from four different domains, where the violet shapes denotes the unseen domain *cartoon*. Bottom row shows the distributions of feature representations from all seven PACS classes for four domains, where the unseen domain (green) is *art painting*. MetaVIB reduces the domain gap to achieve domain-invariant yet discriminative representations, which enables accurate predictions. MetaVIB fills the gap between domains (c), while maximally separating samples of different classes (f).

Success and Failure Cases. We show some success and failure cases in Fig. 4. MetaVIB successfully predicts the labels for ambiguous images. The dog in the

       (a) Success cases   (b) Failure cases

Fig. 4. Success and failure cases of MetaVIB. The numbers associated with each image are the top two prediction probabilities of MetaVIB, with ground truth labels in red. MetaVIB successfully distinguishes ambiguous cases in (a). For more challenging cases in (b), MetaVIB provides a high probability for the true label, but fails to make the correct prediction.

Table 4. State-of-the-Art comparison on VLCS, in classification accuracy (%).

	VOC2007	LabelMe	Caltech-101	SUN09	Mean
D'Innocente & Caputo [11]	66.06	57.45	94.95	65.87	71.08
Li et al. [24]	69.99	63.49	93.63	61.32	72.11
Li et al. [25]	67.70	62.60	94.40	64.40	72.28
Li et al. [26]	67.10	64.30	94.10	65.90	72.90
Carlucci et al. [8]	**70.62**	60.90	96.93	64.30	73.19
Dou et al.[10]	69.14	**64.90**	94.78	67.64	74.11
MetaVIB	70.28±0.21	62.66±0.35	**97.37**±0.23	**67.85**±0.17	**74.54**

second image in Fig. 4(a) wears human clothes, showing strong characteristics of a person. Yet, MetaVIB correctly predicts it with a high confidence probability of 0.732. The sketch of the horse looks like a dog in the fourth image, but MetaVIB predicts it correctly with a high probability of 0.636. In the failure cases (b), MetaVIB fails to make the correct prediction, but provides reasonable probabilities for both a person and a dog, which shows the effectiveness in handling uncertainty. It is hard to distinguish which object needs to be predicted in these images, as shown in the first image in Fig. 4(b).

4.4 State-of-the-Art Comparison

We compare with regular and meta-learning methods for domain generalization. The results on the three datasets are reported in Tables 4, 5, and 6. On the **VLCS** dataset [49], our MetaVIB achieves high recognition accuracy, surpassing the second best method, i.e., MASF [10], by a margin of 0.43%. Note that on all domains, our MetaVIB consistently outperforms MLDG [25], which is a gradient-based meta-learning algorithm. On the **PACS** dataset [24], our MetaVIB again achieves the best overall performance. It outperforms most of the previous methods, showing clear performance advantages over JiGen [8]. Again, our MetaVIB performs better than other meta-learning based methods, e.g., MetaReg [4], Reptile [33], MLDG [25], Feature-Critic [29], and MASF [10]. It is worth highlighting that our MetaVIB exceeds those meta-learning methods

Table 5. State-of-the-Art comparison on PACS, in classification accuracy (%).

	Photo	Art painting	Cartoon	Sketch	Mean
Ghifary et al. [17]	91.12	60.27	58.65	47.68	64.48
Bousmalis et al. [7]	83.25	61.13	66.54	58.58	67.37
Li et al. [24]	89.50	62.86	66.97	57.51	69.21
Shankar et al. [42]	89.48	64.84	67.69	57.52	69.63
Li et al. [25]	88.00	66.23	66.88	58.96	70.01
Nichol et al. [33]	88.78	64.35	70.09	59.91	70.78
Li et al. [26]	86.10	64.70	72.30	65.00	72.00
Li et al. [29]	89.94	64.89	71.72	61.85	72.10
Balaji et al. [4]	91.70	69.82	70.35	59.26	72.62
Carlucci et al. [8]	89.00	67.63	71.71	65.18	73.38
Dou et al.[10]	90.68	70.35	72.46	**67.33**	75.21
MetaVIB	**91.93**±0.23	**71.94**±0.34	**73.17**±0.21	65.94±0.24	**75.74**

Table 6. State-of-the-Art comparison on Rotated MNIST, in averaged classification accuracy (%) of different methods over 10 runs. MetaVIB consistently achieves the best performance on different domains with different rotation angles.

	$M_{0°}$	$M_{15°}$	$M_{30°}$	$M_{45°}$	$M_{60°}$	$M_{75°}$	Mean
Shankar et al. [42]	86.03±0.69	98.92±0.53	98.60±0.51	98.38±0.29	98.68±0.28	88.94±0.47	94.93
Balaji et al. [4]	85.70±0.31	98.87±0.41	98.32±0.44	98.58±0.28	98.93±0.32	89.44±0.37	94.97
Li et al. [27]	86.42±0.24	98.61±0.27	99.19±0.19	98.22±0.24	99.48±0.19	88.92±0.43	95.15
Nichol et al. [33]	87.78±0.30	99.44±0.24	98.42±0.24	98.80±0.20	99.03±0.28	87.42±0.33	95.15
Li et al. [29]	89.23±0.25	99.68±0.24	99.20±0.20	99.24±0.18	99.53±0.23	91.44±0.34	96.39
MetaVIB	**91.28**±0.21	**99.90**±0.02	**99.29**±0.11	**99.78**±0.10	**99.57**±0.13	**92.75**±0.31	**97.08**

on the "Cartoon" domain by phenomenal margins. On the **Rotated MNIST** dataset [42], the proposed MetaVIB achieves consistently high performance on the test domains, exceeding the alternative methods. It is worthwhile to mention that our MetaVIB outperforms the meta-learning algorithms MetaReg [4], and Reptile [33] showing its effectiveness as a meta-learning method for domain generalization. To conclude, on all datasets, our MetaVIB accomplishes better performance than previous methods based on both regular learning and meta-learning. The best results on all benchmarks validate the effectiveness of our method for domain generalization.

5   Conclusion

In this work, we propose a new probabilistic model for domain generalization under the meta-learning framework. To address prediction uncertainty, we model the parameters of the classifiers shared across domains by a probabilistic distribution, which is inferred from the source domain and directly used for the target domains. To reduce domain shift, our method learns domain-invariant representations by a new Meta Variational Information Bottleneck principle, derived from a variational bound of mutual information. MetaVIB integrates the strengths of meta-learning, variational inference and probabilistic modeling for domain generalization. Our MetaVIB has been evaluated by extensive experiments on three benchmark datasets for cross-domain visual recognition. Ablation studies validate the benefits of our contributions. MetaVIB consistently achieves high performance and advances the state of the art on all three benchmarks.

References

1. Alemi, A.A., Fischer, I., Dillon, J.V., Murphy, K.: Deep variational information bottleneck. In: International Conference on Learning Representations (2017)
2. Amjad, R.A., Geiger, B.C.: Learning representations for neural network-based classification using the information bottleneck principle. In: IEEE Transactions on Pattern Analysis and Machine Intelligence (2019)
3. Andrychowicz, M., et al.: Learning to learn by gradient descent by gradient descent. In: Advances in Neural Information Processing Systems (2016)
4. Balaji, Y., Sankaranarayanan, S., Chellappa, R.: MetaReg: towards domain generalization using meta-regularization. In: Advances in Neural Information Processing Systems, pp. 998–1008 (2018)
5. Bertinetto, L., Henriques, J.F., Valmadre, J., Torr, P.H.S., Vedaldi, A.: Learning feed-forward one-shot learners. In: Advances in Neural Information Processing Systems (2016)
6. Blanchard, G., Lee, G., Scott, C.: Generalizing from several related classification tasks to a new unlabeled sample. In: Advances in Neural Information Processing Systems, pp. 2178–2186 (2011)
7. Bousmalis, K., Trigeorgis, G., Silberman, N., Krishnan, D., Erhan, D.: Domain separation networks. In: Advances in Neural Information Processing Systems, pp. 343–351 (2016)
8. Carlucci, F.M., D'Innocente, A., Bucci, S., Caputo, B., Tommasi, T.: Domain generalization by solving jigsaw puzzles. In: IEEE Conference on Computer Vision and Pattern Recognition (2019)
9. Choi, M.J., Lim, J.J., Torralba, A., Willsky, A.S.: Exploiting hierarchical context on a large database of object categories. In: 2010 IEEE Computer Society Conference on Computer Vision and Pattern Recognition, pp. 129–136. IEEE (2010)
10. Dou, Q., de Castro, D.C., Kamnitsas, K., Glocker, B.: Domain generalization via model-agnostic learning of semantic features. In: Advances in Neural Information Processing Systems, pp. 6447–6458 (2019)
11. D'Innocente, A., Caputo, B.: Domain generalization with domain-specific aggregation modules. In: Brox, T., Bruhn, A., Fritz, M. (eds.) GCPR 2018. LNCS, vol. 11269, pp. 187–198. Springer, Cham (2019). https://doi.org/10.1007/978-3-030-12939-2_14
12. Erfani, S., et al.: Robust domain generalisation by enforcing distribution invariance. In: Proceedings of the International Joint Conference on Artificial Intelligence, pp. 1455–1461 (2016)
13. Everingham, M., Van Gool, L., Williams, C.K., Winn, J., Zisserman, A.: The Pascal visual object classes (VOC) challenge. Int. J. Comput. Vis. **88**(2), 303–338 (2010)

14. Finn, C., Abbeel, P., Levine, S.: Model-agnostic meta-learning for fast adaptation of deep networks. In: Proceedings of International Conference on Machine Learning, pp. 1126–1135 (2017)
15. Finn, C., Levine, S.: Meta-learning and universality: deep representations and gradient descent can approximate any learning algorithm. In: International Conference on Learning Representations (2018)
16. Finn, C., Xu, K., Levine, S.: Probabilistic model-agnostic meta-learning. In: Advances in Neural Information Processing Systems, pp. 9516–9527 (2018)
17. Ghifary, M., Bastiaan Kleijn, W., Zhang, M., Balduzzi, D.: Domain generalization for object recognition with multi-task autoencoders. In: The IEEE International Conference on Computer Vision, pp. 2551–2559 (2015)
18. Gordon, J., Bronskill, J., Bauer, M., Nowozin, S., Turner, R.E.: Meta-learning probabilistic inference for prediction. arXiv preprint arXiv:1805.09921 (2018)
19. Griffin, G., Holub, A., Perona, P.: Caltech-256 object category dataset (2007)
20. Kingma, D.P., Welling, M.: Auto-encoding variational Bayes. In: International Conference on Learning Representations (2014)
21. Kolchinsky, A., Tracey, B.D., Van Kuyk, S.: Caveats for information bottleneck in deterministic scenarios. arXiv preprint arXiv:1808.07593 (2018)
22. Krizhevsky, A., Sutskever, I., Hinton, G.E.: ImageNet classification with deep convolutional neural networks. In: Advances in Neural Information Processing Systems, pp. 1097–1105 (2012)
23. LeCun, Y., Bottou, L., Bengio, Y., Haffner, P., et al.: Gradient-based learning applied to document recognition. Proc. IEEE **86**(11), 2278–2324 (1998)
24. Li, D., Yang, Y., Song, Y.Z., Hospedales, T.M.: Deeper, broader and artier domain generalization. In: Proceedings of the IEEE International Conference on Computer Vision, pp. 5542–5550 (2017)
25. Li, D., Yang, Y., Song, Y.Z., Hospedales, T.M.: Learning to generalize: meta-learning for domain generalization. In: 32nd AAAI Conference on Artificial Intelligence (2018)
26. Li, D., Zhang, J., Yang, Y., Liu, C., Song, Y.Z., Hospedales, T.M.: Episodic training for domain generalization. In: IEEE International Conference on Computer Vision (2019)
27. Li, H., Jialin Pan, S., Wang, S., Kot, A.C.: Domain generalization with adversarial feature learning. In: Proceedings of the IEEE Conference on Computer Vision and Pattern Recognition, pp. 5400–5409 (2018)
28. Li, Y., et al.: Deep domain generalization via conditional invariant adversarial networks. In: Ferrari, V., Hebert, M., Sminchisescu, C., Weiss, Y. (eds.) ECCV 2018. LNCS, vol. 11219, pp. 647–663. Springer, Cham (2018). https://doi.org/10.1007/978-3-030-01267-0_38
29. Li, Y., Yang, Y., Zhou, W., Hospedales, T.M.: Feature-critic networks for heterogeneous domain generalization. In: Proceedings of International Conference on Machine Learning (2019)
30. Maaten, L., Hinton, G.: Visualizing data using t-SNE. J. Mach. Learn. Res. **9**, 2579–2605 (2008)
31. Muandet, K., Balduzzi, D., Schölkopf, B.: Domain generalization via invariant feature representation. In: Proceedings of International Conference on Machine Learning, pp. 10–18 (2013)
32. Munkhdalai, T., Yu, H.: Meta networks. In: Proceedings of International Conference on Machine Learning (2017)
33. Nichol, A., Achiam, J., Schulman, J.: On first-order meta-learning algorithms. arXiv preprint arXiv:1803.02999 (2018)

34. Peng, X.B., Kanazawa, A., Toyer, S., Abbeel, P., Levine, S.: Variational discriminator bottleneck: Improving imitation learning, inverse RL, and GANs by constraining information flow. arXiv preprint arXiv:1810.00821 (2018)
35. Ravi, S., Larochelle, H.: Optimization as a model for few-shot learning. In: International Conference on Learning Representations (2017)
36. Rezende, D.J., Mohamed, S., Wierstra, D.: Stochastic backpropagation and approximate inference in deep generative models. arXiv preprint arXiv:1401.4082 (2014)
37. Russell, B.C., Torralba, A., Murphy, K.P., Freeman, W.T.: LabelMe: a database and web-based tool for image annotation. Int. J. Comput. Vis. **77**(1–3), 157–173 (2008)
38. Satorras, V.G., Estrach, J.B.: Few-shot learning with graph neural networks. In: International Conference on Learning Representations (2018)
39. Saxe, A.M., et al.: On the information bottleneck theory of deep learning. In: International Conference on Learning Representations (2018)
40. Schmidhuber, J.: Learning to control fast-weight memories: an alternative to dynamic recurrent networks. Neural Comput. **4**(1), 131–139 (1992)
41. Schmidhuber, J., Zhao, J., Wiering, M.: Shifting inductive bias with success-story algorithm, adaptive Levin search, and incremental self-improvement. Mach. Learn. **28**(1), 105–130 (1997)
42. Shankar, S., Piratla, V., Chakrabarti, S., Chaudhuri, S., Jyothi, P., Sarawagi, S.: Generalizing across domains via cross-gradient training. arXiv preprint arXiv:1804.10745 (2018)
43. Shwartz-Ziv, R., Tishby, N.: Opening the black box of deep neural networks via information. arXiv preprint arXiv:1703.00810 (2017)
44. Snell, J., Swersky, K., Zemel, R.: Prototypical networks for few-shot learning. In: Advances in Neural Information Processing Systems, pp. 4077–4087 (2017)
45. Sung, F., Yang, Y., Zhang, L., Xiang, T., Torr, P.H., Hospedales, T.M.: Learning to compare: relation network for few-shot learning. In: IEEE Conference on Computer Vision and Pattern Recognition, pp. 1199–1208 (2018)
46. Thrun, S., Pratt, L.: Learning to Learn. Springer, New York (2012). https://doi.org/10.1007/978-1-4615-5529-2
47. Tishby, N., Pereira, F.C., Bialek, W.: The information bottleneck method. arXiv preprint physics/0004057 (2000)
48. Tishby, N., Zaslavsky, N.: Deep learning and the information bottleneck principle. In: 2015 IEEE Information Theory Workshop (ITW) (April 2015). https://doi.org/10.1109/itw.2015.7133169
49. Torralba, A., Efros, A.A., et al.: Unbiased look at dataset bias. In: IEEE Conference on Computer Vision and Pattern Recognition (2011)
50. Vilalta, R., Drissi, Y.: A perspective view and survey of meta-learning. Artif. Intell. Rev. **18**(2), 77–95 (2002)
51. Vinyals, O., Blundell, C., Lillicrap, T., Kavukcuoglu, K., Wierstra, D.: Matching networks for one shot learning. In: Advances in Neural Information Processing Systems, pp. 3637–3645 (2016)
52. Xie, Q., Dai, Z., Du, Y., Hovy, E., Neubig, G.: Controllable invariance through adversarial feature learning. In: Advances in Neural Information Processing Systems, pp. 585–596 (2017)
53. Zhen, X., et al.: Learning to learn kernels with variational random features. In: International Conference on Machine Learning (2020)

Deep Positional and Relational Feature Learning for Rotation-Invariant Point Cloud Analysis

Ruixuan Yu[1,2], Xin Wei[1], Federico Tombari[2,3], and Jian Sun[1(✉)]

[1] Xi'an Jiaotong University, Xi'an, China
{yuruixuan123,wxmath}@stu.xjtu.edu.cn, jiansun@xjtu.edu.cn
[2] Technical University of Munich, Munich, Germany
tombari@google.com
[3] Google, Zürich, Switzerland

Abstract. In this paper we propose a rotation-invariant deep network for point clouds analysis. Point-based deep networks are commonly designed to recognize roughly aligned 3D shapes based on point coordinates, but suffer from performance drops with shape rotations. Some geometric features, e.g., distances and angles of points as inputs of network, are rotation-invariant but lose positional information of points. In this work, we propose a novel deep network for point clouds by incorporating positional information of points as inputs while yielding rotation-invariance. The network is hierarchical and relies on two modules: a positional feature embedding block and a relational feature embedding block. Both modules and the whole network are proven to be rotation-invariant when processing point clouds as input. Experiments show state-of-the-art classification and segmentation performances on benchmark datasets, and ablation studies demonstrate effectiveness of the network design.

Keywords: Rotation-invariance · Point cloud · Deep feature learning

1 Introduction

Point clouds are widely employed as a popular 3D representation for objects and scenes. They are generated by most current acquisition techniques and 3D sensors, and used within well-studied application fields such as autonomous driving, archaeology, robotics, augmented reality, to name a few. Among these applications, shape recognition and segmentation are two fundamental tasks focusing on automatically recognizing and segmenting 3D objects or object parts [1–3].

The majority of 3D object recognition approaches are currently based on deep learning [1,2,4–7]. Most of the point-based methods take positional information,

---

Electronic supplementary material The online version of this chapter (https://doi.org/10.1007/978-3-030-58607-2_13) contains supplementary material, which is available to authorized users.

© Springer Nature Switzerland AG 2020
A. Vedaldi et al. (Eds.): ECCV 2020, LNCS 12355, pp. 217–233, 2020.
https://doi.org/10.1007/978-3-030-58607-2_13

such as point coordinates or normal vectors on aligned 3D objects, as inputs for the network, then learn deep features suitable for the task at hand. These methods now achieve state-of-the-art performance for 3D recognition. PointNet [8] firstly designed a network to process point clouds by taking point coordinates as inputs. Following works such as [1,2,9–11] developed various convolution operations on point clouds which brought performance improvements. These advances justify that designing networks based on the positional information of 3D points on aligned object shapes is an effective way for shape recognition.

Nevertheless, in many scenarios such as, e.g., 6D pose estimation for robotics/AR [12,13] and CAD models [14] in industrial environments, or analysis of molecules [15,16] where small scale objects are uncontrolled, a major limitation of above point-based methods is that they tend to be rotation-sensitive, and their performance drops dramatically when tested on shapes under arbitrary rotations in the 3D rotation group SO(3). A remedy for this is to develop robustness against rotations by augmenting training dataset with arbitrary rotations, e.g., the SO(3)/SO(3) mode in Spherical CNN [17]. However, it is not efficient to use data augmentation for learning rotation-invariance, since the enlarged dataset requires a large computational cost. Also, the developed robustness to rotations of the network will be up to the seen augmentations during training.

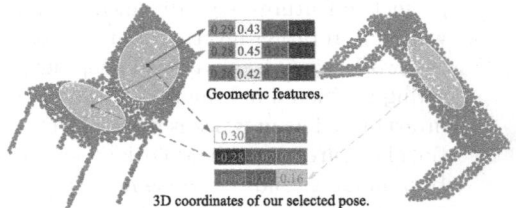

Geometric features.

3D coordinates of our selected pose.

To deal with rotation-sensitivity, an alternative way is to represent shapes with geometric features such as distances and angles. Spherical CNN [17] and a^3SCNN [19] are representative works that take distances and angles as spherical functions. They learn rotation-equivariant features by defining convolutions on spherical functions, and then aggregate features by global average pooling for rotation-invariance. Note that

Fig. 1. The three circles highlight examples of local planar surfaces. Their center points are similar with geometric features [18], but distinguishable by point coordinates of selected pose as features in our approach. Features of each center point are shown in rows of tables.

these representations are not rigorously rotation-invariant due to discretization on sphere. ClusterNet [18] and RIConvNet [20] also take rotation-invariant geometric features as inputs and design specific convolutions on local point cloudsan. However, directly transforming point coordinates to rotation-invariant geometric features may lose positional information of point cloud, which is essential to recognize 3D shapes when they are (roughly) aligned. For example, in Fig. 1, three local surfaces within the circles are flat surfaces belonging to different parts of two shapes. If we represent the center points of these local surfaces by geometric features (e.g., in ClusterNet [18]) agnostic to their positional information, these features may not distinguish different parts of the same shape or different shapes.

To achieve rotation-invariant shape recognition with high accuracy, we propose a novel deep architecture by learning positional and relational features of point cloud. It takes both point coordinates and geometric features as network inputs, and achieves rotation-invariance by designing a *Positional Feature Embedding block (PFE-block)* and a *Relational Feature Embedding block (RFE-block)*, both of which are rotation-invariant. For both shape classification and segmentation, invariant features on point cloud guarantee that classification label of shape and segmentation label of each point are invariant to shape rotation.

It seems to be contradictory to learn rotation-invariant features with point coordinates as input. We design the PFE-block as composition of a pose expander, a pose selector and a positional feature extractor. The PFE-block is proven to be able to produce invariant features for points agnostic to shape rotations. The pose expander maps the shape into a rotation-invariant pose space, then the pose selector selects a unique pose from the space, whose point coordinates are more discriminative than geometric features as shown in Fig. 1. With this selected pose, we extract its positional features by a positional feature extractor. The RFE-block further enhances the deep feature representation of the point cloud with relational convolutions, where the weights are learned based on the relations of neighboring points. This block is also rotation-invariant.

As a summary, we propose two novel rotation-invariant network blocks and a deep hierarchical network jointly learning positional and relational features as shown in Fig. 2. Our network is one of the very few works that achieve rigorous rotation-invariance. For both point cloud shape classification and segmentation, we achieve state-of-the-art performances on commonly used benchmark datasets.

2   Related Work

2.1   Point-Based Deep Learning

Point cloud is a basic representation for 3D shape, and point coordinates are taken as raw features by most point-based networks to carry out tasks on aligned shapes. PointNet [8] is the first effort that takes point coordinates as raw features and embeds positional information of points to deep features followed by max-pooling to be a global shape descriptor. Afterwards, a series of works attempt to improve feature embedding by designing novel deep networks on point clouds. PointNet++ [1] builds hierarchical architecture with PointNet as local encoder. More works such as SpiderCNN [9], PointCNN [2], KCNet [21], PointConv [22], RS-CNN [23] learn point cloud features with various local convolutions starting from point coordinates or additional geometric features. Though these works have achieved state-of-the-art performance for various shape analysis tasks, they are sensitive to shape rotation. In our work, we build a novel network with building blocks being able to achieve rotation-invariance, but with positional raw features as inputs. Our network can explore and encode positional information of 3D shapes while precluding the disadvantage of rotation-sensitiveness.

2.2   Rotation-Robust Representations

There are several ways to improve rotation-robustness. Data augmentation by randomly rotating shapes in training set is widely applied in training 3D

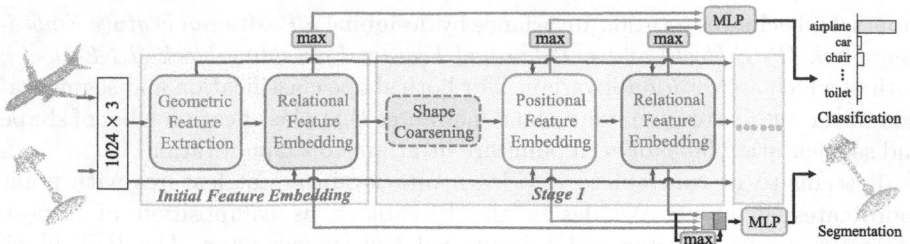

Fig. 2. PR-invNet consists of geometric feature extraction, positional feature embedding block, relational feature embedding block. PR-invNet is designed for classification and segmentation. Shape coarsening is not utilized in segmentation.

networks as in [8,9]. Furthermore, transformer network [24] was generalized and utilized in 3D recognition [8,25,26]. The transformer implicitly learns alignments among shapes either in 3D space or feature space which may reduce the impact of shape rotations. As shown in [18], these techniques commonly improved robustness but can not achieve rigorous invariance to rotations.

Rotation-invariant geometric features can be taken as network inputs. Traditionally, these hand-crafted features are widely utilized to represent 3D shapes in [27–31], and further introduced as inputs of deep networks [18,20,32]. Most of them utilize distances and angles [20,32] and sine/cosin values of the angles [18] as raw point-wise features. They encode relations among points and achieve invariance to arbitrary shape rotations. However, the geometric features may lose discriminative clues that are contained in point positions/orientations.

Another way to achieve rotation-robustness is to learn rotation-equivariant features. [33] built filters on spherical harmonics and learned locally equivariant features to 3D rotations and translations. Group convolution [34] is a generalized convolution to achieve rotation-equivariant feature learning based on rotation-group. This idea is extended to 3D domain [35] with various discretized rotation-groups. Spherical CNN [17] and a^3SCNN [19] defined group convolution on sphere which can be taken as an approximation to infinite group SO(3). They also require the input of the networks to be rotation-equivariant if regarding features as functions over shapes. Commonly, these methods lead to rotation-robustness by global aggregation such as average-pooling or max-pooling, but rigorous rotation-invariance is not ensured due to the discretized rotation groups.

Instead of requiring rotation-invariant geometric features as inputs, our network can directly learn positional features from point coordinates as inputs while achieving rigorous rotation-invariance based on PFE-block. It embeds the input shape into a rotation-invariant pose space, from which we derive a discriminative pose by pose selector to be sent to positional feature extractor, and this operation is rotation-invariant and justified to be effective in experiments.

3   Method

In this section, we introduce our rotation-invariant network, dubbed *PR-InvNet*. It aims at deep positional and relational feature learning, based on, respectively, the PFE-block and RFE-block. As in Fig. 2, it consists of several stages. The initial feature embedding stage is composed of geometric feature extraction and RFE-block. The output features of the PFE and RFE blocks are max-pooled over point cloud and concatenated, then fed to a MLP for shape classification. For point cloud segmentation, we switch off shape coarsening operation, and the concatenated features of PFE-blocks and RFE-blocks are further concatenated with globally max-pooled features before being fed to MLP for point label prediction. Each stage is now detailed in the following.

3.1   Geometric Feature Extraction

PR-invNet takes geometric features similar to [18] as additional raw input features complementary to point coordinates[1]. As shown in Fig. 3, c and o are the centers of the global shape and a local patch respectively. To compute geometric features of point o, we first consider its neighboring points. The feature of each of its neighboring point q is computed as $[|\vec{cq}|, |\vec{oq}|, cos(\alpha), cos(\beta)]$, with $[\cdot]$ being the concatenation operation. Then we concatenate features of all neighboring points together with the distance of $|\vec{co}|$ as the geometric feature of point o, i.e.,

$$g_o = [|\vec{co}|, \{|\vec{cq}|, |\vec{oq}|, cos(\alpha), cos(\beta)\}_{q \in N(o)}],   \tag{1}$$

where $N(o)$ denotes set of neighboring points of o. For simplicity, we denote it as $\{g_i\}_{i=1}^{N}$ with N as number of points. It can be noted that g_i is rotation-invariant, please refer to supplemental material for proof. In our work, for each given point, the above geometric features are extracted and concatenated over a multi-scale neighborhoods (three neighborhoods determined by Euclidean distance with 8, 16, 32 points), and 8 neighboring points are uniformly sampled at each scale. Then the geometric feature of each point is in length of $3 \times 4 \times 8 + 1 = 97$.

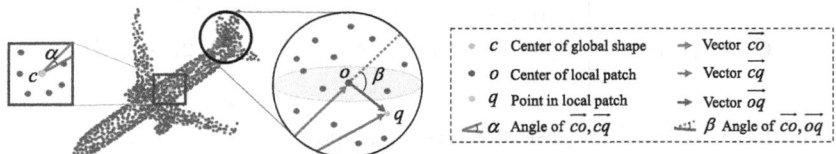

Fig. 3. Illustration of geometric feature extraction for point o which is based on distances and angles. See Subsect. 3.1 for details.

---

[1] Even without geometric features, our network would be still rotation-invariant.

3.2   Positional Feature Embedding Block

The PFE-block aims to perform rotation-invariant feature embedding by incorporating positional information encoded in point coordinates. Since point coordinates are sensitive to shape rotations, one solution is to take all rotated versions (i.e., poses) of a shape into consideration, and fuse extracted features from them by global pooling. However, this is inefficient since there are infinite number of rotations in SO(3) to ensure rigorous rotation-invariance. We propose an idea that first maps input shape to a rotation-invariant pose space by *pose expander*, then selects a representative pose by *pose selector*. Point coordinates of selected pose are utilized to extract positional features by *feature extractor*.

Pose Expander. The pose expander aims to map a shape to produce a rotation-invariant pose space. Given a shape with point cloud $P \in \mathcal{R}^{N \times 3}$, it is obvious that the pose space $\{T_g P\}_{g \in SO(3)}$ containing all possible rotated shapes in SO(3) is rotation-invariant. We aim to derive a compact pose space of input shape guaranteeing rotation-invariance. We achieve this by first normalizing the pose of each shape via Principal Components Analysis (PCA), then applying a discretized rotation-group in SO(3) to the normalized shape to derive a pose space.

We first apply PCA on the point coordinates of a shape to normalize its pose using a coordinate system composed of the three eigen-vectors. We indicate the normalized shape as $\widehat{P}$. Note that pose normalization by PCA is not injective. For example, eigen-decomposition may result in different signs of eigen-vectors, therefore results in different normalized shapes. In Fig. 4, a shape with two rotated versions

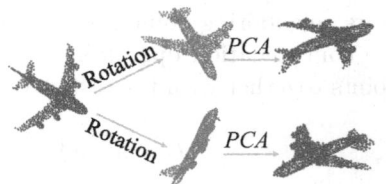

Fig. 4. Two rotated versions of one shape may result in two symmetric and different poses by PCA.

may produce two different normalized shapes, which are symmetric.

To solve the ambiguity of PCA-normalized shape, we enumerate all possible signs of eigen-vectors, and construct a PCA-normalized pose space with eight normalized shapes based on a symmetric group G_S

$$G_S = \{g_s | g_s = \begin{bmatrix} x & 0 & 0 \\ 0 & y & 0 \\ 0 & 0 & z \end{bmatrix}, x, y, z \in \{-1, 1\}, s = 1, 2, \cdots, 8\}, \quad (2)$$

Then the PCA-normalized pose space is obtained as

$$H_S(P) = \{\widehat{P} g_s | g_s \in G_S\}, \quad (3)$$

where $H_S(P)$ contains eight possible PCA-normalized shapes corresponding to different possible signs of eigen-vectors, and this pose space is denoted as *sym-space*. Theorem 1 proves that $H_S(P)$ is rotation-invariant for input shape P.

Though sym-space is rotation-invariant, PCA may not always well align the poses of different shapes even from the same category. We further expand the pose space from $H_S(P)$ to increase the possibility of containing aligned poses for different shapes. By discretizing SO(3) using limited representative rotations, we enlarge sym-space $H_S(P)$ to *rot-space* $H_{SR}(P)$ using rotation group G_R as

$$H_{SR}(P) = \{\widehat{P}g_s g_r | g_s \in G_S, g_r \in G_R\}, \qquad (4)$$

where G_R can be any discretized subgroup of SO(3). $H_{SR}(P)$ is also rotation-invariant for P as proved by Theorem 1. Compared with $H_S(P)$, rot-space $H_{SR}(P)$ contains more poses with higher chances to include the same or similar poses of different shapes. In our implementation, we use rotation group A_5 , i.e., alternating group of a regular dodecahedron (or a regular icosahedron) [36] to construct the rot-space. By deleting duplicate shapes, we finally map the shape with rotation set $A_5 \times Z_2$ into rot-space with 120 poses.

Pose Selector. Given a shape P, we have derived a rotation-invariant pose space $H_{SR}(P)$, i.e., the rot-space. One naive way is to extract features from different poses of the shape in pose space followed by orderless operations, e.g., average- or max-pooling, to aggregate features as a rotation-invariant representation for shape P. However, it is computationally intensive to extract features from multiple poses of shape. We design a simple but effective method by selecting the most representative shape pose using a pose selector, and learn positional features from this single selected shape instead than from all shapes in pose space.

The pose selector is designed as a *multi-head neural network* $\Psi(\cdot)$ over shape poses in $H_{SR}(P)$. We score each pose by $v_s = \Psi(\bar{P}_s)$ for pose $\bar{P}_s \in H_{SR}(P)$, $s = 1, \cdots, |H_{SR}(P)|$. $v_s \in \mathcal{R}^{N_h}$ is a vector generated by N_h heads of $\Psi(\cdot)$. In our implementation, $\Psi(\cdot)$ is designed as a simple network with a point-wise fully connected (FC) layer, a max-pooling layer over all points, followed by an additional FC layer and softmax with N_h output scores for a point cloud. Similar to multi-head attention [37], the multiple elements in vector v_s reflect the responses of $\bar{P}_s$ to different modes of the neural network. For a shape pose $\bar{P}_s$, its final score is set as the largest response in vector v_s, i.e., $\bar{v}_s = \max\{v_s\}$, and $\bar{v}_s$ is a scalar. Then the selected representative shape $\widetilde{P}$ from pose space $H_{SR}(P)$ for shape P is the shape pose with the largest score.

Theorem 1 proves that the sym-space, rot-space and the selected pose are rotation-invariant to P (please see supplementary material for proof).

Theorem 1. *Denoting $P \in \mathcal{R}^{N \times 3}$ as point cloud of a shape, its sym-space $H_S(P)$ in Eq. (3) and rot-space $H_{SR}(P)$ in Eq. (4) are rotation-invariant for P, i.e., for rotated shape $Q = PR$ of P with any rotation matrix $R \in \mathcal{R}^{3 \times 3}$, we have $H_S(P) = H_S(Q)$ and $H_{SR}(P) = H_{SR}(Q)$. Assuming the pose selector is injective, the selected pose of P is rotation-invariant, i.e., $\widetilde{P} = \widetilde{Q}$.*

Feature Extractor. With the selected shape pose $\widetilde{P} \in \mathcal{R}^{N \times 3}$ of input shape P, we can extract its point-wise features based on the point coordinates like the traditional point-based networks, e.g., [1,2,9]. Specifically, given point-wise coordinates $\tilde{p}_i$, geometric feature g_i (extracted from input shape P), and already

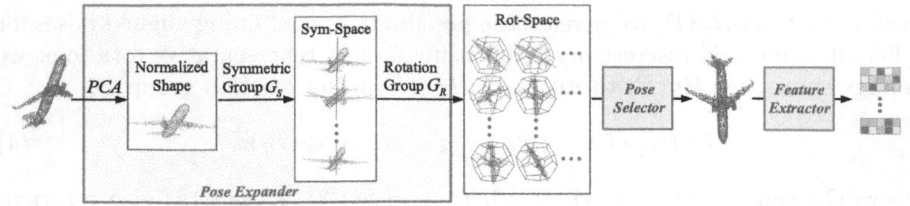

Fig. 5. Overview of the PFE-block. It maps a shape to be rotation-invariant pose space, i.e., rot-space, then selects a discriminative pose via pose selector, followed by feature extractor. This block is rotation-invariant.

extracted point features f_i, we concatenate $[g_i, f_i, \tilde{p}_i]$ as point-wise input features for our feature extractor. Motivated by the structure of PointNet++ [1], for each point i, its point feature is extracted as

$$f_i' = \Gamma\left(\{[g_j, f_j, \tilde{p}_j]\}_{j \in N(i)}\right) \tag{5}$$

where $N(i)$ is the local neighborhood of point i with K points including point i. $\Gamma(\cdot)$ is the feature extractor, which is designed as a shared MLP for points, followed by max-pooling over neighborhood. Figure 5 shows the pipeline of the PFE-block. Since the selected pose is rotation-invariant to input shape by Theorem 1, its point coordinates $\tilde{p}_i$ are also rotation-invariant. Hence, features in Eq. (5) are rotation-invariant because all inputs of Γ are rotation-invariant.

3.3 Relational Feature Embedding Block

The relational feature embedding block (RFE-block) is specifically designed to explore and learn point features by modeling interactions of neighboring points. For each point i, we aggregate the features of its local neighborhood with K points including point i by convolution. Assuming the neighboring points are indexed by k sorted by increasing Euclidean distance to point i, and corresponding point features are $\{f_k \in \mathcal{R}^d\}_{k=1}^K$, the updated feature $f_i' \in \mathcal{R}^{d'}$ for point i is

$$f_{il}' = \sum_{k \in N(i)} \sum_{j=1}^{d} f_{kj} W_{kjl}, \text{ for } l = 1, \cdots, d' \tag{6}$$

where f_{kj} is the j-th feature channel of the k-th neighboring point, f_{il}' is the l-th channel of the updated feature f_i'. W_{kjl} is defined as

$$W_{kjl} = \Phi([C_k^p, C_k^g, C_k^f, g_k])_j \Theta_{kjl}, \tag{7}$$

where $C_k^p, C_k^g, C_k^f \in \mathcal{R}^K$ are K-d vectors denoting correlations of centered point coordinates, geometric features, point features respectively between k-th point and all K points in local neighborhood, followed by l_2-normalization. For example, for centered point coordinates, i.e., coordinates subtracted by that of center pixel i, $C_k^p = \text{Normalize}([p_k^\top p_1, p_k^\top p_2, \cdots, p_k^\top p_K])$, where we use p to represent the centered point coordinates. C_k^g, C_k^f are similarly defined as inner products of corresponding features. $\Phi(\cdot)$ is modeled as MLP, embedding relationships of neighboring points to convolution weight with learnable parameters Θ_{kjl}. It is easy to verify that weights in Eq. (7) are rotation-invariant because the inputs of Φ are rotation-invariant defined by inner products.

3.4 Network Architecture

PR-invNet is designed by concatenating rotation-invariant PFE-block and RFE-block. As shown in Fig. 2, given a shape, we first initialize the point-wise features by initial feature embedding, followed by three stages concatenating PFE-block and RFE-block to extract positional and relational features. For classification, we use an additional shape coarsening operation at each stage to construct a hierarchy of coarsened points, implemented by farthest point sampling with sampling rate of 1/2. The intermediate features generated by PFE-blocks and RFE-blocks of different stages are concatenated and aggregated by a MLP set as two layers of FC+BN+ReLU+Dropout, followed by a FC to output confidence for shape categorization or segmentation. The number of hidden units of the first two FCs are 512, 256, and dropout probability is 0.5. The number of neighboring points in Eqs. (5–6) is 16. For an input shape of PR-invNet, we conduct PCA to normalize shape pose only one time, and all PFE-blocks in different stages derive rot-space by Eq. (4) starting from point cloud of this normalized pose or its coarsened point clouds. More details of pose selector Ψ, feature extractor Γ, convolution filters Φ, Θ in RFE-block are introduced in supplementary material.

4 Experimental Results

In this section we evaluate and compare with state-of-the-art methods for rotated shape classification and segmentation on the following 3D datasets.

ModelNet40 [6] consists of 12,311 shapes from 40 categories, with 9,843 training and 2,468 test objects for shape classification.

ShapenetCore55 [38] contains two subsets: 'normal', 'perturbed', with aligned and randomly rotated shapes in $SO(3)$ respectively. 51,190 models are categorized into 55 classes with training, validation, test sets in ratios of 70%, 10%, 20%. We uniformly sample points from the original mesh data for both subsets.

ShapeNet part [39] contains 16,880 shapes from 16 category of shapes, with 14,006/2,874 shapes for training/test, annotated with 50 parts.

Each shape is represented by 1024 points. To train our PR-invNet, we take Adam optimizer with initial learning rate, epoch number as 0.001, 250, and the learning rate is exponentially decayed with decay rate and decay step as 0.7, 200000. The batch size for shape classification and segmentation are 16 and 8 respectively. It takes 286.6 ms, 672.1 ms in one iteration for shape classification and segmentation respectively on a NVIDIA 1080 Ti GPU.

4.1 3D Shape Classification

We mainly compare with point-based methods and rotation-robust methods.

ModelNet40. As done in Spherical CNN [17], we compare in the following three modes. (1) Both training and test on data augmented by azimuthal rotation (z/z); (2) Training with azimuthal rotation and test with arbitrary rotation (z/SO(3)); (3) Both training and test with arbitrary rotation augmented data (SO(3)/SO(3)). The results are presented in Table 1. The traditional point-based methods, including PointNet [8], PointNet++ [1], PointCNN [2], DGCNN [10], perform best in z/z mode, but decline sharply when testing on data augmented with arbitrary rotations (z/SO(3)). Though using arbitrarily augmented training data in SO(3)/SO(3) mode, their performances still drop with large gaps. For these rotation-robust methods including Spherical CNN [17], a^3SCNN [19], RIConvNet [20], ClusterNet [18] and RRI^2-PointNet++, they are more robust in different modes. Considering that Spherical CNN and a^3SCNN rely on discretized angles in the sphere, they are not rigorously rotation-invariant and performance drops in modes (2)-(3). ClusterNet, RIConvNet and RRI-PointNet++ are rotation-invariant relying on input geometric features. Our PR-invNet is also rotation-invariant, and it achieves highest performance in modes (2–3) and second highest performance in mode (1) than all the rotation-robust methods, demonstrating its superiority for arbitrarily rotated shape classification.

Table 1. Shape classification accuracy on ModelNet40 (in %).

	Method	Input size	z/z	SO(3)/SO(3)	z/SO(3)
Rotation-sensitive	VoxNet [40]	30^3	83.0	87.3	–
	SubVolSup [7]	30^3	88.5	82.7	36.6
	SubVolSup MO [7]	30^3	89.5	85.0	45.5
	MVCNN 12x [4]	12×224^2	89.5	77.6	70.1
	MVCNN 80x [4]	80×224^2	90.2	86.0	**81.5**
	PointNet [8]	1024×3	87.0	80.3	12.8
	PointNet++ [1]	1024×3	89.3	85.0	28.6
	PointCNN [2]	1024×3	91.3	84.5	41.2
	DGCNN [10]	1024×3	**92.2**	**81.1**	20.6
Rotation-robust	Spherical CNN [17]	$2 \times 64 \times 64$	88.9	76.9	86.9
	a^3SCNN [19]	$2 \times 165 \times 65$	**89.6**	87.9	88.7
	RIConvNet [20]	1024×3	86.5	86.4	86.4
	ClusterNet [18]	1024×3	87.1	87.1	87.1
	RRI-PointNet++	1024×3	79.4	79.4	79.4
	Proposed	1024×3	89.2	**89.2**	**89.2**

ShapeNetCore55. We compare with point-based methods including Point-Net [8], PointNet++ [1], DGCNN [10], RS-CNN [23], SpiderCNN [9], and also

---

^{2} RRI is an essential part of ClusterNet, and the codes are provided by the authors.

rotation-robust Spherical CNN [17] and rotation-invariant RIConvNet [20], RRI-PointNet++. The results are presented in Table 2. As shown in Table 2, we achieve best performance in both aligned and perturbed datasets, compared with Spherical CNN, RIConvNet and RRI-PointNet++. Among all methods, we achieve highest accuracy on the perturbed dataset.

4.2   3D Shape Segmentation

Table 2. Shape classification accuracy on ShapeNetCore55 (in %). All the results of compared methods are achieved by running their code.

	Method	Input size	Aligned	Perturbed
Rotation-sensitive	PointNet [8]	1024×3	83.4	74.6
	PointNet++ [1]	1024×3	84.2	70.9
	DGCNN [10]	1024×3	**86.3**	**74.1**
	RS-CNN [23]	1024×3	85.9	73.4
	SpiderCNN [9]	1024×3	79.8	64.4
Rotation-robust	Spherical CNN [17]	2×64^2	76.2	73.8
	RIConvNet [20]	1024×3	78.5	76.9
	RRI-PointNet++	1024×3	70.8	67.9
	Proposed	1024×3	**78.9**	**77.6**

Table 3. Shape segmentation mIoU on ShapeNet part segmentation dataset (in %).

	Method	Input	z/z	SO(3)/SO(3)	z/SO(3)
Rotation-sensitive	PointNet [8]	xyz	76.2	74.4	37.8
	PointNet++ [1]	xyz + normal	80.7	**76.7**	**48.2**
	PointCNN [2]	xyz	81.5	71.4	34.7
	DGCNN [10]	xyz	78.8	73.3	37.4
	SpiderCNN [9]	xyz + normal	**81.8**	72.3	42.9
Rotation-robust	RIConvNet [20]	xyz	75.6	75.5	75.3
	Proposed	xyz	**79.4**	**79.4**	**79.4**

We next apply PR-invNet to point cloud segmentation to predict the part label of each point. We use the same experimental settings as RIConvNet [20], and mean per-class IoU (mIoU, %) are presented in Table 3. Compared with all rotation-sensitive point-based methods and

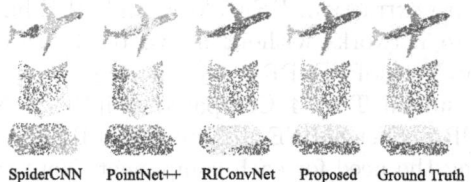

SpiderCNN   PointNet++   RIConvNet   Proposed   Ground Truth

Fig. 6. Shape segmentation results.

rotation-robust methods, our PR-invNet outperforms them significantly in both SO(3)/SO(3) and z/SO(3) modes, i.e., more than 2.7% and 4.1% mIoU improvements. We also report the per-class IoU for above settings in z/SO(3), SO(3)/SO(3) modes respectively in the supplemental material, and our PR-invNet achieves better performance than the rotation-robust RIConvNet on all categories. In Fig. 6, we show the segmentation results in z/SO(3) mode of several objects as well as the corresponding ground truth labels, and our predictions labels are reasonable and close to ground truth.

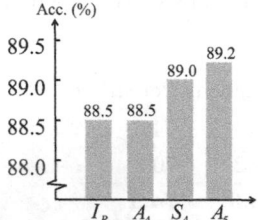

Fig. 7. Rotation groups.   **Fig. 8.** Head numbers.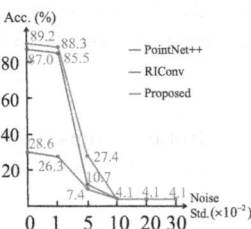
Fig. 9. Noise levels.

Table 4. Classification accuracy on ModelNet40 (%).

Method	Geo-fea	PFE-block	RFE-block	Acc.
PR-invNet-noGeo	×	✓	✓	88.2
PR-invNet-noPFE	✓	×	✓	87.8
PR-invNet-noRFE	✓	✓	×	88.0
PR-invNet	✓	✓	✓	**89.2**

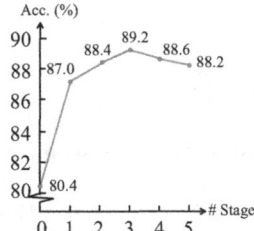

Fig. 10. Stage numbers.

4.3 Ablation Study

In this section, we conduct ablation study on ModelNet40 to justify the effects of our network design, and also test the robustness of PR-invNet to noises.

Effect of Proposed Blocks. To evaluate the effectiveness of geometric feature extraction, PFE-block, and RFE-block, we conduct experiments that utilize networks without above blocks respectively, i.e., PR-invNet-noGeo, PR-invNet-noPFE, PR-invNet-noRFE, on ModelNet40, and present the experiment results in Table 4. Compared with PR-invNet, the networks of PR-invNet-noGeo, PR-invNet-noPFE, PR-invNet-noRFE achieve lower performance, demonstrating the need for each component. Note that all networks of above variants are also rigorously rotation-invariant, and they also achieve better performance than most of the rotation-sensitive and rotation-robust methods whose results are presented in Table 1 in the SO(3)/SO(3) and z/SO(3) modes.

Effect of Stage Number. To evaluate the effect of number of stages in PR-invNet, we compare performance of PR-invNet-i with $i = 0, 1, 2, \cdots, 5$, and i denotes number of stages excluding initial feature embedding stage. As shown in Fig. 10, network with 3 stages achieve the highest accuracy. Deeper architectures have larger capacity but marginally decreased performances. This phenomenon was also observed in other graph CNNs [41], and training of deeper networks on point clouds deserves to be more investigated in future work.

Design of Global Shape Feature. As shown in Fig. 2, learned features from all PFE-blocks and RFE-blocks are aggregated by MLP for classification. We evaluate PR-invNet-PFE and PR-invNet-RFE that only utilize features from PFE-blocks and RFE-blocks respectively, achieving 88.5%, 87.4% classification accuracies on ModelNet40. Result using only features of the last RFE-block is 88.3%. This demonstrates that concatenating all features of PFE-block and RFE-block is more effective.

Effect of PCA-Normalization and Rot-Space. In PR-invNet, we take PCA to normalize shape as network input. We also conduct experiments with networks without PCA-normalization and only with PCA (without using sym-space and rot-space), i.e., PR-invNet-noPCA, PR-invNet-PCA. Their classification accuracies in ModelNet40 with z/z mode are 90.0% and 89.1% respectively, but drop to 44.3%, 74.8% in z/SO(3) mode, which are not rotation-invariant. In SO(3)/SO(3), our pose selector over rot-space upon PCA(89.2%) outperforms pure PCA for alignment(88.3%). Removing both PCA and pose selector achieves 87.3%, showing our pose selection is more effective than PCA.

Effect of Rotation Group G_R. In pose expander of PFE-block, we use the rotation group G_R to construct rot-space, which is taken as alternating group A_5 of a regular dodecahedron (or icosahedron). Other alternating (symmetry) group can also be used, such as identity group (I_R), or A_4, S_4 [36] respectively corresponding to regular tetrahedron, cube (or octahedron). The classification accuracies using these groups are in Fig. 7. Compared with other groups, A_5 has the maximum number of elements, resulting in largest rot-space and achieves the highest accuracy. Operating on this largest space, the pose selector has more probability to select a better pose for shape recognition.

Effect of Pose Selector. In PFE-block, we use a pose selector to select the representative shape pose in rot-space. However, we can also extract features from all shapes from rot-space and then perform max-pooling or average-pooling over them to aggregate features. We compare our pose selector with these aggregation methods and present the classification accuracy and computational cost in Table 5. Since it is infeasible to extract features from all shapes in rot-space containing 120 poses, we compare these variants on the sym-space containing eight shape poses, i.e., rot-space with identity rotation group. We experiment with batch size 12, and as shown in Table 5, our pose selection method achieves higher performance while needing less GPU memory and computational time.

Effect of Head Number in Ψ. For pose selector Ψ, we design it as a multi-head neural network, which has 200 heads. We conduct experiments to demonstrate the effect of head numbers. As shown in Fig. 8, the Ψ with head number as 200 achieves higher performance. Note that Ψ with multi-heads all achieve better accuracies than that with one head.

Table 5. Cla. Acc. on ModelNet40.

Method	Acc. (%)	Memory (GB)	Time (ms)
Average-pooling	88.1	10.2	496.5
Max-pooling	88.3	10.2	512.3
Proposed	**88.5**	**4.4**	**251.0**

Table 6. Cla. Acc. on ModelNet40 (%).

Method	C_k^p	C_k^g	C_k^f	g_k	Acc
PR-invNet-P	×	√	√	√	88.1
PR-invNet-G	√	×	√	√	88.8
PR-invNet-F	√	√	×	√	89.9
PR-invNet-g	√	√	√	×	88.5
PR-invNet	√	√	√	√	**89.2**

Design of RFE-Block. In RFE-block, we design convolution filters based on three terms, i.e., the relations of point position, geometric feature, and point feature in Eq. (7). In Table 6, we show our networks using only one of these terms, resulting in networks of PR-invNet-P, PR-invNet-G, PR-invNet-F respectively. We also present result of PR-invNet-g only using geometric feature in Eq. (7). Their classification accuracies are all inferior compared with full version. We also conduct experiment that without normalization in Eq. (7), achieving classification accuracy as 88.6%.

Robustness to Noise. We train PR-invNet on ModelNet40 training dataset and test it on test data with various levels of noise under the z/SO(3) mode. We add Gaussian noise with different standard deviation (Std) on each point (coordinates within a unit ball) independently. The overall classification accuracies are in Fig. 9. PR-invNet keeps robustness under noise with Std of 0.01.

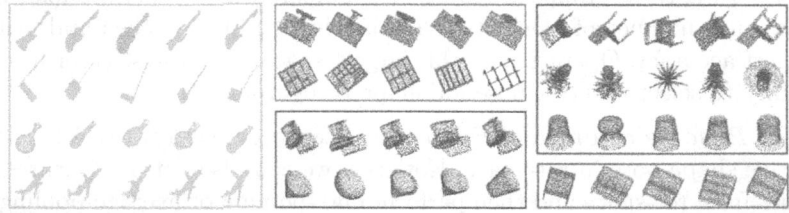

Fig. 11. Illustration of selected shapes corresponding to different heads in multi-head score network. Shapes in a box highlighted by same color correspond to same head.

Visualization for Pose Selector. In PFE-block, we design multi-head score network Ψ to select a pose from rot-space $H_{SR}(P)$ based on scoring each shape pose by its maximum score belonging to multiple heads. Therefore the selected pose from rot-space corresponds to a certain head. Here we illustrate selected shape poses organized by corresponding heads highlighted in different colors in Fig. 11. We observe that shapes corresponding to each head have similar poses. The multi-head score network may enable to learn to align the shapes to clusters of poses using heads in multi-head score network.

5   Conclusions

In this work, we focus on rotation-invariant deep network design on point clouds by proposing two rotation-invariant network blocks. The constructed PR-invNet was extensively justified to be effective for rotated 3D shape classification and segmentation. In future work, we are interested to deeply investigate pose alignment capability of PFE-block, and further improve the network architecture.

Acknowledgement. This work was supported by NSFC (11971373, 11690011, U1811461, 61721002) and National Key R&D Program 2018AAA0102201.

References

1. Qi, C.R., Yi, L., Su, H., Guibas, L.J.: Pointnet++: deep hierarchical feature learning on point sets in a metric space. In: Advances in Neural Information Processing Systems, pp. 5099–5108 (2017)
2. Li, Y., Bu, R., Sun, M., Wu, W., Di, X., Chen, B.: PointCNN: convolution on x-transformed points. In: Advances in Neural Information Processing Systems, pp. 820–830 (2018)
3. Pham, Q.H., Nguyen, T., Hua, B.S., Roig, G., Yeung, S.K.: JSIS3D: joint semantic-instance segmentation of 3D point clouds with multi-task pointwise networks and multi-value conditional random fields. In: IEEE Conference on Computer Vision and Pattern Recognition (CVPR), pp. 8827–8836 (2019)
4. Su, H., Maji, S., Kalogerakis, E., Learned-Miller, E.: Multi-view convolutional neural networks for 3D shape recognition. In: IEEE International Conference on Computer Vision (ICCV), (2015) 945–953
5. Esteves, C., Xu, Y., Allen-Blanchette, C., Daniilidis, K.: Equivariant multi-view networks. In: IEEE International Conference on Computer Vision (ICCV), pp. 1568–1577 (2019)
6. Wu, Z., et al.: 3D shapenets: a deep representation for volumetric shapes. In: CVPR, pp. 1912–1920 (2015)
7. Qi, C.R., Su, H., Nießner, M., Dai, A., Yan, M., Guibas, L.J.: Volumetric and multi-view CNNs for object classification on 3D data. In: CVPR, pp. 5648–5656 (2016)
8. Qi, C.R., Su, H., Mo, K., Guibas, L.J.: Pointnet: deep learning on point sets for 3D classification and segmentation. In: CVPR, pp. 652–660 (2017)
9. Xu, Y., Fan, T., Xu, M., Zeng, L., Qiao, Yu.: SpiderCNN: deep learning on point sets with parameterized convolutional filters. In: Ferrari, V., Hebert, M., Sminchisescu, C., Weiss, Y. (eds.) ECCV 2018. LNCS, vol. 11212, pp. 90–105. Springer, Cham (2018). https://doi.org/10.1007/978-3-030-01237-3_6

10. Wang, Y., Sun, Y., Liu, Z., Sarma, S.E., Bronstein, M.M., Solomon, J.M.: Dynamic graph CNN for learning on point clouds. ACM Trans. Graph. (TOG) **38**(5), 1–12 (2019)
11. Rao, Y., Lu, J., Zhou, J.: Spherical fractal convolutional neural networks for point cloud recognition. In: CVPR, pp. 452–460 (2019)
12. Zhou, Y., Jiang, G., Lin, Y.: A novel finger and hand pose estimation technique for real-time hand gesture recognition. Pattern Recogn. **49**, 102–114 (2016)
13. Xiang, Y., Schmidt, T., Narayanan, V., Fox, D.: PoseCNN: a convolutional neural network for 6D object pose estimation in cluttered scenes. arXiv:1711.00199 (2017)
14. Harald, W., Didier, S.: Tracking of industrial objects by using cad models. J. Virtual Reality Broadcast. **4**(1) (2007)
15. Bero, S.A., Muda, A.K., Choo, Y., Muda, N.A., Pratama, S.F.: Rotation analysis of moment invariant for 2D and 3D shape representation for molecular structure of ATS drugs. In: 4th World Congress on Information and Communication Technologies (WICT), pp. 308–313 (2014)
16. Berenger, F., Voet, A., Lee, X.Y., Zhang, K.Y.J.: A rotation-translation invariant molecular descriptor of partial charges and its use in ligand-based virtual screening. J. Cheminform. **6**(1), 1–12 (2014). https://doi.org/10.1186/1758-2946-6-23
17. Esteves, C., Allen-Blanchette, C., Makadia, A., Daniilidis, K.: Learning SO(3) equivariant representations with spherical CNNs. In: Ferrari, V., Hebert, M., Sminchisescu, C., Weiss, Y. (eds.) ECCV 2018. LNCS, vol. 11217, pp. 54–70. Springer, Cham (2018). https://doi.org/10.1007/978-3-030-01261-8_4
18. Chen, C., Li, G., Xu, R., Chen, T., Wang, M., Lin, L.: Clusternet: deep hierarchical cluster network with rigorously rotation-invariant representation for point cloud analysis. In: CVPR, pp. 4994–5002 (2019)
19. Liu, M., Yao, F., Choi, C., Sinha, A., Ramani, K.: Deep learning 3D shapes using ALT-AZ anisotropic 2-sphere convolution. In: ICLR (2019)
20. Zhang, Z., Hua, B.S., Rosen, D.W., Yeung, S.K.: Rotation invariant convolutions for 3D point clouds deep learning. In: International Conference on 3D Vision (3DV), pp. 204–213 (2019)
21. Shen, Y., Feng, C., Yang, Y., Tian, D.: Mining point cloud local structures by kernel correlation and graph pooling. In: CVPR, pp. 4548–4557 (2018)
22. Wu, W., Qi, Z., Fuxin, L.: Pointconv: deep convolutional networks on 3D point clouds. In: CVPR, pp. 9621–9630 (2019)
23. Liu, Y., Fan, B., Xiang, S., Pan, C.: Relation-shape convolutional neural network for point cloud analysis. In: CVPR, pp. 8895–8904 (2019)
24. Jaderberg, M., Simonyan, K., Zisserman, A., et al.: Spatial transformer networks. In: Advances in Neural Information Processing Systems, pp. 2017–2025 (2015)
25. Bas, A., Huber, P., Smith, W.A., Awais, M., Kittler, J.: 3D morphable models as spatial transformer networks. In: IEEE International Conference on Computer Vision Workshops, pp. 904–912 (2017)
26. Mukhaimar, A., Tennakoon, R., Lai, C.Y., Hoseinnezhad, R., Bab-Hadiashar, A.: PL-net3D: robust 3D object class recognition using geometric models. IEEE Access **7**, 163757–163766 (2019)
27. Stein, F., Medioni, G.: Structural indexing: efficient 3-D object recognition. IEEE Trans. Pattern Anal. Mach. Intell. (2), 125–145 (1992)
28. Sun, Y., Abidi, M.A.: Surface matching by 3D point's fingerprint. In: IEEE International Conference on Computer Vision (ICCV), pp. 263–269 (2001)
29. Zhong, Y.: Intrinsic shape signatures: a shape descriptor for 3D object recognition. In: International Conference on Computer Vision Workshops, pp. 689–696 (2009)

30. Rusu, R.B., Blodow, N., Beetz, M.: Fast point feature histograms (FPFH) for 3D registration. In: IEEE International Conference on Robotics and Automation, pp. 3212–3217 (2009)

31. Tombari, F., Salti, S., Di Stefano, L.: Unique signatures of histograms for local surface description. In: Daniilidis, K., Maragos, P., Paragios, N. (eds.) ECCV 2010. LNCS, vol. 6313, pp. 356–369. Springer, Heidelberg (2010). https://doi.org/10.1007/978-3-642-15558-1_26

32. Deng, H., Birdal, T., Ilic, S.: PPF-FoldNet: unsupervised learning of rotation invariant 3D local descriptors. In: Ferrari, V., Hebert, M., Sminchisescu, C., Weiss, Y. (eds.) ECCV 2018. LNCS, vol. 11209, pp. 620–638. Springer, Cham (2018). https://doi.org/10.1007/978-3-030-01228-1_37

33. Thomas, N., et al.: Tensor field networks: rotation-and translation-equivariant neural networks for 3D point clouds. arXiv:1802.08219 (2018)

34. Cohen, T., Welling, M.: Group equivariant convolutional networks. In: International Conference on Machine Learning (ICML), pp. 2990–2999 (2016)

35. Worrall, D., Brostow, G.: CubeNet: equivariance to 3D rotation and translation. In: Ferrari, V., Hebert, M., Sminchisescu, C., Weiss, Y. (eds.) ECCV 2018. LNCS, vol. 11209, pp. 585–602. Springer, Cham (2018). https://doi.org/10.1007/978-3-030-01228-1_35

36. Zimmermann, B.P.: On finite groups acting on spheres and finite subgroups of orthogonal groups. arXiv:1108.2602 (2011)

37. Vaswani, A., et al.: Attention is all you need. In: Advances in Neural Information Processing Systems, pp. 5998–6008 (2017)

38. Savva, M., et al.: Shrec16 track: large-scale 3D shape retrieval from shapenet core55. In: Eurographics Workshop on 3D Object Retrieval (2016)

39. Chang, A.X., et al.: Shapenet: an information-rich 3D model repository. arXiv preprint arXiv:1512.03012 (2015)

40. Maturana, D., Scherer, S.: Voxnet: a 3D convolutional neural network for real-time object recognition. In: 2015 IEEE/RSJ International Conference on Intelligent Robots and Systems (IROS), pp. 922–928 (2015)

41. Li, G., Muller, M., Thabet, A., Ghanem, B.: DeepGCNs: can GCNs go as deep as CNNs? In: CVPR, pp. 9267–9276 (2019)

Thanks for Nothing: Predicting Zero-Valued Activations with Lightweight Convolutional Neural Networks

Gil Shomron[1]([✉]), Ron Banner[2], Moran Shkolnik[1,2], and Uri Weiser[1]

[1] Faculty of Electrical Engineering, Technion, Haifa, Israel
gilsho@campus.technion.ac.il, uri.weiser@ee.technion.ac.il
[2] Habana Labs, An Intel Company, Caesarea, Israel
{rbanner,mshkolnik}@habana.ai

Abstract. Convolutional neural networks (CNNs) introduce state-of-the-art results for various tasks with the price of high computational demands. Inspired by the observation that spatial correlation exists in CNN output feature maps (ofms), we propose a method to dynamically predict whether ofm activations are zero-valued or not according to their neighboring activation values, thereby avoiding zero-valued activations and reducing the number of convolution operations. We implement the zero activation predictor (ZAP) with a lightweight CNN, which imposes negligible overheads and is easy to deploy on existing models. ZAPs are trained by mimicking hidden layer ouputs; thereby, enabling a parallel and label-free training. Furthermore, without retraining, each ZAP can be tuned to a different operating point trading accuracy for MAC reduction.

Keywords: Convolutional neural networks · Dynamic pruning

1 Introduction

In the past decade, convolutional neural networks (CNNs) have been adopted for numerous applications [27,37,39], introducing state-of-the-art results. Despite being widely used, CNNs involve a considerable amount of computations. For example, classification of a 224×224 colored image requires billions of multiply-accumulate (MAC) operations [4,42]. Such computational loads have many implications, from execution time to power and energy consumption of the underlying hardware.

CNN output feature maps (ofms) have been observed to exhibit spatial correlation, i.e., adjacent ofm activations share close values [32,38]. This observation is particularly true for zero-valued activations, as it is common practice to use

Electronic supplementary material The online version of this chapter (https://doi.org/10.1007/978-3-030-58607-2_14) contains supplementary material, which is available to authorized users.

© Springer Nature Switzerland AG 2020
A. Vedaldi et al. (Eds.): ECCV 2020, LNCS 12355, pp. 234–250, 2020.
https://doi.org/10.1007/978-3-030-58607-2_14

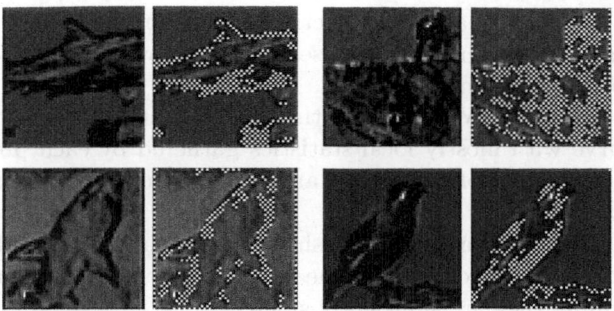

Fig. 1. Exploiting spatial correlation for zero-value prediction of ofm activations with CNN-based predictor. Bright white pixels represent a predicted zero-valued ofm activation.

the ReLU activation function [33], which squeezes all negative values to zero. If it were possible to predict which of the convolution operations will result in a negative value, they could be skipped, their corresponding ofm activations could be set to zero, and many multiply-accumulate (MAC) operations could be saved.

Prediction mechanisms are at the heart of many general-purpose processors (GPPs), leveraging unique application characteristics, such as code semantics and temporal locality, to predict branch prediction outcomes and future memory accesses, for example. Prediction mechanisms may similarly be employed for CNNs. In this paper, we propose a prediction method for CNNs that dynamically classifies ofm activations as zero-valued or non-zero-valued by leveraging the spatial correlation of ofms. The zero activation predictor (ZAP) works in three-steps: first, only a portion of the ofm is fully computed; then, the remaining activations are classified as zero-valued or non-zero-valued using a lightweight convolutional neural network; and finally, the predicted non-zero-valued activations are computed while the zero-valued activations are skipped, thereby saving entire convolution operations (Fig. 1). ZAP imposes negligible overheads in terms of computations and memory footprint, it may be plugged into pretrained models, it is trained quickly, in parallel, and does not require labeled data.

ZAP may be considered as a CNN-based, dynamic, unstructured, and magnitude-based ofm activations pruning strategy. However, as opposed to many pruning techniques, ZAP is tunable on-the-fly. Therefore, ZAP captures a wide range of operating points, trading accuracy for MAC savings. For example, by strictly focusing on zero-valued ofm activations, ZAP can capture a range of operating points that does not require retraining. ZAP is also capable of pruning when set to high speculation levels, as more mispredictions of non-zero-valued activations as zero-valued activations take place. Interestingly, we observe that these mispredictions usually occur with small activation values, which is practically a magnitude-based pruning strategy.

This paper makes the following contributions:

- **Zero activation predictor (ZAP).** We introduce a dynamic, easy to deploy, CNN-based zero-value prediction method that exploits the spatial correlation of output feature map activations. Compared with conventional convolution layers, our method imposes negligible overheads in terms of both computations and parameters.

- **Trade-off control.** We estimate the model's entire accuracy-to-savings trade-off curve with mostly local statistics gathered by each predictor. This provides a projection of the model and the predictor performance for any operating point.
- **Accuracy to error linearity.** We show, both analytically and empirically, that the entire model accuracy is linear with the sum of local misprediction errors, assuming they are sufficiently small.
- **Local tuning given global constraints.** We consider layers variability by optimizing each ZAP to minimize the model MAC operations subject to a global error budget.

2   ZAP: Zero Activation Predictor

In this section, we describe our prediction method and its savings potential. We analyze its overheads in terms of computational cost and memory footprint and show that both are negligible compared with conventional convolution layers.

2.1   Preliminary

A convolution layer consists of a triplet $\langle X_i, X_o, W \rangle$, where X_i and X_o correspond to the input and output activation tensors, respectively, and W corresponds to the set of convolution kernels. Each activation tensor is a three-dimensional tensor of size $w \times h \times c$, where w, h and c represent the tensor width, height, and depth, respectively. For convenience, the dimensions of X_i and X_o are denoted by $[w_i \times h_i \times c_i]$ and $[w_o \times h_o \times c_o]$. Finally, the set of convolution kernels W is denoted by a four-dimensional tensor $[k \times k \times c_i \times c_o]$, where k is the filter width and height. The filter width and height are not necessarily equal, but it is common practice in most conventional CNNs to take them a such. Given the above notations, each output activation value $X_o[x, y, z]$ is computed from the input tensor X_i and weights W as follows:

$$X_o(x, y, z) = \sum_{i,j=0}^{k-1} \sum_{c=0}^{c_i-1} X_i[x+i, y+j, c] \cdot W[i, j, c, z], \qquad (1)$$

where the bias term is omitted for simplicity's sake. We use the above notations throughout this paper.

2.2   Three-Step Method

Conventional convolution layers compute their ofm by applying Eq. (1) for each $[x, y, z]$. It has been observed that ofms accommodate many zero-valued activations due to the widespread usage of the ReLU activation function [2,34,42].

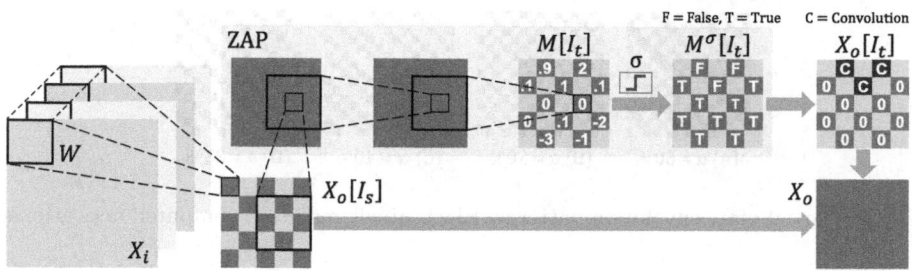

Fig. 2. Illustration of a single ofm channel convolution with ZAP. $X_o[I_s]$ is computed based on a pre-defined pattern. $X_o[I_s]$ is then subjected to ZAP, which produces a prediction map $M[I_t]$, followed by a thresholding step to form the binary prediction map $M^\sigma[I_t]$. $X_o[I_t]$ is created according to $M^\sigma[I_t]$—a portion of the I_t ofm activations are predicted as zero-valued and skipped, whereas the rest are computed using Eq. (1).

For example, with ResNet-18 [13], almost 50% of the ofm activations are zero-valued; therefore, 50% of the MAC operations may be potentially skipped. Moreover, ofm activations exhibit spatial correlation [32,38], meaning that a group of activation values testifies about other adjacent activation values.

We suggest a three-step dynamic prediction mechanism that locates zero-valued ofm activations by exploiting the spatial correlation inherent in CNNs to potentially skip them and reduce the computational burden of the model. Given an ofm, X_o, we divide its indices into two subsets (I_s, I_t) according to a pre-defined pattern. Then, the following three steps are carried out (as illustrated in Fig. 2): (i) the values that belong to indices I_s are fully computed in the conventional manner, resulting in a sparse ofm, $X_o[I_s]$; (ii) this partial ofm ($X_o[I_s]$) is passed through our predictor to yield a binary map, $M^\sigma[I_t]$, which is used to predict the zero values in $X_o[I_t]$; and (iii) all values predicted to be non-zero by $M^\sigma[I_t]$ are computed. We describe this process in detail next.

Computation Pattern. $X_o[I_s]$ is computed based on a pre-defined pattern as depicted in Fig. 3. Since our predictor exploits spatial correlation, we partially compute the ofm so that activations that are not computed in the first step will reside next to a number of computed activations. We use α to denote the ratio between the number of activations computed in the partial ofm and the ofm dimensions. This may be formally formulated as $\alpha \equiv \frac{|I_s|}{w_o h_o c_o}$, where $|I_s|$ is the set cardinality.

By decreasing α, less ofm activations are computed prior to the prediction, which may potentially lead to the saving of more operations. For example, for $\alpha = 40\%$, 60% of the activations may potentially be saved. Less prior data about the ofm may, however, lead to higher misprediction rates, which in turn may decrease model accuracy.

Prediction Process via Lightweight CNN. Given the partial ofm, $X_o[I_s]$, our goal is to produce an output computation mask that predicts which of the remaining activations are zero-valued and may be skipped. Recall that ofm activations are originally computed using Eq. (1) and so the prediction process must

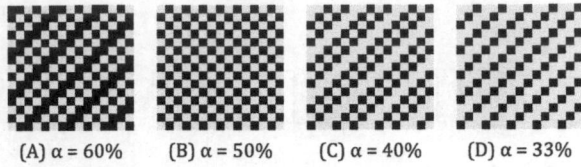

(A) α = 60%   (B) α = 50%   (C) α = 40%   (D) α = 33%

Fig. 3. Partial ofm convolution patterns. Black pixels represent computed activations.

involve less MAC operations than the original convolution operation with as minimal memory footprint as possible.

We use a CNN to implement ZAP. We exploit the spatial correlation inherent in CNNs [9,21,32,38] and use only depthwise convolution (DW-CONV) layers [16], i.e., only spatial filters with no depth ($k \times k \times 1 \times c_o$). As such, we obtain a lightweight model in terms of both MAC operations and parameters (further analyzed in Subsect. 2.3). Our CNN comprises a 3×3 DW-CONV layer followed by a batch normalization (BN) layer [20] followed by ReLU, twice. DW-CONV layer padding and stride are both defined as 1 to achieve equal dimensions throughout the CNN predictor. During training, the last ReLU is capped at 1 [24], whereas during inference we discard the last ReLU activation and use a threshold.

Thresholding. Altough ZAP is trained to output a binary classifier (described in Subsect. 4.1), ZAP naturally outputs $M[I_t]$, which is not a strict binary mask but rather a range of values that corresponds to a prediction confidence [11,43] of whether the ofm activation is zero-valued or not. To binarize ZAP's output, we define a threshold σ that sets the level of prediction confidence; therefore, $M^\sigma[I_t] = M[I_t] > \sigma$ (boolean operation).

According to $M^\sigma[I_t]$, part of the ofm activations in $X_o[I_t]$ are predicted to be non-zero-valued and are computed, whereas the others are predicted to be zero-valued and are skipped. When an ofm activation is predicted to be zero-valued, two types of misprediction may occur. First, an actual zero-valued activation may be predicted as a non-zero-valued activation and so redundant MAC operations may take place. Second, an actual non-zero-valued activation may be predicted as zero. The latter misprediction increases the model error, potentially decreasing model accuracy.

The motivation behind ZAP is clear—reducing computations by skipping convolution operations. Its impact on the model accuracy, number of computations, and amount of parameters has yet, however, to be discussed. We next discuss the overhead of ZAP, and in Sect. 4, we show empirically how ZAP affects the accuracy of different model architectures.

2.3   Overhead Analysis

ZAP is a CNN by itself, which means that it introduces additional computations and parameters. To be beneficial, it must execute less operations per ofm activation than the original convolution operation. A conventional convolution layer requires $k^2 c_i$ MAC operations per ofm activation. On the other hand, the number of MAC operations required by a two-layered DW-CONV ZAP for a single ofm activation is K^2, where K is the filter width and height. Note that ZAP's first layer needs only to consider $|I_s|$ values for computation since, according to the pre-defined pattern, the remaining $|I_t|$ values are zero; the second layer needs only to compute $|I_t|$ ofm activations.

Compared with a standard convolution operation, and for the case of $K = k$,

$$\frac{\text{ZAP ops.}}{\text{standard convolution ops.}} = \frac{1}{c_i}. \tag{2}$$

c_i is usually greater than 10^2 [13, 26, 40], in which case $1/c_i \approx 0$ and ZAP overhead is, therefore, negligible.

Regarding the parameters, a conventional convolution layer requires $k^2 c_i c_o$ parameters and a two-layered DW-CONV requires $2K^2 c_o$ parameters. Given c_i conventional sizes and $K = k$, ZAP's memory footprint is negligible as well.

3   Trade-Off Control

The threshold hyperparameter, σ, represents the prediction confidence of whether an ofm activation is zero or non-zero. Users should, however, address the accuracy and MAC reduction terms rather than using σ, since it is not clear how a specific σ value affects accuracy and savings. In this section, we show that, given some statistics, we can estimate the entire model accuracy and predictor MAC savings, thereby avoiding the need to address the threshold value directly and providing the user with an accuracy-MAC savings trade-off control "knob".

3.1   Accuracy, MAC Savings, and Threshold

Accuracy and Threshold. Consider a DNN with L layers. Each layer i comprises weights w_i, an ifm x_i, and an ofm y_i. When predictions are avoided, layer $i + 1$ input, x_{i+1}, is given by

$$x_{i+1} = y_i = \max(x_i w_i, 0), \tag{3}$$

where $\max(\cdot, 0)$ is the ReLU activation function.

Our predictor is not perfect and may zero out non-zero elements with a small probability ε_i. Therefore, non-zero inputs to layer $i + 1$ have a probability ε_i of becoming zero and a probability $1 - \varepsilon$ of remaining y_i. Using y_i^π to denote the prediction of output y_i, we obtain the following error in the expected activation:

$$E(y_i^\pi) = (1 - \varepsilon_i) \cdot E(y_i). \tag{4}$$

In other words, the prediction at each layer i introduces a multiplicative error of $(1 - \varepsilon_i)$ with respect to the true activation. This multiplicative error builds up across layers. For an L-layer network, the expected network outputs are scaled down with respect to the true network outputs as follows:

$$\text{Scale Error} = \prod_{i=1}^{L} (1 - \varepsilon_i). \tag{5}$$

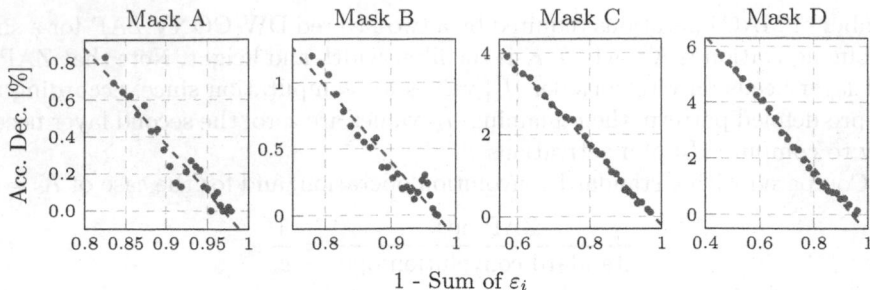

Fig. 4. AlexNet + CIFAR-100 top-1 accuracy decrease as a function of $1 - \sum_{i=1}^{L} \varepsilon_i(\sigma)$. Each dot represents a measurement with a different threshold: the leftmost and rightmost thresholds are 0 and 0.5, respectively. Measurements were taken in steps of 0.02.

Note that for a sufficiently small ε, $1 - \varepsilon = e^{-\varepsilon}$. Therefore, assuming sufficiently small misprediction probabilities, $\{\varepsilon_i\}$, we obtain the following expression

$$\text{Scale Error} = \prod_{i=1}^{L}(1 - \varepsilon_i) \approx \prod_{i=1}^{L} e^{-\varepsilon_i}$$

$$= e^{-\sum_{i=1}^{L} \varepsilon_i} \approx 1 - \sum_{i=1}^{L} \varepsilon_i, \tag{6}$$

where the approximations can easily be extracted from a Taylor expansion to e^{-x}. Eq. (6) shows that the final error due to small mispredictions accumulates along the network in a *linear* fashion when the errors due to mispredictions are small enough.

Denoting the output of layer i for a threshold σ by $y_i^{\pi,\sigma}$, the error is associated with a threshold σ as follows:

$$\text{Scale Error}\,(\sigma) \approx 1 - \sum_{i=1}^{L} \varepsilon_i(\sigma)$$

$$= 1 - \sum_{i=1}^{L} \left(1 - \frac{\sum_{x,y,z} y_i^{\pi,\sigma}[x,y,z]}{\sum_{x,y,z} y_i[x,y,z]} \right), \tag{7}$$

where Eq. (4) is used for the last transition. Figure 4 shows that this analytical observation is in good agreement with our empirical results.

Ideally, we would like to have a scale error that is as close as possible to 1 so as to avoid shifting the network statistics from the learned distribution. When the scale error is 1, network outputs remain unchanged and no accuracy degradation associated with mispredictions occurs. Yet, as σ increases, more ofm activations are predicted as zero-valued, decreasing the scale error below 1, as exhibited by Eq. (7). This scale error decreases monotonically with σ and introduces an inverse mapping, which enables us to define a threshold value for any desired accuracy degradation.

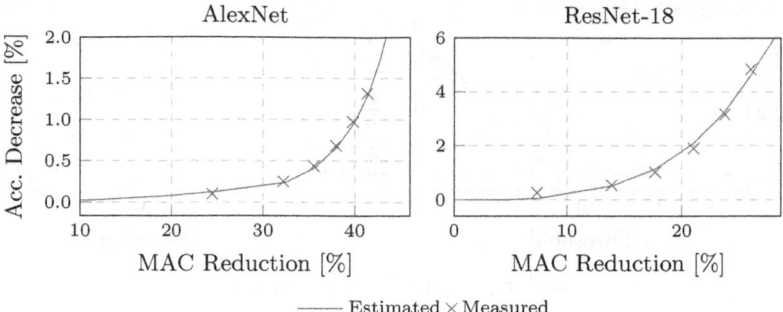

Fig. 5. Estimated top-5 accuracy-MAC savings trade-off curve using mask B and ILSVRC-2012 dataset. The measured operating points correspond to thresholds of 0 to 0.5, in steps of 0.1.

MAC Savings and Threshold. Recall that $M[I_t]$ represents the collection of values predicted by ZAP for a given layer before applying the threshold. For readability, assume $m(x)$ is the probability density function of $M[I_t]$ values (i.e., continuous). Then, the number of ofm activations predicted as zeros relative to I_t can be expressed as follows:

$$\text{Zero Prediction Rate}\,(\sigma) = \int_{-\infty}^{\sigma} m(x)dx\,. \tag{8}$$

To achieve the actual MAC reduction in layer i, the layer dimensions, α, and ZAP overhead should be considered. Clearly, the total MAC reduction equals the sum of the contributions from all layers. Note that the zero prediction rate, and therefore the MAC reduction, increases monotonically, and for a certain range it may be considered a strictly monotonic function. Inverse mapping from MAC reduction to σ is, therefore, possible.

Putting It All Together. Given the derivations so far, it is possible to make an *a priori* choice of any operating point, given estimates about the desired accuracy and MAC reduction, without directly dealing with the threshold. Assume a pre-processing step that consists of collecting statistical information about the prediction values $M[I_t]$ and at least two accuracy measurements of the entire model, to obtain the linear accuracy-error relationship. With this statistical information, we can effectively estimate the desired operating point, as demonstrated in Fig. 5.

3.2 Non-uniform Threshold

Thus far, for the sake of simplicity, σ was set uniformly across all layers. Layers, however, behave differently, and so ZAP error and savings may differ between layers for a given threshold. This is evident in Fig. 6 in which we present the error and total MAC operations of four layers in ResNet-18. Notice how the error of

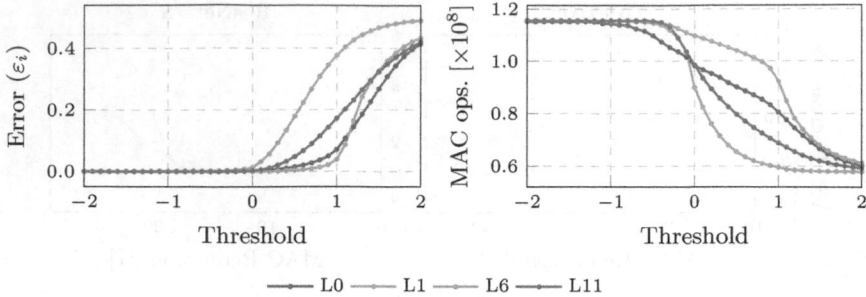

Fig. 6. ResNet-18 + ILSVRC-2012 example of different layers behavior in terms of error and MAC operations as a function of ZAP threshold.

layer 6 (L6) increases earlier than the other layers, for example. Ideally, given L layers, we would like to choose a threshold per layer, σ_i, to save as many MAC operations as possible, given an error (or accuracy) constraint, ϵ, i.e.,

$$
\begin{aligned}
&\text{minimize} \quad \sum_{i=1}^{L} \text{MAC ops.}_i\,(\sigma_i) \\
&\text{subject to} \sum_{i=1}^{L} \varepsilon_i(\sigma_i) \leq \epsilon \propto \text{Accuracy.}
\end{aligned}
\tag{9}
$$

We use curve fitting to define a parameterized sigmoid function for the error and for the MAC operations of each layer and apply standard non-linear optimization methods to solve Eq. (9) (see supplementary material for curve fitting results). It is worth mentioning that Eq. (9) can also be written the other way around, that is, minimizing the error given a computation budget.

4   Experiments

In this section, we evaluate ZAP performance in terms of MAC savings and accuracy degradation using various model architectures and datasets, and compare our results to previous work.

4.1   ZAP Training

ZAPs are deployed at each desired convolution layer and are trained independently. By training in isolation [8,14], ZAPs can be plugged into a model without altering its architecture and trained parameters and may be trained in parallel. First, a batch is fed forward bypassing all predictors. During the feedforward phase, each ZAP saves a copy of its local input feature map (ifm) and corresponding local ofm. Then, each ZAP computes its $M[I_t]$, using its ifm followed by a ReLU activation function which is capped at 1. The ground truth, M_{ideal}, of each ZAP is its local ofm passed through a zero-threshold boolean operation

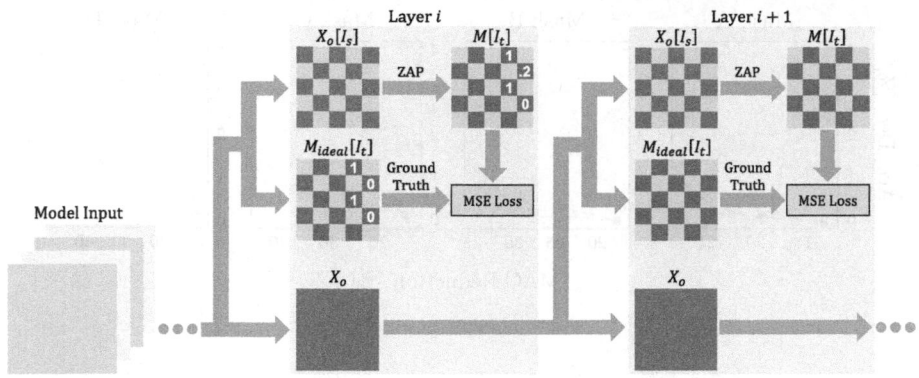

Fig. 7. Illustration of ZAP training. Each ZAP is trained independently in a teacher-student manner, enabling a parallel label-free training. The ground truth is the original layer ofm after a binary threshold operation (>0). The CNN predictor is used with the ReLU activation function capped at 1.

at indices I_t. Finally, the MSE loss is used to minimize each of the predictor errors, as follows:

$$\min \sum_{(x,y,z) \in I_t} (M - M_{ideal})^2. \tag{10}$$

Notice that no labeled data is needed. ZAP training is illustrated in Fig. 7.

4.2   Experimental Setup

We evaluated our method using CIFAR-100 [25] and ILSVRC-2012 [36] datasets, and AlexNet [26], VGG-16 [40], and ResNet-18 [13] CNN architectures. The source code is publicly available.[1]

ZAPs were trained using the Adam [22] optimizer for 5 epochs. When the ILSVRC-2012 dataset was used for ZAPs training, only 32 K training set images were used. After ZAPs were trained, we recalibrated the running mean and variance of the model BN layers; this is not considered fine-tuning since it does not involve backpropagation. BN recalibration was noticeably important with ResNet-18, which has multiple BN layers. When fine-tuning was considered, it was limited to 5 epochs with CIFAR-100 and to 1 epoch with ILSVRC-2012. We did not deploy ZAPs on the first layers of any of the models, since it is not beneficial in terms of potential operation savings.

AlexNet with CIFAR-100 was trained from scratch using the original hyperparameters, achieving top-1 accuracy of 64.4%. AlexNet, VGG-16, and ResNet-18 with ILSVRC-2012 were used with the PyTorch pretrained parameters, achieving top-1/top-5 accuracies of 56.5%/79.1%, 71.6%/90.6%, and 69.8%/89.1%, respectively.

---

[1] https://github.com/gilshm/zap.

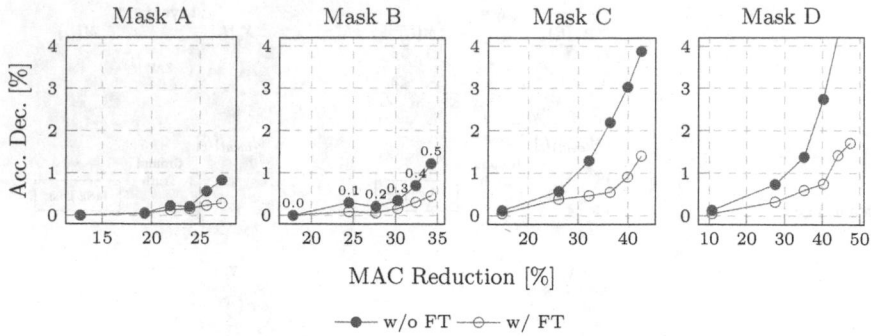

Fig. 8. Demonstrating the different operating points of AlexNet + CIFAR-100 with (w/) and without (w/o) fine-tuning (FT). Accuracy measurements are top-1. Threshold range is set between 0 to 0.5, in steps of 0.1. Each measurement corresponds to a threshold, as presented in "Mask B" plot.

We experimented with four different prediction patterns (Fig. 3). The same prediction pattern was used across all layers and channels. Mixing patterns in layer and channel granularity is an option we leave for future work.

Throughout this section, MAC reduction is defined as $(1 - \text{after/before})$ and accuracy degradation is defined as $(\text{before} - \text{after})$. When discussing MAC reduction, we consider only the relative savings from convolution layers.

4.3   CIFAR-100

Operating Points. We demonstrate different operating points as measured with different masks and uniform thresholds across all layers with AlexNet using the CIFAR-100 dataset. For each operating point, we report the entire model top-1 accuracy degradation and MAC operation savings, with and without fine-tuning (Fig. 8). For example, considering a 1% top-1 accuracy degradation cap, ZAP achieves a 32.4% MAC reduction with 0.7% accuracy degradation at mask B with a 0.4 threshold. In addition, by fine-tuning the model, our predictor achieves 40.3% MAC reduction with 0.8% accuracy degradation at mask D with a 0.3 threshold.

Masks with greater α values lead to ofms with relatively more computed activations, i.e., larger $|I_s|$. We observe that these masks show better accuracy results in the low degradation region (e.g., mask A versus mask D at 20% MAC reduction), whereas for higher MAC reduction requirements, masks with lower α values are preferred. In order to achieve high MAC reductions with the former masks (for example, mask A), σ would have to be cranked up. Since the prediction potential of these masks is low to begin with (for example, the best-case scenario with mask A is 40% activations savings with mask A), high thresholds will lead to pruning of relatively significant values and, as a result, to significant accuracy degradation. On the other hand, for conservative MAC reductions,

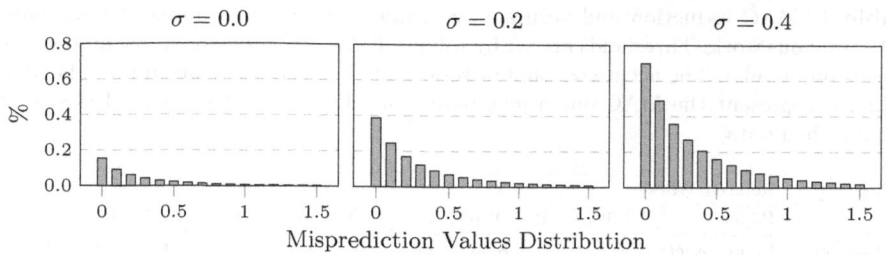

Fig. 9. AlexNet + CIFAR-100 histograms of non-zero values that were predicted as zero using mask B and different uniform thresholds.

these masks are preferred, since their speculation levels are lower and prediction confidence is higher.

Misprediction Breakdown. The model accuracy is not solely dependent on *how many* non-zeros were predicted as zero, but also *which* values were zeroed out. The notion that small values within DNN are relatively ineffectual is at the core of many pruning techniques. In Fig. 9 we present the mispredicted activation values distribution, normalized to the number of ofm activations for value steps of 0.1. For example, when using $\sigma = 0$, 0.15% of ofm activations with original values between 0 to 0.1 were zeroed out. Increasing the threshold level increases the number of predicted and mispredicted ofm activations. It is apparent that insignificant values are more prone to be mispredicted—it is easier to be mistaken about zeroing out a small value than a large value—attesting to the correlation between σ and the prediction confidence level.

4.4   ILSVRC-2012

Comparison with Previous Work. In Table 1 we compare our method with previous works. Shomron and Weiser [38], and Kim et al. [21] focus on predicting zero-valued activations according to nearby zero-valued activations. Figurnov et al. [9], on the other hand, mainly use "nearest neighbor" to interpolate missing activation values. Dong et al. [7] present a network structure with embedded low-cost convolution layers that act as zero-valued activation masks for the original convolution masks.

Using AlexNet and VGG-16, our method shows better results across the board (besides a small difference of 0.07 with VGG-16 top5 compared to Kim et al.)—for more MAC savings, a smaller accuracy drop is observed. Regrading ResNet-18, our method shows better results compared with Shomron and Weiser but falls short when compared with Dong et al. Notice though that the method Dong et al. introduced involves an entire network training with *hundreds* of epochs. Therefore, even though there is some resemblance between our method and theirs, the results themselves are not necessarily comparable.

Table 1. MAC reduction and accuracy with and without fine-tuning (ft) compared with previous work. Thresholds are set by solving Eq. 9 (see supplementary material for execution details). The accuracy columns represent the decrease in accuracy. The MAC columns represent the MAC operations reduction. The minus ('-') symbol represents unpublished data.

Net	Related Work						Ours				
	Paper	Top1	ft	Top5	ft	MAC	Top1	ft	Top5	ft	MAC
AlexNet	Figurnov et al.	-	-	8.50	2.0	50.0%	4.63	1.97	3.04	1.17	51.1%
	Kim et al.	0.48	-	0.40	-	28.6%	0.34	0.33	0.24	0.14	32.4%
	Shomron et al.	4.00	1.6	2.90	1.3	37.8%	1.28	0.78	0.84	0.42	38.0%
VGG-16	Figurnov et al.	-	-	15.6	1.1	44.4%	11.02	1.27	7.02	0.71	44.5%
	Kim et al.	0.68	-	0.26	-	25.7%	0.54	0.24	0.33	0.11	26.2%
	Shomron et al.	3.60	0.7	2.00	0.4	30.7%	1.71	0.31	0.87	0.19	31.3%
ResNet-18	Dong et al. *	-	3.6	-	2.3	34.6%	12.35	7.22	8.37	4.66	34.0%
	Shomron et al.	11.0	2.7	7.60	1.7	22.7%	2.96	1.86	1.70	1.13	23.8%

All MAC saving measurements reported in Table 1 are theoretical, that is, they are not actual speedups. However, it is apparent that the *potential* of ZAP is greater than the other previous works. We discuss related hardware implementations and related work next.

5   Discussion and Related Work

Hardware. It is not trivial to attain true benefits from mainstream compute engines, such as GPUs, when dealing with compute intensive tasks, such as CNNs, and using a conditional compute paradigm of which only a portion of the MAC operations are conducted and the rest performed or skipped according to the previously computed results. However, the implementation of CNN *accelerators*, which are capable of doing so and gain performance, has already been demonstrated. Kim et al. [21] present an architecture based on SCNN [34] which is capable of skipping computations of entire ofm activations based on already computed zero-valued ofm activations. Moreover, Hua et al. [18], Akhlaghi et al. [1] and Asadikouhanjani et al. [3] propose hardware that is capable of saving a portion of the MAC operations needed per ofm activation based on the accumulated partial sum. Akhlaghi et al. also suggest a method to do so in a speculative manner.

Speculative Execution. GPPs make extensive use of speculative execution [15]. They leverage unique application characteristics, such as code semantics and temporal locality, to better utilize the GPP's internal structure to achieve better performance. Researchers have also studied the speculative execution of CNNs to decrease their compute demands. Song et al. [41], Lin et al. [30], and Chang et al. [5] predict whether an entire convolution result is negative according to a partial result yielded by the input MSB bits. Huan et al. [19] avoid convolution multiplications by predicting and skipping near-zero valued data, given certain thresholds. Chen et al. [6] predict future weight updates during training based on Momentum [35] parameters. Zhu et al. [44] use a fully connected layer to predict each ofm activation sign and low-rank approximation to decrease the weight matrix.

Spatial Correlation. The correlation between neighboring activations in CNN feature maps is an inherent CNN characteristic that may be exploited. The works by Shomron and Weiser [38], Kim et al. [21], and Figurnov et al. [9] were described at Subsect. 4.4. In addition, Kligvasser et al. [23] propose nonlinear activations with learnable spatial connection to enable the network capture more complex features, and Mahmoud et al. [32] operate on reduced precision deltas between adjacent activations rather than on true values.

Dynamic Pruning. As opposed to static pruning [12,17,28,31,31], dynamic pruning is input-dependent. Dong et al. [7] present a network structure with embedded low-cost convolution layers that act as zero-valued activation masks for the original convolution masks. In a higher granularity, Lin et al. [29] use reinforcement learning for channel pruning, Gao et al. [10] prune channels according to a channel saliency map followed by a fully connected layer, and He et al. [14] propose a two-step channel pruning algorithm with LASSO regression and fine-tuning. All these works, except [14], involve extensive model training.

Our work is most closely related to the work of Dong et al., Shomron and Weiser, Kim et al., and Figurnov et al., with which we have also compared our results. However, our work provides the user with a continuous range of operating points and offers a prior estimate of the model accuracy degradation and MAC savings. Specifically, in contrast to Dong et al., our approach does not require labeled data (yet, it can be used for fine-tuning) and does not require hundreds of epochs for training. As for Shomron and Weiser, Kim et al., and Figurnov et al., we create the binary prediction masks using a CNN-based approach.

6 Conclusions

We propose a zero activation predictor (ZAP) that dynamically identifies the zero-valued output feature map (ofm) activations prior to their computation, thereby saving their convolution operations. ZAP exploits the spatial correlation of ofm activations inherent in convolution neural networks, meaning that according to a sparsely computed ofm, ZAP determines whether the remaining activations are zero-valued or non-zero-valued. ZAP is a lightweight CNN that imposes negligible computation and parameter overheads and its deployment and training does not require labeled data or modification of the baseline model architecture and parameters. In addition, ZAP speculation level is tunable, allowing an efficient *a priori* control of its accuracy-savings trade-off.

Acknowledgments. We acknowledge the support of NVIDIA Corporation for its donation of a Titan V GPU used for this research.

References

1. Akhlaghi, V., Yazdanbakhsh, A., Samadi, K., Gupta, R.K., Esmaeilzadeh, H.: Sna-PEA: predictive early activation for reducing computation in deep convolutional neural networks. In: International Symposium on Computer Architecture (ISCA), pp. 662–673. IEEE (2018)
2. Albericio, J., Judd, P., Hetherington, T., Aamodt, T., Jerger, N.E., Moshovos, A.: Cnvlutin: ineffectual-neuron-free deep neural network computing. In: International Symposium on Computer Architecture (ISCA), pp. 1–13. IEEE (2016)
3. Asadikouhanjani, M., Ko, S.B.: A novel architecture for early detection of negative output features in deep neural network accelerators. Trans. Circ. Syst. II Express Briefs (2020)
4. Canziani, A., Paszke, A., Culurciello, E.: An analysis of deep neural network models for practical applications. arXiv preprint arXiv:1605.07678 (2016)
5. Chang, J., Choi, Y., Lee, T., Cho, J.: Reducing MAC operation in convolutional neural network with sign prediction. In: International Conference on Information and Communication Technology Convergence (ICTC), pp. 177–182. IEEE (2018)
6. Chen, C.C., Yang, C.L., Cheng, H.Y.: Efficient and robust parallel DNN training through model parallelism on multi-GPU platform. arXiv preprint arXiv:1809.02839 (2018)
7. Dong, X., Huang, J., Yang, Y., Yan, S.: More is less: a more complicated network with less inference complexity. In: Conference on Computer Vision and Pattern Recognition (CVPR), pp. 5840–5848. IEEE (2017)
8. Elthakeb, A.T., Pilligundla, P., Esmaeilzadeh, H.: Divide and conquer: leveraging intermediate feature representations for quantized training of neural networks. In: International Conference on Machine Learning (ICML) Workshop on Understanding and Improving Generalization in Deep Learning (2019)
9. Figurnov, M., Ibraimova, A., Vetrov, D.P., Kohli, P.: PerforatedCNNs: acceleration through elimination of redundant convolutions. In: Advances in Neural Information Processing Systems (NIPS), pp. 947–955 (2016)
10. Gao, X., Zhao, Y., Dudziak, L., Mullins, R., Xu, C.z.: Dynamic channel pruning: feature boosting and suppression. In: International Conference on Learning Representations (ICLR) (2018)
11. Geifman, Y., El-Yaniv, R.: Selective classification for deep neural networks. In: Advances in Neural Information Processing Systems (NIPS), pp. 4878–4887 (2017)
12. Han, S., Mao, H., Dally, W.J.: Deep compression: compressing deep neural networks with pruning, trained quantization and Huffman coding. In: International Conference on Learning Representations (ICLR) (2016)
13. He, K., Zhang, X., Ren, S., Sun, J.: Deep residual learning for image recognition. In: Conference on Computer Vision and Pattern Recognition (CVPR), pp. 770–778. IEEE (2016)
14. He, Y., Zhang, X., Sun, J.: Channel pruning for accelerating very deep neural networks. In: International Conference on Computer Vision (ICCV), pp. 1389–1397. IEEE (2017)
15. Hennessy, J.L., Patterson, D.A.: Computer Architecture: A Quantitative Approach. Elsevier (2011)
16. Howard, A.G., et al.: MobileNets: efficient convolutional neural networks for mobile vision applications. arXiv preprint arXiv:1704.04861 (2017)
17. Hu, H., Peng, R., Tai, Y.W., Tang, C.K.: Network trimming: a data-driven neuron pruning approach towards efficient deep architectures. arXiv preprint arXiv:1607.03250 (2016)

18. Hua, W., Zhou, Y., De Sa, C., Zhang, Z., Suh, G.E.: Boosting the performance of CNN accelerators with dynamic fine-grained channel gating. In: International Symposium on Microarchitecture (MICRO), pp. 139–150. ACM (2019)
19. Huan, Y., Qin, Y., You, Y., Zheng, L., Zou, Z.: A multiplication reduction technique with near-zero approximation for embedded learning in IoT devices. In: International System-on-Chip Conference (SOCC), pp. 102–107. IEEE (2016)
20. Ioffe, S., Szegedy, C.: Batch normalization: accelerating deep network training by reducing internal covariate shift. In: International Conference on Machine Learning (ICML) (2015)
21. Kim, C., Shin, D., Kim, B., Park, J.: Mosaic-CNN: A combined two-step zero prediction approach to trade off accuracy and computation energy in convolutional neural networks. J. Emerg. Sel. Topics Circ. Syst. 8(4), 770–781 (2018)
22. Kingma, D.P., Ba, J.: Adam: a method for stochastic optimization. In: International Conference on Learning Representations (ICLR) (2014)
23. Kligvasser, I., Rott Shaham, T., Michaeli, T.: xUnit: learning a spatial activation function for efficient image restoration. In: Conference on Computer Vision and Pattern Recognition (ECCV), pp. 2433–2442 (2018)
24. Krizhevsky, A., Hinton, G.: Convolutional deep belief networks on CIFAR-10 40(7), 1–9 (2010). Unpublished manuscript
25. Krizhevsky, A., Nair, V., Hinton, G.: CIFAR-10 and CIFAR-100 datasets. http://www.cs.toronto.edu/kriz/cifar.html
26. Krizhevsky, A., Sutskever, I., Hinton, G.E.: ImageNet classification with deep convolutional neural networks. In: Advances in Neural Information Processing Systems (NIPS), pp. 1097–1105 (2012)
27. Levine, S., Finn, C., Darrell, T., Abbeel, P.: End-to-end training of deep visuomotor policies. J. Mach. Learn. Res. 17(1), 1334–1373 (2016)
28. Li, H., Kadav, A., Durdanovic, I., Samet, H., Graf, H.P.: Pruning filters for efficient ConvNets. In: International Conference on Learning Representations (ICLR) (2017)
29. Lin, J., Rao, Y., Lu, J., Zhou, J.: Runtime neural pruning. In: Advances in Neural Information Processing Systems (NIPS), pp. 2181–2191 (2017)
30. Lin, Y., Sakr, C., Kim, Y., Shanbhag, N.: PredictiveNet: an energy-efficient convolutional neural network via zero prediction. In: International Symposium on Circuits and Systems (ISCAS), pp. 1–4. IEEE (2017)
31. Luo, J.H., Wu, J., Lin, W.: ThiNet: a filter level pruning method for deep neural network compression. In: International Conference on Computer Vision (ICCV), pp. 5058–5066. IEEE (2017)
32. Mahmoud, M., Siu, K., Moshovos, A.: Diffy: a déjà vu-free differential deep neural network accelerator. In: International Symposium on Microarchitecture (MICRO), pp. 134–147. IEEE (2018)
33. Nair, V., Hinton, G.E.: Rectified linear units improve restricted Boltzmann machines. In: International Conference on Machine Learning (ICML), pp. 807–814 (2010)
34. Parashar, A., et al.: SCNN: an accelerator for compressed-sparse convolutional neural networks. In: International Symposium on Computer Architecture (ISCA), pp. 27–40. IEEE (2017)
35. Qian, N.: On the momentum term in gradient descent learning algorithms. Neural Netw. 12(1), 145–151 (1999)
36. Russakovsky, O., et al.: ImageNet large scale visual recognition challenge. Int. J. Comput. Vis. (IJCV) 115(3), 211–252 (2015)

37. Sainath, T.N., Mohamed, A.R., Kingsbury, B., Ramabhadran, B.: Deep convolutional neural networks for LVCSR. In: International Conference on Acoustics, Speech and Signal Processing (ICASSP), pp. 8614–8618. IEEE (2013)
38. Shomron, G., Weiser, U.: Spatial correlation and value prediction in convolutional neural networks. Comput. Architect. Lett. (CAL) **18**(1), 10–13 (2019)
39. Silver, D., et al.: Mastering the game of Go with deep neural networks and tree search. Nature **529**(7587), 484 (2016)
40. Simonyan, K., Zisserman, A.: Very deep convolutional networks for large-scale image recognition. In: International Conference on Machine Learning (ICML) (2015)
41. Song, M., Zhao, J., Hu, Y., Zhang, J., Li, T.: Prediction based execution on deep neural networks. In: International Symposium on Computer Architecture (ISCA), pp. 752–763. IEEE (2018)
42. Sze, V., Chen, Y.H., Yang, T.J., Emer, J.S.: Efficient processing of deep neural networks: a tutorial and survey. Proc. IEEE **105**(12), 2295–2329 (2017)
43. Yazdani, R., Riera, M., Arnau, J.M., González, A.: The dark side of DNN pruning. In: International Symposium on Computer Architecture (ISCA), pp. 790–801. IEEE (2018)
44. Zhu, J., Jiang, J., Chen, X., Tsui, C.Y.: Sparsenn: an energy-efficient neural network accelerator exploiting input and output sparsity. In: Design, Automation and Test in Europe Conference (DATE), pp. 241–244. IEEE (2018)

Layered Neighborhood Expansion
for Incremental Multiple Graph Matching

Zixuan Chen[1,2], Zhihui Xie[1,2], Junchi Yan[1,2(✉)] (iD), Yinqiang Zheng[3],
and Xiaokang Yang[2]

[1] Department of Computer Science and Engineering,
Shanghai Jiao Tong University, Shanghai, China
{m13953842591,fffffarmer,yanjunchi}@sjtu.edu.cn
[2] MoE Key Laboratory of Artificial Intelligence, AI Institute,
Shanghai Jiao Tong University, Shanghai, China
xkyang@sjtu.edu.cn
[3] National Institute of Informatics, Chiyoda, Japan
yqzheng@nii.ac.jp

Abstract. Graph matching has been a fundamental problem in computer vision and pattern recognition, for its practical flexibility as well as NP hardness challenge. Though the matching between two graphs and among multiple graphs have been intensively studied in literature, the online setting for incremental matching of a stream of graphs has been rarely considered. In this paper, we treat the graphs as graphs on a super-graph, and propose a novel breadth first search based method for expanding the neighborhood on the super-graph for a new coming graph, such that the matching with the new graph can be efficiently performed within the constructed neighborhood. Then depth first search is performed to update the overall pairwise matchings. Moreover, we show our approach can also be readily used in the batch mode setting, by adaptively determining the order of coming graph batch for matching, still under the neighborhood expansion based incremental matching framework. Experiments on both online and offline matching of graph collections show our approach's state-of-the-art accuracy and efficiency.

Keywords: Multi-graph matching · Clustering · Self-supervised learning

1 Introduction

Over the decades, to fuse the information among two or multiple graphs, the matching of graphs has attracted extensive attention in vision and learning communities. In general, graph matching (GM) aims to establish pairwise node correspondences over two or more graphs, whereby both cross-graph node-to-node and

Work was partly supported by National Key Research and Development Program of China 2018AAA0100704, NSFC (61972250, U19B2035), and SJTU Global Strategic Partnership Fund (2020 SJTU-CORNELL).

© Springer Nature Switzerland AG 2020
A. Vedaldi et al. (Eds.): ECCV 2020, LNCS 12355, pp. 251–267, 2020.
https://doi.org/10.1007/978-3-030-58607-2_15

edge-to-edge affinity are considered. By incorporating geometrical edge information, the graph structure can be effectively explored resulting in better robustness against deformation and noise. This is in contrast to the node-wise information based matching models e.g. RANSAC [10] and Iterative Closet Point (ICP) [40]. However, it meanwhile lifts the node affinity based linear assignment problem to the task of quadratic assignment programming (QAP) [22]. The global optimum for the former problem can be found in polynomial time by Hungarian method, while QAP is known NP-complete [12] in general. Hence, most existing graph matching methods often seek for approximate solutions.

Apart from its mathematical challenge, graph matching is also prone to suffer from the biased modeling of real-world data. In the presence of local noise over the two graphs for matching, the affinity model can be biased such that the mathematically global optimum may not correspond to the perfect matching for the data at hand. Considering the fact that in practice often a collection of graphs are available for matching, a natural idea is to perform joint matching of multiple graphs in one shot [31,34]. The hope is that the local noise among individual graphs can be smoothed over. The so-called cycle-consistency enforcement has been a popular and useful technique which is based on the simple observation that the correct pairwise matching among three graphs form a closed loop.

We take one step further and consider the problem of incremental matching of graph stream over time. In online applications such as video analysis, and event log mining, graph data may be collected sequentially rather than in one shot. Therefore like many online variants of different algorithms, the community calls for effective and efficient online version of multiple graph matching. This setting is in fact rarely studied in literature until a recent work in [38].

This paper departures from the mainstream literature on offline multiple graph [25,27,31–33,35]. Rather, we present a novel algorithm for incremental multiple graph matching (IMGM). The main contributions of the paper are:

(i) We develop a novel and efficient IMGM solver based on maximum spanning tree on the super-graph (i.e. graph for matching is treated as a node) that gradually identifies and expands the neighborhood for the coming graph, by breadth first search to ensure the quality of the neighborhood, and then all the graphs are visited by depth first search for efficiency. In the procedure, the two-graph matchings are updated via matching composition which has been shown cost-effectiveness in previous works [31].

(ii) By creating an adaptive order for sequential matching, we show that our method can be applied in the offline multiple graph matching setting effectively.

(iii) Experiments on both synthetic data and real images clearly show the advantages of our method. In particular, it outperforms the state-of-the-art method [38] for incremental multiple graph matching remarkably, for both accuracy and efficiency. Our method also performs competitively in offline mode.

2   Related Works

There have emerged a series of surveys [1,7,11,29,36]. Our review divides existing works into matching of two-graph, multi-graphs and incremental matching.

Two-Graph Matching. Most works are devoted to the classic setting for two graph matching, which in its general form relates to QAP when up to second-order edge affinity is considered [2,6,9,13,20]. There are two ways of modeling the affinity matrix in QAP: (i) learning-free models: using a fixed and parametric form [17] e.g. Gaussian kernel to model the node-to-node, and edge-to-edge similarity. Due to the limited capacity of such simple affinity model, the complex landscape of the affinity information of real-world data may not be perfectly captured and as mentioned in the introduction part of this paper, the objective function for QAP can be biased which causes the difficulty for finding the correct matching in addition with the mathematical combinatorial problem itself. To improve the model capacity, one way is to lift the affinity matrix to higher-order (often third-order) tensor [4,8,23,37,39]. However the additional cost can be exponential in terms of the number of nodes in graph hurting their applicability.

Another seemingly promising direction is adopting learning to find appropriate parameters for affinity modeling rather simply determined by hand [16]. The key idea is to learn the affinity function either in supervised [2,5,20,21] or unsupervised (or semi-supervised) setting [20,21]. Deep neural networks are employed in recent works [30] to improve the model capacity, and also to enable end-to-end learning supervised by node correspondence information.

Offline and Online Multiple Graph Matching. Beyond two-graph, works [3,15,18,24–27,33,34] tackle the problem of matching a collection of graphs.

For multiple graph matching, or more generally the correspondence problem from multiple views, the so-called cycle-consistency [33] has been a widely adopted concept and metric to evaluate the behavior of the matching solvers. Specifically, here we consider the three graphs G_i, G_j, G_k, and denote the two-graph matching as $\mathbf{X}_{ij}$, $\mathbf{X}_{jk}$, and $\mathbf{X}_{ik}$. Then for ground truth matching, the close loop will establish: $\mathbf{X}_{ik} = \mathbf{X}_{ij}\mathbf{X}_{jk}$, and the deviation signifies the inconsistency incurred by less accurate matchings. In another word, cycle-consistency is the necessary condition for perfect matching, and also an important indicator for the accuracy of matchings for multiple graphs.

We follow the protocol in [38] that categorizes existing multiple graph matching methods into two groups: (i) two-stage methods that separate the local two-graph matching and post consistency based smoothing in two steps; (ii) iterative methods that integrate the consistency and affinity optimization alternately.

In the two-step methods, first the pairwise matchings between two graphs or two node sets (the edge information may not be used) are first calculated by certain means, and then different smoothing techniques are devised to enforce cycle-consistency. Bijection and partial matching are respectively considered in the work [24] and [3]. One particular difficulty is that the number of cycles is exponential regarding with the number of graphs for matching. In a more recent study [14], the authors show that it is possible and theoretically guaranteed that only a subset of cycles need being sampled for joint optimization.

In contrast to the above post-smoothing methods, another line of study combine the optimization of both affinity and consistency in an iterative fashion. In general, it is difficult to incorporate the discrete consistency term for gradient based optimization. The authors in [31] devise a discrete composition based approach to generate new matching solution. The criterion refers to both affinity score and consistency improved by the new solution. In some other works [27, 28, 33, 34], the consistency constraint is strictly obeyed which makes them less flexible, and more sensitive to error accumulation over iterations.

There are little study on the online setting whereby graphs arrive one by one. This setting is nontrivial and calls for efficient mechanism. We only identify one related work as directly termed by incremental multiple graph matching (IMGM) in [38]. The idea of [38] is to partition existing graphs into a few clusters, based on the criterion that each cluster shall maintain certain diversity as such the newly coming graph can be matched to only one cluster which is a good representative of the whole set. The diversity is fulfilled by the determinantal point process (DPP) [19] which sometimes can be more effective than random sampling.

Remarks. We argue that the success of the method in [38] is based on the assumption that a cluster can well cover the variation of the whole set of graphs, such that the new graph only need to match with the graphs in cluster. However it is difficult to ensure especially when the cluster size is small. In fact, there is a tradeoff between efficiency (small cluster) and effectiveness (representative cluster), and the clustering design in [38] essentially suffers such a dilemma and as shown in Fig. 3 (the bottom row) in [38]: its accuracy drops significantly by slightly increasing the cluster number k from 2 to 3 and 4.

We circumvent such a dilemma by avoiding explicit clustering of graphs which is time consuming and lacks flexibility to capture the complex variation of graph collection at hand. Instead, we propose to dynamically form a neighborhood based on breadth first search, allowing more easier and efficient matching for the new arrival graph. In other words, the involved graph subset for matching with the new graph is selected without any clustering step. Then we further use depth first search to cover all the nodes on the super-graph with compositional matching updating (akin to CAO-C [31]) to fulfill the whole matching process.

3   Preliminaries

Notations and Definitions. In this paper, we use n for the number of nodes in each graph, N for the current number of graphs for processing, and M for the upper bound of the neighborhood size for a new graph, respectively. Furthermore, $L(N)$ denotes the number of two-graph matching performed when the N-th graph comes in a certain algorithm. This is useful for evaluating its complexity.

For bijection[1], the matching objective can be defined as [6]:

$$\max_{\mathbf{x}} \mathcal{E}_{ij} = \text{vec}(\mathbf{X}_{ij})^\top \mathbf{K}_{ij} \text{vec}(\mathbf{X}_{ij})$$
$$\text{s.t.} \quad \mathbf{X}_{ij}\mathbf{1}_n = \mathbf{1}_n \quad \mathbf{1}_n^T \mathbf{X}_{ij} = \mathbf{1}_n^T \quad \mathbf{X}_{ij} \in \{0,1\}^{n\times n} \tag{1}$$

where $\mathbf{X}_{ij}$ is the matching (permutation) matrix denoting node correspondences between graph G_i and G_j, and $\mathbf{K}_{ij}$ stands for the affinity matrix whose diagonal and offdiagonal elements encode the node-to-node and edge-to-edge affinity, respectively [6,34]. To be self-contained, we also rewrite the definitions in terms of consistency metric as defined in [31,38] and other literature.

Definition 1. *Given N graphs $\mathbb{G} = \{G_k\}_{k=1}^N$ and the corresponding pairwise matchings $\mathbb{X} = \{\mathbf{X}_{ij}\}_{i=1,j=i+1}^{N-1,N}$, define the unary consistency of G_k as $C_u(k,\mathbb{X}) = 1 - \frac{\sum_{i=1}^{N-1}\sum_{j=i+1}^{N} \|\mathbf{X}_{ij}-\mathbf{X}_{ik}\mathbf{X}_{kj}\|_F/2}{nN(N-1)/2} \in (0,1]$.*

Definition 2. *Given $\mathbb{G}$ and their pairwise matchings $\mathbb{X}$, define the overall consistency as $C(\mathbb{X}) - \frac{\sum_{k=1}^{N} C_u(k,\mathbb{X})}{N} \in (0,1]$.*

Definition 3. *Given $\mathbb{G}$, pairwise matchings $\mathbb{X} = \{\mathbf{X}_{ij}\}_{i=1,j=i+1}^{N-1,N}$ and affinity matrices $\mathbb{K} = \{\mathbf{K}_{ij}\}_{i=1,j=i+1}^{N-1,N}$, the pairwise affinity score between G_i and G_j is defined as $S_{ij} = \text{vec}(\mathbf{X}_{ij})^\top \mathbf{K}_{ij} \text{vec}(\mathbf{X}_{ij})$.*

Definition 4. *A supergraph $\mathcal{H}$ is an undirected complete graph induced by graph set $\mathbb{G}$ and pairwise matchings $\mathbb{X}$. Its nodes, edges and edge weights denote graphs, pairwise matchings, and pairwise matching score, respectively:*

$$\mathcal{H} = \{V = \{G_k\}_{k=1}^N, E = \mathbb{X}, W = \{S_{ij}\}_{i,j=1}^{N,N}\}$$

Definition 5. *Given a supergraph $\mathcal{H}$, a path from G_i to G_j is denoted as $\mathcal{P}_{ij}$, which is a set containing edges from G_i to G_j: $\mathcal{P}_{ij} = \{\mathbf{X}_{ik_1}, \mathbf{X}_{k_1k_2}, ..., \mathbf{X}_{k_sj}\}$. The consistent matching matrix along path $\mathcal{P}_{ij}$ is defined as:*

$$\overline{\mathbf{X}}_{ij} = \mathbf{X}_{ik_1}\mathbf{X}_{k_1k_2}...\mathbf{X}_{k_sj}$$

And the affinity score along path $\mathcal{P}_{ij}$ is defined as:

$$\overline{S}_{ij} = \text{vec}(\overline{\mathbf{X}}_{ij})^\top \mathbf{K}_{ij} \text{vec}(\overline{\mathbf{X}}_{ij})$$

Definition 6. *Given a supergraph $\mathcal{H}$, a spanning tree $\mathcal{T} = \{V = \{G_k\}_{k=1}^N, E = \mathbb{X}' \subsetneq \mathbb{X}\}$ is a sub-supergraph, with $N-1$ edges and satisfies that each two vertices has exactly one path in $\mathcal{T}$. The spanning tree with the highest accumulated pairwise affinity score over all its edges is called maximum spanning tree (MST).*

---

[1] We assume graphs are of equal size in this paper, which can be obtained by adding dummy nodes if needed as widely done in literature [6].

Problem Formulation. The incremental multiple graph matching problem can be summarized as follows: given the $N-1$ graphs $\{G_k\}_{i=1}^{N-1}$ with their matchings $\mathbb{X}_{N-1}$, how to match the new graph G_N and update the existing matchings $\mathbb{X}_{N-1}$ (if necessary) and generate the new overall matching set $\mathbb{X}_N$. In contrast, traditional multiple graph matching is performed in a way that involves all the graphs at offline. Directly applying such joint matching each time a new graph comes is intimidating. Thus, new methods are in demand to address such a nontrivial problem. Our setting is the same with the recent work [38].

4   IMGM by Layered Neighbor Expansion

4.1   Problem Analysis and Approach Overview

To reduce the computing overhead, one natural idea appearing in [38] is to divide the whole graph set $\mathbb{G}$ into k clusters $\mathbb{C}_1, \mathbb{C}_2, \ldots, \mathbb{C}_k$. Let the new coming graph G_N match one of these clusters $\mathbb{C}_i$ according to some similarity metric between the cluster and G_N, and the matchings between $\mathbb{C}_i \cup \{G_N\}$ and the rest clusters $\mathbb{G} \backslash \mathbb{C}_i$ can be generated by certain means e.g. cycle consistency enforcement.

However, we argue such a clustering-oriented strategy may not inherently fit with the online graph matching problem. The reasons include: (i) clustering is not optimized for the purpose of finding the most similar (or representative as in [38]) graphs for matching; (ii) clustering results can be unstable especially for $K > 2$ clusters e.g. using k-means, which means it is difficult for the resulting cluster to effectively fit with the coming graph for matching; (iii) clustering can be time consuming, especially for large-scale and complex techniques e.g. k-DPP (determinantal point process) [19] as used in [38] to ensure the efficacy.

In this paper, we hold a principle to find graphs similar to the new coming one, and the matchings can be conducted in a diffusion manner on the super-graph (see Definition 4), such that the new graph is regarded as a seed and the pairwise matchings are generated over the diffusion path. For efficiency, we first build a maximum spanning tree (MST) (see Definition 6) on the existing super-graph $\mathcal{H}_{N-1}$ as such the pairwise matching can be focused on the tree which also avoids matching inconsistency due to the existence of matching cycles. As shown in Fig. 1(c) based on the formed MST, we first find the most similar graph G_k to G_N in $\mathbb{G}_{N-1}$ and perform breadth first search (BFS) starting from G_k until at most M graphs are reached on $\mathcal{H}_{N-1}$. The hope is that the most similar graphs to G_N can be effectively found along $\mathcal{H}_{N-1}$ such that matchings among these graphs can be more reliable and accurate. Given these accurate early matchings, we then devise a greedier and more cost-effective means to perform depth first search (DFS) to match the rest of graphs on $\mathcal{H}_{N-1}$. Note that DFS can help the matching be efficiently and consistently conducted for each pair of graphs along the search path by reusing the pairwise matching, as shown in Fig. 1(d), (e): after computing matching $\mathbf{X}_{ik}$ and $\mathbf{X}_{kj}$, the skip matching between G_i and G_j can be readily computed by $\mathbf{X}_{ij} = \mathbf{X}_{ik}\mathbf{X}_{ik}$ without redundantly computing $\mathbf{X}_{ij}$ between G_i and G_j, which can further cause cycle inconsistency (see Definition 1). In this way, the local consistency along each DFS path is guaranteed. It is also worth

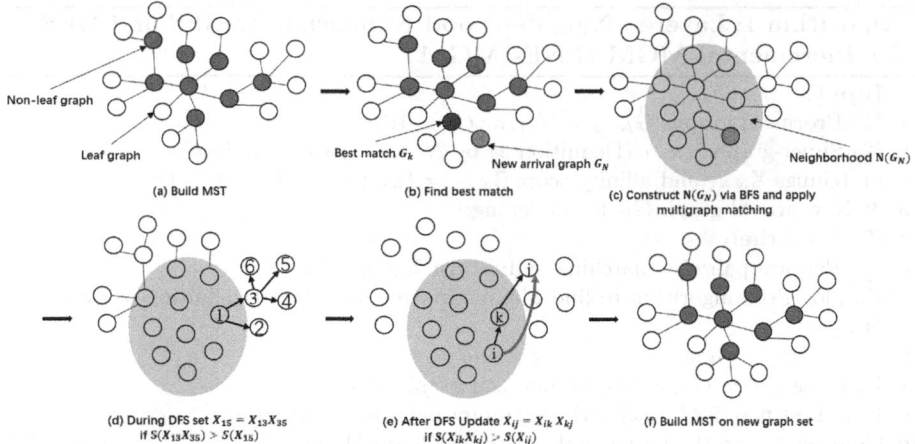

Fig. 1. Illustration of LNE-IMGM. (a) The red leaf nodes denote non-leaf graph set $\mathbb{C}$ and the white nodes denote leaf graph set $\mathbb{G}\backslash\mathbb{C}$. (b) The blue node denotes the new arrival graph G_N for incremental matching and the purple node denote the best match graph $G_k \in \mathbb{C}$. (c) The green ellipse denote the neighborhood $\mathcal{N}(G_N)$ with size $M = 10$. (d) We do DFS in numerical order and update the matchings during the search. (e) $G_i, G_k \in \mathcal{N}(G_N)$ and $G_j \in \mathbb{G}\backslash\mathcal{N}(G_N)$. (Color figure online)

noting that directly using DFS instead of BFS can be efficient but less effective because the error can be accumulated over the DFS path. In contrast, the BFS strategy ensures better matching quality in the beginning, which allows for the aggressive DFS stage later.

We shall emphasize that the above steps are integrated as a whole based on the MST structure. Hence we cannot replace either the BFS stage or DFS stage with other techniques e.g. k-nearest neighbor, clustering. One may also notice that our DFS mechanism ensures the local consistency along each DFS path though the overall consistency cannot be guaranteed by our approach. We call our approach **layered neighborhood expansion** since it involves the above starting graph finding, BFS and DFS to gradually expand the neighborhood.

An overview of our method is illustrated in Fig. 1. Compared with the traditional multi-graph algorithm with time complexity of $O(N^4)$, we reduce the complexity to $O(N^2)$ with two order of scalability improvement. We will cover each step of the algorithm in detail in the following sections.

4.2 Build MST and Find Best Match Graphing as Seed

We first build a Maximum Spanning Tree according to Definition 6. Denote D_i as the degree of node i on MST, and $E_{ij} = 1$ if node i and j are connected. It is clear that all non-leaf nodes have degree greater than 1, and all leaf nodes have only 1 degree. Suppose $\mathbb{C} = \{G_i, D_i > 1\}$ represents all non-leaf graph set. For each new graph G_N, it first matchings with every $G_i, i \in \mathbb{C}$. Let $k = \arg\max_{i \in \mathbb{C}} S_{iN}$ represent the best matched non-leaf graph. G_N is then linked to G_k on MST.

Algorithm 1: Layered Neighborhood Expansion by BFS and DFS for Incremental MGM (LNE-IMGM)

Input: *//The only hyerparameter: size of the neighbourhood M*

1 (1) Processed graphs $\mathbb{G}_{N-1} = \{G_1, ..., G_{N-1}\}$;

2 (2) Super-graph $\mathcal{H}_{N-1}$ (Definition 4) by $N-1$ existing graphs $\mathbb{G}_{N-1}$, matchings $\mathbb{X}_{N-1}$ and affinity score $\mathbb{S}_{N-1} = \{S_{ij}\}(i, j = 1, ..., N-1)$;

3 3) New arrival graph G_N for matching;

4 **if** $N = 2$ **then**

5 | Perform pairwise matching and return $\mathbb{X}_N$ and $\mathbb{S}_N$;

6 Employ Prim algorithm to find Maximum Spanning Tree (Definition 6) over $\mathcal{H}_{N-1}$

7 *// Build MST and Find Best Matching Graph:*

8 Pairwise match G_N with each non-leaf graph $G_i \in \mathbb{C}$;

9 Find best match $G_k \in \mathbb{C}$ with maximum pairwise affinity score S_{Nk};

10 Connect G_N to the best matching graph G_k on MST;

11 *// Neighbourhood Construction by BFS:*

12 Apply breadth first search (BFS) on MST with root G_N, get neighbourhood $\mathcal{N}(G_N)$ with size at most M or early stop due to end of search;

13 Apply a multi-graph solver e.g. CAO-C [31] to obtain multi-graph matchings $\mathbb{X}_{bfs}$ on $\mathcal{N}(G_N)$;

14 Update $\mathbb{X}_N$ with $\mathbb{X}_{bfs}$;

15 *// Local Optimization along each DFS path:*

16 **for** *each* $G_i \in \mathcal{N}(G_N)$ **do**

17 | Set G_i as root node and apply depth first search within $\mathbb{G}\backslash\mathcal{N}(G_N)$;

18 | **for** *each* G_s *along DFS path* $\mathcal{P}_{is}$ **do**

19 | | Update $\mathbf{X}_{is} = \overline{X}_{is}$, $S_{is} = \overline{S}_{is}$ if $\overline{S}_{is} > S_{is}$;

20 *// Global Optimization along after DFS:*

21 **for** *each* $G_i \in \mathcal{N}(G_N)$ **do**

22 | **for** *each* $G_j \in \mathbb{G}\backslash\mathcal{N}(G_N)$ **do**

23 | | Find $G_k \in \mathcal{N}(G_N)$;

24 | | Update $\mathbf{X}_{ij} = \mathbf{X}_{ik}\mathbf{X}_{kj}$, $S_{ij} = \overline{S}_{ij}$ if $\overline{S}_{ij} > S_{ij}$;

25 $\mathbb{G} = \mathbb{G} \cup \{G_N\}$;

Output: Multi-graph matchings $\mathbb{X}_N$ and $\mathbb{S}_N$

4.3 Neighbourhood Construction by BFS

On MST, all adjacent nodes are closely connected. To promote similarity, We construct neighbourhood $\mathcal{N}(G_N)$ by applying breadth first search (BFS) on MST rooted in G_N. Through BFS, we can not only search out the neighbourhood with graphs that are mostly similar to G_N, but also control the neighbourhood size. We denote $M = |\mathcal{N}(G_N)|$. After expansion, we perform multi-graph matching in $\mathcal{N}(G_N)$ to further optimize the matching.

Algorithm 2: Layered Neighborhood Expansion for Multiple Graph Matching (LNE-MGM)

Input: (1) Graph streams $\mathbb{G}_N = \{G_1, G_2, ..., G_N\}$,
(2) Pairwise affinity $\mathbf{K}_{ij}(i, j = 1, ..., N)$,

1 Do pairwise matching by RRWM to obtain initial $\mathbb{X}$;
2 Calculate affinity score for $G_i \in \mathbb{G}$;
3 Reorder graph streams $\mathbb{G}' = \{G'_1, G'_2, ..., G'_N\}$ by the graph-wise affinity score (descending order is suggested for better performance);
4 perform pairwise match between G'_1 and G'_2;
5 **for** $n = 3, 4, ..., N$ **do**
6 $\quad \lfloor$ Apply Algorithm 1 to obtain updated $\mathbb{X}_n$ and $\mathbb{S}_n$;

Output: Multi-graph matching $\mathbb{X}$

4.4 Whole Set Coverage and Matching by DFS

By expanding neighbourhood, we cover the whole graph set $\mathbb{G}$. For each graph in $\mathcal{N}(G_N)$, we perform depth first search(DFS) on MST, where it only search graphs in $\mathbb{G}\backslash\mathcal{N}(G_N)$. Assignment X_{rs} is updated to $\overline{X}_{rs}$ along DFS path $\mathcal{P}_{rs}$ if $\overline{S}_{rs} > S_{rs}$ (see Definition 5).

After running DFS, some matchings between $\mathcal{N}(G_N)$ and $\mathbb{G}\backslash\mathcal{N}(G_N)$ are still not updated. To update those match between $G_i \in \mathbb{N}(G_N)$ and $G_j \in \mathbb{G}\backslash\mathcal{N}(G_N)$, suppose match between $G_k \in \mathcal{N}(G_N)$ and G_j has been updated during DFS, $\mathbf{X}_{ij}$ is updated to $\overline{\mathbf{X}}_{ij}$ along path $\mathcal{P}_{ij} = \{\mathbf{X}_{ik}, \mathbf{X}_{kj}\}$ if $\overline{S}_{ij} > S_{ij}$.

4.5 Adaptive Ordering for Batch of Graphs

LNE-IMGM can be applied offline by matching the graph batch one by one, i.e., in a pseudo online setting. Here we aim to improve this baseline strategy by reordering the graph sequence for matching. Specifically, the order is by the graph-wise affinity score over the graph set $\mathbb{G}$. Specifically, for graph G_i, its overall graph-wise affinity score is given by: $S_i = \sum_j S_{ij}$. For those with higher affinity score, we consider to match them first as we assume they are easier to match. Figure 7(a), (b) basically verifies our idea.

4.6 Time Complexity Analysis

The time complexity is compared in Table 1. We discuss each method in detail.

LNE-IMGM. For each step, given $\mathbb{G}_{N-1} = \{G_1, G_2, ..., G_{N-1}\}$ as processed graphs with graph size n, and neighbourhood size M, we analyze the main overhead components as follows.

(i) **Two-graph Matching Solver.** For pairwise matching process, we only match G_N with all non-leaf graphs $G_i \in \mathbb{C} \cup \mathcal{N}(G_N)$. Define the number

Table 1. Time complexity for matching of IMGM per iteration. Note d is the number of clusters in [38]. It is often set to 2 to ensure accuracy, which limits [38]'s efficiency.

Method	Time complexity
CAO-C-INC [31]	$O(N^4n + N^3n^3 + N\tau_{pair})$
CAO-C-RAW [31]	$O(N^4n + N^3n^3 + N^2\tau_{pair})$
IMGM-D, IMGM-R [38]	$O(N^3n^3/d^2 + N^3/d^2 + N\tau_{pair})$
LNE-IMGM (ours)	$O(N^2 + M^2Nn^3 + M^4n + L(N)\tau_{pair})$
LNE-MGM (ours)	$O(N^3 + M^2N^2n^3 + NM^4n + N^2\tau_{pair})$

of pairwise matching for G_N as $L(N)$, then $L(N) = |\mathbb{C} \cup \mathcal{N}(G_N)|$. Clearly $L(N) \leq N$. The overall complexity for pairwise matching is $O(L(N)\tau_{pair})$, where τ_{pair} is the cost for calling a two-graph matching solver e.g. RRWM [6].

(ii) **Multi-graph Matching Solver.** Our method can accept any multi-graph solver. In our experiment we use CAO-C which is the state-of-the-art MGM solver in [31] based on the compositional matching updating over pairwise matchings, whose time complexity is $O(M^4n + M^3n^3)$.

(iii) **Other Overhead.** The time to compute MST is $O(N^2)$. The time for BST is $O(MN)$. The time for **L13-17** is $O((N - M)n^3)$. The complexity for **L18-21** in Algorithm 1 is $O(M^2(N - M)n^3)$.

(iv) **(iv) Overall Complexity.** The overall complexity can be reduced to $O(N^2 + M^2Nn^3 + M^4n + L(N)\tau_{pair})$. As M is constant for each step, the complexity thus can be roughly treated as $O(N^2 + Nn^3 + L(N)\tau_{pair})$.

LNE-MGM. The time to compute pairwise matching is $O(N^2\tau_{pair})$. The time to compute overall affinity score for each graph is $O(N^2n^3)$. The time to reorder graph stream is $O(N \log N)$. The overall complexity is $O(N^3 + M^2N^2n^3 + NM^4n + N^2\tau_{pair})$. As M is constant for each step, the complexity thus can be roughly treated as $O(N^3 + N^2n^3 + N^2\tau_{pair})$.

5 Experiments

Experiments run on a laptop with 3.2 GHZ CPU and 16G memory. In synthetic data and real-world images, 50 trials and 20 trials are performed respectively, and the average are reported. For the plots, the settings are given in Table 2. The source code is public available at https://github.com/ffffarmer/LNE_IMGM.

5.1 Protocols and Compared Methods

Three popular evaluation metrics for multiple graph matching [31,34] are used: accuracy (acc), affinity score (scr) and consistency (con, see Eq. 2). Accuracy is computed by comparing solution $\mathbf{X}_{ij}^*$ to ground-truth $\mathbf{X}_{ij}^{GT}$:

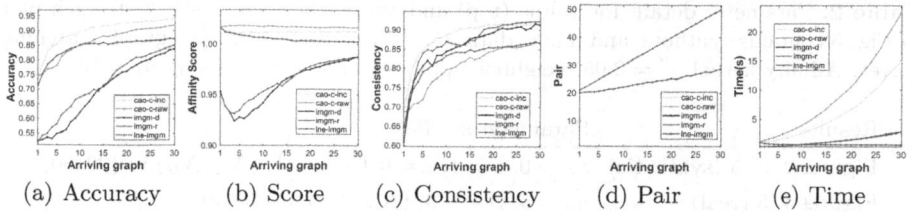

(a) Accuracy (b) Score (c) Consistency (d) Pair (e) Time

Fig. 2. Online evaluation on synthetic deformed graphs. LNE-IMGM is our method.

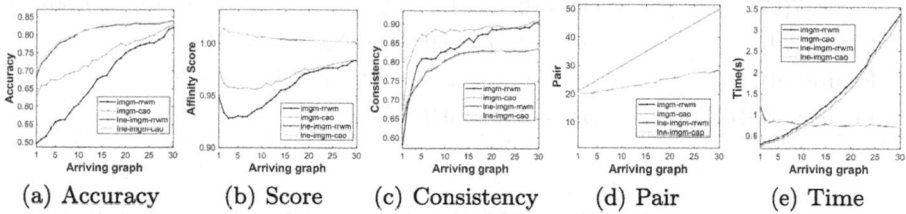

(a) Accuracy (b) Score (c) Consistency (d) Pair (e) Time

Fig. 3. Evaluation on using two-graph solver RRWM and multi-graph matching solver CAO-C for initialization of two IMGM methods.

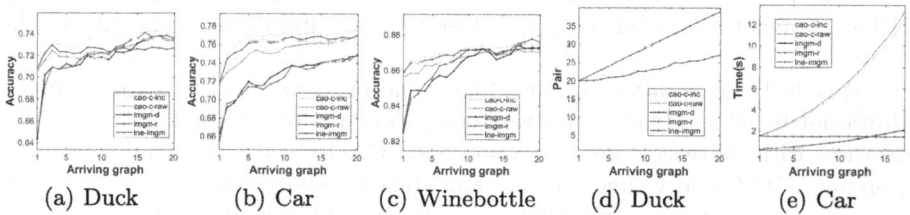

(a) Duck (b) Car (c) Winebottle (d) Duck (e) Car

Fig. 4. Online evaluation on Willow-ObjectClass. CAO-C-INC means rerunning CAO-C initialized by the previous results by CAO-C. CAO-C-RAW denotes run from scratch.

$$\text{acc} = 1 - \sum_{i,j} \|\mathbf{X}_{ij}^* - \mathbf{X}_{ij}^{\text{GT}}\|_F^2 / nN^2 \in [0,1]$$

While the overall affinity score is calculated by:

$$\text{scr} = \frac{1}{N^2} \sum_{i,j} \frac{\text{vec}(\mathbf{X}_{ij}^*)^\top \mathbf{K}_{ij} \text{vec}(\mathbf{X}_{ij}^*)}{\text{vec}(\mathbf{X}_{ij}^{\text{GT}})^\top \mathbf{K}_{ij} \text{vec}(\mathbf{X}_{ij}^{\text{GT}})}$$

It is possible that scr > 1 as the affinity function may not perfectly reach the maximum at ground truth, especially in the presence of outliers. For comparison of time cost with previous works following [38], we leave the pairwise matching cost which is the multiplication of the number of runs $L(N)$ at step N and the unit time τ_{pair} for a calling of a certain two-graph matching solver e.g. RRWM. Then we define the time cost as (without two-graph

Table 2. Parameter details for online (top) and offline (bottom) tests. Note each plot in Fig. 5 contains synthetic and image data. RRWM is used as the two-graph matching solver. Affinity kernel $\sigma^2 = 0.05$, neighbor upper size $M = 20$, inlier # $n_i = 10$.

Results	Parameter settings
Figures 2, 3, 5 (synthetic)	$n_o = 0$, $c = 1$, $\epsilon = 0.15$, $\rho = 1$, $(N_A, N_B) = (20, 50)$
Figures 4, 5 (real)	$n_o = 4$, $\beta = 0.9$, $(N_A, N_B) = (20, 40)$
Figure 7(a)	$n_o = 0$, $c = 1$, $\epsilon = 0.15$, $\rho = 1$, $(N_A, N_B) = (20, 52)$
Figure 7(b)	$n_o = 4$, $\beta = 0.9$, $(N_A, N_B) = (20, 52)$
Figure 7(c)	$n_o = 0$, $c = 1$, $\epsilon = 0.15$, $\rho = 1$, $(N_A, N_B) = (30, 50)$
Figure 7(d)	$n_o = 4$, $\beta = 0.9$, $(N_A, N_B) = (30, 50)$
Figure 6(d), (e)	$n_o = 0$, $c = 1$, $\epsilon = 0.15$, $\rho = 1$
Figure 6(a), (b), (c)	$n_o = 4$, $\beta = 0.9$

matching part): $Time(N) = Total(N) - L(N)\tau_{pair}$. We separate $Total(N)$ into $Pair = L(N)\tau_{pair}$ and $Time(N)$ to have a more insightful study on overhead.

So far we have only identified one peer method [38] for multiple graph matching. This method has two variants termed as **IMGM-D** and **IMGM-R**, with DPP and random sampling for graph clustering over iterations, respectively. The number of clusters are set to 2 for these two methods in all tests (if not otherwise specified). In addition, we also follow the protocol in [38] to compare two additional baselines. One is the vanilla version of Composition Affinity Optimization with pairwise consistency method (CAO-C) [31], i.e., independently applying CAO-C every time a new graph comes with existing ones to form the new collection of graphs. The other is running CAO-C which is initialized by the matching results before the new graph's arrival. These two versions are termed as **CAO-C-RAW** and **CAO-C-INC**, respectively. In the experiments, all the initial two-graph matchings are computed using Reweighted Random Walk base Matching (RRWM) [6] as it has been proved effective and stable for two-graph matching. To be fair, we set up CAO-C as the inner used multi-graph solver for all methods (**IMGM-D, IMGM-R, LNE-IMGM, LNE-MGM**).

5.2   Experiments on Synthetic Dataset

In line with the compared works [31,38], synthetic graphs are generated for each trial. The details are as follows. First, a reference graph of size $n_R = 10$ is randomly created, whose edge weight q_{ab}^R for edge (a, b) is sampled from the uniform distribution $[0, 1]$. Then a derived graph is generated by adding a Gaussian noise sampled from $\mu \sim \mathcal{N}(0, \epsilon)$ on the weight: $q_{ab}^D = q_{ab}^R + \mu$. Meanwhile, a density parameter ρ is used to control the edge density of graphs. For two-graph matching which is adopted as a building block in our method and the compared algorithms, the pairwise edge affinity is set as $\mathbf{K}_{ac;bd} = \exp(-\frac{(q_{ab}-q_{cd})^2}{\sigma^2})$. We denote (N_B, N_A) as number of base graphs and number of arriving graphs.

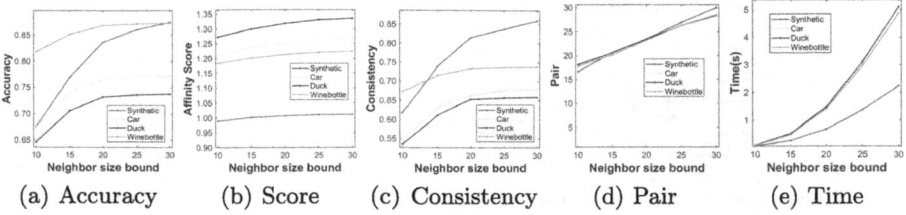

(a) Accuracy   (b) Score   (c) Consistency   (d) Pair   (e) Time

Fig. 5. Sensitivity test under **online IMGM** setting, for hyperparameter M i.e. the upper bound of expanded neighborhood size.

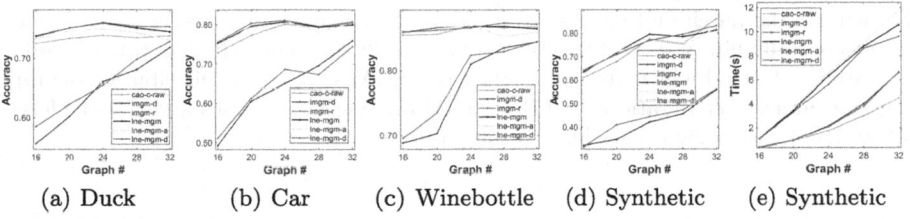

(a) Duck   (b) Car   (c) Winebottle   (d) Synthetic   (e) Synthetic

Fig. 6. Offline evaluation on synthetic graphs and Willow-ObjectClass. For our LNE-MGM, '-d' ('-a') denotes reordering is performed by the graph-wise affinity score in descending (ascending) order. Otherwise the matching order keeps by default.

For N_B based graphs, we make two different initializations for matching the base graphs: by RRWM pairwise matching or by CAO multi-graph matching.

Online Setting. We show the result of **RRWM–based** incremental matching result in Fig. 2. Our algorithm outperforms **IMGM-D** and **IMGM-R** in accuracy and affinity score, meanwhile is very close to **CAO-C-RAW** and its incremental updating version **CAO-C-INC**. Besides, our algorithm need much less times of pairwise matching in each step. In detail, the trend of $Pair$ is a straight line $L(N) = N_B + kN_A$, where $k \ll 1$ in our algorithms. Most importantly, our method almost achieves constant in time, while the time taken by other algorithms increases significantly as more graphs arrive. Note that for each time a new graph comes, **CAO-C-RAW** has no online mechanism and we use it by repeatedly re-running it from scratch every time a new graph comes.

We also study the effects of two initialization strategies for **IMGM-D** and **LNE-IMGM**, i.e. adopting RRWM to match the base graphs and using a more advanced MGM solver CAO-C. In Fig. 3, our method is generally unaffected by initialization, while **IMGM-D** suffers changing from CAO-C to RRWM.

We test the sensitivity on batch processing size and also with different ordering strategies. As shown in Fig. 7(a), (b), the accuracy increases as we rank graph-wise affinity in descending order, which means gradually matching harder graphs can be a better strategy for overall matching accuracy. Meanwhile larger batch size can also lead to better accuracy which also well fits one's intuition.

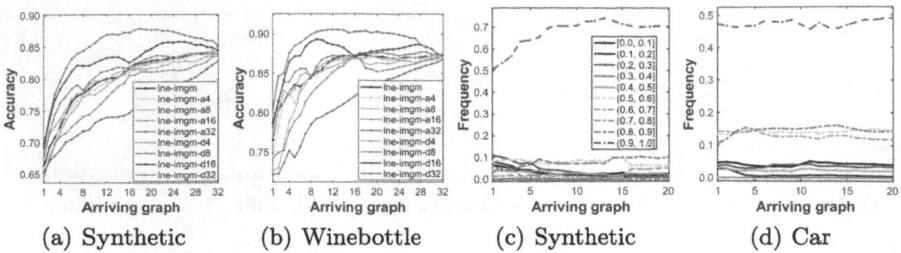

(a) Synthetic   (b) Winebottle   (c) Synthetic   (d) Car

Fig. 7. (a)(b): Sensitivity test for the batch processing size and ordering strategies on the synthetic deform graphs and Willow-ObjectClass Winebottle. The suffix '-a4'/'-d4' denotes the batch of 4 graphs are received in ascending/descending order by each graph's overall affinity score. Likewise for '-a8', '-d32' etc. The default is random ordering with batch size 1 which fits exactly the case for IMGM. (c)(d): Distribution of graph pair's accuracy over iterations by LEN-IMGM on synthetic graphs and Car. Different colors denote accuracy ranges [0, 1] by step 0.1.

Offline Setting. Figure 6 compares our offline versions (LNE-MGM-d and LNE-MGM-a) with CAO-based method CAO-C and IMGM_D and IMGM_R. The proposed method outperforms the baseline IMGM for synthetic random graphs, and performs competitively against CAO. IMGM-based algorithms are highly susceptible to the number of base graphs, resulting unsatisfactory performance in offline setting, while our approach performs more robustly, and even running from scratch without any base graph, it can still achieve strong result. Also, by using descending order, our algorithm gains further improvement.

5.3 Experiments on Real Image Dataset

We first test on the Willow-ObjectClass as provided and released by [5]. It consists of 5 classes of natural images collected from Caltech-256 and PASCAL07: 109 Face, 66 Winebottle, 50 Duck, 40 Car and 40 Motorbike images. There are 10 landmark points which are manually tagged on the object in each image. For object Duck and Car, we randomly permute all images. To verify the robustness of compared methods, four outliers are randomly chosen from the background. Delaunay triangulation is used to sparsify the graphs to construct the adjacency graph and the resulting affinity matrix, which is calculated as $\mathbf{K}_{ac;bd} = \beta \mathbf{K}_{ac;bd}^{len} + (1 - \beta)\mathbf{K}_{ac;bd}^{ang}$. Here both edge length and angle similarity, where $\beta \in [0, 1]$ is a controlling parameter regarding with the weight.

Online Setting. When there are more arriving graphs in Winebottle and Duck tests, IMGM-D outperforms the counterparts on most arriving graphs as shown in Fig. 4. Meanwhile, in Car test with fewer arriving graphs, the proposed method gradually adapts the problem along with the new graphs, and achieves strong accuracy. Moreover we use Fig. 7(c), (d) to show the pairwise matching accuracy distribution over iterations by LEN-IMGM for online MGM.

Offline Setting. As shown in Fig. 6, on Willow-ObjectClass, our methods outperform or perform competitively against the offline solver CAO-C. Among the three variants of our method, the ascending reordering version performs generally best, suggesting the strategy for handling easier graphs first is useful.

6 Conclusions

This paper has presented a novel method for incremental matching of sequentially arriving graphs. For each coming new graph, its neighborhood is expanded in two steps which allows for cost-effective matching updating. This is in contrast to the peer method [38] adopting clustering which is complicated and inefficient. Our method can also serve as an effective offline multi-graph matching solver by sequential matching, except a treatment on determining the processing order by graph-wise affinity score. Experiments show its state-of-the-art accuracy and efficiency on synthetic graphs and images. Future work will explore machine learning especially deep networks for incremental graph matching.

References

1. Bunke, H.: Graph matching: theoretical foundations, algorithms, and applications. In: Vision Interface (2000)
2. Caetano, T., McAuley, J., Cheng, L., Le, Q., Smola, A.J.: Learning graph matching. TPAMI **31**(6), 1048–1058 (2009)
3. Chen, Y., Guibas, L., Huang, Q.: Near-optimal joint object matching via convex relaxation. In: ICML (2014)
4. Chertok, M., Keller, Y.: Efficient high order matching. TPAMI **32**, 2205–2215 (2010)
5. Cho, M., Alahari, K., Ponce, J.: Learning graphs to match. In: ICCV (2013)
6. Cho, M., Lee, J., Lee, K.M.: Reweighted random walks for graph matching. In: Daniilidis, K., Maragos, P., Paragios, N. (eds.) ECCV 2010. LNCS, vol. 6315, pp. 492–505. Springer, Heidelberg (2010). https://doi.org/10.1007/978-3-642-15555-0_36
7. Conte, D., Foggia, P., Sansone, C., Vento, M.: Thirty years of graph matching in pattern recognition. IJPRAI **18**, 265–298 (2004)
8. Duchenne, O., Bach, F., Kweon, I., Ponce, J.: A tensor-based algorithm for high-order graph matching. TPAMI **33**, 2383–2395 (2011)
9. Egozi, A., Keller, Y., Guterman, H.: A probabilistic approach to spectral graph matching. TPAMI **35**, 18–27 (2013)
10. Fischler, M.A., Bolles, R.C.: Random sample consensus: a paradigm for model fitting with applications to image analysis and automated cartography. Commun. ACM **24**, 381–395 (1981)
11. Foggia, P., Percannella, G., Vento, M.: Graph matching and learning in pattern recognition in the last 10 years. IJPRAI **33**(1), 1450001 (2014)
12. Garey, M.R., Johnson, D.S.: Computers and Intractability; A Guide to the Theory of NP-Completeness. W. H. Freeman and Company, New York (1990)
13. Gold, S., Rangarajan, A.: A graduated assignment algorithm for graph matching. TPAMI **18**, 377–388 (1996)

14. Guibas, L.J., Huang, Q., Liang, Z.: A condition number for joint optimization of cycle-consistent networks. In: NeurIPS (2019)
15. Hu, N., Huang, Q., Thibert, B., Guibas, L.J.: Distributable consistent multi-object matching. In: Proceedings of the IEEE Conference on Computer Vision and Pattern Recognition, pp. 2463–2471 (2018)
16. Hu, N., Rustamov, R.M., Guibas, L.: Graph matching with anchor nodes: a learning approach. In: Proceedings of the IEEE Conference on Computer Vision and Pattern Recognition, pp. 2906–2913 (2013)
17. Hu, N., Rustamov, R.M., Guibas, L.: Stable and informative spectral signatures for graph matching. In: Proceedings of the IEEE Conference on Computer Vision and Pattern Recognition, pp. 2305–2312 (2014)
18. Huang, Q., Zhang, G., Gao, L., Hu, S., Butscher, A., Guibas, L.: An optimization approach for extracting and encoding consistent maps in a shape collection. ACM Trans. Graph. (TOG) **31**, 1–11 (2012)
19. Kulesza, A., Taskar, B., Liu, L.: Determinantal point processes for machine learning. Found. Trends Mach. Learn. **5**, 123–286 (2012)
20. Leordeanu, M., Sukthankar, R., Hebert, M.: Unsupervised learning for graph matching. IJCV **96**, 28–45 (2012)
21. Leordeanu, M., Zanfir, A., Sminchisescu, C.: Semi-supervised learning and optimization for hypergraph matching. In: ICCV (2011)
22. Loiola, E.M., de Abreu, N.M., Boaventura-Netto, P.O., Hahn, P., Querido, T.: A survey for the quadratic assignment problem. EJOR **176**, 657–690 (2007)
23. Ngoc, Q., Gautier, A., Hein, M.: A flexible tensor block coordinate ascent scheme for hypergraph matching. In: CVPR (2015)
24. Pachauri, D., Kondor, R., Vikas, S.: Solving the multi-way matching problem by permutation synchronization. In: NIPS (2013)
25. Shi, X., Ling, H., Hu, W., Xing, J., Zhang, Y.: Tensor power iteration for multi-graph matching. In: CVPR (2016)
26. Solé-Ribalta, A., Serratosa, F.: Models and algorithms for computing the common labelling of a set of attributed graphs. CVIU **115**, 929–945 (2011)
27. Solé-Ribalta, A., Serratosa, F.: Graduated assignment algorithm for multiple graph matching based on a common labeling. IJPRAI **27**, 1350001 (2013)
28. Swoboda, P., Mokarian, A., Theobalt, C., Bernard, F., et al.: A convex relaxation for multi-graph matching. In: Proceedings of the IEEE Conference on Computer Vision and Pattern Recognition, pp. 11156–11165 (2019)
29. Vento, M.: A long trip in the charming world of graphs for pattern recognition. Pattern Recogn. **48**(2), 291–301 (2015)
30. Wang, R., Yan, J., Yang, X.: Learning combinatorial embedding networks for deep graph matching. In: ICCV (2019)
31. Yan, J., Cho, M., Zha, H., Yang, X., Chu, S.: Multi-graph matching via affinity optimization with graduated consistency regularization. TPAMI **38**, 1228–1242 (2016)
32. Yan, J., Li, Y., Liu, W., Zha, H., Yang, X., Chu, S.M.: Graduated consistency-regularized optimization for multi-graph matching. In: Fleet, D., Pajdla, T., Schiele, B., Tuytelaars, T. (eds.) ECCV 2014. LNCS, vol. 8689, pp. 407–422. Springer, Cham (2014). https://doi.org/10.1007/978-3-319-10590-1_27
33. Yan, J., Tian, Y., Zha, H., Yang, X., Zhang, Y., Chu, S.: Joint optimization for consistent multiple graph matching. In: ICCV (2013)
34. Yan, J., Wang, J., Zha, H., Yang, X., Chu, S.: Consistency-driven alternating optimization for multigraph matching: a unified approach. IEEE Trans. Image Process. **24**(3), 994–1009 (2015)

35. Yan, J., Xu, H., Zha, H., Yang, X., Liu, H., Chu, S.: A matrix decomposition perspective to multiple graph matching. In: ICCV (2015)
36. Yan, J., Yin, X., Lin, W., Deng, C., Zha, H., Yang, X.: A short survey of recent advances in graph matching. In: ICMR (2016)
37. Yan, J., Zhang, C., Zha, H., Liu, W., Yang, X., Chu, S.: Discrete hyper-graph matching. In: CVPR (2015)
38. Yu, T., Yan, J., Liu, W., Li, B.: Incremental multi-graph matching via diversity and randomness based graph clustering. In: Ferrari, V., Hebert, M., Sminchisescu, C., Weiss, Y. (eds.) ECCV 2018. LNCS, vol. 11217, pp. 142–158. Springer, Cham (2018). https://doi.org/10.1007/978-3-030-01261-8_9
39. Zass, R., Shashua, A.: Probabilistic graph and hypergraph matching. In: CVPR (2008)
40. Zhang, Z.: Iterative point matching for registration of free-form curves and surfaces. IJCV **13**, 119–152 (1994)

SCAN: Learning to Classify Images Without Labels

Wouter Van Gansbeke[1]([⊠]), Simon Vandenhende[1], Stamatios Georgoulis[2], Marc Proesmans[1], and Luc Van Gool[1,2]

[1] KU Leuven/ESAT-PSI, Leuven, Belgium
wouter.vangansbeke@esat.kuleuven.be
[2] ETH Zurich/CVL, TRACE, Zürich, Switzerland

Abstract. Can we automatically group images into semantically meaningful clusters when ground-truth annotations are absent? The task of unsupervised image classification remains an important, and open challenge in computer vision. Several recent approaches have tried to tackle this problem in an end-to-end fashion. In this paper, we deviate from recent works, and advocate a two-step approach where feature learning and clustering are decoupled. First, a self-supervised task from representation learning is employed to obtain semantically meaningful features. Second, we use the obtained features as a prior in a learnable clustering approach. In doing so, we remove the ability for cluster learning to depend on low-level features, which is present in current end-to-end learning approaches. Experimental evaluation shows that we outperform state-of-the-art methods by large margins, in particular +26.6% on CIFAR10, +25.0% on CIFAR100-20 and +21.3% on STL10 in terms of classification accuracy. Furthermore, our method is the first to perform well on a large-scale dataset for image classification. In particular, we obtain promising results on ImageNet, and outperform several semi-supervised learning methods in the low-data regime without the use of any ground-truth annotations. The code is available at www.github.com/wvangansbeke/Unsupervised-Classification.git.

Keywords: Unsupervised learning · Self-supervised learning · Image classification · Clustering

1 Introduction and Prior Work

Image classification is the task of assigning a semantic label from a predefined set of classes to an image. For example, an image depicts a cat, a dog, a car, an

---

W. Van Gansbeke and S. Vandenhende—Contributed equally.

Electronic supplementary material The online version of this chapter (https://doi.org/10.1007/978-3-030-58607-2_16) contains supplementary material, which is available to authorized users.

© Springer Nature Switzerland AG 2020
A. Vedaldi et al. (Eds.): ECCV 2020, LNCS 12355, pp. 268–285, 2020.
https://doi.org/10.1007/978-3-030-58607-2_16

airplane, etc., or abstracting further an animal, a machine, etc. Nowadays, this task is typically tackled by training convolutional neural networks [18,27,43,46, 52] on large-scale datasets [11,29] that contain annotated images, i.e. images with their corresponding semantic label. Under this supervised setup, the networks excel at learning discriminative feature representations that can subsequently be clustered into the predetermined classes. What happens, however, when there is no access to ground-truth semantic labels at training time? Or going further, the semantic classes, or even their total number, are not *a priori* known? The desired goal in this case is to group the images into clusters, such that images within the same cluster belong to the same or similar semantic classes, while images in different clusters are semantically dissimilar. Under this setup, unsupervised or self-supervised learning techniques have recently emerged in the literature as an alternative to supervised feature learning.

Representation learning methods [12,15,34,38,57] use self-supervised learning to generate feature representations solely from the images, omitting the need for costly semantic annotations. To achieve this, they use pre-designed tasks, called pretext tasks, which do not require annotated data to learn the weights of a convolutional neural network. Instead, the visual features are learned by minimizing the objective function of the pretext task. Numerous pretext tasks have been explored in the literature, including predicting the patch context [12,32], inpainting patches [38], solving jigsaw puzzles [34,36], colorizing images [28,57], using adversarial training [13,14], predicting noise [3], counting [35], predicting rotations [15], spotting artifacts [22], generating images [40], using predictive coding [19,37], performing instance discrimination [7,17,31,47,50], and so on. Despite these efforts, representation learning approaches are mainly used as the first pretraining stage of a two-stage pipeline. The second stage includes fine-tuning the network in a fully-supervised fashion on another task, with as end goal to verify how well the self-supervised features transfer to the new task. When annotations are missing, as is the case in this work, a clustering criterion (e.g. K-means) still needs to be defined and optimized independently. This practice is arguably suboptimal, as it leads to imbalanced clusters [4], and there is no guarantee that the learned clusters will align with the semantic classes.

As an alternative, *end-to-end learning* pipelines combine feature learning with clustering. A first group of methods (e.g. DEC [51], DAC [6], DeepCluster [4], DeeperCluster [5], or others [1,16,53]) leverage the architecture of CNNs as a prior to cluster images. Starting from the initial feature representations, the clusters are iteratively refined by deriving the supervisory signal from the most confident samples [6,51], or through cluster re-assignments calculated offline [4,5]. A second group of methods (e.g. IIC [23], IMSAT [20]) propose to learn a clustering function by maximizing the mutual information between an image and its augmentations. In general, methods that rely on the initial feature representations of the network are sensitive to initialization [4–6,16,21,51,53], or prone to degenerate solutions [4,5], thus requiring special mechanisms (e.g. pretraining, cluster reassignment and feature cleaning) to avoid those situations. Most importantly, since the cluster learning depends on the network initialization, they are likely to latch onto low-level features, like color, which is unwanted for the objective of semantic clustering. To partially alleviate this problem, some works [4,20,23] are tied to the use of specific preprocessing (e.g. Sobel filtering).

In this work we advocate a two-step approach for unsupervised image classification, in contrast to recent end-to-end learning approaches. The proposed method, named SCAN (Semantic Clustering by Adopting Nearest neighbors), leverages the advantages of both representation and end-to-end learning approaches, but at the same time it addresses their shortcomings:

- In a first step, we learn feature representations through a pretext task. In contrast to representation learning approaches that require K-means clustering after learning the feature representations, which is known to lead to cluster degeneracy [4], we propose to mine the nearest neighbors of each image based on feature similarity. We empirically found that in most cases these nearest neighbors belong to the same semantic class (see Fig. 2), rendering them appropriate for semantic clustering.
- In a second step, we integrate the semantically meaningful nearest neighbors as a prior into a learnable approach. We classify each image and its mined neighbors together by using a loss function that maximizes their dot product after softmax, pushing the network to produce both consistent and discriminative (one-hot) predictions. Unlike end-to-end approaches, the learned clusters depend on more meaningful features, rather than on the network architecture. Furthermore, because we encourage invariance w.r.t. the nearest neighbors, and not solely w.r.t. augmentations, we found no need to apply specific preprocessing to the input.

Experimental evaluation shows that our method outperforms prior work by large margins across multiple datasets. Furthermore, we report promising results on the large-scale ImageNet dataset. This validates our assumption that separation between learning (semantically meaningful) features and clustering them is an arguably better approach over recent end-to-end works.

2   Method

The following sections present the cornerstones of our approach. First, we show how mining nearest neighbors from a pretext task can be used as a prior for semantic clustering. Also, we introduce additional constraints for selecting an appropriate pretext task, capable of producing semantically meaningful feature representations. Second, we integrate the obtained prior into a novel loss function to classify each image and its nearest neighbors together. Additionally, we show how to mitigate the problem of noise inherent in the nearest neighbor selection with a self-labeling approach. We believe that each of these contributions are relevant for unsupervised image classification.

2.1   Representation Learning for Semantic Clustering

In the supervised learning setup, each sample can be associated with its correct cluster by using the available ground-truth labels. In particular, the mapping between the images $\mathcal{D} = \{X_1, \ldots, X_{|\mathcal{D}|}\}$ and the semantic classes $\mathcal{C}$ can generally be learned by minimizing a cross-entropy loss. However, when we do not have access to such ground-truth labels, we need to define a prior to obtain an estimate of which samples are likely to belong together, and which are not.

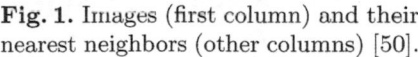

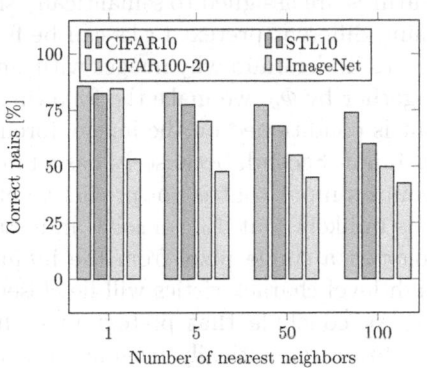

Fig. 1. Images (first column) and their nearest neighbors (other columns) [50].

Fig. 2. Neighboring samples tend to be instances of the same semantic class.

End-to-end learning approaches have utilized the architecture of CNNs as a prior [4–6,16,51,53], or enforced consistency between images and their augmentations [20,23] to disentangle the clusters. In both cases, the cluster learning is known to be sensitive to the network initialization. Furthermore, at the beginning of training the network does not extract high-level information from the image yet. As a result, the clusters can easily latch onto low-level features (e.g. color, texture, contrast, etc.), which is suboptimal for semantic clustering. To overcome these limitations, we employ representation learning as a means to obtain a better prior for semantic clustering.

In representation learning, a pretext task τ learns in a self-supervised fashion an embedding function Φ_θ - parameterized by a neural network with weights θ - that maps images into feature representations. The literature offers several pretext tasks which can be used to learn such an embedding function Φ_θ (e.g. rotation prediction [15], affine or perspective transformation prediction [56], colorization [28], in-painting [38], instance discrimination [7,17,31,50], etc.). In practice, however, certain pretext tasks are based on specific image transformations, causing the learned feature representations to be covariant to the employed transformation. For example, when Φ_θ predicts the transformation parameters of an affine transformation, different affine transformations of the same image will result in distinct output predictions for Φ_θ. This renders the learned feature representations less appropriate for semantic clustering, where feature representations ought to be invariant to image transformations. To overcome this issue, we impose the pretext task τ to also minimize the distance between images X_i and their augmentations $T[X_i]$, which can be expressed as:

$$\min_{\theta} d(\Phi_\theta(X_i), \Phi_\theta(T[X_i])). \tag{1}$$

Any pretext task [7,17,31,50] that satisfies Eq. 1 can consequently be used. For example, Fig. 1 shows the results when retrieving the nearest neighbors under an instance discrimination task [50] which satisfies Eq. 1. We observe that similar features are assigned to semantically similar images. An experimental evaluation using different pretext tasks can be found in Sect. 3.2.

To understand why images with similar high-level features are mapped closer together by Φ_θ, we make the following observations. First, the pretext task output is conditioned on the image, forcing Φ_θ to extract specific information from its input. Second, because Φ_θ has a limited capacity, it has to discard information from its input that is not predictive of the high-level pretext task. For example, it is unlikely that Φ_θ can solve an instance discrimination task by only encoding color or a single pixel from the input image. As a result, images with similar high-level characteristics will lie closer together in the embedding space of Φ_θ.

We conclude that pretext tasks from representation learning can be used to obtain semantically meaningful features. Following this observation, we will leverage the pretext features as a prior for clustering the images.

2.2   A Semantic Clustering Loss

Mining Nearest Neighbors. In Sect. 2.1, we motivated that a pretext task from representation learning can be used to obtain semantically meaningful features. However, naively applying K-means on the obtained features can lead to cluster degeneracy [4]. A discriminative model can assign all its probability mass to the same cluster when learning the decision boundary. This leads to one cluster dominating the others. Instead, we opt for a better strategy.

Let us first consider the following experiment. Through representation learning, we train a model Φ_θ on the unlabeled dataset $\mathcal{D}$ to solve a pretext task τ, i.e. instance discrimination [7,17]. Then, for every sample $X_i \in \mathcal{D}$, we mine its K nearest neighbors in the embedding space Φ_θ. We define the set $\mathcal{N}_{X_i}$ as the neighboring samples of X_i in the dataset $\mathcal{D}$. Figure 2 quantifies the degree to which the mined nearest neighbors are instances of the same semantic cluster. We observe that this is largely the case across four datasets[1] (CIFAR10 [26], CIFAR100-20 [26], STL10 [9] and ImageNet [11]) for different values of K. Motivated by this observation, we propose to adopt the nearest neighbors obtained through the pretext task τ as our prior for semantic clustering.

Loss Function. We aim to learn a clustering function Φ_η - parameterized by a neural network with weights η - that classifies a sample X_i and its mined neighbors $\mathcal{N}_{X_i}$ together. The function Φ_η terminates in a softmax function to perform a soft assignment over the clusters $\mathcal{C} = \{1, \ldots, C\}$, with $\Phi_\eta(X_i) \in$

---

[1] The details for each dataset are provided in the supplementary materials.

$[0,1]^C$. The probability of sample X_i being assigned to cluster c is denoted as $\Phi_\eta^c(X_i)$. We learn the weights of Φ_η by minimizing the following objective:

$$\Lambda = -\frac{1}{|\mathcal{D}|} \sum_{X \in \mathcal{D}} \sum_{k \in \mathcal{N}_X} \log \langle \Phi_\eta(X), \Phi_\eta(k) \rangle + \lambda \sum_{c \in \mathcal{C}} \Phi_\eta'^c \log \Phi_\eta'^c,$$

$$\text{with } \Phi_\eta'^c = \frac{1}{|\mathcal{D}|} \sum_{X \in \mathcal{D}} \Phi_\eta^c(X). \tag{2}$$

Here, $\langle \cdot \rangle$ denotes the dot product operator. The first term in Eq. 2 imposes Φ_η to make consistent predictions for a sample X_i and its neighboring samples $\mathcal{N}_{X_i}$. Note that, the dot product will be maximal when the predictions are one-hot (confident) and assigned to the same cluster (consistent). To avoid Φ_η from assigning all samples to a single cluster, we include an entropy term (the second term in Eq. 2), which spreads the predictions uniformly across the clusters $\mathcal{C}$. If the probability distribution over the clusters $\mathcal{C}$ is known in advance, which is not the case here, this term can be replaced by KL-divergence.

Remember that, the exact number of clusters in $\mathcal{C}$ is generally unknown. However, similar to prior work [6,23,51], we choose C equal to the number of ground-truth clusters for the purpose of evaluation. In practice, it should be possible to obtain a rough estimate of the amount of clusters[2]. Based on this estimate, we can overcluster to a larger amount of clusters, and enforce the class distribution to be uniform. We refer to Sect. 3.4 for a concrete experiment.

Implementation Details. For the practical implementation of our loss function, we approximate the dataset statistics by sampling batches of sufficiently large size. During training we randomly augment the samples X_i and their neighbors $\mathcal{N}_{X_i}$. For the corner case $K = 0$, only consistency between samples and their augmentations is imposed. We set $K \geq 1$ to capture more of the cluster's variance, at the cost of introducing noise, i.e. not all samples and their neighbors belong to the same cluster. Section 3.2 experimentally shows that choosing $K \geq 1$ significantly improves the results compared to only enforcing consistency between samples and their augmentations, as in [20,23].

Discussion. Unlike [2,24,33,39,48,51,58] we do not include a reconstruction criterion into the loss, since this is not explicitly required by our target task. After all, we are only interested in a few bits of information encoded from the input signal, rather than the majority of information that a reconstruction criterion typically requires. It is worth noting that the consistency in our case is enforced at the level of individual samples through the dot product term in the loss, rather than on an approximation of the joint distribution over the classes [20,23]. We argue that this choice allows to express the consistency in a more direct way.

---

[2] As an example, say you want to cluster various animal species observed in a national park. In this case, we can rely on prior domain knowledge to make an estimate.

2.3   Fine-Tuning Through Self-labeling

The semantic clustering loss in Sect. 2.2 imposed consistency between a sample and its neighbors. More specifically, each sample was combined with $K \geq 1$ neighbors, some of which inevitably do not belong to the same semantic cluster. These false positive examples lead to predictions for which the network is less certain. At the same time, we experimentally observed that samples with highly confident predictions ($p_{max} \approx 1$) tend to be classified to the proper cluster. In fact, the highly confident predictions that the network forms during clustering can be regarded as "prototypes" for each class (see Sect. 3.5). Unlike prior work [4,6,51], this allows us to select samples based on the confidence of the predictions in a more reliable manner. Hence, we propose a self-labeling approach [30,42,45] to exploit the already well-classified examples, and correct for mistakes due to noisy nearest neighbors.

Algorithm 1. Semantic Clustering by Adopting Nearest neighbors (SCAN)

1: **Input:** Dataset $\mathcal{D}$, Clusters $\mathcal{C}$, Task τ, Neural Nets Φ_θ and Φ_η, Neighbors $\mathcal{N}_{\mathcal{D}} = \{\}$.
2: Optimize Φ_θ with task τ.   ▷ Pretext Task Step, Sect. 2.1
3: **for** $X_i \in \mathcal{D}$ **do**
4:     $\mathcal{N}_{\mathcal{D}} \leftarrow \mathcal{N}_{\mathcal{D}} \cup \mathcal{N}_{X_i}$, with $\mathcal{N}_{X_i} = K$ neighboring samples of $\Phi_\theta(X_i)$.
5: **end for**
6: **while** SCAN-loss decreases **do**   ▷ Clustering Step, Sect. 2.2
7:     Update Φ_η with SCAN-loss, i.e. $\Lambda(\Phi_\eta(\mathcal{D}), \mathcal{N}_{\mathcal{D}}, C)$ in Eq. 2
8: **end while**
9: **while** $Len(Y)$ increases **do**   ▷ Self-Labeling Step, Sect. 2.3
10:     $Y \leftarrow (\Phi_\eta(\mathcal{D}) >$ threshold$)$
11:     Update Φ_η with cross-entropy loss, i.e. $H(\Phi_\eta(\mathcal{D}), Y)$
12: **end while**
13: **Return:** $\Phi_\eta(\mathcal{D})$ ▷ $\mathcal{D}$ is divided over C clusters

---

In particular, during training confident samples are selected by thresholding the probability at the output, i.e. $p_{max} >$ threshold. For every confident sample, a pseudo label is obtained by assigning the sample to its predicted cluster. A cross-entropy loss is used to update the weights for the obtained pseudo labels. To avoid overfitting, we calculate the cross-entropy loss on strongly augmented versions of the confident samples. The self-labeling step allows the network to correct itself, as it gradually becomes more certain, adding more samples to the mix. We refer to Sect. 3.2 for a concrete experiment.

Algorithm 1 summarizes all the steps of the proposed method. We further refer to it as SCAN, i.e. Semantic Clustering by Adopting Nearest neighbors.

3   Experiments

3.1   Experimental Setup

Datasets. The experimental evaluation is performed on CIFAR10 [26], CIFAR100-20 [26], STL10 [9] and ImageNet [11]. We focus on the smaller datasets first. The results on ImageNet are discussed separately in Sect. 3.5. Some prior works [6,23,51,53] trained and evaluated on the complete datasets. Differently, we train and evaluate using the train and val split respectively. Doing so, allows to study the generalization properties of the method for novel unseen examples. Note that this does not result in any unfair advantages compared to prior work. The results are reported as the mean and standard deviation from 10 different runs. Finally, all experiments are performed using the same backbone, augmentations, pretext task and hyperparameters.

Training Setup. We use a standard ResNet-18 backbone. For every sample, the 20 nearest neighbors are determined through an instance discrimination task based on noise contrastive estimation (NCE) [50]. We adopt the SimCLR [7] implementation for the instance discrimination task on the smaller datasets, and the implementation from MoCo [8] on ImageNet. The selected pretext task satisfies the feature invariance constraint from Eq. 1 w.r.t. the transformations applied to augment the input images. In particular, every image is disentangled as a unique instance independent of the applied transformation. To speed up training, we transfer the weights, obtained from the pretext task to initiate the clustering step (Sect. 2.2). We perform the clustering step for 100 epochs using batches of size 128. The weight on the entropy term is set to $\lambda = 5$. A higher weight avoids the premature grouping of samples early on during training. The results seem to be insensitive to small changes of λ. After the clustering step, we train for another 200 epochs using the self-labeling procedure with threshold 0.99 (Sect. 2.3). A weighted cross-entropy loss compensates for the imbalance between confident samples across clusters. The class weights are inversely proportional to the number of occurrences in the batch after thresholding. The network weights are updated through Adam [24] with learning rate 10^{-4} and weight decay 10^{-4}. The images are strongly augmented by composing four randomly selected transformations from RandAugment [10] during both the clustering and self-labeling steps. The transformation parameters are uniformly sampled between fixed intervals. For more details visit the supplementary materials.

Validation Criterion. During the clustering step, we select the best model based on the lowest loss. During the self-labeling step, we save the weights of the model when the amount of confident samples plateaus. We follow these practices as we do not have access to a labeled validation set.

3.2 Ablation Studies

Method. We quantify the performance gains w.r.t. the different parts of our method through an ablation study on CIFAR10 in Table 1. K-means clustering of the NCE pretext features results in the lowest accuracy (65.9%), and is characterized by a large variance (5.7%). This is to be expected since the cluster assignments can be imbalanced (Fig. 3), and are not guaranteed to align with the ground-truth classes. Interestingly, applying K-means to the pretext features outperforms prior state-of-the-art methods for unsupervised classification based on end-to-end learning schemes (see Sect. 3.3). This observation supports our primary claim, i.e. it is beneficial to separate feature learning from clustering. Updating the network weights through the SCAN-loss - while augmenting the input images through SimCLR transformations - outperforms K-means (+15.9%). Note that the SCAN-loss is somewhat related to K-means, since both methods employ the pretext features as their prior to cluster the images. Differently, our loss avoids the cluster degeneracy issue. We also research the effect of using different augmentation strategies during training. Applying transformations from RandAgument (RA) to both the samples and their mined neighbors further improves the performance (78.7% vs. 81.8%). We hypothesize that strong augmentations help to reduce the solution space by imposing additional invariances.

<table>
<tr><td colspan="2">Table 1. Ablation method CIFAR10</td></tr>
<tr><td>Setup</td><td>ACC (Avg ± Std)</td></tr>
<tr><td>Pretext + K-means</td><td>65.9 ± 5.7</td></tr>
<tr><td>SCAN-loss (SimCLR)</td><td>78.7 ± 1.7</td></tr>
<tr><td>(1) Self-labeling (SimCLR)</td><td>10.0 ± 0</td></tr>
<tr><td>(2) Self-labeling (RA)</td><td>87.4 ± 1.6</td></tr>
<tr><td>SCAN-loss (RA)</td><td>81.8 ± 1.7</td></tr>
<tr><td>(1) Self-labeling (RA)</td><td>87.6 ± 0.4</td></tr>
</table>

Table 2. Ablation pretext CIFAR10

Pretext task	Clustering	ACC (Avg ± Std)
RotNet [15]	K-means	27.1 ± 2.1
	SCAN	74.3 ± 3.9
Inst. discr. [50]	K-means	52.0 ± 4.6
	SCAN	83.5 ± 4.1
Inst. discr. [7]	K-means	65.9 ± 5.7
	SCAN	87.6 ± 0.4

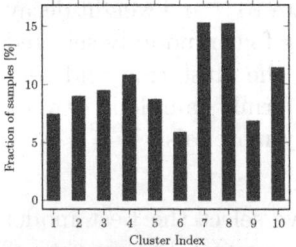
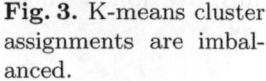
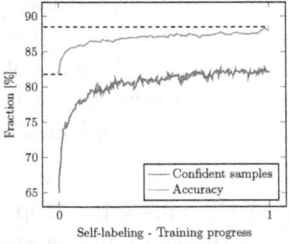
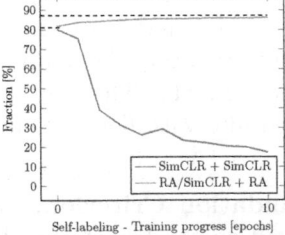

Fig. 3. K-means cluster assignments are imbalanced.

Fig. 4. Acc. and the number of confident samples during self-labeling.

Fig. 5. Self-labeling with SimCLR or RandAugment augmentations.

Fine-tuning the network through self-labeling further enhances the quality of the cluster assignments (81.8% to 87.6%). During self-labeling, the network corrects itself as it gradually becomes more confident (see Fig. 4). Importantly, in order for self-labeling to be successfully applied, a shift in augmentations is required (see Table 1 or Fig. 5). We hypothesize that this is required to prevent the network from overfitting on already well-classified examples. Finally, Fig. 6 shows that self-labeling procedure is not sensitive to the threshold's value.

Pretext Task. We study the effect of using different pretext tasks to mine the nearest neighbors. In particular we consider two different implementations of the instance discrimination task from before [7,50], and RotNet [15]. The latter trains the network to predict image rotations. As a consequence, the distance between an image X_i and its augmentations $T[X_i]$ is not minimized in the embedding space of a model pretrained through RotNet (see Eq. 1). Differently, the instance discrimination task satisfies the invariance criterion w.r.t. the used augmentations. Table 2 shows the results on CIFAR10.

First, we observe that the proposed method is not tied to a specific pretext task. All cases report high accuracy (>70%). Second, pretext tasks that satisfy the invariance criterion are better suited to mine the nearest neighbors, i.e. 83.5% and 87.6% for inst. discr. versus 74.3% for RotNet. This confirms our hypothesis from Sect. 2.1, i.e. it is beneficial to choose a pretext task which imposes invariance between an image and its augmentations.

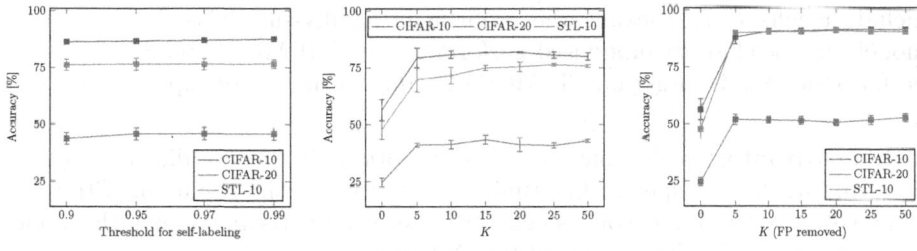

Fig. 6. Ablation threshold during self-labeling step.   **Fig. 7.** Influence of the used number of neighbors K.   **Fig. 8.** Results without false positives in the nearest neighbors.

Number of Neighbors. Figure 7 shows the influence of using a different number of nearest neighbors K during the clustering step. The results are not very sensitive to the value of K, and even remain stable when increasing K to 50. This is beneficial, since we do not have to fine-tune the value of K on very new dataset. In fact, both robustness and accuracy improve when increasing the value of K upto a certain value. We also consider the corner case $K = 0$, when only enforcing consistent predictions for images and their augmentations. The performance decreases on all three datasets compared to $K = 5$, 56.3% vs 79.3% on CIFAR10, 24.6% vs 41.1% on CIFAR100-20 and 47.70% vs 69.8% on STL10.

This confirms that better representations can be learned by also enforcing coherent predictions between a sample and its nearest neighbors.

Convergence. Figure 8 shows the results when removing the false positives from the nearest neighbors, i.e. sample-pairs which belong to a different class. The results can be considered as an upper-bound for the proposed method in terms of classification accuracy. A desirable characteristic is that the clusters quickly align with the ground truth, obtaining near fully-supervised performance on CIFAR10 and STL10 with a relatively small increase in the number of used neighbors K. The lower performance improvement on CIFAR100-20 can be explained by the ambiguity of the superclasses used to measure the accuracy. For example, there is not exactly one way to group categories like omnivores or carnivores together.

3.3   Comparison with the State-of-the-Art

Comparison. Table 3 compares our method to the state-of-the-art on three different benchmarks. We evaluate the results based on clustering accuracy (ACC), normalized mutual information (NMI) and adjusted rand index (ARI). The proposed method consistently outperforms prior work by large margins on all three metrics, e.g. +26.6% on CIFAR10, +25.0% on CIFAR100-20 and +21.3% on STL10 in terms of accuracy. We also compare with the state-of-the-art in representation learning [7] (Pretext + K-means). As shown in Sect. 3.2, our method outperforms the application of K-means on the pretext features. Finally, we also include results when tackling the problem in a fully-supervised manner. Our model obtains close to supervised performance on CIFAR-10 and STL-10. The performance gap is larger on CIFAR100-20, due to the use of superclasses.

Other Advantages. In contrast to prior work [6,20,23], we did not have to perform any dataset specific fine-tuning. Furthermore, the results on CIFAR10 can be obtained within 6 h on a single GPU. As a comparison, training the model from [23] requires at least a day of training time.

3.4   Overclustering

So far we assumed to have knowledge about the number of ground-truth classes. The method predictions were evaluated using a hungarian matching algorithm. However, what happens if the number of clusters does not match the number of ground-truth classes anymore. Table 3 reports the results when we overestimate the number of ground-truth classes by a factor of 2, e.g. we cluster CIFAR10 into 20 rather than 10 classes. The classification accuracy remains stable for CIFAR10 (87.6% to 86.2%) and STL10 (76.7% to 76.8%), and improves for CIFAR100-20 (45.9% to 55.1%)[3]. We conclude that the approach does not require knowledge

---

[3] Since the overclustering case is evaluated using a many-to-one mapping, a direct comparison is not entirely fair. Still, we provide the comparison as an indication.

Table 3. State-of-the-art comparison: We report the averaged results for 10 different runs after the clustering (∗) and self-labeling steps (†), and the best model. Opposed to prior work, we train and evaluate using the train and val split respectively, instead of using the full dataset for both training and testing.

Dataset	CIFAR10			CIFAR100-20			STL10		
Metric	ACC	NMI	ARI	ACC	NMI	ARI	ACC	NMI	ARI
K-means [49]	22.9	8.7	4.9	13.0	8.4	2.8	19.2	12.5	6.1
SC [54]	24.7	10.3	8.5	13.6	9.0	2.2	15.9	9.8	4.8
Triplets [41]	20.5	–	–	9.94	–	–	24.4	–	–
JULE [53]	27.2	19.2	13.8	13.7	10.3	3.3	27.7	18.2	16.4
AEVB [25]	29.1	24.5	16.8	15.2	10.8	4.0	28.2	20.0	14.6
SAE [33]	29.7	24.7	15.6	15.7	10.9	4.4	32.0	25.2	16.1
DAE [48]	29.7	25.1	16.3	15.1	11.1	4.6	30.2	22.4	15.2
SWWAE [58]	28.4	23.3	16.4	14.7	10.3	3.9	27.0	19.6	13.6
AE [2]	31.4	23.4	16.9	16.5	10.0	4.7	30.3	25.0	16.1
GAN [39]	31.5	26.5	17.6	15.1	12.0	4.5	29.8	21.0	13.9
DEC [51]	30.1	25.7	16.1	18.5	13.6	5.0	35.9	27.6	18.6
ADC [16]	32.5	–	–	16.0	–	–	53.0	–	–
DeepCluster [4]	37.4	–	–	18.9	–	–	33.4	–	–
DAC [6]	52.2	40.0	30.1	23.8	18.5	8.8	47.0	36.6	25.6
IIC [23]	61.7	51.1	41.1	25.7	22.5	11.7	59.6	49.6	39.7
Supervised	93.8	86.2	87.0	80.0	68.0	63.2	80.6	65.9	63.1
Pretext [7] + K-means	65.9 ± 5.7	59.8 ± 2.0	50.9 ± 3.7	39.5 ± 1.9	40.2 ± 1.1	23.9 ± 1.1	65.8 ± 5.1	60.4 ± 2.5	50.6 ± 4.1
SCAN∗ (Avg ± Std)	81.8 ± 0.3	71.2 ± 0.4	66.5 ± 0.4	42.2 ± 3.0	44.1 ± 1.0	26.7 ± 1.3	75.5 ± 2.0	65.4 ± 1.2	59.0 ± 1.6
SCAN† (Avg ± Std)	87.6 ± 0.4	78.7 ± 0.5	75.8 ± 0.7	45.9 ± 2.7	46.8 ± 1.3	30.1 ± 2.1	76.7 ± 1.9	68.0 ± 1.2	61.6 ± 1.8
SCAN† (Best)	**88.3**	**79.7**	**77.2**	**50.7**	**48.6**	**33.3**	**80.9**	**69.8**	**64.6**
SCAN† (Overcluster)	86.2 ± 0.8	77.1 ± 0.1	73.8 ± 1.4	55.1 ± 1.6	50.0 ± 1.1	35.7 ± 1.7	76.8 ± 1.1	65.6 ± 0.8	58.6 ± 1.6

of the exact number of clusters. We hypothesize that the increased performance on CIFAR100-20 is related to the higher intra-class variance. More specifically, CIFAR100-20 groups multiple object categories together in superclasses. In this case, an overclustering is better suited to explain the intra-class variance.

3.5 ImageNet

Setup. We consider the problem of unsupervised image classification on the large-scale ImageNet dataset [11]. We first consider smaller subsets of 50, 100 and 200 randomly selected classes. The sets of 50 and 100 classes are subsets of the 100 and 200 classes respectively. Additional details of the training setup can be found in the supplementary materials.

Quantitative Evaluation. Table 4 compares our results against applying K-means on the pretext features from MoCo [8]. Surprisingly, the application of K-means already performs well on this challenging task. We conclude that the pretext features are well-suited for the down-stream task of semantic clustering. Training the model with the SCAN-loss again outperforms the application of K-means. Also, the results are further improved when fine-tuning the model through self-labeling. We do not include numbers for the prior state-of-the-art [23], since we could not obtain convincing results on ImageNet when running the publicly available code. We refer the reader to the supplementary materials for additional qualitative results on ImageNet-50.

Table 4. Validation set results for 50, 100 and 200 randomly selected classes from ImageNet. The results with K-means were obtained using the pretext features from MoCo [8]. We provide the results obtained by our method after the clustering step (*), and after the self-labeling step (†).

ImageNet	50 classes				100 classes				200 classes			
Metric	Top-1	Top-5	NMI	ARI	Top-1	Top-5	NMI	ARI	Top-1	Top-5	NMI	ARI
K-means	65.9	-	77.5	57.9	59.7	-	76.1	50.8	52.5	-	75.5	43.2
SCAN*	75.1	91.9	80.5	63.5	66.2	88.1	78.7	54.4	56.3	80.3	75.7	44.1
SCAN†	76.8	91.4	82.2	66.1	68.9	86.1	80.8	57.6	58.1	80.6	77.2	47.0

Prototypical Behavior. We visualize the different clusters after training the model with the SCAN-loss. Specifically, we find the samples closest to the mean embedding of the top-10 most confident samples in every cluster. The results are shown together with the name of the matched ground-truth classes in Fig. 9. Importantly, we observe that the found samples align well with the classes of the dataset, except for 'oboe' and 'guacamole' (red). Furthermore, the discriminative features of each object class are clearly present in the images. Therefore, we regard the obtained samples as "prototypes" of the various clusters. Notice that the performed experiment aligns well with prototypical networks [44].

Fig. 9. Prototypes obtained by sampling the confident samples. (Color figure online)

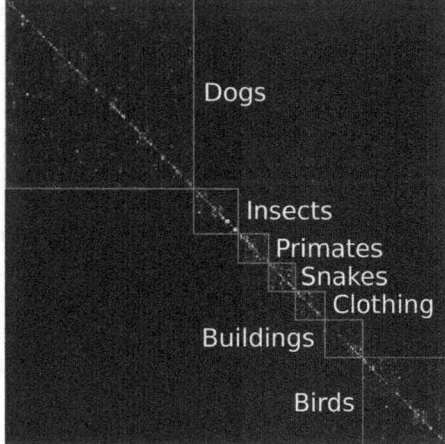

Fig. 10. Zoom on seven superclasses in the confusion matrix on ImageNet.

Fig. 11. Clusters extracted by our model on ImageNet (more in supplementary).

ImageNet - 1000 Classes. Finally, the model is trained on the complete ImageNet dataset. Figure 11 shows images from the validation set which were assigned to the same cluster by our model. The obtained clusters are semantically meaningful, e.g. planes, cars and primates. Furthermore, the clusters capture a large variety of different backgrounds, viewpoints, etc. We conclude that (to a large extent) the model predictions are invariant to image features which do not alter the semantics. On the other hand, based on the ImageNet ground-truth annotations, not all sample pairs should have been assigned to the same cluster. For example, the ground-truth annotations discriminate between different primates, e.g. chimpanzee, baboon, langur, etc. We argue that there is not a single correct way of categorizing the images according to their semantics in case of ImageNet. Even for a human annotator, it is not straightforward to cluster each image according to the ImageNet classes without prior knowledge.

Based on the ImageNet hierarchy we select class instances of the following superclasses: dogs, insects, primates, snake, clothing, buildings and birds. Figure 10 shows a confusion matrix of the selected classes. The confusion matrix has a block diagonal structure. The results show that the misclassified examples tend to be assigned to other clusters from within the same superclass, e.g. the model confuses two different dog breeds. We conclude that the model has learned to group images with similar semantics together, while its prediction errors can be attributed to the lack of annotations which could disentangle the fine-grained differences between some classes.

Finally, Table 5 compares our method against recent semi-supervised learning approaches when using 1% of the images as labelled data. We obtain the following quantitative results on ImageNet: Top-1: 39.9%, Top-5: 60.0%, NMI: 72.0%, ARI: 27.5%. Our method outperforms several semi-supervised learning approaches, without using labels. This further demonstrates the strength of our approach.

Table 5. Comparison with supervised, and semi-supervised learning methods using 1% of the labelled data on ImageNet.

Method	Backbone	Labels	Top-1	Top-5
Supervised baseline	ResNet-50	✓	25.4	48.4
Pseudo-Label	ResNet-50	✓	-	51.6
VAT + Entropy Min. [55]	ResNet-50	✓	-	47.0
InstDisc [50]	ResNet-50	✓	-	39.2
BigBiGAN [14]	ResNet-50(4x)	✓	-	55.2
PIRL [31]	ResNet-50	✓	-	57.2
CPC v2 [19]	ResNet-161	✓	52.7	77.9
SimCLR [7]	ResNet-50	✓	48.3	75.5
SCAN (Ours)	ResNet-50	✗	39.9	60.0

4   Conclusion

We presented a novel framework to unsupervised image classification. The proposed approach comes with several advantages relative to recent works which adopted an end-to-end strategy. Experimental evaluation shows that the proposed method outperforms prior work by large margins, for a variety of datasets. Furthermore, positive results on ImageNet demonstrate that semantic clustering can be applied to large-scale datasets. Encouraged by these findings, we believe that our approach admits several extensions to other related domains.

Acknowledgment. The authors thankfully acknowledge support by Toyota via the TRACE project and MACCHINA (KU Leuven, C14/18/065). Finally, we thank Xu Ji and Kevis-Kokitsi Maninis for their feedback.

References

1. Asano, Y.M., Rupprecht, C., Vedaldi, A.: Self-labelling via simultaneous clustering and representation learning. In: ICLR (2020)
2. Bengio, Y., Lamblin, P., Popovici, D., Larochelle, H.: Greedy layer-wise training of deep networks. In: NIPS (2007)
3. Bojanowski, P., Joulin, A.: Unsupervised learning by predicting noise. In: ICML (2017)
4. Caron, M., Bojanowski, P., Joulin, A., Douze, M.: Deep clustering for unsupervised learning of visual features. In: Ferrari, V., Hebert, M., Sminchisescu, C., Weiss, Y. (eds.) Computer Vision – ECCV 2018. LNCS, vol. 11218, pp. 139–156. Springer, Cham (2018). https://doi.org/10.1007/978-3-030-01264-9_9
5. Caron, M., Bojanowski, P., Mairal, J., Joulin, A.: Unsupervised pre-training of image features on non-curated data. In: ICCV (2019)
6. Chang, J., Wang, L., Meng, G., Xiang, S., Pan, C.: Deep adaptive image clustering. In: ICCV (2017)

7. Chen, T., Kornblith, S., Norouzi, M., Hinton, G.: A simple framework for contrastive learning of visual representations. arXiv preprint arXiv:2002.05709 (2020)
8. Chen, X., Fan, H., Girshick, R., He, K.: Improved baselines with momentum contrastive learning. arXiv preprint arXiv:2003.04297 (2020)
9. Coates, A., Ng, A., Lee, H.: An analysis of single-layer networks in unsupervised feature learning. In: JMLR (2011)
10. Cubuk, E.D., Zoph, B., Shlens, J., Le, Q.V.: Randaugment: practical automated data augmentation with a reduced search space. In: Proceedings of the IEEE/CVF Conference on Computer Vision and Pattern Recognition Workshops, pp. 702–703 (2020)
11. Deng, J., Dong, W., Socher, R., Li, L.J., Li, K., Fei-Fei, L.: ImageNet: a large-scale hierarchical image database. In: CVPR (2009)
12. Doersch, C., Gupta, A., Efros, A.A.: Unsupervised visual representation learning by context prediction. In: ICCV (2015)
13. Donahue, J., Krähenbühl, P., Darrell, T.: Adversarial feature learning. In: ICLR (2017)
14. Donahue, J., Simonyan, K.: Large scale adversarial representation learning. In: NIPS (2019)
15. Gidaris, S., Singh, P., Komodakis, N.: Unsupervised representation learning by predicting image rotations. In: ICLR (2018)
16. Haeusser, P., Plapp, J., Golkov, V., Aljalbout, E., Cremers, D.: Associative deep clustering: training a classification network with no labels. In: Brox, T., Bruhn, A., Fritz, M. (eds.) GCPR 2018. LNCS, vol. 11269, pp. 18–32. Springer, Cham (2019). https://doi.org/10.1007/978-3-030-12939-2_2
17. He, K., Fan, H., Wu, Y., Xie, S., Girshick, R.: Momentum contrast for unsupervised visual representation learning. In: arXiv preprint arXiv:1911.05722 (2020)
18. He, K., Zhang, X., Ren, S., Sun, J.: Deep residual learning for image recognition. In: CVPR (2016)
19. Hénaff, O.J., Razavi, A., Doersch, C., Eslami, S., van den Oord, A.: Data-efficient image recognition with contrastive predictive coding. arXiv preprint arXiv:1905.09272 (2019)
20. Hu, W., Miyato, T., Tokui, S., Matsumoto, E., Sugiyama, M.: Learning discrete representations via information maximizing self-augmented training. In: ICML (2017)
21. Huang, J., Dong, Q., Gong, S., Zhu, X.: Unsupervised deep learning by neighbourhood discovery. In: ICML (2019)
22. Jenni, S., Favaro, P.: Self-supervised feature learning by learning to spot artifacts. In: CVPR (2018)
23. Ji, X., Henriques, J.F., Vedaldi, A.: Invariant information clustering for unsupervised image classification and segmentation. In: ICCV (2019)
24. Kingma, D.P., Ba, J.: Adam: a method for stochastic optimization. arXiv preprint arXiv:1412.6980 (2014)
25. Kingma, D.P., Welling, M.: Auto-encoding variational Bayes. arXiv preprint arXiv:1312.6114 (2013)
26. Krizhevsky, A., Hinton, G., et al.: Learning multiple layers of features from tiny images (2009)
27. Krizhevsky, A., Sutskever, I., Hinton, G.E.: ImageNet classification with deep convolutional neural networks. In: NIPS (2012)
28. Larsson, G., Maire, M., Shakhnarovich, G.: Colorization as a proxy task for visual understanding. In: CVPR (2017)

29. Lin, T.-Y., et al.: Microsoft COCO: common objects in context. In: Fleet, D., Pajdla, T., Schiele, B., Tuytelaars, T. (eds.) ECCV 2014. LNCS, vol. 8693, pp. 740–755. Springer, Cham (2014). https://doi.org/10.1007/978-3-319-10602-1_48

30. McLachlan, G.J.: Iterative reclassification procedure for constructing an asymptotically optimal rule of allocation in discriminant analysis. J. Am. Stat. Assoc. **70**, 365–369 (1975)

31. Misra, I., van der Maaten, L.: Self-supervised learning of pretext-invariant representations. In: CVPR (2020)

32. Nathan Mundhenk, T., Ho, D., Chen, B.Y.: Improvements to context based self-supervised learning. In: CVPR (2018)

33. Ng, A.: Sparse autoencoder. CS294A Lecture notes (2011)

34. Noroozi, M., Favaro, P.: Unsupervised learning of visual representations by solving Jigsaw puzzles. In: Leibe, B., Matas, J., Sebe, N., Welling, M. (eds.) ECCV 2016. LNCS, vol. 9910, pp. 69–84. Springer, Cham (2016). https://doi.org/10.1007/978-3-319-46466-4_5

35. Noroozi, M., Pirsiavash, H., Favaro, P.: Representation learning by learning to count. In: ICCV (2017)

36. Noroozi, M., Vinjimoor, A., Favaro, P., Pirsiavash, H.: Boosting self-supervised learning via knowledge transfer. In: CVPR (2018)

37. van den Oord, A., Li, Y., Vinyals, O.: Representation learning with contrastive predictive coding. arXiv preprint arXiv:1807.03748 (2018)

38. Pathak, D., Krahenbuhl, P., Donahue, J., Darrell, T., Efros, A.A.: Context encoders: feature learning by inpainting. In: CVPR (2016)

39. Radford, A., Metz, L., Chintala, S.: Unsupervised representation learning with deep convolutional generative adversarial networks. arXiv preprint arXiv:1511.06434 (2015)

40. Ren, Z., Jae Lee, Y.: Cross-domain self-supervised multi-task feature learning using synthetic imagery. In: CVPR (2018)

41. Schultz, M., Joachims, T.: Learning a distance metric from relative comparisons. In: NIPS (2004)

42. Scudder, H.: Probability of error of some adaptive pattern-recognition machines. IEEE Trans. Inf. Theory **11**, 363–371 (1965)

43. Simonyan, K., Zisserman, A.: Very deep convolutional networks for large-scale image recognition. In: ICLR (2015)

44. Snell, J., Swersky, K., Zemel, R.: Prototypical networks for few-shot learning. In: NIPS (2017)

45. Sohn, K., et al.: FixMatch: simplifying semi-supervised learning with consistency and confidence. arXiv preprint arXiv:2001.07685 (2020)

46. Szegedy, C., Vanhoucke, V., Ioffe, S., Shlens, J., Wojna, Z.: Rethinking the inception architecture for computer vision. In: CVPR (2016)

47. Tian, Y., Krishnan, D., Isola, P.: Contrastive multiview coding. arXiv preprint arXiv:1906.05849 (2019)

48. Vincent, P., Larochelle, H., Lajoie, I., Bengio, Y., Manzagol, P.A.: Stacked denoising autoencoders: learning useful representations in a deep network with a local denoising criterion. JMLR **11**, 3371–3408 (2010)

49. Wang, J., Wang, J., Song, J., Xu, X.S., Shen, H.T., Li, S.: Optimized Cartesian k-means. IEEE Trans. Knowl. Data Eng. **27**, 180–192 (2015)

50. Wu, Z., Xiong, Y., Yu, S.X., Lin, D.: Unsupervised feature learning via non-parametric instance discrimination. In: CVPR (2018)

51. Xie, J., Girshick, R., Farhadi, A.: Unsupervised deep embedding for clustering analysis. In: ICML (2016)

52. Xie, S., Girshick, R., Dollár, P., Tu, Z., He, K.: Aggregated residual transformations for deep neural networks. In: CVPR (2017)
53. Yang, J., Parikh, D., Batra, D.: Joint unsupervised learning of deep representations and image clusters. In: CVPR (2016)
54. Zelnik-Manor, L., Perona, P.: Self-tuning spectral clustering. In: NIPS (2005)
55. Zhai, X., Oliver, A., Kolesnikov, A., Beyer, L.: S4l: self-supervised semi-supervised learning. In: Proceedings of the IEEE International Conference on Computer Vision, pp. 1476–1485 (2019)
56. Zhang, L., Qi, G.J., Wang, L., Luo, J.: AET vs. AED: unsupervised representation learning by auto-encoding transformations rather than data. In: CVPR (2019)
57. Zhang, R., Isola, P., Efros, A.A.: Colorful image colorization. In: Leibe, B., Matas, J., Sebe, N., Welling, M. (eds.) ECCV 2016. LNCS, vol. 9907, pp. 649–666. Springer, Cham (2016). https://doi.org/10.1007/978-3-319-46487-9_40
58. Zhao, J., Mathieu, M., Goroshin, R., Lecun, Y.: Stacked what-where auto-encoders. arXiv preprint arXiv:1506.02351 (2015)

Graph Convolutional Networks for Learning with Few Clean and Many Noisy Labels

Ahmet Iscen[1(✉)], Giorgos Tolias[2], Yannis Avrithis[3], Ondřej Chum[2],
and Cordelia Schmid[1]

[1] Google Research, Meylan, France
iscen@google.com
[2] VRG, Faculty of Electrical Engineering, Czech Technical University in Prague,
Prague, Czech Republic
[3] Inria, Univ Rennes, CNRS, IRISA, Rennes, France

Abstract. In this work we consider the problem of learning a classifier from noisy labels when a few clean labeled examples are given. The
structure of clean and noisy data is modeled by a graph per class and
Graph Convolutional Networks (GCN) are used to predict class relevance of noisy examples. For each class, the GCN is treated as a binary
classifier, which learns to discriminate clean from noisy examples using a
weighted binary cross-entropy loss function. The GCN-inferred "clean"
probability is then exploited as a relevance measure. Each noisy example
is weighted by its relevance when learning a classifier for the end task.
We evaluate our method on an extended version of a few-shot learning
problem, where the few clean examples of novel classes are supplemented
with additional noisy data. Experimental results show that our GCN-
based cleaning process significantly improves the classification accuracy
over not cleaning the noisy data, as well as standard few-shot classification where only few clean examples are used.

1 Introduction

State-of-the-art deep learning methods require a large amount of manually
labeled data. The need for supervision may be reduced by decoupling representation learning from the end task and/or using additional training data that
is unlabeled, weakly labeled (with noisy labels), or belong to different domains
or classes. Example approaches are *transfer learning* [39], *unsupervised representation learning* [39], *semi-supervised learning* [42], *learning from noisy labels*
[16] and *few-shot learning* [33].

However, for several classes, only very few or even no clean labeled examples might be available at the representation learning stage. *Few-shot learning*

Electronic supplementary material The online version of this chapter (https://
doi.org/10.1007/978-3-030-58607-2_17) contains supplementary material, which is
available to authorized users.

© Springer Nature Switzerland AG 2020
A. Vedaldi et al. (Eds.): ECCV 2020, LNCS 12355, pp. 286–302, 2020.
https://doi.org/10.1007/978-3-030-58607-2_17

severely limits the number of labeled samples on the end task, while the representation is learned on a large training set of different classes [12,33,38]. Nevertheless, in many situations, more data with noisy labels can be acquired or is readily available for the end task.

One interesting mix of few-shot learning with additional large-scale data is the work of Douze *et al.* [5], where labels are propagated from few clean labeled examples to a large-scale collection. This collection is unlabeled and actually contains data for many more classes than the end task. Their method overall improves the classification accuracy, but at an additional computational cost. It is a *transductive* method, *i.e.*, instead of learning a parametric classifier, the large-scale collection is still necessary at inference.

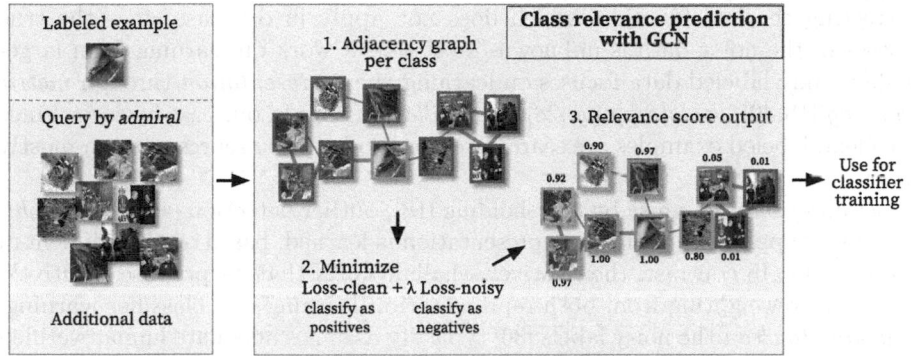

Fig. 1. Overview of our cleaning approach for 1-shot learning with noisy examples. We use the class name *admiral* to crawl noisy images from the web and create an adjacency graph based on visual similarity. We then assign a relevance score to each noisy example with a graph convolutional network (GCN). Relevance scores are displayed next to the images.

In this work, we learn a classifier from a few clean labeled examples and additional weakly labeled data, while the representation is learned on different classes, similarly to few-shot learning. We assume that the class names are known, and we use them to search an existing large collection of images with textual description. The result is a set of images with novel class labels, but potentially incorrect (noisy). As shown in Fig. 1, we clean this data using a *graph convolutional network* (GCN) [17], which learns to predict a class relevance score per image based on connections to clean images in the graph. Both the clean and the noisy images are then used to learn a classifier, where the noisy examples weighted by relevance. Unlike most existing work, our method operates independently per class and applies when clean labeled examples are few or even only one per class.

We make the following contributions:

1. We learn a classifier on a *large-scale weakly-labeled* collection jointly with only a *few clean labeled* examples.

2. To our knowledge, we are the first to use a GCN to clean noisy data: we cast a GCN as a *binary classifier* which learns to discriminate clean from noisy data, and we use its inferred "clean" probabilities as a relevance score per example.
3. We apply our method to two few-shot learning benchmarks and show significant improvement in accuracy, outperforming the method by Douze *et al.* [5] using the same large-scale collection of data without labels.

2   Related Work

Learning with Noisy Labels is often concerned with estimating or learning a *transition matrix* [24,25,34] or *knowledge graph* [19] between labels and correcting the loss function, which does not apply in our case since the true classes in the noisy data is unknown. Most recent work on learning from large-scale weakly-labeled data focuses on learning the *representation* through *metric learning* [18,40], *bootstrapping* [28], or *distillation* [19]. In our case however, since the clean labeled examples are scarce, we need to keep the representation mostly fixed.

Dealing with the noise by thresholding [18], outlier detection [40] or *reweighting* [20], is applicable while the representation is learned, based on the gradient of the loss [30]. In contrast, the relatively-shallow GCN that we propose effectively decouples reweighting from both representation learning and classifier learning. *Learning to clean* the noisy labels [36] typically assumes adequate human verified labels for training, which again is not the case in this work.

Few-Shot Learning. *Meta-learning* [37] refers to learning at two levels, where generic knowledge is acquired before adapting to more specific tasks. In few-shot learning, this translates to learning on a set of *base classes* how to learn from few examples on a distinct set of *novel classes* without overfitting. For instance, *optimization meta-learning* [6,7,27] amounts to learning a model that is easy to fine-tune in few steps. In our work, we study an extension of few-shot learning where more novel class instances are available, reducing the risk of overfitting when fine-tuning the model. *Metric learning* approaches learn how to compare queries for instance to few examples [38] or to the corresponding *class prototypes* [33]. Hariharan and Girshick [12] and Wang *et al.* [41] learn how to *generate* novel-class examples, which is not needed when more data is actually available.

Gidaris and Komodakis [9] learn on base classes a simpler cosine similarity-based parametric classifier, or simply *cosine classifier*, without meta-learning. The same classifier has been introduced independently by Qi *et al.* [26], who further fine-tune the network, assuming access to the base class training set. A recent survey [3] confirms the superiority of the cosine classifier to previous work including meta-learning [6]. We use the cosine classifier in this work, both for base and novel classes.

Making use of *unlabeled data* has been little explored in few-shot learning until recently. Ren *et al.* [29] introduce a semi-supervised few-shot classification task, where some labels are unknown. Liu *et al.* [21] follow the same semi-supervised setup, but use graph-based *label propagation* (LP) [45] for classification and consider all test images jointly. These methods assume a meta-learning scenario, where only small-scale data is available at each training episode; arguably, such a small amount of data limits the representation adaptation and generalization to unseen data. Similarly, Rohrbach *et al.* [31] use label propagation in a *transductive* setting, but at a larger scale assuming that all examples come from a set of known classes. Douze *et al.* [5] extend to an even larger scale, leveraging 100M unlabeled images in a graph without using additional text information. We focus on the latter large-scale scenario using the same 100M dataset. However, we filter by text to obtain *noisy data* and follow an *inductive* approach by training a classifier for novel classes, such that the 100M collection is not needed at inference.

Graph Neural Networks are generalizations of convolutional networks to non-Euclidean spaces [1]. Early *spectral methods* [2,14] have been succeeded by *Chebyshev polynomial* approximations [4], which avoid the high computational cost of computing eigenvectors. *Graph convolutional networks* (GCN) [17] provide a further simplification by a *first-order* approximation of graph filtering and are applied to *semi-supervised* [17] and subsequently *few-shot learning* [8]. Kipf and Welling [17] apply the loss function to labeled examples to make predictions on unlabeled ones. Similarly, Garcia and Bruna [8] use GCNs to make predictions on novel class examples. Gidaris and Komodakis [10] use Graph Neural Networks as denoising autoencoders to generate class weights for novel classes. By contrast, we cast GCNs as *binary classifiers* discriminating clean from noisy examples: we apply a loss function to all examples, and then use the inferred probabilities as a class relevance measure, effectively cleaning the data.

Our counter-intuitive objective of treating all noisy examples as negative can be compared to treating each example as a different class in *instance-level discrimination* [43]. In fact, our loss function is similar to *noise-contrastive estimation* (NCE) [11]. Our experiments show that our GCN-based classifier outperforms classical LP [45] used for a similar purpose by [31].

3 Problem Formulation

We consider a space $\mathcal{X}$ of examples. We are given a set $X_C \subset \mathcal{X}$ of examples, each having a *clean* (manually verified) label in a set C of classes with $|C| = K$. We assume that the number $|X_C^c|$ of examples[1] labeled in each class $c \in C$ is only k, typically in $\{1, 2, 5, 10, 20\}$. We are also given an additional set $X_\mathcal{N}$ of examples, each with a set of *noisy* labels in C. The *extended* set of examples for class c is now $X_\mathcal{E}^c = X_C^c \cup X_\mathcal{N}^c$. Examples or sets of examples having clean (noisy) labels are referred to as clean (noisy) as well. The goal is to train a K-way classifier,

---

[1] For any set $X \subset \mathcal{X}$, we denote by X^c its subset of examples labeled in class $c \in C$.

using the additional noisy set in order to improve the accuracy compared to only using the small clean set.

We assume that we are given a feature extractor $g_\theta : \mathcal{X} \to \mathbb{R}^d$, mapping an example to a d-dimensional vector. For instance, when examples are images, the feature extractor is typically a *convolutional neural network* (CNN) and θ are the parameters of all layers.

In this work, we assume that the noisy set $X_\mathcal{N}$ is collected via web crawling. Examples are images accompanied by free-form text descriptions and/or user tags originating from community photo collections. To make use of text data, we assume that the names of the classes in C are given. An example in $X_\mathcal{N}$ is given a label in class $c \in C$ if its textual information contains the name of class c; it may then have none, one or more labels. In this way, we automatically infer labels for $X_\mathcal{N}$ without human effort, which are however *noisy*.

4   Cleaning with Graph Convolutional Networks

We perform cleaning by predicting a *class relevance* measure for each noisy example in $X_\mathcal{N}^c$, independently for each class $c \in C$. To simplify the notation, we drop superscript c where possible in this subsection and we denote $X_\mathcal{E}^c$ by $\{x_1, \dots, x_k, x_{k+1}, \dots, x_N\}$, where $X_\mathcal{C}^c = \{x_1, \dots, x_k\}$ and $X_\mathcal{N}^c = \{x_{k+1}, \dots, x_N\}$. The features of these examples are similarly represented by matrix $V = [\mathbf{v}_1, \dots, \mathbf{v}_k, \mathbf{v}_{k+1}, \dots, \mathbf{v}_N] \in \mathbb{R}^{d \times N}$, where $\mathbf{v}_i = g_\theta(x_i)$ for $i = 1, \dots, N$.

We construct an affinity matrix $A \in \mathbb{R}^{N \times N}$ with elements $a_{ij} = [\mathbf{v}_i^\top \mathbf{v}_j]_+$ if examples $\mathbf{v}_i$ and $\mathbf{v}_j$ are reciprocal nearest neighbors in $X_\mathcal{E}^c$ and 0 otherwise. Matrix A has zero diagonal, but self-connections are added before A is normalized as $\tilde{A} = D^{-1}(A + I)$ with $D = \mathrm{diag}((A + I)\mathbf{1})$ being the degree matrix of $A + I$ and $\mathbf{1}$ the all-ones vector.

Graph convolutional networks (GCNs) [17] are formed by a sequence of layers. Each layer is a function $f_\Theta : \mathbb{R}^{N \times N} \times \mathbb{R}^{l \times N} \to \mathbb{R}^{n \times N}$ of the form

$$f_\Theta(\tilde{A}, Z) = h(\Theta^\top Z \tilde{A}), \tag{1}$$

where $Z \in \mathbb{R}^{l \times N}$ represents the input features, $\Theta \in \mathbb{R}^{l \times n}$ holds the parameters of the layer to be learned, and h is a nonlinear activation function. Function f_Θ maps l-dimensional input features to n-dimensional output features.

In this work we consider a two-layer GCN with a scalar output per example. This network is a function $F_\Theta : \mathbb{R}^{N \times N} \times \mathbb{R}^{d \times N} \to \mathbb{R}^N$ given by

$$F_\Theta(\tilde{A}, V) = \sigma(\Theta_2^\top [\Theta_1^\top V \tilde{A}]_+ \tilde{A}), \tag{2}$$

where $\Theta = \{\Theta_1, \Theta_2\}$, $\Theta_1 \in \mathbb{R}^{d \times m}$, $\Theta_2 \in \mathbb{R}^{m \times 1}$, $[\cdot]_+$ is the positive part or ReLU function [23] and $\sigma(a) = (1 + e^{-a})^{-1}$ for $a \in \mathbb{R}$ is the sigmoid function. Function F_Θ performs feature propagation through the affinity matrix in an analogy to classical graph-based propagation methods for classification [45] or search [46].

The output $F_\Theta(\tilde{A}, V)$ is a vector of length N, with element $F_\Theta(\tilde{A}, V)_i$ in $[0, 1]$ representing a relevance value of example x_i for class c. To learn the parameters

Θ, we treat the GCN as a *binary classifier* where target output 1 corresponds to clean examples and 0 to noisy. In particular, we minimize the loss function

$$L_{\mathcal{G}}(V, \tilde{A}; \Theta) = -\frac{1}{k} \sum_{i=1}^{k} \log \left(F_{\Theta}(\tilde{A}, V)_i \right) - \frac{\lambda}{N-k} \sum_{i=k+1}^{N} \log \left(1 - F_{\Theta}(\tilde{A}, V)_i \right). \quad (3)$$

This is a binary cross-entropy loss function where noisy examples are given an importance weight λ. Given the propagation on the nearest neighbor graph, and depending on the relative importance λ of the second term, noisy examples that are strongly connected to clean ones are still expected to receive high class relevance, while noisy examples that are not relevant to the current class are expected to get a class relevance near zero.

The impact of parameter λ is validated in Sect. 6, where we show that the fewer the available clean images are (smaller k) the smaller the importance weight should be. As is standard practice for GCNs in classification [17], training is performed in batches of size N, that is the entire set of features.

Figure 2 shows examples of clean images, corresponding noisy ones and the predicted relevance. Using the visual similarity to the clean image, we can use relevance to resolve cases of polysemy, *e.g. black widow (spider)* vs. *black widow (superhero)*, or cases like *pineapple* vs. *pineapple juice*.

Discussion. Loss function (3) is similar to *noise-contrastive estimation* (NCE) [11] as used by We *et al.* [43] for *instance-level discrimination*, whereas we discriminate clean from noisy examples. The semi-supervised learning setup of GCNs [17] uses a loss function that applies only to the labeled examples, and makes discrete predictions on unlabeled examples. In our case, all examples contribute to the loss but with different importance, as we infer real-valued class relevance for the noisy examples, to be used for subsequent learning.

Function F_{Θ} in (2) reduces to a Multi-Layer Perceptron (MLP) when the affinity matrix A is zero, in which case all examples are disconnected. Using an MLP to perform cleaning would take each example into account independently of the others, while the GCN considers the collection of examples as a whole. MLP training is performed identically to GCN by minimizing (3). We compare the two alternatives in our experiments.

5   Learning a Classifier with Few Clean and Many Noisy Examples

Our cleaning process applies when the clean labeled examples are few, but assumes a feature extractor[2] g_θ. That is, representation learning, label cleaning and classifier learning are decoupled. We perform GCN-based cleaning as described in Sect. 4, and learn a classifier by weighting examples according to class relevance. The process of training the classifier is described below.

---

[2] For instance, after training on a different task or a set of classes other than C. Learning of the feature extractor used in our experiments is described in Appendix.

5.1 Cosine-Similarity Based Classifier

We use a *cosine-similarity based classifier* [9,26], or *cosine classifier* for short. Each class $c \in C$ is represented by a learnable parameter $\mathbf{w}_c \in \mathbb{R}^d$. The *prediction* of example $x \in \mathcal{X}$ is the class c of maximum cosine similarity $\hat{\mathbf{w}}_c^\top \hat{g}_\theta(x)^3$

$$\pi_{\theta,W}(x) = \arg\max_c \hat{\mathbf{w}}_c^\top \hat{g}_\theta(x), \tag{4}$$

where $W = [\mathbf{w}_1, \ldots, \mathbf{w}_K] \in \mathbb{R}^{d \times K}$.

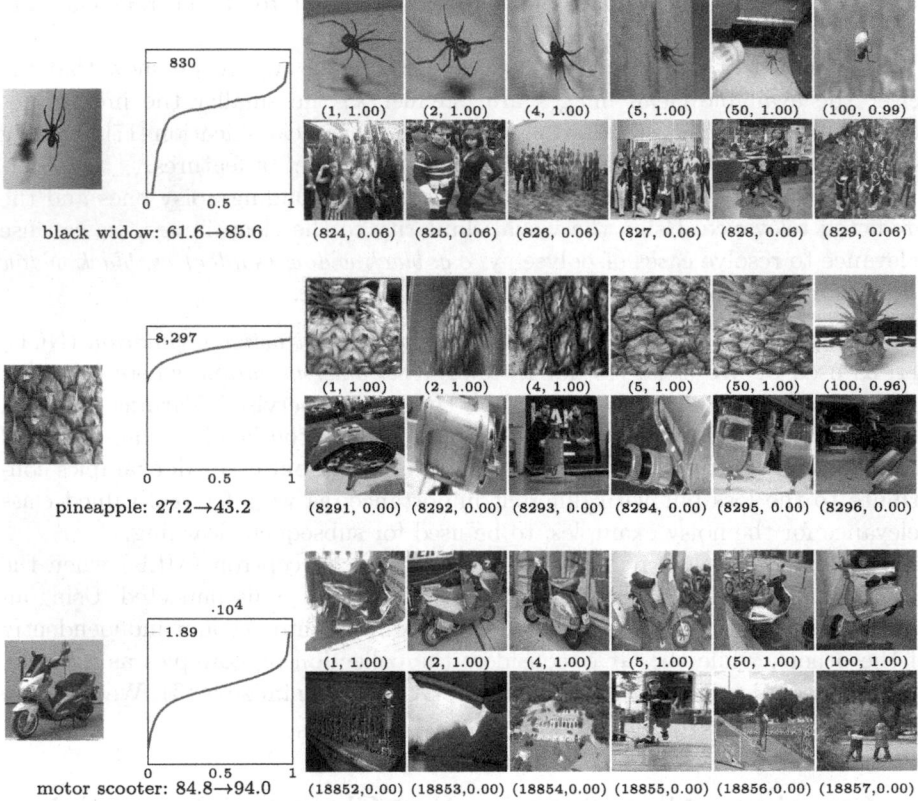

Fig. 2. Examples of clean images from the Low-Shot ImageNet Benchmark (left) for 1-shot classification, cumulative histogram of the predicted relevance for noisy images (middle) and representative noisy images (right) by descending order of relevance, with relevance value reported below. Test accuracy without and with additional data using class prototypes (5) is shown next to class names.

---

³ We denote the ℓ_2-normalized counterpart of vector $\mathbf{x}$ by $\hat{\mathbf{x}}$. Similarly, if $\mathbf{y} = f(x)$, we denote $\hat{\mathbf{y}}$ by $\hat{f}(x)$.

5.2 Classifier Learning

The goal is to learn a K-way classifier for unseen data in $\mathcal{X}$. Unlike the typical few-shot learning task, each class contains a few clean and many noisy examples.

Prior to learning classifiers, training examples $x_i \in X_{\mathcal{E}}^c$ are weighted by their relevance $r(x_i)$ to class c. For a noisy example $x_i \in X_{\mathcal{N}}^c$, we define $r(x_i) = F_\Theta(\tilde{A}, V)_i$ where $F_\Theta(\tilde{A}, V)$ is the output vector of the GCN, while for a clean example $x_i \in X_{\mathcal{C}}^c$ we fix $r(x_i) = 1$. Note that optimizing (3) does not guarantee $F_\Theta(\tilde{A}, V)_i = 1$ for clean examples $x_i \in X_{\mathcal{C}}^c$. We define $r(X) = \sum_{x \in X} r(x)$ for any set $X \subset \mathcal{X}$.

We first assume that the given feature extractor is fixed and consider two different classifiers, namely class prototypes and cosine-similarity based classifier. Then, this assumption is dropped and the classifier and feature representation are learned jointly by fine-tuning the entire network.

Class Prototypes. For each class $c \in C$, we define *prototype* $\mathbf{w}_c$ by

$$\mathbf{w}_c = \frac{1}{r(X_{\mathcal{E}}^c)} \sum_{x \in X_{\mathcal{E}}^c} r(x) g_\theta(x). \tag{5}$$

Prototypes are fixed vectors, not learnable parameters. Collecting them into matrix $W = [\mathbf{w}_1, \ldots, \mathbf{w}_K] \in \mathbb{R}^{d \times K}$, K-way prediction is made by classifier $\pi_{\theta, W}$ (4).

Cosine Classifier Learning. Given examples $X_{\mathcal{E}}$, we learn a parametric cosine classifier with parameters $W = [\mathbf{w}_1, \ldots, \mathbf{w}_K] \in \mathbb{R}^{d \times K}$ by minimizing the weighted cross entropy loss $L(C, X_{\mathcal{E}}, \theta; W)$ over W, given by

$$L(C, X_{\mathcal{E}}, \theta; W) = - \sum_{c \in C} \frac{1}{r(X_{\mathcal{E}}^c)} \sum_{x \in X_{\mathcal{E}}^c} r(x) \log(\sigma(s\hat{W}^\top \hat{g}_\theta(x))_c), \tag{6}$$

where $\sigma : \mathbb{R}^K \to \mathbb{R}^K$ is the softmax function with $\sigma(\mathbf{a})_c = e^{a_c} / \sum_{j \in C} e^{a_j}$ for $\mathbf{a} \in \mathbb{R}^K$, s is a *scale parameter* and $\hat{W} = [\hat{\mathbf{w}}_1, \ldots, \hat{\mathbf{w}}_K]$. The parameters θ of the feature extractor are fixed. The scale parameter s is also fixed according to the training of the feature extractor. Prediction is made as in the previous case.

Deep Network Fine-Tuning. An alternative is to drop the assumption that the feature extractor is fixed. In this case, we jointly learn the parameters θ of the feature extractor and W of the K-way cosine classifier by minimizing the right-hand side of (6). This requires access to examples $X_{\mathcal{E}}$, while for the previous two classifiers, access to features $g_\theta(x)$ is enough. Note that, due to over-fitting on the few available examples, such learning is typically avoided in a few-shot learning setup.

6 Experiments

6.1 Experimental Setup

Datasets and Task Setup. We extend the *Low-Shot ImageNet benchmark* [12] by assuming many noisy examples in addition to the few clean ones. In this benchmark, the 1000 ImageNet classes [32] are split into 389 base classes and 611 novel classes. The validation set contains 193 base and 300 novel classes, and the test set the remaining 196 base and 311 novel classes. The base classes are used to learn the feature extractor (see supplementary material), while the novel classes form the set of classes C on which we apply the cleaning and learn the classifier. We only assume noisy examples for the novel classes, not for the base ones. Additionally, we apply a similar setup to the Places365 dataset [44]. We randomly choose 183 test and 182 validation classes. We use the model learned on the base classes of Low-Shot ImageNet benchmark as the feature extractor. Therefore, all classes in Places365 dataset are considered *novel*. We refer to this setup as *Low-Shot Places365 benchmark*.

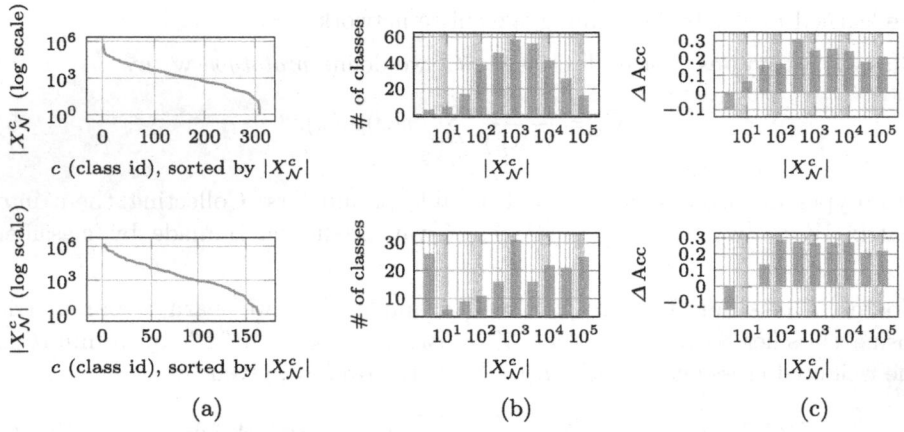

(a)   (b)   (c)

Fig. 3. Noisy data statistics for Low-Shot ImageNet(top) and Low-Shot Places365 (bottom). (a) Number of additional images collected from YFCC-100M per class c for all novel classes. (b) Number of classes per group, when groups are created according to $|X_{\mathcal{N}}^c|$ in logarithmic scale. (c) Accuracy improvement Δ Acc (difference of accuracy between our method with noisy examples and the baseline without noisy examples) for prototype classifier, for same groups as in (b).

The standard benchmark includes k-shot classification, *i.e.* classification on k clean examples per class, with $k \in \{1, 2, 5, 10, 20\}$. We extend it to k clean and many noisy examples per class. Similar to the work of Hariharan and Girshick [12], we perform 5 episodes, each drawing a subset of k clean examples per class. We report the average top-5 accuracy over the 5 episodes on novel classes of the test set. Accuracy over all classes (base and novel) is reported in supplementary material.

Noisy Data and Statistics. We use the YFCC100M dataset [35] as a source of additional data with noisy labels. It contains approximatively 100M images collected from Flickr. Each image comes with a text description obtained from the user title and caption. We use the text description to obtain images with noisy labels, as discussed in Sect. 3.

Figure 3 (top) shows the statistics of noisy examples for Low-Shot ImageNet benchmark. The noisy examples for novel classes are long tailed in log scale (a). Noisy examples per class differ significantly for different classes, with a minimum of zero for classes *maillot* and *missile*, and a maximum of 620,142 for the class *church/church building*. There is a significant number of classes where we obtain less than 1000 extra examples, but we improve nevertheless; see Fig. 3(c). A small exception is 4 very rare classes out of 311, with around 3 additional images per class (leftmost bin in Fig. 3(b) and (c)). One could use more resources like web queries to collect additional data in real world applications.

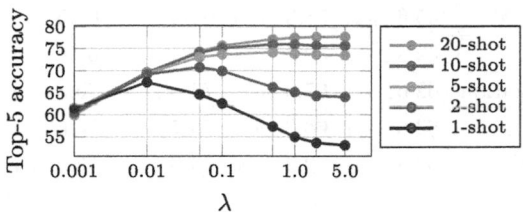

Fig. 4. Impact of λ on the validation set of the extended Low-shot ImageNet benchmark with YFCC-100M for noisy examples using class prototypes (5).

Figure 3 (bottom) presents the same statistics for Low-Shot Places365 benchmark. The trends are similar to those from Fig. 3, except that there are more than 20 classes without any additional noisy data in this task (b). Nevertheless, there is a more consistent improvement in accuracy for classes that do have sufficient noisy data(c).

Representation and Classifier Learning. In most experiments, we use ResNet-10 [13] as feature extractor as in [9]. Classification for novel classes is performed with *class prototypes* (5), *cosine classifier learning* (6) or *deep network fine-tuning*. Hyper-parameters, such as batch size and number of epochs, are tuned on the validation set. We cross-validate the possible values of 512, 1024, 2048, 4096, and 8192 for batchsize and 10, 20, 30 and 50 for number of epochs. The learning rate starts from 0.1 and is reduced to 0.001 at the end of training with *cosine annealing* [22]. We handle the imbalance of the noisy set by normalizing by $r(X_c)$ in (6). Prototypes (5) are used to initialize the weights W of the cosine classifier in (6). We ignore examples x_i with relevance $r(x_i) < 0.1$ to reduce the complexity when fine-tuning the network. We also report results with ResNet-50 as feature extractor, using the model trained on base classes by [12]. Following [5], we apply PCA to the features to reduce their dimensionality to 256. Base classes are represented by class prototypes (5) in this case.

GCN training is performed with the Adam optimizer and a learning rate of 0.1 for 100 iterations. We use dropout with probability 0.5. The dimensionality of the input descriptors is $d = 512$ for ResNet-10 and $d = 256$ for ResNet-50 (after PCA). Dimensionality of the internal representation in (1) is $m = 16$. The affinity matrix is constructed with reciprocal top-50 nearest neighbors.

Table 1. Comparison with baselines using noisy examples on the Low-shot ImageNet benchmark. We report top-5 accuracy on novel classes with classification by class prototypes (5).

Method	$k = 1$	2	5	10	20
FEW CLEAN EXAMPLES					
Class proto. [9]	45.3 ± 0.65	57.1 ± 0.37	69.3 ± 0.32	74.8 ± 0.20	77.8 ± 0.24
FEW CLEAN & MANY NOISY EXAMPLES					
Similarity	49.8 ± 0.29	56.3 ± 0.27	64.2 ± 0.32	68.4 ± 0.14	71.2 ± 0.12
β-weighting, $\beta = 1$	56.1 ± 0.06	56.4 ± 0.08	57.1 ± 0.05	57.7 ± 0.08	58.7 ± 0.06
β-weighting, β^*	55.6 ± 0.24	58.3 ± 0.14	63.4 ± 0.25	67.5 ± 0.34	71.0 ± 0.22
Linear	59.8 ± 0.00	59.3 ± 0.00	58.4 ± 0.00	58.6 ± 0.00	59.4 ± 0.00
Label propagation	62.6 ± 0.35	67.0 ± 0.41	74.6 ± 0.30	76.3 ± 0.23	77.7 ± 0.18
MLP	63.6 ± 0.41	68.8 ± 0.42	73.7 ± 0.25	75.6 ± 0.21	77.6 ± 0.21
Ours	67.8 ± 0.10	70.9 ± 0.30	73.9 ± 0.17	76.1 ± 0.12	78.2 ± 0.14

Baseline Methods. We implement and evaluate several baseline methods:

1. *β-cleaning* assigns $r(x_i) = \beta$ to all additional examples. We report results for $\beta = 1.0$ (unit relevance score) and β^*, the optimal β for all k obtained on the validation set.
2. *Similarity* uses the scaled cosine similarity as the relevance weight, *i.e.* $r(x_i) = (1 + \mathbf{v}_i^\top \mathbf{x})/2$, where $\mathbf{x}$ is the class prototype created with the features of clean examples.
3. *Linear* learns a linear binary classifier where the positive instances are the k labeled examples, and the negative examples are chosen randomly from other classes.
4. *Label Propagation* (LP) [45] propagates information by a linear operation. It solves the linear system $(I - \alpha D^{-1/2} A D^{-1/2}) \mathbf{r}_c = \mathbf{y}_c$ [15] for each class c, where D is the degree matrix of A, $\alpha = 0.9$ and $\mathbf{y}_c \in \mathbb{R}^N$ is a k-hot binary vector indicating the clean (labeled) examples of class c. Relevance $r(x_i)$ is the i-th element $(\mathbf{r}_c)_i$ of the solution.
5. *MLP*, discussed in Sect. 4, learns a nonlinear mapping to assign relevance weights, but does not propagate over the graph. It is trained using (3) and therefore includes part of our contribution.

6.2   Experimental Results

The Impact of the Importance Weight λ is measured on the validation set and the best performing value is used on the test set for each value of k. Results on Low-shot ImageNet benchmark are shown in Fig. 4. The larger the value of λ, the more the loss encourages noisy examples to be classified as negatives. As a consequence, large (small) λ results in smaller (larger) relevance, on average, for noisy examples. The optimal λ per value of k suggests that as the number of clean examples decreases, the need for additional noisy ones increases.

Comparison with Baselines Using Additional Data on Low-shot Imagenet benchmark is presented in Table 1. Qualitative results are presented in Fig. 2. The use of additional data is mostly harmful for β-weighting except for 1 and 2-shot. MLP offers improvements in most cases, implying that it manages to appropriately down-weight irrelevant examples. The consistent improvement of GCN compared to MLP, especially large for small k, suggests that it is beneficial to incorporate relations, with the affinity matrix A modeling the structure of the feature space. LP is a classic approach that also uses A but is a linear operation with no parameters, and is inferior to our method. The gain of cleaning ($\beta = 1$ vs. ours) ranges from 11% to 20%.

Comparison with the State of the Art on Low-shot Imagenet benchmark is presented in Table 2. We significantly improve the performance by using addi-

Table 2. Comparison to the state of the art on the Low-shot ImageNet benchmark. We report top-5 accuracy on novel classes. We use class prototypes (5), cosine classifier learning (6) and deep network fine-tuning for classification with our GCN-based data addition method. † denotes numbers taken from the corresponding papers. All other experiments are re-implemented by us.

METHOD	TOP-5 ACCURACY ON NOVEL CLASSES				
	$k = 1$	2	5	10	20
RESNET-10 – FEW CLEAN EXAMPLES					
Proto.-Nets [33]†	39.3	54.4	66.3	71.2	73.9
Logistic reg. w/H [41]†	40.7	50.8	62.0	69.3	76.5
PMN w/H [41]†	45.8	57.8	69.0	74.3	77.4
Class proto. [9]	45.3 ± 0.65	57.1 ± 0.37	69.3 ± 0.32	74.8 ± 0.20	77.8 ± 0.24
Class proto. w/Att. [9]	45.8 ± 0.74	57.4 ± 0.38	69.6 ± 0.27	75.0 ± 0.29	78.2 ± 0.23
RESNET-10 – FEW CLEAN & MANY NOISY EXAMPLES					
Ours - class proto. (5)	$\mathbf{67.8} \pm 0.10$	$\mathbf{70.9} \pm 0.30$	$\mathbf{73.7} \pm 0.20$	$\mathbf{76.1} \pm 0.16$	$\mathbf{78.2} \pm 0.14$
Ours - cosine (6)	$\mathbf{73.2} \pm 0.14$	$\mathbf{75.3} \pm 0.25$	$\mathbf{75.6} \pm 0.24$	$\mathbf{78.5} \pm 0.32$	$\mathbf{80.7} \pm 0.26$
Ours - fine-tune	$\mathbf{74.1} \pm 0.19$	$\mathbf{76.2} \pm 0.28$	$\mathbf{77.7} \pm 0.23$	$\mathbf{80.6} \pm 0.31$	$\mathbf{82.6} \pm 0.24$
RESNET-50 – FEW CLEAN EXAMPLES					
Proto.-Nets [33]†	49.6	64.0	74.4	78.1	80.0
PMN w/H [41]†	54.7	66.8	77.4	81.4	83.8
RESNET-50 – FEW CLEAN & MANY UNLABELED EXAMPLES					
Diffusion [5]†	63.6 ± 0.61	69.5 ± 0.60	75.2 ± 0.40	78.5 ± 0.34	80.8 ± 0.18
Diffusion - logistic [5]†	64.0 ± 0.70	71.1 ± 0.82	79.7 ± 0.38	83.9 ± 0.10	86.3 ± 0.17
RESNET-50 – FEW CLEAN & MANY NOISY EXAMPLES					
Ours - class proto. (5)	$\mathbf{69.7} \pm 0.44$	$\mathbf{73.7} \pm 0.56$	$\mathbf{77.0} \pm 0.20$	$\mathbf{79.9} \pm 0.30$	$\mathbf{81.9} \pm 0.29$
Ours - cosine (6)	$\mathbf{78.0} \pm 0.38$	$\mathbf{80.2} \pm 0.33$	$\mathbf{80.9} \pm 0.17$	$\mathbf{83.7} \pm 0.19$	$\mathbf{85.7} \pm 0.11$
Ours - fine-tune	$\mathbf{80.2} \pm 0.33$	$\mathbf{82.6} \pm 0.14$	$\mathbf{83.3} \pm 0.26$	$\mathbf{85.9} \pm 0.22$	$\mathbf{88.3} \pm 0.21$

tional data and cleaning compared to a number of different approaches, including the work by Gidaris and Komodakis [9], which is our starting point. As expected, the gain is more pronounced for small k, reaching more than 20% improvement for 1-shot novel accuracy.

Closest to ours is the work by Douze *et al.* [5], who use the same experimental setup and the same additional data, but without filtering by text or using noisy labels. We outperform this approach in all cases, while requiring much less computation: *offline*, we construct a separate small graph per class rather than a single graph over the entire 100M collection; *online*, we perform inference by cosine similarity to one prototype per class or a learned classifier rather than iterative diffusion on the entire collection. By ignoring examples that are not given any noisy label, we are only using a tiny fraction of the 100M collection: in particular, only 3,744,994 images for the 311-class test split of the Low-shot ImageNet benchmark. In contrast to [5], additional data brings improvement even at 20-shot with classifier learning or network fine-tuning. Most importantly, our approach does not require the entire 100M collection at inference.

Analysis of Relevance Weights. We manually label all the noisy examples from 20 classes in order to quantitatively measure the accuracy of the assigned relevance. We measure the noise ratio per class, *i.e.* the ratio of irrelevant (negative) noisy images to all noisy (positive and negative) images. Positive and negative images are defined according to the manual labels. The 20 classes are selected such that 10 of them have the highest 1-shot accuracy, and the rest have the lowest. This allows us to examine success and failure cases.

In the case of 1-shot classification ($k = 1$), the average relevance weight is 0.71 for positive and 0.40 for negative examples. A success case is the "bee eater" class with noise ratio equal to 0.52. Our method achieves 98.4% accuracy for 1-shot classification, compared to 68.8% without any additional data. The average relevance weight is 0.99 for positive examples and 0.25 for negative examples of

Table 3. Comparison with baselines using noisy examples on the Low-shot Places365 benchmark. We report top-5 accuracy on novel classes.

Method	$k = 1$	2	5	10	20
FEW CLEAN EXAMPLES					
Class proto. [9]	$28.7_{\pm 1.12}$	$38.0_{\pm 0.37}$	$50.5_{\pm 0.51}$	$57.9_{\pm 0.35}$	$62.3_{\pm 0.25}$
FEW CLEAN & MANY NOISY EXAMPLES - CLASS PROTO. (5)					
β-weighting, $\beta = 1$	$44.0_{\pm 0.34}$	$45.7_{\pm 0.22}$	$48.4_{\pm 0.31}$	$50.0_{\pm 0.12}$	$50.8_{\pm 0.25}$
Label propagation	$39.6_{\pm 0.78}$	$46.5_{\pm 0.22}$	$54.8_{\pm 0.42}$	$59.6_{\pm 0.11}$	$62.0_{\pm 0.14}$
MLP	$46.9_{\pm 0.78}$	$50.1_{\pm 0.38}$	$55.4_{\pm 0.29}$	$59.2_{\pm 0.26}$	$61.5_{\pm 0.31}$
Ours	$47.1_{\pm 0.70}$	$50.5_{\pm 0.31}$	$55.1_{\pm 0.50}$	$59.0_{\pm 0.32}$	$61.9_{\pm 0.22}$
FEW CLEAN & MANY NOISY EXAMPLES - OTHER CLASSIFIERS					
Ours - cosine (6)	$50.7_{\pm 0.61}$	$53.5_{\pm 0.49}$	$57.0_{\pm 0.54}$	$59.8_{\pm 0.22}$	$62.3_{\pm 0.12}$
Ours - fine-tune	$51.8_{\pm 0.69}$	$54.8_{\pm 0.57}$	$59.5_{\pm 0.63}$	$62.9_{\pm 0.39}$	$66.0_{\pm 0.27}$

this class. One failure case is the "muzzle" class; it corresponds to the muzzle of an animal. The noise ratio is high; 94% of the 980 collected images are not relevant with most being animals without a muzzle or a firearm. The 1-shot classification accuracy without noisy data is 4%. Our method offers only a small increase to 8%. This can be explained by inaccurate relevance weights, which are on average 0.18 for positive and 0.30 for negative examples.

Experiments in Low-Shot Places365 are reported in Table 3. Our results indicate that our method consistently outperforms the baselines on this benchmark as well. Note that *MLP*, which is also competitive for this task, is trained with our proposed loss function 3. This is our contribution as well as the use of GCN. These methods significantly improve over existing methods, such as Label Propagation [45]. Further improvements are brought by cosine classifier learning (6) and deep network fine-tuning.

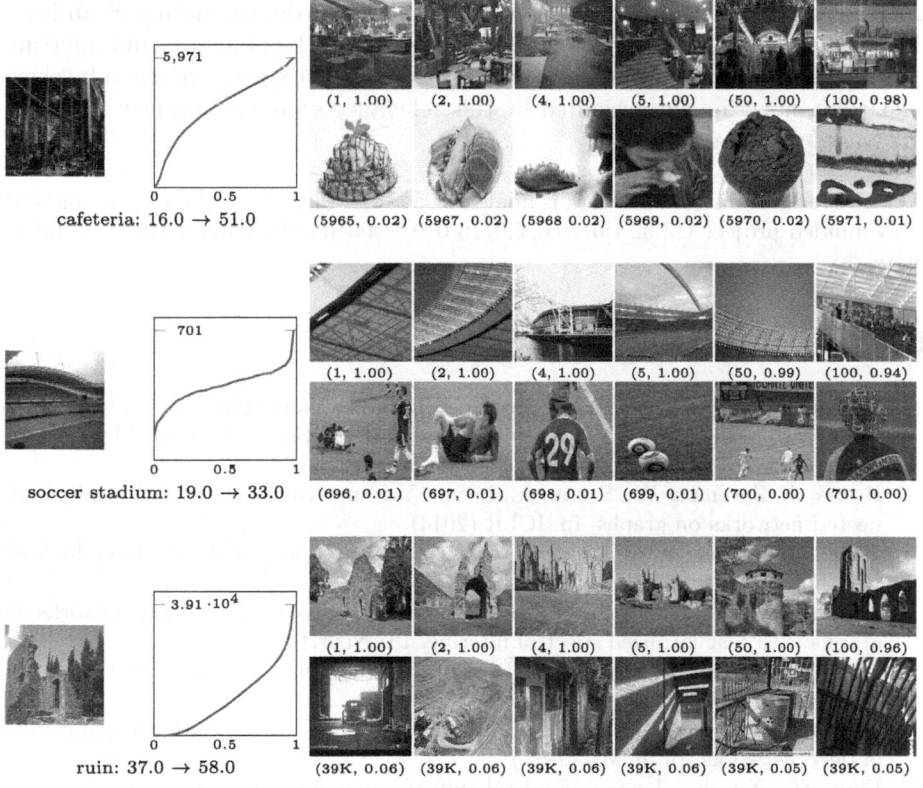

Fig. 5. Examples of clean images on Low-Shot Places365 Benchmark (left) for 1-shot classification, cumulative histogram of the predicted relevance for noisy images (middle), and representative noisy images (right), each having its position in the descending ranked list according to relevance value reported below. Test accuracy without and with additional data using prototypes (5) is shown next to class names.

We also present qualitative results on Low-Shot Places365 in Fig. 5. The first example at the top shows that top-ranked images by relevance depict different views of cafeterias for the *cafeteria* class, while bottom-ranked images depict food served in a cafeteria, which are irrelevant to our task. Similarly, our method assigns high relevance to images of soccer stadiums and low relevance to soccer players for the *soccer* class. Finally, our method finds similar images to the clean example for the *ruin* class. In general, top-ranking images exhibit diversity and are not just near-duplicates.

7   Conclusions

In this paper we have introduced a new method for assigning class relevance to noisy images obtained by textual queries with class names. Our approach leverages one or a few labeled images per class and relies on a graph convolutional network (GCN) to propagate visual information from the labeled images to the noisy ones. The GCN is trained as a binary classifier discriminating clean from noisy examples using a weighted binary cross-entropy loss function and inferring "clean" probability as a relevance score for that class. Experimental results show that using noisy images weighted by this relevance score significantly improves the classification accuracy.

Acknowledgements. This work is funded by MSMT LL1901 ERC-CZ grant and OP VVV funded project CZ.02.1.01/0.0/0.0/16_019/0000765 "Research Center for Informatics".

References

1. Bronstein, M.M., Bruna, J., LeCun, Y., Szlam, A., Vandergheynst, P.: Geometric deep learning: going beyond Euclidean data. IEEE Signal Process. Mag. **34**(4), 18–42 (2017)
2. Bruna, J., Zaremba, W., Szlam, A., Lecun, Y.: Spectral networks and locally connected networks on graphs. In: ICLR (2014)
3. Chen, W.Y., Liu, Y.C., Kira, Z., Wang, Y.C.F., Huang, J.B.: A closer look at few-shot classification. In: ICLR (2019)
4. Defferrard, M., Bresson, X., Vandergheynst, P.: Convolutional neural networks on graphs with fast localized spectral filtering. In: NeurIPS (2016)
5. Douze, M., Szlam, A., Hariharan, B., Jégou, H.: Low-shot learning with large-scale diffusion. In: CVPR (2018)
6. Finn, C., Abbeel, P., Levine, S.: Model-agnostic meta-learning for fast adaptation of deep networks. In: ICML (2017)
7. Finn, C., Xu, K., Levine, S.: Probabilistic model-agnostic meta-learning. In: NeurIPS (2018)
8. Garcia, V., Bruna, J.: Few-shot learning with graph neural networks. In: ICLR (2018)
9. Gidaris, S., Komodakis, N.: Dynamic few-shot visual learning without forgetting. In: CVPR (2018)

10. Gidaris, S., Komodakis, N.: Generating classification weights with GNN denoising autoencoders for few-shot learning. In: CVPR (2019)
11. Gutmann, M., Hyvärinen, A.: Noise-contrastive estimation: a new estimation principle for unnormalized statistical models. In: International Conference on Artificial Intelligence and Statistics (2010)
12. Hariharan, B., Girshick, R.: Low-shot visual recognition by shrinking and hallucinating features. In: CVPR (2017)
13. He, K., Zhang, X., Ren, S., Sun, J.: Deep residual learning for image recognition. In: CVPR (2016)
14. Henaff, M., Bruna, J., LeCun, Y.: Deep convolutional networks on graph-structured data. arXiv preprint arXiv:1506.05163 (2015)
15. Iscen, A., Tolias, G., Avrithis, Y., Furon, T., Chum, O.: Efficient diffusion on region manifolds: recovering small objects with compact CNN representations. In: CVPR (2017)
16. Joulin, A., van der Maaten, L., Jabri, A., Vasilache, N.: Learning visual features from large weakly supervised data. In: Leibe, B., Matas, J., Sebe, N., Welling, M. (eds.) ECCV 2016. LNCS, vol. 9911, pp. 67–84. Springer, Cham (2016). https://doi.org/10.1007/978-3-319-46478-7_5
17. Kipf, T.N., Welling, M.: Semi-supervised classification with graph convolutional networks. In: ICLR (2017)
18. Lee, K.H., He, X., Zhang, L., Yang, L.: CleanNet: transfer learning for scalable image classifier training with label noise. In: CVPR (2018)
19. Li, Y., Yang, J., Song, Y., Cao, L., Luo, J., Li, L.J.: Learning from noisy labels with distillation. In: ICCV (2017)
20. Liu, T., Tao, D.: Classification with noisy labels by importance reweighting. IEEE Trans. PAMI 38(3), 447–461 (2015)
21. Liu, Y., et al.: Learning to propagate labels: transductive propagation network for few-shot learning. In: ICLR (2019)
22. Loshchilov, I., Hutter, F.: SGDR: Stochastic gradient descent with warm restarts. In: ICLR (2017)
23. Nair, V., Hinton, G.E.: Rectified linear units improve restricted Boltzmann machines. In: ICML (2010)
24. Natarajan, N., Dhillon, I.S., Ravikumar, P.K., Tewari, A.: Learning with noisy labels. In: NeurIPS (2013)
25. Patrini, G., Rozza, A., Krishna Menon, A., Nock, R., Qu, L.: Making deep neural networks robust to label noise: a loss correction approach. In: CVPR (2017)
26. Qi, H., Brown, M., Lowe, D.G.: Low-shot learning with imprinted weights. In: CVPR (2018)
27. Ravi, S., Larochelle, H.: Optimization as a model for few-shot learning. In: ICLR (2017)
28. Reed, S., Lee, H., Anguelov, D., Szegedy, C., Erhan, D., Rabinovich, A.: Training deep neural networks on noisy labels with bootstrapping. In: ICLR (2015)
29. Ren, M., et al.: Meta-learning for semi-supervised few-shot classification. In: ICLR (2018)
30. Ren, M., Zeng, W., Yang, B., Urtasun, R.: Learning to reweight examples for robust deep learning. In: ICML (2018)
31. Rohrbach, M., Ebert, S., Schiele, B.: Transfer learning in a transductive setting. In: NeurIPS (2013)
32. Russakovsky, O., et al.: ImageNet large scale visual recognition challenge. Int. J. Comput. Vision 115(3), 211–252 (2015)

33. Snell, J., Swersky, K., Zemel, R.: Prototypical networks for few-shot learning. In: NeurIPS (2017)
34. Sukhbaatar, S., Bruna, J., Paluri, M., Bourdev, L., Fergus, R.: Training convolutional networks with noisy labels. arXiv preprint arXiv:1406.2080 (2014)
35. Thomee, B., et al.: YFCC100M: the new data in multimedia research. Commun. ACM **59**(2), 64–73 (2016)
36. Veit, A., Alldrin, N., Chechik, G., Krasin, I., Gupta, A., Belongie, S.: Learning from noisy large-scale datasets with minimal supervision. In: CVPR (2017)
37. Vilalta, R., Drissi, Y.: A perspective view and survey of meta-learning. Artif. Intell. Rev. **18**(2), 77–95 (2002)
38. Vinyals, O., Blundell, C., Lillicrap, T., Wierstra, D., et al.: Matching networks for one shot learning. In: NeurIPS (2016)
39. Wang, X., Gupta, A.: Unsupervised learning of visual representations using videos. In: CVPR (2015)
40. Wang, Y., et al.: Iterative learning with open-set noisy labels. In: CVPR (2018)
41. Wang, Y.X., Girshick, R., Hebert, M., Hariharan, B.: Low-shot learning from imaginary data. In: CVPR (2018)
42. Weston, J., Ratle, F., Mobahi, H., Collobert, R.: Deep learning via semi-supervised embedding. In: Montavon, G., Orr, G.B., Müller, K.-R. (eds.) Neural Networks: Tricks of the Trade. LNCS, vol. 7700, pp. 639–655. Springer, Heidelberg (2012). https://doi.org/10.1007/978-3-642-35289-8_34
43. Wu, Z., Xiong, Y., Yu, S., Lin, D.: Unsupervised feature learning via non-parametric instance-level discrimination. In: CVPR (2018)
44. Zhou, B., Lapedriza, A., Khosla, A., Oliva, A., Torralba, A.: Places: a 10 million image database for scene recognition. IEEE Trans. PAMI **40**(6), 1452–1464 (2017)
45. Zhou, D., Bousquet, O., Lal, T.N., Weston, J., Schölkopf, B.: Learning with local and global consistency. In: NeurIPS (2003)
46. Zhou, D., Weston, J., Gretton, A., Bousquet, O., Schölkopf, B.: Ranking on data manifolds. In: NeurIPS (2003)

Object-and-Action Aware Model
for Visual Language Navigation

Yuankai Qi[1], Zizheng Pan[1], Shengping Zhang[2,3], Anton van den Hengel[1],
and Qi Wu[1(✉)]

[1] The University of Adelaide, Adelaide, Australia
qykshr@gmail.com, zizhpan@gmail.com,
{anton.vandenhengel,qi.wu01}@adelaide.edu.au
[2] Harbin Institute of Technology, Weihai, China
s.zhang@hit.edu.cn
[3] Aipixel Inc., Shenzhen, China

Abstract. Vision-and-Language Navigation (VLN) is unique in that it requires turning relatively general natural-language instructions into robot agent actions, on the basis of visible environments. This requires to extract value from two very different types of natural-language information. The first is object description (e.g., 'table', 'door'), each presenting as a tip for the agent to determine the next action by finding the item visible in the environment, and the second is action specification (e.g., 'go straight', 'turn left') which allows the robot to directly predict the next movements without relying on visual perceptions. However, most existing methods pay few attention to distinguish these information from each other during instruction encoding and mix together the matching between textual object/action encoding and visual perception/orientation features of candidate viewpoints. In this paper, we propose an Object-and-Action Aware Model (OAAM) that processes these two different forms of natural language based instruction separately. This enables each process to match object-centered/action-centered instruction to their own counterpart visual perception/action orientation flexibly. However, one side-issue caused by above solution is that an object mentioned in instructions may be observed in the direction of two or more candidate viewpoints, thus the OAAM may not predict the viewpoint on the shortest path as the next action. To handle this problem, we design a simple but effective path loss to penalize trajectories deviating from the ground truth path. Experimental results demonstrate the effectiveness of the proposed model and path loss, and the superiority of their combination with a 50% SPL score on the R2R dataset and a 40% CLS score on the R4R dataset in unseen environments, outperforming the previous state-of-the-art.

Keywords: Vision-and-Language Navigation · Modular network · Reward shaping

© Springer Nature Switzerland AG 2020
A. Vedaldi et al. (Eds.): ECCV 2020, LNCS 12355, pp. 303–317, 2020.
https://doi.org/10.1007/978-3-030-58607-2_18

Object-Aware (OA) Module: walk through the first doorway out the three - the one all the way to the left , walk straight through the doorway directly across from in , in front of the mirror . turn right , and stop before the long carpet .

Action-Aware (AA) Module: walk through the first doorway out the three - the one all the way to the left , walk straight through the doorway directly across from in , in front of the mirror . turn right , and stop before the long carpet .

Envdrop: walk through the first doorway out the three - the one all the way to the left , walk straight through the doorway directly across from in , in front of the mirror . turn right , and stop before the long carpet .

Target Action: 5   OA Module Prediction: 5   AA Module Prediction: 1   Final Prediction: 5   Envdrop Prediction: 4

Fig. 1. A snapshot of navigating action predicted by the proposed model and our baseline navigator EnvDrop [18]. Our model is able to more flexibly utilize object and action phrases thanks to the object-/action- aware modules. The numbered circles denote navigable viewpoints, and the blue one is our final decision. (Color figure online)

1   Introduction

Vision-and-language navigation (VLN) has attracted increasing attention, partly due to the prospect that the capability to interpret general spoken instructions might represent a significant step toward enabling intelligent robots [2,4,10,17]. The goal of VLN is for a robot to interpret a navigation instruction expressed in natural language, and carry out the associated actions. Typically this involves an agent navigating through a 3D photo-realistic simulator [2] to a goal location, which is not visible from the start point. The natural language instructions involved are of the form of 'Go left down the hallway toward the exit sign until the end. Turn right and go down the hallway. Go into the door on the left and stop by the table.'. The simulator in this scenario provides a set of panoramic images of a real environment, and a limited set of navigation choices that can be taken for each. Although it is related to other Vision-and-Language problems that have been extensively studied, VLN remains an open problem due to the difficulty of navigating general real environments, and the complexity of the instructions that humans give for doing so.

A range of approaches have been proposed to address the vision-and-language guided navigation problem [4,5,15–18,20,21]. For instance, to progressively process long navigation instructions, Ma et al. [16] propose a progress monitor network to identify the completed part of an instruction and the part associated with the next action. To expand training data, the Speaker-Follower (SF) [4] and EnvDrop [18] are proposed to generate new trajectories and 'unseen' scenes from seen ones, respectively. To mimic human behaviors when navigating, the Regretful model [17] introduces a backtracking mechanism into the navigation process to enable the agent to retrace its steps. In FAST model [13], a strategy that compromises between greedy search and beam search is developed to balance search efficiency against accuracy. However, all of these approaches entangle the encoding of object descriptions with that of action specifications, instead of processing them separately. Most action specifications (e.g., 'go straight ahead' or 'turn right'), closely relating to orientations[1] rather than visual perceptions of each navigable candidate viewpoint, are able to directly lead to the correct next action. By contrast, the object descriptions (e.g., 'the stairs' or 'the table') correspond to visual perceptions, instead of the orientations, in the visible scene. Therefore, the mixed encoding scheme may limit the similarity/grounding learning in the decoding phase between instructions and visual perceptions as well as orientations.

To address the above mentioned problem, we propose here an object-and-action aware model (OAAM) for robust navigation that reflects to exploit the important distinction. Specifically, we first utilize two learnable attention modules to highlight language relating to objects and actions within a given instruction. Then, the resulting attention maps guide an object-vision matching module and an action-orientation matching module, respectively. Finally, the action to be taken is identified by combining the outcomes of both modules using weights derived by an additional attention module taking the instruction and visual context as input. Figure 1 provides an example of the VLN process that demonstrates that our design enables the agent to more flexibly utilize object descriptions and action specifications, and finally leads to the correct prediction compared against the strong baseline navigator EnvDrop [18].

The proposed OAAM is able to improve the navigation success as demonstrated later in the experiment. However, its trajectory might not be the shortest because the focused object in the instruction may be observed in the direction of multiple candidate viewpoints. To handle this problem, we design a simple but effective path loss to encourage the agent to stay on the shortest path instead of merely picking alternative viewpoints containing the instruction mentioned object. In particular, the proposed path loss is based on distances calculated at each agent step to its nearest viewpoint on the ground-truth path. Note that this differs from the Coverage weighted by Length Score (CLS) award [12] that computes a normalised score by inversely finding the nearest viewpoint in the agent trajectory to each viewpoint on the ground-truth path. Experimental results show that this loss aids the OAAM to generalise in unseen scenarios.

The main contributions of this work are summarized as follows:

1. We propose an object-and-action aware model, which better reflects the nature of the associated natural language instructions and responds more flexibly.
2. We design a path loss that encourages the agent to closely follow navigation instructions.

---

[1] 'orientation' means the encoding of the angle that an agent should rotate in order to find a navigable viewpoint from its front direction as in [13, 16, 17].

3. Extensive experimental results demonstrate the effectiveness of the proposed method and set new state-of-the-art on the R4R dataset with a CLS score of 0.40.

2 Related Work

Vision-and-Language Navigation. Numerous methods have been proposed to address the VLN problem. Most of them employ the CNN-LSTM architecture with attention mechanism to first encode instructions and then decode the embedding to a series of actions. Together with the proposing of the VLN task, Anderson et al. [2] develop the teacher-forcing and student-forcing training strategy. The former equips the network with basic ability for navigating using ground truth action at each step, while the latter mimics the test scenarios, where the agent may predict wrong actions, by sampling actions instead of using ground truth actions. Deep learning based methods always benefit from massive training data. To generate more training data, Fried et al. [4] propose a speaker model to synthesize new instructions for randomly selected robot trajectories. By contrast, Tan et al. [18] augment the training data by additionally removing objects from the original training data to generate new 'unseen' environments. To further enhance the generalization ability, they also propose to train the model using both imitation learning and reinforcement learning so as to take advantage of both off-policy and on-policy optimization. Not all chunks of an instruction are useful to predict the next action. Ma et al. [16] propose a progress monitor to locate the completed sub-instructions and to be aware of the ones for predicting the next action. Another way to improve navigation success is to equip the agent with backtracking. In [17], Ma et al.propose to treat the navigation as a graph search problem and predict to move forward or roll back to a previous viewpoint. In [13], each passed viewpoint is viewed as a goal candidate, and the final decision is the viewpoint with the highest local and global matching score.

However, the above mentioned methods neglect to distinguish the object descriptions and the action specifications within the focused sub-instruction. This may limit the learning of matching between object-/action-centered instructions and their counterpart visual perceptions/orientations. To address this problem, we propose to separately learn the object attention and action attention, and so the learning of object-vision matching and action-orientation matching.

Modular Language Process Networks. Modular language decomposition has been widely adopted in question answering [3], visual reasoning [7], referring expression comprehension [9,22], etc. Most methods are based on hard parsers or learned parsers. For example, Andreas et al. [3] decompose each question into a sequence of modular sub-problems with the help of an fixed off-the-shelf syntactic parsers. Such hard parsers are not able to analyse semantic relationships between entities. By contrast, the learned parses can be flexibly designed according to parsing purposes. For instance, Hu et al. [9] design a attention-based network to learn to decompose expressions into (Subject, Relationship, Object) triplets, which facilitates to ground language to visual regions. In [22],

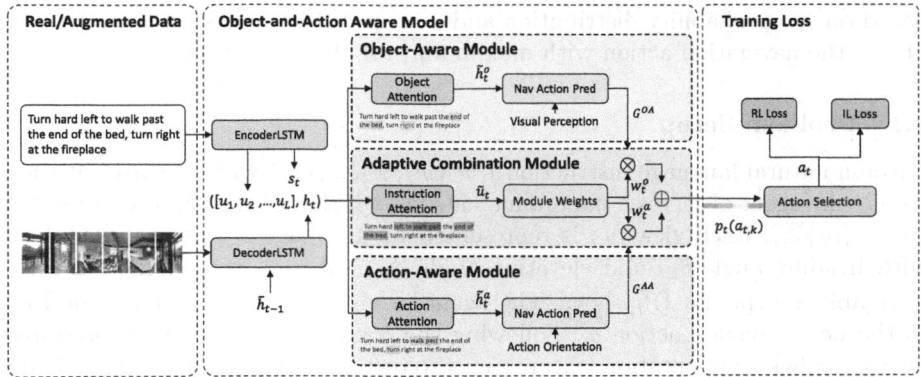

Fig. 2. Main steps of the proposed object-and-action aware model, which consists of three modules: the object-aware module that predicts the next action based on object-centered instructions and visual perceptions; the action-aware module that predicts the next action based on action-centered instructions and orientations of candidate viewpoints; and the adaptive combination module that predicts weights to combine predictions obtained by the other two modules.

Yu *et al.* propose the (Subject, Location, Relationship) triplet to additionally taking object position into consideration.

Inspired by the above modular decomposition mechanism, we propose to decompose an instruction into object and action components for the VLN task because two fundamental different type of information of candidate viewpoints are used to match to instructions, namely visual perceptions and orientations. Differ from the above mentioned methods, our modular decomposition model takes navigation progress into consideration, i.e., the decomposition should take place on a certain part of the instruction, which is closely related to the current agent location, instead of the whole instruction.

3   Method

In this section, we first describe the symbols that will be used later and briefly introduce the baseline navigator, EnvDrop [18], to put our method into a proper context. EnvDrop is adopted due to its good performance. Then, we detail the proposed object-and-action aware model (OAAM).

Figure 2 shows the pipeline of the proposed method in training phase. An instruction is first encoded by a bi-direction LSTM. Then our OAAM model decomposes the instruction encoding into object- and action-centered representations using two attention-based modules. These representations are further used to predict navigation actions via matching to visual perceptions and orientations, respectively. The OAAM model also predicts combination weights to compute the final navigation action probability distribution over candidate viewpoints. Lastly, imitation learning and reinforcement learning losses are calculated based on the probability distribution and a proposed path loss. In the inference phase, the navigation action with maximum probability is selected.

3.1   Problem Setup

Given a natural language instruction $I = \{w_1, w_2, ..., w_L\}$ with L words, at each step t, the agent observes a panoramic view o_t, which contains 36 discrete single views $\{o_t\}_{i=1}^{36}$. Each view $o_{t,i}$ is represented by an image $v_{t,i}$ at an orientation with heading angle $\theta_{t,i}$ and elevation angle $\phi_{t,i}$. At each step t, there are N_t navigable viewpoints $\{P_{t,k}\}_{k=1}^{N_t}$. The agent needs to select one viewpoint $P_{t,k}$ as the next navigate action a_t. Following the common practice, each navigable viewpoint has an orientation feature $n_{t,k} = (cos\theta_{t,k}, sin\theta_{t,k}, cos\phi_{t,k}, sin\phi_{t,k})$ and a visual feature $m_{t,k} = ResNet(v_{t,k})$.

3.2   Baseline–EnvDrop

Recent works show that data augmentation is able to significantly improve the generalization ability in unseen environment [4,18]. We make use of this strategy by adopting EnvDrop [18] as our baseline, which simultaneously benefits from the back translation technique [4] to generate new (trajectory, instruction) pairs in existing environments and from its global dropout technique to generate new environments.

EnvDrop first uses a bidirectional LSTM to encode instruction I:

$$[u_1, u_2, ..., u_L] = \text{Bi-LSTM}(e_1, ..., e_L) \tag{1}$$

where $e_j = \text{embedding}(w_j)$ is the embedded j-th word in the instruction, and u_j is the feature containing context information for the j-th word. Then, a soft attention is imposed on visual feature m_t to get attentive feature $\tilde{f}_t = \Sigma_i \alpha_{t,i} m_{t,i}$, where $\alpha_{t,i} = \text{softmax}_i(m_{t,i}^\top W_F \tilde{h}_{t-1})$. The concatenation of $\tilde{f}_t$ and the previous action embedding $\tilde{a}_{t-1}$ is fed into the decoder LSTM:

$$h_t = \text{LSTM\_Decoder}([\tilde{f}_t; \tilde{a}_{t-1}], \tilde{h}_{t-1}). \tag{2}$$

The decoder input also includes the previous instruction-aware hidden output $\tilde{h}_{t-1}$, which is updated based on the attentive instruction feature $\tilde{u}_t$ and the newly obtained h_t:

$$\tilde{h}_t = \tanh(W_L[\tilde{u}_t; h_t]), \tag{3}$$

$$\tilde{u}_t = \Sigma_j \beta_{t,j} u_j, \tag{4}$$

where $\beta_{t,j} = \text{softmax}_j(u_j^\top W_I h_t)$, and W_L is trainable parameter. Finally, EnvDrop predicts navigation action by selecting a navigable view with the biggest probability

$$a_t^* = \arg\max_k P(a_{t,k}), \tag{5}$$

where $P(a_{t,k}) = \text{softmax}_k([m_{t,k}; n_{t,k}]^\top W_B \tilde{h}_t)$.

Different from EnvDrop, our navigator calculates the probability $P(a_{t,k})$ using the proposed object-and-action aware model as detailed in the next section.

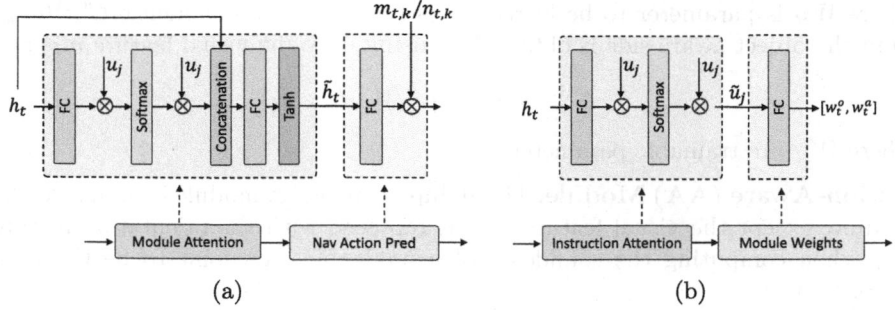

Fig. 3. Pipeline and configuration of the proposed object-/action-aware module (a) and the adaptive combination module (b).

3.3 Object-and-Action Aware Model

To disentangle the encoding of object- and action-related instruction, as well as the matching to their counterpart visual perceptions and orientations of candidate viewpoints, we propose the object-and-action aware model (OAAM). OAAM consists of three key modules: an object-aware (OA) module that is aware of object-related instruction and predicts action using visual perceptions; an action-aware (AA) module that is aware of action-related instruction and predicts action using orientations of candidate viewpoints; and an adaptive combination module that learns weights to combine the action predictions from the other two modules based on the attentive instructions with the consideration of the current panoramic views.

Object-Aware (OA) Module. Figure 3(a) shows the pipeline and configuration of the proposed OA module. Different from the subject/object module in referring expression comprehension methods, such as [9,22], which highlight all objects in an expression, our OA module is designed to highlight object phrase *just for the next navigation step* instead of *all objects* in an instruction. This is essential for the VLN task because the long instruction should be carried out step-by-step, which indicates objects not related to the current step may be noise and mislead the action predicting. To this end, our OA module calculates the attentive object feature $\tilde{u}_t^o$ by taking the decoder hidden state h_t as input for navigation progress reference:

$$\gamma_{t,j} = \text{softmax}_j(u_j^\top W_O h_t), \tag{6}$$

$$\tilde{u}_t^o = \Sigma_j \gamma_{t,j} u_j, \tag{7}$$

where W_O is learnable parameters. Then, the object-aware hidden output $\tilde{h}_t^o$ related to the current navigation is computed via

$$\tilde{h}_t^o = \tanh(W_P[\tilde{u}_t^o; h_t]), \tag{8}$$

where W_P is parameter to be learned. Lastly, the action confidence $G^{OA}(a_{t,k})$ from the object-aware side is obtained by using only the visual feature $m_{t,k}$:

$$G^{OA}(a_{t,k}) = m_{t,k}^\top W_H \tilde{h}_t^o, \tag{9}$$

where W_H are trainable parameters.

Action-Aware (AA) Module. The architecture of AA module is similar to OA module, except the visual feature $m_{t,k}$ is replaced with the orientation feature $n_{t,k}$ when computing the confidence of a navigable viewpoint to be the next action:

$$\delta_{t,j} = \text{softmax}_j(u_j^\top W_A h_t) \tag{10}$$

$$\tilde{u}_t^a = \Sigma_j \delta_{t,j} u_j \tag{11}$$

$$\tilde{h}_t^a = \tanh(W_K[\tilde{u}_t^a; h_t]) \tag{12}$$

$$G^{AA}(a_{t,k}) = n_{t,k}^\top W_F \tilde{h}_t^a, \tag{13}$$

where $\delta_{t,j}$ is the action attention on j-th word, $\tilde{h}_t^a$ is action-aware hidden state, and W_A, W_K, W_F are trainable parameters. Both $\delta_{t,j}$ and $\tilde{h}_t^a$ have taken the navigation progress into consideration.

Adaptive Combination Module. Figure 3(b) shows the pipeline and configuration of the proposed adaptive combination module. The final probability $P(a_{t,k})$ of navigable view k is a softmax of weighted sum of the object-aware confidence $G^{OA}(a_{t,k})$ and action-aware probability $G^{AA}(a_{t,k})$:

$$P(a_{t,k}) = \text{softmax}([G^{OA}(a_{t,k}); G^{AA}(a_{t,k})]w_t), \tag{14}$$

where w_t is a predicted weight vector. w_t should vary as the navigation goes because the importance of an object description and an action specification may change at different processing point of the instruction. Thus, to adaptively combine $G^{OA}(a_{t,k})$ and $G^{AA}(a_{t,k})$ in terms of the processing state, we utilize a trainable layer to predict weights $w_t = W_T \tilde{u}_t$, where W_T is trainable parameter, $\tilde{u}_t$ is the vision-aware attentive instruction feature.

3.4   Training Loss

Following the training process of our baseline [18], the model is trained using both imitation learning (IL) and reinforcement learning (RL) with original training data and augmented data. In addition to the losses in the baseline, we introduce a Nearest Point Loss (NPL) to encourage the agent to stay on ground-truth paths. NPL is based on the distance to the nearest viewpoint on the ground-truth path (see Fig. 4(b))

$$\mathcal{L}^{NP} = \sum_t \log(p_t(a_t)) * D_t^{NP}, \tag{15}$$

where $D_t^{NP} = \min_{P_i \in Q} d(P_t, P_i)$, $d(P_t, P_i)$ is the shortest trajectory distance between the current viewpoint P_t and each viewpoint P_i on the ground truth path, Q is the set of viewpoints on the ground-truth path. If an agent stays on the ground-truth path, D_t^{NP} would be zero; otherwise, the farther the larger.

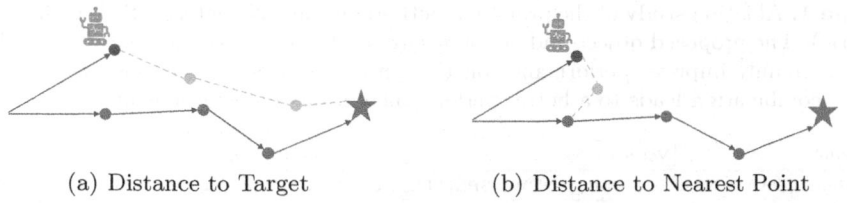

(a) Distance to Target   (b) Distance to Nearest Point

Fig. 4. Illustration of distance to target (a) and distance to nearest point(b). The trajectory of the agent is in red and the ground-truth path is in blue. The star indicates the target viewpoint. The brown dot line indicates the shortest trajectory length. (Color figure online)

4   Experiments

4.1   Dataset and Implementations

Dataset. Experiments are conducted on the widely used indoor R2R [2] and the R4R [12] VLN datasets. R2R dataset consists of train/seen validation/unseen validation/test splits, involving 7,189 paths with 21,567 human annotated instructions with an average length of 29 words. In particular, these four splits contains 14,025/1,020/4,173/2,349 instructions, respectively. R4R aims to evaluate whether an agent is able to follow instructions by concatenating several trajectories and thus instructions of R2R (the shortest path is therefore no longer the ground-truth path) into long ones. Note that the R4R dataset only contains train/seen validation/unseen validation splits.

Implementation Details. Following the common practice, we use the precomputed ResNet [6] feature to represent percepted images. We adopt the same training strategy as our baseline [18]: First, we train the agent using real data (i.e., the training split); Then, we train the agent using augmented data generated by the speaker and environment dropout techniques. We implement the proposed method with PyTorch, and all the experiments are carried out on NVIDIA GeForce RTX 2080 Ti.

4.2   Evaluation Metrics

To evaluate the proposed method on R2R, we adopt four metrics from [1,2]: Success Rate (SR), Trajectory Length (TL), Oracle Success Rate (OSR), and Success rate weighted by Path Length (SPL). Among the four metrics, SPL is the main metric because it emphasizes the trade-off between SR and TL, which is also a recommended primary measure of navigation performance by the official VLN Challenge [1]. To measure the performance on R4R, we additionally adopt the Coverage weighted by Length Score (CLS) metric as recommended by the builder of this dataset [12] and the Success weighted by normalized Dynamic Time Warping (SDTW) metric as recommended in [11]. These two metrics focus on navigation fidelity using the ground-truth path as reference.

Table 1. Ablation study of the proposed method on the R2R dataset (SPL is the main metric). The proposed object-and-action aware model (OAAM) and nearest point loss (NPL) mainly improve performance on the Unseen and Seen scenarios, respectively. Their combination leads to a better performance in unseen environments.

Model			Val Seen						Val Unseen					
Baseline	OAAM	NPL	SR↑	OSR↑	SDTW↑	SPL↑	TL↓	CLS↑	SR↑	OSR↑	SDTW↑	SPL↑	TL↓	CLS↑
✓			0.63	0.70	0.53	0.60	10.17	0.70	0.50	0.57	0.37	0.47	9.27	0.60
✓	✓		0.65	0.72	0.53	0.62	10.21	0.71	0.51	0.59	0.37	0.47	10.05	0.60
✓		✓	0.68	0.74	0.57	0.66	10.06	0.73	0.48	0.54	0.35	0.45	9.04	0.60
✓	✓	✓	0.65	0.73	0.53	0.62	10.20	0.73	0.54	0.61	0.39	0.50	9.95	0.61

4.3 Ablation Study

We conduct the ablation study to find out the effectiveness of the proposed object-and-action aware model (OAAM) and the nearest point loss (NPL). The results are presented in Table 1. The results show that: (I) Both OAAM and NPL improve the performance on the Val Seen split with about 2% and 4% increase in SPL, respectively. (II) The phenomenon on Val Unseen is a bit complicated. When OAAM or NPL works alone with the baseline, OAAM brings about 1% improvement in SR and NPL harms the SR about 2%. When OAAM and NPL work together, the performance is significantly improved about 4% in SR and 3% in SPL. This can be attributed to that NPL is able to help OAAM to find viewpoints on the ground-truth path and therefore improves the SR as well as shortens the trajectory length compared to the case that they work separately. Overall, both OAAM and NPL facilitate our method to achieve better performance, especially in the unseen scenario.

We further study the importance of the object-aware (OA) module and the action-aware (AA) module within the trained OAAM. As these two sub-modules contribute to the final navigation decision via a weighted sum (14), we test the performance of each module by setting its weight to 1 and the other weight to 0. The results are presented in Table 2. There is about 20% performance drop in SR when OA or AA works alone. This indicates that both modules contribute to the final performance and the adaptive combination module plays a crucial role (also see visualized samples in Fig. 5 and 6). Furthermore, the AA module performs consistently better than the object-aware module on ValSeen, ValUnSeen, and Test splits, in terms of SPL, SR, or OSR. For example, when AA module is removed, the SR is about 20% lower than that when OA module is removed on the Unseen split. This indicates the AA module is more generalizable than the OA, which is roughly consistent with the claim that visual feature may hurt models in unseen environments [8]. Fortunately, when OA and AA are adaptively combined, a much better performance is achieved (10% ~ 28% improvement in SPL on the Val Unseen split). Additionally, we calculate the mean of w_t of all steps on ValSeen and ValUnseen. Results show that OA and AA are asigned 0.18 and 0.82 on average, respectively. This also reflects AA contributes more to the final results. Lastly, we make a try to conduct quantitative evaluation of these

Table 2. Comparison of object-aware module (OA) and action-aware module (AA) on the R2R dataset. 'w/o' denotes to remove the module from the full model. The AA module contributes more than the OA module.

Model	Val Seen						Val Unseen					
	SR↑	OSR↑	SDTW↑	SPL↑	TL↓	CLS↑	SR↑	OSR↑	SDTW↑	SPL↑	TL↓	CLS↑
Full model	0.65	0.73	0.53	0.62	10.20	0.73	0.54	0.61	0.39	0.50	9.95	0.61
w/o AA module	0.42	0.52	0.31	0.39	9.26	0.59	0.26	0.34	0.15	0.22	8.86	0.46
w/o OA module	0.45	0.53	0.32	0.42	10.63	0.56	0.44	0.52	0.30	0.40	10.46	0.54

two modules based on NLTK tags, although it is not perfect. An attention is considered success if the top3 words attended by OA contain nouns (verbs for AA). OA and AA achieve accuracy of about 80% and 75% on average, respectively. This at some extent indicates improvement room for these modules.

4.4 Comparison to State-of-the-Art Navigators

In this section, we compare our model against six state-of-the-art navigating methods, including FAST [13], RCM [19], EnvDrop [18], Speaker-Follower (SF) [4], RegretAgent (RA) [17], and Self-Monitor (SM) [16]. Results on the R2R and R4R datasets are presented in Table 3 and 4, respectively.

Table 3. Comparison against several state-of-the-art VLN methods on the R2R dataset. SPL is the main metric. The best three results are highlighted in red, green, and blue fonts, respectively.

Model	Val Seen				Val Unseen				Test			
	SR↑	OSR↑	SPL↑	TL↓	SR↑	OSR↑	SPL↑	TL↓	SR↑	OSR↑	SPL↑	TL↓
SF [4]	0.67	0.74	0.61	11.73	0.35	0.45	0.28	14.56	0.35	0.44	0.28	14.82
SM [16]	0.70	0.80	0.61	12.90	0.43	0.54	0.29	17.09	0.48	0.59	0.35	18.04
RA [17]	0.69	0.77	0.63	-	0.50	0.59	0.41	-	0.48	0.56	0.40	13.69
RCM [19]	0.67	0.75	-	10.65	0.43	0.50	-	11.46	0.43	0.50	0.38	11.97
FAST [13]	0.70	0.80	0.64	12.34	0.56	0.67	0.44	20.45	0.54	0.64	0.41	22.08
EnvDrop [18]	0.63	0.70	0.60	10.17	0.50	0.57	0.47	9.27	0.50	0.57	0.47	9.70
Ours	0.65	0.73	0.62	10.20	0.54	0.61	0.50	9.95	0.53	0.61	0.50	10.40

Table 4. Results on the R4R dataset. CLS is the main metric. The best three results are highlighted in red, green, and blue fonts, respectively.

Model	Val Seen					Val Unseen				
	SR↑	SDTW↑	SPL↑	TL↓	CLS↑	SR↑	SDTW↑	SPL↑	TL↓	CLS↑
SF [4]	0.52	-	0.37	15.40	0.46	0.24	-	0.12	19.90	0.30
RCM goal-oriented [12]	0.56	-	0.32	24.50	0.40	0.29	-	0.10	32.50	0.20
RCM fidelity-oriented [12]	0.53	-	0.31	18.80	0.55	0.26	-	0.08	28.50	0.35
PTA high-level [14]	0.58	0.41	0.39	16.50	0.60	0.24	0.10	0.10	17.70	0.37
EnvDrop [18]	0.52	0.27	0.41	19.85	0.53	0.29	0.09	0.18	26.97	0.34
Ours	0.56	0.32	0.49	11.75	0.54	0.31	0.11	0.23	13.80	0.40

As shown in Table 3, our model achieves the best performance on both the Val UnSeen and Test splits in terms of the main evaluation metric, SPL, which is up to 50%. As analysed in the ablation study, the performance of our model is the result of both the OAAM and the NPL loss. We also observe that on the Val Seen split, our model ranks third falling behind FAST and RA. This indicates that our model may not fit the training data as well as FAST and RA, and there

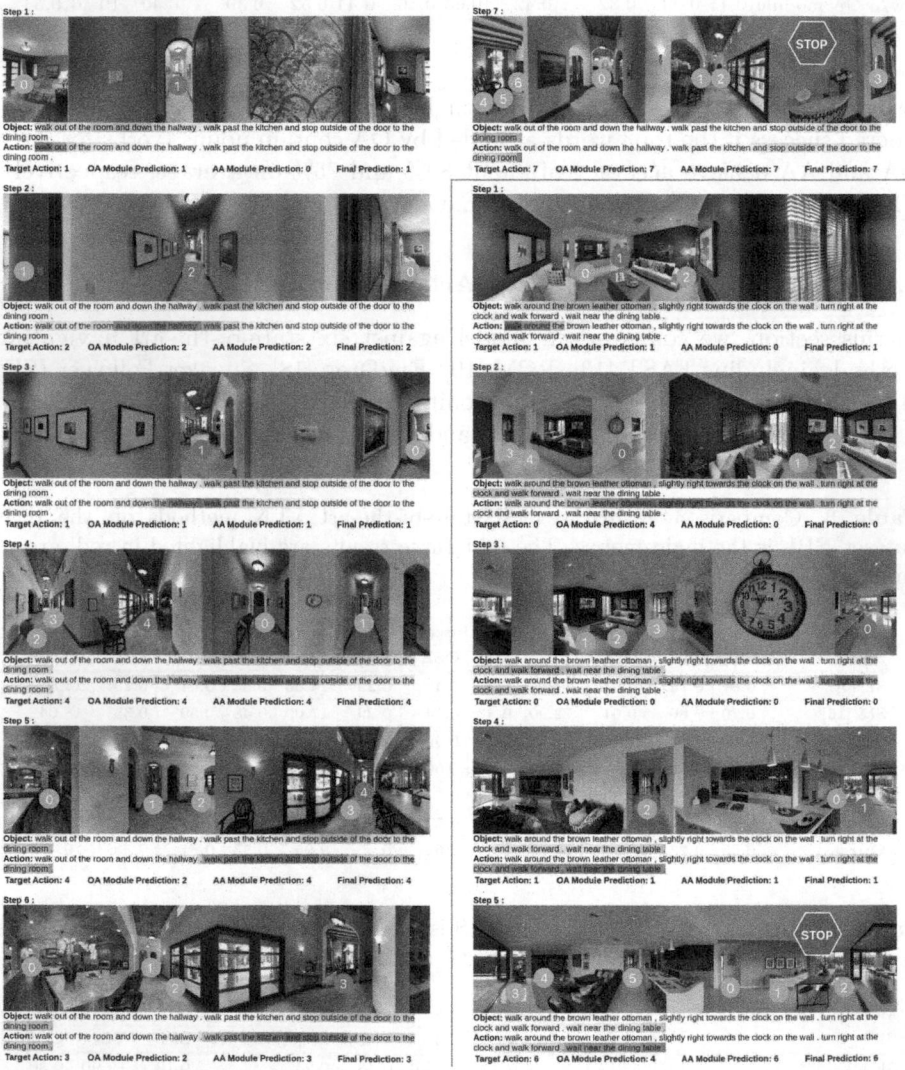

Fig. 5. Navigation samples of the proposed method in two unseen environments. The dark or light color on the instruction denotes the relative attention value (the darker the larger). The numbered circles denote navigable viewpoints, and the blue ones denote the final decision. (Color figure online)

are more information can be learned from the training data for our model. We leave this for the future exploration.

Table 4 shows the result on the R4R dataset, where CLS is the recommended metric [12]. On one side, the proposed method performs consistently better than our baseline, namely Envdrop, with up to 6% improvement in CLS on the unseen split. On the other side, the proposed method achieves the best performance with a 0.40 CLS score in unseen environments, which is 3% higher than the

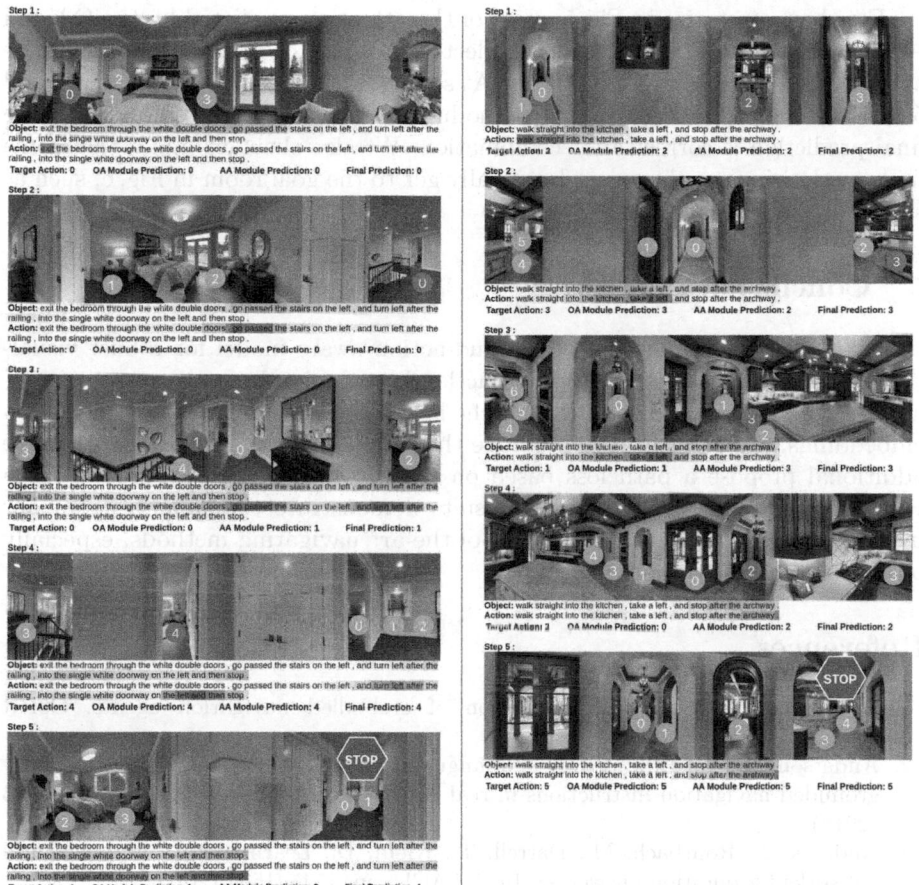

Fig. 6. Two more navigation samples of the proposed method in unseen environments. On the left panel, at step 3, our model predicts an incorrect action but gets to the goal room in end. It is worth noting that at step 5, both OA and AA modules give wrong prediction, but after combination our model predicts the correct action. On the right panel, the final decision at each step is correct, but we could observe that the OA or AA module not always gives correct prediction, such as at step 2 and step 3. These indicate that all the OA and AA modules as well as the adaptive combination module are crucial to the final success.

second best and thus set the new SoTA. Similar to the phenomenon on the R2R dataset, we also observe that the proposed model ranks top three in the seen environments, which indicates more information could be learned.

4.5 Qualitative Results

In this section, we visualize several navigation process at each step in Fig. 5 and Fig. 6, including key information, such as attention distribution and navigation decision.

For the trajectories in Fig. 5, most of the attention predicted by the OA and AA modules are able to correctly reflect the object or action that should be considered to make correct decisions. At some midway steps, such as step 1 and 5 on the left panel of Fig. 5, only one module gives the correct prediction but the final prediction is correct after combination. We also show examples that some midway decisions are incorrect but finally get to the goal room in Fig. 6, such as step 3 in the left panel.

5   Conclusion

In this paper, we propose an object-and-action aware model for robust visual-and-language navigation. Object and action information in instructions are separately highlighted, and are then matched to visual perceptions and orientation embeddings, respectively. To encourage the robot agent to stay on the path, we additional propose a path loss based on the distance to nearest ground-truth viewpoint. Extensive experimental results demonstrate the superiority of our model compared against several state-of-the-art navigating methods, especially on the unseen test scenarios.

References

1. Anderson, P., et al.: On evaluation of embodied navigation agents. CoRR abs/1807.06757 (2018)
2. Anderson, P., et al.: Vision-and-language navigation: interpreting visually-grounded navigation instructions in real environments. In: CVPR, pp. 3674–3683 (2018)
3. Andreas, J., Rohrbach, M., Darrell, T., Klein, D.: Learning to compose neural networks for question answering. In: NAACL, pp. 1545–1554 (2016)
4. Fried, D., et al.: Speaker-follower models for vision-and-language navigation. In: NeurIPS, pp. 3318–3329 (2018)
5. Fu, T., Wang, X., Peterson, M., Grafton, S., Eckstein, M.P., Wang, W.Y.: Counterfactual vision-and-language navigation via adversarial path sampling. CoRR abs/1911.07308 (2019)
6. He, K., Zhang, X., Ren, S., Sun, J.: Deep residual learning for image recognition. In: CVPR, pp. 770–778 (2016)
7. Hu, R., Andreas, J., Rohrbach, M., Darrell, T., Saenko, K.: Learning to reason: end-to-end module networks for visual question answering. In: ICCV, pp. 804–813 (2017)

8. Hu, R., Fried, D., Rohrbach, A., Klein, D., Darrell, T., Saenko, K.: Are you looking? Grounding to multiple modalities in vision-and-language navigation. In: Proceedings of the 57th Conference of the Association for Computational Linguistics, Long Papers, ACL 2019, Florence, Italy, 28 July–2 August 2019, vol. 1, pp. 6551–6557 (2019)

9. Hu, R., Rohrbach, M., Andreas, J., Darrell, T., Saenko, K.: Modeling relationships in referential expressions with compositional modular networks. In: CVPR, pp. 4418–4427 (2017)

10. Huang, H., et al.: Transferable representation learning in vision-and-language navigation. In: ICCV, pp. 7403–7412 (2019)

11. Ilharco, G., Jain, V., Ku, A., Ie, E., Baldridge, J.: General evaluation for instruction conditioned navigation using dynamic time warping. In: Visually Grounded Interaction and Language (ViGIL), NeurIPS 2019 Workshop, Vancouver, Canada, 13 December 2019 (2019)

12. Jain, V., Magalhães, G., Ku, A., Vaswani, A., Ie, E., Baldridge, J.: Stay on the path: instruction fidelity in vision-and-language navigation. In: ACL, pp. 1862–1872 (2019)

13. Ke, L., et al.: Tactical rewind: self-correction via backtracking in vision-and-language navigation. In: CVPR, pp. 6741–6749 (2019)

14. Landi, F., Baraldi, L., Cornia, M., Corsini, M., Cucchiara, R.: Perceive, transform, and act: multi-modal attention networks for vision-and-language navigation. CoRR abs/1911.12377 (2019)

15. Li, X., et al.: Robust navigation with language pretraining and stochastic sampling. In: Inui, K., Jiang, J., Ng, V., Wan, X. (eds.) EMNLP, pp. 1494–1499 (2019)

16. Ma, C.Y., et al.: Self-monitoring navigation agent via auxiliary progress estimation. In: ICLR (2019)

17. Ma, C., Wu, Z., AlRegib, G., Xiong, C., Kira, Z.: The regretful agent: heuristic-aided navigation through progress estimation. In: CVPR, pp. 6732–6740 (2019)

18. Tan, H., Yu, L., Bansal, M.: Learning to navigate unseen environments: back translation with environmental dropout. In: NAACL, pp. 2610–2621 (2019)

19. Wang, X., et al.: Reinforced cross-modal matching and self-supervised imitation learning for vision-language navigation. In: CVPR, pp. 6629–6638 (2019)

20. Wang, X., Jain, V., Ie, E., Wang, W.Y., Kozareva, Z., Ravi, S.: Environment-agnostic multitask learning for natural language grounded navigation. CoRR abs/2003.00443 (2020)

21. Wang, X., Xiong, W., Wang, H., Wang, W.Y.: Look before you leap: bridging model-free and model-based reinforcement learning for planned-ahead vision-and-language navigation. In: Ferrari, V., Hebert, M., Sminchisescu, C., Weiss, Y. (eds.) ECCV 2018. LNCS, vol. 11220, pp. 38–55. Springer, Cham (2018). https://doi.org/10.1007/978-3-030-01270-0_3

22. Yu, L., et al.: MattNet: modular attention network for referring expression comprehension. In: CVPR, pp. 1307–1315 (2018)

A Comprehensive Study of Weight Sharing in Graph Networks for 3D Human Pose Estimation

Kenkun Liu[1], Rongqi Ding[2], Zhiming Zou[1], Le Wang[3], and Wei Tang[1(✉)]

[1] University of Illinois at Chicago, Chicago, IL, USA
{kliu44,zzou6,tangw}@uic.edu
[2] Northwestern University, Evanston, IL, USA
rongqiding2020@u.northwestern.edu
[3] Xi'an Jiaotong University, Xi'an, Shaanxi, People's Republic of China
lewang@xjtu.edu.cn

Abstract. Graph convolutional networks (GCNs) have been applied to 3D human pose estimation (HPE) from 2D body joint detections and have shown encouraging performance. One limitation of the vanilla graph convolution is that it models the relationships between neighboring nodes via a shared weight matrix. This is suboptimal for articulated body modeling as the relations between different body joints are different. The objective of this paper is to have a comprehensive and systematic study of weight sharing in GCNs for 3D HPE. We first show there are two different ways to interpret a GCN depending on whether feature transformation occurs before or after feature aggregation. These two interpretations lead to five different weight sharing methods, and three more variants can be derived by decoupling the self-connections with other edges. We conduct extensive ablation study on these weight sharing methods under controlled settings and obtain new conclusions that will benefit the community.

1 Introduction

The task of 3D human pose estimation (HPE) means to predict the locations of human body joints in the camera coordinate system from a single RGB image. It has attracted a lot of attention in recent years [5,8,19,22,26,30,37,43] due to its broad applications in human-computer interaction, action recognition and robotics. 3D HPE is an ill-posed problem since multiple 3D poses may explain the same 2D projection in the image space. Fortunately, this ambiguity could be largely resolved as the human body is a highly structured object [21,40].

K. Liu and R. Ding—The first two authors contributed equally to this work.

Electronic supplementary material The online version of this chapter (https://doi.org/10.1007/978-3-030-58607-2_19) contains supplementary material, which is available to authorized users.

© Springer Nature Switzerland AG 2020
A. Vedaldi et al. (Eds.): ECCV 2020, LNCS 12355, pp. 318–334, 2020.
https://doi.org/10.1007/978-3-030-58607-2_19

Previous research on 3D HPE can be divided into two streams. The first one is to regress the 3D human pose directly from the input image [25,35]. Early work [1,41] rely on handcrafted features but they are prone to fail in case of depth ambiguity, rare viewpoints and occlusion. Recent approaches [25,31,32, 39,44] exploit convolutional neural networks (CNNs) to learn powerful visual representations from large-scale image data [3,15] and significantly improve the regression accuracy. The second stream follows a two-stage pipeline, i.e., 2D human pose detection [6,23,33,34] followed by 2D-to-3D pose lifting [19,21,40]. For example, Martinez et al. [21] use a fully connected network to regress the 3D body joint locations from the output of an off-the-shelf 2D pose detector. This simple baseline is effective and outperforms state-of-the-art one-stage methods.

Recently graph convolutional networks (GCNs) [17,42] have been applied to solve the 2D-to-3D pose lifting problem [5,8,40]. They generalize CNNs by performing convolutions on graph data. As illustrated in Fig. 1, the articulated body skeleton naturally forms a graph wherein body joints and bones respectively correspond to the nodes and edges. A GCN then repeatedly transforms and aggregates features of neighboring body joints and learns their relational patterns which are critical to resolve the depth ambiguity. Compared with a fully connected network [21], a GCN not only learns a compact representation defined on graph nodes but also explicitly captures their structural relationships.

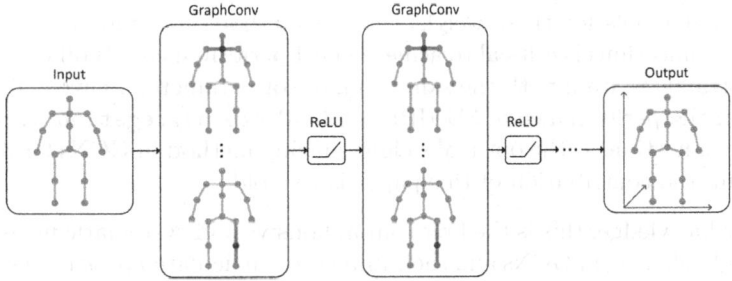

Fig. 1. Illustration of a graph convolutional network (GCN) for 3D human pose estimation. The input is the 2D body joint locations predicted by an off-the-shelf 2D pose detector. A GCN repeatedly transforms and aggregates features of neighboring body joints to learn an increasingly powerful representation. The output 3D pose is predicted by the last layer

One limitation of the vanilla GCN, which was originlly proposed for graph or node classification, is that it shares a feature transformation for each node within a graph convolutional layer. While weight sharing leads to a more compact model and promotes its generalization ability, it is suboptimal for articulated body modeling. On one hand, the relations between different body joints are different. For example, the ankles of a standing, walking or sitting person are always below their knees while the relational pattern between wrists and elbows are more complex. On the other hand, it is actually the feature transformation that captures the relations between each node and their neighboring nodes. Thus, this kind of weight sharing can prevent the GCN from learning diverse models specific to different relations and therefore adversely affect 3D HPE.

The objective of this paper is to have a comprehensive and systematic study of weight sharing in GCNs for 3D HPE. Specifically, we consider five different weight sharing strategies: `full-sharing`, `pre-aggregation`, `post-aggregation`, `convolution-style` and `no-sharing`. `Full-sharing` corresponds to the vanilla graph convolution. We show that there are two ways to interpret the graph convolution depending on whether the feature transformation occurs before or after features are aggregated from the neighborhood of each node. `Pre-aggregation` and `post-aggregation` are obtained by unsharing the feature transformations for each node in these two equivalent forms respectively. `Convolution-style` is motivated by the convolution operation used in CNNs, but the displacement between two entities are defined on the graph. `No-sharing` is on the other extreme of `full-sharing` as it defines a different feature transformation between any two nodes. Furthermore, we notice that the affinity matrix used in a GCN usually includes self-connections, i.e., edges connecting each node and itself. Since they do not model relations between different nodes, we consider decoupling them with the edges connecting each node to their neighbors. This leads to three more variants of `full-sharing`, `pre-aggregation` and `post-aggregation`. After conducting extensive ablation study by controlling the number of parameters, computational complexity and number of channels for these weight sharing methods, we find that (1) decoupling self-connections is critical to achieve good performance, (2) different weight sharing strategies, even with the same number of parameters, have a significant impact on the performance of 3D HPE, and (3) `pre-aggregation` with decoupled self-connections is the optimal weight sharing method in GCNs for 3D HPE.

In sum, the contribution of this paper is twofold.

– To our knowledge, this is the first comprehensive and systematic investigation of weight sharing in GCNs and their impact on articulated pose regression. We study five different weight sharing strategies derived from two perspectives of a graph convolution as well as three more variants based on decoupling self-connections.
– We conduct extensive experiments to compare the different weight sharing methods under controlled settings. We make new conclusions that we believe will benefit not only the research community of human pose estimation but also that of deep learning on graphs.

2   Related Work

3D Human Pose Estimation. The development of 3D HPE has gone through a long time. In the beginning, researchers build 3D pose models based on hand-crafted features and geometric constraints [2,14,28]. Recent approaches exploit deep neural networks [19,21,31,32,39,40,44] for end-to-end learning and significantly push forward the state-of-the-art performance. Zhou et al. [43] augment a 2D pose estimation sub-network with a 3D depth regression sub-network and introduce a weakly-supervised transfer learning method to make full use of mixed 2D and 3D labels. Sun et al. [32] introduce a simple integral operation to relate and unify the heat map representation and body joint regression. Yang et al. [39] design an adversarial learning framework, which distills the 3D human pose structures learned from the fully annotated dataset to in-the-wild images with only 2D pose annotations. 3D HPE from videos have been studied in [7, 26]. There is also research on multi-person 3D pose detection [22].

Some researchers divide the 3D HPE task into two sub-tasks, i.e., 2D human pose estimation from an image and 2D-to-3D pose lifting. Our approach falls into this category. The most related work to ours are [5, 8, 40], which also apply GCNs for 3D pose regression. Zhao et al. [40] propose a semantic GCN to capture local and global node relationships not explicitly represented in the graph. Ci et al. [8] extend the GCN to a locally connected network to improve its representation capability. This model is actually equivalent to the no-sharing method discussed in this paper. Cai et al. [5] incorporate domain knowledge about the articulated body configurations into the graph convolutional operations and introduce a local-to-global network to learn multi-scale features for the graph-based representations. They classify neighboring nodes according to their semantic meanings and use different kernels for different neighboring nodes. Their form is similar to that of our convolution-style method but our derivation is inspired by the spatial convolution and is more general. Moreover, we also consider new weight sharing methods based on two different interpretations of the graph convolution and decoupling self-connections. Although decoupling self-connections in a GCN has been studied in [38] and [40], we investigate it in different weight sharing methods. To our knowledge, this is the first systematic study of weight sharing in GCNs for 3D human pose estimation.

Graph Convolutional Networks. GCNs generalize CNNs by performing convolutions on graphs. They have been widely used to solve problems involving graph data like the citation network [17], news network [13], molecular property prediction [11] and information retrieval [29]. There are two categories of GCNs: spectral approaches and non-spectral (spatial) approaches [42]. The former are defined in the Fourier domain by calculating eigen-decomposition of graph Laplacian [4], and the latter apply neural message passing to features defined on a graph [11]. Our approach falls into the second category. GCNs are conventionally used for graph or node classification and share the feature transformation for each node so that they could work on graphs with arbitrary structures. By contrast, the human body skeleton has a fixed structure consisting of diverse relations. Thus, it is important to study weight sharing for 3D HPE.

3   Our Approach

We first revisit a vanilla GCN and show two different ways to interpret it (Sect. 3.1). We introduce and compare different weight sharing methods in

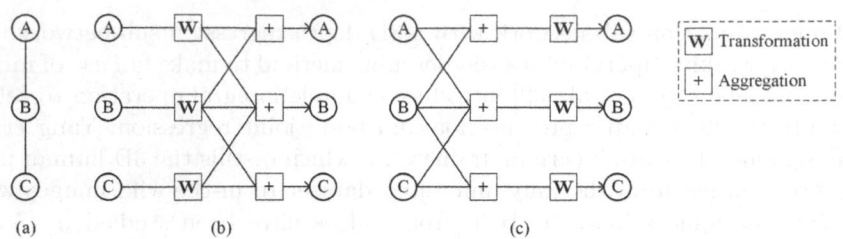

Fig. 2. Illustration of two different ways to interpret a graph convolution. (a) A simple graph consisting of three nodes. (b) The features of each node are updated via feature transformation followed by neighborhood aggregation. (c) The features of each node are updated via neighborhood aggregation followed by feature transformation

Sect. 3.2. Sect 3.3 discusses weight sharing based on decoupled self-connections. Finally, we detail the network architecture for 3D HPE in Sect. 3.4.

3.1   Understand GCN

A GCN generalizes CNNs by learning representations on graph data. Let $\mathcal{G} = (\mathcal{V}, \mathcal{E})$ denote a graph where $\mathcal{V}$ is a set of N nodes and $\mathcal{E}$ is the collection of all edges. We can encode the edges in an adjacency matrix $\mathbf{A} \in \{0, 1\}^{N \times N}$. Let $\mathbf{h}_i \in \mathcal{R}^D$ denote a D-dimensional feature vector associated with each node i. $\mathbf{H} \in \mathcal{R}^{D \times N}$ is the collection of all feature vectors, and its i-th column is $\mathbf{h}_i$. Then a graph convolutional layer [17], the building block of a GCN, updates features defined on the nodes via the following operation:

$$\mathbf{H}' = \sigma(\mathbf{W}\mathbf{H}\hat{\mathbf{A}}) \tag{1}$$

where $\mathbf{H}' \in \mathbb{R}^{D' \times N}$ is the updated feature matrix, D' is the dimension of the updated feature vector of each node, $\sigma(\cdot)$ is an activation function, e.g.., ReLU, $\mathbf{W} \in \mathbb{R}^{D' \times D}$ is a learnable weight matrix. $\hat{\mathbf{A}}$ is a normalized version of $\mathbf{A}$:

$$\hat{\mathbf{A}} = \tilde{\mathbf{D}}^{-\frac{1}{2}}(\mathbf{A} + \mathbf{I})\tilde{\mathbf{D}}^{-\frac{1}{2}} \tag{2}$$

Adding an identity matrix $\mathbf{I}$ to $\mathbf{A}$ means to include self-connections in the graph so that the update of a node feature vector also depends on itself. $\tilde{\mathbf{D}}$ is the diagonal node degree matrix of $\mathbf{A} + \mathbf{I}$ and helps the graph convolution to retain the scale of features. A GCN takes as input a feature vector associated with each node and repeatedly transforms them via a composition of multiple graph convolutions to get increasingly more powerful representations, which are used by the last layer to predict the output.

Let $\hat{a}_{ij}$ be the entry of $\hat{\mathbf{A}}$ at (i, j). $\mathcal{N}_i$ and $\hat{\mathcal{N}}_i \equiv \mathcal{N}_i \cup \{i\}$ denote the neighbors of node i excluding and including the node itself respectively. This means $j \in \hat{\mathcal{N}}_i$

if and only if $\hat{a}_{ij} \neq 0$. Then Eq. (1) can be written equivalently as below.

$$\mathbf{h}'_i = \sigma\left(\sum_{j \in \hat{\mathcal{N}}_i} \mathbf{W}\mathbf{h}_j \hat{a}_{ij}\right) \tag{3}$$

$$= \sigma\left(\mathbf{W} \sum_{j \in \hat{\mathcal{N}}_i} \mathbf{h}_j \hat{a}_{ij}\right) \tag{4}$$

where $i \in \{1, ..., N\}$, $\mathbf{h}'_i$ is the i-th column of $\mathbf{H}'$ and also the updated feature vector of node i.

Table 1. Comparison of different weight sharing methods

Method	Definition	Parameters	Complexity
Full-sharing	$\mathbf{h}'_i = \sigma(\sum_{j \in \hat{\mathcal{N}}_i} \mathbf{W}\mathbf{h}_j \hat{a}_{ij})$	$D' \times D$	$D' \times D \times \sum_{i=1}^{N} |\hat{\mathcal{N}}_i|$
Conv-style	$\mathbf{h}'_i = \sigma(\sum_{j \in \hat{\mathcal{N}}_i} \mathbf{W}_{d(i,j)}\mathbf{h}_j \hat{a}_{ij})$	$D' \times D \times 3$	$D' \times D \times \sum_{i=1}^{N} |\hat{\mathcal{N}}_i|$
Pre-agg	$\mathbf{h}'_i = \sigma(\sum_{j \in \hat{\mathcal{N}}_i} \mathbf{W}_j \mathbf{h}_j \hat{a}_{ij})$	$D' \times D \times N$	$D' \times D \times \sum_{i=1}^{N} |\hat{\mathcal{N}}_i|$
Post-agg	$\mathbf{h}'_i = \sigma(\mathbf{W}_i \sum_{j \in \hat{\mathcal{N}}_i} \mathbf{h}_j \hat{a}_{ij})$	$D' \times D \times N$	$D' \times D \times \sum_{i=1}^{N} |\hat{\mathcal{N}}_i|$
No-sharing	$\mathbf{h}'_i = \sigma(\sum_{j \in \hat{\mathcal{N}}_i} \mathbf{W}_{ij}\mathbf{h}_j \hat{a}_{ij})$	$D' \times D \times \sum_{i=1}^{N} |\hat{\mathcal{N}}_i|$	$D' \times D \times \sum_{i=1}^{N} |\hat{\mathcal{N}}_i|$

This equivalence indicates we can interpret the graph convolution in two different ways. Specifically, Eq. (3) updates the feature vector of each node by first transforming the features of their neighboring nodes via $\mathbf{W}$ and then aggregating those transformed features via a summation. Alternatively, Eq. (4) first aggregates features of neighboring nodes and then transforms the aggregated features via a linear projection. These two interpretations are illustrated in Fig. 2. We will show how they can be used to derive different weight sharing methods.

3.2 Weight Sharing

The transformation matrix in a graph convolution captures the relationships between nodes. It is conventionally shared by all nodes, i.e., Eqs. (3) and (4). This weight sharing method, which we call `full-sharing`, has several advantages. First, it leads to a compact model potentially with better generalization ability. Second, it allows us to apply the same GCN to graphs with arbitrary structures, which is critical to graph or node classification tasks. However, `full-sharing` can be suboptimal for human pose estimation as the relations among different sets of body joints are different. To resolve this potential issue, we try to *unshare* a portion of the weights, which leads to different weight sharing methods.

Pre-aggregation. Motivated by Eq. (3), we consider applying different transformations to the input features of each node before they are aggregated:

$$\mathbf{h}'_i = \sigma\left(\sum_{j \in \hat{\mathcal{N}}_i} \mathbf{W}_j \mathbf{h}_j \hat{a}_{ij}\right) \tag{5}$$

where $\mathbf{W}_j \in \mathcal{R}^{D' \times D}$ $(j \in \{1, ..., N\})$ is the weight matrix applied to $\mathbf{h}_j$. Since the weight unsharing occurs before feature aggregation, we call this method `pre-aggregation`.

Post-aggregation. Alternatively, we can also unshare the weights to get the output features of each node after the aggregation step. Equation (4) is reformulated:

$$\mathbf{h}'_i = \sigma(\mathbf{W}_i \sum_{j \in \hat{\mathcal{N}}_i} \mathbf{h}_j \hat{a}_{ij}) \tag{6}$$

where $\mathbf{W}_i \in \mathcal{R}^{D' \times D}$ $(i \in \{1, ..., N\})$ is the transformation to get the output features of node i from its neighbors. We call it `post-aggregation` as the weight unsharing occurs after feature aggregation.

No-sharing. `Pre-aggregation` and `post-aggregation` differ in whether the weights are unshared for the input or output features of each node. It is straightforward to combine them and unshare the weights between any pair of input and output feature vectors:

$$\mathbf{h}'_i = \sigma(\sum_{j \in \hat{\mathcal{N}}_i} \mathbf{W}_{ij} \mathbf{h}_j \hat{a}_{ij}) \tag{7}$$

where $\mathbf{W}_{ij} \in \mathcal{R}^{D' \times D}$ is the weight matrix corresponding to the input features of node j and the output features of node i. We call this method `no-sharing`. Note the number of different weight matrices is $\sum_{i=1}^{N} |\hat{\mathcal{N}}_i|$ instead of N^2.

Convolution-Style. An image is a special kind of graph with its nodes or pixels arranged in a grid. This makes it possible to define the *displacement* between any two pixels by subtracting their 2D coordinates on the grid. Then the spatial convolution on an image can be considered as a weight sharing method by assigning different feature transformations to each displacement value between two nodes. Thus, if we can define the displacement $d(i, j)$ between two nodes i and j on a graph, we can develop a `convolution-style` weight sharing method:

$$\mathbf{h}'_i = \sigma(\sum_{j \in \hat{\mathcal{N}}_i} \mathbf{W}_{d(i,j)} \mathbf{h}_j \hat{a}_{ij}) \tag{8}$$

where $\mathbf{W}_{d(i,j)} \in \mathcal{R}^{D' \times D}$ is the weight matrix corresponding to each displacement value $d(i, j)$. Motivated by the fact that the skeleton graph as shown in Fig. 1 has a star shape and body joints farther away from the body center have larger degrees of freedom, we define the *coordinate* of a body joint node as the length of the shortest path between it and the body center node. Thus for a pair of neighboring nodes $i \in \{1, ..., N\}$ and $j \in \hat{\mathcal{N}}_i$, we have $d(i, j) \in \{-1, 0, 1\}$. In other words, the relationships between a node and (1) itself, (2) a neighboring body joint farther from the body center and (3) a neighboring body joint closer to the body center are modeled separately.

Table 1 compares definitions of the five weight sharing methods as well as their parameters and computational complexities based on a unified implementation. Possible ways to reduce the computational complexity are discussed in the supplementary material. With the same dimensions of input and output features, `full-sharing` has the smallest number of parameters while `no-sharing` is on the other extreme. Figure 3 illustrates different weight sharing methods.

3.3 Decouple Self-connections

The normalized affinity matrix $\hat{\mathbf{A}}$ used in a GCN usually includes self-connections, i.e., edges connecting each node and itself. Unlike edges connecting nodes to their neighbors, self-connections do not involve relational modeling between different nodes. This motivates us to decouple their feature transformations, which leads to variants of `full-sharing`, `pre-aggregation` and `post-aggregation`:

$$\mathbf{h}'_i = \sigma(\mathbf{Th}_i \hat{a}_{ii} + \sum_{j \in \mathcal{N}_i} \mathbf{Wh}_j \hat{a}_{ij}) \tag{9}$$

$$\mathbf{h}'_i = \sigma(\mathbf{T}_i \mathbf{h}_i \hat{a}_{ii} + \sum_{j \in \mathcal{N}_i} \mathbf{W}_j \mathbf{h}_j \hat{a}_{ij}) \tag{10}$$

$$\mathbf{h}'_i = \sigma(\mathbf{T}_i \mathbf{h}_i \hat{a}_{ii} + \mathbf{W}_i \sum_{j \in \mathcal{N}_i} \mathbf{h}_j \hat{a}_{ij}) \tag{11}$$

where $\mathbf{T} \in \mathcal{R}^{D' \times D}$ and $\mathbf{T}_i \in \mathcal{R}^{D' \times D}$ denote feature transformations for self-connections, $\mathcal{N}_i \equiv \hat{\mathcal{N}}_i - \{i\}$. For decoupled `full-sharing`, i.e., Eq. (9), the weight

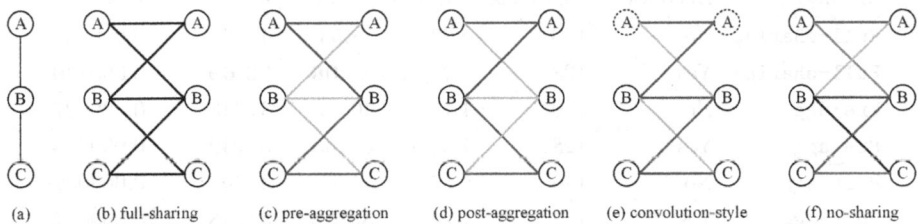

(a)   (b) full-sharing   (c) pre-aggregation   (d) post-aggregation   (e) convolution-style   (f) no-sharing

Fig. 3. Illustration of the five weight sharing methods discussed in Sect. 3.2. Weight unsharing is encoded via different colors. For `convolution-style`, we assume the coordinate of a node is defined as its graph distance to node A

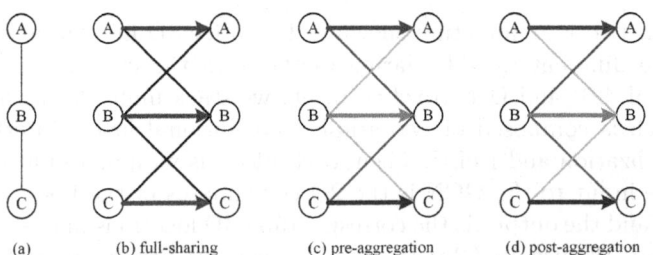

(a)   (b) full-sharing   (c) pre-aggregation   (d) post-aggregation

Fig. 4. Illustration of decoupled weight sharing methods. Weight unsharing is encoded via different colors. Arrows denote weights corresponding to self-connections

matrix $\mathbf{T}$ is fully shared by all self-connections. For decoupled `pre-aggregation` and decoupled `post-aggregation`, i.e., Eqs. (10) and (11), we modify their respective original formulations so that a different weight matrix is assigned to each self-connection and they are different from weight matrices for other connections. Note `convolution-style` and `no-sharing` decouple self-connections by definition. Figure 4 illustrates these three decoupled weight sharing methods.

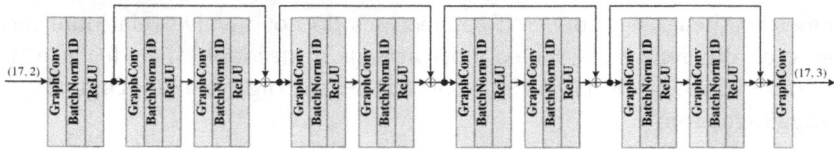

Fig. 5. An example GCN architecture for 2D-to-3D pose lifting. The building block is a residual block composed of two graph convolutional layers with 128 channels. This block is repeated four times. Each graph convolutional layer (except for the last one) is followed by a batch normalization layer and a ReLU activation

Table 2. Ablation study on the impact of decoupling self-connections. We adjust the channels so that each pair of comparing methods have similar model sizes. All errors are measured in millimeters (mm)

Method	Decouple?	Channels	Params	MPJPE	P-MPJPE	Loss
Full-sharing	No	180	0.27 M	53.53	43.37	0.000630
Full-sharing	Yes	128	0.27 M	**41.96**	**33.69**	0.000140
Pre-agg	No	180	4.17 M	40.34	31.59	0.000027
Pre-agg	Yes	128	4.22 M	**37.83**	**30.09**	0.000016
Post-agg	No	180	4.17 M	41.39	33.68	0.000052
Post-agg	Yes	128	4.22 M	**38.92**	**31.33**	0.000022

3.4 Network Architecture

We use the network architecture shown in Fig. 5 for 3D human pose estimation and compare different weight sharing methods in the experiments. Following Martinez et al. [21] and Defferrard et al. [9], we stack multiple cascaded blocks, each of which is composed of two graph convolutional layers interleaved with batch normalization and ReLU. Then, each block is wrapped in a residual connection. The input to the GCN is the 2D coordinates of the body joints in the image space and the output is the corresponding 3D locations in the camera coordinate system. We use an $L2$-norm loss between the prediction and the ground truth. The network can be trained end-to-end.

4 Experiments

4.1 Datasets and Evaluation Protocols

We conduct our experiments on the widely used Human 3.6M dataset [15] and follow the standard evaluation procedure.

Dataset. The Human 3.6M dataset is currently the largest public dataset for 3D HPE. It contains 3.6 million images filmed by 4 synchronized high-resolution progressive scan cameras 50 Hz [15]. 11 subjects perform 15 different daily activities in the film like eating, phoning, sitting and walking, but only 7 subjects are annotated with 3D poses. We follow previous work [8,26,40] for fair and effective comparison. The 7 annotated subjects are divided into 5 subjects (S1, S5, S6, S7, S8) for training and 2 subjects (S9 and S11) for testing. A single model is trained and tested on all 15 actions.

Table 3. Ablation study on different weight sharing methods (controlled number of channels and computational complexity). All errors are measured in millimeters (mm)

Method	Channels	Params	MPJPE	P-MPJPE	Loss
Full-sharing	128	0.27 M	41.96	33.69	0.000140
Conv-style	128	0.40 M	42.85	33.32	0.000078
Pre-agg	128	4.22 M	**37.83**	**30.09**	0.000016
Post-agg	128	4.22 M	38.92	31.33	0.000022
No-sharing	128	6.86 M	39.88	31.02	0.000013

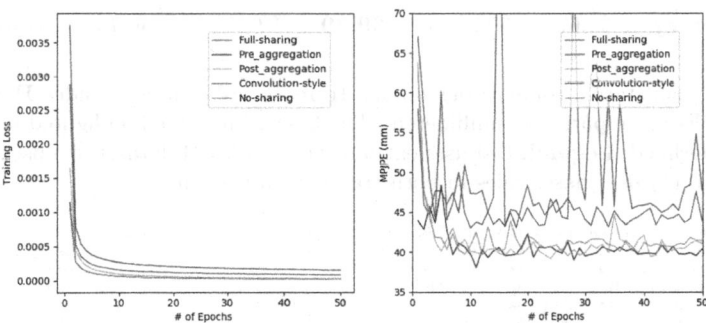

Fig. 6. Training curves (left) and validation errors (right) of different methods (controlled number of channels and computational complexity). Curves corresponding to controlled model size can be found in the supplementary material

Evaluation Protocols. There are two protocols for evaluation. **Protocol-1** uses the mean per-joint position error (MPJPE) as the evaluation metric. It computes the mean Euclidean distance error per-joints between the prediction and the ground truth in millimeters. **Protocol-2** computes the error after aligning the root joint of the prediction with ground truth via rigid transformation. This metric is abbreviated as P-MPJPE.

4.2 Ablation Study

We conduct ablation study to compare the five different weight sharing methods and the three variants in controlled settings. To avoid the influence of 2D human pose detector, we utilize the 2D ground truth as the input for all models. We adopt Adam [16] as our optimization method with an initial learning rate 0.001 and a decay rate 0.96 every 100 K iterations. We train each model for 50 epochs using a batch size 64. The weights of GCNs are initialized using the method proposed in [12]. Following Zhao et al. [40], we use 128 as the default number of channels of each graph convolutional layer.

Decouple Self-connections. We first study the effect of decoupling self-connections in `full-sharing`, `pre-aggregation` and `post-aggregation`. We

Table 4. Ablation study on different weight sharing methods (controll the model size to be 4.2 M, 2.1 M or 1.05 M). All errors are measured in millimeters (mm)

Method	4.2 M		2.1 M		1.05 M	
	MPJPE	P-MPJPE	MPJPE	P-MPJPE	MPJPE	P-MPJPE
`Full-sharing`	41.70	33.02	42.20	33.19	42.00	33.37
`Conv-style`	41.19	32.20	43.14	33.32	42.73	34.09
`Pre-agg`	**37.83**	**30.09**	39.86	**31.14**	**40.14**	**31.17**
`Post-agg`	38.92	31.33	39.99	32.06	40.41	32.51
`No-sharing`	39.62	30.93	**39.49**	31.15	40.75	31.31

Table 5. Quantitative comparisons on the Human 3.6M dataset under **Protocol-1**. The MPJPEs are reported in millimeters. The best results are highlighted in bold and second underlined. **Legend:** (+) uses extra data from MPII dataset. (†) uses temporal information. (*) uses pose scales in both training and testing

Protocol # 1	Direct.	Discuss	Eating	Greet	Phone	Photo	Pose	Purch.	Sitting	SittingD.	Smoke	Wait	WalkD.	Walk	WalkT.	Avg.
Lee et al. [18] ECCV'18 (†)	40.2	49.2	47.8	52.6	50.1	75.0	50.2	43.0	55.8	73.9	54.1	55.6	58.2	43.3	43.3	52.8
Hossain et al. [27] ECCV'18 (†)	44.2	46.7	52.3	49.3	59.9	59.4	47.5	46.2	59.9	65.6	55.8	50.4	52.3	43.5	45.1	51.9
Pavllo et al. [26] CVPR'19 (†)	45.2	46.7	43.3	45.6	48.1	55.1	44.6	44.3	57.3	65.8	47.1	44.0	49.0	32.8	33.9	46.8
Cai et al. [5] ICCV'19 (†)	44.6	47.4	45.6	48.8	50.8	59.0	47.2	43.9	57.9	61.9	49.7	46.6	51.3	37.1	39.4	48.8
Martinez et al. [21] ICCV'17	51.8	56.2	58.1	59.0	69.5	78.4	55.2	58.1	74.0	94.6	62.3	59.1	65.1	49.5	52.4	62.9
Tekin et al. [36] ICCV'17	54.2	61.4	60.2	61.2	79.4	78.3	63.1	81.6	70.1	107.3	69.3	70.3	74.3	51.8	63.2	69.7
Martinez et al. [21] ICCV'17	51.8	56.2	58.1	59.0	69.5	78.4	55.2	58.1	74.0	94.6	62.3	59.1	65.1	49.5	52.4	62.9
Sun et al. [31] ICCV'17 (+)	52.8	54.8	54.2	54.3	61.8	67.2	53.1	53.6	71.7	86.7	61.5	53.4	61.6	47.1	53.4	59.1
Yang et al. [39] CVPR'18 (+)	51.5	58.9	50.4	57.0	62.1	65.4	49.8	52.7	69.2	85.2	57.4	58.4	43.6	60.1	47.7	58.6
Fang et al. [10] AAAI'18	50.1	54.3	57.0	57.1	66.6	73.3	53.4	55.7	72.8	88.6	60.3	57.7	62.7	47.5	50.6	60.4
Pavlakos et al. [24] CVPR'18 (+)	48.5	54.4	54.4	52.0	59.4	65.3	49.9	52.9	65.8	71.1	56.6	52.9	60.9	44.7	47.8	56.2
Luvizon et al. [20] CVPR'18 (+)	49.2	51.6	47.6	50.5	51.8	60.3	48.5	51.7	61.5	70.9	53.7	48.9	57.9	44.4	48.9	53.2
Zhao et al. [40] CVPR'19	48.2	60.8	51.8	64.0	64.6	53.6	51.1	67.4	88.7	57.7	73.2	65.6	48.9	64.8	51.9	60.8
Li et al. [19] CVPR'19	43.8	48.6	49.1	49.8	57.6	61.5	45.9	48.3	62.0	73.4	54.8	50.6	56.0	43.4	45.5	52.7
Zhou et al. [40] CVPR'19	47.3	60.7	51.4	60.5	61.1	49.9	47.3	68.1	86.2	55.0	67.8	61.0	42.1	60.6	45.3	57.6
Sharma et al. [30] ICCV'19	48.6	54.5	54.2	55.7	62.2	72.0	50.5	54.3	70.0	78.3	58.1	55.4	61.4	45.2	49.7	58.0
Ci et al. [8] ICCV'19 (+)(*)	46.8	52.3	44.7	50.4	52.9	68.9	49.6	46.4	60.2	78.9	51.2	50.0	54.8	40.4	43.3	52.7
Ours	46.3	52.2	47.3	50.7	55.5	67.1	49.2	46.0	60.4	71.1	51.5	50.1	54.5	40.3	43.7	52.4

Table 6. Quantitative comparisons on the Human 3.6M dataset under **Protocol-2**. The P-MPJPEs are reported in millimeters. The best results are highlighted in bold and second underlined. **Legend:** (+) uses extra data from MPII dataset. (†) uses temporal information. (*) uses pose scales in both training and testing

Protocol # 2	Dire.	Disc.	Eat	Greet	Phone	Photo	Pose	Purch.	Sit	SitD.	Smoke	Wait	WalkD.	Walk	WalkT.	Avg.
Lee et al. [18] ECCV'18 (†)	34.9	35.2	43.2	42.6	46.2	55.0	37.6	38.8	50.9	67.3	48.9	35.2	50.7	31.0	34.6	43.4
Hossain et al. [27] ECCV'18 (†)	36.9	37.9	42.8	40.3	46.8	46.7	37.7	36.5	48.9	52.6	45.6	39.6	43.5	35.2	38.5	42.0
Pavllo et al. [26] CVPR'19 (†)	34.2	36.8	33.9	37.5	37.1	43.2	34.4	33.5	45.3	52.7	37.7	34.1	38.0	25.8	27.7	36.8
Cai et al. [5] ICCV'19 (†)	35.7	37.8	36.9	40.7	39.6	45.2	37.4	34.5	46.9	50.1	40.5	36.1	41.0	29.6	33.2	39.0
Sun et al. [31] ICCV'17	42.1	44.3	45.0	45.4	51.5	53.0	43.2	41.3	59.3	73.3	51.0	44.0	48.0	38.3	44.8	48.3
Martinez et al. [21] ICCV'17	39.5	43.2	46.4	47.0	51.0	56.0	41.4	40.6	56.5	69.4	49.2	45.0	49.5	38.0	43.1	47.7
Fang et al. [10] AAAI'18	38.2	41.7	43.7	44.9	48.5	55.3	40.2	38.2	54.5	64.4	47.2	44.3	47.3	36.7	41.7	45.7
Pavlakos et al. [24] CVPR'18	**34.7**	**39.8**	41.8	**38.6**	42.5	**47.5**	38.0	36.6	50.7	56.8	42.6	39.6	43.9	32.1	36.5	41.8
Li et al. [19] CVPR'19	35.5	39.8	41.3	42.3	46.0	48.9	**36.9**	37.3	51.0	60.6	44.9	40.2	44.1	33.1	36.9	42.6
Ci et al. [8] ICCV'19 (+)(*)	36.9	41.6	**38.0**	41.0	**41.9**	51.1	38.2	37.6	49.1	62.1	43.1	39.9	43.5	32.2	37.0	42.2
Ours	35.9	40.0	**38.0**	41.5	42.5	51.4	37.8	36.0	48.6	56.6	41.8	38.3	42.7	31.7	36.2	41.2

do not include `convolution-style` or `no-sharing` here as their self-connections are decoupled by definition. Since introducing a separate weight matrix for self-connections will bring more parameters, we increase the number of channels of the models without decoupling so that each pair of comparing methods have similar model sizes. Table 2 shows the results[1]. It is obvious that all these three weight sharing methods benefit from decoupling self-connections, and among them `full-sharing` benefits the most. This demonstrates that decoupling self-connections in GCN is very important for 3D HPE. Thus, we will use decoupled weight sharing methods in the remaining experiments.

Weight Sharing Methods (Controlled Number of Channels and Computational Complexity). Then we study the impact of different weight sharing methods on the 3D HPE performance. We first fix the number of channels of each graph convolutional layer to be 128 so that the shape of each weight matrix is the same for different weight sharing methods. This also means the computational complexities of all models are the same according to Table 1. Note we decouple the self-connections for `full-sharing`, `pre-aggregation` and `post-aggregation` for better performance. As we can see in Table 3, the weight sharing methods have a great impact on the localization error. Among them, `pre-aggregation` performs the best. We can observe that `no-sharing` has the smallest training loss, but does not perform as well as `pre-aggregation`. We conjecture that unsharing weights between any pair of input and output feature vectors gives it too much freedom and thus leads to overfitting. The vanilla graph convolution, i.e., `full-sharing`, has the smallest model size, which may bring it some disadvantage. Thus, we will fix the number of parameters of each model in the next ablation study.

Figure 6 plots the loss and validation error of each method in the training phase. Compared with `full-sharing`, the training losses of other methods decrease very fast. `Pre-aggregation`, `post-aggregation` and `no-sharing` have

---

[1] `Pre-agg`, `post-agg` and `conv-style` are short for `pre-aggregation`, `post-aggregation` and `convolution-style` respectively.

significantly lower validations errors as the training goes on than `full-sharing` and `convolution-style`.

Weight Sharing Methods (Controlled Model Size). Next, we fix the number of parameters to be about 4.2 M, 2.1 M or 1.05 M by merely changing the number of channels of each model. For example, to have a model size of about 4.2 M, the channels of the five methods listed in Table 4 are 512, 415, 128, 128 and 100, respectively. We decouple the self-connections for `full-sharing`, `pre-aggregation` and `post-aggregation`. The result is shown in Table 4. Given the same model size, `pre-aggregation` achieves the overall best performance. The performance of `full-sharing` and `convolution-style` do not improve consistently with the increase of model size.

Table 7. Quantitative comparisons on the Human 3.6M dataset under **Protocol-1**. All approaches take 2D ground truth as input. The MPJPEs are reported in millimeters. **Legend:** (+) uses extra data from MPII dataset. (*) uses pose scales in both training and testing

Protocol # 1	Direct.	Discuss	Eating	Greet	Phone	Photo	Pose	Purch.	Sitting	SittingD.	Smoke	Wait	WalkD.	Walk	WalkT.	Avg.
Zhou et al. [43] ICCV'19 (+)	34.4	42.4	36.6	42.1	38.2	39.8	34.7	40.2	45.6	60.8	39.0	42.6	42.0	29.8	31.7	39.9
Ci et al. [8] ICCV'19 (+)(*)	36.3	38.8	29.7	37.8	34.6	42.5	39.8	32.5	36.2	39.5	34.4	38.4	38.2	31.3	34.2	36.3
Zhao et al. [40] CVPR'19	37.8	49.4	37.6	40.9	45.1	41.4	40.1	48.3	50.1	42.2	53.5	44.3	40.5	47.3	39.0	43.8
Ours	36.8	40.3	33.0	36.3	37.5	45.0	39.7	34.9	40.3	47.7	37.4	38.5	38.6	29.6	32.0	37.8

Why `Pre-aggregation` Performs Best? As mentioned, `full-sharing` is inferior because the shared feature transformation prevents it from learning different relational models between different body joints. On the other extreme is `no-sharing`, which assigns a different weight matrix to each pair of related body joints. This can be too much freedom as some common relational patterns do exist, especially as the human body is symmetric and has a star-shape. `Convolution-style`, `pre-aggregation` and `post-aggregation` are between these two extremes. `Convolution-style` mimics the image convolution and shares weights according to the displacement between two nodes on the graph. However, unlike image pixels, the relation between two nodes is not strictly *translation equivariant*, e.g.., hand and elbow versus neck and head. `Pre-aggregation` provides the freedom to transform each node independently so that the transformed nodes will affect their neighbors in a unified way (via summation). It overcomes the limitation of `full-sharing` due to the independent transformation of each node. Compared with `no-sharing`, it requires the transformed nodes to share relations. `Post-aggregation` sums the features first, which will unavoidably lose information. By contrast, transforming the features first, as in `pre-aggregation`, provides a chance to retain or extract the most important features that are suitable for aggregation.

Our ablation study proves that using different weight sharing methods has a great impact on 3D HPE performance. It also reveals that choosing an appropriate weight sharing method according to the property of a problem is very important when applying GCN models (Table 7).

4.3   Comparison with the State of the Art

Following Pavllo et al. [26], we use 2D poses provided by a pre-trained 2D cascaded pyramid network detector (CPN) [6] for benchmark evaluation. We use `pre-aggregation` as our weight sharing method as it outperforms the others in our ablation study. We set the initial learning rate 0.0001, the decay factor 0.95 per 4 epochs and the batch size 256. We add dropout with a factor 0.2 after each graph convolutional layer to prevent overfitting. Following Zhao et al. [40], we integrate non-local blocks into our network to boost its performance. Note we do not use this kind of complementary tools in our ablation study to exclude their inference and ensure fairness. It takes about 10 h to train our model for 30 epochs on a single Nvidia RTX 2080Ti GPU.

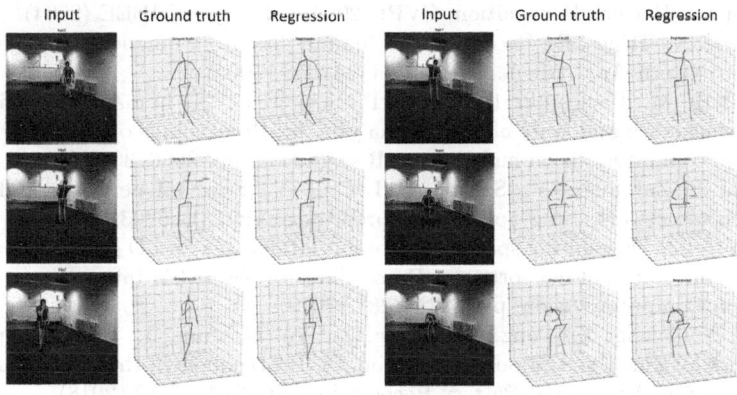

Fig. 7. Qualitative results of our approach on Human 3.6M

Table 5 and Table 6 show the results under two protocols respectively. There are work that exploiting temporal information [5,18,26,27] to assist 3D regression and some using extra data to boost the performance [8,20,24,31,39]. By contrast, we aim to find the weight sharing method that is optimal for 3D HPE. Therefore, their ideas and strategies are complementary to ours and can also benefit our model. While our approach only takes 2D detections as input, it achieves the state-of-the-art performance by applying the optimal weight sharing method. This indicates that our model can effectively utilize relationships between different joints in the graph. Figure 7 demonstrates some qualitative results of our approach on the Human3.6M dataset.

5   Conclusions

This paper has had a comprehensive and systematic study of weight sharing in GCNs for 3D HPE. After extensive ablation study and benchmark comparison, we make the following conclusions. (1) Weight sharing methods in GCNs have a great impact on the HPE performance. More parameters do not necessarily lead to better performance. (2) It is always beneficial to decouple self-connections. (3) Among all the variants of graph convolutions discussed in this paper, `pre-aggregation` is the optimal weight sharing method for 3D HPE.

Acknowledgments. This work was supported in part by Wei Tang's start-up funds from the University of Illinois at Chicago and the National Science Foundation (NSF) award CNS-1828265.

References

1. Agarwal, A., Triggs, B.: 3D human pose from silhouettes by relevance vector regression. In: Proceedings of the 2004 IEEE Computer Society Conference on Computer Vision and Pattern Recognition, CVPR 2004, vol. 2, p. II. IEEE (2004)
2. Agarwal, A., Triggs, B.: Recovering 3D human pose from monocular images. IEEE Trans. Pattern Anal. Mach. Intell. **28**(1), 44–58 (2005)
3. Andriluka, M., Pishchulin, L., Gehler, P., Schiele, B.: 2D human pose estimation: new benchmark and state of the art analysis. In: Proceedings of the IEEE Conference on computer Vision and Pattern Recognition, pp. 3686–3693 (2014)
4. Bruna, J., Zaremba, W., Szlam, A., LeCun, Y.: Spectral networks and locally connected networks on graphs. arXiv preprint arXiv:1312.6203 (2013)
5. Cai, Y., et al.: Exploiting spatial-temporal relationships for 3D pose estimation via graph convolutional networks. In: Proceedings of the IEEE International Conference on Computer Vision, pp. 2272–2281 (2019)
6. Chen, Y., Wang, Z., Peng, Y., Zhang, Z., Yu, G., Sun, J.: Cascaded pyramid network for multi-person pose estimation. In: Proceedings of the IEEE Conference on Computer Vision and Pattern Recognition, pp. 7103–7112 (2018)
7. Cheng, Y., Yang, B., Wang, B., Yan, W., Tan, R.T.: Occlusion-aware networks for 3D human pose estimation in video. In: Proceedings of the IEEE International Conference on Computer Vision, pp. 723–732 (2019)
8. Ci, H., Wang, C., Ma, X., Wang, Y.: Optimizing network structure for 3D human pose estimation. In: Proceedings of the IEEE International Conference on Computer Vision, pp. 2262–2271 (2019)
9. Defferrard, M., Bresson, X., Vandergheynst, P.: Convolutional neural networks on graphs with fast localized spectral filtering. In: Advances in Neural Information Processing Systems, pp. 3844–3852 (2016)
10. Fang, H.S., Xu, Y., Wang, W., Liu, X., Zhu, S.C.: Learning pose grammar to encode human body configuration for 3D pose estimation. In: Thirty-Second AAAI Conference on Artificial Intelligence (2018)
11. Gilmer, J., Schoenholz, S.S., Riley, P.F., Vinyals, O., Dahl, G.E.: Neural message passing for quantum chemistry. In: Proceedings of the 34th International Conference on Machine Learning, vol. 70, pp. 1263–1272. JMLR.org (2017)
12. Glorot, X., Bengio, Y.: Understanding the difficulty of training deep feedforward neural networks. In: Proceedings of the Thirteenth International Conference on Artificial Intelligence and Statistics, pp. 249–256 (2010)
13. Hamilton, W., Ying, Z., Leskovec, J.: Inductive representation learning on large graphs. In: Advances in Neural Information Processing Systems, pp. 1024–1034 (2017)

14. Ionescu, C., Li, F., Sminchisescu, C.: Latent structured models for human pose estimation. In: 2011 International Conference on Computer Vision, pp. 2220–2227. IEEE (2011)
15. Ionescu, C., Papava, D., Olaru, V., Sminchisescu, C.: Human3.6M: large scale datasets and predictive methods for 3D human sensing in natural environments. IEEE Trans. Pattern Anal. Mach. Intell. **36**(7), 1325–1339 (2013)
16. Kingma, D.P., Ba, J.: Adam: a method for stochastic optimization. arXiv preprint arXiv:1412.6980 (2014)
17. Kipf, T.N., Welling, M.: Semi-supervised classification with graph convolutional networks. arXiv preprint arXiv:1609.02907 (2016)
18. Lee, K., Lee, I., Lee, S.: Propagating LSTM: 3D pose estimation based on joint interdependency. In: Ferrari, V., Hebert, M., Sminchisescu, C., Weiss, Y. (eds.) ECCV 2018. LNCS, vol. 11211, pp. 123–141. Springer, Cham (2018). https://doi.org/10.1007/978-3-030-01234-2_8
19. Li, C., Lee, G.H.: Generating multiple hypotheses for 3D human pose estimation with mixture density network. In: Proceedings of the IEEE Conference on Computer Vision and Pattern Recognition, pp. 9887–9895 (2019)
20. Luvizon, D.C., Picard, D., Tabia, H.: 2D/3D pose estimation and action recognition using multitask deep learning. In: Proceedings of the IEEE Conference on Computer Vision and Pattern Recognition, pp. 5137–5146 (2018)
21. Martinez, J., Hossain, R., Romero, J., Little, J.J.: A simple yet effective baseline for 3D human pose estimation. In: Proceedings of the IEEE International Conference on Computer Vision, pp. 2640–2649 (2017)
22. Moon, G., Chang, J.Y., Lee, K.M.: Camera distance-aware top-down approach for 3D multi-person pose estimation from a single RGB image. In: Proceedings of the IEEE International Conference on Computer Vision, pp. 10133–10142 (2019)
23. Newell, A., Yang, K., Deng, J.: Stacked hourglass networks for human pose estimation. In: Leibe, B., Matas, J., Sebe, N., Welling, M. (eds.) ECCV 2016. LNCS, vol. 9912, pp. 483–499. Springer, Cham (2016). https://doi.org/10.1007/978-3-319-46484-8_29
24. Pavlakos, G., Zhou, X., Daniilidis, K.: Ordinal depth supervision for 3D human pose estimation. In: Proceedings of the IEEE Conference on Computer Vision and Pattern Recognition, pp. 7307–7316 (2018)
25. Pavlakos, G., Zhou, X., Derpanis, K.G., Daniilidis, K.: Coarse-to-fine volumetric prediction for single-image 3D human pose. In: Proceedings of the IEEE Conference on Computer Vision and Pattern Recognition, pp. 7025–7034 (2017)
26. Pavllo, D., Feichtenhofer, C., Grangier, D., Auli, M.: 3D human pose estimation in video with temporal convolutions and semi-supervised training. In: Proceedings of the IEEE Conference on Computer Vision and Pattern Recognition, pp. 7753–7762 (2019)
27. Hossain, M.R.I., Little, J.J.: Exploiting temporal information for 3D human pose estimation. In: Ferrari, V., Hebert, M., Sminchisescu, C., Weiss, Y. (eds.) ECCV 2018. LNCS, vol. 11214, pp. 69–86. Springer, Cham (2018). https://doi.org/10.1007/978-3-030-01249-6_5
28. Rogez, G., Rihan, J., Ramalingam, S., Orrite, C., Torr, P.H.: Randomized trees for human pose detection. In: 2008 IEEE Conference on Computer Vision and Pattern Recognition, pp. 1–8. IEEE (2008)
29. Schlichtkrull, M., Kipf, T.N., Bloem, P., van den Berg, R., Titov, I., Welling, M.: Modeling relational data with graph convolutional networks. In: Gangemi, A.A., et al. (eds.) ESWC 2018. LNCS, vol. 10843, pp. 593–607. Springer, Cham (2018). https://doi.org/10.1007/978-3-319-93417-4_38

30. Sharma, S., Varigonda, P.T., Bindal, P., Sharma, A., Jain, A.: Monocular 3D human pose estimation by generation and ordinal ranking. In: Proceedings of the IEEE International Conference on Computer Vision, pp. 2325–2334 (2019)
31. Sun, X., Shang, J., Liang, S., Wei, Y.: Compositional human pose regression. In: Proceedings of the IEEE International Conference on Computer Vision, pp. 2602–2611 (2017)
32. Sun, X., Xiao, B., Wei, F., Liang, S., Wei, Y.: Integral human pose regression. In: Ferrari, V., Hebert, M., Sminchisescu, C., Weiss, Y. (eds.) ECCV 2018. LNCS, vol. 11210, pp. 536–553. Springer, Cham (2018). https://doi.org/10.1007/978-3-030-01231-1_33
33. Tang, W., Wu, Y.: Does learning specific features for related parts help human pose estimation? In: Proceedings of the IEEE Conference on Computer Vision and Pattern Recognition, pp. 1107–1116 (2019)
34. Tang, W., Yu, P., Wu, Y.: Deeply learned compositional models for human pose estimation. In: Ferrari, V., Hebert, M., Sminchisescu, C., Weiss, Y. (eds.) ECCV 2018. LNCS, vol. 11207, pp. 197–214. Springer, Cham (2018). https://doi.org/10.1007/978-3-030-01219-9_12
35. Tekin, B., Katircioglu, I., Salzmann, M., Lepetit, V., Fua, P.: Structured prediction of 3D human pose with deep neural networks. arXiv preprint arXiv:1605.05180 (2016)
36. Tekin, B., Márquez-Neila, P., Salzmann, M., Fua, P.: Learning to fuse 2D and 3D image cues for monocular body pose estimation. In: Proceedings of the IEEE International Conference on Computer Vision, pp. 3941–3950 (2017)
37. Wang, J., Huang, S., Wang, X., Tao, D.: Not all parts are created equal: 3D pose estimation by modeling bi-directional dependencies of body parts. In: Proceedings of the IEEE International Conference on Computer Vision, pp. 7771–7780 (2019)
38. Yan, S., Xiong, Y., Lin, D.: Spatial temporal graph convolutional networks for skeleton-based action recognition. In: Thirty-Second AAAI Conference on Artificial Intelligence (2018)
39. Yang, W., Ouyang, W., Wang, X., Ren, J., Li, H., Wang, X.: 3D human pose estimation in the wild by adversarial learning. In: Proceedings of the IEEE Conference on Computer Vision and Pattern Recognition, pp. 5255–5264 (2018)
40. Zhao, L., Peng, X., Tian, Y., Kapadia, M., Metaxas, D.N.: Semantic graph convolutional networks for 3D human pose regression. In: Proceedings of the IEEE Conference on Computer Vision and Pattern Recognition, pp. 3425–3435 (2019)
41. Zhao, X., Ning, H., Liu, Y., Huang, T.: Discriminative estimation of 3D human pose using Gaussian processes. In: 2008 19th International Conference on Pattern Recognition, pp. 1–4. IEEE (2008)
42. Zhou, J., et al.: Graph neural networks: a review of methods and applications. arXiv preprint arXiv:1812.08434 (2018)
43. Zhou, K., Han, X., Jiang, N., Jia, K., Lu, J.: Hemlets pose: learning part-centric heatmap triplets for accurate 3D human pose estimation. In: Proceedings of the IEEE International Conference on Computer Vision, pp. 2344–2353 (2019)
44. Zhou, X., Huang, Q., Sun, X., Xue, X., Wei, Y.: Towards 3D human pose estimation in the wild: a weakly-supervised approach. In: Proceedings of the IEEE International Conference on Computer Vision, pp. 398–407 (2017)

MuCAN: Multi-correspondence Aggregation Network for Video Super-Resolution

Wenbo Li[1(✉)], Xin Tao[2], Taian Guo[3], Lu Qi[1], Jiangbo Lu[4], and Jiaya Jia[1,4]

[1] The Chinese University of Hong Kong, Sha Tin, Hong Kong
{wenboli,luqi,leojia}@cse.cuhk.edu.hk
[2] Kuaishou Technology, Beijing, China
jiangsutx@gmail.com
[3] Tsinghua University, Beijing, China
gta17@mails.tsinghua.edu.cn
[4] Smartmore Technology, Shenzhen, China
jiangbo@smartmore.com

Abstract. Video super-resolution (VSR) aims to utilize multiple low-resolution frames to generate a high-resolution prediction for each frame. In this process, inter- and intra-frames are the key sources for exploiting temporal and spatial information. However, there are a couple of limitations for existing VSR methods. First, optical flow is often used to establish one-on-one temporal correspondences. But flow estimation itself is error-prone and hence largely affects the ultimate recovery result. Second, similar patterns existing in natural images are rarely exploited for the VSR task. Motivated by these findings, we propose a temporal multi-correspondence aggregation strategy to leverage most similar patches across frames, and also a cross-scale nonlocal-correspondence aggregation scheme to explore self-similarity of images across scales. Based on these two novel modules, we build an effective multi-correspondence aggregation network (MuCAN) for VSR. Our method achieves state-of-the-art results on multiple benchmark datasets. Extensive experiments justify the effectiveness of our method.

Keywords: Video super-resolution · Correspondence aggregation

1 Introduction

Super-resolution (SR) is a fundamental task in image processing and computer vision, which aims to reconstruct high-resolution (HR) images from low-resolution (LR) ones. While single-image super-resolution methods design natural and clear structures mostly based on spatial information, video super-

Electronic supplementary material The online version of this chapter (https://doi.org/10.1007/978-3-030-58607-2_20) contains supplementary material, which is available to authorized users.

© Springer Nature Switzerland AG 2020
A. Vedaldi et al. (Eds.): ECCV 2020, LNCS 12355, pp. 335–351, 2020.
https://doi.org/10.1007/978-3-030-58607-2_20

resolution (VSR) extends to exploit temporal information from multiple neighboring frames to recover missing details. Nowadays, VSR is widely applied in video surveillance, satellite imagery, etc.

Early methods [24, 26] for VSR propose delicate image models, which are solved via various optimization techniques. Recent deep neural network based VSR methods [2, 11, 19, 22, 23, 26, 32, 37, 38, 41] further push the limits and set new state-of-the-arts.

In contrast to previous methods that model VSR as separate alignment and regression stages, we view this problem as a kind of inter- and intra-frame correspondence aggregation task. Based on the fact that consecutive frames share similar content, and different locations within a single frame may contain similar structures (known as self-similarity [9, 20, 29]), we propose to aggregate these similar contents from multiple correspondences to better restore HR results.

Inter-frame Correspondence. Motion compensation (or alignment) is usually an important component for most video tasks to handle displacements between frames. A majority of methods [2, 32, 37] design specific sub-networks for optical flow estimation. In [14, 15, 19, 22], motion is implicitly handled using Conv3D or recurrent networks. Recent methods [38, 41] utilize deformable convolution layers [3] to explicitly align feature maps using learnable offsets. All the methods establish explicit or implicit one-on-one pixel correspondences between frames. However, motion estimation may suffer from inevitable errors and there is no chance for wrongly estimated mapping to locate correct pixels. Thus, we advocate that a better solution may be possible when considering multiple candidate correspondences for a pixel at a time, as illustrated in Fig. 1(a).

In order to validate this point, we estimate optical flow with a simple patch-matching strategy on the MPI Sintel Flow dataset. After obtaining top-K most similar patches as candidate correspondences for the objective, we calculate the Euclidean distance between the best-performing one and ground-truth flow. As shown in Fig. 1(b), it is clear that a better result is obtained by taking into consideration more correspondences for a pixel. Inspired by this, we propose a *temporal multi-correspondence aggregation module* (TM-CAM) for alignment. It uses top-K most similar feature patches as supplement. More specifically, we design a pixel-adaptive aggregation strategy, which will be detailed in Sect. 3. Our module is lightweight and, more interestingly, can be easily integrated into common frameworks. It is robust to visual artifact production, as shown in Sect. 4.

Intra-frame Correspondence. From another perspective, similar patterns within each frame as shown in Fig. 1(c) can also benefit detail restoration, which has been verified in several previous low-level tasks [9, 13, 20, 29, 44, 47]. This line is still new for VSR. For existing methods in VSR, the commonly used way to explore intra-frame information is to introduce a U-net-like [31] or deep structure, so that a large but still local receptive field is covered. We notice that valuable information may not always come from neighboring positions. Similar patches within nonlocal locations or across scales may also be beneficial.

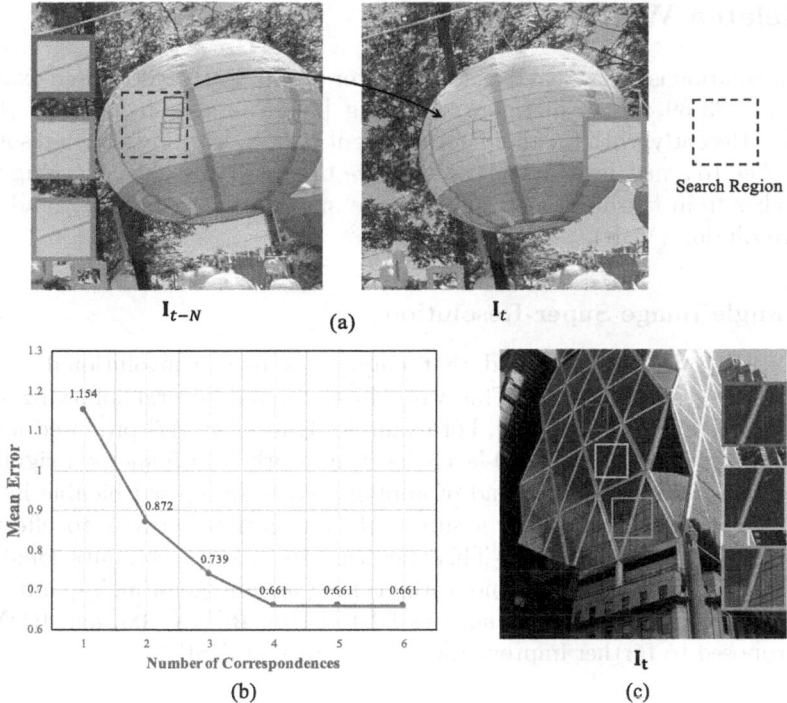

Fig. 1. Inter- and intra-frame correspondence. (a) Inter-frame correspondence estimated from temporal frames (e.g., $\mathbf{I}_{t-N}$ at time $t - N$ and $\mathbf{I}_t$ at time t) can be leveraged for VSR. For a patch in $\mathbf{I}_t$, there are actually multiple similar patterns within a co-located search region in $\mathbf{I}_{t-N}$. (b) Mean error of optical flow estimated by different numbers of inter-frame correspondences on MPI Sintel Flow dataset. (c) Similar patterns existing over different scales in an image $\mathbf{I}_t$.

Accordingly, we in this paper design a new *cross-scale nonlocal-correspondence aggregation module* (CN-CAM) to exploit the multi-scale self-similarity property of natural images. It aggregates similar features across different levels to recover more details. The effectiveness of this module is verified in Sect. 4.

The contribution of this paper is threefold.

- We design a multi-correspondence aggregation network (MuCAN) to deal with video super-resolution in an end-to-end manner. It achieves state-of-the-art performance on multiple benchmark datasets.
- Two effective modules are proposed to make good use of temporal and spatial information. The temporal multi-correspondence aggregation module (TM-CAM) conducts motion compensation in a more robust way. The cross-scale nonlocal-correspondence aggregation module (CN-CAM) explores similar features from multiple spatial scales.
- We introduce an edge-aware loss that enables the proposed network to generate better refined edges.

2   Related Work

Super-resolution is a classical task in computer vision. Early works used example-based [7–9,33,39,40,46], dictionary learning [28,45] and self-similarity [13,44] methods. Recently, with the rapid development of deep learning, super-resolution has reached to a new level. In this section, we briefly discuss deep learning based approaches from two lines, i.e., single-image super-resolution (SISR) and video super-resolution (VSR).

2.1   Single-Image Super-Resolution

SRCNN [4] is the first method that employs a deep convolutional network in the super-resolution task. This work has inspired several following methods [5,10,17,18,21,34,36,48,49]. For example, Kim *et al.* [17] proposed a residual learning strategy using a 20-layer depth network, which shows a significant improvement in accuracy. Instead of applying commonly used bicubic interpolation, Shi *et al.* [34] designed a sub-pixel convolution network to effectively upsample low-resolution inputs. This operation reduces the computational complexity and enables a real-time network. Taking advantage of high-quality large image datasets, more networks such as DBPN [10], RCAN [48], and RDN [49] were proposed to further improve the performance of SISR.

2.2   Video Super-Resolution

Video super-resolution takes multiple frames into consideration. Based on the way to aggregate temporal information, previous methods can be roughly grouped into three categories.

The first group of methods process video sequences without any explicit alignment. For example, methods of [19,22] utilize 3D convolutions to directly extract features from multiple frames. Although this approach is simple, the computational cost is typically high. Jo *et al.* [15] proposed dynamic upsampling filters to avoid explicit motion compensation. However, it stands the chance of ignoring informative details of neighboring frames. Noise in the misaligned regions can also be harmful.

The second line [2,11,16,23,25,26,32,37] is to use optical flow to compensate motion between frames. Methods of [16,23] first obtain optical flow using classical algorithms and then build a network for high-resolution image reconstruction. Caballero *et al.* [2] integrated these two steps into a single framework and trained it in an end-to-end way. Tao *et al.* [37] further proposed sub-pixel motion compensation to reveal more details. No matter optical flow is predicted independently or not, this category of methods needs to handle two relatively separated tasks. Besides, the estimated optical flow critically affects the quality of reconstruction. Because optical flow itself is a challenging task especially for large motion scenes, the resulting accuracy cannot be guaranteed.

The last line [38,41] conducts deformable convolution networks [3] to accomplish video super-resolution. For example, EDVR proposed in [41] extracts and

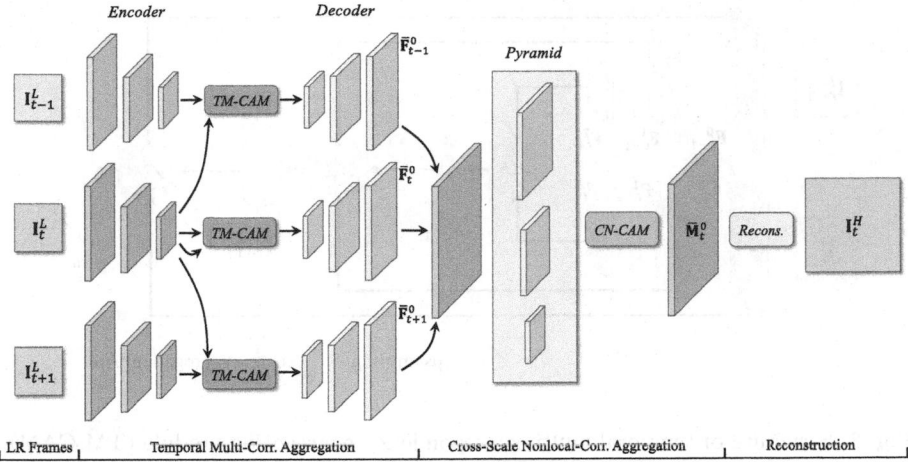

Fig. 2. Architecture of our multi-correspondence aggregation network (MuCAN). It contains two novel modules: temporal multi-correspondence aggregation module (TM-CAM) and cross-scale nonlocal-correspondence aggregation module (CN-CAM).

aligns features at multiple levels, and achieves reasonable performance. The deformable network is however sensitive to the input patterns, and may give rise to noticeable reconstruction artifacts due to unreasonable offsets.

3   Our Method

The architecture of our proposed multi-correspondence aggregation network (MuCAN) is illustrated in Fig. 2. Given $2N + 1$ consecutive low-resolution frames $\{\mathbf{I}_{t-N}^{L}, \dots, \mathbf{I}_{t}^{L}, \dots, \mathbf{I}_{t+N}^{L}\}$, our framework predicts a high-resolution central image $\mathbf{I}_{t}^{H}$. It is an end-to-end network consisting of three modules: a temporal multi-correspondence aggregation module (TM-CAM), a cross-scale nonlocal-correspondence aggregation module (CN-CAM), and a reconstruction module. The details of each module are given in the following subsections.

3.1   Temporal Multi-correspondence Aggregation Module

Camera or object motion between neighboring frames has its pros and cons. On the one hand, large motion needs to be eliminated to build correspondences among similar contents. On the other hand, the accuracy of small motion (at sub-pixel level) is very important, which is the source to draw details. Inspired by the work of [30,35], we design a hierarchical correspondence aggregation strategy to handle large and subtle motion simultaneously.

As shown in Fig. 3, given two neighboring LR images $\mathbf{I}_{t-1}^{L}$ and $\mathbf{I}_{t}^{L}$, we first encode them into lower resolutions (level $l = 0$ to $l = 2$). Then, the aggregation starts in the high-level/low-resolution stage (i.e., from $\overline{\overline{\mathbf{F}}}_{t-1}^{l=2}$) compensating large

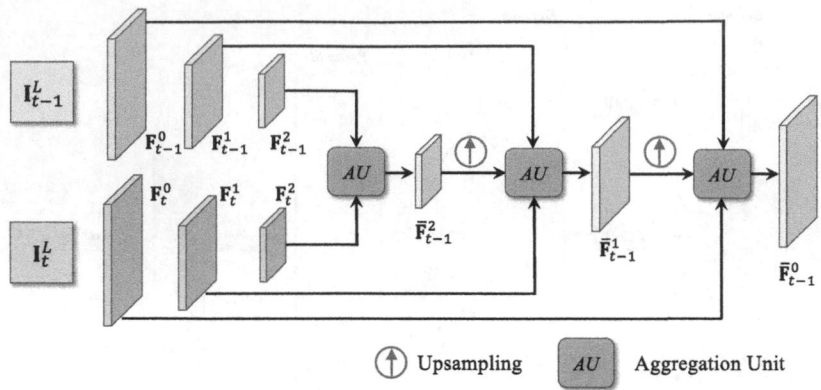

Fig. 3. Structure of temporal multi-correspondence aggregation module (TM-CAM).

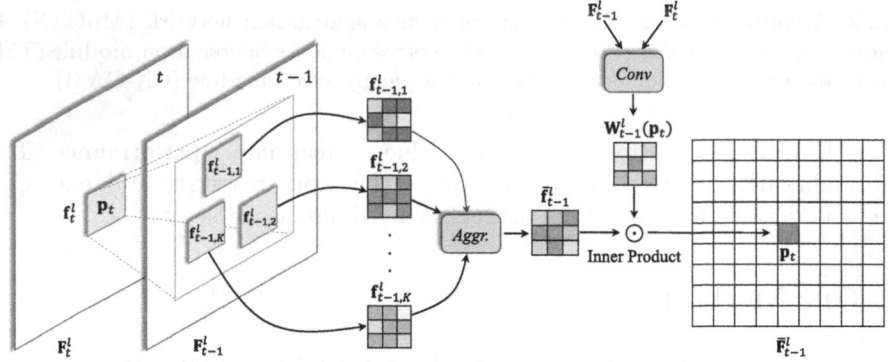

Fig. 4. Aggregation unit in TM-CAM. It aggregates multiple inter-frame correspondences to recover a given pixel at $\mathbf{p}_t$.

motion, while progressively moving up to low-level/high-resolution stages (i.e., to $\overline{\mathbf{F}}_{t-1}^{l=0}$) for subtle sub-pixel shift. Different from many methods [2,32,37] that directly regress flow fields in the image space, our module functions in the feature space. It is more stable and robust to noise [35].

The aggregation unit in Fig. 3 is detailed in Fig. 4. A patch-based matching strategy is used since it naturally contains structural information. As aforementioned in Fig. 1(b), one-on-one mapping may not be able to capture the true correspondences between frames. We thus aggregate multiple candidates to obtain sufficient context information as in Fig. 4.

In details, we first locally select top-K most similar feature patches, and then utilize a pixel-adaptive aggregation scheme to fuse them into one pixel to avoid boundary problems. Taking aligning $\mathbf{F}_{t-1}^{l}$ to $\mathbf{F}_t^{l}$ as an example, given an image patch $\mathbf{f}_t^{l}$ (represented as a feature vector) in $\mathbf{F}_t^{l}$, we first find its nearest neighbors on $\mathbf{F}_{t-1}^{l}$. For efficiency, we define a local search area satisfying $\left|\mathbf{p}_t - \mathbf{p}_{t-1}\right| \leq \mathbf{d}$, where $\mathbf{p}_t$ is the position vector of $\mathbf{f}_t^l$. $\mathbf{d}$ means the maximum displacement. We use correlation as a distance measure as in Flownet [6]. For $\mathbf{f}_{t-1}^l$ and $\mathbf{f}_t^l$, their correlation is computed as the normalized inner product of

$$corr(\mathbf{f}_{t-1}^l, \mathbf{f}_t^l) = \frac{\mathbf{f}_{t-1}^l}{||\mathbf{f}_{t-1}^l||} \cdot \frac{\mathbf{f}_t^l}{||\mathbf{f}_t^l||}. \tag{1}$$

After calculating correlations, we select top-K most correlated patches (i.e., $\vec{\mathbf{f}}_{t-1,1}^l, \vec{\mathbf{f}}_{t-1,2}^l, \dots, \vec{\mathbf{f}}_{t-1,K}^l$) in a descending order from $\mathbf{F}_{t-1}^l$, and concatenate and aggregate them as

$$\vec{\mathbf{f}}_{t-1}^l = Aggr\left(\left[\vec{\mathbf{f}}_{t-1,1}^l, \vec{\mathbf{f}}_{t-1,2}^l, \dots, \vec{\mathbf{f}}_{t-1,K}^l\right]\right), \tag{2}$$

where $Aggr$ is implemented as convolution layers. Instead of assigning equal weights (e.g., $\frac{1}{9}$ when the patch size is 3), we design a pixel-adaptive aggregation strategy to enable varying aggregation patterns in different locations. The weight map is obtained by concatenating $\mathbf{F}_{t-1}^l$ and $\mathbf{F}_t^l$ and going through a convolution layer, which has a size of $H \times W \times s^2$ when the patch size is $s \times s$. More precisely, the adaptive weight map takes the form of

$$\mathbf{W}_{t-1}^l = Conv\left(\left[\mathbf{F}_{t-1}^l, \mathbf{F}_t^l\right]\right). \tag{3}$$

As shown in Fig. 4, the final value at position $\mathbf{p}_t$ on the aligned neighboring frame $\bar{\mathbf{F}}_{t-1}^l$ is obtained as

$$\bar{\mathbf{F}}_{t-1}^l(\mathbf{p}_t) = \vec{\mathbf{f}}_{t-1}^l \cdot \mathbf{W}_{t-1}^l(\mathbf{p}_t). \tag{4}$$

After repeating the above steps for $2N$ times, we obtain a set of aligned neighboring feature maps $\{\bar{\mathbf{F}}_{t-N}^0, \dots, \bar{\mathbf{F}}_{t-1}^0, \bar{\mathbf{F}}_{t+1}^0, \dots, \bar{\mathbf{F}}_{t+N}^0\}$. To handle all frames at the same feature level, as shown in Fig. 2, we employ an additional TM-CAM, which performs self-aggregation with $\mathbf{I}_t^L$ as the input and produces $\bar{\mathbf{F}}_t^0$. Finally, all these feature maps are fused into a double-spatial-sized feature map by a convolution and PixelShuffle operation, which is to keep sub-pixel details.

3.2 Cross-scale Nonlocal-Correspondence Aggregation Module

Similar patterns exist widely in natural images that can provide abundant texture information. Self-similarity [9,20,29,44,47] can help detail recovery. In this part, we design a cross-scale aggregation strategy to capture nonlocal correspondences across different feature resolutions, as illustrated in Fig. 5.

To distinguish from Sect. 3.1, we use $\mathbf{M}_t^s$ to denote feature maps at time t with scale level s. We first downsample the input feature maps $\mathbf{M}_t^0$ and obtain a feature pyramid as

$$\mathbf{M}_t^{s+1} = AvgPool\left(\mathbf{M}_t^s\right), \ s = \{0, 1, 2\}, \tag{5}$$

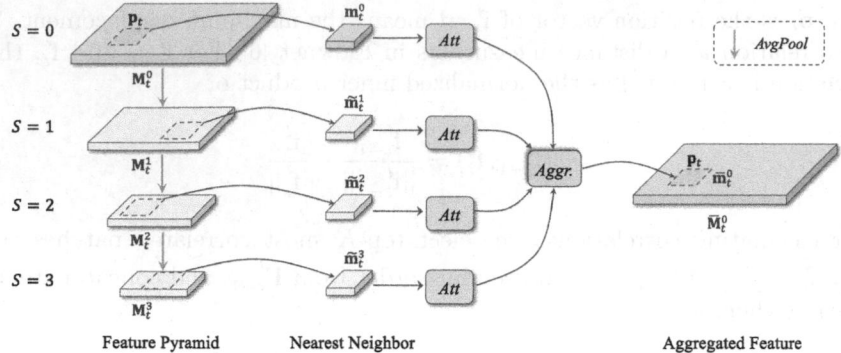

Fig. 5. Cross-scale nonlocal-correspondence aggregation module (CN-CAM).

where *AvgPool* is the average pooling with stride 2. Given a query patch $\mathbf{m}_t^0$ in $\mathbf{M}_t^0$ centered at position $\mathbf{p}_t$, we implement a non-local search on other three scales to obtain

$$\tilde{\mathbf{m}}_t^s = NN\left(\mathbf{M}_t^s, \mathbf{m}_t^0\right), \ s = \{1,2,3\}, \tag{6}$$

where $\tilde{\mathbf{m}}_t^s$ denotes the nearest neighbor (the most correlated patch) of $\mathbf{m}_t^0$ in $\mathbf{M}_t^s$. Before merging, a self-attention module [41] is applied to determine whether the information is useful or not. Finally, the aggregated feature $\bar{\mathbf{m}}_t^0$ at position $\mathbf{p}_t$ is calculated as

$$\bar{\mathbf{m}}_t^0 = Aggr\left(\left[Att\left(\mathbf{m}_t^0\right), Att\left(\tilde{\mathbf{m}}_t^1\right), Att\left(\tilde{\mathbf{m}}_t^2\right), Att\left(\tilde{\mathbf{m}}_t^3\right)\right]\right), \tag{7}$$

where *Att* is the attention unit and *Aggr* is implemented as convolution layers. Our results presented in Sect. 4.3 demonstrate that CN-CAM reveals more details.

3.3 Edge-Aware Loss

Usually, reconstructed high-resolution images produced by VSR methods suffer from jagged edges. To alleviate this problem, we propose an edge-aware loss to obtain better refined edges. First, an edge detector is used to extract edge information of ground-truth HR images. Then, the detected edge areas are weighted more in loss calculation, enforcing the network to pay more attention to these areas during the learning.

In this paper, we choose the Laplacian filter as the edge detector. Given the ground-truth $\mathbf{I}_t^H$, the edge map $\mathbf{I}_t^E$ is obtained from the detector and the binary mask value at $\mathbf{p}_t$ is represented as

$$\mathbf{B}_t\left(\mathbf{p}_t\right) = \begin{cases} 1, & \mathbf{I}_t^E\left(\mathbf{p}_t\right) \geq \delta \\ 0, & \mathbf{I}_t^E\left(\mathbf{p}_t\right) < \delta, \end{cases} \tag{8}$$

where δ is a predefined threshold. Suppose the size of a high-resolution image is $H \times W$. The edge mask is also a $H \times W$ map filled with binary values. The areas marked as edges are 1 while others being 0.

During training, we adopt the Charbonnier Loss, which is defined as

$$L = \sqrt{\left\| \hat{\mathbf{I}}_t^H - \mathbf{I}_t^H \right\|^2 + \epsilon^2}, \tag{9}$$

where $\hat{\mathbf{I}}_t^H$ is the predicted high-resolution result, and ϵ is a small constant. The final loss is formulated as

$$L_{final} = L + \lambda \left\| \mathbf{B}_t \circ \left(\hat{\mathbf{I}}_t^H - \mathbf{I}_t^H \right) \right\|, \tag{10}$$

where λ is a coefficient to balance the two terms and $\circ$ is element-wise multiplication.

4   Experiments

4.1   Dataset and Evaluation Protocol

REDS. [27] is a realistic and dynamic scene dataset published in NTIRE 2019 challenge. There are a total of 30K images extracted from 300 video sequences. The training, validation and test subsets contain 240, 30 and 30 sequences, respectively. Each sequence has equally 100 images with resolution 720×1280. Similar to that of [41], we merge the training and validation parts and divide the data into new training (with 266 sequences) and testing (with 4 sequences) datasets. The new testing part contains the $000, 011, 015$ and 020 sequences.

Vimeo-90K. [43] is a large-scale high-quality video dataset designed for various video tasks. It consists of 89,800 video clips which cover a broad range of actions and scenes. The super-resolution subset has 91,701 7-frame sequences with fixed resolution 448×256, among which training and testing splits contain 64,612 and 7,824 sequences respectively.

Peak signal-to-noise ratio (PSNR) and structural similarity index (SSIM) [42] are used as metrics in our experiments.

4.2   Implementation Details

Network Settings. The network takes 5 (or 7) consecutive frames as input. In feature extraction and reconstruction modules, 5 and 40 (20 for 7 frames) residual blocks [12] are implemented respectively with channel size 128. In Fig. 3, the patch size is 3 and the maximum displacements are set to $\{3, 5, 7\}$ from low to high resolutions. The K value is set to 4. In the cross-scale aggregation module, we define patch size as 1 and fuse information from 4 scales as shown in Fig. 5. After reconstruction, both the height and width of images are quadrupled.

Table 1. Ablation Study of our proposed modules and loss on the REDS testing dataset. 'Baseline' is without using the proposed modules and loss. 'TM-CAM' represents the temporal multi-correspondence aggregation module. 'CN-CAM' means the cross-scale nonlocal-correspondence aggregation module. 'EAL' is the proposed edge-aware loss.

Components				PSNR(dB)	SSIM
Baseline	TM-CAM	CN-CAM	EAL		
✓				28.98	0.8280
✓	✓			30.13	0.8614
✓	✓	✓		30.25	0.8641
✓	✓	✓	✓	**30.31**	**0.8648**

Table 2. Results of TM-CAM with different numbers (K) of aggregated temporal correspondences on the REDS testing dataset.

K	PSNR(dB)	SSIM
1	30.19	0.8624
2	30.24	0.8640
4	**30.31**	0.8648
6	30.30	**0.8651**

Training. We train our network using eight NVIDIA GeForce GTX 1080Ti GPUs with mini-batch size 3 per GPU. The training takes 600K iterations for all datasets. We use Adam as the optimizer and cosine learning rate decay strategy with an initial value $4e-4$. The input images are augmented with random cropping, flipping and rotation. The cropping size is 64×64 corresponding to an output 256×256. The rotation is selected as $90°$ or $-90°$. When calculating the edge-aware loss, we set both δ and λ as 0.1.

Testing. During testing, the output is evaluated without boundary cropping.

4.3 Ablation Study

To demonstrate the effectiveness of our proposed method, we conduct experiments for each individual design. For convenience, we adopt a lightweight setting in this section. The channel size of network is set to 64 and the reconstruction module contains 10 residual blocks. Meanwhile, the amount of training iterations is reduced to 200K.

Temporal Multi-correspondence Aggregation Module. To make fair comparison, we first build a baseline without the proposed ideas. As shown in Table 1, the baseline only yields 28.98 dB PSNR and 0.8280 SSIM, a relatively poor result. Our designed module brings about a 1.15 dB improvement on PSNR.

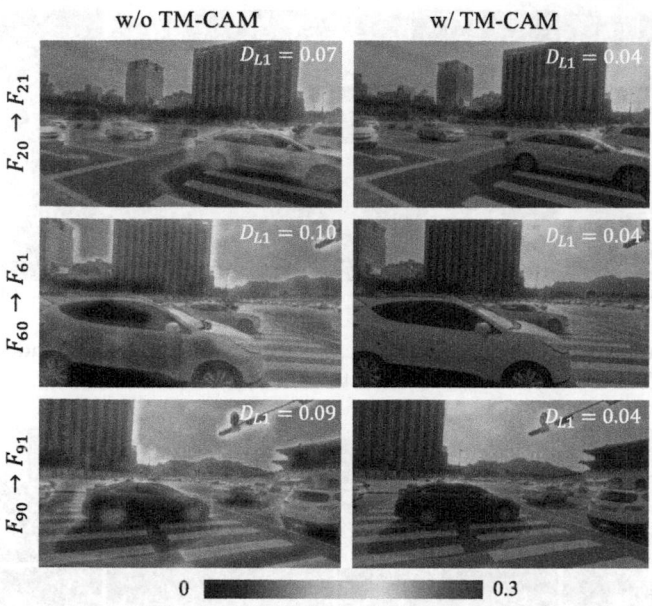

Fig. 6. Residual maps between aligned neighboring feature maps and reference feature maps without and with temporal multi-correspondence aggregation module (TM-CAM) on the REDS dataset. Values on the upper right represent the average $L1$ distance between aligned neighboring feature maps and reference feature maps.

To show the effectiveness of TM-CAM in a more intuitive way, we visualize residual maps between aligned neighboring feature maps and reference feature maps in Fig. 6. After aggregation, it is clear that feature maps obtained with the proposed TM-CAM are smoother and cleaner. The mean $L1$ distance between aligned neighboring and reference feature maps are smaller. All these facts manifest the great alignment performance of our method.

Then, we evaluate how the number of aggregated temporal correspondences affects performance. Table 2 shows that the capability of TM-CAM rises at first and drops with the increasing number of correspondences. Compared with taking only one candidate, the four-correspondence setting obtains more than 0.1 dB gain on PSNR. It demonstrates that highly correlated correspondences can provide useful complementary details. However, once saturated, it is not necessary to include more correspondences, since weakly correlated correspondences actually bring unwanted noise. We further verify this point by estimating optical flow using a KNN strategy for the MPI Sintel Flow dataset [1]. From Fig. 1(b), we find that the four-neighbor setting is also the best choice. Therefore, we set K as 4 in our implementation.

Finally, we verify the performance of pixel-adaptive weights. Based on the experiments, we find that a larger patch in TM-CAM usually gives a better result. It is reasonable since neighboring pixels usually have similar information and are likely to complement each other. Also, structural information is embed-

Fig. 7. Examples without and with the cross-scale nonlocal-correspondence aggregation module (CN-CAM) on the REDS dataset.

Fig. 8. Examples without and with the proposed edge-aware loss (EAL) on the REDS dataset.

ded. To balance between performance and computing cost, we set the size to 3. When using fixed wieghts (at $K = 4$), we obtain the resulting PSNR/SSIM as 30.12 dB/0.8614. From Table 2, the proposed pixel-adaptive weighting scheme achieves 30.31 dB/0.8648, which is superior to the fixed counterpart by nearly 0.2 dB on PSNR, which demonstrates that different aggregating patterns are necessary for consideration of spatial variance.

More experiments of TM-CAM with regard to patch size and maximum displacements are provided in the supplementary file.

Cross-scale Nonlocal-Correspondence Aggregation Module In Sect. 4.3, we already notice that highly correlated temporal correspondences can serve as a supplement in motion compensation. To handle cases with different scales, we proposed a cross-scale nonlocal-correspondence aggregation module (CN-CAM).

As listed in Table 1, CN-CAM improves PSNR by 0.12 dB. Besides, from Fig. 7, we observe that this module enables the network to reveal more details when images contain repeated patterns such as windows and buildings within the spatial domain or across scales. All these results show that the proposed CN-CAM method further enhances the quality of reconstructed images.

Table 3. Comparisons of PSNR(dB)/SSIM results on the REDS dataset for ×4 setting. '*' denotes without pretraining.

Method	Frames	Clip_000	Clip_011	Clip_015	Clip_020	Average
Bicubic	1	24.55/0.6489	26.06/0.7261	28.52/0.8034	25.41/0.7386	26.14/0.7292
RCAN [48]	1	26.17/0.7371	29.34/0.8255	31.85/0.8881	27.74/0.8293	28.78/0.8200
TOFlow [43]	7	26.52/0.7540	27.80/0.7858	30.67/0.8609	26.92/0.7953	27.98/0.7990
DUF [15]	7	27.30/0.7937	28.38/0.8056	31.55/0.8846	27.30/0.8164	28.63/0.8251
EDVR* [41]	5	27.78/0.8156	31.60/0.8779	33.71/0.9161	29.74/0.8809	30.71/0.8726
MuCAN (Ours)	5	**27.99/0.8219**	**31.84/0.8801**	**33.90/0.9170**	**29.78/0.8811**	**30.88/0.8750**

Table 4. Comparisons of PSNR(dB)/SSIM results on the Vimeo-90K dataset for ×4 setting. '–' indicates results not available.

Method	Frames	RGB	Y
Bicubic	1	29.79/0.8483	31.32/0.8684
RCAN [48]	1	33.61/0.9101	35.35/0.9251
DeepSR [23]	7	25.55/0.8498	
BayesSR [24]	7	24.64/0.8205	–
TOFlow [43]	7	33.08/0.9054	34.83/0.9220
DUF [15]	7	34.33/0.9227	36.37/0.9387
RBPN [10]	7	–	37.07/0.9435
MuCAN (Ours)	7	**35.49/0.9344**	**37.32/0.9465**

Edge-Aware Loss. In this part, we evaluate the proposed edge-aware loss (EAL). Table 1 lists the statistics. A few visual results in Fig. 8 indicate that EAL improves the proposed network further, yielding more refined edges. The textures on the wall and edges of lights are clearer and sharper, which demonstrates the effectiveness of the proposed edge-aware loss.

4.4 Comparison with State-of-the-Art Methods

We compare our proposed multi-correspondence aggregation network (MuCAN) with previous state-of-the-arts including TOFlow [43], DUF [15], RBPN [10], EDVR [41], etc., on REDS [27], Vimeo-90K [43], Vid4 [24] and SPMCS [37] datasets. The quantitative results in Tables 3 and 4 are from the original publications. Especially, original EDVR [41] is initialized with a well-trained model. For fairness, we use the author-released code to train EDVR without pretraining.

On the REDS dataset, results are shown in Table 3. It is clear that our method outperforms other methods by at least **0.17 dB**. As for Vimeo-90K, the results are reported in Table 4. Our MuCAN method works better than DUF [15] with nearly **1.2 dB** enhancement on RGB channels. Meanwhile, it obtains **0.25 dB** improvement on the Y channel compared with RBPN [10]. All of these results demonstrate the effectiveness of our method. Besides, the performance on the Vid4 and SPMCS datasets are reported in the supplementary file. Several examples are visualized in Fig. 9.

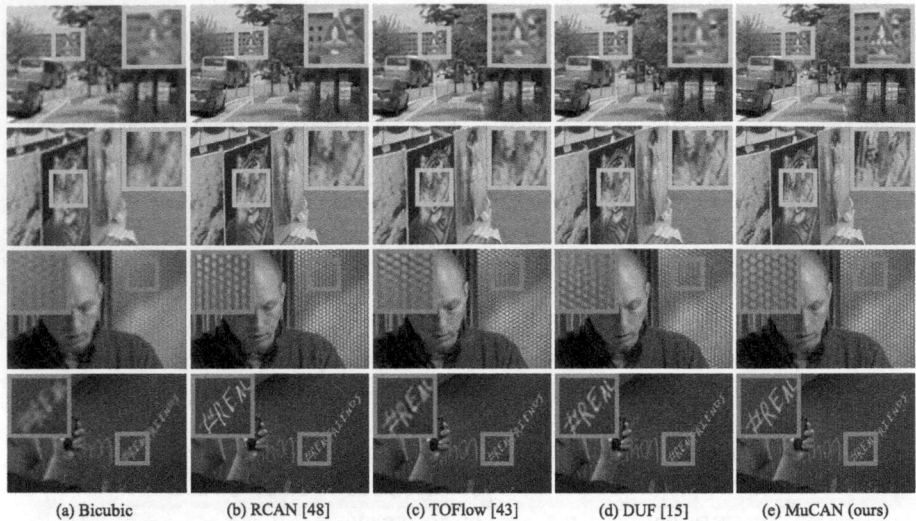

(a) Bicubic   (b) RCAN [48]   (c) TOFlow [43]   (d) DUF [15]   (e) MuCAN (ours)

Fig. 9. Examples of REDS (top two rows) and Vimeo-90K (bottom two rows) datasets.

4.5   Generalization Analysis

To evaluate the generality of our method, we apply our model trained on the REDS dataset to test video frames in the wild. In addition, we test EDVR with the author-released model[1] on the REDS dataset. Some visual results are shown in the supplementary file. We remark that EDVR may generate visual artifacts in some cases due to the variance of data distributions between training and testing. In contrast, our MuCAN demonstrates its decent generality in the real world setting.

5   Conclusion

In this paper, we have proposed a novel multi-correspondence aggregation network (MuCAN) for the video super-resolution task. We showed that the proposed temporal multi-correspondence aggregation module (TM-CAM) takes advantage of highly correlated patches to achieve a better alignment-based frame recovery. Additionally, we verified that the cross-scale nonlocal-correspondence aggregation module (CN-CAM) utilizes multi-scale information and further boosts the performance of our network. Also, the edge-aware loss enforces the network to obtain more refined edges on the high-resolution output. Extensive experiments have demonstrated the effectiveness and generality of our proposed method.

---

[1] https://github.com/xinntao/EDVR.

References

1. Butler, D.J., Wulff, J., Stanley, G.B., Black, M.J.: A naturalistic open source movie for optical flow evaluation. In: Fitzgibbon, A., Lazebnik, S., Perona, P., Sato, Y., Schmid, C. (eds.) ECCV 2012. LNCS, vol. 7577, pp. 611–625. Springer, Heidelberg (2012). https://doi.org/10.1007/978-3-642-33783-3_44
2. Caballero, J., et al.: Real-time video super-resolution with spatio-temporal networks and motion compensation. In: Proceedings of the IEEE Conference on Computer Vision and Pattern Recognition, pp. 4778–4787 (2017)
3. Dai, J., et al.: Deformable convolutional networks. In: Proceedings of the IEEE International Conference on Computer Vision, pp. 764–773 (2017)
4. Dong, C., Loy, C.C., He, K., Tang, X.: Learning a deep convolutional network for image super-resolution. In: Fleet, D., Pajdla, T., Schiele, B., Tuytelaars, T. (eds.) ECCV 2014. LNCS, vol. 8692, pp. 184–199. Springer, Cham (2014). https://doi.org/10.1007/978-3-319-10593-2_13
5. Dong, C., Loy, C.C., Tang, X.: Accelerating the super-resolution convolutional neural network. In: Leibe, B., Matas, J., Sebe, N., Welling, M. (eds.) ECCV 2016. LNCS, vol. 9906, pp. 391–407. Springer, Cham (2016). https://doi.org/10.1007/978-3-319-46475-6_25
6. Dosovitskiy, A., et al.: FlowNet: learning optical flow with convolutional networks. In: Proceedings of the IEEE International Conference on Computer Vision, pp. 2758–2766 (2015)
7. Freedman, G., Fattal, R.: Image and video upscaling from local self-examples. ACM Trans. Graph. (TOG) **30**(2), 12 (2011)
8. Freeman, W.T., Jones, T.R., Pasztor, E.C.: Example-based super-resolution. IEEE Comput. Graph. Appl. **2**, 56–65 (2002)
9. Glasner, D., Bagon, S., Irani, M.: Super-resolution from a single image. In: 2009 IEEE 12th International Conference on Computer Vision, pp. 349–356. IEEE (2009)
10. Haris, M., Shakhnarovich, G., Ukita, N.: Deep back-projection networks for super-resolution. In: Proceedings of the IEEE Conference on Computer Vision and Pattern Recognition, pp. 1664–1673 (2018)
11. Haris, M., Shakhnarovich, G., Ukita, N.: Recurrent back-projection network for video super-resolution. In: Proceedings of the IEEE Conference on Computer Vision and Pattern Recognition, pp. 3897–3906 (2019)
12. He, K., Zhang, X., Ren, S., Sun, J.: Deep residual learning for image recognition. In: Proceedings of the IEEE Conference on Computer Vision and Pattern Recognition, pp. 770–778 (2016)
13. Huang, J.B., Singh, A., Ahuja, N.: Single image super-resolution from transformed self-exemplars. In: Proceedings of the IEEE Conference on Computer Vision and Pattern Recognition, pp. 5197–5206 (2015)
14. Huang, Y., Wang, W., Wang, L.: Bidirectional recurrent convolutional networks for multi-frame super-resolution. In: Advances in Neural Information Processing Systems, pp. 235–243 (2015)
15. Jo, Y., Wug Oh, S., Kang, J., Joo Kim, S.: Deep video super-resolution network using dynamic upsampling filters without explicit motion compensation. In: Proceedings of the IEEE Conference on Computer Vision and Pattern Recognition, pp. 3224–3232 (2018)
16. Kappeler, A., Yoo, S., Dai, Q., Katsaggelos, A.K.: Video super-resolution with convolutional neural networks. IEEE Trans. Comput. Imaging **2**(2), 109–122 (2016)

17. Kim, J., Kwon Lee, J., Mu Lee, K.: Accurate image super-resolution using very deep convolutional networks. In: Proceedings of the IEEE Conference on Computer Vision and Pattern Recognition, pp. 1646–1654 (2016)
18. Kim, J., Kwon Lee, J., Mu Lee, K.: Deeply-recursive convolutional network for image super-resolution. In: Proceedings of the IEEE Conference on Computer Vision and Pattern Recognition, pp. 1637–1645 (2016)
19. Kim, S.Y., Lim, J., Na, T., Kim, M.: 3DSRnet: video super-resolution using 3D convolutional neural networks. arXiv preprint arXiv:1812.09079 (2018)
20. Kindermann, S., Osher, S., Jones, P.W.: Deblurring and denoising of images by nonlocal functionals. Multiscale Model. Simul. 4(4), 1091–1115 (2005)
21. Lai, W.S., Huang, J.B., Ahuja, N., Yang, M.H.: Deep Laplacian pyramid networks for fast and accurate super-resolution. In: Proceedings of the IEEE Conference on Computer Vision and Pattern Recognition, pp. 624–632 (2017)
22. Li, S., He, F., Du, B., Zhang, L., Xu, Y., Tao, D.: Fast residual network for video super-resolution. arXiv preprint arXiv:1904.02870 (2019)
23. Liao, R., Tao, X., Li, R., Ma, Z., Jia, J.: Video super-resolution via deep draft-ensemble learning. In: Proceedings of the IEEE International Conference on Computer Vision, pp. 531–539 (2015)
24. Liu, C., Sun, D.: On Bayesian adaptive video super resolution. IEEE Trans. Pattern Anal. Mach. Intell. 36(2), 346–360 (2013)
25. Liu, D., et al.: Robust video super-resolution with learned temporal dynamics. In: Proceedings of the IEEE International Conference on Computer Vision, pp. 2507–2515 (2017)
26. Ma, Z., Liao, R., Tao, X., Xu, L., Jia, J., Wu, E.: Handling motion blur in multi-frame super-resolution. In: Proceedings of the IEEE Conference on Computer Vision and Pattern Recognition, pp. 5224–5232 (2015)
27. Nah, S., et al.: NTIRE 2019 challenge on video deblurring and super-resolution: dataset and study. In: Proceedings of the IEEE Conference on Computer Vision and Pattern Recognition Workshops, pp. 0–0 (2019)
28. Pérez-Pellitero, E., Salvador, J., Ruiz-Hidalgo, J., Rosenhahn, B.: PSyCo: manifold span reduction for super resolution. In: Proceedings of the IEEE Conference on Computer Vision and Pattern Recognition, pp. 1837–1845 (2016)
29. Protter, M., Elad, M., Takeda, H., Milanfar, P.: Generalizing the nonlocal-means to super-resolution reconstruction. IEEE Trans. Image Process. 18(1), 36–51 (2008)
30. Ranjan, A., Black, M.J.: Optical flow estimation using a spatial pyramid network. In: Proceedings of the IEEE Conference on Computer Vision and Pattern Recognition, pp. 4161–4170 (2017)
31. Ronneberger, O., Fischer, P., Brox, T.: U-Net: convolutional networks for biomedical image segmentation. In: Navab, N., Hornegger, J., Wells, W.M., Frangi, A.F. (eds.) MICCAI 2015. LNCS, vol. 9351, pp. 234–241. Springer, Cham (2015). https://doi.org/10.1007/978-3-319-24574-4_28
32. Sajjadi, M.S., Vemulapalli, R., Brown, M.: Frame-recurrent video super-resolution. In: Proceedings of the IEEE Conference on Computer Vision and Pattern Recognition, pp. 6626–6634 (2018)
33. Schulter, S., Leistner, C., Bischof, H.: Fast and accurate image upscaling with super-resolution forests. In: Proceedings of the IEEE Conference on Computer Vision and Pattern Recognition, pp. 3791–3799 (2015)
34. Shi, W., et al.: Real-time single image and video super-resolution using an efficient sub-pixel convolutional neural network. In: Proceedings of the IEEE Conference on Computer Vision and Pattern Recognition, pp. 1874–1883 (2016)

35. Sun, D., Yang, X., Liu, M.Y., Kautz, J.: PWC-Net: CNNs for optical flow using pyramid, warping, and cost volume. In: Proceedings of the IEEE Conference on Computer Vision and Pattern Recognition, pp. 8934–8943 (2018)
36. Tai, Y., Yang, J., Liu, X.: Image super-resolution via deep recursive residual network. In: Proceedings of the IEEE Conference on Computer Vision and Pattern Recognition, pp. 3147–3155 (2017)
37. Tao, X., Gao, H., Liao, R., Wang, J., Jia, J.: Detail-revealing deep video super-resolution. In: Proceedings of the IEEE International Conference on Computer Vision, pp. 4472–4480 (2017)
38. Tian, Y., Zhang, Y., Fu, Y., Xu, C.: TDAN: temporally deformable alignment network for video super-resolution. arXiv preprint arXiv:1812.02898 (2018)
39. Timofte, R., De Smet, V., Van Gool, L.: Anchored neighborhood regression for fast example-based super-resolution. In: Proceedings of the IEEE International Conference on Computer Vision, pp. 1920–1927 (2013)
40. Timofte, R., De Smet, V., Van Gool, L.: A+: adjusted anchored neighborhood regression for fast super-resolution. In: Cremers, D., Reid, I., Saito, H., Yang, M.-H. (eds.) ACCV 2014. LNCS, vol. 9006, pp. 111–126. Springer, Cham (2015). https://doi.org/10.1007/978-3-319-16817-3_8
41. Wang, X., Chan, K.C., Yu, K., Dong, C., Change Loy, C.: EDVR: video restoration with enhanced deformable convolutional networks. In: Proceedings of the IEEE Conference on Computer Vision and Pattern Recognition Workshops (2019)
42. Wang, Z., Bovik, A.C., Sheikh, H.R., Simoncelli, E.P., et al.: Image quality assessment: from error visibility to structural similarity. IEEE Trans. Image Process. **13**(4), 600–612 (2004)
43. Xue, T., Chen, B., Wu, J., Wei, D., Freeman, W.T.: Video enhancement with task-oriented flow. Int. J. Comput. Vis. **127**(8), 1106–1125 (2019)
44. Yang, C.-Y., Huang, J.-B., Yang, M.-H.: Exploiting self-similarities for single frame super-resolution. In: Kimmel, R., Klette, R., Sugimoto, A. (eds.) ACCV 2010. LNCS, vol. 6494, pp. 497–510. Springer, Heidelberg (2011). https://doi.org/10.1007/978-3-642-19318-7_39
45. Yang, J., Wang, Z., Lin, Z., Cohen, S., Huang, T.: Coupled dictionary training for image super-resolution. IEEE Trans. Image Process. **21**(8), 3467–3478 (2012)
46. Yang, J., Wright, J., Huang, T.S., Ma, Y.: Image super-resolution via sparse representation. IEEE Trans. Image Process. **19**(11), 2861–2873 (2010)
47. Zhang, X., Burger, M., Bresson, X., Osher, S.: Bregmanized nonlocal regularization for deconvolution and sparse reconstruction. SIAM J. Imaging Sci. **3**(3), 253–276 (2010)
48. Zhang, Y., Li, K., Li, K., Wang, L., Zhong, B., Fu, Y.: Image super-resolution using very deep residual channel attention networks. In: Ferrari, V., Hebert, M., Sminchisescu, C., Weiss, Y. (eds.) ECCV 2018. LNCS, vol. 11211, pp. 294–310. Springer, Cham (2018). https://doi.org/10.1007/978-3-030-01234-2_18
49. Zhang, Y., Tian, Y., Kong, Y., Zhong, B., Fu, Y.: Residual dense network for image super-resolution. In: Proceedings of the IEEE Conference on Computer Vision and Pattern Recognition, pp. 2472–2481 (2018)

Efficient Semantic Video Segmentation with Per-Frame Inference

Yifan Liu[1], Chunhua Shen[1], Changqian Yu[1,2], and Jingdong Wang[3(✉)]

[1] The University of Adelaide, Adelaide, Australia
[2] Huazhong University of Science and Technology, Wuhan, China
[3] Microsoft Research, Redmond, USA
jingdw@microsoft.com

Abstract. For semantic segmentation, most existing real-time deep models trained with each frame independently may produce inconsistent results when tested on a video sequence. A few methods take the correlations in the video sequence into account, e.g., by propagating the results to the neighbouring frames using optical flow, or extracting frame representations using multi-frame information, which may lead to inaccurate results or unbalanced latency. In contrast, here we explicitly consider the temporal consistency among frames as extra constraints during training and process each frame independently in the inference phase. Thus no computation overhead is introduced for inference. Compact models are employed for real-time execution. To narrow the performance gap between compact models and large models, new temporal knowledge distillation methods are designed. Weighing among accuracy, temporal smoothness and efficiency, our proposed method outperforms previous keyframe based methods and corresponding baselines which are trained with each frame independently on benchmark datasets including Cityscapes and Camvid. Code is available at: https://git.io/vidseg.

Keywords: Semantic video segmentation · Temporal consistency

1 Introduction

Semantic segmentation, a fundamental task in computer vision, aims to assign a semantic label to each pixel in an image. In recent years, the development of deep learning has brought significant success to the task of image semantic segmentation [5, 31, 37] on benchmark datasets, but often with a high computational cost. This task becomes computationally more expensive when extending to video. For a few real-world applications, e.g., autonomous driving and robotics, it is challenging but crucial to build a fast and accurate video semantic segmentation system.

Electronic supplementary material The online version of this chapter (https://doi.org/10.1007/978-3-030-58607-2_21) contains supplementary material, which is available to authorized users.

© Springer Nature Switzerland AG 2020
A. Vedaldi et al. (Eds.): ECCV 2020, LNCS 12355, pp. 352–368, 2020.
https://doi.org/10.1007/978-3-030-58607-2_21

Previous works for semantic video segmentation can be categorized into two groups. The first group focuses on improving the performance for video segmentation by performing post-processing among frames [18], or employing extra modules to use multi-frames information during inference [8]. The high computational cost makes it difficult for mobile applications. The second group uses keyframes to avoid processing of each frame, and then propagate [32,38,39] the outputs or the feature maps to other frames (non-key frames) using optical flows. Keyframe based methods indeed accelerate inference. However, it requires different inference time for keyframes and non-key frames, leading to an unbalanced latency, thus being not friendly for real-time processing. Moreover, accuracy cannot be guaranteed for each frame due to the cumulative warping error, for example, the first row in Fig. 1(a).

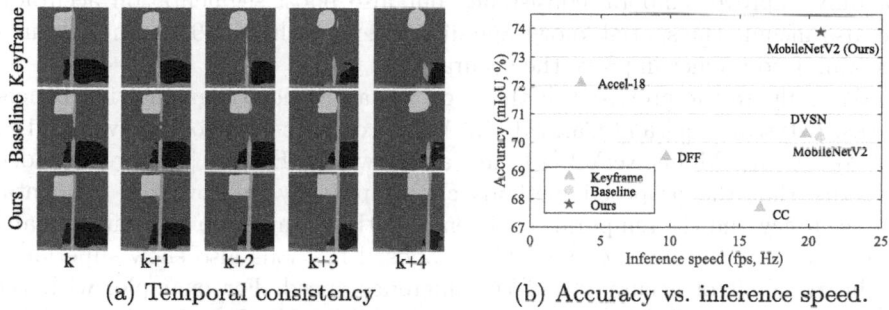

(a) Temporal consistency   (b) Accuracy vs. inference speed.

Fig. 1. (a) Visualization results on consecutive frames: *Keyframe*: Accel18 [13] propagates and fuses the results from the keyframe (k) to non-key frames ($k + 1, \ldots$), which may lead to poor results on non-key frames. *Baseline*: PSPNet18 [37] trains the model on single frames. Inference on single frames separately can produce temporally inconsistent results. *Ours*: training the model with the correlations among frames and inferring on single frames separately lead to high quality and smooth results. (b) Comparing our enhanced MobileNetV2 model with previous keyframe based methods: Accel [13], DVSN [32], DFF [39] and CC [27]. The inference speed is evaluated on a single GTX 1080Ti.

Efficient semantic segmentation methods on 2D images [20,23,34] have draw much attention recently. Clearly, applying compact networks to each frame of a video sequence independently may alleviate the latency and enable real-time execution. However, directly training the model on each frame independently often produces temporally inconsistent results on the video as shown in the second row of Fig. 1(a). To address the above problems, we explicitly consider the temporal consistency among frames as extra constraints during the training process and employ compact networks with per-frame inference to ease the problem of latency and achieve real-time inference.

A motion guided *temporal loss* is employed with the motivation of assigning a consistent label to the same pixel along the time axis. A motion estimation network is introduced to predict the motion (e.g., optical-flow) of each pixel from the current frame to the next frame based on the input frame-pair. Predicted semantic labels are propagated to the next frame to supervise predictions of the next frame. Thus, the temporal consistency is encoded into the segmentation network through this constraint.

To narrow the performance gap between compact models and large models, we design a new *temporal consistency knowledge distillation* strategy to help the training of compact models. Distillation methods are widely used in image recognition tasks [11,16,19], and achieve great success. Different from previous distillation methods, which only consider the spatial correlations, we embed the temporal consistency into distillation items. We extract the pair-wise frames dependency by calculating the pair-wise similarities for different locations between two frames, and further encode the multi-frames dependency into a latent embedding by using a recurrent unit, ConvLSTM [28]. The new distillation methods not only improve temporal consistency but also boost segmentation accuracy. We also include the spatial knowledge distillation methods [19] of single frames in training to further improve the accuracy.

We evaluate the proposed methods on semantic video segmentation benchmarks: Cityscapes [6] and Camvid [3]. A few compact backbone networks, i.e., PSPNet18 [37], MobileNetV2 [26] and a lightweight HRNet [30], are included to verify that the proposed methods can empirically improve the segmentation accuracy and the temporal consistency, without any extra computation and post-processing during inference. The proposed methods also show superiority in the trade-off of accuracy and the inference speed. For example, with the per-frame inference fashion, our enhanced MobileNetV2 [26] can achieve higher accuracy with a faster inference speed compared with state-of-the-art keyframe based methods as shown in Fig. 1(b). We summarize our main contributions as follows.

- We process semantic video segmentation with compact models by per-frame inference, without introducing post-processing and computation overhead, enabling real-time inference without latency.
- We explicitly consider the temporal consistency in the training process by using a temporal loss and newly designed temporal consistency knowledge distillation methods.
- Empirical experiment results on Cityscapes and Camvid show that with the help of proposed training methods, the compact models outperform previous state-of-the-art semantic video segmentation methods weighing among accuracy, temporal consistency and inference speed.

1.1   Related Work

Semantic Video Segmentation. Semantic video segmentation requires dense labeling for all pixels in each frame of a video sequence into a few semantic categories. Previous work can be summarized into two streams.

The first one focuses on improving the accuracy by exploiting the temporal relations and the unlabelled data in the video sequence. Nilsson and

Sminchiesescu [22] employ a gated recurrent unit to propagate semantic labels to unlabeled frames. Other works like NetWarp [8], STFCN [7], and SVP [18] also employ optical-flow or recurrent units to fuse the results of several frames during inferring to improve the segmentation accuracy. Recently, Zhu et al. [40] propose to use a motion estimation network to propagate labels to unlabeled frames as data augmentation and achieve state-of-the-art performance with the segmentation accuracy. These methods can achieve significant performance but can be difficult to be deployed on mobile devices.

The second line of works pay attention to reduce the computational cost by re-using the feature maps in the neighbouring frames. ClockNet [27] proposes to copy the feature map to the next frame directly, thus reducing the computational cost. DFF [39] employs the optical flow to warp the feature map between the keyframe and non-key frames. Xu et al. [32] further propose to use an adaptive keyframe selection policy while Zhu et al. [38] find out that propagating partial region in the feature map can get better performance. Li et al. [17] propose a low-latency video segmentation network by optimizing both the keyframe selection and the adaptive feature propagation. Accel [13] proposes a network fusion policy to use a large model to predict the keyframe and use a compact one in non-key frames. Keyframe based methods require different inference time and may produce different quantity results between keyframes and other frames. In this work, we solve the real-time video segmentation by per-frame inference with a compact network and propose a temporal loss and the temporal consistency knowledge distillation to ensure both good accuracy and temporal consistency.

Temporal Consistency. Applying image processing algorithms to each frame of a video may lead to inconsistent results. The temporal consistency problem has draw much attention in low-level and mid-level applications, such as task-specific methods including colorization [15], style transfer [9], and video depth estimation [1,2] and task agnostic approaches [14,33]. Temporal consistency is also essential in semantic video segmentation. Miksik et al. [21] employ a post-processing method that learns a similarity function between pixels of consecutive frames to propagate predictions across time. Nilsson and Sminchiesescu [22] insert the optical flow estimation network into the forward pass and employ a recurrent unit to make use of neighbouring predictions. Our method is more efficient than theirs as we employ per-frame inference. The warped previous predictions work as a constraint *only* during training.

Knowledge Distillation. The effectiveness of knowledge distillation has been verified in classification [12,25,35]. The output of the large teacher net, including the final logits and the intermediate feature maps, are treated as soft targets to supervise the compact student net. Previous knowledge distillation methods in semantic segmentation [11,19] design distillation strategies only for improving the segmentation accuracy. To our knowledge, to date no distillation methods consider to improve temporal consistency. In this work, we focus on encoding the motion information into the distillation terms to make the segmentation networks more suitable for the semantic video segmentation tasks.

2   Approach

In this section, we show how we exploit the temporal information during training. As shown in Fig. 2(a), we introduce two terms: a simple temporal loss (Fig. 2(b)) and newly designed temporal consistency knowledge distillation strategies (Fig. 2(c) and (d)). The temporal consistency of the single-frame models can be significantly improved by employing temporal loss. However, if compact models are employed for real-time execution, there is still a performance gap between large models and small ones. We design new temporal consistency knowledge distillation to transfer the temporal consistency from large models to small ones. With the help of temporal information, the segmentation accuracy can also be boosted.

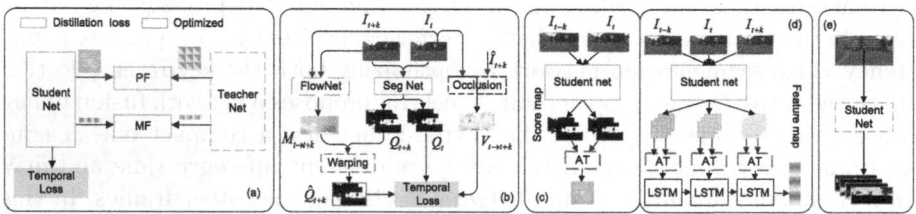

Fig. 2. (a) **Overall of proposed training scheme:** We consider the temporal information by the temporal consistency knowledge distillation (c and d) and the temporal loss (b) during training. (b) **Temporal loss (TL)** encode the temporal consistency through motion constraints. Both the teacher net and the student net are enhanced by the temporal loss. (c) **Pair-wise frame dependency (PF):** encode the motion relations between two frames. (d) **multi-frame dependency (MF):** extract the correlations of the intermediate feature maps among multi-frames. We only show the forward pass of the student net here and apply the same operations on the teacher net to get the dependency cross frames as soft targets. (e) **The inference process.** All the proposed methods are only applied during training. We can improve the temporal consistency as well as the segmentation accuracy without any extra parameters or post-processing during inference.

2.1   Motion Guided Temporal Consistency

Training semantic segmentation networks independently on each frame of a video sequence often leads to undesired inconsistency. Conventional methods include previous predictions as an extra input, which introduces extra computational cost during inference. We employ previous predictions as supervised signals to assign consistent labels to each corresponding pixel along the time axis.

As shown in Fig. 2(b), for two input frames $\mathbf{I}_t$, $\mathbf{I}_{t+k}$ from time t and $t + k$, we have:

$$\ell_{tl}(\mathbf{I}_t, \mathbf{I}_{t+k}) = \frac{1}{N} \sum_{i=1}^{N} V_{t \Rightarrow t+k}^{(i)} \left\| \mathbf{q}_t^i - \hat{\mathbf{q}}_{t+k \Rightarrow t}^i \right\|_2^2 \tag{1}$$

where $\mathbf{q}_t^i$ represents the predicted class probability at the position i of the segmentation map $\mathbf{Q_t}$, and $\hat{\mathbf{q}}_{t+k\Rightarrow t}^i$ is the warped class probability from frame $t+k$ to frame t, by using a motion estimation network (e.g., FlowNet) $f(\cdot)$. Such an $f(\cdot)$ can predict the amount of motion changes in the x and y directions for each pixel: $f(\mathbf{I}_{t+k}, \mathbf{I}_t) = \mathbf{M}_{t\rightarrow t+k}$, where $\delta i = \mathbf{M}_{t\rightarrow t+k}(i)$, indicating the pixel on the position i of the frame t moves to the position $i + \delta i$ in the frame $t+k$. Therefore, the segmentation maps between two input frames are aligned by the motion guidance. An occlusion mask $\mathbf{V}_{t\Rightarrow t+k}$ is designed to remove the noise caused by the warping error: $\mathbf{V}_{t\Rightarrow t+k} = \exp(-\left|\mathbf{I}_t - \hat{\mathbf{I}}_{t+k}\right|)$, where $\hat{\mathbf{I}}_{t+k}$ is the warped input frame. We employ a pre-trained optical flow prediction network as the motion estimation net in implementation. We directly consider the temporal consistency during the training process through the motion guided temporal loss by constraining a moving pixel along the time steps to have a consistent semantic label. Similar constraints are proposed in image processing tasks [14, 33], but rarely discussed in semantic segmentation. We find that the straightforward temporal loss can improve the temporal consistency of single-frame models significantly.

2.2 Temporal Consistency Knowledge Distillation

Inspired by [19], we build a distillation mechanism to effectively train the compact student net S by making use of the cumbersome teacher net T. The teacher net T is already well trained with the cross-entropy loss and the temporal loss to achieve a high temporal consistency as well as the segmentation accuracy. Different from previous single frame distillation methods, two new distillation strategies are designed to transfer the temporal consistency from T to S: pair-wise-frames dependency (PF) and multi-frame dependency (MF).

Pair-wise-Frames Dependency. Following [19], we denote an attention (AT) operator to calculate the pair-wise similarity map $\mathbf{A}_{\mathbf{X}_1, \mathbf{X}_2}$ of two input tensors $\mathbf{X}_1, \mathbf{X}_2$, where $\mathbf{A}_{\mathbf{X}_1, \mathbf{X}_2} \in \mathbb{R}^{N \times N \times 1}$ and $\mathbf{X}_1, \mathbf{X}_2 \in \mathbb{R}^{N \times C}$. For the pixel a_{ij} in $\mathbf{A}$, we calculate the cosine similarity between $\mathbf{x}_1^i$ and $\mathbf{x}_2^j$ from $\mathbf{X}_1$ and $\mathbf{X}_2$, respectively: $a_{ij} = \mathbf{x}_1^{i\top}\mathbf{x}_2^j/(\|\mathbf{x}_1^i\|_2\|\mathbf{x}_2^j\|_2)$. It is an efficient and easy way to encode the correlations between two input tensors.

As shown in Fig. 2(c), we encode the pair-wise dependency between the prediction of every two neighbouring frame pairs by using the AT operator, and get the similarity map $\mathbf{A}_{\mathbf{Q}_t, \mathbf{Q}_{t+k}}$, where $\mathbf{Q}_t$ is the segmentation map of frame t and a_{ij} of $\mathbf{A}_{\mathbf{Q}_t, \mathbf{Q}_{t+k}}$ denotes the similarity between the class probabilities on the location i of the frame t and the location j of the frame $t+k$. If a pixel on the location i of frame t moves to location j of frame $t+k$, the similarity a_{ij} may be higher. Therefore, the pair-wise dependency can reflect the motion correlation between two frames.

We align the pair-wise-frame (PF) dependency between the teacher net T and the student net S,

$$\ell_{PF}(\mathbf{Q_t}, \mathbf{Q_{t+k}}) = \frac{1}{N^2} \sum_{i=1}^{N} \sum_{j=1}^{N} (a_{ij}^{\mathsf{S}} - a_{ij}^{\mathsf{T}})^2, \tag{2}$$

where $\forall a_{ij}^{\mathsf{S}} \in \mathbf{A}_{\mathbf{Q_t},\mathbf{Q_{t+k}}}^{\mathsf{S}}$ and $\forall a_{ij}^{\mathsf{T}} \in \mathbf{A}_{\mathbf{Q_t},\mathbf{Q_{t+k}}}^{\mathsf{T}}$.

Multi-frame Dependency. As shown in Fig. 2(d), for a video sequence $\mathcal{I} = \{\dots I_{t-1}, I_t, I_{t+1} \dots\}$, the corresponding feature maps $\mathcal{F} = \{\dots \mathbf{F}_{t-1}, \mathbf{F}_t, \mathbf{F}_{t+1} \dots\}$ are extracted from the output of the last convolutional block before the classification layer. Then, the self-similarity map, $\mathbf{A}_{\mathbf{F}_t,\mathbf{F}_t}$, for each frame are calculated by using AT operator in order to: (1) capture the structure information among pixels, and (2) align the different feature channels between the teacher net and student net.

We employ a ConvLSTM unit to encode the sequence of self-similarity maps into an embedding $\mathbf{E} \in \mathbb{R}^{1 \times D_e}$, where D_e is the length of the embedding space. For each time step, the ConvLSTM unit takes $\mathbf{A}_{\mathbf{F}_t,\mathbf{F}_t}$ and the hidden state which contains the information of previous $t-1$ frames as input and gives an output embedding $\mathbf{E}_t$ along with the hidden state of the current time step. We align the final output embedding[1] at the last time step, $\mathbf{E}^{\mathsf{T}}$ and $\mathbf{E}^{\mathsf{S}}$ from T and S, respectively. The output embedding encodes the relations of the whole input sequence, named multi-frame dependency (MF). The distillation loss based on multi-frame dependency is termed as: $\ell_{MF}(\mathcal{F}) = \left\| \mathbf{E}^{\mathsf{T}} - \mathbf{E}^{\mathsf{S}} \right\|_2^2$.

The parameters in the ConvLSTM unit are optimized together with the student net. To extract the multi-frame dependency, both the teacher net and the student net share the weight of the ConvLSTM unit. Note that there exists a model collapse point when the weights and bias in the ConvLSTM are all equal to zero. We clip the weights of ConvLSTM between a certain range and enlarges the $\mathbf{E}^{\mathsf{T}}$ as a regularization to prevent the model collapse.

2.3   Optimization

We pre-train the teacher net with the segmentation loss and the temporal loss to attain a segmentation network with a high semantic accuracy and temporal consistency. When optimizing the student net, we fix the weight of the motion estimation net (FlowNet) and the teacher net. These two parts are only used to calculate the temporal loss and the distillation terms, which can be seen as extra regularization terms during the training of the student net. During training, we also employ conventional cross-entropy loss, and the single frame distillation method (SF) proposed in [21] on every single frame to improve the segmentation accuracy. Details can be found in Section S1.1 in supplementary materials. The whole objective function for a sampled video sequence consists

---

[1] The details of calculations in ConvLSTM is referred in [28], and we also include the key equations in Section S1.2 in supplementary materials.

of the conventional cross-entropy loss ℓ_{ce}, the single-frame distillation loss ℓ_{SF}, temporal loss, and the temporal consistency distillation terms:

$$\ell = \sum_{t=1}^{T'} \ell_{ce}^{(t)} + \lambda\left(\sum_{t=1}^{T} \ell_{SF}^{(t)} + \sum_{i=1}^{T-1} \ell_{tl}(\mathbf{Q}_t, \mathbf{Q}_{t+1}) + \sum_{i=1}^{T-1} \ell_{PF}(\mathbf{Q}_t, \mathbf{Q}_{t+1}) + \ell_{MF}\right), \quad (3)$$

where T is the number of all the frames in one training sequence, and T' is the number of labeled frames. Due to the high labeling cost in semantic video segmentation tasks [3,6], most of the datasets are only annotated with sparse frames. Our methods can be easily applied to the sparse-labeled dataset, because (1) we can make use of large teacher models to generate soft targets; and (2) we care about the temporal consistency between two frames, which can be self-supervised through motion. The loss weight for all regularization terms λ is set to 0.1.

After training the compact network, all the motion-estimation net, teacher net, and the distillation modules can be removed. We only keep the student net as the semantic video segmentation network. Thus, both the segmentation accuracy and the temporal consistency can be improved with no extra computational cost in the per-frame inference process.

3   Implementation Details

Dataset. We evaluate our proposed method on Camvid [3] and Cityscapes [6], which are standard benchmarks for semantic video segmentation [13,22,27]. More details of the training and evaluation can be found in Section S2 of the supplementary materials. **Network structures.** Different from the keyframe based method, which takes several frames as input during inferring, we apply our training methods to a compact segmentation model with per-frame inference. There are three main parts while training the system:

- A light-weight segmentation network. We conduct most of the experiments on ResNet18 with the architecture of PSPnet [37], namely PSPNet18. We also employ MobileNetV2 [26] and a light-weight HRNet-w18 [30] to verify the effectiveness and generalization ability.
- A motion estimation network. We use a pre-trained FlowNetV2 [24] to predict the motion between two frames. Because this module can be removed during inferring, we do not need to consider employing a lightweight flownet for acceleration, like in DFF [39] and GRFP [22].
- A teacher network. We adopt widely-used segmentation architecture PSPNet [37] with a ResNet101 [10] as the teacher network, namely PSPNet101, which is used to calculate the soft targets in distillation items. We train the teacher net with the temporal loss to enhance the temporal consistency of the teacher.

Random Sampled Policy. In order to reduce the computational cost while training video data, and make use of more unlabeled frames, we randomly sample frames in front of the labelled frame, named 'frame_f' and behind of the labelled frame, named 'frame_b' to form a training triplet (frame_f, labelled frame, frame_b), instead of only using the frames right next to the labelled ones. The random sampled policy can take both long term and short term correlations into consideration and achieve better performance. Training on a longer sequence may show better performance with more expensive computation.

Evaluation Metrics. We evaluate our method on three aspects: accuracy, temporal consistency, and efficiency. The accuracy is evaluated by widely-used mean Intersection over Union (mIoU) and pixel accuracy for semantic segmentation [19]. We report the model parameters (#Param) and frames per second (fps) to show the efficiency of employed networks. We follow [14] to measure the temporal stability of a video based on the mean flow warping error between every two neighbouring frames. Different from [14], we use the mIoU score instead of the mean square error to evaluate the semantic segmentation results, and more details can be found in the supplementary materials.

Table 1. Accuracy and temporal consistency on Cityscapes validation set. SF: single-frame distillation methods, PF: our proposed pair-wise-frame dependency distillation method. MF: our proposed multi-frame dependency distillation method, TL: the temporal loss. The proposed distillation methods and temporal loss can improve both the temporal consistency and accuracy, and they are complementary to each other.

Scheme index	SF	PF	MF	TL	mIoU	Pixel accuracy	Temporal consistency
a					69.79	77.18	68.50
b	✓				70.85	78.41	69.20
c		✓			70.32	77.96	70.10
d			✓		70.38	77.99	69.78
e				✓	70.67	78.46	70.46
f		✓	✓		71.16	78.69	70.21
g	✓			✓	71.36	78.64	70.13
h		✓	✓	✓	71.57	78.94	70.61
i	✓	✓	✓		72.01	79.21	69.99
j	✓	✓	✓	✓	**73.06**	**80.75**	**70.56**

4 Experiments

4.1 Ablations

All the ablation experiments are conducted on the Cityscapes dataset with the PSPNet18.

Effectiveness of Proposed Methods. In this section, we verify the effectiveness of the proposed training scheme. Both the accuracy and temporal consistency are shown in Table 1. We build the baseline scheme a, which is trained on

Table 2. Impact of the random sample policy. RS: random sample policy, TC: temporal consistency, TL: temporal loss, Dis: distillation terms, ALL: combine TL with Dis. The proposed random sample policy can improve the accuracy and temporal consistency.

Method	RS	mIoU	TC
PSPNet18 + TL		70.04	70.21
PSPNet18 + TL	✓	70.67	70.46
PSPNet18 + Dis		71.24	69.48
PSPNet18 + Dis	✓	72.01	69.99
PSPNet18 + ALL		72.87	70.05
PSPNet18 + ALL	✓	73.06	70.56

Table 3. Influence of the teacher net. TL: temporal loss. TC: temporal consistency. We use the pair-wise-frame distillation to show our design can transfer the temporal consistency from the teacher net.

Method	Teacher model	mIoU	TC
PSPNet101	None	78.84	69.71
PSPNet101 + TL	None	79.53	71.68
PSPNet18	None	69.79	68.50
PSPNet18	PSPNet101	70.26	69.27
PSPNet18	PSPNet101 + TL	**70.32**	**70.10**

every single labelled frame. Then, we apply three distillation terms: the single-frame dependency (SF), the pair-wise-frame dependency (PF) and multi-frame dependency (MF), separately, to get the scheme b, c and d. The temporal loss is employed in the scheme e. Compared with the baseline scheme, all the schemes can improve accuracy as well as temporal consistency. To compare scheme b with c and d, one can see that the newly designed distillation scheme across frames can improve the temporal consistency to a greater extent. From the scheme e, we can see the temporal loss is most effective for the improvement of temporal consistency. To compare scheme f with i, we can see that single frame distillation methods [19] can improve the segmentation accuracy but may harm the temporal consistency.

To further improve the performance, we combine the distillation terms with the temporal loss and achieve the mIoU of 73.06% and temporal consistency of 70.56%. We do not increase any parameters or extra computational cost with per-frame inference. Both the distillation terms and the temporal loss can be seen as regularization terms, which can help the training process. Such regularization terms introduce extra knowledge from the pre-trained teacher net and the motion estimation network. Besides, performance improvement also benefits from temporal information and unlabelled data from the video.

Impact of the Random Sample Policy. We apply the random sample (RS) policy when training with video sequence in order to make use of more unlabelled images, and capture the long-term dependency. Experiment results are shown in Table 2. By employing the random sampled policy, both the temporal loss and distillation terms can benefit from more sufficient training data in the video sequences, and obtain an improvement on mIoU from 0.24% to 0.69% as well as the temporal consistency from 0.19% to 0.63%. We employ such a random sampled policy considering the memory cost during training.

Table 4. We compare our methods with recent efficient image/video semantic segmentation networks on three aspects: accuracy (mIoU, %), smoothness (TC, %) and inference speed (fps, Hz). TL: temporal loss, ALL: all proposed terms, TC: temporal consistency, #Param: parameters of the networks.

Method	Backbone	#Params	Cityscapes			Camvid		
			mIoU	TC	fps	mIoU	TC	fps
Video-based methods: Train and infer on multi frames								
CC [27]	VGG16	–	67.7	71.2	16.5	–	–	–
DFF [39]	ResNet101	–	68.7	71.4	9.7	66.0	78.0	16.1
GRFP [22]	ResNet101	–	69.4	–	3.2	66.1	–	6.4
DVSN [32]	ResNet101	–	70.3	–	19.8	–	–	–
Accel [13]	ResNet101/18	–	72.1	70.3	3.6	66.7	76.2	7.1
Single frame methods: Train and infer on each frame independently								
PSPNet [37]	ResNet101	68.1	78.8	69.7	1.7	77.6	77.1	4.1
SKD-MV2 [19]	MobileNetV2	8.3	74.5	68.2	14.4	–	–	–
SKD-R18 [19]	ResNet18	15.2	72.7	67.6	8.0	72.3	75.4	13.3
PSPNet18 [37]	ResNet18	13.2	69.8	68.5	9.5	–	–	–
HRNet-w18 [29,30]	HRNet	3.9	75.6	69.1	18.9	–	–	–
MobileNetV2 [26]	MobileNetV2	3.2	70.2	68.4	20.8	74.4	76.8	27.8
Ours: Train on multi frames and infer on each frame independently								
Teacher Net	ResNet101	68.1	**79.5**	**71.7**	1.7	**79.4**	**78.6**	4.1
PSPNet18 + TL	ResNet18	13.2	71.1	70.0	9.5	–	–	–
PSPNet18 + ALL	ResNet18	13.2	73.1	70.6	9.5	–	–	–
HRNet-w18 + TL	HRNet	3.9	76.4	69.6	18.9	–	–	–
HRNet-w18 + ALL	HRNet	3.9	76.6	70.1	18.9	–	–	–
MobileNetV2 + TL	MobileNetV2	3.2	70.7	70.4	20.8	76.3	77.6	27.8
MobileNetV2 + ALL	MobileNetV2	**3.2**	73.9	69.9	**20.8**	78.2	77.9	**27.8**

Impact of the Teacher Net. The temporal loss can improve the temporal consistency of both cumbersome models and compact models. We compare the performance of the student net training with different teacher net (i.e., with and without the proposed temporal loss) to verify that the temporal consistency can be transferred with our designed distillation term. The results are shown in Table 3. The temporal consistency of the teacher net (PSPNet101) can be enhanced by training with temporal loss by 1.97%. Meanwhile, the mIoU can also be improved by 0.69%. By using the enhanced teacher net in the distillation framework, the segmentation accuracy is comparable (70.26 **vs.** 70.32), but the temporal consistency has a significant improvement (69.27 **vs.** 70.10), indicating that the proposed distillation methods can transfer the temporal consistency from the teacher net.

Discussions. We focus on improving the accuracy and temporal consistency for real-time models by making use of temporal correlations. Thus, we do not introduce extra parameters during inference. A series of work [23,34,36] focus on designing network structures for fast segmentation on single images and achieve promising results. They do not contradict to our work. We will verify that our methods can generalize to different network structures, e.g. ResNet18, MobileNetV2 and HRNet in the next session. Besides, large models [37,40] can achieve high segmentation accuracy but have low inference speed. The temporal loss is also effective when applying to large models, e.g., our teacher net.

4.2   Results on Cityscapes

Comparison with Single-Frame Based Methods. Single-frame methods are trained and inferred on each frame independently. Directly apply such methods to video sequences will produce inconsistent results. We apply our training schemes to several efficient single-frame semantic segmentation networks: PSP-Net18 [37], MobileNetV2 [26] and HRNet-w18 [29,30]. Metrics of mIoU, temporal consistency, inference speed, and model parameters are shown in Table 4. As Table 4 shows, the proposed training scheme works well with a few compact backbone networks (e.g., PSPNet18, HRNet-w18 and MobileNetV2). Both temporal consistency and segmentation accuracy can be improved using the temporal information among frames.

We also compare our training methods with the single-frame distillation method [19]. According to our observation, GAN based distillation methods proposed in [19] can produce inconsistent results. For example, with the same backbone ResNet18, training with the GAN based distillation methods (SKD-R18) achieves higher mIoU: 72.7 vs. 69.8, and a lower temporal consistency: 67.6 vs. 68.5 compared with the baseline PSPNet18, which is trained with cross-entropy loss on each single frame. We replace the GAN based distillation term with our temporal consistency distillation terms and the temporal loss, denoted as "PSPNet18 + ALL". Both accuracy and smoothness are improved. Note that we also employ a smaller structure of the PSPNet with half channels than in [19].

Comparison with Video-Based Methods. Video-based methods are trained and inferred on multi frames, we list current methods including keyframe based methods: CC [27], DFF [39], DVSN [32], Accel [13] and multi-frame input method: GRFP [22] in Table 4. The compact networks with per-frame inference can be more efficient than video-based methods. Besides, with per-frame inference, semantic segmentation networks have no unbalanced latency and can handle every frame independently. Table 4 shows the proposed training schemes can

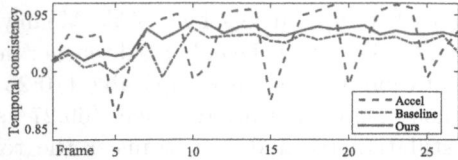

Fig. 3. The temporal consistency between neighbouring frames in one sampled sequence on Cityscapes. The keyframe based method Accel shows severe jitters between keyframes and others.

achieve a better trade-off between the accuracy and the inference speed compared with other state-of-the-art semantic video segmentation methods, especially the MobileNetV2 with the fps of 20.8 and mIoU of 73.9. Although keyframe methods can achieve a high average temporal consistency score, the predictions beyond the keyframe are in low quality. Thus, the temporal consistency will be quiet low between keyframe and non-key frames, as shown in Fig. 3. The high average temporal consistency score is mainly from the low-quality predictions on non-key frames. In contrast, our method can produce stable segmentation results on each frame.

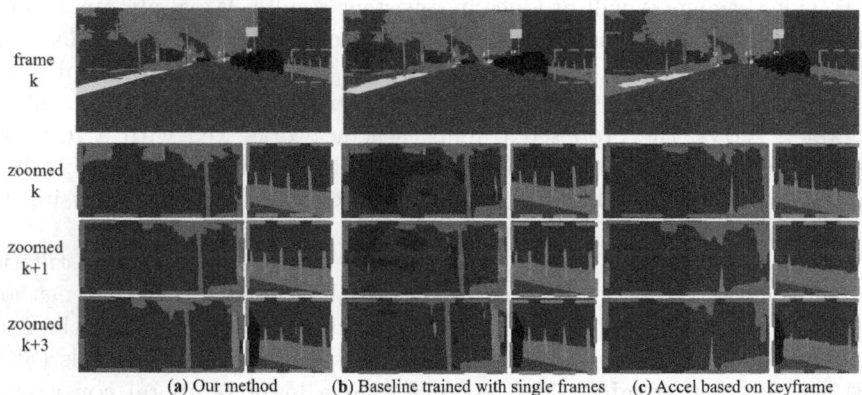

Fig. 4. Qualitative outputs. (a): PSPNet18, training on multi frames and inferring on each frame. (b): PSPNet18, training and inferring on each frame. (c): Accel-18 [13], training and inferring on multiple frames. The keyframe is selected in every five frames. For better visualization, we zoom the region in the red and orange box. The proposed method can give more consistent labels to the moving train and the trees in the red box. In the orange boxes, we can see our methods have similar quantity results in each frame while the keyframe based methods may generate worse results in the frame (e.g., $k + 3$) which is far from the keyframe (i.e., k). (Color figure online)

Qualitative Visualization. Qualitative visualization results are shown in Fig. 4, in which, we can see, the keyframe-based method Accel-18 will produce unbalanced quality segmentation results between the keyframe (e.g., the orange box of k) and non-key frames (e.g., the orange box of $k+1$ and $k+3$), due to the different forward-networks it chooses. By contrast, ours can produce stable results on the video sequence because we use the same enhanced network on all frames. Compared with the baseline method trained on single frames, we can see our proposed method can produce more smooth results, e.g., the region in red boxes. *Video results* can be found in the supplementary materials. The improvement of temporal consistency is more clearly shown in the video comparison results. Moreover, we show a case of the temporal consistency between neighbouring frames in a sampled frame sequence in Fig. 3. Temporal consistency between two frames is evaluated by the warping pixel accuracy. The higher, the better. The keyframe based method will produce jitters between keyframe and non-key frames, while our training methods can improve the temporal consistency for every frame. The temporal consistency between non-key frames are higher than our methods, but the segmentation performance is lower than ours.

4.3 CamVid

We provide additional experiments on CamVid. We use MobileNetV2 as the backbone in the PSPNet. In Table 4, the segmentation accuracy, and the temporal consistency are improved compared with the baseline method. We also outperform current state-of-the-art semantic video segmentation methods with a better trade-off between the accuracy and the inference speed. We use the pre-trained weight from cityscapes following VideoGCRF [4], and achieve better segmentation results of 78.2 vs. 75.2. VideoGCRF [4] can achieve 22 fps with 321×321 resolution on a GTX 1080 card. We can achieve 78 fps with the same resolution. The consistent improvements on both datasets verify the value of our training schemes for real-time semantic video segmentation.

5 Conclusions

In this work, we have developed real-time video segmentation methods that consider not only accuracy but also temporal consistency. To this end, we have proposed to use compact networks with per-frame inference. We explicitly consider the temporal correlation during training by using: the temporal loss and the new temporal consistency knowledge distillation. For inference, the model processes each frame separately, which does not introduce latency and avoids post-processing. The compact networks achieve considerably better temporal consistency and semantic accuracy, without introducing extra computational cost during inference. Our experiments have verified the effectiveness of each component that we have designed. They can improve the performance individually and are complement to each other.

Acknowledgements. Correspondence should be addressed to CS. CS was in part supported by ARC DP 'Deep learning that scales'.

References

1. Bian, J.W., Zhan, H., Wang, N., Chin, T.J., Shen, C., Reid, I.: Unsupervised depth learning in challenging indoor video: weak rectification to rescue. arXiv:2006.02708 (2020). Comp. Res. Repository
2. Bian, J., et al.: Unsupervised scale-consistent depth and ego-motion learning from monocular video. In: Proceedings of the Advances in Neural Information Processing Systems, pp. 35–45 (2019)
3. Brostow, G.J., Shotton, J., Fauqueur, J., Cipolla, R.: Segmentation and recognition using structure from motion point clouds. In: Forsyth, D., Torr, P., Zisserman, A. (eds.) ECCV 2008. LNCS, vol. 5302, pp. 44–57. Springer, Heidelberg (2008). https://doi.org/10.1007/978-3-540-88682-2_5
4. Chandra, S., Couprie, C., Kokkinos, I.: Deep spatio-temporal random fields for efficient video segmentation. In: Proceedings of the IEEE Conference on Computer Vision and Pattern Recognition, pp. 8915–8924 (2018)
5. Chen, L.C., Papandreou, G., Kokkinos, I., Murphy, K., Yuille, A.L.: DeepLab: semantic image segmentation with deep convolutional nets, atrous convolution, and fully connected CRFs. IEEE Trans. Pattern Anal. Mach. Intell. **40**(4), 834–848 (2018)
6. Cordts, M., et al.: The cityscapes dataset for semantic urban scene understanding. In: Proceedings of the IEEE Conference on Computer Vision and Pattern Recognition (2016)
7. Fayyaz, M., Saffar, M.H., Sabokrou, M., Fathy, M., Huang, F., Klette, R.: STFCN: spatio-temporal fully convolutional neural network for semantic segmentation of street scenes. In: Chen, C.-S., Lu, J., Ma, K.-K. (eds.) ACCV 2016. LNCS, vol. 10116, pp. 493–509. Springer, Cham (2017). https://doi.org/10.1007/978-3-319-54407-6_33
8. Gadde, R., Jampani, V., Gehler, P.V.: Semantic video CNNs through representation warping. In: Proceedings of the IEEE International Conference on Computer Vision, pp. 4453–4462 (2017)
9. Gupta, A., Johnson, J., Alahi, A., Fei-Fei, L.: Characterizing and improving stability in neural style transfer. In: Proceedings of the IEEE International Conference on Computer Vision, pp. 4067–4076 (2017)
10. He, K., Zhang, X., Ren, S., Sun, J.: Deep residual learning for image recognition. In: Proceedings of the IEEE Conference on Computer Vision and Pattern Recognition, pp. 770–778 (2016)
11. He, T., Shen, C., Tian, Z., Gong, D., Sun, C., Yan, Y.: Knowledge adaptation for efficient semantic segmentation. In: Proceedings of the IEEE Conference on Computer Vision and Pattern Recognition, pp. 578–587 (2019)
12. Hinton, G.E., Vinyals, O., Dean, J.: Distilling the knowledge in a neural network. arXiv:1503.02531 (2015). Comp. Res. Repository
13. Jain, S., Wang, X., Gonzalez, J.E.: Accel: a corrective fusion network for efficient semantic segmentation on video. In: Proceedings of the IEEE Conference on Computer Vision and Pattern Recognition, pp. 8866–8875 (2019)
14. Lai, W.-S., Huang, J.-B., Wang, O., Shechtman, E., Yumer, E., Yang, M.-H.: Learning blind video temporal consistency. In: Ferrari, V., Hebert, M., Sminchisescu, C., Weiss, Y. (eds.) ECCV 2018. LNCS, vol. 11219, pp. 179–195. Springer, Cham (2018). https://doi.org/10.1007/978-3-030-01267-0_11
15. Levin, A., Lischinski, D., Weiss, Y.: Colorization using optimization. ACM Trans. Graph. **23**(3), 689–694 (2004)

16. Li, Q., Jin, S., Yan, J.: Mimicking very efficient network for object detection. In: Proceedings of the IEEE Conference on Computer Vision and Pattern Recognition, pp. 7341–7349 (2017)
17. Li, Y., Shi, J., Lin, D.: Low-latency video semantic segmentation. In: Proceedings of the IEEE Conference on Computer Vision and Pattern Recognition, pp. 5997–6005 (2018)
18. Liu, S., Wang, C., Qian, R., Yu, H., Bao, R., Sun, Y.: Surveillance video parsing with single frame supervision. In: Proceedings of the IEEE Conference on Computer Vision and Pattern Recognition, pp. 413–421 (2017)
19. Liu, Y., Chen, K., Liu, C., Qin, Z., Luo, Z., Wang, J.: Structured knowledge distillation for semantic segmentation. In: Proceedings of the IEEE Conference on Computer Vision and Pattern Recognition, pp. 2604–2613 (2019)
20. Mehta, S., Rastegari, M., Caspi, A., Shapiro, L., Hajishirzi, H.: ESPNet: efficient spatial pyramid of dilated convolutions for semantic segmentation. In: Ferrari, V., Hebert, M., Sminchisescu, C., Weiss, Y. (eds.) ECCV 2018. LNCS, vol. 11214, pp. 561–580. Springer, Cham (2018). https://doi.org/10.1007/978-3-030-01249-6_34
21. Miksik, O., Munoz, D., Bagnell, J.A., Hebert, M.: Efficient temporal consistency for streaming video scene analysis. In: Proceedings of the IEEE International Conference on Robotics and Automation, pp. 133–139. IEEE (2013)
22. Nilsson, D., Sminchisescu, C.: Semantic video segmentation by gated recurrent flow propagation. In: Proceedings of the IEEE Conference on Computer Vision and Pattern Recognition, pp. 6819–6828 (2018)
23. Orsic, M., Kreso, I., Bevandic, P., Segvic, S.: In defense of pre-trained ImageNet architectures for real-time semantic segmentation of road-driving images. In: Proceedings of the IEEE Conference on Computer Vision and Pattern Recognition (2019)
24. Reda, F., Pottorff, R., Barker, J., Catanzaro, B.: FlowNet2-PyTorch: PyTorch implementation of FlowNet 2.0: evolution of optical flow estimation with deep networks (2017). https://github.com/NVIDIA/flownet2-pytorch
25. Romero, A., Ballas, N., Kahou, S.E., Chassang, A., Gatta, C., Bengio, Y.: FitNets: hints for thin deep nets. arXiv:1412.6550 (2014). Comp. Res. Repository
26. Sandler, M., Howard, A., Zhu, M., Zhmoginov, A., Chen, L.C.: MobileNetV2: inverted residuals and linear bottlenecks. In: Proceedings of the IEEE Conference on Computer Vision and Pattern Recognition (2018)
27. Shelhamer, E., Rakelly, K., Hoffman, J., Darrell, T.: Clockwork convnets for video semantic segmentation. In: Hua, G., Jégou, H. (eds.) ECCV 2016. LNCS, vol. 9915, pp. 852–868. Springer, Cham (2016). https://doi.org/10.1007/978-3-319-49409-8_69
28. Shi, X., Chen, Z., Wang, H., Yeung, D.Y., Wong, W.K., Woo, W.C.: Convolutional LSTM network: a machine learning approach for precipitation nowcasting. In: Proceedings of the Advances in Neural Information Processing Systems, pp. 802–810 (2015)
29. Sun, K., Xiao, B., Liu, D., Wang, J.: Deep high-resolution representation learning for human pose estimation. In: Proceedings of the IEEE Conference on Computer Vision and Pattern Recognition (2019)
30. Sun, K., et al.: High-resolution representations for labeling pixels and regions. arXiv:1904.04514 (2019). Comp. Res. Repository
31. Tian, Z., He, T., Shen, C., Yan, Y.: Decoders matter for semantic segmentation: data-dependent decoding enables flexible feature aggregation. In: Proceedings of the IEEE Conference on Computer Vision and Pattern Recognition, pp. 3126–3135 (2019)

32. Xu, Y.S., Fu, T.J., Yang, H.K., Lee, C.Y.: Dynamic video segmentation network. In: Proceedings of the IEEE Conference on Computer Vision and Pattern Recognition, pp. 6556–6565 (2018)

33. Yao, C.H., Chang, C.Y., Chien, S.Y.: Occlusion-aware video temporal consistency. In: Proceedings of the 25th ACM International Conference on Multimedia, pp. 777–785. ACM (2017)

34. Yu, C., Wang, J., Peng, C., Gao, C., Yu, G., Sang, N.: BiSeNet: bilateral segmentation network for real-time semantic segmentation. In: Ferrari, V., Hebert, M., Sminchisescu, C., Weiss, Y. (eds.) ECCV 2018. LNCS, vol. 11217, pp. 334–349. Springer, Cham (2018). https://doi.org/10.1007/978-3-030-01261-8_20

35. Zagoruyko, S., Komodakis, N.: Paying more attention to attention: Improving the performance of convolutional neural networks via attention transfer. In: Proceedings of the International Conference on Learning Representations (2017)

36. Zhao, H., Qi, X., Shen, X., Shi, J., Jia, J.: ICNet for real-time semantic segmentation on high-resolution images. In: Ferrari, V., Hebert, M., Sminchisescu, C., Weiss, Y. (eds.) ECCV 2018. LNCS, vol. 11207, pp. 418–434. Springer, Cham (2018). https://doi.org/10.1007/978-3-030-01219-9_25

37. Zhao, H., Shi, J., Qi, X., Wang, X., Jia, J.: Pyramid scene parsing network. In: Proceedings of the IEEE Conference on Computer Vision and Pattern Recognition, pp. 2881–2890 (2017)

38. Zhu, X., Dai, J., Yuan, L., Wei, Y.: Towards high performance video object detection. In: Proceedings of the IEEE Conference on Computer Vision and Pattern Recognition, pp. 7210–7218 (2018)

39. Zhu, X., Xiong, Y., Dai, J., Yuan, L., Wei, Y.: Deep feature flow for video recognition. In: Proceedings of the IEEE Conference on Computer Vision and Pattern Recognition, pp. 2349–2358 (2017)

40. Zhu, Y., et al.: Improving semantic segmentation via video propagation and label relaxation. In: Proceedings of the IEEE Conference on Computer Vision and Pattern Recognition, pp. 8856–8865 (2019)

Increasing the Robustness of Semantic Segmentation Models with Painting-by-Numbers

Christoph Kamann[1,2(✉)] and Carsten Rother[2]

[1] Corporate Research, Robert Bosch GmbH, Renningen, Germany
`christoph.kamann@bosch.com`
[2] Visual Learning Lab, Heidelberg University (HCI/IWR), Heidelberg, Germany
`carsten.rother@iwr.uni-heidelberg.de`
`https://vislearn.de`

Abstract. For safety-critical applications such as autonomous driving, CNNs have to be robust with respect to unavoidable image corruptions, such as image noise. While previous works addressed the task of robust prediction in the context of full-image classification, we consider it for dense semantic segmentation. We build upon an insight from image classification that output robustness can be improved by increasing the network-bias towards object shapes. We present a new training schema that increases this shape bias. Our basic idea is to alpha-blend a portion of the RGB training images with faked images, where each class-label is given a fixed, randomly chosen color that is not likely to appear in real imagery. This forces the network to rely more strongly on shape cues. We call this data augmentation technique "Painting-by-Numbers". We demonstrate the effectiveness of our training schema for DeepLabv3+ with various network backbones, MobileNet-V2, ResNets, and Xception, and evaluate it on the Cityscapes dataset. With respect to our 16 different types of image corruptions and 5 different network backbones, we are in 74% better than training with clean data. For cases where we are worse than a model trained without our training schema, it is mostly only marginally worse. However, for some image corruptions such as images with noise, we see a considerable performance gain of up to 25%.

Keywords: Semantic segmentation · Shape-bias · Corruption robustness

1 Introduction

Convolutional Neural Networks (CNNs) have set the state-of-the-art for many computer vision tasks [5,25,29,30,37,40,41,44,49,50,56,57]. The benchmark

---

Electronic supplementary material The online version of this chapter (https://doi.org/10.1007/978-3-030-58607-2_22) contains supplementary material, which is available to authorized users.

© Springer Nature Switzerland AG 2020
A. Vedaldi et al. (Eds.): ECCV 2020, LNCS 12355, pp. 369–387, 2020.
https://doi.org/10.1007/978-3-030-58607-2_22

datasets which are used to measure performance often consist of clean and undistorted images [11]. When networks are trained on clean image data and tested on real-world image corruptions, such as image noise or blur, the performance can decrease drastically [2, 17, 23, 31, 35].

Common image corruptions cannot be avoided in safety-critical applications: Environmental influences, such as adverse weather conditions, may corrupt the image quality significantly. Foggy weather decreases the image contrast, and low-light scenarios may exhibit image noise. Fast-moving objects or camera motion cause image blur. Such influences cannot be fully suppressed by sensing technology, and it is hence essential that CNNs are robust against common image corruptions. Obviously a CNN should also be robust towards adversarial perturbations (e.g., [3, 4, 10, 27, 33, 47, 58]).

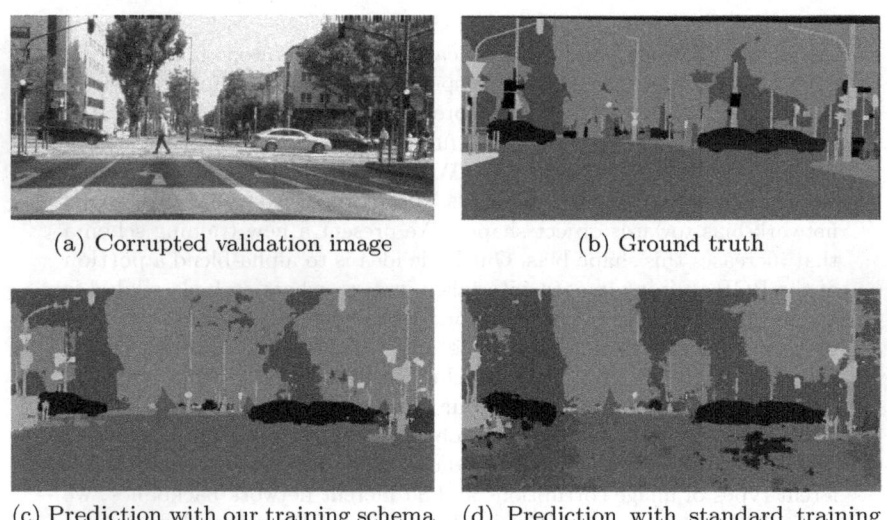

(a) Corrupted validation image   (b) Ground truth

(c) Prediction with our training schema   (d) Prediction with standard training schema

Fig. 1. Results of a semantic segmentation model that is trained with our data augmentation schema. (a) An image crop of the Cityscapes validation set is corrupted by severe image noise. (b) Corresponding ground-truth. (c) Prediction of a model that is trained with our schema. (d) Prediction of the same model with reference training schema, where training images are not augmented with noise. The prediction with our training schema (c) is clearly superior to the prediction of the reference training schema (d), though our model is not trained with image noise. In particular the classes *road*, *traffic signs*, *cars*, *persons* and *poles*, are more accurately predicted

Training CNNs directly on image corruptions is generally a possibility to increase the performance on the respective type of image corruption, however, this approach comes at the cost of increased training time. It is also possible that a CNN overfits to a specific type of image corruption trained on [23, 60].

Recent work deals with the robustness against common image corruptions for the task of full-image classification, and less effort has been dedicated to semantic segmentation. Whereas other work utilizes, e.g., a set of data augmentation operations [32] we propose a new, robustness increasing, data augmentation schema (see Fig. 1) that does: a) not require any additional image data, and b) is easy to implement and c) can be used within any supervised semantic segmentation network, and d) is robust against many common image corruptions.

For this, we build upon the work of Geirhos et al. [22], where it has been shown that increasing the network bias towards the shape of objects does make the task of full-image classification more robust with respect to common image corruptions. We applied the style-transfer technique of Geirhos et al. to Cityscapes, but found the resulting images to be quite noisy (see Fig. 2). Training on such data might, therefore, increase robustness not solely due to an increased shape bias, but rather due to increased image corruption. Our aim is to find a training schema that does not have any type of image corruption added.

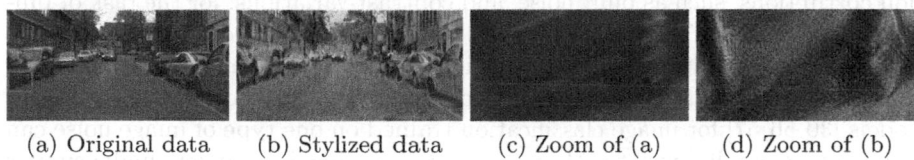

(a) Original data   (b) Stylized data   (c) Zoom of (a)   (d) Zoom of (b)

Fig. 2. Illustration of the style transfer technique of [22]. An original training image (a) of the Cityscapes dataset is stylized by a painting (b). (c) and (d) show the image content of the red rectangle of (a), where (d) is clearly noisier compared to the original data (c)

Whereas the method of [22] delivers high-quality results, their approach requires a computationally intensive style transfer technique and additional image data. We propose a simple, yet effective, data augmentation scheme, that decreases the amount of texture in the training data, and does not need additional data. The basic idea is to alpha-blend some training images with a texture-free representation, as illustrated in Fig. 3(b). By doing so, the texture-based appearance of a training image is less reliable, forcing the network to develop additional shape-based cues for the segmentation. In this way, our schema does not require additional training data, as we directly use the available semantic segmentation ground-truth. It can be easily utilized for training any supervised semantic segmentation model. We demonstrate our data augmentation scheme's effectiveness on a broad range of common image corruptions, evaluated on the Cityscapes dataset.

In summary, we give the following contributions:

– We propose a simple, yet effective, data augmentation scheme that increases the robustness of well-established semantic segmentation models for a broad range of image corruptions, through increasing the model's shape-bias. Our

new training schema requires no additional data, can be utilized in any supervised semantic segmentation model, and is computationally efficient.
- We validate our training schema through a series of validation experiments. With respect to our 16 different types of image corruptions and five different network backbones, we are in 74% better than training with clean data. We are able to increase the mean IoU by up to 25%.

2   Related Work

Recent work has dealt with the robustness of CNNs for common image corruptions. We discuss the most recent work in the following.

Benchmarking Robustness with Respect to Common Corruptions. The work in [2,18] demonstrates that shifting input pixels can change the outcome significantly. Dodge and Karam [17] show that CNNs are prone to common corruptions, such as blur, noise, and contrast variations, for the task of full-image classification. The authors further show in [16] that the CNN performance of classifying corrupted images is significantly lower than human performance. Zhou [68] et al. find similar results. Geirhos et al. [23] show that established models [30,56,57] for image classification trained on one type of image noise can struggle to generalize well to other noise types. Vasiljevic et al. [60] find a similar result w.r.t image blur, and further, a reduced performance for clean data.

Hendrycks and Dietterich [31] corrupt the ImageNet dataset [14] by many common image corruptions and image perturbations. In this work, we apply the proposed image corruptions to the Cityscapes dataset. Michaelis et al. [48] benchmark the robustness in object detection and find a significant performance drop for corrupted input data.

For the task of semantic segmentation, Vasiljevic et al. [60] find that model performance of a VGG-16 [56] is decreasing for an increasing amount of blur in the test data. Kamann and Rother [35] ablate the state-of-the-art semantic segmentation DeepLabv3+ architecture and show that established architectural design choices affect model robustness with respect to common image corruptions. Other work deals with robustness towards adverse weather conditions [53,54,61], night scenes [13], or geometric transformations [20,51].

Increasing Robustness with Respect to Common Corruptions. The research interest in increasing the robustness of CNN models with respect to common image corruptions grows. Most methods have been proposed for the task of full-image classification. Mahajan et al. [46] and Xie et al. [62] show that using more training data increases the robustness. The same result is found when more complex network backbones are used, also for object detection [48] and semantic segmentation [35]. Hendrycks et al. [31] show that adversarial logit pairing [36] increases the robustness for adversarial and common perturbations. The authors of [38,66] increase model robustness through stability training methods.

Several other works apply data augmentation techniques to increase generalization performance. Whereas some work occludes parts of images [15,67], crops, replaces and mixes several images [59,63,64], or applies various (learned) sets of distortions [12,32], other methods augment with artificial noise to increase robustness [24,45,52].

Geirhos et al. [22] demonstrate that classifiers trained on ImageNet tend to classify images based on an image's texture. They further show that increasing the shape-bias of a classifier (through style transfer [21]), also increases the robustness for common image corruptions. This work builds upon this finding to increase the shape-bias of semantic segmentation models and, thus, the robustness for common image corruptions.

3   Training Schema: Painting-by-Numbers

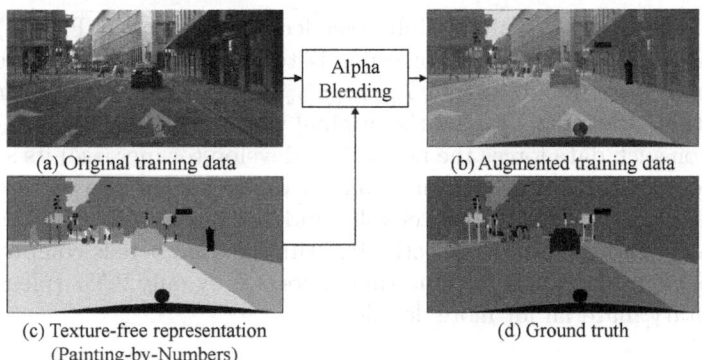

(a) Original training data

(b) Augmented training data

(c) Texture-free representation
(Painting-by-Numbers)

(d) Ground truth

Fig. 3. Overview of our proposed training schema, which we refer to as Painting-by-Numbers. (a) An RGB image of the Cityscapes training set and the respective ground-truth in (d). We paint the *numbers*, i.e., ground-truth IDs of (d) randomly, leading to the texture-free representation shown in (c). Painting the numbers randomly is essential since these colors are not likely to appear in real imagery. The final training image (b) is then generated by alpha-blending (a) and (c). A fraction of training data is augmented as in b), which is used as training data that increases the robustness against common corruptions

Our goal is to generically increase the robustness of semantic segmentation models for common image corruptions. Here, *robustness* refers to training a model on clean data and subsequently validating it on corrupted data. Simply adding corrupted data to the training set does certainly increase the robustness against common corruptions. However, this approach comes along with drawbacks: Firstly, a significantly increased training time. Secondly, the possibility to overfit to specific image corruptions [23,60] and reduced performance on clean data [60]. Thirdly, it further may be hard to actually identify all sources of corruption for new test scenarios. For our training schema, we build on the finding of [22]. We propose an augmentation schema (Painting-by-Numbers) that modifies the training process so that the model develops shape-based cues for the decision of how to segment a pixel, resulting in a generic increase of model robustness.

The basis of our schema is that we treat the segmentation ground-truth as a texture-free representation of the original training data (see Fig. 3). We then colorize (or *paint*) the ground-truth labels (or *numbers*) randomly (Painting-by-Numbers) to generate a representation as shown in Fig. 3(c). We uniformly sample the color from the sRGB color gamut with range $[0, 255]$, similar to the images of the Cityscapes dataset. Painting the numbers randomly is essential since these colors are not likely to appear in real imagery. Finally, we alpha-blend this this representation with the original training image, according to Eq. 1,

$$I_{blended} = \alpha \times I_{painting-by-numbers} + (1 - \alpha) \times I_{original} \qquad (1)$$

where $I_{blended}$ is the resulting alpha-blended training image (Fig. 3b), α is the blend parameter (where $\alpha = 1$ corresponds to a representation where original training input is entirely blended), $I_{painting-by-numbers}$ is the texture-free representation (Fig. 3c) and $I_{original}$ is the original training image (Fig. 3a). Training a network on such data forces the network to develop (or increase) its shape-bias since we actively corrupt the textural content of the image. The texture features of the image are, therefore, less reliable, and a model needs to develop additional cues to segment pixels correctly. Painting-by-Numbers is computationally efficient. For our setup, the training time increases by only 2.5% (please see the supplementary material for more details).

Motivation Blending with $0 < \alpha < 1$. We conducted the following analysis. We trained a model solely on texture-free images, as shown in Fig. 3 c, meaning that the blend parameter α is fixed to 1. This network achieved a decent performance when tested on a texture-free variant of the Cityscapes validation set. This is a positive signal because it means that the model is able to learn from entirely texture-free training data.

When we augmented only half of a training batch, instead of every image, (α is still fixed to 1), the performance on both, the original validation set and texture-free validation set was, again, considerably high; However, the robustness of the new model with respect to common image corruptions was not increased. We hypothesize that such a model learns to predict well for two different domains, which are the original data and the texture-free data. This motivates us to choose $\alpha < 1$ for some training images. As we will see, with a varying degree of alpha-blending, the robustness of the model towards common image corruptions increases significantly and, at the same time, keeps a consistently good performance on clean data.

Training Protocol. We use the state-of-the-art DeepLabv3+ [5–8] semantic segmentation architecture as baseline model. We show the effectiveness of Painting-by-Numbers for many network backbones: MobileNet-V2 [55], ResNet-50 [30], ResNet-101, Xception-41, Xception-71 [9]. We augment exactly half of a batch by our Painting-by-Numbers approach and leave the remaining images unchanged. Doing so ensures that the performance on clean data is comparable to a network that is trained regularly on clean data only. We kindly refer to the next section for reasonable choices of the hyperparameters. We apply a similar training protocol as in [8]: crop size 513×513^1, initial learning rate 0.01, "poly" [43] learning rate schedule, using the Atrous Spatial Pyramid Pooling (ASPP) module [5,26,28,39,65], fine-tuning batch normalization [34] parameters, output stride 16, random scale data augmentation and random flipping during training. As suggested by [8], we apply no global average pooling [42]. We train every model using TensorFlow [1].

Evaluation Protocol. We use the image transformations provided by the ImageNet-C [31] dataset to generate Cityscapes-C, similar to [35]. The ImageNet-C corruptions give a huge selection of transformations. They consist of several types of blur (Gaussian, motion, defocus, frosted glass), image noise (Gaussian, impulse, shot, speckle), weather (snow, spatter, fog, frost), and digital transformations (JPEG, brightness, contrast). Please see the supplementary material for examples. Each corruption type (e.g., Gaussian noise) is parameterized in five severity levels. We evaluate the mean-IoU [19] of many variants of the Cityscapes validation set, which is corrupted by the ImageNet-C transformations.

4 Experimental Evaluation and Validation

In this section, we demonstrate the effectiveness of Painting-by-Numbers. In Sect. 4.1 we discuss implementation details. We then show the results w.r.t the Cityscapes dataset in Sect. 4.2. We conduct a series of experiments to validate the increased shape-bias of a model trained with Painting-by-Numbers in Sect. 4.3.

4.1 Implementation Details

We experiment with varying implementations and augmentation schemes, which we discuss next.

Parameters for Alpha-Blending. Our experiments show that a fixed value for α does not yield the best results. Instead, we use two parameters for alpha-blending, α_{min} and α_{max}. These values define an interval from which α is

---

[1] Due to hardware limitations we are not able to train on the suggested crop size of 769.

drawn. They are the essential hyperparameters needed to achieve the best results towards common image corruptions. If α_{min} is too low, i.e., the amount of texture in the image is high, the robustness increase for common corruptions is minor. If α_{min} is too high, i.e., the amount of texture in the image is further diminished, the robustness decreases with respect to common corruptions (as discussed previously). We observe that the models only connect learned features from the two domains (original data domain and alpha-blended data domain) if the latter's texture is present, i.e., $0 < \alpha < 1$.

Batch Augmentation Schemes. We always augment exactly the half of a batch by Painting-By-Numbers for each iteration of the forward path. To summarize, the only parameters to be optimized are α_{min} and α_{max}. We do not observe better results when for every image in the mini-batch is individually decided if it shall be augmented by Painting-by-Numbers.

Incorporating Instance Labels. Beside semantic segmentation ground-truth, the Cityscapes dataset also contains instance labels for several classes. We additionally utilize them in our augmentation scheme to paint each instance with a randomly chosen color (instead of painting each instance of a class with the same color), as illustrated in Fig. 4(a). This produces promising results with respect to further increasing network robustness. Since Painting-by-Numbers is targeted for semantic segmentation task, we base our schema on the more general semantic labels, which are available for all reference datasets.

 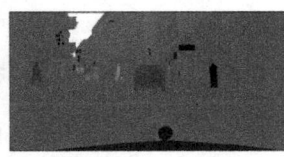 

(a) Instances are painted randomly   (b) Instances are painted by RGB-mean   (c) Instances are painted by RGB-median

Fig. 4. Examples of several coloring schemes used for Painting-by-Numbers

Paint with Mean and Median RGB. We further paint the images with a more consistent color, such as the mean and median RGB value of the class or instance (instead of painting the semantic classes randomly), as illustrated in Fig. 4(b) and (c). This approach does, as expected, not increase the model robustness. Instead of forcing a model to not rely on texture and color appearance, by corrupting these very properties, the network learns to assign a mean or median value to classes and instances, contrary to the effect of random painting. Hence, there is no need to increase the shape-bias for predicting the segmentation map when the colors are likely to appear in real imagery.

Best Setup. We train MobileNet-V2, ResNet-50, ResNet-101, Xception-41, and Xception-71 with Painting-by-Numbers. We evaluate the models on Gaussian noise to select the final values for α. For ResNet-50, and Xception-41, we observe the best results when we draw α uniformly from the interval $\alpha_{min} = 0.70$ and $\alpha_{max} = 0.99$. For the remaining networks, we observe the best results for $\alpha_{min} = 0.50$ and $\alpha_{max} = 0.99$.

4.2   Results on Cityscapes

In the following, we refer to a network that is trained with standard training schema as the reference model (i.e., trained on clean data only), and to a model that is trained with Painting-by-Numbers as our model. Figure 5 shows qualitative and quantitative results on corrupted variants of the Cityscapes dataset,

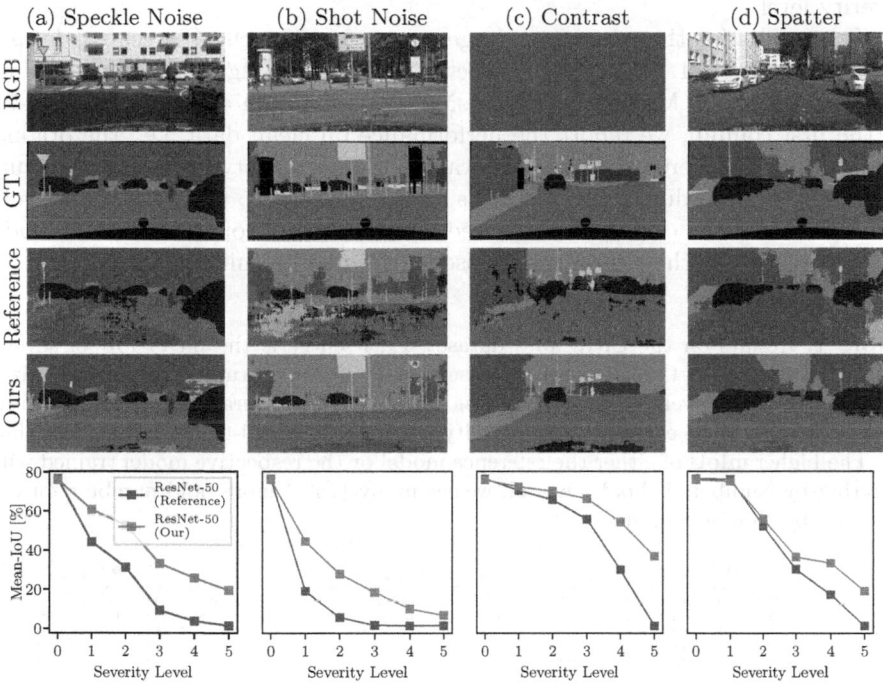

Fig. 5. (top) Qualitative results by the ResNet-50 backbone on four corrupted images of the Cityscapes validation dataset for both the reference model and our model (i.e., trained with Painting-by-Numbers). **(bottom)** Quantitative results on the corrupted variants of the Cityscapes dataset. Each image corruption is parameterized with five severity levels, where severity level 0 corresponds to clean (i.e., original) data. While for clean data, both models' performance is more or less the same, we see that our model is clearly superior for all types of noise added. For consistent performance on clean data, the performance on corrupted data increases when the model is trained with Painting-by-Numbers. For the first severity level of shot noise, the mIoU of our model is higher by 25%

when a network (ResNet-50) is trained with both training schemes. Every image corruption is parameterized with five severity levels. Severity level 0 corresponds to the clean data.

The reference model (third row) struggles to predict well in the presence of image corruptions (Fig. 5 top). It segments large parts of *road* wrongly as *building* for *spatter* and *image noise*. When the same model is trained with Painting-by-Numbers, the predictions are clearly superior (fourth row). With respect to quantitative results (Fig. 5 bottom), our model performs significantly better for image corruptions of category *speckle noise*, *shot noise*, and *contrast*. Corruption *contrast* decreases the contrast of the full image, corrupting hence the textural image content strongly. A network that is able to rely also on shape-based cues for the image segmentation is hence a well-performing model for *contrast reduction*. The mean IoU on *spatter* is for both models comparable for the first severity level, but it is for our model higher by almost 15% for the fourth severity level.

The results for the remaining image corruptions for the Cityscapes dataset are listed in Table 1. We show the effectiveness of Painting-by-Numbers besides ResNet-50 also for MobileNet-V2, ResNet-101, Xception-41, and Xception-71. In the first column, we report the performance on clean data, i.e., the original Cityscapes validation set. The mIoU evaluated on several types of image corruptions is listed accordingly. Each value is the average for up to five severity levels. We report for both clean and corrupted data, the result of the reference model and our model. In the following, we discuss the main results of Table 1.

Table 1. Results on the Cityscapes dataset. Each entry is the mean IoU of several corrupted variants of the Cityscapes dataset. Every image corruption is parameterized with five severity levels, and the resulting mean IoU are averaged. For image noise-based corruption, we exclude every severity level whose signal-to-noise ratio less than 10. The higher mIoU of either the reference model or the respective model trained with Painting-by-Numbers is bold. Overall, we see many (74%) more bold numbers for our Painting-by-Numbers model

Network	Clean	Blur				Noise				Digital				Weather			
		Motion	Defocus	Frosted Glass	Gaussian	Gaussian	Impulse	Shot	Speckle	Brightness	Contrast	Saturate	JPEG	Snow	Spatter	Fog	Frost
MobileNet-V2	73.0	52.4	47.0	44.7	48.1	9.6	14.2	9.8	25.6	50.4	43.8	32.5	20.3	10.8	43.3	47.7	16.1
ResNet-50	76.6	57.1	55.2	45.3	56.5	10.7	13.4	12.1	37.7	59.8	52.7	41.7	23.4	12.9	39.8	56.2	19.0
ResNet-101	76.0	58.9	55.3	47.8	56.3	22.9	22.9	23.1	45.5	57.7	56.8	41.6	32.5	11.9	45.5	55.8	23.2
Xception-41	77.8	61.6	54.9	51.0	54.7	27.9	28.4	27.2	53.5	63.6	56.9	51.7	38.5	18.2	46.6	57.6	20.6
Xception-71	77.9	62.5	58.5	52.6	57.7	22.0	11.5	21.6	48.7	67.0	57.2	45.7	36.1	16.0	48.0	63.9	20.5
Painting-by-Numbers																	
MobileNet-V2	72.2	49.5	41.4	40.7	43.0	17.4	18.4	16.8	35.7	62.5	50.8	51.0	17.6	12.1	46.9	56.5	22.4
ResNet-50	76.1	58.1	53.5	50.3	55.1	35.7	34.3	36.1	56.7	68.8	64.2	60.5	21.3	10.6	46.1	61.0	22.9
ResNet-101	76.3	58.1	54.2	48.7	54.7	41.6	44.3	40.6	57.4	70.5	64.4	65.0	25.6	10.8	50.1	56.9	28.0
Xception-41	78.5	65.5	54.2	51.1	51.8	46.9	44.9	46.9	64.3	73.4	60.2	68.8	15.7	19.3	55.8	65.7	28.2
Xception-71	78.6	63.0	53.6	48.6	52.2	35.5	38.4	34.2	57.6	74.9	63.9	69.1	22.2	18.2	57.4	65.4	25.5

Performance w.r.t Clean Data. Even though we paint the exact half of the training data and train both models for the same amount of iterations, the performance on clean data is oftentimes barely affected.

Performance w.r.t Image Blur. The robustness of our model with respect to image blur does not notably increase. We assume that Painting-by-Numbers does not increase the performance for this category of image corruptions because blur corrupts the object shapes by smearing the object boundaries. Hence, our learned shape-bias does not work well.

Performance w.r.t Image Noise. Painting-by-Numbers increases the robustness with respect to image noise the most (see figures above). For example, the absolute mIoU of Xception-41 for Gaussian noise, impulse noise, shot noise, and speckle noise increases by 19.0%, 16.5%, 19.7%, and 11.0%, respectively.

Performance w.r.t Digital Corruptions. A network trained with Painting-by-Numbers increases significantly the robustness against the corruptions *brightness*, *contrast*, and *saturation*–but not JPEG artifacts. The reason is that *JPEG compression* corrupts the boundary of objects and incorporates new boundaries through posterization artifacts. Our network cannot hence profit from its increased shape-bias. We refer to the supplement for an illustration.

Performance w.r.t Weather Corruptions. Xception-71 and Xception-41 increases the performance with respect to *spatter* by 9.4% and 9.2%, respectively. Xception-41 further increases the mIoU against *frost* by 7.6%. Every model increases the performance against *fog*. We cannot observe a significant performance increase for *snow*.

Though the performance increase on image corruptions of category *weather* is less than, e.g., for image noise, the predictions of a network trained with Painting-by-Numbers are improved for key-classes such as *cars*, *persons*, and *traffic signs* than for a regularly trained network. Please see the supplementary material for more results.

4.3   Understanding Painting-by-Numbers

We explain the increased robustness towards common image corruptions, i.e., when a network is trained with Painting-by-Numbers, by an increased shape-bias. To validate this assumption, we conduct a series of experiments that are based on the following consideration: Classes that either have a) no texture at all or b) texture that is strongly corrupted should be more reliably segmented by a network trained with Painting-by-Numbers. In more detail, we generate numerous, on class-level corrupted, variants of the Cityscapes validation set, as illustrated in Fig. 6. In (a), we remove the texture of *cars* and replace it by the dataset-wide RGB-mean of the training set of the respective class. The respective class does, in this way, not contain any texture but homogeneous color information. In (b) and (c) we corrupt *building* and *car* by a high degree of additive Gaussian noise and Gaussian blur, respectively. Please note that Fig. 6 shows only a small set of examples. We apply these corruptions for every class.

We test the models on such images to evaluate if they are capable of segmenting the respective class when they cannot rely on the class texture. To achieve this, a network needs to utilize other cues, such as shape-based cues.

(a) Replaced *car* by RGB-mean (b) Corrupted *building* by severe noise (c) Corrupted *car* by severe blur

Fig. 6. Examples of image data to validate an increasing shape-bias when models are trained with Painting-by-Numbers. We remove, or strongly corrupt, the texture of each class in the Cityscapes dataset and evaluate the segmentation performance when a network cannot rely on the class texture. (a) Texture is fully replaced by the dataset-wide RGB-mean value of the respective class. (b) Class is corrupted by severe noise. (c) Class is corrupted by severe blur

Instead of IoU, we use the sensitivity s ($s = TP/(TP + FN)$, where TP are true-positives, and FN are false-negatives) as evaluation metric. The sensitivity is for these experiments more appropriate than IoU ($IoU = TP/(TP + FN + FP)$) since we are solely interested in the segmentation performance on the class-level. Because all classes but one is clean (i.e., not corrupted), false-positively (FP) segmented pixels are of less interest. Utilizing IoU could, especially for classes covering fewer image regions, result in misleading scores. The results of these experiments are listed in Table 2.

Table 2. Sensitivity score per class for several corrupted variants on the class-level of the Cityscapes datasets. **Clean:** The performance on clean (i.e. original, non-corrupted) data. **RGB-mean:** The texture of a class is replaced by the dataset-wide RGB mean of that class. **Noise:** The texture of a class is corrupted by severe additive Gaussian noise. **Blur:** The texture of a class is corrupted by severe Gaussian blur. The higher sensitivity score of a network backbone of either the reference (top) or our model (bottom) is bold. Overall, we see many more bold numbers for our Painting-by-Numbers model

	road	sidewalk	building	wall	fence	pole	traffic light	traffic sign	vegetation	terrain	sky	person	rider	car	truck	bus	train	motorcycle	bicycle
Reference																			
Clean	98.8	93.1	96.6	53.3	69.6	74.5	81.7	85.7	96.7	74.1	97.8	91.5	76.9	97.6	85.1	92.8	70.7	79.2	88.7
RGB-mean	92.7	21.1	88.9	40.7	5.4	68.9	12.8	31.5	1.4	3.3	97.7	73.4	62.5	24.5	13.6	16.3	9.0	2.9	0.9
Noise (scale = 0.5)	5.8	0.8	95.0	0.2	1.7	4.7	6.4	39.2	0.1	1.4	2.8	8.1	2.9	4.5	0.0	0.0	7.1	0.2	3.4
Noise (scale = 1.0)	2.9	0.0	94.0	0.1	1.2	2.0	6.4	40.2	0.0	0.5	0.2	4.4	1.2	3.6	0.0	0.0	3.0	0.2	2.0
Blur ($\sigma = 20$)	94.6	42.8	89.3	38.0	1.8	63.6	18.4	19.1	0.6	7.3	94.0	55.4	55.5	56.7	32.5	24.0	7.7	9.0	0.9
Blur ($\sigma = 30$)	94.1	42.1	89.4	33.2	1.2	62.3	14.0	16.2	0.6	2.3	93.8	54.6	51.8	44.2	29.8	18.6	8.1	4.2	1.1
Painting-by-Numbers																			
Clean	99.0	90.3	96.3	56.0	67.1	68.9	76.5	81.1	96.2	66.3	97.1	89.5	74.0	96.8	89.7	86.0	59.6	72.2	87.8
RGB-mean	97.9	53.8	51.2	34.2	14.9	79.7	38.4	40.5	1.8	2.3	97.4	78.4	66.3	78.6	37.6	3.5	0.4	9.1	4.6
Noise (scale = 0.5)	97.4	50.9	92.1	8.4	37.4	34.1	8.2	11.1	23.3	30.6	32.3	50.1	19.7	49.8	31.5	1.9	0.0	0.3	26.7
Noise (scale = 1.0)	95.9	51.7	91.3	9.6	29.4	32.3	7.1	9.9	12.2	27.2	33.6	52.7	21.3	40.6	25.8	1.1	0.0	0.4	23.3
Blur ($\sigma = 20$)	49.3	43.5	86.5	18.7	4.7	73.6	55.1	29.8	1.0	0.8	94.3	75.5	73.2	71.9	56.6	7.9	0.5	20.2	3.5
Blur ($\sigma = 30$)	46.3	48.0	83.2	14.1	4.5	73.6	49.7	25.4	1.0	0.5	94.7	74.6	71.1	73.7	47.9	3.8	0.2	18.2	3.8

Quantitative Results. The results in Table 2 are created by DeepLabv3+ with ResNet-50 as network backbone. As previously, we refer to a network that is trained with the standard training schema as the reference model (i.e., only clean data used), and to a model that is trained with Painting-by-Numbers as our model. The top (bottom) part of the Table contains the sensitivity score for each class of the reference model (our model). Each line shows the sensitivity for the corrupted data as described previously (the performance on clean data is also listed). The higher sensitivity of a network backbone of either the reference model (top) or our model (bottom) is bold. We separately discuss in the following the quantitative results for class categories "stuff" and "things".

Both networks perform well for classes "stuff" since the amount of texture is often poor, such as for *road, wall, sidewalk,* and *sky.* The sensitivity of both models differs for *road* by 5.2%, for *wall* by 6.5%, and for sky by 0.3%. Whereas the absolute sensitivity for both models is above 90.0% for *road* and *sky,* it is less than 41% for *wall.* Our model performs for *sidewalk* better by 32.7%.

Painting-by-Numbers performs worse than the reference for classes "stuff" with a large amount of textual information, such as *building, vegetation,* and *terrain.* For example, the sensitivity score of our model for *building* is 37.7% less. Classes "stuff" have no distinct shape, hence, Painting-by-Numbers does not aid performance. When, additionally, the amount of texture of a class is large, the sensitivity of our model is less than of the reference model.

The reference model performs well when the texture of the category "things" is replaced by RGB-mean. Its sensitivity for *person* is 73.4%, which is only 5.0% less than for our model. The result for class *rider* is similar.

However, our model performs often significantly better than the reference model for most of the remaining "things" such as *car.* The sensitivity score of our model for this class is $s_{ours} = 78.6\%$, which is 54.1% higher than the sensitivity score of the reference model. We explain this high score with a large shape-bias due to both the distinct shape of *cars* and the comparatively large number of *cars* in the training set [11]. Our model performs for other classes of "things" also better than the reference model. For example, the sensitivity score for classes *traffic light, traffic sign* and *pole* is higher by 25.6%, 9.0%, and 9.8%, respectively. Both models perform poorly on "vehicles" that are, compared to *cars,* less frequent present in the training set (e.g., *truck, motorcycle, train*).

In the presence of severe Gaussian noise, the reference model is struggling to segment classes. The sensitivity is poor for every class, except for *traffic signs* and *building.* In the presence of image noise, the reference model tends to segment pixels oftentimes as these very classes, as illustrated in Fig. 5 and Fig. 7. The sensitivity scores of our model are often significantly higher. Similar to the previously discussed results, the sensitivity with respect to "stuff" with less texture is often high (e.g., $s_{ours} = 95.9\%$ for *road*). The sensitivity scores are also high for "things" such as *persons* and *cars* ($s_{ours} = 52.7\%$, and $s_{ours} = 40.6\%$, respectively). Our model segments many classes well that are corrupted by severe image noise, even though our model has not seen image noise during the training.

Fig. 7. Qualitative results of our experiments to understand the effect of Painting-by-Numbers. We train the ResNet-50 network backbone on Cityscapes with a standard training schema (i.e., with clean data only, reference model) and with Painting-by-Numbers (our model). **(top)** The first row shows the original validation image and the corrupted variants for class *car* and the respective ground truth in the second row. We replace either the class texture by the dataset-wide RGB-mean, strongly low-pass filtered the class, or added severe Gaussian image noise. The third row shows the predictions of the reference model. The fourth row shows the predictions of our model. The predictions in the fourth row (our model) are superior to the third row (reference model). Our model is able to withstand the image noise based corruption (last column) for which the reference model confuses *cars* with *traffic signs* mostly. **(bottom)** For *persons*, the reference model predicts well, when the RGB-mean replaces the texture of the class. Both models are relatively robust when the classes are low-pass filtered by severe Gaussian blur. Similar to the results with respect to class *car*, the reference model struggles to predict well for severe image noise and confuses *persons* also with *traffic signs* mostly

The reference model generally performs well when classes are low-pass filtered by severe Gaussian blur. This result is in accordance with [35], where the authors found semantic segmentation models to be relatively robust towards image blur. Again, for class category "things", our model outperforms the reference model in most cases. For example, the sensitivity score of our model for *person, rider,* and *car* is by approx. 20.0% higher.

Qualitative Results. See Fig. 7 for qualitative results of the previously discussed experiments. Please see the caption of Fig. 7 for discussion.

5   Conclusions

We proposed a simple, yet effective, data augmentation schema (Painting-by-Numbers) for semantic image segmentation in this work. This training schema increases the robustness for a wealth of common image corruptions in a generic way. Painting-by-Numbers corrupts training data so that the texture of image classes becomes less reliable, forcing the neural network to develop and increase its shape-bias to segment the image correctly. Painting-by-Numbers' benefits are that it does not require any additional data, is easy to implement in any supervised segmentation model, and is computationally efficient. It would be interesting to enforce other network biases, such as context bias or layout bias, and even to combine these with a shape bias, to further increase the robustness of semantic segmentation models with respect to common image corruptions.

References

1. Abadi, M., Barham, P., et al.: TensorFlow: a system for large-scale machine learning. In: 12th USENIX Symposium on Operating Systems Design and Implementation (OSDI 16), pp. 265–283 (2016). https://www.usenix.org/system/files/conference/osdi16/osdi16-abadi.pdf
2. Azulay, A., Weiss, Y.: Why do deep convolutional networks generalize so poorly to small image transformations? J. Mach. Learn. Res. **20**(184), 1–25 (2019). http://jmlr.org/papers/v20/19-519.html
3. Carlini, N., Wagner, D.: Adversarial examples are not easily detected: bypassing ten detection methods. In: Proceedings of the 10th ACM Workshop on Artificial Intelligence and Security (AISec 2017), pp. 3–14. ACM, New York, NY, USA (2017). https://doi.org/10.1145/3128572.3140444
4. Carlini, N., Wagner, D.A.: Towards evaluating the robustness of neural networks. In: 2017 IEEE Symposium on Security and Privacy (SP) (2017)
5. Chen, L.C., Papandreou, G., Kokkinos, I., Murphy, K., Yuille, A.L.: Semantic image segmentation with deep convolutional nets and fully connected CRFs. In: ICLR. vol. abs/1412.7062 (2015). http://arxiv.org/abs/1412.7062
6. Chen, L.C., Papandreou, G., Kokkinos, I., Murphy, K., Yuille, A.L.: Deeplab: semantic image segmentation with deep convolutional nets, atrous convolution, and fully connected CRFs. In: TPAMI (2017). http://arxiv.org/abs/1606.00915

7. Chen, L.C., Papandreou, G., Schroff, F., Adam, H.: Rethinking atrous convolution for semantic image segmentation (2017). http://arxiv.org/abs/1706.05587
8. Chen, L.-C., Zhu, Y., Papandreou, G., Schroff, F., Adam, H.: Encoder-decoder with atrous separable convolution for semantic image segmentation. In: Ferrari, V., Hebert, M., Sminchisescu, C., Weiss, Y. (eds.) ECCV 2018. LNCS, vol. 11211, pp. 833–851. Springer, Cham (2018). https://doi.org/10.1007/978-3-030-01234-2_49
9. Chollet, F.: Xception: deep learning with depthwise separable convolutions. In: CVPR (2017). https://doi.org/10.1109/CVPR.2017.195, http://ieeexplore.ieee.org/document/8099678/
10. Cisse, M., Bojanowski, P., Grave, E., Dauphin, Y., Usunier, N.: Parseval networks: improving robustness to adversarial examples. In: Precup, D., Teh, Y.W. (eds.) Proceedings of the 34th International Conference on Machine Learning. Proceedings of Machine Learning Research, PMLR, International Convention Centre, Sydney, Australia (2017). http://proceedings.mlr.press/v70/cisse17a.html
11. Cordts, M., et al.: The cityscapes dataset for semantic urban scene understanding. In: CVPR (2016)
12. Cubuk, E.D., Zoph, B., Mane, D., Vasudevan, V., Le, Q.V.: Autoaugment: learning augmentation strategies from data. In: The IEEE Conference on Computer Vision and Pattern Recognition (CVPR), June 2019
13. Dai, D., Van Gool, L.: Dark model adaptation: semantic image segmentation from daytime to nighttime. In: ITSC, pp. 3819–3824. IEEE (2018)
14. Deng, J., Dong, W., Socher, R., Li, L.J., Li, K., Fei-Fei, L.: ImageNet: a large-scale hierarchical image database. In: CVPR (2009)
15. DeVries, T., Taylor, G.W.: Improved regularization of convolutional neural networks with cutout. arXiv preprint arXiv:1708.04552 (2017)
16. Dodge, S., Karam, L.: A study and comparison of human and deep learning recognition performance under visual distortions. In: 2017 26th International Conference on Computer Communication and Networks (ICCCN), pp. 1–7. IEEE (2017)
17. Dodge, S.F., Karam, L.J.: Understanding how image quality affects deep neural networks. In: Quomex (2016)
18. Engstrom, L., Tran, B., Tsipras, D., Schmidt, L., Madry, A.: Exploring the landscape of spatial robustness. In: Chaudhuri, K., Salakhutdinov, R. (eds.) Proceedings of the 36th International Conference on Machine Learning. Proceedings of Machine Learning Research, vol. 97, pp. 1802–1811. PMLR, Long Beach, California, USA, June 2019. http://proceedings.mlr.press/v97/engstrom19a.html
19. Everingham, M., Van Gool, L., Williams, C.K.I., Winn, J., Zisserman, A.: The pascal visual object classes (VOC) challenge. In: IJCV (2010). https://doi.org/10.1007/s11263-009-0275-4
20. Fawzi, A., Frossard, P.: Manitest: are classifiers really invariant? In: BMVC (2015)
21. Gatys, L.A., Ecker, A.S., Bethge, M.: A neural algorithm of artistic style. arXiv http://arxiv.org/abs/1508.06576 (2015)
22. Geirhos, R., Rubisch, P., Michaelis, C., Bethge, M., Wichmann, F.A., Brendel, W.: Imagenet-trained CNNs are biased towards texture; increasing shape bias improves accuracy and robustness. In: ICLR, May 2019. https://openreview.net/forum?id=Bygh9j09KX
23. Geirhos, R., Temme, C.R.M., Rauber, J., Schütt, H.H., Bethge, M., Wichmann, F.A.: Generalisation in humans and deep neural networks. In: Advances in Neural Information Processing Systems, vol. 31 (2018). https://arxiv.org/abs/1808.08750

24. Gilmer, J., Ford, N., Carlini, N., Cubuk, E.: Adversarial examples are a natural consequence of test error in noise. In: Chaudhuri, K., Salakhutdinov, R. (eds.) Proceedings of the 36th International Conference on Machine Learning. Proceedings of Machine Learning Research, vol. 97, pp. 2280–2289. PMLR, Long Beach, California, USA, June 2019. http://proceedings.mlr.press/v97/gilmer19a.html
25. Goodfellow, I., Bengio, Y., Courville, A.: Deep Learning. MIT Press, Cambridge (2016)
26. Grauman, K., Darrell, T.: The pyramid match kernel: discriminative classification with sets of image features. In: ICCV (2005)
27. Gu, S., Rigazio, L.: Towards deep neural network architectures robust to adversarial examples. In: NIPS Workshop on Deep Learning and Representation Learning abs/1412.5068 (2014)
28. He, K., Zhang, X., Ren, S., Sun, J.: Spatial pyramid pooling in deep convolutional networks for visual recognition. In: Fleet, D., Pajdla, T., Schiele, B., Tuytelaars, T. (eds.) ECCV 2014. LNCS, vol. 8691, pp. 346–361. Springer, Cham (2014). https://doi.org/10.1007/978-3-319-10578-9_23
29. He, K., Zhang, X., Ren, S., Sun, J.: Delving deep into rectifiers: surpassing human-level performance on imagenet classification. In: ICCV, pp. 1026–1034 (2015)
30. He, K., Zhang, X., Ren, S., Sun, J.: Deep residual learning for image recognition. In: CVPR (2016). https://doi.org/10.1109/CVPR.2016.90, http://icccxplore.ieee.org/document/7780459/
31. Hendrycks, D., Dietterich, T.: Benchmarking neural network robustness to common corruptions and perturbations. In: ICLR (2019)
32. Hendrycks, D., Mu, N., Cubuk, E.D., Zoph, B., Gilmer, J., Lakshminarayanan, B.: AugMix: a simple data processing method to improve robustness and uncertainty. In: ICLR (2020)
33. Huang, X., Kwiatkowska, M., Wang, S., Wu, M.: Safety verification of deep neural networks. In: Majumdar, R., Kunčak, V. (eds.) CAV 2017. LNCS, vol. 10426, pp. 3–29. Springer, Cham (2017). https://doi.org/10.1007/978-3-319-63387-9_1
34. Ioffe, S., Szegedy, C.: Batch normalization: accelerating deep network training by reducing internal covariate shift. In: ICML (2015)
35. Kamann, C., Rother, C.: Benchmarking the robustness of semantic segmentation models with respect to common corruptions. Int. J. Comput. Vis. 1–22 (2020). https://doi.org/10.1007/s11263-020-01383-2
36. Kannan, H., Kurakin, A., Goodfellow, I.: Adversarial logit pairing. arXiv preprint arXiv:1803.06373 (2018)
37. Krizhevsky, A., Sutskever, I., Hinton, G.E.: Imagenet classification with deep convolutional neural networks. In: Advances in Neural Information Processing Systems, pp. 1097–1105 (2012)
38. Laermann, J., Samek, W., Strodthoff, N.: Achieving generalizable robustness of deep neural networks by stability training. In: Fink, G.A., Frintrop, S., Jiang, X. (eds.) DAGM GCPR 2019. LNCS, vol. 11824, pp. 360–373. Springer, Cham (2019). https://doi.org/10.1007/978-3-030-33676-9_25
39. Lazebnik, S., Schmid, C., Ponce, J.: Beyond bags of features: spatial pyramid matching for recognizing natural scene categories. In: CVPR, Washington, DC, USA (2006)
40. LeCun, Y., Bengio, Y., Hinton, G.E.: Deep learning. Nature (2015). https://doi.org/10.1038/nature14539
41. Lecun, Y., Bottou, L., Bengio, Y., Haffner, P.: Gradient-based learning applied to document recognition. In: Proceedings of the IEEE (1998)

42. Lin, M., Chen, Q., Yan, S.: Network in network. In: ICLR (2014)
43. Liu, W., Rabinovich, A., Berg, A.C.: Parsenet: Looking wider to see better. arXiv:1506.04579 [cs.CV] (2015)
44. Long, J., Shelhamer, E., Darrell, T.: Fully convolutional networks for semantic segmentation. In: CVPR. vol. abs/1411.4038 (2015)
45. Lopes, R.G., Yin, D., Poole, B., Gilmer, J., Cubuk, E.D.: Improving robustness without sacrificing accuracy with patch gaussian augmentation. arXiv preprint arXiv:1906.02611 (2019)
46. Mahajan, D., et al.: Exploring the limits of weakly supervised pretraining. In: Ferrari, V., Hebert, M., Sminchisescu, C., Weiss, Y. (eds.) ECCV 2018. LNCS, vol. 11206, pp. 185–201. Springer, Cham (2018). https://doi.org/10.1007/978-3-030-01216-8_12
47. Metzen, J.H., Genewein, T., Fischer, V., Bischoff, B.: On detecting adversarial perturbations. In: ICLR (2017). https://arxiv.org/abs/1702.04267
48. Michaelis, C., et al.: Benchmarking robustness in object detection: autonomous driving when winter is coming. In: Machine Learning for Autonomous Driving Workshop (NeurIPS 2019), vol. 190707484, Jul 2019. https://arxiv.org/abs/1907.07484
49. Noh, H., Hong, S., Han, B.: Learning deconvolution network for semantic segmentation. In: ICCV, pp. 1520–1528 (2015)
50. Redmon, J., Divvala, S.K., Girshick, R.B., Farhadi, A.: You only look once: unified, real-time object detection. In: CVPR, pp. 779–788 (2016)
51. Ruderman, A., Rabinowitz, N.C., Morcos, A.S., Zoran, D.: Pooling is neither necessary nor sufficient for appropriate deformation stability in CNNs. arXiv preprint arXiv:1804.04438 (2018)
52. Rusak, E., et al.: Increasing the robustness of DNNs against image corruptions by playing the Game of Noise. arXiv https://arxiv.org/abs/2001.06057 (2020)
53. Sakaridis, C., Dai, D., Van Gool, L.: Semantic foggy scene understanding with synthetic data. IJCV **126**(9), 973–992 (2018)
54. Sakaridis, C., Dai, D., Van Gool, L.: Guided curriculum model adaptation and uncertainty-aware evaluation for semantic nighttime image segmentation. In: ICCV (2019)
55. Sandler, M., Howard, A., Zhu, M., Zhmoginov, A., Chen, L.C.: MobileNetV2: inverted residuals and linear bottlenecks. In: CVPR (2018)
56. Simonyan, K., Zisserman, A.: Very deep convolutional networks for large-scale image recognition. In: ICLR (2015). http://arxiv.org/abs/1409.1556
57. Szegedy, C., et al.: Going deeper with convolutions. In: CVPR (2015). https://doi.org/10.1109/CVPR.2015.7298594, http://ieeexplore.ieee.org/document/7298594/
58. Szegedy, C., et al.: Intriguing properties of neural networks. arXiv preprint arXiv:1312.6199 (2013)
59. Takahashi, R., Matsubara, T., Uehara, K.: Data augmentation using random image cropping and patching for deep CNNs. IEEE Trans. Circ. Syst. Video Technol. **30**, 2917–2931 (2019)
60. Vasiljevic, I., Chakrabarti, A., Shakhnarovich, G.: Examining the impact of blur on recognition by convolutional networks. arXiv:1611.05760 [cs.CV] abs/1611.05760 (2016). http://arxiv.org/abs/1611.05760
61. Volk, G., Stefan, M., von Bernuth, A., Hospach, D., Bringmann, O.: Towards robust CNN-based object detection through augmentation with synthetic rain variations. In: ITSC (2019)
62. Xie, Q., Hovy, E., Luong, M.T., Le, Q.V.: Self-training with noisy student improves imagenet classification. arXiv preprint arXiv:1911.04252 (2019)

63. Yun, S., Han, D., Oh, S.J., Chun, S., Choe, J., Yoo, Y.: Cutmix: regularization strategy to train strong classifiers with localizable features. In: ICCV, pp. 6023–6032 (2019)
64. Zhang, H., Cisse, M., Dauphin, Y.N., Lopez-Paz, D.: mixup: beyond empirical risk minimization. In: ICLR (2017)
65. Zhao, H., Shi, J., Qi, X., Wang, X., Jia, J.: Pyramid scene parsing network. In: Proceedings of the IEEE Conference on Computer Vision and Pattern Recognition (2017). http://arxiv.org/abs/1612.01105
66. Zheng, S., Song, Y., Leung, T., Goodfellow, I.J.: Improving the robustness of deep neural networks via stability training. In: CVPR, pp. 4480–4488 (2016)
67. Zhong, Z., Zheng, L., Kang, G., Li, S., Yang, Y.: Random erasing data augmentation. In: AAAI (2017)
68. Zhou, Y., Song, S., Cheung, N.M.: On classification of distorted images with deep convolutional neural networks. In: International Conference on Acoustics, Speech, and Signal Processing (ICASSP) (2017)

Deep Spiking Neural Network: Energy Efficiency Through Time Based Coding

Bing Han[(✉)] and Kaushik Roy

Purdue University, West Lafayette, IN 47907, USA
{han183,kaushik}@purdue.edu

Abstract. Spiking Neural Networks (SNNs) are promising for enabling low-power event-driven data analytics. The best performing SNNs for image recognition tasks are obtained by converting a trained deep learning Analog Neural Network (ANN) composed of Rectified Linear Unit (ReLU) activation to SNN consisting of Integrate-and-Fire (IF) neurons with "proper" firing thresholds. However, this has come at the cost of accuracy loss and higher inference latency due to lack of a notion of time. In this work, we propose an ANN to SNN conversion methodology that uses a time-based coding scheme, named Temporal-Switch-Coding (TSC), and a corresponding TSC spiking neuron model. Each input image pixel is presented using two spikes and the timing between the two spiking instants is proportional to the pixel intensity. The real-valued ReLU activations in ANN are encoded using the spike-times of the TSC neurons in the converted TSC-SNN. At most two memory accesses and two addition operations are performed for each synapse during the whole inference, which significantly improves the SNN energy efficiency. We demonstrate the proposed TSC-SNN for VGG-16, ResNet-20 and ResNet-34 SNNs on datasets including CIFAR-10 (93.63% top-1), CIFAR-100 (70.97% top-1) and ImageNet (73.46% top-1 accuracy). It surpasses the best inference accuracy of the converted rate-encoded SNN with 7–14.5× lesser inference latency, and 30–60× fewer addition operations and memory accesses per inference across datasets.

Keywords: Spiking Neural Network · ANN-SNN conversion · Temporal coding · Energy efficiency · Deep learning · Machine learning

1 Introduction

Deep neural networks, referred to as Analog Neural Networks (ANNs) in this article (to distinguish them from the digital spiking counterpart), composed of several layers of interconnected neurons, have achieved state-of-the-art performance in various Artificial Intelligence (AI) tasks including image localization and recognition [18,33], video analytics [29], and natural language processing [16], among other tasks. For instance, ResNet [12] that won the ImageNet Large Scale Visual Recognition Challenge in 2015 consists of 152 layers with over 60 million parameters, and incurs 11.3 billion FLOPS per classification. In an effort

© Springer Nature Switzerland AG 2020
A. Vedaldi et al. (Eds.): ECCV 2020, LNCS 12355, pp. 388–404, 2020.
https://doi.org/10.1007/978-3-030-58607-2_23

to explore more power efficient neural architectures, recent research efforts have been directed towards devising computing models inspired from biological neurons that compute and communicate using spikes. These emerging class of networks with increased bio-fidelity are known as Spiking Neural Networks (SNNs) [22]. The intrinsic power-efficiency of SNNs stems from their sparse spike-based computation and communication capability, which can be exploited to achieve higher computational efficiency in specialized neuromorphic hardware [2,4,24].

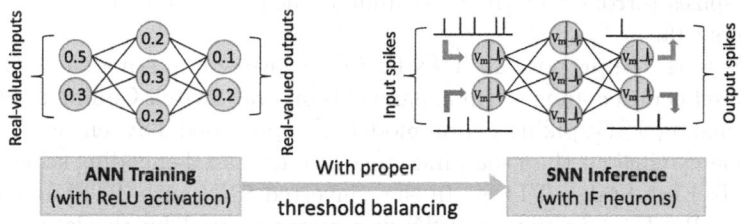

Fig. 1. Illustration of the ANN-SNN conversion methodology.

Considering the rapid strides in accuracy achieved by ANNs over the past few years, SNN training algorithms are much less mature and are an active field of research. The ANN to SNN conversion based training approaches have yielded the best performing SNNs (typically composed of Integrate-and-Fire (IF) neurons), which are converted from a trained non-spiking ANN (consisting of Rectified Linear Units (ReLUs) as the neural activation) [3,6,7,31,37] [47] as illustrated in Fig. 1. However, this has come at the cost of large inference latency (time-steps) and accuracy degradation. Recent work has shown that, the soft-reset membrane potential [35,36] in SNN can alleviate the information loss that occurs during ANN-SNN conversion by retaining the membrane potential above threshold at the firing instants. Near loss-less ANN-SNN conversion has been achieved using the "soft-reset" Residual-Membrane-Potential (RMP) spiking neuron and the required RMP-SNN firing threshold initialization [10]. The conversion schemes intelligently assign "appropriate" firing thresholds to the neurons at different layers of the network, thereby, ensuring that the IF spiking rates (number of spikes over large enough time interval) are proportional to the corresponding analog ReLU activations. However, it still requires sizeable number of inference time-steps, and the spiking activity is relatively high due to the rate-based neural coding for SNNs. The number of spikes for encoding a real-valued activation increases with both the ANN ReLU activation value and the SNN inference time-steps performed. A large number of spikes are fired to achieve accuracy comparable to the ANN accuracy, which leads to high computational cost [6,36,37]. Although several recent methods [34,45,46] reduced the number of spikes by employing more efficient neural coding, these methods relied on complex neuron models that continually perform expensive operations and the computational costs remain high (will be discussed in Sect. 2). The benefits of using spike-times as an additional dimension for computation has not been fully explored due to lack of general learning algorithms for SNNs. The Spike Timing Dependent Plasticity (STDP) based supervised [5,23,40,43] and semi-supervised learning algorithms [17,19,26,42] have thus far been restricted to shallow SNNs (with $\leq$5 layers) yielding considerably lower than acceptable accuracy on complex datasets like CIFAR-10 [9,41]. In order to scale the networks much deeper, the spike-based error backpropagation algorithms have been proposed for supervised training of SNNs [1,15,20,21,28,30,32,38,44]. However the training complexity incurred for performing backpropagation of the rate-encoded spikes (error) over time has limited their scalability for SNNs beyond 9–11 layers [20].

In this work, we propose an ANN to SNN conversion methodology that uses a time-based neural coding scheme, named Temporal-Switch-Coding (TSC), and a corresponding TSC spiking neural model. The proposed TSC encoding scheme is more energy efficient than the First-spike latency based encoding schemes such as Time-To-First-Spike (TTFS). In the converted SNN with TTFS encoding, a real-valued ReLU activation in ANN was approximated by the latency to the first spike of the corresponding spike train in the SNN, and at most one spike needs to be fired for each activation. Even though total spikes are reduced, the memory access and computational costs remain high, because the spiking neuron needs to keep track of a synapse, at every time-step afterwards, ever since the synapse received its first spike. In SNN with the proposed TSC encoding scheme, at most two spikes are fired for each activation, but the spiking neuron keeps track of a synapse only at the instant of an input-spike to reduce the memory access and computational costs (details discussed in Sect. 3).

2   Related Work

Recent ANN to SNN conversion methods reduced the number of spikes used to encode activations by employing more efficient neural coding. In [45], an ANN was converted to an Adapting SNN (AdSNN) based on synchronous Pulsed Sigma-Delta coding. When driven by a strong stimulus, an Adaptive Spiking Neuron (ASN) adaptively raises its dynamic firing threshold every time it fires a spike, reducing its firing rate. However, an ASN has to perform four multiplications every time step to update its postsynaptic current, firing threshold, and refractory response. In [34], an ANN was converted to an SNN based on the Time-To-First-Spike (TTFS) temporal coding, where an activation in the ANN was approximated by the latency to the first spike of the corresponding spike train in the SNN. Thus, at most one spike needs to be fired for each activation, which reduces the number of spikes in inference. However, the spiking neuron needs to keep track of a synapse, at every time-step till the end of the inference, ever since this synapse received its first spike. At each time-step, a large number of synapses including those that receive an input-spike at the current time-step and those that have received an input-spike at any prior time-step are added to the membrane potential of the spiking neuron, which incurs expensive memory access and computational costs. In [25], each activation of an ANN was approximated with a power of two, where the exponents of the powers were constrained within a set of several consecutive integers. The error tolerance of an ANN allows it to compensate for approximation errors in the corresponding SNN during the training phase, which in turn helps close the performance gap between the SNN and the ANN. Authors in [46] proposed Logarithmic Temporal Coding (LTC), where the number of spikes used to encode an activation value grows logarithmically with activation. The Exponentiate-and-Fire (EF) spiking neuron only involves bit-shift and addition operations. However, the energy benefit comes at the cost of large accuracy loss due to the approximation error introduced by LTC, and requires constrained ANN training to compensate for the loss. The method is implemented for shallow network consisting of 2 convolutional layers and evaluated on MNIST dataset. The performance on deeper architectures such as VGG and more complex datasets such as CIFAR-10 are not clear.

3   Temporal Switch Coding Scheme

The real-valued pixel intensities of input image are mapped to the spike-times over a large enough time interval for SNN during inference. The time-step dt is used to keep track of the discrete time, and the total time-steps (latency) required are dictated by the desired inference accuracy. Note that the input images fed to ANN are typically normalized to zero mean and unit standard deviation, yielding pixel intensities between ± 1, and bipolar spikes are used to represent the positive and negative pixels. In our proposed TSC time-based coding scheme, at most a pair of spikes with opposite signs are used to encode one real-valued pixel in time. Suppose $N(N \geq 2)$ time-steps are used to encode a pixel p $(-1 \leq p \leq 1)$. The magnitude of p is first quantized into N levels as described by Eq. 1, where $p^*(0 \leq p^* \leq N)$ is the pixel magnitude after quantization. As described by Eq. 2, two spikes will be produced at time $t = 1$ and $t = p^*$, if p^* is greater or equal to 2; no spike will be produced otherwise. As shown in Fig. 2(a), the real-valued pixel p $(p \neq 0)$ is encoded using the spike-times (t_s^+, t_s^-) of a pair of spikes. The first spike which occurs at $t_s^+ = 1$ always has the same sign as p, and the second spike that occurs at $t_s^- = p^*$ always has the opposite sign as p.

$$p^* = \lfloor |p| \, (N - 1) \rfloor + 1$$

$$(-1 \leq p \leq 1, 1 \leq p^* \leq N, and \, \lfloor \, \rfloor \, is \, the \, floor \, operation) \tag{1}$$

$$T(t) = \begin{cases} sgn(p), & if \,\, (p^* \geq 2, \, t = 1) \\ -sgn(p), & if \,\, (p^* \geq 2, \, t = p^*) \\ 0, & else \end{cases} \tag{2}$$

$(where \,\, "sgn" \,\, is \,\, the \,\, sign \,\, function, \,\, sgn(p) = \frac{|p|}{p})$

We use time-based TTFS and rate-based Poisson coding schemes as benchmarks to evaluate the performance of our proposed TSC encoding. In time-based TTFS, the real-valued pixel p $(p \neq 0)$ is encoded using the spike time t_s of a

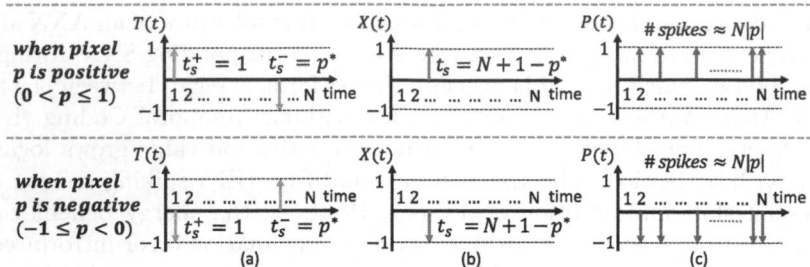

Fig. 2. Illustration of encoding a real-valued pixel p $(-1 \leq p \leq 1)$ of static image to spike trains for SNN using: (a) Temporal-Switch-Coding (TSC), (b) Time-To-First-Spike (TTFS), and (c) Poisson rate-based encoding.

single spike, which always has the same sign as p. The spike-time $t_s = N+1-p^*$, where p^* is the quantized pixel intensity as described by Eq. 1. As shown in Fig. 2 (b), larger the quantized pixel intensity p^*, earlier the spike occurs. In Poisson rate coding, pixels are mapped to spike trains firing at a rate (number of spikes over time) proportional to the corresponding pixel intensities as shown in [13]. The pixel intensity is first mapped to instantaneous spiking probability of the corresponding input neuron. We use Poisson process to generate the input-spike in a stochastic manner as explained below. At every time-step of SNN operation, we generate a uniform random number between 0 and 1, which is compared against the magnitude of the pixel intensity $|p|$ ($|p| \leq 1$). A spike is produced if the random number is lesser than $|p|$. As shown in Fig. 2(c), the spikes produced with Poisson rate coding always have the same sign as p, and total number of spikes over N time-steps is proportional to the magnitude $|p|$.

3.1   Computation Reduction

In this section, we first formalize the derivation of the proposed TSC coding scheme, which is obtained from modifying the TTFS, and explain reasons for the increased performances and decreased computation in SNN inference. Let us assume spike-trains $X_1(t)$ to $X_m(t)$ are encoded from an input image consisting of m pixels using TTFS coding as shown in Fig. 3(a). The spike-trains are fed to a spiking neuron through real-valued synaptic weights w_1 to w_m. The total number of inference time-steps is N. For simplicity, let us assume all pixels of the input image are of different values (between 0 and 1), and the m spike-trains from $X_1(t)$ to $X_m(t)$ have been sorted according to the spike-time (from early to late). As shown in Fig. 3(a), at time-step t, the spiking neuron receives only one spike from the input image through weight w_j. However, computing the weighted-sum of spike-input at t requires summing up synaptic weights from w_1 to w_j. Hence, both the TTFS spike-trains in Fig. 3(a) and the modified TTFS spike-trains in Fig. 3(c) incur the same amount of addition operations as shown in Fig. 3(b) and (d).

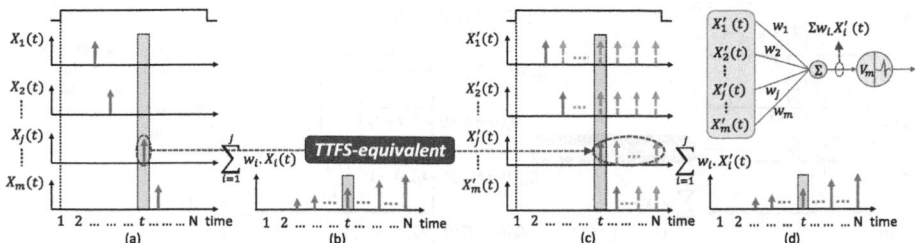

Fig. 3. (a) TTFS coding fires one spike for each pixel. (b) Modified TTFS fires multiple spike for one pixel. (c) Weighted-sum of the TTFS spikes. (d) Weighted-sum of the modified TTFS spikes.

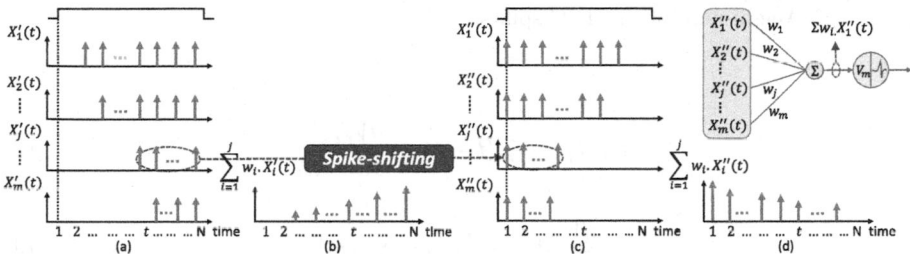

Fig. 4. (a) Modified TTFS fires "late" spikes. (b) Shifted TTFS fires "early" spikes. (c) Weighted-sum of the "late" spikes. (d) Weighted-sum of the "early" spikes.

Now let us transform the modified TTFS spike-trains in Fig. 3(c) to the proposed TSC spike-trains using the "spike-shifting" (shown in Fig. 4) and "frame-subtracting" (shown in Fig. 5) operations. First the "spike-shifting" operation is performed, in which, all "late" spikes in Fig. 4(a) are shifted in time to become the "early" spikes in Fig. 4(c), and the number of spikes for encoding the pixel does not change. The corresponding weighted-sum of input-spikes are shown in Fig. 4(b) and (d). Larger activation arrives earlier due to the "spike-shifting" operation. Next the "frame-subtracting" operation is performed to transform the shifted TTFS spike-trains in Fig. 5(a) to the proposed TSC spike-trains in Fig. 5(c). Suppose $X_j''(t)$ is one of the shifted TTFS spike-trains that consists of t consecutive spikes as highlighted in Fig. 5(a). Every spike in the spike-train is subtracted by the previous spike (except for the first spike) as described by $X_j''(t) - X_j''(t-1)$. As shown in Fig. 5(c), only one positive spike (at time-step 1) and one negative spike (at time-step $t+1$) remain in the resulting TSC spike-train $T_j(t)$. All spikes from time-step 2 to time-step t become zeros. At each time-step, membrane potential $V_m(t)$ in the spiking neuron is updated as described by Eq. 3. Computing the weighted-sum of input-spike using the shifted TTFS spike-trains at t requires j addition operations as described by Eq. 4. However, by reusing the computation at $t-1$ as described by Eq. 5, the addition operations required for computing the weighted-sum of input-spike at time t is reduced to 1 using TSC spike-trains as described by Eq. 6.

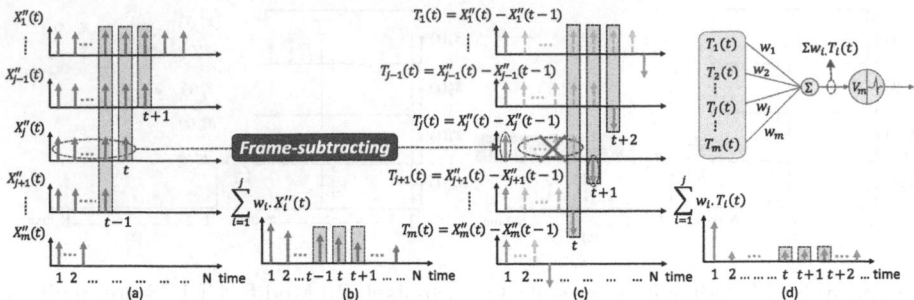

Fig. 5. (a) Shifted TTFS fires multiple consecutive spikes for one pixel. (b) Subtracted TTFS fires a pair of bipolar spikes for one pixel. (c) Weighted-sum of the shifted TTFS spikes. (d) Weight-sum of the TSC spikes.

$$V_m(t) = V_m(t-1) + \left.\frac{dV_m}{dt}\right|_{(t)} \tag{3}$$

$$\left.\frac{dV_m}{dt}\right|_{(t)} = \sum_{i=1}^{j} w_i.X_i^{''}(t) \tag{4}$$

$$\left.\frac{dV_m}{dt}\right|_{(t)} = \left.\frac{dV_m}{dt}\right|_{(t-1)} + \left.\frac{d^2V_m}{dt^2}\right|_{(t)} \tag{5}$$

$$\left.\frac{d^2V_m}{dt^2}\right|_{(t)} = \sum_{i=1}^{j} w_i.T_i(t) = w_j.T_j(t) \tag{6}$$

4   ANN to TSC-SNN Conversion

The fundamental distinction between ANN and SNN is the notion of time. In ANNs, input and output of neurons in all the layers are real-valued as shown in Fig. 6(a), and inference is performed with single feed-forward pass through the network. On the other hand, input and output of the TSC spiking neurons are encoded temporally using sparse spiking events over certain time period as shown in Fig. 6(b). Hence, inference in TSC-SNN is carried out over multiple feed-forward passes or time-steps (also known as inference latency), where each pass entails sparse spike-based computations. Achieving close to ANN accuracy with minimal inference latency is key to obtaining favorable trade-off between accuracy and computational efficiency. The proposed conversion methodology significantly advances the state-of-the-art in this regard as will be detailed in this section.

ANNs used for conversion to SNNs are typically trained with ReLU non-linearity [27] as shown in Fig. 6(a), where Y is the output of ReLU-based artificial neruon, $\sum_i w_i.p_i + b$ is the weighted sum of input p_i with weight w_i and bias

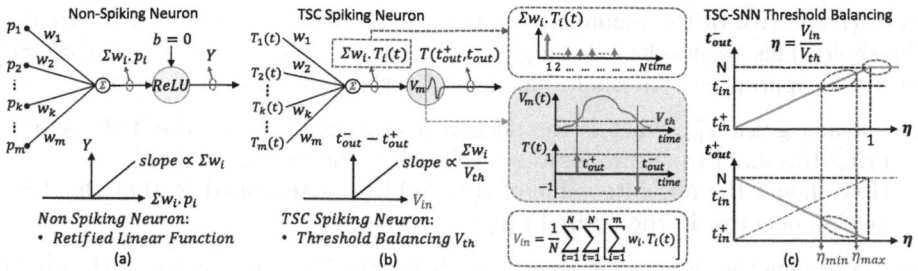

Fig. 6. (a) Non-spiking ReLU neuron driven by a set of analog input pixels via weights (w). (b) TSC spiking neuron driven by a set of time-encoded spikes via weights (w). (c) TSC-SNN requires finding the appropriate firing threshold V_{th} to balance the spike-times across layers to achieve the best performance.

b. The bias is usually set to zero for effective ANN-SNN conversion [37]. The ReLU ouput varies linearly with the input for positive inputs. On the other hand, $\sum_i w_i.T_i(t)$ is the weighted-sum of spike-input received by the TSC spiking neuron as shown in Fig. 6(b). The TSC spiking neuron integrates the weighted-sum of spike-input into the membrane potential as described by Eq. 5 and Eq. 6. The average input V_{in} to the spiking neuron equals to the total amount of potential integrated by the TSC spiking neuron divided by the inference time steps N as described by Eq. 7. The membrane potential update mechanism in the TSC spiking neuron is similar to the "soft-reset" IF neuron. At any time-step, if the membrane potential $V_m(t)$ is higher than the firing threshold V_{th} ($V_{th} >$ 0), the firing threshold is subtracted from the membrane potential $V_m(t) = V_m(t) - V_{th}$. However, a positive spike is produced only at time t^+_{out} when its membrane potential exceeds the firing threshold V_{th} ($V_{th} > 0$), and a negative spike is produced only at time t^-_{out} when its membrane potential drops below the firing threshold V_{th} ($V_{th} > 0$); otherwise, no spike is fired during the whole inference. The linear ReLU input-output dynamics are roughly mimicked using the input potential V_{in} and the output spike-times $T(t^+_{out}, t^-_{out})$ of the proposed TSC spiking neuron as illustrated in Fig. 6(b).

$$V_{in} = \frac{1}{N} \sum_{t=1}^{N} \sum_{t=1}^{N} \sum_{i=1}^{m} w_i.T_i(t) \tag{7}$$

4.1 Threshold Balancing for TSC-SNN

Setting threshold too high causes no spike to be fired in the spiking neuron, whereas setting threshold too low causes the spiking neuron to operate in the non-linear regime, both lead to significant accuracy loss in ANN-SNN conversion. The extended linear input-output relationship of TSC spiking neuron (see Fig. 6(b)) provides "wider operating range" for the neuronal firing threshold compared to that for the IF neuron which "hard reset" the membrane potential to 0 irrespective of the amount by which the membrane potential exceeds the threshold. This begets the following couple of questions that need to be answered to ensure appropriate threshold balancing for the TSC spiking neuron.

1. For any given V_{in}, what is the desired operating range for the TSC neuron firing threshold to ensure loss-less ANN-SNN conversion?
2. How should the absolute value of threshold be determined so that the TSC neuron operates in the desired range?

We determine the upper and lower bounds for the TSC neuron firing threshold based on the desired output spike-time $T(t_{out}^+, t_{out}^-)$. Figure 6(c) indicates that the output spike time t_{out}^- must be larger than the input spike-time t_{in}^+, and smaller than the total inference time steps N. This is because the membrane potential integration does not start until it receives the first input spike at t_{in}^+, and the negative spike can not be fired if the membrane potential does not drop below the firing threshold by the end of time-step N. The desirable range for t_{out}^- is $[t_{in}^-, N)$. Satisfying $t_{out}^- \leq N$ requires $\eta = \frac{V_{in}}{V_{th}} \leq 1$ or $V_{th} \geq V_{in}$ as highlighted in Fig. 6(c), which ensures the linearity in TSC activation. Using smaller η or larger V_{th} helps to reduce the output spike-time t_{out}^-, which intends to improve the inference latency. However, it also delays the spike time t_{out}^+, which causes more delay to the successive layers. Hence, setting appropriate firing thresholds to balance the spike-times t_{out}^+ and t_{out}^- across layers is the key to achieve the best latency in TSC-SNN.

Let us now address the second question concerning the precise V_{th} estimation methodology. In our analysis thus far, we estimated V_{th} using V_{in} as described by Eq. 7, which is the average weighted input sum to the TSC neuron over time. Prior works proposed setting V_{th} to the maximum weighted input sum to the neuron across time-steps [6,37]. Note that, rate encoding was used for the estimation. In this work, we followed a similar procedure to estimate the V_{in}^{max} for each layer of the TSC-SNN. The maximum estimate V_{in}^{max} can enable the TSC neuron to operate in the linear region (where $t_{in}^- < t_{out}^- < N$ as highlighted in Fig. 6(c)). We initialize the thresholds of each layer to the estimated V_{in}^{max} times a scaling factor $\alpha (\alpha \in [0,1])$. According to our simulation, setting $\alpha \approx 0.8$ helps the TSC-SNN to achieve the best accuracy with minimal latency. Before presenting the results, we describe the methodology, originally proposed in [37], used to initialize the layer-wise threshold of deep SNN using the ANN-trained weights and SNN spiking statistics. We transfer the trained weights from ANN to SNN, and feed the TSC spike-inputs (for the entire training set) to the first layer of the SNN. We record the weighted input sum to all the neurons in the first layer across time-steps. We set the threshold of TSC neurons in the first layer to the maximum weighted input sum, across neurons and time-steps, over the training dataset. We then freeze the threshold of the first layer, and estimate the threshold of the second layer using the same procedure outlined previously. The threshold estimation process is carried out sequentially in a layer-wise manner for all the layers.

ResNet-20 SNN, with its layer-wise threshold assigned to V_{in}^{max}, achieved 91.36% on CIFAR-10 using 1024 time-steps, which is comparable to that

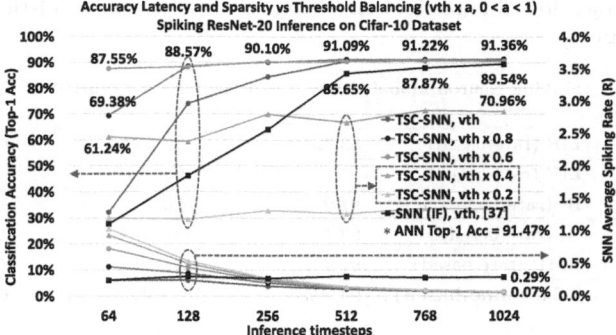

Fig. 7. Threshold balancing for ResNet-20 TSC-SNN inference on CIFAR-10 dataset.

(91.47%) achieved by the corresponding ANN as illustrated in Fig. 7. The x-axis is SNN inference latency, the y-axis on the left measures the SNN top-1 inference accuracy, and the y-axis on the right measures the percentage of neurons those fire spikes per time-step. We thereafter scaled the threshold by a factor of up to 0.6× and found that the TSC-SNN, with scaled threshold, converged to the same accuracy obtained using $V_{th}=V_{in}^{max}$. This corroborates our hypothesis that the TSC neuron operates in the linear region for a wide range of firing thresholds, thereby, causing the TSC-SNN to yield higher accuracy using fewer time-steps as depicted in Fig. 7. As the threshold is scaled further by up to 0.2×, we notice significant drop in accuracy. At such low thresholds, the TSC neuron operates in the non-linear regime, leading to higher accuracy loss during inference. We propose initializing the threshold of TSC-SNN with scaled version of V_{in}^{max} (scaling factor $\alpha \approx 0.8$ in this example) to achieve the optimal accuracy-latency trade-off. We validate the presented threshold initialization scheme across different SNN architectures and datasets. Improving the inference latency by reducing the firing threshold do not increase the spiking activity in TSC-SNN. In an effort to quantify the spiking activity of TSC-SNN for different thresholds, we measure the average spike rate as defined by the following equation.

$$R = \frac{total\ spikes}{total\ neurons \times inference\ time\text{-}steps} \times 100\% \tag{8}$$

The spike rate R in (8) indicates the average percentage of neurons that spike per time-step. Our analysis indicates that the TSC-SNN, with scaled thresholds, provides significant benefits in accuracy and latency with no increase in spiking activity as shown in Fig. 7.

5   Results

We evaluated TSC-SNNs on standard visual object recognition benchmarks, namely the CIFAR-10, CIFAR-100 and ImageNet datasets. We use VGG-16

Table 1. Accuracy loss due to ANN-SNN conversion of the state-of-the-art SNNs on CIFAR-10 dataset

Network Architecture	Spiking Neuron Model	ANN (Top-1 Acc)	SNN (Top-1 Acc)	Accuracy Loss
8-layered [14]	LIF (rate-based)	83.72%	83.54%	0.18%
3-layered [8]	LIF (rate-based)	–	89.32%	–
6-layered [36]	IF (rate-based)	91.91%	90.85%	1.06%
ResNet-20 [37]	IF (rate-based)	89.1%	87.46%	1.64%
ResNet-20 [10]	RMP (rate-based)	91.47%	91.36%	0.11%
ResNet-20 [This work]	**TSC (time-based)**	**91.47%**	**91.42%**	**0.05%**
VGG-16 [37]	IF (rate-based)	91.7%	91.55%	0.15%
VGG-16 [10]	RMP (rate-based)	93.63%	93.63%	<0.01%
VGG-16 [This work]	**TSC (time-based)**	**93.63%**	**93.63%**	**<0.01%**

architecture [39] for all three datasets. ResNet-20 configuration outlined in [12] is used for the CIFAR-10 and CIFAR-100 datasets while ResNet-34 is used for experiments on the ImageNet dataset. Our implementation is derived from the Facebook ResNet implementation code for CIFAR and ImageNet datasets. The code can be found online at https://github.com/facebookarchive/fb.resnet.torch. Proper weight initialization is crucial to achieve convergence in such deep networks without batch-normalization. Similar weights initialization was done as outlined in [11] although their networks were trained without both dropout and batch-normalization. For VGG networks, a dropout layer is used after every ReLU layer except for those layers which are followed by a pooling layer. For Residual networks, we use dropout only for the ReLUs at the non-identity parallel paths but not at the junction layers. We found this to be crucial for achieving training convergence. We found this to be crucial for achieving training convergence. The most recent state-of-the-art ANN-SNN conversion works are provided for comparison as shown in Tables 1, 2 and 3. Note that authors in [36] reported a top-1 SNN error rate of 25.04% for an Inception-V3 network, with their ANN trained to an error rate of 23.88%. The resulting accuracy loss is 1.52% which is much higher than our proposal. The Inception-V3 network conversion was also optimised by a voltage clamping method, that was found to be specific for the Inception network and did not apply to the VGG network [36]. In addition, the results reported on ImageNet in [36] are on a subset of 1382 image samples for Inception-V3 network and 2570 samples for VGG-16 network. Hence, the performance on the entire dataset is unclear. Our proposed TSC-SNN achieved not only the best SNN inference accuracy but also the lowest accuracy loss in ANN-SNN conversion across all network architectures and datasets we evaluated.

The VGG-16 TSC-SNN inference performance on CIFAR-10, CIFAR-100 and ImageNet datasets are shown in Fig. 8(a) (c) and (e). In each figure, x-axis is the SNN inference latency, the y-axis on the left measures the SNN top-1 inference accuracy, and the y-axis on the right measures the percentage of

Table 2. Accuracy loss due to ANN-SNN conversion of the state-of-the-art SNNs on CIFAR-100 dataset

Network Architecture	Spiking Neuron Model	ANN (Top-1 Acc)	SNN (Top-1 Acc)	Accuracy Loss
ResNet-20 [37]	IF (rate-based)	68.72%	64.09%	4.63%
ResNet-20 [10]	RMP (rate-based)	68.72%	67.82%	0.9%
ResNet-20 [This work]	**TSC (time-based)**	**68.72%**	**68.18%**	**0.54%**
VGG-16 [37]	IF (rate-based)	71.22%	70.77%	0.45%
VGG-16 [10]	RMP (rate-based)	71.22%	70.93%	0.29%
VGG-16 [This work]	**TSC (time-based)**	**71.22%**	**70.97%**	**0.25%**

Table 3. Accuracy loss due to ANN-SNN conversion of the state-of-the-art SNNs on ImageNet dataset

Network Architecture	Spiking Neuron Model	ANN (Top-1 Acc)	SNN (Top-1 Acc)	Accuracy Loss
ResNet-34 [37]	IF (rate-based)	70.69%	65.47%	5.22%
ResNet-34 [10]	RMP (rate-based)	70.64%	69.89%	0.75%
ResNet-34 [This work]	**TSC (time-based)**	**70.64%**	**69.93%**	**0.71%**
VGG-16 [36]	RMP (rate-based)	63.89%	49.61%	14.28%
VGG-16 [37]	IF (rate-based)	70.52%	69.96%	0.56%
VGG-16 [10]	RMP (rate-based)	73.49%	73.09%	0.4%
VGG-16 [This work]	**TSC (time-based)**	**73.49%**	**73.46%**	**0.03%**

neurons those fire spikes per time-step. As shown in Fig. 8 (a), TSC-SNN (green curve) achieved the same accuracy 93.63% as the trained ANN, whereas the SNN with IF neurons achieved 93.50% using 2048 time-steps. TSC-SNN reaches an accuracy 92.79% using only 64 time-steps, which is 3 times faster than the RMP-SNN (blue curve) that uses about 200 time-steps, and 10 times faster than the SNN with IF neurons (black curve) that uses about 640 time-steps. The TSC-SNN attains a spike rate around 0.03%, which is 66.3 times lower than the RMP-SNN, and 20.3 times lower than the SNN with IF neuron. As mentioned above, lower spiking rate does not guarantee low computation in temporal SNNs. Hence, the number of addition operations performed in SNNs inference are also provided in Fig. 8(b) (d) and (f). In each figure, x-axis is the SNN inference latency, the y-axis measures the number of addition operations performed for computing the weighted sum of spike-input and updating the membrane potential in SNN inference. As shown in Fig. 8(b). The proposed TSC-SNN reduces the number of addition computation by one order of magnitude than SNN with IF neuron in [37], and two orders of magnitude than the RMP-SNN in [10]. The VGG-16 TSC-SNN inference performance on CIFAR-100 and ImageNet datasets are shown in Fig. 8 (c) (d) and Fig. 8 (e) (f) respectively. Note, no VGG-16 SNN

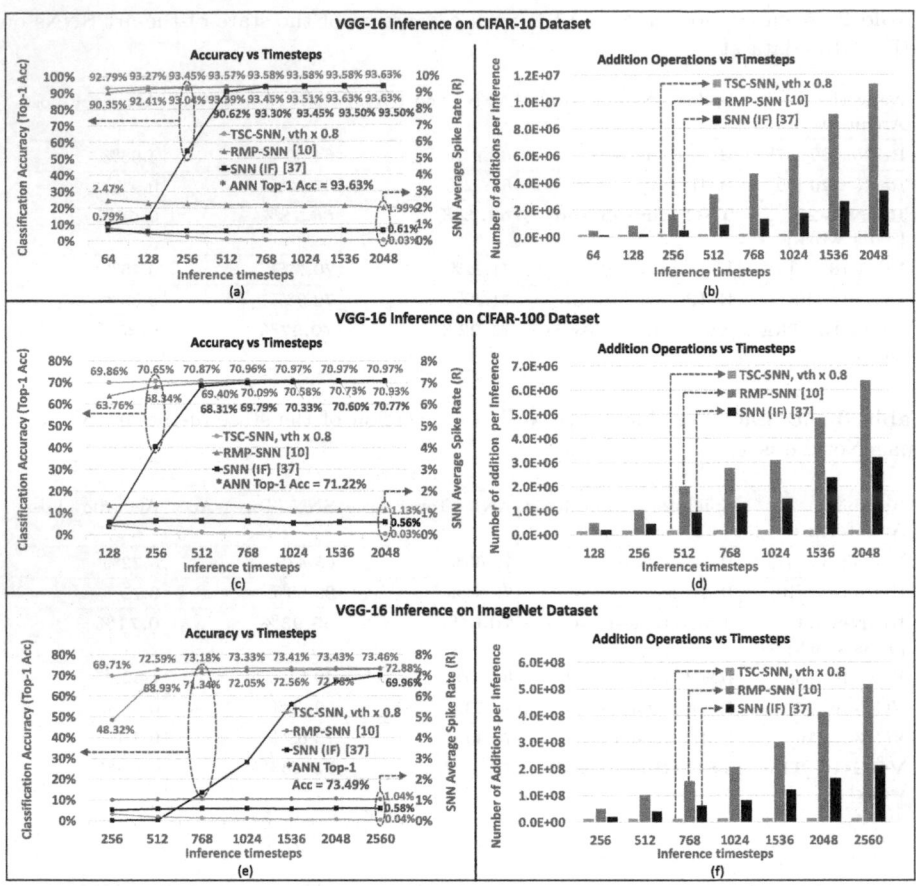

Fig. 8. Inference accuracy ((a) (c) and (e)) and computational cost ((b) (d) and (f)) comparisons between TSC-SNN and the two baseline SNNs (RMP-SNN [10] and SNN(IF) [37]) using VGG-16 architecture on CIFAR-10, CIFAR-100 and ImageNet datasets.

was evaluated on CIFAR-100 dataset in [37]. In this work, the results of VGG-16 on CIFAR-100 using the TSC-SNN, RMP-SNN and the baseline SNN with IF neurons were converted from our trained ANN with top-1 inference accuracy of 71.22%. The ResNet-20 and ResNet-34 TSC-SNNs inference performance on the CIFAR-10, CIFAR-100 and ImageNet datasets are also provided in Fig. 9.

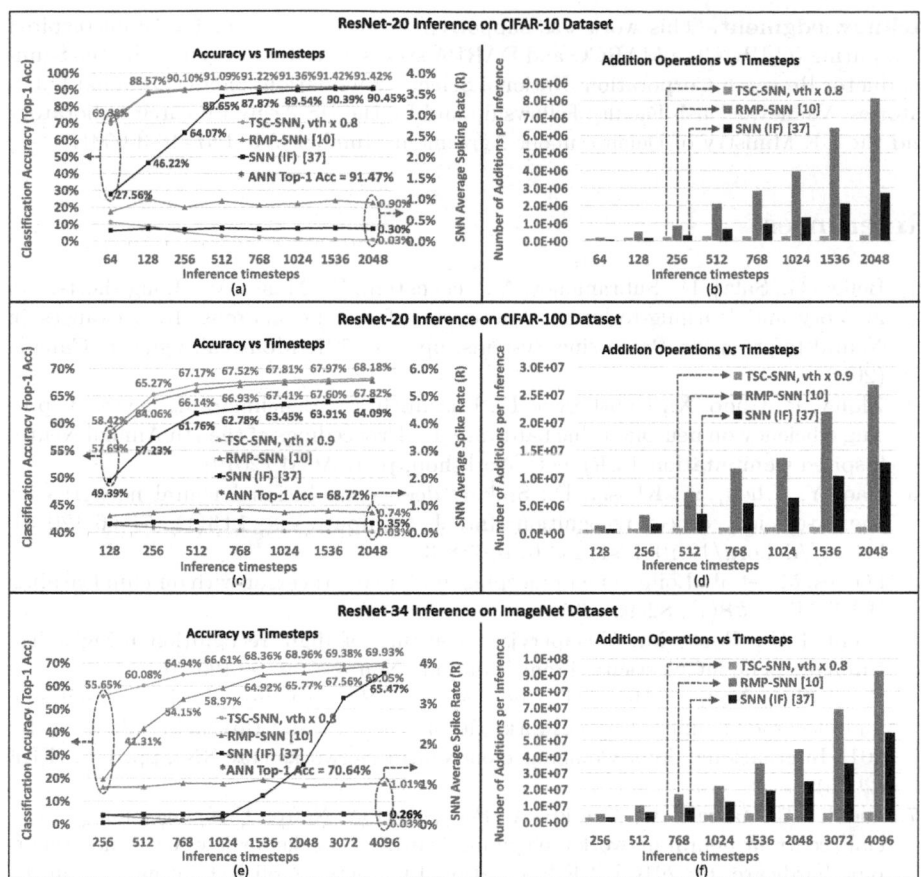

Fig. 9. Inference accuracy ((a) (c) and (e)) and computational cost ((b) (d) and (f)) comparisons between TSC-SNN and the two baseline SNNs (RMP-SNN [10] and SNN(IF) [37]) using ResNet architectures on CIFAR-10, CIFAR-100 and ImageNet datasets.

6   Conclusion and Discussion

In this work, we propose an ANN to SNN conversion technique. It uses a novel time-based coding scheme (TSC) and TSC spiking neuron model. We also propose a threshold balancing technique which alleviates the ANN-SNN conversion accuracy loss and significantly improved the latency and scalability of TSC-SNNs to deep architectures. We implemented large scale deep network architectures such as VGG and Residual networks using the proposed conversion based training and evaluated performance on cifar-10, cifar-100 and ImageNet datasets. Our proposed TSC-SNNs achieve the best accuracies and latencies, the lowest accuracy loss and the lowest computational cost than the state-of-the-art across all network architectures and datasets we tested.

Acknowledgment. This work was supported in part by Center for Brain-Inspired Computing (C-BRIC), a MARCO and DARPA sponsored StarNet center, by the Semiconductor Research Corporation, National Science Foundation, Sandia National Laboratories, Vannevar Bush Faculty Fellowship and by the US Army Research Laboratory and the UK Ministry of Defense under Agreement Number W911NF-16-3-0001.

References

1. Bellec, G., Salaj, D., Subramoney, A., Legenstein, R., Maass, W.: Long short-term memory and learning-to-learn in networks of spiking neurons. In: Advances in Neural Information Processing Systems, pp. 787–797. Montréal, Quebec, Canada (2018)
2. Blouw, P., Choo, X., Hunsberger, E., Eliasmith, C.: Benchmarking keyword spotting efficiency on neuromorphic hardware. In: Proceedings of the 7th Annual Neuro-inspired Computational Elements Workshop, p. 1. ACM (2019)
3. Cao, Y., Chen, Y., Khosla, D.: Spiking deep convolutional neural networks for energy-efficient object recognition. Int. J. Comput. Vis. **113**(1), 54–66 (2015). https://doi.org/10.1007/s11263-014-0788-3
4. Davies, M., et al.: Loihi: a neuromorphic manycore processor with on-chip learning. IEEE Micro **38**(1), 82–99 (2018)
5. Diehl, P.U., Cook, M.: Unsupervised learning of digit recognition using spike-timing-dependent plasticity. Front. Comput. Neurosci. **9**, 99 (2015)
6. Diehl, P.U., Neil, D., Binas, J., Cook, M., Liu, S.C., Pfeiffer, M.: Fast-classifying, high-accuracy spiking deep networks through weight and threshold balancing. In: 2015 International Joint Conference on Neural Networks (IJCNN), pp. 1–8. IEEE (2015)
7. Diehl, P.U., Zarrella, G., Cassidy, A., Pedroni, B.U., Neftci, E.: Conversion of artificial recurrent neural networks to spiking neural networks for low-power neuromorphic hardware. In: 2016 IEEE International Conference on Rebooting Computing (ICRC), pp. 1–8. IEEE (2016)
8. Esser, S.K., et al.: Convolutional networks for fast, energy-efficient neuromorphic computing. CoRR abs/1603.08270 (2016). http://arxiv.org/abs/1603.08270
9. Ferré, P., Mamalet, F., Thorpe, S.J.: Unsupervised feature learning with winner-takes-all based STDP. Front. Comput. Neurosci. **12**, 24 (2018)
10. Han, B., Srinivasan, G., Roy, K.: RMP-SNN: residual membrane potential neuron for enabling deeper high-accuracy and low-latency spiking neural network. In: Proceedings of the IEEE/CVF Conference on Computer Vision and Pattern Recognition (CVPR), June 2020
11. Hardt, M., Ma, T.: Identity matters in deep learning. CoRR abs/1611.04231. http://arxiv.org/abs/1611.04231 (2016)
12. He, K., Zhang, X., Ren, S., Sun, J.: Deep residual learning for image recognition. CoRR abs/1512.03385. http://arxiv.org/abs/1512.03385 (2015)
13. Heeger, D.: Poisson model of spike generation. Stanford Univ. Handout **5**, 1–13 (2000)
14. Hunsberger, E., Eliasmith, C.: Training spiking deep networks for neuromorphic hardware. CoRR abs/1611.05141. http://arxiv.org/abs/1611.05141 (2016)
15. Jin, Y., Zhang, W., Li, P.: Hybrid macro/micro level backpropagation for training deep spiking neural networks. In: Advances in Neural Information Processing Systems, pp. 7005–7015. Montréal, Quebec, Canada (2018)

16. Johnson, M., et al.: Google's multilingual neural machine translation system: enabling zero-shot translation. Trans. Assoc. Comput. Linguit. **5**, 339–351 (2017)
17. Kheradpisheh, S.R., Ganjtabesh, M., Thorpe, S.J., Masquelier, T.: STDP-based spiking deep convolutional neural networks for object recognition. Neural Netw. **99**, 56–67 (2018). https://doi.org/10.1016/j.neunet.2017.12.005. http://www.sciencedirect.com/science/article/pii/S0893608017302903
18. Krizhevsky, A., Sutskever, I., Hinton, G.E.: Imagenet classification with deep convolutional neural networks. In: Advances in Neural Information Processing Systems, pp. 1097–1105 (2012)
19. Lee, C., Srinivasan, G., Panda, P., Roy, K.: Deep spiking convolutional neural network trained with unsupervised spike timing dependent plasticity. IEEE Trans. Cogn. Dev. Syst. pp. 1–1 (2018). https://doi.org/10.1109/TCDS.2018.2833071
20. Lee, C., Sarwar, S.S., Panda, P., Srinivasan, G., Roy, K.: Enabling spike-based backpropagation for training deep neural network architectures. Front. Neurosci. **14**, 119 (2020). https://doi.org/10.3389/fnins.2020.00119
21. Lee, J.H., Delbruck, T., Pfeiffer, M.: Training deep spiking neural networks using backpropagation. Front. Neurosci. **10**, 508 (2016)
22. Maass, W.: Networks of spiking neurons: the third generation of neural network models. Neural Netw. **10**(9), 1659–1671 (1997)
23. Masquelier, T., Thorpe, S.J.: Unsupervised learning of visual features through spike timing dependent plasticity. PLoS Comput. Biol. **3**(2), e31 (2007)
24. Merolla, P.A., et al.: A million spiking-neuron integrated circuit with a scalable communication network and interface. Science **345**(6197), 668–673 (2014)
25. Miyashita, D., Lee, E.H., Murmann, B.: Convolutional neural networks using logarithmic data representation. CoRR abs/1603.01025. http://arxiv.org/abs/1603.01025 (2016)
26. Mozafari, M., Ganjtabesh, M., Nowzari-Dalini, A., Thorpe, S.J., Masquelier, T.: Combining STDP and reward-modulated STDP in deep convolutional spiking neural networks for digit recognition. arXiv preprint arXiv:1804.00227 (2018)
27. Nair, V., Hinton, G.E.: Rectified linear units improve restricted boltzmann machines. In: Proceedings of the 27th International Conference on Machine Learning (ICML-10), pp. 807–814 (2010)
28. Neftci, E.O., Mostafa, H., Zenke, F.: Surrogate gradient learning in spiking neural networks. arXiv preprint arXiv:1901.09948 (2019)
29. Ngiam, J., Khosla, A., Kim, M., Nam, J., Lee, H., Ng, A.Y.: Multimodal deep learning. In: Proceedings of the 28th International Conference on Machine Learning (ICML-11), pp. 689–696 (2011)
30. Panda, P., Roy, K.: Unsupervised regenerative learning of hierarchical features in spiking deep networks for object recognition. In: 2016 International Joint Conference on Neural Networks (IJCNN), pp. 299–306. IEEE, Vancouver, British Columbia, Canada (2016)
31. Pérez-Carrasco, J.A., et al.: Mapping from frame-driven to frame-free event-driven vision systems by low-rate rate coding and coincidence processing-application to feedforward ConvNets. IEEE Trans. Pattern Anal. Mach. Intell. **35**(11), 2706–2719 (2013)
32. Rathi, N., Srinivasan, G., Panda, P., Roy, K.: Enabling deep spiking neural networks with hybrid conversion and spike timing dependent backpropagation. In: International Conference on Learning Representations. https://openreview.net/forum?id=B1xSperKvH (2020)

33. Redmon, J., Divvala, S., Girshick, R., Farhadi, A.: You only look once: unified, real-time object detection. In: Proceedings of the IEEE Conference on Computer Vision and Pattern Recognition, pp. 779–788 (2016)
34. Rueckauer, B., Liu, S.: Conversion of analog to spiking neural networks using sparse temporal coding. In: 2018 IEEE International Symposium on Circuits and Systems (ISCAS), pp. 1–5 (2018)
35. Rueckauer, B., Lungu, I.A., Hu, Y., Pfeiffer, M.: Theory and tools for the conversion of analog to spiking convolutional neural networks. arXiv preprint arXiv:1612.04052 (2016)
36. Rueckauer, B., Lungu, I.A., Hu, Y., Pfeiffer, M., Liu, S.C.: Conversion of continuous-valued deep networks to efficient event-driven networks for image classification. Front. Neurosci. **11**, 682 (2017)
37. Sengupta, A., Ye, Y., Wang, R., Liu, C., Roy, K.: Going deeper in spiking neural networks: VGG and residual architectures. Front. Neurosci. **13**, 95 (2019)
38. Shrestha, S.B., Orchard, G.: Slayer: spike layer error reassignment in time. In: Advances in Neural Information Processing Systems, pp. 1412–1421. Montréal, Quebec, Canada (2018)
39. Simonyan, K., Zisserman, A.: Very deep convolutional networks for large-scale image recognition. In: International Conference on Learning Representations (2015)
40. Srinivasan, G., Panda, P., Roy, K.: STDP-based unsupervised feature learning using convolution-over-time in spiking neural networks for energy-efficient neuromorphic computing. J. Emerg. Technol. Comput. Syst. **14**(4), 1–12 (2018). https://doi.org/10.1145/3266229. https://doi.org/10.1145/3266229
41. Srinivasan, G., Roy, K.: ReStoCNet: residual stochastic binary convolutional spiking neural network for memory-efficient neuromorphic computing. Front. Neurosci. **13**, 189 (2019)
42. Tavanaei, A., Kirby, Z., Maida, A.S.: Training spiking convnets by STDP and gradient descent. In: 2018 International Joint Conference on Neural Networks (IJCNN), pp. 1–8. Rio de Janeiro, Brazil, July 2018. https://doi.org/10.1109/IJCNN.2018.8489104
43. Thiele, J.C., Bichler, O., Dupret, A.: Event-based, timescale invariant unsupervised online deep learning with STDP. Front. Comput. Neurosci. **12**, 46 (2018). https://doi.org/10.3389/fncom.2018.00046. https://www.frontiersin.org/article/10.3389/fncom.2018.00046
44. Wu, Y., Deng, L., Li, G., Zhu, J., Shi, L.: Spatio-temporal backpropagation for training high-performance spiking neural networks. Front. Neurosci. **12**, 331 (2018)
45. Zambrano, D., Nusselder, R., Scholte, H.S., Bohte, S.M.: Efficient computation in adaptive artificial spiking neural networks. CoRR abs/1710.04838. http://arxiv.org/abs/1710.04838 (2017)
46. Zhang, M., Zheng, N., Ma, D., Pan, G., Gu, Z.: Efficient spiking neural networks with logarithmic temporal coding. CoRR abs/1811.04233. http://arxiv.org/abs/1811.04233 (2018)
47. Zhao, B., Ding, R., Chen, S., Linares-Barranco, B., Tang, H.: Feedforward categorization on AER motion events using cortex-like features in a spiking neural network. IEEE Trans. Neural Netw. Learn. Syst. **26**(9), 1963–1978 (2014)

InfoFocus: 3D Object Detection for Autonomous Driving with Dynamic Information Modeling

Jun Wang[1]($\boxtimes$), Shiyi Lan[1], Mingfei Gao[2], and Larry S. Davis[1]

[1] University of Maryland, College Park, MD 20742, USA
{junwang,lsd}@umiacs.umd.edu, sylan@cs.umd.edu
[2] Salesforce Research, Palo Alto, CA 94301, USA
mingfei.gao@salesforce.com

Abstract. Real-time 3D object detection is crucial for autonomous cars. Achieving promising performance with high efficiency, voxel-based approaches have received considerable attention. However, previous methods model the input space with features extracted from equally divided sub-regions without considering that point cloud is generally non-uniformly distributed over the space. To address this issue, we propose a novel 3D object detection framework with dynamic information modeling. The proposed framework is designed in a coarse-to-fine manner. Coarse predictions are generated in the first stage via a voxel-based region proposal network. We introduce InfoFocus, which improves the coarse detections by adaptively refining features guided by the information of point cloud density. Experiments are conducted on the large-scale nuScenes 3D detection benchmark. Results show that our framework achieves the state-of-the-art performance with 31 FPS and improves our baseline significantly by 9.0% mAP on the nuScenes test set.

Keywords: 3D object detection · Point cloud

1 Introduction

With growing interests in autonomous vehicles, 3D object detection has received considerable attention. Due to the superior capability of modeling 3D objects, point cloud is the most popular type of data source. Most existing 3D detectors are point-based [11,17,21,25,27] and voxel-based [7,12,26,28,30]. Point-based approaches generate features from raw point cloud data directly. Although achieving promising performance, these methods suffer from high computational

---

J. Wang and S. Lan—Equal contribution.

Electronic supplementary material The online version of this chapter (https://doi.org/10.1007/978-3-030-58607-2_24) contains supplementary material, which is available to authorized users.

© Springer Nature Switzerland AG 2020
A. Vedaldi et al. (Eds.): ECCV 2020, LNCS 12355, pp. 405–420, 2020.
https://doi.org/10.1007/978-3-030-58607-2_24

complexity which discourages their application in real-time scenarios. Voxel-based approaches [7,12,26,28,30] firstly convert point cloud into voxels and then employ deep convolutional neural networks (DCNN) to conduct object detection. Taking advantage of the advanced DCNN architecture, voxel-based approaches achieve the state-of-the-art performance with low computational cost. Our work follows the setting of voxel-based methods for their advanced balance of efficiency and effectiveness.

| Statistics in Training Set | RGB Image | Bird-eye-view Point Cloud |

Fig. 1. Left: we calculate the average point density across different parts of objects in BEV of nuScenes training set. *E1–E4* indicate four edges sorted by their normalized density scores (sum to 100%) and *others* denotes areas inside objects. We set each edge width as 10% of the length along the object size and only objects over more than 100 points are counted. Middle and right: we visualize an example of the LiDAR point cloud in 2D image and its corresponding bird's eye view (BEV). Clearly, most of the point clouds locate on the contour of the object

Although much progress has been made in improving the performance of voxel-based detectors, an important characteristic of point cloud is not well explored: input data points are usually not uniformly distributed over the space. The density of point cloud can be affected by different factors, e.g., the distance of objects from LiDAR sensor and object self-occlusion. As illustrated in Fig. 1, the density of point cloud over objects highly depends on the relative locations of different parts. It is also intuitive that the amount of information is highly related to the point density. However, existing voxel-based detectors extract features from uniformly divided sub-regions, regardless of the actual distribution of the points. We believe that this will lead to loss of useful information and ultimately result in sub-optimal detection performance.

To fully exploit the non-uniform distribution of point cloud, we propose a novel 3D object detection framework, to adaptively model the rich feature of 3D objects according to the information density of points. Illustrated in Fig. 2, our framework contains two stages. Coarse detection results are obtained in the first stage via voxel-based region proposal network. In the second stage, we introduce InfoFocus, to model and extract the informative features from regions of interest

(RoI) (formed by the coarse predictions) according to the distribution of point cloud, and the predictions are improved with the help of the refined features.

The InfoFocus is the core structure of our framework which contains three sequentially connected modules including the Point-of-interest (PoI) Pooling, the Visibility Attentive Module, and the Adaptive Point-wise Attention.

PoI Pooling. Unlike 2D objects which contain densely distributed information over the whole RoI, more of the points of 3D objects locate on the their surfaces. Therefore, we hypothesize that most informative feature concentrates on the edge of RoI. Motivated by this intuition, we propose PoI Pooling which densely samples features on the edge and sparsely samples feature in the middle of RoI to accommodate the non-uniform information distribution of point cloud.

Visibility Attentive Module. Heavy self-occlusion is presented because of the nature of LiDAR data that is no point cloud exists on the backside of object relatively to the sensor. To mitigate this issue, our proposed Visibility Attentive Module applies hard attention to emphasize the visible parts of objects and eliminate the features from invisible points.

Adaptive Point-Wise Attention. PoIs may contain different amount of information, although they are all visible. We introduce Adaptive Point-wise Attention to re-weight the features to improve the modeling of 3D objects.

We conduct extensive experiments on the largest public 3D object detection benchmark, i.e, nuScenes [1]. Experimental results show that our approach significantly outperforms the baselines, achieving 39.5% mAP with 31 FPS. Results of comprehensive ablation studies demonstrate the effectiveness of our InfoFocus and that each sub-module makes considerable contributions to our framework.

2   Related Work

Point-Based Detectors. Inspired by the powerful feature learning capability of PointNet [18,19] and the advanced modeling structure of 2D object detectors [4,5,20], Frustum PointNets [17] extrude the 2D object proposals into frustums to generate the 3D bounding boxes from raw point cloud. Lan et al. [11] add a decomposition-aggregation module modeling local geometry to extract the global feature descriptor of point cloud. Limited by initial 2D box proposals, those methods yield low performance when objects are occluded. In contrast, PointRCNN [21] generates 3D proposals directly from point cloud instead of 2D images. The recent STD [27] attempts to refine the detection boxes in a coarse-to-fine manner. However, all those methods are computationally expensive due to the large amount of data points to be processed.

Multi-view 3D Detectors. MV3D [2] is proposed to fuse multi-view feature maps for the generation of 3D box proposals. Following [2], Ku et al. [10] explore high resolution feature maps to compensate the information loss for small objects. These methods address the feature alignment between multi-modality in a coarse level and are typically slow. Liang et al. [14] design a continuous fusion layer to deal with the continuous state of LiDAR and the discrete state of images. Later, [13,24] leverage different strategies to jointly fuse related tasks to improve feature representation.

Voxel-Based Detectors. Recently, there is a trend of using regular 3D voxel grids to represent point cloud such that the input data can be easily processed by the 3D/2D convolution networks. Among those, VoxelNet [30] is the pioneering work of performing voxelization on the raw 3D point cloud. To improve its efficiency, Second [26] adopts Sparse Convolution and speeds up detection process without compromising the detection accuracy. PointPillars [12] dynamically converts the 3D point cloud into a 2D pseudo image, making it more suitable for the application of the existing 2D object detection techniques. In [28], Ye et al. design a new voxel generator to preserve the information loss along the vertical direction. Building upon voxel-based detectors, our model captures richer information of objects by refining their feature representations at a second stage guided by the point cloud density and ultimately improves the detection results.

There are several recent studies [3,16] focusing on fusing the voxel-based features with PointNet-based features in order to extract more fine-grained 3D features. InfoFocus is complementary to these techniques and can be further applied on top of them. WYSIWYG [7] is the most related method to our approach since we both drive the model to encode visibility information. However, instead of using a separate branch to generate the hidden invisibility representation, our method directly aggregates the valuable point-wise features together from existing backbone network to refine the proposals in an end-to-end manner.

3   Proposed Approach

The proposed framework is illustrated in Fig. 2, which consists of a deep feature extractor followed by a two-stage architecture. The deep feature extractor containing a Pillar Feature Network and a DCNN, converts the input point cloud to representative feature maps. Specifically, the Pillar Feature Network divides the whole space into equal pillars and generates the so-called pseudo images [12]. The pseudo images are then processed by the DCNN to obtain the feature maps which are shared by the two stages, i.e., Region Proposal Network (RPN) and InfoFocus. The RPN generates the initial coarse bounding box proposals that are refined by InfoFocus, with dynamic information modeling. Note that our Deep Feature Extractor and RPN follow the setting of [12].

3.1   Deep Feature Extractor

Deep Feature Extractor is composed of two parts: 1) voxelization using Pillar Feature Network that converts the orderless point cloud into a sparse pseudo image via a simplified PointNet-like architecture and 2) feature extraction using DCNN to learn informative feature maps.

Pillar Feature Network. The Pillar Feature Network operates on the raw point cloud, and learns point-wise features for each pillar. After voxelizing raw

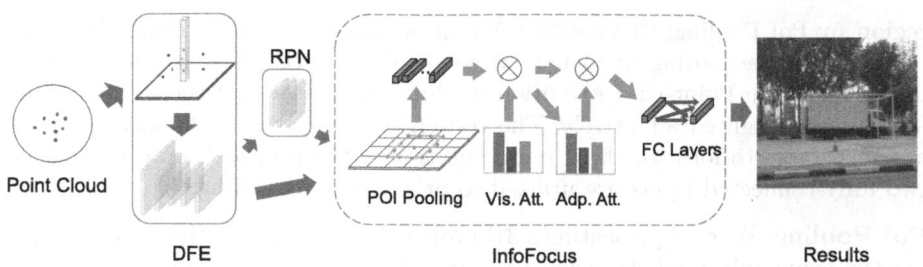

Fig. 2. The proposed 3D object detection framework. It consists of three parts: Deep Feature Extractor (DFE), Region Proposal Network, and InfoFocus. InfoFocus contains three modules: PoI Pooling, Visibility Attentive Module, and Adaptive Point-wise Attention Module

point cloud into evenly spaced pillars, we randomly sample N points from each non-empty pillar and then obtain a dense tensor with the size of $D \times P \times N$, where D indicates the information dimension of each point, P denotes the number of non-empty pillars, and N denotes the number of points in each pillar. The Pillar Feature Network utilizes a PointNet-like block to learn a multi-dimensional feature vector for each pillar. The pillar-wise features are encoded into a 2D pseudo image with the shape of $W \times L \times C$, where W and L indicate the width and length of the pseudo image, and C is the channel of the feature map.

Deep Convolution Neural Network (DCNN). DCNN learns feature maps from the generated pseudo 2D image. The DCNN uses conv-deconv layers to extract features of different levels, and concatenates them to get the final features from different strides.

3.2 Region Proposal Network (RPN)

The RPN takes the feature maps provided by DCNN as inputs and produces high-quality 3D object proposals. Similar to the proposal generation in 2D object detection, anchor boxes are predefined at each position and proposals are generated by learning the offsets between anchors and the ground truths. To handle different scales of objects, a dual-head strategy is adopted. Specifically, the small-scale head takes features from the first conv-deconv phase of the DCNN, while the large-scale head takes the features from its concatenation phase.

3.3 InfoFocus

The InfoFocus serves as the second stage of our framework, which takes the candidate proposals from RPN and extracts features of objects in a hierarchical manner from the feature maps produced by the DCNN. Specifically, given each 3D object proposal, InfoFocus dynamically focuses on the informative parts of the feature maps by gradually emphasizing the representative PoIs in the following three steps: 1) the edge points are selected out from the whole proposal region by PoI Pooling; 2) Visibility Attention module emphasizes on the informative points according to their relative visibility to the LiDAR sensor and 3) in the Adaptive Point-wise Attention module, the features of the visible points are further weighted adaptively. The re-weighted features of the visible points are then fused to form the final representation of the proposal, on top of which two fully-connected layers are utilized to predict the refined box.

PoI Pooling. When representing a 3D proposal, the most intuitive way is adopting the commonly used strategy in the two-stage 2D object detectors, i.e., RoI Pooling (see Fig. 3 left). However, unlike the 2D images that have densely distributed information over the region proposals, the 3D point cloud mostly resides on the object surface which results in non-uniform information over the regions (most information locates on the edges of proposals).

The proposed PoI pooling is illustrated in Fig. 3 (right). Instead of equally sampling points over a region of the feature maps, we focus on sampling the points on the informative parts including four corners, the center point and key-points on the edges. Note that we consider the center position as an additional useful signal since it is likely to capture the semantic-level information.

 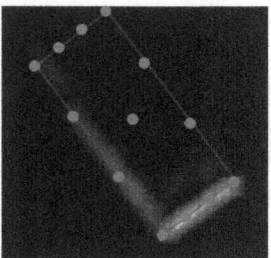

Fig. 3. RoI Pooling *vs.* PoI Pooling. The grid represents the feature map, and the dots denotes sampling points of interest. RoI Pooling samples the whole box, while PoI Pooling focuses on the key-points from edge-of-interest

We first project the 3D proposal to the birds' view coordinate system. Let p_0, p_1, p_2 and p_3 represent the positions of top-left, top-right, bottom-right, and bottom-left corners of a proposal on the pseudo image, respectively and p_c denotes the center point. Along each edge, n more key-points are uniformly sampled. For example, for the top edge between p_0 and p_1, the position of a sampled key-point $kp_j = (p_0 \frac{j}{n+1} + p_1 \frac{n+1-j}{n+1})$, where j is an integer and $1 \leq j \leq n$. To this end, $(5 + 4 * n)$ PoIs are obtained. A high-dimensional feature is extracted for each PoI according to its relative position on the feature map and then we obtain a feature set $F_{poi} = \{f_1^{poi}, f_2^{poi}, ..., f_{N_{poi}}^{poi}\}$, where $N_{poi} = (5 + 4 * n)$ representing the number of selected PoIs within the considered region.

Visibility Attentive Module. Severe self-occlusion typically occurs in point cloud, but is ignored by most of the existing methods. The Visibility Attentive Module (see Fig. 4 left) is proposed to mitigate this issue by focusing on the information provided by the visible parts of objects. We argue that visible regions contain more useful information than the occluded ones. Formally, we propose to re-weight features of PoIs according to their corresponding visibility by exploiting the geometric relationship between the proposals and the LiDAR sensor in bird's eye view. As shown in Eq. 1, F_{vis} denotes the updated feature set, where v_i^{poi} indicates the visibility score of the ith PoI. Different weighting strategies can be used and we use a hard attention strategy in this work for its simplicity, that is assigning $v_i^{poi} = 1$ if the ith PoI is visible and $v_i^{poi} = 0$ otherwise. In other words, we only take PoIs on the visible edges to represent the proposal.

$$F_{vis} = \{f_1^{poi} * v_1^{poi}, f_2^{poi} * v_2^{poi}, ..., f_{N_{poi}}^{poi} * v_{N_{poi}}^{poi}\} \tag{1}$$

For the consideration of model efficiency, a simple yet effective method is used to estimate the visibility of points in the bird's eye view. To figure out the sides of proposals facing to the sensor, we first compute the distance of each corner to the LiDAR sensor and determine the one that is closest to the sensor. Then, we consider the two edges passing this closest corner as the visible edges and the other two as the occluded ones.

Adaptive Point-Wise Attention Module. PoI Pooling and Visibility Attentive Module are motivated by the nature of the non-uniform density of point cloud. However, two points may offer different amount of information even though they are all visible by the sensor. Adaptive Point-wise Attention Module provides the flexibility for the visible PoIs to contribute unequally to the prediction. Suppose $F_{vis} = \{f_1^{vis}, f_2^{vis}, ..., f_{N_{vis}}^{vis}\}$ indicates the feature set of visible PoIs. Adaptive Point-wise Attention Module learns an attention weight, w_i, for each f_i^{vis} adaptively for the next-step feature aggregation. Specifically, a shared fully connected (FC) layer with sigmoid as the activation function is used to learn the attention weights, formally expressed as $v_i^{vis} = Sigmoid(\mathbf{W}f_i^{vis} + b)$. We use $F_{att} = \{f_1^{att}, f_2^{att}, ..., f_{N_{vis}}^{att}\}$ to represent the re-weighted feature set of visible PoIs updated using F_{vis} and the attention weights, where $f_i^{att} = f_i^{vis} * v_i^{vis}$.

The final representation of each proposal aggregates the features of its visible PoIs. Let e_0, e_1, e_2 and e_3 denote the top, right, down, left edges of a proposal, respectively. We first compute f_i^e by applying max pooling to all the visible points on e_i. Then, the final representation is obtained by $f_0^e || f_1^e || f_2^e || f_3^e || f_c^p$, where f_c^p indicates the feature of the center point and $||$ indicates concatenation.

3.4   Loss Function

Given the output PoI feature representation from the aforementioned three modules topped by fully-connected layers, the head network consists of three branches predicting the box class, localization and direction. The ground truth and anchor boxes are parameterized as $(x, y, z, w, l, h, \theta)$, where (x, y, z) is the center of box, (w, l, h) is the dimension of box, and θ is the heading along the z-axis in the LiDAR coordinate system. The box regression target is computed as the residuals between the ground truth and the anchors as:

$$\triangle x = \frac{x^{gt} - x^a}{d^a}, \triangle y = \frac{y^{gt} - y^a}{d^a}, \triangle z = \frac{z^{gt} - z^a}{h^a},$$
$$\triangle w = \log(\frac{w^{gt}}{w^a}), \triangle l = \log(\frac{l^{gt}}{l^a}), \triangle h = \log(\frac{h^{gt}}{h^a}), \tag{2}$$
$$\triangle \theta = \theta_{gt} - \theta_a$$

where x^{gt} and x^a refer to ground truth and anchor box respectively, and $d^a = \sqrt{(w^a)^2 + (l^a)^2}$. To deal with severe class imbalance problem in the dataset, we adopt the focal loss [15] for the classification loss. Smooth L1 loss [5] is used for the regression loss. In addition, to compensate for direction prediction missing in the regression, we adopt a softmax classification loss on orientation prediction.

Similar with that of the vanilla PointPillars network [12], we formally define a multi-task loss for both stages as threefold,

$$L_{stage\_i} = \frac{1}{N_{pos}}(\beta_{cls}L_{cls\_i} + \beta_{reg}L_{reg\_i} + \beta_{dir}L_{dir\_i}), \tag{3}$$

where i could be either RPN or InfoFocus stage, N_{pos} refers to the number of positive anchors and $\beta_{cls}, \beta_{reg}, \beta_{dir}$ are chosen to balance the weights among classification loss, regression loss and direction loss.

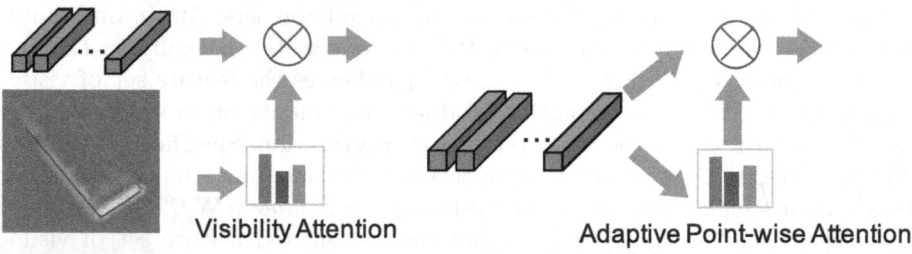

Visibility Attention   Adaptive Point-wise Attention

Fig. 4. Left: illustration of the Visibility Attentive Module. We compute hard attention for each sampled point depending on whether it is visible to the sensor. We also show the visibility map on the bottom left. Points on the blue line are visible while points on the orange line are invisible. Right: the architecture of the Adaptive Point-wise Attention Module. The point-wise attention is generated using a fully connected (FC) layer followed by a Sigmoid function. The input of FC layer is the feature of each point

3.5   Comparisons with Existing Approaches

Point-Based Approaches. Our framework uses PointNet to extract features from equally divided sub-grids and employs a DCNN to generate 2D feature maps while point-based techniques [11,17,21,25] only use PointNet as its backbone. Both our approach and point-based approaches apply two-stage architecture to infer objects. Meanwhile, we both sample features considering the distribution of point cloud. However, compared to PointNet, InfoFocus is more computationally efficient without performance degradation.

Fusion-Based Approaches. Fusion-based detectors [3,16] make use of both RGB images and point cloud data for 3D object detection. InfoFocus is much faster than fusion-based approaches, since they contain two backbones to process multi-view sources and are heavily engineered. On the other hand, InfoFocus also achieves competitive results compared to fusion-based approaches.

Traditional Voxel-Based Approaches. Our method shares the similar backbone as the existing voxel-based architectures [12,26,28,30]. However, previous voxel-based detectors pay less attention to the distribution of LiDAR data that most 3D point cloud locates on the surface of the objects. Our proposed PoI Pooling, Visibility Attentive Module, and Adaptive Point-wise Attention model the non-uniform point cloud using dynamic information focus. First, the PoI Pooling decreases the sampling from the inside of objects where few points locate. Next, the Visibility Attentive Module eliminates the noise from the back of objects where points are occluded. Last, we apply the Adaptive Point-wise Attention to learn the focus on each sampled points. Jointly, these modules contribute significantly to the superior performance of InfoFocus.

4 Experiments

Our method is mainly evaluated on the nuScenes dataset [1] which is considered as the most challenging 3D object detection benchmark. We first present our implementation details. We compare with the existing approaches both quantitatively and qualitatively. Then, extensive ablation studies are conducted to demonstrate the effectiveness of each designed module. Last, we analyze the inference time and the desired speed accuracy trade-off provided by our method.

4.1 Dataset and Evaluation Metric

NuScenes [1] is one of the largest datasets for autonomous driving. There are 1000 scenes of 20 s duration each, including 23 object classes annotated with 28,130 training, and 6,019 validation samples. We use the LiDAR point cloud as the only input to our method and all the experiments follow the standard protocol on the training and validation sets. Officially, nuScenes evaluates the detection accuracy across different classes, based on the average precision metric (AP) which is computed based on 2D center distance between ground truth and the detection box on the ground plane. In details, the AP score is determined as the normalized area under the precision recall curve above 10%. The final mean AP (mAP) is the average among the set of ten classes over matching thresholds of $\mathbb{D} = \{0.5, 1, 2, 4\}$ m.

4.2 Implementation Details

We integrate InfoFocus into a state-of-the-art real-time 3D object detector [12] to improve the detection performance without largely compromising speed.

Closely following the codebase[1] recommended by the authors of PointPillars [12], we use PyTorch to implement our InfoFocus modules and integrate it into vanilla PointPillars network. More details will be introduced in the supplementary materials.

RPN. For each class of objects, the RPN anchor size is set by calculating the average of all objects from the corresponding class in training set of nuScenes. In addition, the matching thresholds are based on the custom configuration following the suggested codebase. 1,000 proposals are obtained from RPN, on which NMS with a threshold of 0.5 is applied to remove the overlapping proposals for both training and inference. The final top-ranked 300 proposals are kept for the InfoFocus stage to simultaneously predict the category, location and direction of objects during both the training and inference.

InfoFocus. The second stage is our proposed InfoFocus. The three novel modules process object-centric feature sequentially based on the initial bounding box proposals from RPN. The number of sampled key-points for each edge, n, is set to be 2. Thus, the total number of PoIs, N_{poi}, is 13, including a center, 4 corners and 2 key-points on each edge. Similar to RoIAlign [6], bi-linear interpolation is used to compute the deep feature from four neighboring regular locations of each point.

As mentioned before, we apply a max-pool layer to summarize the features of points along each edge, resulting in 5 features for each proposal, including features from top, right, down, left edges and the center. When concatenating these features, we always treat the edge that is closest to the sensor as the top edge. A fully connected layer with a single node is used to generate point-wise attention weight for each point.

The feature of each proposal is transformed by two consecutive FC layers with 512 nodes each and passed to three sibling linear layers, a box-regression branch, a box-classification branch and a box-direction branch. For the regression target assignment, anchors having Intersection over Union (IoU) bigger than 0.6 with the ground truth are considered positive, and smaller than 0.55 are assigned negative labels.

Training Parameters. Experiments are conducted on a single NVIDIA 1080Ti GPU. The weight decay is set to be 0.01. We adopt the Adam optimizer [9], and use a one-cycle scheduler proposed in [23]. We train our model with a total of 20 epochs as a default choice, taking about 40 h from scratch. For the first 8 epochs, the learning rate progressively increases from 3×10^{-4} to 3×10^{-3} with decreasing momentum from 0.95 to 0.85, while in the remaining 12 epochs learning rate decreases from 3×10^{-3} to 3×10^{-6} with increasing momentum from 0.85 to 0.95. The focal loss [15] with $\alpha = 0.25$ and $\gamma = 2.0$ is adopted for the classification loss. The balancing weights for the classification, box regression, and direction loss $\beta_{cls}, \beta_{reg}, \beta_{dir}$ of both stages are 1, 2 and 0.2, respectively.

---

[1] https://github.com/traveller59/second.pytorch.

4.3   Main Results

First, we compare our framework with the state-of-the-art methods on the nuScenes validation set, including the vanilla PointPillars [12] as our baseline, and recently published WYSIWYG [7]. As can be seen from Table 1, the baseline has an mAP of 29.5% with a single stage, while InfoFocus improves it by a massive 6.9%. This demonstrates the effectiveness of InfoFocus. We also visualize the detection results of our framework on 2D and 3D BEV images in Fig. 5. As shown in Fig. 6, compared to the vanilla PointPillars qualitatively, InfoFocus helps remove the false positives significantly and obtains better results.

Table 1. Object detection results (%) on nuScenes validation set

Method	car	peds.	barri.	traff.	truck.	bus.	trail.	const.	motor.	bicyc.	mAP
PointPillars [12]	70.5	59.9	33.2	29.6	25.0	34.3	16.7	4.5	20.0	1.6	29.5
WYSIWYG [7]	80.0	66.9	34.5	27.9	35.8	54.1	28.5	7.5	18.5	0	35.4
Ours	77.6	61.7	43.4	33.4	35.4	50.5	25.6	8.3	25.2	2.5	**36.4**

In addition, we submit the detection results of test set on the nuScenes test server. The results show that our method achieves the state-of-the-art performance with inference speed of 31 FPS, improving the baseline performance by 7% mAP. Note that all methods listed in Table 2 are LiDAR-based except that MonoDIS [22] and CenterNet[29] are camera-based methods. Without bells and whilstles, our approach works better than WYSIWYG [7]. Considering that our model contains more parameters than the vanilla PointPillars, we empirically increase the number of the training epoch by 2 times. With all the others settings the same, our method is improved by 2% mAP on the nuScenes test set as shown in Table 2 (Ours 2×). In total, our method outperforms WYSIWYG[7] by 4.5% mAP on the nuScenes test set. In the rest of paper, the default setting of training epochs is adopted. To the best of our knowledge, our framework is superior than all the published real-time methods with respect to mAP.

4.4   Ablation Studies

To understand the contribution of our major component to the success of InfoFocus, Table 3 summarizes the performance of our framework when a certain module is disabled, including PoI Pooling, Visibility Attention Module and Adaptive Attention Module.

PoI Pooling. To investigate the effect of PoI Pooling, we simply add the PoI Pooling on top of the vanilla PointPillar. This baseline introduces 3.0% mAP improvement. However, when we vary the number of pooling key-points on each edge, we see that our framework with four key-points ($n = 4$) on each edge degrades slightly by 0.8% mAP than that of two key-points ($n = 2$). A possible

Table 2. Object detection results (%) on nuScenes test set. Note that MonoDIS and CenterNet are camera based methods, and the rest are LiDAR based. Ours 2× indicates 2× training time with other settings being the same with Ours

Method	car	peds.	barri.	traff.	truck.	bus.	trail.	const.	motor.	bicyc.	mAP
MonoDIS [22]	47.8	37.0	51.1	48.7	22.0	18.8	17.6	7.4	29.0	24.5	30.4
PointPillars [12]	68.4	59.7	38.9	30.8	23.0	28.2	23.4	4.1	27.4	1.1	30.5
SARPNET [28]	59.9	69.4	38.3	44.6	18.7	19.4	18.0	11.6	29.8	14.2	32.4
CenterNet [29]	53.6	37.5	53.3	58.3	27.0	24.8	25.1	8.6	29.1	20.7	33.8
WYSIWYG [7]	79.1	65.0	34.7	28.8	30.4	46.6	40.1	7.1	18.2	0.1	35.0
Ours	77.2	61.5	45.3	40.4	31.5	44.1	35.9	9.8	25.1	4.0	**37.5**
Ours 2×	77.9	63.4	47.8	46.5	31.4	44.8	37.3	10.7	29.0	6.1	**39.5**

Table 3. Ablation studies on nuScenes validation set. "Vis. Att" and "Adp. Att." refer to Visibility Attention Module and Adaptive Attention Module, respectively

PoIPool	Vis. Att.	Adp. Att.	mAP
			29.5
✓			32.5
✓	✓		34.8
✓		✓	34.8
✓	✓	✓	36.4

reason is that the higher number of samples along each edge might bring more noise which harms the detection performance.

Visibility Attention. We further add the Visibility Attention module to filter out invisible edges before PoI pooling. Table 3 shows that when using the features from two visible edges, the mAP result is improved by 2.3% mAP compared to *baseline+PoIPool*. Generally, the visible parts of objects correspond to their sides closer to the LiDAR sensor, thus they may capture richer information. By applying visibility attention, our method focuses more on the representative information which results in better performance.

Adaptive Point-Wise Attention. Without the Adaptive Point-wise Attention module, the framework naturally allows the same weight for each PoI feature. As we can see in Table 3, when adding this module, the result of *baseline+PoIPool* improves by 2.3% mAP and that of *baseline+PoIPool+Vis.Att.* improves by 1.6%. These results suggest that the Adaptive Point-wise Attention module helps emphasize on useful points which leads to a better performance.

Rotated RoIAlign Comparison. One widely considered way to extract the region-wise features in the two-stage architecture is RoIAlign [6]. So, it is intuitive to compare with this strategy under the setting of 3D object detection. We implement rotated RoIAlign (RRoI) operation [8] to compensate for the

Table 4. Inference time of 3D object detectors. Note that inference time for the baseline here is the network reproduced by ourselves

Method	Input format	mAP	Inference time (ms)
Baseline [12]	LiDAR	30.5	26.9
MonoDIS [22]	RGB	30.4	29.0
SARPNET [28]	LiDAR	32.4	70.0
Ours	LiDAR	37.5	32.9

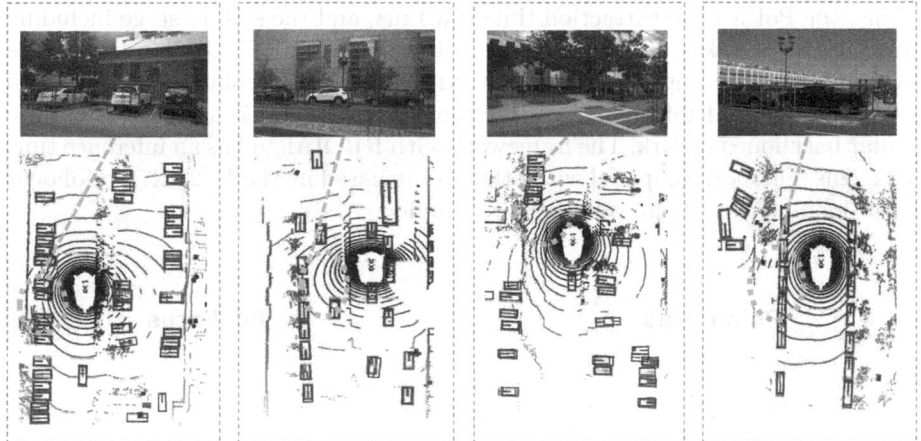

Fig. 5. We visualize the detection results on nuScenes with 2D and 3D BEV images. On the top, we demonstrate the 2D images with the 3D bounding box annotated, while the BEV of LiDAR with ground truth (red) and detection (blue) box are shown on the bottom. Note that the line in the frame denotes the direction of the object (Color figure online)

rotated bounding box, since in our case they are often not axis-aligned. We conduct experiments exploring two different pooling sizes, 4×4 (pooled length and pooled width), and 8×4 with 4 sampled points in each bin. One of the reasons that we use 8×4 is that most of the objects like car and bus's length is larger than their width. With all other implementations the same as InfoFocus, Table 5 presents detection results utilizing the rotated-RoI with different pooling sizes. Compared with the vanilla PointPillars [12], adding the RoIAlign layer with size of 4×4 increases the mAP performance by 4.4%. However, InfoFocus still outperforms RoIAlign by 2.5% with the better information modeling scheme.

4.5   Real-Time Inference Analysis

As indicated in Table 4, our framework takes about 32.9 ms to perform detection on an example of point cloud in the nuScenes, compared with 26.9 ms of the vanilla PointPillars when both are evaluated on a single NVIDIA 1080Ti GPU. In details, the pillar feature extraction time is 12.6 ms, the DCNN costs 1.1 ms,

Table 5. Comparison with rotated RoIAlign feature extraction results (%) on the nuScenes validation set

Method	car	peds.	barri.	traff.	truck.	bus.	trail.	const.	motor.	bicyc.	mAP
RRoI 4 × 4	76.9	60.1	37.6	29.5	32.4	50.6	22.4	5.0	20.8	**3.8**	33.9
RRoI 8 × 4	77.0	59.5	36.7	29.2	33.2	**51.5**	25.4	4.5	24.0	1.8	34.3
Ours	**77.6**	**61.7**	**43.4**	**33.4**	**35.4**	50.5	**25.6**	**8.3**	**25.2**	2.5	**36.4**

RPN takes 7.3 ms to generate proposals, and the InfoFocus stage takes 11.9 ms. Specifically, the proposal generation for the InfoFocus stage including NMS is 5.1 ms, the PoI feature extraction time is 3.1 ms, and the second stage including three branches takes 0.7 ms. We also note that WYSIWYG [7] provides the overhead of computing visibility over a 32-beam LiDAR point to be 24.4 ± 3.5 ms on average and InfoFocus is faster than WYSIWYG [7] since we share the similar backbone network. The framework with RROIAlign has an inference time of 32.2 ms. Further, compared with other point-based methods [21,27], InfoFocus is considerably faster and conceptually simpler.

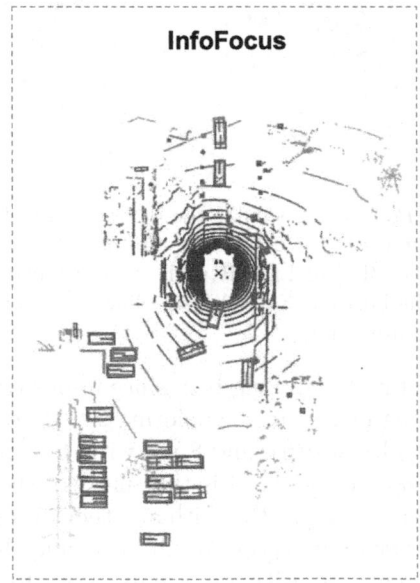

Fig. 6. We visualize the BEV detection results for the same point cloud sample on nuScenes with the vanillar PointPillars (left) and InfoFocus (right)

5 Conclusions

Non-uniform distribution of point cloud causes varying amount of information at different locations. Therefore, we argue that this imbalance distribution of information may result in degradation on previous 3D voxel-based detectors when modeling 3D objects. To address this issue, we propose a 3D object detection framework with InfoFocus to dynamically conduct information modeling. InfoFocus contain three effective modules including PoI Pooling, the Visibility Attentive Module, and the Adaptive Point-wise Attention. Demonstrated by the comprehensive experiments, our framework achieves the state-of-art performance among all the real-time detectors on the challenging nuScenes dataset.

Acknowledgement. This work was supported by the Intelligence Advanced Research Projects Activity (IARPA) via DOI/IBC contract numbers D17PC00345 and D17PC00287. The U.S. Government is authorized to reproduce and distribute reprints for Governmental purposes not withstanding any copyright annotation thereon. The authors would like to thank Zuxuan Wu and Xingyi Zhou for proofreading the manuscript.

References

1. Caesar, H., et al.: nuScenes: a multimodal dataset for autonomous driving. arXiv preprint arXiv:1903.11027 (2019)
2. Chen, X., Ma, H., Wan, J., Li, B., Xia, T.: Multi-view 3D object detection network for autonomous driving. In: Proceedings of the IEEE Conference on Computer Vision and Pattern Recognition, pp. 1907–1915 (2017)
3. Chen, Y., Liu, S., Shen, X., Jia, J.: Fast point R-CNN. In: Proceedings of the IEEE International Conference on Computer Vision, pp. 9775–9784 (2019)
4. Girshick, R.: Fast R-CNN. In: The IEEE International Conference on Computer Vision (ICCV), December 2015
5. Girshick, R., Donahue, J., Darrell, T., Malik, J.: Rich feature hierarchies for accurate object detection and semantic segmentation. In: The IEEE Conference on Computer Vision and Pattern Recognition (CVPR), June 2014
6. He, K., Gkioxari, G., Dollár, P., Girshick, R.: Mask R-CNN. In: Proceedings of the IEEE International Conference on Computer Vision, pp. 2961–2969 (2017)
7. Hu, P., Ziglar, J., Held, D., Ramanan, D.: What you see is what you get: exploiting visibility for 3D object detection. arXiv preprint arXiv:1912.04986 (2019)
8. Huang, J., Sivakumar, V., Mnatsakanyan, M., Pang, G.: Improving rotated text detection with rotation region proposal networks. arXiv preprint arXiv:1811.07031 (2018)
9. Kingma, D.P., Ba, J.: Adam: a method for stochastic optimization. arXiv preprint arXiv:1412.6980 (2014)
10. Ku, J., Mozifian, M., Lee, J., Harakeh, A., Waslander, S.L.: Joint 3D proposal generation and object detection from view aggregation. In: 2018 IEEE/RSJ International Conference on Intelligent Robots and Systems (IROS), pp. 1–8. IEEE (2018)
11. Lan, S., Yu, R., Yu, G., Davis, L.S.: Modeling local geometric structure of 3D point clouds using Geo-CNN. In: The IEEE Conference on Computer Vision and Pattern Recognition (CVPR), June 2019
12. Lang, A.H., Vora, S., Caesar, H., Zhou, L., Yang, J., Beijbom, O.: PointPillars: fast encoders for object detection from point clouds. In: Proceedings of the IEEE Conference on Computer Vision and Pattern Recognition, pp. 12697–12705 (2019)

13. Liang, M., Yang, B., Chen, Y., Hu, R., Urtasun, R.: Multi-task multi-sensor fusion for 3D object detection. In: Proceedings of the IEEE Conference on Computer Vision and Pattern Recognition, pp. 7345–7353 (2019)
14. Liang, M., Yang, B., Wang, S., Urtasun, R.: Deep continuous fusion for multi-sensor 3D object detection. In: Ferrari, V., Hebert, M., Sminchisescu, C., Weiss, Y. (eds.) ECCV 2018. LNCS, vol. 11220, pp. 663–678. Springer, Cham (2018). https://doi.org/10.1007/978-3-030-01270-0_39
15. Lin, T.Y., Goyal, P., Girshick, R., He, K., Dollár, P.: Focal loss for dense object detection. In: Proceedings of the IEEE International Conference on Computer Vision, pp. 2980–2988 (2017)
16. Liu, Z., Tang, H., Lin, Y., Han, S.: Point-voxel CNN for efficient 3D deep learning. In: Advances in Neural Information Processing Systems, pp. 963–973 (2019)
17. Qi, C.R., Liu, W., Wu, C., Su, H., Guibas, L.J.: Frustum pointnets for 3D object detection from RGB-D data. In: Proceedings of the IEEE Conference on Computer Vision and Pattern Recognition, pp. 918–927 (2018)
18. Qi, C.R., Su, H., Mo, K., Guibas, L.J.: Pointnet: deep learning on point sets for 3D classification and segmentation. In: Proceedings of the IEEE Conference on Computer Vision and Pattern Recognition, pp. 652–660 (2017)
19. Qi, C.R., Yi, L., Su, H., Guibas, L.J.: PointNet++: deep hierarchical feature learning on point sets in a metric space. In: Advances in Neural Information Processing Systems, pp. 5099–5108 (2017)
20. Ren, S., He, K., Girshick, R., Sun, J.: Faster R-CNN: towards real-time object detection with region proposal networks. In: Advances in Neural Information Processing Systems, pp. 91–99 (2015)
21. Shi, S., Wang, X., Li, H.: PointRCNN: 3D object proposal generation and detection from point cloud. In: Proceedings of the IEEE Conference on Computer Vision and Pattern Recognition, pp. 770–779 (2019)
22. Simonelli, A., Bulo, S.R., Porzi, L., López-Antequera, M., Kontschieder, P.: Disentangling monocular Ddetection. In: Proceedings of the IEEE International Conference on Computer Vision, pp. 1991–1999 (2019)
23. Smith, L.N.: A disciplined approach to neural network hyper-parameters: part 1-learning rate, batch size, momentum, and weight decay. arXiv preprint arXiv:1803.09820 (2018)
24. Vora, S., Lang, A.H., Helou, B., Beijbom, O.: PointPainting: sequential fusion for 3D object detection. arXiv preprint arXiv:1911.10150 (2019)
25. Wang, Z., Jia, K.: Frustum ConvNet: sliding frustums to aggregate local point-wise features for amodal 3D object detection. arXiv preprint arXiv:1903.01864 (2019)
26. Yan, Y., Mao, Y., Li, B.: Second: sparsely embedded convolutional detection. Sensors 18(10), 3337 (2018)
27. Yang, Z., Sun, Y., Liu, S., Shen, X., Jia, J.: STD: sparse-to-dense 3D object detector for point cloud. In: Proceedings of the IEEE International Conference on Computer Vision. pp. 1951–1960 (2019)
28. Ye, Y., Chen, H., Zhang, C., Hao, X., Zhang, Z.: SARPNET: shape attention regional proposal network for LiDAR-based 3D object detection. Neurocomputing 379, 53–63 (2020)
29. Zhou, X., Wang, D., Krähenbühl, P.: Objects as points. arXiv preprint arXiv:1904.07850 (2019)
30. Zhou, Y., Tuzel, O.: VoxelNet: end-to-end learning for point cloud based 3D object detection. In: Proceedings of the IEEE Conference on Computer Vision and Pattern Recognition, pp. 4490–4499 (2018)

Utilizing Patch-Level Category Activation Patterns for Multiple Class Novelty Detection

Poojan Oza$^{(\boxtimes)}$ and Vishal M. Patel

Johns Hopkins University, 3400 N. Charles Street, Baltimore, MD 21218, USA
{poza,vp36}@jhu.edu

Abstract. For any recognition system, the ability to identify novel class samples during inference is an important aspect of the system's robustness. This problem of detecting novel class samples during inference is commonly referred to as Multiple Class Novelty Detection. In this paper, we propose a novel method that makes deep convolutional neural networks robust to novel classes. Specifically, during training one branch performs traditional classification (referred to as global inference), and the other branch provides patch-level information to keep track of the class-specific activation patterns (referred to as local inference). Both global and local branch information are combined to train a novelty detection network, which is used during inference to identify novel classes. We evaluate the proposed method on four datasets (Caltech256, CUB-200, Stanford Dogs and FounderType-200) and show that the proposed method is able to identify novel class samples better compared to the other deep convolutional neural network-based methods.

Keywords: Multiple class novelty detection · Class activation patterns

1 Introduction

Improving the robustness of recognition models has been one of the primary research topics in computer vision and machine learning in recent years. Specifically, problems such as adversarial attacks [8,12,21,30,34,37], recognition bias [16,36,40], out-of-distribution detection [9,14,19], open-set recognition [2,23,26], outlier removal [42,43] and novelty/anomaly detection [1,3,5,20,25,28,32] have received tremendous interest. In this paper, we focus on one such aspect of robustness, referred to as multi-class novelty detection.

Typically, in a recognition problem, the goal is to learn a model that can identify the underlying features using data samples from a given set of classes (i.e., known classes). Later, these features can be used at inference stage to

Electronic supplementary material The online version of this chapter (https:// doi.org/10.1007/978-3-030-58607-2_25) contains supplementary material, which is available to authorized users.

© Springer Nature Switzerland AG 2020
A. Vedaldi et al. (Eds.): ECCV 2020, LNCS 12355, pp. 421–437, 2020.
https://doi.org/10.1007/978-3-030-58607-2_25

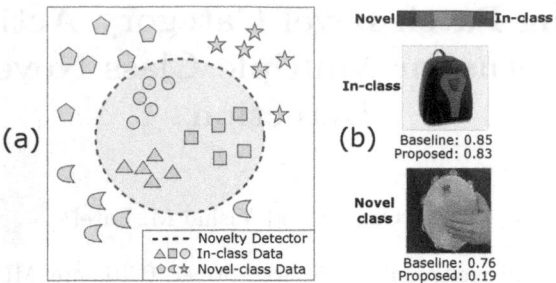

Fig. 1. (a) Typical example of a multiple class novelty detection scenario, where a novelty detector is used to differentiate between in-class and novel class data. (b) Baseline and the proposed method are able to produce high scores for in-class data. However, for novel class data the proposed approach does is better at assigning low scores compared to the baseline. Here, the "Baseline" refers to the novelty detection using traditional deep convolutional neural network with penultimate layer scores.

identify data samples into a given set of known classes. The problem arises when samples from novel classes (i.e. samples that do not belong to any of the known classes) are observed during inference. In this case, the network misidentifies the sample from a novel class as one of the known classes. Novelty detection was specifically introduced to address this issue [15,22,22,27,29,32]. Generally, a novelty detector attempts to identify whether a sample during inference is either from in-class (i.e, one of the known classes) or is from a novel class. When the number of known classes are more than one, the problem is also referred to as *multi-class novelty detection* [5,20,24,28]. When employed, the multi-class novelty detection module allows data samples only from known classes to pass through the recognition model, which results in increased robustness for the model. This is useful in many real-world vision applications. For example, in the case of autonomous navigation systems, it is important to stop and re-plan the navigation path by detecting a novel class as obstacle rather than misclassifying it and risking a potential crash (Fig. 1).

The major challenge in developing multi-class novelty detector is the unavailability of novel class samples during training. Since the knowledge or data samples of novel classes are impossible to attain beforehand, the majority of novelty detection algorithms rely on how well they can encode the in-class data. There have been a few multi-class novelty detection methods proposed in recent years that try to overcome this challenge. Some of the earlier methods such as [5,20] use the feature encoding of in-class data to learn a subspace (referred to as null space of training data in [5,20]), and during inference the novelty score is calculated based on the distance of a test sample projected onto that subspace with the learned in-class data projections. However, these methods can not be integrated with deep convoluitonal neural networks (DCNN) to perform end-to-end training.

Recently, Perera and Patel [28] proposed a DCNN-based multi-class novelty detection method that can be trained in an end-to-end fashion. Specifically, to improve the novelty detection capability of a DCNN, they proposed a fine-tuning approach, where a *reference dataset* is used as a proxy for novel-class data. The authors argue that, since novelty detection methods often operate on features extracted from DCNN models which are pre-trained on the reference dataset, it would be beneficial, especially for novelty detection, to utilize the samples from a reference dataset as well. However, that argument does not always hold true. There are many cases where access to such reference datasets might not be possible. For example, consider a dataset having biometric information of users. Such datasets have high privacy risk associated with them and hence might not be available for public use. Additionally, for many private companies it is a competitive advantage to keep their datasets only for internal use, e.g., recently Google released state of the art neural network recognition models[1] trained on their internal datasets which are not publicly released. Also, in the case of Federated Learning [6] based applications, sharing dataset across devices is restricted to promote data privacy. However, in such scenario sharing a trained model parameters is possible as it contains very little risk on the privacy of the corresponding data. Hence, for the cases described above, it is not possible to access the reference dataset. Moreover, the reference dataset as described in [28] has to be fully labeled and hence can not be replaced by any randomly collected set of images. Ideally, we would want a novelty detection method that is flexible enough to work on scenarios where the reference dataset is not available, and when available it should be able to utilize the reference dataset to improve the novelty detection capability of the model.

In this paper, we propose a multiple class novelty detection to address the above mentioned concerns. Specifically, we use two parallel DCNN branches, where one branch learns features for identifying what class is present in the image and the second branch learns class-wise activations in the image patches. The information from both branches are combined in proposed training strategy to train a novelty detection network, without requiring a reference dataset. Moreover, to increase the flexibility of the approach, we also extend the method for the cases where reference dataset is available to further improve the performance. The advantage of this approach is that, as opposed to previous methods [28], it does not rely heavily on the availability of a reference dataset. We show that this proposed approach performs well on the novelty detection task compared to the other methods in the literature.

In summary, this paper makes the following contributions:

- We propose multiple class novelty detection approach, trained using a novel training strategy which utilizes both image-level and patch-level information.
- The proposed approach does not rely heavily on the availability of reference dataset, but when reference dataset is accessible, it can be easily extended to further improve the novelty detection performance.
- The performance is evaluated on four benchmark datasets and is shown to achieve improvements over several recent novelty detection methods.

---

[1] github.com/tensorflow/tpu/tree/master/models/official/efficientnet.

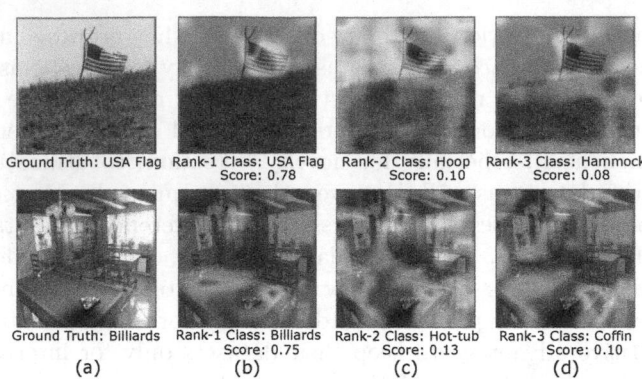

Ground Truth: USA Flag   Rank-1 Class: USA Flag   Rank-2 Class: Hoop   Rank-3 Class: Hammock
                          Score: 0.78   Score: 0.10   Score: 0.08

Ground Truth: Billiards   Rank-1 Class: Billiards   Rank-2 Class: Hot-tub   Rank-3 Class: Coffin
                           Score: 0.75   Score: 0.13   Score: 0.10
        (a)   (b)   (c)   (d)

Fig. 2. (a) Original image with corresponding ground truth label. (b), (c) and (d) represent grad-cam visualizations for rank-1, rank-2 and rank-3 classes and predicted probability scores.

2   Related Work

Over the years many novelty detection methods have been proposed some the earliest methods include principle component analysis-based [15,39], support vector machine-based [31,38], sparse representation-based [41,44], nearest neighbors-based [11,13,17]. In some of the recent works, Bodesheim et al. [5] proposed a kernel-based method that projects all in-class data onto a subspace (referred to as null-space of training data), where all in-class categories are forced to have zero intra-class variance. Specifically, they employ a special case of linear discriminant analysis formulation, called Null-space Foley-Shannon Transform (NFST), to achieve zero intra-class variance. The smallest distance between the test sample projection with the class projections is used to decide whether an input is from a known class or a novel class. Liu et al. [20] pointed out that NFST training does not scale well with the increase in dataset size due to its high computation cost. To counter that, they proposed an incremental addition of classes to learn NFST subspace, which results in improved scalability with increased dataset size. Bodesheim et al. [4] proposed another variant of NFST-based novelty detection method which rather than using all in-class data samples, learns the NFST model based on the k nearest neighbor samples. This selective sampling helps to locate the local manifold on the feature space and learn specific models for each test sample.

However, all of these methods provide a general framework for novelty detection and none of them are specifically designed for DCNNs. Schultheiss et al. [32] proposed a DCNN-based novelty detection method by examining the extreme signatures observed in the penultimate layer. More precisely, depending on the input data there are specific dimensions in the penultimate layer of DCNNs, which produce high activation values (referred to as extreme value signatures) if the input is from novel class. Recently, Perera et al. [28] proposed a DCNN-based training method using a reference dataset. Instead of just utilizing pre-trained models trained on some reference dataset, they propose to use samples from the reference dataset as well. They show that having access to these additional data samples acts as a novel class proxy and benefits the novelty detection aspect of DCNNs. The reference dataset used during training, enables learning of negative filters which forces low activations at penultimate layer, when the input data is not from a novel class.

3   Proposed Approach

Deep convolutional neural networks have the ability to learn high-quality representations that are class-discriminative, making them the most successful tool for image recognition. These representations are learned by an end-to-end training and are computed by aggregating patch-level convolution responses (or activation maps) through non-linear activation functions and pooling process. Furthermore, these activation maps are aggregated depending on the strength of the activation to predict the probability scores for each class. The classes are ranked based on the predicted probability score and the class having the maximum score (i.e. rank-1 class) is predicted as the label. Figure 2 illustrates this point with grad-cam [33] visualizations of top-3 classes. Here, the classes are ranked based on the predicted probability scores. The visualizations in Fig. 2 are not limited to top-3 classes and can be shown for all categories in the training set. This figure shows that given an image, a DCNN produces activation maps that has some contribution from all known classes.

For novel class test samples, none of the predictions would be correct, since the training set did not contain these classes. Furthermore, as shown in Fig. 3, often the rank-1 prediction scores for novel classes are very high, making it difficult for DCNNs to identify them as novel. However, looking at the examples

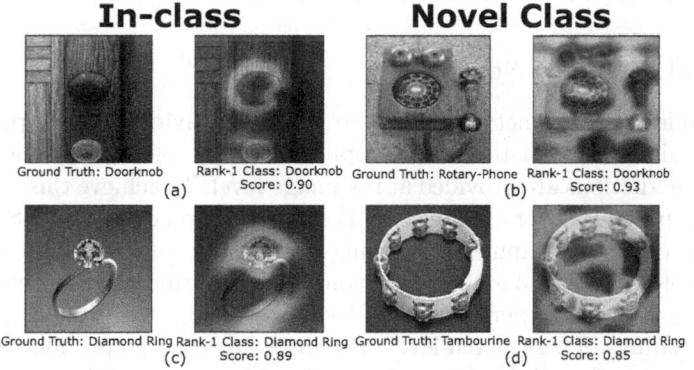

Fig. 3. (a)-(b) In-class samples from Doorknob and Diamond Ring classes with grad-cam visualizations and the predicted scores. (c)-(d) Novel class samples from Rotary-Phone and Tambourine are mis-classified as Doorknob and Diamond Ring as shown with grad-cam visualizations and predicted scores.

shown in Fig. 3, one can notice that the patch-level activation patterns for both known class samples and novel class samples are different, even when both images are classified as the same class with high scores. The activation patterns for in-class (i.e. known class) samples are focused on the underlying object, whereas for novel class data the patterns are spread out across the image producing high activations at multiple image-patch locations. Given this information, we make an assumption that this type of discrepancy in the patch-level activation pattern exists across all novel class samples. Based on this assumption, we propose a novelty detection algorithm that learns to detect novel class samples by identifying discrepancy in the patch-level activation patterns.

Typically, for multi-class novelty detection we have access to only in-class data samples, $\{x_i, y_i\}_{i=1}^{i=n}$, where $y_i \in \{1, 2, ..., K\}$ is the class label corresponding to the data point x_i, n is the total number of data samples and K is the total number of classes. In the following subsections, we provide details of the proposed novelty detection method.

3.1   Global Inference Network

The global inference network can be decomposed in to two parts, feature extractor ($\mathcal{G}$) and classifier ($\mathcal{C}$). The feature extractor ($\mathcal{G}$), processes the image through stacked convolutional, pooling and activation layers to produce a global feature encoding of the object present in the image, as shown in Fig. 4(a). The classifier ($\mathcal{C}$), uses this global feature encoding to classify the image into one of K classes. The cross entropy loss used to train such network can be defined as follows

$$\mathcal{L}_{global} = \frac{1}{n} \sum_{i=1}^{n} L_{ce}(\mathcal{C}(\mathcal{G}(x_i)),\ y_i), \tag{1}$$

where y_i is the ground truth class label for the input x_i, n is total number of images from known classes and $\mathcal{C}(\mathcal{G}(x_i))$ is the predicted probability vector.

3.2   Local Inference Network

For local inference, the network needs to process individual image patches and provide predictions at patch-level as opposed to the global inference network where the predictions are provided at the image level. To achieve this, we utilize a recently proposed BagNet architecture [7] as local inference network. Specifically, BagNet processes the input image using a series of convolutional layers with 1×1 convolutions and 3×3 convolutions. The limiting of receptive field size restricts the network to perform patch-level processing and produce patch-level feature encodings. These patch-level encodings are used to produce patch-level prediction scores for all K classes, here referred to as local feature encodings. All these predictions are average pooled to produce the final prediction score, which is trained using the cross entropy loss in an end-to-end fashion. This process is illustrated in Fig. 4(b). The local feature encodings provide us with information regarding what each image-patch corresponds to and also the details

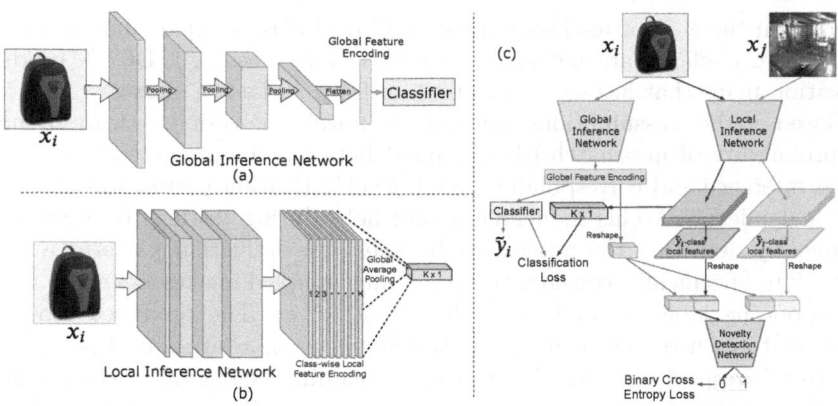

Fig. 4. (a) The global inference network processes the image to produce a global feature encoding which is used by the classifier to predict the class label. (b) The local inference network architecture provides patch-level features which are used to produce class-wise local feature encoding for all K classes, providing information regarding the presence of all classes at the patch-level. (c) Both global and local network information are combined in a novel training strategy for novelty detection, specifically to model mismatch between local activations and global predictions. For given any image x_i, the global and local features of the predicted class $\tilde{y}_i$ are concatenated to create a positive example. Local feature of the predicted class $\tilde{y}_i$ for another randomly sampled image x_j from a different class is combined with the same global feature to create a negative example. The novelty detection network is trained to distinguish between these positive and negative examples. The Global and Local inference networks are trained using the cross entropy classification loss on their respective predictions. *Note that, both x_i and x_j are sampled from in-class data.*

regarding patch-level activation patterns for a particular class. This information is particularly useful in our approach and is utilized in the next section to train the novelty detection network. The local inference network is trained using the following loss function

$$\mathcal{L}_{local} = \frac{1}{n} \sum_{i=1}^{n} L_{ce}(gap(\mathcal{R}(x_i)), \ y_i), \tag{2}$$

where $\mathcal{R}$ denotes the local inference network, $\mathcal{R}(x_i)$ denotes the prediction map having all patch-level prediction scores corresponding to all K classes and *gap* represents global average pooling operation along the height and width of the prediction map (shown in Fig. 4).

3.3 Novelty Detection Network

The proposed novelty detection method utilizing global and local inference is illustrated in Fig. 4(c). As discussed earlier, the proposed approach relies on two assumptions, *1)* the activation patterns for a particular global predictions are different in the case of in-class sample and novel class sample, and *2)* for each image from in-class data belonging to a particular class (y_i), DCNN produces activation maps that has some contribution from all known classes.

Based on these assumptions, we train the novelty detection network to model the probability of mis-match (discrepancy) between the predicted label by the global inference and corresponding patch-level activation patterns predicted by the local inference. This modeling should help during testing to detect novel samples by detecting the mis-match between the activation patterns and the prediction. Specifically, consider two randomly sampled images x_i and x_j having corresponding labels y_i and y_j, such that $y_i \neq y_j$. The predicted label and global feature encoding for image x_i is denoted as $\tilde{y}_i = \arg\max_i \mathcal{C}(\mathcal{G}(x_i))$ and $g_i = \mathcal{G}(x_i)$, respectively. The local feature encoding belonging to the predicted class $\tilde{y}_i$ for both images x_i and x_j are denoted as $r_i = \mathcal{R}(x_i)_{\tilde{y}_i}$ and $r_j = \mathcal{R}(x_j)_{\tilde{y}_i}$, respectively. This process is illustrated in Fig. 4(c). The following loss is used for training the novelty detection network

$$\mathcal{L}_{novelty} = \frac{1}{n} \sum_{\substack{i=1, y_i \neq y_j \\ j \sim \{1,..,n\}}}^{n} L_{ce}(\mathcal{N}(cat(g_i, r_i)),\ 0)$$
$$+ L_{ce}(\mathcal{N}(cat(g_i, r_j)),\ 1), \tag{3}$$

where $\mathcal{N}$ denotes the novelty detection network and *cat* represents reshape and concatenation operations. Also, $j \sim \{1,..,n\}$ and $y_i \neq y_j$ denote that for every training image x_i an index j is randomly sampled from the given in-class data, such that both x_j and x_i have different labels. During, testing the novel samples are identified by using predictions from network $\mathcal{N}$. The overall objective for the proposed approach can be written by combining Eq. (1)-(3) as follows

$$\min_{\mathcal{N},\ \mathcal{G},\ \mathcal{R},\ \mathcal{C}} \mathcal{L}_{global} + \mathcal{L}_{local} + \mathcal{L}_{novelty}. \tag{4}$$

Details regarding the network architectures and training procedures are provided in supplementary material.

3.4   Leveraging a Reference Dataset

The proposed method can be easily extended in the case where the reference dataset is available. We apply regularization on penultimate activations of the global inference network, similar to the loss function proposed in [10]. Such regularization of the final layer activations penalizes the high activations of any input from the reference dataset. Let us denote the reference dataset as $\mathcal{D}_{ref}$ having m number of images, then the regularization loss can be expressed as follows

$$\mathcal{L}_{reg} = \frac{1}{m} \sum_{x \in \mathcal{D}_{ref}} \|\mathcal{C}(\mathcal{G}(x))\|_2. \tag{5}$$

The final objective function in this case is updated by adding $\mathcal{L}_{reg}$, in Eq. 4 as,

$$\min_{\mathcal{N},\ \mathcal{G},\ \mathcal{R},\ \mathcal{C}} \mathcal{L}_{global} + \mathcal{L}_{local} + \mathcal{L}_{novelty} + \lambda \mathcal{L}_{reg}. \tag{6}$$

Here, the parameter λ controls the effect of regularization on the final activations, and is chosen using the validation accuracy of the dataset. In experiments, we set parameter λ equal to 0.001.

4   Experiments and Results

4.1   Novelty Detection Datasets

Caltech-256. The Caltech-256 dataset contains 256 object classes and a total of 30607 images. The dataset has a minimum of 80 images to a maximum of 827 images per category. Based on the protocol defined in [28], we first sort all classes into the alphabetical order according to their class name. The first 128 classes and the last 128 classes are considered as in-class and novel categories, respectively. The in-class categories are further divided into 50-50 splits to create training and test sets.

Table 1. Novelty detection performance measured using the Area Under the receiver operating characteristic Curve evaluation metric (AUC). The best performing method for each dataset is shown in bold. The second best method is shown in italics. Here, symbol [†] indicate that reference dataset was used during training for that method.

Method	Caltech		CUB		Stanford dogs		FounderType		Overall performance
	VGG16	AlexNet	VGG16	AlexNet	VGG16	AlexNet	VGG16	AlexNet	
Fine-tune	0.827	0.785	0.931	0.909	0.766	0.702	0.841	0.650	0.801
K-extremes [32]	0.546	0.521	0.520	0.514	0.610	0.592	0.557	0.512	0.546
OC-SVM [31]	0.576	0.561	0.554	0.532	0.542	0.520	0.627	0.612	0.567
KNFST [5]	0.743	0.688	0.891	0.748	0.633	0.602	0.870	0.678	0.732
Local KNFST [4]	0.712	0.628	0.820	0.690	0.626	0.600	0.673	0.633	0.673
OpenMax [2]	0.831	0.787	0.935	0.915	0.776	0.711	0.852	0.667	0.809
Fine-tune[†] [28]	0.848	0.788	0.921	0.899	0.780	0.692	0.754	0.723	0.800
DTMND[†] [28]	*0.869*	0.807	0.958	0.947	0.825	0.748	*0.893*	0.741	0.848
Proposed	0.859	*0.826*	*0.972*	*0.952*	*0.827*	*0.751*	0.876	*0.798*	*0.857*
Proposed[†]	**0.870**	**0.847**	**0.979**	**0.965**	**0.873**	**0.812**	**0.898**	**0.801**	**0.879**

Caltech-UCSD Birds-200. The Caltech-UCSD Birds (CUB-200) is a fine-grained bird classification dataset. It contains 200 distinct bird categories and 6033 images in total. Similar to the protocol used before, the first 100 classes in the alphabetical order are picked as in-class categories and the last 100 classes in the alphabetical order are considered as the novel classes. The in-class categories are further divided into 50-50 splits to create training and test sets. As before, we make sure that both novel and in-class categories have equal number of images.

Stanford Dogs. This is another fine-grained classification dataset, containing 120 distinct dog breeds and a total of 20580 images. After sorting the dog breed classes in the alphabetical order, we pick the first and the last 60 breed categories as in-class and novel class, respectively. The in-class categories are further divided into 50-50 splits to create training and test sets. The number of images are the same for both in-class and novel classes during testing.

FounderType-200. The FounderType-200 dataset contains 200 different font types corresponding to the Chinese characters. Each font type category contains 6763 images. Similar to the other datasets, the first 100 font types are used as in-class categories and the last 100 font types are used as the novel class categories. We keep 50% of the image samples per category as the training set and the remaining 50% are used for testing. The number of images are the same for both in-class and novel classes during testing.

4.2   Quantitative Analysis

Novelty Detection Performance. We evaluate the performance of our method and compare it with several recent novelty detection methods. Each method provides a score to quantify the novelty of a test image. The lower the score, the higher the probability of input being from a novel class and vice versa. Following the protocol proposed in [28], we compare all methods using AlexNet [18] and VGG16 [35] as the global inference network architectures. In our approach, BagNet-33 [7] is used as the local inference network. Below is the list of methods used for comparison:

- **Fine-tune:** In this baseline, the pre-trained DCNN models are fine-tuned on the in-class data samples. The scores from penultimate layer of the models are used to evaluate novelty detection performance.
- **OC-SVM:** One-class SVM [31] is trained on the fine-tuned features and the SVM scores are used to evaluate the novelty detection performance.
- **KNFST:** KNFST as proposed in [4]. It uses fine-tuned deep features to learn a subspace for in-class data. The distance from the subspace is used to evaluate the performance.
- **Local KNFST:** Local KNFST [4] is an extension of the previous baseline, where a local region of in-class data are used to compute the score for performance evaluation.
- **OpenMax:** OpenMax [2] uses penultimate layer scores of a fine-tuned DCNN and distance from class-wise mean vectors combined with extreme value modeling for performance evaluation.
- **K-extremes:** This baseline focuses on the penultimate activations where top 10% of the sorted activations are binarized to find extreme signatures, which are later used to compute the normalized scores for performance evaluation.
- **Fine-tune†:** This is another fine-tuning baseline proposed in [28]. Here, during fine-tuning DCNN on any given novelty detection dataset, a *reference dataset* is used to improve the quality of the features. During testing, the maximum score from the penultimate layer of a DCNN, extracted from the in-class categories (excluding the reference dataset) is used for performance evaluation.

- **DTMND:** Recently proposed novelty detection method, where a *reference dataset* is utilized in a novel training strategy to learn better model that can respond negatively to the novel classes. Maximum activation from the penultimate layer of the model is used for evaluating the novelty detection performance.

The evaluation protocol proposed by [28] considered two more baselines, namely KNFST-*pre* and Local KNFST-*pre*. However, we excluded these from comparison here as they do not observe any improvement over the KNFST and Local KNFST baselines. More details regarding these baselines are provided in [28]. For the proposed method, we use addition of scores from the global inference and the novelty detection networks to evaluate the performance.

The performance of different methods are evaluated using the area under the receiver operating characteristic curve (AUC) metric. The results are reported in Table 1. As can be seen from this table, OC-SVM and K-extremes methods have the lowest performances. Local KNFST performs better than both OC-SVM and K-extremes for all four datasets. KNFST provides better performance compared to Local KNFST on average, and has consistently better performance on all datasets. On average Fine-tune and Fine-tune† have similar performances. However, their performances are inconsistent across datasets and network architectures. For the Caltech-256 dataset, Fine-tune† performs better than Fine-tune for both AlexNet and VGG16, while for CUB-200 the trend is reversed. For both the Stanford Dogs and the FounderType-200 datasets, Fine-tune† performs better when the VGG16 architecture is used and the reverse trend is observed when the AlexNet architecture is used. The performance obtained by Fine-tune† baseline shows that simple fine-tuning is not an efficient way to utilize a reference dataset for novelty detection. OpenMax performs better than both Fine-tune and Fine-tune† baselines, resulting in 1% overall improvement. Except for the FounderType-200 dataset using the VGG16 architecture, Open-Max consistently performs better than OC-SVM, K-extremes, Local KNFST, KNFST, Fine-tune and Fine-tune† baselines. Out of all the baselines, DTMND yields the best performance. DTMND on average performs 3% better than the next best performing baseline and performs approximately 5% better than Fine-tune† on average. Even-though both of these baselines have access to a reference dataset, DTMND utilizes this additional data more efficiently, resulting in the better performance. The performance of DTMND is largely attributed to their approach for fine-tuning using the reference dataset.

In the absence of reference dataset, the best method in the literature DTMND would become similar to that of fine-tune baseline and the performance will drop by $\sim$5% to 0.80. Whereas the proposed approach without the reference dataset during training provides approximately 6% improvement over the DTMND without reference dataset. This is due to the fact that the performance gain for DTMND is mainly due to the fact that it uses an external reference dataset for training the network. When the reference dataset is utilized during the training of the proposed approach (described in Eq. 5), the proposed approach consistently performs better than DTMND for all datasets and network architectures.

Overall, when the proposed approach is trained with the help of reference dataset it improves by ∼2% and provides ∼4% improvement over the DTMND. The performance improvement with the proposed[†] method shows that our approach can be easily extended to a scenario where a reference dataset is available to further enhance the novelty detection performance. On the other hand, DTMND becomes sub-optimal for the cases where a reference dataset is not available. Especially in such cases the proposed approach is a better alternative for DCNN-based multi-class novelty detection compared to DTMND.

Ablation Analysis. In this section, we provide an ablation analysis showing the significance of combining patch-level information with global in our approach. For ablation experiments, we consider all four novelty detection datasets and the corresponding protocol proposed in Sect. 4.1. For all experiments, VGG16 is used as the global inference network. The following ablation baselines are considered:

- **Global Only:** This baseline is similar to Fine-tune as described in Sect. 4.2. The in-class data samples are used to fine-tune the VGG16 network. The maximum activation score from the penultimate layer of VGG16 is used to evaluate the novelty detection performance.
- **Local Only:** Fine-tuning only the local inference network using the given in-class data. The maximum activation score from the penultimate layer of the local inference network is used to evaluate the novelty detection performance.
- **Global+Local:** Here, we perform a straight forward concatenation of information from the global and local inference networks. The novelty detection performance is evaluated based on the addition of scores from both networks.
- **Proposed:** This is the method proposed in the paper, where instead of a straight-forward fusion we utilize novel training strategy proposed in Sect. 3, to train a novelty detector network, which can better identify the mismatch of local activity patterns for global feature of a given category.

Table 2. Ablation analysis using AUC. The best performing method is shown in bold.

Method	Caltech	CUB	Stanford dogs	FounerType	Overall performance
Global Only	0.827	0.931	0.766	0.841	0.841
Local Only	0.799	0.785	0.598	0.773	0.739
Global+Local	0.831	0.943	0.741	0.835	0.837
Proposed	**0.859**	**0.972**	**0.827**	**0.876**	**0.883**

The performance of all three ablation baselines are reported in Table 2. The lowest performance is obtained by local only baseline. The local inference network processes image patches and classifies images based on the local image features. This leads to relatively poor classification of in-class samples, which in turn hurts the novelty detection performance. On the other hand, the global inference network processes the entire image with a cascade of convolutional, pooling and fully connected layers to get a feature encoding for the entire image. This helps the global only baseline perform better classification and generates high prediction scores for the in-class samples. However, the problem with the global only baseline is that it ends up providing high prediction scores for the novel class samples as well, hurting the novelty detection performance. In the proposed approach, the novelty detection network is trained using both local and global inference networks. The combined information and novel training strategy helps the trained novelty detection network to perform better in identifying novel classes. Specifically, the local inference network provides patch-level activation information corresponding to the prediction provided by the global inference network. The novelty detection network identifies the mismatch between the patch-level activation patterns and global feature encoding to predict whether the input image belongs to either in-class or novel class. As a result, the proposed method performs approximately 14% and 4% better than the local and the global baselines, respectively. We also compare the performance of our method with a *naive* fusion baseline, i.e. Global+Local, where the information from global and local networks are directly concatenated and the performance evaluation is done using the added scores. From Table 2, it can be observed that the proposed approach is able to perform better than the Global+Local baseline.

4.3 Qualitative Analysis

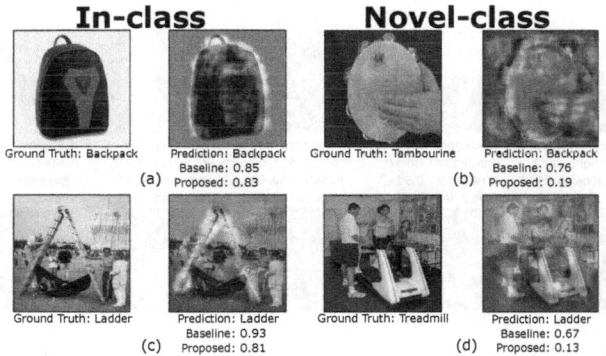

Fig. 5. Image examples of in-class (a) & (c) and novel class (b) & (d) data with corresponding class activation heat-maps as predicted by local inference network and scores assigned using both baseline and proposed.

Fine-Tune Baseline vs Proposed Method. To show the effectiveness of the proposed approach, we provide a qualitative comparison with the Fine-tune baseline (i.e. traditional DCNN) in Fig. 5. Specifically, we provide image examples, prediction from the global inference network, their corresponding local class-activation heat-maps and scores assigned by both baseline and the proposed method. The heat-maps are generated by normalizing the local feature encodings of the class predicted by the global inference network. The images presented here are from two novel classes, namely, 'Tambourine' and 'Treadmill', as shown in Fig. 5(b), Fig. 5(d), respectively. These images are wrongly identified by the baseline as in-class data, and assigned the category 'Backpack', and 'Ladder' with high scores. Additionally, we show the images from the corresponding in-class categories 'Backpack' and 'Ladder' and their corresponding class activation heat-maps in Fig. 5(a) and Fig. 5(c), respectively. This figure shows the difference in class activation heat-maps for the case where the image samples are from in-class data and the case where the image samples are from novel classes. For example, in Fig. 5(a), the image sample is from a known class with category label 'Backpack' and the network is able to correctly identify it by assigning a high score. The patch-level class activation patterns shown in heat-map focuses on highly discriminative patch locations providing strong presence of the given class. On the other hand, in Fig. 5(b), the image sample is from a novel class, but the network wrongly identifies it as 'Backpack' with a high score. However, if we look at the class activation patterns, there are moderate to high activations all over the image, as opposed to in-class image in Fig. 5(a). The novelty detector of the proposed method is specifically trained to identify this mis-match in activation patterns and predicted label. This helps the proposed approach correctly predict a high score for the image sample of 'Backpack' and a low score for the image sample of a novel class, 'Tambourine'. Similar observations can be made for the other example provided for 'Ladder' in Fig. 5(c) and Fig. 5(d).

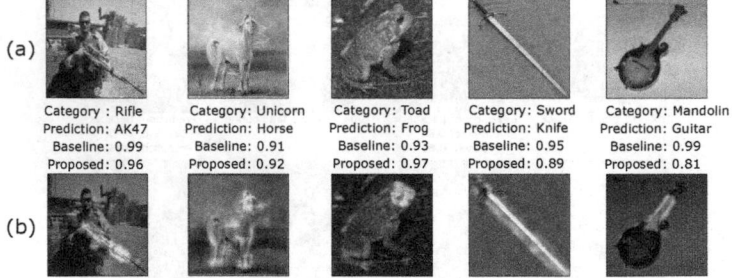

(a)

Category : Rifle	Category: Unicorn	Category: Toad	Category: Sword	Category: Mandolin
Prediction: AK47	Prediction: Horse	Prediction: Frog	Prediction: Knife	Prediction: Guitar
Baseline: 0.99	Baseline: 0.91	Baseline: 0.93	Baseline: 0.95	Baseline: 0.99
Proposed: 0.96	Proposed: 0.92	Proposed: 0.97	Proposed: 0.89	Proposed: 0.81

(b)

Fig. 6. Examples of images from novel classes that are wrongly identified as in-class samples with high scores.

Examples of Wrong Prediction. Though the proposed approach exhibits reasonable novelty detection performance, there are some cases where it fails to predict low scores when the samples are from novel classes. Some of these examples are illustrated in Fig. 6 with their corresponding class activation heat-maps and the predicted scores using the Fine-tune baseline (i.e. traditional DCNN) and the proposed method. The image sample from novel category 'Toad' is identified as in-class category 'Frog'. In this case, the novelty detector network fails to detect any mis-match between the local patch-wise activation patterns and the predicted label. Similarly, the novel categories 'Unicorn', 'Rifle' and 'Mandolin' are identified as in-class categories 'Horse', 'AK47' and 'Guitar', respectively. For all of these examples presented here, the reason for failure can be due to very subtle differences between these novel categories with their respective misclassified in-class categories.

5   Conclusion

We proposed a novel DCNN-based multi-class novelty detection method, that is end-to-end trainable. Unlike recent methods, the proposed approach does not rely on the availability of a reference dataset and is flexible enough to work on both scenarios, when the reference dataset is available and when it is not. We discussed assumptions regarding patch-level activation patterns of DCNNs when the test image is from novel classes. Based on these assumptions, we proposed a novel training methodology which utilizes both global level predictions from the traditional DCNNs and a local inference network, which processes image at patch level. Furthermore, we show how the proposed approach can be extended when a reference dataset is accessible by regularizing the reference data penultimate activations. Experimental results, evaluated on four multi-class novelty detection datasets, show that the proposed method is able to identify novel class samples better compared to the other DCNN-based methods.

Acknowledgement. This work was supported by the NSF grant 1910141.

References

1. Baweja, Y., Oza, P., Perera, P., Patel, V.M.: Anomaly detection-based unknown face presentation attack detection. In: International Joint Conference on Biometrics (IJCB), Houston, TX (2020)
2. Bendale, A., Boult, T.E.: Towards open set deep networks. In: Proceedings of the IEEE Conference on Computer Vision and Pattern Recognition, pp. 1563–1572 (2016)
3. Bhattacharjee, S., Mandal, D., Biswas, S.: Multi-class novelty detection using mixup technique. In: The IEEE Winter Conference on Applications of Computer Vision, pp. 1400–1409 (2020)
4. Bodesheim, P., Freytag, A., Rodner, E., Denzler, J.: Local novelty detection in multi-class recognition problems. In: 2015 IEEE Winter Conference on Applications of Computer Vision, pp. 813–820. IEEE (2015)
5. Bodesheim, P., Freytag, A., Rodner, E., Kemmler, M., Denzler, J.: Kernel null space methods for novelty detection. In: Proceedings of the IEEE Conference on Computer Vision and Pattern Recognition, pp. 3374–3381 (2013)
6. Bonawitz, K., et al.: Practical secure aggregation for privacy-preserving machine learning. In: Proceedings of the 2017 ACM SIGSAC Conference on Computer and Communications Security, pp. 1175–1191 (2017)

7. Brendel, W., Bethge, M.: Approximating cnns with bag-of-local-features models works surprisingly well on imagenet. arXiv preprint arXiv:1904.00760 (2019)
8. Carlini, N., Wagner, D.: Towards evaluating the robustness of neural networks. In: 2017 IEEE Symposium on Security and Privacy (SP), pp. 39–57. IEEE (2017)
9. DeVries, T., Taylor, G.W.: Learning confidence for out-of-distribution detection in neural networks. arXiv preprint arXiv:1802.04865 (2018)
10. Dhamija, A.R., Günther, M., Boult, T.E.: Improving deep network robustness to unknown inputs with objectosphere (2019)
11. Eskin, E., Arnold, A., Prerau, M., Portnoy, L., Stolfo, S.: A geometric framework for unsupervised anomaly detection. In: Barbará, D., Jajodia, S. (eds.) Applications of data mining in computer security. Advances in Information Security, vol. 6, pp. 77–101. Springer, Boston (2002). https://doi.org/10.1007/978-1-4615-0953-0_4
12. Goodfellow, I.J., Shlens, J., Szegedy, C.: Explaining and harnessing adversarial examples. arXiv preprint arXiv:1412.6572 (2014)
13. Hautamaki, V., Karkkainen, I., Franti, P.: Outlier detection using k-nearest neighbour graph. In: Proceedings of the 17th International Conference on Pattern Recognition, ICPR 2004, vol. 3, pp. 430–433. IEEE (2004)
14. Hendrycks, D., Gimpel, K.: A baseline for detecting misclassified and out-of-distribution examples in neural networks. arXiv preprint arXiv:1610.02136 (2016)
15. Hoffmann, H.: Kernel PCA for novelty detection. Pattern Recogn. **40**(3), 863–874 (2007)
16. Kim, B., Kim, H., Kim, K., Kim, S., Kim, J.: Learning not to learn: training deep neural networks with biased data. In: The IEEE Conference on Computer Vision and Pattern Recognition (CVPR), June 2019
17. Knorr, E.M., Ng, R.T., Tucakov, V.: Distance-based outliers: algorithms and applications. VLDB J. Int. J. Very Large Data Bases **8**(3-4), 237–253 (2000)
18. Krizhevsky, A., Sutskever, I., Hinton, G.E.: Imagenet classification with deep convolutional neural networks. In: Advances in Neural Information Processing Systems, pp. 1097–1105 (2012)
19. Liang, S., Li, Y., Srikant, R.: Enhancing the reliability of out-of-distribution image detection in neural networks. arXiv preprint arXiv:1706.02690 (2017)
20. Liu, J., Lian, Z., Wang, Y., Xiao, J.: Incremental kernel null space discriminant analysis for novelty detection. In: Proceedings of the IEEE Conference on Computer Vision and Pattern Recognition, pp. 792–800 (2017)
21. Madry, A., Makelov, A., Schmidt, L., Tsipras, D., Vladu, A.: Towards deep learning models resistant to adversarial attacks. arXiv preprint arXiv:1706.06083 (2017)
22. Markou, M., Singh, S.: Novelty detection: a review—part 1: statistical approaches. Signal Process. **83**(12), 2481–2497 (2003)
23. Neal, L., Olson, M., Fern, X., Wong, W.-K., Li, F.: Open set learning with counterfactual images. In: Ferrari, V., Hebert, M., Sminchisescu, C., Weiss, Y. (eds.) ECCV 2018. LNCS, vol. 11210, pp. 620–635. Springer, Cham (2018). https://doi.org/10.1007/978-3-030-01231-1_38
24. Oza, P., Nguyen, H.V.N., Patel, V.M.: Multiple class novelty detection under data distribution shift. In: ECCV 2020. Springer, Cham (2020)
25. Oza, P., Patel, V.M.: One-class convolutional neural network. IEEE Signal Process. Lett. **26**(2), 277–281 (2018)
26. Perera, P., et al.: Generative-discriminative feature representations for open-set recognition. In: Proceedings of the IEEE/CVF Conference on Computer Vision and Pattern Recognition, pp. 11814–11823 (2020)

27. Perera, P., Nallapati, R., Xiang, B.: OCGAN: one-class novelty detection using GANs with constrained latent representations. In: Proceedings of the IEEE Conference on Computer Vision and Pattern Recognition, pp. 2898–2906 (2019)
28. Perera, P., Patel, V.M.: Deep transfer learning for multiple class novelty detection. In: Proceedings of the IEEE Conference on Computer Vision and Pattern Recognition, pp. 11544–11552 (2019)
29. Perera, P., Patel, V.M.: Learning deep features for one-class classification. IEEE Trans. Image Process. **28**(11), 5450–5463 (2019)
30. Samangouei, P., Kabkab, M., Chellappa, R.: Defense-GAN: protecting classifiers against adversarial attacks using generative models. arXiv preprint arXiv:1805.06605 (2018)
31. Schölkopf, B., Smola, A.J., Bach, F., et al.: Learning with Kernels: Support Vector Machines, Regularization, Optimization, and Beyond. MIT Press, Cambridge (2002)
32. Schultheiss, A., Käding, C., Freytag, A., Denzler, J.: Finding the unknown: novelty detection with extreme value signatures of deep neural activations. In: Roth, V., Vetter, T. (eds.) GCPR 2017. LNCS, vol. 10496, pp. 226–238. Springer, Cham (2017). https://doi.org/10.1007/978-3-319-66709-6_19
33. Selvaraju, R.R., Cogswell, M., Das, A., Vedantam, R., Parikh, D., Batra, D.: Grad-CAM: visual explanations from deep networks via gradient-based localization. In: Proceedings of the IEEE International Conference on Computer Vision, pp. 618–626 (2017)
34. Shao, R., Perera, P., Yuen, P.C., Patel, V.M.: Open-set adversarial defense. In: ECCV 2020. Springer, Cham (2020)
35. Simonyan, K., Zisserman, A.: Very deep convolutional networks for large-scale image recognition. arXiv preprint arXiv:1409.1556 (2014)
36. Srinivas, N., Ricanek, K., Michalski, D., Bolme, D.S., King, M.: Face recognition algorithm bias: Performance differences on images of children and adults. In: Proceedings of the IEEE Conference on Computer Vision and Pattern Recognition Workshops (2019)
37. Szegedy, C., et al.: Intriguing properties of neural networks. arXiv preprint arXiv:1312.6199 (2013)
38. Tax, D.M., Duin, R.P.: Support vector data description. Mach. Learn. **54**(1), 45–66 (2004)
39. Turk, M., Pentland, A.: Eigenfaces for recognition. J. Cogn. Neurosci. **3**(1), 71–86 (1991)
40. Vera-Rodriguez, R., Blazquez, M., Morales, A., Gonzalez-Sosa, E., Neves, J.C., Proenca, H.: Facegenderid: exploiting gender information in dcnns face recognition systems. In: Proceedings of the IEEE Conference on Computer Vision and Pattern Recognition Workshops (2019)
41. Wright, J., Yang, A.Y., Ganesh, A., Sastry, S.S., Ma, Y.: Robust face recognition via sparse representation. IEEE Trans. Pattern Anal. Mach. Intell. **31**(2), 210–227 (2008)
42. Xia, Y., Cao, X., Wen, F., Hua, G., Sun, J.: Learning discriminative reconstructions for unsupervised outlier removal. In: Proceedings of the IEEE International Conference on Computer Vision, pp. 1511–1519 (2015)
43. You, C., Robinson, D.P., Vidal, R.: Provable self-representation based outlier detection in a union of subspaces. In: The IEEE Conference on Computer Vision and Pattern Recognition (CVPR), July 2017
44. Zhang, H., Patel, V.M.: Sparse representation-based open set recognition. IEEE Trans. Pattern Anal. Mach. Intell. **39**(8), 1690–1696 (2016)

People as Scene Probes

Yifan Wang[✉], Brian L. Curless, and Steven M. Seitz

University of Washington, Seattle, USA
{yifan1,curless,seitz}@cs.washington.edu

Abstract. By analyzing the motion of people and other objects in a scene, we demonstrate how to infer depth, occlusion, lighting, and shadow information from video taken from a single camera viewpoint. This information is then used to composite new objects into the same scene with a high degree of automation and realism. In particular, when a user places a new object (2D cut-out) in the image, it is automatically rescaled, relit, occluded properly, and casts realistic shadows in the correct direction relative to the sun, and which conform properly to scene geometry. We demonstrate results (best viewed in supplementary video) on a range of scenes and compare to alternative methods for depth estimation and shadow compositing.

1 Introduction

The presence of people in an image reveals much about scene structure. Each pedestrian effectively acts as a *depth probe*, whose image height is inversely proportional to distance. Similarly, people act as *occlusion probes*, revealing which parts of the scene are in front of others, as they pass in front of or behind signs, trees, cars, fences, and other structures. They also act as *light probes*, revealing both how the scene casts light on them (shade vs. sun), as well as how they cast shadows on the scene. Taken together (and over many observations), these cues capture a great deal of information about the scene.

This paper presents techniques for inferring depth, occlusion, and lighting/shadow information from image sequences of a scene, through analysis of people (and other objects such as cars). A key property of our approach is that it is completely *passive* – unlike prior use of light probes [7], depth probes [4], or shadow probes [5] which require actively placing and/or moving special objects in the scene; we recover all of this information purely from the images themselves.

As an application, we focus on geometry- and lighting-aware image compositing, i.e., pasting new people or other objects into an image in a way that automatically accounts for depth, occlusions, lighting, and shadows. For example, when you drag a segmented image of a person onto the image, it automatically resizes her to be larger in the foreground and smaller in the background.

Electronic supplementary material The online version of this chapter (https://doi.org/10.1007/978-3-030-58607-2_26) contains supplementary material, which is available to authorized users.

© Springer Nature Switzerland AG 2020
A. Vedaldi et al. (Eds.): ECCV 2020, LNCS 12355, pp. 438–454, 2020.
https://doi.org/10.1007/978-3-030-58607-2_26

Placing her on the stairs will correctly occlude the car behind, and the system will add a realistic shadow that bends over the stairs and onto the pavement below. Dragging her behind the tree close to a building automatically adds partial occlusion from the branches in front, and the part of her you see is darker due to the shadow cast by the building. All of these effects occur in real-time, as you move her to different locations in the image.

Our technical contributions include (1) An automatic method for estimating occlusion maps from objects (e.g., people and cars) moving through a scene, (2) A network that learns from a video of a scene how to cast shadows of newly inserted objects into that scene, including warping and occlusion of shadows due to scene geometry, and (3) A method for implicitly estimating a ground plane based on heights of people observed throughout the scene without camera calibration or explicit depth estimation, enabling depth-dependent scaling of newly inserted objects based on their locations. Combined with a technique for estimating approximate illumination – modeled by just scaling whole-object brightness depending on placement in the image – we demonstrate a novel system for compositing objects into the scene with plausible occlusions, object scaling, lighting, and cast shadows. We show that components of the system outperform alternatives such as single-view depth estimation for occlusions and standard GANs for shadow insertion.

We note that the method does have limitations: it works for a single scene at a time for which stationary camera video is available, assumes a single ground plane, and does not handle complex re-shading of inserted objects or their reflections off of specular surfaces in the scene, and the shadow generation works when inserting in-class objects that are observed in typical places in the scene (people on sidewalks and cars on streets, but not cars on sidewalks or, say, sharks placed anywhere). Despite these restrictions, we show that much can be learned about the geometry and lighting of a scene simply by observing the effects of everyday people and cars passing through, thus enabling new image compositing capabilities.

2   Related Work

Conditional Image Synthesis. Deep generative models can learn to synthesize images, including generative adversarial networks (GANs) [10] and variational autoencoders (VAE) [19]. Conditional GANs [3,28–31] are used to synthesize images given category labels. [17,34,39] focus on converting segmentation masks to photo-realistic images. They offer users an interactive GUI to draw their own segmentation masks and output a realistic image based on the given segmentation masks. However, these GANs do not leverage scene-specific geometry and lighting information, derived from many images. Our work embeds the scene's geometry and lighting into the GAN, to generate more realistic compositions.

Image Composition. Lalonde *et al.* [20] proposed a system for inserts new objects into existing photographs by querying a vast image-based object library. Several authors have explored use of GANs to transform a foreground object to better match a background. ST-GAN [26] learns a homography of a foreground object conditioned on the background image. Compositional GAN [1] additionally learns the correct occlusion for the foreground object. SF-GAN [40] warps and adjusts the color, brightness, and styles of the foreground objects and embeds them into background images harmoniously. However, a realistic composition should also consider the foreground object's effect on the background (including shadows).

Some approaches aim to compose an object by rendering its appearance. [16] inserts an object into a scene based on a specified location and bounding box. [24] learns the joint distribution of the location and shape of an object conditioned on the semantic label map. PS-GAN [32] replaces a pedestrian's bounding box by random noise and infills with a new pedestrian based on the surrounding context. [25] blends the object with the background image in the bounding box, and learns a mapping to synthesize realistic images using both real and fake pairs. These works all train on images without hard shadows, and focus on person rather than shadow synthesis. For example, they only synthesize an area around the person's bounding box (not including long shadows), and don't take into account shadow casting information from other images of the same scene.

Shadow Matting. Matting [35] is an effective tool to handle shadows. [5] enables synthesizing correct cast shadows, by estimating a shadow displacement map obtained by *manually* waving a shadow-casting stick over every part of the scene. Given an object to be composited, they can then synthesize correct shadows based on the object shape and shadow displacement map. The related problem of shadow *removal* has also been explored by a number of authors, e.g., [11,22,41]. We present the first shadow matting (synthesis) method that is completely *passive*, i.e., does not require manually waving a stick, but instead learns from the movement of objects (people and cars) in the scene itself.

Image Layering. Our work was inspired in part by [4], who first proposed using the motion of people (and other objects) to infer scene occlusions relationships. As the technology in the 1990's was more limited, their approach required manual intervention and made a number of simplifying assumptions. Less related to our work, but also worth mentioning is the use of layered representation for view synthesis, e.g. [8,36–38,42]. Like [4], our approach infers occlusion order purely from the movement of objects in the scene, but is entirely automated and leverages modern techniques for object detection and tracking.

3   Problem Definition

We start with a video of a scene, taken by a stationary camera. As objects – people, cars, bicycles – pass through the scene, they occlude and are occluded by scene elements, pass into and out of shadowed regions, cast shadows into the scene, and, due to perspective, appear larger or smaller in an image depending on their position in the scene. From the video sequence, we seek to extract occlusion layering, shadowing, and position-dependent scale to enable realistically compositing new objects (of similar classes) into the scene.

We design a fully automatic pipeline to tackle this problem. Our key idea is that the occurrence and motion of existing objects (aka *scene probes*) through the video is the primary cue for inferring properties of the scene. These properties include depth, occlusion ordering, lighting, and shadows. Unlike some related methods, our pipeline does not require active scanning for shadow matting [5], or manual annotation for layering [4]. Furthermore, our pipeline does not require the camera to be calibrated.

4   Technical Approach

4.1   People as Occlusion Probes

Occlusion is key for realistic image composition. An inserted object should be occluded by the foreground and occlude the background properly. Cars driving on the street are occluded by the trees on the sidewalk nearer to the viewer, and road signs occlude people walking behind them. We propose a method to estimate the occlusion order by *analyzing the occlusion relationships between people, other moving objects in the video, and static scene structures and objects.* Our method records the occlusion relationship between object and the scene to yield an occlusion map $\tilde{z}(x, y)$, similar to a depth map, for determining which pixels of an object occlude or are occluded by the scene, depending on the location of the object. To make the problem tractable, we approximate the scene as a single ground plane, with moving objects and occluders represented as planar sprites (on vertical planes parallel to the image plane) that are in contact with the ground plane. Based on this simplification, we can assume a monotonic relationship between object location and occlusion order; the closer the object, the lower in the image its ground contact occurs.

Algorithm. We first calculate a median image within a local temporal window of one second to serve as a background plate; we have found the one second window to work well for scenes that are not densely crowded, and with objects (especially people) moving at a natural pace. For each frame in this temporal window, we apply Mask-RCNN [12] to estimate segmentation masks for people, cars, bikes, trucks, buses, and related categories. For each individual object O_i, Mask-RCNN returns a binary mask M_i, and we record the lowest point y_i of the mask. We refine this mask to avoid accidental inclusion of background pixels: each pixel in M_i whose color difference with the median image is greater than a threshold is assigned to refined mask M_i'.

Now we construct the occlusion map. We set the image origin $(x, y) = (0, 0)$ at the lower left corner of the image. The key idea is that if an object O_i with bottom pixel y_i occludes a background pixel, then another object O_j with $y_j < y_i$ is likely to be closer to the camera and would then also occlude this pixel. We initialize the occlusion map with $\tilde{z}(x, y) = -1$ at all pixels and then iteratively update the map for each object O_i:

$$\tilde{z}(x, y) = \begin{cases} y_i, & \text{if } (x, y) \in M_i' \text{ and } y_i > \tilde{z}(x, y) \\ \tilde{z}(x, y), & \text{otherwise.} \end{cases} \tag{1}$$

To create a new composite, we initialize image I_{comp} with one of the median images. For a new object O_j (e.g., cropped from another photo) with mask M_j and bottom coordinate y_j, we update I_{comp}:

$$I_{comp}(x,y) = \begin{cases} O_j(x,y), & \text{if } (x,y) \in M_j \text{ and } y_j < \tilde{z}(x,y) \\ I_{comp}(x,y), & \text{otherwise.} \end{cases} \quad (2)$$

where $O_j(x,y)$ is the color of the object at a given pixel (x,y). Note that this composite image lacks shadows cast by O_j. Further, if O_j is inserted into an area that is itself in shadow, then O_j should be darkened before compositing. We discuss these shadowing effects in the next section.

4.2   People as Light Probes

People appear brighter in direct sunlight and darker in shadow. Hence, we can potentially use people to *probe* lighting variation in different parts of a scene. Based on this cue, we compute a lighting map that enables automatically adjusting overall brightness of new objects as a function of position in the image. We do not attempt to recover an environment map to relight objects, or to cast complex/partial shadows on objects (areas for future work). Instead, we simply estimate a darkening/lightening factor to apply to each object depending on its location in the scene, approximating the effect of the object being in shadow or in open illumination. We call this factor, stored at each pixel, the lighting map $L(x,y)$. This lighting map is a *spatially varying* illumination map across the image, whereas the prior work [9,14,15,33] generally solves for a single *directionally varying* illumination model for the entire scene. From the input video, we observe that people walking in well-lit areas tend to have higher pixel intensity than people in shadowed areas. We further assume there is no correlation between the color of people's clothing and where they appear in the image; e.g., people wearing red do not walk along different paths than those wearing blue. Given these conditions, we estimate the lighting map from statistics of overall changes in object colors as they move through the scene. Note that this lighting map is a combination of average illumination and reflection from the surface; it does not give absolute brightness of illumination, but gives a measure of relative illumination for different parts of the scene.

Algorithm. Starting with the detected objects $\{O_i\}$ and associated masks $\{M_i'\}$ described in Sect. 4.1, we compute the mean color C_i per object across all pixels in its mask. The lighting map is then the average of the C_i that cover a given pixel, i.e.:

$$L(x,y) = \frac{1}{|\{i \mid (x,y) \in M_i'\}|} \sum_{i|(x,y)\in M_i'} C_i \quad (3)$$

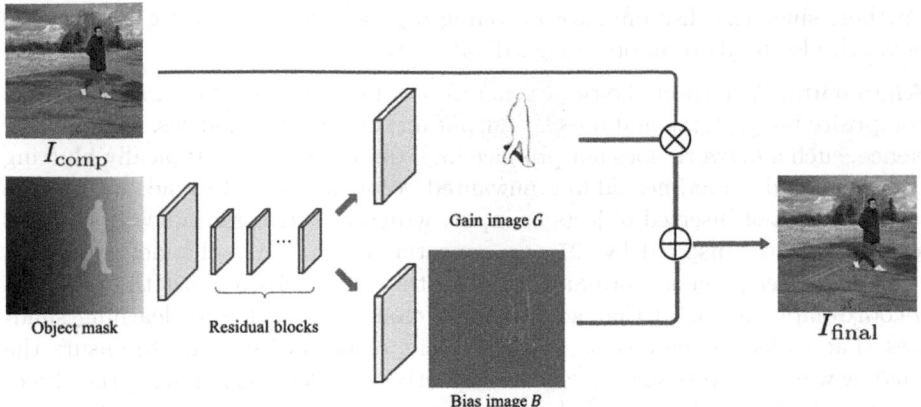

Fig. 1. The generator network takes the object mask, x, and y coordinates as input (visualized here in red, green, and blue channels) and outputs a scalar gain image G and color bias image B (mid-gray corresponds to zero bias as shown). Given the shadow-free, composite image I_{comp}, we synthesize the final image $I_{\mathrm{final}} = G \cdot I_{\mathrm{comp}} + B$. (Color figure online)

When compositing a new object, O_j with mask M_j into the background plate, we first compute the average lighting L_j for the pixels covered by M_j:

$$L_j = \frac{1}{|\{(x,y) \in M_j\}|} \sum_{(x,y) \in M_j} L(x,y) \tag{4}$$

and apply this color factor component-wise to all of the colors in O_j. As noted above, this lighting factor makes the most sense as a relative measure. Thus, when compositing a new object into the scene in our application scenario, the user would first set the brightness of the object at a given point in the scene (with the lighting multiplied in), and can then move the object to different parts of the scene with plausible changes to the brightness then occurring automatically.

4.3 People as Shadow Probes

Shadows are one of the most interesting and complex ways that moving objects interact with a scene. Predicting shadows is challenging, as their shapes and locations depend on the position of the sun in the sky, the weather, and the geometry of both the object casting the shadow and the scene receiving it. Furthermore, unlike other lighting effects, shadows are not additive, as a surface already in shadow does not darken further when a second shadow is cast on it from the same light source. We propose using observations of objects passing through the scene to recover these shadowing effects, using a deep network – a pix2pix [17] GAN with improved losses [39] – trained on the given scene to learn how objects cast shadows depending on their shapes and locations in scene.

Further, since the discriminator encourages generation of realistic images, the network also tends to improve jagged silhouettes.

Algorithm. A natural choice of generator would take as input a shadow-free, composite image I_{comp} and directly output an image with shadows. In our experience, such a network does not produce high quality shadows, typically blurring them out and sometimes adding unwanted color patterns. Instead, we use the object masks of inserted objects as input, which are stronger indicators of cast shadow shapes. Inspired by [27], we concatenate an image channel comprised of just the per-pixel x-coordinate, and another channel with just the per-pixel y-coordinate; we found that adding these channels was key to learning shadows that varied depending on the placement of the object, e.g., to ensure the shadow warped across surfaces or was correctly occluded when moving the object around. As in Fig. 1, we feed this x-y augmented object mask through a deep residual convolutional neural network to generate a scalar gain image G and color bias image B, similar to the formulation in [22,23]. The final image is then $I_{final} = G \cdot I_{comp} + B$. We found that having the generator produce I_{final} directly resulted in repetitive pattern artifacts that were alleviated by indirectly generating the result through bias and gain images.

For training, we take each input image I and follow the procedure in Sect. 4.1 to extract objects $\{O_i\}$ and masks $\{M_i'\}$ from an image and then composite the objects directly back onto the local median image to create the shadow-free image I_{comp}. The resulting I_{final}, paired with the ground truth I, can then be used to supervise training of the generator and discriminator, following the method described in [39].

4.4   People as Depth Probes

The size of a person (or other object) in an image is inversely proportional to depth. Hence, the presence of people and their motion through a scene provides a strong depth cue. Using this cue, we can infer how composited people should be resized as a function of placement in the scene. We propose a method to estimate how the scale of an object should vary across an image without directly estimating scene depth or camera focal length, but based instead on the sizes of people at different positions in the scene. Our problem is related to [2] who rectify a planar image by tracking moving objects, although they require constant velocity assumptions, which we avoid. [6] determines the height of a person using a set of parallel planes and a reference direction, which we do not require. We make two assumptions: (1) The ground (on which people walk) can be approximated by a single plane, and (2) All the people in the video are roughly the same height. While the second assumption is not strictly true, it facilitates scale estimation, essentially treating individual height differences among people as Gaussian noise, as in [13], and solving via least squares.

Algorithm. According to our first assumption, all ground plane points (X, Y, Z) in the world coordinate should fit a plane equation:

$$aX + bY + cZ = 1 \qquad (5)$$

Under the second assumption, all people are roughly the same height H in world coordinates. Under perspective projection, we have:

$$x = X \cdot \frac{f}{Z}, y = Y \cdot \frac{f}{Z}, h = H \cdot \frac{f}{Z} \tag{6}$$

where f is the focal length of the camera. Multiplying both sides of Eq. 5 by $H \cdot \frac{f}{Z}$, we arrive at a linear relation between pixel coordinates and height:

$$a'x + b'y + c' = h \tag{7}$$

where a', b', c' are constants. Because people in the scene are grounded, Eq. 7 suggests that any person's bottom middle point (x_i, y_i) and her height h_i follow this linear relationship.

Given the input video, we use the same segmentation network as in Sect. 4.1 to segment out all the people in the video. For each person in the video, we record her height h_i and bottom middle point (x_i, y_i) in camera coordinates. After collecting all the (x_i, y_i) and h_i from the image segmentation network, we use the least squares method to solve for the (a', b', c') in Eq. 7.

When inserting a new object into the scene at (x_j, y_j), we apply Eq. 7 to estimate height h_j. The inserted object will then be resized accordingly and translated to (x_j, y_j). In our application, if the user requires a different height for an inserted object, then she can simply place the object and rescale as desired, and the system will then apply this rescaling factor on top of the height factor from Eq. 7 when moving the object around the scene.

4.5   Implementation Details

We use Mask-RCNN [12] as the instance segmentation network. Inspired by [18], our shadow network uses a deep residual generator. The generator has 5 residual blocks, followed by two different transposed convolution layers to output the bias and gain maps. The loss function is the same as in [39]. We use ADAM with an initial learning rate of 1e-4, and decays linearly after 25 epochs to optimize the objectives. More details can be found in supplementary.

5   Results and Evaluation

In this section, we first introduce our collected datasets, and then evaluate our entire pipeline, including individual components.

5.1   Data

We collected 11 videos with an iPhone camera on a monopod. These videos cover a range of scenes including city streets, parks, plazas, beaches, etc., under lighting conditions from clear sky to cloudy day. The videos are 25 min long on average, during which the ambient lighting changes little. We center-crop to 800×800 at 15 fps in training. We use the first 95% of the video for training and the last 5% for test.

pix2pix   Ours   Ground Truth

Fig. 2. Shadow synthesis results on the test set. The images synthesized by a conventional pix2pix approach [39] (left) lack details inferred by our network (middle) which more closely resembles ground truth (right). In addition, the pix2pix method injects color patterns above the inserted person in the bottom row. Note that both networks learn not to further darken existing shadows (bottom row, sidewalk near the feet).

Reference image   Ours   Ground truth   Reference image   Ours   Ground truth

Fig. 3. Ground plane estimation for height scaling. Given the person's reference height (taken from person in reference image), our algorithm accurately estimates the height in a different location (middle composite in each set). The difference between our estimate and the ground truth is small. (Each of these images is a composite before adding shadows.)

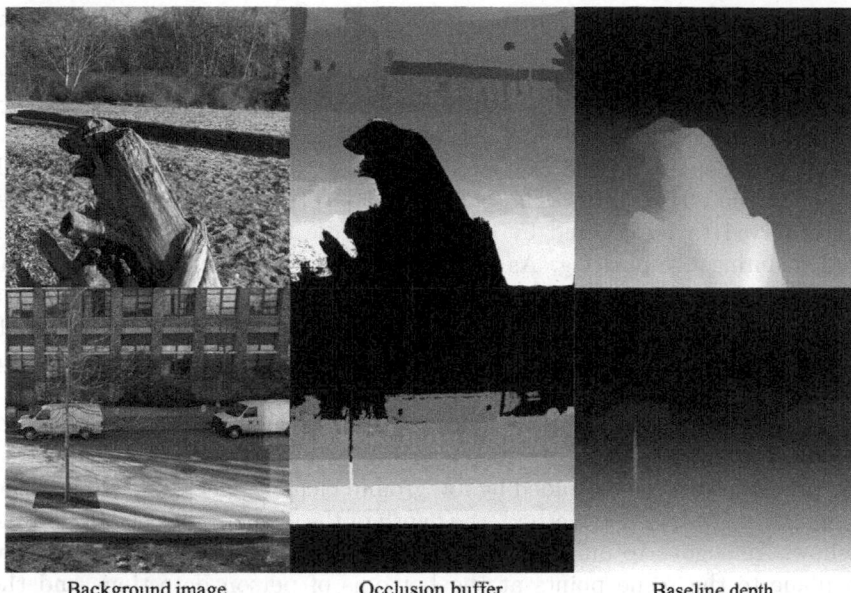

Background image   Occlusion buffer   Baseline depth

Fig. 4. From left to right: the background image, our estimated occlusion buffer, and the depth predicted by [21]. In our occlusion buffer, black pixels are never occluded. Pixels toward yellow were occluded only by smaller y-value objects, and pixels toward red were occluded by larger y-value objects. Some quantization and noise arises in our occlusion map due, respectively, to common object placements (cars in the road) and object mask errors (arising from object/background color similarity at a given pixel). (Color figure online)

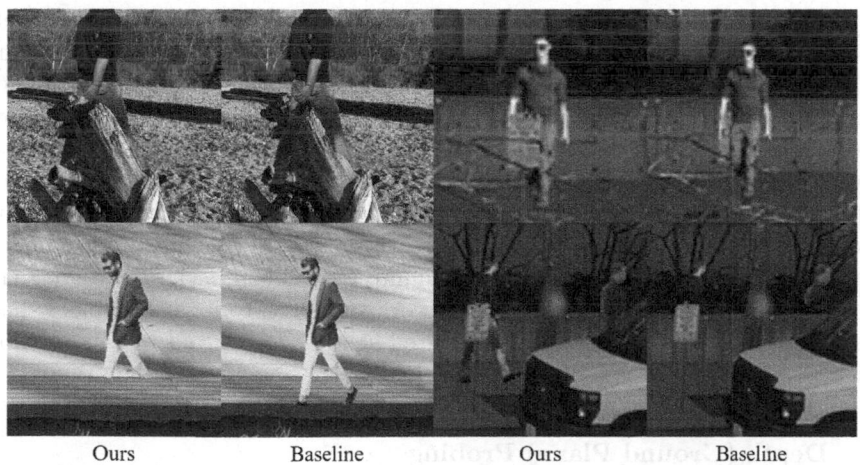

Ours   Baseline   Ours   Baseline

Fig. 5. Qualitative results on occlusion order estimation. People are reasonably well-occluded by foreground objects using our occlusion buffer, while errors in the depth map approach [21] (e.g., sign not reconstructed, bench reconstructed at ground level) result in incorrect occlusions. (Each of these images is a composite before adding shadows.)

5.2   Occlusion Probing

Following Sect. 4.1, we generated occlusion maps for each scene; two of them are illustrated in Fig. 4 in yellow to red pseudocolor. The quantization in colors corresponds to how objects moved through the scene; e.g., the two tones in the street correspond to the restricted placement of cars, which are generally centered in one of two lanes. The black regions correspond to pixels that were never observed to be covered by an object; these are treated as never-to-be-occluded during compositing. As a baseline, we also constructed depth maps using the state-of-the-art, depth-from-single-image MiDaS network [21]. MiDaS produces visually pleasing depth maps, but misses details that are crucial for compositing, such as the street signs toward the back of the scene in the second row of Fig. 4.

Figure 5 shows several (shadow-free) composites. For our method, we simply place an object (such as a person, scaled by the method in Sect. 4.4) into the scene, and it is correctly occluded by foreground elements such as trees, benches, and signs. For the baseline method, the depth of the element must be determined somehow. Analogous to our plane estimation method for height prediction, we fit a plane to the scene points at the bottoms of person detections and then placed new elements at the depths found at the bottom-middle pixel of each inserted element. In a number of cases, elements inserted into the MiDaS depth map were not correctly occluded as shown in the figure, due to erroneous depth estimates and the difficulty of placing the element at a meaningful depth given the reconstruction.

5.3   Shadow Probing

We trained our shadow estimation network (Sect. 4.3) on each scene separately, i.e, one network per scene. On average, each scene had 17, 000 images for training with 900 images held out for testing. Figure 2 shows example results for shadow estimation using (1) a baseline pix2pix-style method [39] that takes a shadow-free image and directly generates a shadowed image and (2) our method that takes an x-y-mask image and produces bias and gain maps which are applied to the shadow-free image. Both networks had similar capacity (with 5 residual blocks). In this case, we also had ground truth, as we could segment out a person from one of the test images and copy them into the median background image for processing. The conventional pix2pix network tends to produce "blobbier" shadows when compared to the more structured shadows produced by our method, which is generally more similar to ground truth.

5.4   Depth (Ground Plane) Probing

For each input video, we predict the plane parameters from the training images using the method described in Sect. 4.4. When inserting a new object into the scene, we apply Eq. 7 with regressed plane parameters to get its estimated height.

We then resize it based on the estimated height, and copy-paste it onto the background frame.

To numerically evaluate the accuracy of the plane estimation as height predictor, we use it to measure relative, rather than absolute, height variation across the image. This measure factors out errors due to, e.g., children not being of average adult height as the absolute model would predict. In particular, we take one image as reference and another as a test image with the same person at two different positions in the images. Suppose Eq. 7 predicts height h in the reference image, but the actual height of the object is observed to be $\hat{h}$. The prediction ratio is then $r = \hat{h}/h$. For the same person in the test image, we then predict the new height h' again using Eq. 7 and rescale the extracted person by $r \cdot h'$ before compositing again. We compared this rescaled height to the actual height of the person in the test image and found that on a small set of selected reference/test image pairs, the estimates were within 3% of ground truth. Figure 3 illustrates this accuracy qualitatively.

Note that without relative height prediction, i.e., instead using Eq. 7 to predict absolute heights, the height prediction error was 13.28%, reasonable enough for inserting an adult of near-average height, though of course more objectionable when inserting, say, a young child. In our demo application, we allow the user to change the initial height of the inserted element.

5.5   Inserting New Objects

We have developed an interactive image compositing application (see suppl. video) that leverages the elements of our system. With this tool, a user can take an object (e.g., a person or car) downloaded from the internet or segmented from another image and drag it to a desired location in one of our captured background plates. The system both resizes the object and adjusts its brightness depending on where it is placed, applies our occlusion map, and synthesizes any cast shadows. We do not fully re-light or re-orient objects, so we rely on the user to select objects with generally compatible lighting and orientation. We provide the user with the option of adjusting the height and overall brightness of the object after initially placing it, but afterward the height and brightness are updated automatically as the user moves the object around in the scene.

Figure 6 shows several results for object insertion using our tool. Here we again compare to using the pix2pix variant just for the final shadow generation step. Our method produces crisper shadows whereas the pix2pix method sometimes produces no shadow at all, generalizing poorly on some of the newly inserted objects and sometimes injecting undesirable color patterns. We conducted human studies to quantify the realism of the synthesized shadows and found that our synthesized images were preferred by users 70.0% of the time to baseline pix2pix, demonstrating a clear advantage for novel composites. Details of the study appear in the supplementary material.

In Fig. 7, we demonstrate the effect of moving a person around in the scene. Note how the brightness and height changes when moved from the lit front area to the back shadowed area, and how the person is occluded by the foreground

I_{comp} pix2pix   Ours

Fig. 6. Inserting new objects. From left to right: the shadow-free composite image I_{comp}, image synthesized by pix2pix [39], and image synthesized by our shadow network. After applying our automatic scaling, lighting, and occlusion handling, we can see that our shadow network performs better than pix2pix on the final shadow compositing step; pix2pix generates less-detailed shadows and sometimes none at all and can introduce new artifacts (e.g., color patterning in the branches above the inserted car in the second row). Our method warps detailed shadows over surfaces. Both methods successfully avoid double-darkening of shadows (man in tree shadow in bottom row)

bench with shadow wrapped over the bench when bringing the person closer to the camera. We also show in Fig. 8 how the shadow network reduces aliasing artifacts arising from the object's binary mask when initially inserted.

Fig. 7. Our system adjusts the height, illumination, occlusion, and shadow for the same person based where he is placed in the image.

I_{comp} Ours

I_{comp} Ours I_{comp} Ours

Fig. 8. Our shadow network reduces aliasing artifacts in I_{comp}, smoothing out the boundary.

Fig. 9. Our shadow network does not perform well on misplaced objects or objects not observed in the training set (left). On the right, the person should be reflected in the puddle, but is not.

6   Conclusion

In this paper, we have introduced a fully automatic pipeline for inferring depth, occlusion, and lighting/shadow information from image sequences of a scene. The central contributions of this work are recognizing that so much information can be extracted just by using people (and other objects such as cars) as scene probes to passively scan the scene. We show that the inferred depth, occlusion ordering, lighting, and shadows are plausible, with the occlusion layering and shadow casting methods outperforming single-image depth estimation and traditional pix2pix shadow synthesis baselines. Further, we show results using a tool for image compositing based on our synthesis pipeline.

As noted earlier, our method is not without limitations, requiring a single scene video as input, assumes a ground plane, does not model advanced shading effects, and cannot composite arbitrary objects at arbitrary locations. Figure 9, e.g., highlights two failure modes; objects either placed in unusual locations or objects in previously unseen categories do not result in plausible shadows, and reflections of objects off of reflective surfaces in the scene are not handled correctly. These limitations point to a number of fruitful areas for future work.

Acknowledgement. This work was supported by the UW Reality Lab, Facebook, Google, and Futurewei.

References

1. Azadi, S., Pathak, D., Ebrahimi, S., Darrell, T.: Compositional GAN: learning conditional image composition. arXiv preprint arXiv:1807.07560 (2018)
2. Bose, B., Grimson, E.: Ground plane rectification by tracking moving objects. In: Proceedings of the Joint IEEE International Workshop on Visual Surveillance and Performance Evaluation of Tracking and Surveillance (2003)
3. Brock, A., Donahue, J., Simonyan, K.: Large scale GAN training for high fidelity natural image synthesis. arXiv preprint arXiv:1809.11096 (2018)
4. Brostow, G.J., Essa, I.A.: Motion based decompositing of video. In: Proceedings of the Seventh IEEE International Conference on Computer Vision, vol. 1, pp. 8–13. IEEE (1999)
5. Chuang, Y.Y., Goldman, D.B., Curless, B., Salesin, D.H., Szeliski, R.: Shadow matting and compositing. ACM Trans. Graph. **22**(3), 494–500 (2003). Sepcial Issue of the SIGGRAPH 2003 Proceedings
6. Criminisi, A., Reid, I., Zisserman, A.: Single view metrology. Int. J. Comput. Vis. **40**(2), 123–148 (2000)
7. Debevec, P.: Rendering synthetic objects into real scenes: bridging traditional and image-based graphics with global illumination and high dynamic range photography. In: Proceedings of the 25th Annual Conference on Computer Graphics and Interactive Techniques, SIGGRAPH 1998, pp. 189–198. Association for Computing Machinery, New York, NY, USA (1998). https://doi.org/10.1145/280814.280864
8. Dhamo, H., Tateno, K., Laina, I., Navab, N., Tombari, F.: Peeking behind objects: layered depth prediction from a single image. Pattern Recogn. Lett. **125**, 333–340 (2019)
9. Georgoulis, S., Rematas, K., Ritschel, T., Fritz, M., Tuytelaars, T., Van Gool, L.: What is around the camera? In: Proceedings of the IEEE International Conference on Computer Vision, pp. 5170–5178 (2017)
10. Goodfellow, I., et al.: Generative adversarial nets. In: NIPS (2014)
11. Guo, R., Dai, Q., Hoiem, D.: Paired regions for shadow detection and removal. IEEE Trans. Pattern Anal. Mach. Intell. **35**(12), 2956–2967 (2012)
12. He, K., Gkioxari, G., Dollár, P., Girshick, R.: Mask R-CNN. In: Proceedings of the IEEE International Conference on Computer Vision, pp. 2961–2969 (2017)
13. Hoiem, D., Efros, A.A., Hebert, M.: Putting objects in perspective. IJCV **80**(1), 3–15 (2008)
14. Hold-Geoffroy, Y., Athawale, A., Lalonde, J.F.: Deep sky modeling for single image outdoor lighting estimation. In: Proceedings of the IEEE Conference on Computer Vision and Pattern Recognition, pp. 6927–6935 (2019)
15. Hold-Geoffroy, Y., Sunkavalli, K., Hadap, S., Gambaretto, E., Lalonde, J.F.: Deep outdoor illumination estimation. In: Proceedings of the IEEE Conference on Computer Vision and Pattern Recognition, pp. 7312–7321 (2017)
16. Hong, S., Yan, X., Huang, T.S., Lee, H.: Learning hierarchical semantic image manipulation through structured representations. In: Advances in Neural Information Processing Systems, pp. 2708–2718 (2018)
17. Isola, P., Zhu, J.Y., Zhou, T., Efros, A.A.: Image-to-image translation with conditional adversarial networks. In: Proceedings of the IEEE Conference on Computer Vision and Pattern Recognition, pp. 1125–1134 (2017)

18. Johnson, J., Alahi, A., Fei-Fei, L.: Perceptual losses for real-time style transfer and super-resolution. In: Leibe, B., Matas, J., Sebe, N., Welling, M. (eds.) ECCV 2016. LNCS, vol. 9906, pp. 694–711. Springer, Cham (2016). https://doi.org/10.1007/978-3-319-46475-6_43

19. Kingma, D.P., Welling, M.: Auto-encoding variational Bayes. In: ICLR (2014)

20. Lalonde, J.F., Hoiem, D., Efros, A.A., Rother, C., Winn, J., Criminisi, A.: Photo clip art. ACM Trans. Graph. (TOG) **26**(3), 3-es (2007)

21. Lasinger, K., Ranftl, R., Schindler, K., Koltun, V.: Towards robust monocular depth estimation: Mixing datasets for zero-shot cross-dataset transfer. arXiv preprint arXiv:1907.01341 (2019)

22. Le, H., Samaras, D.: Shadow removal via shadow image decomposition. In: Proceedings of the IEEE International Conference on Computer Vision, pp. 8578–8587 (2019)

23. Le, H., Yago Vicente, T.F., Nguyen, V., Hoai, M., Samaras, D.: A+ d net: training a shadow detector with adversarial shadow attenuation. In: Ferrari, V., Hebert, M., Sminchisescu, C., Weiss, Y. (eds.) Proceedings of the European Conference on Computer Vision (ECCV), vol. 11206, pp. 662–678. Springer, Cham (2018). https://doi.org/10.1007/978-3-030-01216-8_41

24. Lee, D., Liu, S., Gu, J., Liu, M.Y., Yang, M.H., Kautz, J.: Context-aware synthesis and placement of object instances. In: Advances in Neural Information Processing Systems, pp. 10393–10403 (2018)

25. Lee, D., Pfister, T., Yang, M.H.: Inserting videos into videos. In: Proceedings of the IEEE Conference on Computer Vision and Pattern Recognition, pp. 10061–10070 (2019)

26. Lin, C.H., Yumer, E., Wang, O., Shechtman, E., Lucey, S.: ST-GAN: spatial transformer generative adversarial networks for image compositing. In: Proceedings of the IEEE Conference on Computer Vision and Pattern Recognition, pp. 9455–9464 (2018)

27. Liu, R., et al.: An intriguing failing of convolutional neural networks and the Coord-Conv solution. In: Advances in Neural Information Processing Systems, pp. 9605–9616 (2018)

28. Mescheder, L., Geiger, A., Nowozin, S.: Which training methods for gans do actually converge? arXiv preprint arXiv:1801.04406 (2018)

29. Mirza, M., Osindero, S.: Conditional generative adversarial nets. arXiv preprint arXiv:1411.1784 (2014)

30. Miyato, T., Koyama, M.: cGSNs with projection discriminator. arXiv preprint arXiv:1802.05637 (2018)

31. Odena, A., Olah, C., Shlens, J.: Conditional image synthesis with auxiliary classifier gans. In: Proceedings of the 34th International Conference on Machine Learning, vol. 70, pp. 2642–2651. JMLR. org (2017)

32. Ouyang, X., Cheng, Y., Jiang, Y., Li, C.L., Zhou, P.: Pedestrian-synthesis-GAN: generating pedestrian data in real scene and beyond. arXiv preprint arXiv:1804.02047 (2018)

33. Park, J.J., Holynski, A., Seitz, S.: Seeing the world in a bag of chips. arXiv preprint arXiv:2001.04642 (2020)

34. Park, T., Liu, M.Y., Wang, T.C., Zhu, J.Y.: Semantic image synthesis with spatially-adaptive normalization. In: Proceedings of the IEEE Conference on Computer Vision and Pattern Recognition, pp. 2337–2346 (2019)

35. Porter, T., Duff, T.: Compositing digital images. In: Proceedings of the 11th Annual Conference on Computer Graphics and Interactive Techniques, pp. 253–259 (1984)

36. Shade, J., Gortler, S., He, L.w., Szeliski, R.: Layered depth images. In: SIGGRAPH, pp. 231–242. ACM (1998)
37. Srinivasan, P.P., Tucker, R., Barron, J.T., Ramamoorthi, R., Ng, R., Snavely, N.: Pushing the boundaries of view extrapolation with multiplane images. In: Proceedings of the IEEE Conference on Computer Vision and Pattern Recognition, pp. 175–184 (2019)
38. Tulsiani, S., Tucker, R., Snavely, N.: Layer-structured 3D scene inference via view synthesis. In: Ferrari, V., Hebert, M., Sminchisescu, C., Weiss, Y. (eds.) ECCV 2018. LNCS, vol. 11211, pp. 311–327. Springer, Cham (2018). https://doi.org/10.1007/978-3-030-01234-2_19
39. Wang, T.C., Liu, M.Y., Zhu, J.Y., Tao, A., Kautz, J., Catanzaro, B.: High-resolution image synthesis and semantic manipulation with conditional GANs. In: Proceedings of the IEEE Conference on Computer Vision and Pattern Recognition, pp. 8798–8807 (2018)
40. Zhan, F., Zhu, H., Lu, S.: Spatial fusion GAN for image synthesis. In: Proceedings of the IEEE Conference on Computer Vision and Pattern Recognition, pp. 3653–3662 (2019)
41. Zhang, L., Zhang, Q., Xiao, C.: Shadow remover: image shadow removal based on illumination recovering optimization. IEEE Trans. Image Process. 24(11), 4623–4636 (2015)
42. Zhou, T., Tucker, R., Flynn, J., Fyffe, G., Snavely, N.: Stereo magnification: learning view synthesis using multiplane images. arXiv preprint arXiv:1805.09817 (2018)

Mapping in a Cycle: Sinkhorn Regularized Unsupervised Learning for Point Cloud Shapes

Lei Yang[1], Wenxi Liu[2,1], Zhiming Cui[1], Nenglun Chen[1], and Wenping Wang[1(✉)]

[1] Department of Computer Science, The University of Hong Kong, Hong Kong, China
{lyang,zmcui,nlchen,wenping}@cs.hku.hk
[2] College of Mathematics and Computer Science, Fuzhou University, Fuzhou, China
wenxi.liu@hotmail.com

Abstract. We propose an unsupervised learning framework with the pretext task of finding dense correspondences between point cloud shapes from the same category based on the cycle-consistency formulation. In order to learn discriminative pointwise features from point cloud data, we incorporate in the formulation a regularization term based on Sinkhorn normalization to enhance the learned pointwise mappings to be as bijective as possible. Besides, a random rigid transform of the source shape is introduced to form a triplet cycle to improve the model's robustness against perturbations. Comprehensive experiments demonstrate that the learned pointwise features through our framework benefits various point cloud analysis tasks, e.g. partial shape registration and keypoint transfer. We also show that the learned pointwise features can be leveraged by supervised methods to improve the part segmentation performance with either the full training dataset or just a small portion of it.

Keywords: Point cloud · Unsupervised learning · Dense correspondence · Cycle-consistency

1 Introduction

Point clouds are unordered sets of interacting points sampled from surface of objects for 3D shape representation, and have been widely used in computer vision, graphics, robotics, etc. for their accessibility and flexibility. With the recent advancement of deep learning techniques, a spectrum of networks have been proposed to process point cloud data and to learn to perform various tasks, e.g. [25,26,32,33,47], which have achieved tremendous progress. However, a major limitation of deep networks is their data hunger nature that requires a large amount of supervisory signals to learn a satisfactory task-specific model. Therefore, many attempts have been made to alleviate this issue, and among others

Electronic supplementary material The online version of this chapter (https://doi.org/10.1007/978-3-030-58607-2_27) contains supplementary material, which is available to authorized users.

© Springer Nature Switzerland AG 2020
A. Vedaldi et al. (Eds.): ECCV 2020, LNCS 12355, pp. 455–472, 2020.
https://doi.org/10.1007/978-3-030-58607-2_27

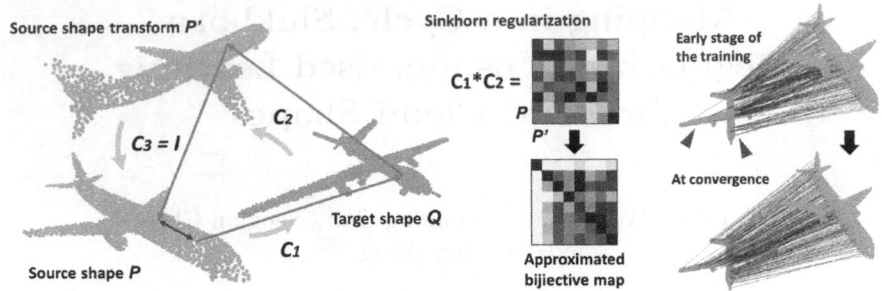

Fig. 1. We train a neural network in an unsupervised manner to derive dense correspondences between point cloud shapes based on the cycle-consistency formulation. Given a source shape $\mathcal{P}$, its rigid transform $\mathcal{P}'$ and a target one $\mathcal{Q}$, the cycle is completed by mapping every point in $\mathcal{P}$, via C_1, C_2, C_3, and finally back to $\mathcal{P}$ (left). The red segment indicates the measure of the cycle deviation which is minimized during the unsupervised training. Within the cycle, the correspondence map formed by the mappings C_1 and C_2 is constrained to approximate a bijective map by Sinkhorn regularization, significantly reducing the number of many-to-one correspondences (right). (Color figure online)

training deep networks in an unsupervised manner (without manually labeled data) shows its potential in many scenarios [5,10,29]. In the case of 3D point clouds, these techniques are in demand as it is prohibitive to attain accurate, densely labeled ground-truth on point clouds for various shape analysis tasks.

As one of unsupervised learning approaches, algorithms based on cycle consistency have attracted interests in many vision-based applications, e.g., video object segmentation [44] and facial landmark detection [39], as well as some recent 3D shape analysis works [13,19,46,55]. Intuitively, a cycle consistent transformation between a pair of data instances shall map one data instance to the other, and then transform it backward with little deviation. With a pretext defined, such as registration [46] or deformation [13], one can leverage the cycle consistency formulation between a pair of unlabeled data, model the transformation with a neural network, and thus optimize the network parameters by minimizing the cycle deviation.

In this work, we leverage such a formulation to pre-train the neural network in an unsupervised manner, and aim to learn pointwise features for subsequent 3D point cloud applications. Specifically, the pretext in our setting is to find dense correspondences between two point cloud shapes using the learned pointwise features. In particular, given a pair of source and target shapes, we intend to find, for each point in the source, its corresponding point in the target. Then, starting from the target ones, we search reversely their corresponding points in the source. During this process we minimize the cycle deviation of each reversely corresponded point from its original location in the source. In this way, the network parameters can be optimized and expected to encode each point to a high-dimensional descriptor for correspondence query.

While dense correspondences between contents have been exploited in many image-based applications (e.g. [38,44]), this self-supervised framework encounters two major challenges when dealing with point cloud data. First, since the point clouds are usually sampled from smooth 3D surfaces, each point embeds very limited information as opposite to image pixels with rich textures. This precludes the network training based on cycle consistency as the obtained correspondence may map a point to a wrong but spatially proximate location, forming a many-to-one mapping while yielding a small loss. Thus, the learned representation may suffer from this sub-optimality and fail to attain sufficient distinctiveness for correspondence query and potential applications. Second, many point-based networks based on cycle consistency assume the shapes are well aligned, and thus are sensitive to rotations. This makes the extracted features unrobust to small perturbations, and may become less applicable in many applications.

To address the first and primary concern, we propose a novel regularization technique to strengthen the pointwise correspondences to be as bijective as possible. We thus impose a bijective constraint on the cycle-back correspondence by adopting the Sinkhorn normalization technique [24,37]. We term this constraint as Sinkhorn regularization in our paper.

We also introduce, into the cycle, an additional shape which is a random rigid transform of the source shape, forming a 3-edge cycle as shown in Fig. 1. In this particular setting, each point starting from the source first finds its corresponding point in the target (i.e. C_1 in Fig. 1), and then arrives at the source transform (i.e. C_2). Since the last transport edge (i.e. C_3) from the source transform to its origin provides us the ground-truth dense correspondences that form a one-to-one map, we can safely impose the bijective constraint by Sinkhorn regularization on this particular edge without assuming any shape pair should meet the bijective constraint. Further, unlike traditional cycle consistency methods on shapes, the introduction of a transformed shape allows the network and the learned pointwise features to be less sensitive against non-aligned point cloud data. This partially addresses the second challenge as mentioned before, thus making the learned pointwise features appealing to many downstream tasks.

To demonstrate the effectiveness of our proposed framework, we conduct comprehensive experiments, in which we leverage the pointwise features learned from our model to perform partial shape registration, keypoint transfer, and as an additional pre-trained feature for supervised part segmentation. In these experiments, it is demonstrated that our approach can surpass the state-of-the-art methods or be comparable to their performances. Contributions of this paper are summarized as follows:

1) A novel unsupervised learning framework based on cycle-consistent dense correspondences between point cloud shapes of the same category;
2) The Sinkhorn regularization that brings a large improvement on learning discriminative pointwise features;
3) Extensive evaluation showing the effectiveness of the proposed unsupervised learning strategy in multiple point cloud analysis tasks.

2 Related Work

Deep Unsupervised Methodology and Applications. Unsupervised learning methodology has emerged to address one of the major concerns for data-driven algorithms – the need for a large set of labeled data, and has achieved state-of-the-art performances in many applications in language [10] and images [5,17]. To this end, a pretext is often required for network pretraining and representation learning, such as by contrastive learning [17,29,31,40,50], mutual information maximization [41], reconstruction [36], and correspondence [11,39,44].

Deep Unsupervised Point Cloud Analysis. Point-based networks have demonstrated their capability in many shape analysis tasks, such as classification, segmentation, reconstruction and registration [9,26,32,33,47,48,53]. To enforce the network to learn semantically meaningful and consistent representations, many pretext tasks have been designed such as part re-arranging [36], half-to-half prediction [15], deformation [12,13], and self-supervised classification and clustering [16]. Many of these works rely on the reconstruction metric as an indicator for the unsupervised training process [9,12,54]. In this paper, we provide an alternative viewpoint that is complementary to the prior works. Instead of geometric reconstruction of the content, we consider the pretext of finding dense correspondences between shapes, and solve it as a *soft permutation recovery problem* for the indices of points in point cloud.

Learning from 3D Shape Correspondences. 3D shape correspondence has long been an exciting topic in 3D shape modeling [14,20–22,35,42]. Many state-of-the-art works have leveraged dense correspondences to learn and perform various shape analysis tasks. [6–8,53] design network architectures to learn local contextual descriptors via the task of 3D scan registration. This is amiable especially in the case of scene understanding and processing. As for the analysis of man-made shapes, [45,46] and [2] instill classical methodologies (e.g. iterative closest point) in the neural network design and achieve state-of-the-art performance. In our case, we are more focused on learning pointwise features that are consistent across man-made shapes and thus differ from these studies.

In pursuit of such pointwise latent representations of man-made shapes, [4,18,30] make use of rough dense shape correspondence as supervision and demonstrate promising performance in shape correspondence. Alternatively, cycle consistency, initially proposed in [19], has been widely employed to establish correspondences between diverse data in an unsupervised manner, on images [55,56], videos [11,44], and more recently on point cloud data [13].

In line of these prior works, we build our unsupervised learning framework based on cycle consistency to process point cloud shapes. Different from prior arts [13,46] that evaluate cycle consistency by measuring shape discrepancy, we innovatively cast the problem of finding dense correspondences as solving permutation on point clouds. This particular design provides an alternative view to existing works and allows the network to learn a pointwise representation. While the unsupervised learning works [13,46] focus on their pretexts such as deformation and registration, we show a variety of applications with the proposed network as well as the learned pointwise representation. We further propose a novel Sinkhorn regularization in the cycle consistency framework to enforce the learned pointwise features to be sparsely corresponded for different instances.

3   Methodology

Our overarching goal is to learn, without manual labels, a category-specific point-wise encoding that benefits the downstream applications such as shape registration, keypoint detection and part segmentation. To this end, we train the network via a pretext task of finding dense correspondences between two point cloud shape instances based on the cycle-consistent pointwise encoding features learned through the proposed framework.

3.1   Unsupervised Loss Based on Cycle Consistency

The pretext of finding cycle-consistent dense correspondences is depicted in Fig. 1. We denote the source shape $\mathcal{P}$, its random rigid transform $\mathcal{P}'$, and the target $\mathcal{Q}$, forming a 3-edge cycle from $\mathcal{P}$ to $\mathcal{Q}$ (mapping C_1), then from $\mathcal{Q}$ to $\mathcal{P}'$ (mapping C_2), and finally return to $\mathcal{P}$ from $\mathcal{P}'$ (mapping C_3). In order to formulate it as an optimization problem, with the dense correspondences between shapes, our goal is to minimize the deviation between each cycle-back point and its origin (i.e. the red segment in Fig. 1), thus enforcing the cycle consistency.

Correspondence Query Between Point Cloud Shapes. We use a point-based neural network, denoted as f_θ with trainable parameters θ, to learn the pointwise features, which will be employed for the correspondence query. We denote a point using its index as p_k where $p_k \in \{0,1\}^{|\mathcal{P}|}$ is a one-hot vector with the k-th entry equal to 1 and the rest to 0. The corresponding 3D coordinate of p_k is denoted by $\mathbf{p}_k$. If a particular point q_i from shape $\mathcal{Q}$ is said to correspond to p_k from $\mathcal{P}$, then the associated learned representation $f_\theta(q_i)$ is more similar with $f_\theta(p_k)$ than all other points in $\mathcal{Q}$ as below:

$$i = \arg \max_{q_j \in \mathcal{Q}} S(f_\theta(p_k), f_\theta(q_j)), \tag{1}$$

where $S(\cdot, \cdot)$ measures the similarity between any two pointwise representations and is defined as their inner product. Since the operator arg max is not differentiable, we approximate the solution to the above equation by a scaled softmax function:

$$q_i \approx C(\mathcal{Q}, p_k; f_\theta) = \frac{\exp(f_\theta(p_k)^T f_\theta(q_j)/\tau)}{\sum_j \exp(f_\theta(p_k)^T f_\theta(q_j)/\tau)}, \tag{2}$$

where $C(\mathcal{Q}, p_k; f_\theta)$ is a vector that represents the probability that p_k corresponds to all points in $\mathcal{Q}$. Thus, the dense correspondences from $\mathcal{P}$ to $\mathcal{Q}$ can be approximated as follow:

$$\mathbf{Q} \approx C(\mathcal{Q}, \mathcal{P}; f_\theta). \tag{3}$$

where, ideally, $\mathbf{Q}$ is expected to be a permutation matrix, establishing a one-to-one mapping between two given shapes $\mathcal{P}$ and $\mathcal{Q}$.

Cycle-Consistency Loss. In this paper, we use three shapes to form a 3-edge cycle $\{\mathcal{P} \rightarrow \mathcal{Q} \rightarrow \mathcal{P}' \rightarrow \mathcal{P}\}$, where $\mathcal{P}$ and $\mathcal{Q}$ are termed the source and the target shapes, respectively, and $\mathcal{P}'$ is a random rigid transform of $\mathcal{P}$ that helps increase the robustness of the model. Thus, with the cycle-consistency condition met, this closed cycle should finally bring every point (in terms of index and not spatial coordinates) back to its origin index via the following mappings,

$$C_{cycle}(\mathcal{P}) = C_3(\mathcal{P}, \mathcal{P}')C_2(\mathcal{P}', \mathcal{Q})C_1(\mathcal{Q}, \mathcal{P}) = C_3(\mathcal{P}, \mathcal{P}')C_{1,2}(\mathcal{P}', \mathcal{P}), \qquad (4)$$

where $C_{cycle}(\mathcal{P})$ shall be the identity matrix that brings points in $\mathcal{P}$ back to its origin index via C_1, C_2, and C_3. Similarly, $C_{1,2}(\mathcal{P}', \mathcal{P})$ forms the mapping from the source shape $\mathcal{P}$ to the transformed shape $\mathcal{P}'$ via $\mathcal{Q}$. To measure the cycle deviation from the above formulation, a loss should be defined

$$d_{cycle} = D(\mathbf{I}_{|\mathcal{P}|}, C_{cycle}(\mathcal{P})), \qquad (5)$$

where $\mathbf{I}_{|\mathcal{P}|}$ is the identity matrix of size $|\mathcal{P}|$.

As we introduce a rigid transform to the end of the cycle list, the cycle mapping mainly depends on two parts, i.e., $C_{1,2}(\mathcal{P}', \mathcal{P})$ and $C_3(\mathcal{P}, \mathcal{P}')$, in Eq. 4. First, as rigid transformations in $\mathbb{R}^3$ do not alter the permutation of the point cloud data. So, when it is perfectly estimated, $C_3(\mathcal{P}, \mathcal{P}')$ should be the identity matrix that maintains the original permutation of $\mathcal{P}$. On the other hand, the mapping $C_{1,2}$ from $\mathcal{P}$ to $\mathcal{P}'$ (via $\mathcal{Q}$), in an ideal situation, should be the identity matrix as well. Hence, the cycle loss minimization can be reduced to minimize two terms, $D(\mathbf{I}_{|\mathcal{P}|}, C_{1,2}(\mathcal{P}', \mathcal{P}))$ and $D(\mathbf{I}_{|\mathcal{P}|}, C_3(\mathcal{P}, \mathcal{P}'))$.

One way to concretely define $D(\cdot, \cdot)$ is to use KL-divergence or cross-entropy losses to formulate the problem as classification. However, minimizing such *thousand*-way classification losses may be difficult at the beginning and overlook, during the course of optimization, the underlying geometric relationship of the points cloud shapes. Therefore, we cast the cycle consistency loss in a regression form similar to the losses used in [11,38]. This way, we impose a soft penalty on the wrong cycles relying on the distances from their correct correspondences,

$$\mathcal{L}_C = \|D(\mathcal{P}) \otimes C_{1,2}(\mathcal{P}', \mathcal{P})\|_1, \qquad (6)$$

where $D(\mathcal{P}) = \{d_{p,p'} = d_{Euclid}(\mathbf{p}, \mathbf{p}'), \forall \mathbf{p}, \mathbf{p}' \in \mathcal{P}\}$ measures the Euclidean distance between a pair of points in $\mathcal{P}$ and $\otimes$ is the element-wise product. Here the Euclidean distance is adopted for simplicity and computational efficiency, but one may employ more accurate geodesics distance for training. Note that the diagonals of $D(\mathcal{P})$ are zeros, which makes the loss of Eq. 6 to be zero when $C_{1,2}(\mathcal{P}', \mathcal{P})$ converges to be an identity matrix. This loss is thus equivalent to the classification-based formulation at convergence, while additionally taking the spatial proximity of points into consideration. Similarly, we formulate $D(\mathbf{I}_{|\mathcal{P}|}, C_3(\mathcal{P}, \mathcal{P}'))$ as follow:

$$\mathcal{L}_R = \|D(\mathcal{P}) \otimes C_3(\mathcal{P}, \mathcal{P}')\|_1. \qquad (7)$$

3.2   Sinkhorn Regularization for Bijective Constraint

Optimizing the regression-based cycle loss can converge to the correct correspondences as demonstrated in many image-based applications [11,38]. However, the convergence will be slowed down or even get stuck in the case of 3D point cloud data. This is because the decaying distance-based penalty imposed in Eq. 6 cannot provide a sufficient magnitude of loss that encourages the network to distinguish nearby points as the optimization proceeds. Thus, it may still result in many-to-one mappings and thus wrong cycles, leading to undesirable results.

To address this issue, we introduce a so-called Sinkhorn regularization term, L_S, in addition to the previous ones. This design relies on the fact that $C_{1,2}(\mathcal{P}', \mathcal{P})$ in our setting should ideally form a bijective map. Instead of directly enforcing $C_{1,2}$ to be the identity matrix, we *relax* this constraint to any permutation matrices, retaining the bijective property. The reason of using a relaxed bijective map instead of the identity is that while this relaxation penalizes the deviation of $C_{1,2}$ from a permutation, the synergistic effect of L_S and L_C gradually makes $C_{1,2}$ converge to the identity as the training proceeds. This novel relaxation brings the performance gain by a large margin in terms of the percentage of correct cycle-consistent correspondences, as shown in the ablation study (Sect. 4.2).

We follow the methods proposed in [1,28] to enforce this constraint and describe it to make our paper self-contained. One may compute the optimal approximant to $C_{1,2}$ from the permutation set $\mathbb{P}$ with dimension $|\mathcal{P}|$,

$$X^* = \arg\max_{X \in \mathbb{P}_{|\mathcal{P}|}}\langle X, C_{1,2}\rangle_F, \tag{8}$$

where $\langle X, C_{1,2}\rangle_F$ denotes the Frobenius inner product of the two matrices. As solving the above linear assignment problem (Eq. 8) is generally NP-hard, the constraint can be further relaxed to solve the best approximation of $C_{1,2}$ from the set of doubly stochastic matrices $\mathbb{B}_{|\mathcal{P}|}$,

$$\tilde{X} = \arg\max_{X \in \mathbb{B}_{|\mathcal{P}|}}\langle X, C_{1,2}\rangle_F. \tag{9}$$

Solving the maximization problem of Eq. 9 has been shown to be exceptionally simple by taking row-wise and column-wise softmax normalizations in an alternating fashion. This is known as the Sinkhorn normalization [37] where $\tilde{X}$ shall meet the following conditions at convergence:

$$\tilde{X}\mathbf{1} = \mathbf{1}, \quad \tilde{X}^T\mathbf{1} = \mathbf{1}, \quad \text{and } \tilde{X} \in \mathbb{B}_{|\mathcal{P}|}. \tag{10}$$

While the solution to Eq. 9 can be reached in a limit sense, practically a truncated Sinkhorn normalization [1] is used to obtain a fair approximation,

$$\tilde{X} \approx SH(C_{1,2}; t, l), \tag{11}$$

where two hyper-parameters, i.e., the number of iterations l for the column-wise and row-wise normalization and the temperature t for softmax normalization are to be furnished. We adopt this truncated Sinkhorn normalizaltion and set t and l to be 0.3 and 30 across all our experiments.

Sinkhorn Regularization. Accordingly, during the network optimization we add the following Sinkhorn regularizaton to the loss function:

$$\mathcal{L}_S = \|C_{1,2}(\mathcal{P}', \mathcal{P}) - SH(C_{1,2}; t, l)\|_1. \tag{12}$$

This loss term enforces $C_{1,2}$ to be a bijective map, and thus encourages the neural network f to learn discriminative pointwise features by reducing many-to-one mappings between point clouds $\mathcal{P}$ and $\mathcal{Q}$ which $C_{1,2}$ traverses. As it is derived based on $C_{1,2}$, $SH(C_{1,2}; t, l)$ keeps its closeness to $C_{1,2}$ at every iteration step. Thus, this formulation provides a gradual guidance for $C_{1,2}$ to become a permutation matrix ensuring the bijective property.

3.3 Loss Function

To sum up, the loss function of our unsupervised framework consists of three terms, as below:

$$\mathcal{L} = \lambda_C \mathcal{L}_C + \lambda_R \mathcal{L}_R + \lambda_S \mathcal{L}_S, \tag{13}$$

where λ_C, λ_R, and λ_S are predefined coefficients for balancing these loss terms. By the loss term $\mathcal{L}_C$, we can constrain the chained mapping $C_{1,2}(\mathcal{P}', \mathcal{P})$ to be an identity matrix. In addition, as we explicitly require the last shape to be some random rigid transform $\mathcal{P}'$ of the source $\mathcal{P}$, L_R enforces the learned representation to be robust to mild rotations. Moreover, L_S encourages the correspondence to be as bijective as possible, benefiting the pointwise representation learning.

3.4 Network Architecture

Our network takes 1024 points as input from a point cloud shape sampled by the farthest sampling technique, and outputs pointwise representations of dimension 64. PointNet++ [33] is adopted as the backbone for unsupervised learning, and trained with Eq. 13. Other backbones (e.g. DGCNN [47]) may be applicable but we limit our discussion here to PointNet++.

In addition, we incorporate the multi-head attention module (see [25,43]) in between adjacent layers of the original PointNet++. The motivation of such design is to combine both local information gathered by convolution-like operations and non-local information by self-attention modules to benefit the unsupervised learning process. For details of the network architecture, please refer to our supplementary materials.

4   Experimental Results

4.1   Implementation and Results of the Unsupervised Pretraining

We pre-train the proposed networks on the pretext of finding dense correspondences on *ShapeNet part segmentation* dataset [52]. *ShapeNet part segmentation* dataset contains 16 categories of shapes, each of which is represented by a point

Fig. 2. Visualization of the learned pointwise representations on rotated shapes from different categories, i.e., *Airplane*, *Table*, *Guitar*, *Skateboard*, and *Chair*. Color-codes reflect the consistency of the learned pointwise representations across a variety of shape instances, even if the shapes are under perturbation of rigid transformations

set and associated with normals and the part labels. The number of parts per shape in a category varies from 2 to 6, totaling 50 parts in the dataset. All the point clouds are pre-aligned.

Training data are augmented with random rotations, translations and scalings sampled from a uniform distribution. The rotations and translations along each coordinate axis are sampled from the range $[-15deg, +15deg]$ and $[-0.2, +0.2]$, respectively; and the uniform scaling factor ranges from $[0.8, 1.25]$. These random transformations are applied to each of the training triplet, i.e., source shape, its rigid transform, and the target. We first sample a source shape and a target one from the same category, and then apply two sets of random transformations described above to the source and one set of random transformations to the target, respectively. Thus, three transformed shapes are generated, forming a triplet, i.e. the source, its rigid transform, and the target, for training.

We use a variant [34] of the Adam optimizer [23] with $\beta_1 = 0.900$ and $\beta_2 = 0.999$ across all experiments presented in the paper. The learning rates for bias and the rest of parameters are set to 0.0001 and 0.0005, respectively, without decay during the training process. Balancing coefficients $\lambda_{C,R,S}$ are set to $1.0, 1.0, 0.06$ to weight each loss term for the network pre-training. All network models are trained with an NVIDIA GeForce GTX 1080Ti graphical card.

We randomly sample a set of perturbed shapes with random rigid transformations as described above, and visualize their pointwise features in Fig. 2. The features are dimension-reduced via t-SNE [27] and color-coded to reflect their similarity. Although the shapes are randomly transformed, the visualization shows that our learned representations on various non-aligned shape instances are consistent. More qualitative results can be found in the supplementary.

4.2 Ablation Study

We validate our network design and our proposed training strategy in this subsection. For evaluation, we employ the ratio of correct cycle matches $(CC\%)$

during training and validation as the metrics, which indicates the success rate of completing cycle-consistent correspondences. Point-cloud shapes from three categories, i.e. Airplane, Chair, and Table, from the *ShapeNet part segmentation* dataset are adopted for evaluation.

Different settings are compared to justify our proposed framework with the designed loss function (Eq. 13) and the self-attention module. We first evaluate two variants of the loss functions: 1) removing the bijective constraint enabled by the Sinkhorn regularization (w/o L_S); and 2) enforcing the correspondence matrix to be the identity matrix instead of permutation matrices (i.e. replacing Eq. 11 by $L_I = \|C_{1,2} - \mathbf{I}\|_1$, denoted L_I). The comparison results are depicted in Table 1. As can be seen from the second row block of Table 1, our complete loss function (*Ours*) produces the best result among the three settings. The performances of the other two settings, i.e. w/o L_S and L_I, are similar.

The performance gain by Sinkhorn regularization is mainly due to the penalty it imposes on the many-to-one correspondences, which smoothly increases as the training proceeds and thus drives the resulting mapping as much close to a bijective map as possible. On the contrary, the setting without such a constraint (w/o L_S) would indulge many-to-one mappings; and the setting (L_I) that enforces the mapping to identity would be too difficult for training at the very beginning stage, thus impeding the convergence.

As shown in Fig. 3, we compare the $CC\%$ of testing using the models obtained at different training iterations, in which the higher results are better. As observed, after training for more than 2000 iterations, the results w/ L_S (in solid curves) perform significantly better than the ones w/o L_S (in dashed curves), which shows the advantage of our proposed Sinkhorn regularization.

In addition, we compare our network structure with self-attention modules against the vanilla PointNet++. As observed from Table 1, our results are higher than those produced by the vanilla PointNet++. This is primarily because the self-attention modules will attend to long-range dependency that convolution-like operations overlook at the entrancing levels. Note that, although using the network structure equipped with self-attention modules, the two settings (L_I and w/o L_S) are generally inferior to the vanilla PointNet++ (w/o *self-attention*) trained with the Sinkhorn regularization, revealing that it is the primary contributor to the performance gain. Besides, we also evaluate the input of our model. As shown in Table 1, the performance will be degraded without normals as inputs. But such a decrease in performance is relatively small, comparing to settings of L_I and w/o L_S that use normals.

4.3   Applications to Shape Analysis Tasks

As the pointwise features learned by the proposed unsupervised framework method are independent of the subsequent tasks, we demonstrate their applicability to the following point cloud analysis tasks: partial-to-partial shape registration, keypoint transfer via correspondence, and supervised part segmentation.

Table 1. Ablation study on different loss terms, network structures, and the input of our model. $CC\%$ denotes the percentage of the correct cycle matches. We compare the metrics on three categories of data: *Airplane, Chair* and *Table*

Category	Airplane		Chair		Table		Mean	
$CC\%$	Train	Val.	Train	Val.	Train	Val.	Train	Val.
Ours	69.4	67.9	68.7	69.4	67.1	65.1	68.4	67.5
w/o L_S	44.8	44.9	40.4	41.0	40.5	39.1	41.9	41.5
L_I (replacing L_S)	40.6	42.0	61.4	62.0	43.4	42.2	48.8	48.7
w/o self-attention	51.5	49.9	51.0	51.4	50.6	48.8	51.0	50.0
w/o normals	57.6	56.6	63.6	64.9	48.3	47.3	56.5	56.3

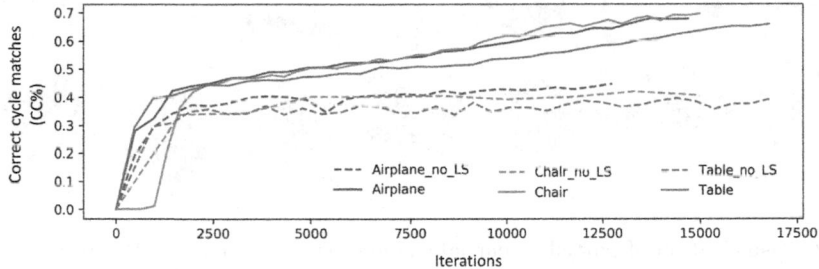

Fig. 3. Performances with the Sinkhorn regularization L_S (solid) or without it (dashed) are compared in terms of the percentages of correct cycle matches ($CC\%$) on three data categories, showing that the Sinkhorn regularization can facilitate the optimization and achieves consistently better results

Partial-to-Partial Shape Registration. To perform partial shape registration between a shape and its rigid transform, we leverage the obtained pointwise correspondence between these two shapes, and compute a rigid transformation [3] to perform shape registration. To this end, we first pre-train our network on the pretext as described above. We then fine-tune it with more emphasis on the rigid transformation term L_R by setting $\lambda_{C,R,S} = 0.0001, 1.0, 0.06$.

We compare, in a category-specific manner, our results to those produced by PRNet [46] on five categories of shapes from *ModelNet40* [49]. We follow the training settings in [46] by using 1024 points to train our network and PRNet with respect to each category data. It is worthy noting that different from their training strategy where a portion of points are subtracted from input data to mimic partial point clouds, we do not apply this specialized data augmentation to our training data. During test time, a shape with 1024 points is truncated to 768 points to produce a partial point cloud. Both our method and PRNet perform 3 iterative estimations for pose registration. Same random transformations are applied to generating a consistent testing set, ensuring a fair, category-specific comparison between our method and PRNet.

We evaluate the comparison results using the metrics Root Mean Square Error (RMSE) and Mean Absolute Error (MAE). As shown in Table 2, our

Table 2. Category-specific comparison with PRNet [46] for partial-to-partial registration on unseen point clouds. Bold values refer to the better performance.

Category		Aeroplane		Car		Chair		Table		Lamp	
Metric		[46]	Ours	[46]	Ours	[46]	Ours	[46]	Ours	[46]	Ours
Rotation	RMSE	7.206	**4.287**	15.42	**4.678**	**4.93**	6.202	39.6	**3.13**	37.1	**21.85**
	MAE	3.78	**3.532**	7.58	**3.876**	**3.09**	5.279	23.7	**2.71**	23.1	**18.22**
Translation	RMSE	0.047	**0.018**	0.127	**0.018**	0.027	**0.015**	0.175	**0.017**	0.174	**0.0476**
	MAE	0.030	**0.016**	0.096	**0.015**	0.019	**0.013**	0.124	**0.015**	0.125	**0.0418**

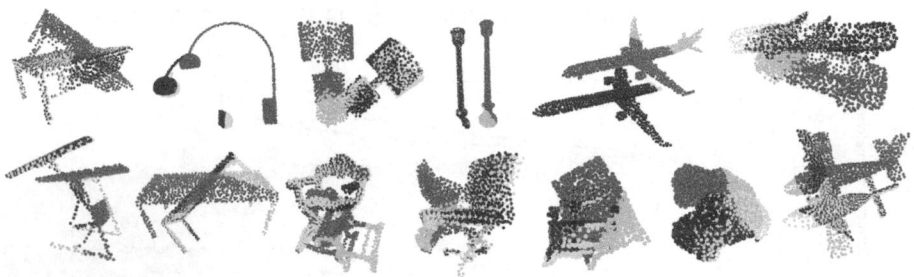

Fig. 4. Visualization of partial-to-partial shape registration results. Purple and green point clouds are the source and target poses of a shape; the blue are the obtained results via three iterative match-and-transform; and the grey parts are those randomly truncated during the testing stage (Color figure online)

network can achieve results better than or at least comparable to PRNet (trained in a category-specific manner) across the listed categories. An exception is the *Chair* category in terms of the rotation metrics. Some registration results are randomly selected and visualized in Fig. 4 where shapes in purple, green and blue represent the source pose, target pose and our result, respectively.

Keypoint Transfer via Correspondences. Keypoints are a group of sparsely defined landmarks on a shape, crucial for many shape analysis applications. In this part, we demonstrate the learned pointwise representations can be leveraged to transfer a set of keypoints defined on a shape to other shapes alike. We compare our results to several state-of-the-art unsupervised learning methods for 3D shapes, i.e. [9,51] based on autoencoder structures and [4,30] based on pointwise feature learning (similar to ours). All methods are trained on the *Airplane, Chair*, and *Bike* data from the *ShapeNet part segmentation* dataset in a category-specifc, unsupervised manner. Shapes are pre-aligned for training and testing to conduct fair comparison. Evaluation is made on the test set in [18] where ground-truth keypoints of around 100 shapes per category are provided and each shape may contains 6 to 12 keypoints.

Table 3. Results of keypoint transfer comparing with the state-of-the-art methods. The results are measured by the percentage of the keypoints with the distance error less than 0.05. Bold values refer to the top performance

	LMVCNN [18]	AtlasNet [9]	FoldingNet [51]	EdgeNet [4]	ShapeUnicode [30]	Ours
Airplane	30.3	51.1	26.6	33.5	30.8	**57.9**
Chair	12.0	37.3	16.2	12.6	25.4	**40.4**
Bike	17.4	34.2	31.7	27.2	**58.3**	49.8
Mean	19.9	40.9	24.9	24.4	38.2	**49.4**

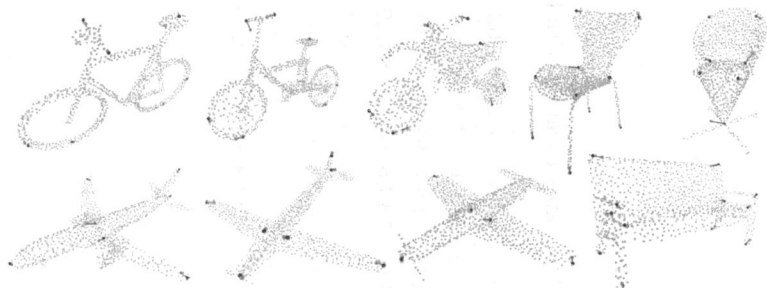

Fig. 5. Visualization of the key point transfer task. Blue points are the ground-truth landmarks while points in magenta are estimated by our network (Color figure online)

Given a point cloud shape, $\mathcal{P}$, with several 3D keypoints, we find their corresponding points in another given shape $\mathcal{Q}$. As the ground-truth keypoints are not given as a particular point in the point cloud data, we first sample 5 neighboring points from the point cloud and then search for each of the neighbors its correspondence point in $\mathcal{Q}$ via the learned pointwise features. Finally, we simply average the correspondence points to predict the corresponding keypoints in $\mathcal{Q}$.

We measure the distance error between the ground-truth keypoints and the predicted ones with the Euclidean metric. Noticing that the distance error greater than 0.05 is a relatively large value for a shape whose size is normalized with respect to its shape diameter, we show the percentage of keypoints with the distance error smaller than this threshold in Table 3. As shown in the table, our result generally outperforms the other existing methods, except a slight fall behind ShapeUnicode [30] on the category of *Bike*, showing the effectiveness of the learned pointwise representations in correspondence query. Some qualitative results are shown in Fig. 5.

Supervised Part Segmentation. To demonstrate the ability of the learned pointwise representations as a feature to boost subsequent applications, we also use them as additional features to train a supervised part segmentation network. In particular, we adopt the PointNet++ [33] as a baseline for this supervised task.

Table 4. Comparison of the segmentation results on *ShapeNet part segmentation* dataset trained with full and 10% of the dataset

Full train	aero.	bag	cap	car	chair	ear.	guitar	knife	lamp	laptop	motor	mug	pistol	rocket	skate.	table	mean
[32]	83.40	78.70	82.50	74.90	89.60	**73.00**	91.50	85.90	80.80	95.30	65.20	93.00	81.20	57.90	72.80	80.60	83.7
[33]	82.30	79.00	**87.70**	77.30	**90.80**	71.80	91.00	85.90	**83.70**	95.30	71.60	94.10	81.30	58.70	**76.40**	82.60	85.1
Ours	82.66	**81.97**	79.96	**78.03**	85.77	70.12	**91.61**	**86.53**	81.81	**96.03**	**73.55**	**95.57**	**83.49**	**59.10**	75.39	**88.23**	**85.5**
10% train	aero	bag	cap	car	chair	ear	guitar	knife	lamp	laptop	motor	mug	pistol	rocket	skate	table	mean
[32]	76.10	69.80	62.60	61.40	86.00	62.10	86.20	79.70	73.60	93.30	59.10	83.40	75.90	41.80	57.70	74.80	77.3
[33]	76.40	43.40	77.80	**75.52**	**87.50**	67.70	87.40	77.40	71.40	94.10	61.30	90.40	72.80	**51.40**	**68.70**	75.30	78.6
Ours	**77.09**	**73.24**	**81.80**	74.39	84.71	**70.23**	**88.37**	**84.23**	**76.63**	**94.12**	**62.98**	**91.29**	**80.60**	51.25	65.02	**77.94**	**79.8**

During this supervised training for part segmentation, the proposed network pre-trained on the dense correspondence pretext is frozen and serves as a feature extractor. We compare the part segmentation results obtained with our additional input features and with the original inputs containing point coordinates and normals only. As can be seen from Table 4, the results with our pointwise features are improved in most categories. The part-averaged mean IoU (Intersection-over-Union) reaches 85.5%, higher than the performance obtained by the PointNet++.

On the other hand, when we train the network with 10% of the labeled training data (without fine-tuning the pre-trained network), the performance gains are observed in 12 out of 16 categories, many of which outperforms the original results by a large margin (i.e. up to 7%). In this setting, we achieve a part-averaged mean IoU of 79.8%.

5   Conclusions and Future Work

This paper proposes a pretext of finding dense correspondences between two different shapes for unsupervised learning of pointwise features for point cloud shapes and formulates a cycle-consistency based framework to solve this problem. In order to learn discriminative pointwise features, we force the cycle correspondences to be as bijective as possible using the Sinkhorn regularization. Ablation study validates the design and effectiveness of the proposed unsupervised framework. Furthermore, we demonstrate the applicability of acquired pointwise features in downstream tasks: partial-to-partial shape registration, unsupervised keypoint transfer, and supervised part segmentation.

While geometric correspondences can be effectively learned by the proposed approach, such correspondences learned in this unsupervised manner may fail to capture the semantic meaning of the shapes. As future work, we would like to explore solutions to this problem based on the proposed unsupervised framework.

Acknowledgement. We acknowledge valuable comments from anonymous reviewers. Our work is supported in part by Hong Kong Innovation and Technology Fund ITS/457/17FP.

References

1. Adams, R.P., Zemel, R.S.: Ranking via Sinkhorn propagation. arXiv preprint arXiv:1106.1925 (2011)
2. Aoki, Y., Goforth, H., Srivatsan, R.A., Lucey, S.: PointNetLK: robust & efficient point cloud registration using PointNet. In: Proceedings of the IEEE Conference on Computer Vision and Pattern Recognition, pp. 7163–7172 (2019)
3. Arun, K.S., Huang, T.S., Blostein, S.D.: Least-squares fitting of two 3-D point sets. IEEE Trans. Pattern Anal. Mach. Intell. **9**(5), 698–700 (1987)
4. Chen, M., Zou, Q., Wang, C., Liu, L.: EdgeNet: deep metric learning for 3D shapes. Comput. Aided Geom. Des. **72**, 19–33 (2019)

5. Chen, T., Kornblith, S., Norouzi, M., Hinton, G.: A simple framework for contrastive learning of visual representations. arXiv preprint arXiv:2002.05709 (2020)
6. Choy, C., Park, J., Koltun, V.: Fully convolutional geometric features. In: Proceedings of the IEEE International Conference on Computer Vision, pp. 8958–8966 (2019)
7. Deng, H., Birdal, T., Ilic, S.: PPF-FoldNet: unsupervised learning of rotation invariant 3D local descriptors. In: Ferrari, V., Hebert, M., Sminchisescu, C., Weiss, Y. (eds.) ECCV 2018. LNCS, vol. 11209, pp. 620–638. Springer, Cham (2018). https://doi.org/10.1007/978-3-030-01228-1_37
8. Deng, H., Birdal, T., Ilic, S.: PPFNet: global context aware local features for robust 3D point matching. In: Proceedings of the IEEE Conference on Computer Vision and Pattern Recognition, pp. 195–205 (2018)
9. Deprelle, T., Groueix, T., Fisher, M., Kim, V., Russell, B., Aubry, M.: Learning elementary structures for 3D shape generation and matching. In: Advances in Neural Information Processing Systems, pp. 7433–7443 (2019)
10. Devlin, J., Chang, M.W., Lee, K., Toutanova, K.: BERT: pre-training of deep bidirectional transformers for language understanding. arXiv preprint arXiv:1810.04805 (2018)
11. Dwibedi, D., Aytar, Y., Tompson, J., Sermanet, P., Zisserman, A.: Temporal cycle-consistency learning. In: Proceedings of the IEEE Conference on Computer Vision and Pattern Recognition, pp. 1801–1810 (2019)
12. Groueix, T., Fisher, M., Kim, V.G., Russell, B.C., Aubry, M.: AtlasNet: a papier-mâché approach to learning 3D surface generation. In: Proceedings of the IEEE Conference on Computer Vision and Pattern Recognition (CVPR), pp. 216–224 (2018)
13. Groueix, T., Fisher, M., Kim, V.G., Russell, B.C., Aubry, M.: Unsupervised cycle-consistent deformation for shape matching. In: Computer Graphics Forum, vol. 38, pp. 123–133. Wiley Online Library (2019)
14. Halimi, O., Litany, O., Rodola, E., Bronstein, A.M., Kimmel, R.: Unsupervised learning of dense shape correspondence. In: Proceedings of the IEEE Conference on Computer Vision and Pattern Recognition, pp. 4370–4379 (2019)
15. Han, Z., Wang, X., Liu, Y.S., Zwicker, M.: Multi-angle point cloud-VAE: unsupervised feature learning for 3D point clouds from multiple angles by joint self-reconstruction and half-to-half prediction. arXiv preprint arXiv:1907.12704 (2019)
16. Hassani, K., Haley, M.: Unsupervised multi-task feature learning on point clouds. In: Proceedings of the IEEE International Conference on Computer Vision, pp. 8160–8171 (2019)
17. He, K., Fan, H., Wu, Y., Xie, S., Girshick, R.: Momentum contrast for unsupervised visual representation learning. arXiv preprint arXiv:1911.05722 (2019)
18. Huang, H., Kalogerakis, E., Chaudhuri, S., Ceylan, D., Kim, V.G., Yumer, E.: Learning local shape descriptors from part correspondences with multiview convolutional networks. ACM Trans. Graph. (TOG) **37**(1), 1–14 (2017)
19. Huang, Q.X., Guibas, L.: Consistent shape maps via semidefinite programming. In: Computer Graphics Forum, vol. 32, pp. 177–186. Wiley Online Library (2013)
20. Huang, Q.X., Su, H., Guibas, L.: Fine-grained semi-supervised labeling of large shape collections. ACM Trans. Graph. (TOG) **32**(6), 1–10 (2013)
21. Kim, V.G., Li, W., Mitra, N.J., Chaudhuri, S., DiVerdi, S., Funkhouser, T.: Learning part-based templates from large collections of 3D shapes. ACM Trans. Graph. (TOG) **32**(4), 1–12 (2013)

22. Kim, V.G., Li, W., Mitra, N.J., DiVerdi, S., Funkhouser, T.: Exploring collections of 3D models using fuzzy correspondences. ACM Trans. Graph. (TOG) **31**(4), 1–11 (2012)
23. Kingma, D.P., Ba, J.: Adam: a method for stochastic optimization. arXiv preprint arXiv:1412.6980 (2014)
24. Knight, P.A.: The Sinkhorn-Knopp algorithm: convergence and applications. SIAM J. Matrix Anal. Appl. **30**(1), 261–275 (2008)
25. Lee, J., Lee, Y., Kim, J., Kosiorek, A.R., Choi, S., Teh, Y.W.: Set transformer: A framework for attention-based permutation-invariant neural networks. arXiv preprint arXiv:1810.00825 (2018)
26. Li, Y., Bu, R., Sun, M., Wu, W., Di, X., Chen, B.: PointCNN: convolution on X-transformed points. In: Advances in Neural Information Processing Systems, pp. 820–830 (2018)
27. van der Maaten, L., Hinton, G.: Visualizing data using t-SNE. J. Mach. Learn. Res. **9**, 2579–2605 (2008)
28. Mena, G., Belanger, D., Linderman, S., Snoek, J.: Learning latent permutations with Gumbel-Sinkhorn networks. arXiv preprint arXiv:1802.08665 (2018)
29. Misra, I., van der Maaten, L.: Self-supervised learning of pretext-invariant representations. arXiv preprint arXiv:1912.01991 (2019)
30. Muralikrishnan, S., Kim, V.G., Fisher, M., Chaudhuri, S.: Shape unicode: a unified shape representation. In: Proceedings of the IEEE Conference on Computer Vision and Pattern Recognition, pp. 3790–3799 (2019)
31. van den Oord, A., Li, Y., Vinyals, O.: Representation learning with contrastive predictive coding. arXiv preprint arXiv:1807.03748 (2018)
32. Qi, C.R., Su, H., Mo, K., Guibas, L.J.: PointNet: deep learning on point sets for 3D classification and segmentation. In: Proceedings of the IEEE Conference on Computer Vision and Pattern Recognition, pp. 652–660 (2017)
33. Qi, C.R., Yi, L., Su, H., Guibas, L.J.: PointNet++: deep hierarchical feature learning on point sets in a metric space. In: Advances in Neural Information Processing Systems, pp. 5099–5108 (2017)
34. Reddi, S.J., Kale, S., Kumar, S.: On the convergence of Adam and beyond. arXiv preprint arXiv:1904.09237 (2019)
35. Sahillioğlu, Y.: Recent advances in shape correspondence. Vis. Comput. **36**, 1705–1721 (2019). https://doi.org/10.1007/s00371-019-01760-0
36. Sauder, J., Sievers, B.: Self-supervised deep learning on point clouds by reconstructing space. In: Advances in Neural Information Processing Systems, pp. 12942–12952 (2019)
37. Sinkhorn, R.: A relationship between arbitrary positive matrices and doubly stochastic matrices. Ann. Math. Stat. **35**(2), 876–879 (1964)
38. Thewlis, J., Albanie, S., Bilen, H., Vedaldi, A.: Unsupervised learning of landmarks by descriptor vector exchange. In: Proceedings of the IEEE International Conference on Computer Vision, pp. 6361–6371 (2019)
39. Thewlis, J., Bilen, H., Vedaldi, A.: Unsupervised learning of object landmarks by factorized spatial embeddings. In: Proceedings of the IEEE International Conference on Computer Vision, pp. 5916–5925 (2017)
40. Tian, Y., Krishnan, D., Isola, P.: Contrastive multiview coding. arXiv preprint arXiv:1906.05849 (2019)
41. Tschannen, M., Djolonga, J., Rubenstein, P.K., Gelly, S., Lucic, M.: On mutual information maximization for representation learning. arXiv preprint arXiv:1907.13625 (2019)

42. Van Kaick, O., Zhang, H., Hamarneh, G., Cohen-Or, D.: A survey on shape correspondence. In: Computer Graphics Forum, vol. 30, pp. 1681–1707. Wiley Online Library (2011)
43. Vaswani, A., et al.: Attention is all you need. In: Advances in Neural Information Processing Systems, pp. 5998–6008 (2017)
44. Wang, X., Jabri, A., Efros, A.A.: Learning correspondence from the cycle-consistency of time. In: Proceedings of the IEEE Conference on Computer Vision and Pattern Recognition, pp. 2566–2576 (2019)
45. Wang, Y., Solomon, J.M.: Deep closest point: learning representations for point cloud registration. In: Proceedings of the IEEE International Conference on Computer Vision, pp. 3523–3532 (2019)
46. Wang, Y., Solomon, J.M.: PRNet: self-supervised learning for partial-to-partial registration. In: Advances in Neural Information Processing Systems, pp. 8814–8826 (2019)
47. Wang, Y., Sun, Y., Liu, Z., Sarma, S.E., Bronstein, M.M., Solomon, J.M.: Dynamic graph CNN for learning on point clouds. ACM Trans. Graph. (TOG) **38**(5), 1–12 (2019)
48. Wu, W., Qi, Z., Fuxin, L.: PointConv: deep convolutional networks on 3D point clouds. In: Proceedings of the IEEE Conference on Computer Vision and Pattern Recognition, pp. 9621–9630 (2019)
49. Wu, Z., et al.: 3D ShapeNets: a deep representation for volumetric shapes. In: Proceedings of the IEEE Conference on Computer Vision and Pattern Recognition, pp. 1912–1920 (2015)
50. Wu, Z., Xiong, Y., Yu, S.X., Lin, D.: Unsupervised feature learning via non-parametric instance discrimination. In: Proceedings of the IEEE Conference on Computer Vision and Pattern Recognition, pp. 3733–3742 (2018)
51. Yang, Y., Feng, C., Shen, Y., Tian, D.: FoldingNet: point cloud auto-encoder via deep grid deformation, pp. 206–215 (2018)
52. Yi, L., et al.: A scalable active framework for region annotation in 3D shape collections. ACM Trans. Graph. (TOG) **35**(6), 1–12 (2016)
53. Zeng, A., Song, S., Nießner, M., Fisher, M., Xiao, J., Funkhouser, T.: 3DMatch: learning local geometric descriptors from RGB-D reconstructions. In: Proceedings of the IEEE Conference on Computer Vision and Pattern Recognition, pp. 1802–1811 (2017)
54. Zhao, Y., Birdal, T., Deng, H., Tombari, F.: 3D point capsule networks. In: Proceedings of the IEEE Conference on Computer Vision and Pattern Recognition, pp. 1009–1018 (2019)
55. Zhou, T., Krahenbuhl, P., Aubry, M., Huang, Q., Efros, A.A.: Learning dense correspondence via 3D-guided cycle consistency. In: Proceedings of the IEEE Conference on Computer Vision and Pattern Recognition, pp. 117–126 (2016)
56. Zhu, J.Y., Park, T., Isola, P., Efros, A.A.: Unpaired image-to-image translation using cycle-consistent adversarial networks. In: Proceedings of the IEEE International Conference on Computer Vision (2017)

Label-Efficient Learning on Point Clouds Using Approximate Convex Decompositions

Matheus Gadelha$^{(\boxtimes)}$, Aruni RoyChowdhury, Gopal Sharma,
Evangelos Kalogerakis, Liangliang Cao, Erik Learned-Miller, Rui Wang,
and Subhransu Maji

University of Massachusetts Amherst, Amherst, USA
{mgadelha,aruni,gopal,kalo,llcao,elm,ruiwang,smaji}@cs.umass.edu

Abstract. The problems of shape classification and part segmentation
from 3D point clouds have garnered increasing attention in the last few
years. Both of these problems, however, suffer from relatively small training sets, creating the need for statistically efficient methods to learn 3D
shape representations. In this paper, we investigate the use of Approximate Convex Decompositions (ACD) as a self-supervisory signal for
label-efficient learning of point cloud representations. We show that using
ACD to approximate ground truth segmentation provides excellent self-
supervision for learning 3D point cloud representations that are highly
effective on downstream tasks. We report improvements over the state-
of-the-art for unsupervised representation learning on the ModelNet40
shape classification dataset and significant gains in few-shot part segmentation on the ShapeNetPart dataset. Our source code is publicly available
(https://github.com/matheusgadelha/PointCloudLearningACD).

1   Introduction

The performance of current neural network models on tasks such as classification and semantic segmentation of point cloud data is limited by the amount of
labeled training data. Since collecting high quality annotations on 3D shapes is
usually expensive and time consuming, there have been increasing efforts to train
on noisy or weakly labeled datasets [42,53,83], or via completely unsupervised
training [11,19,25,75,76]. An alternative strategy is to train the network on one
task through *self-supervision* with automatically generated labels to initialize its
parameters, then fine-tune it on the final task. Examples of such self-supervised

---

M. Gadelha and A. RoyChowdhury—Equal contribution.

A. RoyChowdhury—Now at Amazon, work done prior to joining.

Electronic supplementary material The online version of this chapter (https://
doi.org/10.1007/978-3-030-58607-2_28) contains supplementary material, which is
available to authorized users.

© Springer Nature Switzerland AG 2020
A. Vedaldi et al. (Eds.): ECCV 2020, LNCS 12355, pp. 473–491, 2020.
https://doi.org/10.1007/978-3-030-58607-2_28

approaches for network initialization include clustering [6,7], solving jigsaw puzzles [44], and image colorization [78]. A key question in our problem setting is *"What makes for a good self-supervision task in the case of 3D shapes?"* That is, what tasks induce inductive biases that are beneficial to the downstream shape understanding tasks.

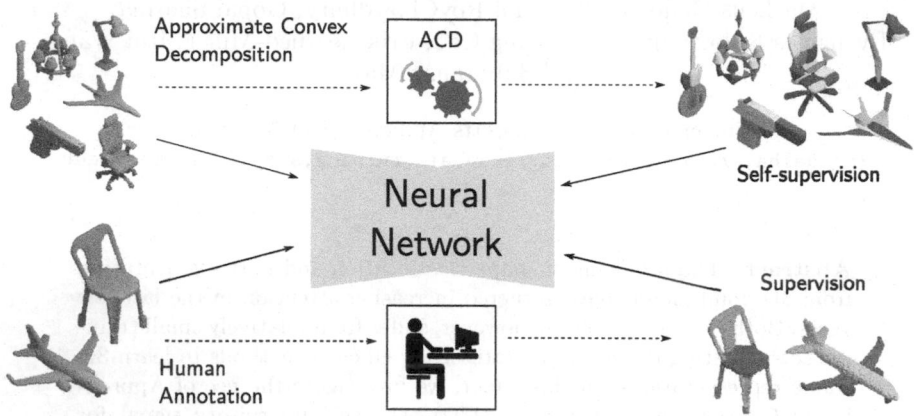

Fig. 1. Overview of our method versus a fully-supervised approach. ***Top:*** Approximate Convex Decomposition (ACD) can be applied on a large repository of unlabeled point clouds, yielding a *self-supervised* training signal for the neural network without involving any human annotators. ***Bottom:*** the usual *fully-supervised* setting, where human annotators label the semantic parts of shapes, which are then used as supervision for the neural network. The unsupervised ACD task results in learning useful representations from unlabeled data, significantly improving performance in shape classification and semantic segmentation, especially when labeled data is scarce or unavailable.

We posit that decomposing shapes into geometrically simple constituent parts provides an excellent self-supervisory learning signal for downstream 3D segmentation and classification tasks. Specifically, we propose using a classical shape decomposition method, Approximate Convex Decomposition (ACD), as the self-supervisory signal to pre-train neural networks for processing 3D data. Our approach is motivated by the observation that convexity provides cues to capture structural components related to human perception [30,37], and object manufacturability [14,38]. However, strict convex decomposition often leads to highly over-segmented shapes, leading to our choice of *approximate* convex decomposition [37]. As shown in the Fig. 2, ACD decomposes shapes into segments that roughly align with instances of different parts. For example, two wings of an airplane are decomposed into two separate, approximately convex parts.

Our approach is illustrated in Fig. 1. The main idea is to automatically generate training data by decomposing unlabeled 3D shapes into convex components. Since ACD relies solely on geometric information to perform its decomposition, the process does not require any human intervention. We formulate ACD as a metric learning problem on point embeddings and train the model using a contrastive loss [12,24]. We demonstrate the effectiveness of our approach on standard 3D shape classification and segmentation benchmarks. In classification, we show that the representation learned from performing shape decomposition leads to features that achieve state-of-the-art performance for *unsupervised shape classification* on ModelNet40 [73] (**89.8%**). For *few-shot shape segmentation* on ShapeNet [8], our model outperforms the state-of-the-art by **7.5%** mIoU when using 1% of the available labeled training data. Moreover, differently from other unsupervised approaches, our method can be applied to any of the well-known neural network backbones for point cloud processing. Finally, we provide thorough experimental analysis and visualizations demonstrating the role of the ACD self-supervision on representations learned by neural networks.

2 Related Work

Learning Representations on 3D Data. Shape representations using neural networks have been widely studied in computer vision and graphics. An early approach was the use of *occupancy grids* to represent shapes for classification or segmentation tasks [40,73]; however these representations suffered from computational and memory inefficiency. These problems were mitigated by architectures that use spatial partitioning data structures [32,49,66,67]. *Multi-view approaches* [27,31,56,58,60] learn representations by using order invariant pooling of features from multiple rendered views of a shape. Another class of methods take *point cloud representations* (*i.e.*, a set of (x, y, z) coordinate triples) as input, and learn permutation invariant representations [18,19,25,47, 48,55,70,75]. Using point sets as a 3D representation does not suffer from the memory constraints of volumetric representations nor the self-occlusion issues of multi-view approaches. Still, all the above approaches rely on massive amounts of labeled 3D data. In this paper, we develop a technique to enable the learning of label-efficient representations from point clouds. Our approach is architecture-agnostic and relies on learning from approximate convex decompositions, which can be automatically computed from a 3D shapes.

Approximate Convex Decompositions. Studies in the cognitive science literature have argued that humans tend to reason about 3D shapes as the union of convex components [26]. However, performing exact convex decomposition is an NP-Hard problem that leads to an impractically high number of shape components [5]. An alternative class of decomposition techniques, named *Approximate Convex Decomposition* (ACD) [30,37,39,82], compute approximate decompositions up to a concavity tolerance ϵ. This tolerance makes the computation significantly more efficient and leads to shape approximations containing a smaller number of components. Apart from shape segmentation [4,30], these approximations are useful for a variety of tasks like mesh generation [37] and collision detection [71]. Furthermore, ACD-based decompositions has been shown to have a high degree of similarity to human segmentations, as indicated by segmentation evaluation measures, such as the Rand Index in the PSB benchmark [9,30]. This indicates that ACD can provide useful cues for discovering shape parts.

There have been various techniques to compute ACD for shapes based on either geometric analysis [30,37,39,82], and recently with deep networks [10,15]. In this work, we used a particular type of ACD named Volumetric Hierachical Approximate Convex Decomposition (V-HACD) [39] (more details in Sect. 3.1.) Unlike previous methods, our goal is to apply ACD to automatically supervise a convex decomposition task as an initialization step for learning point cloud representations. We show that the training signal provided by ACD leads to improvements in semantic segmentation as well as unsupervised shape classification.

Self-supervised Learning. In many situations, unlabeled images or videos contain useful information that can be leveraged to automatically create a training loss for learning useful representations. *Self-supervised learning* explores this idea, using unlabeled data to train deep networks by solving tasks that do not require any human annotation effort.

Learning to colorize grayscale images was among the first approaches to training modern deep neural networks in a self-supervised fashion [35,78,79]. Estimating the color for a pixel from a black-and-white image requires some understanding of a pixel's meaning (*e.g.*, skies are blue, grass is green, etc.). Thus training a network to estimate pixel colors leads to the learning of representations that are useful in downstream tasks like object classification. The contextual information in an image also lends itself to the design of proxy tasks. These include learning to estimate the relative positions of cropped image patches [16], the similarity of patches tracked across videos [68,69], the appearance of missing patches in an image [46,63], or learning from image modalities in RGBD data [23,58]. Motion from unlabeled videos also provides a useful pre-training signal. Pathak et al. [45] used motion segmentation to learn how to segment images, and Jiang et al. [29] estimate relative depth as a proxy task for pre-training a network for scene understanding tasks. Other approaches include solving jigsaw puzzles with permuted image patches [44], and training a generative adversarial model [17]. An empirical comparison of various self-supervised tasks may be found in [21,33]. In the case of limited samples, *i.e.*, the *few-shot classification* setting, including self-supervised losses along with the usual supervised training is shown to be beneficial [59]. Recent work has also focused on learning unsupervised representations for 3D shapes using tasks such as clustering [25] and reconstruction [52,76], which we compare against in our experiments.

Label-Efficient Representation Learning on Point Clouds. Several recent approaches [11,25,43,53,83] have been proposed to alleviate expensive labeling of shapes. Muralikrishnan et al. [43] learn a per-point representation by training a network to predict shape-level tags. Yi et al. [77] embed pre-segmented parts in descriptor space by jointly learning a metric for clustering parts, assigning tags to them, and building a consistent part hierarchy. Chen et al. [11] proposed a branched auto-encoder, where each branch learns coarse part level features, which are further used to reconstruct the shape by producing implicit fields

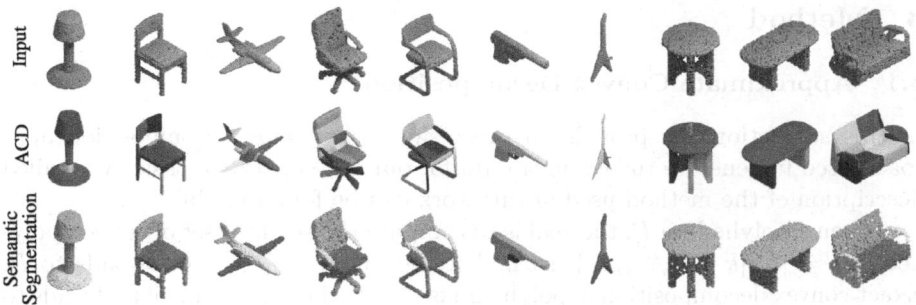

Fig. 2. Input point clouds (first row), convex components *automatically* computed by ACD (second row) and *human-labeled* point clouds (last row) from the ShapeNet [8] part segmentation benchmark. Note – *(i)* different colors for the ACD components only signify different parts – no semantic meaning or inter-shape correspondence is inferred by this procedure; *(ii)* for the human labels, colors do convey semantic meaning: *e.g.*, the backs of chairs are always orange; *(iii)* while the ACD decompositions tend to oversegment the shapes, they contain most of the boundaries present in the human annotations, suggesting that the model has similar criteria for decomposing objects into subparts; *e.g.*, the chair's legs are separated from the seat, wings and engines are separated from the airplane boundary, pistol trigger is separated from the rest.

for each part. However, this approach requires one decoder for every different part, which restricts their experiments to category-specific models. On the other hand, our approach can be directly applied to any of the well known point-based architectures, is capable of handling multiple categories at once for part segmentation, and additionally learns useful features for unsupervised shape classification. Furthermore, Chen et al. [11] show experiments on single shot semantic segmentation on manually selected shapes, whereas we show results on randomly selected training shapes in a few-shot setting. Most similar to our work, Hassani et al. [25] propose a novel architecture for point clouds, which is trained on multiple tasks at the same time: clustering, classification and reconstruction. In our experiments, we demonstrate that we outperform their method on few-shot segmentation by **7.5%** IoU and achieve the same performance on unsupervised ModelNet40 classification by using *only ACD as a proxy task*. If we further add a reconstruction term, our method achieves state-of-the-art performance in unsupervised shape classification. Finally, Sharma et al. [53] proposed learning point embeddings by using noisy part labels and semantic tags available on the 3DWarehouse dataset [62]. Their model is used for few-shot semantic segmentation. In this work, we instead gather part labels using approximate convex decomposition, whose computation is automatic and can be applied to any mesh regardless of the existence of semantic tags.

3   Method

3.1   Approximate Convex Decomposition

In this subsection, we provide an overview of the shape decomposition approach used to generate the training data for our self-supervised task. A detailed
description of the method used in this work can be found in [39].

Given a polyhedron P, the goal is to compute the smallest set of convex poly-
hedra $\mathcal{C} = \{C_k | k = 1, \ldots, K\}$, such that the union $\cup_{k=1}^{K} C_i$ corresponds to P.
Exact convex decomposition of polyhedra is an NP-Hard problem [5] and leads to
decompositions containing too many components, rendering it impractical for use
in most applications (ours included). This can be circumvented by Approximate
Convex Decomposition (ACD) techniques. ACD relaxes the convexity constraint
of exact convex decomposition by allowing every component to be *approximately
convex* up to a concavity ϵ. The way concavity is computed and how the components are split varies according to different methods [20,30,37,39,82]. In this
work, we use an approach called Volumetric Hierarchical Approximate Convex
Decomposition (V-HACD) [39]. The reasons for using this approach are three-
fold. First, as the name suggests, V-HACD performs computations using volumetric representations, which can be easily computed from dense point cloud
data or meshes and lead to good results without having to resort to costly mesh
decimation and remeshing procedures. Second, the procedure is reasonably fast
and can be applied to open surfaces of arbitrary genus. Third, V-HACD guarantees that no two components overlap, which means that there is no part of
the surface that is approximated by more than one component. In the next
paragraph, we describe V-HACD in detail.

V-HACD. Since the method operates on volumetric representations, the first
step is to convert a shape into an occupancy grid. If the shape is represented
as a point cloud, one can compute an occupancy grid by selecting which cells
are occupied by the points and filling its interior. In our case, since our training shapes are from ShapeNet [8] that includes meshes, we chose to compute the
occupancy grid by voxelizing the meshes using [28]. Once the voxelization is computed, the algorithm proceeds on computing convex components by recursively
splitting the volume into two parts. First, the volume is centered and aligned
in the coordinate system according to its principal axis. Then, one of the three
axis aligned planes is selected as a splitting plane that separates the volume in
two different parts. This procedure is applied multiple times until we reach the
maximum number of desired components or the concavity tolerance is reached.
The concavity $\eta(\mathcal{C})$ of a set of components $\mathcal{C}$ is computed as

$$\eta(\mathcal{C}) = \max_{k=1,\ldots,K} d(C_k, \text{CH}(C_k)),   \tag{1}$$

where $d(X, Y)$ is the difference between the volumes X and Y; $\text{CH}(X)$ is the
convex hull of X; and C_k is the kth element of the set $\mathcal{C}$. The splitting plane
selection is performed by choosing the axis-aligned plane that minimizes an

energy $E(V, \mathbf{p})$, where V is the volume we are aiming to split and $\mathbf{p}$ is the splitting plane. This energy is defined as:

$$E(V, \mathbf{p}) = E_{con}(V, \mathbf{p}) + \alpha E_{bal}(V, \mathbf{p}) + \beta E_{sym}(V, \mathbf{p}), \tag{2}$$

where E_{con} is a component connectivity term, which measures the sum of the normalized concavities between both sides of volume; E_{bal} is a balance component term, which measures the dissimilarity between both sides; and E_{sym} is a symmetry component term, which penalizes planes that are orthogonal to a potential revolution axis. The parameters α and β are weights for the last two terms. In all our experiments, we used the default values of $\alpha = \beta = 0.05$. We refer the reader to [39] for a detailed description of the components in the energy term.

Assigning Component Labels to Point Clouds. The output of ACD for every shape is a set of approximately convex components represented as meshes. For each shape, we sample points on the original ShapeNet mesh and on the mesh of every ACD component. We then propagate component labels to every point in the original point cloud by using nearest neighbor matching with points used in the decomposition. More precisely, given an unlabeled point cloud $\{p_i\}_{i=1}^N$, this assigns a component label $\Gamma(p_i, \mathcal{C})$ to each point p_i via:

$$\Gamma(p_i, \mathcal{C}) = \operatorname*{argmin}_{k=1...|\mathcal{C}|} \left[\min_{p_j \in C_k} ||p_i - p_j|| \right]. \tag{3}$$

3.2 Self-supervision with ACD

The component labels generated by the ACD algorithm are not consistent across point clouds, *i.e.*, "component 5" may refer to the *seat* of a chair in one point cloud but the *leg* of the chair in another. Therefore, the usual cross-entropy loss, which is generally used to train networks for tasks such as semantic part labeling, is not applicable in our setting. We formulate the learning of ACDs as a metric learning problem on point embeddings via a *pairwise* or *contrastive loss* [24].

We assume that each point $p_i = (x_i, y_i, z_i)$ in a point cloud $\mathbf{x}$ is encoded as $\Phi(\mathbf{x})_i$ in some embedding space by a neural network encoder $\Phi(\cdot)$, *e.g.* Point-Net [57] or PointNet++ [48]. Let the embeddings of a pair of points p_i and p_j from a shape be $\Phi(\mathbf{x})_i$ and $\Phi(\mathbf{x})_j$, normalized to unit length (*i.e.* $||\Phi(\mathbf{x})_i|| = 1$), and the set of convex components as described above be $\mathcal{C}$. The pairwise loss is then defined as

$$\mathcal{L}^{pair}(\mathbf{x}, p_i, p_j, \mathcal{C}) = \begin{cases} 1 - \Phi(\mathbf{x})_i^\top \Phi(\mathbf{x})_j, & \text{if } [\Gamma(p_i, \mathcal{C}) = \Gamma(p_j, \mathcal{C})] \\ \max(0, \Phi(\mathbf{x})_i^\top \Phi(\mathbf{x})_j - m), & \text{if } [\Gamma(p_i, \mathcal{C}) \neq \Gamma(p_j, \mathcal{C})]. \end{cases} \tag{4}$$

This loss encourages points belonging to the same component to have a high similarity $\Phi(\mathbf{x})_i^\top \Phi(\mathbf{x})_j$, and encourages points from different components to have low similarity, subject to a margin m (set to $m = 0.5$ as in [34]). $[\cdot]$ denotes the Iverson bracket.

Joint Training with ACD. Formally, let us consider samples $\mathcal{X} = \{\mathbf{x}_i\}_{i \in [n]}$, divided into two parts: $\mathcal{X}^{\mathcal{L}}$ and $\mathcal{X}^{\mathcal{U}}$ of sizes l and u respectively. Now $\mathcal{X}^{\mathcal{L}} :=$ $\{\mathbf{x}_1, \ldots, \mathbf{x}_l\}$ consist of point clouds that are provided with human-annotated labels $\mathcal{Y}^{\mathcal{L}} := \{\mathbf{y}_1, \ldots, \mathbf{y}_l\}$, while we do not know the labels of the samples $\mathcal{X}^{\mathcal{U}} :=$ $\{\mathbf{x}_{l+1}, \ldots, \mathbf{x}_{l+u}\}$. By running ACD on the samples in $\mathcal{X}^{\mathcal{U}}$, we can obtain a set of components for each shape. The pairwise contrastive loss $\mathcal{L}^{pair}$ (Eq. 4) can then be defined over $\mathbf{x}_i \in \mathcal{X}^{\mathcal{U}}$ as a self-supervised objective. For the samples $\mathbf{x}_i \in \mathcal{X}^{\mathcal{L}}$, we have access to their ground-truth labels $\mathcal{Y}^{\mathcal{L}}$, which may for example, be semantic part labels. In that case, the standard choice of training objective is the *cross-entropy loss* $\mathcal{L}^{CE}$, defined over the points in an input point cloud. Thus, we can train a network on both $\mathcal{X}^{\mathcal{L}}$ and $\mathcal{X}^{\mathcal{U}}$ via a ***joint loss*** that combines both the supervised ($\mathcal{L}^{CE}$) and self-supervised ($\mathcal{L}^{pair}$) objectives,

$$\mathcal{L} = \mathcal{L}^{CE} + \lambda \cdot \mathcal{L}^{pair}. \tag{5}$$

The scalar hyper-parameter λ controls the relative strength between the supervised and self-supervised training signals. In the ***pretraining*** scenario, when we *only* have the unlabeled dataset $\mathcal{X}^{\mathcal{U}}$ available, we can train a neural network purely on the ACD parts by optimizing the $\mathcal{L}^{pair}$ objective.

4   Experiments

We demonstrate the effectiveness of the ACD-based self-supervision across a range of experimental scenarios. For all the experiments in this section we use ACDs computed on all shapes from the ShapeNetCore data [8], which contains 57,447 shapes across 55 categories. The decomposition was computed using a concavity tolerance of 1.5×10^{-3} and a volumetric grid of resolution 128^3. All the other parameters are set to their default values according to a publicly available implementation[1] of [39]. The resulting decompositions have an average of 17 parts per shape. The ACD computation takes 1.6 s per shape on an Intel i7-2600 3.4 GHz using 8 cores.

4.1   Shape Classification on ModelNet

In this set of experiments, we show that the representations learned by a network trained on ACD are useful for discriminative downstream tasks such as classifying point clouds into shape categories.

Dataset. We report results on the ModelNet40 shape classification benchmark, which consists of 12,311 shapes from 40 shape categories in a train/test split of 9,843/2,468. A linear SVM is trained on the features extracted on the training set of ModelNet40. This setup mirrors other approaches for unsupervised learning on point clouds, such as FoldingNet [76] and Hassani et al. [25].

Experimental Setup. A PointNet++ network is trained on the unlabeled ShapeNet-Core data using the pairwise contrastive loss on the ACD task, using

---

[1] https://github.com/kmammou/v-hacd.

the Adam optimizer, initial learning rate of 10^{-3} and halving the learning rate every epoch. This network architecture creates an embedding for each of the N points in an input shape, while for the shape classification task we require a single global descriptor for the entire point cloud. Therefore, we aggregate the per-point features of PointNet++ at the first two set aggregation layers (SA1 and SA2) and the last fully connected layer (fc), resulting in 128, 256 and 128 dimensional feature vectors, respectively. Since features from different layers may have different scales, we normalize each vector to unit length before concatenating them, and apply element-wise signed square-rooting [50], resulting in a final 512-dim descriptor for each point cloud. The results are presented in Table 1.

Comparison with Baselines. As an initial naïve baseline, we use a Point-Net++ network with random weights as our feature extractor, and then perform the usual SVM training. This gives 78% accuracy on ModelNet40 – while surprisingly good, the performance is not entirely unexpected: randomly initialized convolutional neural networks are known to provide useful features by virtue of their architecture, as studied in Saxe et al. [51]. Training this network with ACD, on the other hand, gives a significant boost to performance (78% → **89.1%**), demonstrating the effectiveness of our proposed self-supervision task. This indicates some degree of generalization across datasets and tasks – from distinguishing convex components on ShapeNet to classifying shapes on ModelNet40. Inspired by [25], we also investigated if adding a reconstruction component to the loss would further improve accuracy. Reconstruction is done by simply adding an AtlasNet [22] decoder to our model and using Chamfer distance as reconstruction loss. Without the reconstruction term (i.e. trained only to perform ACD using contrastive loss), our accuracy (89.1%) is the same as the multi-task learning approach presented in [25]. After adding a reconstruction term, we achieve an improved accuracy of **89.8%**. On the other hand, having just reconstruction without ACD yields an accuracy of 86.2%. This shows not only that ACD is a useful task when learning representations for shape classification, but that it can also be combined with shape reconstruction to yield complementary benefits.

Comparison with Previous Work. Approaches for *unsupervised* or *self-supervised* learning on point clouds are listed in the upper portion of Table 1. Our method achieves **89.1%** classification accuracy from purely using the ACD loss, which is met only by the unsupervised multi-task learning method of Hassani et al. [25] (adding a reconstruction loss to our method slightly improves over the state-of-the-art: 89.1% → **89.8%**). We note that our method merely adds a contrastive loss to a standard architecture (PointNet++), without requiring a custom architecture and multiple pretext tasks as in [25], which uses clustering, pseudo-labeling and reconstruction.

4.2   Few-Shot Segmentation on ShapeNet

Dataset. We report results on the **ShapeNetSeg** part segmentation benchmark [8], which is a subset of the ShapeNetCore database with manual

Table 1. Unsupervised shape classification on the ModelNet40 dataset. The representations learned in the intermediate layers by a network trained for the ACD task on ShapeNet data are general enough to be useful for discriminating between shape categories on ModelNet40.

Method	Accuracy (%)
VConv-DAE [52]	75.5
3D-GAN [72]	83.3
Latent-GAN [1]	85.7
MRTNet [19]	86.4
PointFlow [75]	86.8
FoldingNet [76]	88.4
PointCapsNet [80]	88.9
Multi-task [25]	89.1
Our baseline (with Random weights)	78.0
With reconstruction term only	86.2
Ours with ACD	89.1
Ours with ACD + Reconstruction	**89.8**

Table 2. Few-shot segmentation on the ShapeNet dataset (*class avg. IoU* over 5 rounds). The number of shots or samples per class is denoted by k for each of the 16 ShapeNet categories used for supervised training. Jointly training with the ACD task reduces overfitting when labeled data is scarce, leading to significantly better performance over a purely supervised baseline.

Samples/cls.	$k = 1$	$k = 3$	$k = 5$	$k = 10$
Baseline	53.15 ± 2.49	59.54 ± 1.49	68.14 ± 0.90	71.32 ± 0.52
w/ACD	61.52 ± 2.19	69.33 ± 2.85	72.30 ± 1.80	74.12 ± 1.17
	$k = 20$	$k = 50$	$k = 100$	$k = \text{inf}$
Baseline	75.22 ± 0.82	78.79 ± 0.44	79.67 ± 0.33	81.40 ± 0.44
w/ACD	76.19 ± 1.18	78.67 ± 0.72	78.76 ± 0.61	81.57 ± 0.68

annotations (train/val/test splits of 12,149/1,858/2,874). It consists of 16 man-made shape categories such as airplanes, chairs, and tables, with manually labeled semantic parts (50 in total), such as wings, tails, and engines for airplanes; legs, backs, and seats for chairs, and so on. Given a point cloud at test time, the goal is to assign each point its correct part label out of the 50 possible parts. Few-shot learning tasks are typically described in terms of "n-way k-shot" – the task is to discriminate among n classes and k samples per class are provided as training data. We modify this approach to our setup as follows – we select k samples from each of the $n = 16$ shape categories as the labeled training data, while the task remains semantic part labeling over the 50 part categories.

Table 3. Comparison with state-of-the-art semi-supervised part segmentation methods on ShapeNet. Performance is evaluated using *instance-averaged IoU*.

Method	1% labeled	5% labeled
	IoU	IoU
SO-Net [36]	64.0	69.0
PointCapsNet [80]	67.0	70.0
MortonNet [61]	-	77.1
JointSSL [2][a]	71.9	77.4
Multi-task [25]	68.2	77.7
ACD (*ours*)	**75.7**	**79.7**

[a]Concurrent work.

Experimental Setup. For this task, we perform *joint training* with two losses – the usual cross-entropy loss over labeled parts for the training samples from ShapeNetSeg, and an additional contrastive loss over the ACD components for the samples from ShapeNetCore (Eq. 5), setting $\lambda = 10$. In our initial experiments, we found joint training to be more helpful than pre-training on ACD and then fine-tuning on the few-shot task (an empirical phenomenon also noted in [74]), and thereafter consistently used joint training for the few-shot experiments. All overlapping point clouds between the human-annotated ShapeNetSeg and the unlabeled ShapeNetCore were removed from the self-supervised training set. The (x, y, z) coordinates of the points in each point cloud are used an the input to the neural network; we do not include any additional information such as normals or category labels in these experiments.

Comparison with Baselines. Table 2 shows the few-shot segmentation performance of our method, versus a fully-supervised baseline. Especially in the cases of very few labeled training samples ($k = 1, \ldots, 10$), having the ACD loss over a large unlabeled dataset provides a consistent and significant gain in performance over purely training on the labeled samples. As larger amounts of labeled training samples are made available, naturally there is limited benefit from the additional self-supervised loss – *e.g.* when using all the labeled data, our method is within standard deviation of the purely supervised baseline. Qualitative results are shown in Fig. 3.

Comparison with Previous Work. The performance of recent *unsupervised* and *self-supervised* methods on ShapeNet segmentation are listed in Table 3. Consistent with the protocol followed by the multi-task learning approach of Hassani et al. [25], we provide 1% and 5% of the training samples of ShapeNetSeg as the labeled data and report instance-average IoU. Our method clearly outperforms the state-of-the-art unsupervised learning approaches, improving over [25] at both the 1% and 5% settings (68.2 → **75.7**% and 77.7 → **79.7**%, respectively).

Fig. 3. Qualitative comparison on 5-shot ShapeNet [8] part segmentation. The baseline method in the first row corresponds to training using only 5 examples per class, whereas the ACD results in the second row were computed by performing joint training (cross-entropy from 5 examples + contrastive loss over ACD components from ShapeNetCore). The network backbone architecture is the same for both approaches – PointNet++ [48]. The baseline method merges parts that should be separated, *e.g.*, engines of the airplane, details of the rocket, top of the table, and seat of the motorcycle.

4.3   Analysis of ACD

Effect of Backbone Architectures. Differently from [11,25,76], the ACD self-supervision does not require any custom network design and should be easily applicable across various backbone architectures. To this end, we use two recent high-performing models – *PointNet++* (with multi-scale grouping [48]) and *DGCNN* [70] – as the backbones, reporting results on ModelNet40 shape classification and few-shot segmentation ($k = 5$) on ShapeNetSeg (Table 4).

On shape classification, both networks show large gains from ACD pre-training: 11% for PointNet++ (as reported earlier) and 14% for DGCNN. On few-shot segmentation with 5 samples per category (16 shape categories), PointNet++ improves from 68.14% IoU to 72.3% with the inclusion of the ACD loss. The baseline DGCNN performance with only 5 labeled samples per class is relatively lower (64.14%), however with the additional ACD loss on unlabeled samples, the model achieves 73.11% IoU, which is comparable to the corresponding PointNet++ performance (72.30%).

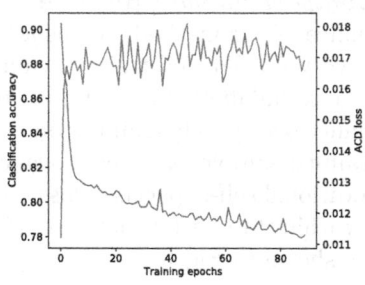

Fig. 4. Classification accuracy of a linear SVM on the ModelNet40 *validation set* v.s. the ACD *validation loss* over training epochs. (Color figure online)

Role of ACD in Shape Classification. Figure 4 shows the reduction in validation loss on learning ACD (red curve) as training progresses on the unlabeled ShapeNet data. Note that doing well on ACD (in terms of the validation loss) also leads to learning representations that are useful for the downstream tasks of shape classification (in terms of SVM accuracy on a validation subset of

Table 4. Comparing embeddings from PointNet++ [48] and DGCNN [70] backbones: shape classification accuracy on ModelNet40 (*Class./MN40*) and few-shot part segmentation performance in terms of class-averaged IoU on ShapeNet (*Part Seg./ShapeNet*).

Task/dataset	Method	PointNet++	DGCNN
Class./MN40	Baseline	77.96	74.11
	w/ACD	**89.06**	**88.21**
5-shot Seg./ShapeNet	Baseline	68.14 ± 0.90	64.14 ± 1.43
	w/ACD	**72.30** ± 1.80	**73.11** ± 0.95

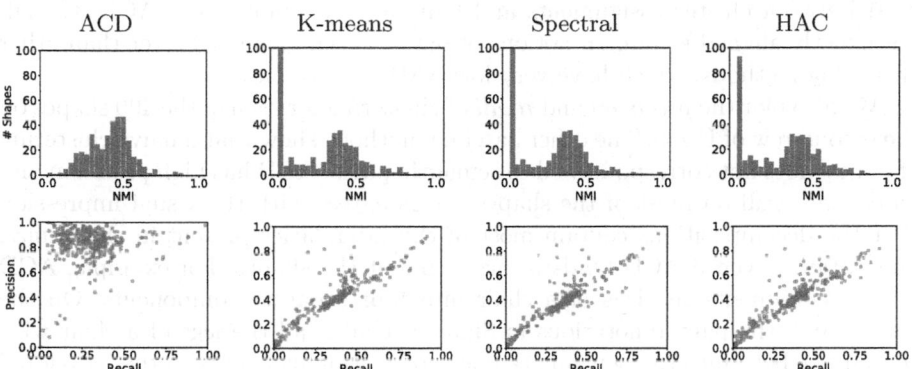

Fig. 5. Correspondence between human part labels and shape decompositions: comparing ACD with basic clustering algorithms – K-means, spectral clustering and hierarchical agglomerative clustering (HAC). ***Row-1:*** histogram of *normalized mutual information* (NMI) between human labels and clustering – ACD is closer to the ground-truth parts than others (y-axes clipped at 100 for clarity). ***Row-2:*** plotting *precision v.s. recall* for each input shape, ACD has high precision and moderate recall (tendency to over-segment parts), while other methods are usually lower in both metrics.

ModelNet40 data, shown in blue). However, the correlation between the two quantities is not very strong (Pearson $\rho = 0.667$) – from the plots it appears that after the initial epochs, where we observe a large gain in classification accuracy as well as a large reduction in ACD loss, continuing to be better at the pretext task does not lead to any noticeable gains in the ability to classify shapes: training with ACD gives the model some useful notion of grouping and parts, but it is not intuitively obvious if *perfectly* mimicking ACD will improve representations for classifying point-clouds into shape categories.

Comparison with Clustering Algorithms. We quantitatively analyse the connection between convex decompositions and semantic object parts by comparing ACD with human part annotations on 400 shapes from ShapeNet, along with simple clustering baselines – K-means [3], spectral clustering [54,65] and hierarchical agglomerative clustering (HAC) [41] on (x, y, z) coordinates of the point clouds. For the baselines, we set the number of clusters to be the number of ground-truth parts in each shape. For each sample shape, given the set of M part categories $\Omega = \{\omega_1, \omega_2, \dots \omega_M\}$ and the set of N clusters $\mathcal{C} = \{C_1, C_2, \dots C_N\}$, clustering performance is evaluated using *normalized mutual information* (NMI) [64], defined as

$$\mathrm{NMI}(\Omega, \mathcal{C}) = \frac{I(\Omega; \mathcal{C})}{[H(\Omega) + H(\mathcal{C})]/2}, \tag{6}$$

where $I(\cdot; \cdot)$ denotes the mutual information between classes Ω and clusters $\mathcal{C}$, and $H(\cdot)$ is the entropy [13]. A better clustering results in *higher* NMI w.r.t. the ground-truth part labels. The first row of Fig. 5 shows the histograms of NMI between cluster assignments and human part annotations: ACD, though not exactly aligned to human notions of parts, is significantly better than other clustering methods, which have very low NMI in most cases.

We also plot the *precision* and *recall* of clustering for each of the 400 shapes on the second row of Fig. 5. The other baseline methods show that a naïve clustering of points does not correspond well to semantic parts. ACD has high precision and moderate recall on most of the shapes – this agrees with the visual impression that the decompositions contain most of the boundaries present in the human annotations, even if ACD tends to oversegment the shapes. For example, ACD typically segments the legs of a chair into four separate components. On the other hand, the part annotations in ShapeNet label all the legs of a chair with the same label, since the benchmark does not distinguish between the individual legs of a chair. We note that the correspondence of ACD to human part labels is not perfect, and this opens an interesting avenue for further work – exploring other decomposition methods like generalized cylinders [81] that may correspond more closely to human-defined parts.

5   Conclusion

Self-supervision using approximate convex decompositions (ACD) has been shown to be effective across multiple tasks and datasets – few-shot part segmentation on ShapeNet and shape classification on ModelNet, consistently surpassing existing self-supervised and unsupervised methods in performance. A simple pairwise contrastive loss is sufficient for introducing the ACD task into a network training framework, without dependencies on any custom architectures. The method can be easily integrated into existing state-of-the-art architectures operating on point clouds such as PointNet++ and DGCNN, yielding significant improvements in both cases. Given the demonstrated effectiveness of ACD in self-supervision, this opens the door to incorporating other shape decomposition methods from the classical geometry processing literature into deep neural network models operating on point clouds.

Acknowledgements. The project is supported in part by the National Science Foundation (NSF) through grants #1908669, #1749833, #1617333. Our experiments used the UMass GPU cluster obtained under the Collaborative Fund managed by the Massachusetts Technology Collaborative.

References

1. Achlioptas, P., Diamanti, O., Mitliagkas, I., Guibas, L.: Representation learning and adversarial generation of 3D point clouds. arXiv preprint arXiv:1707.02392 (2017)
2. Alliegro, A., Boscaini, D., Tommasi, T.: Joint supervised and self-supervised learning for 3D real-world challenges (2020). https://arxiv.org/abs/2004.07392
3. Arthur, D., Vassilvitskii, S.: k-means++: The advantages of careful seeding. Technical report (2007)
4. Au, O.K.C., Zheng, Y., Chen, M., Xu, P., Tai, C.L.: Mesh segmentation with concavity-aware fields. IEEE Trans. Vis. Comput. Graph. 18(7), 1125–1134 (2011). https://doi.org/10.1109/TVCG.2011.131
5. Bernard, C.: Convex partitions of polyhedra a lower bound and worst-case optimal algorithm. SIAM J. Comput. 13(3), 488–507 (1984). https://dl.acm.org/doi/10.1137/0213031
6. Caron, M., Bojanowski, P., Joulin, A., Douze, M.: Deep clustering for unsupervised learning of visual features. In: Ferrari, V., Hebert, M., Sminchisescu, C., Weiss, Y. (eds.) Computer Vision – ECCV 2018. LNCS, vol. 11218, pp. 139–156. Springer, Cham (2018). https://doi.org/10.1007/978-3-030-01264-9_9
7. Caron, M., Bojanowski, P., Mairal, J., Joulin, A.: Unsupervised pre-training of image features on non-curated data. In: Proceedings of the IEEE International Conference on Computer Vision, pp. 2959–2968 (2019)
8. Chang, A.X., et al.: ShapeNet: An information-rich 3D model repository. CoRR abs/1512.03012 (2015)
9. Chen, X., Golovinskiy, A., Funkhouser, T.: A benchmark for 3D mesh segmentation. ACM Trans. Graph. (Proc. SIGGRAPH) 28(3), 1–12 (2009)
10. Chen, Z., Tagliasacchi, A., Zhang, H.: BSP-Net: generating compact meshes via binary space partitioning. In: Proceedings of the IEEE Conference on Computer Vision and Pattern Recognition (2019)
11. Chen, Z., Yin, K., Fisher, M., Chaudhuri, S., Zhang, H.: BAE-NET: branched autoencoder for shape co-segmentation. In: Proceedings of the IEEE International Conference on Computer Vision, pp. 8490–8499 (2019)
12. Chopra, S., Hadsell, R., LeCun, Y.: Learning a similarity metric discriminatively, with application to face verification. In: 2005 IEEE Computer Society Conference on Computer Vision and Pattern Recognition, CVPR 2005, vol. 1, pp. 539–546. IEEE (2005)
13. Cover, T.M., Thomas, J.A.: Elements of Information Theory. Wiley, Hoboken (2012)
14. Demir, İ., Aliaga, D.G., Benes, B.: Near-convex decomposition and layering for efficient 3D printing. Addit. Manuf. 21, 383–394 (2018). https://doi.org/10.1016/j.addma.2018.03.008. http://www.sciencedirect.com/science/article/pii/S2214860417300386
15. Deng, B., Genova, K., Yazdani, S., Bouaziz, S., Hinton, G., Tagliasacchi, A.: CvxNet: learnable convex decomposition. In: Proceedings of the IEEE Conference on Computer Vision and Pattern Recognition (2020)
16. Doersch, C., Gupta, A., Efros, A.A.: Unsupervised visual representation learning by context prediction. In: Proceedings of the IEEE International Conference on Computer Vision, pp. 1422–1430 (2015)
17. Donahue, J., Simonyan, K.: Large scale adversarial representation learning. In: Advances in Neural Information Processing Systems, pp. 10541–10551 (2019)

18. Gadelha, M., Maji, S., Wang, R.: 3D shape generation using spatially ordered point clouds. In: British Machine Vision Conference (BMVC) (2017)
19. Gadelha, M., Wang, R., Maji, S.: Multiresolution tree networks for 3D point cloud processing. In: Ferrari, V., Hebert, M., Sminchisescu, C., Weiss, Y. (eds.) ECCV 2018. LNCS, vol. 11211, pp. 105–122. Springer, Cham (2018). https://doi.org/10.1007/978-3-030-01234-2_7
20. Ghosh, M., Amato, N.M., Lu, Y., Lien, J.M.: Fast approximate convex decomposition using relative concavity. Comput. Aided Des. **45**, 494–504 (2013)
21. Goyal, P., Mahajan, D., Gupta, A., Misra, I.: Scaling and benchmarking self-supervised visual representation learning. arXiv preprint arXiv:1905.01235 (2019)
22. Groueix, T., Fisher, M., Kim, V.G., Russell, B., Aubry, M.: AtlasNet: a Papier-Mâché approach to learning 3D surface generation. In: Proceedings IEEE Conference on Computer Vision and Pattern Recognition (CVPR) (2018)
23. Gupta, S., Hoffman, J., Malik, J.: Cross modal distillation for supervision transfer. In: Proceedings of the IEEE Conference on Computer Vision and Pattern Recognition, pp. 2827–2836 (2016)
24. Hadsell, R., Chopra, S., LeCun, Y.: Dimensionality reduction by learning an invariant mapping. In: 2006 IEEE Computer Society Conference on Computer Vision and Pattern Recognition, CVPR 2006, vol. 2, pp. 1735–1742. IEEE (2006)
25. Hassani, K., Haley, M.: Unsupervised multi-task feature learning on point clouds. In: Proceedings of the IEEE International Conference on Computer Vision, pp. 8160–8171 (2019)
26. Hoffman, D.D., Richards, W.: Parts of recognition. Cognition **18**, 65–96 (1983)
27. Huang, H., Kalogerakis, E., Chaudhuri, S., Ceylan, D., Kim, V.G., Yumer, E.: Learning local shape descriptors from part correspondences with multiview convolutional networks. ACM Trans. Graph. **37**(1), 1–14 (2018)
28. Huang, J., Yagel, R., Filippov, V., Kurzion, Y.: An accurate method for voxelizing polygon meshes. In: IEEE Symposium on Volume Visualization (October 1998)
29. Jiang, H., Larsson, G., Maire, M., Shakhnarovich, G., Learned-Miller, E.: Self-supervised relative depth learning for urban scene understanding. In: Ferrari, V., Hebert, M., Sminchisescu, C., Weiss, Y. (eds.) ECCV 2018. LNCS, vol. 11215, pp. 20–37. Springer, Cham (2018). https://doi.org/10.1007/978-3-030-01252-6_2
30. Kaick, O.V., Fish, N., Kleiman, Y., Asafi, S., Cohen-OR, D.: Shape segmentation by approximate convexity analysis. ACM Trans. Graph. **34**(1), 1–11 (2014)
31. Kalogerakis, E., Averkiou, M., Maji, S., Chaudhuri, S.: 3D shape segmentation with projective convolutional networks. In: Proceedings of the CVPR (2017)
32. Klokov, R., Lempitsky, V.: Escape from cells: deep Kd-networks for the recognition of 3D point cloud models. In: Proceedings of the ICCV (2017)
33. Kolesnikov, A., Zhai, X., Beyer, L.: Revisiting self-supervised visual representation learning. arXiv preprint arXiv:1901.09005 (2019)
34. Kong, S., Fowlkes, C.C.: Recurrent pixel embedding for instance grouping. In: Proceedings of the IEEE Conference on Computer Vision and Pattern Recognition, pp. 9018–9028 (2018)
35. Larsson, G., Maire, M., Shakhnarovich, G.: Learning representations for automatic colorization. In: Leibe, B., Matas, J., Sebe, N., Welling, M. (eds.) ECCV 2016. LNCS, vol. 9908. Springer, Cham (2016). https://doi.org/10.1007/978-3-319-46493-0_35
36. Li, J., Chen, B.M., Hee Lee, G.: SO-Net: self-organizing network for point cloud analysis. In: Proceedings of the IEEE Conference on Computer Vision and Pattern Recognition, pp. 9397–9406 (2018)

37. Lien, J.M., Amato, N.M.: Approximate convex decomposition of polyhedra. In: Proceedings of the 2007 ACM Symposium on Solid and Physical Modeling, SPM 2007 (2007)
38. Luo, L., Baran, I., Rusinkiewicz, S., Matusik, W.: Chopper: Partitioning models into 3D-printable parts. ACM Trans. Graph. **31**(6), 1–9 (2012)
39. Mamou, K.: Volumetric approximate convex decomposition, chap. 12. In: Lengyel, E. (ed.) Game Engine Gems, vol. 3, pp. 141–158. A K Peters/CRC Press (2016)
40. Maturana, D., Scherer, S.: 3D convolutional neural networks for landing zone detection from LiDAR. In: Proceedings of the ICRA (2015)
41. Müllner, D., et al.: fastcluster: fast hierarchical, agglomerative clustering routines for R and Python. J. Stat. Softw. **53**(9), 1–18 (2013)
42. Muralikrishnan, S., Kim, V.G., Chaudhuri, S.: Tags2parts: Discovering semantic regions from shape tags. CoRR abs/1708.06673 (2017)
43. Muralikrishnan, S., Kim, V.G., Chaudhuri, S.: Tags2Parts: discovering semantic regions from shape tags. In: Proceedings of the CVPR. IEEE (2018)
44. Noroozi, M., Favaro, P.: Unsupervised learning of visual representations by solving jigsaw puzzles. In: Leibe, B., Matas, J., Sebe, N., Welling, M. (eds.) ECCV 2016. LNCS, vol. 9910, pp. 69–84. Springer, Cham (2016). https://doi.org/10.1007/978-3-319-46466-4_5
45. Pathak, D., Girshick, R., Dollár, P., Darrell, T., Hariharan, B.: Learning features by watching objects move. In: Proceedings of the IEEE Conference on Computer Vision and Pattern Recognition, pp. 2701–2710 (2017)
46. Pathak, D., Krahenbuhl, P., Donahue, J., Darrell, T., Efros, A.A.: Context encoders: feature learning by inpainting. In: Proceedings of the IEEE Conference on Computer Vision and Pattern Recognition, pp. 2536–2544 (2016)
47. Qi, C.R., Su, H., Mo, K., Guibas, L.J.: PointNet: deep learning on point sets for 3D classification and segmentation. In: Proceedings of the CVPR (2017)
48. Qi, C.R., Yi, L., Su, H., Guibas, L.: PointNet++: deep hierarchical feature learning on point sets in a metric space. In: Proceedings of the NIPS (2017)
49. Riegler, G., Ulusoys, A.O., Geiger, A.: OctNet: learning deep 3D representations at high resolutions. In: Proceedings of the CVPR (2017)
50. Sánchez, J., Perronnin, F., Mensink, T., Verbeek, J.: Image classification with the fisher vector: theory and practice. Int. J. Comput. Vis. **105**(3), 222–245 (2013)
51. Saxe, A.M., Koh, P.W., Chen, Z., Bhand, M., Suresh, B., Ng, A.Y.: On random weights and unsupervised feature learning. In: ICML, vol. 2, p. 6 (2011)
52. Sharma, A., Grau, O., Fritz, M.: VConv-DAE: deep volumetric shape learning without object labels. In: Hua, G., Jégou, H. (eds.) ECCV 2016. LNCS, vol. 9915, pp. 236–250. Springer, Cham (2016). https://doi.org/10.1007/978-3-319-49409-8_20
53. Sharma, G., Kalogerakis, E., Maji, S.: Learning point embeddings from shape repositories for few-shot segmentation. In: 2019 International Conference on 3D Vision (3DV), pp. 67–75 (2019)
54. Shi, J., Malik, J.: Normalized cuts and image segmentation. IEEE Trans. Pattern Anal. Mach. Intell. **22**(8), 888–905 (2000)
55. Su, H., et al.: SPLATNet: sparse lattice networks for point cloud processing. In: Proceedings of the IEEE Conference on Computer Vision and Pattern Recognition (2018)
56. Su, H., Maji, S., Kalogerakis, E., Learned-Miller, E.G.: Multi-view convolutional neural networks for 3D shape recognition. In: Proceedings of the ICCV (2015)
57. Su, H., Qi, C., Mo, K., Guibas, L.: PointNet: deep Learning on point sets for 3D classification and segmentation. In: CVPR (2017)

58. Su, J.C., Gadelha, M., Wang, R., Maji, S.: A deeper look at 3D shape classifiers. In: Leal-Taixé, L., Roth, S. (eds.) ECCV 2018. LNCS, vol. 11131. Springer, Cham (2019). https://doi.org/10.1007/978-3-030-11015-4_49

59. Su, J.C., Maji, S., Hariharan, B.: When does self-supervision improve few-shot learning? arXiv preprint arXiv:1910.03560 (2019)

60. Tatarchenko, M., Park, J., Koltun, V., Zhou., Q.Y.: Tangent convolutions for dense prediction in 3D. In: CVPR (2018)

61. Thabet, A., Alwassel, H., Ghanem, B.: MortonNet: Self-Supervised Learning of Local Features in 3D Point Clouds. arXiv (March 2019). https://arxiv.org/abs/1904.00230

62. Trimble Inc.: Trimble 3D Warehouse (2008). https://3dwarehouse.sketchup.com/

63. Trinh, T.H., Luong, M.T., Le, Q.V.: Selfie: Self-supervised pretraining for image embedding. arXiv preprint arXiv:1906.02940 (2019)

64. Vinh, N.X., Epps, J., Bailey, J.: Information theoretic measures for clusterings comparison: variants, properties, normalization and correction for chance. J. Mach. Learn. Res. **11**, 2837–2854 (2010)

65. Von Luxburg, U.: A tutorial on spectral clustering. Stat. Comput. **17**(4), 395–416 (2007)

66. Wang, P.S., Liu, Y., Guo, Y.X., Sun, C.Y., Tong, X.: O-CNN: octree-based convolutional neural networks for 3D shape analysis. ACM Trans. Graph. **36**(4), 1–11 (2017)

67. Wang, P.S., Sun, C.Y., Liu, Y., Tong, X.: Adaptive O-CNN: a patch-based deep representation of 3D shapes. ACM Trans. Graph. **37**(6), 1–11 (2018)

68. Wang, X., Gupta, A.: Unsupervised learning of visual representations using videos. In: Proceedings of the IEEE International Conference on Computer Vision, pp. 2794–2802 (2015)

69. Wang, X., He, K., Gupta, A.: Transitive invariance for self-supervised visual representation learning. In: Proceedings of the IEEE International Conference on Computer Vision, pp. 1329–1338 (2017)

70. Wang, Y., Sun, Y., Liu, Z., Sarma, S.E., Bronstein, M.M., Solomon, J.M.: Dynamic graph CNN for learning on point clouds. ACM Trans. Graph. (TOG) **38**(5), 1–12 (2019)

71. Weller, R.: A brief overview of collision detection. In: Ferre, M., Ernst, M.O., Wing, A. (eds.) New Geometric Data Structures for Collision Detection and Haptics. Springer Series on Touch and Haptic Systems. Springer, Heidelberg (2013). https://doi.org/10.1007/978-3-319-01020-5_2

72. Wu, J., Zhang, C., Xue, T., Freeman, B., Tenenbaum, J.: Learning a probabilistic latent space of object shapes via 3D generative-adversarial modeling. In: Advances in Neural Information Processing Systems, pp. 82–90 (2016)

73. Wu, Z., et al.: 3D ShapeNets: a deep representation for volumetric shapes. In: Proceedings of the IEEE Conference on Computer Vision and Pattern Recognition, pp. 1912–1920 (2015)

74. Xie, Q., Hovy, E., Luong, M.T., Le, Q.V.: Self-training with noisy student improves imagenet classification. arXiv preprint arXiv:1911.04252 (2019)

75. Yang, G., Huang, X., Hao, Z., Liu, M.Y., Belongie, S., Hariharan, B.: PointFlow: 3D point cloud generation with continuous normalizing flows. In: Proceedings of the IEEE International Conference on Computer Vision, pp. 4541–4550 (2019)

76. Yang, Y., Feng, C., Shen, Y., Tian, D.: FoldingNet: point cloud auto-encoder via deep grid deformation. In: Proceedings of the IEEE Conference on Computer Vision and Pattern Recognition, pp. 206–215 (2018)

77. Yi, L., Guibas, L., Hertzmann, A., Kim, V.G., Su, H., Yumer, E.: Learning hierarchical shape segmentation and labeling from online repositories. ACM Trans. Graph. **36**, 1–12 (2017)
78. Zhang, R., Isola, P., Efros, A.A.: Colorful image colorization. In: Leibe, B., Matas, J., Sebe, N., Welling, M. (eds.) ECCV 2016. LNCS, vol. 9907. Springer, Cham (2016). https://doi.org/10.1007/978-3-319-46487-9_40
79. Zhang, R., Isola, P., Efros, A.A.: Split-brain autoencoders: unsupervised learning by cross-channel prediction. In: Proceedings of the IEEE Conference on Computer Vision and Pattern Recognition, pp. 1058–1067 (2017)
80. Zhao, Y., Birdal, T., Deng, H., Tombari, F.: 3D point capsule networks. In: Proceedings of the IEEE Conference on Computer Vision and Pattern Recognition, pp. 1009–1018 (2019)
81. Zhou, Y., Yin, K., Huang, H., Zhang, H., Gong, M., Cohen-Or, D.: Generalized cylinder decomposition. ACM Trans. Graph. **34**, 6 (2015)
82. Ren, Z., Yuan, J., Li, C., Liu, W.: Minimum near-convex decomposition for robust shape representation. In: 2011 International Conference on Computer Vision (November 2011)
83. Zhu, C., Xu, K., Chaudhuri, S., Yi, L., Guibas, L.J., Zhang, H.: AdaCoSeg: Adaptive shape co-segmentation with group consistency loss. CoRR abs/1903.10297 (2019). http://arxiv.org/abs/1903.10297

TexMesh: Reconstructing Detailed Human Texture and Geometry from RGB-D Video

Tiancheng Zhi[1], Christoph Lassner[2], Tony Tung[2], Carsten Stoll[2],
Srinivasa G. Narasimhan[1], and Minh Vo[2(✉)]

[1] Carnegie Mellon University, Pittsburgh, USA
{tzhi,srinivas}@cs.cmu.edu
[2] Facebook Reality Labs, Sausalito, USA
{classner,tony.tung,carsten.stoll,minh.vo}@fb.com

Abstract. We present TexMesh, a novel approach to reconstruct detailed human meshes with high-resolution full-body texture from RGB-D video. TexMesh enables high quality free-viewpoint rendering of humans. Given the RGB frames, the captured environment map, and the coarse per-frame human mesh from RGB-D tracking, our method reconstructs spatiotemporally consistent and detailed per-frame meshes along with a high-resolution albedo texture. By using the incident illumination we are able to accurately estimate local surface geometry and albedo, which allows us to further use photometric constraints to adapt a synthetically trained model to real-world sequences in a self-supervised manner for detailed surface geometry and high-resolution texture estimation. In practice, we train our models on a short example sequence for self-adaptation and the model runs at interactive framerate afterwards. We validate TexMesh on synthetic and real-world data, and show it outperforms the state of art quantitatively and qualitatively.

Keywords: Human shape reconstruction · Human texture generation

1 Introduction

An essential component of VR communication, modern game and movie production is the ability to reconstruct accurate and detailed human geometry with high-fidelity texture from real world data. This allows us to re-render the captured character from novel viewpoints. This is challenging even when using complex multi-camera setups [12,20,29,47]. Recent works such as Tex2Shape [4] and Textured Neural Avatars [41] (TNA) have shown how to reconstruct geometry and texture respectively using nothing but a single RGB image/video as input.

Electronic supplementary material The online version of this chapter (https://doi.org/10.1007/978-3-030-58607-2_29) contains supplementary material, which is available to authorized users.

© Springer Nature Switzerland AG 2020
A. Vedaldi et al. (Eds.): ECCV 2020, LNCS 12355, pp. 492–509, 2020.
https://doi.org/10.1007/978-3-030-58607-2_29

Figure 1 shows examples of novel viewpoint synthesis using Tex2Shape for geometry reconstruction and TNA for texture estimation. Tex2Shape is a single view method trained only on synthetic images without adaptation to real data. Hence, it generates the rough shape of the actor but misses some of the finer geometric details that appear in the real data (Fig. 1(b)), and often hallucinates incorrect deformation memorized from its training data especially in occluded parts. As TNA does not consider the input lighting, the estimated texture contains the baked-in lighting of the original input sequence. Besides, due to small geometric misalignments, the estimated texture is blurry.

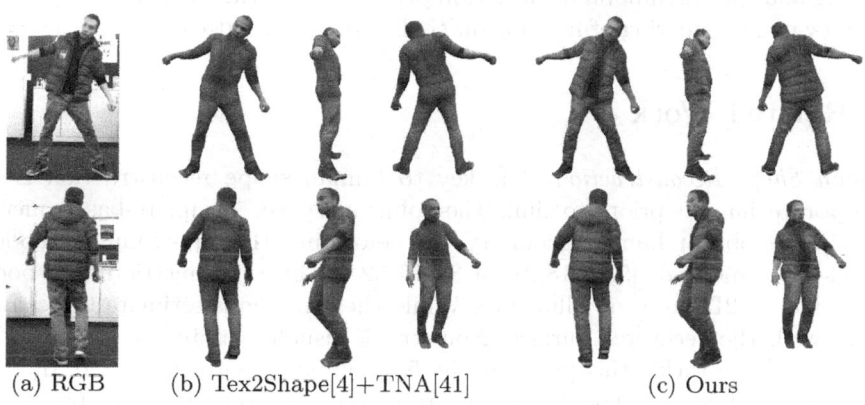

(a) RGB   (b) Tex2Shape[4]+TNA[41]   (c) Ours

Fig. 1. Tex2Shape [4] + TNA [41] vs. Our Result. The mesh with texture is rendered from different viewpoints. Our approach reconstructs more detailed geometry, such as the moving jacket, as well as more accurate texture.

To address these issues, we introduce TexMesh, a novel framework to reconstruct both significantly higher quality mesh and texture from a real world video (see Fig. 1(c)). Our model takes an RGB video, a corresponding environment map, and a per-frame coarse mesh as inputs, and produces a per-frame fine mesh and a high-resolution texture shared across the whole video that can be used for free-viewpoint rendering. The coarse mesh is a parametric human model obtained by 3D tracking from an RGB-D camera [49]. We use a short real video clip for self-adaptation after which TexMesh runs at 18 fps (not including human segmentation). In the pipeline, depth is used only for obtaining the coarse mesh.

Concretely, for texture generation, we parameterize the texture using a CNN and optimize it on real data by comparing the rasterized images with a limited number of selected key albedo images. Our design offers three benefits: no shading and texture mixing, less geometric misalignment leading to less blur, and built-in CNN structure prior for noise and artifact removal [46]. For mesh reconstruction, we propose to first pre-train a displacement map prediction model on synthetic images with supervision, and later optimize it on a real sequence in a self-supervised manner using photometric perceptual loss and spatiotemporal deformation priors to obtain detailed clothing wrinkles even for occluded parts.

Experiments show that the proposed method provides clear texture with high perceptual quality, and detailed dynamic mesh deformation in both the visible and occluded parts. The resulting mesh and texture can produce realistic free-viewpoint rendering (Fig. 11) and relighting results (Fig. 12).

Contributions: (1) We present a self-supervised framework to adapt the training on synthetic data to real data for high quality texture and mesh reconstruction. This framework is based on (2) a texture generation method including albedo estimation, frame selection, and CNN refinement and (3) a mesh reconstruction method that faithfully reconstructs clothing details even in invisible regions using shading and spatiotemporal deformation priors. Our method enables state of art free-viewpoint rendering of humans on challenging real videos.

2 Related Work

Human Shape Reconstruction. The key to human shape reconstruction is to incorporate human priors to limit the solution space. Template-based methods [15,51] obtain human geometry by deforming the pre-scanning model. Model-based methods [9,16,18,21,24,33,36,52,58] fit a parametric naked-body model [28] to 2D poses or silhouette. While these methods estimate the coarse shape well, the recovered surface geometry is usually limited to tight clothing only [8]. To tackle this problem, [54,55] combine depth fusion [30,31] and human priors [28] and show highly accurate reconstruction in visible parts but not occluded regions. With multiple images, [1–3] model clothing by deforming a parametric model [28] to obtain an animatable avatar, which enables powerful VR applications. However, the clothing details are inconsistent across frames, making the re-targeting result not faithful to the observation. Some methods treat clothing as separate meshes, providing strong possibilities for simulation, but are limited to a single clothing [23], pre-defined categories [6], or mechanical properties [56]. Recently, single image methods utilizes deep learning for recovering detailed shapes, including UV space methods [4,23], volumetric methods [57], implicit surface [17,38], and method combining learning and shading [59]. They provide excellent details in visible regions, but hallucinate invisible parts rather than using temporal information for faithful reconstruction. In contrast to the above methods, we exploit photometric and spatiotemporal deformation cues to obtain detailed mesh, even in occluded regions.

Human Texture Generation. The key of texture generation is to fuse information from multiple images. Sampling based methods [2,3] sample colors from video frames and merge them together. TNA [41] uses photometric supervision from rendering. These methods work well for videos with limited deformation but fail when the misalignment caused by large clothing deformation is significant. Single view methods [14,32] avoid the problem of fusing multi-view information by hallucinating the occluded part. Yet, the hallucinated texture may not match the real person. Different from these methods, our method handles large deformation and provides high quality albedo texture.

Face Reconstruction. Face modeling is closely related to body modeling but with limited self-occlusions. Methods using photometric cues reconstruct detailed geometry and albedo via self-supervision [44,45]. Deep learning also provides the opportunity for learning face geometry from synthetic data [39] or both synthetic data and real data [40]. These methods achieve high quality results but cannot be trivially extended to full body, especially for occluded parts.

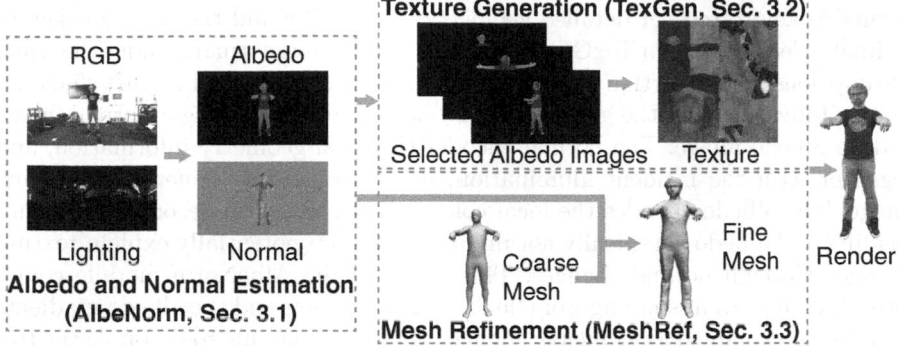

Fig. 2. Framework overview. Our method consists of three modules: Albedo and Normal Estimation (AlbeNorm) pre-precosses RGB images to estimate albedo and normal; Texture Generation (TexGen) selects key albedo frames and recovers a texture map; Mesh Refinement (MeshRef) takes a coarse mesh and a normal image as input and outputs a fine mesh. We pre-train AlbeNorm and MeshRef on synthetic data. Then given a short clip of the real video, we optimize TexGen to obtain texture and finetune MeshRef via self-supervision. Finally, we run AlbeNorm and MeshRef on the whole video for fine meshes. (Color figure online)

3   Method

As in Fig. 2, our framework consists of three modules: Albedo and Normal Estimation (AlbeNorm), Texture Generation (TexGen), and Mesh Refinement (MeshRef). AlbeNorm takes an RGB image and the lighting, represented using Spherical Harmonics [35], and estimates texture and geometry information in the form of albedo and normal images. This is used consecutively to refine the texture and geometry estimates: TexGen selects albedo key frames and generates a high-resolution texture map from them. MeshRef takes a coarse mesh from RGB-D tracking and a normal image and estimates a refined mesh. Ground truth data for these tasks is naturally scarce. However, we observe that (1) synthetic data can be used to train the AlbeNorm and MeshRef. In synthetic settings we can use datasets with detailed person models to obtain highly detailed geometry estimates; (2) TexGen and MeshRef can be finetuned on a short sequence using perceptual photometric loss and the spatiotemporal deformation priors in a *self-supervised* manner. This makes training on large annotated video datasets obsolete. While we train AlbeNorm using only synthetic data, the model empirically generalizes well to real data. The final results are a single high-resolution full-body texture for the whole sequence and fine body geometry predicted at every frame. We describe our method in details in the following sections.

3.1 Albedo and Normal Estimation

The cornerstone for our method is a good albedo and normal estimation: the normal is key to recover detailed geometry in MeshRef and the albedo is key to estimate clear texture in TexGen. To extract albedo and normals, under the usual assumptions of Lambertian materials, distant light sources, and no cast shadows, we can fully represent the geometry and color of an image using a normal image and an albedo image. The normal encodes the local geometry information, and together with the incident illumination, it can be used to generate a shading image. The albedo encodes the local color and texture. The decomposition into shading and albedo is typically not unique, as we can potentially explain texture changes through normal changes. This is where the AlbeNorm module comes into play: to prevent shading from 'leaking' into texture and the albedo gradients from being explained as geometry change, we use the module to decouple the two components. Unlike [2], we resolve the scale ambiguity with the known lighting.

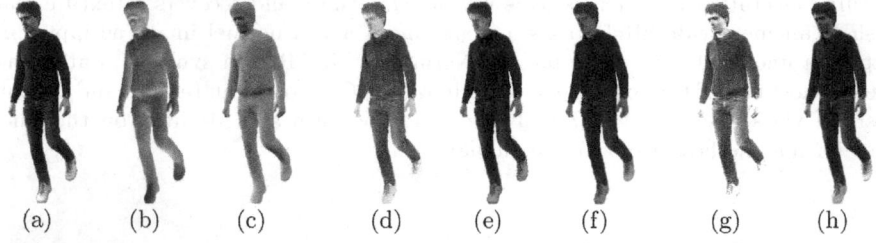

(a)   (b)   (c)   (d)   (e)   (f)   (g)   (h)

Fig. 3. Intermediate results of AlbeNorm. (a) original RGB image; (b) predicted normal; (c) calculated shading; (d) albedo directly from CNN; (e) albedo from dividing RGB by shading; (f) final albedo; (g) rendering using (d); (h) rendering using (f). The final albedo (f) includes less shading information than (e) (e.g., the face region), and (h) resembles the original RGB (a) better than (g). (Color figure online)

The AlbeNorm module uses a CNN to predict albedo and normal images. The inputs to this module are a segmented human image [11,34] and the incident illumination represented as Spherical Harmonics [35]. Knowing the lighting information, we omit the scene background and process the masked human region. Concretely, let A_p and A_g be the predicted and ground truth albedo images, N_p and N_g be the predicted and ground truth normal images, and M the human mask, respectively. Then, our supervised loss L_{AN} with weights λ_a^{an} and λ_n^{an} is:

$$L_{AN} = \lambda_a^{an}||(A_p - A_g) \cdot M||_1 + \lambda_n^{an}||(N_p - N_g) \cdot M||_1, \tag{1}$$

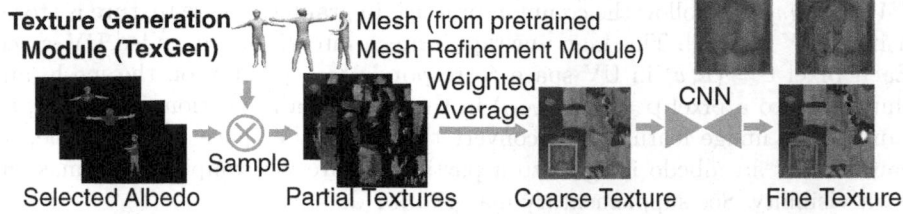

Fig. 4. Texture Generation Module (TexGen). TexGen selects K albedo images and converts them into partial textures. A coarse full texture is constructed by averaging the partial textures with weights. The texture is then refined by a CNN optimized from scratch for each video. The supervision comes from rasterizing the texture to the image space and comparing it with the input albedo images.

To faithfully recover the color and texture for rendering applications, the albedo and normal should be consistent. In other words, the image synthesized using the albedo and normal should match the original image. However, as shown in Fig. 3, due to the domain gap between real and synthetic data, the synthesized image (g) does not have a similar appearance as the original one (a). Another way to obtain consistent albedo is to use the normal N_p and the input illumination to estimate the shading [35] (c), and estimate the albedo (e) by dividing the image (a) by this normal estimated shading. This albedo (e) is consistent with the estimated normal N_p, and thus has the correct color and global scale. Yet it does not have a "flat" appearance, which means there is residual shading information included due to incorrectly estimated normals. The estimated albedo A_p in (d) on the other hand correctly factored out the shading, but is not consistent with the normal image. To consolidate the two estimates, we modify (d) by taking the color and scale from (e), to obtain an albedo (f) which is consistent with the normal image and at the same time has a "flat" appearance.

Concretely, let I be the per-pixel intensity of R, G, B channels: $I = (R + G + B)/3$, and $med(I)$ be the median intensity within human mask. We first take the color from (e) as $R' = I_d/I_e \times R_e$ and globally scale it to (e) as $R = med(I_e)/med(I') \times R'$. B and G are obtained similarly. The resulting albedo (f) is consistent with the normal image (b) and the newly synthesized image (h) better matches the original image (a).

3.2 Texture Generation

TexGen is used to encode and refine the person texture. Inspired by TNA [41], the texture is obtained by optimizing the photometric loss between rendered images and the original ones. We propose to (1) use albedo instead of the original image to prevent shading leaking into texture, (2) select keyframes to mitigate geometric misalignment, and (3) use a CNN to parameterize the texture to reduce noise and artifacts. We assume the availability of MeshRef (Sect. 3.3) pre-trained on synthetic data. Figure 4 shows the TexGen pipeline.

UV Mapping. We follow the common practice in graphics where texture is stored using a UV map [7]. This map unwraps a mesh into 2D space, called UV space. Each pixel $\mathbf{t} = (u, v)$ in UV space corresponds to a point $\mathbf{v}$ on the mesh, and thus maps to a pixel $\mathbf{p} = (x_{2D}, y_{2D})$ in the image via projection. Therefore, we can sample image features and convert them into UV space. For example, we can convert an albedo image into a partial texture via sampling and masking with visibility. See supplementary material for details.

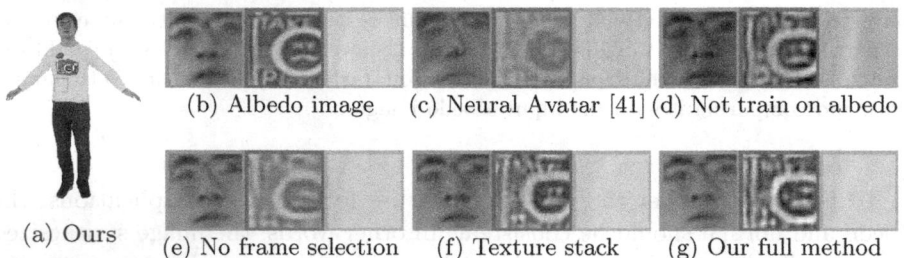

(a) Ours

(b) Albedo image   (c) Neural Avatar [41] (d) Not train on albedo

(e) No frame selection   (f) Texture stack   (g) Our full method

Fig. 5. Rasterized albedo using generated texture. (b) is the albedo from AlbeNorm, which can be seen as "ground truth". Training on the original image rather than albedo (d) causes the texture to include shading. No frame selection (e) makes the result blurry. Using a texture stack instead of a CNN (f) creates a noisy face. (c) is TNA [41] (trained on original images using a texture stack, without frame selection). These issues are addressed by our full method (a)(g).

Key Frame Selection. We aim to extract a sharp texture from a short video sequence. Inherently, this is difficult because of misalignments. We aim to address these issues through selection of a few, particularly well suited frames for this task. Our selection should cover the whole body using a small number (K) of albedo frames based on the visibility of the partial texture image. More concretely, let V_i be the visibility UV map for the i-th selected frame and V_0 be the visibility map of the rest pose mesh. Since most salient parts (e.g., faces) are visible in the rest pose, we first select the frame closest to the rest pose by minimizing $||V_1 - V_0||_1$. We then greedily add the i-th frame by maximizing the total visibility $|| \max_{j=1}^{i} V_j ||_1$, until K frames are selected. We also assign a sampling frequency weight of $W_i = 1/K + w_i / \sum_{i=1}^{K} w_i$, where $w_i = ||V_i - \max_{j=1}^{i-1} V_j||_1$, to every i-th frame. These weights bias the training to more visible frames and speed up the convergence. In practice, we add two adjacent frames with $w = w_i/2$ of the i-th frame for denoising. Figure 5 shows the benefit of our selection scheme which leads to more detailed and accurate reconstructions.

Texture Refinement CNN. From the key albedo frames, we generate partial textures and obtain a coarse texture using a weighted average, where the weight is $w_i V_i$. The coarse texture is processed by a CNN for generating a fine texture, using a deep image prior [46] for denoising and artifact removal (see faces in

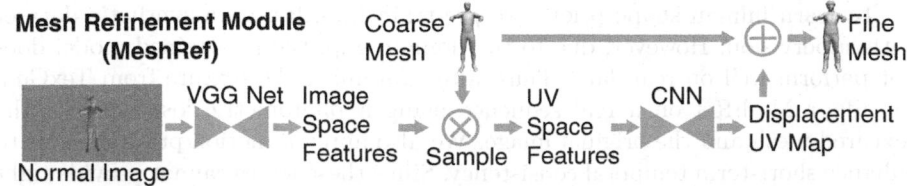

Fig. 6. Mesh Refinement Pipeline (MeshRef). MeshRef first extracts features from a normal image, then convert those features to UV space. The UV space features are then sent to a CNN to predict a 3D displacement map. We obtain the fine mesh by adding the displacements to the coarse mesh. This module is first trained using synthetic data with ground truth and later self-adapted on a short real sequence via photometric and temporal losses.

Fig. 5(f) and (g) for the benefit of our CNN-based texture paramaterization over the texture stack of TNA [41]). The loss comes from rasterizing the texture to the image space and comparing it with the selected albedo images. The gradients are also back-propagated to the mesh and thus MeshRef for a better alignment. This mesh adjustment scheme is a crucial component of the TexGen module.

Concretely, let R be the albedo image rasterized using SoftRas [27], A be the albedo image from AlbeNorm, and M be the human mask from segmentation [11,34]. We use an L_1 photometric loss and a perceptual loss [19] to compare R and A within M. We further regularize the mesh deformation by an L_1 loss between the Laplacian coordinates [43] of the current vertices and the vertices from the initial pre-trained MeshRef model. Our total loss L_{TG} is written as:

$$L_{TG} = \lambda_{L1}^{tg}||(R-A)\cdot M||_1 + \lambda_{pct}^{tg}l_{pct}(R\cdot M, A\cdot M) + \lambda_{lap}^{tg}\sum_{i\in V}||\mathbf{v}'_{p,i}-\mathbf{v}'_{o,i}||_1, \quad (2)$$

where V is the vertex index set and $\mathbf{v}'_{p,i}$ and $\mathbf{v}'_{o,i}$ are the Laplacian coordinates of the i-th predicted vertex and original vertex, respectively. $l_{pct}^{tg}(x,y)$ computes an adaptive robust loss function [5] over the VGG features [42] as perceptual loss [19]. λ_{L1}^{tg}, λ_{pct}^{tg}, and λ_{lap}^{tg} are weights. In practice, we empirically limit the deformation of small structures such as the head and hands by locally disabling gradients, because of possible large mesh registration errors in these regions.

3.3 Mesh Refinement

The MeshRef module is used to refine the coarse mesh. Figure 6 gives an overview of its design. Inspired by the effectiveness of predicting human shape deformation in UV space [4], MeshRef converts the image features into UV space to predict 3D displacement vectors. Our design takes the normal map from AlbeNorm and extracts VGG features [42] to obtain a better encoding, before converting the features to UV space. The features can be further augmented by other information such as vertex positions (see supplementary material for details).

To learn human shape priors, we pre-train MeshRef on a synthetic dataset with supervision. However, due to the domain gap, the pre-trained model does not perform well on real data. Thus, after obtaining the texture from TexGen, we adapt MeshRef on a real sequence using a photometric loss between the textured mesh and the original image. We also apply a motion prior loss [48] to enhance short-term temporal consistency. Since these losses cannot provide tight supervision for invisible regions, we further use a deformation loss to propagate the deformation from frames where those regions are visible to frames where they are not. This model is trained on batches of consecutive video frames.

Supervised Training on Synthetic Images. We supervise the 3D displacement maps using L_1 and SSIM losses and regularize the 3D vertices using a Laplacian loss. Let D_p and D_g be the predicted and ground truth displacement maps and $DSSIM = (1 - SSIM)/2$ be the structural dissimilarity function [50]. Our loss L_{MR1} is defined as:

$$L_{MR1} = \lambda_{L1}^{mr1}||D_p - D_g||_1 + \lambda_{ssim}^{mr1} DSSIM(D_p, D_g) + \lambda_{lap}^{mr1} \sum_{i \in V} ||\mathbf{v}'_{p,i} - \mathbf{v}'_{g,i}||_1, \quad (3)$$

where $\mathbf{v}'_{p,i}$ and $\mathbf{v}'_{g,i}$ are Laplacian coordinates defined similar to Eq. 2, and λ_{L1}^{mr1}, λ_{ssim}^{mr1}, and λ_{lap}^{mr1} are the weights between different losses.

Self-supervised Training on Real Video Data. For self-supervised training, we render the images using the SoftRas differentiable renderer [27] and compare with the original images. Our self-supervised loss is defined as:

$$\begin{aligned} L_{MR2} = \; & \lambda_{pct}^{mr2} L_{pct} + \lambda_{sil}^{mr2} L_{sil} + \lambda_{temp}^{mr2} L_{temp} + \\ & \lambda_{pos}^{mr2} L_{pos} + \lambda_{lap}^{mr2} L_{lap} + \lambda_{deform}^{mr2} L_{deform}, \end{aligned} \quad (4)$$

where $L_{pct}, L_{sil}, L_{temp}, L_{pos}, L_{lap}, L_{deform}$ are the perceptual loss, the silhouette loss, the motion consistency loss, the vertex position loss, Laplacian loss, deformation propagation loss, and $\lambda_{pct}^{mr2}, \lambda_{sil}^{mr2}, \lambda_{temp}^{mr2}, \lambda_{pos}^{mr2}, \lambda_{lap}^{mr2}, \lambda_{deform}^{mr2}$ are their corresponding weights, respectively. We introduce the losses below. For simplicity, we present the losses for one frame, omitting the summation over all frames.

Perceptual Loss. Let R be the rendered image, I be the original image, M_R be the rasterized silhouette and M_I be the segmented human mask, and $M = M_R \cdot M_I$. The loss is defined as $L_{pct} = l_{pct}(R \cdot M, I \cdot M)$, where l_{pct} is the robust perceptual loss function [5,19].

Silhouette Loss. This loss compares the rasterized silhouette and the segmented human mask is defined as $L_{sil} = ||(M_R - M_I) \cdot C||_1$, where C is the confidence map given by the segmentation algorithm [11,34].

Motion Consistency Loss. Let t be the current frame index and $\mathbf{v}_{p,i}^{(t)}$ be the position of the i-th vertex in frame t. Our motion consistency loss favors constant velocity in adjacent frames [48] and is written as $L_{temp} = \sum_{i \in V} ||\mathbf{v}_{p,i}^{(t-1)} + \mathbf{v}_{p,i}^{(t+1)} - 2\mathbf{v}_{p,i}^{(t)}||_1$, where V is the set of vertex indices.

Vertex Position Loss. This loss prevents large deformation from the original position predicted by the model pre-trained on synthetic data and is defined as $L_{pos} = \sum_{i \in V'} ||\mathbf{v}_{p,i} - \mathbf{v}_{o,i}||_2$, where $\mathbf{v}_{p,i}$ and $\mathbf{v}_{o,i}$ are the positions of the i-th predicted vertex and original vertex, and V' be the set of visible vertex indices.

Laplacian Loss. This loss is not only applied to visible vertices but also head and hand vertices regardless of their visibility because noisy deformation of these vertices can significantly affect the perceptual result, and is defined as $L_{lap} = \sum_{i \in V} ||(\mathbf{v}_{p,i}' - \mathbf{v}_{o,i}') \cdot u_i||_1$, where $\mathbf{v}_{p,i}'$ and $\mathbf{v}_{o,i}'$ are the Laplacian coordinates of the i-th predicted and original vertices, and u_i be the weight of the i-th vertex. We set $u_i = 100$ for head and hand, 1 for other visible vertices, and 0 for the rest.

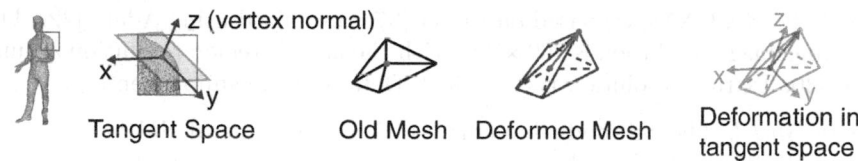

Tangent Space   Old Mesh   Deformed Mesh   Deformation in tangent space

Fig. 7. Deformation in tangent space. At a local point, the z-axis points to the vertex normal direction and the x and y axes complete the orthogonal basis, forming a local coordinate system. We use this coordinate system to represent the vertex deformation. This representation is invariant to pose change, propagating deformation of the same vertex in different frames.

Deformation Propagation Loss. To reconstruct an vertex invisible in the current frame, we find a visible counterpart in the set of keyframes computed in Sect. 3.2 and propagate the deformation from it. This is similar in spirit to the canonical shape model [30]. However, because the human in the source frame and target frame may have different poses, we can not simply force the deformation in the global coordinates to be similar. We adopt the local tangent space [25] (Fig. 7) to solve this problem.

Let $\mathbf{d}_i^{(s)}$ and $\mathbf{d}_i^{(t)}$ be the deformation in tangent space of the i-th source vertex visible in one of the selected keyframes and occluded target vertex at the current frame. The deformation loss is defined as $L_{deform} = \sum_{i \in V''} ||\mathbf{d}_i^{(t)} - \mathbf{d}_i^{(s)}||_1$, where V'' is the set of invisible vertex indices in target frame. $\mathbf{d}_i^{(s)}$ does not receive gradients, and is stored in a buffer updated when the source frame is sampled during training. In practice, we extend V'' to include head vertices, to enhance head rigidity. Our deformation propagation scheme provides more realistic details on invisible surfaces as shown in Fig. 8.

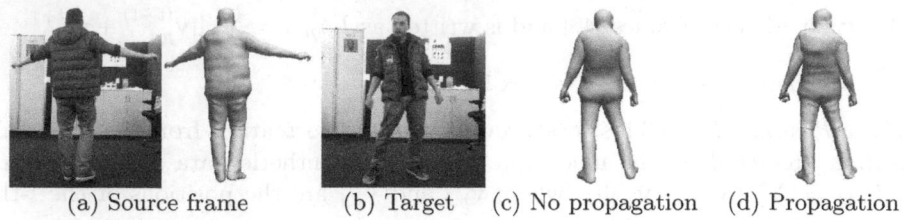

(a) Source frame   (b) Target   (c) No propagation   (d) Propagation

Fig. 8. Effect of deformation propagation. (a) is a source frame propagating defor-mation to frame (b) where the back is not visible. The back of (b) is reconstructed without (c) and with (d) deformation propagation. The one with propagation shows more clothing details.

4   Experimental Analysis

4.1   Implementation Details

Deep Networks. CNNs are based on U-Net [37], optimized using Adam [22]. The full-frame image resolution is 960×540 with the human region resolution around 200×430. Texture resolution is 512×512. Details are in supplementary.

Human Model. The full-body human model is a variant of SMPL [28]. The original SMPL model has about 7k vertices, which is too large for the coarse mesh representation, and insufficient to represent fine details such as clothing wrinkles. Thus, we construct a body model with two levels of resolution: the coarse level has 1831 vertices and 3658 faces, and the fine level has 29,290 vertices and 58,576 faces obtained by subdividing the coarse mesh topology. The vertices of the coarse mesh are a subset of the vertices of the fine mesh and share identical vertex indices. Both representations also share a unique skeletal rig that contains 74 joints. This design reduces the overhead for generating the coarse mesh, and preserves the fine mesh capability to represent geometric details.

4.2   Datasets

Our method requires lighting information, which is not provided by most public datasets. Thus we capture and render our own data to perform experiments.

Synthetic Images for Pre-training. We synthesize 18,282 images using 428 human 3D scans from RenderPeople[1] and Our Dataset under the lighting from Laval Dataset [13]. Our Dataset was captured with a 3dMD scanner and contains 48 subjects. We registered the fine level Human Model to the 3D scans using non-rigid ICP [26], initialized with a 3D pose estimator [9]. To generate the coarse mesh, Gaussian noise scaled by a random factor sampled from uniform distribution is added to the pose and shape parameters, and the position of the character. The registered model can be set in arbitrary pose with skeletal rig.

---

[1] http://renderpeople.com/.

We render the 3D scans into images of various poses sampled from the Motion Capture data. No video sequences are synthesized due to its high computational demand. Our final dataset contains coarse meshes, fine meshes, displacement maps, environment maps, RGB images, albedos, normals, and human masks.

Synthetic Videos for Quantitative Evaluation. We synthesize 6 videos with ground truth measurements that contain dynamic clothing deformation for higher realism. Our clothing is modeled as separate meshes on top of human body scans as in DeepWrinkles [23]. However, we obtain deformation by physics-based simulation. We use the human bodies from AXYZ dataset[2] and the lighting from HDRI Heaven[3]. The videos represent subjects performing different motions such as walking or dancing and has about 3.8k frames each. In each video, we use about half of the frames for model adaptation and do inference on the rest. We treat the naked body as coarse mesh and the clothed body as fine mesh.

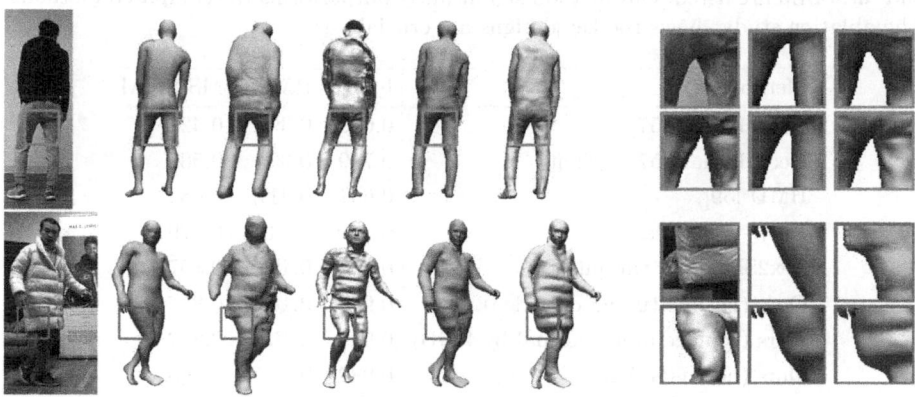

Fig. 9. Comparing mesh with coarse mesh (grey), DeepHuman [57] (red), HMD [59] (yellow), Tex2Shape [4]. Our method (green) outperforms them in shape and details: DeepHuman is coarse in head and hands. HMD has artifacts in head and body regions. Tex2Shape does not obtain realistic wrinkles. (Color figure online)

Real Videos for Qualitative Evaluation. We capture 8 videos (~4 min each) using a Kinect along with lighting captured using a ThetaS. The cameras are geometrically and radiometrically calibrated. We use the first 2k frames for model adaption and infer on the whole video. We obtain the coarse mesh in real-time by solving an inverse kinematic problem to fit the posed body shape to the 3D point cloud and detected body keypoints [10] using an approach similar to [49].

4.3   Results

Texture. We compare our texture with a sampling-based method (SBM) [3] variant and a Textured Neural Avatars (TNA) [41] variant re-implemented with our

---

[2] http://secure.axyz-design.com/.

[3] http://hdrihaven.com/.

Human Model, which map between image and UV spaces using the mesh. We render albedo images on synthetic videos, and evaluate average RMSE within valid mask and MS-SSIM [50] within human bounding box over subsampled videos. Our method outperforms SBM and TNA on (RMSE, MS-SSIM): (0.124, 0.800) for SBM, (0.146, 0.809) for TNA, and (**0.119, 0.831**) for ours, respectively. See Fig. 5 and the supplementary material for qualitative results.

Mesh. We compare our method with DeepHuman [57], HMD [59], and a variant of Tex2Shape [4] trained on our synthetic images for our Human Model, predicting 3D displacements on top of the posed coarse mesh, using our network and loss settings. For fairness, we compare with both the original version and the variants of DeepHuman and HMD where the initial mesh is replaced by our coarse mesh.

Table 1. Evaluation of mesh reconstruction. Silhouette IoU, rasterized normal RMSE and MS-SSIM are listed. Our method significantly outperforms the compared methods. The ablation study shows the key designs are crucial

Method	IoU	RMSE	MS-SSIM
DeepHuman [57]	0.650	0.399	0.421
DeepHuman [57] variant	0.779	0.309	0.587
HMD [59]	0.667	0.417	0.684
HMD [59] variant	0.790	0.344	0.779
Tex2Shape [4] variant	0.926	0.192	0.857
Ours (no fine-tuning on video)	0.940	0.186	0.857
Ours (replace input normal by RGB)	0.928	0.190	0.852
Ours (no VGG feature)	0.932	0.185	0.865
Ours (no deformation propagation)	**0.941**	0.174	0.869
Our full method	**0.941**	**0.173**	**0.870**

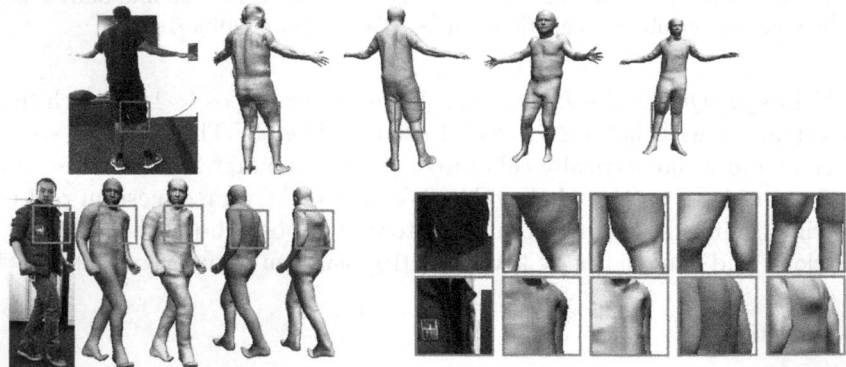

Fig. 10. Viewing from front and back. Tex2Shape (blue), HMD (yellow), Ours (green). Ours captures the shape of occluded jacket hood and shorts deformation. (Color figure online)

See the supplementary material about how to resolve the mismatch of camera parameters and human models. In Fig. 9, while DeepHuman and HMD provide unrealistic heads and Tex2Shape fails to produce faithful clothing details, our method is shape-preserving and generates better fine geometry. We also recover the geometry of shorts and jacket in occluded regions (Fig. 10). The supplemental video shows our result is temporal consistent. Quantitatively, we evaluate on the synthetic videos by rasterizing 2D normal images. The metrics are silhouette IoU, RMSE, and MS-SSIM[50] within human mask/bounding box. Table 1 shows that our method outperforms the others on all metrics.

Ablation Study. We quantify the effect of domain finetuning, replacing the normal image by RGB image in MeshRef, removing the VGGNet, and removing the deformation propagation scheme in Table 1. Evidently, the first three components are crucial and ignoring them hurts the performance. As expected, removing deformation propagation has little effect because it focuses mainly on the occluded regions (see Fig. 8 for its qualitative effect).

Applications. We show rendering from novel viewpoints (Fig. 11) and relighting in a different environment (Fig. 12) using our outputs. The results have clear textures and realistic shading variation around clothing wrinkles.

Fig. 11. Rendering results. The right-most scene is from synthetic video. The rendering has both high fidelity and perceptual quality, from different viewpoints. The clothing wrinkles, logo, and text are clearly recovered.

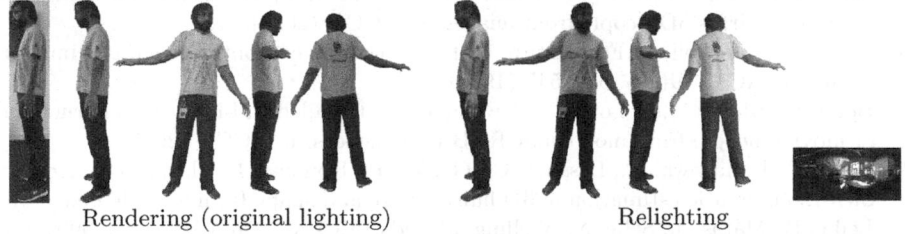

Rendering (original lighting)   Relighting

Fig. 12. Free-viewpoint rendering and relighting. The detailed pattern on the shirt is clearly reconstructed. The shading varies in the clothing wrinkles implying that the wrinkles are correctly estimated as geometry rather than texture.

5   Conclusion

In summary, we present TexMesh, a state of art method for high fidelity human texture and geometry reconstruction, enabling high quality free-viewpoint human rendering on real videos. Our key idea is a self-supervised learning framework to adapt a synthetically-trained model to real videos. After adaptation, our model runs at interactive frame rate. In the future, we will train the model on many real videos concurrently to learn a generic shape prior as it could allow faster adaptation to new sequences or even require no adaptation at all.

Besides, we will address two limitations of our method in the future. First, we rely on a spherical camera to capture the lighting and represent it using only low frequency Spherical Harmonics. Exploring recent techniques on using a single narrow FOV image to estimate high frequency environmental lighting [13,40] together with subtle lighting cues from human appearance [53] is an exciting future direction to tackle this problem. Second, we assume the deformation in invisible regions is the same or similar as in the keyframes, which is not always true. We will consider using clothing simulation [56] to alleviate this problem.

Acknowledgements. This work was done during Tiancheng Zhi's internship at Facebook Reality Labs, Sausalito, CA, USA. We thank Junbang Liang, Yinghao Huang, and Nikolaos Sarafianos for their help with data generation.

References

1. Alldieck, T., Magnor, M., Bhatnagar, B.L., Theobalt, C., Pons-Moll, G.: Learning to reconstruct people in clothing from a single RGB camera. In: CVPR (2019)
2. Alldieck, T., Magnor, M., Xu, W., Theobalt, C., Pons-Moll, G.: Detailed human avatars from monocular video. In: 3DV (2018)
3. Alldieck, T., Magnor, M., Xu, W., Theobalt, C., Pons-Moll, G.: Video based reconstruction of 3D people models. In: CVPR (2018)
4. Alldieck, T., Pons-Moll, G., Theobalt, C., Magnor, M.: Tex2shape: detailed full human body geometry from a single image. In: CVPR (2019)
5. Barron, J.T.: A general and adaptive robust loss function. In: CVPR (2019)
6. Bhatnagar, B.L., Tiwari, G., Theobalt, C., Pons-Moll, G.: Multi-Garment Net: learning to dress 3D people from images. In: ICCV (2019)
7. Blinn, J.F., Newell, M.E.: Texture and reflection in computer generated images. Commun. ACM **19**(10), 542–547 (1976)
8. Bogo, F., Black, M.J., Loper, M., Romero, J.: Detailed full-body reconstructions of moving people from monocular RGB-D sequences. In: ICCV (2015)
9. Bogo, F., Kanazawa, A., Lassner, C., Gehler, P., Romero, J., Black, M.J.: Keep it SMPL: automatic estimation of 3D human pose and shape from a single image. In: Leibe, B., Matas, J., Sebe, N., Welling, M. (eds.) ECCV 2016. LNCS, vol. 9909, pp. 561–578. Springer, Cham (2016). https://doi.org/10.1007/978-3-319-46454-1_34
10. Cao, Z., Hidalgo, G., Simon, T., Wei, S.E., Sheikh, Y.: Openpose: realtime multi-person 2D pose estimation using part affinity fields. TPAMI (2019)
11. Chen, L.C., Papandreou, G., Schroff, F., Adam, H.: Rethinking atrous convolution for semantic image segmentation. arXiv preprint arXiv:1706.05587 (2017)

12. Collet, A., et al.: High-quality streamable free-viewpoint video. TOG **34**, 1–13 (2015)
13. Gardner, M.A., et al.: Learning to predict indoor illumination from a single image. TOG (SIGGRAPH Asia) **9**(4) (2017)
14. Grigorev, A., Sevastopolsky, A., Vakhitov, A., Lempitsky, V.: Coordinate-based texture inpainting for pose-guided human image generation. In: CVPR (2019)
15. Habermann, M., Xu, W., Zollhoefer, M., Pons-Moll, G., Theobalt, C.: Livecap: real-time human performance capture from monocular video. TOG **38**(2), 1–17 (2019)
16. Huang, Y., et al.: Towards accurate marker-less human shape and pose estimation over time. In: 3DV (2017)
17. Huang, Z., Xu, Y., Lassner, C., Li, H., Tung, T.: ARCH: animatable reconstruction of clothed humans. In: CVPR (2020)
18. Jain, A., Thormählen, T., Seidel, H.P., Theobalt, C.: MovieReshape: tracking and reshaping of humans in videos. TOG **29**(6), 1–10 (2010)
19. Johnson, J., Alahi, A., Fei-Fei, L.: Perceptual losses for real-time style transfer and super-resolution. In: Leibe, B., Matas, J., Sebe, N., Welling, M. (eds.) ECCV 2016. LNCS, vol. 9906, pp. 694–711. Springer, Cham (2016). https://doi.org/10.1007/978-3-319-46475-6_43
20. Kanade, T., Rander, P., Narayanan, P.: Virtualized reality: constructing virtual worlds from real scenes. IEEE Multimed. **4**(1), 34–47 (1997)
21. Kanazawa, A., Black, M.J., Jacobs, D.W., Malik, J.: End-to-end recovery of human shape and pose. In: CVPR (2018)
22. Kingma, D.P., Ba, J.: Adam: a method for stochastic optimization. In: ICLR (2015)
23. Lähner, Z., Cremers, D., Tung, T.: DeepWrinkles: accurate and realistic clothing modeling. In: Ferrari, V., Hebert, M., Sminchisescu, C., Weiss, Y. (eds.) ECCV 2018. LNCS, vol. 11208, pp. 698–715. Springer, Cham (2018). https://doi.org/10.1007/978-3-030-01225-0_41
24. Lassner, C., Romero, J., Kiefel, M., Bogo, F., Black, M.J., Gehler, P.V.: Unite the people: closing the loop between 3D and 2D human representations. In: CVPR (2017)
25. Lengyel, E.: Mathematics for 3D Game Programming and Computer Graphics. Cengage Learning, Boston (2012)
26. Li, H., Sumner, R.W., Pauly, M.: Global correspondence optimization for non-rigid registration of depth scans. In: CGF (2008)
27. Liu, S., Li, T., Chen, W., Li, H.: Soft Rasterizer: a differentiable renderer for image-based 3d reasoning. In: ICCV (2019)
28. Loper, M., Mahmood, N., Romero, J., Pons-Moll, G., Black, M.J.: SMPL: a skinned multi-person linear model. TOG **34**(6), 1–16 (2015)
29. Matsuyama, T., Takai, T.: Generation, visualization, and editing of 3D video. In: 3DPVT (2002)
30. Newcombe, R.A., Fox, D., Seitz, S.M.: DynamicFusion: reconstruction and tracking of non-rigid scenes in real-time. In: CVPR (2015)
31. Newcombe, R.A., et al.: KinectFusion: real-time dense surface mapping and tracking. In: 2011 10th IEEE International Symposium on Mixed and Augmented Reality, pp. 127–136. IEEE (2011)
32. Oechsle, M., Mescheder, L., Niemeyer, M., Strauss, T., Geiger, A.: Texture fields: learning texture representations in function space. In: ICCV (2019)
33. Omran, M., Lassner, C., Pons-Moll, G., Gehler, P., Schiele, B.: Neural body fitting: unifying deep learning and model based human pose and shape estimation. In: 3DV (2018)

34. Piccardi, M.: Background subtraction techniques: a review. In: 2004 IEEE International Conference on Systems, Man and Cybernetics (IEEE Cat. No. 04CH37583), vol. 4, pp. 3099–3104. IEEE (2004)
35. Ramamoorthi, R., Hanrahan, P.: An efficient representation for irradiance environment maps. In: SIGGRAPH (2001)
36. Rhodin, H., Robertini, N., Casas, D., Richardt, C., Seidel, H.-P., Theobalt, C.: General automatic human shape and motion capture using volumetric contour cues. In: Leibe, B., Matas, J., Sebe, N., Welling, M. (eds.) ECCV 2016. LNCS, vol. 9909, pp. 509–526. Springer, Cham (2016). https://doi.org/10.1007/978-3-319-46454-1_31
37. Ronneberger, O., Fischer, P., Brox, T.: U-Net: convolutional networks for biomedical image segmentation. In: Navab, N., Hornegger, J., Wells, W.M., Frangi, A.F. (eds.) MICCAI 2015. LNCS, vol. 9351, pp. 234–241. Springer, Cham (2015). https://doi.org/10.1007/978-3-319-24574-4_28
38. Saito, S., Huang, Z., Natsume, R., Morishima, S., Kanazawa, A., Li, H.: PIFu: pixel-aligned implicit function for high-resolution clothed human digitization. In: ICCV (2019)
39. Sela, M., Richardson, E., Kimmel, R.: Unrestricted facial geometry reconstruction using image-to-image translation. In: ICCV (2017)
40. Sengupta, S., Kanazawa, A., Castillo, C.D., Jacobs, D.W.: SfSNet: learning shape, reflectance and illuminance of faces 'in the wild'. In: CVPR (2018)
41. Shysheya, A., et al.: Textured neural avatars. In: CVPR (2019)
42. Simonyan, K., Zisserman, A.: Very deep convolutional networks for large-scale image recognition. In: ICLR (2015)
43. Sorkine, O.: Differential representations for mesh processing. In: CGF (2006)
44. Tewari, A., et al.: FML: face model learning from videos. In: CVPR (2019)
45. Tewari, A., et al.: Self-supervised multi-level face model learning for monocular reconstruction at over 250 Hz. In: CVPR (2018)
46. Ulyanov, D., Vedaldi, A., Lempitsky, V.: Deep image prior. In: CVPR (2018)
47. Vlasic, D., Peers, P., Baran, I., Debevec, P., Popović, J., Rusinkiewicz, S., Matusik, W.: Dynamic shape capture using multi-view photometric stereo. TOG (SIGGRAPH Asia) 28(5) (2009)
48. Vo, M., Narasimhan, S.G., Sheikh, Y.: Spatiotemporal bundle adjustment for dynamic 3D reconstruction. In: CVPR (2016)
49. Walsman, A., Wan, W., Schmidt, T., Fox, D.: Dynamic high resolution deformable articulated tracking. In: 3DV (2017)
50. Wang, Z., Bovik, A.C., Sheikh, H.R., Simoncelli, E.P.: Image quality assessment: from error visibility to structural similarity. TIP 13(4), 600–612 (2004)
51. Xu, W., et al.: MonoPerfCap: human performance capture from monocular video. TOG 37, 27:1–27:15 (2018)
52. Xu, Y., Zhu, S.C., Tung, T.: DenseRaC: joint 3D pose and shape estimation by dense render and compare. In: ICCV (2019)
53. Yi, R., Zhu, C., Tan, P., Lin, S.: Faces as lighting probes via unsupervised deep highlight extraction. In: Ferrari, V., Hebert, M., Sminchisescu, C., Weiss, Y. (eds.) ECCV 2018. LNCS, vol. 11213, pp. 321–338. Springer, Cham (2018). https://doi.org/10.1007/978-3-030-01240-3_20
54. Yu, T., et al.: BodyFusion: real-time capture of human motion and surface geometry using a single depth camera. In: ICCV (2017)
55. Yu, T., et al.: DoubleFusion: real-time capture of human performances with inner body shapes from a single depth sensor. In: CVPR (2018)

56. Yu, T., et al.: SimulCap: single-view human performance capture with cloth simulation. In: CVPR (2019)
57. Zheng, Z., Yu, T., Wei, Y., Dai, Q., Liu, Y.: DeepHuman: 3D human reconstruction from a single image. In: ICCV (2019)
58. Zhou, S., Fu, H., Liu, L., Cohen-Or, D., Han, X.: Parametric reshaping of human bodies in images. TOG **29**(4), 1–10 (2010)
59. Zhu, H., Zuo, X., Wang, S., Cao, X., Yang, R.: Detailed human shape estimation from a single image by hierarchical mesh deformation. In: CVPR (2019)

Consistency-Based Semi-supervised Active Learning: Towards Minimizing Labeling Cost

Mingfei Gao[1(✉)], Zizhao Zhang[2], Guo Yu[3], Sercan Ö. Arık[2], Larry S. Davis[1],
and Tomas Pfister[2]

[1] University of Maryland, College Park, USA
mgao@cs.umd.edu
[2] Google Cloud AI, Sunnyvale, USA
[3] University of Washington, Seattle, USA

Abstract. Active learning (AL) combines data labeling and model training to minimize the labeling cost by prioritizing the selection of high value data that can best improve model performance. In pool-based active learning, accessible unlabeled data are not used for model training in most conventional methods. Here, we propose to unify unlabeled sample selection and model training towards minimizing labeling cost, and make two contributions towards that end. First, we exploit both labeled and unlabeled data using semi-supervised learning (SSL) to distill information from unlabeled data during the training stage. Second, we propose a consistency-based sample selection metric that is coherent with the training objective such that the selected samples are effective at improving model performance. We conduct extensive experiments on image classification tasks. The experimental results on CIFAR-10, CIFAR-100 and ImageNet demonstrate the superior performance of our proposed method with limited labeled data, compared to the existing methods and the alternative AL and SSL combinations. Additionally, we also study an important yet under-explored problem – "When can we start learning-based AL selection?". We propose a measure that is empirically correlated with the AL target loss and is potentially useful for determining the proper starting point of learning-based AL methods.

Keywords: Active learning · Semi-supervised learning · Consistency-based sample selection

---

M. Gao—Work done while the author was an intern at Google; now at Salesforce Research.

Electronic supplementary material The online version of this chapter (https://doi.org/10.1007/978-3-030-58607-2_30) contains supplementary material, which is available to authorized users.

© Springer Nature Switzerland AG 2020
A. Vedaldi et al. (Eds.): ECCV 2020, LNCS 12355, pp. 510–526, 2020.
https://doi.org/10.1007/978-3-030-58607-2_30

1   Introduction

Deep learning models are improved when trained with more labeled data [19]. A standard deep learning procedure involves constructing a large-scale labeled dataset and optimizing a model on it. Yet, in many real-world scenarios, large-scale labeled datasets can be very costly to acquire, especially when expert annotators are required, as in medical diagnosis. An ideal framework would integrate data labeling and model training to improve model performance with minimal amount of labeled data.

Active learning (AL) [2] assists the learning procedure by judicious selection of unlabeled samples for human labeling, with the goal of maximizing the model performance with minimal labeling cost. We focus on practically-common pool-based AL, where an unlabeled data pool is given initially and the AL mechanism iteratively selects batches to label in conjunction with training.

Learning-based AL methods select a batch of samples for labeling with guidance from the previously-trained model and then add these samples into the labeled dataset for the model training in the next cycle. Existing methods generally start with a randomly sampled labeled set. The size of the starting set affects learning-based AL performance – when the start size is not sufficiently large, the models learned in subsequent AL cycles are highly-biased which results in poor selection, a phenomenon commonly known as the *cold start problem* [23,26]. When cold start issues arise, learning-based selection yields samples that lead to lower performance improvement than naive uniform sampling [26].

To improve the performance at early AL cycles when the amount of labeled data is limited, it is important to address cold-start and ensure high performance later on with low labeling cost. Along this line of research, one natural idea for pool-based AL is integration of abundant unlabeled data into learning using semi-supervised learning (SSL) [48,55]. Recent advances in SSL [5,45,46,50,51] has demonstrated the vast potential of utilizing unlabeled data for learning effective representations. Although "semi-supervised AL" seems natural, only a small portion of AL literature has focused on it. Past works that use SSL for AL [14,36,39,55] treated SSL and AL independently without considering their impact on each other. We on the other hand, hypothesize that a better AL selection criterion should be in coherence with the corresponding objectives of unlabeled data in SSL to select the most valuable samples. A primary reason is that SSL already results in embodiment of knowledge from unlabeled data in a meaningful way, thus AL selection should reflect the value of additionally collected labeled data on top of such embodied knowledge. Based on these motivations, we propose an AL framework that integrates SSL to AL and also a selection metric that is highly related to the training objective.

The proposed AL framework is based on an insight that has driven recent advances in SSL [5,50,51] – a model should be consistent in its decisions between a sample and its meaningfully distorted versions, obtained via appropriate data augmentation. This motivates us to introduce an AL selection strategy: *a sample along with its distorted variants that yields low consistency in predictions indicates that the SSL model may be incapable of distilling useful information from that unlabeled sample – thus human labeling is needed.*

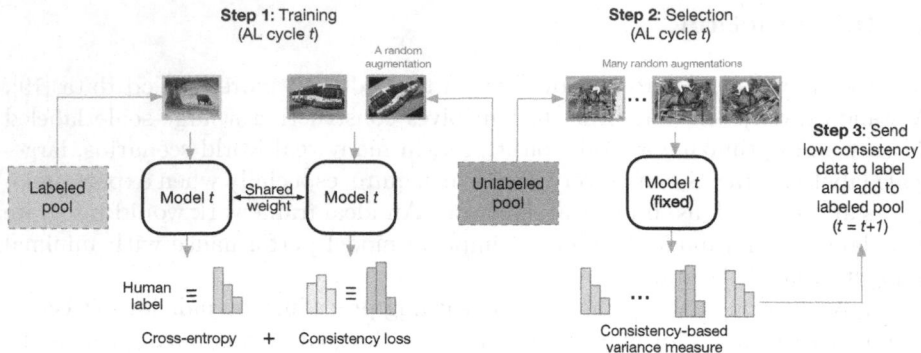

Fig. 1. Illustration of the proposed framework at t^{th} AL cycle. During training, both labeled and unlabeled data are used for the model optimization, with cross-entropy loss encouraging correct predictions for the labeled samples and consistency-based loss encouraging consistent outputs between unlabeled samples and their augmentations. During sample selection, the unlabeled samples and their augmentations are evaluated by the model obtained from the training stage. Their outputs are measured by our proposed consistency-based metric. The samples with low consistency scores are selected for labeling and sent to the labeled pool

Overall, **our contributions** are summarized as follows:

1. We propose to unify model training and sample selection with a semi-supervised AL framework. The proposed framework outperforms the previous AL methods and the baselines of straightforward SSL and AL combinations.
2. We propose a simple yet effective selection metric based on sample consistency which implicitly balances sample uncertainty and diversity during selection. With comprehensive analyses, we demonstrate the rationale behind the proposed consistency-based sampling.
3. We propose a measure that is potentially useful for determining the proper start size to mitigate cold start problems in AL.

2   Related Work

2.1   Active Learning

There exists a broad literature on AL [2,8,11,12]. Most AL methods can be classified under three categories: uncertainty-based methods, diversity-based methods and methods based on model performance change. Most uncertainty-based methods use *max entropy* [30,31] and *max margin* [3,25,37] criteria due to their simplicity. Some others use distances between samples and the decision boundary [6,49]. Most uncertainty-based methods use heuristics, while recent work [53] directly learns the target loss of inputs jointly with the training phase and shows promising results. Diversity-based methods select diverse samples that span the input space maximally [22,32,34,39]. There are also methods that consider uncertainty and diversity in conjunction [15,21,52]. The third category estimates the future model status and selects samples that encourage optimal model improvement [16,38,40].

2.2   Semi-supervised Active Learning

Both AL and SSL aim to improve learning with limited labeled data, thus they are naturally related. Yet, only a few recent works have considered combining AL and SSL. In [14], joint application of SSL and AL is considered for speech understanding, and significant error reduction is demonstrated with limited labeled speech data. Their AL selection criteria is based on a confidence score obtained from the posterior probabilities of the decoded text. Rhee *et al.* [36] propose an semi-supervised AL system which demonstrates superior performance in the pedestrian detection task. Zhu *et al.* [55] combine AL and SSL using Gaussian fields. Sener *et al.* [39] also consider SSL during AL cycles. However, in their setting, the performance improvement is marginal when adding SSL in comparison to their supervised counterpart, potentially due to the sub-optimal SSL method and combination strategy. Recently, Sinha *et al.* propose VAAL in [44], where a variational autoencoder and an adversarial network are learned using both labeled and unlabeled samples to infer the representativeness of unlabeled samples during the sampling process. Although, unlabeled data is not used for model training. The concurrent AL works [42,47] also consider integrating SSL, but their selection procedures are independent from the model training. We demonstrate that our proposed method unifying AL selection with SSL training is superior than the straightforward-combination strategy.

2.3   Agreement-Based Active Learning

Agreement-based methods, also referred as "query-by-committee", base the selection on the opinions of a committee which consists of independent AL metrics or models [4,7,9,24,33,41]. Our method is related to agreement-based AL where samples are determined based on the conformity of different metrics or models. Specifically, our method selects samples that mostly disagree with the predictions of their augmentations.

3   Consistency-Based Semi-supervised AL

We consider the setting of pool-based AL, where an unlabeled data pool is available for selection of samples to label. To minimize the labeling cost, we propose a method that unifies selection and model updates. The proposed semi-supervised AL is depicted in Fig. 1.

Most conventional AL methods base model learning only on the available labeled data, ignoring the useful information in the unlabeled data. While, we incorporate a semi-supervised learning (SSL) objective at training phases of AL

Algorithm 1. A semi-supervised learning based AL framework

Require: Unlabeled data pool $\mathcal{D}$, the total number of steps T, selected sample batch
set B, AL batch size K, start size $K_0 \ll |\mathcal{D}|$
    $B_0 \leftarrow$ uniformly sampling from $\mathcal{D}$ with $|B_0| = K_0$
    $U_0 \leftarrow \mathcal{D} \backslash B_0$
    $L_0 \leftarrow \{(x, \mathcal{J}(x)) : x \in B_0\}$, where $\mathcal{J}(x)$ stands for the assigned label of x.
    for $t = 0, \ldots, T - 1$ **do**
        (training) $M_t \leftarrow \arg\min_M \left\{ \frac{1}{|L_t|} \sum_{(x,y) \in L_t} \mathcal{L}_l(x, y, M) + \frac{1}{|U_t|} \sum_{x \in U_t} \mathcal{L}_u(x, M) \right\}$
        (selection) $B_{t+1} \leftarrow \arg\max_{B \subset U_t} \{ \mathcal{C}(B, M_t), s.t. |B| = K \}$
        (labeling) $L_{t+1} \leftarrow L_t \cup \{(x, \mathcal{J}(x)) : x \in B_{t+1}\}$
        (pool update) $U_{t+1} \leftarrow U_t \backslash B_{t+1}$
    end for
    $M_T \leftarrow \arg\min_M \left\{ \frac{1}{|L_T|} \sum_{(x,y) \in L_T} \mathcal{L}_l(x, y, M) + \frac{1}{|U_T|} \sum_{x \in U_T} \mathcal{L}_u(x, M) \right\}$
    return M_T

---

cycles. The target model M_t at AL selection cycle t is learned by minimizing an objective loss function of the form $\mathcal{L}_l + \mathcal{L}_u$, where L_l and L_u indicate supervised and unsupervised losses, respectively. $\mathcal{L}_l$ is the supervised learning objective, such as the standard cross-entropy loss for classification. The proposed semi-supervised AL framework is presented in Algorithm 1. For $\mathcal{L}_u$, we adopt the recent successful advances in SSL [1,5,50,54], that are based on minimizing the notion of sensitivity to perturbations with the idea of inducing "consistency", i.e., imposing similarity in predictions when the input is perturbed in a way that would not change its perceptual content. For consistency-based SSL, the common choice for the loss is

$$\mathcal{L}_u(x, M) = D(P(\hat{Y} = \ell | x, M), P(\hat{Y} = \ell | \tilde{x}, M)), \tag{1}$$

where D is a distance function such as KL divergence [51], or L2 norm [5,28], M indicates the model and $\tilde{x}$ denotes a distortion (augmentation) of the input x.

The design of the selection criteria is crucial while integrating SSL into AL. The unsupervised objective exploits unlabeled data by encouraging consistent predictions across slightly-distorted versions of each unlabeled sample. We hypothesize that *labeling samples that have highly-inconsistent predictions should be valuable, because these samples are hard to be minimized using $\mathcal{L}_u$.* Human annotations on them can ensure a correct label, to be useful for supervised model training at next cycle. The samples that yield the large performance gains with SSL would not be necessarily the samples with the highest uncertainty, as the most uncertain data could be out-of-distribution examples, and including them in training might be misleading. Based on the intuitions, we argue that, for semi-supervised AL, valuable samples are the ones that demonstrate highly unstable predictions given different input distortions, i.e., the samples that a model can not consistently classify as a certain class.

To this end, we propose a simple metric to quantify the inconsistency of predictions over a random set of data augmentations given a sample:

$$\mathcal{E}(x, M) = \sum_{\ell=1}^{J} \text{Var} \left[P(\hat{Y} = \ell | x, M), P(\hat{Y} = \ell | \tilde{x}_1, M), ..., P(\hat{Y} = \ell | \tilde{x}_N, M) \right],$$

(2)

where J is the number of response classes and N is the number of perturbed samples of the original input data x, $\{\tilde{x}_1, ..., \tilde{x}_N\}$, which can be obtained by standard augmentation operations.

For batch selection, we jointly consider K samples and aim to choose the subset B such that the aggregate metric $\mathcal{C}(B, M) = \sum_{x \in B} \mathcal{E}(x, M)$ is maximized, i.e. the high inconsistency samples can be selected to be labeled by humans.

4 Experiments

In this section, we present experimental results of our proposed method. First, we compare our method to naive AL and SSL combinations, to show the effectiveness of our consistency based selection when all the methods are trained in a semi-supervised way. Second, since most recent AL methods still use only labeled data to conduct model training, we compare our method to recent AL methods and show a large improvement, motivating future research for semi-supervised AL. Third, we present qualitative analyses on several important properties of the proposed consistency based sampling.

4.1 Experimental Setup

Datasets. We demonstrate the performance of our method on CIFAR-10, CIFAR-100 [27] and ImageNet [13] datasets. CIFAR-10 and CIFAR-100 have 60 K images in total, of which 10 K images are for testing. CIFAR-10 consists of 10 classes and CIFAR-100 has 100 classes. ImageNet is a large-scale image dataset with 1.2 M images from 1 K classes.

Implementation Details. Different variants of SSL methods encourage consistency loss in different ways. In our implementation, we focus on the recently-proposed method, Mixmatch [5], which proposes a specific loss term to encourage consistency of unlabeled data. For comparison with selection baselines on CIFAR-10 and CIFAR-100, we use Wide ResNet-28 [35] as the base model and keep the default hyper-parameters for different settings following [5]. In each cycle, the model is initialized with the model trained in the previous cycle. 50 augmentations of each image are obtained by horizontally flipping and random cropping, but we observe that 5 augmentations can produce comparable results. To perform a fair comparison, different selection baselines start from the same initial model. The initial set of labeled data is randomly sampled and is uniformly distributed over classes. When comparing with advanced supervised AL methods, we follow [44] for the settings of start size, AL batch size and backbone architecture (VGG16 [43]). We adopt an advanced augmentation strategy, RandAugment [10], to perform augmentation of unlabeled samples on ImageNet.

Selection Baselines. We consider three representative selection methods. *Uniform* indicates random selection (no AL). *Entropy* is widely considered as an uncertainty-based baseline in previous methods [39,53]. It selects uncertain samples that have maximum entropy of its predicted class probabilities. *k-center* [39] selects representative samples by maximizing the distance between a selected sample and its nearest neighbor in the labeled pool. We use the features from the last fully connected layer of the target model to compute sample distances.

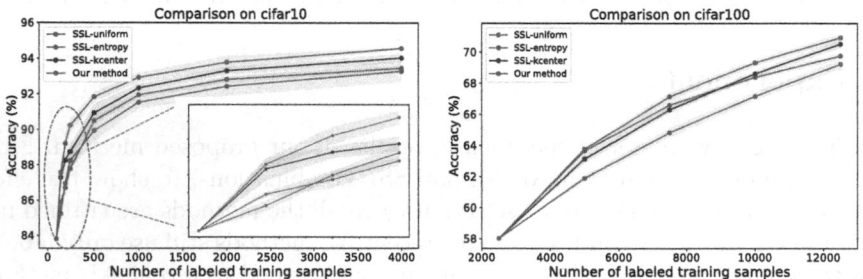

Fig. 2. Model performance comparison with different sample selection methods on CIFAR-10 and CIFAR-100. Solid lines indicate the averaged results over 5 trials. Shadows represent standard deviation

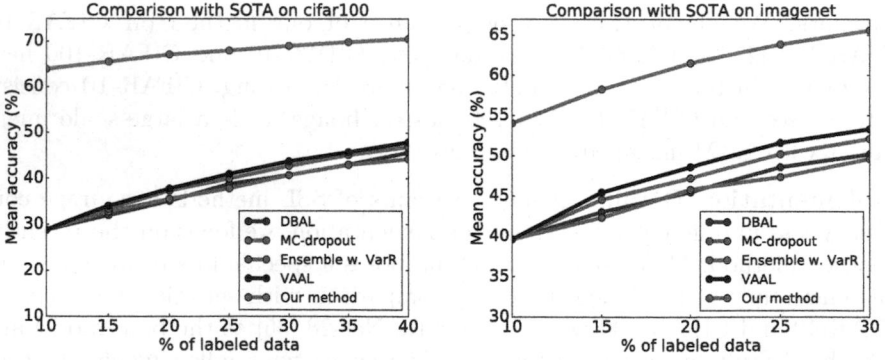

Fig. 3. Comparison with recent AL methods on CIFAR-100 and ImageNet. Our results on CIFAR-100 and ImageNet are averaged over 5 and 3 trials, respectively

4.2   Comparison with Selection Baselines Under SSL

To demonstrate the effectiveness of our method over the straightforward AL and SSL combinations, we focus on comparing with different selection methods in SSL framework. Figure 2 and Table 1 show that when integrated with SSL training, our method outperforms baselines by a clear margin: on CIFAR-10, with 250 labeled images, our method outperforms *uniform* (passive selection) by ∼2.5% and outperforms *k-center*, by ∼1.5%. As the number of labels increases, it is harder to improve model performance, but our method outperforms the *uniform* selection with 4 K labels using only 2 K labels, halving the labeled data requirements for the similar performance. Given access to all the labels (50 K) for the entire training set, a fully-supervised model achieves an accuracy of 95.83% [5]. Our method with 4 K (8%) examples achieves about 30% more error compared to the fully supervised method. CIFAR-100 is a more challenging dataset as it has the same amount of training images of CIFAR-10, but 10× more categories. On CIFAR-100, we observe a consistent outperformance over baselines of our method at all AL cycles.

Table 1. Comparison of different sampling methods on CIFAR-10. Note that all the methods are under the SSL setting and start with 100 labeled samples. When the number of labeled samples reaches 250, AL batch size K is set to be 250 and doubled afterwards. The reported results are averaged over 5 trials

Methods	# of labeled samples in total				
	250	500	1000	2000	4000
Uniform	87.78 ± 0.23	90.50 ± 0.21	91.95 ± 0.15	92.81 ± 0.17	93.45 ± 0.16
Entropy	88.24 ± 0.51	89.95 ± 0.58	91.53 ± 0.35	92.42 ± 0.53	93.28 ± 0.61
k-center	88.75 ± 0.42	90.94 ± 0.53	92.34 ± 0.24	93.30 ± 0.21	94.03 ± 0.25
Ours	**90.23 + 0.39**	**91.84 ± 0.29**	**92.93 ± 0.26**	**93.78 ± 0.38**	**94.57 ± 0.06**

There is typically a trade-off between using a large and a small AL batch sizes. A large batch size will lead to insufficient usage of active learning given a limited budget. However, selecting a small batch of samples would lead to more AL cycles, which is computationally expensive. We conduct experiments on CIFAR-10 following the setting in Fig. 2 using reasonable AL batch sizes. Results show that when consuming 200 labels in total, our methods obtain comparable performance (89.5%, 89.2% and 89.3%) with AL batch size set to be 25, 50 and 100, respectively.

4.3   Comparison with Supervised AL Methods

We have shown that our method clearly outperforms the straightforward AL and SSL combinations in Sect. 4.2. As mentioned, most AL methods focus on learning with only labeled samples. Consequently, it is worth showing the overall gap between our proposed framework and the existing methods to emphasize the benefit of the proposed framework. We choose the following recent methods as baselines: MC-Dropout [17], DBAL [18], Ensembles w. VarR [4] and VAAL [44] and compare with them on CIFAR-100 and ImageNet. The results of the baselines are reprinted from [44].

As can be seen from Fig. 3, our method significantly outperforms the existing supervised AL methods at all AL cycles on both datasets. Specifically, when 40% images are labeled, our method improves the best baseline (VAAL) by 22.62% accuracy on CIFAR100 and by 12.28% accuracy on ImageNet. The large improvements are mostly due to effective utilization of SSL at AL cycles.

Moreover, the performance of our method over the supervised models combined with the selection baselines in the scenario of very few labeled samples is of interest. As shown in Table 2, our method significantly outperforms the methods which only learn from labeled data at each cycle. When 150 samples in total are labeled, our method outperforms *kcenter* by 39.24% accuracy.

Table 2. Comparison between our method (trained in SSL) and our baselines that trained in supervised setting with very few labeled samples on CIFAR-10. All methods start from 100 labeled samples. The following columns are results of different methods with the same selection batch size. The reported results are over 5 trials

Setting	Methods	# of labeled samples in total			
		100	150	200	250
Supervised	Uniform	41.85	46.13 ± 0.38	51.10 ± 0.60	53.45 ± 0.71
	Entropy		46.05 ± 0.34	50.15 ± 0.79	52.83 ± 0.82
	k-center		48.33 ± 0.49	50.96 ± 0.45	53.77 ± 1.01
Semi-supervised	Ours	83.81	$\mathbf{87.57 \pm 0.31}$	$\mathbf{89.20 \pm 0.51}$	$\mathbf{90.23 \pm 0.49}$

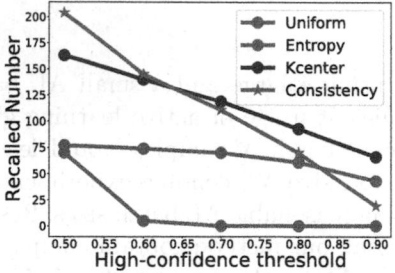 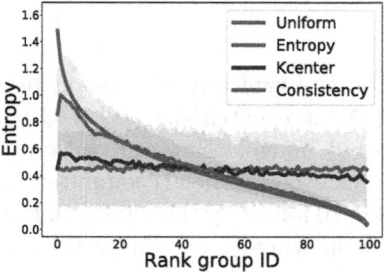

Fig. 4. Left: Number of overconfident mis-classified samples in top 1% samples ranked by different methods. Overconfident samples are defined as those having the highest class probability larger than threshold. Right: the average entropy of unlabeled samples ranked by different selection metrics. The ranked samples are divided into 100 groups for computing average entropy. Shadows represent standard deviation

4.4   Analyses of Consistency-Based Selection

To build insights on the superior performance of our AL selection method, we analyze different attributes of the selected samples, which are considered to be important for AL. Experiments are conducted on CIFAR-10.

Uncertainty and Overconfident Mis-Classification. Uncertainty-based AL methods query the data samples close to the decision boundary. However, deep neural networks yield poorly-calibrated uncertainty estimates when the raw outputs are considered – they tend to be overconfident even when they are wrong [20,29]. Entropy-based AL metrics would not distinguish such overconfident mis-classifications, thus may result in sub-optimal selection. Figure 4(left) demonstrates that our *consistency*-based selection is superior in detecting high-confident mis-classification cases compared to *entropy*-based selection. Figure 4(right) shows the uncertainty in the selected samples with different methods, quantified using entropy. When different AL selection methods are compared, *uniform* and *k-center* methods do not base selection on uncertainty at all, whereas *consistency* tends to select highly-uncertain samples but not necessarily the top ones. Such samples might contribute to our superior performance compared to *entropy*.

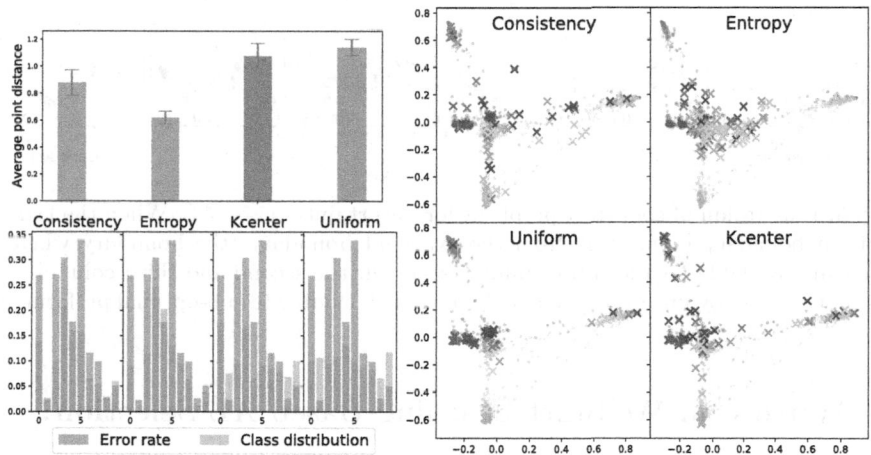

Fig. 5. Average distance between samples (top-left): the average pair-wise L_2 distance of top 1% unlabeled samples ranked by different selection metrics. Per-class error rate vs. the class distribution of the selected samples are shown in bottom-left. Diversity visualization (right): Dots and crosses indicate unlabeled (un-selected) samples and the selected samples (top 100), respectively. Each color represent a ground truth class

Sample Diversity. Diversity has been proposed as a key factor for AL [52]. *k-center* is a diversity based AL method, preferring to select data points that span the whole input space. Towards this end, Fig. 5(right) visualizes the diversity of samples selected by different methods. We use principal component analysis to reduce the dimensionality of embedded samples to a two-dimensional space. *Uniform* chooses samples equally-likely from the unlabeled pool. Samples selected by *entropy* are clustered in certain regions. On the other hand, *consistency* selects data samples as diverse as those selected by *k-center*. The average distances between top 1% samples selected by different methods are shown in Fig. 5(top-left). We can see that *entropy* chooses samples relatively close to each other, while *consistency* yield samples that are separated with much larger distance which are comparable to samples selected by *uniform* and *k-center*.

Class Distribution Complies with Classification Error. Figure 5(bottom-left) shows the per-class classification error and the class distribution of samples selected by different metrics. Samples selected by *entropy* and *consistency* are correlated with per class classification error, unlike the samples selected by *uniform* and *k-center*.

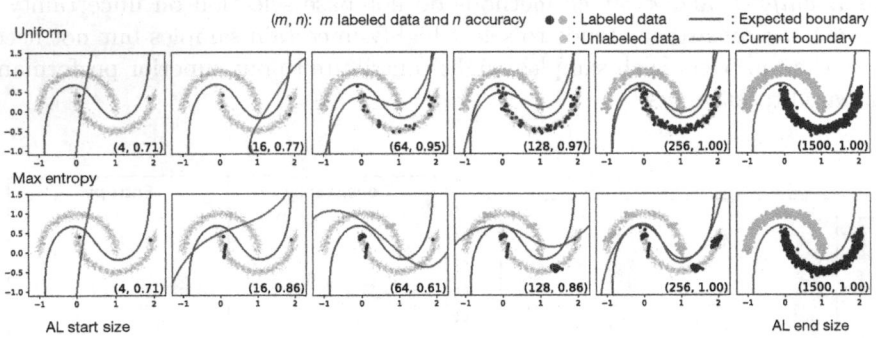

Fig. 6. Illustration of cold-start problems for uncertainty-based AL. When the learned decision boundary is far away from the expected boundary (the boundary when all labels are available for the entire training set), e.g. the second and third columns, the selected samples by uncertainty-based AL is biased, leading to sub-optimal performance

5   When Can We Start Learning-Based AL Selection?

Based on the studies above, our proposed semi-supervised AL framework demonstrates clear advantages. While towards minimizing the labeling cost, a challenging issue, cold start failure, may occur when only a extreme small labeled set is available, which leads to sub-optimal AL performance. The proper study of this problem is essential for scenarios especially when labels are very expensive or challenging to collect.

5.1   Cold-Start Failure

When the size of the initial labeled dataset is too small, the learned decision boundaries could be far away from the real boundaries and AL selection based on the model outputs could be biased. To illustrate the problem, Fig. 6 shows the toy two-moons dataset using a simple support vector machine model with an RBF kernel, trained in supervised setting to learn the decision boundary [35]. As can be seen, the naive uniform sampling approach achieves better predictive accuracy by exploring the whole space. On the other hand, the samples selected by *max entropy* concentrate around the poorly-learned boundary.

Next, we study the cold start phenomenon for our proposed semi-supervised AL method. We focus on CIFAR-10 with small labeled initial sets, shown in Fig. 7. Using uniform sampling to select different starting sizes, AL methods achieve different accuracies. For example, the model starting with $K_0 = 50$ data points clearly under-performs the model starting with $K_0 = 100$ samples, when both models reach 150 labeled samples. It may be due to the cold start problem encountered when $K_0 = 50$. On the other hand, given a limited labeling budget, naively choosing a large start size is also not practically desirable, because it may lead to under-utilization of learning-based selection. For example, starting with $K_0 = 100$ labeled samples has better performance than starting from 150 or 200, since we have more AL cycles in the former case given the same label budget. The semi-supervised nature of our learning proposal encourages the practice of initiating learning-based sample selection from a much smaller start size. However, the initial model can still have poorly-learned boundary when started with extremely small labeled data. If there is a sufficiently large validation dataset, this problem can be relieved by tracking validation performance. However, in

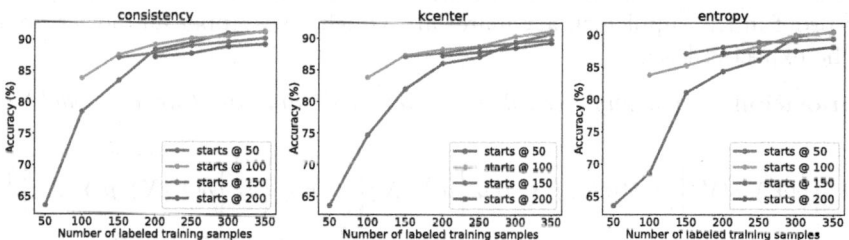

Fig. 7. Comparison of different sampling methods trained with SSL framework on CIFAR-10 when AL starts from different number of labeled samples

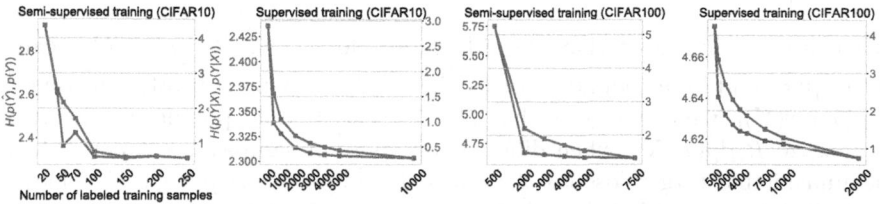

Fig. 8. Empirical risk (i.e. the target loss) on the entire training data (in blue) and cross-entropy between $p(\hat{Y})$ and $p(Y)$ show strong correlations in both semi-supervised and supervised settings (Color figure online)

practice, such a validation set typically doesn't exist. These motivate us to conduct an exploration to systematically infer a proper starting size.

5.2   An Exploratory Analysis in Start Size Selection

Recall from the last step of Algorithm 1, if T is set such that $U_T = \emptyset$, i.e., if the entire dataset is labeled, then the final model M_T is trained to minimize the purely supervised loss $\mathcal{L}_l$ on the total labeled dataset L_T. Consider the cross-entropy loss for any classifier $p(\hat{Y}|X)$, which we call the *AL target loss*:

$$\mathcal{L}_l\left[L_T, p(\hat{Y}|X)\right] = -\frac{1}{|L_T|} \sum_{(x,y) \in L_T} \log p(\hat{Y} = y|X = x). \tag{3}$$

Note that the goal of an AL method can be viewed as minimizing the AL target loss of the entire training set L_T [55] with the small subset of labeled data available. In any intermediate AL step, we expect our model can minimize the target loss. If the model do a poor job in approximating and minimizing Eq. 3 (cold start problem occurs), the quality of the samples selected in the subsequent AL cycles could be consequently poor. Therefore, it is crucial to assess the performance of the currently-learned model in minimizing the criterion in Eq. 3. However, since the labeled data set L_t at cycle t is a strict subset of the entire training set L_T, it is impossible to simply plug the most recently-learned model $\hat{Y}$ in Eq. 3 for direct calculation.

To this end, we approximate the target loss based on the following proposition (see proof in the supplementary material), which gives upper and lower bounds on the expected loss:

Proposition 1. *For any given distribution of Y, and any learned model $\hat{Y}$, we have*

$$H\left[p(Y), p(\hat{Y})\right] - H[p(X)] \le R_H\left[p(\hat{Y}|X)\right] = \mathbb{E}_X\left\{H\left[p(Y|X), p(\hat{Y}|X)\right]\right\}$$

$$\le H\left[p(Y), p(\hat{Y})\right] - H[p(X)] - \log \hat{Z}, \tag{4}$$

where $H[p, q]$ is the cross-entropy between two distributions p and q, $H[p(X)]$ is the entropy of the random variable X, and $\hat{Z} = \min_{x,y} p(X = x|\hat{Y} = y)$.

Proposition 1 indicates that the AL target loss, *i.e.*, $R_H\left[p(\hat{Y}|X)\right]$, can be both upper and lower bounded. In particular, both bounds involve the quantity $H[p(Y), p(\hat{Y})]$, which suggests that $H[p(Y), p(\hat{Y})]$ could potentially be tracked to analyze $R_H[p(\hat{Y}|X)]$ when different numbers of samples are labeled. Unlike the unavailable target loss on the entire training set, $H[p(Y), p(\hat{Y})]$ does not need all data to be labeled. In fact, to compute $H[p(Y), p(\hat{Y})]$, we just need to specify a distribution for Y, which could be assumed from prior knowledge or estimated using all of the labels in the starting cycle.

As shown in Fig. 8, we observe a strong correlation between the target loss and $H[p(Y), p(\hat{Y})]$, where Y is assumed to be uniformly distributed. In practice, a practitioner can trace the difference of $H[p(Y), p(\hat{Y})]$ between two consecutive points and empirically stop expanding the start set when the difference is within a pre-defined threshold. Particularly, in SSL setting, 100 or 150 labeled samples may be used as start set on CIFAR-10, as the value of $H[p(Y), p(\hat{Y})]$ essentially ceases decreasing, which coincides with the oracle stopping points if we were given access to the target loss. In contrast, a start size of 50 may not be favorable since the difference of $H[p(Y), p(\hat{Y})]$ between the points of 50 and 20 are relatively large. A similar pattern in the supervised learning setting is also shown in Fig. 8.

6   Weaknesses of Our Method

We explore how well our AL selection method would perform with supervised learning using only labeled samples. Following [53], we start with 1000 labeled samples on CIFAR-10. As shown in Table 3, after 4 AL cycles ($B = 500$, totaling 3000 labels), *uniform, k-center, entropy* and our method (*consistency*) achieve accuracy of 80.81%, 81.70%, 82.67% and 82.75%, respectively. It shows that *consistency* sampling performs comparable with the baseline metrics without significant improvement. This discourages the direct application of our selection metric in the supervised setting. Mixmatch is mainly used as the target model in this work and we experiment with two more SSL methods (see results in the supplementary material). However, comprehensive analyses with extensive SSL methods are desirable to further understand the advantages/disadvantages of our approach. As an exploratory analysis, we propose a measure that is shown to be strongly correlated with the AL target loss, but exact determination of the optimal start size is yet to be addressed.

Table 3. Comparison of different sampling methods in the supervised setting on CIFAR-10. All methods start from 1000 labeled samples. The reported results are over 5 trials

Methods	# of labeled samples in total				
	1000	1500	2000	2500	3000
Uniform	72.93	75.38 ± 0.17	77.46 ± 0.3	78.79 ± 0.38	80.81 ± 0.28
Entropy		76.31 ± 0.18	79.50 ± 0.29	81.30 ± 0.31	82.67 ± 0.55
k-center		74.25 ± 0.29	77.56 ± 0.30	79.50 ± 0.20	81.70 ± 0.32
Ours		76.63 ± 0.17	79.39 ± 0.31	80.99 ± 0.39	82.75 ± 0.26

7   Conclusion

We present a consistency-based semi-supervised AL framework and a simple pool-based AL selection metric to select data for labeling by leveraging unsupervised information of unlabeled data during training. Our experiments demonstrate that our semi-supervised AL method outperforms the state-of-the art

AL methods and also alternative SSL and AL combinations. Through quantitative and qualitative analyses, we show that our proposed metric implicitly balances uncertainty and diversity when making selection. In addition, we study and address the practically-valuable and fundamentally-challenging question – "When can we start learning-based AL selection?". We present a measure to assist determining proper start size. Our experimental analysis demonstrates that the proposed measure correlates well with the AL target loss (i.e. the ultimate supervised loss on all labeled data), thus is potentially useful to evaluate target models without extra labeling effort. Overall, semi-supervised AL opens new horizons for training with very limited labeling budget, and we highly encourage future research along this direction to further analyze SSL and cold-start impacts on AL.

Acknowledgment. Discussions with Giulia DeSalvo, Chih-kuan Yeh, Kihyuk Sohn, Chen Xing, and Wei Wei are gratefully acknowledged.

References

1. Athiwaratkun, B., Finzi, M., Izmailov, P., Wilson, A.G.: There are many consistent explanations of unlabeled data: why you should average. In: ICLR (2019)
2. Balcan, M.F., Beygelzimer, A., Langford, J.: Agnostic active learning. J. Comput. Syst. Sci. **75**(1), 78–89 (2009)
3. Balcan, M.F., Broder, A., Zhang, T.: Margin based active learning. In: International Conference on Computational Learning Theory (2007)
4. Beluch, W.H., Genewein, T., Nürnberger, A., Köhler, J.M.: The power of ensembles for active learning in image classification (2018)
5. Berthelot, D., Carlini, N., Goodfellow, I., Papernot, N., Oliver, A., Raffel, C.: Mixmatch: a holistic approach to semi-supervised learning. arXiv preprint arXiv:1905.02249 (2019)
6. Brinker, K.: Incorporating diversity in active learning with support vector machines. In: ICML (2003)
7. Cohn, D., Atlas, L., Ladner, R.: Improving generalization with active learning. Mach. Learn. **15**(2), 201–221 (1994)
8. Cortes, C., DeSalvo, G., Mohri, M., Zhang, N.: Agnostic active learning without constraints. In: ICML (2019)
9. Cortes, C., DeSalvo, G., Mohri, M., Zhang, N., Gentile, C.: Active learning with disagreement graphs. In: ICML (2019)
10. Cubuk, E.D., Zoph, B., Shlens, J., Le, Q.V.: Randaugment: practical automated data augmentation with a reduced search space. arXiv preprint arXiv:1909.13719 (2019)
11. Dasgupta, S., Hsu, D.: Hierarchical sampling for active learning. In: ICML (2008)
12. Dasgupta, S., Hsu, D.J., Monteleoni, C.: A general agnostic active learning algorithm. In: NIPS (2008)
13. Deng, J., Dong, W., Socher, R., Li, L.J., Li, K., Fei-Fei, L.: Imagenet: a large-scale hierarchical image database. In: CVPR (2009)
14. Drugman, T., Pylkkonen, J., Kneser, R.: Active and semi-supervised learning in ASR: benefits on the acoustic and language models. arXiv preprint arXiv:1903.02852 (2019)

15. Elhamifar, E., Sapiro, G., Yang, A., Shankar Sasrty, S.: A convex optimization framework for active learning. In: CVPR (2013)
16. Freytag, A., Rodner, E., Denzler, J.: Selecting influential examples: active learning with expected model output changes. In: Fleet, D., Pajdla, T., Schiele, B., Tuytelaars, T. (eds.) ECCV 2014. LNCS, vol. 8692, pp. 562–577. Springer, Cham (2014). https://doi.org/10.1007/978-3-319-10593-2_37
17. Gal, Y., Ghahramani, Z.: Dropout as a Bayesian approximation: representing model uncertainty in deep learning. In: ICML (2016)
18. Gal, Y., Islam, R., Ghahramani, Z.: Deep Bayesian active learning with image data. In: ICML (2017)
19. Goodfellow, I., Bengio, Y., Courville, A.: Deep Learning. MIT Press (2016). http://www.deeplearningbook.org
20. Guo, C., Pleiss, G., Sun, Y., Weinberger, K.Q.: On calibration of modern neural networks. In: ICML (2017)
21. Guo, Y.: Active instance sampling via matrix partition. In: NIPS (2010)
22. Hasan, M., Roy-Chowdhury, A.K.: Context aware active learning of activity recognition models. In: CVPR (2015)
23. Houlsby, N., Hernández-Lobato, J.M., Ghahramani, Z.: Cold-start active learning with robust ordinal matrix factorization. In: ICML (2014)
24. Iglesias, J.E., Konukoglu, E., Montillo, A., Tu, Z., Criminisi, A.: Combining generative and discriminative models for semantic segmentation of CT scans via active learning. In: Székely, G., Hahn, H.K. (eds.) IPMI 2011. LNCS, vol. 6801, pp. 25–36. Springer, Heidelberg (2011). https://doi.org/10.1007/978-3-642-22092-0_3
25. Joshi, A.J., Porikli, F., Papanikolopoulos, N.: Multi-class active learning for image classification. In: CVPR (2009)
26. Konyushkova, K., Sznitman, R., Fua, P.: Learning active learning from data. In: NIPS (2017)
27. Krizhevsky, A., Hinton, G., et al.: Learning multiple layers of features from tiny images. Technical report. Citeseer (2009)
28. Laine, S., Aila, T.: Temporal ensembling for semi-supervised learning. In: ICLR (2017)
29. Lakshminarayanan, B., Pritzel, A., Blundell, C.: Simple and scalable predictive uncertainty estimation using deep ensembles. In: NIPS (2017)
30. Lewis, D.D., Catlett, J.: Heterogeneous uncertainty sampling for supervised learning. In: Machine Learning Proceedings 1994, pp. 148–156. Elsevier (1994)
31. Lewis, D.D., Gale, W.A.: A sequential algorithm for training text classifiers. In: SIGIR 1994, pp. 3–12 (1994)
32. Mac Aodha, O., Campbell, N.D., Kautz, J., Brostow, G.J.: Hierarchical subquery evaluation for active learning on a graph. In: CVPR (2014)
33. McCallumzy, A.K., Nigamy, K.: Employing EM and pool-based active learning for text classification. In: ICML (1998)
34. Nguyen, H.T., Smeulders, A.: Active learning using pre-clustering. In: ICML (2004)
35. Oliver, A., Odena, A., Raffel, C.A., Cubuk, E.D., Goodfellow, I.: Realistic evaluation of deep semi-supervised learning algorithms. In: NeurIPS (2018)
36. Rhee, P.K., Erdenee, E., Kyun, S.D., Ahmed, M.U., Jin, S.: Active and semi-supervised learning for object detection with imperfect data. Cogn. Syst. Res. **45**, 109–123 (2017)
37. Roth, D., Small, K.: Margin-based active learning for structured output spaces. In: ECML (2006)
38. Roy, N., McCallum, A.: Toward optimal active learning through Monte Carlo estimation of error reduction. In: ICML (2001)

39. Sener, O., Savarese, S.: Active learning for convolutional neural networks: a core-set approach. In: ICLR (2018)
40. Settles, B., Craven, M., Ray, S.: Multiple-instance active learning. In: NIPS (2008)
41. Seung, H.S., Opper, M., Sompolinsky, H.: Query by committee. In: Proceedings of the Workshop on Computational Learning Theory (1992)
42. Siméoni, O., Budnik, M., Avrithis, Y., Gravier, G.: Rethinking deep active learning: using unlabeled data at model training. arXiv preprint arXiv:1911.08177 (2019)
43. Simonyan, K., Zisserman, A.: Very deep convolutional networks for large-scale image recognition. arXiv preprint arXiv:1409.1556 (2014)
44. Sinha, S., Ebrahimi, S., Darrell, T.: Variational adversarial active learning. arXiv preprint arXiv:1904.00370 (2019)
45. Sohn, K., et al.: Fixmatch: simplifying semi-supervised learning with consistency and confidence. arXiv preprint arXiv:2001.07685 (2020)
46. Sohn, K., Zhang, Z., Li, C.L., Zhang, H., Lee, C.Y., Pfister, T.: A simple semi-supervised learning framework for object detection. arXiv preprint arXiv:2005.04757 (2020)
47. Song, S., Berthelot, D., Rostamizadeh, A.: Combining mixmatch and active learning for better accuracy with fewer labels. arXiv preprint arXiv:1912.00594 (2019)
48. Tomanek, K., Hahn, U.: Semi-supervised active learning for sequence labeling. In: ACL (2009)
49. Tong, S., Koller, D.: Support vector machine active learning with applications to text classification. JMLR **2**, 45–66 (2001)
50. Verma, V., Lamb, A., Kannala, J., Bengio, Y., Lopez-Paz, D.: Interpolation consistency training for semi-supervised learning. In: International Joint Conferences on Artifical Intelligence (2019)
51. Xie, Q., Dai, Z., Hovy, E., Luong, M.T., Le, Q.V.: Unsupervised data augmentation for consistency training. arXiv preprint arXiv:1904.12848 (2019)
52. Yang, Y., Ma, Z., Nie, F., Chang, X., Hauptmann, A.G.: Multi-class active learning by uncertainty sampling with diversity maximization. IJCV **113**(2), 113–127 (2015)
53. Yoo, D., Kweon, I.S.: Learning loss for active learning. In: CVPR (2019)
54. Zhang, Z., Zhang, H., Arik, S.O., Lee, H., Pfister, T.: Distilling effective supervision from severe label noise. In: CVPR (2020)
55. Zhu, X., Lafferty, J., Ghahramani, Z.: Combining active learning and semi-supervised learning using Gaussian fields and harmonic functions. In: ICML Workshops (2003)

Point-Set Anchors for Object Detection, Instance Segmentation and Pose Estimation

Fangyun Wei[1]([✉]), Xiao Sun[1], Hongyang Li[2], Jingdong Wang[1],
and Stephen Lin[1]

[1] Microsoft Research Asia, Beijing, China
{fawe,xias,jingdw,stevelin}@microsoft.com
[2] Peking University, Beijing, China
lhy_ustb@pku.edu.cn

Abstract. A recent approach for object detection and human pose estimation is to regress bounding boxes or human keypoints from a central point on the object or person. While this center-point regression is simple and efficient, we argue that the image features extracted at a central point contain limited information for predicting distant keypoints or bounding box boundaries, due to object deformation and scale/orientation variation. To facilitate inference, we propose to instead perform regression from a set of points placed at more advantageous positions. This point set is arranged to reflect a good initialization for the given task, such as modes in the training data for pose estimation, which lie closer to the ground truth than the central point and provide more informative features for regression. As the utility of a point set depends on how well its scale, aspect ratio and rotation matches the target, we adopt the anchor box technique of sampling these transformations to generate additional point-set candidates. We apply this proposed framework, called Point-Set Anchors, to object detection, instance segmentation, and human pose estimation. Our results show that this general-purpose approach can achieve performance competitive with state-of-the-art methods for each of these tasks.

Keywords: Object detection · Instance segmentation · Human pose estimation · Anchor box · Point-based representation

1 Introduction

A basic yet effective approach for object localization is to estimate keypoints. This has been performed for object detection by detecting points that can define a bounding box, e.g., corner points [22], and then grouping them together. An even simpler version of this approach that does not require grouping is to extract the center point of an object and regress the bounding box size from it.

F. Wei and X. Sun—Equal contribution.

© Springer Nature Switzerland AG 2020
A. Vedaldi et al. (Eds.): ECCV 2020, LNCS 12355, pp. 527–544, 2020.
https://doi.org/10.1007/978-3-030-58607-2_31

This method, called CenterNet [48], can be easily applied to human pose estimation as well, by regressing the offsets of keypoints instead.

While CenterNet is highly practical and potentially has broad application, its regression of keypoints from features at the center point can be considered an important drawback. Since keypoints might not lie in proximity of the center point, the features extracted at the center may provide little information for inferring their positions. This problem is exacerbated by the geometric variations an object can exhibit, including scale, orientation, and deformations, which make keypoint prediction even more challenging.

In this paper, we propose to address this issue by acquiring more informative features for keypoint regression. Rather than extract them at the center point, our approach is to obtain features at a set of points that are likely to lie closer to the regression targets. This point set is determined according to task. For instance segmentation, the points are placed along the edges of an implicit bounding box. For pose estimation, the arrangement of points follows modes in the pose distribution of the training data, such as that in Fig. 1b). As a good task-specific initialization, the point set can yield features that better facilitate keypoint localization.

It can be noted that a point set best serves its purpose when it is aligned in scale and aspect ratio with the target. To accomplish this, we adapt the anchor box scheme commonly used in object detection by expressing point sets as *point-set anchors*. Like their anchor box counterparts, point-set anchors are sampled at multiple scales, aspect ratios, and image positions. In addition, different point-set configurations may be enumerated, such as different modes in a pose estimation training set. With the generated point-set candidates, keypoint regression is conducted to find solutions for the given task.

The main contributions of this work can be summarized as:

- A new object representation named *Point-Set Anchors*, which can be seen as a generalization and extension of classical box anchors. Point-set anchors can further provide informative features and better task-specific initializations for shape regression.
- A network based on point-set anchors called PointSetNet, which is a modification of RetinaNet [25] that simply replaces the anchor boxes with the proposed point-set anchors and also attaches a parallel regression branch. Variants of this network are applied to object detection, human pose estimation, and also instance segmentation, for which the problem of defining specific regression targets is addressed.

It is shown that the proposed general-purpose approach achieves performance competitive with state-of-the-art methods on object detection, instance segmentation and pose estimation.

2   Related Work

Object Representations. In object detection, rectangular anchors [24,25,36] are the most common representation used in locating objects. These anchors

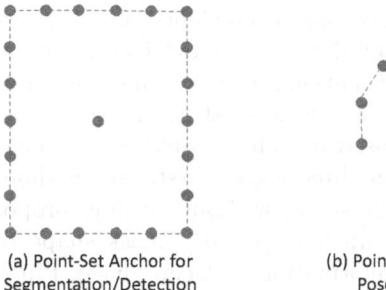

(a) Point-Set Anchor for
Segmentation/Detection

(b) Point-Set Anchor for
Pose Estimation

Fig. 1. Illustration of our point-set anchors for instance segmentation, object detection and pose estimation. Instance mask point-set anchors contain an implicit bounding box, and n anchor points are uniformly sampled from the corresponding bounding box. Pose point-set anchors are initialized as the most frequent poses in the training set.

serve as initial bounding boxes, and an encoding is learned to refine the object localization or to provide intermediate proposals for top-down solutions [10,17]. However, the anchor box is a coarse representation that is insufficient for finer degrees of localization required in tasks such as instance segmentation and pose estimation. An alternative is to represent objects in terms of specific points, including center points [40,48], corner points [14,22], extreme points [49], octagon points [34], point sets [44,45], and radial points [43]. These point representations are designed to solve one or two tasks among object detection, instance segmentation and pose estimation. Polygon point based methods, such as corner points [14,22] and extreme points [49], are hard to apply to instance segmentation and pose estimation due to their restricted shape. While center point representations [40,48] are more flexible, as offsets from the object center to the corresponding bounding box corners or human joints can be directly predicted, we argue that features extracted from center locations are not as informative as from our task-specific point sets, illustrated in Fig. 1. In addition, how to define regression targets for instance segmentation is unclear for these representations. Another way to perform instance segmentation from a center point is by regressing mask boundary points in radial directions [43]; however, radial regressions at equal angular intervals are unsuitable for pose estimation. Other representations such as octagon points or point sets [44,45] are specifically designed for one or two recognition tasks. The proposed point-set anchors combine benefits from anchor boxes and point representations, and its flexibility makes them applicable to object detection, instance segmentation and pose estimation.

Instance Segmentation. Two-stage methods [17,19,23] formulate instance segmentation in a 'Detect and Segment' paradigm, which detects bounding boxes and then performs instance segmentation inside the boxes. Recent research has focused on single-stage approaches since two-stage methods are often slow in practice. PolarMask [43] emits n rays at equal angular intervals from a center point for dense distance regression. YOLACT [1] generates a set of prototype masks and predicts per-instance mask coefficients for linearly combining the prototype masks. ExtremeNet [49] detects four extreme points and a center point using a standard keypoint estimation network, which requires lengthy training, and then coarse octagonal masks are formed by grouping. Deep Snake [34] proposes a two-stage pipeline based on initial contours and contour deformation. Our method differs from it in three ways. First, our method for instance segmentation operates in a single stage, without needing proposals generated by detectors. Second, Point-Set Anchors perform mask shape regression directly, in contrast to the iterative deformation in Deep Snake. Finally, our method is evaluated on the challenging MS COCO dataset [26] and is compared to state-of-the-art methods in object detection, instance segmentation and pose estimation.

Pose Estimation. In pose estimation, most previous works follow the paradigm of estimating a heat map for each joint [2,3,6,8,9,16,17,20,30,35,42]. The heat map represents the confidence of a joint existing at each position in the image. Despite its good performance, a heat map representation has a few drawbacks such as no end-to-end training, a need for high resolution [39], and separate steps for joint localization and association. The joint association problem is typically addressed by an early stage of human bounding box detection [17,42] or a post-processing step that groups the detected joints together with additionally learned joint relations [3,29]. Recently, a different approach has been explored of directly regressing the offsets of joints from a center or root point [48]. In contrast to the heat map based approaches, the joint association problem is naturally addressed by conducting a holistic regression of all joints from a single point. However, holistic shape regression is generally more difficult than part based heat map learning due to optimization on a large, high-dimensional vector space. Nie et al. [31] address this problem by factorizing the long-range displacement with respect to the center position into accumulative shorter ones based on the articulated kinematics of human poses. They argue that modeling short-range displacements can alleviate the learning difficulty of mapping from an image representation to the vector domain. We follow the regression based paradigm and propose to address the long-range displacement problem by regressing from a set of points placed at more advantageous positions.

3   Our Method

In this section, we first formulate the proposed task-specific point-set anchors. Next, we show how to make use of these point-set anchors for regression-based instance segmentation and pose estimation. Finally, we introduce our PointSet-Net, which is an extension of RetinaNet with a parallel branch attached for keypoint regression.

3.1   Point-Set Anchors

The point-set anchor $\mathbf{T}$ contains an ordered set of points that are defined according to the specific task. We describe the definitions for the tasks of human pose estimation and instance segmentation that we will handle.

Pose Point-Set Anchor. We naturally use the human keypoints to form the pose point-set anchor. For example, in the COCO [26] dataset, there are 17 keypoints, and the pose point-set anchor is represented by a 34-dimensional vector. At each image position, we use several point-set anchors. We initialize the point-set anchors as the most frequent poses in the training set. We use a standard k-means clustering algorithm [28] to partition all the training poses into k clusters, and the mean pose of each cluster is used to form a point-set anchor. Figure 1(b) illustrates one of the point-set anchors for pose estimation.

Instance Mask Point-Set Anchor. This anchor has two parts: one center point and n ordered anchor points which are uniformly sampled from an implicit bounding box as illustrated in Fig. 1(a). n is a hyper-parameter to control sampling density. Corner points in a mask point-set anchor can also serve as a reference for object detection. At each image position, we form 9 point-set anchors by varying the scale and aspect ratios of the implicit bounding box.

3.2   Shape Regression

In this work, instance segmentation, object detection and pose estimation are treated as a shape regression problem. We represent the object by a shape S, i.e., a set of n_s ordered points $S = \{S_i\}_{i=1}^{n_s}$, where S_i represents the i-th *polygon vertex* for an instance mask, i-th *corner vertex* for a bounding box, or the i-th *keypoint* for pose estimation. Instead of regressing the shape point locations from the object center, we employ T as a reference for shape regression. Our goal is to regress the offsets ΔT from the point-set anchor T to the shape S.

Offsets for Pose Estimation. Each keypoint in the human pose estimation task represents a joint with semantic meaning, e.g., head, right elbow or left knee. We use 17 keypoints as the shape S and the offsets are simply the difference: $\Delta T = S - T$.

Offsets for Instance Segmentation. The shape S of an instance mask also contains a set of ordered points, and the number of points might be different for different object instances. The point-set anchor T is defined for all instances and contains a fixed number of points. To compute the offsets ΔT, we find the matching points T^*, each of which has a one-to-one correspondence to each point in T, from the shape S, and then $\Delta T = T^* - T$. The matching strategies, illustrated in Fig. 2, are described as follows.

- **Nearest Point.** The matching target of each point in the point-set anchor T is defined as the nearest polygon point in S based on L_1 distance. Thus, a single polygon point may be assigned to several anchor points, one anchor point, or none of them.
- **Nearest Line.** We treat the mask contour S as a sequence of n_s line segments instead of n_s discrete polygon vertices. Each of the anchor points is projected to all the polygon edges, and the closest projection point is assigned to the corresponding anchor point.

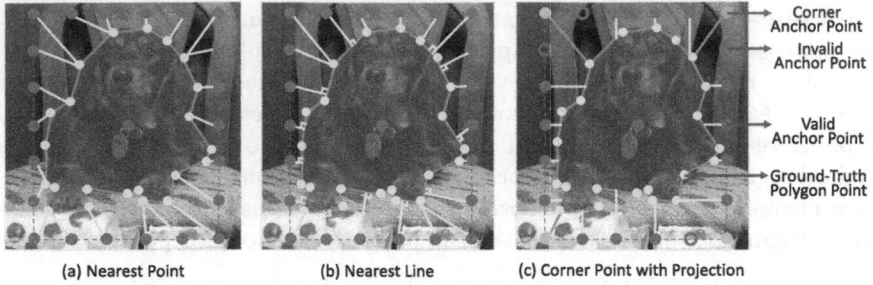

(a) Nearest Point   (b) Nearest Line   (c) Corner Point with Projection

Fig. 2. Illustration of three matching strategies between a point-set anchor and a ground-truth mask contour for instance segmentation. Yellow solid dots represent polygon points of the ground-truth mask. Green solid dots and green hollow dots denote valid and invalid anchor points, respectively. Orange and yellow lines indicate correspondences for corner and non-corner anchor points, respectively. Only valid anchor points are considered for training and inference. (Color figure online)

- **Corner Point with Projection.** We first find the targets of the four corner anchor points by the Nearest Point strategy, which are then used to subdivide the mask contour into four parts, i.e., top, right, bottom and left parts, that are to be matched with anchor points on the corresponding side. For each of the four parts, the target of each anchor point is the nearest intersection point between the horizontal (for left and right parts) or vertical (for top and bottom parts) projection line and the line segments of the mask contour. If a matched point lies outside of the corresponding contour segment delimited by the matched corner points, we mark it as invalid and it is ignored in training and testing. The remaining anchor points and their matches are marked as valid for mask regression learning.

Offsets for Object Detection. The bounding box shape $\mathbf{S}$ in object detection can be denoted as two keypoints, i.e., the top-left and bottom-right point. The offsets $\Delta\mathbf{T}$ are the distance from the target points to the corresponding corner points in mask point-set anchors.

Positive and Negative Samples. In assigning positive or negative labels to point-set anchors, we directly employ IoU for object detection and instance segmentation, and Object Keypoint Similarity (OKS) for pose estimation. Formally, in instance segmentation and object detection, a point-set anchor is assigned a positive label if it has the highest IoU for a given ground-truth box or an IoU over 0.6 with any ground-truth box, and a negative label if it has an IoU lower than 0.4 for all ground-truth boxes. In practice, we use the IoU between the implicit bounding box of the mask point-set anchors and ground-truth bounding boxes instead of masks in instance segmentation, for reduced computation. For human pose estimation, a point-set anchor is assigned a positive label if it has the highest OKS for a given ground-truth pose or an OKS over 0.5 with any ground-truth pose, and a negative label if it has OKS lower than 0.4 for all ground-truth poses.

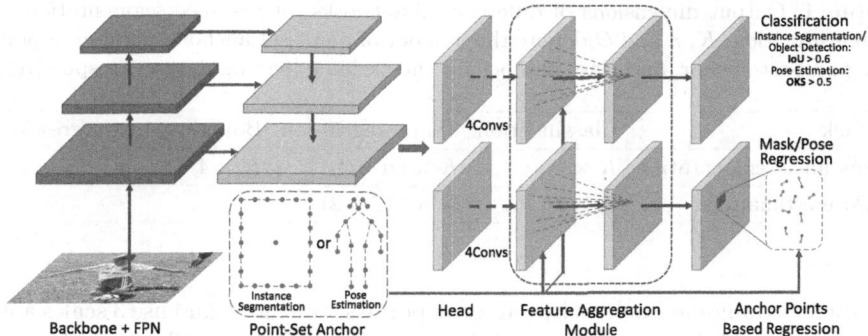

Fig. 3. Network architecture. The left part represents the backbone and feature pyramid network to extract features from different levels. The right part shows the shared heads for classification and mask/pose estimation with point-set anchors. We omit the bounding box regression branch for clearer illustration.

Mask Construction. In instance segmentation, a mask is constructed from the regressed anchor points as a post-processing step during inference. For the matching methods Nearest Point and Nearest Line, we choose an arbitrary point as the origin and connect adjacent points sequentially. For Corner Point with Projection, a mask is similarly constructed from only the valid points.

3.3   PointSetNet

Architecture. PointSetNet is an intuitive and natural extension of RetinaNet [25]. Conceptually, it simply replaces the classical rectangular anchor with the proposed point-set anchor, and attaches a parallel regression branch for instance segmentation or pose estimation in the head. Figure 3 illustrates its network structure. Following RetinaNet, we use a multi-scale feature pyramid for detecting objects at different scales. Specifically, we make use of five levels of feature maps, denoted as $\{P_3, P_4, P_5, P_6, P_7\}$. P_3, P_4 and P_5 are generated by backbone feature maps C_3, C_4 and C_5 followed by a 1×1 convolutional layer and lateral connections as in FPN [24]. P_6 and P_7 are generated by a 3×3 stride-2 convolutional layer on C_5 and P_6, respectively. As a result, the stride of $\{P_3, P_4, P_5, P_6, P_7\}$ is $\{8, 16, 32, 64, 128, 256\}$. The head contains several subnetworks for classification, mask or pose regression, and bounding box regression. Each subnetwork contains four 3×3 stride-1 convolutional layers, a feature aggregation layer which is used only for the pose estimation task, and an output layer. Table 1 lists the output dimensions from the three subnetworks for instance segmentation and pose estimation. Following [24,25], we also share the head among $P3 - P7$.

Point-Set Anchor Density. One of the most important design factors in anchor based detection frameworks [24,25,27,36] is how densely the space of possible anchors is sampled. For instance segmentation, following [25], we simply replace

Table 1. Output dimensions of different subnetworks for instance segmentation and pose estimation. K, n and C denote the number of point-set anchors, number of points per point-set anchor, and class number for the training/testing dataset, respectively.

Task	Classification	Shape regression	Bounding box regression
Instance segmentation	$K \times C$	$K \times (n \times 2)$	$K \times 4$
Pose estimation	$K \times 2$	$K \times (17 \times 2)$	-

classical rectangular anchors by our mask point-set anchors, and use 3 scales and 3 aspect ratios per location on each of the feature maps. Specifically, we make use of the implicit bounding box in point-set anchors, where each bounding box has three octave scales $2^{k/3}(k \leq 3)$ and three aspect ratios $[0.5, 1, 2]$, and the base scale for feature maps $P3 - P7$ is $\{32, 64, 128, 256, 512\}$. The combination of octave scales, aspect ratios and base scales will generate 9 bounding boxes per location on each of the feature maps. Anchor points are uniformly sampled on the four sides of the generated bounding boxes. For pose estimation, we use 3 mean poses generated by the k-means clustering algorithm. Then we translate them to each position of the feature maps as the point-set anchors. We further use 3 scales and 3 rotations for each anchor, yielding 27 anchors per location. The other feature map settings are the same as in instance segmentation.

Loss Function. We define our training loss function as follows:

$$L = \frac{1}{N_{pos}} \sum_{x,y} L_{cls}(p_{x,y}, c^*_{x,y}) + \frac{\lambda}{N_{pos}} \sum_{x,y} \mathbb{1}_{\{c^*_{x,y}\}>0} L_{reg}(t_{x,y}, t^*_{x,y}), \qquad (1)$$

where L_{cls} is the Focal loss in [25] and L_{reg} is the L1 loss for shape regression. $c^*_{x,y}$ and $t^*_{x,y}$ represent classification and regression targets, respectively. N_{pos} denotes the number of positive samples and λ is the balance weight, which is set to 0.1 and 10.0 for instance segmentation and pose estimation, respectively. $\mathbb{1}_{\{c^*_{x,y}\}>0}$ denotes the indicator function, being 1 if $\{c^*_{x,y}\} > 0$ and 0 otherwise. The loss is calculated over all locations and all feature maps.

Elements Specific to Pose Estimation. Besides target normalization and the embedding of prior knowledge in the anchor shapes, we further show how feature aggregation with point-set anchors achieves a certain feature transformation invariance and how point-set anchors can be extended to multi-stage learning.

– Deep Shape Indexed Features. Learning of shape/transformation invariant features has been a fundamental problem in computer vision [13,38], as they provide consistent and robust image information that is independent of geometric configuration. A point-set anchor acts as a shape hypothesis of the object to be localized. Though it reflects a coarse estimate of the target object shape, it still achieves a certain feature invariance to object shape, as it extracts the feature in accordance with the ordered point-set. The blue dashed rectangle in Fig. 3 depicts the feature aggregation module. In principle, the closer the anchor

Table 2. Comparison of different matching strategies between anchor points and mask contours on the instance segmentation task.

Matching strategy	AP	AP_{50}	AP_{75}	AP_S	AP_M	AP_L
Nearest Point	21.9	42.1	20.6	11.4	24.6	29.8
Nearest Line	23.2	46.5	21.0	12.5	26.2	32.0
Corner Point with Projection	**27.0**	**49.1**	**26.6**	**13.8**	**30.6**	**36.7**

points are to the object shape, the better shape invariance of the feature. The deep shape indexed feature is implemented by DCN [11]. Specifically, we replace the learnable offset in DCN with the location of points in a point-set anchor.

– **Multi-stage Refinement.** Holistic shape regression is generally more difficult than part based heat map learning [39]. This is on one hand because of the large and continuous solution space of poses. On the other hand, it is due to the extremely unbalanced transformation variance between different keypoints. To address this, a classic paradigm is to estimate the pose progressively via a sequence of weak regressors where each weak regressor uses features that depend on the estimated pose from the previous stage [13,38].

To this end, we use an additional refinement stage for pose estimation. While the k mean poses in the training set are used as the initial anchors for the first stage, we can directly use the pose predictions of the first stage as the point-set anchors for the second stage. Since the joint positions in the point-set anchors are well-initialized in the first stage, the point-set anchors for the second stage are much closer to the ground truth shapes. This facilitates learning since the distance of the regression target becomes much smaller and better shape-invariant features can be extracted by using the more accurate anchor shapes.

Conceptually, this head network can be stacked for multi-stage refinement, but we find the use of a single refinement to be most effective. Hence, we use one-step refinement for simplicity and efficiency.

4   Experiments

4.1   Instance Segmentation Settings

Dataset. We present experimental results for instance segmentation and object detection on the MS-COCO [26] benchmark. We use COCO `trainval35k` (115 k images) for training and the `minival` split (5 k images) for ablations. Comparisons to the state-of-the-art are reported on the `test-dev` split (20 k images).

Training Details. All our ablation experiments, except when specifically noted, are conducted on the `minival` split with ResNet-50 [18] and FPN. Our network is trained with synchronized stochastic gradient descent (SGD) over 4 GPUs with a mini-batch of 16 images (4 images per GPU). We adopt the 1× training setting, with 12 epochs in total and the learning rate initialized to 0.01 and then

Table 3. Comparison on different numbers of anchor points.

n	AP	AP_{50}	AP_{75}	AP_S	AP_M	AP_L
24	26.7	48.8	26.1	13.6	30.2	36.4
36	27.0	49.1	26.6	13.8	30.6	36.7
48	27.2	49.2	26.8	13.9	30.7	36.7
60	28.0	**49.8**	27.9	13.9	31.4	38.6
72	**28.0**	49.6	**27.9**	**14.6**	**31.5**	**38.8**

Table 4. Comparison of two regression origins.

Origin	AP	AP_{50}	AP_{75}	AP_S	AP_M	AP_L
Center point	26.0	48.4	24.8	13.6	29.3	35.4
Anchor points	**27.0**	**49.1**	**26.6**	**13.8**	**30.6**	**36.7**

divided by 10 at epochs 8 and 11. The weight decay and momentum parameters are set to 10^{-4} and 0.9, respectively. We initialize our backbone network with the weights pre-trained on ImageNet [12]. For the newly added layers, we keep the same initialization as in [25]. Unless specified, the input images are resized to have a shorter side of 800 and a longer side less than or equal to 1333. Samples with IoU higher than 0.6 and lower than 0.4 are defined as positive samples and negative samples, respectively. We use the Corner Point with Projection matching strategy and set the number of anchor points to 36 by default.

Inference Details. The input image is sent through the network to obtain classification scores and corresponding predicted classes. Based on the classification scores, the top-1 k anchors from each feature map level are sent for mask construction. Then the top predictions from all levels are merged and non-maximum suppression (NMS)[1] with a threshold of 0.5 is applied as post-processing.

4.2 Experiments on Instance Segmentation

Mask Matching Strategies. First, we compare the three strategies for matching between a point-set anchor and the corresponding mask contour. As shown in Table 2, Nearest Point has the worst performance, perhaps because each polygon point may be assigned to multiple anchor points and this inconsistency may misguide training. Both Nearest Line and Corner Point with Projection treat the ground-truth mask as a whole contour instead of as discrete polygon points in the mask matching step. However, there still exist ambiguous anchor points for the Nearest Line method as shown in Fig. 2(b). Corner Point with Projection

---

[1] IoU is calculated from predicted bounding boxes and ground-truth rectangles due to the high computation of mask IoU. If there is no bounding box branch in the network, we use the smallest rectangle that encompasses the predicted mask instead.

eliminates inconsistency, as the subdivision of the mask contour into segments leads to better-defined matches, and it achieves the best performance.

Effect of Point-Set Anchors. The number of anchor points can greatly affect instance segmentation. Table 3 shows that greater accuracy from more anchor points leads to better performance. Also, the performance is seen to saturate beyond a certain number of anchor points, e.g., 72 points. We also demonstrate the benefits of using point-set anchors as the regression origin as shown in Table 4. It can be seen that with the same regression targets, using point-set anchors as the regression origin outperforms center point based regression by 1.0 AP.

Table 5. Results on the MS COCO `test-dev` compared to state-of-the-art **instance segmentation** and **object detection** methods. '*' denotes multi-scale testing.

Method	Backbone	Regression Based	Segmentation			Detection		
			AP	AP_{50}	AP_{75}	AP	AP_{50}	AP_{75}
Mask RCNN [17]	ResNeXt-101	✗	37.1	60.0	39.4	39.8	62.3	43.4
TensorMask [4]	ResNet-101	✗	37.1	59.3	39.4	–	–	–
FCIS [23]	ResNet-101	✗	29.2	49.5	–	–	–	–
YOLACT [1]	ResNet-101	✗	31.2	50.6	32.8	33.7	54.3	35.9
ExtremeNet*[49]	Hourglass-104	✗	18.9	44.5	13.7	43.7	60.5	47.0
CornerNet* [22]	Hourglass-104	✗	–	–	–	42.2	57.8	45.2
RetinaNet [25]	ResNext-101	✓	–	–	–	40.8	61.1	44.1
FCOS [40]	ResNext-101	✓	–	–	–	44.7	64.1	48.4
CenterNet*[48]	Hourglass-104	✓	–	–	–	45.1	63.9	49.3
RepPoints*[44]	ResNeXt-101-DCN	✓	–	–	–	46.5	67.4	50.9
PolarMask [43]	ResNeXt-101-DCN	✓	36.2	59.4	37.7	–	–	–
Dense RepPoints [45]	ResNeXt-101-DCN	✓	41.8	65.7	45.0	48.9	69.2	53.4
ATSS* [47]	ResNeXt-101-DCN	✓	–	–	–	50.7	68.9	56.3
Ours	ResNeXt-101-DCN	✓	34.6	60.1	34.9	45.1	66.1	48.9
Ours*	ResNeXt-101-DCN	✓	36.0	61.5	36.6	46.2	67.0	50.5

Comparison with State-of-the-Art Methods. We evaluate PointSetNet on the COCO `test-dev` split and compare with other state-of-the-art object detection and instance segmentation methods. We use 60 anchor points for contour representation and ResNext-101 with DCN [11] as backbone. For data augmentation, we randomly scale the shorter side of images in the range of 480 to 960 during training and increase the number of training epochs to 24 (2× training setting). An image pyramid with a shorter side of $\{400, 600, 800, 100, 1200\}$ is applied during inference. As shown in Table 5, PointSetNet achieves performance competitive with the state-of-the-art in both object detection and instance segmentation. The gap between TensorMask and PointSetNet arises from the tensor bipyramid head which brings a +5.1 AP improvement. We do not plug this into our framework due to its heavy time and memory cost. Although the AP is 0.2

lower than PolarMask on instance segmentation, our proposed point-set anchor has the benefit of being applicable to human pose estimation.

4.3   Pose Estimation Settings

Dataset. We conduct comprehensive comparison experiments on the MS COCO Keypoint dataset [26] to evaluate the effectiveness of point-set anchors on multi-person human pose estimation. The COCO train, validation, and test sets contain more than 200 k images and 250 k person instances labeled with keypoints. 150 k of the instances are publicly available for training and validation. Our models are trained only on the COCO `train2017` dataset (which includes 57 K images and 150 K person instances) with no extra data. Ablations are conducted on the `val2017` set, and final results are reported on the `test-dev2017` set for a fair comparison to published state-of-the-art results [3,15,17,29,31–33,48].

Training Details. For pose estimation, we use the Adam [21] optimizer for training. The base learning rate is 1e-4. It drops to 1e-5 at 80 epochs and 1e-6 at 90. There are 100 epochs in total. Samples with OKS higher than 0.5 and lower than 0.4 are defined as positive samples and negative samples, respectively. The other training details are the same as for instance segmentation including the backbone network, network initialization, batch size and image resolution.

Table 6. Comparing different point-set anchors. Results are better when anchors more *efficiently* cover ground truth shapes with larger positive/negative sample ratio.

Anchor type	Matched GT (%)	Pos/Neg (‰₀)	AP	AP_{50}	AP_{75}
Center point	0	4.5	16.9	48.7	6.0
Rectangle	4.0	7.7	12.0	33.9	5.9
Mean Pose	18.0	6.6	**40.9**	**69.4**	**42.0**
K-means_3	27.7	6.4	43.3	70.7	45.5
K-means_5	32.1	6.1	**43.8**	**71.3**	**46.6**
K-means_7	34.6	6.0	43.8	71.2	46.5
Scale (0.8:0.2:1.2)	25.2	6.5	42.6	69.8	44.9
Scale (0.6:0.2:1.4)	27.6	6.2	**42.6**	**69.7**	**44.5**
Scale (0.4:0.2:1.6)	29.6	5.9	39.4	65.4	41.2
Rotation (−10:10:10)	27.2	9.0	42.6	70.6	44.2
Rotation (−20:10:20)	36.0	6.6	**43.5**	**71.6**	**45.9**
Rotation (−30:10:30)	40.5	6.2	42.6	70.6	44.4

4.4   Experiments on Pose Estimation

Effect of Point-Set Anchors. We first compare the proposed point-set anchors with strong prior knowledge of pose shapes to other point-based anchors like the center point and points on a rectangle. We denote as *mean pose* the use of the average pose in the training set as the canonical shape. Then we translate this *mean pose* to every position in the image as the point-set anchors for pose estimation. No other transformation is used to augment the anchor distribution for a fair comparison to the *center point* and *rectangle* anchors. A ground truth pose is assigned to anchors with OKS higher than 0.5. If no anchor is found higher than OKS 0.5, the ground truth is assigned to the closest anchor.

In Table 6, it is shown that the mean pose anchor outperforms the *center point* and *rectangle* anchors by a large margin with more ground truth poses assigned with OKS greater than 0.5. Specifically, it surpasses *center point* anchors by 24 AP and *rectangle* anchors by 28.9 AP. This indicates that an anchor that better approximates the target shape is more effective for shape regression.

We obtain further improvements by using additional canonical pose shapes generated by K-Means clustering or by augmenting the *mean pose* shape with additional sampling of rotation and scaling transformations. However, more anchor shapes and transformation augmentations also introduce more negative anchors not assigned to any of the ground truth poses, which makes learning less efficient. Better performance can be attained with a better trade-off between covering more ground truth shapes and incurring fewer negative samples. Empirically, we achieve the best performance by using 5 canonical pose shapes (+2.9 AP), 5 scale transformations (+1.7 AP) and 5 rotation transformations (+2.6 AP).

Table 7. Deep shape indexed feature compared with other feature extraction methods. Deep-SIF-n denotes deep shape indexed feature with n points for feature extraction.

Feature types	Loss_cls	Loss_reg	AP	AP_{50}	AP_{75}
Center feature	0.31	5.92	40.9	69.4	42.0
Box corner feature	0.31	6.22	42.6	68.2	45.6
Box region feature	0.30	5.99	42.8	69.0	46.0
Deep-SIF-9 for Cls	0.30	6.29	41.6	68.2	44.0
Deep-SIF-9 for Reg	0.32	5.93	45.5	69.6	49.1
Deep-SIF-9 for Cls & Reg	0.29	5.92	46.0	71.7	49.1
Deep-SIF-25 for Cls & Reg	**0.29**	**5.79**	**47.5**	**72.0**	**51.6**

Table 8. Effect of multi-stage refinement.

Stage	OKS	Matched GT (%)	Pos/Neg (%ₒₒₒ)	Loss_cls	Loss_reg	AP	AP_{50}	AP_{75}
Stage-1	0.5	45.7	12.7	0.25	5.52	48.3	74.3	52.5
Stage-2	0.99	81.5	11.5	0.23	4.28	58.0	80.8	62.4

Effect of Deep Shape Indexed Feature. Table 7 compares the deep shape indexed feature with other feature extraction methods. First, three regular feature extraction methods, namely from the center point, 4 corner points of the bounding box and 9 grid points in the bounding box region are compared. With more feature extraction points, slightly better performance is obtained.

Then, we use the deep shape indexed feature which uses the point set in the anchors for feature extraction. A point set based on pose shape priors extracts more informative features that greatly improve learning and performance. Specifically, with the same number of points (part of the 17 joints) as in the box region feature (i.e., 9), the deep shape indexed feature improves the AP from 42.8 to 46.0 (+3.2 AP, relative 7.5% improvement). Further improvement can be obtained by using more joint points for feature extraction. Note that if the shape indexed feature is used only for the person classification sub-network, the improvement is not as great as using it only in the pose regression sub-network. This indicates that it mainly enhances pose regression learning.

Effect of Multi-stage Refinement. Table 8 shows the result of using a second stage for refinement. Since the anchors for the second stage are much closer to the ground truth, we use a much higher OKS threshold (0.99) for positive sample selection. Even though the second stage uses a much higher OKS threshold, it is found that many more ground truth poses are covered. Both the person classification and the pose regression losses are decreased. We thus obtain significant improvement from the second stage, specifically, 9.7 AP (relative 20.1% improvement) over the first stage.

Effect of Stronger Backbone Network and Multi-scale Testing. Table 9 shows the result of using stronger backbones and multi-scale testing. Specifically, we obtain 4.5 AP improvement from using the ResNeXt-101-DCN backbone network. A 3.2 AP improvement is found from using multi-scale testing. We obtain further improvement by using HRNet [37] as the backbone (+4.1 AP).

Comparison with State-of-the-Art Methods. Finally, we test our model (with HRNet backbone and multi-scale testing) on the MSCOCO `test-dev2017` dataset and compare to the state-of-the-art in Table 10. PointSetNet outperforms CenterNet [48] by 5.7 AP and achieves competitive results to the state-of-the-art.

Table 9. Effect of backbone network and multi-scale testing.

Backbone	Multi-Test	AP	AP_{50}	AP_{75}
ResNet-50	✗	58.0	80.8	62.4
ResNeXt-101-DCN	✗	62.5	83.1	68.3
ResNeXt-101-DCN	✓	65.7	85.4	71.8
HRNet-W48	✓	69.8	88.8	76.3

Table 10. State-of-the-art **pose estimation** comparisons on COCO `test-dev2017`.

Method	Backbone	AP	AP_{50}	AP_{75}	AP_M	AP_L
Heat map based						
CMU-Pose [3]	3CM-3PAF (102)	61.8	84.9	67.5	57.1	68.2
RMPE [15]	Hourglass-4 stacked	61.8	83.7	69.8	58.6	67.6
Mask-RCNN [17]	ResNet-50	63.1	87.3	68.7	57.8	71.4
G-RMI [33]	ResNet-101+ResNet-50	64.9	85.5	71.3	62.3	70.0
AE [29]	Hourglass-4 stacked	65.5	86.8	72.3	60.6	72.6
PersonLab [32]	ResNet-152	68.7	89.0	75.4	64.1	75.5
HigherHRNet [7]	HRNet-W48	70.5	89.3	77.2	66.6	75.8
CPN [5]	ResNet-Inception	72.1	91.4	80.0	68.7	77.2
SimpleBaseline [42]	ResNet-152	73.7	91.9	81.1	70.3	80.0
HRNet [37,41]	HRNet-W48	75.5	92.5	83.3	71.9	81.5
DARK [46]	HRNet-W48	76.2	92.5	83.6	72.5	82.4
Regression based						
CenterNet [48]	Hourglass-2 stacked (104)	63.0	86.8	69.6	58.9	70.4
SPM [31]	Hourglass-8 stacked	66.9	88.5	72.9	62.6	73.1
Integral [39]	ResNet-101	67.8	88.2	74.8	63.9	74.0
Ours	HRNet-W48	68.7	89.9	76.3	64.8	75.3

5 Conclusion

We proposed Point-Set Anchors, which generalize and extend classical anchors to high-level recognition tasks such as instance segmentation and pose estimation. Point-set anchors provide informative features and good task-specific initializations which are beneficial for keypoint regression. Moreover, we propose PointSetNet by simply replacing the anchor boxes with the proposed point-set anchors in RetinaNet and attaching a parallel branch for keypoint regression. Competitive experimental results on object detection, instance segmentation and human pose estimation show the generality of our point-set anchors.

References

1. Bolya, D., Zhou, C., Xiao, F., Lee, Y.J.: Yolact: real-time instance segmentation. In: Proceedings of the IEEE International Conference on Computer Vision, pp. 9157–9166 (2019)
2. Bulat, A., Tzimiropoulos, G.: Human pose estimation via convolutional part heatmap regression. In: Leibe, B., Matas, J., Sebe, N., Welling, M. (eds.) ECCV 2016. LNCS, vol. 9911, pp. 717–732. Springer, Cham (2016). https://doi.org/10.1007/978-3-319-46478-7_44
3. Cao, Z., Simon, T., Wei, S.E., Sheikh, Y.: Realtime multi-person 2D pose estimation using part affinity fields. In: CVPR (2017)

4. Chen, X., Girshick, R., He, K., Dollár, P.: Tensormask: a foundation for dense object segmentation. In: Proceedings of the IEEE International Conference on Computer Vision, pp. 2061–2069 (2019)
5. Chen, Y., Wang, Z., Peng, Y., Zhang, Z., Yu, G., Sun, J.: Cascaded pyramid network for multi-person pose estimation. In: Proceedings of the IEEE Conference on Computer Vision and Pattern Recognition, pp. 7103–7112 (2018)
6. Chen, Y., Shen, C., Wei, X.S., Liu, L., Yang, J.: Adversarial posenet: a structure-aware convolutional network for human pose estimation. arXiv preprint arXiv:1705.00389 (2017)
7. Cheng, B., Xiao, B., Wang, J., Shi, H., Huang, T.S., Zhang, L.: Bottom-up higher-resolution networks for multi-person pose estimation. arXiv preprint arXiv:1908.10357 (2019)
8. Chou, C.J., Chien, J.T., Chen, H.T.: Self adversarial training for human pose estimation. arXiv preprint arXiv:1707.02439 (2017)
9. Chu, X., Yang, W., Ouyang, W., Ma, C., Yuille, A.L., Wang, X.: Multi-context attention for human pose estimation. arXiv preprint arXiv:1702.07432 (2017)
10. Dai, J., He, K., Sun, J.: Instance-aware semantic segmentation via multi-task network cascades. In: Proceedings of the IEEE Conference on Computer Vision and Pattern Recognition, pp. 3150–3158 (2016)
11. Dai, J., et al.: Deformable convolutional networks. In: Proceedings of the IEEE International Conference on Computer Vision, pp. 764–773 (2017)
12. Deng, J., Dong, W., Socher, R., Li, L.J., Li, K., Fei-Fei, L.: Imagenet: a large-scale hierarchical image database. In: 2009 IEEE Conference on Computer Vision and Pattern Recognition, pp. 248–255. IEEE (2009)
13. Dollár, P., Welinder, P., Perona, P.: Cascaded pose regression. In: 2010 IEEE Computer Society Conference on Computer Vision and Pattern Recognition, pp. 1078–1085. IEEE (2010)
14. Duan, K., Bai, S., Xie, L., Qi, H., Huang, Q., Tian, Q.: Centernet: keypoint triplets for object detection. In: Proceedings of the IEEE International Conference on Computer Vision, pp. 6569–6578 (2019)
15. Fang, H.S., Xie, S., Tai, Y.W., Lu, C.: RMPE: regional multi-person pose estimation. In: Proceedings of the IEEE International Conference on Computer Vision, pp. 2334–2343 (2017)
16. Gkioxari, G., Toshev, A., Jaitly, N.: Chained predictions using convolutional neural networks. In: Leibe, B., Matas, J., Sebe, N., Welling, M. (eds.) ECCV 2016. LNCS, vol. 9908, pp. 728–743. Springer, Cham (2016). https://doi.org/10.1007/978-3-319-46493-0_44
17. He, K., Gkioxari, G., Dollar, P., Girshick, R.: Mask R-CNN. In: International Conference on Computer Vision (2017)
18. He, K., Zhang, X., Ren, S., Sun, J.: Deep residual learning for image recognition. In: Proceedings of the IEEE Conference on Computer Vision and Pattern Recognition, pp. 770–778 (2016)
19. Huang, Z., Huang, L., Gong, Y., Huang, C., Wang, X.: Mask scoring R-CNN. In: Proceedings of the IEEE Conference on Computer Vision and Pattern Recognition, pp. 6409–6418 (2019)
20. Insafutdinov, E., Pishchulin, L., Andres, B., Andriluka, M., Schiele, B.: DeeperCut: a deeper, stronger, and faster multi-person pose estimation model. In: Leibe, B., Matas, J., Sebe, N., Welling, M. (eds.) ECCV 2016. LNCS, vol. 9910, pp. 34–50. Springer, Cham (2016). https://doi.org/10.1007/978-3-319-46466-4_3
21. Kingma, D., Ba, J.: Adam: a method for stochastic optimization. arXiv preprint arXiv:1412.6980 (2014)

22. Law, H., Deng, J.: CornerNet: detecting objects as paired keypoints. In: Ferrari, V., Hebert, M., Sminchisescu, C., Weiss, Y. (eds.) Computer Vision – ECCV 2018. LNCS, vol. 11218, pp. 765–781. Springer, Cham (2018). https://doi.org/10.1007/978-3-030-01264-9_45

23. Li, Y., Qi, H., Dai, J., Ji, X., Wei, Y.: Fully convolutional instance-aware semantic segmentation. In: Proceedings of the IEEE Conference on Computer Vision and Pattern Recognition, pp. 2359–2367 (2017)

24. Lin, T.Y., Dollár, P., Girshick, R., He, K., Hariharan, B., Belongie, S.: Feature pyramid networks for object detection. In: Proceedings of the IEEE Conference on Computer Vision and Pattern Recognition, pp. 2117–2125 (2017)

25. Lin, T.Y., Goyal, P., Girshick, R., He, K., Dollár, P.: Focal loss for dense object detection. In: Proceedings of the IEEE International Conference on Computer Vision, pp. 2980–2988 (2017)

26. Lin, T.-Y., et al.: Microsoft COCO: common objects in context. In: Fleet, D., Pajdla, T., Schiele, B., Tuytelaars, T. (eds.) ECCV 2014. LNCS, vol. 8693, pp. 740–755. Springer, Cham (2014). https://doi.org/10.1007/978-3-319-10602-1_48

27. Liu, W., et al.: SSD: single shot multibox detector. In: Leibe, B., Matas, J., Sebe, N., Welling, M. (eds.) ECCV 2016. LNCS, vol. 9905, pp. 21–37. Springer, Cham (2016). https://doi.org/10.1007/978-3-319-46448-0_2

28. Lloyd, S.: Least squares quantization in PCM. IEEE Trans. Inf. Theory **28**(2), 129–137 (1982)

29. Newell, A., Huang, Z., Deng, J.: Associative embedding: end-to-end learning for joint detection and grouping. In: Advances in Neural Information Processing Systems, pp. 2277–2287 (2017)

30. Newell, A., Yang, K., Deng, J.: Stacked hourglass networks for human pose estimation. In: Leibe, B., Matas, J., Sebe, N., Welling, M. (eds.) ECCV 2016. LNCS, vol. 9912, pp. 483–499. Springer, Cham (2016). https://doi.org/10.1007/978-3-319-46484-8_29

31. Nie, X., Feng, J., Zhang, J., Yan, S.: Single-stage multi-person pose machines. In: Proceedings of the IEEE International Conference on Computer Vision, pp. 6951–6960 (2019)

32. Papandreou, G., Zhu, T., Chen, L.-C., Gidaris, S., Tompson, J., Murphy, K.: PersonLab: person pose estimation and instance segmentation with a bottom-up, part-based, geometric embedding model. In: Ferrari, V., Hebert, M., Sminchisescu, C., Weiss, Y. (eds.) Computer Vision – ECCV 2018. LNCS, vol. 11218, pp. 282–299. Springer, Cham (2018). https://doi.org/10.1007/978-3-030-01264-9_17

33. Papandreou, G., et al.: Towards accurate multi-person pose estimation in the wild. arXiv preprint arXiv:1701.01779 (2017)

34. Peng, S., Jiang, W., Pi, H., Bao, H., Zhou, X.: Deep snake for real-time instance segmentation. arXiv preprint arXiv:2001.01629 (2020)

35. Pishchulin, L., et al.: Deepcut: joint subset partition and labeling for multi person pose estimation. In: Proceedings of the IEEE Conference on Computer Vision and Pattern Recognition, pp. 4929–4937 (2016)

36. Ren, S., He, K., Girshick, R., Sun, J.: Faster R-CNN: towards real-time object detection with region proposal networks. In: Advances in Neural Information Processing Systems (NIPS) (2015)

37. Sun, K., Xiao, B., Liu, D., Wang, J.: Deep high-resolution representation learning for human pose estimation. In: Proceedings of the IEEE Conference on Computer Vision and Pattern Recognition, pp. 5693–5703 (2019)

38. Sun, X., Wei, Y., Liang, S., Tang, X., Sun, J.: Cascaded hand pose regression. In: Proceedings of the IEEE Conference on Computer Vision and Pattern Recognition, pp. 824–832 (2015)

39. Sun, X., Xiao, B., Wei, F., Liang, S., Wei, Y.: Integral human pose regression. In: Ferrari, V., Hebert, M., Sminchisescu, C., Weiss, Y. (eds.) ECCV 2018. LNCS, vol. 11210, pp. 536–553. Springer, Cham (2018). https://doi.org/10.1007/978-3-030-01231-1_33

40. Tian, Z., Shen, C., Chen, H., He, T.: FCOS: fully convolutional one-stage object detection. In: Proceedings of the IEEE International Conference on Computer Vision, pp. 9627–9636 (2019)

41. Wang, J., et al.: Deep high-resolution representation learning for visual recognition. IEEE Trans. Pattern Anal. Mach. Intell. (2020)

42. Xiao, B., Wu, H., Wei, Y.: Simple baselines for human pose estimation and tracking. arXiv preprint arXiv:1804.06208 (2018)

43. Xie, E., et al.: Polarmask: single shot instance segmentation with polar representation. arXiv preprint arXiv:1909.13226 (2019)

44. Yang, Z., Liu, S., Hu, H., Wang, L., Lin, S.: Reppoints: point set representation for object detection. In: Proceedings of the IEEE International Conference on Computer Vision, pp. 9657–9666 (2019)

45. Yang, Z., et al.: Dense reppoints: representing visual objects with dense point sets. arXiv preprint arXiv:1912.11473 (2019)

46. Zhang, F., Zhu, X., Dai, H., Ye, M., Zhu, C.: Distribution-aware coordinate representation for human pose estimation. In: Proceedings of the IEEE/CVF Conference on Computer Vision and Pattern Recognition, pp. 7093–7102 (2020)

47. Zhang, S., Chi, C., Yao, Y., Lei, Z., Li, S.Z.: Bridging the gap between anchor-based and anchor-free detection via adaptive training sample selection. In: Proceedings of the IEEE/CVF Conference on Computer Vision and Pattern Recognition, pp. 9759–9768 (2020)

48. Zhou, X., Wang, D., Krähenbühl, P.: Objects as points. arXiv preprint arXiv:1904.07850 (2019)

49. Zhou, X., Zhuo, J., Krahenbuhl, P.: Bottom-up object detection by grouping extreme and center points. In: Proceedings of the IEEE Conference on Computer Vision and Pattern Recognition, pp. 850–859 (2019)

Modeling 3D Shapes by Reinforcement Learning

Cheng Lin[1,2], Tingxiang Fan[1], Wenping Wang[1(✉)], and Matthias Nießner[2]

[1] The University of Hong Kong, Pok Fu Lam, Hong Kong
wenping@cs.hku.hk
[2] Technical University of Munich, Munich, Germany

Abstract. We explore how to enable machines to model 3D shapes like human modelers using deep reinforcement learning (RL). In 3D modeling software like Maya, a modeler usually creates a mesh model in two steps: (1) approximating the shape using a set of primitives; (2) editing the meshes of the primitives to create detailed geometry. Inspired by such artist-based modeling, we propose a two-step neural framework based on RL to learn 3D modeling policies. By taking actions and collecting rewards in an interactive environment, the agents first learn to parse a target shape into primitives and then to edit the geometry. To effectively train the modeling agents, we introduce a novel training algorithm that combines heuristic policy, imitation learning and reinforcement learning. Our experiments show that the agents can learn good policies to produce regular and structure-aware mesh models, which demonstrates the feasibility and effectiveness of the proposed RL framework.

1 Introduction

Enabling machines to learn the behavior of humans in visual arts, such as teaching machines to paint [5,7,15], has aroused researchers' curiosity in recent years. The 3D modeling, a process of preparing geometric data of 3D objects, is also an important form of visual and plastic arts and has wide applications in computer vision and computer graphics. Human modelers are able to form high-level interpretations of 3D objects, and use them for communicating, building memories, reasoning and taking actions. Therefore, for the purpose of enabling machines to understand 3D artists' behavior and developing a modeling-assistant tool, it is a meaningful but under-explored problem to teach intelligent agents to learn 3D modeling policies like human modelers.

Generally, there are two steps for a 3D modeler to model a 3D shape in mainstream modeling software. First, the modeler needs to perceive the part-based structure of the shape, and starts with basic geometric primitives to approximate the shape. Second, the modeler edits the mesh of the primitives using specific

Electronic supplementary material The online version of this chapter (https://doi.org/10.1007/978-3-030-58607-2_32) contains supplementary material, which is available to authorized users.

© Springer Nature Switzerland AG 2020
A. Vedaldi et al. (Eds.): ECCV 2020, LNCS 12355, pp. 545–561, 2020.
https://doi.org/10.1007/978-3-030-58607-2_32

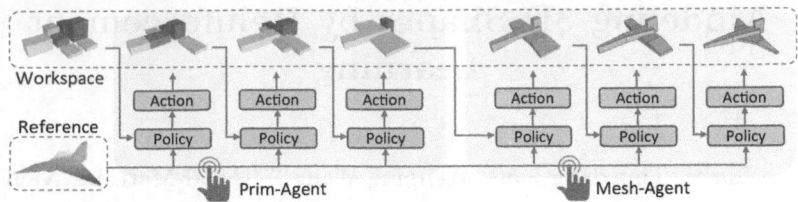

Fig. 1. The RL agents learn policies and take actions to model 3D shapes like human modelers. Given a reference, the Prim-Agent first approximates the shape using primitives, and then the Mesh-Agent edits the mesh to create detailed geometry.

operations to create more detailed geometry. These two steps embody humans' hierarchical understanding and preserve high-level regularity within a 3D shape, which is more accessible compared to predicting low-level points.

Inspired by such artist-based modeling, we propose a two-step deep reinforcement learning (RL) framework to learn 3D modeling policies. RL is a decision-making framework, where an agent interacts with the environment by executing actions and collecting rewards. As visualized in Fig. 1, in the first step, we propose Prim-Agent which learns to parse a target shape into a set of primitives. In the second step, we propose Mesh-Agent to edit the meshes of the primitives to create more detailed geometry.

There are two major challenges to teach RL agents to model 3D shapes. The first one is the environment setting of RL for shape analysis and geometry editing. The Prim-Agent is expected to understand the shape structure and decompose the shape into components. For this task, however, the interaction between agent and environment is not intuitive and naturally derived. To motivate the agent to learn, rather than directly predicting the primitives, we break down the main task into small steps; that is, we make the agent operate a set of pre-defined primitives step-by-step to approximate the target shape, which finally results in a primitive-based shape representation. For the Mesh-Agent, the challenge lies in preserving mesh regularity when editing geometry. Instead of editing single vertices, we propose to operate the mesh based on edge loops [14]. Edge loop is a widely used technique in 3D modeling software to manage complexity, by which we can edit a group of vertices and control an integral geometric unit. The proposed settings capture the insights of the behavior of modeling artists and are also tailored to the properties of the RL problem.

The second challenge is, due to the complex operations and huge action space in this problem, off-the-shelf RL frameworks are unable to learn good policies. Gathering demonstration data from human experts to guide the agents would help, but this modeling data is expensive to obtain, while the demonstrations are far from covering most scenarios the agent will experience in real-world 3D modeling. To address this challenge, innovations are made on the following two points. First, we design a heuristic algorithm as a "virtual expert" to generate demonstrations, and show how to interactively incorporate the heuristics into an imitation learning (IL) process. Second, we introduce a novel scheme to effectively combine IL and RL for modeling 3D shapes. The agents are first trained by IL to learn an initial policy, and then they learn in an RL paradigm by collecting the rewards. We show that the combination of IL and RL gives better performance than either does on its own, and it also outperforms the existing related algorithms on the 3D modeling task.

To demonstrate our method, we condition the modeling agents mainly on the shape references from single depth maps. Note, however, the architecture of our agents is agnostic to the shape reference, while we also test RGB images. The contributions of this paper are three-fold:

- We make the first attempt to study how to teach machines to model real 3D shapes like humans using deep RL. The agents can learn good modeling policies by interacting with the environment and collecting feedback.
- We introduce a two-step RL formulation for shape analysis and geometry editing. Our agents can produce regular and structure-aware mesh models to capture the fundamental geometry of 3D shapes.
- We present a novel algorithm that combines heuristic policy, imitation learning and reinforcement learning. We show a considerable improvement compared to the related training algorithms on the 3D modeling task.

2   Related Work

Imitation Learning and Reinforcement Learning. Imitation learning (IL) aims to mimic human behavior by learning from demonstrations. Classical approaches [1, 34] are based on training a classifier or regressor to predict behavior using demonstrations collected from experts. However, since policies learned in this way can easily fail in theory and practice [16], some interactive strategies for IL are introduced such as DAagger [18] and AggreVaTe [17].

Reinforcement learning (RL) is to train an agent by making it explore in an environment and collect rewards. With the development of the scalability of deep learning [10], a breakthrough of deep reinforcement learning (DRL) is made by the introduction of Deep Q-learning (DQN) [12]. Afterward, a series of approaches have been continuously proposed to improve the DQN, such as Dueling DQN [30], Double DQN [28] and Prioritized experience replay [20].

Typically, an RL agent can find a reasonable action only after numerous steps of poor performance in exploration, which leads to low learning efficiency and accuracy. Thus, there has been interest in combining IL with RL to achieve better performance [4, 22, 23]. For example, Hester et al. proposed Deep Q-learning from Demonstrations (DQfD) [6], in which they initially pre-train the networks solely on the demonstration data to accelerate the RL process. However, our experiments show that directly using these approaches for 3D modeling does not produce good performance; thus we introduce a novel variant algorithm that enables the modeling agents to learn considerably better policies.

Shape Generation by RL. Painting is an important form for people to create shapes. There is a series of methods using RL to learn how to paint by generating strokes [5,7,32] or drawing sketc.hes [15,33]. Some works explore to use grammar parsing for shape analysis and modeling. Teboul et al. [25] use RL to parse the shape grammar of the building facade. Ruiz-Montiel et al. [19] propose an approach to complement the generative power of shape grammars with RL techniques. These methods all focus on the 2D domain, while our method targets 3D shape modeling, which is under-explored and more challenging. Sharma et al. [21] present CSG-Net, which is a neural architecture to parse a 2D or 3D input into a collection of modeling primitives with operations. However, it only handles synthetic 3D shapes composed of the most basic geometries, while our method is evaluated on ShapeNet [3] models.

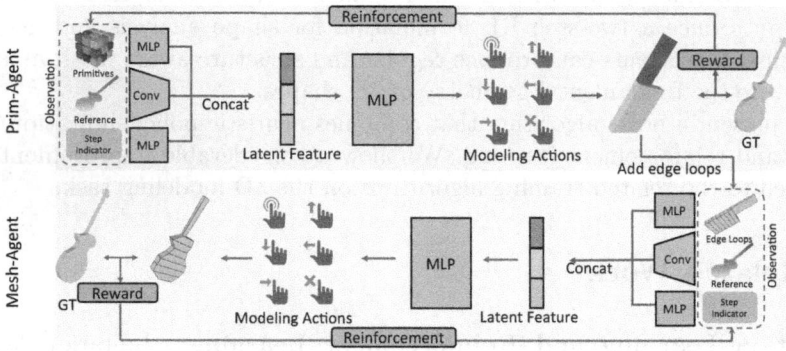

Fig. 2. The architecture of our two-step pipeline for 3D shape modeling. First, given a shape reference and pre-defined primitives, the Prim-Agent predicts a sequence of actions to operate the primitives to approximate the target shape. Then the edge loops are added to the output primitives. Second, the Mesh-Agent takes as input the shape reference and the primitive-based representation, and predicts actions to edit the meshes to create detailed geometry.

High-Level Shape Understanding. There has been growing interest in high-level shape analysis, where the ideas are central to part-based segmentation [8,9] and structure-based shape understanding [11,29]. Primitive-based shape abstraction [13,27,31,35], in particular, is well-researched for producing structurally simple representation and reconstruction. Zou et al. [35] introduce a supervised method that uses a generative RNN to predict a set of primitives step-by-step to synthesize a target shape. Li et al. [11] and Sun et al. [24] propose neural architectures to infer the symmetry hierarchy of a 3D shape. Tian et al. [26] propose a neural program generator to represent 3D shapes as 3D programs, which can reflect shape regularity such as symmetry and repetition. These methods capture higher-level shape priors but barely consider geometric details. Instead, our method performs joint primitive-based shape understanding and mesh detail editing. In essence, these methods have different goals with our work. They aim to directly minimize the reconstruction loss using end-to-end networks, while we focus on enabling machines to understand the environment, learn policies and take actions like human modelers.

3   Method

In this section, we first give the detailed RL formulations of the Prim-Agent (Sect. 3.1) and the Mesh-Agent (Sect. 3.2). Then, we introduce an algorithm to efficiently train the agents (Sect. 3.3 and 3.4). We will discuss and evaluate these designs in the next section.

3.1   Primitive-Based Shape Abstraction

The Prim-Agent is expected to understand the part-based structure of a shape by interacting with the environment. We propose to decompose the task into small steps, where the agent constantly tweaks the primitives based on the feedback to achieve the goal. The detailed formulation of the Prim-Agent is given below.

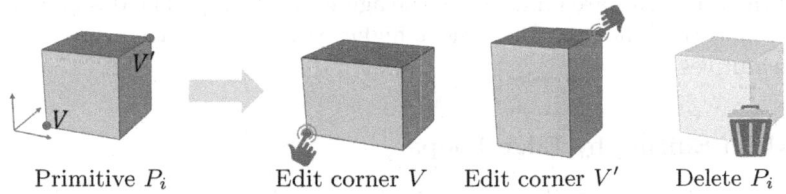

| Primitive P_i | Edit corner V | Edit corner V' | Delete P_i |

Fig. 3. Visualization of the three types of actions to operate a primitive.

State. At the beginning, we arrange m^3 cubes that are uniformly distributed in the canonical frame (m cubes for each axis), denoted as $\mathcal{P} = \{P_i \mid i = 1, ..., m^3\}$. We use $m = 3$ in this paper. Each cuboid is defined by a six-tuple (x, y, z, x', y', z') which specifies its two diagonal corner points $V = (x, y, z)$ and $V' = (x', y', z')$ (see Fig. 3). We define the state by: (1) the input shape reference; (2) the updated cuboid primitives at each iteration; (3) the step number represented by one-hot encoding. The agent will learn to predict the next action by observing the current state.

Action. As shown in Fig. 3, we define three types of actions to operate a cuboid primitive P_i: (1) drag the corner V; (2) drag the corner V'; (3) delete P_i. For each type of action, we use four parameters $-2, -1, 1, 2$ to control the range of movement on the axis directions (for the delete action, these parameters all lead to deleting the primitive). In total, there are 27 cuboids, 3 types of actions, 3 moving directions (x, y and z) for the drag actions, and 4 range parameters, which leads to an action space of 756.

Reward Function. The reward function reflects the quality of an executed action, while the agent is expected to be inspired by the reward to generate simple but expressive shape abstractions. The primary goal is to encourage the consistency between the generated primitive-based representation $\cup_i P_i$ and the target shape O. We measure the consistency by the following two terms based on the intersection over union (IoU):

$$\mathcal{I}_1 = IoU(\cup_i P_i, O) \qquad \mathcal{I}_2 = \frac{1}{\mathcal{K}} \sum_{P_i \in \overline{\mathcal{P}}} IoU(P_i, O), \tag{1}$$

where $\mathcal{I}_1$ is the global IoU term and $\mathcal{I}_2$ is the local IoU term to encourage the agent to make each primitive cover more valid parts of the target shape; $\overline{\mathcal{P}}$ ($|\overline{\mathcal{P}}| = \mathcal{K}$) is the set of primitives that are not deleted yet. To favor simplicity, i.e., small number of primitives, we introduce a parsimony reward measured by the number of deleted primitives denoted by $\mathcal{N}$. Therefore, the reward function at the kth step is defined as

$$R_k = (\mathcal{I}_1^k - \mathcal{I}_1^{k-1}) + \alpha_1(\mathcal{I}_2^k - \mathcal{I}_2^{k-1}) + \alpha_2(\mathcal{N}^k - \mathcal{N}^{k-1}), \tag{2}$$

where α_1 and α_2 are the weights to balance the last two terms. We set $R_k = -1$ once all the primitives are removed by the agent at k^{th} step. The designed reward function motivates the agent to achieve higher volume coverage using larger and fewer primitives.

3.2   Mesh Editing by Edge Loops

An edge loop is a series of connected edges on the surface of an object that runs completely around the object and ends up at the starting point. It is an effective tool that plays a vital role in modeling software [14]. Using edge loops, modelers can jointly edit a group of vertices and control an integral geometric unit instead of editing each vertex separately, which preserves the mesh regularity and improves the efficiency. Therefore, we make the Mesh-Agent learn mesh editing based on edge loops to produce higher mesh quality.

Edge Loop Assignment. The output primitives from the last step do not have any edge loops. Thus we need to define edge loops on these primitives. For a primitive P_i, we choose the axis in which the longest cuboid side (principle direction) lies to assign the loop, while the loop planes are vertical to the chosen axis. We assign n loops to $\mathcal{K}$ (not removed) cuboids; the number of loops assigned to a cuboid is proportional to its volume, while a larger cuboid will be assigned more loops. Each cuboid is assigned at least two loops on the boundaries. An example of edge loop assignment is shown in Fig. 4(a).

State. We define the state by: (1) the input shape reference; (2) the updated edge loops at each iteration; (3) the step number represented by one-hot encoding. An edge loop L_i is a rectangle defined by a six-tuple $(x_l, y_l, z_l, x_l', y_l', z_l')$ which specifies its two diagonal corner points $V_L = (x_l, y_l, z_l)$, $V_L' = (x_l', y_l', z_l')$.

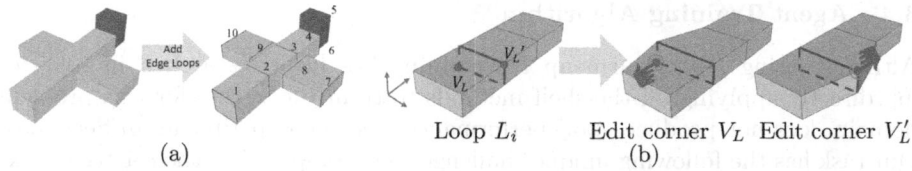

Loop L_i Edit corner V_L Edit corner V_L'
(a)   (b)

Fig. 4. (a) We assign edge loops to the output primitives of the Prim-Agent for further mesh editing. Here, we show an example of adding $n = 10$ edge loops to 3 primitives. (b) Two types of actions to operate an edge loop.

Action. As shown in Fig. 4(b), we define two types of actions to operate a loop L_i: (1) drag the corner V_L; (2) drag the corner V_L'. For each type of action, we use six parameters $-3, -2, -1, 1, 2, 3$ to control the range of movement on three axis directions. The number of edge loops we use is $n = 10$ in this paper. In total, there are 10 edge loops, 2 types of actions, 3 moving directions and 6 range parameters, which leads to an action space of 360.

Reward Function. The goal of this step is to encourage visual similarity of the edited mesh with the target shape, which can be measured by IoU. Accordingly, the reward is defined by the increments of IoU after executing an action.

3.3   Virtual Expert

Given such a huge action space, complex environment and long operation steps in this task, it is extremely difficult to train the modeling agents from scratch. However, collecting large scale sequence demonstration data from real experts can be expensive and the data are far from covering most scenarios. To address this problem, we propose an efficient heuristic algorithm as a virtual expert to generate the demonstration data. Note that the proposed algorithm is not for producing perfect actions used as ground-truth, but it can help the agents start the exploration with relatively better performance. More importantly, the agents are able to learn even better policies than imitating the virtual expert by the self-exploration in the RL phase (see the evaluation in Sect. 4.3).

For the primitive-based shape abstraction, we design an algorithm that outputs the actions as the following heuristics. We iteratively visit each primitive, test all the potential actions for the primitive and execute the one which can obtain the best reward. During the first half of the process, we do not consider any delete operations but only adjust the corners. This is to encourage all the primitives to fit the target shape first. Then in the second half, we allow deleting the primitives to eliminate redundancy.

Similarly, for the edge loop editing, we iteratively visit each edge loop, test all the potential actions for the edge loop, and execute the one which can obtain the best reward.

3.4   Agent Training Algorithm

Although using IL to warm up RL training has been researched in robotics [6], directly applying off-the-shelf methods to train the agents for this problem domain does not produce good performance (see the experiments in Sect. 4.3). Our task has the following unique challenges: (1) compared to the robotics tasks [2] of which action space is usually less than 20, our agents need to handle over 1000 actions in a long sequence for modeling a 3D shape. This requires that the data from both "expert" and self-exploration should be organized and exploited effectively by the experience replay buffer. (2) The modeling demonstrations are generated by heuristics which are imperfect and monotonous, and thus the training scheme should not only use the "expert" to its fullest potential, but also enable the agents to escape from local optimum.

Therefore, in this section, we introduce a variant algorithm to train the modeling agents. The architecture of our training scheme is illustrated in Fig. 5.

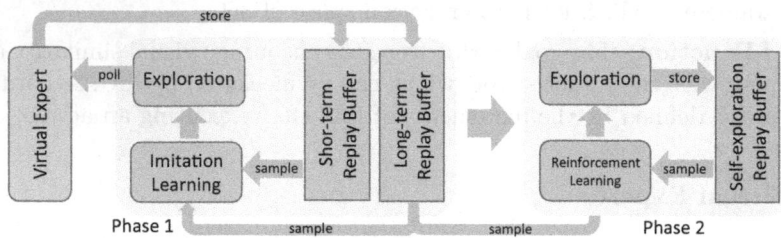

Fig. 5. Illustration of the architecture and the data flow of our training scheme.

Basic Network. The basic network is based on the Double DQN (DDQN) [28] to predict the Q-values of the potential actions. The network outputs a set of action values $Q(s, \cdot; \theta)$ for an input state s, where θ are the parameters of the network. DDQN uses two separate Q-value estimators, i.e., current and target network, each of which is used to update the other. An experience is denoted as a tuple $\{s_k, a, R, s_{k+1}\}$ and the experiences will be stored in a replay buffer $\mathcal{D}$; the agent is trained by the data sampled from $\mathcal{D}$. The loss function for training DDQN is determined by temporal difference (TD) update:

$$\mathcal{L}_{TD}(\theta) = ((R + \gamma Q(s_{k+1}, a_{k+1}^{max}; \theta') - Q(s_k, a_k; \theta))^2, \tag{3}$$

where R is the reward, γ the discount factor, $a_{k+1}^{max} = argmax_a Q(s_{k+1}, a; \theta)$, θ and θ' the parameters of current and target network respectively.

Imitation Learning by Dataset Aggregation. Our imitation learning process benefits from the idea of data aggregation (DAgger) [18] which is an interactive guiding method. A notable limitation of DAgger is that an expert has to be always available during training to provide additional feedback to the agent, making the training expensive and troublesome. However, benefiting from the developed virtual expert, we are able to guide the agent without additional cost by integrating the virtual expert into the training process.

Different from the original DAgger, we use two replay buffers, named $\mathcal{D}_{short}^{demo}$ and $\mathcal{D}_{long}^{demo}$ for storing short-term and long-term experiences respectively. The $\mathcal{D}_{short}^{demo}$ only stores the experiences at the current iteration and will be emptied once an iteration is completed, while the $\mathcal{D}_{long}^{demo}$ stores all the accumulated experiences. At iteration k, we train a policy π_k that mimics the "expert" on these demonstrations by equally sampling from both $\mathcal{D}_{short}^{demo}$ and $\mathcal{D}_{long}^{demo}$. Then we use the policy π_k to generate new demonstrations, but re-label the actions using the heuristics of the virtual expert described in Sect. 3.3.

Incorporating the virtual expert into DAgger, we poll the "expert" policy outside its original state space to make it iteratively produce new policies. Using double replay buffers provides a trade-off between learning and reviewing in the long sequence of decisions for shape modeling. The algorithm is detailed in Algorithm 1 with pseudo-code.

Algorithm 1: DAgger with virtual expert using double replay buffers

---

Use the virtual expert algorithm to generate demonstrations
$\mathcal{D}_0 = \{(s_1, a_1), ..., (s_M, a_M)\}$.
Initialize $\mathcal{D}_{short}^{demo} \leftarrow \mathcal{D}_0$, $\mathcal{D}_{long}^{demo} \leftarrow \mathcal{D}_0$.
Initialize π_1.
for $k = 1$ *to* N **do**
    Train policy π_k by equally sampling on both $\mathcal{D}_{short}^{demo}$ and $\mathcal{D}_{long}^{demo}$.
    Get dataset $\mathcal{D}_k = \{(s'_1), (s'_2), ..., (s'_M)\}$ by π_k.
    Label $\mathcal{D}_k$ with the actions given by the virtual expert algorithm.
    Empty short-term memory $\mathcal{D}_{short}^{demo} \leftarrow \varnothing$.
    Aggregate dataset $\mathcal{D}_{long}^{demo} \leftarrow \mathcal{D}_{long}^{demo} \cup \mathcal{D}_k$, $\mathcal{D}_{short}^{demo} \leftarrow \mathcal{D}_k$

Similar to [6], we apply a supervised loss to force the Q-value of the actions of "expert" to be higher than the other actions by at least a margin:

$$\mathcal{L}_S(\theta) = \max_{a \in A}(Q(s, a; \theta) + l(s, a_E, a)) - Q(s, a_E; \theta), \tag{4}$$

where a_E is the action taken by the "expert" in state s and $l(s, a_E, a)$ is a margin function that is a positive number when $a \neq a_E$ and is 0 when $a = a_E$. The final loss function used to update the network in the imitation learning phase is defined by jointly applying TD-loss and supervised loss:

$$\mathcal{L}(\theta) = \mathcal{L}_{TD}(\theta) + \lambda \mathcal{L}_S(\theta). \tag{5}$$

Reinforcement Learning by Self-exploration. Once the imitation learning is completed, the agents will have learned a reasonable initial policy. Nevertheless, the heuristics of the virtual expert suffer from the local minimum and the demonstrations cannot cover all the situations the agents will encounter in the real system. Therefore, we make the agents interact with the environment and learn from their own experiences in a reinforcement paradigm. In this phase, we create a separate experience replay butter $\mathcal{D}^{self}$ to store only self-generated data during the exploration, and maintain the demonstration data in $\mathcal{D}^{demo}_{long}$. In each mini-batch, similar to the last step, we equally sample the experiences from $\mathcal{D}^{self}$ and $\mathcal{D}^{demo}_{long}$, and update the network only using TD-loss $\mathcal{L}_{TD}$. In this way, the agents retain a part of the memory from the "expert" but also gain new experiences by their own exploration. This allows the agents to potentially compare the actions learned from the "expert" and explored by themselves, and then make better decisions based on the accumulated reward in the practical environment.

4   Experiments

4.1   Implementation Details

Network Architecture. As shown in Fig. 2, for the Prim-Agent, the encoder is composed of three parallel streams: three 2D convolutional layers for the shape reference, two fully-connected (FC) layers followed by ReLU non-linearities for the primitive parameters, and one FC layer with ReLU for the step indicator. The three streams are concatenated and input to three FC layers with ReLU non-linearities for the first two layers, and the final layer outputs the Q-values for all actions. The Mesh-Agent adopts a similar architecture. The Prim-Agent is unrolled for 300 steps to operate the primitives and the Mesh-Agent 100 steps, while we have observed that more steps do not result in further improvement.

Agent Training. We first train the Prim-Agent and then use its output to train the Mesh-Agent. To learn a relatively consistent mapping from the modeling actions to the edge loops, we sort the edge loops into a canonical order. Each network is first trained by imitation and then by a reinforcement paradigm. The capacities of the replay buffer $\mathcal{D}^{demo}_{long}$ and $\mathcal{D}^{self}$ are 200,000 and 100,000 respectively, while the agents will over-write the old data in the buffers when they are full. Two agent networks are trained with batch size 64 and learning rate $8e^{-5}$. In the IL process, we perform DAgger for 4 iterations for each shape and the network is updated with 4000 mini-batches in each DAgger iteration. In the RL, we use $\epsilon = 0.02$ for ϵ-greedy exploration, $\tau = 4000$ for the frequency at which to update the target network, and $\gamma = 0.9$ for the discount factor.

We use $\alpha_1 = 0.1$ and $\alpha_2 = 0.01$ to balance the terms in the reward function Eq. 2, and $\lambda = 1.0$ in the loss function Eq. 5. The expert margin $l(s, a_E, a)$ in Eq. 4 is set to 0.8 when $a \neq a_E$. We observe sometimes the agents are stuck at a state and output repetitive actions; therefore, at each step, we force the agents to edit a different object, i.e., editing the ith ($i \in \{1, 2, ..., m\}$) primitive or loop at the kth step, where $i = k \bmod m$. Also, the output of the Prim-Agent may have redundant or small primitives contained in the large ones, while we merge them to make the results cleaner and simpler.

4.2   Experimental Results

Following the works for part-based representation of 3D shapes [13,24,27], we train our modeling agents on three shape categories separately. We collect a set of 3D shapes from ShapeNet [3], i.e., airplane(800), guitar(600) and car(800), to train our network. We render a 128*128 depth map for each shape to serve as the reference. We use 10% shapes from each category to generate the demonstrations for imitation learning. To show the exploration as well as the generalization ability, in each category, we randomly select 100 shapes that are either without demonstrations(50) or unseen(50) for testing.

We show a set of qualitative results in Fig. 6. Given a depth map as shape reference, the Prim-Agent first approximates the target shape using primitives; then the Mesh-Agent takes as input the primitives and edits the meshes of the primitives to produce more detailed geometry. The procedure of the agents'

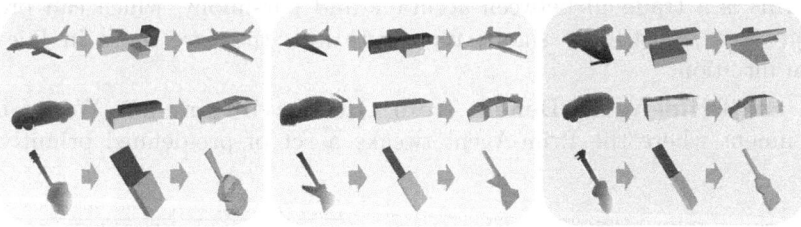

Fig. 6. Qualitative results of Prim-Agent and Mesh-Agent. Given a shape reference, the Prim-Agent first approximates the target shape using primitives and then the Mesh-Agent edits the meshes to create detailed geometry.

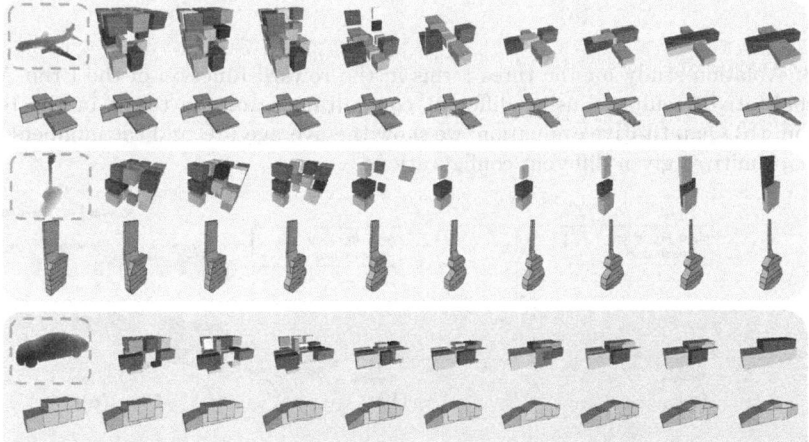

Fig. 7. The step-by-step procedure of 3D shape modeling. The first row of each subfigure shows how the Prim-Agent approximates the target shape by operating the primitives (step 5, 10, 20, 40, 60, 80, 100, 200, 300). The second row shows the process of mesh editing by the Mesh-Agent (step 10, 20, 30, 40, 50, 60, 70, 80, 90, 100).

modeling operation is visualized in Fig. 7. The agents show the power in understanding the part-based structure and capturing the fundamental geometry of the target shapes, and they are able to express such understanding by taking a sequence of interpretable actions. Also, the part-aware regular mesh can provide human modelers a reasonable initialization for further editing.

4.3   Discussions

Reward Function. Reward function is a key component for RL framework design. There are three terms in the reward function Eq. 2 for the Prim-Agent. To demonstrate the necessity of each term, we conduct an ablation study by alternatively removing each one and evaluating the performance of the agent. Figure 8(a) shows the qualitative results for different configurations. We also quantitatively report the average IoU and the average amount of the output primitives in Fig. 8(b). Both qualitative and quantitative results show that using full terms is a trade-off between accuracy and parsimony, which can produce accurate but structurally simple representations that are more in line with human intuition.

Does the Prim-Agent Benefit from Our Environment? We set up an environment where the Prim-Agent tweaks a set of pre-defined primitives to

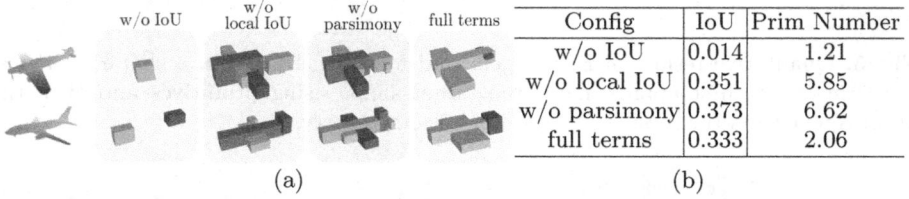

Config	IoU	Prim Number
w/o IoU	0.014	1.21
w/o local IoU	0.351	5.85
w/o parsimony	0.373	6.62
full terms	0.333	2.06

(a)   (b)

Fig. 8. Ablation study for the three terms in the reward function of the Prim-Agent. (a) Qualitative results of using different configurations of the terms in the reward function. (b) Quantitative evaluation; we show the average IoU and the numbers of the output primitives given different configurations.

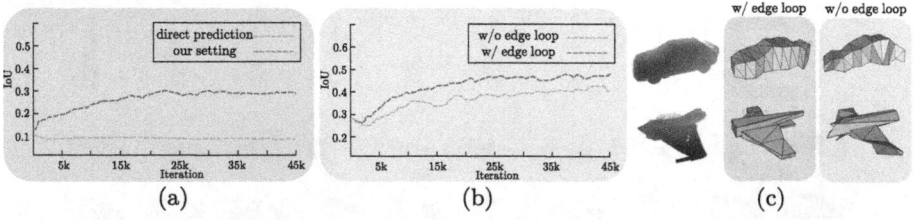

(a)   (b)   (c)

Fig. 9. Evaluations on the environment setting for Prim-Agent and Mesh-Agent. (a) IoU over the course of training the Prim-Agent in different environment settings. (b) IoU over the course of training the Mesh-Agent with and without using edge loops. (c) Qualitative results produced by the Mesh-Agent with and without using edge loops; we show the triangulated meshes of the generated wireframes.

approximate the target shape step-by-step. A more straightforward way, how-ever, is to make the agent directly predict the parameters of each primitive in a sequence. We evaluate the effect of these two environment settings on the agent for understanding the primitive-based structure. As shown in Fig. 9(a), the agent is unable to learn reasonable policies by directly predicting the primitives. The reason behind this is, in such an environment, the effective attempts are too sparse during exploration and the agent cannot be rewarded very often. Instead, in our environment setting, the task is decomposed into small action steps that the agent can simply do. The agent obtains gradual feedback and can be aware that the policy is getting better and closer. Therefore, the learning is progressive and smooth, which is advantageous to incentivize the agent to achieve the goal.

Do the Edge Loops Help? We use edge loops as the tool for geometry editing. To evaluate the advantages of our environment setting for the Mesh-Agent, we train a variant of the Mesh-Agent without using edge loops, where the agent edits each vertex separately. This leads to a doubled action space and uncorrelated operations between vertices. As shown in Fig. 9(b) and (c), the agent using edge loops yields a lower modeling error and better mesh quality.

Is Our Learning Algorithm Better than the Others for 3D Modeling? In Sect. 3.4, we introduce an algorithm to train the agents by combining heuristics, interactive IL and RL. Here, we provide an evaluation of the proposed learning algorithm with a comparison to using different related learning

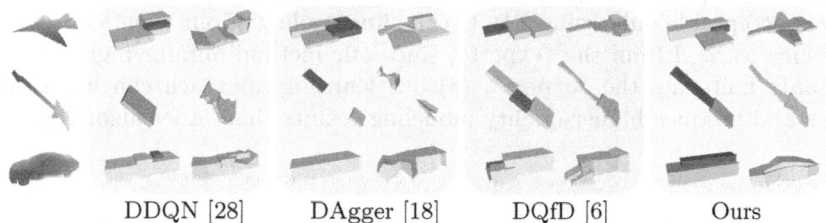

DDQN [28]   DAgger [18]   DQfD [6]   Ours

Fig. 10. Qualitative comparison with related RL algorithms on the 3D modeling task. Our method gives better results, i.e., more structurally meaningful primitive-based representations and more regular and accurate meshes.

Table 1. Comparison with related learning algorithms. We report the average accumulated rewards gained by the agents on each category.

	Prim-Agent			Mesh-Agent		
	Airplane	Guitar	Car	Airplane	Guitar	Car
DDQN (only RL)	0.377	0.214	0.703	−0.013	−0.025	0.002
DAgger (only interactive IL)	0.574	0.802	0.755	0.046	0.089	0.059
DQfD (non-interactive IL + RL)	0.685	0.723	0.789	0.019	0.042	0.055
DAgger* (double replay buffers)	0.725	0.954	0.897	0.048	0.105	0.065
Ours (interactive IL + RL)	**0.764**	**0.987**	**0.956**	**0.134**	**0.204**	**0.134**

Table 2. Quantitative evaluation on the shape reconstruction quality using additional metrics: IoU and Chamfer distance (CD).

	Prim-Agent						Mesh-Agent					
	Airplane		Guitar		Car		Airplane		Guitar		Car	
	IoU	CD	IoU	CD	IoU	CD	IoU	CD	IoU	CD	IoU	CD
DDQN	0.082	0.1165	0.094	0.1010	0.382	0.0812	0.069	0.1177	0.069	0.1092	0.384	0.0864
DAgger	0.133	0.1068	0.202	0.0890	0.406	0.0761	0.179	0.0926	0.291	0.0804	0.466	0.0763
DQfD	0.132	0.1112	0.196	0.0937	0.415	0.0749	0.151	0.1047	0.238	0.0796	0.471	0.0729
DAgger*	0.131	0.1104	0.275	0.0808	0.449	0.0778	0.179	0.0986	0.381	0.0598	0.514	0.0670
Ours	**0.179**	**0.0966**	**0.308**	**0.0595**	**0.481**	**0.0669**	**0.313**	**0.0917**	**0.512**	**0.0476**	**0.614**	**0.0532**

schemes. Table 1 shows the average accumulated rewards across categories of different algorithms: (1) using the basic setting of DDQN [28] without an IL phase; (2) using the original DAgger [18] algorithm with only supervised loss without an RL phase; (3) using DQfD algorithm [6], which also combines IL and RL but the agent learns on fixed demonstrations rather than being interactively guided; (4) only using our improved DAgger with double replay buffers; (5) our training strategy described in Sect. 3.4. Table 2 shows the evaluation on the shape reconstruction quality measured by the Chamfer distance (CD) and IoU. Also, we show the qualitative comparison results with these algorithms in Fig. 10.

Based on the qualitative and quantitative experiments, we can arrive at the following conclusions: (1) introducing simple heuristics of the virtual expert by IL significantly improves the performance, since the results show the modeling quality is unacceptable only using RL; (2) the final policy of our agents outperform the policy learned from the "expert", since our method obtains higher rewards than only imitating the "expert"; (3) our learning approach can learn better polices and produce higher-quality modeling results than other algorithms.

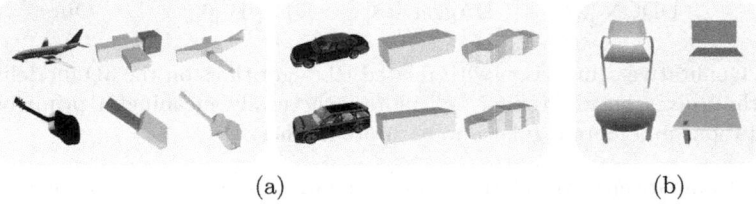

(a)   (b)

Fig. 11. (a) Modeling results using RGB images as reference. (b) Failure cases.

Can the Agents Work with Other Shape References? We train the agents on a different type of reference, i.e., RGB images, without any modification. The average accumulated rewards obtained on different categories are 0.721, 0.877, 0.991 (Prim-Agent) and 0.120, 0.197, 0.135 (Mesh-Agent), which are similar to using depth maps. We also give some qualitative results in Fig. 11(a).

Limitations. A limitation of our method is, it fails to capture very detailed parts and thin structures of shapes. Figure 11(b) shows the results on a chair and a table model. Since the reward is too small when exploring the thin parts, the agent tends to neglect these parts to favor parsimony. A potential solution could be to develop a reward shaping scheme to increase the rewards at the thin parts.

5   Conclusion

In this work, we explore how to enable machines to model 3D shapes like human modelers using deep reinforcement learning. Mimicking the behavior of 3D artists, we propose a two-step RL framework, named Prim-Agent and Mesh-Agent respectively. Given a shape reference, the Prim-Agent first parses the target shape into a primitive-based representation, and then the Mesh-Agent edits the meshes of the primitives to create fundamental geometry. To effectively train the modeling agents, we introduce an algorithm that jointly combines heuristic policy, IL and RL. The experiments demonstrate that the proposed RL framework is able to learn good policies for modeling 3D shapes.

Overall, we believe that our method is an important first stepping stone towards learning modeling actions in artist-based 3D modeling. Ultimately, we hope to achieve conditional and purely generative agents that cover various modeling operations, which can be integrated into modeling software as an assistant to guide real modelers, such as giving step-wise suggestions for beginners or interacting with modelers to edit the shape cooperatively, thus significantly reducing content creation cost, for instance in games, movies, or AR/VR settings.

Acknowledgements. We thank Roy Subhayan and Agrawal Dhruv for their help on data preprocessing and Angela Dai for the voice-over of the video. We also thank Armen Avetisyan, Changjian Li, Nenglun Chen, Zhiming Cui for their discussions and comments. This work was supported by a TUM-IAS Rudolf Mößbauer Fellowship, the ERC Starting Grant *Scan2CAD* (804724), and the German Research Foundation (DFG) Grant *Making Machine Learning on Static and Dynamic 3D Data Practical*.

References

1. Abbeel, P., Ng, A.Y.: Apprenticeship learning via inverse reinforcement learning. In: Proceedings of the Twenty-First International Conference on Machine Learning, p. 1. ACM (2004)
2. Brockman, G., et al.: OpenAI gym. arXiv preprint arXiv:1606.01540 (2016)
3. Chang, A.X., et al.: Shapenet: an information-rich 3D model repository. arXiv preprint arXiv:1512.03012 (2015)
4. Cruz Jr., G.V., Du, Y., Taylor, M.E.: Pre-training neural networks with human demonstrations for deep reinforcement learning. arXiv preprint arXiv:1709.04083 (2017)
5. Ganin, Y., Kulkarni, T., Babuschkin, I., Eslami, S.A., Vinyals, O.: Synthesizing programs for images using reinforced adversarial learning. In: International Conference on Machine Learning, pp. 1666–1675 (2018)

6. Hester, T., et al.: Deep q-learning from demonstrations. In: Thirty-Second AAAI Conference on Artificial Intelligence (2018)
7. Huang, Z., Heng, W., Zhou, S.: Learning to paint with model-based deep reinforcement learning. In: Proceedings of the IEEE International Conference on Computer Vision, pp. 8709–8718 (2019)
8. Kalogerakis, E., Averkiou, M., Maji, S., Chaudhuri, S.: 3D shape segmentation with projective convolutional networks. In: Proceedings of the IEEE Computer Vision and Pattern Recognition (CVPR) (2017)
9. Kalogerakis, E., Hertzmann, A., Singh, K.: Learning 3D mesh segmentation and labeling. ACM Trans. Graph. (TOG) **29**, 102 (2010). ACM
10. LeCun, Y., Bengio, Y., Hinton, G.: Deep learning. Nature **521**(7553), 436 (2015)
11. Li, J., Xu, K., Chaudhuri, S., Yumer, E., Zhang, H., Guibas, L.: Grass: Generative recursive autoencoders for shape structures. ACM Trans. Graph. (TOG) **36**(4), 52 (2017)
12. Mnih, V., et al.: Human-level control through deep reinforcement learning. Nature **518**(7540), 529 (2015)
13. Paschalidou, D., Ulusoy, A.O., Geiger, A.: Superquadrics revisited: learning 3D shape parsing beyond cuboids. In: Proceedings of the IEEE Conference on Computer Vision and Pattern Recognition, pp. 10344–10353 (2019)
14. Raitt, B., Minter, G.: Digital sculpture techniques. Interact. Mag. **4**(5) (2000)
15. Riaz Muhammad, U., Yang, Y., Song, Y.Z., Xiang, T., Hospedales, T.M.: Learning deep sketch abstraction. In: Proceedings of the IEEE Conference on Computer Vision and Pattern Recognition, pp. 8014–8023 (2018)
16. Ross, S., Bagnell, D.: Efficient reductions for imitation learning. In: Proceedings of the Thirteenth International Conference on Artificial Intelligence and Statistics, pp. 661–668 (2010)
17. Ross, S., Bagnell, J.A.: Reinforcement and imitation learning via interactive no-regret learning. arXiv preprint arXiv:1406.5979 (2014)
18. Ross, S., Gordon, G., Bagnell, D.: A reduction of imitation learning and structured prediction to no-regret online learning. In: Proceedings of the Fourteenth International Conference on Artificial Intelligence and Statistics, pp. 627–635 (2011)
19. Ruiz-Montiel, M., Boned, J., Gavilanes, J., Jiménez, E., Mandow, L., PéRez-De-La-Cruz, J.L.: Design with shape grammars and reinforcement learning. Adv. Eng. Inform. **27**(2), 230–245 (2013)
20. Schaul, T., Quan, J., Antonoglou, I., Silver, D.: Prioritized experience replay. arXiv preprint arXiv:1511.05952 (2015)
21. Sharma, G., Goyal, R., Liu, D., Kalogerakis, E., Maji, S.: CSGNet: neural shape parser for constructive solid geometry. In: Proceedings of the IEEE Conference on Computer Vision and Pattern Recognition, pp. 5515–5523 (2018)
22. Silver, D., et al.: Mastering the game of go with deep neural networks and tree search. Nature **529**(7587), 484 (2016)
23. Subramanian, K., Isbell Jr., C.L., Thomaz, A.L.: Exploration from demonstration for interactive reinforcement learning. In: Proceedings of the 2016 International Conference on Autonomous Agents & Multiagent Systems, pp. 447–456. International Foundation for Autonomous Agents and Multiagent Systems (2016)
24. Sun, C., Zou, Q., Tong, X., Liu, Y.: Learning adaptive hierarchical cuboid abstractions of 3D shape collections. ACM Trans. Graph. (SIGGRAPH Asia) **38**(6) (2019)
25. Teboul, O., Kokkinos, I., Simon, L., Koutsourakis, P., Paragios, N.: Shape grammar parsing via reinforcement learning. In: CVPR 2011, pp. 2273–2280. IEEE (2011)
26. Tian, Y., et al.: Learning to infer and execute 3D shape programs. In: International Conference on Learning Representations (2019)

27. Tulsiani, S., Su, H., Guibas, L.J., Efros, A.A., Malik, J.: Learning shape abstractions by assembling volumetric primitives. In: Proceedings of the IEEE Conference on Computer Vision and Pattern Recognition, pp. 2635–2643 (2017)
28. Van Hasselt, H., Guez, A., Silver, D.: Deep reinforcement learning with double q-learning. In: Thirtieth AAAI Conference on Artificial Intelligence (2016)
29. Wang, Y., et al.: Symmetry hierarchy of man-made objects. Comput. Graph. Forum **30**, 287–296 (2011). Wiley Online Library
30. Wang, Z., Schaul, T., Hessel, M., Hasselt, H., Lanctot, M., Freitas, N.: Dueling network architectures for deep reinforcement learning. In: International Conference on Machine Learning, pp. 1995–2003 (2016)
31. Wu, J., Kobbelt, L.: Structure recovery via hybrid variational surface approximation. J. Comput. Graph. Forum **24**, 277–284 (2005). Wiley Online Library
32. Xie, N., Hachiya, H., Sugiyama, M.: Artist agent: a reinforcement learning approach to automatic stroke generation in oriental ink painting. IEICE Trans. Inf. Syst. **96**(5), 1134–1144 (2013)
33. Zhou, T., et al.: Learning to sketch with deep Q networks and demonstrated strokes. arXiv preprint arXiv:1810.05977 (2018)
34. Ziebart, B.D., Maas, A., Bagnell, J.A., Dey, A.K.: Maximum entropy inverse reinforcement learning (2008)
35. Zou, C., Yumer, E., Yang, J., Ceylan, D., Hoiem, D.: 3D-PRNN: generating shape primitives with recurrent neural networks. In: Proceedings of the IEEE International Conference on Computer Vision, pp. 900–909 (2017)

LST-Net: Learning a Convolutional Neural Network with a Learnable Sparse Transform

Lida Li[1], Kun Wang[1,2], Shuai Li[1,3], Xiangchu Feng[2],
and Lei Zhang[1,3]

[1] Department of Computing, The Hong Kong Polytechnic University,
Hong Kong, China
{cslli,csshuaili,cslzhang}@comp.polyu.edu.hk
[2] School of Mathematics and Statistics, Xidian University, Xi'an, China
[3] DAMO Academy, Alibaba Group, Hangzhou, China
kwang96@stu.xidian.edu.cn, xcfeng@mail.xidian.edu.cn

Abstract. The 2D convolutional (Conv2d) layer is the fundamental element to a deep convolutional neural network (CNN). Despite the great success of CNN, the conventional Conv2d is still limited in effectively reducing the spatial and channel-wise redundancy of features. In this paper, we propose to mitigate this issue by learning a CNN with a learnable sparse transform (LST), which converts the input features into a more compact and sparser domain so that the spatial and channel-wise redundancy can be more effectively reduced. The proposed LST can be efficiently implemented with existing CNN modules, such as point-wise and depth-wise separable convolutions, and it is portable to existing CNN architectures for seamless training and inference. We further present a hybrid soft thresholding and ReLU (ST-ReLU) activation scheme, making the trained network, namely LST-Net, more robust to image corruptions at the inference stage. Extensive experiments on CIFAR-10/100, ImageNet, ImageNet-C and Places365-Standard datasets validated that the proposed LST-Net can obtain even higher accuracy than its counterpart networks with fewer parameters and less overhead.

Keywords: CNN · Network architecture · Learnable sparse transform

1 Introduction

The past decade has witnessed a great success of deep convolutional neural netowrk (CNN) in various computer vision problems, such as visual object

L. Li and K. Wang—The first two authors contribute equally in this work.
This work is supported by HK RGC General Research Fund (PolyU 152216/18E).

Electronic supplementary material The online version of this chapter (https://doi.org/10.1007/978-3-030-58607-2_33) contains supplementary material, which is available to authorized users.

© Springer Nature Switzerland AG 2020
A. Vedaldi et al. (Eds.): ECCV 2020, LNCS 12355, pp. 562–579, 2020.
https://doi.org/10.1007/978-3-030-58607-2_33

recognition [14, 34], object detection [35, 43, 44], face recognition [25, 30], scene understanding [56, 64], etc. The 2D convolutional (Conv2d) layer [34] is one of the key elements in a CNN to extract powerful features from the input image. Despite the great success of CNN, the conventional Conv2d is limited in effectively reducing the spatial and channel-wise redundancy of features. When image features are propagated through Conv2d, it usually requires a large number of kernels to model the data and hence introduces exaggerated parameters and overhead. Meanwhile, Conv2d simply sums up all convolutional responses along the channel dimension regarding to the same kernel and takes little advantage of inter-channel cues [9, 24], which is less effective.

A lot of efforts have been devoted to improving the performance of Conv2d. Recent works can be roughly categorized into two categories. The first category of works aim to enhance what a Conv2d layer sees in the spatial domain. For representative works in this category, dilated convolution [58] effectively expands its receptive field by applying predefined gaps, while deformable convolutional networks [8, 65] improve the performance of Conv2d by learning internal parameters to model geometric transformation or variations so as to adaptively focus on some more important areas. Though these methods make better use of spatial information, they fail to take advantage of the channel-wise cues. The second category of works strengthen the performance of Conv2d by combining both spatial and channel-wise attentions. Representative works in this category can be found in [4, 16, 24, 54]. For example, squeeze-and-excitation networks (SENet) [24] re-weights the features along the channel dimension using an efficient squeeze-and-excitation block. Usually, these works rely on an extra network path to adjust spatial and channel-wise attentions after the conventional Conv2d is computed. The redundancy of conventional Conv2d remains but it requires additional network parameters and overhead. It is interesting to investigate whether we can develop a new convolutional module, which can better describe the local features, reduce the spatial and channel-wise feature redundancies, and reduce the parameters and overhead while keeping the accuracy unchanged or even improved.

We propose to mitigate these issues by learning a CNN with a learnable sparse transform (LST). We are motivated by the classical harmonic analysis works such as discrete cosine transform (DCT) [52] and discrete wavelet transform (DWT) [5, 21, 45], which can convert the given image into a more compact and sparse domain to reduce the spatial and channel redundancy of features. In DCT and DWT, the sparser transforms are manually pre-designed, while in our proposed LST, the sparse transform is learned from training data together with the process of CNN training. The proposed LST learning can be efficiently implemented with existing CNN modules, such as point-wise convolutions [36] (PWConvs) and depth-wise separable convolutions [23] (DWConvs). This makes LST compatible with existing CNN architectures for seamless training and inference without additional operations.

The proposed LST promotes sparser features. In light of the sparsity priors [2, 3, 50], we further present a hybrid soft thresholding [13] and ReLU [40] (ST-ReLU) activation scheme. Compared with the standard ReLU, the ST-ReLU

564 L. Li et al.

activation can suppress the noise and trivial features in the learning process, making the trained network more robust to image corruptions, such as noise, blur, digital compression, etc. Overall, the proposed LST module can be applied to existing state-of-the-art network architectures such as ResNet and VGGNet. The obtained new network, namely LST-Net, achieves more robust and accurate performance with fewer parameters and less overhead. Our major contributions are summarized as follows.

- A novel learnable sparse transform based Conv2d module is developed, which can be efficiently implemented and seamlessly integrated into existing CNN learning process, producing sparser features and improving the effectiveness of learned CNN models.
- A new activation function is presented by properly combining soft-thresholding and ReLU operations, which endows the proposed LST-Net better robustness to image trivial features and corruptions.

2 Related Work

2.1 Network Bottleneck

To save parameters and overhead of Conv2d layers, group convolution [34] (GConv) and PWConv [36] are popularly employed in the design of bottle-necks. PWConv employs a 1×1 window, performing a linear combination of the input from all channels. It is often used to align a set of feature maps with different number of channels [49]. GConv assumes that the input features can be decomposed into several groups along the channel dimension, where features from different groups are independent. A successful application of GConv is ResNeXt [57]. DWConv [23] is a special case of GConv when there is only one input channel per group. It is widely used to build lightweight models for mobile devices, such as MobileNet [23,47], ShuffleNet [37,62], etc.

Xie *et al.* [57] improved ResNet bottleneck [19] by substituting the conventional 3×3 Conv2d in the middle with a GConv of slightly more channels. One problem of this method is how to set the group number. A larger number of groups can easily cause loss of inter-channel cues while a smaller number of groups can hardly reduce redundancy of Conv2d. Recently, Res2Net [17] was developed by fusing the group with the intermediate results obtained from the latest group in a recursive manner. Though Res2Net demonstrates higher accuracy, it actually sacrifices parallel execution on devices such as GPUs. In this paper, we naturally incorporate DWConvs and PWConvs to facilitate transforms in spatial and channel-wise fields.

2.2 Learning Space

The conventional Conv2d layer is less effective in reducing the spatial and channel-wise feature redundancies because each Conv2d kernel interacts with input features locating in a local grid of limited size and cannot take features outside the grid into consideration. To mitigate this issue, dilated convolution [58] applies predefined gaps to enlarge spatial receptive field of Conv2d. Deformable convolutional networks [8,65] learn to adaptively focus on some more important areas by modelling geometric transformation or variations with internal parameters; however, they fail to further consider the channel-wise cues of features and require sophisticated implementation skills. SENet [24] and its variants [4,16,54] focus on designing lightweight network paths to fuse channel-wise and spatial features to improve the attention of the conventional Conv2d. Though these methods is effective to boost accuracy, they remain inefficient as they use more parameters and require extra overhead.

To improve the performance of Conv2d layer, it's more straightforward to perform convolution in a more compact and sparser domain. The classical DCT [52] and DWT [5,21,45] transform the input image into a sparse space for manipulation and they have a wide range of successful applications [1,5,15,26,52,61]. The sparse coding [41] techniques encode the image patches as a sparse linear combination of learned atoms. However, the transformation filters used in DCT and DWT are manually designed and they are not effective enough to represent image structures, while sparse coding is computationally inefficient and is hard to be extended for deep feature extraction. In this paper, we propose to learn a sparse transformation together with the deep CNN learning so that the network can be more efficiently and effectively learned in a sparser space.

2.3   Activation Function

Non-linearity introduced by the activation function is among the most critical factors to the success of a CNN model in various computer vision tasks. ReLU [40] is a pioneer and the most popular non-linear activation function in deep CNN. It is a simple yet highly effective segmented function, forcing the input negative valued features to zeros and keeping only the non-negative features. To make use of the information of negative features, parametric ReLU [18], leaky ReLU [51], ELU [7] and SELU [31] are proposed to allow adaptive negative activation with learnable parameters. However, negative activation functions need to be carefully designed and they only exhibit better performance in specific applications.

One problem of ReLU and its variants is that they are not very robust to noise or other corruptions in the input image. It is well-known that by soft-thresholding the image features in some sparse domain, such as DWT domain [5,21,45] and sparse coding domain [41], the latent image features can be well recovered. In our proposed LST, we adaptively learn a sparse transform together with the CNN learning, which can make the CNN features sparser. This motivates us to develop a new activation scheme, i.e., hybrid soft-thresholding and ReLU (ST-ReLU), to better exploit the merit of sparser features. The ST-ReLU further enhances the robustness of learned CNN models to various types of corruptions.

3   Proposed Method

3.1   Learnable Sparse Transform (LST)

Denote by $\mathcal{I} \in \mathcal{R}^{H_{in} \times W_{in} \times C_{in}}$ the input feature and $\mathcal{O} \in \mathcal{R}^{H_{out} \times W_{out} \times C_{out}}$ the output feature of a Conv2D layer, where H_{in}/H_{out}, W_{in}/W_{out}, C_{in}/C_{out} denote the height, the width, and the channel number of the input/output feature, respectively. The sliding window Ω of the Conv2D can be parameterized by the kernel size $s_H \times s_W$ (for simplicity of expression, we omit the subscripts H and W in the remaining of this paper), number of kernels C_{out}, stride, as well as padding. We denote the kth kernel by $\mathcal{K}^{(k)}$.

The Conv2d output feature is redundant in both spatial and channel dimensions. When the sliding window Ω is centered at spatial location (i,j) of $\mathcal{I}$, the output $\mathcal{O}_{i,j,k}$ by convolving $\mathcal{I}$ with kernel $\mathcal{K}^{(k)}$ is computed as

$$\mathcal{O}_{i,j,k} = \sum_{x=1}^{s} \sum_{y=1}^{s} \sum_{z=1}^{C_{in}} \Omega(\mathcal{I}; i, j)_{x,y,z} \cdot \mathcal{K}^{(k)}_{x,y}, \tag{1}$$

where $\Omega(\mathcal{I}; i, j)_{x,y,z}$ is the pixel at (x, y, z) of the tensor extracted from $\mathcal{I}$ by Ω, and $\mathcal{K}^{(k)}_{x,y}$ means the pixel at (x, y) of $\mathcal{K}^{(k)}$.

We have two observations from Eq. 1. First, all feature pixels in the local neighborhood at spatial location (i,j) are involved in the computation. While this is helpful to extract the high frequency features, it is redundant for extracting the low frequency features, which usually occupy most of the pixels in a feature map. Second, the subscript z does not follow $\mathcal{K}$ but only comes up with Ω. That is to say, all pixels in the same channel are equally weighted to produce $\mathcal{O}_{i,j,k}$. It has been found that the input features have strong similarities along the channel dimension [20,53]. Therefore, there exists much redundant channel-wise computations. All these motivate us to develop a learnable sparse transform (LST), with which the redundancy of conventional Conv2D can be reduced and hence a more efficient CNN can be learned.

Overview of LST. Our LST consists of three transforms: a spatial transform T_s, a channel-wise transform T_c, and a resize transform T_r. T_s and T_c strive to reduce the spatial and channel-wise redundancies by transforming the corresponding field into a more compact domain, while T_r aims resize the input to obtain the desired shape of output. T_r can be placed either before or after T_s and T_c. The LST, denoted by T_{LST}, can be implemented as

$$T_{LST} \circ \mathcal{I} = T_r \circ T_s \circ T_c \circ \mathcal{I}, \tag{2}$$

or in the form of

$$T_{LST} \circ \mathcal{I} = T_s \circ T_c \circ T_r \circ \mathcal{I}. \tag{3}$$

The Spatial Transform T_s**.** We propose to reduce the spatial redundancies of local features by using a learnable spatial transform T_s with associated weights $\mathcal{W}_s \in \mathcal{R}^{a^2 \times 1 \times s \times s}$ (dimensions are organized in PyTorch [42] style). Inspired by the success of classical 2D-DCT [39], which decomposes the image local region into different frequency bands by using sequential column and row transforms, we can implement T_s by applying column and row transforms, denoted by T_{column} and T_{row}, respectively. Mathematically, the corresponding weights W_s can be expressed as:

$$\mathcal{W}_s = \mathcal{W}_{column} \otimes \mathcal{W}_{row}, \tag{4}$$

where $\otimes$ means the Kronecker product with necessary dimension insertion and removal, $\mathcal{W}_{column} \in \mathcal{R}^{a \times 1 \times s \times 1}$ and $\mathcal{W}_{row} \in \mathcal{R}^{a \times 1 \times 1 \times s}$ are the weights of T_{column} and T_{row}, respectively, and a is a hyper parameter specifying the number of coefficients to keep.

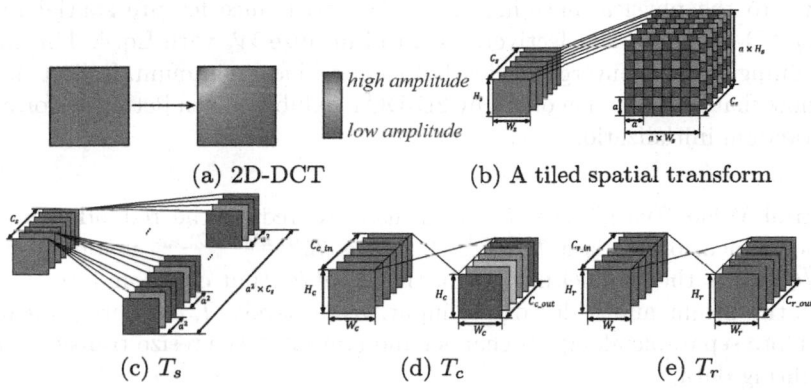

(a) 2D-DCT   (b) A tiled spatial transform

(c) T_s (d) T_c (e) T_r

Fig. 1. Illustration of different transforms.

As illustrated in Fig. 1a, a 2D-DCT transforms a local region into different frequencies. The low frequency coefficients concentrate at the top left corner and they dominate the energy (high amplitude), while many high frequency coefficients are close to zero (low amplitude) and can be neglected. Based on this fact, to save unnecessary parameters and computation, we set $1 \le a < s$ so that the low amplitude trivial features can be excluded from calculation. Since for almost all existing CNN architectures, it is true that the kernel size $s \ge 3$, we set $a = \lceil \frac{s}{2} \rceil$ by default in this paper.

Figure 1c depicts our implementation of T_s. One can see that the output of T_s is arranged along the channel dimension (this will ease much the implementation of our resize transform T_r). For each $s \times s$ local region, by convolving it with W_s, we obtain an a^2-*dim* output vector. Thus, for each input feature map, it is transformed into a number of a^2 feature maps by aggregating the a^2-*dim* output vectors. That is, T_s maps $\mathcal{R}^{H_{s\_in} \times W_{s\_in} \times C_s}$ to $\mathcal{R}^{H_{s\_out} \times W_{s\_out} \times (a^2 \times C_s)}$, where C_s is the channel number of the input argument of T_s, and H_{s_in}/H_{s_out}

and W_{s_in}/W_{s_out} are the input/output height and width, respectively. In contrast, the conventional spatial transform organizes the output in the height and width fields, instead of the channel domain. We term the conventional spatial transform as tiled spatial transform, which maps $\mathcal{R}^{H_{s\_in} \times W_{s\_in} \times C_s}$ to $\mathcal{R}^{(a \times H_{s\_in}) \times (a \times W_{s\_in}) \times C_s}$, as illustrated in Fig. 1b. Comparing our T_s with tiled spatial transform, we can obtain three findings.

First, T_s is simpler to implement than tiled spatial transform. In practice, we can adopt a DWConv operation to implement it. Second, T_s only affects the channel dimension, which allows us to easily use the existing efficient implementations for the resize transform T_r. (Please see the following section of resize transform for details.) In contrast, a tiled spatial transform increases both the height and width of feature maps so that T_r must be changed to deal with the enlarged spatial dimensions. Third, our T_s always holds memory continuity, making it faster in both training and inference. In contrast, a tiled spatial transform needs channel shuffle, which requires extra memory alignment.

Owe to the physical meaning of T_s (i.e., to reduce feature spatial redundancy), 2D-DCT can be effectively used to initialize W_s with Eq. 4. This makes the training of LST converge efficiently to a good local minimum. In Sect. 4.2, we will show that initialization of W_s by 2D-DCT exhibits much better performance than random initialization.

Channel-Wise Transform T_c. T_c is used to reduce the redundancy along channel dimension. It is a $\mathcal{R}^{H_c \times W_c \times C_{c\_in}} \rightarrow \mathcal{R}^{H_c \times W_c \times C_{c\_out}}$ mapping, where C_{c_in}/C_{c_out} is the channel number of the input/output of T_c, and H_c and W_c denote the height and width of the input, respectively. T_c encourages features to be more separable along the channel and simplifies the resize transform T_r in reweighting data.

A PWConv operation can be naturally leveraged for T_c with its associated weights $W_c \in \mathcal{R}^{C_{c\_out} \times C_{c\_in} \times 1 \times 1}$. Similar to T_s, 2D-DCT can be used to initialize T_c for compact features. We fill W_c with the 2D-DCT basis functions shaped as $C_{c\_in} \times C_{c\_out}$ and expand its dimensions where necessary. Figure 1d illustrates the implementation of T_c. One can see that the output of T_c is organized in order by the expected feature amplitude like 2D-DCT. It should be noted that T_c is similar to the resize transform T_r since both of them adopt PWConv for implementation. However, they are initialized in different ways.

The Resize Transform T_r. A conventional Conv2d equally treats all the samples in the window without considering their importance. To fill this gap, the resize transform T_r is designed as a $\mathcal{R}^{H_r \times W_r \times C_{r\_in}} \rightarrow \mathcal{R}^{H_r \times W_r \times C_{r\_out}}$ mapping, where H_r/W_r is the height/width of the input, and C_{r_in} and C_{r_out} are the channel number of the input and output, respectively. T_r is learned to adaptively reweight the input features with its weights $W_r \in \mathcal{R}^{C_{r\_out} \times C_{r\_in} \times 1 \times 1}$. Figure 1e illustrates how T_r works. With the help of our design of T_s and T_c, T_r can be implemented by directly leveraging a normal PWConv operation in our paper.

Discussions. To better understand the role of LST, in Fig. 2 we visualize the learned features by the standard ResNet50 (with conventional Conv2d) and our LST-Net with a ResNet50 architecture on ImageNet [11]. (The details of the model can be found in our supplementary material.) Once trained, a validation image is randomly selected and its center crop is fed into the two models. Figure 2 visualizes 16 channels of the features (other channels are similar) from the first bottleneck (the features after the T_s transform are visualized for our LST-Net). We clip the amplitude of the feature in the range of $[0, 0.1]$ and stretch the features in each channel as a vector. Each column in Fig. 2 represents the vectorized features of a channel.

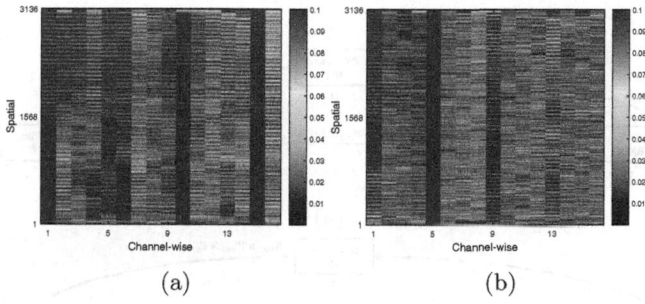

(a)   (b)

Fig. 2. Visualization of output features obtained by (a) a conventional Conv2d layer in ResNet50 and (b) our LST-Net after T_s. One can see that the features output by LST-Net are sparser and well-structured along the channel dimension.

One can see that the output features of conventional Conv2d in ResNet50 are mixed up along the channel dimension. In contrast, the features output by LST-Net are sparser (with lower amplitude) and well-structured along channel dimension. Specifically, every $a^2 = 2^2 = 4$ channels form a unit where the four channel features are de-correlated into different frequency bands (please also refer to Fig. 1c). Such kind of sparser and structured features are highly suited to the successive channel-wise operations such as PWConv (used by resize transform T_r) or a sequential of global average pooling (GAP) [36] plus a dense layer.

3.2 Hybrid ReLU-ST Activation Scheme

By using the proposed LST introduced in Subsect. 3.1, we are able to generate more compact and sparser features than the conventional Conv2D layers in a CNN, as illustrated in Fig. 2. It has been shown in the many works of WT [12,13] and sparse coding [41] that a soft-thresholding (ST) operation in the sparse feature domain can increase the robustness to noise and trivial features. The ST operation for the input feature x can be written as

$$y = \begin{cases} sgn(x)(|x| - \tau), & |x| \geq \tau, \\ 0, & otherwise. \end{cases} \tag{5}$$

where τ is a hyper parameter for the threshold. To exploit the merit of sparser features brought by LST, we propose a new activation scheme for our LST-Net by jointly using ST and ReLU, namely ST-ReLU.

Specifically, ST is adopted at two places in LST-Net; otherwise, ReLU is used. First, ST is inserted in the middle of T_c and T_s. It not only reduces the noises along the channel dimension but also further forces sparsity and suppresses trivial features in the spatial domain. Second, ST is used as the last activation function for an LST to allow adaptive negative activation. Unlike existing methods such as parametric ReLU [18], leaky ReLU [51], ELU [7] and SELU [31], ST is a natural selection of activation in the sparse feature domain, and it accords with the findings on spiking states of neurons in neuroscience [10,27,28,46,60].

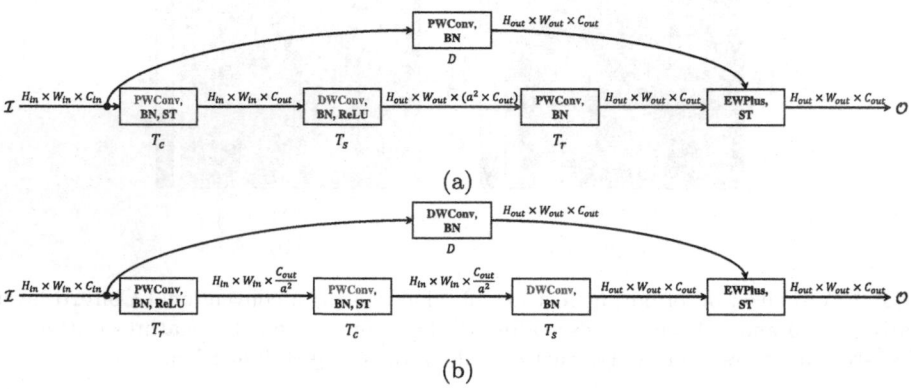

Fig. 3. Illustration of the two LST bottlenecks with downsample operators. (a): LST-I; (b): LST-II. EWPlus means element-wise plus. Red font indicates initialization with 2D-DCT while blue font suggests random initialization.

3.3　The Bottleneck

We construct a novel bottleneck, namely LST bottleneck, to wrap LST and the hybrid ST-ReLU activation scheme. A shortcut path is introduced in our LST bottleneck to avoid gradient exploding or vanishing when a model goes deeper. As a result, an LST bottleneck can be written as follows when the shape of input feature $\mathcal{I}$ is the same as that of output $\mathcal{O}$:

$$\mathcal{O} = T_{LST} \circ \mathcal{I} + \mathcal{I} \tag{6}$$

If the input shape is different from the output shape, the bottleneck becomes

$$\mathcal{O} = T_{LST} \circ \mathcal{I} + D \circ \mathcal{I}, \tag{7}$$

where D is a downsample operator to adjust the shape of features. D is adopted when the stride of Ω is greater than 1 or $C_{in} \neq C_{out}$.

According to the arrangement of T_s, T_c and T_r defined in Eq. 2 and Eq. 3, we design two bottleneck structures, namely LST-I and LST-II, as illustrated in Fig. 3. One difference between LST-I and LST-II lies in how the bottleneck expands. LST-I is similar to the basic bottleneck in [19]. It first expands the number of channels by a^2 times with T_s; then, it reduces the number of channels back to C_{out} with T_r. The expansion factor of LST-I is 1. In contrast, LST-II adopts a similar ideology to the ResNet bottleneck [19]. It starts to reduce the channel number to $\frac{C_{out}}{a^2}$ with T_r and then increases it to C_{out} with T_s. Like ResNet bottleneck [19], we refer the planes (core number of channels) of an LST-II bottleneck to C_{ch_out}, i.e., $\frac{C_{out}}{a^2}$. Meanwhile, the expansion factor of LST-II is determined by T_s, which equals to a^2.

Another difference between the two bottlenecks lies in the implementation of D. LST-I adopts the widely used structure, i.e., a PWConv followed by a BN. In contrast, we propose to leverage a 1×1 DWConv followed by BN for the downsample operator D of LST-II by assuming that C_{out} is divisible by C_{in}. Such an assumption usually holds in many modern architectures, e.g., VGG [48], ResNet [19], ResNeXt [57], etc. It shifts the original definition of "identity" in such cases to a group-wise mapping by expanding one channel to $\frac{C_{out}}{C_{in}}$ channels. Each input feature map only interacts with its $\frac{C_{out}}{C_{in}}$ associated output feature maps regarding to the DWConv, making it very efficient to handle hundreds or even thousands of feature maps. With LST-I or LST-II, one can easily build an LST-Net by using existing network architectures with fewer parameters and less overhead. Code is available at: https://github.com/lld533/LST-Net.

4 Experiments

4.1 Experiment Setup and Datasets

To evaluate our method, we build up LST-Nets by replacing conventional Conv2d operations with our proposed LST bottlenecks w.r.t. some widely used CNN architectures. The datasets used include CIFAR-10/100 [33] and ImageNet [11]. Besides, ImageNet-C [22] dataset is used to demonstrate the robustness of LST-Net to common image corruptions. Ablation studies are performed to discuss the initialization, the selection of parameter τ in ST-ReLU, the difference between LST-I and LST-II and comparison of ReLU-ST to other activations. Results on Places365-Standard [64] can be found in the supplementary material.

4.2 Ablation Study

Initialization. As discussed in Sect. 3, 2D-DCT is used to initialize our spatial and channel-wise transforms W_s and W_c to reduce the feature redundancy. It is wondering whether random initialization (R.I.) can achieve similar results. We build LST-Nets of 20~164 layers in depth using the vanilla ResNet architecture [19] to test this (LST-II bottleneck is used). We use the uniform distribution within $[-\sqrt{u}, \sqrt{u}]$ to randomly initialize W_s and W_c, where $u = \frac{1}{C_{in} \times a^2 \times s^2}$ for W_s and $u = \frac{1}{C_{in} \times a \times s}$ for W_c.

Table 1. Comparison (error rates, %) on CIFAR-100.

(a) Different initialization methods.

Method/Depth	20	56	110	164
ResNet [19] (R.I.)	30.88	27.62	26.23	26.07
LST-Net (R.I.)	31.12	29.92	28.95	28.94
LST-Net (2D-DCT)	**28.21**	**24.09**	**22.66**	**21.94**

(b) Different bottlenecks.

Method/Depth	20	56	110	164
ResNet [19]	30.88	27.62	26.23	26.07
LST-I	**27.64**	25.08	23.76	23.15
LST-II	28.21	**24.09**	**22.66**	**21.94**

(c) Different activation methods.

Depth	ReLU-ST	LReLU [38]	SELU [31]	ReLU [40]	PReLU [18]	ELU [7]
20	**28.21**	28.37	28.69	28.92	29.35	31.60
164	**21.94**	22.44	22.84	22.86	23.91	29.94

Table 1a summarizes the error rates on CIFAR-100 (similar conclusions can be obtained on CIFAR-10). One can see that 2D-DCT initialization obtains much better performance than R.I., which lags behind the former by 2.7%~7.0%. Besides, an LST-Net with R.I. is even worse than the baseline vanilla ResNet. This is because LST-Net will drop a certain amount of trivial frequencies after 2D-DCT initialization, while R.I. is difficult to transform the channel and spatial fields of the input feature into different frequencies with PWConv and DWConv operations, resulting in unnecessary loss of some crucial information.

The Selection of Parameter τ. We study the effect of parameter τ (refer to Eq. 5) on LST-Net. We built a 20-layer LST-Net in favor of ResNet architecture, and tested on CIFAR100. We search for the optimal value of τ in the range of $\{0, 10^{-1}, 10^{-2}, 10^{-3}, 10^{-4}, 10^{-5}, 10^{-6}\}$. The error rates are $\{28.92\%, 28.32\%, 28.28\%, 28.86\%, 28.21\%, 28.43\%, 28.70\%\}$, where the best result is 28.21% when $\tau = 10^{-4}$. Thus, we set $\tau = 10^{-4}$ by default in all experiments of this paper. Note that when $\tau = 0$, ST-ReLU is reduced to standard ReLU, but its error rate is larger than other values of τ. This validates that our hybrid ReLU-ST activation scheme works better than ReLU for LST-Net.

LST-I Vs LST-II. We discuss the pros and cons of our proposed LST-I and LST-II bottlenecks in building up a LST-Net. For LST-I, one is free to replace a conventional Conv2d with it in many existing architectures, such as ResNet [19], AlexNet [32], VGG [48], etc. For example, a basic ResNet bottleneck can be replaced by a pair of LST-I bottlenecks as it has two Conv2d operations. For LST-II, due to the expansion factor of LST-II, parameters and overhead of the associated PWConv operation in the shortcut path are increased by a^2 times compared to LST-I. Thus, LST-II is not suitable to architectures with larger spatial size at earlier layers, such as AlexNet and VGG. LST-II will also increase the output channel number of the last bottleneck, but this issue can be easily solved with an extra PWConv operation, which is cheap compared to the entire CNN model in terms of number of parameters and computational cost. When building a deeper CNN model, such as ResNet-50 or ResNet-101, it is more suitable to use LST-II than LST-I. In Table 1b, we construct LST-Nets with LST-I and LST-II bottlenecks *w.r.t.* ResNet architecture and compare them on CIFAR-100. The vanilla ResNet is included as the baseline. Both LST-I and LST-II outperform the baseline by a large margin, while LST-II performs better than its LST-I counterpart. In the remaining experiments of this paper, if not specified, we adopt LST-II bottleneck to build ResNet models by default.

Comparison of ST-ReLU to Other Activations. We use a 20-layer and a 164-layer LST-Net to compare our ReLU-ST with ReLU [40], leaky ReLU (LReLU) [38], parametric ReLU (PReLU) [18], ELU [7] and SELU [31] on CIFAR-100. For comparison, we remove ST operations in LST bottleneck and replace ReLU by other activations. Table 1 presents the Top-1 error rates achieved by different activations. One can see that ReLU-ST outperforms other activations for both 20- and 164-layer LST-Nets. The gain is higher for deeper models.

Table 2. Results (error rates, %) by different networks on CIFAR-10/100.

(a) ResNet family.

Depth	Model	Param/FLOPs	C10/C100
20	ResNet [19]	0.27M/40.8M	7.7/30.9
	PreactResNet [19]	0.27M/40.8M	7.7/30.8
	ShiftResNet [55]	**0.16M/27M**	9.0/31.4
	FE-Net [6]	**0.16M/27M**	8.3/30.8
	SENet [24]	0.28M/40.8M	7.6/30.5
	CBAM [54]	0.28M/40.8M	7.3/30.3
	LST-Net	0.20M/34M	**6.7/28.2**
56	ResNet [19]	0.86M/126M	6.6/27.6
	PreactResNet [19]	0.86M/126M	6.5/27.6
	ShiftResNet [55]	**0.55M/84M**	7.3/27.9
	FE-Net [6]	**0.55M/84M**	8.3/30.8
	SENet [24]	0.87M/126M	6.4/27.5
	CBAM [54]	0.87M/126M	6.0/27.1
	LST-Net	0.59M/94M	**5.6/24.1**
110	ResNet [19]	1.73M/253M	6.6/25.2
	PreactResNet [19]	1.73M/253M	6.2/24.1
	ShiftResNet [55]	1.18M/187M	6.8/27.4
	FE-Net [6]	N.A.	N.A.
	SENet [24]	1.74M/253M	5.2/23.9
	CBAM [54]	1.74M/253M	5.1/23.5
	LST-Net	**1.17M/183M**	**5.0/22.7**

(b) WRN.

Depth	Multiplier	Model	Param/FLOPs	C10/C100
16	8	WRN [59]	10.96M/2.00G	4.80/22.03
		LST-Net	6.03M/0.98G	**4.70/20.88**
	10	WRN [59]	17.12M/3.12G	4.49/21.52
		LST-Net	9.36M/1.52G	**4.46/20.21**
22	8	WRN [59]	17.16M/2.91G	4.56/21.21
		LST-Net	8.87M/1.40G	**4.40/19.33**
	10	WRN [59]	26.80M/4.54G	4.44/20.75
		LST-Net	16.99M/2.79G	**4.31/18.57**
28	10	WRN [59]	36.48M/5.95G	4.17/20.50
		LST-Net	22.47M/3.60G	**4.03/18.23**
	12	WRN [59]	43.42M/8.56G	4.33/20.41
		LST-Net	26.06M/4.03G	**3.94/17.93**
40	4	WRN [59]	8.91M/1.41G	4.97/22.89
		LST-Net	4.98M/0.72G	**4.31/19.14**
	8	WRN [59]	35.75M/5.63G	4.66/19.38
		LST-Net	19.88M/3.16G	**3.76/18.56**

4.3   Evaluation on CIFAR-10 and CIFAR-100

We build our LST-Net models *w.r.t.* the popular architectures, including ResNet [19] and Wide Residual Networks (WRN) [59], and compare LST-Net with state-of-the-art CNNs in those families, e.g. Pre-activation ResNet [19], SENet [24], CBAM [54], and two other models, i.e., ShiftResNet [55] and FE-Net [6].

Table 2 presents the results on CIFAR-10/100. We can have the following findings. First, LST-Net achieves the lowest error rates under different network depths with almost the least number of parameters and FLOPs (very close to ShiftResNet and FE-Net). This validates its effectiveness and efficiency. LST-Net outperforms ResNet and PreactResNet while reducing over 40% parameters and 35% overhead. Compared to SENet and CBAM, LST-Net does not need extra paths while it achieves even better results. For instance, a 110-layer LST-Net improves SENet/CBAM of the same depth by 0.2%/0.1% and 1.2%/0.8% on CIFAR-10 and CIFAR-100, respectively. Besides, LST-Net outperforms both ShiftResNet and FENet by a large margin with comparable parameters and overhead. For example, a 20-layer LST-Net reduces the error rates of ShiftResNet and FE-Net by 2.3/3.2% and 1.6/2.6% on CIFAR-10/100, respectively.

Second, when we switch to wider CNN models, our bottleneck can save more parameters and computational cost because the computation of PWConv dominates an entire LST bottleneck when it is wide enough (the cost of DWConv can be neglected). We can obtain consistent performance boost of our LST-Net with the increase of width and/or depth. In contrast, the corresponding WRN architecture is less effective to improve its results with more channels and/or layers. For example, for a 28-layer WRN, the error rates will rise by 4.17%~4.33% on CIFAR-10 when the width multiplier is increased from 10 to 12.

Table 3. Results (error rates, %) by different networks on ImageNet.

(a) ResNet family.

Depth	Model	Param/FLOPs	Top-1/Top-5
18	ResNet [19]	11.69M/1.81G	30.24/10.92
	SENet [24]	11.78M/1.81G	29.41/10.22
	CBAM [54]	11.78M/1.82G	29.31/10.17
	LST-Net	8.03M/1.48G	26.55/8.59
34	ResNet [19]	21.79M/3.66G	26.70/8.58
	SENet [24]	21.96M/3.66G	26.13/8.35
	CBAM [54]	21.96M/3.67G	26.01/8.40
	LST-Net	13.82M/2.56G	23.92/7.24
50	ResNet [19]	25.56M/4.09G	23.85/7.13
	SENet [24]	28.09M/4.09G	23.14/6.70
	CBAM [54]	28.09M/4.10G	22.98/6.68
	LST-Net	23.33M/4.05G	22.78/6.66
101	ResNet [19]	44.55M/7.80G	22.63/6.44
	SENet [24]	49.29M/7.81G	22.35/6.19
	CBAM [54]	49.29M/7.81G	21.65/5.95
	LST-Net	42.36M/7.75G	21.63/5.94

(b) WRN.

Depth	Mulp.	Model	Param/FLOPs	Top-1/Top-5
18	1	WRN [59]	11.69M/1.81G	30.24/10.92
		LST-Net	8.03M/1.48G	26.55/8.59
	1.5	WRN [59]	25.88M/3.87G	27.06/9.00
		LST-Net	14.40M/2.49G	24.44/7.51
	2	WRN [59]	45.62M/6.70G	25.58/8.06
		LST-Net	25.12M/4.31G	23.49/6.93
	3	WRN [59]	101.78M/14.72G	24.06/7.33
		LST-Net	55.44M/9.43G	22.33/6.52
34	1	WRN [59]	21.79M/3.66G	26.70/8.58
		LST-Net	13.82M/2.56G	23.92/7.24
	1.5	WRN [59]	48.61M/8.03G	24.50/7.58
		LST-Net	24.78M/4.41G	22.29/6.30
	2	WRN [59]	86.04M/14.09G	23.39/7.00
		LST-Net	43.44M/7.69G	21.44/6.11
50	1	WRN [59]	25.56M/4.09G	23.85/7.13
		LST-Net	23.33M/4.05G	22.78/6.66
	2	WRN [59]	68.88M/11.40G	21.90/6.03
		LST-Net	66.10M/11.09G	20.89/5.76

(c) Other CNNs.

Model	Param/FLOPs	Top-1/Top-5
AlexNet [32]	61.10M/0.71G	43.45/20.91
AlexNet (BN)	61.10M/0.71G	41.93/20.02
AlexNet (GAP)	2.73M/0.66G	51.13/26.33
LST-Net (FC)	60.30M/0.62G	39.32/17.40
LST-Net (GAP)	2.25M/0.60G	39.91/17.86
VGG [48]	132.86M/7.61G	30.98/11.37
VGG (BN)	132.86M/7.61G	29.62/10.19
VGG (GAP)	9.73M/7.49G	33.40/12.20
LST-Net (FC)	128.63M/5.89G	28.56/9.79
LST-Net (GAP)	6.63M/5.04G	29.23/10.26
ShiftNet-A [55]	4.1M/1.4G	29.9/10.3
ShiftNet-B [55]	1.1M/N.A.	38.8/16.4
ShiftNet-C [55]	0.78M/N.A.	41.2/18.0
LST-Net (A)	4.3M/1.2G	29.3/10.0
LST-Net (B)	1.2M/389.5M	36.9/14.8
LST-Net (C)	0.84M/342.5M	38.9/16.3
MobileNet V2 [47]	3.4M/300M	28.1%/N.A.
LST-Net (M-V2)	3.4M/300M	27.7%/9.4%

4.4   Evaluation on ImageNet

We then evaluate LST-Net on ImageNet [11] for large-scale image classification. We construct LST-Nets regarding to the widely used network architectures, including ResNet [19], WRN [59], AlexNet [32] and VGG (with 11 layers) [48]. We also build LST-Nets *w.r.t.* ShiftNet [55] and MobileNet V2 [47].

Specifically, for ResNet or WRN architecture, we construct LST-Net using LST-II bottleneck, and for AlexNet/VGG, we build LST-Net (FC) by replacing Conv2d layers with LST-I bottlenecks. We also change the original classifier layer in AlexNet/VGG into GAP [36] plus a dense layer following [63], resulting in LST-Net (GAP). Similarly, the standard AlexNet/VGG can be modified in the same way, resulting in AlexNet (GAP)/VGG (GAP). Since BN [29] is used in our bottleneck, we further insert a BN layer after each Conv2d of AlexNet/VGG, termed as AlexNet/VGG (BN). For ShiftNet architecture, we build the LST-Nets by adjusting the stride, kernel size, number of stages, etc., according to its variants A, B, and C with different depth and width. For MobileNet V2, we build LST-Net (M-V2) by replacing Inverted Residual bottlenecks with our modified LST-I bottlenecks. Details can be found in our supplementary material.

Table 3 summarizes the results. One can see that LST-Net consistently surpasses ResNet, SENet and CBAM of the same depth with fewer parameters and less overhead. An 18-layer LST-Net even achieves lower Top-1 error rates than the standard ResNet-34 on ImageNet. Despite of different depth, increasing width of LST-Net with WRN architecture steadily increases its accuracy. Meanwhile, LST-Net saves larger proportion of parameters and overhead compared to WRN. LST-Net with AlexNet or VGG architecture is much more robust to different classifier structures than the standard AlexNet or VGG because LST-Net learns structured features, which are well suited for channel-wise operations (see our discussion in Sect. 3.1). Meanwhile, LST-Net (FC) can reduce Top-1/Top-5 error rates of AlexNet (BN) and VGG (BN) by 2.61%/2.62% and 1.06%/0.40%, respectively. LST-Net also shows better performance under the ShiftNet architecture. Compared with all the three variants, our LST-Net reduces the Top-1 error rate of its corresponding counterpart by 0.6%~2.3% with similar number of parameters. LST-Net (M-V2) achieves a 72.3% Top-1 accuracy, outperforming MobileNet V2 by 0.4% using the same number of parameters and computational cost. This again validates the generality and superiority of our LST method.

Table 4. Comparison of robustness to common corruptions on ImageNet-C.

Network	mCE	Noise			Blur				Weather				Digital				Extra			
		Gauss	Shot	Impulse	Defocus	Glass	Motion	Zoom	Snow	Frost	Fog	Bright	Contrast	Elastic	Pixel	JPEG	Saturate	Spatter	Gaus. blur	Speckle
ResNet-18 [19]	85.29	87	89	89	88	93	90	88	88	87	81	73	81	93	81	89	72	81	86	86
SENet-18 [24]	83.97	85	86	87	87	93	88	88	85	85	79	73	82	92	84	92	71	81	86	82
CBAM-18 [54]	84.97	86	88	87	88	93	89	90	85	86	80	74	82	92	81	89	71	81	87	85
LST-Net-18 (w/o ST)	80.34	81	82	85	85	91	83	85	82	83	75	68	79	90	74	85	66	75	84	78
LST-Net-18 (w/ ST)	79.89	80	81	83	84	91	83	85	82	82	75	68	78	90	73	85	66	74	83	76
ResNet-50 [19]	77.01	78	80	80	79	90	81	80	80	78	69	62	75	88	76	78	62	74	78	76
SENet-50 [24]	74.47	76	77	76	77	89	79	82	75	76	70	59	75	85	71	74	58	69	76	71
CBAM-50 [54]	72.56	69	71	71	80	86	77	78	75	76	69	61	74	85	63	70	58	68	78	66
LST-Net-50 (w/o ST)	70.85	71	72	71	77	85	77	75	73	72	66	58	70	82	61	72	56	65	76	67
LST-Net-50 (w/ ST)	70.54	71	72	71	76	84	77	75	73	72	65	58	70	81	61	72	56	65	75	67

4.5 Evaluation on ImageNet-C

We study the robustness of LST-Net to common corruptions in input by using the ImageNet-C dataset [22]. The mean corruption error (mCE) defined in [22] is used as our criteria. We construct LST-Net according to the ResNet architecture and compare it with the vanilla ResNet [19], SENet [24] and CBAM [54]. To examine the role of ST (please refer to Sect. 3.2) in improving the robustness of LST-Net, we also test LST-Net without ST in activation.

Table 4 lists the mCE and corruption errors for each type of corruption. One can see that LST-Net achieves lower mCE than its competitors of the same depth. It significantly reduces the mCE of the vanilla ResNet by 3.69% (18-layer)/6.47% (50-layer), and also improves SENet and CBAM by at least 2.76% (18-layer)/2.02% (50-layer). Though SENet and CBAM use extra paths which work well on clean images, the pooling operations in these paths may produce biased results in the existence of corruptions when the model is shallow. In contrast, LST does not need such extra paths and its robustness comes from the compact and sparser features. In addition, the ST operation in our ST-ReLU activation function can strengthen the robustness of LST-Net to most types of corruptions. With ST, the mCE of LST-Net-18/50 is reduced by 0.45%/0.31%.

5   Conclusion

In this paper, we proposed to train deep CNNs with a learnable sparse transform (LST), which learns to convert the input features into a more compact and sparser domain together with the CNN training process. LST can more effectively reduce the spatial and channel-wise feature redundancies than the conventional Conv2d. It can be efficiently implemented with existing CNN modules, and is portable to existing CNN architectures for seamless training and inference. We further presented a hybrid ST-ReLU activation to enhance the robustness of the learned CNN models to common types of corruptions in the input. Extensive experiments validated that the proposed LST-Net achieves even higher accuracy than its counterpart networks of the same family with lower cost.

References

1. Cai, J.F., Dong, B., Osher, S., Shen, Z.: Image restoration: total variation, wavelet frames, and beyond. J. Am. Math. Soc. **25**(4), 1033–1089 (2012)
2. Candes, E.J., Romberg, J., Tao, T.: Robust uncertainty principles: exact signal reconstruction from highly incomplete frequency information. IEEE Trans. Inf. Theory **52**(2), 489–509 (2006)
3. Candes, E.J., Wakin, M.B., Boyd, S.: Enhancing sparsity by reweighted ℓ_1 minimization. J. Fourier Anal. Appl. **14**, 877–905 (2008)
4. Cao, Y., Xu, J., Lin, S., Wei, F., Hu, H.: GCNet: non-local networks meet squeeze-excitation networks and beyond. arXiv preprint arXiv:1904.11492 (2019)
5. Chang, T., Kuo, C.C.: Texture analysis and classification with tree-structured wavelet transform. IEEE Trans. Image Process. **2**(4), 429–441 (1993)
6. Chen, W., Xie, D., Zhang, Y., Pu, S.: All you need is a few shifts: designing efficient convolutional neural networks for image classification. In: Proceedings of the CVPR (2019)
7. Clevert, D., Unterthiner, T., Hochreiter, S.: Fast and accurate deep network learning by exponential linear units (ELUs). In: Proceedings of the ICLR (2016)
8. Dai, J., et al.: Deformable convolutional networks. In: Proceedings of the ICCV (2017)
9. Dai, T., Cai, J., Zhang, Y., Xia, S.T., Zhang, X.P.: Second-order attention network for single image super-resolution. In: Proceedings of the CVPR (2019)

10. Denève, S., Alemi, A., Bourdoukan, R.: The brain as an efficient and robust adaptive learner. Neuron **94**(5), 969–977 (2017)
11. Deng, J., Dong, W., Socher, R., Li, L.J., Li, K., Fei-Fei, L.: ImageNet: a large-scale hierarchical image database. In: Proceedings of the CVPR. IEEE (2009)
12. Donoho, D.L.: De-noising by soft-thresholding. IEEE Trans. Inf. Theory **41**(3), 613–627 (1995)
13. Donoho, D.L., Johnstone, J.M.: Ideal spatial adaptation by wavelet shrinkage. Biometrika **81**(3), 425–455 (1994)
14. Everingham, M., Eslami, S.M.A., Van Gool, L., Williams, C.K.I., Winn, J., Zisserman, A.: The Pascal visual object classes challenge: a retrospective. Int. J. Comput. Vis. **111**(1), 98–136 (2015)
15. Fracastoro, G., Fosson, S.M., Magli, E.: Steerable discrete cosine transform. IEEE Trans. Image Process. **26**(1), 303–314 (2017)
16. Fu, J., et al.: Dual attention network for scene segmentation. In: Proceedings of the CVPR (2019)
17. Gao, S.H., Cheng, M.M., Zhao, K., Zhang, X.Y., Yang, M.H., Torr, P.: Res2Net: a new multi-scale backbone architecture. IEEE Trans. Pattern Anal. Mach. Intell. (2020). https://doi.org/10.1109/TPAMI.2019.2938758
18. He, K., Zhang, X., Ren, S., Sun, J.: Delving deep into rectifiers: surpassing human-level performance on imagenet classification. In: Proceedings of the ICCV (2015)
19. He, K., Zhang, X., Ren, S., Sun, J.: Identity mappings in deep residual networks. In: Leibe, B., Matas, J., Sebe, N., Welling, M. (eds.) ECCV 2016. LNCS, vol. 9908, pp. 630–645. Springer, Cham (2016). https://doi.org/10.1007/978-3-319-46493-0_38
20. He, Y., Zhang, X., Sun, J.: Channel pruning for accelerating very deep neural networks. In: Proceedings of the ICCV (2017)
21. Heil, C., Walnut, D.F.: Continuous and discrete wavelet transforms. SIAM Rev. **31**(4), 628–666 (1989)
22. Hendrycks, D., Dietterich, T.: Benchmarking neural network robustness to common corruptions and perturbations. In: Proceedings of the ICLR (2019)
23. Howard, A.G., et al.: MobileNets: efficient convolutional neural networks for mobile vision applications. In: Proceedings of the CVPR (2017)
24. Hu, J., Shen, L., Sun, G.: Squeeze-and-excitation networks. In: Proceedings of the CVPR (2018)
25. Huang, G.B., Ramesh, M., Berg, T., Learned-Miller, E.: Labeled faces in the wild: a database for studying face recognition in unconstrained environments. Technical report 07-49. University of Massachusetts, Amherst (2007)
26. Huang, K., Aviyente, S.: Wavelet feature selection for image classification. IEEE Trans. Image Process. **17**(9), 1709–1720 (2008)
27. Hubel, D.H., Wiesel, T.N.: Receptive fields of single neurones in the cat's striate cortex. J. Physiol. **148**(3), 574–591 (1959)
28. Huys, R., Jirsa, V.K., Darokhan, Z., Valentiniene, S., Roland, P.E.: Visually evoked spiking evolves while spontaneous ongoing dynamics persist. Front. Syst. Neurosci. **9**, 183 (2016)
29. Ioffe, S., Szegedy, C.: Batch normalization: accelerating deep network training by reducing internal covariate shift. In: Proceedings of the ICML (2015)
30. Kemelmacher-Shlizerman, I., Seitz, S.M., Miller, D., Brossard, E.: The megaface benchmark: 1 million faces for recognition at scale. In: Proceedings of the CVPR (2016)
31. Klambauer, G., Unterthiner, T., Mayr, A., Hochreiter, S.: Self-normalizing neural networks. In: Proceedings of the NeurIPS (2017)

32. Krizhevsky, A.: One weird trick for parallelizing convolutional neural networks. arXiv preprint arXiv:1404.5997 (2014)
33. Krizhevsky, A., Hinton, G.: Learning multiple layers of features from tiny images. Technical report. University of Toronto (2009)
34. Krizhevsky, A., Sutskever, I., Hinton, G.E.: ImageNet classification with deep convolutional neural networks. In: Proceedings of the NeurIPS (2012)
35. Li, S., Yang, L., Huang, J., Hua, X.S., Zhang, L.: Dynamic anchor feature selection for single-shot object detection. In: Proceedings of the ICCV (2019)
36. Lin, M., Chen, Q., Yan, S.: Network in network. In: Proceedings of the ICLR (2014)
37. Ma, N., Zhang, X., Zheng, H.-T., Sun, J.: ShuffleNet V2: practical guidelines for efficient CNN architecture design. In: Ferrari, V., Hebert, M., Sminchisescu, C., Weiss, Y. (eds.) Computer Vision – ECCV 2018. LNCS, vol. 11218, pp. 122–138. Springer, Cham (2018). https://doi.org/10.1007/978-3-030-01264-9_8
38. Maas, A., Hannun, A., Ng, A.: Rectifier nonlinearities improve neural network acoustic models. In: Proceedings of the ICML (2013)
39. Makhoul, J.: A fast cosine transform in one and two dimensions. IEEE Trans. Acoust. Speech Signal Process. 28(1), 27–34 (1980)
40. Nair, V., Hinton, G.E.: Rectified linear units improve restricted Boltzmann machines. In: Proceedings of the ICML (2010)
41. Olshausen, B.A., Field, D.J.: Emergence of simple-cell receptive field properties by learning a sparse code for natural images. Nature 381(6583), 607–609 (1996)
42. Paszke, A., et al.: Automatic differentiation in PyTorch. In: Proceedings of the NeurIPS-W (2017)
43. Redmon, J., Divvala, S., Girshick, R., Farhadi, A.: You only look once: unified, real-time object detection. In: Proceedings of the CVPR (2016)
44. Ren, S., He, K., Girshick, R., Sun, J.: Faster R-CNN: towards real-time object detection with region proposal networks. In: Proceedings of the NeurIPS (2015)
45. Rioul, O., Duhamel, P.: Fast algorithms for discrete and continuous wavelet transforms. IEEE Trans. Inf. Theory 38(2), 569–586 (1992)
46. Roland, P.E.: Space-time dynamics of membrane currents evolve to shape excitation, spiking, and inhibition in the cortex at small and large scales. Neuron 94(5), 934–942 (2017)
47. Sandler, M., Howard, A., Zhu, M., Zhmoginov, A., Chen, L.C.: MobileNetV2: inverted residuals and linear bottlenecks. In: Proceedings of the CVPR (2018)
48. Simonyan, K., Zisserman, A.: Very deep convolutional networks for large-scale image recognition. In: Proceedings of the ICLR (2015)
49. Szegedy, C., Ioffe, S., Vanhoucke, V., Alemi, A.A.: Inception-v4, Inception-ResNet and the impact of residual connections on learning. In: AAAI (2017)
50. Tibshirani, R.: Regression shrinkage and selection via the lasso. J. Roy. Stat. Soc. Ser. B (Methodol.) 58(1), 267–288 (1996)
51. Wang, S.H., Phillips, P., Sui, Y., Liu, B., Yang, M., Cheng, H.: Classification of Alzheimer's disease based on eight-layer convolutional neural network with leaky rectified linear unit and max pooling. J. Med. Syst. 42(5), 85 (2018)
52. Watson, A.B.: Image compression using the discrete cosine transform. Math. J. 4(1), 81 (1994)
53. Wen, W., Wu, C., Wang, Y., Chen, Y., Li, H.: Learning structured sparsity in deep neural networks. In: Proceedings of the NeurIPS (2016)
54. Woo, S., Park, J., Lee, J.-Y., Kweon, I.S.: CBAM: convolutional block attention module. In: Ferrari, V., Hebert, M., Sminchisescu, C., Weiss, Y. (eds.) ECCV 2018. LNCS, vol. 11211, pp. 3–19. Springer, Cham (2018). https://doi.org/10.1007/978-3-030-01234-2_1

55. Wu, B., et al.: Shift: a zero flop, zero parameter alternative to spatial convolutions. In: Proceedings of the CVPR (2018)
56. Xiao, J., Ehinger, K.A., Hays, J., Torralba, A., Oliva, A.: Sun database: exploring a large collection of scene categories. Int. J. Comput. Vision **119**(1), 3–22 (2016)
57. Xie, S., Girshick, R., Dollár, P., Tu, Z., He, K.: Aggregated residual transformations for deep neural networks. In: Proceedings of the CVPR. IEEE (2017)
58. Yu, F., Koltun, V.: Multi-scale context aggregation by dilated convolutions. In: Proceedings of the ICLR (2016)
59. Zagoruyko, S., Komodakis, N.: Wide residual networks. In: Proceedings of the BMVC (2016)
60. Zerlaut, Y., Destexhe, A.: Enhanced responsiveness and low-level awareness in stochastic network states. Neuron **94**(5), 1002–1009 (2017)
61. Zhang, L., Bao, P., Wu, X.: Multiscale lmmse-based image denoising with optimal wavelet selection. IEEE Trans. Circuits Syst. Video Technol. **15**(4), 469–481 (2005)
62. Zhang, X., Zhou, X., Lin, M., Sun, J.: ShuffleNet: an extremely efficient convolutional neural network for mobile devices. In: Proceedings of the CVPR (2018)
63. Zhou, B., Khosla, A., Lapedriza, A., Oliva, A., Torralba, A.: Learning deep features for discriminative localization. In: Proceedings of the CVPR (2016)
64. Zhou, B., Lapedriza, A., Khosla, A., Oliva, A., Torralba, A.: Places: a 10 million image database for scene recognition. IEEE Trans. Pattern Anal. Mach. Intell. **40**(6), 1452–1464 (2018)
65. Zhu, X., Hu, H., Lin, S., Dai, J.: Deformable ConvNets v2: more deformable, better results. In: Proceedings of the CVPR (2019)

Learning What Makes a Difference from Counterfactual Examples and Gradient Supervision

Damien Teney[(✉)], Ehsan Abbasnedjad, and Anton van den Hengel

Australian Institute for Machine Learning, University of Adelaide,
North Terrace, Adelaide, SA 5005, Australia
damien.teney@adelaide.edu.au

Abstract. One of the primary challenges limiting the applicability of deep learning is its susceptibility to learning spurious correlations rather than the underlying mechanisms of the task of interest. The resulting failure to generalise cannot be addressed by simply using more data from the same distribution. We propose an auxiliary training objective that improves the generalization capabilities of neural networks by leveraging an overlooked supervisory signal found in existing datasets. We use pairs of minimally-different examples with different labels, a.k.a counterfactual or contrasting examples, which provide a signal indicative of the underlying causal structure of the task. We show that such pairs can be identified in a number of existing datasets in computer vision (visual question answering, multi-label image classification) and natural language processing (sentiment analysis, natural language inference). The new training objective orients the gradient of a model's decision function with pairs of counterfactual examples. Models trained with this technique demonstrate improved performance on out-of-distribution test sets.

1 Introduction

Most of today's machine learning methods rely on the assumption that the training and testing data are drawn from a same distribution [72]. One implication is that models are susceptible to poor real-world performance when the test data differs from what is observed during training. This limited capability to generalise partly arises because supervised training essentially amounts to identifying correlations between given examples and their labels. However, correlations can be spurious, in the sense that they may reflect dataset-specific biases or sampling artifacts, rather than intrinsic properties of the task of interest [44,70]. When spurious correlations do not hold in the test data, the model's predictive performance suffers and its output becomes unreliable and unpredictable.

Electronic supplementary material The online version of this chapter (https://doi.org/10.1007/978-3-030-58607-2_34) contains supplementary material, which is available to authorized users.

© Springer Nature Switzerland AG 2020
A. Vedaldi et al. (Eds.): ECCV 2020, LNCS 12355, pp. 580–599, 2020.
https://doi.org/10.1007/978-3-030-58607-2_34

For example, an image recognition system may rely on common co-occurrences of objects, such as people together with a dining table, rather visual evidence for each recognized object. This system could then hallucinate people when a table is observed (Fig. 4).

Fig. 1. The traditional supervised learning process treats each training example individually. We use counterfactual *relations* between examples as an additional supervisory signal. In some datasets, the relations are provided explicitly, as in sentiment analysis (top) with sentences edited by annotators to flip their label between positive and negative. In other datasets (COCO, middle, and VQA v2, bottom), we show that counterfactual examples can be generated from existing annotations, by masking relevant regions. Our method then leverages the *relations* between the original and edited examples, which proves superior to simple data augmentation.

A model capable of generalization and extrapolation beyond its training distribution should ideally capture the causal mechanisms at play behind the data. Acquiring additional training examples from the same distribution cannot help in this process [52]. Rather, we need either to inject strong prior assumptions in the model, such as inductive biases encoded in the architecture of a neural network, or a different type of training information. Ad hoc methods such as data augmentation and domain randomization fall in the former category, and they only defer the limits of the system by hand-designed rules.

In this paper, we show that many existing datasets contain an overlooked signal that is informative about their causal data-generating process. This information is present in the form of groupings of training examples, and it is often discarded by the shuffling of points occurring during stochastic training. We show that this information can be used to learn a model that is more faithful to the causal model behind the data. This training signal is fundamentally different and complementary to the labels of individual points. We use pairs of minimally-dissimilar, differently-labeled training examples, which we interpret as counterfactuals of one another. In some datasets, such pairs are provided explicitly [10,15,50,51]. In others, they can be identified from existing annotations [21,28,39,64,65,73].

The intuition for our approach is that relations between pairs of counterfactual examples indicate what changes in the input space map to changes in the space of labels. In a classification setting, this serves to constrain the geometry of a model's decision boundary between classes. Loosely speaking, we complement the traditional "curve fitting" to individual training points of standard supervised learning, with "aligning the curve" with pairs of training counterfactuals.

We describe a novel training objective (gradient supervision) and its implementation on various architectures of neural networks. The vector difference in input space between pairs of counterfactual examples serves to supervise the orientation of the gradient of the network. We demonstrate the benefits of the method on four tasks in computer vision and natural language processing (NLP) that are notoriously prone to poor generalization due to dataset biases: visual question answering (VQA), multi-label image classification, sentiment analysis, and natural language inference. We use annotations from existing datasets that are usually disregarded, and we demonstrate significant improvements in generalization to out-of-distribution test sets for all tasks.

In summary, the contributions of this paper are as follows.

1. We propose to use relations between training examples as additional information in the supervised training of neural networks (Subsect. 3.1). We show that they provide a fundamentally different and complementary training signal to the fitting of individual examples, and explain how they improve generalization (Subsect. 3.3).
2. We describe a novel training objective (gradient supervision) to use this information and its implementation on multiple architectures of neural networks (Sect. 4).
3. We demonstrate that the required annotations are present in a number of existing datasets in computer vision and NLP, although they are usually discarded. We show that our technique brings improvements in out-of-distribution generalization on VQA, multi-label image classification, sentiment analysis, and natural language inference.

2   Related Work

This work proposes a new training objective that improves the generalization capabilities of models trained with supervision. This touches a number of core concepts in machine learning.

The predictive performance of machine learning models rests on the fundamental assumption of statistical similarity of the distributions of training and test data. There is a growing interest for evaluating and addressing the limits of this assumption. Evaluation on **out-of-distribution data** is increasingly common in computer vision [5, 11, 30] and NLP [36, 81]. These evaluations have shown that some of the best models can be right for the wrong reasons [5, 24, 28, 70, 71]. This happens when they rely on dataset-specific biases and artifacts rather than intrinsic properties of the task of interest. When these biases do not hold in the test data, the predictive performance of the models can drop dramatically [5, 11].

When poor generalization is viewed as a deficiency of the training data, it is often referred to as **dataset biases**. They correspond to correlations between inputs and labels in a dataset that can be exploited by a model to exhibit strong performance on a test set containing these same biases, without actually solving the task of interest. Several popular datasets used in vision-and-language [27] and NLP [81] have been shown to exhibit strong biases, leading to an inflated sense of progress on these tasks.

Recent works have discussed generalization from a **causal perspective** [2, 9, 32, 53, 57]. This sheds light on the possible avenues for addressing the issue. In order to generalize perfectly, a model should ideally capture the real-world causal mechanisms at play behind the data. The limits of identifiability of causal models from observational data have been well studied [52]. In particular, additional data from a single biased training distribution can not solve the problem. The alternative options are to use strong assumptions (*e.g.* inductive biases, engineered architectures, hand-designed data augmentations), or additional data, collected in controlled conditions and/or of a different type than labeled examples. This work uses the latter option, using pairings of training examples that represent counterfactuals of one another. Recent works that follow this line include the principle of invariant risk minimization (IRM [9]). IRM uses multiple training environments, *i.e.* non-IID training distributions, to discover generalizable invariances in the data. Teney *et al.* [20] showed that existing datasets could be automatically partitioned to create these environments, and demonstrated improvements in generalization for visual question answering (VQA).

Generalization is also related to the wide area of **domain adaptation** [25]. Our objective in this paper is not to adapt to a particular new domain, but rather to learn a model that generalizes more broadly by using annotations indicative of the causal mechanisms of the task of interest. In domain adaptation, the idea of finding a data representation that is invariant across domains is limiting, because the true causal factors that our model should rely on may differ in their distribution across training domains. We refer the reader to [9] for a formal discussion of these issues.

The growing popularity of high-level tasks in **vision-and-language** [3,7, 8,22] has brought the issue of dataset biases to the forefront. In VQA, language biases cause models to be overly reliant on the presence of particular words in a question. Improving the data collection process can help [27,83] but it only addresses precisely identified biases and confounders. Controlled evaluations for VQA now include out-of-distribution test sets [5,68]. Several models and training methods [14,18,19,29,30,43,55] have been proposed with significant improvements. They all use strong prior knowledge about the task and/or additional annotations (question types) to improve generalization. Some methods also supervise the model's attention [40,54,60] with ground truth human attention maps [21]. All of these methods are specific to VQA or to captioning [33,40] whereas we describe a much more general approach.

Evaluating generalization overlaps with the growing interest in **adversarial examples** for evaluation [12,16,34,36,45,49,74]. The term has been used to refer both to examples purposefully generated to fool existing models [46,47], but also to hard natural examples that current models struggle with [12,16,74,82]. Our method is most related to the use of these examples for **adversarial training**. Existing methods focus mostly on the generation of these examples then mix them with the original data in a form of data augmentation [37,61,78]. We argue that this shuffling of examples destroys valuable information. In many datasets, we demonstrate that relations between training points contain valuable information. The above methods also aim at improving robustness to targeted adversarial attacks, which often use inputs outside the manifold of natural data. Most of them rely on prior knowledge and unsupervised regularizers [35,38,77] whereas we seek to exploit additional supervision to improve generalization on natural data.

3   Proposed Approach

We start with an intuitive motivation for our approach, then describe its technical realization. In Subsect. 3.3, we analyze more formally how it can improve generalization. In Sect. 4, we demonstrate its application to a range of tasks.

3.1   Motivation

Training a machine learning model amounts to fitting a function $f(\cdot)$ to a set of labeled points. We consider a binary classification task, in which the model is a neural network f of parameters $\boldsymbol{\theta}$ such that $f_{\boldsymbol{\theta}} : \mathbb{R}^d \to \{0,1\}$, and a set of training points[1] $\mathcal{T} = \{(\boldsymbol{x}_i, y_i)\}_i$, with $\boldsymbol{x}_i \in \mathbb{R}^d$ and $y_i \in [0,1]$. By training the model, we typically optimize $\boldsymbol{\theta}$ such that the output of the network $\tilde{y}_i = f_{\boldsymbol{\theta}}(\boldsymbol{x}_i)$ minimizes a loss $\mathcal{L}_{\text{Main}}(\tilde{y}_i, y_i)$ on the training points. However, this does not specify the behaviour of f between these points, and the decision boundary

---

[1] By *input space*, we refer to a space of feature representations of the input, *i.e.* vector representations ($\boldsymbol{x}$) obtained with a pretrained CNN or text encoder.

could take an arbitrary shape (Fig. 3). The typical practice is to restrain the space of functions $\mathcal{F} \supset f$ (e.g. a particular architecture of neural networks) and of parameters $\Theta \supset \theta$ (e.g. with regularizers [35,38,77]). The capability of the model to interpolate and extrapolate beyond the training points depends on these choices (Fig. 2).

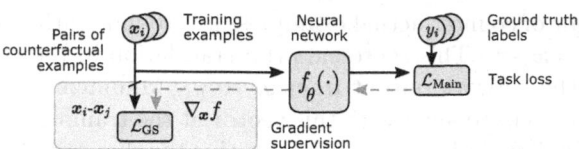

Fig. 2. The proposed gradient supervision (GS) is an auxiliary loss on the gradient of a neural network with respect to its inputs, which is simply computed by backpropagation (dashed lines). Supervision for this gradient is generated from pairs of training examples identified as counterfactuals of one another. The loss $\mathcal{L}_{\mathrm{GS}}$ is a cosine distance that encourages the gradient of the network to align with the vector between pairs of counterfactual examples.

Our motivating intuition is that many datasets contain information that is indicative of the shape of an ideal f (in the sense of being faithful to the data-generating process, see Subsect. 3.3) between training points. In particular, we are interested in pairs of training examples that are **counterfactuals** of one another. Given a labeled example (x_1, y_1), we define its counterfactuals as examples such as (x_2, y_2) that represents an alternative premise x_2 ("counter to the facts") that lead to different outcome y_2. These points represent "minimal changes" ($\|x_1 - x_2\| \ll$, in a semantic sense) such that their label $y_1 \neq y_2$. All possible counterfactuals to a given example x_1 constitute a distribution. We assume the availability of samples from it, forming pairs such as $\{(x_1, y_1), (x_2, y_2)\}$. The counterfactual relation is undirected.

Obtaining Pairs of Counterfactual Examples. Some existing datasets explicitly contain pairs of counterfactual examples [10,15,37,50,51]. For example, [37] contains sentences (movie reviews) with positive and negative labels. Annotators were instructed to edit a set of sentences to flip the label, thus creating counterfactual pairs (see examples in Fig. 1). Existing works simply use these as additional training point. Our contribution is to use the *relation* between these pairs, which is usually discarded. In other datasets, counterfactual examples can be created by masking parts of the input, thus creative negative examples. In Sect. 4, we apply this approach to the COCO and VQA v2 datasets.

3.2 Gradient Supervision

To exploit relations between counterfactual examples, we introduce an auxiliary loss that supervises the gradient of the network f_θ. We denote the gradient of the network with respect to its input at a point x_i with $g_i = \nabla_x f(x_i)$. Our new gradient supervision (GS) loss encourages g_i to align with a "ground truth" gradient vector $\hat{g}_i$:

$$\mathcal{L}_{\text{GS}}(g_i, \hat{g}_i) = 1 - (g_i \cdot \hat{g}_i) / (\|g_i\| \|\hat{g}_i\|) . \tag{1}$$

This definition is a cosine distance between g_i and $\hat{g}_i$. Assuming $\{(x_i, y_i), (x_j, y_j)\}$ is a pair of counterfactual examples, a "ground truth" gradient at x_i is obtained as $\hat{g}_i = x_j\text{-}x_i$. This represents the translation in the input space that should change the network output from y_i to y_j. Minimizing Eq. 1 encourages the network's gradient to align with this vector at the training points. Assuming f is continuously differentiable, it also constrains the shape of f *between* training points. This makes f more faithful to the generating process behind the training data (see Subsect. 3.3). Also note that the GS loss uses a local linearization of the network. Although deep networks are highly non-linear globally, first-order approximations have found multiple uses, for example in providing explanations [56, 59] and generating adversarial examples [26]. In our application, this approximation is reasonable since pairs of counterfactual examples lie close to one another and to the classification boundary, by definition.

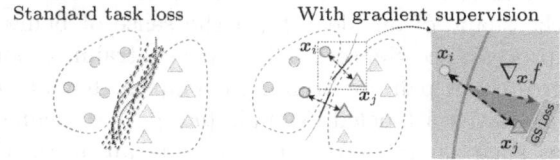

Fig. 3. The proposed gradient supervision constrains the geometry of a model's decision boundary between classes. (Left) We show possible decision boundaries consistent with a conventional supervised loss for two classes (circles and triangles representing training points of each). (Right) The gradient supervision uses pairs of counterfactual examples (x_i, x_j) to constrain classifier f such that its local gradient aligns with the vector between these points. When the gradient supervision counterfactuals are included with the GS loss, the boundary is clearer between two classes. On the right, we show the GS loss for a pair of counterfactuals.

The network is optimized for a combination of the main and GS losses, $\mathcal{L} = \mathcal{L}_{\text{Main}} + \lambda \mathcal{L}_{\text{GS}}$, where λ is a scalar hyperparameter. The optimization of the GS loss requires backpropagating second-order derivatives through the network. The computational cost over standard supervised training is of two extra backpropagations through the whole model for each mini-batch.

Multiclass Output. In cases where the network output y is a vector, a ground truth gradient is only available for classes for which we have positive examples. Denoting such a class gt, we apply the GS loss only on the gradient of this class, using $g_i = \nabla_x f_i(x_i)$. If a softmax is used, the output for one class depends on that of the others, so the derivative of the network is taken on its logits to make it dependent on one class only.

3.3 How Gradient Supervision Improves Generalization

By training a machine learning model f_θ, we seek to approximate an ideal $\mathcal{F}$ that represents the real-world process attributing the correct label $y = \mathcal{F}(x)$ to any possible input x. Let us considering the Taylor expansion of f at a training point x_j:

$$f(x_j) \;=\; f(x_i) \;+\; f'(x_i)\,(x_i - x_j) \;+\; \underbrace{\frac{1}{2}\,f''(x_i)\,(x_i - x_j)^2 \;+\; \dots}_{\approx 0} \tag{2}$$

Our definition of a pair of counterfactual examples (x_i, x_j) (Subsect. 3.1) implies that $(x_i\text{-}x_j)^m$ approaches 0 ($m > 1$). For such a pair of nearby points, the terms beyond the first order virtually vanish. It follows that the distance between $f(x_j)$ and $f(x_i)$ is maximized when the dot product $\nabla_x f(x_i)\,.\,(x_i\text{-}x_j)$ is maximum. This is precisely the desired behavior of f in the vicinity of x_i and x_j, since their ground truth labels y_i and y_j are different by our definition of counterfactuals. This leads to the definition of the GS loss in Eq. 1. Geometrically, it encourages the gradient of f to align with the vector pointing from a point to its counterfactual, as illustrated in Fig. 3.

The conventional empirical risk minimization with non-convex functions leads to large numbers of local minimas. They correspond to multiple plausible decision boundaries with varied capability for generalization. Our approach essentially modifies the optimization landscape for the parameters θ of f such that the minimizer found after training is more likely to reflect the ideal $\mathcal{F}$.

4 Applications

The proposed method is applicable to datasets with counterfactual examples in the training data. They are sometimes provided explicitly [10,15,37,50,51]. Most interestingly, we show that they can be also be generated from existing annotations [21,28,39,64,65,73].

We selected four classical tasks in vision and language that are notoriously subject to poor generalization due to dataset biases. Our experiments aim (1) to measure the impact of gradient supervision on performance for well-known tasks, and (2) to demonstrate that the necessary annotations are available in a variety of existing datasets. We therefore prioritized the breadth of experiments and the use of simple models (details in supplementary material) rather than chasing the state of the art on any particular task. The method should readily apply to more complex models for any of these tasks.

4.1 Visual Question Answering

The task of visual question answering (VQA) involves an image and a related question, to which the model must determine the correct answer among a set of approximately 2,000 candidate answers. Models trained on existing datasets (*e.g.* VQA v2 [27]) are notoriously poor at generalization because of dataset biases. These models rely on spurious correlations between the correct answer and certain words in the question. We use the training/test splits of VQA-CP [5] that were manually organized such that the correlation between the questions' prefixes (first few words) and answers differ at training/test time. Most methods evaluated on VQA-CP **use the explicit knowledge of this fact** [5,14,18,20, 29,55,69,79] or even of the ground truth set of prefixes, which defeats the purpose of evaluating generalization. As discussed in the introduction, strong background assumptions are one of the two options to improve generalization beyond a set of labels. Our method, however, follows the other option of using a different type of data, and **does not rest on the knowledge of the construction of VQA-CP** (Table 1).

Table 1. Application to VQA-CP v2. Existing methods all rely on built-in knowledge of the construction procedure of the dataset, defeating some of the claimed improvements in robustness. Using counterfactual data with the proposed gradient supervision (GS) improve performance on most question types on the out-of-distribution test sets (see text for discussion).

Test data →	Val.				Test				Test "focused"			
	All	YesNo	Nb	Other	All	YesNo	Nb	Other	All	YesNo	Nb	Other
SAN [79]	–	–	–	–	25.0	38.4	11.1	21.7	–	–	–	–
GVQA [5]	–	–	–	–	31.3	58.0	13.7	22.1	–	–	–	–
UpDown [67]	–	–	–	–	39.1	62.4	15.1	34.5				
Ramakrishnan *et al.* 2018 [55]	–	–	–	–	42.0	**65.5**	15.9	36.6	–	–	–	–
Grand and Belinkov, 2019 [29]	–	–	–	–	42.3	59.7	14.8	40.8	–	–	–	–
RUBi [14]	–	–	–	–	47.1	68.7	20.3	43.2	–	–	–	–
Teney *et al.* 2019 [69]	–	–	–	–	46.0	58.2	**29.5**	44.3	–	–	–	–
Unshuffling [20]	–	–	–	–	42.39	47.72	14.43	47.24	–	–	–	–
Strong baseline [20] + CF data	63.3	79.4	45.5	53.7	46.0	61.3	15.6	**46.0**	44.2	57.3	9.2	**42.2**
+ CF data + GS	62.4	77.8	43.8	53.6	**46.8**	64.5	15.3	45.9	**46.2**	**63.5**	**10.5**	41.4
Weak baseline (BUTD [67]), trained on 'Other' only	–	–	–	54.7	–	–	–	43.3	–	–	–	40.6
+ CF data	–	–	–	55.9	–	–	–	45.0	–	–	–	40.6
+ CF data + GS	–	–	–	56.1	–	–	–	44.7	–	–	–	38.3

Generating Counterfactual Examples. We build counterfactual examples for VQA-CP using annotations of human attention from [21]. Given a question/image/answer triple (q, I, a), we build its counterfactual counterpart (q, I', a') by editing the image and answer. The image I is a set of features pre-extracted with a bottom-up attention model [6] (typically a matrix of dimensions $N \times 2048$). We build I' ($N' \times 2048$, $N' \leq N$) by masking the features whose bounding boxes overlap with the human attention map past a certain threshold (details in supplementary material). The vector a is a binary vector of correct answers over all candidates. We simply set all entries in a' to zero.

Experimental Setting. For training, we use the training split of VQA-CP, minus 8,000 questions held out as an "in-domain" validation set (as in [20]). We generate counterfactual versions of the training examples that have a human attention map (approx. 7% of them). For evaluation, we use (1) our "in-domain" validation set (held out from the training set), (2) the official VQA-CP test set (which has a different correlation between prefixes and answers), and (3) a new *focused* test set.

The *focused* test set contains the questions from VQA-CP test from which we only keep image features of regions looked at by humans to answer the questions. We essentially perform the opposite of the building of counterfactual examples, and mask regions where the human attention is **below** a low threshold. Answering questions from the *focused* test set should intuitively be easier, since the background and distracting image regions have been removed. However, a model that relies on context (question or irrelevant image regions) rather than strictly on the relevant visual evidence will do poorly on the focused test set. This serves to measure robustness beyond the question biases that VQA-CP was specifically designed for.

Results. We present results of our method applied on top of two existing models. The first (*weak baseline*) is the popular BUTD model [6,67]. The second (*strong baseline*) is the "unshuffling" method of [20], which was specifically tuned to address the language biases evaluated with VQA-CP. We compare the baseline model with the same model trained with the additional counterfactual data, and then with the additional GS loss. The performance improves on most question types with each of these additions. The "focused" provides an out-of-distribution evaluation complementary to the VQA-CP test set (which only accounts for language biases). It shows the improvements expected from our method to a larger extent that the VQA-CP test set. This suggests that evaluating generalization in VQA is still not completely addressed with the current benchmarks. Importantly, the improvements over both the weak and strong baselines indicate that **the proposed method is not redundant with existing methods that specifically address the language biases measured by VQA-CP**, like the strong baseline. Additional details are provided in the supplementary material.

4.2 Multi-label Image Classification

We apply our method to the COCO dataset [39]. Its images feature objects from 80 classes. They appear in common situations such that the patterns of co-occurrence are highly predictable: a bicycle often appears together with a person, and a traffic light often appears with cars, for example. These images serve as the basis of a number of benchmarks for image detection [39], captioning [17], visual question answering [8], etc. They all inherit the biases inherent to the COCO images [5,33,75] which is an increasing cause of concern. A method to improve generalization in this context has a wide potential impact.

Experimental Setting. We consider a simple multi-label classification task that captures the core issue of dataset biases that affect higher-level tasks (captioning for example [33]). Each image is associated with a binary vector of size 80 that represents the presence of at least one object of the corresponding class in the image. The task is to predict this binary vector. Performance is measured with the mean average precision (mAP) over all classes. The model is a feed-forward neural network that performs an 80-class binary classification with sigmoid outputs, over pre-extracted ResNet-based visual features. We pre-extract these features with the bottom-up attention model of Anderson *et al.* [6]. They are spatially pooled into a 2048-dimensional vector. The model is trained with a standard binary cross-entropy loss (details in the supplementary material).

Table 2. Application to multi-label classification on COCO. We use counterfactual examples generated by masking objects with the inpainter GAN [4,62]. Our method allows to train a model that is less reliant less on common object co-occurrences of the training set. The most striking improvements are measurable with images that feature sets of objects that appear rarely ("Edited") or never ("Hard edited") during training.

Test data →	$\mathcal{N}(C)$OCO Multi-label classification		
	Original	Edited images	Hard edited
	Images	Images	Images
Random predictions (chance)	5.1	3.9	7.8
Baseline w/o edited tr. examples	71.8	58.1	54.8
Baseline w/ edited tr. examples	72.1	64.0	56.0
+ GS, counterfactual relations	**72.9**	**65.2**	**57.7**
+ GS, random relations	71.8	63.9	56.1

Generating Counterfactual Examples. Counterfactual examples can be generated using existing annotation in COCO. Agarwal *et al.* [4] used the inpainter GAN [1,62] to edit images by masking selected objects. This only requires the original labels and bounding boxes. The edited images represent a "minimal change" that makes the corresponding label negative, which agrees with our definition of counterfactuals. The vector of ground truth labels for edited images are edited accordingly. For training, we use all images produced by [4] from the COCO *train2014* split (original and edited versions). For evaluation, we use their images from the *val2014* split (original and edited version, evaluated separately). We also create an additional evaluation split named "Hard edited images". It contains a subset of edited images with patterns of classes that **never** appear in the training set.

Results. We first compare the baseline model trained with the original images, and then with the original and edited images (Table 2). The performance

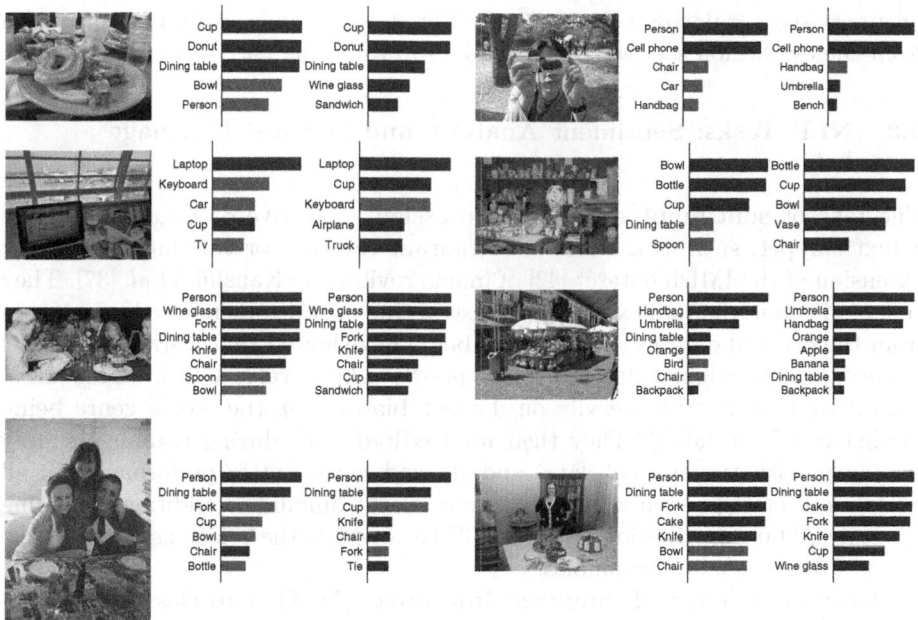

Fig. 4. Qualitative examples of multi-label classification on COCO. We show the input image and the scores of the top predicted labels by the baseline and by our method (blue: correct, red: incorrect). The baseline can erroneously predict common co-occurring objects, such as a *person* with food items (top left) even though there is no visual evidence for the former. Our method is better at predicting unusual combinations, such as as a *donut* with a *wineglass* (first row, left) or a *laptop* with an *airplane* (second row, left). (Color figure online)

improves (71.8→72.1%), which is particularly clear when evaluated on edited images (58.1→64.0%). This is because the patterns of co-occurrence in the training data cannot blindly relied on with the edited images. The images in this set depict situations that are unusual in the training set, such as a surfboard without a person on top, or a man on a tennis court who is not holding a racquet. A model that relies on common co-occurrences in the training set rather than strictly on visual evidence can do well on the original images, but not on edited ones. An improvement from additional data is not surprising. It is still worth emphasizing that the edited images were generated "for free" using existing annotations in COCO.

Training the model with the proposed gradient supervision (GS) further improves the precision (72.1→72.9%). This is again more significant on the edited images (64.0→65.2%). The improvement is highest on the set of "hard edited images" (56.0→57.7%). As an ablation, we train the GS model with random pairwise relations instead of relations between counterfactual pairs. The performance is clearly worse, showing that the value of GS is in leveraging an additional training signal, rather than setting arbitrary constraints on the gradient like existing unsupervised regularizers [35,38,77]. In Fig. 4, we provide qualitative examples from the evaluation sets where our model improves the baseline.

4.3   NLP Tasks: Sentiment Analysis and Natural Language Inference

The task of **sentiment analysis** is to assign a positive or negative label to a text snippet, such as a movie or restaurant review. For training, we use the extension of the IMDb dataset [42] of movie reviews by Kaushik *et al.* [37]. They collected counterfactual examples by instructing crowdworkers to edit sentences from the original dataset to flip their label. They showed that a standard model trained on the original data performs poorly when evaluated on edited data, indicating that it relies heavily on dataset biases (*e.g.* the movie genre being predictive of the label). They then used edited data during training (simply mixing it with the original data) and showed much better performance in all evaluation settings, even when controlling for the amount of additional training examples. Our contribution is to use GS to leverage the relations between the pairs of original/edited examples.

The task of **natural language inference (NLI)** is to classify a pair of sentences, named the premise and the hypothesis, into {*entailment, contradiction, neutral*} according to their logical relationship. We use the extension of the SNLI dataset [13] by Kaushik *et al.* [37]. They instructed crowdworkers to edit

Table 3. Application to sentiment analysis (top) and natural language inference (bottom), trained resp. on the subsets of the IMDb and SNLI datasets augmented with "edited" counterfactual examples [37]. Our technique brings clear improvements over mere data augmentation baseline (accuracy in %), in particular when evaluated on the edited test data (on which biases from the original training data cannot be relied on) and on test data from other datasets (no fine-tuning is used).

Test data →	IMDb with counterfactuals			Zero-shot transfer		
	Val.	Test original	Test edited	Amazon	Twitter	Yelp
Random predictions (chance)	51.4	47.7	49.2	47.3	53.3	45.4
Baseline w/o edited tr. data	71.2	82.6	55.3	78.6	61.0	82.8
Baseline w/ edited tr. data	85.7	82.0	88.7	80.8	63.1	87.4
+ **GS**, counterfactual rel.	**89.8**	**83.8**	**91.2**	**81.6**	**65.4**	**88.8**
+ **GS**, random relations	50.8	49.2	52.0	47.4	61.2	57.4

Test data →	SNLI with counterfactuals			Zero-shot transfer
	Val.	Test original	Test edited	MultiNLI dev.
Random predictions (chance)	30.8	34.6	32.9	31.9
Baseline w/o edited tr. data	61.8	42.0	59.0	46.0
Baseline w/ edited tr. data	61.3	39.1	57.8	42.4
+ **GS**, counterfactual relations	**64.8**	**44.4**	**61.2**	**46.8**
+ **GS**, random relations	58.5	40.4	58.6	45.7

original examples to change their labels. Each original example is supplemented with versions produced by editing the premise or the hypothesis, to either of the other two classes. The original and edited data together are therefore four times as large as the original data alone.

Results on Sentiment Analysis. We first compare a model trained with the original data, and with the original and edited data as simple augmentation (Table 3). The improvement is significant when tested on edited data (55.3→88.7%). We then train the model with our GS loss. The added improvement is visible on both the original data (82.0→83.8%) and on the edited data (88.7→91.2%). The evaluation on edited examples is the more challenging setting, because spurious correlations from the original training data cannot be relied on. The ablation that uses GS with random relations completely fails, confirming the value of the supervision with relations between pairs of related examples.

We additionally evaluate the model on out-of-sample data with three additional test sets: Amazon Reviews [48], Semeval 2017 (Twitter data) [58], and Yelp reviews [80]. The model trained on IMDb is applied **without any fine-tuning** to these, which constitutes a significant challenge in terms of generalization. We observe a clear gain over the data augmentation baseline on all three.

Results on NLI. We perform the same set of experiments on NLI. The fairest point of comparison is again the model trained with the original and edited data. Using the GS loss on top of it brings again a clear improvement (Table 3), both when evaluated on standard test data and on edited examples. As an additional measure of generalization, we also evaluate the same models on the dev. set of MultiNLI [76] without any fine-tuning.

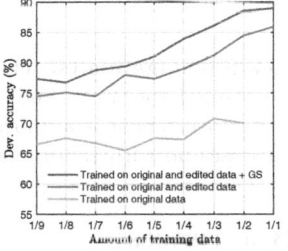

There is a significant domain shift between the datasets. Using the edited examples for data augmentation actually hurts the performance here, most likely because they constitute very "unnatural" sentences, such that easy-to-pick-up language cues cannot be relied on. Using GS (with always uses the edited data as augmentations as well) brings back the performance higher, and above the baseline trained only on the original data (Fig. 5).

Fig. 5. Training on different amounts of data for sentiment analysis. The proposed gradient supervision (GS) brings a clear improvement over a model trained with edited examples for simple data augmentation, and even more so over a model trained with the same number of original training examples.

Limitations. Our NLP experiments were conducted with simple models and relatively little data. The current state of the art in sentiment analysis and NLI is achieved by transformer-based models [23] trained on vastly more data. Kaushik *et al.* [37] showed that counterfactual examples are much more valuable than the same amount of standard data, including for fine-tuning a BERT model for NLI. The application of our technique to the extremely-large data regime, including with large-scale language models, is an exciting direction for future work.

5 Conclusions

We proposed a new training objective that improves the generalization capabilities of neural networks by supervising their gradient, and using an unused training signal found in many datasets. While most machine learning models rely on identifying correlations between inputs and output, we showed that relations between counterfactual examples provide a fundamentally different, complementary type of information. We showed theoretically and empirically that our technique can shape the decision boundary of the model to be more faithful to the causal mechanisms that generated the data. Practically speaking, the model is then more likely to be "right for the right reasons". We showed that this effect brings significant improvements on a number of tasks when evaluated with out-of-distribution test data. We demonstrated that the required annotations can be extracted from existing datasets for a number of tasks.

There is a number of additional tasks and datasets on which our method can readily apply [10,15,50,51,64,65,73]. Scaling up the technique to state-of-the-art models in vision and NLP [23,31,41,63,66] is another exciting direction for future work.

Acknowledgements. This material is based on research sponsored by Air Force Research Laboratory and DARPA under agreement number FA8750-19-2-0501. The U.S. Government is authorized to reproduce and distribute reprints for Governmental purposes notwithstanding any copyright notation thereon.

References

1. Abbasnejad, E., Shi, Q., van den Hengel, A., Liu, L.: A generative adversarial density estimator. In: Proceedings of the IEEE Conference on Computer Vision and Pattern Recognition (2019)
2. Abbasnejad, E., Teney, D., Parvaneh, A., Shi, J., van den Hengel, A.: Counterfactual vision and language learning. In: Proceedings of the IEEE Conference on Computer Vision and Pattern Recognition (2020)
3. Abbasnejad, E., Wu, Q., Shi, Q., van den Hengel, A.: What's to know? Uncertainty as a guide to asking goal-oriented questions. In: Proceedings of the IEEE Conference on Computer Vision and Pattern Recognition (2019)
4. Agarwal, V., Shetty, R., Fritz, M.: Towards causal VQA: revealing and reducing spurious correlations by invariant and covariant semantic editing. arXiv preprint arXiv:1912.07538 (2019)
5. Agrawal, A., Batra, D., Parikh, D., Kembhavi, A.: Don't just assume; look and answer: overcoming priors for visual question answering. In: Proceedings of the IEEE Conference on Computer Vision and Pattern Recognition, pp. 4971–4980 (2018)

6. Anderson, P., et al.: Bottom-up and top-down attention for image captioning and VQA. In: Proceedings of the CVPR (2018)
7. Anderson, P., et al.: Vision-and-language navigation: interpreting visually-grounded navigation instructions in real environments. In: Proceedings of the IEEE Conference on Computer Vision and Pattern Recognition, pp. 3674–3683 (2018)
8. Antol, S., et al.: VQA: visual question answering. In: Proceedings of the IEEE Conference on Computer Vision (2015)
9. Arjovsky, M., Bottou, L., Gulrajani, I., Lopez-Paz, D.: Invariant risk minimization. arXiv preprint arXiv:1907.02893 (2019)
10. Baradel, F., Neverova, N., Mille, J., Mori, G., Wolf, C.: CoPhy: Counterfactual learning of physical dynamics. arXiv preprint arXiv:1909.12000 (2019)
11. Barbu, A., et al.: ObjectNet: a large-scale bias-controlled dataset for pushing the limits of object recognition models. In: Proceedings of the Advances in Neural Information Processing Systems, pp. 9448–9458 (2019)
12. Bartolo, M., Roberts, A., Welbl, J., Riedel, S., Stenetorp, P.: Beat the AI: investigating adversarial human annotations for reading comprehension. arXiv preprint arXiv:2002.00293 (2020)
13. Bowman, S.R., Angeli, G., Potts, C., Manning, C.D.: A large annotated corpus for learning natural language inference. In: Proceedings of the Conference on Empirical Methods in Natural Language Processing (2015)
14. Cadene, R., Dancette, C., Ben-younes, H., Cord, M., Parikh, D.: RUBi: reducing unimodal biases in visual question answering. arXiv preprint arXiv:1906.10169 (2019)
15. Camburu, O.M., Rocktäschel, T., Lukasiewicz, T., Blunsom, P.: e-SNLI: natural language inference with natural language explanations. In: Proceedings of the Advances in Neural Information Processing Systems, pp. 9539–9549 (2018)
16. Chen, M., D'Arcy, M., Liu, A., Fernandez, J., Downey, D.: CODAH: an adversarially-authored question answering dataset for common sense. In: Proceedings of the 3rd Workshop on Evaluating Vector Space Representations for NLP, pp. 63–69 (2019)
17. Chen, X., et al.: Microsoft COCO captions: data collection and evaluation server. arXiv preprint arXiv:1504.00325 (2015)
18. Clark, C., Yatskar, M., Zettlemoyer, L.: Don't take the easy way out: ensemble based methods for avoiding known dataset biases. arXiv preprint arXiv:1909.03683 (2019)
19. Teney, D., Abbasnejad, E., van den Hengel, A.: On incorporating semantic prior knowledge in deep learning through embedding-space constraints. arXiv preprint arXiv:1909.13471 (2019)
20. Teney, D., Abbasnejad, E., van den Hengel, A.: Unshuffling data for improved generalization. arXiv preprint arXiv:2002.11894 (2020)
21. Das, A., Agrawal, H., Zitnick, C.L., Parikh, D., Batra, D.: Human attention in visual question answering: do humans and deep networks look at the same regions? In: Proceedings of the Conference on Empirical Methods in Natural Language Processing (2016)
22. Das, A., et al.: Visual dialog. In: Proceedings of the CVPR (2017)
23. Devlin, J., Chang, M.W., Lee, K., Toutanova, K.: BERT: pre-training of deep bidirectional transformers for language understanding. arXiv preprint arXiv:1810.04805 (2018)
24. Feng, S., Wallace, E., Boyd-Graber, J.: Misleading failures of partial-input baselines. arXiv preprint arXiv:1905.05778 (2019)

25. Ganin, Y., et al.: Domain-adversarial training of neural networks. J. Mach. Learn. Res. **17**, 1–35 (2016)
26. Goodfellow, I.J., Shlens, J., Szegedy, C.: Explaining and harnessing adversarial examples. arXiv preprint arXiv:1412.6572 (2014)
27. Goyal, Y., Khot, T., Summers-Stay, D., Batra, D., Parikh, D.: Making the V in VQA matter: elevating the role of image understanding in visual question answering. arXiv preprint arXiv:1612.00837 (2016)
28. Goyal, Y., Khot, T., Summers-Stay, D., Batra, D., Parikh, D.: Making the V in VQA matter: elevating the role of image understanding in visual question answering. In: Proceedings of the IEEE Conference on Computer Vision and Pattern Recognition, pp. 6904–6913 (2017)
29. Grand, G., Belinkov, Y.: Adversarial regularization for visual question answering: strengths, shortcomings, and side effects. arXiv preprint arXiv:1906.08430 (2019)
30. Guo, Y., Cheng, Z., Nie, L., Liu, Y., Wang, Y., Kankanhalli, M.: Quantifying and alleviating the language prior problem in visual question answering. arXiv preprint arXiv:1905.04877 (2019)
31. He, K., Zhang, X., Ren, S., Sun, J.: Deep residual learning for image recognition. In: Proceedings of the IEEE Conference on Computer Vision and Pattern Recognition (2016)
32. Heinze-Deml, C., Meinshausen, N.: Conditional variance penalties and domain shift robustness. arXiv preprint arXiv:1710.11469 (2017)
33. Hendricks, L.A., Burns, K., Saenko, K., Darrell, T., Rohrbach, A.: Women also snowboard: overcoming bias in captioning models. In: Ferrari, V., Hebert, M., Sminchisescu, C., Weiss, Y. (eds.) ECCV 2018. LNCS, vol. 11207, pp. 793–811. Springer, Cham (2018). https://doi.org/10.1007/978-3-030-01219-9_47
34. Iyyer, M., Wieting, J., Gimpel, K., Zettlemoyer, L.: Adversarial example generation with syntactically controlled paraphrase networks. arXiv preprint arXiv:1804.06059 (2018)
35. Jakubovitz, D., Giryes, R.: Improving DNN robustness to adversarial attacks using Jacobian regularization. In: Ferrari, V., Hebert, M., Sminchisescu, C., Weiss, Y. (eds.) ECCV 2018. LNCS, vol. 11216, pp. 525–541. Springer, Cham (2018). https://doi.org/10.1007/978-3-030-01258-8_32
36. Jia, R., Liang, P.: Adversarial examples for evaluating reading comprehension systems. arXiv preprint arXiv:1707.07328 (2017)
37. Kaushik, D., Hovy, E., Lipton, Z.C.: Learning the difference that makes a difference with counterfactually-augmented data. arXiv preprint arXiv:1909.12434 (2019)
38. Li, Y., Cohn, T., Baldwin, T.: Learning robust representations of text. In: Proceedings of the Conference on Empirical Methods in Natural Language Processing, pp. 1979–1985. Association for Computational Linguistics (2016)
39. Lin, T.-Y., et al.: Microsoft COCO: common objects in context. In: Fleet, D., Pajdla, T., Schiele, B., Tuytelaars, T. (eds.) ECCV 2014. LNCS, vol. 8693, pp. 740–755. Springer, Cham (2014). https://doi.org/10.1007/978-3-319-10602-1_48
40. Liu, C., Mao, J., Sha, F., Yuille, A.: Attention correctness in neural image captioning. In: Proceedings of the Conference on AAAI (2017)
41. Liu, Y., et al.: CBNet: a novel composite backbone network architecture for object detection. arXiv preprint arXiv:1909.03625 (2019)
42. Maas, A.L., Daly, R.E., Pham, P.T., Huang, D., Ng, A.Y., Potts, C.: Learning word vectors for sentiment analysis. In: Proceedings of the 49th Annual Meeting of the Association for Computational Linguistics: Human Language Technologies, vol. 1, pp. 142–150. Association for Computational Linguistics (2011)

43. Mahabadi, R.K., Henderson, J.: Simple but effective techniques to reduce biases. arXiv preprint arXiv:1909.06321 (2019)
44. Mitchell, T.M.: The need for biases in learning generalizations. Department of Computer Science, Laboratory for Computer Science Research (1980)
45. Miyato, T., Dai, A.M., Goodfellow, I.: Adversarial training methods for semi-supervised text classification. arXiv preprint arXiv:1605.07725 (2016)
46. Moosavi-Dezfooli, S.M., Fawzi, A., Fawzi, O., Frossard, P.: Universal adversarial perturbations. In: Proceedings of the IEEE Conference on Computer Vision and Pattern Recognition, pp. 1765–1773 (2017)
47. Nguyen, A., Yosinski, J., Clune, J.: Deep neural networks are easily fooled: high confidence predictions for unrecognizable images. In: Proceedings of the IEEE Conference on Computer Vision and Pattern Recognition, pp. 427–436 (2015)
48. Ni, J., Li, J., McAuley, J.: Justifying recommendations using distantly-labeled reviews and fine-grained aspects. In: Proceedings of the Conference on Empirical Methods in Natural Language Processing, pp. 188–197. Association for Computational Linguistics (2019)
49. Nie, Y., Williams, A., Dinan, E., Bansal, M., Weston, J., Kiela, D.: Adversarial NLI: a new benchmark for natural language understanding. arXiv preprint arXiv:1910.14599 (2019)
50. Park, D.H., Darrell, T., Rohrbach, A.: Robust change captioning. In: Proceedings of the IEEE Conference on Computer Vision and Pattern Recognition, pp. 4624–4633 (2019)
51. Park, D.H., Darrell, T., Rohrbach, A.: Viewpoint invariant change captioning. arXiv preprint arXiv:1901.02527 (2019)
52. Didelez, V., Pigeot, I.: *Judea Pearl*: Causality: models, reasoning, and inference. Politische Vierteljahresschrift **42**(2), 313–315 (2001). https://doi.org/10.1007/s11615-001-0048-3
53. Peters, J., Bühlmann, P., Meinshausen, N.: Causal inference by using invariant prediction: identification and confidence intervals. J. Roy. Stat. Soc.: Ser. B (Stat. Methodol.) **78**, 947–1012 (2016)
54. Qiao, T., Dong, J., Xu, D.: Exploring human-like attention supervision in visual question answering. In: Proceedings of the Conference on AAAI (2018)
55. Ramakrishnan, S., Agrawal, A., Lee, S.: Overcoming language priors in visual question answering with adversarial regularization. In: Proceedings of the Advances in Neural Information Processing Systems, pp. 1541–1551 (2018)
56. Ribeiro, M.T., Singh, S., Guestrin, C.: "Why should i trust you ?" Explaining the predictions of any classifier. In: Proceedings of the ACM SIGKDD International Conference on Knowledge Discovery and Data Mining (2016)
57. Rojas-Carulla, M., Schölkopf, B., Turner, R., Peters, J.: Invariant models for causal transfer learning. J. Mach. Learn. Res. **19**, 1309–1342 (2018)
58. Rosenthal, S., Farra, N., Nakov, P.: SemEval-2017 task 4: sentiment analysis in twitter. In: Proceedings of the 11th International Workshop on Semantic Evaluation (SemEval 2017), pp. 502–518. Association for Computational Linguistics (2017)
59. Selvaraju, R.R., Das, A., Vedantam, R., Cogswell, M., Parikh, D., Batra, D.: Grad-CAM: why did you say that? arXiv preprint arXiv:1611.07450 (2016)
60. Selvaraju, R.R., et al.: Taking a hint: leveraging explanations to make vision and language models more grounded. In: Proceedings of the IEEE International Conference on Computer Vision (2019)
61. Shafahi, A., et al.: Adversarial training for free! In: Proceedings of the Advances in Neural Information Processing Systems, pp. 3353–3364 (2019)

62. Shetty, R.R., Fritz, M., Schiele, B.: Adversarial scene editing: automatic object removal from weak supervision. In: Proceedings of the Advances in Neural Information Processing Systems, pp. 7706–7716 (2018)
63. Su, W., et al.: VL-BERT: pre-training of generic visual-linguistic representations. arXiv preprint arXiv:1908.08530 (2019)
64. Suhr, A., Lewis, M., Yeh, J., Artzi, Y.: A corpus of natural language for visual reasoning. In: Proceedings of the Conference on Association for Computational Linguistics, vol. 2, pp. 217–223 (2017)
65. Suhr, A., Zhou, S., Zhang, A., Zhang, I., Bai, H., Artzi, Y.: A corpus for reasoning about natural language grounded in photographs. arXiv preprint arXiv:1811.00491 (2018)
66. Tan, H., Bansal, M.: LXMERT: learning cross-modality encoder representations from transformers. arXiv preprint arXiv:1908.07490 (2019)
67. Teney, D., Anderson, P., He, X., van den Hengel, A.: Tips and tricks for visual question answering: learnings from the 2017 challenge. In: Proceedings of the CVPR (2018)
68. Teney, D., van den Hengel, A.: Zero-shot visual question answering. arXiv preprint arXiv:1611.05546 (2016)
69. Teney, D., van den Hengel, A.: Actively seeking and learning from live data. In: The IEEE Conference on Computer Vision and Pattern Recognition (CVPR) (2019)
70. Torralba, A., Efros, A.A., et al.: Unbiased look at dataset bias. In: Proceedings of the CVPR, vol. 1, p. 7 (2011)
71. Vapnik, V., Izmailov, R.: Rethinking statistical learning theory: learning using statistical invariants. Mach. Learn. 108, 381–423 (2019)
72. Vapnik, V.N.: An overview of statistical learning theory. IEEE Trans. Neural Netw. 10(5), 988–999 (1999)
73. Vo, N., et al.: Composing text and image for image retrieval-an empirical Odyssey. In: Proceedings of the IEEE Conference on Computer Vision and Pattern Recognition, pp. 6439–6448 (2019)
74. Wallace, E., Boyd-Graber, J.: Trick me if you can: adversarial writing of trivia challenge questions. In: ACL Student Research Workshop (2018)
75. Wang, T., Zhao, J., Yatskar, M., Chang, K.W., Ordonez, V.: Balanced datasets are not enough: estimating and mitigating gender bias in deep image representations. In: Proceedings of the IEEE International Conference on Computer Vision, pp. 5310–5319 (2019)
76. Williams, A., Nangia, N., Bowman, S.R.: A broad-coverage challenge corpus for sentence understanding through inference. arXiv preprint arXiv:1704.05426 (2017)
77. Woods, W., Chen, J., Teuscher, C.: Adversarial explanations for understanding image classification decisions and improved neural network robustness. Nat. Mach. Intell. 1(11), 508–516 (2019)
78. Xie, C., Tan, M., Gong, B., Wang, J., Yuille, A., Le, Q.V.: Adversarial examples improve image recognition. arXiv preprint arXiv:1911.09665 (2019)
79. Yang, Z., He, X., Gao, J., Deng, L., Smola, A.: Stacked attention networks for image question answering. In: Proceedings of the IEEE Conference on Computer Vision and Pattern Recognition (2016)
80. Yelp: Yelp dataset challenge. http://www.yelp.com/dataset_challenge
81. Zellers, R., Bisk, Y., Schwartz, R., Choi, Y.: SWAG: a large-scale adversarial dataset for grounded commonsense inference. arXiv preprint arXiv:1808.05326 (2018)

82. Zellers, R., Holtzman, A., Bisk, Y., Farhadi, A., Choi, Y.: HellaSwag: can a machine really finish your sentence? arXiv preprint arXiv:1905.07830 (2019)
83. Zhang, P., Goyal, Y., Summers-Stay, D., Batra, D., Parikh, D.: Yin and Yang: balancing and answering binary visual questions. In: Proceedings of the IEEE Conference on Computer Vision and Pattern Recognition (2016)

CN: Channel Normalization for Point Cloud Recognition

Zetong Yang[1]([✉]), Yanan Sun[2], Shu Liu[3], Xiaojuan Qi[4], and Jiaya Jia[1,3]

[1] The Chinese University of Hong Kong, Shatin, The People's Republic of China
tomztyang@gmail.com, leojia@cse.cuhk.edu.hk
[2] Hong Kong University of Science and Technology, Kowloon, Hong Kong
now.syn@gmail.com
[3] SmartMore, Shenzhen, China
sliu@smartmore.com
[4] The University of Hong Kong, Pokfulam, Hong Kong
xjqi@eee.hku.hk

Abstract. In 3D recognition, to fuse multi-scale structure information, existing methods apply hierarchical frameworks stacked by multiple fusion layers for integrating current relative locations with structure information from the previous level. In this paper, we deeply analyze these point recognition frameworks and present a factor, called difference ratio, to measure the influence of structure information among different levels on the final representation. We discover that structure information in deeper layers is overwhelmed by information in shallower layers in generating the final features, which prevents the model from understanding the point cloud in a global view. Inspired by this observation, we propose a novel channel normalization scheme to balance structure information among different layers and avoid excessive accumulation of shallow information, which benefits the model in exploiting and integrating multilayer structure information. We evaluate our channel normalization in several core 3D recognition tasks including classification, segmentation and detection. Experimental results show that our channel normalization further boosts the performance of state-of-the-art methods effectively.

Keywords: 3D recognition · Point cloud · Object detection · Classification

1 Introduction

Recently, 3D point cloud recognition has attracted much attention in computer vision, since it benefits many real-life applications, such as autonomous driving [4] and robot manipulation. Compared to 2D recognition, this task is challenging because of several unique characteristics of point cloud for its sparse, unordered and locality sensitive properties.

Z. Yang and Y. Sun—Equal Contribution.

© Springer Nature Switzerland AG 2020
A. Vedaldi et al. (Eds.): ECCV 2020, LNCS 12355, pp. 600–616, 2020.
https://doi.org/10.1007/978-3-030-58607-2_35

To deal with raw point-cloud data, PointNet [19] extracts features for each point and aggregates them by max-pooling. Though effective, this method does not capture multi-scale structure information, which is of great importance in point cloud recognition considering the diversity of 3D object size.

To fill this gap, later methods utilize a hierarchical structure stacked by several fusion layers to exploit multi-scale structure information. There are a variety of fusion layers. In general, they can be classified into two main streams. The first one is explicit fusion layer who applies concatenation, multiplication or summation to explicitly fuse current relative locations with previous features. *Set Abstraction* (SA) layers [20] and RS-CNN [14] are two representative structures of this track who apply concatenation or multiplication after multi-layer perceptron (MLP) encoding network to fuse current relative locations with previous features. Another track is implicit fusion layer. These layers [11,16,26,29] utilize continuous convolution to encode relative locations to dynamic weights and merge previous features by matrix multiplication.

These fusion layers yield consistent performance boost for classification [14,16,26,30], segmentation [16,20,30], and object detection [2,18,22]. Albeit performance improvement, existing fusion layers either require heavy computation [14,16,26,29] or have their performance bottlenecks [20]. In this paper, we instead aim at a light-weight parameter-free and yet effective fusion layer.

Motivation. Despite intensive research on fusion layer structures [13,14,16, 20,26], it is rare to see systematic analysis to understand these operations for principled design. Importantly, we propose to evaluate its ability in aggregating multilayer structure information by a quantitative metric, called **difference ratio**. We note that difference ratio reflects the contribution of relative locations in various fusion layers on the final generated feature. If the difference ratio of a fusion layer is greater than a threshold, information of this layer generally dominates and consequently overwhelms information of other layers, which hampers the model from capturing multilayer structure information. Our empirical observation in Table 1 manifests that fusion layers with difference ratio closer to 1 tend to yield better performance since they fill the gap of influence among different layers.

Although existing methods are capable of alleviating the imbalance, the difference ratio of these fusion layers is still large and they introduce computational overhead. In this paper, we propose a simple and effective mechanism, called channel normalization, to fully utilize multilayer structure information. In each fusion layer, we rescale previous features by their difference ratios so as to enforce the model to treat location information from each fusion layer equally.

Our channel normalization does *not* introduce any extra parameters but yields impressive improvement in several 3D recognition tasks of classification, segmentation, and detection. Experimental results on multiple datasets including ModelNet40 [30], ShapeNet3D [30], and KITTI [4] prove that our CN pushes the performance of state-of-the-art (SOTA) recognition models further. Our overall contribution is the following.

- We propose to analyze fusion layers by difference ratio, which can reflect the effect of relative locations from different fusion layers on the final generated 3D representation features.
- We analyze the bottleneck of 3D recognition frameworks by difference ratio and raise the imbalance issue between shallower and deeper layers, which hampers the model from extracting proper multilayer structure information.
- We propose channel normalization, to accomplish considerable improvement on SOTA methods for all vital 3D recognition tasks without using extra parameters.

2   Related Work

View- and Voxel-Based Methods. View-based methods [3,5,25] treat 3D shape as a set of 2D images from different views and use deep neural networks to recognize them. These methods ignore the structure information in the point cloud and demand other operations to ensure performance, which may lead to considerable computation cost.

Voxel-based methods [17,30] subdivide the raw point cloud to equally distributed voxels and employ CNN to extract their 3D representations. These methods are straightforward and efficient; but quantization during voxelization may cause information loss and performance bottleneck. In this paper, we focus on methods dealing with raw point cloud directly.

PointNet-Based Methods. To extract 3D representations from the raw point cloud data, PointNet [19] applies MLP network to learn features for each point and aggregates them by a symmetric function of max-pooling to extract 3D representation. Nonetheless, it ignores multi-scale structure information that is common and effective in 2D recognition.

To address this issue, later SOTA methods utilize hierarchical structures stacked by different types of fusion layers to fuse multi-scale structure information. In general, a fusion layer consists of two steps. The first one receives relative locations of points within a specific range as structure information. It also uses previous features as shallow structure information and merges them together. In the second step, merged features are sent to a MLP network to extract high-level representation. In the following subsection, we review these different fusion layers in current PointNet-based recognition frameworks.

Fusion Layers in PointNet-Based Methods. There are a variety of fusion layers that differ mainly in the first step. In general, they can be classified into two types. The first type is explicit fusion layer, who applies concatenation, summation or multiplication to explicitly fuse current relative locations and former features. The most straightforward one is direct concatenation, which is used in the SA layer of PointNet++ [20]. Other methods adopt an extra MLP network to encode relative locations and aggregate these encoded results with previous features by summation, concatenation or multiplication, like RS-CNN [14]. These methods achieve SOTA recognition performance but double the computation compared to direct concatenation.

The second type is implicit fusion layer. The most representative operation among these types of layers is continuous convolution, which is utilized in [11,16, 26,29]. For each point, these methods employ the relative location to generate the unique kernel weight and apply matrix multiplication based on the previous feature and the kernel weight. Multilayer structure information is obtained in an implicit way.

The recognition performance between these two types of fusion layers are comparable. In this paper, we mainly analyze the explicit ones systematically since their effectiveness and simpleness, and give an explanation behind the discrepancy of performance. We also develop a parameter-free normalization module to further boost the performance of these explicit SOTA recognition models.

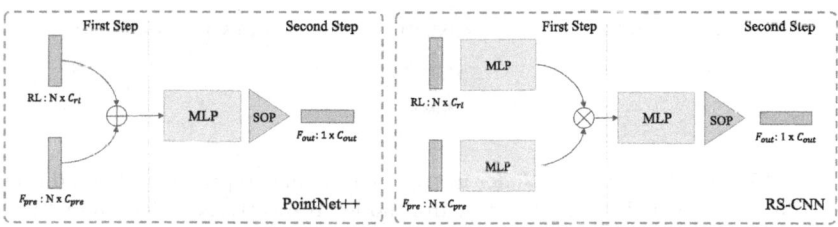

Fig. 1. Examples of explicit fusion layers. "RL", "N", F_{pre}, and F_{out} represent current relative locations, the number of interior points, previous features and output features respectively. "SOP" means symmetric operations, like max-pool.

3   Systematic Analysis

3.1   Background

Current 3D recognition frameworks are all hierarchical networks stacked by many fusion layers [16,20,26,29]. The fusion layer is responsible for generating local structure features for target points and has a unique spherical range to cover structure information on a specific scale. The spherical range is similar to the receptive field of CNNs. Shallower fusion layers usually have smaller spherical ranges to extract local detail information, and those in deeper layers retain larger spherical ranges to capture structure information for the whole object. In this paper, we mainly focus on explicit fusion layers since they are simple and effective. All fusion layers below represent for explicit ones.

Normally, there are two parts in a fusion layer. The first combines relative locations of interior points in the current layer with features from the previous fusion layer. The second is an MLP network to extract high-dimension features. We illustrate two representative ones in Fig. 1.

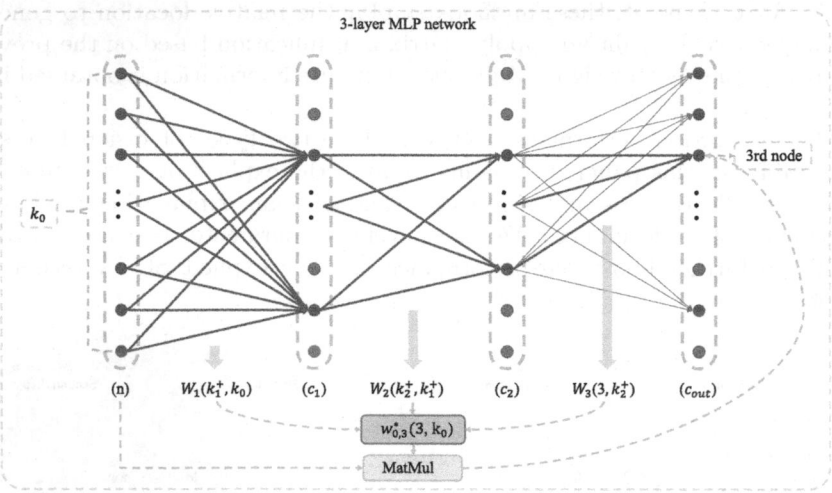

Fig. 2. A 3-layer MLP network. Nodes in "red" and "blue" represent activated (greater than 0) and inactivated (equal to 0) neuron nodes respectively. "Red" and "Yellow" lines illustrate the complete computation flow as Eq. (2) and merged computation flow as Eq. (3) respectively from input features to the certain activated node (the 3rd node) in final generated features. W_i and $W_{0,3}^\star$ stand for activated kernel weight in layer i and merged kernel weight computed by Eq. (3) respectively. (Color figure online)

3.2 Analysis

In this subsection, we analyze the fusion layers considering the impact of relative locations in different fusion layers on the final extracted representation since it directly reflects the relative importance of different fused structure information. Our analysis further enables us to understand and explain how different fusion layers work and why they lead to varying performance. To quantify the impact, we propose an impact factor. It is followed by our development of "difference ratio" to measure impact rates, so as to compute the relative importance.

Impact Factor. Since all kinds of fusion layers consist of an MLP network in the second step, we first consider a small MLP network with 3 layers in Fig. 2. Generally, a layer in an MLP network is composed of three parts: kernel multiplication, batch normalization and the non-linear unit. Since the batch normalization is a linear transformation, we can merge it with kernel multiplication (in the inference stage) and define the output of a 3-layer MLP network as

$$M_3 = \sigma(W_3 \cdot \sigma(W_2 \cdot \sigma(W_1 \cdot X))), \tag{1}$$

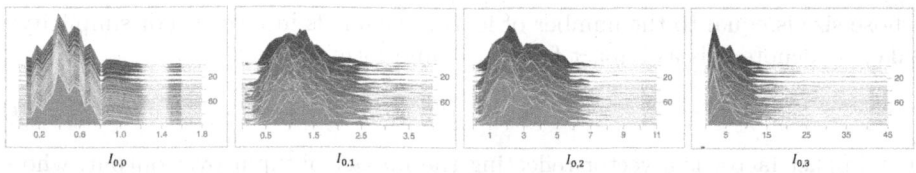

Fig. 3. We illustrate distributions of values in $I_{0,j}$ among different input features, where 0 and j represent indexes of different layers within an MLP network with 4 layers. The X-axis means the impact value. The Y-axis shows the number of channels with this impact value. The Z-axis contains indexes of different features within an MLP network.

where W_i, X and σ represent merged kernel weight in layer i, input feature and the non-linear unit "ReLU" respectively.

For any channel in M_3, if its value is greater than 0, there must be non-zero channels in M_2 multiplied with their corresponding kernel weights. This fact also holds for features M_2 and M_1. Generally, for an MLP network, for each non-zero channel in the final feature, there must be a computation flow from the original input X to current channel value as illustrated by "red" lines in Fig. 2.

This makes it possible to estimate the concrete contribution of input from a certain layer to each channel in the last generated features. For example, we assume that the list with k_i^+, k_i^- and k_i contains activated channel indexes (channels with positive values), inactivated channel indexes and total channel indexes for layer i respectively. This computation flow can be formulated as

$$
\begin{aligned}
M_1(k_1^+) &= W_1(k_1^+, k_0) \cdot X \\
M_2(k_2^+) &= W_2(k_2^+, k_1^+) \cdot M_1(k_1^+) \\
M_3(k_3^+) &= W_3(k_3^+, k_2^+) \cdot M_2(k_2^+)
\end{aligned}
\tag{2}
$$

where (k_1, k_2) means "index operation" that gathers values by query indexes.

Based on Eq. (2), we merge these multiplication matrices, and build up a merged computation flow as

$$
\begin{aligned}
M_3(k_3^+) &= W_3(k_3^+, k_2^+) \cdot W_2(k_2^+, k_1^+) \cdot W_1(k_1^+, k_0) \cdot X \\
&= \mathbf{W_{0,3}} \cdot X \\
W_{0,3}^\star(k_3^+, k_0) &= \mathbf{W_{0,3}}, \ W_{0,3}^\star(k_3^-, k_0) = 0 \\
M_3 &= W_{0,3}^\star \cdot X
\end{aligned}
\tag{3}
$$

which is highlighted by yellow lines in Fig. 2. Suppose X has n input channels, $W_{0,3}^\star$ should have a shape of $[c_{out}, n]$ to transform X to features with c_{out} dimensions in a straightforward way.

Equation (3) enables us to directly link the input to each output feature channel. Thus, we propose to use $\|W_{0,i}^\star\|$ to measure the impact of input in layer 0 on each channel imposed on the output feature in layer i, where $\|\cdot\|$ is an operation to calculate the L2-norm of each row of the matrix. $\|W_{0,i}^\star\|$ is a vector whose size is equal to the number of feature channels in layer i. For simplicity's sake, we denote this as impact factor $I_{0,i}$ and form it as

$$I_{0,i} = \left\| W_{0,i}^\star \right\| \tag{4}$$

The impact factor is a vector reflecting the impact of input over output, whose size equals to the output channel number. Each value in this vector represents the input influence on the corresponding channel of the output feature.

In Fig. 3, we count $I_{0,i}$ among a 4-layer MLP network with different input features, which illustrates that the influence of input grows rapidly with the increase of depth of layer i.

Similarly, the impact of relative locations in a certain fusion layer on different generated features can also be calculated. We adopt PointNet++ in our study since it has been widely adopted in multiple 3D computer vision tasks of detection [33], generation [9], scene flow [12], etc.

In a SA layer, it directly concatenates relative locations with the previous feature, and adopts an MLP network to extract high-level representation. In order to analyze the effect of relative locations in the current layer and previous features respectively, we rewrite the computation process in the SA layer as

$$F_i^l = W_i^l \cdot X_i$$
$$F_i^f = W_i^f \cdot F_{i-1} \tag{5}$$
$$F_i = M_i(F_i^l + F_i^f)$$

In each SA layer, it first transforms relative locations X_i and previous features F_{i-1} by weights W_i^l and W_i^f to obtain F_i^l and F_i^f, and then employ an MLP network M_i based on the sum of F_i^l and F_i^f to generate final features F_i.

F_i^f in Eq. (5) is derived from F_{i-1}^l and F_{i-1}^f while F_{i-1}^f is derived from F_{i-2}^l and F_{i-2}^f. In the beginning, F_0^f equals to 0, since there is no previous features in the first layer. We eliminate all F_i^f in Eq. (5) in a recursive way. Based on Eqs. (5) and (3), the recursion formula is given as

$$\begin{aligned} F_i^f &= W_i^f \cdot F_{i-1} = W_i^f \cdot M_{i-1}(F_{i-1}^l + F_{i-1}^f) \\ &= W_i^f \cdot W_{i-1,i}^\star \cdot W_{i-1}^l \cdot X_{i-1} + W_i^f \cdot W_{i-1,i}^\star \cdot F_{i-1}^f \end{aligned} \tag{6}$$

where $W_{i-1,i}^\star$ is the merged multiplication matrix in MLP network M_{i-1} by Eq. (3). This iteration process makes it possible to calculate features F_i^f generated by X_{i-1}.

We then calculate $I_{i-1,i}$ and $I_{i,i}$ as

$$\begin{aligned} I_{i-1,i} &= \left\| W_i^f \cdot W_{i-1,i}^\star \cdot W_{i-1}^l \right\|, \\ I_{i,i} &= \left\| W_i^l \right\|, \end{aligned} \tag{7}$$

and repeat the process above to obtain $I_{i,j}$ where $(i \leq j)$ for any fusion layers i and j in PointNet++ network.

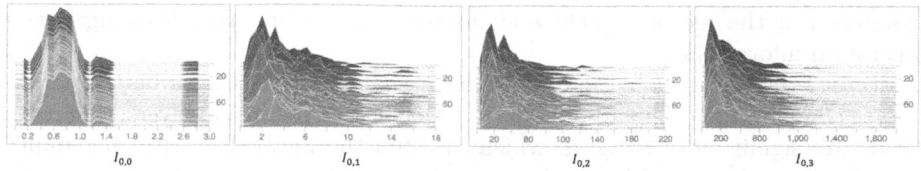

Fig. 4. Illustration of distributions of values in $I_{0,j}$ among different SA layers. The X-axis means the impact value. The Y-axis shows the number of channels with this impact value. The Z-axis represents indexes of different input points for an SA layer.

Table 1. Comparison among different methods in terms of average $D_{0,j}$ and classification accuracy, where 0 indexes the first layer and j indexes other fusion layers.

Methods		PointNet++ [20]	RS-CNN [14]	CN
Layer j	0	1	1	1
	1	16.35	1.22	1.04
	2	116.31	19.21	1.33
Accuracy (%)		90.7	92.9	93.3

In Fig. 4, we illustrate distributions of $I_{0,j}$, which measure the impact of input relative locations in fusion layer 0 imposed upon output features of fusion layer j. The contribution of relative locations in the first fusion layer grows even faster with the increase of index j.

Difference Ratio. The impact factor quantifies the importance of input towards each channel of output, we now analyze the relative influence of input features from different layers towards the same output feature, which determines their relative importance in the final fusion result. We propose difference ratio $D_{i,j}$, which is the quotient between $I_{i,j}$ and $I_{j,j}$ as

$$D_{i,j} = \frac{I_{i,j}}{I_{j,j}}, \tag{8}$$

to judge if the relative location information from certain layer i overwhelms information from layer j. This can help us verify the quality of multilayer feature fusion. For example, if $D_{i,j}$ is close to 1 for any $(i \leq j)$, it means that all fused information is equally used, which makes the optimal fusion results.

This parameter reflects the contribution of relative location in different layers on the final generated features. In Table 1, we test $D_{0,j}$ between the first SA layer and others indexed by j in PointNet++ and average them in channels to get an overall value. As illustrated, when the network goes deeper, the influence of relative locations in the first layer not only increases on values but also enhances rapidly their proportions. That is, the features from the last SA layer mainly contain relative locations in the first SA layer, and ignore structure information from the current new neighborhood. This phenomenon is not conducive to the expansion of the receptive field and impedes the model from learning better structural information.

Table 1 also reveals the potential reason that RS-CNN draws better performance compared to original PointNet++. Because of the fusion layers, difference ratios are significantly reduced, which benefits the network in utilizing multiscale structure hints and boost the recognition performance.

4   Channel Normalization

4.1   Approximate Difference Ratio Calculation

Even though current SOTA methods diminish difference ratios between previous and current structure information on the generated features, the gap between these two types of effect is still very large. In order to help the model exploit multiple structure information from different layers better and take full advantage of model capacity, it is a decent choice to rescale previous features i by $D_{i,j}$ to enforce this value to be 1.

However, it is intractable to calculate $D_{i,j}$ during training or inference directly because of the difficulty in calculating $W_{i,j}^{\star}$. Due to the application of ReLU, differently activated neurons lead to varying computation flow, which requires to obtain $W_{i,j}^{\star}$ for each of the flow. In a normal case, suppose there are N_t target points and for each point there are N_n interior points for calculating relative locations, we need to calculate $W_{i,j}^{\star}$ for $N_t \times N_n$ times, which is extremely large computation cost. Therefore, our main concern is to find a way to approximate the unique $W_{i,j}^{\star}$ for different points.

To this end, we propose a global approximation of $W^{\star}$. We treat all neurons to be activated. To simulate the activation of neuron nodes during inference, we utilize the probability of a to-active neuron to re-weight the corresponding weights. The probability is estimated as the ratio between the number of points whose neuron n is activated and total points in the whole scene. This approximation shares similar intuition with Dropout [23] where the not-activated neuron corresponds to the dropped neuron.

To be more specific, in order to approximate $W_{i,j}^{\star}$, for a certain layer m of the MLP network in the SA layer i, we multiply its weight matrix W_{i_m} with probability vector P_{i_m} to simulate activation of neuron nodes during inference. Considering a 3-layer MLP network in SA layer i, we approximate calculation of $W_{i,i+1}^{\star}$ by

$$M_i = (P_{i_3} \odot (W_{i_3} \cdot (P_{i_2} \odot (W_{i_2} \cdot (P_{i_1} \odot W_{i_1}))))) \cdot X = W_{i,i+1}^{\star} \cdot X, \qquad (9)$$

in which $\cdot$ and $\odot$ represent matrix- and element-wise multiplication.

Similarly, we estimate $W_{i-1,i}^{\star}$ and take it into Eq. (7) to calculate $I_{i-1,i}$ and $D_{i-1,i}$ with almost no extra effort.

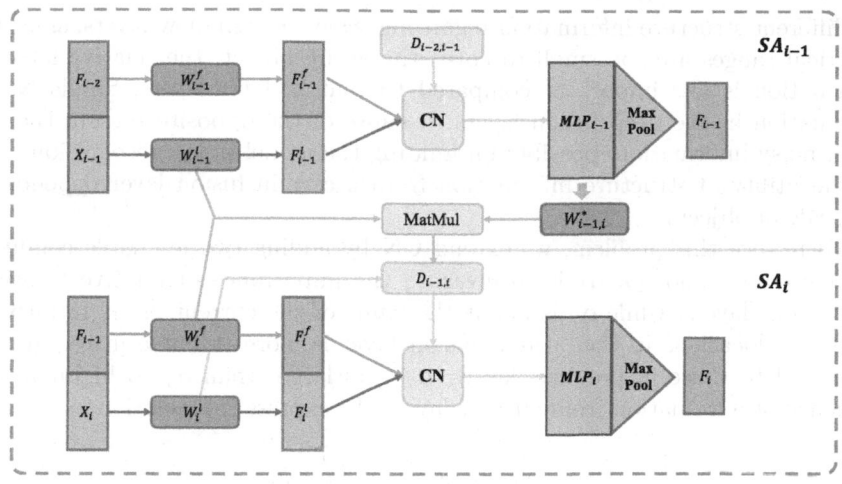

Fig. 5. Illustration of CN module in SA layer i.

4.2   Channel Normalization

After deriving $D_{i,j}$, we detail our channel normalization as follows. The main purpose of calculating $D_{i,j}$ is to balance the influence of structural information from different fusion layers on the final 3D representation. Apparently, if for all fusion layers $(i \geq 1)$, $D_{i-1,i}$ equals to 1, $D_{i,j}$ always reaches 1 for all $i,j(i \leq j)$. Therefore, the best choice to align the influence is to calculate F_i as

$$D_{i-1,i} = \frac{I_{i-1,i}}{I_{i,i}} = \frac{\left\| W_i^f \cdot W_{i-1,i}^\star \cdot W_{i-1}^l \right\|}{\left\| W_i^l \right\|},$$

$$F_i = M_i(F_i^l + \frac{F_i^f}{D_{i-1,i}}),$$

(10)

in which we enforce $D_{i-1,i}$ to be 1.

We name this new operation as channel normalization (CN), which is visualized in Fig. 5. There are two main advantages of our proposed CN compared to former SOTA modules. First, compared to original SA layers in PointNet++, we do not introduce extra parameters. Second, for any fusion layer i in the network, our solution greatly reduces the gap between the values of all $D_{i,j}$ and 1, which is illustrated in Table 1.

Put differently, in any SA layer, the effect of relative locations from the current layer is the same as those from previous layers. Since relative locations from all fusion layers in the network contribute the same in the final features, they maintain structure information from every fusion layer, which benefits the model in recognizing objects with a variety of scales.

It may be ideal to set $D_{i-1,i}$ close to 1. But in this case, not all structure information from different fusion layers is equal. Actually, fusion layers are bound for different structure information regarding scales. For shallow layers, since the spherical ranges are too small to cover the entire object, the relative location information is less important compared to that in later layers. Similarly, for information in the deep fusion layers, because of the opposite reason, there is much noisy information, possibly misguiding the model in the recognition task. So the utility of structure information from a certain fusion layer depends on the scale of objects.

To resolve this problem, we extend CN by adding two learnable condition parameters α_1 and α_2. α_1 is to measure the importance of relative locations in previous layers, while α_2 is about the value of the current layer. Intuitively, if relative locations in the current fusion layer is more valuable in recognition compared to those in previous layers, α_2 gets larger than α_1 to highlight the influence of information from current layer. We express this relation as

$$F_i = M_i(\alpha_2 F_i^l + \alpha_1 \frac{F_i^f}{D_{i-1,i}}), \tag{11}$$

where F_i is the result after channel normalization in the i-th fusion layer.

5   Experiments

We conduct extensive experiments on a series of core 3D recognition tasks to verify the effectiveness of our CN and prove that reducing $D_{i,j}$, where $(i \leq j)$, is helpful for learning structure information at different scales. These experiments consist of classification on ModelNet40 [30] dataset, part segmentation on ShapeNet [30] and detection on KITTI [4] dataset. If not specified otherwise, all fusion layers in our model are the combination of SA layers and CN.

5.1   Classification on ModelNet40

We evaluate the classification accuracy of our model on the ModelNet40 dataset. This dataset contains 12,311 CAD models with 9,843 training shapes and 2,468 testing shapes in 40 different classes. For fair comparison, we follow the configuration in former papers by sampling 1,024 points uniformly for each model and by normalizing them to a unit ball. During training, we apply random translation and scaling on the point cloud, and keep the same training schedule as PointNet++. We do not apply any voting operation in the testing phase and compare our model with SOTA 3D recognition frameworks in Table 2.

It shows that our CN module outperforms the PointNet++ baseline by a large margin and achieves the new SOTA results on recognition by raw point cloud data. We also provide a light-weight single scale grouping (SSG) model, in which there is only one spherical range for a single fusion layer. It also draws great improvement compared to PointNet++ baseline and outperforms RS-CNN (SSG) by 0.7%. These results clearly demonstrate the power of our CN module.

Table 2. Classification accuracy compared with SOTA methods on the ModelNet40 dataset. "PN2", "MSG", and "SSG" represent PointNet++ baseline, multi-scale grouping and single-scale grouping respectively. "norm" means using the normal vectors from the mesh models as input.

Methods	Input	Point numbers	Accuracy (%)
PointNet [19]	xyz	1024	89.2
Spec-GCN [27]	xyz	1024	91.5
PointCNN [10]	xyz	1024	91.7
DGCNN [28]	xyz	1024	92.2
PointConv [29]	xyz, norm	1024	92.5
RS-CNN [14] (SSG)	xyz	1024	92.2
RS-CNN [14] (MSG)	xyz	1024	92.9
PN2 [20]	xyz	1024	90.7
PN2 + CN (SSG)	xyz	1024	92.9
PN2 + CN (MSG)	xyz	1024	**93.3**

5.2   Segmentation on ShapeNet

We also expriment with 3D segmentation on the ShapeNet part segmentation dataset [30]. We take PointNet++ as our baseline and add the CN module to each SA layer. The comparison between CN models and other 3D recognition methods are listed in Table 3. We use two CN baseline models here. In the "CN" model, we directly apply CN to each SA layer in the original PointNet++ model. In "CN2", two more long-range skip connections are added to the "CN" model as that of [14] – it is for structure information loss during upsampling. The experiments show that our CN module promotes the PointNet++ baseline by 2% in terms of class mIoU without any extra parameters.

5.3   Detection on KITTI Dataset

The KITTI [4] dataset contains 7,481 training point clouds and 7,518 testing point clouds in three different categories of Car, Pedestrian and Cyclist. In each class, there are three difficulty levels of "Easy", "Moderate" and "Hard", for distinguishing among objects with regard to depth to camera and occlusion. Our baseline model is 3DSSD [32], which is the SOTA single-stage 3D object detector presented in Table 4. It uses PointNet++ with multiple SA layers as the backbone.

For fair comparison, our model is trained under the same configuration as 3DSSD, including time schedule, data augmentation, input point cloud size etc. As shown in Table 4, our CN module significantly improves the detection accuracy of 3DSSD, especially on easy cases, which mainly contain cars close to the camera. For these cars with a shorter range, the LiDAR camera captures their

612   Z. Yang et al.

Table 3. Comparison among different 3D segmentation methods. "CN" is modified based on original PointNet++ baseline and "CN2" adds two more long-range connections as [14].

Methods	Types	Numbers	Class mIoU (%)	Instance mIoU (%)
Kd-Net [6]	Points	4k	77.4	82.3
PointNet [19]	Points	2k	80.4	83.7
SPLATNet [24]	–	–	82.0	84.6
KCNet [21]	Points	2k	82.2	84.7
PointConv [29]	Points, normal	2k	82.8	85.7
RS-CNN [14]	Points	2k	84.0	**86.2**
PN2 [20]	Points, normal	2k	81.9	85.1
CN	Points	2k	83.9	85.8
CN2	Points	2k	**84.3**	**86.2**

Table 4. Results on KITTI test set in class "Car". State-of-the-art single-stage object detector results are drawn from official benchmark. "Sens." means sensors used by the method. "L" and "R" represent using LiDAR and RGB images respectively.

Methods	Sens.	AP_{BEV}(%)			AP_{3D}(%)		
		Easy	Mod	Hard	Easy	Mod	Hard
ContFuse [11]	R + L	94.07	85.35	75.88	83.68	68.78	61.67
SECOND [31]	L	91.81	86.37	81.04	84.65	75.96	68.71
PointPillars [8]		90.07	86.56	82.81	82.58	74.31	68.99
TANet [15]		91.58	86.54	81.19	84.39	75.94	68.82
HRI-VoxelFPN [7]		92.75	87.21	79.82	85.64	76.70	69.44
OHS [1]		93.59	87.95	83.21	88.12	78.34	73.49
3DSSD [32]	L	92.66	89.02	**85.86**	88.36	79.57	74.55
3DSSD [32] + CN		**94.51**	**90.50**	**85.86**	**90.55**	**79.89**	**76.31**

surface points well and brings good-quality information in multiple structure levels of wheel, door, and car, for example.

The original SA layers in PointNet++ only focus on the relative locations in shallower level, which mainly include small hints like wheel or door. Larger structure information such as the whole car, is more likely to be ignored. This procedure does not make full use of the high-quality information given by the LiDAR camera and hampers the model from further improvement. With our CN module, the network exploits both local tiny structure and global objects. It greatly benefits the model in boosting detection performance.

We also compare the performance of 3DSSD with PointNet++, RS-CNN and CN. Their 3D mAPs are 82.37%, 82.88% and 85.01% respectively among KITTI moderate val set on class "Car". As listed, our CN model draws much better performance compared to its RS-CNN counterpart. We analyze its reason as below. As illustrated in Table 1, in these fusion layers, $D_{0,j}$ consistently increases with regard to j. It means the deeper the fusion layer is, the less effective its relative locations are. Since $D_{0,j}$ in RS-CNN increases rapidly, they have their limitation in gathering structure information from deep layers. In contrast, our CN rescales previous features by $D_{i-1,i}$, making the model much more capable to gather information of deep neural networks and bringing better performance compared to other fusion layers.

5.4 Effect of Condition Parameters

This ablation study is conducted on the KITTI dataset since the detection task can well reflect the model's ability in extracting multi-scale structure information. All AP results in this subsection are calculated in class "Car".

In our channel normalization, after rescaling previous features by $D_{i-1,i}$, we use two extra learnable condition parameters α_1 and α_2 to enable the model to gather structure information in a certain fusion layer. The consequence is the following. If previous structure information plays an important role in recognition, α_1 becomes large. Otherwise, if the current relative location works better, α_2 is greater.

Table 5. Condition parameters in different fusion layers. "Spherical Range" means the scale of structure information for this layer, which is usually expressed by the radius of the ball.

	Layer1	Layer2	Layer3	Layer4
Spherical range (m)	0.8	1.6	3.2	6.4
α_1	0.148	0.721	1.392	1.295
α_2	0.686	0.868	0.293	0.143

We train a 4-layer 3DSSD with our CN module, and list the learned condition parameters in Table 5. In the first layer, since there is no structure information in previous features, α_2 is greater than α_1 to capture more relative location information in the current layer. In layer 2, since the mean size of a car in the KITTI dataset is ($l = 3.9\,\text{m}, h = 1.6\,\text{m}, w = 1.6\,\text{m}$). With radius 1.6 m, the layer covers the whole object. Therefore, α_2 is still greater than α_1 to capture features for the whole object. Differently, in layers 3 and 4, spherical ranges are much larger than those of cars, making α_1 much greater than α_2 to avoid these unnecessary features. We also compare the mAP performance between pure CN and CN with condition parameters. Their performances are 84.60% and 85.01% respectively which demonstrates the effectiveness of the condition parameters and manifests that always balancing is not optimal.

6   Conclusion

In this paper, we have analyzed the bottleneck of explicit fusion layers in SOTA hierarchical 3D recognition networks regarding extracting multilayer structure information. We provided "difference ratio" to measure the contribution of relative locations among different fusion layers on the final generated features. By comparing difference ratios among different SOTA methods, we find that when this factor is closer to 1, the learned features can maintain more structure information from different levels and extract more powerful 3D representations. Based on this observation, we developed a new technique "channel normalization", which enables the recognition models to fully exploit multilayer structure information and further boosts their performance without extra parameters.

References

1. Chen, Q., Sun, L., Wang, Z., Jia, K., Yuille, A.: Object as hotspots: an anchor-free 3D object detection approach via firing of hotspots (2019)
2. Chen, Y., Liu, S., Shen, X., Jia, J.: Fast point R-CNN. In: Proceedings of the ICCV (2019)
3. Feng, Y., Zhang, Z., Zhao, X., Ji, R., Gao, Y.: GVCNN: group-view convolutional neural networks for 3D shape recognition. In: Proceedings of the CVPR (2018)
4. Geiger, A., Lenz, P., Stiller, C., Urtasun, R.: Vision meets robotics: the KITTI dataset. Int. J. Robot. Res. **32**, 1231–1237 (2013)
5. Guo, H., Wang, J., Gao, Y., Li, J., Lu, H.: Multi-view 3D object retrieval with deep embedding network. IEEE Trans. Image Process. **25**, 5526–5537 (2016)
6. Klokov, R., Lempitsky, V.S.: Escape from cells: deep Kd-networks for the recognition of 3D point cloud models. In: Proceedings of the ICCV (2017)
7. Kuang, H., Wang, B., An, J., Zhang, M., Zhang, Z.: Voxel-FPN: multi-scale voxel feature aggregation in 3D object detection from point clouds. Sensors **20**, 704 (2020)
8. Lang, A.H., Vora, S., Caesar, H., Zhou, L., Yang, J., Beijbom, O.: PointPillars: fast encoders for object detection from point clouds. In: Proceedings of the CVPR (2019)
9. Li, R., Li, X., Fu, C., Cohen-Or, D., Heng, P.: PU-GAN: a point cloud upsampling adversarial network. CoRR (2019)
10. Li, Y., Bu, R., Sun, M., Chen, B.: PointCNN. CoRR (2018)
11. Liang, M., Yang, B., Wang, S., Urtasun, R.: Deep continuous fusion for multisensor 3D object detection. In: Ferrari, V., Hebert, M., Sminchisescu, C., Weiss, Y. (eds.) ECCV 2018. LNCS, vol. 11220, pp. 663–678. Springer, Cham (2018). https://doi.org/10.1007/978-3-030-01270-0_39
12. Liu, X., Qi, C.R., Guibas, L.J.: FlowNet3D: learning scene flow in 3D point clouds. In: Proceedings of the CVPR (2019)
13. Liu, Y., Fan, B., Meng, G., Lu, J., Xiang, S., Pan, C.: DensePoint: learning densely contextual representation for efficient point cloud processing. In: Proceedings of the ICCV (2019)
14. Liu, Y., Fan, B., Xiang, S., Pan, C.: Relation-shape convolutional neural network for point cloud analysis. In: Proceedings of the CVPR (2019)

15. Liu, Z., Zhao, X., Huang, T., Hu, R., Zhou, Y., Bai, X.: TANet: robust 3D object detection from point clouds with triple attention. AAAI (2020)
16. Mao, J., Wang, X., Li, H.: Interpolated convolutional networks for 3D point cloud understanding. In: Proceedings of the ICCV (2019)
17. Maturana, D., Scherer, S.: VoxNet: a 3D convolutional neural network for real-time object recognition. In: Proceedings of the IROS (2015)
18. Qi, C.R., Liu, W., Wu, C., Su, H., Guibas, L.J.: Frustum pointnets for 3D object detection from RGB-D data. CoRR (2017)
19. Qi, C.R., Su, H., Mo, K., Guibas, L.J.: PointNet: deep learning on point sets for 3D classification and segmentation. In: Proceedings of the CVPR (2017)
20. Qi, C.R., Yi, L., Su, H., Guibas, L.J.: PointNet++: deep hierarchical feature learning on point sets in a metric space. In: Proceedings of the NIPS (2017)
21. Shen, Y., Feng, C., Yang, Y., Tian, D.: Mining point cloud local structures by kernel correlation and graph pooling. In: Proceedings of the CVPR (2018)
22. Shi, S., Wang, X., Li, H.: PointRCNN: 3D object proposal generation and detection from point cloud. In: Proceedings of the CVPR (2019)
23. Srivastava, N., Hinton, G.E., Krizhevsky, A., Sutskever, I., Salakhutdinov, R.: Dropout: a simple way to prevent neural networks from overfitting. J. Mach. Learn. Res. **15**, 1929–1958 (2014)
24. Su, H., et al.: SPLATNet: sparse lattice networks for point cloud processing. In: Proceedings of the CVPR (2018)
25. Su, H., Maji, S., Kalogerakis, E., Learned-Miller, E.G.: Multi-view convolutional neural networks for 3D shape recognition. In: Proceedings of the ICCV (2015)
26. Thomas, H., Qi, C.R., Deschaud, J., Marcotegui, B., Goulette, F., Guibas, L.J.: KPConv: flexible and deformable convolution for point clouds. In: Proceedings of the ICCV (2019)
27. Wang, C., Samari, B., Siddiqi, K.: Local spectral graph convolution for point set feature learning. In: Ferrari, V., Hebert, M., Sminchisescu, C., Weiss, Y. (eds.) ECCV 2018. LNCS, vol. 11208, pp. 56–71. Springer, Cham (2018). https://doi.org/10.1007/978-3-030-01225-0_4
28. Wang, Y., Sun, Y., Liu, Z., Sarma, S.E., Bronstein, M.M., Solomon, J.M.: Dynamic graph CNN for learning on point clouds. ACM Trans. Graph. **38**, 1–12 (2019)
29. Wu, W., Qi, Z., Li, F.: PointConv: deep convolutional networks on 3D point clouds. In: Proceedings of the CVPR (2019)
30. Wu, Z., et al.: 3D shapeNets: a deep representation for volumetric shapes. In: Proceedings of the CVPR (2015)

31. Yan, Y., Mao, Y., Li, B.: Second: sparsely embedded convolutional detection. Sensors **18**, 3337 (2018)
32. Yang, Z., Sun, Y., Liu, S., Jia, J.: 3DSSD: point-based 3D single stage object detector (2020)
33. Yang, Z., Sun, Y., Liu, S., Shen, X., Jia, J.: STD: sparse-to-dense 3D object detector for point cloud. In: Proceedings of the ICCV (2019)

Rethinking the Defocus Blur Detection Problem and a Real-Time Deep DBD Model

Ning Zhang[1,2] and Junchi Yan[1,2(✉)]

[1] Department of Computer Science and Engineering, Shanghai Jiao Tong University,
Shanghai , China
ningzh6610@gmail.com, yanjunchi@sjtu.edu.cn
[2] MoE Key Lab of Artificial Intelligence, AI Institute, Shanghai Jiao Tong
University, Shanghai, China

Abstract. Defocus blur detection (DBD) is a classical low level vision task. It has recently attracted attention focusing on designing complex convolutional neural networks (CNN) which make full use of both low level features and high level semantic information. The heavy networks used in these methods lead to low processing speed, resulting difficulty in applying to real-time applications. In this work, we propose novel perspectives on the DBD problem and design convenient approach to build a real-time cost-effective DBD model. First, we observe that the semantic information does not always relate to and sometimes mislead the blur detection. We start from the essential characteristics of the DBD problem and propose a data augmentation method accordingly to inhibit the semantic information and enforce the model to learn image blur related features rather than the semantic features. A novel self-supervision training objective is proposed to enhance the model training consistency and stability. Second, by rethinking the relationship between defocus blur detection and salience detection, we identify two previously ignored but common scenarios, based on which we design a hard mining strategy to enhance the DBD model. By using the proposed techniques, our model that uses a slightly modified U-Net as backbone, improves the processing speed by more than 3 times and performs competitively against state of the art methods. Ablation study is also conducted to verify the effectiveness of each part of our proposed methods.

Keywords: Defocus blur detection · Self-supervision · Hard-mining

1 Introduction

Deep learning techniques have promoted explosive growth of many computer vision tasks including but not restricted to image classification [17], object location and detection [14], semantic segmentation [1], salience detection [5]. However,

Work was partly supported by National Key Research and Development Program of China 2018AAA0100704, NSFC (61972250, U19B2035), and SJTU Global Strategic Partnership Fund (2020 SJTU-CORNELL).

© Springer Nature Switzerland AG 2020
A. Vedaldi et al. (Eds.): ECCV 2020, LNCS 12355, pp. 617–632, 2020.
https://doi.org/10.1007/978-3-030-58607-2_36

Fig. 1. Examples of blurry images from [16] (zoom in for details). The left half shows the motion blur with a mask (black area denotes blur). This paper focuses on the right half case: defocus blur detection. As highlighted around the red bounding box, yellow leaves show similar semantics, while both in-focus and defocused regions appear. (Color figure online)

the performance of above algorithms are related to the quality of images and blur images with lots of noise can lead to a sharp decline in accuracy. Thus blur detection is an fundamental yet challenging topic in computer vision area. It detects the degraded area with loss of image details, which is the basic and critical pre-process step for deblurring. As shown in Fig. 1, image blur can be generally classified into two types: motion blur and out of focus blur (or defocus blur) [16]. Object moving definitely accounts for motion blur. The defocus blur is caused by the limited depth of fields of camera lens. Objects located in too remote or too close distance are out of focus and blurry. The defocus blur is ubiquitous for pictures captured by digital cameras, especially by cell phone cameras. In this paper, we pay attention to the detection of defocus blur areas. Our work is motivated by two important insights which have been ignored and probably misused by previous works. 1) the semantic information does not always relate to and sometimes mislead the blur detection. 2) the salience detection, which is a related topic with DBD, can be used to help the mining of hard occasions in DBD. Based on these two important insights, we designed clever and convenient approaches to solve the DBD problem.

Defocus blur detection methods can generally be divided into two categories: traditional algorithms based on handcrafted features [10–12,15,16,18,20,22,26, 27,30,31] and deep learning algorithms based on CNN [6,21,25,28,29]. The former ones usually apply statistics of gradient or high frequency information to differentiate blur, considering that blur areas are usually smoother than clear areas. They can work for simple cases effectively and endure lousy results for complex scenes. The phenomena are related to the following reasons.

At first, although smoothing or filtering images can unavoidably lead to image blur, we could not judge the clarity just by gradients. Some objects such as sky and ground are always with low gradients all the time, no matter they are focused or not. Besides, some areas with complex texture and high frequency could be out of focus. There are lots of leaves marked in a red rectangle in the second row of Fig. 1. These leaves have similar textures and gradient information, however parts of leaves are out of focused and parts are not. Thus it is unreasonable and not the case for practical application to distinguish focus area just using gradient distributions or frequency information.

Secondly, CNN based methods are more flexible to combine multi-scale of information and multi-level of features together to detect blurry. Multi branches and shortcut fuel information flow and information fusion in deep networks. CNN can fuse the results of different filters and extract discriminative features. These characteristics of CNN lead to more powerful feature extracting than traditional algorithms based on handcrafted features.

The authors in [28] propose a multi-stream bottom-top-bottom fully convolutional network (BTBnet) to detect defocus blur. They design a recurrent reconstruction strategy which fuses low level cues and high level information to improve the performance. Although the BTBnet achieves impressive results, their large computation cost hinders their wide applications. In [25], a dilated fully convolutional neural network is applied to widen the network without increasing the parameters. A deep defocus blur detector cross ensemble network (CEnet) is proposed in [29]. Two groups of defocus blur detectors are alternatively optimized to enhance diversity in CEnet. While in [21], a deep neural network is devised which recurrently fuses and refines multi-scale deep features (DeFusionnet) for defocus blur detection.

Most of the existing works try to improve the accuracy of the DBD models by designing deeper or wider networks, while other works tried to decrease the computational cost and increase the processing speed of those models. These approaches emphasize too much on the structure of the network and employ the semantic information to detect the defocus blur region. However, we have an insight that the semantic information in the images does not always relate to the blur region. We can observe from Fig. 1 that the regions of similar semantic (yellow leaves) can be either blur or clear. This results in unsatisfactory performance of those approaches. In this paper, we rethink the DBD problem, explore its characteristics and its relationship with related topics. To enforce the neural network to learn the defocus blur related features, rather than the semantic features, we propose a novel data augmentation method by taking advantage of the transition-invariant property of the defocus blur region. A self-supervision objective is proposed to enhance the robustness of the model. In addition, we have another insight that the salient detection can help the mining of the hard occasions in the DBD. It is difficult to detect the in-focus region in the non-salient region, and to detect the defocus region in the salient region, especially when a single object contains both the in-focus part and defocus part. Based on this insight, we proposed a novel hard mining policy to train the neural network. With the proposed method, a simple U-Net [13] with slight modification performed competitively and even better than most of the state of the arts. In addition, our method achieves notable improvement on the processing speed.

Conclusively, the contributions of this paper are as follows.

- We put forward two basic observations, which have been relatively ignored in previous research. First, the semantic information does not always relate to, and sometimes even can mislead the DBD. Existing deep learning based methods are mostly devoted to designing wider and/or deeper networks to learn the semantic features. While little study has been made to consider the inherent mechanism of the DBD problem. Second, we take a closer look at the connection between the salience detection and DBD, and find that the salient information can help to locate the hard occasions in DBD.

- Based on the first observation, we propose a novel data augmentation technique to inhibit the semantic information and enforce the neural network to learn the blur related features rather than semantic features. A self-supervision objective is devised to enhance the consistency of training. To our best knowledge, this is the first work to incorporate the blur related constraints into the objective for deep learning.
- Based on the second observation, we design a hard mining approach to cope with two hard occasions, which are previously overlooked while practically common: 1) defocus and salient region; 2) in-focus but non-salient region. These two scenarios are more difficult to identify from other scenarios. We propose a hard mining strategy for these two cases. Our resulting method can handle these two cases effectively without sacrificing the performance on other scenarios. It is empirically shown that the hard mining policy can improve the performance notably, especially on the regions of depth boundary.
- With the proposed objective, even by using a simple network, i.e. a slightly modified U-Net, we can achieve competitive and even superior performances, with improved processing speed by more than 3 times. Experimental results show that the proposed method performs competitively. We also conducted an ablation study to verify the effectiveness of self-supervision objective and our hard mining technique.

2   Related Works

In general, defocus blur detectors can be divided into two categories: traditional methods using hand-designed features and deep learning methods.

2.1   Traditional Methods

The blurry images are relatively smoother in some scenes. Inspired from that, some researchers made full use of gradient information or frequency information to detect blur. The works [2,19] detect the DBD using the radio of strong gradient components in an image patch. The authors in [11] design special kernels to measure image sharpness. In [18], singular value distribution and gradient distribution work together for blur detection. Multi-scale high frequency information and sorted transform of coefficients of gradient magnitudes are fused to detect blur in [3]. Fourier domain features are applied to detect image sharpness and a public blur detection dataset has been built in [16]. The authors in [20] obtain coarse-to-fine blurred region using spectral and spatial information. In [23], image patch ranks are fully used to estimate blur map.

Although hand designed features have made contributions to detect blur regions, they often fail in complex scenes. Compared with traditional algorithms, CNN methods can fuse multi-scale multi-level information to different blurred and clear image regions and outperform most of hand designed methods.

2.2   Deep Network Based Methods

In [12], hand designed features and deep learning features are used together to estimate blur region. However, these deep learning features are extracted in local patches and time consuming. Subsequently, more carefully-designed CNN structures are proposed for DBD. The authors in [28] propose a multi-stream bottom-top-bottom fully convolutional networks to estimate the probability of each pixel being out-of-focus and blurry. It is a fusion and recurrent reconstruction network which is deep and wide. It integrates both low-level and high-level information to handle blur images. [25] apply a dilated fully convolutional neural network which increases the field-of-view without increasing parameters. The cross-ensemble network is designed to obtain multiple defocus blur detectors with less computation cost [29]. In [21], a novel network which fuses deep features and suppressed background clutter is also devised.

3   Proposed Method

3.1   Approach Overview

It is sometimes assumed that CNN can make full use of semantic information and this information benefit detection performance [21, 28]. While this assumption may not always hold. Image regions with similar semantic information can be easily broken into in-focused and out-of-focus parts, which is a common occurrence for images captured by macro lens. As shown in the right half in Fig. 1, there is a clear boundary between the focused paper glass and defocus leaves. In this respect, semantic information is beneficial to distinguish sharp object from the blur. However the leaves in red rectangle are blurry due to out of focus and other leaves are clear. All of them are considered as leaves and can not be distinguished according to semantic information. It means that there is no necessary relation between the semantic information and the defocus detection. The semantic information sometimes disturb the judgment of defocus or not. We should pay attention to the image clarity itself. In addition, we identify two hard occasions for the DBD problem: 1) detection of the defocus blur region at the salient region, 2) detection of the in-focus region at the non-salient region. Based on the two insights, we propose 1) a novel data augmentation method to inhibit the semantic information, and a self-supervision objective to enhance the model consistency. The proposed strategy not only expands the training but also reduces the affect of semantic information. 2) a hard mining strategy by taking advantage of the relation between the salience detection and DBD.

We expound our algorithm in the following three parts. First, we explain the data augmentation strategy and the self-supervision loss. Then the hard mining strategy is introduced by analyzing the relation of blur detection and the salience detection. Finally, we present our network which is a slightly modified U-Net.

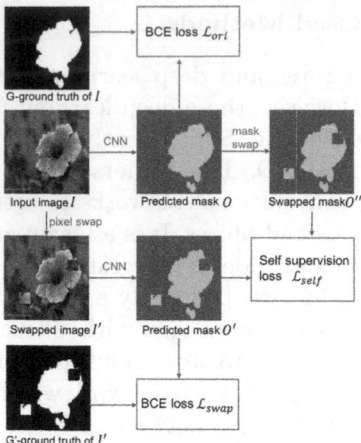

Fig. 2. Self-supervision learning scheme. For input image I, we obtain the swapped input I' by swapping the pixel values of two patches. The predicted mask of swapped input image O' should be same with O'' which is the swapped mask of original image.

3.2 Data Augmentation and Self-supervision Loss

As our goal is to detect the blur region, rather than the blur objects, it is more important to learn the image clarity features than the semantic features. For a patch in a given image, whether it is blur or not is irrelevant to its location in the image, neither relevant to what object it belongs to. A clear patch remains to be clear wherever we move it in an image. Similarly, a blur patch is still blur even we paste it to a clear region.

Take Fig. 2 as an example, it gets the focus on the flower, and all the background areas are out of focus and blurry. If we move the position of flower, it would lead to some artifacts and sharpness on the boundary. However, this action did not cause the flower to be blurry or the backgrounds to be clear. If we moved parts of flower, it would break the integrity of flower and inhibit the semantic information. However, this action still would not change the clarity of the flower parts.

Formally speaking, for an input image I, we randomly choose two patches with the same size and swapped the pixel value of one patches for the other. Then we got the swapped image I', as shown in Fig. 2. G and G' are corresponding ground truth of the image I and the swapped image I', respectively. O and O' represent the predicted masks for the image I and the swapped image I'.

Most existing DBD works train models to minimize the distance between the groudtruth G and the predicted blurry mask O. The distance is computed as the binary cross entropy (BCE) between G and O. This can be expressed as:

$$\mathcal{L}_{ori} = \sum_{i=1}^{h} \sum_{j=1}^{w} -G(x,y) * \log(O(x,y)) \tag{1}$$

where, h and w stand for the height and width of images respectively. While (x, y) represents the coordinates of images.

In this paper, we enlarge the training set tremendously by swapping the image patches. In this way, we should also train the model on the augmented data to minimize the distance between the swapped ground truth G' and the swapped predicted mask O'. This is represented as Eq. (2).

$$\mathcal{L}_{aug} = \sum_{i=1}^{h} \sum_{j=1}^{w} -G'(x, y) * \log(O'(x, y)) \tag{2}$$

In addition, according to our analysis, the predicted mask O' should be a derivative of predicted mask O. For robustness, the transition of input images should lead to the same transition of the output mask. This can be stated as:

$$O = \Phi_\theta(I); \quad f(O) = \Phi_\theta(f(I)) \tag{3}$$

where Φ_θ is a neural network of DBD parametered by θ. $f(I) = I'$ and $f(O) = O''$ are the patch transition operation. In our case, the swapped output O'' and the output of the swapped image O' should be same for a robust DBD system. Inspired by this, we introduced the self-supervision loss to enhance the robustness of our model. The similarity of the output O'' and the output O' are calculated by L1 loss.

$$\mathcal{L}_{self} = \frac{1}{h * w} \sum_{i=1}^{h} \sum_{j=1}^{w} |O'(x, y)) - O''(x, y)| \tag{4}$$

The total loss for the proposed self-supervision method is the weighted sum of the above losses.

$$\mathcal{L}_{ts} = \mathcal{L}_{ori} + \mathcal{L}_{aug} + \lambda_s \mathcal{L}_{self} \tag{5}$$

where λ_s is the weight for the self-supervision term. As in our training settings, the number of input original image I and the number of input augmented image I' are always equal, we simply keep the weights of $\mathcal{L}_{ori}$ and $\mathcal{L}_{aug}$ to be 1. And we only adjust the weight λ_s for $\mathcal{L}_{self}$. The patch size used in this paper is 64×64.

3.3   Hard Mining

It is hard to identify the blur of the boundary area, when the clear and the blurred area mingle, especially when a single object contains both focused part and defocus part. DBD algorithms do not have satisfactory performances in above two cases [28,29]. In this paper, we propose a hard mining algorithm to improve the performances.

By analyzing the DBD related topics, we observe that the salient detection is closely related to but inconsistent with the DBD problem. Salient detection can help to locate the regions of the above difficult scenarios.

Specifically, salience detection is to identify the most visually distinctive regions in images. Figure 3 shows the difference between the focused area and

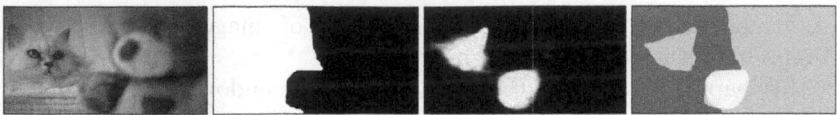

Fig. 3. The relation between the focus detection and salience detection. From the first column to the last column are: the input images (collected in [28]), the ground truth of DBD (black area denotes blur), the salience detection result of [5] (black area denotes non-salient), and the difference between the focused detection and salience detection (yellow area denotes 'salient but out-of-focus', and red area denotes 'in-focus but not salient', blue area denotes 'salient and in-focus' and 'non-salient and out-of-focus'). (Color figure online)

salient area. The first column shows the image with out-of-focus area collected by [28]. The second column is the in-focus area of this image. Both the cat and its background are in-focus. The third column contains the salience detection result of one of state of the art [5]. The face of the cat and the paw of the bear is detected as salient. The last column shows the difference of the focus area and the salient area. This difference help us to locate the depth boundary and ignore the semantic information.

According to the above analysis, we creatively proposed a region based hard mining method for DBD. At first, we calculate the salient detection areas by the algorithms in [5], which is a state of the art salient detection method. Secondly, we compute the hard mining region H as 1) the out-of-focus and salient region 2) in-focus but not salient region. Formally, $H = (S \cup F) - (S \cap F)$, where H denotes the hard mining region, S and F denote the salient region and in-focus region, respectively.

By giving different weights to the intersection and the union, we realize a hard mining algorithm based on pixel position. In this way, the loss functions in Eq. (1) and Eq. (2) should be changed into Eq. (6) and Eq. (7), respectively.

$$\mathcal{L}_{weighted} = \sum_{i=1}^{h} \sum_{j=1}^{w} -W(x,y) * G(x,y) * \log(O(x,y)) \tag{6}$$

$$\mathcal{L}_{weightedaug} = \sum_{i=1}^{h} \sum_{j=1}^{w} -W'(x,y) * G'(x,y) * \log(O'(x,y)) \tag{7}$$

where $W(x,y)$ represents the weights based on intersection and difference. $W'(x,y)$ means the swapped weights according to pixel value swap of input images.

In this way, the final loss function of proposed algorithm is defined as follows.

$$\mathcal{L}_{total} = \mathcal{L}_{weighted} + \mathcal{L}_{weightedaug} + \lambda_s \mathcal{L}_{self} \tag{8}$$

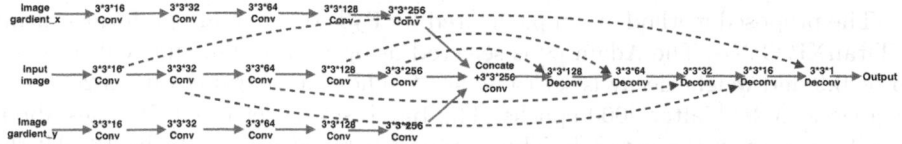

Fig. 4. The backbone network used in this paper. This is a modified U-Net to facilitate the flow of the horizontal and vertical gradient information.

3.4 Backbone Network

We briefly introduce the network used in this paper. As shown in Fig. 4, it is inspired by the design of U-Net [13]. The "$3*3*t$ Conv" module consists of two convolutional filers, two Relu [9] layers and two BN [7] layers and one pooling layer. The convolution kernel size of this module is 3×3 and the number of filters is t. The strides of all the "$3*3*t$ Conv" modules are 2 except for the one before concatenation. Many traditional algorithms apply gradient information for DBD. Inspired that, partial derivatives in both X and Y direction are encoded in our network. Both encoded partial derivatives and the image are concatenated at the end of the encoding part. "$3*3*256$" module reduces the number of redundant filters and fuses features. After that, a dropout layer [4] is added and the dropout rate is set to be 0.2.

The dotted arrows in Fig. 4 represent a shortcut from a encoder layer to a decoder layer. "$3*3*t$ Deconv" means that the kernel size for each deconvolution layer [24] is 3×3 and the number of filters is t. The stride of each deconvolution is 2. Since our proposed algorithm is focused on loss design instead of network design, we just apply this popular network for experiments.

4 Experiments

4.1 Experimental Setup

We use two public and popular defocus blur detection datasets for evaluation.

The CUHK dataset [16] consists of 1000 blurry images. Among these, 296 blur images are caused by object motion and 704 images are defocus blur images. We divide the 704 images into training set and testing set, as many researchers do [21,28,29]. There are 604 images randomly selected for training, and the rest are applied to measure the performance in [28,29]. [21] applied top 604 images for training and the last 100 images for testing. To compare with state of the arts, we share the same training set and testing set with [28,29].

The DUT dataset appears in [28]. It contains 1100 images with pixel-wise annotations. 600 images belongs to the training set and 500 images belongs to the testing set. It is relatively more challenging dataset.

The proposed method are implemented by PyTorch, and are performed using 4 TitanXP GPUs. The Adam [8] is selected as optimizer. The momentum is set to be 0.9 and weight decay is set to be $5e^{-4}$. The start learning rate is $2e^{-5}$ and decreases to $2e^{-6}$ after 2000 epochs. The batch size is set to 64. It takes about two days to train the network. The swapped patch size is set to be 16. All the weights of hard mining regions are set to be double weights of other areas.

The training images are resized into 320×320 at first step. After that, we apply horizon mirroring and rotating to augment data. Different from other works [21, 28], no extra data is used to pretrain our model.

Evaluation Metrics. Three metrics are applied to evaluate the performance of proposed method: F-measure, mean absolute error (MAE), F-measure curve by all the thresholds and the Precision-Recall (PR) curve. The output need to be binarized to calculated F-measure and MAE. F-measure is defined by:

$$F_\beta = \frac{(1 + \beta^2) * Precision * Recall}{\beta^2 * Precision + Recall} \tag{9}$$

where $\beta^2 = 0.3$ is employed to emphasize the importance of precision, which represents for the percentage of correctly detected pixels which are focused. The correctly detected pixels is divided by the ground truth number of focused pixels to get Recall. Bigger F-measure means better performance.

The metric MAE denote the average pixel-wise difference between the output results and the ground truth. It is defined as the follow.

$$MAE = \frac{1}{h * w} \sum_{i=1}^{h} \sum_{j=1}^{w} |O(x,y) - G(x,y)| \tag{10}$$

where, O stands for the binarized output and G stands for the ground truth. Smaller MAE represented smaller difference between output and ground truth.

Both F-measure and MAE evaluate the performance of different methods by binarized the outputs at the specific threshold. The F-measure curve and the Precision-Recall curve provide more comprehensive displays of performances. The output are binarized at each point in range of [0, 255] to display the F-measure curve and Precision-Recall curve.

4.2 Comparison with Peer Methods

Compared with traditional methods, deep learning methods achieve better performance for DBD [21, 28, 29]. In this way, we just compare our method with these state-of-the-art algorithms. BTBnet is devised in [28]. BTBnet handles input images with different scales and combines all these information to calculate the possibility of blur. It is complex network and high time costing. After that, the work [29] proposes a deep cross ensemble network (CEnet) which reduces the time cost comparable with BTBnet. As the name implies, CEnet makes full use of diversity of networks to produce accurate results. The authors in [21] present

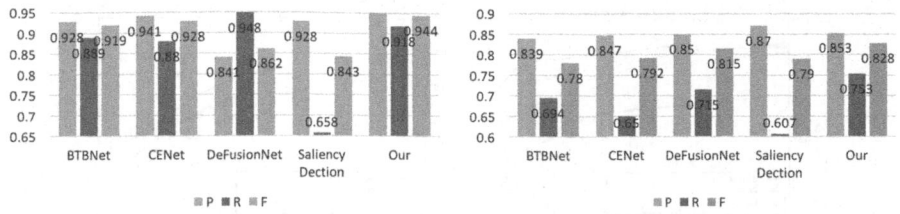

Fig. 5. F-measure of different algorithms. The left plot shows the results over the CUHK dataset. The right plot shows the results over the DUT dataset. P and R stand for precision and recall, respectively. F stands for the F-measure.

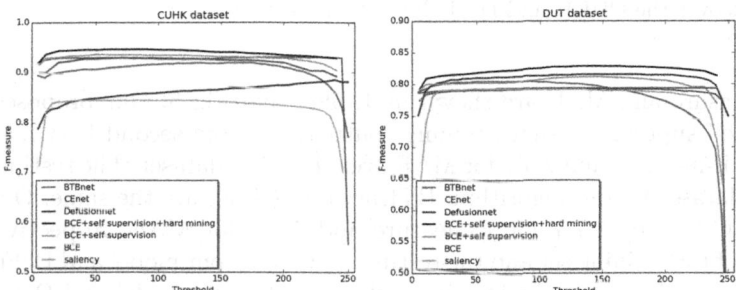

Fig. 6. F-measure by different thresholds of different algorithms. The left plot shows the result over the CUHK dataset. The right plot shows the result over DUT dataset.

Table 1. Comparison of F-measure (the higher the better) and MAE (the lower the better) of different approaches. Two networks (CENet, DeFusionNet) have not released their models hence the exact sizes are unknown and not reported. Best in bold.

Dataset	Metric	Models							
		BTBNet [28]	CENet [29]	DeFusionNet [21]	Salience Detection [5]	BCE+self-supervision+ hard mining	BCE+self-supervision	BCE	BCE without image gradient
CUHK	F-measure↑	0.919	0.928	0.862	0.843	**0.944**	0.933	0.927	0.918
	MAE↓	0.060	0.057	0.111	0.125	**0.053**	0.060	0.066	0.078
DUT	F-measure↑	0.780	0.792	0.815	0.791	**0.828**	0.811	0.793	0.754
	MAE↓	0.127	0.136	0.118	0.151	**0.115**	0.127	0.140	0.163
DUT & CUHK	FPS↑	0.04	15.63	17.86	22.20	**58.82**	**58.82**	**58.82**	112.35
	Model size	200M	–	–	238M	26.73M	26.73M	26.73M	**7.79M**

the DeFusionnet which recurrently fuses and refines multi-scale deep features to detect out-of-focus regions. We just download their results from their project website since they have not released their implementation. As mentioned above, our testing dataset of CUHK dataset is the same with [28,29] and different from [21]. All the above approaches adopt complex networks and their models are pretrained using ImageNet data [9].

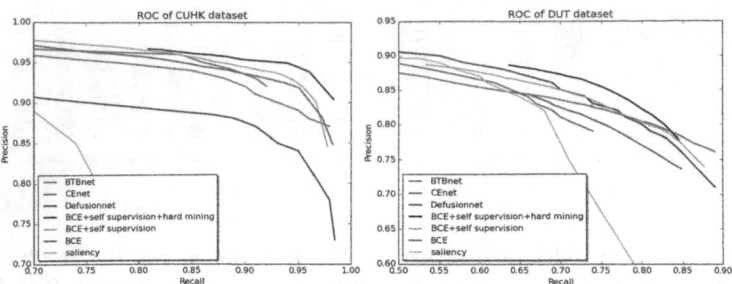

Fig. 7. Precision-Recall curves of different algorithms. The left and right plot shows the result over the CUHK and DUT dataset, respectively.

F-measure and MAE are shown in Table 1 and Fig. 5. Our proposed model (BCE+self supervision+hard mining) outperforms the second best method by 1.6% for F-measure and 2.5% for MAE over the DUT dataset. The testing data of CUHK dataset for our algorithm, BTBnet and CEnet are the same. Our model exceeds CEnet by 1.7% for F-measure and 7.0% for MAE, respectively. The number of the training set and the testing set used by our model and DeFusionnet are the same. However, the images in these set for our model and DeFusionnet are different. Our model beats DeFusionNet by 9.5% for F-measure and 52.3% for MAE. For reference, we also present the salience detection performance on the DBD task, although the salience detection is a different task with the DBD. The salience detection performance is poor on the DBD task over all the metrics.

The F-measure curve and the Precision-Recall curves are shown in and Fig. 6 and Fig. 7, respectively. Our model shows superior performance over most parts of the F-measure curves. Besides, our model generates better results compared with other models over most parts of the Precision-Recall curves.

Figure 8 and Fig. 9 show some comparison examples of different algorithms. Images in Fig. 8 come from the testing set of the DUT dataset and images in Fig. 9 come from the testing set of the CUHK dataset. We can see that the hard mining method help us to identify the boundary of the focus and defocus regions despite whether they belonging to a same object or not. All the algorithms can detect the main parts of focused area. While the competitors can not get accurate boundary in areas where the focus and defocus changed in high frequency. What's worse, the competitors usually fail to detect the focused part of one object which consists of the focused area and defocus area at the same time.

In the testing phase, each input image is resized into 320 × 320 pixels to obtain the final defocus blur map. We and [21] both use a single Nvidia GTX Titan Xp GPU for inference, while [28] and [29] use a GTX1080Ti GPU. These two GPUs have similar processing power. As shown in Table 1, our model is highly efficient with the speed of 58.82 FPS (frames per second), which is 3.29 times faster than the second fastest method named Defusionnet.

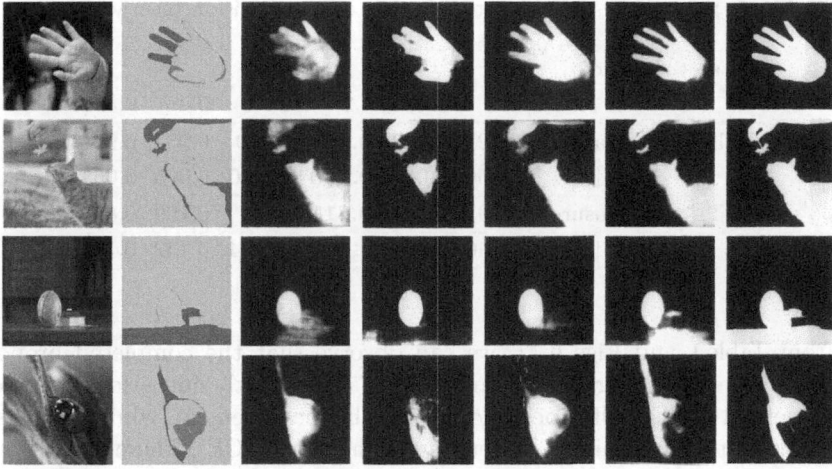

Fig. 8. Examples on DUT (by column): input images, hard mining regions, outputs of BTBnet, CEnet, DeFusionnet, and proposed methods, respectively, and ground truth.

Fig. 9. Examples on CUIIK (left to right): input images, hard mining regions, outputs of BTBnet, outputs of CEnet, outputs of DeFusionnet (the bottom two are not public available), outputs of proposed methods, and ground truth.

4.3   Ablation Analysis

We conduct ablation study to test the effectiveness of the proposed self-supervision objective and the hard mining method. The completed proposed method is denoted as 'BCE+self-supervision+hard mining'. While 'BCE+self-supervision' denotes the comparison method which we remove the hard mining part from the whole proposed method. 'BCE' means that we only use the common BCE objective to train our backbone network. 'BCE without image gradient' denotes that the image input gradient information is removed from the backbone network, and only the U-net trained by the common BCE objective is used.

Table 2. Parameter sensitivity test for the self-supervision term weight λ_s.

Dataset	Metric	λ_s					
		0.0	0.1	0.2	0.3	0.4	0.5
CUHK	F-meature↑	0.927	0.932	**0.933**	0.929	0.932	0.928
	MAE↓	0.066	0.063	**0.060**	**0.060**	0.065	0.065
DUT	F-measure↑	0.793	0.807	**0.811**	0.807	0.799	0.805
	MAE↓	0.140	0.131	0.127	**0.124**	0.132	0.131

From Table 1 and Figs. 6, 7, we can observe that the completed proposed method 'BCE+self-supervision+hard mining' significantly outperforms the compared method 'BCE+self-supervision' in all the measurement, while 'BCE+self-supervision' steadily achieves better results than the 'BCE'. These results verify that both the proposed self-supervision objective and the hard mining method are effective for defocus blur detection. In addition, we also show that the if the image gradient is not used, the performance drops obviously, though the model size is much smaller and the process speed is much higher.

4.4 Parameter Sensitive Test

In the above experiments, the weight coefficient λ_s in Eq. 5 is set to 0.2. To test the sensitive of the value for λ_s, we test the model 'BCE+self supervision' performance when λ_s is with a set of different values. The testing results are shown in Table 2. We can observe that the performance varies a little as the value of λ_s changes. When $\lambda_s = 0.0$, this model boils down to BCE model, and when $\lambda_s = 0.2$, it is equal to the model $BCE + self\ supervision$ in Table 1.

5 Conclusion

Different from most existing works focusing on designing complex network, in this paper we propose a light model to cope with the DBD problem. We reanalyze the DBD problem and identify that the semantic information may harm the blur detection. Starting from the DBD problem itself, we propose a novel data augmentation method to inhibit the semantic information and enforce the neural network to learn the blur related features rather than the semantic features. A novel self-supervision objective is used to enhance the training. In addition, by analyzing the relation between the salience detection and defocus blur detection, we identify two hard occasions for DBD models, and based on the difference of salience detection and focus detection, we design a hard mining method and give different weights to various parts in image. With the proposed objective function, a simple and slightly modified U-Net can achieve competitive and even better results than competitors whose network are complex, carefully designed and also pretrained on the ImageNet dataset. In addition, our method achieves more than 3 times improvement on processing speed.

References

1. Chen, L., Zhu, Y., Papandreou, G., Schroff, F., Adam, H.: Encoder-decoder with atrous separable convolution for semantic image segmentation. arXiv: Computer Vision and Pattern Recognition (2018)
2. Elder, J.H., Zucker, S.W.: Local scale control for edge detection and blur estimation. IEEE Trans. Pattern Anal. Mach. Intell. **20**(7), 699–716 (1998)
3. Golestaneh, S.A., Karam, L.J.: Spatially-varying blur detection based on multiscale fused and sorted transform coefficients of gradient magnitudes. In: Computer Vision and Pattern Recognition, pp. 596–605 (2017)
4. Hinton, G.E., Srivastava, N., Krizhevsky, A., Sutskever, I., Salakhutdinov, R.: Improving neural networks by preventing co-adaptation of feature detectors. arXiv: Neural and Evolutionary Computing (2012)
5. Hou, Q., Cheng, M., Hu, X., Borji, A., Tu, Z., Torr, P.H.S.: Deeply supervised salient object detection with short connections. IEEE Trans. Pattern Anal. Mach. Intell. **41**(4), 815–828 (2019)
6. Huang, R., Feng, W., Fan, M., Wan, L., Sun, J.: Multiscale blur detection by learning discriminative deep features. Neurocomputing **285**, 154–166 (2018)
7. Ioffe, S., Szegedy, C.: Batch normalization: accelerating deep network training by reducing internal covariate shift. arXiv: Learning (2015)
8. Kingma, D.P., Ba, J.: Adam: a method for stochastic optimization. arXiv: Learning (2014)
9. Krizhevsky, A., Sutskever, I., Hinton, G.E.: ImageNet classification with deep convolutional neural networks. Neural Inf. Process. Syst. **141**(5), 1097–1105 (2012)
10. Liu, R., Li, Z., Jia, J.: Image partial blur detection and classification. Comput. Vis. Pattern Recognit., 1–8 (2008)
11. Pang, Y., Zhu, H., Li, X., Li, X.: Classifying discriminative features for blur detection. IEEE Trans. Syst. Man Cybern. **46**(10), 2220–2227 (2016)
12. Park, J., Tai, Y.W., Cho, D., Kweon, I.S.: A unified approach of multi-scale deep and hand-crafted features for defocus estimation. In: Computer Vision and Pattern Recognition (2017)
13. Ronneberger, O., Fischer, P., Brox, T.: U-net: convolutional networks for biomedical image segmentation. In: Navab, N., Hornegger, J., Wells, W.M., Frangi, A.F. (eds.) MICCAI 2015. LNCS, vol. 9351, pp. 234–241. Springer, Cham (2015). https://doi.org/10.1007/978-3-319-24574-4_28
14. Rutishauser, U., Walther, D., Koch, C., Perona, P.: Is bottom-up attention useful for object recognition? In: Computer Vision and Pattern Recognition, vol. 2, pp. 37–44 (2004)
15. Saad, E., Hirakawa, K.: Defocus blur-invariant scale-space feature extractions. IEEE Trans. Image Process. **25**(7), 3141–3156 (2016)
16. Shi, J., Li, X., Jia, J.: Discriminative blur detection features. In: Computer Vision and Pattern Recognition (2014)
17. Simonyan, K., Zisserman, A.: Very deep convolutional networks for large-scale image recognition. arXiv: Computer Vision and Pattern Recognition (2014)
18. Su, B., Lu, S., Tan, C.L.: Blurred image region detection and classification. In: ACM Multimedia, pp. 1397–1400 (2011)
19. Tai, Y., Brown, M.S.: Single image defocus map estimation using local contrast prior. In: International Conference on Image Processing, pp. 1777–1780 (2009)
20. Tang, C., Wu, J., Hou, Y., Wang, P., Li, W.: A spectral and spatial approach of coarse-to-fine blurred image region detection. IEEE Signal Process. Lett. **23**(11), 1652–1656 (2016)

21. Tang, C., Zhu, X., Liu, X., Wang, L., Zomaya, A.: DeFusionNET: defocus blur detection via recurrently fusing and refining multi-scale deep features. In: Proceedings of the IEEE Conference on Computer Vision and Pattern Recognition, pp. 2700–2709 (2019)
22. Vu, C.T., Phan, T.D., Chandler, D.M.: S3: a spectral and spatial measure of local perceived sharpness in natural images. IEEE Trans. Image Process. **21**(3), 934–945 (2012)
23. Xu, G., Quan, Y., Ji, H.: Estimating defocus blur via rank of local patches. In: Computer Vision and Pattern Recognition, pp. 5381–5389 (2017)
24. Zeiler, M.D., Krishnan, D., Taylor, G.W., Fergus, R.: Deconvolutional networks. In: Computer Vision and Pattern Recognition (2010)
25. Zhang, S., Shen, X., Lin, Z., Mech, R., Costeira, J.P., Moura, J.M.F.: Learning to understand image blur. In: Computer Vision and Pattern Recognition, pp. 6586–6595 (2018)
26. Zhang, Y., Hirakawa, K.: Blur processing using double discrete wavelet transform. In: Computer Vision and Pattern Recognition, pp. 1091–1098 (2013)
27. Zhao, J., Feng, H., Xu, Z., Li, Q., Tao, X.: Automatic blur region segmentation approach using image matting. Signal Image Video Process. **7**(6), 1173–1181 (2012). https://doi.org/10.1007/s11760-012-0381-6
28. Zhao, W., Zhao, F., Wang, D., Lu, H.: Defocus blur detection via multi-stream bottom-top-bottom network. IEEE Trans. Pattern Anal. Mach. Intell. (2019)
29. Zhao, W., Zheng, B., Lin, Q., Lu, H.: Enhancing diversity of defocus blur detectors via cross-ensemble network. In: Computer Vision and Pattern Recognition, pp. 8905–8913 (2019)
30. Zhu, X., Cohen, S., Schiller, S.N., Milanfar, P.: Estimating spatially varying defocus blur from a single image. IEEE Trans. Image Process. **22**(12), 4879–4891 (2013)
31. Zhuo, S., Sim, T.: Defocus map estimation from a single image. Pattern Recognit. **44**(9), 1852–1858 (2011)

AutoMix: Mixup Networks for Sample Interpolation via Cooperative Barycenter Learning

Jianchao Zhu[1]⬤, Liangliang Shi[2]⬤, Junchi Yan[2(✉)]⬤, and Hongyuan Zha[3]

[1] School of Software Engineering, East China Normal University, Shanghai, China
1486013862@qq.com
[2] Department of Computer Science and Engineering, Shanghai Jiao Tong University,
Shanghai, China
851636947@qq.com, yanjunchi@sjtu.edu.cn
[3] Shenzhen Research Institute of Big Data, The Chinese University of Hong Kong,
Shenzhen, China
zha@cc.gatech.edu

Abstract. This paper proposes new ways of sample mixing by think-
ing of the process as generation of barycenter in a metric space for data
augmentation. First, we present an optimal-transport-based mixup technique to generate Wasserstein barycenter which works well on images
with clean background and is empirically shown complementary to existing mixup methods. Then we generalize mixup to an AutoMix technique by using a learnable network to fit barycenter in a cooperative
way between the classifier (a.k.a. discriminator) and generator networks.
Experimental results on both multi-class and multi-label prediction tasks
show the efficacy of our approach, which is also verified in the presence
of unseen categories (open set) and noise.

Keywords: Image mixing · Generative model · Image classification

1 Introduction and Related Work

Deep networks have achieved unprecedented performance in various tasks, such
as image classification [18], speech recognition [13], natural language processing [30], etc. The researches on improving network performance mainly focus on
backbone design [26,31], regularization [28] and data augmentation [36], etc.

Orthogonal to improvement on network backbone side, data augmentation [25,36,42] has been widely used for improving (neural network) model training. If a model is trained with a tiny dataset, over-fitting problem tends to occur.

Part of the work was done when Junchi Yan was with Tencent AI Lab as visiting scholar. Hongyuan Zha is on leave from Georgia Institute of Technology. Work
was partly supported by National Key Research and Development Program of China
2018AAA0100704, NSFC (61672231, U1609220), and SJTU Global Strategic Partnership Fund (2020 SJTU-CORNELL).

© Springer Nature Switzerland AG 2020
A. Vedaldi et al. (Eds.): ECCV 2020, LNCS 12355, pp. 633–649, 2020.
https://doi.org/10.1007/978-3-030-58607-2_37

The model overly fits to the training data domain and results in poor generalization performance on data out of that domain. As a consequence, a large number of methods of data augmentation have been proposed to solve over-fitting. For images, typical operations include rotation, scaling and cropping, as well as adding noise and performing affine and other geometrical transformation. However, such augmentation methods inherently involve human knowledge to define the vicinity or neighborhood around each sample in the training dataset [8], and other potential techniques have not been fully explored.

There is emerging trend on data augmentation using the so-called mixup strategy [42]. It basically involves interpolating raw samples into a synthetic one with a new label, resulting in an augmented dataset. SamplePairing [15] randomly samples two images and mixes them with ratio $\lambda = 0.5$. The first image's label is used to train the network. Mixup [42] uses a randomly selected mixing ratio λ from β distribution to weigh the two images and their corresponding labels respectively. The Between-Class (BC) model [32] randomly selects two images from two distinctive classes and mixes them by a method in [33].

There are other methods do the mixing in Latent space (a.k.a. feature space). The MixFeat [38] and Manifold Mixup [35] seeks to interpolate the feature maps extracted by a convolutional network. While AdaMixUp [11] aims to determine the sample's ratio for interpolation via network learning. However, the interpolation of the methods mentioned above is still a predefined one, e.g., bilinear interpolation. The ACAI [7] uses an auto-encoder to learn mixed encoding of two images and a discriminator network to predict the mixing ratio from the decoded output of mixed encoding. These two parts are trained adversarially. Different from ACAI, the AMR [5] uses the discriminator to predict whether the mix is real or fake and a channel-wise binary mask $m \in \{0,1\}$ sampled from Bernoulli distribution to randomly activate the feature maps.

In the following, we discuss some basic background related to our approach.

Barycenter Learning. Recently image mixing methods [11,15,32,33,35,38,42] are emerging, which simply mix two images or two feature maps to achieve the purpose of data augmentation. In this paper, we view such methods as instances of barycenter learning. While such a perspective in fact has not been adopted in literature to our knowledge. We can find data points' mean value, i.e., barycenter via unsupervised learning as studied in optimal transport [1,2]. As a variational problem, a weighted barycenter $\hat{x}$ can be defined for some points $\{x_i\}_{i=1}^n$ in a metric space $(X, d(\cdot, \cdot))$ with weights $\{\lambda_i\}_{i=1}^n$:

$$\min_x \sum_{i=1}^{n} \lambda_i d(x_i, x)^p, \tag{1}$$

here $d(\cdot, \cdot)$ is a distance function or more generally divergence, p is a constant, $\lambda_i > 0$ and $\sum_{i=1}^n \lambda_i = 1$. Different metric space according to $d(\cdot, \cdot)$ can lead to different results of barycenter. For instance, by setting $p = 2$, $X = \mathbb{R}^n$ and $d(x, y) = \|x - y\|_2$ in Euclidean space, we get its solution directly with $\hat{x} = \sum_{i=1}^n \lambda_i x_i$. Recent data augmentation methods by mixing two images (i.e., $n = 2$, $\hat{x} = \lambda x_1 + (1 - \lambda)x_2$) can be viewed as finding barycenters in this way.

Table 1. Comparison of mixup methods for classification. Note that the mixing space refers to the space in which the relevant distance is calculated during the mixing phase. Therefore, Manifold Mixup and MixFeat are still bilinear interpolation methods that mix feature maps in Euclidean space. Our OptTransMix is based on optimal transport theory which works in Wasserstein space, and AutoMix directly adopts a network to learn the barycenter as interpolation for input samples in Latent space. Both of them are different from the recent mixup methods.

Method	Mixing way	Mixing phase	Mixing space	Sample ratio	Label ratio
OptTransMix (ours)	Optimal transport	Raw image	Wasserstein	Fixed ratio	Fixed ratio (1:0/0:1)
AutoMix (ours)	Deep neural networks	Feature map	Latent	Random ratio	Same as sample's
AMR [5]	Combine by mask	Feature map	Euclidean	Random ratio	Same as sample's
ACAI [7]	Bilinear interpolation	Feature map	Euclidean	Generated by NN	Same as sample's
AdaMixup [11]	Bilinear interpolation	Raw image	Euclidean	Generated by NN	Same as sample's
SamplePairing [15]	Bilinear interpolation	Raw image	Euclidean	Half-half (1:1)	Fixed ratio (1:0)
Between-Class [32]	Bilinear interpolation	raw image	Euclidean	Random ratio	Same as sample's
Manifold Mixup [35]	Bilinear interpolation	Feature map	Euclidean	Random ratio	Same as sample's
MixFeat [38]	Bilinear interpolation	Feature map	Euclidean	Random ratio	Fixed ratio (1:0/0:1)
Mixup [42]	Bilinear interpolation	Raw image	Euclidean	Random ratio	Same as sample's

Wasserstein Barycenter. Optimal transport [1,2] has gained its popularity in learning and graphics. Regarding pixels as samples and viewing the images as histograms (i.e., probability measure), we can get the Wasserstein distance between images. So by replacing Euclidean space with Wasserstein space and setting $d(x,y) = W(x,y)$, $p = 1$, $n = 2$, we can find Wasserstein barycenters $\hat{x} = \arg\min_x [\lambda W(x_1, x) + (1 - \lambda)W(x_2, x)]$, in which the Wasserstein distance between two images $W(x,y)$ can be calculated iteratively in some way. One technique for calculating barycenter in Wasserstein space can be found in [9].

KL$_{D*}$ Barycenter. As a way of data augmentation, all these methods do have some effect on improving robustness and accuracy, compared with Empirical Risk Minimization (ERM). However, the way of mixing is limited and requires human interference on the specific design of mixup mechanism. On the basis of Euclidean barycenter and Wasserstein barycenter, we choose to use a neural network to automatically fit barycenters in latent space, instead of manual calculation. Recall that the goal of data augmentation is to improve the classifier's accuracy and in fact we can view the cross-entropy loss in classification as a divergence. Specifically, it equals to KL-divergence between the mixed (as generated by mixup techniques e.g. [32]) and true labels. Hence we propose a barycenter generator network to fit the KL$_{D*}$ barycenter and a discriminator network (or called classifier) to control the quality of the generator network. We train both of the networks cooperatively such that we can get them better simultaneously. Note that different from the generator and discriminator in GANs [3,10,20], their relation is not adversarial but cooperative to make both better. Similar to the Euclidean (Wasserstein) distance in Euclidean (Wasserstein) space, we define a KL$_{D*}$ divergence to calculate KL$_{D*}$ barycenter in Sect. 2.3.

Contributions. Table 1 shows the comparison of different methods, w.r.t. the way of mixing, the mixing phase (mix with raw images or feature maps), the different mixing space and mixing ratios for sample and label. AutoMix is the only one using the network to find the barycenter in Latent space, and more broadly speaking, sample mixup by end-to-end network learning. We use Fig. 1 and Table 2 to better summarize the position and results of our approaches: **OptTransMix, AutoMix**. The main highlights of our work are:

i) We apply the barycenter theory to view data augmentation and find that many previous studies on image mixing can be viewed as finding Euclidean barycenters to make the discriminator better.

ii) Under this perspective, we propose OptTransMix, whereby Wasserstein distance is used to find the barycenters in contrast to linear interpolation in Euclidean space, as implemented by the optimal-transport-based transformation technique [27]. Though the tool is originally for graphics, while we show it is complementary to bilinear interpolation for mixup-based data augmentation, especially given images with relatively clean backgrounds.

iii) One step further, the cross-entropy loss for image classifier can be viewed as KL divergence between label distribution based on the classifier given two images as input. By this divergence, we devise an AutoMix technique to generate barycenter images with a deep network. It is more general compared with parameters' learning-free mixing methods. Specifically, we have tried to implement such a barycenter generator network with pixel-level processing model U-Net [22] based on SE [14] attention mechanism.

iv) Experimental results on multi-class and multi-label prediction show our method's effectiveness. It also performs robustly against noise, and on the openset problem whereby unseen categories emerge. The source code will be released.

In this paper, we mainly discuss two-image-based barycenter generation for efficiency, while it is straightforward to generalize to multiple images with a larger batch-size. We leave for future work for its necessity and advantage.

2   Proposed Barycenter Learning Method

We first present the main idea of our method, followed by two embodiments named OptTransMix and AutoMix, which is based on fixed Wasserstein distance and learnable network induced space based on training data, respectively.

2.1   Main Idea and Approach Overview

The barycenter learning, especially Wasserstein barycenter learning has been studied in recent years with its common definition in Eq. 1. For data augmentation, we use the barycenter $\hat{x}$ calculated in Eq. 1 as the augmented training set. So we can get the objective for training:

$$\min_{D} \mathbb{E}_{x_i \sim p(x)} \sum_{i=1}^{n} \lambda_i KL\big(y_i \| D(\hat{x})\big), \tag{2}$$

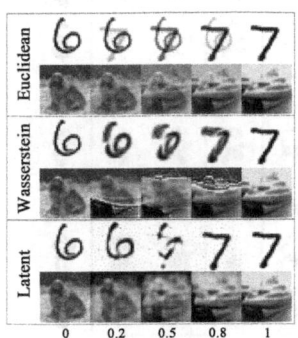

Fig. 1. Different barycenters on MNIST and CIFAR-10.

Table 2. The main observation of this paper: viewing mixup methods from the distance induced space perspective. The proposed method AutoMix enjoys the capability of learning a barycenter from training data tailored to a specific prediction task. In contrast, the Euclidean-distance-based models and Wasserstein-distance-based methods are all learning-free.

Space	Distance and equations	Methods
Euclidean	Euclidean distance, Eq. 3	AdaMixup [11] etc.
Wasserstein	Wasserstein distance, Eq. 5	OptTransMix (ours)
Latent	KL_{D^*} divergence, Eq. 7	AutoMix (ours)

where $\hat{x} = \arg\min_x \sum_{i=1}^n \lambda_i d(x_i, x)^p$ if given n samples as $x_1, x_2, ..., x_n$ as referred in Eq. 1, $D(\cdot)$ is the target label distribution output by discriminator D, $p(x)$ is the distribution of real images, y_i is the real-label distribution, i.e., one-hot encoding, and $\mathbb{E}[\cdot]$ denotes the expectation. The above object is actually equal to weighted cross-entropy loss. For $p = 2$ and $n = 2$, the barycenter $\hat{x}$ in Euclidean space (i.e., with Euclidean distance) is simplified as:

$$\hat{x} = \arg\min_x \lambda \|x_1 - x\|_2^2 + (1 - \lambda)\|x_2 - x\|_2^2, \tag{3}$$

and the solution is $\hat{x} = \lambda x_1 + (1 - \lambda)x_2$, which is exactly the linear mixup methods [15,32,42]. For simplicity, barycenter learning is done with different distances $d(\cdot, \cdot)$ and the number of images $n = 2$ in Eq. 1.

Our main approach is based on barycenter learning which relates to optimal transport. We first propose our baseline method called OptTransMix in Sect. 2.2. We extend the optimal transport based barycenter computing to a neural network and propose our main approach AutoMix in Sect. 2.3, which enables learning of barycenter instead of fixed computing.

2.2 OptTransMix: Barycenter Computing by Wasserstein Distance

Although previous studies have partly explained the effectiveness of mixup-like models and achieve good results, while to some extent these methods are basically linear models (either mixing with raw images or feature maps) which is restrictive and equivalent to finding barycenters in Euclidean space. Here we provide a non-linear alternative that leverages the fast optimal-transport-based barycenter computation technique as developed in [27]. The Wasserstein distance in optimal transport can evaluate two probability measures, as given by [1]:

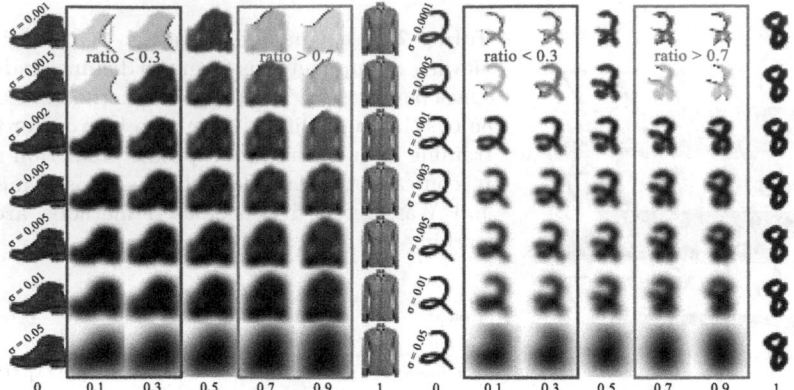

Fig. 2. Results by OptTransMix under smoothing parameter value (y-axis) and ratios (x-axis). We choose the sample whose mixing ratio $[0.1, 0.3]$ or $[0.7, 0.9]$ for training.

$$W(a_1, a_2) = \min_{\pi \in U(a_1, a_2)} \mathbb{E}_{(x,y) \sim \pi} ||x - y||, \tag{4}$$

where a_1 and a_2 are two probability measures, $U(a_1, a_2)$ is the set of all joint distributions π whose marginals are a_1 and a_2. By viewing a_1 and a_2 as two images, x and y are their pixels, we can calculate the distance between images.

With Wasserstein distance used for Wasserstein barycenter, one can find image barycenters in Wasserstein space as new inputs instead of linear barycenters in Euclidean space for training a classifier (namely discriminator). By setting $p = 1$ in Eq. 1, we can get the Wasserstein barycenter:

$$\min_{a} \sum_{i=1}^{n} \lambda_i W_\sigma(a, a_i), \tag{5}$$

where a_i is the discrete probability measure (i.e., input images), a is the Wasserstein barycenter. For high-resolution input images, we use entropic approximation of barycenters [9] to make it a smooth convex minimization problem which can be calculated by gradient descent. To put it in a same setting with existing mixup methods, we specify $n = 2$ as a nonlinear mixup method.

We call such a geometrical image mixing up method OptTransMix. It considers the global layout of the image content and aims to warp an intermediate one between the two inputs, in a sense of more realistic interpolation in appearance. For synthetic image's label for OptTransMix, we resort to a simple strategy that if the ratio between two input images is under 0.5, then the label is set to the first image's label, otherwise we use the second's label. The samples in the middle (i.e., ratio around 0.5) are not generated for training due to vagueness.

The results generated by OptTransMix are shown in Fig. 2 from MNIST and FASHION-MNIST. Given a set of weights $\lambda = \{\lambda\}_{i=1}^{k} \in \mathbb{R}_+^k$, we can compute any synthetic one between the two images by re-weighting. Moreover, the

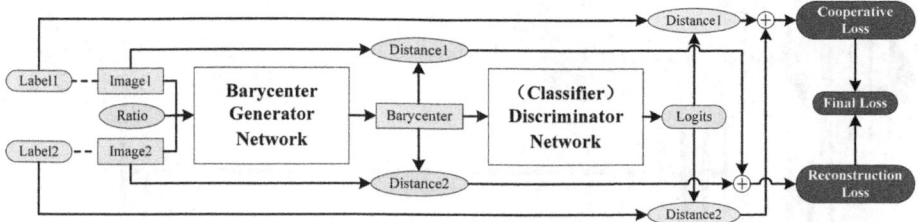

Fig. 3. Our barycenter-based network architecture. Unlike GAN's adversarial training which is time consuming, the two networks in AutoMix reinforce each other and are trained simultaneously thus being much more efficient.

regularization strength scalar value σ in the formula, i.e., the smoothing parameter, controls the smoothness of optimal-transport-based interpolation.

In short, OptTransMix aims to obtain the intermediate states, as a new way of data augmentation. Compared with mixup-like methods' synthetic images (refer to their papers), the ones generated by OptTransMix are more visually meaningful for human and the experimental results also prove the advantages for computer image recognition. However, we find this method has limitations in that it is only applicable to images with clean backgrounds, i.e., the images need to highlight the foreground and ignore the background such that the shape of the image content can be meaningfully interpolated. The failure case of OptTransMix on CIFAR-10 can be seen in the middle of Fig. 1. In fact, the technique is originally applied for graphics with little background noise [27]. Meanwhile, we also note the recent advance on generative adversarial networks (GAN) [10] and Wasserstein GAN [3] related to OT techniques have pushed forward the realistic interpolation of image for specific objects e.g., face [16].

2.3 AutoMix: Barycenter Learning with Learnable Deep Networks

The pipeline of AutoMix is shown in Fig. 3, which is mainly composed of a barycenter generator network and a discriminator network. We input two raw images and the related mixing ratio to get the weighted barycenter, and then feed it into the discriminator to output logits. We use the reconstruction loss of generation process and the cooperative loss of classification process to optimize both of the networks simultaneously. Here we define KL_{D^*} divergence and KL_{D^*} barycenter analogous to the measure rules in Euclidean and Wasserstein space.

Barycenter Generator Network. We start with the barycenter generator network according to Fig. 3 to introduce our AutoMix technique. Specifically, we adopt U-Net [22] as the baseline generative model. This network is known to be state-of-the-art architecture for image segmentation, which we believe is suitable for our pixel-level transformation task. Figure 4 illustrates the improved U-Net architecture for our barycenter generation task. SE (Squeeze-and-Excitation) [14] module is embedded as an attention mechanism before each downsampling layer

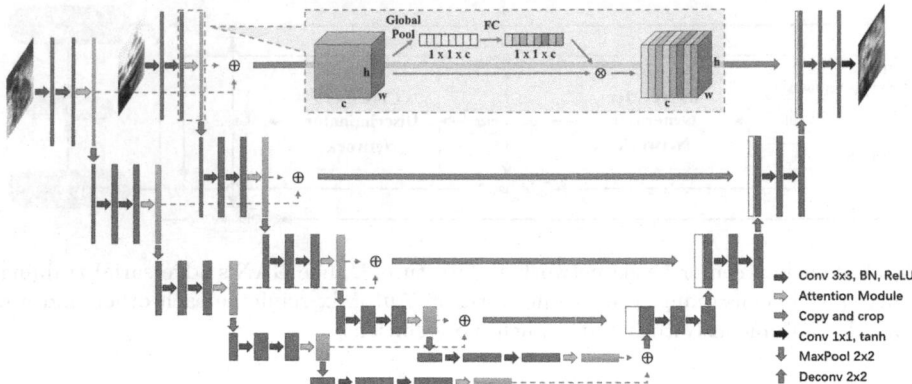

Fig. 4. The improved U-Net with SE modules. Weighted feature maps at various scales of each image are activated by λ and then concatenated with up-sampled feature maps to fuse multi-scale information for the final generation of high-quality barycenters.

in the feature extraction phase based on the original U-Net structure. SE module is divided into three stages, that is, the global pooling layer to generate the embedding of channel-wise feature responses, the fully connected layers to produce a collection of per-channel modulation weights and finally the channel-wise multiplication operation to obtain the weighted feature maps.

We input two raw images and extract their weighted feature maps at multiple scales after passing through the SE modules as shown by the blue dotted arrows in the figure. For feature maps of each scale, the $\oplus$ denotes the channel-wise concatenation of two activated feature maps according to the mixing ratio λ. The operation can be summarized as $\left[f^{(l)}(x_1) \times \lambda\right] \oplus \left[f^{(l)}(x_2) \times (1-\lambda)\right]$, where x_i denotes the input image, $f^{(l)}(x_i)$ represents the output of SE module at l_{th} scale in U-Net and $l \in [1,5]$. So we attribute the outstanding performance of AutoMix to our U-Net's excellent feature extraction and feature screening capabilities. With an attention-like module in U-Net, AutoMix can better retain feature maps of two images and mix them appropriately rather than mixup's fixed mixing way.

Although we are not the first to integrate the attention mechanism into U-Net [21,41], it is worth noting that we may be the first to apply the integration of U-Net and SE module to the field of image generation and achieve good performance according to the experimental results. Besides, our model can accept more than two inputs to generate barycenters of multiple images after expanding.

KL_{D*} Divergence. Similar to Euclidean and Wasserstein barycenters based on their respective distances, the divergence in Latent space for barycenter learning needs to be defined and we call it KL_{D*} divergence. In fact, the corresponding barycenter can be derived from the cross-entropy, i.e., KL-divergence for the classifier. For an image x, let $D(x)$ denotes the prediction probability with a discriminator D, which is exactly the distribution of x in Latent space. If x comes from the original data domain, we set $D(x) = y$, otherwise $D(x)$. Here we define an optimal discriminator D^* to combine these two cases, and based on this observation, we then define the KL_{D^*} divergence given two images x_1, x_2:

$$D^*(x) = \begin{cases} y, & \text{if } x \text{ is a raw image} \\ D(x), & \text{if } x = G(x_1, x_2, \lambda) \end{cases}, KL_{D^*}(x_1||x_2) \overset{\text{def}}{=} KL\big(D^*(x_1)||D^*(x_2)\big). \tag{6}$$

KL_{D^*} Barycenter. Different from Euclidean barycenter and Wasserstein barycenter, the barycenter based on KL_{D^*} divergence can not be calculated directly by iterations but gradient descent as it is based on deep-net discriminator. So we use barycenter generator network G, specifically a U-Net [22] architecture to generate the barycenter given two images x_1, x_2 and their ratio λ, as expressed by $\hat{x} = G(x_1, x_2, \lambda)$. So we can get the KL_{D^*} barycenter by optimizing

$$\min_G \lambda KL_{D^*}(x_1||\hat{x}) + (1-\lambda)KL_{D^*}(x_2||\hat{x}). \tag{7}$$

Cooperative Loss. The generated barycenter $\hat{x}$ is input into discriminator D for training as the augmented sample. Akin to Euclidean (Wasserstein) distance for Euclidean (Wasserstein) barycenter, KL_{D^*} divergence is used for KL_{D^*} barycenter, which is also the loss for discriminator (recall it is image classifier). Hence our optimization for barycenter generator network and discriminator network refers to minimizing the KL divergence between real label distribution and Latent distribution output by D:

$$L_{G,D}(x_1, x_2) = \lambda KL\big(y_1||D(\hat{x})\big) + (1-\lambda)KL\big(y_2||D(\hat{x})\big), \tag{8}$$

where $D(\hat{x})$ is the target distribution in view of discriminator D with barycenter $\hat{x}$, and $\lambda \sim U(0,1)$ is the mixing ratio. Different from GANs [3,10], here the loss for G and D is cooperative. When D reaches optimum, the optimization goal changes from Eq. 8 to Eq. 7. While given optimized G, we just need to optimize Eq. 2, to get discriminator $D \to D^*$ and the generated barycenter closer to the theoretical optimum.

Reconstruction Loss. In line with CGAN [20], in order to prevent the generated image from being too far from the original ones, L1 regularization is imposed by a reconstruction loss to train the barycenter generator network:

$$L_G(x_1, x_2) = \lambda||x_1 - \hat{x}||_1 + (1-\lambda)||x_2 - \hat{x}||_1, \tag{9}$$

where x_1 and x_2 are two input images, and $\hat{x} = G(x_1, x_2, \lambda)$ is the barycenter generated by G. The reason for using L1 instead of L2 is that L1 produces images with relatively higher definition.

Final Loss. Unlike GAN's adversarial training process, the two networks in AutoMix reinforce each other and are trained jointly with a factor α controlling the weight of two loss terms (not the difference to min max in GAN):

$$\min_D \min_G \mathbb{E}_{x_1, x_2 \sim p(x)} L_{G,D}(x_1, x_2) + \alpha L_G(x_1, x_2). \tag{10}$$

where $p(x)$ is the distribution of real images. We find the performance by setting different α from 0.5 to 2 with a step 0.1 is very small. We finally set $\alpha = 1.5$. The barycenters generated by OptTransMix and AutoMix are compared in Fig. 1.

Table 3. Sampling and training protocols. We use 10-fold cross-validation for MIML because of its small size and we train for 10 trials for other datasets. We train models on both sampling and full set of some of the datasets and test models on their official testing set respectively to explore how these methods perform on small scale datasets. CIFAR-100 and Tiny-ImageNet are only trained with full dataset.

Label	Dataset	#cls.	Sampling	Sub/full training set	Testing set	Training strategy
Single	MNIST [19]	10	50 per class	500/60,000	Official 10,000	10 trials
	F-MNIST [37]	10	50 per class	500/60,000	Official 10,000	
	CIFAR-10 [17]	10	500 per class	5,000/50,000	Official 10,000	
	CIFAR-100 [17]	100	500 per class	−/50,000	Official 10,000	
	GTSRB [29]	43	50 per class	2,150/39,209	Official 12,630	
	T-IMAGENET [39]	200	500 per class	−/100,000	Official 10,000	
Multi	MIML [44]	5	train:test = 1:1	1000	1000	10-fold CV

We also have tried alternating optimization strategy for two networks while the convergence become slower with worse final performance. Besides the standard classification setting, we also explore the possibility of applying our OptTransMix and AutoMix to other common tasks. The first one is multi-label prediction [34,43], the other is the so-called openset problem [6,24] whereby there exist new categories in the testing set which are unseen in the training set. Especially for the second problem, this is still considered as an open problem and a simple but effective treatment is to adopt a threshold-based strategy to decide if the test sample shall be regarded as an unseen one that does not belong to any of the existing categories in training set. Precisely, if the highest inference score (or the top 2 or so) is under a given threshold, this sample will be classified as an unseen sample. Note the threshold can be determined in more diverse and adaptive ways e.g., depending on the specific label of samples. In this paper, for simplicity and generality, we use a fixed threshold for all labels in experiments.

3 Experiment and Discussion

Experiments are conducted on a desktop with Nvidia GeForce GTX1080Ti GPU and 32G memory. We verify our model on public datasets including MNIST [19], FASHION-MNIST [37], the traffic sign benchmark GTSRB [29], CIFAR-10 [17], CIFAR-100 [17] for image classification. The reason for using these datasets is that they have a relatively small size such that the effects of different mixup strategies can be more pronounced as a way of data augmentation. This is also practically common in front of small data for network learning. Besides, for larger dataset, we choose Tiny-ImageNet [39] instead of ImageNet [23] due to our hardware limitation. To further evaluate the behavior of our methods on different tasks, we also adopt the MIML [44] dataset for image multi-label prediction.

Table 4. Top-1 error rate (mean ± standard deviation) on MNIST/FASHION-MNIST by 10 trials. Underline denotes best results.

Method	MNIST (full)	MNIST (sub)	F-MNIST (full)	F-MNIST (sub)
Baseline	0.271 ± 0.012	10.83 ± 0.61	5.202 ± 0.087	20.95 ± 0.97
BC [32]	0.257 ± 0.032	5.93 ± 0.59	4.905 ± 0.071	16.69 ± 0.31
Mixup [42]	0.268 ± 0.015	6.17 ± 0.85	4.788 ± 0.066	17.38 ± 0.59
Manifold Mixup [35]	0.258 ± 0.021	4.98 ± 0.34	4.910 ± 0.079	17.47 ± 0.38
OptTransMix	0.260 ± 0.031	4.86 ± 0.48	5.021 ± 0.068	16.97 ± 0.65
OptTransMix+Mixup	0.265 ± 0.018	8.12 ± 0.48	4.869 ± 0.078	17.10 ± 0.76
OptTransMix+BC	0.257 ± 0.028	4.37 ± 0.44	4.872 ± 0.059	16.67 ± 0.53
AutoMix	0.256 ± 0.036	4.58 ± 0.57	4.769 ± 0.064	16.79 ± 0.75

Note for our OptTransMix, it is only tested on classification benchmark MNIST and FASHION-MNIST as we find it requires clean background. The dataset sampling and training protocols are detailed in Table 3.

For discriminator backbone, we use a simple 11-layer CNN (2conv + pool + 2conv + pool + 4conv + pool + 3fc) according to [32] and ResNet-18 [12]. The 11-layer CNN is used for MNIST and FASHION-MNIST, while ResNet-18 is used for the other datasets.

We compare the baseline (namely without mixing method) and three mixup methods including Between-Class (BC) learning [32], Mixup [42] and Manifold Mixup [35]. Regarding the details of training, we apply data pre-processing including random cropping, horizontal flipping and normalization on the raw data. We choose Stochastic Gradient Descent with *momentum* = 0.9 as our optimizer and the learning rate is set to 0.1 at the beginning and decays as the training process continues. For classification (single-label prediction), we adopt the log-softmax cross-entropy as loss. For multi-label prediction, as it can be arguably treated as a binary classification problem by selecting one label as positive and the others negative [34], we use sigmoid activation function as the last layer of discriminator network and the sigmoid cross-entropy as the loss function, for simplicity. Note the effectiveness of such a one vs. rest binary classification treatment has been also verified [4,40].

Single-Label Classification. We first apply OptTransMix and AutoMix on two simple image classification datasets: MNIST and FASHION-MNIST. In addition, since OptTransMix is orthogonal to Between-Class learning [32] and Mixup [42], we also apply it to generate additional samples for these two methods. We averagely sample 50 images per class to form a training set with a total of 500 images, which is relatively small and thus calls for data augmentation. We also train with full data to figure out how these methods actually work. For testing, we use the official 10,000-image testing set for both MNIST and FASHION-MNIST. To eliminate the impact of random initialization, we train each model for 10 trials. An 11-layer CNN is used as the backbone and is trained

Table 5. Top-1 error rate (mean ± standard deviation), and mAP for MIML using ResNet-18 trained by 200 epochs for 10 trials. Underline denotes best results.

Dataset	Baseline	BC [32]	Mixup [42]	M-Mixup [35]	**AutoMix**
CIFAR10 (full)	4.59 ± 0.09	4.03 ± 0.34	3.96 ± 0.10	3.99 ± 0.06	<u>3.72 ± 0.10</u>
CIFAR10 (sub)	18.79 ± 0.33	15.97 ± 0.18	15.76 ± 0.33	15.38 ± 0.22	<u>15.17 ± 0.41</u>
CIFAR100 (full)	22.39 ± 0.17	21.19 ± 0.24	21.05 ± 0.24	20.25 ± 0.17	<u>20.04 ± 0.14</u>
GTSRB (full)	0.44 ± 0.06	0.41 ± 0.04	0.54 ± 0.05	<u>0.38 ± 0.11</u>	0.41 ± 0.08
GTSRB (sub)	4.52 ± 0.69	2.38 ± 0.22	2.98 ± 0.27	2.38 ± 0.21	<u>2.34 ± 0.18</u>
T-ImageNet (full)	40.35 ± 0.25	38.71 ± 0.27	38.77 ± 0.19	37.75 ± 0.46	<u>37.15 ± 0.26</u>
MIML (full)	72.14 ± 1.08	72.92 ± 0.85	73.02 ± 0.80	74.56 ± 1.02	<u>74.80 ± 0.92</u>

for 100 epochs. The learning rate is divided by 10 at the epoch in $\{50, 75\}$. Top-1 accuracy is used as the evaluation metric for single-label classification tasks.

We show the results of 10 trials on MNIST and FASHION-MNIST in Table 4. Improvement is made by using OptTransMix and AutoMix. Besides, using Opt-TransMix to generate more diverse samples can further improve the performance of Mixup and BC. Moreover, OptTransMix performs better on small datasets, while AutoMix outperforms on relatively bigger ones.

We then apply AutoMix to some of the bigger and more difficult datasets. Similarly, we still averagely sample training images, namely 500 images per class for CIFAR-10 and 50 images per class for GTSRB, so the total amount of training set is 5,000 images and 2,150 images respectively. Full data training is also conducted. Since CIFAR-100 and Tiny-ImageNet only have 500 images per class, we only train with full data on them. ResNet-18 is used to train 100 epochs for GTSRB and 200 epochs for CIFAR-10/100 and Tiny-ImageNet. The learning rate is divided by 10 at the epoch in $\{50, 75\}$, $\{100, 150\}$ and $\{100, 150\}$ respectively. We test the model on the official 10,000-image testing set for CIFAR-10/100 and Tiny-ImageNet, and the official 12,630-image testing set for GTSRB.

The average of 10 trials are reported in Table 5, showing that AutoMix outperforms baseline and other mixup-like methods on all datasets except GTSRB.

Multi-label Classification. MIML [44] is a multi-instance multi-label dataset, which has a total of 2,000 landscape images. Due to its small amount of data, we divide it into a training set and a testing set with the ratio of 1:1. We use 10-fold cross-validation to evaluate whether our methods perform well on multi-label image classification tasks compared with baseline and other image mixing methods. ResNet-18 is used to train 100 epochs and the learning rate is divided by 10 at the epoch in $\{50, 75\}$. Mean average precision (mAP) is used for multi-label classification tasks, which is calculated in a similar way to mAP in object detection. As shown in Table 5, AutoMix outperforms as well.

Openset Problem. The openset problem can be defined as there exist unseen categories in testing set but not in training set. In this part, we train the model

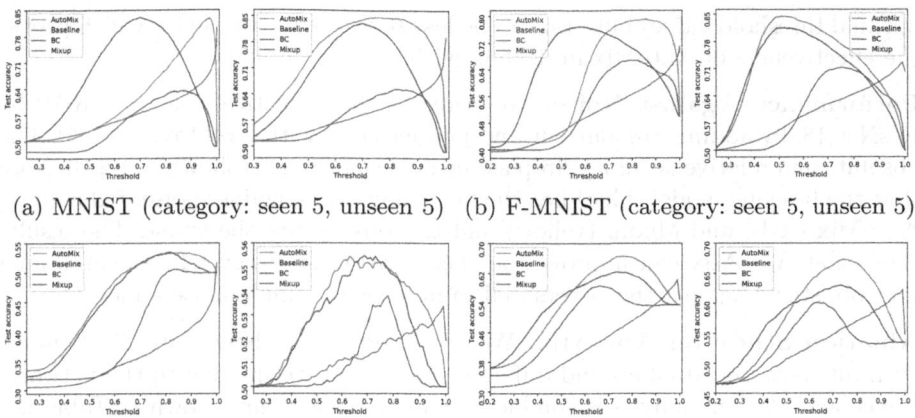

(a) MNIST (category: seen 5, unseen 5)   (b) F-MNIST (category: seen 5, unseen 5)

(c) CIFAR-10 (category: seen 5, unseen 5)   (d) GTSRB (category: seen 12, unseen 31)

Fig. 5. Top-1 accuracy as threshold grows on the openset problem. Left in each pair: setting a). Right in each pair: setting b). See main test for details of the two settings.

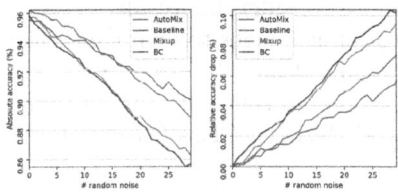

Fig. 6. Absolute accuracy (left) and relative accuracy drop (right) as noise increases. The higher (lower) the better. (Color figure online)

Table 6. Ablation study on AutoMix using ResNet-18 on CIFAR-10 by top-1 error rate (mean ± standard deviation of 10 trials). Underline denotes best results.

Comparison	Setting	CIFAR10 (full)	CIFAR10 (sub)
Label strategy for synthetic sample	(a)	5.38 ± 0.11	16.32 ± 0.43
	(b)	3.91 ± 0.17	15.44 ± 0.34
	(c)	3.86 ± 0.11	15.35 ± 0.31
	(d)	3.72 ± 0.10	15.17 ± 0.41
Label conflict	Same	4.21 ± 0.18	16.10 ± 0.39
	Different	3.98 ± 0.15	15.67 ± 0.32
	Random	3.72 ± 0.10	15.17 ± 0.41

by a subset of categories and test by whole categories. In testing phase, 'threshold' is used to compare with the confidence to control whether a sample will be classified as a known or unknown category. We conduct results in two settings here: **a) normal openset setting (n seen categories + 1 'unknown' category)** and **b) binary classification setting (1 'known' category + 1 'unknown' category).** The results are reported in Fig. 5, illustrating the relationship between accuracy and threshold. The left figures in each subplot correspond to setting a) and the right figures correspond to b). Intuitively, the bigger the area under the curve is, the more robust the model is, which means we can get high performance in a wide range of threshold values. By a closer study, one can find our method not only achieves a higher peak of accuracy (with optimal threshold value) but also can be less sensitive to threshold, which proves the effectiveness of AutoMix in dealing with openset problems.

Performance Against Noise. We evaluate the robustness on CIFAR-10 by ResNet-18, by adding random salt-and-pepper noise with level from 0 to 30. The absolute and relative accuracy drop as the noise increases is shown in Fig. 6. Note that the baseline model (blue) has the best robustness against noise, followed by AutoMix (red), and Mixup (yellow) and BC (green) are the worst. The results show that AutoMix can improve the classification accuracy while maintaining the robustness against the adversarial samples with simple noise added.

Ablation Study on AutoMix. We are interested in how AutoMix behaves with different mixed labels and different sample constraints fed to the network. Hence an ablation analysis is conducted and the results are shown in Table 6.

We investigate the relationship between the performance and the label settings. We attempt to treat it as a multi-class classification task, either **taking the first image's label (a)** or the **half-half mix of two labels (b)** as the final label. According to the experimental results, treating it as a **multi-label classification task (c)**, i.e., simply add the two labels and constrain it between 0 and 1, is more effective. Furthermore, our proposed AutoMix using **random ratios for label weighting (d)** achieves a more considerable result.

We also study how the categories of the two input images to be mixed affects performance. We find that the performance degrades if the given images have the same label. The best results come from two randomly selected samples, which means AutoMix can learn both within-class and Between-Class features by the barycenter generated in Latent space.

Discussion. The reason why OptTransMix excels on small datasets (Table 4) may be that the optimal-transport-based Wasserstein barycenter can be calculated with any amount of data. Compared to the U-Net in AutoMix, OptTransMix does not need a large amount of data for training to achieve good performance.

Regarding the computational complexity of the models, although the Wasserstein barycenter is computationally intensive (especially for high-dimensional data), we can separate this generation process before the training stage. Thus to some extent, the complexity has not increased for OptTransMix. For AutoMix, the U-Net introduces ~ 1.96 million additional parameters beyond the ~ 11.27 million parameters required by ResNet18, corresponding to $\sim 17\%$ increase.

4   Conclusion

This paper aims to learn the interpolation model for data augmentation which is a general and fundamental building block for practical learning systems. Differing from most existing mixup methods that interpolate the raw images or their feature maps in the Euclidean space by linear or bilinear interpolation, we first explore a more advanced interpolation technique called OptTransMix, which seeks the Wasserstein barycenter between two images, and show their usefulness on small datasets. Then we generalize the fixed Wasserstein-distance-based model to the new approach called AutoMix, which stands out on large datasets. It trains an attention-based barycenter generator network and a discriminator network concurrently with the cooperative loss.

Experiments have shown the efficacy of both our proposed techniques on traditional classification, multi-label prediction, openset problems, and the robustness test against noise. Limited by our hardware device, we leave the experiments on large scale datasets for our future work.

References

1. Agueh, M., Carlier, G.: Barycenters in the Wasserstein space. SIAM J. Math. Anal. **43**, 904–921 (2011)
2. Anderes, E., Borgwardt, S., Miller, J.: Discrete Wasserstein barycenters: optimal transport for discrete data. Math. Methods Oper. Res. **84**, 389–409 (2016)
3. Arjovsky, M., Chintala, S., Bottou, L.: Wasserstein generative adversarial networks. In: International Conference on Machine Learning (2017)
4. Babbar, R., Schölkopf, B.: DiSMEC: distributed sparse machines for extreme multi-label classification. In: Proceedings of the Tenth ACM International Conference on Web Search and Data Mining, pp. 721–729 (2017)
5. Beckham, C., et al.: On adversarial mixup resynthesis. In: Advances in Neural Information Processing Systems, pp. 4348–4359 (2019)
6. Bendale, A., Boult, T.E.: Towards open set deep networks. In: Proceedings of the IEEE Conference on Computer Vision and Pattern Recognition, pp. 1563–1572 (2016)
7. Berthelot, D., Raffel, C., Roy, A., Goodfellow, I.: Understanding and improving interpolation in autoencoders via an adversarial regularizer. In: International Conference on Learning Representations (2018)
8. Chapelle, O., Weston, J., Bottou, L., Vapnik, V.: Vicinal risk minimization. In: Advances in Neural Information Processing Systems, pp. 416–422 (2001)
9. Cuturi, M., Doucet, A.: Fast computation of Wasserstein barycenters. In: International Conference on Machine Learning, pp. 685–693 (2014)
10. Goodfellow, I., et al.: Generative adversarial nets. In: Advances in Neural Information Processing Systems, pp. 2672–2680 (2014)
11. Guo, H., Mao, Y., Zhang, R.: Mixup as locally linear out-of-manifold regularization. In: Proceedings of the AAAI Conference on Artificial Intelligence, vol. 33, pp. 3714–3722 (2019)
12. He, K., Zhang, X., Ren, S., Sun, J.: Deep residual learning for image recognition. In: Proceedings of the IEEE Conference on Computer Vision and Pattern Recognition, pp. 770–778 (2016)
13. Hinton, G., et al.: Deep neural networks for acoustic modeling in speech recognition: the shared views of four research groups. IEEE Signal Process. Mag. **29**, 82–97 (2012)
14. Hu, J., Shen, L., Sun, G.: Squeeze-and-excitation networks. In: Proceedings of the IEEE Conference on Computer Vision and Pattern Recognition, pp. 7132–7141 (2018)
15. Inoue, H.: Data augmentation by pairing samples for images classification. arXiv preprint arXiv:1801.02929 (2018)

16. Karras, T., Laine, S., Aila, T.: A style-based generator architecture for generative adversarial networks. In: Proceedings of the IEEE Conference on Computer Vision and Pattern Recognition, pp. 4401–4410 (2019)
17. Krizhevsky, A., Hinton, G., et al.: Learning multiple layers of features from tiny images. Technical report (2009)
18. Krizhevsky, A., Sutskever, I., Hinton, G.E.: ImageNet classification with deep convolutional neural networks. In: Advances in Neural Information Processing Systems, pp. 1097–1105 (2012)
19. LeCun, Y., Bottou, L., Bengio, Y., Haffner, P.: Gradient-based learning applied to document recognition. Proc. IEEE **86**, 2278–2324 (1998)
20. Mirza, M., Osindero, S.: Conditional generative adversarial nets. arXiv preprint arXiv:1411.1784 (2014)
21. Oktay, O., et al.: Attention U-Net: Learning where to look for the pancreas. arXiv preprint arXiv:1804.03999 (2018)
22. Ronneberger, O., Fischer, P., Brox, T.: U-Net: convolutional networks for biomedical image segmentation. In: Navab, N., Hornegger, J., Wells, W.M., Frangi, A.F. (eds.) MICCAI 2015. LNCS, vol. 9351, pp. 234–241. Springer, Cham (2015). https://doi.org/10.1007/978-3-319-24574-4_28
23. Russakovsky, O., et al.: ImageNet large scale visual recognition challenge. Int. J. Comput. Vis. **115**, 211–252 (2015)
24. Scheirer, W.J., de Rezende Rocha, A., Sapkota, A., Boult, T.E.: Toward open set recognition. IEEE Trans. Pattern Anal. Mach. Intell. **35**, 1757–1772 (2013)
25. Simard, P.Y., LeCun, Y.A., Denker, J.S., Victorri, B.: Transformation invariance in pattern recognition — tangent distance and tangent propagation. In: Orr, G.B., Müller, K.-R. (eds.) Neural Networks: Tricks of the Trade. LNCS, vol. 1524, pp. 239–274. Springer, Heidelberg (1998). https://doi.org/10.1007/3-540-49430-8_13
26. Simonyan, K., Zisserman, A.: Very deep convolutional networks for large-scale image recognition. In: International Conference on Learning Representations (2015)
27. Solomon, J., et al.: Convolutional Wasserstein distances: efficient optimal transportation on geometric domains. ACM Trans. Graph. (TOG) **34**, 1–11 (2015)
28. Srivastava, N., Hinton, G., Krizhevsky, A., Sutskever, I., Salakhutdinov, R.: Dropout: a simple way to prevent neural networks from overfitting. J. Mach. Learn. Res. **15**, 1929–1958 (2014)
29. Stallkamp, J., Schlipsing, M., Salmen, J., Igel, C.: The German traffic sign recognition benchmark: a multi-class classification competition. In: IEEE International Joint Conference on Neural Networks (2011)
30. Sutskever, I., Vinyals, O., Le, Q.V.: Sequence to sequence learning with neural networks. In: Advances in Neural Information Processing Systems, pp. 3104–3112 (2014)
31. Szegedy, C., et al.: Going deeper with convolutions. In: Proceedings of the IEEE Conference on Computer Vision and Pattern Recognition, pp. 1–9 (2015)
32. Tokozume, Y., Ushiku, Y., Harada, T.: Between-class learning for image classification. In: Proceedings of the IEEE Conference on Computer Vision and Pattern Recognition, pp. 5486–5494 (2018)
33. Tokozume, Y., Ushiku, Y., Harada, T.: Learning from between-class examples for deep sound recognition. In: International Conference on Learning Representations (2018)
34. Tsoumakas, G., Katakis, I., Vlahavas, I.: Mining multi-label data. In: Maimon, O., Rokach, L. (eds.) Data Mining and Knowledge Discovery Handbook, pp. 667–685. Springer, Boston (2009). https://doi.org/10.1007/978-0-387-09823-4_34

35. Verma, V., Lamb, A., Beckham, C., Najafi, A., Bengio, Y.: Manifold mixup: better representations by interpolating hidden states. In: International Conference on Machine Learning, pp. 6438–6447 (2019)
36. Wong, S.C., Gatt, A., Stamatescu, V., McDonnell, M.D.: Understanding data augmentation for classification: when to warp? In: International Conference on Digital Image Computing: Techniques and Applications, pp. 1–6 (2016)
37. Xiao, H., Rasul, K., Vollgraf, R.: Fashion-MNIST: a novel image dataset for benchmarking machine learning algorithms. arXiv preprint arXiv:1708.07747 (2017)
38. Yaguchi, Y., Shiratani, F., Iwaki, H.: MixFeat: mix feature in latent space learns discriminative space. Submission at International Conference on Learning Representations (2019)
39. Yao, L., Miller, J.: Tiny ImageNet classification with convolutional neural networks. CS 231N, p. 8 (2015)
40. Yen, I.E.H., Huang, X., Ravikumar, P., Zhong, K., Dhillon, I.: PD-sparse: a primal and dual sparse approach to extreme multiclass and multilabel classification. In: International Conference on Machine Learning, pp. 3069–3077 (2016)
41. Yue, D., Hua-jun, F., Zhi-hai, X., Yue-ting, C., Qi, L.: Attention Res-Unet: an efficient shadow detection algorithm. J. Zhejiang Univ. (Eng. Sci.) **53**, 373 (2019)
42. Zhang, H., Cisse, M., Dauphin, Y.N., Lopez-Paz, D.: mixup: Beyond empirical risk minimization. In: International Conference on Learning Representations (2018)
43. Zhang, W., Yan, J., Wang, X., Zha, H.: Deep extreme multi-label learning. In: Proceedings of the 2018 ACM on International Conference on Multimedia Retrieval, pp. 100–107 (2018)
44. Zhou, Z.H., Zhang, M.L.: Multi-instance multi-label learning with application to scene classification. In: Advances in Neural Information Processing Systems, pp. 1609–1616 (2007)

Scene Text Image Super-Resolution in the Wild

Wenjia Wang[1], Enze Xie[2], Xuebo Liu[1], Wenhai Wang[3], Ding Liang[1],
Chunhua Shen[4(✉)], and Xiang Bai[5]

[1] SenseTime Research, Shatin, Hong Kong
wangwenjia@sensetime.com
[2] The University of Hong Kong, Shatin, Hong Kong
[3] Nanjing University, Nanjing, China
[4] The University of Adelaide, Adelaide, Australia
chunhua.shen@adelaide.edu.au
[5] Huazhong University of Science and Technology, Wuhan, China

Abstract. Low-resolution text images are often seen in natural scenes such as documents captured by mobile phones. Recognizing low-resolution text images is challenging because they lose detailed content information, leading to poor recognition accuracy. An intuitive solution is to introduce super-resolution (SR) techniques as pre-processing. However, previous single image super-resolution (SISR) methods are trained on synthetic low-resolution images (*e.g.* Bicubic down-sampling), which is simple and not suitable for real low-resolution text recognition. To this end, we propose a real scene text SR dataset, termed TextZoom. It contains paired real low-resolution and high-resolution images which are captured by cameras with different focal length in the wild. It is more authentic and challenging than synthetic data, as shown in Fig. 1. We argue improving the recognition accuracy is the ultimate goal for Scene Text SR. In this purpose, a new Text Super-Resolution Network, termed TSRN, with three novel modules is developed. (1) A sequential residual block is proposed to extract the sequential information of the text images. (2) A boundary-aware loss is designed to sharpen the character boundaries. (3) A central alignment module is proposed to relieve the misalignment problem in TextZoom. Extensive experiments on TextZoom demonstrate that our TSRN largely improves the recognition accuracy by over 13% of CRNN, and by nearly 9.0% of ASTER and MORAN compared to synthetic SR data. Furthermore, our TSRN clearly outperforms 7 state-of-the-art SR methods in boosting the recognition accuracy of LR images in TextZoom. For example, it outperforms LapSRN by over 5% and 8% on the recognition accuracy of ASTER and CRNN. Our results suggest that low-resolution text recognition in the

---

W. Wang and E. Xie—Equal Contribution.

Electronic supplementary material The online version of this chapter (https://doi.org/10.1007/978-3-030-58607-2_38) contains supplementary material, which is available to authorized users.

© Springer Nature Switzerland AG 2020
A. Vedaldi et al. (Eds.): ECCV 2020, LNCS 12355, pp. 650–666, 2020.
https://doi.org/10.1007/978-3-030-58607-2_38

wild is far from being solved, thus more research effort is needed. The codes and models will be released at: github.com/JasonBoy1/TextZoom

Keywords: Scene text recognition · Super-resolution · Dataset · Sequence · Boundary

1   Introduction

Scene text recognition is a fundamental and important task in computer vision, since it is usually a key step towards many downstream text-related applications, including document retrieval, card recognition, license plate recognition, etc. [3,34,35,43]. Scene Text recognition has achieved remarkable success due to the development of Convolutional Neural Network (CNN) (Table 1).

Many accurate and efficient methods have been proposed for most constrained scenarios (e.g., text in scanned copies or network images). Recent works focus on texts in natural scenes [6,25,26,28,37,41,42,44], which is much more

Fig. 1. Comparison between synthetic LR, real LR, and HR images in TextZoom. 'Syn LR' denotes BICUBIC down-sampled image of HR. 'Real LR' and 'HR' denotes LR and HR images captured by camera with different focal lengths. From the images we can find that the real LR images are much more challenging than the synthetic LR images.

Table 1. Statistics of TextZoom. The testing set is divided into 3 different subsets: easy, medium and hard. The recognition accuracy is tested by ASTER [37]. We see the recognition accuracy of LR images decreases when the difficulty increases. Our main purpose is to increase the recognition accuracy of the LR images by super-resolution.

TextZoom	Train	Test		
		Easy	Medium	Hard
Image number	17367	1619	1411	1343
Accuracy (LR)	35.7%	62.4%	42.7%	31.6%
Accuracy (HR)	81.2%	94.2%	87.7%	76.2%
Gap	45.5%	31.8%	45.0%	44.6%

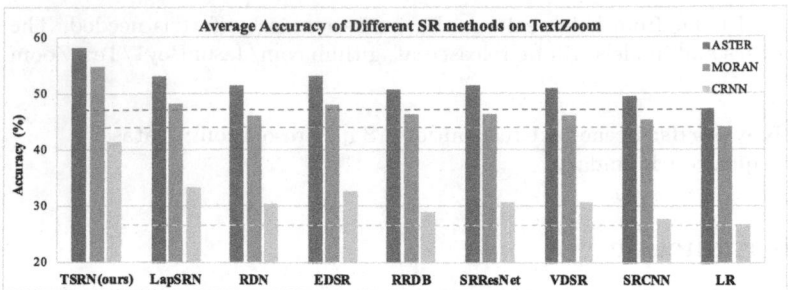

Fig. 2. Average recognition accuracy of the super-resolved images of LR images in TextZoom. We first super-resolve LR images with different SR methods, then directly test the SR results with the official released model of ASRER [37], MORAN [28] and CRNN [36]. We compare our TSRN with 7 state-of-the-art deep learning networks and show ours outperforms them clearly. Dotted lines means accuracy of LR inputs.

challenging due to the high diversity of texts in blur, orientation, shape, and low-resolution. A thorough survey of recent advantages of text recognition can be found in [27]. Modern text recognizers have achieved impressive results on clear text images. However, their performances drop sharply when recognizing low-resolution text images [1]. The main difficulty to recognize LR text is that the optical degradation blurred the shape of the characters. **Therefore, it would be promising if we introduce SR methods as a pre-processing procedure before recognition.** To our surprise, none of the real dataset and corresponding methods focus on scene text SR (Fig. 2).

In this paper, we propose a paired scene text SR dataset, termed TextZoom, which is the **first dataset focus on real text SR**. Previous Super-Resolution methods [7,20–24,47] generate LR counterparts of the high-resolution (HR) images by simply applying uniform degradation like bicubic interpolation or blur kernels. Unfortunately, real blur scene text images are more varied in degradation formation. Scene texts are of arbitrary shapes, distributed illumination, and different backgrounds. Super-resolution on scene text images is much more challenging. Therefore, the proposed TextZoom, which contains paired LR and HR text images of the same text content, is very necessary. The TextZoom dataset is cropped from the newly proposed SISR datasets [4,46]. Our dataset has three main advantages. **(1)** This dataset is well annotated. We provide the direction, the text content and the original focal length of the text images. **(2)** The dataset contains abundant text from different natural scenes, including street views, libraries, shops, vehicle interiors and so on. **(3)** The dataset is carefully divided into three subsets by difficulty. Experiments on TextZoom demonstrate that our TSRN largely improves the recognition accuracy of CRNN by over 13% compared to synthetic SR data. The annotation and allocation strategy will be briefly introduced in Sect. 3 and demonstrated in detail in supplementary materials.

Moreover, to reconstruct low-resolution text images, we propose a text-oriented end-to-end method. Traditional SISR methods only focus on reconstruct the detail of texture and only satisfy human's visual perception. However, scene text SR is quite a special task since it contains high-level text content. The fore-and-aft characters have information relations with each other. Obviously, a single blur character will not disable human to recognize the whole word if other characters are clear. To solve this task, firstly, we present a Sequential Residual Block to model recurrent information in text lines, which enabling us to build a correlation in the fore-and-aft characters. Secondly, we propose a boundary-aware loss termed gradient profile loss to reconstructing the sharp boundary of the characters. This loss helps us to distinguish between the characters and backgrounds better and generate a more explicit shape. Thirdly, the misalignment of the paired images is inevitable due to the inaccuracy of the cameras. We propose a central alignment module to make the corresponding pixels more aligned. We evaluate the recognition accuracy by two steps: **(1)** Do super-resolution with different methods on LR text images; **(2)** Evaluate the SR text images with trained Text Recognizers *e.g.* ASTER, MOCAN and CRNN. Extensive experiments show our TSRN clearly outperforms 7 state-of-the-art SR methods in boosting the recognition accuracy of LR images in TextZoom. For example, it outperforms LapSRN by over 5% and 8% on recognition accuracy of ASTER and CRNN. Our results suggest that low-resolution text recognition in the wild is far from being solved, thus more research effort is needed.

The contributions of this work are therefore three-fold:

1. We introduce the first **real** paired scene text SR dataset TextZoom with different focal lengths. We annotate and allocate the dataset with three subsets: easy, medium and hard, respectively.
2. We prove the superiority of the proposed dataset TextZoom by comparing and analyzing the models trained on synthetic LR and proposed LR images. We also prove the necessity of scene text SR from different aspects.
3. We propose a new text super-resolution network with three novel modules. It surpasses 7 representative SR methods clearly by training and testing them on TextZoom for fair comparisons.

2   Related Work

Super-Resolution. Super-resolution aims to output a plausible high-resolution image that is consistent with a given low-resolution image. Traditional approaches, such as bilinear, bicubic or designed filtering, leverage the insight that neighboring pixels usually exhibit similar colors and generate the output by interpolating between the colors of neighboring pixels according to a predefined formula. In the deep learning era, super-resolution is treated as a regression problem, where the input is the low-resolution image, and the target output is the high-resolution image [7,20–24,47]. A deep neural net is trained on the input and target output pairs to minimize some distance metric between the prediction and the ground truth. These works are mainly trained and evaluated on those popular datasets [2,14,30,31,40,45]. In these datasets, LR images are generated by a down-sample interpolation or Gaussian blur filter. Recently, several works capture LR-HR images pairs by adjusting the focal length of the cameras [4,5,46]. In [4,5], a pre-processing method is applied to reduce the misalignment between the captured LR and HR images While in [46], a contextual bilateral loss is proposed to leverage the misalignment. In this work, a new dataset TextZoom is proposed, which fills in the absence of paired scene text SR dataset. It is well annotated and allocated with difficulty. We hope it can serve as a challenging benchmark.

Text Recognition. Early work adopts a bottom-up fashion [18] which detects individual characters firstly and integrates them into a word, or a top-down manner [16], which treats the word image patch as a whole and recognizes it as a multi-class image classification problem. Considering that scene text generally appears as a character sequence, CRNN [36] regard it as a sequence recognition problem and employs Recurrent Neural Network (RNNs) to model the sequential features. CTC [10] loss is often combined with the RNN outputs for calculating the conditional probability between the predicted sequences and the target [25,26]. Recently, an increasing number of recognition approaches based on the attention mechanism have achieved significant improvements [6,28]. ASTER [37] rectified oriented or curved text based on Spatial Transformer Network(STN) [17] and then performed recognition using an attentional sequence-to-sequence model. In this work, we choose state-of-the-art recognizer ASTER [37], MORAN [28] and CRNN [36] as baseline recognizers to evaluate the recognition accuracy of the SR images.

Scene Text Image Super-Resolution. Some previous works conducted on scene text image super-resolution are aimed at improving the recognition accuracy and image quality evaluation metrics. [29] compared the performance of several artificial filters on down-sampled text images. [32] propose a convolution-transposed convolution architecture to deal with binary document SR. [8] adapt SRCNN [7] in text image SR in the ICDAR 2015 competition TextSR [33] and achieved a good performance, but no text-oriented method was proposed.

These works take a step on low-resolution text recognition, but they only train on down-sampled images, learning to regress a simple mapping function of inverse-bicubic (or bilinear) interpolation. Since all the LR images are identically generated by a simple down-sample formulation, it is not well-generalized to real text images.

3   TextZoom Dataset

Data Collection and Annotation. Our proposed dataset TextZoom comes from two state-of-the-art SISR datasets: RealSR [4] and SRRAW [46]. These two newly proposed datasets consist of paired LR-HR images captured by digital cameras.

RealSR [4] is captured by four focal lengths with two digital cameras: Canon 5D3 and Nikon D810. In RealSR [4], these four focal lengths of images are allocated as ground truth, 2X LR images, 3X LR images, 4X LR images separately. For RealSR, we annotate the bounding box of the words on the 105 mm focal length images. SR-RAW is collected by seven different focal lengths with SONY FE camera, range from 24–240 mm. The images captured in shorted focal lengths could be used as LR images while those captured in longer lengths as corresponding ground truth. For SR-RAW, we annotate the bounding box of the words on the 240 mm focal length images.

We labeled the images with the largest focal length of each group and cropped the text boxes from the rest following the same rectangle. So the misalignment is unavoidable. There are some top-down or vertical text boxes in the annotated results. In this task, we rotate all of these images to horizontal for better recognition. There are only a few curved text images in our dataset. For each pair of LR-HR images, we provide the annotation of the case sensitive character string (including punctuation), the type of the bounding box, and the original focal lengths. We demonstrate the detailed annotation principle of the text images cropped from SR-RAW and RealSR in detail in supplementary materials.

The size of the cropped text boxes is diverse, *e.g.* height from 7 to 1700 pixels, so it is not suitable to treat the text images cropped from the same focal lengths as a same domain. We define our principle following these considerations. **(1) No patching.** In SISR, data are usually generated by cropping patches from the original images [4,9,22,23,46]. Text images could not be cut into patches since the shape of the characters should maintain completed. **(2) Accuracy distribution.** We divide the text images by height and test the accuracy (Refer to the Tables showed in supplementary materials). We found that the accuracy does not increase obviously when the height is larger than 32 pixels. Setting images to 32 pixels height is also a customary rule in scene text recognition research [6,28,36]. The accuracy of the images smaller than 8 pixels are too low, which hardly has any value for super-resolution, so we discard the images the height of which is less than 8 pixels. **(3) Number.** We found that in the cropped text images, the height range from 8 to 32 claim the majority. **(4) No downsample.** Since the interpolation degradation should not be introduced into real blur images, we could only up-sample the LR images to a relatively bigger size.

Following these 4 considerations, we up-sample the images ranging from 16–32 pixels height to 32 pixels height, and up-sample the images ranging from 8–16 pixels height to 16 pixels height. We conclude that (16, 32) should be a good pair to form a 2X train set for scene text SR task. For example, the text images taken from 150 mm focal length and height sized in 16–32 pixels would be taken as a ground truth for the 70 mm counterpart. So we selected all the images the height of which range from 16 pixels to 32 pixels as our ground truth image and up-sample them to the size of 128×32 (width $\times$ height), and the corresponding 2X LR images to the size of 64×16 (width $\times$ height). For this task, we only generate this 2X LR-HR pair dataset from the annotated text images mainly due to the special characteristics of text recognition. Other scale of factors of our annotated images could be used for different purpose.

Allocation of TextZoom. The SR-RAW and RealSR are collected by different cameras with different focal lengths. The distance from the objects also affect the legibility of the images. So the dataset should be further divided following their distribution.

The train-set and test-set are cropped from the original train-set and test-set in SR-RAW and RealSR separately. The author of SR-RAW used larger distance from the camera to the subjects to minimize the perspective shift [46]. So the accuracy of text images from SR-RAW is relatively lower under the similar focal lengths compared to RealSR. The accuracy of the images cropped from 100mm focal lengths in SR-RAW is 52.1% tested by ASTER [37], while the accuracy of those from 105mm in RealSR is 75.0% tested by ASTER [37] (Refer to the Tables showed in supplementary materials). With the same height, the images of smaller focal lengths are more blurred. With this in mind, we allocate our dataset into three subsets by difficulty. The LR images cropped from RealSR render **easy**. The LR images from SR-RAW and the focal lengths of which larger than 50 mm are viewed as **medium**. The rest are as **hard**.

In this task, our main purpose is to increase the **recognition accuracy** of the easy, medium and hard subsets. We also show the results of peak signal to noise ratio (PSNR) and structural similarity index (SSIM) in the supplementary materials.

Dataset Statistics. The detailed statistics of TextZoom is shown in supplementary materials.

4   Method

In this section, we present our proposed method TSRN in detail. Firstly, we briefly describe our pipeline in Sect. 4.1. Then we demonstrate the proposed Sequential Residual Block. Thirdly, we introduce our central alignment module. Finally, we introduce a new gradient profile loss to sharpen the text boundaries.

4.1   Pipeline

Our baseline is SRResNet [23]. As shown in Fig. 3, we mainly make two modifications to the structure of SRResNet: 1) add a central alignment module in front of the network; 2) replace the original basic blocks with the proposed Sequential Residual Blocks (SRBs). In this work, we concatenate the binary mask with RGB image as our input. The binary masks are simply generated by calculating the mean gray scale of the image. The detailed information of masks is shown in supplementary materials. During training, firstly, the input is rectified by central alignment module. Then we use CNN layers to extract shallow features from the rectified image. Stacking five SRBs, we extract deeper and sequential dependent feature and do shortcut connection following ResNet [12]. The SR images are

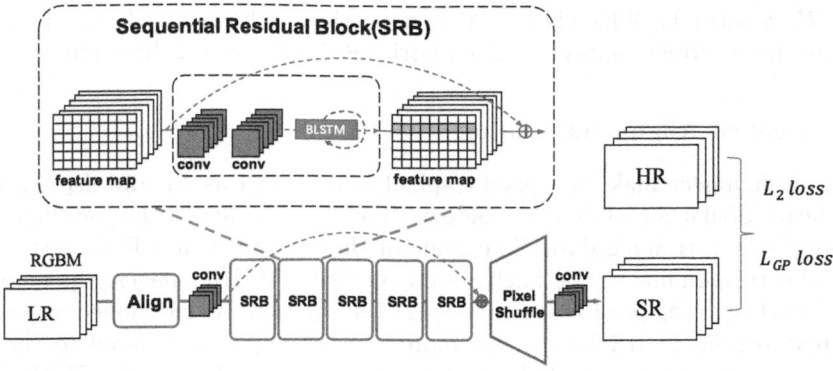

Fig. 3. The illustration of our proposed TSRN. We concatenate binary mask with RGB channels as a RGBM 4-channel input. The input is recitified by central alignment module and then fed into our pipeline. The output is the super-resolved RGB image. The outputs are supervised by $L_2 loss$. The RGB channels of the outputs are supervised by L_{GP} loss.

finally generated by up-sampling block and CNN. We also design a gradient prior loss (L_{GP}) aiming at enhancing the shape boundary of the characters. The output of the network is supervised by MSELoss (L_2) and our proposed gradient profile loss (L_{GP}).

4.2 Sequential Residual Block

Previous state-of-the-art SR methods mainly pursue better performance in PSNR and SSIM. Traditional SISR only cares about texture reconstruction while text images have strong sequential characteristics. In text recognition tasks, scene text images encode the context information for text recognition by Recurrent Neural Network (RNN) [13]. Inspired from them, we modified the residual blocks [23] by adding Bi-directional LSTM (BLSTM) mechanism. Inspired by [39], we build sequence connectionist in horizontal lines and fused the feature into deeper channels. Different from [39], we build the in-network recurrence architecture not for detecting but for low-level reconstruction, so we only adapt the idea of building text line sequence dependence. In Fig. 3, the SRB is briefly illustrated. Firstly, we extract feature by CNN. Then permute and resize the feature map as the horizontal text line can be encoded into sequence. Then the BLSTM can propagate error differentials [36], and invert the feature maps into feature sequences, and feed them back to the convolutional layers. To make the sequence dependent robust for tilted text images, we introduce the BLSTM from two directions, horizontal and vertical. BLSTM takes the horizontal and vertical convolutional feature as sequential inputs, and updates its internal state recurrently in the hidden layer.

$$H_{t_1} = \phi_1(X_{t_1}, H_{t_1-1}), \quad t_1 = 1, 2, ..., W$$
$$H_{t_2} = \phi_1(X_{t_2}, H_{t_2-1}), \quad t_2 = 1, 2, ..., H$$

$$(1)$$

Here H_t denotes the hidden layers, X_t denotes the input features, t_1, t_2 separately denote the recurrent connection from horizontal and vertical direction.

4.3 Central Alignment Module

The misalignment make the pixel-to-pixel losses, such as L_1 and L_2 generate significant artifacts and double shadows. This mainly due to the misalignment of the pixels in training data. Sine some of the text pixels in LR images are in spatial corresponding to the background pixels in the HR images, the network could learn a wrong pixel-wise counterpart information. As mentioned in Sect. 3, the text regions in HR images are more central aligned compared to the LR images. So we introduce STN[17] as our central alignment module. The STN is a spatial transform network which can rectify the images and be learned end-to-end. To rectify spatial variation flexibly, we adopt TPS transformation as the transform manipulation. Once the text regions in LR images are aligned adjacent the center, the pixel-wise losses would make better performance and the artifacts could be relieved. We show more detailed information of central alignment module in supplementary materials.

4.4 Gradient Profile Loss

Gradient Profile Prior (GPP) is proposed in [38] to generate sharper edge in SISR task. Gradient field means the spatial gradient of the RGB values of the pixels.

Since we have a paired text super-resolution dataset, we could use the gradient field of HR images as ground truth. Generally, the color of characters in text images contrast strongly with the backgrounds. So sharpening the boundaries rather than smooth ones of characters could make the characters more explicit (Fig. 4).

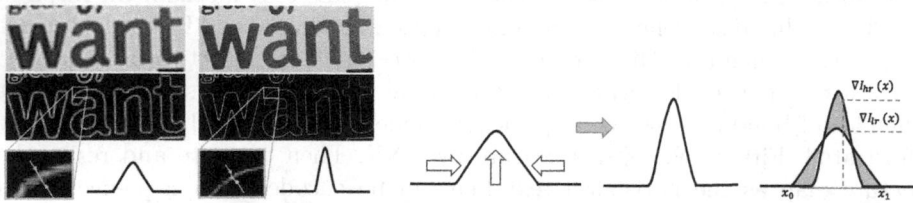

Fig. 4. The illustration of gradient field and Gradient Prior Loss.

We revisit the GPP and generate ground truth from HR images, then we define the loss function as below:

$$L_{GP} = \mathbb{E}_x ||\nabla I_{hr}(x) - \nabla I_{sr}(x)||_1 \qquad (x \in [x_0,\ x_1]) \tag{2}$$

$\nabla I_{hr}(x)$ denotes the gradient field of HR images, and $\nabla I_{sr}(x)$ denotes that of SR images.

Our proposed L_{GP} exhibits two advantageous properties: (1) The gradient field vividly show the characteristics of text images: the texts and backgrounds. (2) The LR images always come with wider curve of gradient field, while HR images mean thinner curve. And the curve of gradient field could be easily generated through mathematical calculation. This ensures a confidential supervision label.

5 Experiments

5.1 Datasets

We train the SR methods on our proposed TextZoom (see Sect. 3.) training set. We evaluate our models on our three subsets **easy**, **medium** and **hard**. To avoid down-sample degradation, all the LR images are up-sampled to 64×16, and HR images to 128×32.

5.2 Implementation Details

During training, we set the trade-off weight of L_2 loss as 1 and L_{GP} as $1e-4$. We use the Adam optimizer with momentum term 0.9. When evaluating recognition accuracy, we use the official Pytorch version code and the released model of ASTER: aster.pytorch, MORAN: MORAN_v2.pytorch, CRNN: crnn.pytorch from github.

All the SR models are trained by 500 epochs with 4 NVIDIA GTX 1080ti GPUs. The batch-size is adapted as the setting in the original papers.

5.3 Is SR Necessary for Text Recognition?

We further quantitatively analyzed the necessity of super-resolution from three aspects.

It is assumed that we could achieve better performance on recognizing low-resolution (LR) text images if we directly train the recognition networks on small size images, and then the super-resolution procedure could be removed. This query is reasonable because the deep neural networks have a strong robustness on the training domains. To refute this query and prove the necessity of super-resolution for text images, we compare the recognition accuracy of 4 methods:

- **Released.** Recognize with ASTER [37] model trained on customary size (no less than 32 pixels in height, We use official released model here).
- **ReIm.** Recognize with model trained on low-resolution images (In this work, we re-implemented ASTER [37] on Syn90K [15] and SynthText [11] at the size of 64×16, All the training details are the same as the original paper except the input sizes

Table 2. Comparison between different methods. **Released** means official released model from github. **ReIm** means our re-implemented model trained on Syn90K [15] and SynthText [11] at the size of 64 × 16.

Method	Recognition accuracy	
	TextZoom	CommonLR
Released	47.2%	75.3%
ReIm	52.6%	79.3%
Fine-tune	**59.3%**	73.2%
Ours	58.3%	**80.3%**

- **Fine-tune.** Fine-tune released ASTER [37] model on our TextZoom training set.
- **Ours.** Choose the low resolution images by size, then use our proposed TSRN to generate the SR images and then recognize them with ASTER [37] official released model.

To verify the robustness, we select all the images smaller than 64 × 16 from 7 common scene text testing sets, IC13, IC15, CUTE, IC03, SVT, SVTP, CUTE and IIIT5K and get 436 images in total. We term this testing set **CommonLR**. We compare these 4 methods on our dataset TextZoom and CommonLR. From Table 2, we can figure that the re-implemented model do increase the accuracy sharply on the LR images. The average accuracy of TextZoom can be increased by 5.4%, from 47.2% to 52.6%. And the accuracy of CommonLR could also be improved for 5%. The result of re-implemented model is still lower than the accuracy of our results (TSRN(ours) + ASTER(Released)).

When we fine-tune the Aster on our TextZoom training set, the accuracy of TextZoom testing set would be even higher than our method. But TextZoom is a small sized dataset for recognition task, its different distribution would make the recognizer over-fit on it. The accuracy of CommonLR of fine-tune method is the lowest. Moreover, on this fine-tune Aster model the other testing sets like IC13, IC15, etc. would drop sharply for more than 10.0% points.

Actually, our method is superior to fine-tune and re-Im methods in following aspects. (1). The fine-tuned model over-fit on TextZoom. It achieves highest performance on TextZoom while lowest on CommomLR because the number of TextZoom is far from enough for text recognition task. Super-resolution, a low-level task, usually needs less data to converge. Our method could directly choose SR or not by the size and get better overall performance.

(2). Our SR method can also produce better visual results for people to read (see Fig. 5). (3). While re-Im and fine-tune method need 2 recognition models for big and small size images separately, our method only need a tiny SR model, introducing marginal computation cost. This part could be found in supplementary materials.

So the SR methods could be a effective and convenient pre-processing procedure of scene text recognition.

5.4   Synthetic LR vs. TextZoom LR

To demonstrate the superiority of paired scene text SR images, we compare the performance of the models trained on synthetic datasets and our TextZoom dataset. The quantitative results are shown in the supplementary materials.

Table 3. Ablation study for different settings of our method TSRN. The recognition accuracies are tested by the official released model of ASTER [37].

Configuration		Accuracy of ASTER [37]			
Method	Loss function	Easy	Medium	Hard	Average
0	SRResNet	$L_2 + L_{tv} + L_p$	69.6%	47.6%	34.3%	51.3%
1	5 × SRBs	L_2	74.5%	53.3%	37.3%	56.2%
2	5 × SRBs + align	L_2	74.8%	55.7%	39.6%	57.8%
3	5 × SRBs + align (**Ours**)	$L_2 + L_{GP}$	**75.1%**	**56.3%**	**40.1%**	**58.3%**

5.5   Ablation Study on TSRN

In order to study the effect of each component in TSRN, we gradually modify the configuration of our network and compare their differences to build a best network. For brevity, we only compare the accuracy of ASTER [37].

Fig. 5. Visual comparisons for showing the effects of each component in our proposed TSRN. The recognition result strings of ASTER are displayed under each image. Those characters in red denote wrong recognition.

1) SRBs. We add BLSTM mechanism to the basic residual block in SRResNet [23] and get the proposed SRB. The SRB is the essential component in TSRN. Comparing # 0 and # 1 in Table 3, stacking 5 SRBs, we can boost up the average accuracy by 4.9% compared to SRResNet [23].

2) Central Alignment Module. Central alignment module can boost the average accuracy by 1.5%, as shown in Table 3 method 2. From Fig. 5, we can find that without central alignment module, the artifacts are strong, and the characters are twisted. While with more appropriate alignment, we could generate higher quality images since the pixel-wise loss function could supervise the training better.

3) Gradient Profile Loss. From Table 3 method 3, we can find the proposed gradient profile loss can boost the average accuracy by 0.5%. Although the increase is slight, the visual results are better (Fig. 5 method 3).

In supplementary materials, we further discuss about the detailed component of our method.

5.6   Comparison with State-of-the-Art SR Methods

Table 4. Performance of state-of-the-art SR methods on the three subsets in TextZoom. For better displaying, we calculated the average accuracy. L_1 denotes Mean Average Error (MAE) Loss. L_2 denotes Mean Squared Error (MSE) Loss. L_{tv} denotes Total Variation Loss. L_p denotes Perceptual Loss proposed in [19]. *Charbonnier* denotes the Charbonnier Loss proposed in LapSRN [21]. L_{GP} denotes our proposed Gradient Prior Loss. The recognition accuracies are tested by the official released model of ASTER [37], MORAN [28] and CRNN [36].

Method	Loss function	Accuracy of ASTER [37]				Accuracy of MORAN [28]				Accuracy of CRNN [36]			
		Easy	Medium	Hard	Average	Easy	Medium	Hard	Average	Easy	Medium	Hard	Average
BICUBIC	–	64.7%	42.4%	31.2%	47.2%	60.6%	37.9%	30.8%	44.1%	36.4%	21.1%	21.1%	26.8%
SRCNN [7]	L_2	69.4%	43.4%	32.2%	49.5%	63.2%	39.0%	30.2%	45.3%	38.7%	21.6%	20.9%	27.7%
VDSR [20]	L_2	71.7%	43.5%	34.0%	51.0%	62.3%	42.5%	30.5%	46.1%	41.2%	25.6%	23.3%	30.7%
SRResNet [23]	$L_2 + L_{tv} + L_p$	69.6%	47.6%	34.3%	51.3%	60.7%	42.9%	32.6%	46.3%	39.7%	27.6%	22.7%	30.6%
RRDB [22]	L_1	70.9%	44.4%	32.5%	50.6%	63.9%	41.0%	30.8%	46.3%	40.6%	22.1%	21.9%	28.9%
EDSR [24]	L_1	72.3%	48.6%	34.3%	53.0%	63.6%	45.4%	32.2%	48.1%	42.7%	29.3%	24.1%	32.7%
RDN [47]	L_1	70.0%	47.0%	34.0%	51.5%	61.7%	42.0%	31.6%	46.1%	41.6%	24.4%	23.5%	30.5%
LapSRN [21]	*Charbonnier*	71.5%	48.6%	35.2%	53.0%	64.6%	44.9%	32.2%	48.3%	46.1%	27.9%	23.6%	33.3%
TSRN(ours)	$L_2 + L_{GP}$	**75.1%**	**56.3%**	**40.1%**	**58.3%**	**70.1%**	**53.3%**	**37.9%**	**54.8%**	**52.5%**	**38.2%**	**31.4%**	**41.4%**
Improvement of TSRN		10.4%	13.9%	8.9%	11.1%	9.5%	15.4%	7.1%	10.7%	16.1%	17.1%	10.3%	14.6%

To prove the effectiveness of TSRN, we compare it with 7 SISR methods on our TextZoom dataset, including SRCNN [7], VDSR [20], SRResNet [23], RRDB [22], EDSR [24], RDN [47] and LapSRN [21]. All of the networks are trained on our TextZoom training set and evaluated on our three testing subsets.

In Table 4, we list the recognition accuracy tested by ASTER [37], MORAN [28], and CRNN [36] of all the mentioned 7 methods, along with BICUBIC and the proposed TSRN. In Table 4, it can be observed that TSRN outperforms all the 7 SISR methods in recognition accuracy sharply. Although these 7 SISR methods could achieve a relatively good accuracy, what we should pay attention to is the gap between SR results and BICUBIC. These methods could improve the average accuracy 2.3%–5.8%, while ours could improve 10.7%–14.6%. We can also find that our TSRN could improve the accuracy on all of the three state-of-the-art recognizers. In the supplementary materials, we show the results of PSNR and SSIM and show that our TSRN could also surpass most of the state-of-the-art methods in PSNR and SSIM.

	heights	FORMULAS	minimum	guardrails	naturelles	supervisor	While
HR	heights	formulas	minimum	guardrails	naturelles	supervisor	while
BICUBIC	has	power	and	from	naturalles	superniser	what
SRCNN	the	formular	able	was	naturalies	superniser	what
VDSR	topic	formulad	and	quartnt	naturallos	supervisor	wh3s
SRResNet	helpm	formulad	am	goardish	naturalies	superrisor	while
RRDB	less	formulad	and	with	naturolog	superniser	what
EDSR	leigh(s)	formulad	when	youndnt	naturallos	supervisor	what
RDN	leigh(ts)	formulad	anun	young	naturalies	supervisor	wh3s
LapSRN	telpo	formulad	man	youd	naturallos	supervisor	what
Ours	heights	formulas	minimum	guardrails	naturelles	supervisor	while

Fig. 6. Visualization results of state-of-the-art SR methods on our proposed dataset TextZoom. The character strings under the images are recognition results of ASTER [37]. Those in red denote wrong recognition.

6   Conclusion and Discussion

In this work, we verify the importance of scene text image super-resolution task. We proposed the TextZoom dataset, which is, to the best of our knowledge, the first real paired scene text image super-resolution dataset. The TextZoom is well annotated and allocated and divided into three subset: easy, medium and hard. Through extensive experiments, we demonstrated the superiority of real data over synthetic data. To tackle text images super-resolution task, we build a new text-oriented SR method TSRN. Our TSRN clearly outperforms 7 SR methods. It also shows low-resolution text SR and recognition is far from being solved, thus more research effort is needed (Fig. 6).

In the future, we will capture more appropriately distributed text images. Extremely large and small images will be avoided. The images should also contain more kinds of languages, such as Chinese, French and Germany. We will also focus on new methods such as introducing recognition attention into the text super-resolution task.

Acknowledgement. Xiang Bai was supported by the Program for HUST Academic Frontier Youth Team 2017QYTD08.

References

1. Baek, J., et al.: What is wrong with scene text recognition model comparisons? Dataset and model analysis. arXiv preprint arXiv:1904.01906 (2019)

2. Bevilacqua, M., Roumy, A., Guillemot, C., Alberi-Morel, M.: Low-complexity single-image super-resolution based on nonnegative neighbor embedding. In: BMVC (2012)
3. Björklund, T., Fiandrotti, A., Annarumma, M., Francini, G., Magli, E.: Robust license plate recognition using neural networks trained on synthetic images. Pattern Recognit. **93**, 134–146 (2019)
4. Cai, J., Zeng, H., Yong, H., Cao, Z., Zhang, L.: Toward real-world single image super-resolution: a new benchmark and a new model. In: ICCV (2019)
5. Chen, C., Xiong, Z., Tian, X., Zha, Z., Wu, F.: Camera lens super-resolution. In: CVPR (2019)
6. Cheng, Z., Bai, F., Xu, Y., Zheng, G., Pu, S., Zhou, S.: Focusing attention: towards accurate text recognition in natural images. In: Proceedings of the IEEE International Conference on Computer Vision (2017)
7. Dong, C., Loy, C.C., He, K., Tang, X.: Image super-resolution using deep convolutional networks. TPAMI (2015)
8. Dong, C., Zhu, X., Deng, Y., Loy, C.C., Qiao, Y.: Boosting optical character recognition: a super-resolution approach. arXiv preprint arXiv:1506.02211 (2015)
9. Ferrari, V., Hebert, M., Sminchisescu, C., Weiss, Y. (eds.): ECCV 2018. LNCS, vol. 11211. Springer, Cham (2018). https://doi.org/10.1007/978-3-030-01234-2
10. Graves, A., Fernández, S., Gomez, F., Schmidhuber, J.: Connectionist temporal classification: labelling unsegmented sequence data with recurrent neural networks. In: Proceedings of the International Conference on Machine Learning (2006)
11. Gupta, A., Vedaldi, A., Zisserman, A.: Synthetic data for text localisation in natural images. In: Proceedings of the IEEE Conference on Computer Vision and Pattern Recognition (2016)
12. He, K., Zhang, X., Ren, S., Sun, J.: Deep residual learning for image recognition. In: CVPR (2016)
13. He, P., Huang, W., Qiao, Y., Loy, C.C., Tang, X.: Reading scene text in deep convolutional sequences. In: AAAI (2016)
14. Huang, J.B., Singh, A., Ahuja, N.: Single image super-resolution from transformed self-exemplars. In: CVPR (2015)
15. Jaderberg, M., Simonyan, K., Vedaldi, A., Zisserman, A.: Synthetic data and artificial neural networks for natural scene text recognition. arXiv preprint arXiv:1406.2227 (2014)
16. Jaderberg, M., Simonyan, K., Vedaldi, A., Zisserman, A.: Reading text in the wild with convolutional neural networks. IJCV **116**, 1–20 (2016)
17. Jaderberg, M., Simonyan, K., Zisserman, A., et al.: Spatial transformer networks. In: Proceedings of the Advances in Neural Information Processing Systems (2015)
18. Jaderberg, M., Vedaldi, A., Zisserman, A.: Deep features for text spotting. In: Fleet, D., Pajdla, T., Schiele, B., Tuytelaars, T. (eds.) ECCV 2014. LNCS, vol. 8692, pp. 512–528. Springer, Cham (2014). https://doi.org/10.1007/978-3-319-10593-2_34
19. Johnson, J., Alahi, A., Fei-Fei, L.: Perceptual losses for real-time style transfer and super-resolution. In: Leibe, B., Matas, J., Sebe, N., Welling, M. (eds.) ECCV 2016. LNCS, vol. 9906, pp. 694–711. Springer, Cham (2016). https://doi.org/10.1007/978-3-319-46475-6_43
20. Kim, J., Lee, J.K., Lee, K.M.: Accurate image super-resolution using very deep convolutional networks. In: CVPR (2016)
21. Lai, W., Huang, J., Ahuja, N., Yang, M.: Deep Laplacian pyramid networks for fast and accurate super-resolution. In: CVPR (2017)

22. Leal-Taixé, L., Roth, S. (eds.): ECCV 2018, Part III. LNCS, vol. 11131. Springer, Cham (2019). https://doi.org/10.1007/978-3-030-11015-4
23. Ledig, C., et al.: Photo-realistic single image super-resolution using a generative adversarial network. In: Proceedings of the IEEE Conference on Computer Vision and Pattern Recognition (2017)
24. Lim, B., Son, S., Kim, H., Nah, S., Lee, K.M.: Enhanced deep residual networks for single image super-resolution. In: CVPR (2017)
25. Liu, W., Chen, C., Wong, K.Y.K., Su, Z., Han, J.: Star-net: a spatial attention residue network for scene text recognition. In: Proceedings of the British Machine Vision Conference (2016)
26. Liu, Z., Li, Y., Ren, F., Goh, W.L., Yu, H.: SqueezedText: a real-time scene text recognition by binary convolutional encoder-decoder network. In: Proceedings of the AAAI Conference on Artificial Intelligence (2018)
27. Long, S., He, X., Ya, C.: Scene text detection and recognition: the deep learning era. arXiv preprint arXiv:1811.04256 (2018)
28. Luo, C., Jin, L., Sun, Z.: Moran: a multi-object rectified attention network for scene text recognition. Pattern Recognit. **90**, 109–118 (2019)
29. Mancas-Thillou, C., Mirmehdi, M.: An introduction to super-resolution text. In: Chaudhuri, B.B. (ed.) Digital Document Processing. Advances in Pattern Recognition, pp. 305–327. Springer, London (2007). https://doi.org/10.1007/978-1-84628-726-8_14
30. Martin, D.R., Fowlkes, C.C., Tal, D., Malik, J.: A database of human segmented natural images and its application to evaluating segmentation algorithms and measuring ecological statistics. In: ICCV (2001)
31. Matsui, Y., Ito, K., Aramaki, Y., Fujimoto, A., Ogawa, T., Yamasaki, T., Aizawa, K.: Sketch-based manga retrieval using manga109 dataset. Multimed. Tools Appl. **76**(20), 21811–21838 (2016). https://doi.org/10.1007/s11042-016-4020-z
32. Pandey, R.K., Vignesh, K., Ramakrishnan, A., et al.: Binary document image super resolution for improved readability and OCR performance. arXiv preprint arXiv:1812.02475 (2018)
33. Peyrard, C., Baccouche, M., Mamalet, F., Garcia, C.: ICDAR 2015 competition on text image super-resolution. In: ICDAR (2015)
34. Ray, A., et al.: An end-to-end trainable framework for joint optimization of document enhancement and recognition. In: ICDAR (2019)
35. Sánchez, J., Romero, V., Toselli, A.H., Villegas, M., Vidal, E.: A set of benchmarks for handwritten text recognition on historical documents. Pattern Recognit. **94**, 122–134 (2019)
36. Shi, B., Bai, X., Yao, C.: An end-to-end trainable neural network for image-based sequence recognition and its application to scene text recognition. IEEE Trans. Pattern Anal. Mach. Intell. **39**, 2298–2304 (2017)
37. Shi, B., Yang, M., Wang, X., Lyu, P., Yao, C., Bai, X.: ASTER: an attentional scene text recognizer with flexible rectification. IEEE Trans. Pattern Anal. Mach. Intell. **41**, 2035–2048 (2018)
38. Sun, J., Sun, J., Xu, Z., Shum, H.: Gradient profile prior and its applications in image super-resolution and enhancement. TIP **20**, 1529–1542 (2011)
39. Tian, Z., Huang, W., He, T., He, P., Qiao, Yu.: Detecting text in natural image with connectionist text proposal network. In: Leibe, B., Matas, J., Sebe, N., Welling, M. (eds.) ECCV 2016. LNCS, vol. 9912, pp. 56–72. Springer, Cham (2016). https://doi.org/10.1007/978-3-319-46484-8_4
40. Timofte, R., Agustsson, E., Van Gool, L., Yang, M.H., Zhang, L.: NTIRE 2017 challenge on single image super-resolution: methods and results. In: CVPRW (2017)

41. Wang, W., et al.: Shape robust text detection with progressive scale expansion network. In: CVPR (2019)
42. Wang, W., et al.: Efficient and accurate arbitrary-shaped text detection with pixel aggregation network (2019)
43. Wu, Y., Yin, F., Liu, C.: Improving handwritten Chinese text recognition using neural network language models and convolutional neural network shape models. Pattern Recognit. **65**, 251–264 (2017)
44. Xie, E., Zang, Y., Shao, S., Yu, G., Yao, C., Li, G.: Scene text detection with supervised pyramid context network. In: AAAI (2019)
45. Zeyde, R., Elad, M., Protter, M.: On single image scale-up using sparse-representations. In: Boissonnat, J.-D., Chenin, P., Cohen, A., Gout, C., Lyche, T., Mazure, M.-L., Schumaker, L. (eds.) Curves and Surfaces 2010. LNCS, vol. 6920, pp. 711–730. Springer, Heidelberg (2012). https://doi.org/10.1007/978-3-642-27413-8_47
46. Zhang, X., Chen, Q., Ng, R., Koltun, V.: Zoom to learn, learn to zoom. In: CVPR (2019)
47. Zhang, Y., Tian, Y., Kong, Y., Zhong, B., Fu, Y.: Residual dense network for image super-resolution. In: CVPR (2018)

Coupling Explicit and Implicit Surface Representations for Generative 3D Modeling

Omid Poursaeed[1,2]($\boxtimes$), Matthew Fisher[3], Noam Aigerman[3],
and Vladimir G. Kim[3]

[1] Cornell University, New York, USA
op63@cornell.edu
[2] Cornell Tech, New York, USA
[3] Adobe Research, San Jose, USA

Abstract. We propose a novel neural architecture for representing 3D surfaces, which harnesses two complementary shape representations: (i) an explicit representation via an atlas, i.e., embeddings of 2D domains into 3D; (ii) an implicit-function representation, i.e., a scalar function over the 3D volume, with its levels denoting surfaces. We make these two representations synergistic by introducing novel consistency losses that ensure that the surface created from the atlas aligns with the level-set of the implicit function. Our hybrid architecture outputs results which are superior to the output of the two equivalent single-representation networks, yielding smoother explicit surfaces with more accurate normals, and a more accurate implicit occupancy function. Additionally, our surface reconstruction step can directly leverage the explicit atlas-based representation. This process is computationally efficient, and can be directly used by differentiable rasterizers, enabling training our hybrid representation with image-based losses.

1 Introduction

Many applications rely on a neural network to generate a 3D geometry [8,12], where early approaches used point clouds [1], uniform voxel grids [18], or template mesh deformations [2] to parameterize the outputs. The main disadvantage of these representations is that they rely on a pre-selected discretization of the output, limiting network's ability to focus its capacity on high-entropy regions. Several recent geometry learning techniques address this limitation by representing 3D shapes as *continuous* mappings over vector spaces. Neural networks learn over a manifold of these mappings, creating a mathematically elegant and visually compelling generative models. Two prominent alternatives have been proposed recently.

Electronic supplementary material The online version of this chapter (https://doi.org/10.1007/978-3-030-58607-2_39) contains supplementary material, which is available to authorized users.

© Springer Nature Switzerland AG 2020
A. Vedaldi et al. (Eds.): ECCV 2020, LNCS 12355, pp. 667–683, 2020.
https://doi.org/10.1007/978-3-030-58607-2_39

The explicit surface representation defines the surface as an atlas – a collection of *charts*, which are maps from 2D to 3D, $\{f_i : \Omega_i \subset \mathbb{R}^2 \to \mathbb{R}^3\}$, with each chart mapping a 2D patch Ω_i into a part of the 3D surface. the surface S is then defined as the union of all 3D patches, $S = \cup_i f_i(\Omega_i)$. In the context of neural networks, this representation has been explored in a line of works considering atlas-based architectures [11,34] which exactly represent surfaces by having the network predict the charts $\{f_i^{\mathbf{x}}\}$, where the network also takes latent code, $\mathbf{x} \in \mathcal{X}$, as input, to describe the target shape. These predicted charts can then be queried at arbitrary 2D points, enabling approximating the resulting surface with, e.g., a polygonal mesh, by densely sampling the 2D domain with the vertices of a mesh, and then mapping the resulting mesh to 3D via $f_i^{\mathbf{x}}$. This reconstruction step is suitable for an end-to-end learning pipeline where the loss is computed over the resulting surface. It can also be used as an input to a differentiable rasterization layer in case image-based losses are desired. On the other hand, the disadvantage of atlas-based methods is that the resulting surfaces tend to have visual artifacts due to inconsistencies at patch boundaries.

The implicit surface representation defines a volumetric function $g : \mathbb{R} \to \mathbb{R}^3$. This function is called an implicit function, with the surface S defined as its zero level set, $S = \{p \in \mathbb{R}^3 | g(p) = 0\}$. Many works train networks to predict implicit functions, either as signed distance fields [5,25], or simply occupancy values [24]. They also typically use shape descriptor, $\hat{\mathbf{x}} \in \hat{\mathcal{X}}$, as additional input to express different shapes: $g^{\hat{\mathbf{x}}}$. These methods tend to produce visually appealing results since they are smooth with respect to the 3D volume. They suffer from two main disadvantages; first, they do not immediately produce a surface, making them less suitable for end-to-end pipeline with surface-based or image-based losses; second, as observed in [5,24,25], their final output tends to produce a higher surface-to-surface distance to ground truth than atlas-based methods.

In this paper we propose to use both representations in a hybrid manner, with our network predicting both an explicit atlas $\{f_i\}$ and an implicit function g. For the two branches of the two representations we use the AtlasNet [11] and OccupancyNet [24] architectures. We use the same loses used to train these two networks (chamfer distance and occupancy, respectively) while adding novel consistency losses that couple the two representations during joint training to ensure that the atlas embedding aligns with the implicit level-set. We show the two representations reinforce one another: OccupancyNet learns to shift its level-set to align it better with the ground truth surface, and AtlasNet learns to align the embedded points and their normals to the level-set. This results in smoother normals that are more consistent with the ground truth for the atlas representation, while also maintaining lower chamfer distance in the implicit representation. Our framework enables a straightforward extraction of the surface from the explicit representation, as opposed to the more intricate marching-cube-like techniques required to extract a surface from the implicit function. This enables us to add image-based losses on the output of a differentiable rasterizer. Even though these losses are only measured over AtlasNet output, we observe that they further improve the results for *both* representations, since the improvements propagate to

OccupancyNet via consistency losses. Another advantage of reconstructing surfaces from the explicit representation is that it is an order of magnitude faster than running marching cubes on the implicit representation. We demonstrate the advantage of our joint representation by using it to train 3D-shape autoencoders and reconstruct a surface from a single image. The resulting implicit and explicit surfaces are consistent with each other and quantitatively and qualitatively superior to either of the branches trained in isolation.

2   Related Work

We review existing representations for shape generation that are used within neural network architectures. While target application and architecture details might vary, in many cases an alternative representation can be seamlessly integrated into an existing architecture by modifying the layers of the network that are responsible for generating the output.

Generative networks designed for images operate over regular 2D grids and can directly extend to 3D voxel occupancy grids [3,8,9,18]. These models tend to be coarse and blobby, since the size of the output scales cubically with respect to the desired resolution. Hierarchical models [13,27] alleviate this problem, but they still tend to be relatively heavy in the number of parameters due to multiple levels of resolution. A natural remedy is to only focus on surface points, hence point-based techniques were proposed to output a tensor with a fixed number of 3D coordinates [1,29]. Very dense point clouds are required to approximate high curvature regions and fine-grained geometric details, and thus, point-based architectures typically generate coarse shapes. While polygonal meshes allow non-even tessellation, learning over this domain even with modest number of vertices remains a challenge [7]. One can predict vertex positions of a template [30], but this can only apply to analysis of very homogeneous datasets. Similarly to volumetric cases, one can adaptively refine the mesh [31,33] using graph unpooling layers to add more mesh elements or iteratively refine it via graph convolutional networks [32]. This refinement can be conditioned on images [31,32] or 3D volumes [33]. The main limitation of these techniques is that they discretize the domain in advance and allocate same network capacity to each discrete element. Even hierarchical methods only provide opportunity to save time by not exploring finer elements in feature-less regions. In contrast, continuous, functional representations enable the network to learn the discretization of the output domain.

The explicit continuous representations view 3D shapes as 2D charts embedded in 3D [11,34]. These atlas-based techniques tend to have visual artifacts related to non-smooth normals and patch misalignments. For homogeneous shape collections, such as human bodies, this can be remedied by replacing 2D charts with a custom template (e.g., a human in a T-pose) and enforce strong regularization priors (e.g., isometry) [10], however, the choice of such a template and priors limits expressiveness and applicability of the method to non-homogeneous collections with diverse geometry and topology of shapes.

Another alternative is to use a neural network to model a space probing function that predicts occupancy [24] or clamped signed distance field [5,25] for each point in a 3D volume. Unfortunately, these techniques cannot be trained with surface-based losses and thus tend to perform worse with respect to surface-to-surface error metrics.

Implicit representations also require marching cubes algorithm [23] to reconstruct the surface. Note that unlike explicit representation, where every sample lies on the surface, marching cubes requires sampling off-surface points in the volume to extract the level set. We found that this leads to a surface reconstruction algorithm that is about an order of magnitude slower than an explicit technique. This additional reconstruction step, also makes it impossible to plugin the output of the implicit representation into a differentiable rasterizer (e.g., [15,19,22]. We observe that using differentiable rasterizer to enforce additional image-based losses can improve the quality of results. Moreover, adding these losses just for the explicit output, still propagates the improvements to the implicit representation via the consistency losses.

In theory, one could use differentiable version of marching cubes [17] for reconstructing a surface from an implicit representation, however, this has not been used by prior techniques due to cubic memory requirements of this step (essentially, it would limit the implicit formulation to 32^3 grids as argued in prior work [24]). Several recent techniques use ray-casting to sample implicit functions for image-based losses. Since it is computationally intractable to densely sample the volume, these methods either interpolate a sparse set of samples [21] or use LSTM to learn the ray marching algorithm [28]. Both solutions are more computationally involved than simply projecting a surface point using differentiable rasterizer, as enabled by our technique.

3   Approach

We now detail the architecture of the proposed network, as well as the losses used within the training to enforce consistency across the two representations.

3.1   Architecture

Our network simultaneously outputs two surface representations. These two representations are generated from two branches of the network, where each branch uses a state-of-the-art architecture for the target representation.

For the explicit branch, we use AtlasNet [11]. AtlasNet represents K charts with neural functions $\{f_i^{\mathbf{x}}\}_{i=1}^{K}$, where each function takes a shape descriptor vector, $\mathbf{x} \in \mathcal{X}$, and a query point in the unit square, $\mathbf{p} \in [0,1]^2$, and outputs a point in 3D, i.e., $f_i^{\mathbf{x}} : [0,1]^2 \to \mathbb{R}^3$. We also denote the set of 3D points achieved by mapping all 2D points in $\mathcal{A} \subset [0,1]^2$ as $f^{\mathbf{x}}(\mathcal{A})$.

For the implicit branch, we use OccupancyNet [24], learning a neural function $g^{\hat{\mathbf{x}}} : \mathbb{R}^3 \to [0,1]$, which takes a query point $q \in \mathbb{R}^3$ and a shape descriptor vector $\hat{\mathbf{x}} \in \hat{\mathcal{X}}$ and outputs the occupancy value. The point q is considered occupied

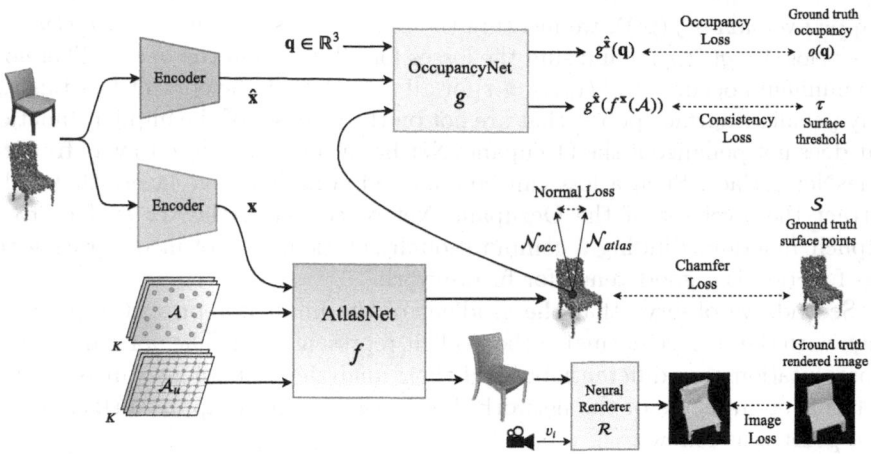

Fig. 1. Model architecture. AtlasNet and OccupancyNet branches of the hybrid model are trained with Chamfer and occupancy losses as well as consistency losses for aligning surfaces and normals. A novel image loss is introduced to further improve generation quality.

(i.e., inside the shape) if $g^{\hat{\mathbf{x}}} \geq \tau$, where we set $\tau = 0.2$ following the choice of OccupancyNet.

3.2   Loss Functions

Our approach centers around losses that ensure geometric consistency between the output of the OccupancyNet and AtlasNet modules. We employ these consistency loses along with each branch's original fitting loss (Chamfer and occupancy loss) that was used to train the network in its original paper. Furthermore, we take advantage of AtlasNet's output lending itself to differentiable rendering in order to incorporate a rendering-based loss. These losses are summarized in Fig. 1 and detailed below.

Consistency Losses. First, to favor consistency between the explicit and implicit representations, we observe that the surface generated by AtlasNet should align with the τ-level set of OccupancyNet:

$$g^{\hat{\mathbf{x}}} \left(f_i^{\mathbf{x}}(\mathbf{p}) \right) = \tau, \tag{1}$$

for all charts $f_i^{\mathbf{x}}$ and at every point $\mathbf{p} \in [0,1]^2$. Throughout this subsection we assume that $\mathbf{x}$ and $\hat{\mathbf{x}}$ are describing the same shape.

This observation motivates the following surface consistency loss:

$$\mathcal{L}_{\text{consistency}} = \sum_{\mathbf{p} \in \mathcal{A}} \mathcal{H}\big(g^{\hat{\mathbf{x}}}(f_i^{\mathbf{x}}(\mathbf{p})), \tau\big). \tag{2}$$

where $\mathcal{H}(\cdot, \cdot)$ is the cross entropy function, and $\mathcal{A}$ is the set of sample points in $[0,1]^2$. More specifically, for each point p_i sampled on a 2D patch and its mapped version $g(f(p_i))$, we measure the binary cross-entropy $\tau \log(g(f(p_i))) + (1-\tau) \log(1 - g(f(p_i)))$ and sum the losses for all points in the batch. Therefore, the minimum occurs at $g(f(p_i)) = \tau$ for all i. Note that the current loss function only penalizes surface points that are not on the level set of the implicit function, but does not penalize if the OccupancyNet has a zero level set far away from the AtlasNet surface. Such a loss can be added via differentiable layers that either extract the level set of the OccupancyNet or convert AtlasNet surface to an implicit function. Finding a computationally efficient way of incorporating this loss function is a good venue for future work.

Second, we observe that the gradient of the implicit representation should align with the surface normal of the explicit representation. The normals for both representations are differentiable and their analytic expressions can be defined in terms of gradients of the network. For AtlasNet, we compute surface normal at a point $\mathbf{p}$ as follows:

$$\mathcal{N}_{\text{atlas}} = \frac{\partial f_i^{\mathbf{x}}}{\partial u} \times \frac{\partial f_i^{\mathbf{x}}}{\partial v}\bigg|_{\mathbf{p}} \tag{3}$$

The gradient of OccupancyNet's at a point $\mathbf{q}$, is computed as:

$$\mathcal{N}_{\text{occ}} = \nabla_{\mathbf{q}} g^{\hat{\mathbf{x}}}(\mathbf{q}) \tag{4}$$

We now define the normal consistency loss by measuring the misalignment in their directions (note that the values are normalized to have unit magnitude):

$$\mathcal{L}_{\text{norm}} = \left| 1 - \frac{\mathcal{N}_{\text{atlas}}}{\|\mathcal{N}_{\text{atlas}}\|} \cdot \frac{\mathcal{N}_{\text{occ}}}{\|\mathcal{N}_{\text{occ}}\|} \right| \tag{5}$$

We evaluate this loss only at surface points predicted by the explicit representation (i.e., $\mathcal{N}_{\text{occ}}$ is evaluated at $\mathbf{q} = f^{\mathbf{x}}(\mathbf{p}), \mathbf{p} \in \mathcal{A}$).

Fitting Losses. Each branch also has its own fitting loss, ensuring it adheres to the input geometry. We use the standard losses used to train each of the two surface representations in previous works.

For the explicit branch, we measure the distance between the predicted surface and the ground truth in standard manner, using Chamfer distance:

$$\mathcal{L}_{\text{chamfer}} = \sum_{\mathbf{p} \in \mathcal{A}} \min_{\hat{\mathbf{p}} \in S} |f^{\mathbf{x}}(\mathbf{p}) - \hat{\mathbf{p}}|^2 + \sum_{\hat{\mathbf{p}} \in S} \min_{\mathbf{p} \in \mathcal{A}} |f^{\mathbf{x}}(\mathbf{p}) - \hat{\mathbf{p}}|^2, \tag{6}$$

where $\mathcal{A}$ be a set of points randomly sampled from the K unit squares of the charts (here $f^{\mathbf{x}}$ uses one of the neural functions f_i depending on which of the K charts the point $\mathbf{p}$ came from). S is a set of points that represent the ground truth surface.

For the implicit branch, given a set of points $\{\mathbf{q}_i\}_{i=1}^N$ sampled in 3D space, with $o(\mathbf{q}_i)$ denoting their ground-truth occupancy values, the occupancy loss is defined as:

$$\mathcal{L}_{\text{occ}} = \sum_{i=1}^{N} \mathcal{H}(g^{\hat{\mathbf{x}}}(\mathbf{q}_i), o(\mathbf{q}_i)) \tag{7}$$

Finally, for many applications visual quality of a rendered 3D reconstruction plays a very important role (e.g., every paper on this subject actually presents a rendering of the reconstructed model for qualitative evaluations). Rendering implicit functions requires complex probing of volumes, while output of the explicit representation can be directly rasterized into an image. Thus, we chose to only include an image-space loss for the output of the explicit branch, comparing its differentiable rendering to the image produced by rendering the ground truth shape. Note that this loss to still improves the representation learned by the implicit branch due to consistency losses.

To compute the image-space loss we first reconstruct a mesh from the explicit branch. In particular, we sample a set of 2D points $\mathcal{A}_u$ on a regular grid for each of the K unit squares. Each grid defines topology of the mesh, and mapping the corners of all grids with $f^{\mathbf{x}}$ gives a triangular 3D mesh that can be used with most existing differentiable rasterizers $\mathcal{R}$ (we use our own implementation inspired by SoftRas [20]). We render 25 images from different viewpoints produced by the cross product of 5 elevation and 5 azimuth uniformly sampled angles.

The image loss is defined as:

$$\mathcal{L}_{\text{img}} = \frac{1}{25} \sum_{i=1}^{25} \|\mathcal{R}(f^{\mathbf{x}}(\mathcal{A}_u), v_i) - \mathcal{R}(\mathcal{M}_{gt}, v_i)\|^2 \tag{8}$$

in which v_i is the ith viewpoint and $\mathcal{M}_{gt}$ represents the ground truth mesh. Our renderer $\mathcal{R}$ outputs a normal map image (based on per-face normals), since they capture the shape better than silhouettes or gray-shaded images.

Our final loss is a weighted combination of the fitting and consistency losses:

$$\mathcal{L}_{\text{total}} = \mathcal{L}_{\text{occ}} + \alpha \cdot \mathcal{L}_{\text{chamfer}} + \beta \cdot \mathcal{L}_{\text{img}} + \gamma \cdot \mathcal{L}_{\text{consistency}} + \delta \cdot \mathcal{L}_{\text{norm}} \tag{9}$$

Since the loss functions measure different quantities with vastly different scales, we set the weights empirically to get the best qualitative and quantitative results on the validation set. We use $\alpha = 2.5 \times 10^4$, $\beta = 10^3$, $\gamma = 0.04$, and $\delta = 0.05$ in all experiments.

3.3   Pipeline and Training

Figure 1 illustrates the complete pipeline for training and inference: given an input image or a point cloud, the two encoders encode the input to shape features, $\mathbf{x}$ and $\hat{\mathbf{x}}$. For the AtlasNet branch, a set of points $\mathcal{A} \subset [0,1]^2$ is randomly sampled from K unit squares. These points are concatenated with the shape feature $\mathbf{x}$ and passed to AtlasNet. The Chamfer loss is computed between $f^{\mathbf{x}}(\mathcal{A})$ and the ground truth surface points, per Eq. 6. For the OccupancyNet branch, similarly to [24], we uniformly sample a set of points $\{q_i\}_{i=1}^{N} \subset \mathbb{R}^3$ inside the bounding box of the object and use them to train OccupancyNet with respect to the fitting losses. To compute the image loss, the generated mesh $f^{\mathbf{x}}(\mathcal{A}_u)$ and the ground truth mesh $\mathcal{M}_{gt}$ are normalized to a unit cube prior to rendering.

For the consistency loss, the occupancy function $g^{\hat{x}}$ is evaluated at the points generated by AtlasNet, $f^x(\mathcal{A})$ and then penalized as described in Eq. (2). AtlasNet's normals are evaluated at the sample points $\mathcal{A}$. OccupancyNet's normals are evaluated at the corresponding points, $f^x(\mathcal{A})$. These are then plugged into the loss described in Eq. (5). We train AtlasNet and OccupancyNet jointly with the loss function in Eq. (9), thereby coupling the two branches to one-another via the consistency losses.

Since we wish to show the merit of the hybrid approach, we keep the two branches' networks' architecture and training setup identical to the one used in the previous works that introduced those two networks. For AtlasNet, we sample random 100 points from each of $K = 25$ patches during training. At inference time, the points are sampled on 10×10 regular grid for each patch. For OccupancyNet, we use the 2500 uniform samples provided by the authors [24]. We use the Adam optimizer [16] with learning rates of 6×10^{-4} and 1.5×10^{-4} for AtlasNet (f) and OccupancyNet (g) respectively.

4   Results

We evaluate our network's performance on single view reconstruction as well as on point cloud reconstruction, using the same subset of shapes from ShapeNet [4] as used in Choy et al. [6]. For both tasks, following prior work (e.g., [11,24]), we use simple encoder-decoder architectures. Similarly to [24], we quantitatively evaluate the results using the chamfer-L_1 distance and normal consistency score. The chamfer-L_1 distance is the mean of the accuracy and completeness metrics, with accuracy being the average distance of points on the output mesh to their nearest neighbors on the ground truth mesh, and completeness similarly with switching the roles of source and target point sets. Note that we use the chamfer-L_2 distance for training in order to be consistent with the AtlasNet paper [11]. For evaluation, we use the chamfer-L_1 distance since it is adopted as the evaluation metric in OccupancyNet [24]. The normal consistency score is the mean absolute dot product of normals in the predicted surface and normals at the corresponding nearest neighbors on the true surface.

Single View Reconstruction. To reconstruct geometry from a single-view image, we use a ResNet-18 [14] encoder for each of the two branches to encode an input image into a shape descriptor which is then fed to the branch. Using distinct encoders enables model-specific feature extraction, and we found this to slightly outperform a shared encoder. We then train end-to-end with the loss (9), on the dataset of images provided by Choy et al. [6], using batch size of 7. Note that with our method the surface can be reconstructed from either the explicit AtlasNet (AN) branch or the implicit OccupancyNet (ON) branch. We show qualitative results (Fig. 2) and error metrics (Table 1) for both branches. The surface generated by our AtlasNet branch, "Hybrid (AN)," provides a visually smoother surface than vanilla AtlasNet (AN), which is also closer to the ground truth – both in terms of chamfer distance, as well as its normal-consistency score. The surface generated by our OccupancyNet branch, "Hybrid (ON)", similarly

Table 1. Quantitative results on single-view reconstruction. Variants of our hybrid model, with AtlasNet (AN) and OccupancyNet (ON) branches, are compared with vanilla AtlasNet and OccupancyNet using Chamfer-L_1 distance and Normal Consistenty score.

Metric	Chamfer-L_1 ($\times 10^{-1}$)									
Model	AN	ON	Hybrid		No $\mathcal{L}_{img}$		No $\mathcal{L}_{norm}$		No $\mathcal{L}_{img}, \mathcal{L}_{norm}$	
Branch			AN	ON	AN	ON	AN	ON	AN	ON
Airplane	1.05	1.34	**0.91**	1.03	0.96	1.10	0.95	1.08	1.01	1.17
Bench	1.38	1.50	**1.23**	1.26	1.27	1.31	1.26	1.29	1.32	1.38
Cabinet	1.75	1.53	1.53	**1.47**	1.57	1.49	1.55	1.49	1.61	1.50
Car	1.41	1.49	**1.28**	1.31	1.33	1.37	1.33	1.36	1.37	1.42
Chair	2.09	2.06	1.96	**1.95**	2.02	2.01	1.99	1.99	2.04	2.03
Display	1.98	2.58	**1.89**	2.14	1.92	2.24	1.90	2.19	1.94	2.29
Lamp	3.05	3.68	**2.91**	3.02	2.93	3.09	2.91	3.06	2.99	3.21
Sofa	1.77	1.81	**1.56**	1.58	1.61	1.63	1.59	1.61	1.68	1.71
Table	1.90	1.82	1.73	**1.72**	1.80	1.78	1.78	1.76	1.83	1.79
Telephone	1.28	1.27	**1.17**	1.18	1.22	1.21	1.19	1.19	1.24	1.24
Vessel	1.51	2.01	**1.42**	1.53	1.46	1.60	1.46	1.58	1.48	1.69
Mean	1.74	1.92	**1.60**	1.65	1.64	1.71	1.63	1.69	1.68	1.77
Metric	Normal consistency ($\times 10^{-2}$)									
Model	AN	ON	Hybrid		No $\mathcal{L}_{img}$		No $\mathcal{L}_{norm}$		No $\mathcal{L}_{img}, \mathcal{L}_{norm}$	
Branch			AN	ON	AN	ON	AN	ON	AN	ON
Airplane	83.6	84.5	85.5	**85.7**	85.3	85.6	84.8	85.3	84.3	85.0
Bench	77.9	81.4	81.4	**82.5**	80.9	82.2	80.4	81.9	79.9	81.7
Cabinet	85.0	88.4	88.3	**89.1**	88.1	89.0	87.2	88.7	86.8	88.6
Car	83.6	85.2	86.2	**86.8**	85.8	86.5	85.3	86.0	84.9	85.8
Chair	79.1	82.9	83.5	**84.0**	83.1	83.7	82.4	83.4	82.0	83.2
Display	85.8	85.7	**87.0**	86.9	86.7	86.6	86.3	86.1	86.0	85.9
Lamp	69.4	75.1	74.9	**76.0**	74.7	75.9	73.3	75.6	72.8	75.4
Sofa	84.0	86.7	87.2	**87.5**	86.9	87.4	86.4	87.1	85.9	86.9
Table	83.2	85.8	86.3	**87.4**	86.0	87.1	85.3	86.4	84.9	86.1
Telephone	92.3	93.9	94.0	**94.5**	93.8	94.4	93.6	94.2	93.3	94.1
Vessel	75.6	79.7	79.2	**80.6**	78.9	80.4	77.7	80.0	77.4	79.9
Mean	81.8	84.5	84.9	**85.5**	84.6	85.4	83.9	85.0	83.5	84.8

Input	AtlasNet	OccNet	Hybrid (AN)	Hybrid (ON)	Ground truth

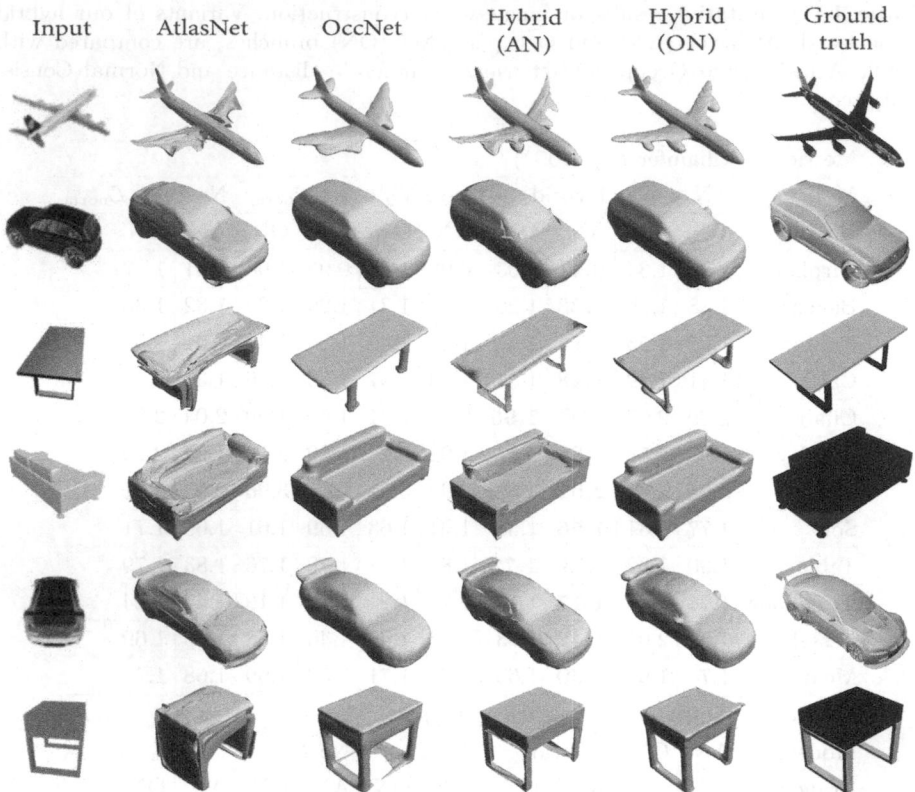

Fig. 2. Comparison of meshes generated by vanilla AtlasNet and OccupancyNet with the AtlasNet (AN) and OccupancyNet (ON) branches of our hybrid model. Compared to their vanilla counterparts, our AtlasNet branch produces results with significantly less oscillatory artifacts, and our OccupancyNet branch produces results that better preserve thin features such as the chair legs.

yields a more accurate surface in comparison to vanilla OccupancyNet (ON). We observe that the hybrid implicit representation tends to be better at capturing thinner surfaces (e.g., see table legs in Fig. 2) than its vanilla counterpart; this improvement is exactly due to having the implicit branch indirectly trained with the chamfer loss propagated from the AtlasNet branch.

Point Cloud Reconstruction. As a second application, we train our network to reconstruct a surface for a sparse set of 2500 input points. We encode the set of points to a shape descriptor using a PointNet [26] encoder for each of the two branches, and train the encoder-decoder architecture end-to-end with the loss (9). We train with the same points as [24] with a batch size of 10. See results in Fig. 3 and Table 2. As in the single view reconstruction task, the hybrid method surpasses the vanilla, single-branch architectures on average. While there are three categories in which vanilla OccupancyNet performs

Table 2. Quantitative results on auto-encoding. Variants of our hybrid model are compared with vanilla AtlasNet and OccupancyNet.

| Metric | Chamfer-L_1($\times 10^{-3}$) | | | | | | | | | |
| Model | AN | ON | Hybrid | | No $\mathcal{L}_{img}$ | | No $\mathcal{L}_{norm}$ | | No $\mathcal{L}_{img},\mathcal{L}_{norm}$ | |
Branch			AN	ON	AN	ON	AN	ON	AN	ON
Airplane	0.17	0.19	**0.15**	0.16	0.16	0.17	0.16	0.17	0.17	0.18
Bench	0.49	**0.23**	0.31	0.25	0.34	0.25	0.33	0.24	0.37	0.24
Cabinet	0.73	0.56	0.55	**0.51**	0.58	0.52	0.61	0.54	0.63	0.54
Car	0.49	0.54	**0.42**	0.44	0.46	0.47	0.44	0.47	0.47	0.50
Chair	0.52	**0.30**	0.36	0.33	0.39	0.33	0.38	0.33	0.41	0.32
Display	0.61	0.45	0.47	**0.39**	0.50	0.41	0.48	0.40	0.52	0.42
Lamp	1.53	1.35	1.42	**1.31**	1.46	1.33	1.44	1.31	1.49	1.34
Sofa	0.32	0.34	**0.25**	0.26	0.28	0.29	0.26	0.27	0.30	0.31
Table	0.58	0.45	0.46	**0.41**	0.48	0.42	0.47	0.42	0.50	0.43
Telephone	0.22	0.12	0.14	**0.10**	0.15	0.10	0.16	0.11	0.18	0.11
Watercraft	0.74	**0.38**	0.53	0.42	0.57	0.41	0.54	0.42	0.61	0.40
Mean	0.58	0.45	0.46	**0.41**	0.49	0.43	0.48	0.43	0.51	0.44
Metric	Normal consistency ($\times 10^{-2}$)									
Model	AN	ON	Hybrid		No $\mathcal{L}_{img}$		No $\mathcal{L}_{norm}$		No $\mathcal{L}_{img},\mathcal{L}_{norm}$	
Branch			AN	ON	AN	ON	AN	ON	AN	ON
Airplane	85.4	89.6	88.3	**90.1**	88.1	90.0	87.5	89.7	87.1	89.6
Bench	81.5	**87.1**	85.6	86.7	85.3	86.8	85.0	86.8	84.7	86.9
Cabinet	87.0	90.6	89.3	**91.1**	89.1	91.0	88.4	90.8	88.1	90.8
Car	84.7	87.9	87.5	**88.6**	87.1	88.5	86.7	88.1	86.1	88.0
Chair	84.7	**94.9**	88.7	94.3	88.2	94.5	87.6	94.5	87.1	94.6
Display	89.7	91.9	91.8	**92.4**	91.5	92.3	91.0	92.2	90.8	92.1
Lamp	73.1	79.5	77.1	**79.8**	76.9	79.7	76.4	79.6	76.0	79.5
Sofa	89.1	92.2	91.8	**92.8**	91.6	92.7	91.3	92.5	91.0	92.4
Table	86.3	91.0	88.8	**91.4**	88.6	91.3	88.3	91.3	88.0	91.2
Telephone	95.9	97.3	97.4	**98.0**	97.2	97.8	96.8	97.6	96.5	97.5
Watercraft	82.1	**86.7**	84.9	86.5	84.7	86.5	84.3	86.7	84.0	86.7
Mean	85.4	89.8	88.3	**90.2**	88.0	90.1	87.6	90.0	87.2	89.9

Input	AtlasNet	OccNet	Hybrid (AN)	Hybrid (ON)	Ground truth

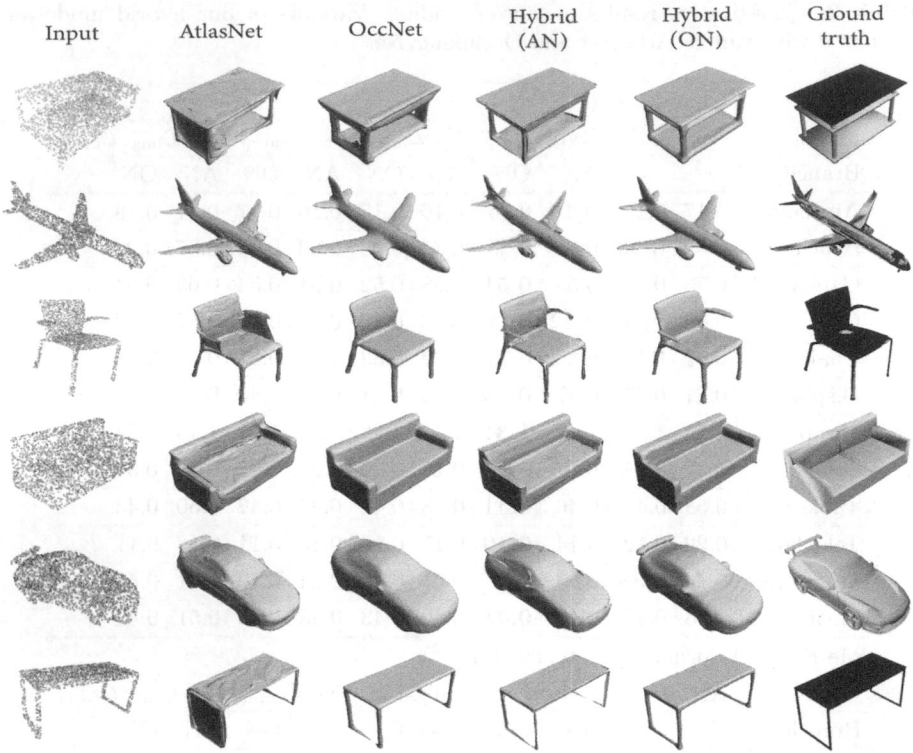

Fig. 3. Reconstructing surfaces from point clouds. Our hybrid approach better reproduces fine features and avoids oscillatory surface normals.

better, we note that Hybrid AtlasNet consistently outperforms vanilla AtlasNet on all categories. This indicates that the hybrid training is mostly beneficial for the implicit representation, and *always* beneficial for the explicit representation; this in turn offers a more streamlined surface reconstruction process. Additional examples are shown in the supplementary material.

Ablation Study on the Loss Functions. We evaluate the importance of the different loss terms via an ablation study for both tasks (see Tables 1, 2). First, we exclude the image-based loss function $\mathcal{L}_{\mathrm{img}}$. Note that even without this loss, hybrid AtlasNet still outperforms vanilla AtlasNet, attributing these improvements mainly to the consistency losses. Removing the normal-consistency loss $\mathcal{L}_{\mathrm{norm}}$ results in decreased quality of reconstructions, especially the accuracy of normals in the predicted surface. Finally, once both terms $\mathcal{L}_{\mathrm{img}}, \mathcal{L}_{\mathrm{norm}}$ are removed, we observe that still, the single level-set consistency term is sufficient to boost the performance within the hybrid training.

We also provide qualitative examples on how each loss term affects the quality of generated point clouds and meshes. Figure 4 illustrates impact of the image loss. Generated meshes from the AN branch are rendered from different viewpoints as shown in Fig. 1. Rendered images are colored based on per-face normals. As we observe, the image loss reduces artifacts such as holes, resulting in more accurate generation. Note that our differentiable renderer uses backface culling, so the back side is not visible as the surface is oriented away from the camera.

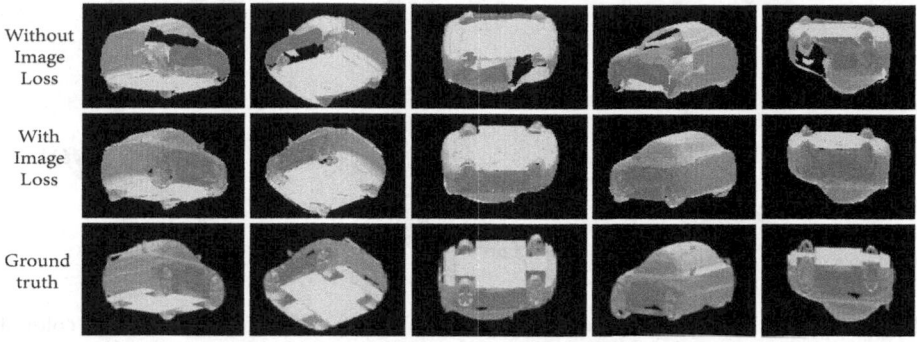

Fig. 4. Impact of the image loss. Rendered images from different viewpoints are shown for models trained with and without the image loss. Evidently, the image loss significantly improves the similarity of the output to the ground truth.

Table 3. Average surface reconstruction time (in seconds) for the explicit (AN) and implicit (ON) representations. Our approach enables to pick the appropriate reconstruction routine at inference time depending on the application needs, where the quality of the reconstructed surfaces increases due to dual training.

	AN (explicit)	ON (implicit)
Single-view reconstruction	0.037	0.400
Auto-encoding	0.025	0.428

We next demonstrate the importance of the normal consistency loss in Fig. 5. We colorize the generated point clouds (from the AN branch) with ground truth normals as well as normals computed from the AN and ON branches (Eq. 3 and 4). We show the change in these results between two models trained with and without normal consistency loss (Eq. 5). As we observe, AN's normals are inaccurate for models without the normal loss. This is since the normals consistency loss drives AN's normals to align with ON's normals, which are generally close to the ground truth's.

Finally, Fig. 6 exhibits the effect of the consistency loss. We evaluate the resulting consistency by measuring the deviation from the constraint in Eq. 1, i.e., the deviation of the predicted occupancy probabilities from the threshold τ, sampled on the predicted AtlasNet surface. We then color the point cloud such that the larger the deviation the redder the point is. Evidently, for models

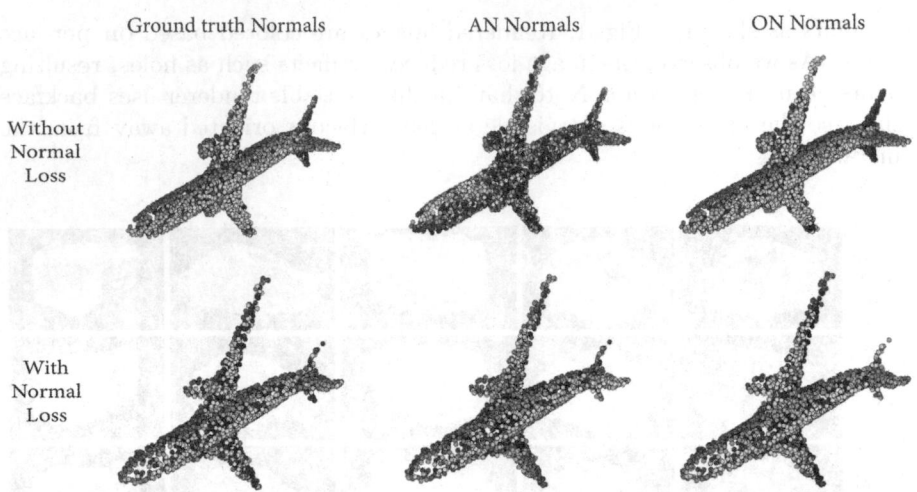

Fig. 5. Impact of the normal consistency loss. The generated point clouds are colored based on the ground truth normals, AtlasNet's (AN) normals, and OccupancyNet's (ON) normals. The results are then compared between a model trained with the normal consistency loss and a model trained without that loss; AN's normals significantly improve when the loss is incorporated, as it encourages alignment with ON's normals which tend to be close to the ground truth normals.

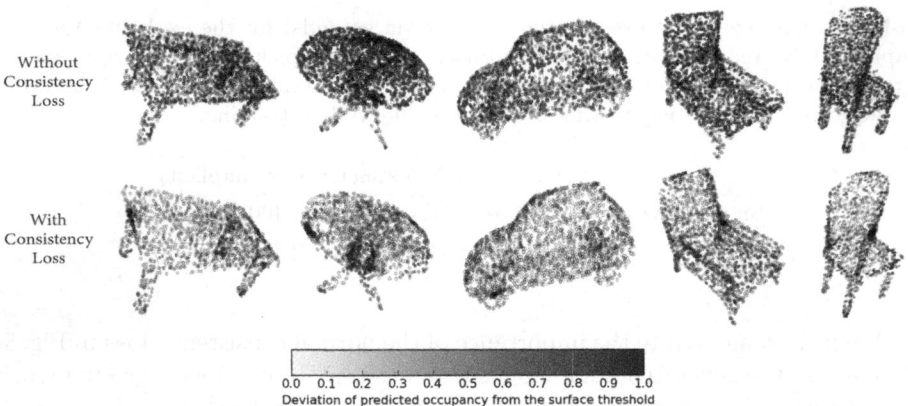

Fig. 6. Impact of the consistency loss. Each point in the generated point cloud is colored based on deviation of its predicted occupancy probability from the threshold τ, with red indicating deviation. (Color figure online)

trained without the consistency loss this deviation is significantly larger, than when the consistency loss is incorporated.

Surface Reconstruction Time. One drawback of the implicit representations is the necessary additional step of extracting the level set. Current approaches require sampling a large number of points near the surface which can be computationally expensive. Our approach allows to circumvent this issue by using the reconstruction from the explicit branch (which is trained to be consistent with the level set of the implicit representation). We see that the surface reconstructing time is about order of magnitude faster for explicit representation (Table 3). Our qualitative and quantitative results suggest that the quality of the explicit representation improves significantly when trained with the consistency losses.

5 Conclusion and Future Work

We presented a dual approach for generating consistent implicit/explicit surface representations using AtlasNet and OccupancyNet in a hybrid architecture via novel consistency losses that encourage this consistency. Various tests demonstrate that surfaces generated by our network are of higher quality, namely smoother and closer to the ground truth compared with vanilla AtlasNet and OccupancyNet. A main shortcoming of our method is that it only penalizes inconsistency of the branches, but does not guarantee perfect consistency; nonetheless, the experiments conducted show that both representations significantly improve by using this hybrid approach during training.

We believe this is an important step in improving neural surface generation, and are motivated to continue improving this hybrid approach, by devising tailor-made encoders and decoders for both representations, to optimize their synergy. In terms of applications, we see many interesting future directions that leverage strengths of each approach, such as using AtlasNet to texture OccupancyNet's implicit level set, or using OccupancyNet to train AtlasNet's surface to encapsulate specific input points.

References

1. Achlioptas, P., Diamanti, O., Mitliagkas, I., Guibas, L.J.: Learning representations and generative models for 3D point clouds. ICML (2018)
2. Ben-Hamu, H., Maron, H., Kezurer, I., Avineri, G., Lipman, Y.: Multi-chart generative surface modeling. In: SIGGRAPH Asia (2018)
3. Brock, A., Lim, T., Ritchie, J.M., Weston, N.: Generative and discriminative voxel modeling with convolutional neural networks. CoRR abs/1608.04236 (2016). http://arxiv.org/abs/1608.04236
4. Chang, A.X., et al.: ShapeNet: an information-rich 3D model repository. arXiv preprint arXiv:1512.03012 (2015)
5. Chen, Z., Zhang, H.: Learning implicit fields for generative shape modeling. In: IEEE Computer Vision and Pattern Recognition (CVPR) (2019)
6. Choy, C.B., Xu, D., Gwak, J.Y., Chen, K., Savarese, S.: 3D-R2N2: a unified approach for single and multi-view 3D object reconstruction. In: Leibe, B., Matas, J., Sebe, N., Welling, M. (eds.) ECCV 2016. LNCS, vol. 9912, pp. 628–644. Springer, Cham (2016). https://doi.org/10.1007/978-3-319-46484-8_38
7. Dai, A., Nießner, M.: Scan2Mesh: from unstructured range scans to 3D meshes. In: Proceedings of the Computer Vision and Pattern Recognition (CVPR). IEEE (2019)

8. Dai, A., Qi, C.R., Nießner, M.: Shape completion using 3D-encoder-predictor CNNs and shape synthesis. In: Proceedings of the Computer Vision and Pattern Recognition (CVPR). IEEE (2017)
9. Girdhar, R., Fouhey, D.F., Rodriguez, M., Gupta, A.: Learning a predictable and generative vector representation for objects. CoRR abs/1603.08637 (2016). http://arxiv.org/abs/1603.08637
10. Groueix, T., Fisher, M., Kim, V.G., Russell, B.C., Aubry, M.: 3D-CODED: 3D correspondences by deep deformation. In: Ferrari, V., Hebert, M., Sminchisescu, C., Weiss, Y. (eds.) ECCV 2018. LNCS, vol. 11206, pp. 235–251. Springer, Cham (2018). https://doi.org/10.1007/978-3-030-01216-8_15
11. Groueix, T., Fisher, M., Kim, V.G., Russell, B.C., Aubry, M.: AtlasNet: a Papier-Mache approach to learning 3D surface generation. arXiv preprint arXiv:1802.05384 (2018)
12. Han, X., Laga, H., Bennamoun, M.: Image-based 3D object reconstruction: state-of-the-art and trends in the deep learning era. CoRR abs/1906.06543 (2019). http://arxiv.org/abs/1906.06543
13. Häne, C., Tulsiani, S., Malik, J.: Hierarchical surface prediction for 3D object reconstruction. In: International Conference on 3D Vision (3DV), pp. 412–420. IEEE (2017)
14. He, K., Zhang, X., Ren, S., Sun, J.: Deep residual learning for image recognition. In: Proceedings of the IEEE Conference on Computer Vision and Pattern Recognition, pp. 770–778 (2016)
15. Kato, H., Ushiku, Y., Harada, T.: Neural 3D mesh renderer (2018)
16. Kingma, D.P., Ba, J.: Adam: a method for stochastic optimization. arXiv preprint arXiv:1412.6980 (2014)
17. Liao, Y., Donné, S., Geiger, A.: Deep marching cubes: learning explicit surface representations. In: Conference on Computer Vision and Pattern Recognition (CVPR) (2018)
18. Liu, J., Yu, F., Funkhouser, T.: Interactive 3D modeling with a generative adversarial network. In: International Conference on 3D Vision (3DV) (2017)
19. Liu, S., Li, T., Chen, W., Li, H.: Soft rasterizer: a differentiable renderer for image-based 3D reasoning. In: The IEEE International Conference on Computer Vision (ICCV), October 2019
20. Liu, S., Li, T., Chen, W., Li, H.: Soft rasterizer: a differentiable renderer for image-based 3D reasoning. In: Proceedings of the IEEE International Conference on Computer Vision, pp. 7708–7717 (2019)
21. Liu, S., Saito, S., Chen, W., Li, H.: Learning to infer implicit surfaces without 3D supervision. In: Neural Information Processing Systems (NeurIPS), October 2019
22. Loper, M.M., Black, M.J.: OpenDR: an approximate differentiable renderer. In: Fleet, D., Pajdla, T., Schiele, B., Tuytelaars, T. (eds.) ECCV 2014. LNCS, vol. 8695, pp. 154–169. Springer, Cham (2014). https://doi.org/10.1007/978-3-319-10584-0_11
23. Lorensen, W., Cline, H.: Marching cubes: a high resolution 3D surface construction algorithm. In: SIGGRAPH (1987)
24. Mescheder, L., Oechsle, M., Niemeyer, M., Nowozin, S., Geiger, A.: Occupancy networks: learning 3D reconstruction in function space. In: Proceedings of the IEEE Conference on Computer Vision and Pattern Recognition, pp. 4460–4470 (2019)
25. Park, J.J., Florence, P., Straub, J., Newcombe, R.A., Lovegrove, S.: DeepSDF: learning continuous signed distance functions for shape representation. In: CVPR (2019)

26. Qi, C.R., Su, H., Mo, K., Guibas, L.J.: PointNet: deep learning on point sets for 3D classification and segmentation. In: Proceedings of the IEEE Conference on Computer Vision and Pattern Recognition, pp. 652–660 (2017)
27. Riegler, G., Osman Ulusoy, A., Geiger, A.: OctNet: learning deep 3D representations at high resolutions. In: Proceedings of the IEEE Conference on Computer Vision and Pattern Recognition, pp. 3577–3586 (2017)
28. Sitzmann, V., Zollhöfer, M., Wetzstein, G.: Scene representation networks: continuous 3D-structure-aware neural scene representations. In: Advances in Neural Information Processing Systems (2019)
29. Su, H., Fan, H., Guibas, L.: A point set generation network for 3D object reconstruction from a single image. In: CVPR (2017)
30. Tan, Q., Gao, L., Lai, Y.K., Xia, S.: Variational autoencoders for deforming 3D mesh models. In: Proceedings of the IEEE Conference on Computer Vision and Pattern Recognition (2018)
31. Wang, N., Zhang, Y., Li, Z., Fu, Y., Liu, W., Jiang, Y.G.: Pixel2Mesh: generating 3D mesh models from single RGB images. In: Proceedings of the European Conference on Computer Vision (ECCV), pp. 52–67 (2018)
32. Wen, C., Zhang, Y., Li, Z., Fu, Y.: Pixel2Mesh++: multi-view 3D mesh generation via deformation. In: Proceedings of the IEEE International Conference on Computer Vision, pp. 1042–1051 (2019)
33. Wickramasinghe, U., Remelli, E., Knott, G., Fua, P.: Voxel2Mesh: 3D mesh model generation from volumetric data. arXiv e-prints arXiv:1912.03681 December 2019
34. Yang, Y., Feng, C., Shen, Y., Tian, D.: FoldingNet: point cloud auto-encoder via deep grid deformation. In: Proceedings of the IEEE Conference on Computer Vision and Pattern Recognition (CVPR), vol. 3 (2018)

Learning Disentangled Representations with Latent Variation Predictability

Xinqi Zhu[✉], Chang Xu, and Dacheng Tao

UBTECH Sydney AI Centre, School of Computer Science, Faculty of Engineering,
The University of Sydney, Darlington, NSW 2008, Australia
{xzhu7491,c.xu,dacheng.tao}@uni.sydney.edu.au

Abstract. Latent traversal is a popular approach to visualize the disentangled latent representations. Given a bunch of variations in a single unit of the latent representation, it is expected that there is a change in a single factor of variation of the data while others are fixed. However, this impressive experimental observation is rarely explicitly encoded in the objective function of learning disentangled representations. This paper defines the *variation predictability* of latent disentangled representations. Given image pairs generated by latent codes varying in a single dimension, this varied dimension could be closely correlated with these image pairs if the representation is well disentangled. Within an adversarial generation process, we encourage variation predictability by maximizing the mutual information between latent variations and corresponding image pairs. We further develop an evaluation metric that does not rely on the ground-truth generative factors to measure the disentanglement of latent representations. The proposed variation predictability is a general constraint that is applicable to the VAE and GAN frameworks for boosting disentanglement of latent representations. Experiments show that the proposed variation predictability correlates well with existing ground-truth-required metrics and the proposed algorithm is effective for disentanglement learning.

1 Introduction

Nowadays learning interpretable representations from high-dimensional data is of central importance for downstream tasks such as classification [10,13,20], domain adaptation [38,43,46], fair machine learning [11,30], and reasoning [42]. To achieve this goal, a series of work have been conducted [9,10,13,18,20,24] under the subject of *disentangled representation learning*. Although there is not a widely adopted mathematical definition for disentanglement, a conceptually agreed definition can be expressed as that each unit of a disentangled representation should capture a single interpretable variation of the data [5].

Electronic supplementary material The online version of this chapter (https://doi.org/10.1007/978-3-030-58607-2_40) contains supplementary material, which is available to authorized users.

© Springer Nature Switzerland AG 2020
A. Vedaldi et al. (Eds.): ECCV 2020, LNCS 12355, pp. 684–700, 2020.
https://doi.org/10.1007/978-3-030-58607-2_40

$\Delta z = z_1 - z_2$	$[x_1, x_2] = [G_{dis}(z_1), G_{dis}(z_2)]$	$[x_1, x_2] = [G_{ent}(z_1), G_{ent}(z_2)]$
$\Delta z = (1,0,0)$	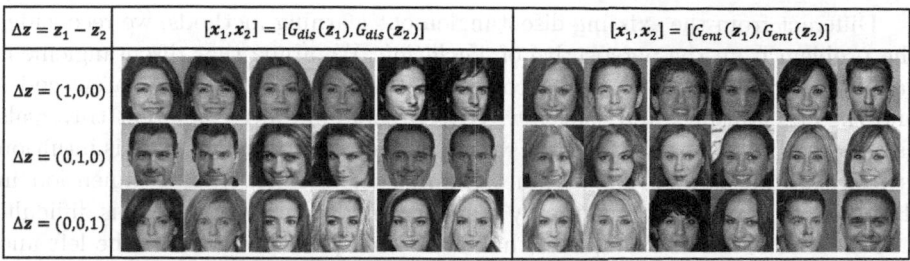	
$\Delta z = (0,1,0)$		
$\Delta z = (0,0,1)$		

Fig. 1. This is a table showing generated image pairs $[x_1, x_2]$ whose latent codes $[z_1, z_2]$ have difference in a single dimension $\Delta z = z_1 - z_2$. Left: image pairs generated by a disentangled generator G_{dis}. Right: image pairs generated by an entangled generator G_{ent}. In each row, the latent code difference Δz is kept fixed with only one dimension modified. For the disentangled image pairs (left), it is not difficult to tell that each row represents the semantics of *fringe*, *smile*, and *hair color* respectively. However, for entangled ones (right) the semantics are not clear although the image pairs are also generated with a single dimension varied in the latent codes just like the left ones.

One line of current most promising disentanglement methods derives from β-VAE [18], with its variants such as FactorVAE [24] and β-TCVAE [9] developed later. This series of works mainly realize disentanglement by enforcing the independence in the latent variables. Although independence assumption is an effective proxy for the learning of disentanglement, this assumption can be unrealistic for real-world data as the underlying distribution of the semantic factors may not be factorizable. Additionally since these models are defined based upon the Variational Autoencoder (VAE) framework [25] which intrinsically causes blurriness in the generated data, their applications are mostly limited to synthetic data and real-world data of small sizes. Another line of work to achieve disentanglement purpose is by using InfoGAN [10], which encourages disentanglement through maximizing the mutual information between the generated data and a subset of latent codes. This model inherits merits from GAN [15] so that sharper and more realistic images can be synthesized thus can be applied to more complex datasets. However, we show in the experiments that the disentanglement performance of InfoGAN is limited and the training of InfoGAN is less stable compared with our proposed GAN-based models. A problem in existing disentanglement learning community is the lack of evaluation metrics that can give a quantitative measurement of the performance of disentanglement. Existing metrics depends on the existence of ground-truth generative factors and an encoder network [9,14,18,24,40,43], thus the quantitative measurements are usually done on synthetic data with VAE framework, leaving latent traversal inspection by human the only evaluation method for experiments on real-world data, and this to an extent discourages the development of GAN-based models, which are known to be effective in photorealistic image synthesis, from disentangled representation learning.

Different from the existing disentanglement learning methods, we reconsider the problem from the perspective of *Variation*. We argue that disentanglement can be naturally described by the correlated variations between the latent codes and the observations, and that is why researchers initially use latent traversals as a method to evaluate whether a representation is disentangled. This intuition is based on an assumption that determining the semantics of a dimension in disentangled representations is easy but in entangled representations is difficult. In Fig. 1 we show an example of this interesting phenomenon. On the left and right parts of Fig. 1, there are image pairs generated by two models (one disentangled and one entangled). All these image pairs are generated by varying a single dimension in the latent codes, and the varied dimension is the same for each row (the varied dimension is indicated by Δz on the left by onehot representation). However, as there can be multiple different latent code pairs $[z_1, z_2]$ that cause the same Δz, the generated image pairs can be diverse. In Fig. 1, it is not difficult to tell from the image pairs that the rows for the left model control the semantics of *fringe*, *smile*, and *hair color* respectively, while for the right model the semantics are not clear. This *easy-to-tell* property for the left model is due to the consistent pattern in the shown image pairs, while there is not a clear pattern for the right model so we cannot tell what each row is controlling.

This phenomenon for distinguishing disentangled and entangled representations motivates us to model the latent *variation predictability* as a proxy to achieve disentanglement, which is defined based on the difficulty of predicting the varied dimension in latent codes from the corresponding image pairs. Taking the case in Fig. 1 as an example, we say the left model has a higher latent variation predictability than the right one, which corresponds with the fact that we only need very small number of image pairs to tell what semantics each row is controlling for the left model. Note that rows in the entangled model (right one) may also contain stable patterns (may not correspond to a specific semantics), but it is difficult for us to tell what they are from such few images. By exploiting the variation predictability, our contributions in this paper can be summarized as follows:

- By regarding the variation predictability as a proxy for achieving disentanglement, we design a new objective which is general and effective for learning disentangled representations.
- Based on the definition of variation predictability, we propose a new disentanglement evaluation metric for quantitatively measuring the performance of disentanglement models, without the requirement of the ground-truth generative factors.
- Experiments on various datasets are conducted to show the effectiveness of our proposed metric and models.

2   Related Work

Generative Adversarial Networks. Since the introduction of the initial GAN by Goodfellow et al. [15], the performance of GANs have been thoroughly improved from various perspectives, e.g. generative quality [7,21–23,39,47], and training stability [1,6,16,23,26,35]. However, the study of semantics learned in the latent space is less exploited. Chen et al. [10] propose InfoGAN which successfully learns disentangled representations by maximizing the mutual information between a subset of latent variables and the generated samples. Donahue et al. [12] introduce Semantically Decomposed GANs which encourage a specified portion of the latent space to correspond to a known source of variation, resulting in the decomposition of identity and other contingent aspects of observations. In [44], Tran et al. introduce DR-GAN containing an encoder-decoder structure that can disentangle the pose information in face synthesis. Karras et al. [22] introduce an intermediate latent space derived by non-linear mapping from the original latent space and conduct disentanglement study on this space with perceptual path length and linear separability. In [37], HoloGANs are introduced by combining inductive bias about the 3D world with GANs for learning a disentangled representation of pose, shape, and appearance. Recently, Lin et al. introduce a contrastive regularization to boost InfoGAN for disentanglement learning, and also propose a ModelCentrality scheme to achieve unsupervised model selection [28]. By looking into well-trained GANs, Bau et al. conducts GAN dissection in [4]. They show that neurals in GANs actually learn interpretable concepts, and can be used for modifying contents in the generated images. In a similar spirit, Shen et al. [41] introduces InterFaceGAN showing GANs spontaneously learn various latent subspaces corresponding to specific interpretable attributes. Besides the existing works, unsupervisedly learning disentangled representations with GANs and quantifying their performance of disentanglement are still unsolved problems.

Variational Autoencoders and Variants. There are more systematic works of disentanglement learning based on the VAE framework [8,25], and the most common method for approaching disentanglement is by modeling the independence in the latent space. As an early attempt of extending VAEs for learning independent latent factors, Higgins et al. [18] pointed out that modulating the KL-term in the learning objective of VAEs (known as evidence lower bound (ELBO)) with a single hyper-parameter $\beta > 1$ can encourage the model to learn independent latent factors:

$$\mathcal{L}(\theta, \phi; \boldsymbol{x}, \boldsymbol{z}, \beta) = \mathbb{E}_{q_\phi(\boldsymbol{z}|\boldsymbol{x})}[\log p_\theta(\boldsymbol{x}|\boldsymbol{z})] - \beta D_{KL}(q_\phi(\boldsymbol{z}|\boldsymbol{x}) \| p(\boldsymbol{z})). \qquad (1)$$

Later based on the decomposition of the KL term $D_{KL}(q_\phi(\boldsymbol{z}|\boldsymbol{x}) \| p(\boldsymbol{z}))$ [19,32], it has been discovered that the KL divergence between the aggregated posterior $q_\phi(\boldsymbol{z}) \equiv \mathbb{E}_{p_{data}(\boldsymbol{x})}[q_\phi(\boldsymbol{z}|\boldsymbol{x})]$ and its factorial distribution $\mathrm{KL}(q_\phi(z) \| \prod_j q_\phi(z_j))$ (known as the total correlation (TC) of the latent variables) contributes most to the disentanglement purpose, leading to the emergence of models enforcing penalty on this term. Kim et al. [24] introduce FactorVAE to minimize this TC term through adopting a discriminator in the latent space [15,33] with density-ratio trick [3,36]. Chen et al. [9] introduce β-TCVAE to employ a mini-bath weighted sampling for the TC estimation. Kumar et al. [27] use moment matching to penalize the divergence between aggregated posterior and the prior.

These works have been shown effective for disentangled representation learning, especially after the introduction of various quantitative disentanglement metric [9,14,18,24,40,43]. Dupont [13] introduces JointVAE for learning continuous and discrete latent factors under the VAE framework for stable training and a principled inference network. Later Jeong et al. [20] introduce CascadeVAE which handles independence enforcing through information cascading and solves discrete latent codes learning by an alternating minimization scheme. However, these works model disentanglement only from the independence perspective, which may not be practical for real-world data.

3   Methods

In this section, we first introduce the Variation Predictability objective in Sect. 3.1, a general constraint which encourages disentanglement from the perspective of predictability for the latent variations, and also show its integration with the GAN framework. We then introduce the proposed Variation Predictability Evaluation Metric in Sect. 3.2, a general evaluation method quantifying the performance of disentanglement without relying on the ground-truth generative factors. Our code is available at: https://github.com/zhuxinqimac/stylegan2vp.

3.1   Variation Predictability Loss

We first introduce the concept of *variation predictability*, defined as follows:

Definition 1. *If image pairs are generated by varying a single dimension in the latent codes, the* variation predictability *represents how easy the prediction of the varied latent dimension from the image pairs is.*

Here we also need to define what *easy* is in this context: a prediction is called easy if the required number of training examples is small.

A high variation predictability means predicting the varied latent dimension from the image pairs is easy, i.e. only a small number of training image pairs are needed to identify this dimension (consider the left part of Fig. 1), while a low predictability means the prediction is hard (consider the right part of Fig. 1). As this concept corresponds well with our determination of disentanglement (the left model in Fig. 1 is disentangled while the right one is not), we propose to utilize it as a proxy for achieving the disentanglement objective. Note that traditionally the assumption of *independence* in latent variables works as another proxy for the learning of disentangled representation [9,13,18,20,24,27], which we think is a stronger assumption than the proposed variation predictability and it may not hold for real-world data.

In order to model the variation predictability from observations to the varied latent dimension, we adopt a straightforward implementation by directly maximizing the mutual information between the varied latent dimension d and the paired images $(\boldsymbol{x}_1, \boldsymbol{x}_2)$ derived by varying dimension d in latent codes:

$I(\boldsymbol{x}_1, \boldsymbol{x}_2; d)$, where we name this mutual information as the Variation Predictability objective (VP objective) and the negative of this term as the Variation Predictability loss (VP loss). We instantiate our VP objective by integrating it within the generative adversarial network (GAN) framework.

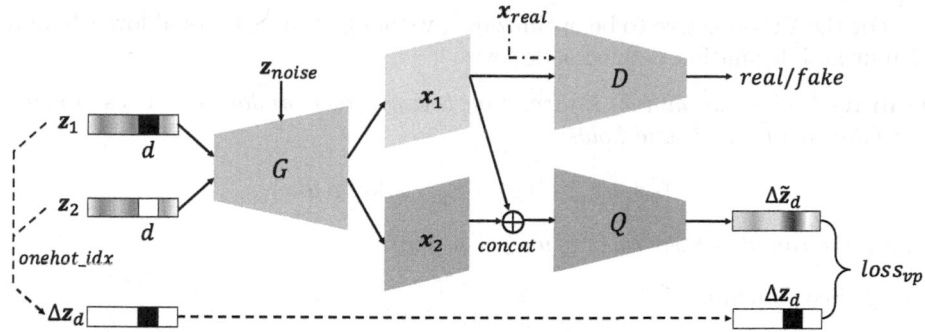

Fig. 2. Overall architecture of our proposed model. The model first samples two latent codes z_1 and z_2 from the latent space that only differs in a single dimension d, and this index d also serves as the target for the recognition network Q after being transformed into onehot representation Δz_d. Two images are then generated with the generator $\boldsymbol{x}_1 = G(z_1)$, $\boldsymbol{x}_2 = G(z_2)$. $\boldsymbol{x}_1$ is fed to the discriminator to get the *real/fake* learning signal same as in the standard GANs. We then concatenate both images along the channel axis and feed them to the recognition network Q for the prediction of d.

As for a brief introduction, GAN is a generative model introduced by Goodfellow et al. [15] for learning the distribution of training data. A generator network G is trained to map a random noise $\boldsymbol{z}$ to an output image $\boldsymbol{x}$: $G(\boldsymbol{z}) : \boldsymbol{z} \rightarrow \boldsymbol{x}$. At the meantime, a discriminator network D is trained to predict whether the generated image $\boldsymbol{x}$ matches the real data distribution $p_{data}(\boldsymbol{x})$. The training strategy of G and D follows a minimax game where G tries to minimize while D tries to maximize the following objective:

$$\min_G \max_D V(G, D) = \mathbb{E}_{\boldsymbol{x} \sim p_{data}}[\log D(\boldsymbol{x})] + \mathbb{E}_{\boldsymbol{z} \sim p_{noise}}[\log(1 - D(G(\boldsymbol{z})))]. \quad (2)$$

After convergence, the generator G can generate images look similar to the real data, while the discriminator D cannot tell whether a generated image is real or not.

The VP loss can be easily integrated into a GAN as:

$$\min_G \max_D V_{vp}(G, D) = V(G, D) - \alpha I(\boldsymbol{x}_1, \boldsymbol{x}_2; d), \quad (3)$$

where α is a hyper-parameter to balance the generative quality and disentanglement quality. This model is named as Variation Predictability GAN (VPGAN). By optimizing the VP objective, the generator is encouraged to synthesize images having a strong correspondence with the latent codes so that the changes in data controlled by each latent dimension is distinguishable from each other, and the changes controlled by a single dimension is consistent all the time. In other words, after the training converges the variations in data should be naturally grouped into as many classes as the number of dimensions in the latent space. In Appendix 6 we show the relation between our objective and the InfoGAN [10] objective.

For the VP objective to be optimizable, we adopt the variational lower bound of mutual information defined as follows.

Lemma 1. *For the mutual information between two random variables* $I(\boldsymbol{x}; \boldsymbol{y})$, *the following lower bound holds:*

$$I(\boldsymbol{x}; \boldsymbol{y}) \geq H(\boldsymbol{y}) + \mathbb{E}_{p(\boldsymbol{x},\boldsymbol{y})} \log q(\boldsymbol{y}|\boldsymbol{x}), \tag{4}$$

where the bound is tight when $q(\boldsymbol{y}|\boldsymbol{x}) = p(\boldsymbol{y}|\boldsymbol{x})$.

Proof. See Appendix 7. $\qquad\qquad\qquad\qquad\qquad\qquad\qquad\qquad\qquad\qquad\square$

Based on Lemma 1, we can get the lower bound of our VP objective:

$$\mathcal{L}_{vp}(\theta, \phi; \boldsymbol{x}_1, \boldsymbol{x}_2, d) \tag{5}$$
$$= \mathbb{E}_{\boldsymbol{x}_1, \boldsymbol{x}_2, d \sim p_\theta(\boldsymbol{x}_1, \boldsymbol{x}_2, d)} \log q_\phi(d|\boldsymbol{x}_1, \boldsymbol{x}_2) + H(d) \tag{6}$$
$$\leq I(\boldsymbol{x}_1, \boldsymbol{x}_2; d). \tag{7}$$

For the sampling of d, $\boldsymbol{x}_1$, $\boldsymbol{x}_2$, we first sample the dimension index d out of the number of continuous latent variables (in this paper we focus on continuous latent codes and leave the modeling for discrete latent codes for future works), then we sample a latent code and sample twice on dimension d so we get a paired latent codes $[\boldsymbol{z}_1, \boldsymbol{z}_2]$ differing only on dimension d. The images $\boldsymbol{x}_1$ and $\boldsymbol{x}_2$ are generated by $G(\boldsymbol{z}_1)$ and $G(\boldsymbol{z}_2)$. The conditional distribution $q_\phi(d|\boldsymbol{x}_1\boldsymbol{x}_2)$ in Eq. 6 is modeled as a recognizor Q. This recognizor network takes the concatenation of the two generated images as inputs to predict the varied dimension d in the latent codes. The architecture of our model is shown in Fig. 2.

3.2   Variation Predictability Disentanglement Metric

As the variation predictability naturally defines a way to distinguish disentangled representations and entangled representations by the difficulty of predicting the varied latent dimensions, we can propose a method to quantitatively measure the performance of disentanglement once we quantify the difficulty of the prediction. In this paper we quantify this difficulty by the performance of doing few-shot learning [45]. The intuition is that a prediction can be seen as easy if only a small number of training examples are needed for the prediction. From another viewpoint, only requiring a small number of training examples means the representation can generalize well for the prediction task, which is also a property of *disentanglement*, so this modeling is also consistent with disentanglement itself. We name our proposed metric as Variation Predictability metric (VP metric), which is defined as follows:

1. For a generative model, sample N indices denoting which dimension to modify in the latent codes: $\{d^1, d^2, ..., d^N\}$.
2. Sample N pairs of latent codes that each pair only differs in the dimension sampled by step 1: $\{[\boldsymbol{z}_1^1, \boldsymbol{z}_2^1], [\boldsymbol{z}_1^2, \boldsymbol{z}_2^2], ..., [\boldsymbol{z}_1^N, \boldsymbol{z}_2^N] \mid \text{Dim}_{\neq 0}(\boldsymbol{z}_1^i - \boldsymbol{z}_2^i) = d^i\}$.
3. For each latent code pair $[\boldsymbol{z}_1^i, \boldsymbol{z}_2^i]$, generate the corresponding image pair $[\boldsymbol{x}_1^i = G(\boldsymbol{z}_1^i), \boldsymbol{x}_2^i = G(\boldsymbol{z}_2^i)]$ and their difference $\Delta \boldsymbol{x}^i = \boldsymbol{x}_1^i - \boldsymbol{x}_2^i$. This forms a dataset $\{(\Delta \boldsymbol{x}^1, d^1), (\Delta \boldsymbol{x}^2, d^2), ..., (\Delta \boldsymbol{x}^N, d^N)\}$ with the difference of image pairs as inputs and the varied dimension as labels.
4. Randomly divide the dataset into a training set and a test set with example numbers ηN and $(1 - \eta)N$ respectively, where η is the ratio of training set.
5. Train a recognition network taking $\Delta \boldsymbol{x}^i$ as input for predicting d^i on the training set. Report the accuracy acc_s on test set.
6. Repeat step 1 to step 5 S times to get accuracies $\{acc_1, acc_2, ..., acc_S\}$.
7. Take the average of the accuracies $Score_{dis} = \frac{1}{S} \sum_{s=1}^{S} acc_s$ as the disentanglement score for the model. Higher is better.

The training set ratio η should not be large since we need to keep this setting as a few-shot learning so that the prediction is sufficiently difficult to distinguish disentangled representations and entangled representations. The reason we use the data difference $\Delta \boldsymbol{x}$ as inputs is that this enforces the model to focus on difference features in data caused by the varied dimension rather than contents in the images, and we also found this implementation can achieve a better correlation with other metrics like the FactorVAE score. In our experiments, we choose $N = 10,000$ and $S = 3$. For Dsprites and 3DShapes datasets we choose $\eta = 0.01$ and for CelebA and 3DChairs datasets we choose $\eta = 0.1$ as there are more dimensions in latent codes used for CelebA and 3DChairs. The main differences between our proposed metric and other disentanglement metrics [9,14,18,24,40,43] are that ours does not require the existence of ground-truth generative factors (which is not available in real-world data), and our metric does not require an encoder so GAN-based models can also be evaluated.

3.3 Implementations

As discovered by the recent works of StyleGANs [22,23] that the latent codes of a generator can be treated as style codes modifying a learned constant for achieving a higher-quality generation and stabler training than transitional GANs, we adopt a similar strategy to ease the training procedure of GANs in our experiments. However, unlike StyleGANs which take a side mapping network to transform the input codes into multiple intermediate latent codes, we directly feed the latent codes sampled from the prior distribution into the generator network without a mapping network to learn the disentangled representation in the prior latent space. The network architectures and parameters for different experiments are shown in Appendix 10.

4 Experiments

We first conduct experiments on popular disentanglement evaluation datasets Dsprites [34] and 3DShapes [24] to validate the effectiveness of our proposed VP disentanglement metric. Second we evaluate our method with VAE framework to show its complementarity to independence modeling for achieving disentanglement. Then we equip our models with GAN framework to conduct experiments on datasets without ground-truth generative factors 3DChairs [2] and CelebA [29], and use our proposed VP metric to quantitatively evaluate the disentanglement performance of our models.

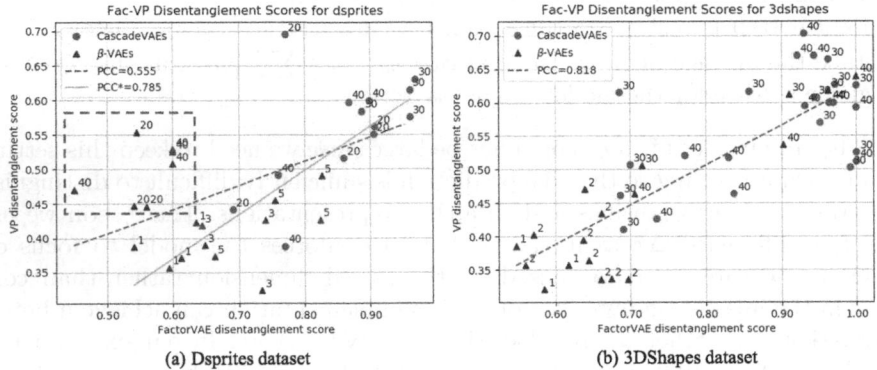

(a) Dsprites dataset   (b) 3DShapes dataset

Fig. 3. These are scatter plots shown between the FactorVAE disentanglement metric and our proposed VP disentanglement metric on Dsprites dataset and 3DShapes dataset. The *PCC* denotes the Pearson's Correlation Coefficient, and the green dash line is the linear regression line. See the main text for discussion. (Color figure online)

4.1 VP Disentanglement Evaluation Metric

In this section, we evaluate the effectiveness of our proposed VP disentanglement metric. Specifically, we reimplement a relatively basic disentanglement model β-VAE [8] and a more advanced model CascadeVAE [20], and train them with different hyper-parameters and random seeds to cover a large range of model performance. Then we obtain their FactorVAE disentanglement metric scores, a widely-used disentanglement measurement shown to be correlated well with other disentanglement metrics and with qualitative evaluation [24,31]. We then obtain the VP metric scores of the trained models and see if these scores have correlation with the ones calculated based on the FactorVAE metric. Note that the FactorVAE metric requires the existence of ground-truth generative factors of each data point in the training dataset for the performance measurement, while our VP metric does not use the ground-truth factors. This experiment is repeated on Dsprites dataset and 3DShapes dataset, which are two most popular datasets for the learning of disentangled representations. The correlation results for both datasets are shown in Fig. 3(a) and (b) respectively. The β hyper-parameter in β-VAE is sampled from $\{1, 2, 3, 5, 20, 30, 40\}$, and the hyper-parameters β_{low} and β_{high} in CascadeVAE are sampled from $\{2, 3, 4\}$ and $\{20, 30, 40\}$ respectively. The models are run with multiple random seeds.

Table 1. Disentanglement scores on Dsprites dataset.

Model	VP score	FacVAE score
CasVAE	59.2 (4.6)	91.3 (7.4)
CasVAE-VP	**65.5** (5.1)	**91.7 (6.9)**

Table 2. Disentanglement scores on 3DShapes dataset.

Model	VP score	FacVAE score
CasVAE	62.3 (4.9)	94.7 (2.1)
CasVAE-VP	**66.4** (5.6)	**95.6** (2.4)

From Fig. 3(a) and (b), we can see there is an evident correlation between our VP metric and the FactorVAE metric. Note that the training of these models are not guided by the VP objective, and there is no relation between the design of FactorVAE metric and our proposed metric. Considering our metric requires no ground-truth factors and the performances of these models suffer from the impact of randomness during training, this correlation is already very strong. For Dsprites dataset, the Pearson's Correlation Coefficient 0.555 is not as high as the one calculated on 3DShapes dataset $PCC = 0.818$. If we take a closer look, we can see the abnormal events happen when β is high in β-VAE models. This is because when β is high (the ones in the red box in Fig. 3(a)), the model tends to ignore the *shape* and *rotation* information in the Dsprites dataset while keeping *xy-shift* and *scaling* disentangled, which leads to a low FactorVAE metric score. However, this ignorance of information is not known by our VP metric as it takes nothing from the ground-truth factors. This causes our metric only take into account the other remaining factors which are well-disentangled so high VP scores are obtained. If we omit the high-β models (in the red box), we get a much higher $PCC = 0.785$ that is close to the one obtained on 3DShapes dataset.

In summary, our proposed VP disentanglement metric correlates well with FactorVAE disentanglement metric even though ours does not rely on the ground-truth generative factors. This property makes our metric a general evaluation method for all disentanglement models with a generator, and it is applicable to datasets with or without ground-truth generative factors. In Appendix Sect. 8, we conducts experiments to show why small η is preferable in our proposed VP metric.

4.2   VP Models with VAE Framework

In this section we apply our VP models to popular disentanglement datasets Dsprites and 3DShapes with VAE framework. We equip our VP loss to the state-of-the-art disentanglement model CascadeVAE [20] to see if our variation predictability is complementary to the statistical independence modeling and

Table 3. Ablation studies of implementation and hyper-parameter α on CelebA.

Model	VP score	FID
VPGAN-flat $\alpha = 0.001$	58.4	**22.3**
VPGAN-flat $\alpha = 0.01$	62.1	27.8
VPGAN-flat $\alpha = 0.1$	64.5	32.8
VPGAN-hierar $\alpha = 0.001$	64.6	53.6
VPGAN-hierar $\alpha = 0.01$	66.8	47.4
VPGAN-hierar $\alpha = 0.1$	**70.3**	56.9

Table 4. Disentanglement models comparison on CelebA dataset.

Model	VP score	FID
GAN	12.9	**20.4**
InfoGAN $\lambda = 0.001$	34.5	24.1
InfoGAN $\lambda = 0.01$	25.3	43.3
FactorVAE	**75.0**	73.9
VPGAN-flat $\alpha = 0.1$	64.5	32.8
VPGAN-hierar $\alpha = 0.1$	**70.3**	56.9

can boost disentangled representation learning. The averaged disentanglement scores of 10 random seeds on two datasets are shown in Table 1 and Table 2. From the tables we can see our model can boost the disentanglement performance of CascadeVAE, but the performance improvement is not very significant. We believe this is because on datasets like Dsprites and 3DShapes the independence assumption is crucial for the disentanglement learning, which has the most impact on the learning of disentangled representations. However, this experiment still shows our VP loss is complementary to the statistical independence modeling, and is beneficial for disentanglement. In Appendix Sect. 9, we show more quantitative comparisons on these two datasets.

4.3   VP Models and Metric on CelebA with GAN Framework

In this section, we apply our VP models and metric to the challenging CelebA [29] human face dataset. This dataset consists of over 200,000 images of cropped real-world human faces of various poses, backgrounds and facial expressions. We crop the center 128×128 area of the images as input for all models.

We first conduct ablation studies on two factors that influence the performance of disentanglement in our models: 1) hierarchical inputs and 2) the hyper-parameter α. The hierarchical latent input impact is a phenomenon discovered in [22,23,48] that when feeding the input latent codes into different layers of the generator, the learned representations tend to capture different levels of semantics. We compare this hierarchical implementation with models with a traditional flat-input implementation to see its impact on disentanglement. The number of network layers and the latent codes are kept the same. In our experiments, we use the VP metric and FID [17] to give a quantitative evaluation on how these two factors impact the disentanglement and the image quality. The results are shown in Table 3. The latent traversals of VPGAN-flat $\alpha = 0.1$, InfoGAN $\lambda = 0.001$, VPGAN-hierarchical $\alpha = 0.1$, and FactorVAE $\gamma = 6.4$ are shown in Fig. 4, and Fig. 5, and more latent traversals can be found in Appendix 11, 12, and 13.

From Table 3, we can see the VP disentanglement score has a positive correlation with the hyper-parameter α. We can also summarize that the hierarchical inputs can boost the disentanglement score by an evident margin, indicating the hierarchical nature in deep neural networks can be a good ingredient for the learning of disentangled representations. On the other hand, the hyper-parameter α has a slight negative impact on FID, therefore it is better to choose a relatively small α to keep a balanced tradeoff between disentanglement and image quality. Nevertheless, the hierarchical input implementation seems to have a more significant negative impact on the FID, which we believe this technique should be better used with larger number of latent codes and more advanced architectures as in [22, 23] to take full advantage of it.

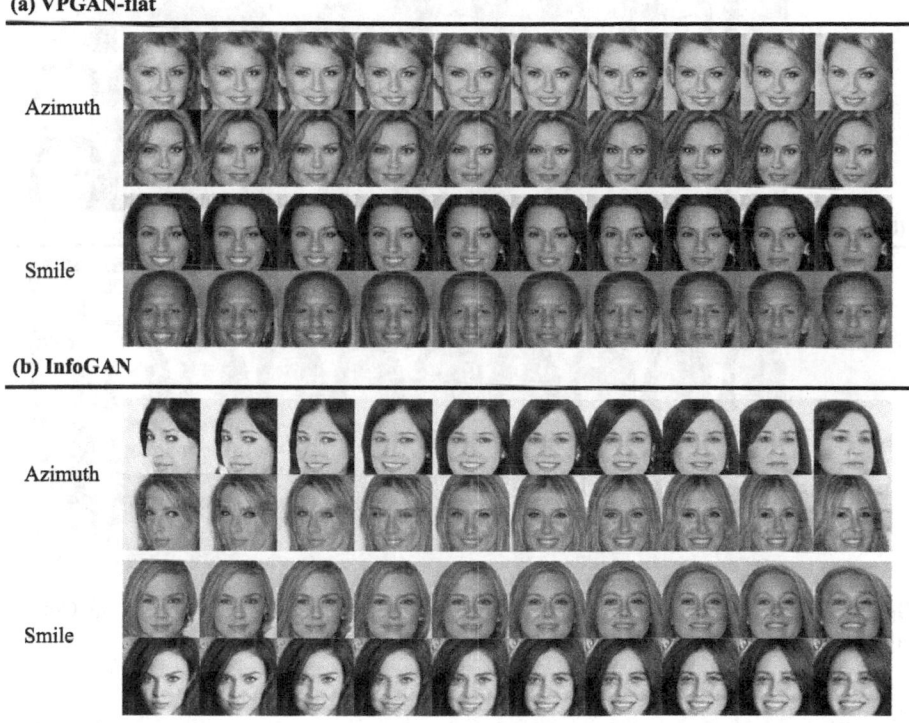

Fig. 4. Latent traversals of VPGAN-flat and InfoGAN models on CelebA dataset. More latent traversals can be found in Appendix 11 and 12.

From Table 4, we can see our VPGANs can achieve highest disentanglement scores among GAN-based models and can even achieve close performance as FactorVAE which models independence in the latent space. However, the FactorVAE has a bad FID score, meaning the generated images are lack of fidelity significantly. On the contrary, our VPGANs can keep a better FID especially the flat-input version. We can see InfoGANs can achieve a certain level of disentanglement, but their performance is significantly lower than VPGANs. In practice, we also found the training of InfoGANs are less stable than our VPGANs where InfoGANs may result in generating all-black images, even though both types of models are using the same generative and discriminative networks. As a summary, our VPGANs keep a more balanced tradeoff between the disentanglement and generation quality than the compared models.

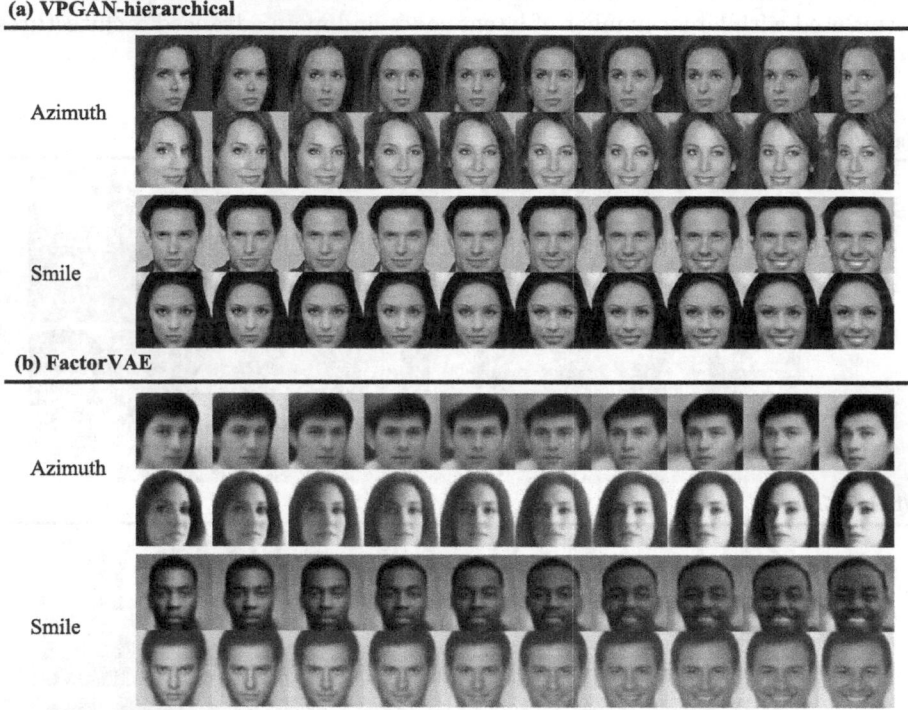

Fig. 5. Latent traversals of VPGAN-hierarchical and FactorVAE models on CelebA dataset. More latent traversals can be found in Appendix 13.

In Fig. 5 and Fig. 4 we qualitatively show the performance of our VPGANs, InfoGAN and FactorVAE baselines in disentanglement by latent traversals. From Fig. 4, we can see our model learns a cleaner semantics of azimuth while Info-GAN entangles azimuth with smile. Our model also learns a better latent code for controlling smile, while InfoGAN entangles smile and elevation into a single unit. In Appendix 11, 12 and 13, we show our VPGANs can learn more semantics (azimuth, brightness, hair color, makeup, smile, fringe, saturation, elevation, gender, lighting) than InfoGANs (azimuth, brightness, hair color, fringe, saturation, smile, gender, lighting). From Fig. 5, we can see the FactorVAE entangles smile with some level of skin texture information, while our model achieves a

Table 5. Experiments on 3DChairs dataset comparing InfoGAN and VPGAN.

Model	VP Score	FID
InfoGAN $\lambda = 0.1$	36.7	30.4
VPGAN $\alpha = 100$	**42.0**	32.1

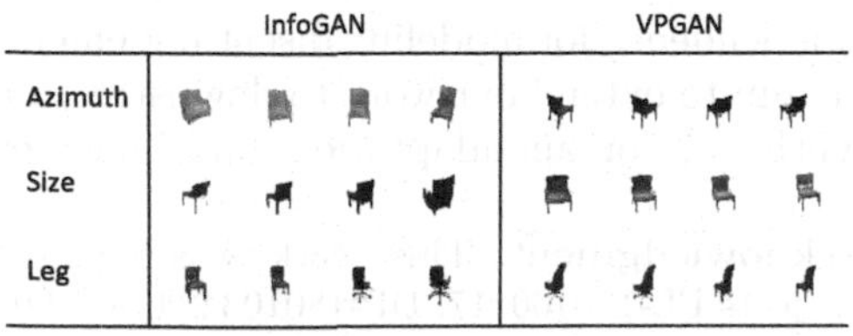

Fig. 6. Latent traversals on 3DChairs.

cleaner disentanglement. Also the results from FactorVAE are highly blurred, resulting in low FID.

There is an interesting phenomenon that for the learned disentangled representations in our models, not all dimensions encode variations. We find there are around 1/3 of dimensions capturing no information (or too subtle to observe by eyes). Disentanglement prefers this property because it means the model does not randomly encode entangled information into the rest of the dimensions but instead deactivates them. When the number of latent factors is set to 25–30, the learning is stable and almost all semantics shown can be learned. For latent factors less than 15, we observe some semantics are absent or entangled.

4.4 Experiments on 3D Chairs

We compare InfoGAN and VPGAN on 3D Chairs dataset. Quantitative results are shown in Table 5 and the latent traversals are shown in Fig. 6. As we can see, VPGAN achieves a higher disentanglement score than InfoGAN at the cost of a slight increase in FID, which agrees with what we found in the CelebA experiments. From the traversals, our VPGAN learns a cleaner latent code on controlling azimuth semantics while InfoGAN entangles it with some shape information. However, the performance of VPGAN on this dataset is not as impressive as on CelebA, indicating a more delicate modeling than the variation predictability assumption is required for this dataset to achieve a perfect disentanglement.

5 Conclusions

In this paper, we introduced the latent *Variation Predictability* as a new proxy for learning disentangled representations. By exploiting the latent variation predictability, we introduced the VP objective, which maximizes the mutual information between the varied dimension in the latent codes and the corresponding generated image pairs. Apart from the VP objective, we also proposed a new evaluation metric for quantitative measurement of disentanglement, which exploits the prediction difficulty of the varied dimension in the latent codes to quantify disentanglement. Different from other disentanglement metrics, our proposed VP metric does not require the existence of ground-truth generative factors. Experiments confirm the effectiveness of our model and metric, indicating the variation predictability can be exploited as a feasible alternative to statistical independence for modeling disentanglement in real-world data. For future works, we aim to extend our work to downstream applications like photorealistic image synthesis, domain adaptation, and image editing.

Acknowledgment. This work was supported by Australian Research Council Projects FL-170100117, DP-180103424 and DE180101438. We thank Jiaxian Guo and Youjian Zhang for their constructive discussions.

References

1. Arjovsky, M., Chintala, S., Bottou, L.: Wasserstein generative adversarial networks. In: ICML (2017)
2. Aubry, M., Maturana, D., Efros, A.A., Russell, B.C., Sivic, J.: Seeing 3D chairs: exemplar part-based 2D-3D alignment using a large dataset of cad models. In: IEEE Conference on Computer Vision and Pattern Recognition, pp. 3762–3769 (2014)
3. Banerjee, A., Merugu, S., Dhillon, I.S., Ghosh, J.: Clustering with Bregman divergences. J. Mach. Learn. Res. **6**, 1705–1749 (2004)
4. Bau, D., et al.: Gan dissection: visualizing and understanding generative adversarial networks. In: Proceedings of the International Conference on Learning Representations (ICLR) (2019)
5. Bengio, Y., Courville, A.C., Vincent, P.: Representation learning: a review and new perspectives. IEEE Trans. Pattern Anal. Mach. Intell. **35**, 1798–1828 (2012)
6. Berthelot, D., Schumm, T., Metz, L.: Began: boundary equilibrium generative adversarial networks. arXiv preprint arXiv:1703.10717 (2017)
7. Brock, A., Donahue, J., Simonyan, K.: Large scale GAN training for high fidelity natural image synthesis (2019)
8. Burgess, C.P., et al.: Understanding disentangling in beta-VAE. ArXiv abs/1804.03599 (2018)
9. Chen, R.T.Q., Li, X., Grosse, R., Duvenaud, D.: Isolating sources of disentanglement in variational autoencoders. In: Advances in Neural Information Processing Systems (2018)
10. Chen, X., Duan, Y., Houthooft, R., Schulman, J., Sutskever, I., Abbeel, P.: Info-GAN: interpretable representation learning by information maximizing generative adversarial nets. In: NIPS (2016)
11. Creager, E., et al.: Flexibly fair representation learning by disentanglement. In: ICML (2019)
12. Donahue, C., Lipton, Z.C., Balsubramani, A., McAuley, J.J.: Semantically decomposing the latent spaces of generative adversarial networks (2018)
13. Dupont, E.: Learning disentangled joint continuous and discrete representations. In: NeurIPS (2018)
14. Eastwood, C., Williams, C.K.I.: A framework for the quantitative evaluation of disentangled representations. In: ICLR (2018)
15. Goodfellow, I.J., et al.: Generative adversarial networks. In: NIPS (2014)
16. Gulrajani, I., Ahmed, F., Arjovsky, M., Dumoulin, V., Courville, A.C.: Improved training of Wasserstein GANs. In: NIPS (2017)
17. Heusel, M., Ramsauer, H., Unterthiner, T., Nessler, B., Hochreiter, S.: GANs trained by a two time-scale update rule converge to a local Nash equilibrium. In: NIPS (2017)

18. Higgins, I., et al.: Beta-VAE: learning basic visual concepts with a constrained variational framework. In: ICLR (2017)
19. Hoffman, M.D., Johnson, M.J.: ELBO surgery: yet another way to carve up the variational evidence lower bound. In: Workshop in Advances in Approximate Bayesian Inference, NIPS, vol. 1 (2016)
20. Jeong, Y., Song, H.O.: Learning discrete and continuous factors of data via alternating disentanglement. In: ICML (2019)
21. Karras, T., Aila, T., Laine, S., Lehtinen, J.: Progressive growing of gans for improved quality, stability, and variation (2018)
22. Karras, T., Laine, S., Aila, T.: A style-based generator architecture for generative adversarial networks. IEEE Trans. Pattern Anal. Mach. Intell. (2020)
23. Karras, T., Laine, S., Aittala, M., Hellsten, J., Lehtinen, J., Aila, T.: Analyzing and improving the image quality of styleGAN. ArXiv abs/1912.04958 (2019)
24. Kim, H., Mnih, A.: Disentangling by factorising. In: ICML (2018)
25. Kingma, D.P., Welling, M.: Auto-encoding variational Bayes. In: ICLR (2013)
26. Kodali, N., Hays, J., Abernethy, J.D., Kira, Z.: On convergence and stability of GANs (2018)
27. Kumar, A., Sattigeri, P., Balakrishnan, A.: Variational inference of disentangled latent concepts from unlabeled observations. In: ICLR (2018)
28. Lin, Z., Thekumparampil, K.K., Fanti, G., Oh, S.: InfoGAN-CR and modelcentrality: self-supervised model training and selection for disentangling GANs. In: ICML (2020)
29. Liu, Z., Luo, P., Wang, X., Tang, X.: Deep learning face attributes in the wild. In: IEEE International Conference on Computer Vision (ICCV), pp. 3730–3738 (2014)
30. Locatello, F., Abbati, G., Rainforth, T., Bauer, S., Schölkopf, B., Bachem, O.: On the fairness of disentangled representations. In: NeurIPS (2019)
31. Locatello, F., et al.: Challenging common assumptions in the unsupervised learning of disentangled representations. In: ICML (2019)
32. Makhzani, A., Frey, B.J.: PixelGAN autoencoders. In: NIPS (2017)
33. Makhzani, A., Shlens, J., Jaitly, N., Goodfellow, I.J.: Adversarial autoencoders. ArXiv abs/1511.05644 (2015)
34. Matthey, L., Higgins, I., Hassabis, D., Lerchner, A.: dSprites: disentanglement testing sprites dataset. https://github.com/deepmind/dsprites-dataset/ (2017)
35. Miyato, T., Kataoka, T., Koyama, M., Yoshida, Y.: Spectral normalization for generative adversarial networks (2018)
36. Nguyen, X., Wainwright, M.J., Jordan, M.I.: Estimating divergence functionals and the likelihood ratio by convex risk minimization. IEEE Trans. Inf. Theory **56**, 5847–5861 (2010)
37. Nguyen-Phuoc, T., Li, C., Theis, L., Richardt, C., Yang, Y.: HoloGAN: unsupervised learning of 3D representations from natural images. In: IEEE/CVF International Conference on Computer Vision (ICCV), pp. 7587–7596 (2019)
38. Peng, X., Huang, Z., Sun, X., Saenko, K.: Domain agnostic learning with disentangled representations. In: ICML (2019)
39. Radford, A., Metz, L., Chintala, S.: Unsupervised representation learning with deep convolutional generative adversarial networks. In: ICLR (2016)
40. Ridgeway, K., Mozer, M.C.: Learning deep disentangled embeddings with the f-statistic loss. In: NeurIPS (2018)
41. Shen, Y., Gu, J., Tang, X., Zhou, B.: Interpreting the latent space of GANs for semantic face editing. ArXiv abs/1907.10786 (2019)
42. van Steenkiste, S., Locatello, F., Schmidhuber, J., Bachem, O.: Are disentangled representations helpful for abstract visual reasoning? In: NIPS (2019)

43. Suter, R., Miladinovic, D., Schölkopf, B., Bauer, S.: Robustly disentangled causal mechanisms: Validating deep representations for interventional robustness. In: Proceedings of the 36th International Conference on Machine Learning (ICML). Proceedings of Machine Learning Research, vol. 97, pp. 6056–6065. PMLR, June 2019. http://proceedings.mlr.press/v97/suter19a.html

44. Tran, L., Yin, X., Liu, X.: Disentangled representation learning GAN for pose-invariant face recognition. In: 2017 IEEE Conference on Computer Vision and Pattern Recognition (CVPR), pp. 1283–1292 (2017)

45. Wang, Y., Yao, Q., Kwok, J.T., Ni, L.M.: Generalizing from a few examples: a survey on few-shot learning (2019)

46. Yang, J., Dvornek, N.C., Zhang, F., Chapiro, J., Lin, M.D., Duncan, J.S.: Unsupervised domain adaptation via disentangled representations: application to cross-modality liver segmentation. In: Shen, D., et al. (eds.) MICCAI 2019. LNCS, vol. 11765, pp. 255–263. Springer, Cham (2019). https://doi.org/10.1007/978-3-030-32245-8_29

47. Zhang, H., Goodfellow, I., Metaxas, D., Odena, A.: Self-attention generative adversarial networks. In: ICML (2019)

48. Zhao, S., Song, J., Ermon, S.: Learning hierarchical features from generative models. In: ICML (2017)

Deep Space-Time Video Upsampling Networks

Jaeyeon Kang[1], Younghyun Jo[1], Seoung Wug Oh[1], Peter Vajda[2],
and Seon Joo Kim[1,2]

[1] Yonsei University, Seoul, South Korea
seonjookim@yonsei.ac.kr
[2] Facebook, Menlo Park, USA

Abstract. Video super-resolution (VSR) and frame interpolation (FI) are traditional computer vision problems, and the performance have been improving by incorporating deep learning recently. In this paper, we investigate the problem of jointly upsampling videos both in space and time, which is becoming more important with advances in display systems. One solution for this is to run VSR and FI, one by one, independently. This is highly inefficient as heavy deep neural networks (DNN) are involved in each solution. To this end, we propose an end-to-end DNN framework for the space-time video upsampling by efficiently merging VSR and FI into a joint framework. In our framework, a novel weighting scheme is proposed to fuse all input frames effectively without explicit motion compensation for efficient processing of videos. The results show better results both quantitatively and qualitatively, while reducing the computation time (×7 faster) and the number of parameters (30%) compared to baselines. Our source code is available at https://github.com/JaeYeonKang/STVUN-Pytorch.

Keywords: Video super-resolution · Video frame interpolation · Joint space-time upsampling

1 Introduction

In this paper, we introduce a method of upsampling both the spatial resolution and the frame rate of a video simultaneously. This is an important problem as more high-performance TV displays are being introduced with higher resolution and frame rate, but the video contents have not yet caught up with the capabilities of displays. For example, new UHD displays now come with 4K or even 8K resolution, and the frame rate of 120 fps. On the other hand, most available contents are still HD (1080p) or less in resolution, with the frame rate of 30 fps. Another potential application of this problem is the video replay for sports and

Electronic supplementary material The online version of this chapter (https://doi.org/10.1007/978-3-030-58607-2_41) contains supplementary material, which is available to authorized users.

© Springer Nature Switzerland AG 2020
A. Vedaldi et al. (Eds.): ECCV 2020, LNCS 12355, pp. 701–717, 2020.
https://doi.org/10.1007/978-3-030-58607-2_41

security videos. In order to inspect a video in much detail, videos are spatially magnified in slow motion. As shown by these examples, there is definitely a major need for a framework that can convert a given video into a video with higher resolution and frame rate.

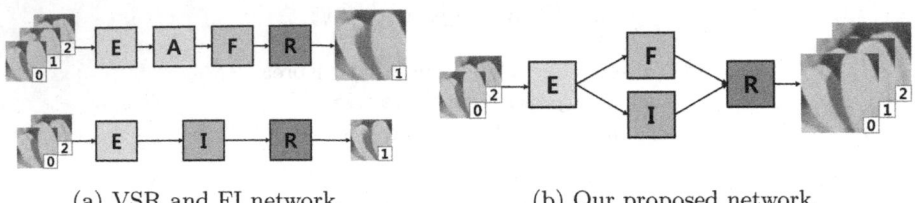

(a) VSR and FI network.   (b) Our proposed network.

Fig. 1. Common pipelines for VSR/FI and the design scheme for our proposed network. By efficiently merging the pipelines for the two tasks with new mechanisms for feature fusion and interactions between modules, we can accurately upsample videos both in space and time in a very efficient fashion. E: extraction, A: alignment, F: fusion, R: reconstruction, I: interpolation.

Deep neural networks (DNN) have become common solutions for video super-resolution (VSR) and frame interpolation (FI) recently. With DNN, an obvious solution for the joint upsampling problem would be to sequentially run a VSR network followed by a FI network or vice versa. However, running the two algorithms independently is computationally expensive and inefficient, as the state-of-the-art methods for each task employ heavy DNNs. The goal of this paper is to design an efficient DNN for the joint space-time upsampling problem by investigating shareable components between the spatial and the temporal upsamping tasks.

While there are many different DNN architecture for VSR [23,29,32,34] and FI [2,9,20,34], the common design schemes can be summarized as in Fig. 1(a). In VSR, most methods employ four stages – feature extraction, alignment, fusion and reconstruction. For FI, the process can be divided into feature extraction, feature interpolation and reconstruction.

To jointly upsample videos both in space and time, we propose to combine the two tasks in an efficient manner as shown in Fig. 1(b) by sharing the common modules in feature extraction and reconstruction. The modules are designed to interact and learn simultaneously for accurate and efficient reconstruction of jointly upsampled videos.

Furthermore, we propose a novel way to efficiently fuse the features of individual frames for VSR without explicit motion compensation. Most VSR methods rely on aligning many input frames through optical flows [8,23,29,34] or deformable convolutions [32] before fusing the extracted features. As many methods use up to 7 input frames, aligning that many frames takes up a large portion of the computation. To remove the computational burden of motion compensation, we fuse the feature maps without explicit alignment step (Fig. 1(b)). In our feature fusion process, we propose Early Fusion with Spatio-Temporal weights (EFST) module that learns to fuse information by considering spatio-temporal relationship between input frames in an implicit manner. In this module, learnable spatio-temporal weights are computed in order to combine rich information from all frames instead of focusing too much on the target frame.

There are no public datasets available for the joint space-time upsampling, as it is a relatively a new topic. While there are many datasets for VSR and FI separately, they are not ideal for the joint upsampling task. To this end, we collected a new dataset called the Space-Time Video Test (STVT) dataset that can be used to evaluate joint upsampling methods. This dataset will be publicly available.

In summary, the main contributions of our paper are as follows:

- By efficiently merging two networks of VSR and FI, we propose a novel framework called the Space-Time Video Upsampling Networks (STVUN) for joint space-time video upsampling. With careful design of each module and their interactions, we produce better results while reducing the computation time (×7 faster) and the number of parameters (30%) compared to sequentially connected state-of-the-art VSR and FI networks.
- We propose Early Fusion with Spatio-Temporal weights (EFST) to fuse input features efficiently without explicit motion compensation for VSR.
- Our framework can deal with more challenging upsampling tasks as it can upsample 4 × 4 in space and ×∞ in time. In comparison, recent works on joint upsampling have only shown results on doubling the resolution both in space and time (2 × 2 × 2).
- We collected Space-Time Video Test (STVT) dataset for evaluating the joint space-time upsampling task. This can be very useful for future work in this topic.

2   Related Work

2.1   Video Super-Resolution

After Dong et al. [6] have successfully achieved the high performance by incorporating deep learning into the single image SR task, deep learning approaches have also become prevalent in solving the VSR problem [4,11,13,16,23,29].

DUF [10] used dynamic up-sampling filters to improve the resolution while reducing the flickering artifact which is prevalent in VSR task. Their method takes the advantage of the implicit motion computed within the network, and additionally used the learned residual image to enhance the sharpness. RBPN [8] used an iterative refinement framework, which forwards the input frame with other frames at multiple times. They use the idea of back-projection, which computes a residual image for each time step to reduce the error between the target and the output. In EDVR [32], input frames are first aligned with the target frame using the deformable convolution [5]. Aligned frames are then fused using the temporal and spatial attention (TSA) mechanism.

2.2   Video Frame Interpolation

Video frame interpolation can be roughly divided into two categories: kernel-based methods and optical flow-based methods. As an interpolation kernel based approach, Niklaus et al. [21] proposed AdaConv, which produces interpolation kernels to generate intermediate frame. In [22], they extended the method to reduce the computational cost, which is named as SepConv using 1D kernels instead of 2D kernels.

With the introduction of CNN-based optical flow algorithms [7], several frame interpolation algorithms using the optical flow have been developed. Liu et al. [18] produce intermediate frames by the trilinear sampling based on the estimated deep voxel flows called DVF. Xue et al. [35] used the bi-directional flow to warp both input frames using the backward warping function. Jiang et al. [9] obtained the bi-directional flow through the network and then linearly transformed two flows with respect to the time value to generate multiple intermediate frames. Niklaus and Liu [20] used the forward warping and further designed a refinement network in order to fill the holes caused by the forward warping. Liu et al. [17] used cycle consistency loss to enhance synthesized frames to be more reliable as input frames. To deal with the occlusion problem which is a common issue in optical flows, additional depth information was used to refine the optical flows in DAIN [2].

2.3   Space-Time Upsampling

In [26], Shechtman et al. first proposed a space-time super-resolution framework by using multiple low resolution (LR) videos of the same dynamic scene. Different from the frame interpolation methods mentioned above, they explicitly deal with the motion blur to generate sharp interpolated frames. In [24], Shahar et al. extended the work in [26] with a method that only uses a single video to enhance the resolution. Sharma et al. [25] first used a DNN architecture for the joint space-time upsampling. They used the auto-encoder to learn the mapping between LR and high resolution (HR) frames, and the frame interpolation was simply done by the tri-cubic interpolation. Another deep joint upsampling method called FISR [12] was recently introduced, which targets for estimating 4K, 60 fps video from 2K, 30 fps video. They regularized their joint upsampling network by forwarding multiple chunks of frames into one iteration and set multiple temporal losses at the output of each chunk. Note that, FISR only generates 8 pixels (space ×2, time ×2) per input pixel, while our work aims at more challenging task of generating more pixels (e.g. 64 pixels for space ×4, time ×4).

3   Space-Time Video Upsampling Algorithm

Given a sequence of LR frames X_t, our method produces HR frames $\hat{Y}_t$ of inputs as well as the intermediate HR frames $\hat{Y}_T$ in-between the input frames. The term

t denotes the input time index, and T indicates the newly created time index. The size of a LR frame is $H \times W \times C$, where H, W, and C are the height, the width, and the number of channels respectively. The output size is $rH \times rW \times C$, with r being the spatial upscaling factor. We can generate N multiple upsampled intermediate frames in-between the two input frames. The problem is very challenging as the algorithm has to generate $r^2 \times (N + 1)$ pixels per pixel in the input frame. For example, we need to generate 64 pixels in the output per input pixel with $r = 4$ and $N = 3$.

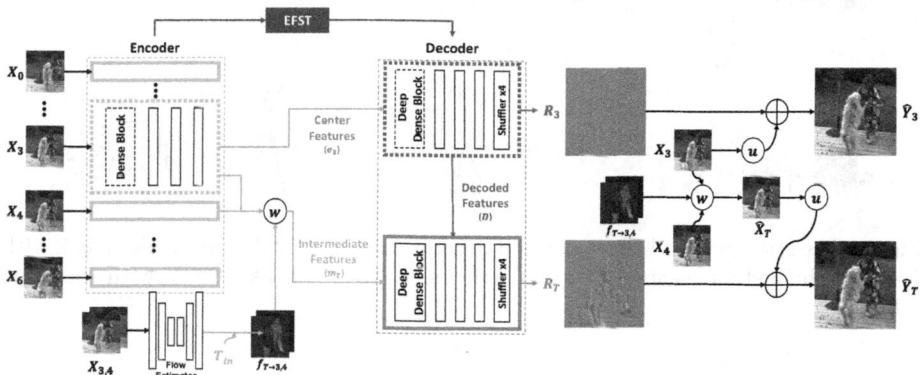

Fig. 2. Overview of our space-time upsampling network. The network is composed of several interacting modules to produce the HR frames of the center frame $\hat{Y}_3$ and the intermediate frames $\hat{Y}_T$, where $T \in [3, 4]$. The term w and u indicate backward warping and bilinear upsampling respectively.

3.1 Network Overview

The overview of our network is shown in Fig. 2. Our network is composed of multiple modules: encoder, feature fusion for spatial upsampling (EFST), flow estimator for frame interpolation, and decoder. Our framework takes 7 LR frames as inputs, for example $X_{[0,1,2,3,4,5,6]}$. Then, it produces the HR frames for the center frame $\hat{Y}_3$ as well as N HR intermediate frames $\hat{Y}_T$, where $T \in [3, 4]$.

The encoders that share weights are first used to extract features per frame. The encoded features are fused using EFST for the spatial upsampling, and interpolated using the computed flows for the temporal upsampling. The decoding block that consists of decoders with shared weights produces residual images for the spatial and the temporal upsampling, both of which are added to the bilinearly upsampled images to produce the final output frames.

3.2 Network Details

Encoder. Structure of the encoder is shown in Fig. 3. The encoder extracts feature representations for each frame and consists of multiple dense convolution blocks. Each dense block is connected to the corresponding block in decoder through EFST. This allows the decoder to keep considering the temporal relationship of inputs. The encoded features are expressed as e_t^i, where i is the block index and t is the time index of the input frame.

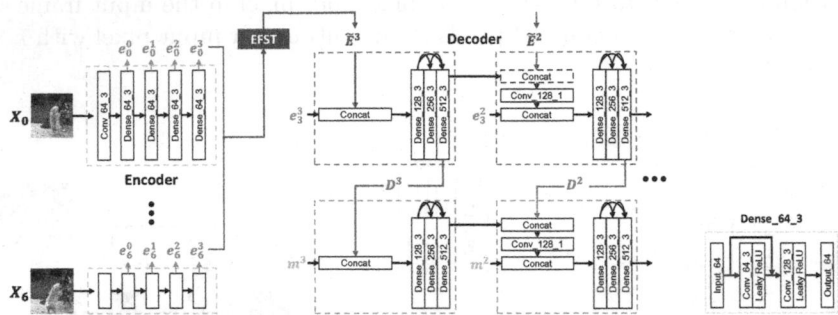

Fig. 3. The structure of the encoder and decoder. Dense_64_3 denotes dense block with 64 input channel dimension and 3×3 kernel size. We use Leaky ReLU with the slope value 0.1.

Early Fusion with Spatio-Temporal Weights (EFST). In most VSR methods, features from multiple frames are aligned before fusion using explicit motion compensation by optical flows or deformable convolutions. However, aligning multiple frames (6 in most cases including ours) to the center frame is computationally expensive. Therefore, we exclude explicit alignment process by devising the EFST module for implicit feature alignment and fusion for spatial upsampling.

To merge input features from the encoders, we first apply early fusion to reduce the computational cost. Early fused features E^i are defined as $Conv(Concat \ [e_0^i, ..., e_6^i])$ where $Conv$ reduces the channel dimension by the factor of 7 with an 1×1 convolution filter. However, since the early fusion will collapse all temporal information in the first layer, the features of the target (center) frame will be mainly used as mentioned in [27]. Some information in other frames may vanish due to the bottleneck. This is because most information for reconstructing the HR target frame is contained in the input LR center frame.

In order to use valuable information in the features from all the input frames without explicit alignment, we propose the EFST module that computes spatio-temporal weights to compensate E^i. The structure of EFST is shown in Fig. 4. In the early fusion result E^i, most input features are not considered equally since E^i will be computed to mainly focus on the center frame. Therefore, we design a confidence score to effectively fuse informative features from the neighbor frames as well as the center frame. We estimate the confidence score by computing dot-product between E^i and all the e_t^i. We use this confidence score as a temporal attention to find which frames need to be more referred. The confidence score is computed as follows:

$$s_t^i = \text{sigmoid}(\theta(e_t^i) \circ \delta(E^i)), \qquad (1)$$

where $\circ$ is dot-product and s is the confidence score. θ and δ are single convolutional layer with filter size 1×1. s_t^i has the same spatial size as e_t^i and the values of s_t^i are in $[0,1]$. To pay more attention to the frames with high confidence score, we multiply this value to the original encoded features e_t^i as follows:

$$\bar{e}_t^{\,i} = s_t^i \odot e_t^i, \qquad (2)$$

where $\odot$ denote element-wise multiplication.

All temporally weighted encoded features $\bar{e}_t^{\,i}$ are then concatenated and forwarded to pyramid designed convolutional layers to further consider spatio-temporal information. Pyramid convolution can effectively enlarge the receptive field with just few convolution layers. Afterwards, we generate learnable spatio-temporal weights α, β. It is a tensor with same size of E^i. It transform the initial early fusion result to learn the alignment in an implicit way. The final fused features is computed as follows:

$$\tilde{E}^i = \alpha \odot E^i + \beta. \qquad (3)$$

Our EFST module is similar to Fusion with Temporal and Spatial Attention called TSA in [32]. TSA measures similarity distance between aligned frames and target frame to temporally weight more on well-aligned frames, since misalignment can severely interfere with learning. In comparison, we use confidence score as a way to involve more features from more input frames, which eventually works as a joint alignment and fusion process without explicit alignment.

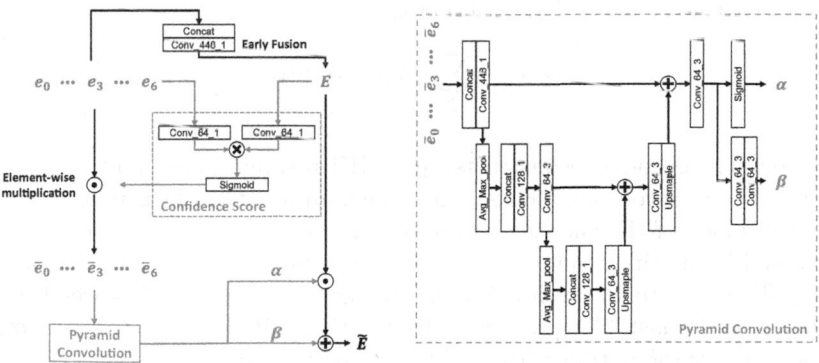

Fig. 4. Early Fusion with Spatio-Temporal weights (EFST) module. Avg_Max_pool means pooling separately with average pooling and max pooling. For temporally attending more frames, the confidence score is computed from early fusion result E^i and e_t^i. Then, the spatio-temporal weights α and β are computed and applied. For simplicity, we omit the superscript i, and see text for details.

Intermediate Feature Interpolation. The feature interpolation process is shown in green in Fig. 2. Features m_T^i of an intermediate frame are synthesized by warping the features of the input frames (X_3, X_4) using the optical flow estimated by the flow estimator. To reduce the computational cost, we warp the encoded features of the two inputs to produce the target intermediate features instead of first creating the intermediate frame and encoding it again. Note that explicit alignment is only used for intermediate frames but not for merging all input features (EFST). We first use the optical flow computed by the PWC-Net [28]. Then, we use the following formulation [9] to estimate the flow between the input frames and the intermediate frame:

$$
\begin{aligned}
f_{T\to3} &= -(1 - T_{in})T_{in}f_{3\to4} + T_{in}^2 f_{4\to3}, \\
f_{T\to4} &= (1 - T_{in})^2 f_{3\to4} - T_{in}(1 - T_{in})f_{4\to3},
\end{aligned}
\tag{4}
$$

where f indicates the optical flow and T_{in} is a relative scalar value (e.g. when we want to get $\hat{Y}_{3.5}$, then T_{in} is set to 0.5). Note that T_{in} is given as an input to the network to provide the time index of the intermediate frame.

Finally, the features of the intermediate frame are computed as follows:

$$
m_T^i = \frac{w(e_3^i, f_{T\to3}) + w(e_4^i, f_{T\to4})}{2},
\tag{5}
$$

where w stands for the backward warping.

At the same time, we generate LR intermediate frames X_T for the subsequent process of bilinear upsampling with

$$
\hat{X}_T = \frac{w(X_3, f_{T\to3}) + w(X_4, f_{T\to4})}{2},
\tag{6}
$$

and for finetuning PWC-net with ground-truth intermediate frames during training whole network, we set loss function as:

$$
\mathcal{L}_{\mathcal{M}} = \sum_T \|\hat{X}_T - X_T\|_1.
\tag{7}
$$

Decoder. The decoder reconstructs target HR residual image and it consists of multiple dense convolution blocks. The same number of blocks is used to connect with each block of the encoder. We design a more deeper dense block which is shown in Fig. 3, since more layers and connections could boost performance [14,33]. To generate the residual image of the target frame, features from the last layer of the last block are convolved with a filter having $C \cdot r \cdot r$ output channels, where the output is then reshaped to the size of $rH \times rW \times C$ through the pixel shuffler [27] with the scale factor of 4.

For space upsampling, features of target (center) frame e_3 and fused features from EFST $\tilde{E}$ are used as inputs. Output residual image R_3 is added to the upsampled target frame to generate final HR output as follows:

$$
\hat{Y}_3 = u(X_3) + R_3,
\tag{8}
$$

where $u(\cdot)$ is the bilinear upsampling function. The loss function for space upsampling is defined as:

$$\mathcal{L}_{\mathcal{S}} = ||\hat{Y}_3 - Y_3||_1. \tag{9}$$

Since the decoder consists of more deeply stacked convolution layers, it creates more refined spatio-temporal information from the EFST features. Therefore, during the space upsampling task, the decoded features D^i are generated at the end of each dense block and forwarded to the space-time upsampling task to supplement with more rich information. For space-time upsampling, the intermediate features m_T are passed to another decoder that shares weights. Here, different from space upsampling, decoded features D^i are fed instead of feeding $\tilde{E}$.

Then, HR residual image R_T of the intermediate frame is generated and the final HR intermediate frame is computed as follows:

$$\hat{Y}_T = u(\hat{X}_T) + R_T, \tag{10}$$

where $\hat{X}_T$ is from Eq. (6). Our loss function to train space-time upsampling is:

$$\mathcal{L}_{\mathcal{F}} = \sum_T ||\hat{Y}_T - Y_T||_1, \tag{11}$$

where T can be any values in $[3, 4]$. Note that we can generate arbitrary number of intermediate frames using Eq. (4).

3.3   Training

Vimeo septuplets dataset [35] is usually used to train VSR and FI tasks. But the length of video frames in Vimeo dataset is too short for our task. It consists of 7 frames per clip, but we need at least 8 frames for training. Therefore, we collect training videos of 240 fps from YouTube. This training dataset consists of various scenes with global camera motions and local object motions. In total, the dataset contains about 1800 video clips and 220K frames. To make LR frames, HR frames are first smoothed with a Gaussian filter and then subsampled with respect to the scaling factor $r = 4$. For the data augmentation, we randomly flip left-right and rotate $90/180°$. We also reverse the order of the sequence to enlarge the training dataset. The whole training and test is processed in RGB channels.

It is difficult to train all the networks in our framework simultaneously from scratch, as there are many interactions between the components. We first pre-train the encoder and the spatial decoder by minimizing $\mathcal{L}_{\mathcal{S}}$ (VSR part only). For this pretraining, we use 7 frames $Y_{[0,1,2,3,4,5,6]}$ in the training dataset and 128×128 patches are cropped. We use the Adam optimizer for 300K iterations with the mini-batch size of 32. The learning rate is initialized to 0.0001 and decreased by a factor of 2 every 100K iterations.

After pretraining the VSR part, we train the whole network using the following total loss function:

$$\mathcal{L} = \lambda_{\mathcal{M}}\mathcal{L}_{\mathcal{M}} + \lambda_{\mathcal{S}}\mathcal{L}_{\mathcal{S}} + \lambda_{\mathcal{F}}\mathcal{L}_{\mathcal{F}}, \tag{12}$$

where $\lambda_{\mathcal{M}}$, $\lambda_{\mathcal{S}}$, and $\lambda_{\mathcal{F}}$ are the weight parameters. In our experiment, we empirically set $\lambda_{\mathcal{M}} = 1, \lambda_{\mathcal{S}} = 1$, and $\lambda_{\mathcal{F}} = 1$ for the best results. For the joint training, 256×256 patches are used rather than 128×128 in order to deal with large motions. Intermediate frames in-between Y_3, Y_4 (e.g. $Y_{3.5}$) as well as the 7 frames are used for training VSR and FI part together. We train the whole network for 400K iterations and the initial learning rate is set to 0.00005. The same learning rate decay is used.

4   Experiments

In this section, we provide both quantitative and qualitative evaluations of our algorithm.

Testsets. While there are some datasets for VSR and FI separately, they are not ideal for the joint space-time upsampling task. For example, the Vid4 testset [15] for VSR have a lot of details, but the motion between the frames is too small. This limits the assessment of FI performance. MPI Sintel testset [3] is synthetic dataset which dose not have much detail to assess VSR performance. REDS-VTSR dataset [19] is used for VSR and FI separately, but it contains unnatural camera movements. In addition, the Vimeo [34], Middleburry [1] and FISR [12] testset are not available, since at least 15 frames are required for each scene to evaluate the performance.

To this end, we use Vid4, MPI Sintel and REDS-VTSR [19] for testing the generalization our performance. In addition, we create Space-Time Video Test (STVT) dataset that consists of 12 dynamic scenes with both natural motions and spatial details for the joint upsampling evaluation. Each scene has at least 50 frames, and we will make STVT dataset publicly available to promote more research in this topic.

Baselines. We make two baseline methods ($V \rightarrow F$ and $F \rightarrow V$) that combine VSR and FI, which run consequently. V and F indicate VSR and FI respectively. For example, $F \rightarrow V$ indicates running FI first and then VSR. For V and F, we use EDVR [32] and DAIN [2] respectively, which are the state-of-the-art methods with publicly available codes. As the bias of the dataset affect the evaluation performance [30], for fair comparison, we try to finetune the baseline methods with our YouTube training dataset. However, since their weights are already highly finetuned, we find that the performance is rather reduced when we jointly train both networks at the same time (0.15 dB is reduced for Vid4 testset). Therefore, we fix their weights to produce the results. We also compare our method with FISR [12], the only deep learning based work that we can compared to at this moment.

4.1   Comparisons

For the evaluation, we extract odd numbered frames in the testset and set them as ground-truth frames. Only the even numbered frames are used to generate the space-time upsampled results. We first compare our method with the two baseline methods. We set $T_{in} = 1/2$ for generating the HR intermediate frame. Table 1 shows the quantitative results of different approaches for ×4 space and ×2 time. In every testset, $F \rightarrow V$ consistently shows the worst performance, because FI works better on HR input frames due to sufficient details. On the other hand, in the case of $V \rightarrow F$, FI can access sufficient details from VSR, thus it can generate sharper results. However, the improvement in the resolution increases the amount of computation for FI (×4 slower).

Table 1. Quantitative evaluation of the joint space-time upsampling on multiple test-sets. We compare our method with the two baseline approaches by measuring the PSNR and SSIM. We set $T_{in} = 1/2$ for comparison. We also write down the number of parameters and the running time for each method. The running time is measured when generating the results with the resolution 960 × 540. The best is shown in bold.

		$F \rightarrow V$	$V \rightarrow F$	Ours
Dataset	Vid4	25.22/0.7506	26.39/0.8163	**26.49/0.8231**
	Sintel	26.99/0.7986	27.56/**0.8185**	**27.58**/0.8134
	REDS-VTSR	23.70/0.6541	23.63/0.6533	**23.78/0.6601**
	STVT	26.43/0.8435	26.96/0.8619	**27.23/0.8644**
#Params		44.7M	44.7M	**30.9M**
Running time		0.52 s	2.14 s	**0.30 s**

Table 2. Comparison with FISR [12]. We train our model with the upsampling factor space ×2 and time ×2 which is the same as FISR.

		FISR [12]	Ours
Dataset	Vid4	26.93/0.8534	**30.60/0.9369**
	Sintel	27.17/0.8115	**28.36/0.8329**
	REDS-VTSR	**23.89/0.6601**	23.66/0.6550
	STVT	26.49/0.8514	**28.01/0.8895**
#Params		62.3M	**30.9M**
Running time		1.10 s	**0.98 s**

Our results show better performance for all datasets as shown in Table 1. The performance difference in Vid4, Sintel and REDS-VTSR testset is not that big because those testsets are not constructed for this particular tasks and not optimal for evaluating the joint upsampling task. The performance gap between our method and the baselines become larger with the STVT dataset, which is specifically designed for the joint upsampling.

Table 1 also shows the number of parameters and the computation time of different methods. In this experiment, our total parameters and computational times does include PWC-Net [28]. We run the methods on Nvidia Geforce Titan X and measure the time taken to generate one 960×540 jointly upsampled frame. The number of parameters is reduced by more than 30% compared to the baseline methods, and the speed is 7 times faster than $V \rightarrow F$ and 1.7 times faster than $F \rightarrow V$. Although ours is lighter than the baseline methods, it exceeds the performance of baseline methods, indicating that our network is designed efficiently.

Additionally, we compare our model with FISR [12] in Table 2. As the upsampling factor of FISR is space $\times 2$ and time $\times 2$, we train our network with the same settings. Note that only the number of output channels of the last convolutional layer in the decoder is changed. As can be seen in Table 2, our method outperforms FISR by a large margin except for REDS-VTSR. In addition, our method runs faster than FISR with fewer parameters.

Figure 5 visually compares our method with the two baseline methods and FISR. In Fig. 5(a), we generate multiple frame ($T_{in} = 0.25, 0.5, 0.75$) in-between two input frames. To better illustrate the results, we enlarge the corresponding red areas. As STVT dataset has a large motion, two baseline methods have difficulty in handling the large motion. In the soccer scene, $F \rightarrow V$ shows more pleasing result than $V \rightarrow F$ because it is easier to estimate the motion at smaller input size. Except for the large motion scene, $V \rightarrow F$ is clearer than $F \rightarrow V$. Overall, our method is more accurate in estimating the motion and shows less artifacts. In Fig. 5(b), we generate one intermediate frame ($T_{in} = 0.5$) for comparison with FISR. The results in FISR show ghost artifact due to wrong motion estimation, but ours restore sharper edge details. However, due to the unnatural movement of REDS-VTSR testset, most center frames are not in the middle of the front and rear frames. So, only for this testset, the blurry results of FISR reduce average pixel error than ours. We recommend watching our demo video in the supplementary material to see the difference more clearly.

Beside the STVUN, our network can be used for VSR. As our main objective is the space-time upsampling, the experiments on VSR will be shown in the supplementary material.

Table 3. Ablation studies on the EFST and our network structure. STVT dataset is used for comparison.

	w/o EFST	w/o D	w/A& F	Ours
PSNR/SSIM	27.06/0.8613	27.15/0.8615	27.20/**0.8652**	**27.23**/0.8644
#Params	**30.5M**	30.9M	32.4M	30.9M
Running time	**0.27 s**	0.30 s	0.75 s	0.30 s

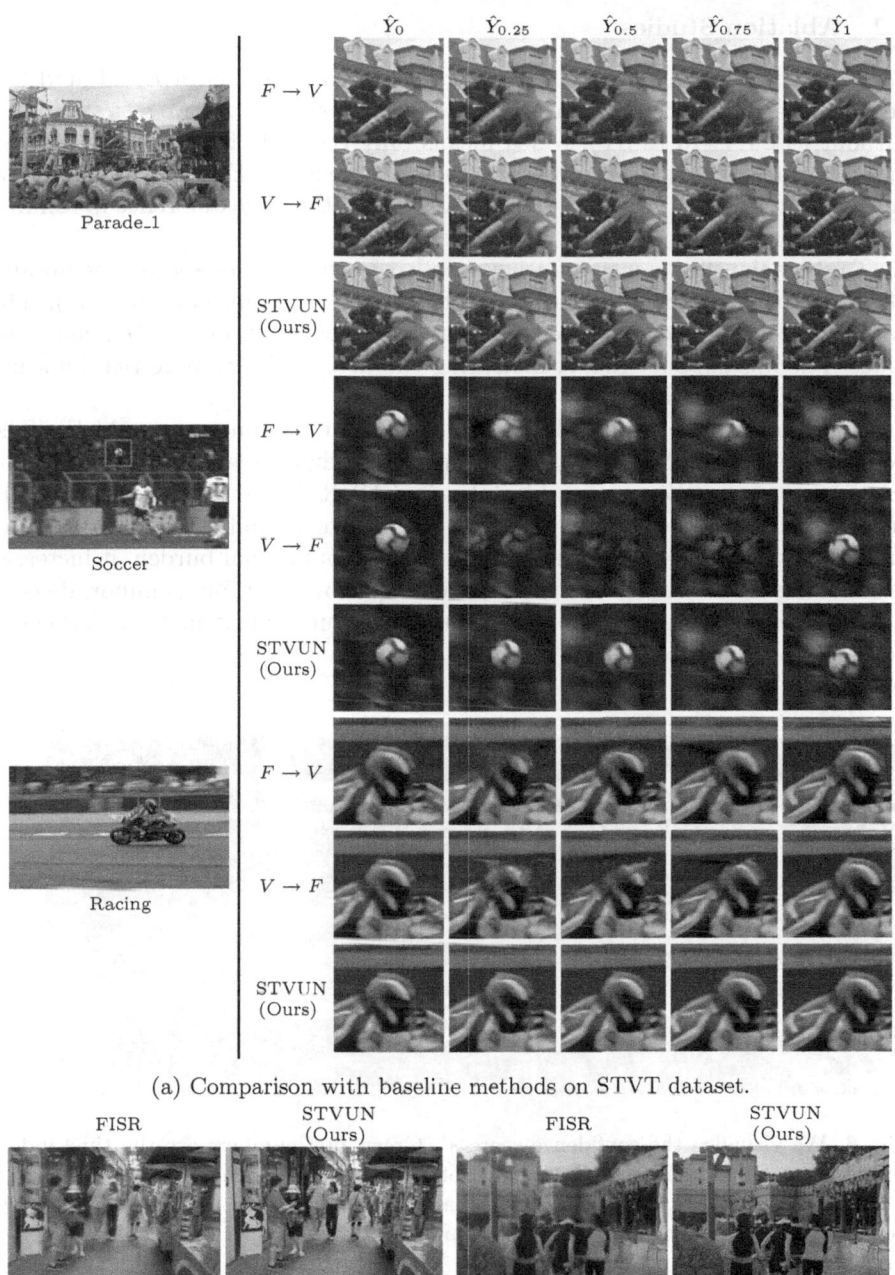

(a) Comparison with baseline methods on STVT dataset.

(b) Comparison with FISR on REDS-VTSR testset.

Fig. 5. Visual comparisons of the space-time upsampling results. In (a), we generate a total of 5 frames that consist of 2 space upsampling and 3 intermediate frames. *Parade_1, Soccer, Racing* scenes are used in our *STVT* dataset. In (b), we generate one intermediate frame. *002* and *007* in REDS-VTSR testset are used.

4.2   Ablation Studies

We conduct ablation studies to investigate the contribution of EFST and our network design. Table 3 summarizes the ablation results. First, we test our model without EFST (w/o EFST), which means only the early fusion is used to fuse input features. This test demonstrates the effectiveness of EFST as it shows that our final model improves the performance without the large difference in running time.

To show the effectiveness of using decoded features D^i for space-time upsampling, we test our model when EFST features is used instead (w/o D). The performance gain shows learned features from space upsampling enhance the space-time upsampling results, indicating the decoder learn more rich information from EFST features.

We also evaluate our model with the explicit alignment (w/ A&F). The overall structure is the same as our proposed method except for the alignment and fusion parts. We use two modules in EDVR [31] – Pyramid, Cascading and Deformable Convolution (PCD) for the alignment and TSA for the feature fusion. As the explicit alignment process is a computational burden, it increases the running time by about 2.5 times. But the performance gap is minor, demonstrating EFST can effectively fuse features without explicit motion compensation.

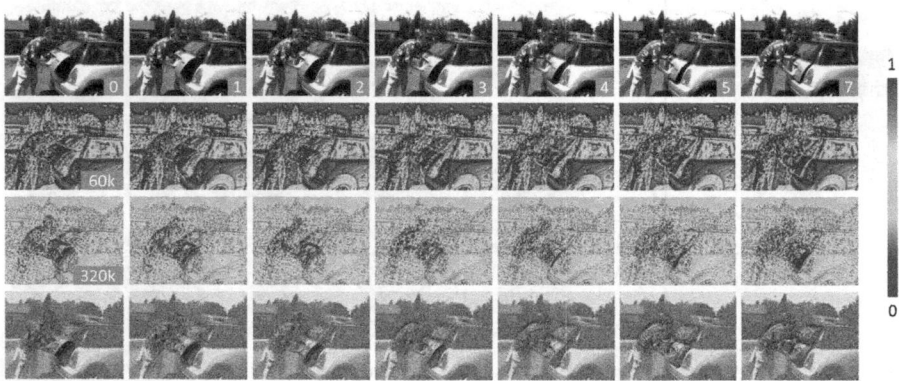

Fig. 6. We visualize the confidence score s^i. Green box numbers are the time index, and the blue box numbers are the number of iterations. High confidence score is shown in red, and this means to be more referred and dark blue is vice versa. In the last row, we overlap results of the input and color map of 320k iterations. Zoom in to see better visualization. (Color figure online)

Figure 6 shows the visualization of the confidence score to analyze how confidence score changes with learning in EFST. In the early stages of training, confidence scores are ambiguous to determine where to concentrate more. Therefore, the overall scores are high and shown in dark red. As the learning progresses, the confidence score gets the ability to determine the important parts among all inputs. High confidence scores remain for the regions which are helpful for reconstructing the center frame. On the other hand, occluded regions such as under the trunk lid in frame 0 have low confidence score because they are unnecessary for reconstructing center frame. It demonstrates that our confidence score effectively fuses features from all frames without explicit alignment.

5 Conclusion

In this paper, we present a deep Space-Time Video Upsampling Networks (STVUN) for joint space-time video upsampling by merging VSR and FI network efficiently. This task has many practical applications, yet a challenging task as the network has to perform two tasks in an efficient manner. In addition, we propose Early Fusion with Spatio-Temporal weights (EFST) modules that learns to fuse information by considering spatio-temporal relationship without any explicit alignment. Our network can generate visually pleasing results with reduced computational time ($\times 7$) and number of parameters (30%) compared to sequentially connected VSR and FI networks. Our method also outperforms a previous space-time upsampling task by a large margin.

Acknowledgements. This work was supported by Institute of Information & Communications Technology Planning & Evaluation (IITP) grant funded by the Korea government (MSIT) (No. 2014-0-00059, Development of Predictive Visual Intelligence Technology).

References

1. Baker, S., Scharstein, D., Lewis, J., Roth, S., Black, M.J., Szeliski, R.: A database and evaluation methodology for optical flow. Int. J. Comput. Vision **92**(1), 1–31 (2011)
2. Bao, W., Lai, W.S., Ma, C., Zhang, X., Gao, Z., Yang, M.H.: Depth-aware video frame interpolation. In: Proceedings of the IEEE Conference on Computer Vision and Pattern Recognition, pp. 3703–3712 (2019)
3. Butler, D.J., Wulff, J., Stanley, G.B., Black, M.J.: A naturalistic open source movie for optical flow evaluation. In: Fitzgibbon, A., Lazebnik, S., Perona, P., Sato, Y., Schmid, C. (eds.) ECCV 2012. LNCS, vol. 7577, pp. 611–625. Springer, Heidelberg (2012). https://doi.org/10.1007/978-3-642-33783-3_44
4. Caballero, J., Ledig, C., Aitken, A., Acosta, A., Totz, J., Wang, Z., Shi, W.: Real-time video super-resolution with spatio-temporal networks and motion compensation. In: Proceedings of the IEEE Conference on Computer Vision and Pattern Recognition (2017)
5. Dai, J., et al.: Deformable convolutional networks. In: Proceedings of the IEEE International Conference on Computer Vision, pp. 764–773 (2017)
6. Dong, C., Loy, C.C., He, K., Tang, X.: Learning a deep convolutional network for image super-resolution. In: Fleet, D., Pajdla, T., Schiele, B., Tuytelaars, T. (eds.) ECCV 2014. LNCS, vol. 8692, pp. 184–199. Springer, Cham (2014). https://doi.org/10.1007/978-3-319-10593-2_13

7. Fischer, P., et al.: FlowNet: learning optical flow with convolutional networks. arXiv preprint arXiv:1504.06852 (2015)
8. Haris, M., Shakhnarovich, G., Ukita, N.: Recurrent back-projection network for video super-resolution. In: Proceedings of the IEEE Conference on Computer Vision and Pattern Recognition, pp. 3897–3906 (2019)
9. Jiang, H., Sun, D., Jampani, V., Yang, M.H., Learned-Miller, E., Kautz, J.: Super SloMo: high quality estimation of multiple intermediate frames for video interpolation. In: Proceedings of the IEEE Conference on Computer Vision and Pattern Recognition, pp. 9000–9008 (2018)
10. Jo, Y., Wug Oh, S., Kang, J., Joo Kim, S.: Deep video super-resolution network using dynamic upsampling filters without explicit motion compensation. In: Proceedings of the IEEE Conference on Computer Vision and Pattern Recognition, pp. 3224–3232 (2018)
11. Kappeler, A., Yoo, S., Dai, Q., Katsaggelos, A.K.: Video super-resolution with convolutional neural networks. IEEE Trans. Comput. Imaging 2(2), 109–122 (2016)
12. Kim, S.Y., Oh, J., Kim, M.: FISR: deep joint frame interpolation and super-resolution with a multi-scale temporal loss. In: AAAI, pp. 11278–11286 (2020)
13. Liao, R., Tao, X., Li, R., Ma, Z., Jia, J.: Video super-resolution via deep draft-ensemble learning. In: Proceedings of the IEEE International Conference on Computer Vision, pp. 531–539 (2015)
14. Lim, B., Son, S., Kim, H., Nah, S., Mu Lee, K.: Enhanced deep residual networks for single image super-resolution. In: Proceedings of the IEEE Conference on Computer Vision and Pattern Recognition Workshops, pp. 136–144 (2017)
15. Liu, C., Sun, D.: On Bayesian adaptive video super resolution. IEEE Trans. Pattern Anal. Mach. Intell. 36(2), 346–360 (2014)
16. Liu, D., Wang, Z., Fan, Y., Liu, X., Wang, Z., Chang, S., Huang, T.: Robust video super-resolution with learned temporal dynamics. In: Proceedings of the IEEE International Conference on Computer Vision (2017)
17. Liu, Y.L., Liao, Y.T., Lin, Y.Y., Chuang, Y.Y.: Deep video frame interpolation using cyclic frame generation. In: Proceedings of the AAAI Conference on Artificial Intelligence, vol. 33, pp. 8794–8802 (2019)
18. Liu, Z., Yeh, R.A., Tang, X., Liu, Y., Agarwala, A.: Video frame synthesis using deep voxel flow. In: Proceedings of the IEEE International Conference on Computer Vision, pp. 4463–4471 (2017)
19. Nah, S., et al.: NTIRE 2019 challenge on video deblurring and super-resolution: dataset and study. In: Proceedings of the IEEE Conference on Computer Vision and Pattern Recognition Workshops (2019)
20. Niklaus, S., Liu, F.: Context-aware synthesis for video frame interpolation. In: Proceedings of the IEEE Conference on Computer Vision and Pattern Recognition, pp. 1701–1710 (2018)
21. Niklaus, S., Mai, L., Liu, F.: Video frame interpolation via adaptive convolution. In: Proceedings of the IEEE Conference on Computer Vision and Pattern Recognition, pp. 670–679 (2017)
22. Niklaus, S., Mai, L., Liu, F.: Video frame interpolation via adaptive separable convolution. In: Proceedings of the IEEE International Conference on Computer Vision, pp. 261–270 (2017)
23. Sajjadi, M.S., Vemulapalli, R., Brown, M.: Frame-recurrent video super-resolution. In: Proceedings of the IEEE Conference on Computer Vision and Pattern Recognition, pp. 6626–6634 (2018)

24. Shahar, O., Faktor, A., Irani, M.: Space-time super-resolution from a single video. In: Proceedings of the IEEE Conference on Computer Vision and Pattern Recognition, pp. 3353–3360 (2011)
25. Sharma, M., Chaudhury, S., Lall, B.: Space-time super-resolution using deep learning based framework. In: Shankar, B.U., Ghosh, K., Mandal, D.P., Ray, S.S., Zhang, D., Pal, S.K. (eds.) PReMI 2017. LNCS, vol. 10597, pp. 582–590. Springer, Cham (2017). https://doi.org/10.1007/978-3-319-69900-4_74
26. Shechtman, E., Caspi, Y., Irani, M.: Space-time super-resolution. IEEE Trans. Pattern Anal. Mach. Intell. **4**, 531–545 (2005)
27. Shi, W., et al.: Real-time single image and video super-resolution using an efficient sub-pixel convolutional neural network. In: Proceedings of the IEEE Conference on Computer Vision and Pattern Recognition, pp. 1874–1883 (2016)
28. Sun, D., Yang, X., Liu, M.Y., Kautz, J.: PWC-Net: CNNs for optical flow using pyramid, warping, and cost volume. In: Proceedings of the IEEE Conference on Computer Vision and Pattern Recognition, pp. 8934–8943 (2018)
29. Tao, X., Gao, H., Liao, R., Wang, J., Jia, J.: Detail-revealing deep video super-resolution. In: Proceedings of the IEEE International Conference on Computer Vision (2017)
30. Tommasi, T., Patricia, N., Caputo, B., Tuytelaars, T.: A deeper look at dataset bias. In: Csurka, G. (ed.) Domain Adaptation in Computer Vision Applications. ACVPR, pp. 37–55. Springer, Cham (2017). https://doi.org/10.1007/978-3-319-58347-1_2
31. Wang, X., Girshick, R., Gupta, A., He, K.: Non-local neural networks. In: Proceedings of the IEEE Conference on Computer Vision and Pattern Recognition, pp. 7794–7803 (2018)
32. Wang, X., Chan, K.C., Yu, K., Dong, C., Change Loy, C.: EDVR: video restoration with enhanced deformable convolutional networks. In: Proceedings of the IEEE Conference on Computer Vision and Pattern Recognition Workshops (2019)
33. Wang, X., et al.: ESRGAN: enhanced super-resolution generative adversarial networks. In: Proceedings of the European Conference on Computer Vision (ECCV) (2018)
34. Xue, T., Chen, B., Wu, J., Wei, D., Freeman, W.T.: Video enhancement with task-oriented flow. arXiv (2017)
35. Xue, T., Chen, B., Wu, J., Wei, D., Freeman, W.T.: Video enhancement with task-oriented flow. Int. J. Comput. Vision **127**(8), 1106–1125 (2019)

Large-Scale Few-Shot Learning via Multi-modal Knowledge Discovery

Shuo Wang[1,3], Jun Yue[3(✉)], Jianzhuang Liu[3], Qi Tian[4], and Meng Wang[1,2]

[1] School of Computer Science and Information Engineering,
Hefei University of Technology, Hefei, China
`shuowang.hfut@gmail.com, eric.mengwang@gmail.com`
[2] Institute of Artificial Intelligence, Hefei Comprehensive National Science Center,
Hefei, China
[3] Noah's Ark Lab, Huawei Technologies, Shenzhen, China
`jyue1991@gmail.com, liu.jianzhuang@huawei.com`
[4] Huawei Cloud BU, Shenzhen, China
`tian.qi1@huawei.com`

Abstract. Large-scale few-shot learning aims at identifying hundreds of novel object categories where each category has only a few samples. It is a challenging problem since (1) the identifying process is susceptible to over-fitting with limited samples of an object, and (2) the sample imbalance between a base (known knowledge) category and a novel category is easy to bias the recognition results. To solve these problems, we propose a method based on multi-modal knowledge discovery. First, we use the visual knowledge to help the feature extractors focus on different visual parts. Second, we design a classifier to learn the distribution over all categories. In the second stage, we develop three schemes to minimize the prediction error and balance the training procedure: (1) Hard labels are used to provide precise supervision. (2) Semantic textual knowledge is utilized as weak supervision to find the potential relations between the novel and the base categories. (3) An imbalance control is presented from the data distribution to alleviate the recognition bias towards the base categories. We apply our method on three benchmark datasets, and it achieves state-of-the-art performances in all the experiments.

Keywords: Large-scale few-shot learning · Multi-modal knowledge discovery

1 Introduction

In the past few years, convolutional neural networks (CNNs) have shown a powerful ability on a number of visual tasks, such as classification [8,13], translation [6,31,34], detection [22,23], reconstruction [17], and segmentation [37].

Electronic supplementary material The online version of this chapter (https://doi.org/10.1007/978-3-030-58607-2_42) contains supplementary material, which is available to authorized users.

© Springer Nature Switzerland AG 2020
A. Vedaldi et al. (Eds.): ECCV 2020, LNCS 12355, pp. 718–734, 2020.
https://doi.org/10.1007/978-3-030-58607-2_42

Although CNNs have strong robustness to object and background variations, they can hardly show a good performance without large amounts of training data. Meanwhile, it is time-consuming and expensive to collect and label these data. On the contrary, a human can recognize and remember a new object from only a few samples (or even one) of it. Therefore, few-shot learning (FSL) is proposed to imitate this human ability. The FSL task can be divided into two categories, traditional FSL [20,21,25,30] and large-scale FSL (LS-FSL) [5,7,15,32]. Different from the traditional FSL which recognizes small N ($N \leqslant 20$) classes of novel objects, LS-FSL is a more realistic task that aims to identify hundreds of novel categories without forgetting those categories (called base categories) that have been recognized.

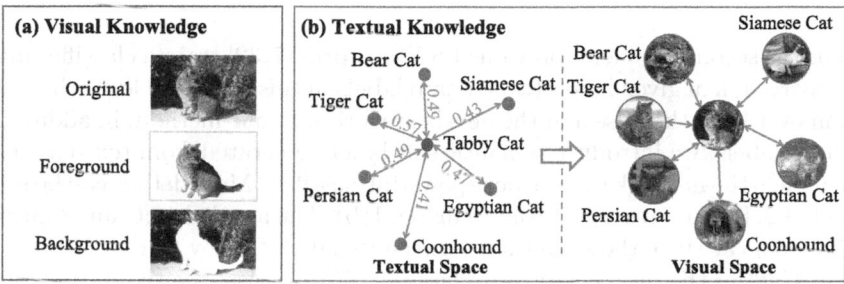

Fig. 1. (a) Given an image, we define its three visual parts, where the foreground focuses on the object, the background describes the environment related to the object, and the original image includes both the foreground and the background. (b) Given a novel label "Tabby Cat", we show the similarities between it and other labels from the base in the textual space. The similarity scores (in orange) are calculated by the word2vec method. This textual knowledge can be effectively used to help the recognition of novel objects as soft supervision information. For example, these scores are the largest among those between "Tabby Cat" and all the labels in the base. Based on them, these objects listed in (b) are considered as most similar to tabby cat, and their similarities with tabby cat can be exploited to help the recognition of a tabby cat image. (Color figure online)

For the task of FSL or LS-FSL, we believe that the key problems are (1) how to extract more information from the available images, and (2) how to effectively use the base objects to help the recognition of novel objects. For the first problem, a popular strategy is using a CNN trained on the base categories to extract the global features of novel objects directly [7,32]. It aims to yield a transferable feature representation (textures and structures) to describe a novel category. However, it is insufficient to represent the novel samples since their global features cannot well describe the distribution of their category with the limited samples. Therefore, to discover more information from the images, we define three visual parts (shown in Fig. 1(a)) computed by an unsupervised saliency detection method. They are used as the network input for training and inference. The effectiveness of this scheme will be elaborated in Sect. 3.1.

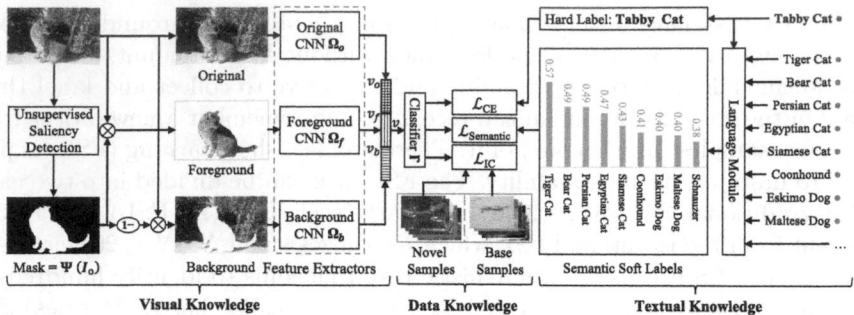

Fig. 2. The overview of the proposed framework, where $\mathcal{L}_{CE}$, $\mathcal{L}_{Semantic}$, and $\mathcal{L}_{IC}$ are three losses.

For the second problem, previous LS-FSL works [7,32] train a classifier under the supervision of given labels (called hard labels in this paper) to learn the distribution over both the base and the novel categories. In our method, in addition to the hard labels, we introduce semantic soft labels generated from textual knowledge to help the network learn a more powerful classifier. More details can be found in Sect. 3.2. Here is an example shown in Fig. 1(b). The novel object can be guessed similar to a cat since the similarity between its label "Tabby Cat" and the label "Tiger Cat" in the base is relatively large (0.57). Besides, the score (0.41) gives the information that the input would be more similar to "Coonhound" than to other categories not shown in Fig. 1(b), such as "Car".

The overview of our framework is depicted in Fig. 2. First, we use the three visual parts of a given image as the input to three independently trained CNNs to extract the features from this image. Second, we calculate the similarities between the hard label of this image and other known labels in the base from the textual knowledge, and use these similarities to generate the semantic soft labels. Third, we design a classifier and train it with both the hard label and the soft labels. The main contributions of our method are fourfold.

(1) We introduce the strategy of extracting more visual information from images, and analyze its advantage for FSL and LS-FSL.
(2) We extract textual knowledge to help the classifier learn from language, which can also be used to improve existing LS-FSL methods.
(3) Two novel losses are designed for semantic knowledge discovery and sample imbalance control during training.
(4) Our method is simple yet powerful; it achieves state-of-the-art performances on popular LS-FSL and FSL datasets.

2   Related Work

2.1   Traditional Few-Shot Learning (FSL)

The methods [20,21,25,30] based on meta-learning are proposed to solve the problem of FSL. They train a meta-learner from many FSL tasks (with base categories) without relying on ad hoc knowledge to suit for new FSL tasks (with novel categories). Metric-learning is another popular approach; it attempts to train a network which can make samples of the same class closer and samples of different classes farther in the feature space [28,30]. Sample hallucination is also useful to generate more training data [36,38]. All the above methods consider small datasets like Omniglot [14], CIFAR [12], and Mini-ImageNet [30], and focus on the N-way-K-shot recognition problem that identifies N ($N \leqslant 20$) novel classes and each class has K ($K = 1$ or 5 usually) samples.

2.2 Large-Scale Few-Shot Learning (LS-FSL)

Recent works [4,5,7,15,32] start to pay attention to the more practical LS-FSL problem that learns hundreds of novel categories without forgetting the base categories. Specifically, [7] hallucinates new samples in the feature space by using a separate Multilayer Perceptron (MLP) to model the relationships between the foregrounds and the backgrounds of images. Wang *et al.* train a meta-learner with hallucination to expand the training set and to classify the samples simultaneously [32]. The work in [15] clusters hierarchical textual labels both from the base and the novel categories to train a feature extractor, and uses the learned features to search the novel labels by the nearest neighbor (NN) method. Gidaris *et al.* design a sample classification weight generator with attention mechanism and modify the classifier with the cosine similarity [4]. Peng *et al.* imprint the weights of the FSL classifier from both visual and textual features [19]. The work in [33] hallucinates novel samples by a generative adversarial network (GAN) which transfers the textual features to the novel image features. The work in [5] combines meta-learning with a graph neural network (GNN) to model the relationships of different categories and predicts the parameters of novel classes.

Different from the sample hallucination methods [7,32,33,36,38], we do not generate hallucinated training samples; instead, we aim to extract more information from each image for training and inference. Compared with the most related method [15] that uses the knowledge to train the feature extractor (with NN as the classifier), we exploit the textual knowledge to train the classifier (with a pre-trained feature extractor). Besides, we discover the knowledge from data distribution and use it to balance the recognition processing.

3 The Proposed Approach

3.1 Visual Knowledge Discovery

For visual representation, [27] visualizes the responses on images from trained CNNs via gradient-based localization. The results show that CNNs trained with large-scale samples tend to use the object regions for the representation. In LS-FSL, the base categories usually have large-scale training samples (*e.g.*, about 1300 samples in one category). Therefore, a CNN trained on the base data is more inclined to focus on the textures and structures of the objects it learns.

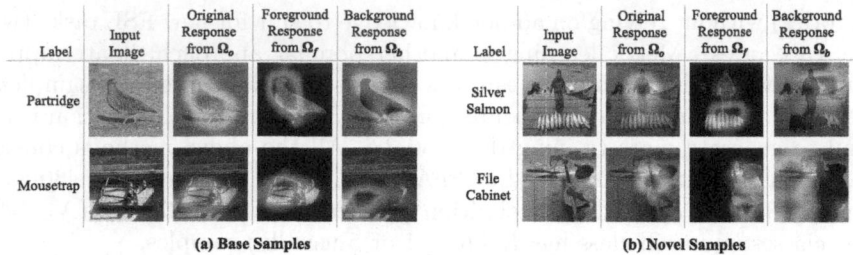

Fig. 3. The responsive regions of three CNNs (ResNets-50) visualized by Grad-CAM [27] from several samples in ImageNet-FS [7].

As shown in the column of "Original Response"[1] in Fig. 3(a), given a base sample in the "Partridge" category, the responsive regions on the original image focus on the body of the bird since the CNN is trained with many partridge images. Similar result can be found for the mousetrap image. However, this CNN may deviate the responses from novel objects and overlook them. For example, it concentrates on the fisherman but not the fishes in the image with label "Silver Salmon" (Fig. 3(b)). Thus, it is important to make the responses more accurate or to enlarge the response regions of novel samples. However, it is difficult to make the responses focus on novel objects since there are no (or only a few) novel samples in the training procedure of a CNN.

Inspired by the work in [9] that humans have a remarkable ability to interpret a complex scene by selecting a subset (foreground) of the available sensory information primarily and then enlarging the vision to the other part (background) of the scene, we extract more visual knowledge from available samples to imitate this human behavior to enrich the representation. First, we employ an off-the-shelf unsupervised saliency detection network [37] to segment the salient region (foreground) from the background of an image. Let the unsupervised saliency detection network be Ψ and the original image be I_o. Then the mask of the saliency regions is denoted as $\Psi(I_o)$ (see Fig. 2 for example, where $\Psi(I_o)$ is of the same size as I_o with 1 for the foreground and 0 for the background). Thus, the foreground I_f and the background I_b are calculated by

$$I_f = \Psi(I_o) \otimes I_o, \quad I_b = (1 - \Psi(I_o)) \otimes I_o, \tag{1}$$

where $\otimes$ denotes the Hadamard product.

Second, we train three independent CNNs, Ω_o, Ω_f, and Ω_b, to learn the representation of the three visual parts I_o, I_f, and I_b, respectively, from all the base samples under the supervision of their hard labels. The reason to use three independent CNNs is because those parts have different distributions. To analyze the effectiveness of the visual knowledge discovery, we visualize the responsive regions of the foregrounds and backgrounds from the trained CNNs using the visualization method Grad-CAM [27] in Fig. 3. For the base samples, it is easy to

---

[1] The response on the original image is called original response.

see that Ω_o and Ω_f focus on the regions of the bird and the mousetrap. Although there is no object in the background I_b, the responses of Ω_b still concentrate on the edges of the bird and the mousetrap. In contrast, these CNNs perform differently on the novel samples. For the two novel samples in Fig. 3(b), if only Ω_o is used, then the responses are mainly on the fisherman and the man for the "Silver Salmon" and "File Cabinet" images, respectively. Obviously, the extracted feature representations are very likely to cause failure recognition. When Ω_f is used, we can see that the response of "Silver Salmon" is shifted to the fishes, which is what we need. Why Ω_b is required is because in many cases, such as the "File Cabinet" image, the result of the unsupervised saliency detection does not give the main object corresponding to the label; instead, the object is considered as the background. Therefore, Ω_b is necessary to extract useful features in these cases, as shown in the lower-right sub-image of Fig. 3(b).

In our framework, the features extracted by Ω_o, Ω_f, and Ω_b are denoted as

$$v_o = \Omega_o(I_o), \quad v_f = \Omega_f(I_f), \quad v_b = \Omega_b(I_b), \tag{2}$$

which are then concatenated together as $v = [v_o, v_f, v_b]$ to describe a sample and for the training of the classifier.

3.2 Textual Knowledge Discovery

Humans can recognize a new category with a few samples of it because they have seen many other related objects or learnt them from textual knowledge, and thus are already familiar with their salient features. Inspired by this, to help the recognition of a novel category, we find its similar categories from the base by using textual knowledge. For example, in Fig. 1(b), the similarity scores between the novel label "Tabby Cat" and the labels from the base in the textual space can describe their similarities to a large extent. Compared with the hard labels of the novel categories, these scores provide more diverse and informative supervision for recognizing the novel samples. To effectively use this textual knowledge to help our network learn a better classifier, we extract the semantic knowledge to enrich the supervision information.

The classifier in our method has two purposes: (1) learning the novel categories without forgetting the base categories, and (2) using the base knowledge to help learn the novel categories. To achieve these, we design a C-way classifier Γ to learn the prediction distribution from both the base and the novel categories, where C is the total number of the base and the novel categories.

Given a feature v extracted by the trained CNNs, the prediction by the classifier is denoted as $p = \Gamma(v)$, where p is a C-dimensional vector. We design our semantic soft label supervision based on the textual knowledge. Given the labels of a novel sample k and the base samples, we first express these labels as vectors by the available word2vec method [15]. Second, we compute the similarities between the novel label and the base labels using the cosine similarity with their vector representations. Then, we obtain a C_{base}-dimensional vector ℓ^k, where C_{base} is the number of the base categories, and the components of ℓ^k are the similarity scores. $\ell^k \in \mathbb{R}^{C_{\text{base}}}$ provides non-sparse supervision measurements to describe the similarities between the novel and the base objects. We call ℓ^k the semantic soft label for the novel sample k. Next, we design a semantic soft loss based on ℓ^k.

In this work, the classifier Γ is a simple network, e.g., as simple as one fully-connected layer. Its prediction (for the novel sample k) $p^k \in \mathbb{R}^C$ is normalized by the sigmoid function, generating a normalized prediction vector $s^k \in \mathbb{R}^C$ with $s_i^k = \text{sigmoid}(p_i^k)$, where $s_i^k \in (0,1)$ and p_i^k, $i = 1, \ldots, C$, are the components of s^k and p^k, respectively. We then define the semantic soft loss for the novel sample k as

$$\mathcal{L}_k = -\frac{1}{|C_{\text{base}}|} \sum_{j \in \text{base}} \gamma \log s_j^k, \quad \gamma = \begin{cases} 1, \text{if } \ell_j^k \geqslant \alpha, \\ 0, \text{if } \ell_j^k < \alpha, \end{cases} \tag{3}$$

where ℓ_j^k is the similarity score between the label of the novel sample k and the jth base category label, and α is a threshold controlling the usage of the textual knowledge. Minimizing $\mathcal{L}_k$ can be loosely considered as maximizing the normalized log likelihood of s_j^k's under $\ell_j^k \geqslant \alpha$, implying that these normalized predictions s_j^k's should be large because they are more similar to the novel label. During training, if there are N novel samples in a training batch, the semantic soft loss for this batch is

$$\mathcal{L}_{\text{Semantic}} = \sum_{k=1}^{N} \mathcal{L}_k. \tag{4}$$

3.3 Imbalance Control from Data Distribution

In LS-FSL, [7] shows that a classifier trained under the supervision of hard labels without other assistant strategies bias the recognition towards the base categories. Specifically, the mean accuracy of the novel categories is much worse than that of the base categories. This is because each base category can use many samples to well describe its feature distribution, while a novel category has only a few training samples. To alleviate the effect of the imbalanced samples between the novel and the base categories, we first oversample the samples from the novel categories in each training batch. Second, we regard the distribution of the dataset as the prior knowledge and then design an imbalance control strategy to bias the predictions towards novel samples.

Given a training batch with B base samples and N novel samples, the predictions of these samples from the classifier are denoted as $\{p^b\}_{b=1}^B$ and $\{p^n\}_{n=1}^N$, where $p^b \in \mathbb{R}^C$ and $p^n \in \mathbb{R}^C$ are the predictions of the bth base sample and the nth novel sample, respectively. Then, the imbalance control loss $\mathcal{L}_{\text{IC}}$ is defined as

$$\mathcal{L}_{\text{IC}} = \sum_{n=1}^{N} \sum_{b=1}^{B} \max\left(\frac{\langle p^b, p^n \rangle}{\|p^b\| \cdot \|p^n\|} + \beta, 0\right), \tag{5}$$

where $\beta \in [0, 1]$ is a hyper-parameter to determine the strength of the imbalance control, and $\langle \cdot, \cdot \rangle$ is the inner product between two vectors.

Without the imbalance control, due to much more training data from the base categories, both p^b and p^n have relatively large predictions for the base categories, meaning that p^b and p^n have a relatively large correlation. Using the proposed imbalance control by minimizing $\mathcal{L}_{\text{IC}}$, we can reduce these correlations, thus making the prediction towards the novel categories when the input is a novel sample. Note that imposing this loss has little effect on base samples because there are much more training data in the base categories.

3.4   Hard Label Supervision and Total Loss

The hard labels are also used to train the classifier with the cross-entropy loss. Given a training batch with $B + N$ samples, the cross-entropy loss between the predictions $\{p^h\}_{h=1}^{B+N}$ and their hard labels $\{L^h\}_{h=1}^{B+N}$ is calculated by

$$\mathcal{L}_{\text{CE}} = \sum_{h=1}^{B+N} \text{CrossEntropy}(\text{softmax}(p^h), L^h). \tag{6}$$

Finally, the total loss for a training batch is defined as

$$\mathcal{L} = \mathcal{L}_{\text{CE}} + \mu_1 \mathcal{L}_{\text{Semantic}} + \mu_2 \mathcal{L}_{\text{IC}}, \tag{7}$$

where μ_1 and μ_2 are two weighting factors.

4   Experiments

In this section, we evaluate our method on three tasks, LS-FSL, traditional FSL, and improving other LS-FSL methods. We use the pre-trained unsupervised saliency detection network [37] to split an image into three visual parts, and use the pre-trained word2vec [15] to represent the labels with vectors. In our experiments, the three feature extractors are of the same structure. It should be mentioned that this saliency detection network [37] is trained unsupervisedly on the MSRA-B dataset [16] without using any object masks and category labels; in other words, no extra visual supervision information is introduced to help the FSL and LS-FSL tasks.

4.1   Large-Scale Few-Shot Learning

4.1.1   Experiments on the ImageNet-FS Benchmark

Dataset and Evaluation. ImageNet-FS [7] contains 1000 categories from the ImageNet dataset [24]. It is divided into 389 base categories and 611 novel categories, where 193 base categories and 300 novel categories are used for validating the hyper-parameters, and the remaining 196 base categories and 311 novel categories are used for classifier learning and testing. Denote the former 493 categories as ALL-S_1 and the latter 507 categories as ALL-S_2. There are about 1300

Table 1. Data partitions of ImageNet-FS [7] for different experiments, where 389 base categories are used to train the feature extractors, ALL-S_1 and ALL-S_2 are used for the ablation studies and the comparisons with other methods, respectively.

	ALL-S_1 (493)	ALL-S_2 (507)
Base categories (389)	BASE-S_1: 193	BASE-S_2: 196
Novel categories (611)	NOVEL-S_1: 300	NOVEL-S_2: 311

samples in a base category. For novel categories, there are 5 settings with $K = 1$, 2, 5, 10, and 20 training samples per category. The evaluation of this benchmark contains two parts: (1) NOVEL-S_2: the Top-5 recognition accuracy of the 311 testing novel categories, and (2) ALL-S_2: the Top-5 recognition accuracy of the 507 (both the base and the novel) categories. More details of the settings can be found from [7]. In Table 1, we summarize the data partitions for different experiments in this section.

Training the Feature Extractors. To compare with other methods, we use ResNets-10 [8] or ResNets-50 [8] as the feature extractors Ω_o, Ω_f, and Ω_b. We respectively train Ω_o, Ω_f, and Ω_b using the original images, the foreground images, and the background images with their hard labels from all the 389 base categories ([7] also uses all the 389 base categories to train its feature extractor). During this training, we optimize the parameters of these feature extractors with the squared gradient magnitude (SGM) loss [7] using SGD [1] for 200 epochs with a batch size = 256. The learning rate starts at 1 and is divided by 10 for every 50 epochs. The weight decay is fixed at 0.0001. Note that the three classifiers for training the three feature extractors are discarded after this training, which are different from the classifier discussed next.

Training the Classifier. Our classifier Γ has only one fully-connected layer with normalized weights [26]. It classifies the features from both the base and the novel categories. It is trained with our loss $\mathcal{L}$ in Eq. (7) for 90 epochs. The batch size $(B + N)$ is set to 1000 with $B = 500$ and $N = 500$. We use the Adam optimization [10] with the starting learning rate of 0.001 and the weight decay of 0.0001. The learning rate is divided by 10 after every 30 epochs.

Ablation Study—The Effectiveness of the Visual Knowledge Discovery. In this ablation study, the classifier is trained with only the $\mathcal{L}_{\mathrm{CE}}$ loss. To evaluate the effectiveness of the visual knowledge discovery, we train seven classifiers with the features of v_o, v_f, v_b, v_{of}, v_{ob}, v_{fb}, or v from ALL-S_1, where v_{of}, v_{ob}, v_{fb}, and v represent the concatenations $[v_o, v_f]$, $[v_o, v_b]$, $[v_f, v_b]$, and $[v_o, v_f, v_b]$, respectively. These features are extracted by the ResNet-10 feature extractors. The recognition performances on the $K = 1$, 2, 5, 10, and 20 settings and on the evaluations of NOVEL-S_1 and ALL-S_1 are shown in Fig. 4. Figure 4(a) indicates that both the foregrounds and the backgrounds can help the network classify the novel and the base samples. As expected, the foregrounds are more useful than the backgrounds, and the original images give more information than either

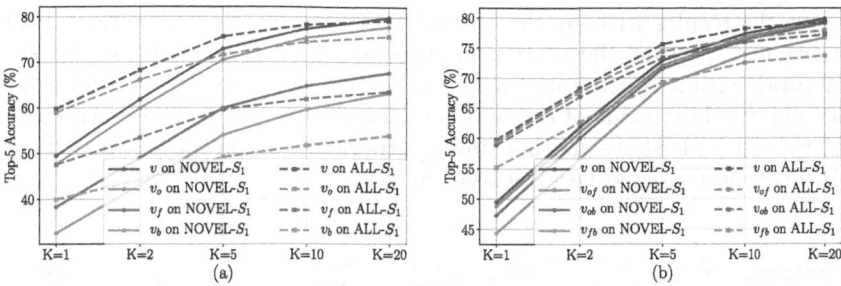

Fig. 4. Top-5 accuracies (%) using different visual parts (v_o, v_f, or v_b) and their concatenations (v_{of}, v_{ob}, v_{fb}, or v) on NOVEL-S_1 and ALL-S_1. The feature extractors are ResNets-10.

foregrounds or backgrounds. Comparing Fig. 4(a) with Fig. 4(b), we can see that the performances of different concatenations are better than their individual features. More importantly, the combination v of v_o, v_f, and v_b provides the best performance, which validates the effectiveness of our visual knowledge discovery.

Table 2. Top-5 accuracies (%) on NOVEL-S_1 and ALL-S_1 with different α in the textual knowledge discovery. The feature extractors are ResNets-10. "$\mathcal{L}_{CE}$ Only" denotes the network without using the textual knowledge.

	NOVEL-S_1/ALL-S_1				
	$K = 1$	$K = 2$	$K = 5$	$K = 10$	$K = 20$
$\alpha = 0.0$	50.2/59.7	61.8/68.3	72.7/75.7	78.4/78.7	80.0/80.0
$\alpha = 0.1$	50.6/59.8	62.1/68.4	72.9/75.9	78.6/78.8	79.9/80.2
$\alpha = 0.2$	51.0/59.7	62.2/68.2	73.0/75.9	78.6/78.9	80.1/80.2
$\alpha = 0.3$	50.9/59.8	**62.3**/68.2	73.0/75.9	78.5/78.8	79.9/80.1
$\alpha = 0.4$	51.0/59.9	62.1/68.2	73.0/75.9	78.5/78.8	79.8/80.0
$\alpha = 0.5$	**51.1/60.1**	62.2/**68.7**	**73.8**/76.0	**78.8/79.0**	**80.9**/80.3
$\alpha = 0.6$	50.6/59.9	62.0/68.3	73.0/75.9	78.5/78.8	80.1/80.2
$\alpha = 0.7$	50.5/59.7	61.8/68.2	72.7/75.7	78.5/78.8	80.3/80.3
$\alpha = 0.8$	50.1/59.5	61.7/68.1	72.9/75.9	78.4/78.7	80.2/**80.4**
$\alpha = 0.9$	50.2/59.6	61.8/68.2	73.2/**76.2**	78.4/78.8	80.1/80.2
$\mathcal{L}_{CE}$ only	49.5/59.7	61.8/68.2	72.9/75.6	77.3/78.3	79.8/79.3

Ablation Study—The Textual Knowledge Discovery. In this ablation study, the classifier is trained with the combined features v and with $\mathcal{L}_{CE}$ and $\mathcal{L}_{Semantic}$ losses ($\mu_1 = 1$, $\mu_2 = 0$). Since the threshold α controls the strength of the textual knowledge usage, we conduct an experiment with different α on NOVEL-S_1 and ALL-S_1. The results are shown in Table 2. For comparison, we also give the results without the textual knowledge in the last row of Table 2. First, we can see that the textual knowledge discovery is effective and stable; the network with it consistently outperforms the network without it for different α. Second, the best value of $\alpha = 0.5$ is selected when the feature extractors are ResNets-10. We also have another similar experiment when the feature extractors are ResNets-50 (omitted here), where the best value of α is 0.3.

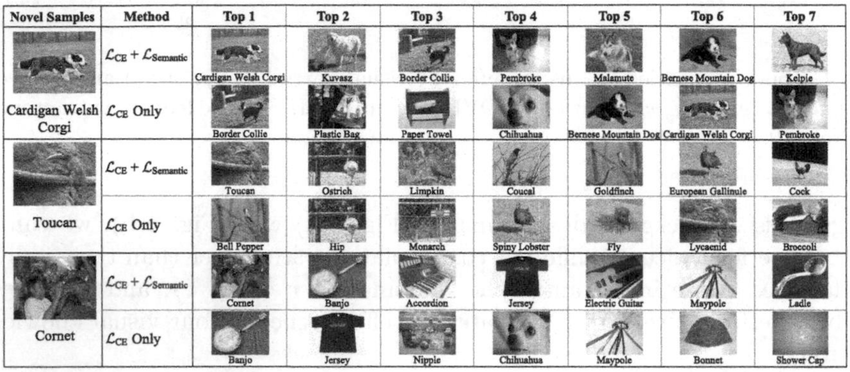

Novel Samples	Method	Top 1	Top 2	Top 3	Top 4	Top 5	Top 6	Top 7
Cardigan Welsh Corgi	$\mathcal{L}_{CE} + \mathcal{L}_{Semantic}$	Cardigan Welsh Corgi	Kuvasz	Border Collie	Pembroke	Malamute	Bernese Mountain Dog	Kelpie
	$\mathcal{L}_{CE}$ Only	Border Collie	Plastic Bag	Paper Towel	Chihuahua	Bernese Mountain Dog	Cardigan Welsh Corgi	Pembroke
Toucan	$\mathcal{L}_{CE} + \mathcal{L}_{Semantic}$	Toucan	Ostrich	Limpkin	Coucal	Goldfinch	European Gallinule	Cock
	$\mathcal{L}_{CE}$ Only	Bell Pepper	Hip	Monarch	Spiny Lobster	Fly	Lycaenid	Broccoli
Cornet	$\mathcal{L}_{CE} + \mathcal{L}_{Semantic}$	Cornet	Banjo	Accordion	Jersey	Electric Guitar	Maypole	Ladle
	$\mathcal{L}_{CE}$ Only	Banjo	Jersey	Nipple	Chihuahua	Maypole	Bonnet	Shower Cap

Fig. 5. The recognition results of several novel samples by the networks with and without the textual knowledge discovery, denoted as "$\mathcal{L}_{CE} + \mathcal{L}_{Semantic}$" and "$\mathcal{L}_{CE}$ Only", respectively. In this experiment, $K = 1$. We randomly select one image from each label category for easy understanding of the objects corresponding to the labels.

In Fig. 5, we show several examples of the results by the network with the textual knowledge discovery (denoted as "$\mathcal{L}_{CE} + \mathcal{L}_{Semantic}$") and the network without it (denoted as "$\mathcal{L}_{CE}$ Only"). It is easy to see that "$\mathcal{L}_{CE} + \mathcal{L}_{Semantic}$" obtains the top-ranked results that are more relevant to the input objects. For example, when the input novel image is a kind of dog ("Cardigan Welsh Corgi" here), all the top 7 results by "$\mathcal{L}_{CE} + \mathcal{L}_{Semantic}$" are dog labels, but the second and the third results ("Plastic Bag" and "Paper Towel") by "$\mathcal{L}_{CE}$ Only" are not relevant. This figure clearly shows the effectiveness of the textual knowledge discovery.

Table 3. Top-5 accuracies (%) in the evaluation of the imbalance control on NOVEL-S_1 and ALL-S_1. The feature extractors are ResNets-10.

	Method	$K = 1$	$K = 2$	$K = 5$	$K = 10$	$K = 20$
NOVEL-S_1	$\mathcal{L}_{CE} + \mathcal{L}_{IC}$	**50.1**	**62.0**	**73.4**	**78.1**	**80.7**
	$\mathcal{L}_{CE}$ only	49.5	61.8	72.9	77.3	79.8
ALL-S_1	$\mathcal{L}_{CE} + \mathcal{L}_{IC}$	**60.1**	**68.5**	**75.9**	**78.6**	**79.9**
	$\mathcal{L}_{CE}$ only	59.7	68.2	75.6	78.3	79.3

Ablation Study—Imbalance Control from Data Distribution. In this ablation study, the classifier is trained with the combined features v and with the $\mathcal{L}_{CE}$ and $\mathcal{L}_{IC}$ losses ($\mu_1 = 0$, $\mu_2 = 1$). We try different values of $\beta \in [0, 1]$, and find that the network performance is insensitive to them. Thus, we set $\beta = 1$. In Table 3, we compare the network using the imbalance control ("$\mathcal{L}_{CE} + \mathcal{L}_{IC}$") and the network without it ("$\mathcal{L}_{CE}$ Only"). In all the cases, "$\mathcal{L}_{CE} + \mathcal{L}_{IC}$" outperforms "$\mathcal{L}_{CE}$ Only", indicating the usefulness of the imbalance control.

Table 4. Top-5 accuracies (%) by different methods on NOVEL-S_2 and ALL-S_2 [7]. Here, "from [32]" means the accuracy numbers of the corresponding method are from [32]. "$H.$" means data hallucination.

	NOVEL-S_2					ALL-S_2				
	$K = 1$	$K = 2$	$K = 5$	$K = 10$	$K = 20$	$K = 1$	$K = 2$	$K = 5$	$K = 10$	$K = 20$
Method with ResNet-10										
Prototypical Nets (from [32])	39.3	54.4	66.3	71.2	73.9	49.5	61.0	69.7	72.9	74.6
Matching Networks (from [32])	43.6	54.0	66.0	72.5	76.9	54.4	61.0	69.0	73.7	76.5
Logistic Regression + $H.$ [7]	40.7	50.8	62.0	69.3	76.5	52.2	59.4	67.6	72.8	76.9
SGM + $H.$ [7]	44.3	56.0	69.7	75.3	78.6	54.8	62.6	71.6	76.0	78.2
PMN + $H.$ [32]	45.8	57.8	69.0	74.3	77.4	57.6	64.7	71.9	75.2	77.5
LwoF [4]	46.2	57.5	69.2	74.8	78.1	58.2	65.2	72.7	76.5	78.7
wDAE-GNN [5]	48.0	59.7	70.3	75.0	77.8	59.1	66.3	73.2	76.1	77.5
Ours	**51.8**	**63.1**	**73.6**	**78.1**	**80.9**	**60.1**	**68.5**	**75.9**	**78.9**	**80.5**
Method with ResNet-50										
Nearest Neighbor (from [15])	49.5	59.9	70.1	75.1	77.6	–	–	–	–	–
Prototypical Nets (from [32])	49.6	64.0	74.4	78.1	80.0	61.4	71.4	78.0	80.0	81.1
Matching Networks (from [32])	53.5	63.5	72.7	77.4	81.2	64.9	71.0	77.0	80.2	82.7
SGM + $H.$ [7]	52.8	64.4	77.3	82.0	84.9	63.7	71.6	80.2	83.3	85.2
PMN + $H.$ [32]	54.7	66.8	77.4	81.4	83.8	65.7	73.5	80.2	82.8	84.5
LSD [2]	57.7	66.9	73.8	77.6	80.0	–	–	–	–	–
KTCH [15]	58.1	67.3	77.6	81.8	84.2	–	–	–	–	–
Ours	**58.5**	**69.7**	**79.2**	**83.0**	**85.5**	**66.7**	**74.8**	**81.5**	**83.4**	**85.5**

Comparisons with Other LS-FSL Methods. In this experiment, we compare our method with state-of-the-art LS-FSL ones. The hyper-parameters of our model are set to $\alpha = 0.5$ when ResNets-10 are used as the feature extractors, $\alpha = 0.3$ when ResNets-50 are used, $\beta = 1$, $\mu_1 = 1$, and $\mu_2 = 1$. The compared methods include Prototypical Nets (PN) [28], Matching Networks (MN) [30], Logistic Regression [7], Prototype Matching Nets (PMN) [7], SGM [7], LwoF [4], wDAE-GNN [5], Nearest Neighbor (NN) [15], LSD [2], and KTCH [15].

All the results on NOVEL-S_2 and ALL-S_2 are listed in Table 4. Our method outperforms others in all the cases. Compared with these methods, our improvements for novel categories (NOVEL-S_2) are larger than those for both the base and the novel categories (ALL-S_2). Besides, our improvements when using ResNets-10 as the feature extractors are more significant than those when using ResNets-50. With ResNets-10, compared with the best previous method wDAE-GNN, ours outperforms it by at least 3.1% in accuracy for $K = 1, 2, 5, 10$, and 20 on NOVEL-S_2, which is significant for LS-FSL.

4.1.2   Experiments on the ImNet Benchmark

Dataset and Evaluation. ImNet [11] is another LS-FSL dataset, which is also selected from ImageNet. It contains 1000 base categories and 360 novel categories. For novel categories, there are 5 settings with $K = 1, 2, 3, 4$, and 5 training samples per category. The evaluation of this benchmark is to recognize the samples from these 360 novel categories. More details are described in [11].

Training the Feature Extractors and the Classifier. The feature extractors are three ResNets-50. The training of them is similar to that in the experiments on ImageNet-FS. Besides, the training of the classifier Γ is also similar to that in the experiments on ImageNet-FS.

Table 5. Top-5 accuracies (%) by different methods on the novel categories from ImNet [11]. All the methods use ResNet-50 for feature extraction. All the accuracy numbers of other methods are from [15].

Method	Novel categories				
	$K = 1$	$K = 2$	$K = 3$	$K = 4$	$K = 5$
Nearest Neighbor (from [15])	34.2	43.6	48.7	52.3	54.0
SGM (from [15])	31.6	42.5	49.0	53.5	56.8
PPA (from [15])	33.0	43.1	48.5	52.5	55.4
LSD (from [15])	33.2	44.7	50.2	53.4	57.6
KTCH [15]	39.0	48.9	54.9	58.7	60.5
Ours	**43.4**	**54.6**	**60.8**	**64.6**	**67.2**

Comparisons with Other LS-FSL Methods. The compared methods include Nearest Neighbor (NN) [15], SGM [7], PPA [21], LSD [2], and KTCH [15]. The Top-5 accuracies by our and these methods on the novel categories are listed in Table 5. We can see that our method again performs best on this dataset in all the cases. Compared with the previous best model KTCH, our improvements for $K = 1, 2, 3, 4$, and 5 are 4.4%, 5.7%, 5.9%, 5.9%, and 6.7%, respectively, showing the power of our approach.

4.2   Traditional Few-Shot Learning

Dataset and Evaluation. For traditional FSL, we apply our model on the Mini-ImageNet dataset [30]. Mini-ImageNet consists of 100 categories from ImageNet and each category has 600 images. It is divided into three parts: 64 base categories, 16 novel categories for validation, and the remaining 20 novel categories for testing. This dataset is evaluated on several 5-way-K-shot classification tasks. In each task, 5 novel categories are sampled first, then K samples in each of the 5 categories are sampled for training, and finally 15 samples (different from the previous K samples) in each of the 5 categories are sampled for testing. To report the results, we sample 2000 such tasks and compute the mean accuracies over all the tasks.

Table 6. Top-1 accuracies (%) by different methods on the testing novel categories of Mini-ImageNet with 95 confidence intervals. †: Using the validation set (in addition to the base set) for feature extractor training.

Method	Feature extractor	$K = 1$	$K = 5$
MAML [3]	Conv-4-64	48.70 ± 1.84%	63.10 ± 0.92%
PN [28]	Conv-4-64	49.42 ± 0.78%	68.20 ± 0.66%
RelationNet [29]	Conv-4-64	50.40 ± 0.80%	65.30 ± 0.70%
MetaGAN [38]	Conv-4-64	52.71 ± 0.64%	68.63 ± 0.67%
SalNet [36]	Conv-4-64	57.45 ± 0.88%	72.01 ± 0.67%
MetaNet [18]	ResNets-12	57.10 ± 0.70%	70.04 ± 0.63%
PPA† [21]	WRN-28-10	59.60 ± 0.41%	73.74 ± 0.19%
LEO† [25]	WRN-28-10	61.76 ± 0.08%	77.59 ± 0.12%
LwoF (from [5])	WRN-28-10	60.06 ± 0.14%	76.39 + 0.11%
wDAE-GNN† [5]	WRN-28-10	62.96 ± 0.15%	78.85 ± 0.10%
Ours	WRN-28-10	**64.40 ± 0.43%**	**83.05 ± 0.28%**

Training the Feature Extractors. We use the 2-layer wide residual networks (WRN-28-10) [35] as the feature extractors. They are trained with the cross-entropy loss using the Adam optimization for 200 epochs with a batch size = 256 on all the 64 base categories. The learning rate starts at 0.001 and is divided by 10 for every 50 epochs. The weight decay is fixed at 0.0001.

Training the Classifier. The training of the classifier Γ on this dataset is similar to that in the experiments on previous datasets. It is trained with our loss $\mathcal{L}$ in Eq. (7) for 40 epochs. The batch size $(B + N)$ is set to 100 with $B = 50$ and $N = 50$. We use the Adam optimization with the starting learning rate of 0.001 and the weight decay of 0.0001. The learning rate is divided by 10 after every 10 epochs. We conduct an experiment with different α on the validation set (omitted here) and find the best value of α is 0.2.

Comparisons with Other Traditional FSL Methods. As shown in Table 6, we compare our method with MAML [3], PN [28], RelationNet [29], Meta-GAN [38], SalNet [36], MetaNet [18], PPA [21], LEO [25], LwoF [4], and wDAE-GNN [5]. Again, our method outperforms them. Specifically, compared with the best previous method wDAE-GNN, we obtain 1.44% and 4.2% accuracy improvements for $K = 1$ and $K = 5$, respectively. Note that wDAE-GNN uses both the base and the validation categories for feature extractor training, while ours are trained with only the base categories.

Table 7. Top-5 accuracies (%) on ImNet.

Method	Novel categories				
	$K = 1$	$K = 2$	$K = 3$	$K = 4$	$K = 5$
SGM [7]	31.4	42.7	49.1	53.2	56.4
SGM + $\mathcal{T}$	**33.5**	**44.1**	**50.1**	**54.5**	**57.3**
KTCH [15]	36.0	47.0	52.9	57.2	60.4
KTCH + $\mathcal{T}$	**40.1**	**50.5**	**56.6**	**60.8**	**63.3**

4.3 Textual Knowledge Discovery on Other Methods

Our textual knowledge discovery can be used to improve other LS-FSL methods. In this section, we show two examples based on SGM [7] and KTCH [15]. We train our classifier (with the $\mathcal{L}_{CE}$ and $\mathcal{L}_{Semantic}$ losses) using the features[2] extracted by SGM or KTCH on the ImNet dataset. The two new models are denoted as SGM + $\mathcal{T}$ and KTCH + $\mathcal{T}$, respectively, where "$\mathcal{T}$" means the textual knowledge discovery. The recognition results by SGM, KTCH, and the two new models are shown in Table 7. We can see that the new models SGM + $\mathcal{T}$ and KTCH + $\mathcal{T}$ respectively improve SGM and KTCH by significant margins.

5 Conclusion

In this paper, we have proposed three schemes to tackle the problem of large-scale few-shot learning (LS-FSL): (1) visual knowledge discovery for better object representation, (2) textual knowledge discovery for finding the relations between novel and base categories, and (3) imbalance control from data distribution to alleviate the recognition bias towards the base categories. Our method is simple yet effective. The extensive experiments have shown that our model achieves state-of-the-art results on both LS-FSL and traditional FSL benchmarks. Besides, the proposed textual knowledge discovery can also be used to improve other LS-FSL methods.

Acknowledgments. This work is supported by the National Key Research and Development Program of China under grant 2018YFB0804205, and National Nature Science Foundation of China (NSFC) under grants 61732008 and 61725203.

References

1. Bottou, L.: Large-scale machine learning with stochastic gradient descent. In: Lechevallier, Y., Saporta, G. (eds.) COMPSTAT, pp. 177–186. Springer (2010). https://doi.org/10.1007/978-3-7908-2604-3_16

---

[2] The SGM features are obtained from the released code by the authors of [7], while the KTCH features are provided by an author of [15].

2. Douze, M., Szlam, A., Hariharan, B., Jégou, H.: Low-shot learning with large-scale diffusion. In: CVPR (2018)
3. Finn, C., Abbeel, P., Levine, S.: Model-agnostic meta-learning for fast adaptation of deep networks. In: ICML (2017)
4. Gidaris, S., Komodakis, N.: Dynamic few-shot visual learning without forgetting. In: CVPR (2018)
5. Gidaris, S., Komodakis, N.: Generating classification weights with gnn denoising autoencoders for few-shot learning. In: CVPR (2019)
6. Guo, D., Wang, S., Tian, Q., Wang, M.: Dense temporal convolution network for sign language translation. In: IJCAI (2019)
7. Hariharan, B., Girshick, R.: Low-shot visual recognition by shrinking and hallucinating features. In: ICCV (2017)
8. He, K., Zhang, X., Ren, S., Sun, J.: Deep residual learning for image recognition. In: CVPR (2016)
9. Itti, L., Koch, C., Niebur, E.: A model of saliency-based visual attention for rapid scene analysis. TPAMI **20**(11), 1254–1259 (1998)
10. Kingma, D.P., Ba, J.: Adam: a method for stochastic optimization. In: ICLR (2015)
11. Kodirov, E., Xiang, T., Gong, S.: Semantic autoencoder for zero-shot learning. In: CVPR (2017)
12. Krizhevsky, A., Hinton, G., et al.: Learning multiple layers of features from tiny images. Technical report, Citeseer (2009)
13. Krizhevsky, A., Sutskever, I., Hinton, G.E.: ImageNet classification with deep convolutional neural networks. In: NeurIPS (2012)
14. Lake, B.M., Salakhutdinov, R., Tenenbaum, J.B.: Human-level concept learning through probabilistic program induction. Science **350**(6266), 1332–1338 (2015)
15. Li, A., Luo, T., Lu, Z., Xiang, T., Wang, L.: Large-scale few-shot learning: knowledge transfer with class hierarchy. In: CVPR (2019)
16. Liu, T., et al.: Learning to detect a salient object. TPAMI **33**(2), 35–367 (2010)
17. Meng, N., Wu, X., Liu, J., Lam, E.Y.: High-order residual network for light field super-resolution. In: AAAI (2020)
18. Munkhdalai, T., Yu, H.: Meta networks. In: ICML (2017)
19. Peng, Z., Li, Z., Zhang, J., Li, Y., Qi, G.J., Tang, J.: Few-shot image recognition with knowledge transfer. In: ICCV (2019)
20. Qi, H., Brown, M., Lowe, D.G.: Low-shot learning with imprinted weights. In: CVPR (2018)
21. Qiao, S., Liu, C., Shen, W., Yuille, A.L.: Few-shot image recognition by predicting parameters from activations. In: CVPR (2018)
22. Redmon, J., Divvala, S., Girshick, R., Farhadi, A.: You only look once: unified, real-time object detection. In: CVPR (2016)
23. Ren, S., He, K., Girshick, R., Sun, J.: Faster R-CNN: towards real-time object detection with region proposal networks. In: NeurIPS (2015)
24. Russakovsky, O., et al.: ImageNet large scale visual recognition challenge. IJCV **115**(3), 211–252 (2015)
25. Rusu, A.A., et al.: Meta-learning with latent embedding optimization. In: ICLR (2019)
26. Salimans, T., Kingma, D.P.: Weight normalization: a simple reparameterization to accelerate training of deep neural networks. In: NeurIPS (2016)
27. Selvaraju, R.R., Cogswell, M., Das, A., Vedantam, R., Parikh, D., Batra, D.: Grad-CAM: visual explanations from deep networks via gradient-based localization. In: ICCV (2017)

28. Snell, J., Swersky, K., Zemel, R.: Prototypical networks for few-shot learning. In: NeurIPS (2017)
29. Sung, F., Yang, Y., Zhang, L., Xiang, T., Torr, P.H., Hospedales, T.M.: Learning to compare: relation network for few-shot learning. In: CVPR (2018)
30. Vinyals, O., Blundell, C., Lillicrap, T., Wierstra, D., et al.: Matching networks for one shot learning. In: NeurIPS (2016)
31. Wang, S., Guo, D., Zhou, W.g., Zha, Z.J., Wang, M.: Connectionist temporal fusion for sign language translation. In: ACM MM (2018)
32. Wang, Y.X., Girshick, R., Hebert, M., Hariharan, B.: Low-shot learning from imaginary data. In: CVPR (2018)
33. Xian, Y., Sharma, S., Schiele, B., Akata, Z.: F-VAEGAN-D2: a feature generating framework for any-shot learning. In: CVPR (2019)
34. You, Q., Jin, H., Wang, Z., Fang, C., Luo, J.: Image captioning with semantic attention. In: CVPR (2016)
35. Zagoruyko, S., Komodakis, N.: Wide residual networks. In: BMVC (2016)
36. Zhang, H., Zhang, J., Koniusz, P.: Few-shot learning via saliency-guided hallucination of samples. In: CVPR (2019)
37. Zhang, J., Zhang, T., Dai, Y., Harandi, M., Hartley, R.: Deep unsupervised saliency detection: a multiple noisy labeling perspective. In: CVPR (2018)
38. Zhang, R., Che, T., Ghahramani, Z., Bengio, Y., Song, Y.: MetaGAN: an adversarial approach to few-shot learning. In: NeurIPS (2018)

Fast Video Object Segmentation Using the Global Context Module

Yu Li[1(✉)], Zhuoran Shen[2], and Ying Shan[1]

[1] Applied Research Center (ARC), Tencent PCG, Shenzhen, China
ianyli@tencent.com
[2] The University of Hong Kong, Pokfulam, Hong Kong
cmsflash@connect.hku.hk

Abstract. We developed a real-time, high-quality semi-supervised video object segmentation algorithm. Its accuracy is on par with the most accurate, time-consuming online-learning model, while its speed is similar to the fastest template-matching method with sub-optimal accuracy. The core component of the model is a novel global context module that effectively summarizes and propagates information through the entire video. Compared to previous approaches that only use one frame or a few frames to guide the segmentation of the current frame, the global context module uses all past frames. Unlike the previous state-of-the-art space-time memory network that caches a memory at each spatio-temporal position, the global context module uses a fixed-size feature representation. Therefore, it uses constant memory regardless of the video length and costs substantially less memory and computation. With the novel module, our model achieves top performance on standard benchmarks at a real-time speed.

Keywords: Video object segmentation · Global context module

1 Introduction

Video object segmentation [1,21,31,37] aims to segment a foreground object from the background on all frames in a video. The task has numerous applications in computer vision. An important one is intelligent video editing. As videos become the most popular form of media on mass content platforms, video content creation is getting increasing levels of attention. Object segmentation on each frame with image segmentation tools is time-consuming and has poor temporal consistency. Semi-supervised video object segmentation tries to solve the problem by segmenting the object in the whole video given only a fine object

---

Y. Li and Z. Shen—contributed equally. This work was done during Zhuoran's internship at Tencent.

Electronic supplementary material The online version of this chapter (https://doi.org/10.1007/978-3-030-58607-2_43) contains supplementary material, which is available to authorized users.

© Springer Nature Switzerland AG 2020
A. Vedaldi et al. (Eds.): ECCV 2020, LNCS 12355, pp. 735–750, 2020.
https://doi.org/10.1007/978-3-030-58607-2_43

mask on the first frame. This problem is challenging since object appearance might vary drastically over time in a video due to pose changes, motion, and occlusions, *etc.*

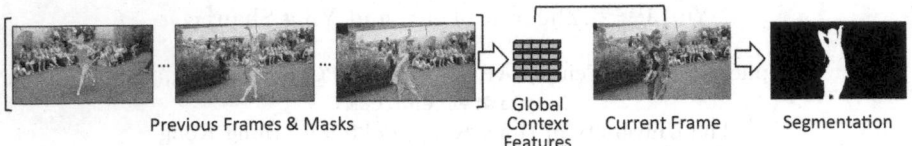

Previous Frames & Masks   Global Context Features   Current Frame   Segmentation

Fig. 1. Our video object segmentation method creates and maintains fixed-size global context features for previous frames and their object masks. These global context features can guide the segmentation on the incoming frame. The global context module is efficient in both memory and computation and achieves high segmentation accuracy. See more details below.

With the success in many computer vision tasks, deep learning techniques are widely used in video object segmentation recently. The essence is to learn an invariant representation that accounts for the variation of object appearance across frames. Some early works [4,25,28,35] in semi-supervised video object segmentation use the first frame to train a model using various data augmentation strategies, which are commonly referred to as online learning-based methods. These methods usually obtain accurate segmentation that are robust to occlusions. However, online learning incurs huge computational costs that lead to several seconds of processing per frame. Another direction is propagation-based methods, *e.g.* [6], which rely on the segmentation of the previous frame to infer for the current frame. These methods are simple and fast, but usually have suboptimal segmentation accuracies. These methods cannot handle occlusions and may suffer from error drifts. Some later works take the advantages of both directions, use both the first frame and the previous frame [26,34,39,42], and achieve both high accuracy and fast processing speed.

A recent work [27] makes a further step to use all previous frames with the corresponding object segmentation results to infer the object mask on the current frame. It proposes a novel space-time memory (STM) module that stores the segmentation information at each processed frame, *i.e.*, this memory module saves information at all spatio-temporal locations on all previous frames. When working on a new frame, a read operation is used to retrieve relevant information from the memory by performing a dense feature correlation operation in both temporal and spatial dimensions. By using this memory that saves all guidance information, the method is robust against drastic object appearance changes and occlusions. It produces promising results and achieves state-of-the-art performance on multiple benchmark datasets.

While STM achieved state-of-the-art performance by making full use of the information from previous frames, leveraging the space-time memory is costly, especially on long videos. As the space-time memory module keeps creating new memories to save new information and put it together with old memories, the computational cost and memory usage in the feature correlation step increase linearly with the number of frames. This makes the method slower and slower while processing and may easily cause GPU memory overflow. To resolve this issue, the authors propose to reduce the memory saving frequency, *e.g.* saving a new memory every 5 frames. However, the linear complexity with time still exists, and such reduction in memorization frequency defeats the original purpose to utilize information from every previous frame.

In this paper, building upon the idea of STM to use information in all past frames, we develop a compact global representation that summarizes the object segmentation information and guides the segmentation of the next frame. This representation automatically updates when the system moves forward by a frame. The core component of it is a novel global context module (illustrated in Fig. 1). By keeping only a fixed-size set of features, our memory and computational complexities for inference are light and do not increase with time, in comparison to the linear complexities of the STM module. We show that using this highly efficient global context module, our method is about three times faster than STM and do not need to worry about the memory usage. The performance of our method on the single object segmentation benchmark DAVIS 2016 in terms of segmentation accuracy is on par with the state-of-the-art. The results of our method on more challenging multiple object segmentation benchmarks DAVIS 2017 and YouTube-VOS are highly competitive.

The contribution of our paper can be summarized as:

- We propose a novel global context module that reliably maintains segmentation information of the entire video to guide the segmentation of incoming frames.
- We implement the global context module in a light-weight way that is efficient in both memory usage and computational cost.
- Experiments on DAVIS and YouTube-VOS benchmarks show that our proposed global context module can achieve top accuracy in video object segmentation and is highly efficient that runs in real time.

2   Related Works

Online-Learning Methods. Online-learning methods usually fine-tune a general object segmentation network on the object mask of the start frame to teach the network to identify the appearance of the target object in the remaining video frames [4]. They use online adaptation [35], instance segmentation information [25], data augmentation techniques [17], or an integration of multiple techniques [24]. Some methods report that online learning boosts the performance of their model [20,39]. While online learning can achieve high-quality segmentation and is robust against occlusions, it is computationally expensive as it requires fine-tuning for each video. This huge computational burden makes it impractical for most applications.

Offline-Learning Methods Offline-learning methods use strategies like mask propagation, feature matching, tracking, or a hybrid strategy. Propagation-based methods rely on the segmentation mask of the previous frame. It usually takes the previous mask as an input and learns a network to refine the mask to align it with the object in current frame. A representative work is MaskTrack [28]. This strategy of using the previous frame is also used in [2,42]. Many works [7,15,28] also use optical flow [9,14] in the propagation process. Matching-based methods [5,13,26,32,34,39] treat the first frame (or intermediate frames) as a template and match the pixel-level feature embeddings in the new frame with the templates. A more common setup is to use both the first frame and the previous frame [26,34,39], which covers both long-term and short-term object appearance information.

Space-Time Memory Network. The STM network [27] is a special feature matching-based method which performs dense feature matching across the entire spatio-temporal volume of the video. This is achieved by a novel space-time memory mechanism that stores the features at the each spatio-temporal location. The space-time memory module mainly contains two components and two operations. The two components are a key map and a value map where the keys encode the visual semantic embeddings for robust matching against appearance variations, and the values store detailed features for guiding the segmentation. The memory write operation simply concatenates the key and value maps generated on past frames and their object segmentation masks. When processing a new frame, the memory read operation uses the keys to match and find the relevant locations in the spatio-temporal volume in the video. Then the features stored in the value maps at those locations are retrieved to predict the current object mask.

3   Our Method

3.1   Global Context Module

The space-time memory network [27] achieves great success in video object segmentation with the space-time memory module. The STM module is an effective module that queries features from a set of spatio-temporal features encoding previous frames and their object masks to guide the processing of the current frame. In this way, the current frame is able to use the features from semantically related regions and the corresponding segmentation information in past frames to generate its features. However, the STM module has a drawback in efficiency in that it stores a pair of key and value vectors for each location of each frame in the memory. These feature vectors are simply concatenated over time when the system moves forward and their sizes keep increasing. This means its resource usage is highly sensitive to the spatial resolution and temporal length of the video. Consequently, the module is limited to have memories with low spatial resolutions, short temporal spans, or reduced memory saving frequency in practice. To remedy this drawback, we propose the global context (GC) module. Unlike the STM

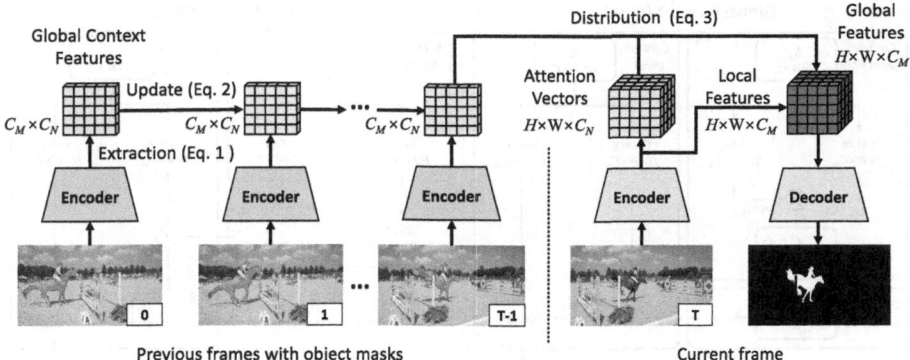

Fig. 2. This is an overview of our pipeline. Our network encodes past frames and their masks to a fixed-size set of global context features. These vectors are updated by a simple rule when the system moves to the next frame. At the current frame, a set of attention vectors are generated from the encoder to retrieve relevant information in the global context to form the global features. Local features are also generated from the encoder output. The global and local features are then concatenated and passed to a decoder to produce the segmentation result for this frame. Note that there are two types of encoders, the blue one for past frames and masks (four input channels), and the orange one for the current frame (three input channels).

module, the global context module keeps only a small set of fixed-size global context features yet retains almost the same representational power compared to the STM module. Figure 2 shows the overall pipeline of our proposed method using the global context module. The main structure is an encoder-decoder and the global context module is built on top of the encoder output, similarly to [27]. There are mainly two operations in our pipeline, namely 1) context extraction and update on a processed frame and its object mask, and 2) context distribution to the current frame under processing. There are two types of encoders used which produce features of $H \times W$ resolution and C channels. One takes a color image and an object mask (ground truth mask for the start frame and segmentation results for intermediate frames) to encode the frame and segmentation information into the feature space. Another encoder encodes the current frame to a feature embedding. We distribute the global context features stored in the global context module and combine the distributed context features with local features. Then, a decoder is used to produce the final object segmentation mask on this frame.

Context Extraction and Update. When extracting the global context features, the global context module first generates the keys and the values, following the same procedure as in the STM module. The keys and the values have size $H \times W \times C_N$ and $H \times W \times C_M$ respectively, where C_N and C_M are the numbers of channels used. Unlike the STM module that directly stores the keys and

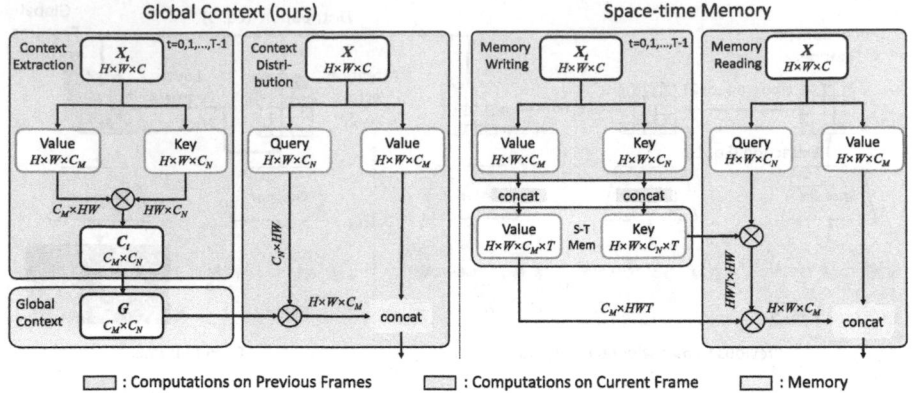

Fig. 3. The detailed implementation of the global context module with a comparison to the space-time memory module in [27].

values, the global context module puts the keys and the values through a further step called global summarization.

The global summarization step treats the keys not as $H \times W$ vectors of size C_M each for a location, but as C_M 1-channel feature maps each as an unnormalized weighting over all locations. For each such weighting, the global context module computes a weighted sum of the values where each value is weighted by the scalar at the corresponding location in the weighting. Each such weighted sum is called a global context vector. The global context module organizes all C_M global context vectors into a global context matrix as the output of global summarization. This step can be efficiently implemented as a matrix product between the transpose of the key matrix and the value matrix. Following is an equation describing the context extraction process of the global context module:

$$C_t = k(X_t)^\mathsf{T} v(X_t), \tag{1}$$

where t is the index of the current frame, C_t is the context matrix of this frame, X_t is the input to the module (output of the encoder), and k, v are the functions that generate the keys and values. Having obtained C_t, the rule for updating the global context feature is simply

$$G_t = \frac{t-1}{t} G_{t-1} + \frac{1}{t} C_t, \tag{2}$$

where G_t is the global context for the first t frames with G_0 being a zero matrix. The weight coefficients before the sum make that each C_p for $1 \leq p \leq t$ contributes equally to G_t.

Context Distribution. At the current frame, our pipeline distributes relevant information stored in the global context module to each pixel. In the distribution process, the global context module first produces the query keys in the same way as the spatce-time memory module. However, the global context module uses the queries differently. At each location, it interprets the query key as a set of weights over the global context features in the memory and computes the weighted sum of the features as the distributed context information. In contrast, the memory read process of the STM module is much more complex. The STM module uses the query to compute a similarity score with the key at each location of each frame in the memory. After that, the module computes the weighted sum of the values in the memory weighted by these similarity scores. Following is an formula that expresses this context distribution process:

$$\boldsymbol{D}_t = q(\boldsymbol{X}_t)\boldsymbol{G}_{t-1}, \tag{3}$$

where $\boldsymbol{D}_t$ is the distributed global features for frame t, and q is the function generating the queries.

Surprisingly, the simple context distribution process of the global context module and the much more complex process of the space-time memory module accomplish the same goal, which is to summarize semantic regions across all past frames that are of interest to the querying location in the current frame. The space-time memory module achieves this by first identifying such regions via query-key matching and then summarizing their values through a weighted sum. The global context module achieves the same much more efficiently since the global context vectors are already global summarizations of regions with similar semantics across all past frames. Therefore, the querying location only needs to determine on an appropriate weighting over the global context vectors to produce a vector that summarizes all the regions of interest to itself. For example, if a pixel is interested in persons, it could place large weights on global context vectors that summarize faces and bodies. Another pixel might be interested in the foreground and could put large weights on vectors that summarize various foreground object categories. We provide a mathematical proof that the global context and space-time memory modules have identical modeling power in the supplementary materials.

Comparison with the Space-Time Memory Module. We have plotted the detailed implementation of our global context module in Fig. 3 and compare with the space-time memory module used in [27]. There are a few places our global context has advantages in efficacy over space-time memory.

The global summarization process is the first way the global context module gains efficiency advantage over the space-time memory module. The global context matrix has size $C_M \times C_N$, which tends to be much smaller than the $H \times W \times C_N$ key and $H \times W \times C_M$ value matrices that the space-time memory module produces. The second way the global context module improves efficiency is that it adds the extracted context matrix to the stored context matrix, thereby keeping constant memory usage however many frames are processed. In contrast, the space-time memory module concatenates the obtained key and value matrices to the original key and value matrices in the memory, thus having a linear growth of memory with the number of frames.

For the computation on the current frame, i.e. the context distribution step, our global context module only needs to perform a light weight matrix product of size $C_M \times C_N$ and $C_N \times HW$ with $C_M C_N HW$ multiplications involved. In contrast, the last step of memory read for the STM module calculate a matrix product of size $HWT \times HW$ and $HW \times C_M$ ($C_M H^2 W^2 T$ multiplications), which has much larger memory usage and computational cost than the global context module and has linear complexities with respect to time T. To get a more intuitive comparison of the two, we calculate the computation and resources needed in this step when the input to the encoder is of size 384×384, $C_M = 512$, and $C_N = 128$ (the default setting in STM). The detailed numbers are listed in Table 1. It is noticeable that our global context module has great advantages over space-time memory in terms of both computation and memory cost, especially when the number of processed frames t becomes large along the processing.

Table 1. The complexity comparison of the memory read operation in space-time memory [27] and context distribution in our global context module. The memory usage is calculated using the float32 data type.

	t	FLOPS	Memory		t	FLOPS	Memory
STM	0	0.2 G	4 MB	GC (ours)	Any	**0.04 G**	**1 MB**
	10	2.1 G	40 MB				
	100	21.2 G	394 MB				

Table 2. Study on the size of global context feature ($C_M \times C_N$). This result is on DAVIS 2016 test set and the $\mathcal{J}\&\mathcal{F}$ is a segmentation accuracy metric (details in Sect. 4).

$C_M \times C_N$	$\mathcal{J}\&\mathcal{F}$	#Params	Time (s)	$C_M \times C_N$	$\mathcal{J}\&\mathcal{F}$	#Params	Time (s)
512×128	**86.6**	38 M	0.040	512×512	86.1	46 M	0.046

3.2   Implementation

Our encoder and decoder design is the same as STM [27]. We use ResNet-50 [12] as the backbone for both the context encoder and current encoder where the context encoder takes four-channel inputs and the current encoder takes three-channel inputs. The feature map at res4 is used to generate the key and value maps. After the context distribution operation, the features are compressed to 256 channels and fed into the decoder. The decoder takes this low-resolution input feature map and gradually upscales it by a scale factor of two each time. A skip connection is used to retrieve and fuse the feature map at the same resolution in the current encoder with the bilinearly upsampled feature map from the previous stage of the decoder. The key and value generation (i.e. k, q, v in Eq. (1) and (3)) are implemented using 3×3 convolutions. In our implementation, we set $C_M = 512$ and $C_N = 128$. We have tested with larger feature sizes which introduce more complexities, but we do not observe accuracy gain in segmentation (see Table 2).

3.3 Training

Our training process mainly contains two stages. We first pre-train the network using simulated videos generated from static images. After that we fine-tune this pre-trained model on the video object segmentation datasets. We minimize the cross-entropy loss and train our model using the Adam [18] optimizer with a learning rate of 10^{-5}.

Pre-training on Images. We follow the successful practice in [26,27,39] that pre-trains the network using simulated video clips with frames generated by applying random transformation to static images. We use the images from the MSRA10K [8], ECSSD [41], and HKU-IS [19] datasets for the saliency detection task [3]. We found these datasets cover more object categories than those semantic segmentation or instance segmentation datasets [10,11,23]. This is more suitable for our purpose to build a general video object segmentation model. There are in total about 15000 images with object masks. A synthetic clip containing three frames is then generated using image transformations. We use random rotation $[-30°, 30°]$, scaling $[-0.75, 1.25]$, thin plate spline (TPS) warping (as in [28]), and random cropping for the video data simulation. We use 4 GPUs and set the batch size to be 8. We run the training for 100 epochs, and it takes one day to finish the pre-training.

Fine-Tuning on Videos. After training on the synthetic video data, we fine-tune our pre-trained model on video object segmentation datasets [29,30] at the 480p resolution. The learning rate is set to 10^{-6} and we run this fine-tuning for 30 epochs. Each training sample contains several temporally ordered frames sampled from the training video. We use random rotation, scaling, and random frame sampling interval in $[1, 3]$ to gain more robustness to the appearance changes over a long time. We have tested different clip lengths (e.g. 3, 6, 9 frames) but did not observe performance gains on lengths greater than three. Therefore, we stick to three-frame clips. In the training, the network infers the object mask on the second frame and back propagates the error. Then, the soft mask from the network output is fed to the encoder to infer the mask on the third frame without thresholding as in [27].

4 Experimental Results

We evaluate our method and compare it with others on the DAVIS [29,30] and YouTube-VOS [40] benchmarks. The object segmentation mask evaluation metrics used in our experiments are the average region similarity ($\mathcal{J}$ mean), the average contour accuracy ($\mathcal{F}$ mean), and the average of the two ($\mathcal{J}\&\mathcal{F}$ mean). DAVIS 2016 [29] is for single object segmentation. DAVIS 2017 [30] and YouTube-VOS [40] contain multiple object segmentation tasks.

Table 3. Quantitative comparison on DAVIS 2016 validation set. The results are sorted for online (OL) and non-online methods respectively according to $\mathcal{J}\&\mathcal{F}$ mean. The highest scores in each category are highlighted in bold.

Method	OL	Time (s)	$\mathcal{J}\&\mathcal{F}$	$\mathcal{J}$ Mean	$\mathcal{F}$ Mean
OSVOS [4]	✓	7	80.2	79.8	80.6
Lucid [17]	✓	–	83.0	83.9	82.0
CINM [2]	✓	>30	84.2	83.4	85.0
OnAVOS [35]	✓	13	85.5	86.1	84.9
OSVOS-S [25]	✓	4.5	86.6	85.6	87.5
PReMVOS [24]	✓	>30	**86.8**	84.9	**88.6**
DyeNet [20]	✓	2.32	–	**86.2**	–
SiamMask [38]		0.03	70.0	71.7	67.8
OSMN [42]		0.13	73.5	74.0	72.9
PML [5]		0.28	77.4	75.5	79.3
VidMatch [13]		0.32	–	81.0	–
FAVOS [6]		1.8	81.0	82.4	79.5
FEELVOS [34]		0.5	81.7	80.3	83.1
RGMP [26]		0.13	81.8	81.5	82.0
AGAME [16]		0.07	81.9	81.5	82.2
RANet [39]		0.13	85.5	85.5	85.4
STM* [27]		0.15	86.5	84.8	**88.1**
GC (ours)		0.04	**86.6**	**87.6**	85.7

4.1   DAVIS 2016 (Single Object)

DAVIS 2016 [29] is a widely used benchmark dataset for single object segmentation in videos. It contains 50 videos among which 30 videos are for training and 20 are for validation. There are in total 3455 frames annotated with a single object mask for each frame. We use the official split for training and validation.

We list the quantitative results for representative works on DAVIS 2016 validation set in Table 3, including the most recent STM [27] and RANet [39]. To show their best performance, we directly quote the numbers posted on the benchmark website or in the papers. We can see that online-learning methods can get higher scores in most metrics. However, recent works of STM [27] and

RANet [39] demonstrate comparable results without online learning. Overall, the scores of our GC are among the top, including getting the highest $\mathcal{J}$ mean score.

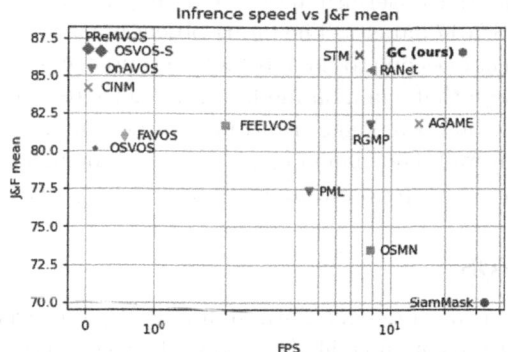

Fig. 4. The speed (FPS) *v.s.* accuracy ($\mathcal{J}\&\mathcal{F}$ mean) comparison on DAVIS 2016 validation set at 480p resolution.

Furthermore, for a more intuitive comparison, we plot the runtime in terms of average FPS and accuracy in terms of $\mathcal{J}\&\mathcal{F}$ mean for different methods in Fig. 4. We test the speed on one Tesla P40. It can be seen that although the online-learning methods (*e.g.* [2,24,25]) can produce highly accurate results, their speeds are extremely slow due to the time consuming online learning process. The methods without online learning (*e.g.* [5,26,42]) are fast but have lower accuracy. The most recent works STM [27] and RANet [39] can get segmentation accuracy comparable to online-learning method while maintaining faster speed (STM [27] 6.7 fps, RANet [39] 8.3 fps for 480p frames[1]). Our GC boosts the speed further (25.0 fps) and still maintains high accuracy. Note that the videos in DAVIS datasets are all short (<100 frames). If running on longer videos, our speed advantage over STM [27] will become more remarkable as STM has a linear time complexity with respect to the video length. While SiamMask [38] is the only method faster than our GC, its accuracy is very unsatisfactory compared to other methods. This demonstrates our GC is both fast and accurate which makes it a practical solution to the video object segmentation problem.

4.2   DAVIS 2017 (Multiple Objects)

DAVIS 2017 is an extension of DAVIS 2016 that contains videos with multiple objects annotated per frame. It has 60 videos for training and 30 videos for testing. We do not use any additional module for multi-object segmentation which [27,39] used, but simply treat each object individually. We still train the

---

[1] RANet [39] reported a faster runtime in the paper using half-precision computation which is disabled in our test for fair comparison.

network to produce a binary mask for the object. In testing, we use the network to get the soft probability map for each object separately and use a softmax operation as post-processing on the maps for all objects in the frame to produce the multi-label segmentation mask.

Table 4 summarizes the performance of existing methods and compare them with ours on DAVIS 2017 dataset. The multi-object scenarios is more challenging than the single object ones due to the interactions and occlusions among multiple objects. It can be seen that again online-learning methods, e.g. [2,24], get decent scores in all metrics, but have longer runtime. For non-online methods, STM [27] ranks the highest overall. Our model can get almost identical performance with STM [27] but with faster speed and much less memory consumption.

4.3   YouTube-VOS

YouTube-VOS [40] is a large-scale dataset for multiple object segmentation in videos. Its training set contains 4453 annotated videos and validation set contains 474 videos. Table 5 compares the performance of different methods on this dataset. Note that there are unseen object categories in the validation set. The unseen objects are tested separately to measure the generalization power of each method. It can be seen that STM [27] gets remarkable high scores. Our GC is among the top performance tier. Further, the results of our method do not show large performance difference between seen and unseen objects.

Table 4. The quantitative comparison on DAVIS 2017 validation set. The results are sorted for online (OL) and non-online methods respectively according to $\mathcal{J}\&\mathcal{F}$ Mean. The highest scores in each category are highlighted in bold.

Method	OL	$\mathcal{J}\&\mathcal{F}$	$\mathcal{J}$ Mean	$\mathcal{F}$ Mean
OSVOS [4]	✓	60.3	56.6	63.9
OnAVOS [35]	✓	65.4	61.6	69.1
OSVOS-S [25]	✓	68.0	64.7	71.3
CINM [2]	✓	70.6	67.2	74.0
PReMVOS [24]	✓	**77.8**	**73.9**	**81.8**
OSMN [42]		54.8	52.5	57.1
SiamMask [38]		56.4	54.3	58.5
FAVOS [6]		58.2	54.6	61.8
VidMatch [13]		–	56.5	–
RANet [39]		65.7	63.2	68.2
RGMP [26]		66.7	64.8	68.6
FEELVOS [34]		69.1	65.9	72.3
AGAME [16]		70.0	67.2	72.7
STM* [27]		**71.6**	69.2	**74.0**
GC (ours)		71.4	**69.3**	73.5

Table 5. The quantitative comparison on YouTube-VOS [40] validation set. The results for other methods are quoted from [22, 27].

	RVOS [33]	OSVOS [4]	S2L(OL) [40]	PreMVOS [24]	AGAME [16]	BoLTVOS [36]	AGSS [22]	STM [27]	GC (ours)
Overall	56.8	58.8	64.4	66.9	66.1	71.1	71.3	79.4	73.2
$\mathcal{J}$ seen	63.6	59.8	71.0	71.4	67.8	71.6	71.3	79.7	72.6
$\mathcal{J}$ unseen	45.5	54.2	55.5	56.5	60.8	64.3	65.5	72.8	68.9
$\mathcal{F}$ seen	67.2	60.5	70.0	75.9	–	–	76.2	84.2	75.6
$\mathcal{F}$ unseen	51.0	60.7	61.2	63.7	–	–	73.1	80.9	75.7

Fig. 5. The visual results of video object segmentation using our global context module.

Notably, the performance gap between STM and our GC does not come from the models. Instead, two external factors are the main cause of the gap:

- an easier testing protocol used by STM;
- a soft-aggregation post-processing module, which is compatible with GC but not implemented due to time constraints.

Table 6 summarized the comparison.

Table 6. Cause of performance gap between STM and our GC on YouTube-VOS.

Model	Soft aggregation	Test input stride	$\mathcal{J}\&\mathcal{F}$ mean
GC		5	73.2
STM		5	73.7
STM	✓	1	79.4

4.4   Qualitative Results

Figure 5 shows visual examples of our segmentation results. As can be seen in the figure, our global context module can effectively handle many challenging cases such as appearance changes (row 1), size changes (row 3, 5, and 6), and occlusions (row 2 and 4).

Fig. 6. Visualization of the global context keys.

4.5   Visualization of the Global Context Module

Figure 6 plots visualization of the global context module. As described in Sect. 3.1, each channel of the global context key (the keys in the blue region in Fig. 3 left) is an attention map (or weight map) over all spatial locations. Our global context module aggregates the features at these locations to form one global context feature vector by a weighted sum. After such aggregation on all C_N channels, C_N feature vectors are generated. Figure 6 shows the visualization of two channels in the global context key at evenly sampled time in a whole video sequence. We can clearly see that it can summarize the segmentation information well, where the keys in the upper row capture parts of the foreground object and the keys in the bottom capture the background. In addition, it shows that the global context module can capture the foreground and background information consistently throughout the video.

5   Conclusion

We have presented a practical solution to the problem of semi-supervised video object segmentation. It is achieved by a novel global context module that effectively and efficiently captures the object segmentation information in all processed frames with a set of fixed-size features. The evaluation on multiple benchmark datasets shows that our method gets top performance, especially on the single object DAVIS 2016 dataset, and runs at a much faster speed than all top-performing methods, including the state-of-the-art STM. Our global context module is also efficient in memory usage and will not have memory issues as with STM for longer video sequences. We believe that our global context module has the potential to become a core module in practical video object segmentation tools. In the future, we want to optimize it further to make it suitable for running on portable devices like tablets and mobile phones. Applying the global context module to other video-related computer vision problems is also of our interest.

References

1. Bai, X., Wang, J., Simons, D.S., Sapiro, G.: Video SnapCut: robust video object cutout using localized classifiers. ACM Trans. Graph. **28**, 70 (2009)
2. Bao, L., Wu, B., Liu, W.: CNN in MRF: video object segmentation via inference in a CNN-based higher-order spatio-temporal MRF. In: CVPR (2018)
3. Borji, A., Cheng, M.M., Jiang, H., Li, J.: Salient object detection: a benchmark. IEEE Trans. Image Process. **24**(12), 5706–5722 (2015)
4. Caelles, S., Maninis, K.K., Pont-Tuset, J., Leal-Taixé, L., Cremers, D., Van Gool, L.: One-shot video object segmentation. In: CVPR (2017)
5. Chen, Y., Pont-Tuset, J., Montes, A., Van Gool, L.: Blazingly fast video object segmentation with pixel-wise metric learning. In: CVPR (2018)
6. Cheng, J., Tsai, Y.H., Hung, W.C., Wang, S., Yang, M.H.: Fast and accurate online video object segmentation via tracking parts. In: CVPR (2018)
7. Cheng, J., Tsai, Y.H., Wang, S., Yang, M.H.: SegFlow: joint learning for video object segmentation and optical flow. In: ICCV (2017)
8. Cheng, M.M., Mitra, N.J., Huang, X., Torr, P.H., Hu, S.M.: Global contrast based salient region detection. TPAMI **37**(3), 569–582 (2014)
9. Dosovitskiy, A., et al.: FlowNet: learning optical flow with convolutional networks. In: ICCV (2015)
10. Everingham, M., Van Gool, L., Williams, C.K.I., Winn, J., Zisserman, A.: The pascal visual object classes (VOC) challenge. IJCV **88**(2), 303–338 (2010)
11. Hariharan, B., Arbelaez, P., Bourdev, L., Maji, S., Malik, J.: Semantic contours from inverse detectors. In: ICCV (2011)
12. He, K., Zhang, X., Ren, S., Sun, J.: Deep residual learning for image recognition. In: CVPR (2016)
13. Hu, Y.-T., Huang, J.-B., Schwing, A.G.: VideoMatch: matching based video object segmentation. In: Ferrari, V., Hebert, M., Sminchisescu, C., Weiss, Y. (eds.) ECCV 2018. LNCS, vol. 11212, pp. 56–73. Springer, Cham (2018). https://doi.org/10.1007/978-3-030-01237-3_4
14. Ilg, E., Mayer, N., Saikia, T., Keuper, M., Dosovitskiy, A., Brox, T.: FlowNet 2.0: evolution of optical flow estimation with deep networks. In: CVPR (2017)
15. Jang, W.D., Kim, C.S.: Online video object segmentation via convolutional trident network. In: CVPR (2017)
16. Johnander, J., Danelljan, M., Brissman, E., Khan, F.S., Felsberg, M.: A generative appearance model for end-to-end video object segmentation. In: CVPR (2019)
17. Khoreva, A., Benenson, R., Ilg, E., Brox, T., Schiele, B.: Lucid data dreaming for video object segmentation. IJCV **127**(9), 1175–1197 (2019)
18. Kingma, D.P., Ba, J.: Adam: a method for stochastic optimization. In: ICLR (2014)
19. Li, G., Yu, Y.: Visual saliency based on multiscale deep features. In: CVPR (2015)
20. Li, X., Loy, C.C.: Video object segmentation with joint re-identification and attention-aware mask propagation. In: Ferrari, V., Hebert, M., Sminchisescu, C., Weiss, Y. (eds.) ECCV 2018. LNCS, vol. 11207, pp. 93–110. Springer, Cham (2018). https://doi.org/10.1007/978-3-030-01219-9_6
21. Li, Y., Sun, J., Shum, H.Y.: Video object cut and paste. In: SIGGRAPH (2005)

22. Lin, H., Qi, X., Jia, J.: AGSS-VOS: attention guided single-shot video object segmentation. In: ICCV (2019)
23. Lin, T.-Y., et al.: Microsoft COCO: common objects in context. In: Fleet, D., Pajdla, T., Schiele, B., Tuytelaars, T. (eds.) ECCV 2014. LNCS, vol. 8693, pp. 740–755. Springer, Cham (2014). https://doi.org/10.1007/978-3-319-10602-1_48
24. Luiten, J., Voigtlaender, P., Leibe, B.: PReMVOS: proposal-generation, refinement and merging for video object segmentation. In: ACCV (2018)
25. Maninis, K.K., et al.: Video object segmentation without temporal information. TPAMI **41**(6), 1515–1530 (2018)
26. Oh, S.W., Lee, J.Y., Sunkavalli, K., Kim, S.J.: Fast video object segmentation by reference-guided mask propagation. In: CVPR (2018)
27. Oh, S.W., Lee, J.Y., Xu, N., Kim, S.J.: Video object segmentation using space-time memory networks. In: ICCV (2019)
28. Perazzi, F., Khoreva, A., Benenson, R., Schiele, B., Sorkine-Hornung, A.: Learning video object segmentation from static images. In: CVPR (2017)
29. Perazzi, F., Pont-Tuset, J., McWilliams, B., Van Gool, L., Gross, M., Sorkine-Hornung, A.: A benchmark dataset and evaluation methodology for video object segmentation. In: CVPR (2016)
30. Pont-Tuset, J., Perazzi, F., Caelles, S., Arbeláez, P., Sorkine-Hornung, A., Van Gool, L.: The 2017 davis challenge on video object segmentation. arXiv:1704.00675 (2017)
31. Price, B.L., Morse, B.S., Cohen, S.: LIVEcut: learning-based interactive video segmentation by evaluation of multiple propagated cues. In: ICCV (2009)
32. Shin Yoon, J., Rameau, F., Kim, J., Lee, S., Shin, S., So Kweon, I.: Pixel-level matching for video object segmentation using convolutional neural networks. In: ICCV (2017)
33. Ventura, C., Bellver, M., Girbau, A., Salvador, A., Marques, F., Giro-i Nieto, X.: RVOS: end-to-end recurrent network for video object segmentation. In: CVPR (2019)
34. Voigtlaender, P., Chai, Y., Schroff, F., Adam, H., Leibe, B., Chen, L.C.: FEELVOS: fast end-to-end embedding learning for video object segmentation. In: CVPR (2019)
35. Voigtlaender, P., Leibe, B.: Online adaptation of convolutional neural networks for video object segmentation. In: BMVC (2017)
36. Voigtlaender, P., Luiten, J., Leibe, B.: BoLTVOS: box-level tracking for video object segmentation. arXiv preprint arXiv:1904.04552 (2019)
37. Wang, J., Bhat, P., Colburn, A., Agrawala, M., Cohen, M.F.: Interactive video cutout. ACM Trans. Graph. **24**, 585–594 (2005)
38. Wang, Q., Zhang, L., Bertinetto, L., Hu, W., Torr, P.H.: Fast online object tracking and segmentation: a unifying approach. In: CVPR (2019)
39. Wang, Z., Xu, J., Liu, L., Zhu, F., Shao, L.: RANet: ranking attention network for fast video object segmentation. In: ICCV (2019)
40. Xu, N., et al.: YouTube-VOS: sequence-to-sequence video object segmentation. In: Ferrari, V., Hebert, M., Sminchisescu, C., Weiss, Y. (eds.) ECCV 2018. LNCS, vol. 11209, pp. 603–619. Springer, Cham (2018). https://doi.org/10.1007/978-3-030-01228-1_36
41. Yan, Q., Xu, L., Shi, J., Jia, J.: Hierarchical saliency detection. In: CVPR (2013)
42. Yang, L., Wang, Y., Xiong, X., Yang, J., Katsaggelos, A.K.: Efficient video object segmentation via network modulation. In: CVPR (2018)

Uncertainty-Aware Weakly Supervised Action Detection from Untrimmed Videos

Anurag Arnab$^{(\boxtimes)}$, Chen Sun, Arsha Nagrani, and Cordelia Schmid

Google Research, Grenoble, France
aarnab@google.com, chensun@google.com, anagrani@google.com,
cordelias@google.com

Abstract. Despite the recent advances in video classification, progress in spatio-temporal action recognition has lagged behind. A major contributing factor has been the prohibitive cost of annotating videos frame-by-frame. In this paper, we present a spatio-temporal action recognition model that is trained with only video-level labels, which are significantly easier to annotate. Our method leverages per-frame person detectors which have been trained on large image datasets within a Multiple Instance Learning framework. We show how we can apply our method in cases where the standard Multiple Instance Learning assumption, that each bag contains at least one instance with the specified label, is invalid using a novel probabilistic variant of MIL where we estimate the uncertainty of each prediction. Furthermore, we report the first weakly-supervised results on the AVA dataset and state-of-the-art results among weakly-supervised methods on UCF101-24.

Keywords: Spatio-temporal action recognition · Weak supervision · Video understanding · Mulitple Instance Learning

1 Introduction

Video classification has witnessed great advances recently due to large datasets such as Kinetics [20] and Moments in Time [30] which have enabled training of specialised neural network architectures for video [5,9]. However, progress in other video understanding tasks, such as spatio-temporal action detection, has lagged behind in comparison. There are fewer datasets for action recognition, which are also significantly smaller than their video-classification counterparts. A reason for this is the exorbitant cost of annotating videos with spatio-temporal labels – each frame of an action has to be manually labelled with a bounding box. Moreover, annotating temporal boundaries of actions is not only arduous, but often ambiguous with annotators failing to reach consensus about the start and end times of an action [6,39].

Electronic supplementary material The online version of this chapter (https://doi.org/10.1007/978-3-030-58607-2_44) contains supplementary material, which is available to authorized users.

© Springer Nature Switzerland AG 2020
A. Vedaldi et al. (Eds.): ECCV 2020, LNCS 12355, pp. 751–768, 2020.
https://doi.org/10.1007/978-3-030-58607-2_44

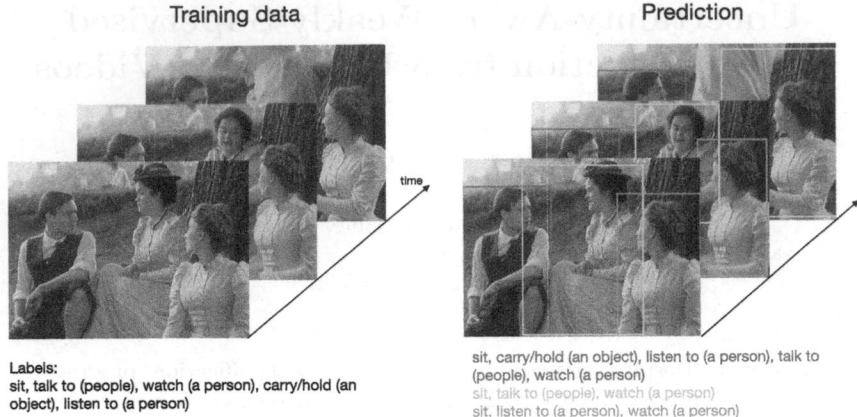

Fig. 1. We propose a method to train a spatio-temporal action detector using only weak, video-level labels on challenging, real-world datasets. Note that the video-level labels that we have may apply to multiple people in the video, and that these labels may only be active for an unannotated time interval of the input clip.

In this paper, we propose a method to train spatio-temporal action detectors using only weak, video-level annotations as shown in Fig. 1. To achieve this, we leverage image-based person detectors which have been trained on large image datasets such as Microsoft COCO [26] and are accurate across large variations in appearance, scene and pose. We adopt a Multiple Instance Learning (MIL) framework, where a person tubelet is an instance, and all person tubelets in the video form a bag. An important consideration in our approach is the presence of label noise: this is introduced from using off-the-shelf person detectors which have not been trained on the video-dataset of interest, and also the fact that we have to sample tubelets from large bags in long videos due to memory constraints. In both of these scenarios, the standard Multiple Instance Learning assumption [7], that each bag contains at least one instance with the bag-level label, may be violated. We are not aware of previous work that has explicitly addressed this problem, and we do so with a probabilistic variant of MIL where we estimate the uncertainty of an instance-level prediction.

Using our approach, we obtain state-of-the-art results among weakly-supervised methods on the UCF101-24 dataset. Furthermore, we report, to our knowledge, the first weakly-supervised results on the AVA dataset (the only large-scale dataset for spatio-temporal action recognition), where we also show the accuracy trade-offs when annotating video-clips for time intervals of varying durations.

2   Related Work

Most prior work on spatio-temporal action recognition has been fully-supervised. Initial approaches in the area used 3D sliding window detectors in conjunction with handcrafted, volumetric features [21,25]. Current state-of-the-art approaches are temporal extensions of object detection architectures [19,35, 41,52] such as Faster-RCNN [37] and SSD [27]. These approaches predict bounding boxes around the action in a frame, using as input either a single frame along with optical flow to capture temporal information [38,41] or multiple frames at the input to provide temporal context [19]. The predicted bounding boxes are then linked over time using an online, greedy algorithm or dynamic programming to create spatio-temporal tracks. Our work builds on these methods by also utilising a detection architecture and spatio-temporal linking. However, these approaches all require bounding box annotations at each frame in the video whilst we only use video-level labels which are significantly cheaper to acquire.

Weakly supervised approaches to spatio-temporal action recognition have also been explored before as they enable a significant reduction in annotation time and cost. Relevant to our approach is the work of [6]. Cheron et al. [6] also use person detections, and infer their action labels using a formulation based on discriminative clustering [2]. Although their approach allows them to incorporate different types of supervision, it effectively learns a linear classifier on top of pretrained, deep features. Our method in contrast is learned fully end-to-end. Mettes et al. [29] also employed Multiple Instance Learning (MIL), but used action proposals [47] instead of the human detections used by our work and [6]. However, [29], rely on additional cheap "point" annotations (a single spatial point annotated for a subset of the frames which constitute the action) which also ensures that the standard MIL assumption is not violated. In follow-up work [28], the authors removed the need for "point" annotations by incorporating biases (i.e. the presence of objects in the video, a bias that actions typically occur in the centre of a frame) instead. Finally, Weinzaepfel et al. [50] also used a Multiple Instance Learning framework in conjunction with human detections. The authors, however, assumed that sparse spatial supervision was present (i.e. bounding boxes for a small subset of frames in the action tube), unlike our method which requires video-level labels alone.

We also note that many approaches have addressed temporal action detection (localising actions in time but not space) with only video-level tags as supervision [31,34,42,48]. UntrimmedNets [48] uses a network with two branches, a classification module to perform action classification and a selection module to select relevant frames. Hide-and-Seek [42] obtains more precise temporal boundaries by forcing the network to attend to more discriminative frames by randomly hiding parts of videos. However, these methods are trained and evaluated on datasets such as ActivityNet [4] and THUMOS14 [18], which contain mostly one action per video, and are thus significantly less challenging than datasets such as AVA [14] which we evaluate on.

Finally, we note that another approach to combat the effort of dataset annotation has been various forms of self-supervised learning, where discriminative feature representations can be learned with unlabelled data. Examples in video include cross-modal self-supervised learning by learning correspondences between the audio and image streams readily available in videos [1,33,51], transcribed speech [44] or using meta-data such as hashtags [10] as a form of weak labelling. Self-supervised approaches, however, are complementary to our approach, as they still require a limited amount of fully-labelled data for the final task of interest. In our weakly-supervised action detection scenario, we never have access to full, spatio-temporal ground-truth annotations for a single training example.

3 Proposed Approach

As shown in Fig. 1, given a set of video clips, with only clip-level annotations of the actions taking place, our goal is to learn a model to recognise and localise these actions in space and time. Our method is based on Multiple Instance Learning (MIL) which we briefly review in Sect. 3.1. Thereafter, we show how we use it for weakly-supervised spatio-temporal action recognition in Sect. 3.2. We then describe how the standard MIL assumption, is often violated in our scenario and describe a method to mitigate this by leveraging uncertainty estimates by our network in Sect. 3.3. Finally, we discuss implementation details of our network in Sect. 3.4.

3.1 Multiple Instance Learning

In the standard Multiple Instance Learning (MIL) [7] formulation, one is given a bag of N instances, denoted as $x = \{x_1, x_2, \ldots, x_N\}$. The class labels for each of the instances is unknown, but the label for the entire bag, x, is known. The standard MIL assumption is that a bag is assigned a class label if at least one instance in the bag is associated with this label. More formally, we consider the multi-label classification case, where the label vector for the bag is $y \in \mathbb{R}^C$, and $y_l = 1$ if there is at least one instance with the lth label is present in the bag, and $y_l = 0$ otherwise. Note that each bag can be labelled with multiple of the C class labels.

Our goal is to train an instance-level classifier (parameterised as a neural network), that predicts $p(y_l = 1|x_j)$, or the label probabilities for the jth instance. However, as we only have the labels for the entire bag, and not each instance, MIL methods aggregate the set of instance-level probabilities, $\{p_{ij}\}$ for a bag i, to bag-level probabilities, p_i, using an aggregation function, $g(\cdot)$, where the probabilities are obtained from a suitable activation function (sigmoid or softmax) on the logits output by the neural network:

$$p(y_{il} = 1|x_1, x_2, \ldots, x_N) = g(p_{i1}, p_{i2}, \ldots, p_{iN}). \tag{1}$$

Once we have bag-level predictions, we can apply a standard classification loss between the bag-level probabilities and bag-level ground truth, and train a neural network with stochastic gradient descent. Since we consider the multi-label classification case, we use the binary cross-entropy:

$$\mathcal{L}_{ce}(x, y) = -\sum_i^{N_b} \sum_l^{C} y_{il} \log p_{il} + (1 - y_{il}) \log(1 - p_{il}) \tag{2}$$

Note that we defined p_{il} as the bag-level probability of the ith bag taking the lth label, which is obtained using Eq. 1, and N_b is the number of bags in the mini-batch.

Aggregation. The aggregation function, $g(\cdot)$, can naturally be implemented in neural networks as a global pooling function over all outputs of the network. Common, permutation-invariant pooling functions include, max-pooling, generalised mean-pooling and log-sum-exponential (LSE) pooling [3] (a smooth and convex approximation of the maximum function) respectively:

$$g(\{p_j\}) = \max_j p_j \tag{3}$$

$$g(\{p_j\}) = \left(\frac{1}{|j|} \sum_j p_j^r \right)^{\frac{1}{r}} \tag{4}$$

$$g(\{p_j\}) = \frac{1}{r} \log \left(\frac{1}{|j|} \sum_j e^{r \cdot p_j} \right) \tag{5}$$

Max-pooling only considers the top-scoring instance in the bag, and thus naturally captures the MIL assumption that at least one instance in the bag has the specified, bag-level label. Moreover, it can also be more robust to instances in the bag that do not have the bag-level label. However, mean and LSE pooling have been employed in applications such as weakly-supervised segmentation [36], object recognition [45] and medical imaging [24] where multiple instances in the bag do typically have the bag-level label. Note that higher values of the r hyperparameter for both these functions increases their "peakiness" and approximates the maximum value. For our scenario, detailed in the next section, we found max-pooling to be the most appropriate.

3.2   Weakly-Supervised Spatio-Temporal Action Recognition as Multiple Instance Learning

Our goal is to learn a model to recognise and localise actions in space and time given only video-level annotations. To facilitate this, we leverage a person detector that has been trained on a large image dataset, *i.e.* Microsoft COCO [26]. Concretely, we run a person detector on our training videos, and create person tubelets which are person detections over K consecutive frames in the video. Our bag for multiple instance learning thus consists of all the tubelets within a video, and is annotated with the video-level labels that we have as supervision, as illustrated in Fig. 2. Note that the size of the bag varies for every video clip, as the bag size is determined by the length of the video and the number of detected people.

As shown in Fig. 2, our network architecture for this task is a Fast-RCNN [12] style detector that has been extended temporally. Given a video clip of K frames, and proposals which in our case are person detections, the network classifies the action(s) taking place at the centre frame of each proposal, given the temporal context of the $K - 1$ frames around it.

Note that the spatio-temporal localisation task is effectively factorised: the spatial localisation capability of the model depends on the quality of the person detections. Temporal localisation, on the other hand, is performed by linking person tubelets through the video as commonly done in the literature [6,19, 41,52], since this method can scale to arbitrarily long videos. We use the same algorithm as Kalogeiton *et al.* [19] which links together detections within a small temporal window greedily based on the spatial intersection over union (IoU) between bounding boxes on consecutive frames.

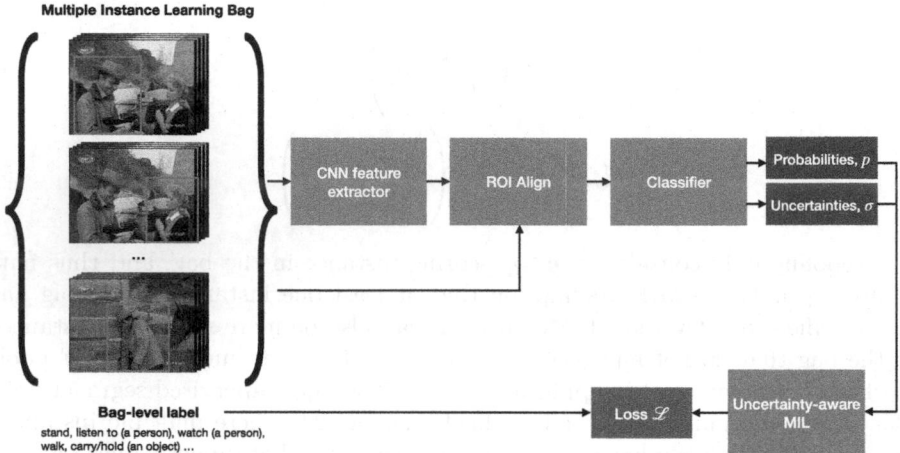

Fig. 2. Overview of our approach for training an action detector in a weakly-supervised manner using multiple instance learning: Each bag consists of all the tubelets that have been extracted from the video-clip. These tubelets are obtained using an off-the-shelf person detector which has not been trained on the dataset of interest. These tubelets act as proposals for a Fast-RCNN style detector operating on a sequence of rgb images. The predictions for each of the tubelets in the bag are then aggregated together, and compared to the bag-level label. Uncertainty estimates produced by the network are used to compensate for noise in the bag-level labels during training.

Finally, note that for a video consisting of T frames, the bag could consist of $T - K + 1$ person tubelets if a person is detected on each frame of the video, and a tubelet is started from each frame. Due to memory limitations, it is infeasible to fit an entire bag onto a GPU for training. As a result, we uniformly sample instances from each bag during training, whilst still retaining the original bag-level label. This introduces additional noise into the problem, as detailed next.

3.3   Label Noise and Violation of the Standard MIL Assumption

The standard MIL assumption, that at least one instance in the bag is assigned the bag-level label is often violated in our scenario. There are two primary factors for this: Firstly, due to computational constraints, we cannot process a whole bag at a time, but must instead sample instances from a bag. It is therefore possible to sample a bag that does not contain any tubelets with the labelled action. The likelihood of this occurring is inversely proportional to the ratio of the duration of the labelled action to the total video length. Secondly, in a weakly-supervised scenario, we use person detectors that are not trained on the video dataset of interest. Consequently, there can be failures in the detector, especially when there is a large domain gap between the detector's training distribution and the video dataset. False negatives (missing detections for people in the scene) are a particular issue because it is possible that we do not have a single person tubelet in the bag that corresponds to the labelled action.

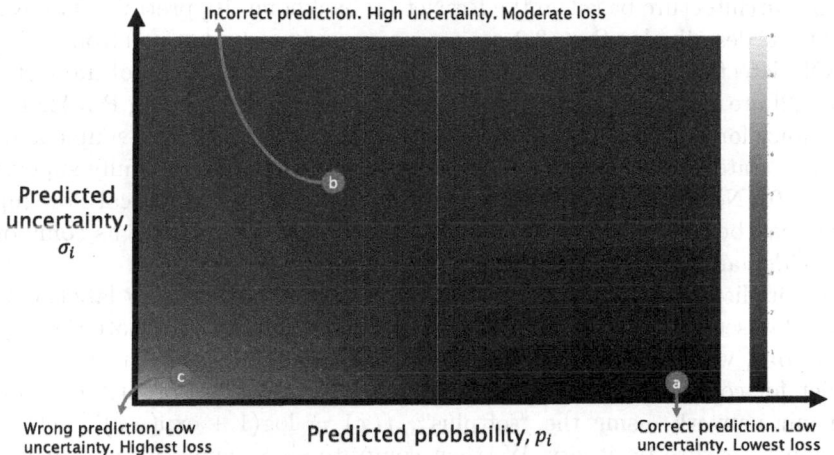

Fig. 3. The loss surface of our uncertainty-based loss (Eq. 6). The ground truth binary label in this example is 1. Hence, the loss is minimised when the network predicts a high probability and a low uncertainty (point "a"). However, making an incorrect prediction with a high uncertainty is not penalised as much (point "b"), and is suitable for cases when the input bags are noisy and the bag-level label is not present in any of the tubelets. Finally, predicting the incorrect label with a low uncertainty is penalised the most (point "c"). Best viewed in colour.

Therefore, there are cases when there is no tubelet which actually has the bag-level label. To handle these cases, inspired by [22,32], we modify the network to additionally predict the uncertainty $\sigma \in \mathbb{R}^C$ for each binary label for all tubelets in the bag. Intuitively, to minimise the training error, the network can predict the bag-level label with low uncertainty or it can predict a high uncertainty to avoid being penalised heavily for noisy bags where the bag-level label is not present in any of the tubelets. The final loss, in conjunction with the original cross entropy, is defined as:

$$\mathcal{L}(x, y, \sigma) = \frac{1}{\sigma^2}\mathcal{L}_{ce}(x, y) + \log \sigma^2 \tag{6}$$

As shown by [23], this corresponds to assuming a Boltzmann distribution on the output of the network with a temperature of σ^2, and approximately minimising its log-likelihood.

The loss surface of this probabilistic loss is visualised in Fig. 3. Note how the loss is the lowest when the predicted label is correct and there is low uncertainty. However, the loss is not excessive if the incorrect label is predicted with a high uncertainty. This is in contrast with the standard cross-entropy loss which penalises incorrect predictions heavily.

3.4   Network Architecture and Implementation

Our action detector is similar to Fast-RCNN [12] using the SlowFast [9] video network architecture based on the ResNet-50 backbone [16] pretrained on Kinetics [20]. As described in Sect. 3.2, we use region proposals obtained from a Faster-RCNN detection model trained with Detectron [13]. Region-of-interest features [12] are extracted from the last feature map of "res5" using RoIAlign [15]. Our choice for this architecture is motivated by the fact that it is simple and has achieved state-of-the-art results on the AVA dataset [14] in a fully-supervised setting [9]. Note that our network does not use additional optical flow inputs (which can be considered as an additional source of supervision) as common in other video architectures [5,6,19,41].

We predict the uncertainty, $\sigma \in \mathbb{R}^C$ for each of the C binary labels defined by the dataset for each tubelet. As we use max-pooling to aggregate the tubelet predictions, we select the uncertainty prediction corresponding to the selected tubelet for computing the loss. For numerical stability, we predict $v := \log \sigma^2$ with our network, using the "softplus", $f(x) = \log(1 + \exp(-x))$, activation function to ensure positivity. We then compute $\frac{1}{\sigma^2} = \exp(-v)$, and avoid the possibility of dividing by 0 which could be the case if we predicted σ^2 directly with the network.

We train our network with synchronous stochastic gradient descent (SGD), using 8 GPUs and a batch size of 4 on each GPU. In our case, each element of a batch is of a bag from Multiple Instance Learning. Each bag samples a maximum of 4 tubelets. Each tubelet itself consists of 16 frames.

4   Experiments

4.1   Experimental Set-Up

We evaluate our method on UCF101-24 and AVA, described in more detail below. Note that other video datasets such as THUMOS [18] and ActivityNet [4] are not suitable for spatiotemporal localisation, as they lack bounding box annotations.

UCF101-24: UCF101-24 is a subset of the UCF101 [43] dataset, consisting of 24 action classes with spatio-temporal localisation annotation, released as bounding box annotations of humans. Although each video contains only a single action class, it may contain multiple individuals performing the action with different spatial and temporal boundaries. Moreover, there may also be people present in the video who are not performing any labelled action. Following standard practice, we use the corrected annotations of [41] and report the mean average precision at a video level (Video AP) for the first split of the dataset. For evaluating the Video AP, we link tubelets together using the algorithm of [19].

Table 1. Ablation study of different variants of our method on the UCF101-24 validation set. We report the Video mAP at IoU thresholds of 0.2 and 0.5 respectively.

	Video AP	
	0.2	0.5
Weakly supervised baseline	54.3	29.7
MIL - LSE pooling	60.1	33.1
MIL - mean pooling	60.3	33.0
MIL - max pooling	60.7	33.5
MIL - max pooling, uncertainty	61.7	35.0
Fully supervised	69.3	43.6

AVA [14]: This dataset consists of 430, 15 min video clips obtained from movies. 80 atomic visual actions are annotated exhaustively for all people in the video, where one person is often simultaneously performing multiple actions. The dataset annotates keyframes at every second in the video. Following standard practice, we report the Frame AP at an IoU threshold of 0.5 using v2.2 annotations.

4.2   Experiments on UCF101-24

We first conduct ablation studies of our model on the UCF101-24 dataset. We discard the spatio-temporal annotations for the whole untrimmed video, and so our bag in multiple instance learning contains tubelets from the whole video.

Ablation Study. Table 1 ablates different variants of our method: The most naïve baseline is to not perform any multiple instance learning, and to simply train in a fully-supervised fashion assuming that the label of a tubelet is the video-level label. As shown in the first row of Table 1, this method performs the worst as the assumed tubelet-level labels are often incorrect. The use of multiple instance learning improves results, with the various aggregation functions performing similarly. Max-pooling, however, performs the best, and we believe this is because the max operation is the most suitable for dealing with the noise present in our tubelets as described in Sect. 3.3. Note that for mean and LSE-pooling, we set $r = 1$. Finally, introducing our uncertainty-based loss function improves results even further, obtaining a Video mAP of 35.0 at a threshold of 0.5. This is 80% of the performance achieved by our fully-supervised baseline.

Person Detections on UCF101-24. Note that for our weakly-supervised experiments, the person tubelets for training are obtained from a Faster-RCNN [37] person detector that has only been trained on Microsoft COCO [26]. There is a significant domain gap between COCO and UCF, and the annotation protocol of person boxes on UCF is also not consistent (for example, the bounding box for a person riding a horse often includes the horse in UCF) with that of COCO. These discrepancies are reflected by the fact that our person detections used during training only have a recall of 46.9% compared to the ground truth person boxes, when using an IoU threshold of 0.5 to signify a correct match. Furthermore, the precision of our person tubelets on the training set is only 21.1%. A major contributing factor to this is that UCF action annotations are not exhaustive – there may be people in the video who are not labelled at all as they are not performing an annotated action. These people will, however, still be detected by a COCO-trained detector and considered as false positives during this evaluation.

The fact that we are able to train our model with these annotations demonstrates the ability of our multiple instance learning method to handle label noise in the training set. The inconsistencies in the UCF101-24 dataset labelling are detailed further in the supplementary, and has also been noted previously by Chéron *et al.* [6].

Noise in the person detections are not a problem for the training of our fully-supervised baseline, as it is trained with ground-truth boxes in addition to predicted boxes. As we have box-level supervision in this case, predicted detections which have an IoU of more than 0.5 with a ground-truth detection are assigned the label of the ground-truth box, or the negative label otherwise, during fully-supervised training.

As the goal of this paper is not to develop a better human detector or tracker for building the person tubelets, we use the Faster-RCNN detector released publicly by Chéron *et al.* [6] for all our evaluations on the UCF101-24 validation set. This detector was originally trained on COCO and then finetuned on the UCF101-24 training set using Detectron [13].

The Effect of Tubelet Sampling. For the tubelets of length $K = 16$ that we use, there is a mean of 33.1 tubelets per video in the UCF101-24 dataset. In computing this, we only consider tubelets which have a spatio-temporal IoU of less than 0.5 with each other. More tubelets would be obtained if we counted one from each frame of the video.

As we can fit a maximum of 16 tubelets onto a 16 GB Nvidia V100 GPU, it is clear that it is necessary to sample the tubelets in each bag. Note that UCF videos often have a high number of tubelets, as there are often many people in the video who are not labelled as performing an action. As described in the previous subsection, this is also a significant source of noise.

Table 2 shows the effect of changing the batch size (number of bags), and the number of tubelets sampled per bag, such that GPU memory usage is maximised. We can see that the uncertainty loss helps in all cases and that accuracy decreases with low batch sizes. We believe this is due to batch normalisation statistics being too correlated when more tubes are from the same video.

Comparison to State-of-the-Art. Table 3 compares our results to the state-of-the-art. The bottom-half of the table shows that we outperform previous weakly-supervised methods by a large margin. The top-half shows that our fully-supervised baseline is also competitive with the fully-supervised state-of-the-art, although that is not the main goal of this work. The fully-supervised methods which outperform our method are based on action detectors which directly predict the person proposals with the network, and are thus able to handle the person annotation peculiarities of the UCF101-24 dataset more effectively. We do not observe any issues with person detections for our experiments on AVA in the next section.

Table 2. The effect of the number of bags in each training batch on accuracy (Video AP at 0.5). The uncertainty loss improves accuracy in all scenarios. Although fewer, but larger, bags can reduce the noise due to sampling, they also cause batch normalisation statistics to be too correlated, reducing accuracy.

Number of bags in batch	Tubelets sampled per bag	Video AP without uncertainty	Video AP with uncertainty
4	4	33.5	35.0
3	5	33.6	34.1
2	8	33.3	34.2
1	16	25.8	26.2

Qualitative Results. Figure 4 presents qualitative results of our method. The first two rows show success cases of our method where the tubelet detection and linking have performed well. The third row shows a failure case, since the basketball player represented by the green track is not actually performing the "Basketball Dunk" action. According to the UCF101-24 annotations, only the player represented with the blue track is performing this action. This video clip is thus an example of a video where there are many people not performing the action annotated for the video, and is especially challenging for our weakly-supervised method. The fourth row shows a different failure case as an error by the online tubelet linking algorithm (we used the same method as [19]) has made the identities of the two cyclists change after they occluded each other.

Table 3. Comparison to state-of-the-art methods on the UCF101-24 dataset in both fully- and weakly-supervised scenarios.

	Video AP at 0.2	Video AP at 0.5
Fully supervised		
Peng *et al.* [35]	42.3	35.9
Hou *et al.* [17]	47.1	–
Weinzaepfel *et al.* [50]	58.9	–
Saha *et al.* [38]	63.1	33.1
Singh *et al.* [41]	73.5	46.3
Zhao *et al.* [52]	78.5	50.3
Singh *et al.* [40]	79.0	50.9
Kalogeiton *et al.* [19]	77.2	51.4
Ours	69.3	43.6
Weakly supervised		
Escorcia *et al.* [8]	45.5	–
Chéron *et al.* [6]	43.9	17.7
Ours	61.7	35.0

Fig. 4. Qualitative examples on UCF101-24. Note that the bounding boxes are coloured according to the identity of the track. The action label, and tube score are labelled from the top-left of the bounding box. Further discussion is included in the text.

4.3   Experiments on AVA

In this section, we report what to our knowledge are the first weakly-supervised action detection experiments on AVA [14]. The AVA dataset labels keyframes in a 15 min video clip, where each keyframe is sampled every second (*i.e.* 1 Hz). The evaluation protocol of the AVA dataset measures the ability of an action detection model to classify the actions occuring in a keyframe given the temporal context around it.

We control the difficulty of the weakly-supervised action recognition problem by combining the annotations from N consecutive keyframes into a single, clip-level annotation. This effectively means that we are obtaining clip-level annotations for sub-clips of N seconds from the original AVA video. The weakly-supervised problem gets more difficult as N increases, as the sub-clips get longer and the number of observed labels within each sub-clip increases. Note that when $N = 1$, only the spatial localisation ability of the model is being tested, as during training, it is unknown which of the subclip-level labels correspond to each person tubelet in the MIL bag. When $N > 1$, the subclip-level labels can correspond to zero, one or many of the person tubelets at different keyframes in the clip, and it is thus a more difficult task. As an AVA video clip consists of 900 s, $N = 900$ represents the most extreme case when spatio-temporal annotations are discarded for the entire 15 min video.

Table 4. Results of our method on the AVA dataset in terms of the Frame mAP at an IoU threshold of 0.5. We vary the length of the sub-clips from which we extract clip-level annotations to control the difficulty of the weakly supervised problems. FS denotes a fully-supervised baseline representing the upper bound on performance. A sub-clip of 900 s is an entire AVA video clip. Results of our method on the AVA dataset in terms of the Frame mAP at an IoU threshold of 0.5. We vary the length of the sub-clips from which we extract clip-level annotations to control the difficulty of the weakly supervised problems. FS denotes a fully-supervised baseline representing the upper bound on performance. A sub-clip of 900 s is an entire AVA video clip.

		Sub-clip duration (seconds)					
Frame AP	FS	1	5	10	30	60	900
	24.9	22.4	18.0	15.8	11.4	9.1	4.2

Table 4 shows the results of our model in this setting. As expected, the performance of our method improves the shorter the sub-clip. For $N = 1$ and $N = 5$, our method obtains 90% and 72% of fully-supervised performance respectively, suggesting that bounding-box level annotations are not required for training action recognition models if the video clips are annotated over short temporal intervals. Understandably, the results from $N = 900$, where we use the video-level annotations over the whole 15 min clip are the worst as it is the most difficult setting.

Table 5. State-of-the-art fully-supervised methods on the AVA dataset.

Method	Frame AP
AVA (with optical flow) [14]	15.6
ARCN (with optical flow) [46]	17.4
Action Transformer [11]	25.0
SlowFast (ResNet 101) [9]	26.8
SlowFast (ResNet 50, Ours)	24.9

Figure 5 further analyses the per-class results for the different levels of supervision presented in Table 4. As expected, stronger levels of supervision (shorter sub-clip durations) result in better per-class accuracy. However, some action classes are affected more than others by weaker labels (longer sub-clips). Examples of this include "sing to" and "listen to" which show a larger difference to the fully-supervised baseline than other classes. Moreover, some classes such as "watch (a person)", "get up", "close (e.g., a door, a box)" and "hand clap" perform reasonably when trained with sub-clips ($N \leq 10$), but much more poorly when trained with longer sub-clips.

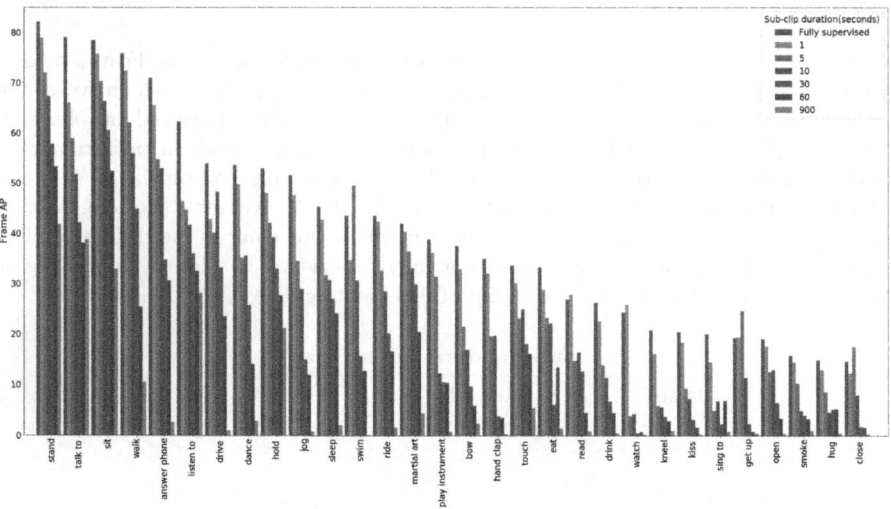

Fig. 5. Per-class results, in terms of the Frame AP, on the AVA dataset under different levels of supervision (the longer the sub-clip duration, the weaker the supervision). For clarity, the first 30 classes, ranked using the fully-supervised model, are shown. As expected, action classes benefit from stronger supervision, while some classes, such as "watch", "get up" and "close" are very difficult to learn from long sub-clips.

Finally, we compare our fully-supervised baseline to the state-of-the-art in Table 5. Note that our weakly-supervised result from sub-clips of 10 s (Table 4) outperforms the original fully-supervised baseline using introduced by the AVA dataset [14] that uses both RGB and optical flow as inputs. Our model, on the other hand, only uses RGB as its input modality. Our SlowFast model performs similarly to the published results of the original authors [9]. Note that we have not used Non-local [49], test-time augmentation or ensembling which are all complementary methods to improve performance [9]. We can see that in contrast to the UCF dataset in the previous section, our person detector is accurate on AVA, and so a Fast-RCNN-style detector using person tubelets as proposals can achieve state-of-the-art results.

5 Conclusion and Future Work

We have proposed a weakly supervised spatio-temporal action detection method based on Multiple Instance Learning (MIL). Our approach incorporates uncertainty predictions made by the network such that it can better handle noise in our bags and violations of the standard MIL assumption by predicting a high uncertainty for noisy bags which cannot be classified correctly. We achieve state-of-the-art results among weakly supervised methods on the UCF101-24 dataset, and also report the first weakly-supervised results on AVA, which is the only large-scale action recognition dataset. Our analysis of the accuracy trade-offs as the time intervals for which sub-clips of the video are annotated will also aid future dataset annotation efforts.

Future work is to incorporate additional sources of noisy, weakly-labelled data, such as data which can be scraped off internet search engines.

References

1. Arandjelovic, R., Zisserman, A.: Look, listen and learn. In: Proceedings of the IEEE International Conference on Computer Vision, pp. 609–617 (2017)
2. Bach, F.R., Harchaoui, Z.: DIFFRAC: a discriminative and flexible framework for clustering. In: Advances in Neural Information Processing Systems, pp. 49–56 (2008)
3. Boyd, S., Boyd, S.P., Vandenberghe, L.: Convex Optimization. Cambridge University Press, Cambridge (2004)
4. Caba Heilbron, F., Escorcia, V., Ghanem, B., Carlos Niebles, J.: ActivityNet: a large-scale video benchmark for human activity understanding. In: Proceedings of the IEEE Conference on Computer Vision and Pattern Recognition, pp. 961–970 (2015)
5. Carreira, J., Zisserman, A.: Quo vadis, action recognition? A new model and the kinetics dataset. In: proceedings of the IEEE Conference on Computer Vision and Pattern Recognition, pp. 6299–6308 (2017)
6. Chéron, G., Alayrac, J.B., Laptev, I., Schmid, C.: A flexible model for training action localization with varying levels of supervision. In: Advances in Neural Information Processing Systems, pp. 942–953 (2018)
7. Dietterich, T.G., Lathrop, R.H., Lozano-Pérez, T.: Solving the multiple instance problem with axis-parallel rectangles. Artif. Intell. **89**(1–2), 31–71 (1997)

8. Escorcia, V., Dao, C.D., Jain, M., Ghanem, B., Snoek, C.: Guess where? Actor-supervision for spatiotemporal action localization. arXiv preprint arXiv:1804.01824 (2018)

9. Feichtenhofer, C., Fan, H., Malik, J., He, K.: SlowFast networks for video recognition. In: Proceedings of the IEEE International Conference on Computer Vision, pp. 6202–6211 (2019)

10. Ghadiyaram, D., Tran, D., Mahajan, D.: Large-scale weakly-supervised pre-training for video action recognition. In: Proceedings of the IEEE Conference on Computer Vision and Pattern Recognition, pp. 12046–12055 (2019)

11. Girdhar, R., Carreira, J., Doersch, C., Zisserman, A.: Video action transformer network. In: Proceedings of the IEEE Conference on Computer Vision and Pattern Recognition, pp. 244–253 (2019)

12. Girshick, R.: Fast R-CNN. In: ICCV (2015)

13. Girshick, R., Radosavovic, I., Gkioxari, G., Dollár, P., He, K.: Detectron (2018). https://github.com/facebookresearch/detectron

14. Gu, C., et al.: AVA: a video dataset of spatio-temporally localized atomic visual actions. In: Proceedings of the IEEE Conference on Computer Vision and Pattern Recognition, pp. 6047–6056 (2018)

15. He, K., Gkioxari, G., Dollár, P., Girshick, R.: Mask R-CNN. In: ICCV (2017)

16. He, K., Zhang, X., Ren, S., Sun, J.: Deep residual learning for image recognition. In: CVPR (2016)

17. Hou, R., Chen, C., Shah, M.: Tube convolutional neural network (T-CNN) for action detection in videos. In: International Conference on Computer Vision, pp. 5822–5831 (2017)

18. Jiang, Y.G., et al.: THUMOS challenge: action recognition with a large number of classes (2014)

19. Kalogeiton, V., Weinzaepfel, P., Ferrari, V., Schmid, C.: Joint learning of object and action detectors. In: Proceedings of the IEEE International Conference on Computer Vision, pp. 4163–4172 (2017)

20. Kay, W., et al.: The kinetics human action video dataset. arXiv preprint arXiv:1705.06950 (2017)

21. Ke, Y., Sukthankar, R., Hebert, M.: Efficient visual event detection using volumetric features. In: International Conference on Computer Vision, vol. 1, pp. 166–173. IEEE (2005)

22. Kendall, A., Gal, Y.: What uncertainties do we need in Bayesian deep learning for computer vision? In: Advances in Neural Information Processing Systems, pp. 5574–5584 (2017)

23. Kendall, A., Gal, Y., Cipolla, R.: Multi-task learning using uncertainty to weigh losses for scene geometry and semantics. In: Computer Vision and Pattern Recognition, pp. 7482–7491 (2018)

24. Kraus, O.Z., Ba, L.J., Frey, B.: Classifying and segmenting microscopy images using convolutional multiple instance learning. arXiv preprint arXiv:1511.05286 (2015)

25. Laptev, I., Pérez, P.: Retrieving actions in movies. In: International Conference on Computer Vision, pp. 1–8. IEEE (2007)

26. Lin, T.-Y., et al.: Microsoft COCO: common objects in context. In: Fleet, D., Pajdla, T., Schiele, B., Tuytelaars, T. (eds.) ECCV 2014. LNCS, vol. 8693, pp. 740–755. Springer, Cham (2014). https://doi.org/10.1007/978-3-319-10602-1_48

27. Liu, W., et al.: SSD: single shot multibox detector. In: Leibe, B., Matas, J., Sebe, N., Welling, M. (eds.) ECCV 2016. LNCS, vol. 9905, pp. 21–37. Springer, Cham (2016). https://doi.org/10.1007/978-3-319-46448-0_2

28. Mettes, P., Snoek, C.G., Chang, S.F.: Localizing actions from video labels and pseudo-annotations. In: British Machine Vision Conference (BMVC) (2017)
29. Mettes, P., van Gemert, J.C., Snoek, C.G.M.: Spot on: action localization from pointly-supervised proposals. In: Leibe, B., Matas, J., Sebe, N., Welling, M. (eds.) ECCV 2016. LNCS, vol. 9909, pp. 437–453. Springer, Cham (2016). https://doi.org/10.1007/978-3-319-46454-1_27
30. Monfort, M., et al.: Moments in time dataset: one million videos for event understanding. arXiv preprint arXiv:1801.03150 (2018)
31. Nguyen, P., Liu, T., Prasad, G., Han, B.: Weakly supervised action localization by sparse temporal pooling network. In: Proceedings of the IEEE Conference on Computer Vision and Pattern Recognition, pp. 6752–6761 (2018)
32. Novotny, D., Albanie, S., Larlus, D., Vedaldi, A.: Self-supervised learning of geometrically stable features through probabilistic introspection. In: Computer Vision and Pattern Recognition, pp. 3637–3645 (2018)
33. Owens, A., Wu, J., McDermott, J.H., Freeman, W.T., Torralba, A.: Ambient sound provides supervision for visual learning. In: Leibe, B., Matas, J., Sebe, N., Welling, M. (eds.) ECCV 2016. LNCS, vol. 9905, pp. 801–816. Springer, Cham (2016). https://doi.org/10.1007/978-3-319-46448-0_48
34. Paul, S., Roy, S., Roy-Chowdhury, A.K.: W-TALC: weakly-supervised temporal activity localization and classification. In: Proceedings of the European Conference on Computer Vision (ECCV), pp. 563–579 (2018)
35. Peng, X., Schmid, C.: Multi-region two-stream R-CNN for action detection. In: Leibe, B., Matas, J., Sebe, N., Welling, M. (eds.) ECCV 2016. LNCS, vol. 9908, pp. 744–759. Springer, Cham (2016). https://doi.org/10.1007/978-3-319-46493-0_45
36. Pinheiro, P.O., Collobert, R.: From image-level to pixel-level labeling with convolutional networks. In: Computer Vision and Pattern Recognition, pp. 1713–1721 (2015)
37. Ren, S., He, K., Girshick, R., Sun, J.: Faster R-CNN: towards real-time object detection with region proposal networks. In: Advances in Neural Information Processing Systems, pp. 91–99 (2015)
38. Saha, S., Singh, G., Sapienza, M., Torr, P.H., Cuzzolin, F.: Deep learning for detecting multiple space-time action tubes in videos. In: BMVC (2016)
39. Sigurdsson, G.A., Russakovsky, O., Gupta, A.: What actions are needed for understanding human actions in videos? In: Proceedings of the IEEE International Conference on Computer Vision, pp. 2137–2146 (2017)
40. Singh, G., Saha, S., Cuzzolin, F.: TraMNet - transition matrix network for efficient action tube proposals. In: Jawahar, C.V., Li, H., Mori, G., Schindler, K. (eds.) ACCV 2018. LNCS, vol. 11366, pp. 420–437. Springer, Cham (2019). https://doi.org/10.1007/978-3-030-20876-9_27
41. Singh, G., Saha, S., Sapienza, M., Torr, P.H., Cuzzolin, F.: Online real-time multiple spatiotemporal action localisation and prediction. In: International Conference on Computer Vision, pp. 3637–3646 (2017)
42. Singh, K.K., Lee, Y.J.: Hide-and-seek: forcing a network to be meticulous for weakly-supervised object and action localization. In: 2017 IEEE International Conference on Computer Vision (ICCV), pp. 3544–3553. IEEE (2017)
43. Soomro, K., Zamir, A.R., Shah, M.: UCF101: a dataset of 101 human actions classes from videos in the wild. arXiv preprint arXiv:1212.0402 (2012)
44. Sun, C., Myers, A., Vondrick, C., Murphy, K., Schmid, C.: VideoBERT: a joint model for video and language representation learning. In: International Conference on Computer Vision, pp. 7464–7473 (2019)

45. Sun, C., Paluri, M., Collobert, R., Nevatia, R., Bourdev, L.: ProNet: learning to propose object-specific boxes for cascaded neural networks. In: The IEEE Conference on Computer Vision and Pattern Recognition (CVPR), June 2016
46. Sun, C., Shrivastava, A., Vondrick, C., Murphy, K., Sukthankar, R., Schmid, C.: Actor-centric relation network. In: Proceedings of the European Conference on Computer Vision (ECCV), pp. 318–334 (2018)
47. Van Gemert, J.C., Jain, M., Gati, E., Snoek, C.G., et al.: APT: action localization proposals from dense trajectories. In: BMVC, vol. 2, p. 4 (2015)
48. Wang, L., Xiong, Y., Lin, D., Van Gool, L.: UntrimmedNets for weakly supervised action recognition and detection. In: Proceedings of the IEEE conference on Computer Vision and Pattern Recognition, pp. 4325–4334 (2017)
49. Wang, X., Girshick, R., Gupta, A., He, K.: Non-local neural networks. In: Proceedings of the IEEE Conference on Computer Vision and Pattern Recognition, pp. 7794–7803 (2018)
50. Weinzaepfel, P., Martin, X., Schmid, C.: Towards weakly-supervised action localization, vol. 2. arXiv preprint arXiv:1605.05197 (2016)
51. Zhao, H., Gan, C., Rouditchenko, A., Vondrick, C., McDermott, J., Torralba, A.: The sound of pixels. In: Proceedings of the European Conference on Computer Vision (ECCV), pp. 570–586 (2018)
52. Zhao, J., Snoek, C.G.: Dance with flow: two-in-one stream action detection. In: Proceedings of the IEEE Conference on Computer Vision and Pattern Recognition, pp. 9935–9944 (2019)

Selecting Relevant Features from a Multi-domain Representation for Few-Shot Classification

Nikita Dvornik[1]([✉]), Cordelia Schmid[2], and Julien Mairal[1]

[1] Univ. Grenoble Alpes, Inria, CNRS, Grenoble INP, LJK, 38000 Grenoble, France
{nikita.dvornik,cordelia.schmid}@inria.fr
[2] Inria, École normale supérieure, CNRS, PSL Research Univ., 75005 Paris, France
julien.mairal@inria.fr

Abstract. Popular approaches for few-shot classification consist of first learning a generic data representation based on a large annotated dataset, before adapting the representation to new classes given only a few labeled samples. In this work, we propose a new strategy based on feature selection, which is both simpler and more effective than previous feature adaptation approaches. First, we obtain a multi-domain representation by training a set of semantically different feature extractors. Then, given a few-shot learning task, we use our multi-domain feature bank to automatically select the most relevant representations. We show that a simple non-parametric classifier built on top of such features produces high accuracy and generalizes to domains never seen during training, leading to state-of-the-art results on MetaDataset and improved accuracy on *mini*-ImageNet.

Keywords: Image recognition · Few-shot learning · Feature selection

1 Introduction

Convolutional neural networks [21] (CNNs) have become a classical tool for modeling visual data and are commonly used in many computer vision tasks such as image classification [19], object detection [8,24,36], or semantic segmentation [8,25,38]. One key of the success of these approaches relies on massively labeled datasets such as ImageNet [39] or COCO [23]. Unfortunately, annotating data at this scale is expensive and not always feasible, depending on the task at hand. Improving the generalization capabilities of deep neural networks and removing the need for huge sets of annotations is thus of utmost importance.

This ambitious challenge may be addressed from different perspectives, such as large-scale unsupervised learning [3], self-supervised learning [6,13], or by

Electronic supplementary material The online version of this chapter (https://doi.org/10.1007/978-3-030-58607-2_45) contains supplementary material, which is available to authorized users.

ⓒ Springer Nature Switzerland AG 2020
A. Vedaldi et al. (Eds.): ECCV 2020, LNCS 12355, pp. 769–786, 2020.
https://doi.org/10.1007/978-3-030-58607-2_45

developing regularization techniques dedicated to deep networks [1,51]. An alternative solution is to use data that has been previously annotated for a different task than the one considered, for which only a few annotated samples may be available. This approach is particularly useful if the additional data is related to the new task [52,54], which is unfortunately not known beforehand. How to use effectively this additional data is then an important subject of ongoing research [9,46,54]. In this paper, we propose to use a multi-domain image representation, *i.e.*, an exhaustive set of semantically different features. Then, by automatically selecting only relevant feature subsets from the multi-domain representation, we show how to successfully solve a large variety of target tasks (Fig. 1).

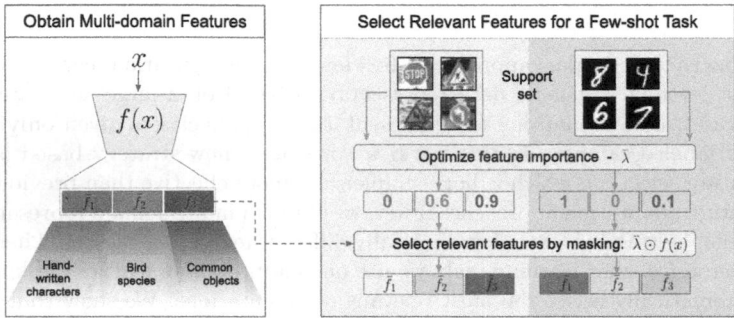

Fig. 1. Illustration of our approach. (Left) First, we obtain a multi-domain feature representation, consisting of feature blocks with different semantics. (Right) Given a few-shot task, we select only the relevant feature blocks from the multi-domain representation, by optimizing masking parameters λ on the support set.

Specifically, we are interested in few-shot classification, where a visual model is first trained from scratch, *i.e.* starting from randomly initialized weights, using a large annotated corpus. Then, we evaluate its ability to transfer the knowledge to new classes, for which only very few annotated samples are provided. Simply fine-tuning a convolutional neural network on a new classification task has been shown to perform poorly [9]. This has motivated the community to develop dedicated techniques, allowing effective adaptation with few samples.

Few-shot classification methods typically operate in two stages, consisting of first pre-training a general feature extractor and then building an adaptation mechanism. A common way to proceed is based on meta-learning [9,33, 42,44,45,47], which is a principle to learn how to adapt to new learning problems. That is, a parametric adaptation module (typically, a neural network) is trained to produce a classifier for new categories, given only a few annotated samples [12,32,40]. To achieve this goal, the large training corpus is split into smaller few-shot classification problems [9,33,47], that are used to train the adaptation mechanism. Training in such episodic fashion is advocated to alleviate overfitting and improve generalization [9,33,47]. However, a more recent work [4] demonstrates that using large training set to train the adapter is not necessary, *i.e.* a linear classifier with similar accuracy can be trained directly from new samples, on top of a fixed feature extractor. Finally, it has been shown that adaptation is not necessary at all [7]; using a non-parametric prototypical classifier [28] combined with a properly regularized feature extractor can achieve better accuracy than recent meta-learning baselines [7,41]. These results suggest that on standard few-shot learning benchmarks [33,35], the little amount of samples in a few-shot task is not enough to learn a meaningful adaptation strategy.

To address the shortcomings of existing few-shot benchmarks, the authors of [46] have proposed MetaDataset, which evaluates the ability to learn across different visual domains and to generalize to new data distributions at test time, given few annotated samples. While methods based solely on pre-trained feature extractors [41] can achieve good results only on test datasets that are similar to the training ones, the adaptation technique [37] performs well across test domains. The method not only predicts a new few-shot classifier but also adapts the filters of a feature extractor, given an input task. The results thus suggest that feature adaptation may be in fact useful to achieve better generalization.

In contrast to these earlier approaches, we show that feature adaptation can be replaced by a simple feature selection mechanism, leading to better results in the cross-domain setup of [46]. More precisely, we propose to leverage a multi-domain representation – a large set of semantically different features that captures different modalities of a training set. Rather than adapting existing features to a new few-shot task, we propose to select features from the multi-domain representation. We call our approach SUR which stands for Selecting from Universal Representations. To be more clear, we say universal because SUR could be applied not only to multi-domain representations, but to any set of representations that are semantically different. In contrast to standard adaptation modules [30,37,46] learned on the training set, selection is performed directly on new few-shot tasks using gradient descent. Approaching few-shot learning with SUR has several advantages over classical adaptation techniques. First, it is simple by nature, *i.e.* selecting features from a fixed set is an easier problem than learning a feature transformation, especially when few annotated images are available. Second, learning an adaptation module on the meta-training set is likely to generalize only to similar domains. In contrast, the selection step in our approach is decoupled from meta-training, thus, it works equally well for any new domain. Finally, we show that our approach achieves better results than current state-of-the-art methods on popular few-shot learning benchmarks. In summary, this work makes the following contributions:

– We propose to tackle few-shot classification by selecting relevant features from a multi-domain representation. While multi-domain representations can be built by training several feature extractors or using a single neural network, the selection procedure is implemented with gradient descent.

- We show that our method outperforms existing approaches in in-domain and cross-domain few-shot learning and sets new state-of-the-art result on Meta-Dataset [46] and improves accuracy on *mini*-ImageNet [33].

Our implementation is available at https://github.com/dvornikita/SUR.

2   Related Work

In this section, we now present previous work on few-shot classification and multi-domain representations, which is a term first introduced in [2].

Few-Shot Classification. Typical few-shot classification problems consist of two parts called meta-training and meta-testing [4]. During the meta-training stage, one is given a large-enough annotated dataset, which is used to train a predictive model. During meta-testing, novel categories are provided along with few annotated examples. The goal is to evaluate the ability of the predictive model to adapt and perform well on these new classes.

Typical few-shot learning algorithms [11,12,32] first pre-train the feature extractor by supervised learning on the meta-training set. Then, they use meta-learning [42,45] to train an adaptation mechanism. For example, in [12,32], adaptation consists of predicting the weights of a classifier for new categories, given a small few-shot training set. The work of [30] goes beyond the adaptation of a single layer on top of a fixed feature extractor, and additionally generates FiLM [31] layers that modify convolutional layers. Alternatively, the work of [4] proposes to train a linear classifier on top of the features directly from few samples from new categories. In the same line of work, [22] performs implanting, *i.e.* learning new convolutional filters within the existing CNN layers.

Other methods do not perform adaptation at all. It has been shown in [7,22,41] that training a regularized CNN for classification on the meta-training set and using these features directly with a nearest centroid classifier produces state-of-the-art few-shot accuracy. To obtain a robust feature extractor, [7] distills an ensemble of networks into a single extractor to obtain low-variance features.

Finally, the methods [37,41] are the most relevant to our work as they also tackle the problem of cross-domain few-shot classification [46]. In [37], the authors propose to adapt each hidden layer of a feature extractor for a new task. They first obtain a task embedding and use conditional neural process [10] to generate parameters of modulation FiLM [31] layers, as well as weights of a classifier for new categories. An adaptation-free method [41] instead trains a CNN on ImageNet, while optimizing for high validation accuracy on other datasets, using hyper-parameter search. When tested on domains similar to ImageNet, the method demonstrates the highest accuracy, however, it is outperformed by adaptation-based methods when tested on other data distributions [41].

Multi-domain Representations. A multi-domain representation (introduced as "universal representation" in [2]) refers to an image representation that works equally well for a large number of visual domains. The simplest way to obtain a multi-domain representation is to train a separate feature extractor for each visual domain and use only the appropriate one at test time. To reduce the computational footprint, [2] investigates if a single CNN can be useful to perform image classification on very different domains. To achieve this goal, the authors propose to share most of the parameters between domains during training and have a small set of parameters that are domain-specific. Such adaptive feature sharing is implemented using conditional batch normalization [16], *i.e.* there is a separate set of batch-norm parameters for every domain. The work of [34] extends the idea of domain-specific computations in a single network and proposes universal parametric network families, which consist of two parts: 1) a CNN feature extractor with universal parameters shared across all domains, and 2) domain-specific modules trained on top of universal weights to maximize the performance on that domain. It has been found important [34] to adapt both shallow and deep layers in a neural network in order to successfully solve multiple visual domains. We use the method of this paper in our work when training a parametric network family to produce a multi-domain representation. In contrast, instead of parallel adapters, in this work, we use much simpler FiLM layers for domain-specific computations. Importantly, parametric networks families [34] and FiLM [31] adapters only provide a way to efficiently compute multi-domain representation; they are not directly useful for few-shot learning. However, using our SUR strategy on this representation produces a useful set of features leading to state-of-the-art results in few-shot learning.

3   Proposed Approach

We now present our approach for few-shot learning, starting with preliminaries.

3.1   Few-Shot Classification with Nearest Centroid Classifier

The goal of few-shot classification is to produce a model which, given a new learning task and a few labeled examples, is able to generalize to unseen examples for that task. In other words, the model learns from a small training set $S = \{(x_i, y_i)\}_{i=1}^{n_S}$, called a *support set*, and is evaluated on a held-out test set $Q = \{(x_j^*, y_j^*)\}_{j=1}^{n_Q}$, called a *query set*. The (x_i, y_i)'s represent image-label pairs while the pair (S, Q) represents the few-shot task. To fulfill this objective, the problem is addressed in two steps. During the meta-training stage, a learning algorithm receives a large dataset D_b, where it must learn a general feature extractor $f(\cdot)$. During the meta-testing stage, one is given a target dataset D_t, used to repeatedly sample few-shot tasks (S, Q). Importantly, meta-training (D_b) and meta-testing (D_t) datasets have no categories in common.

During the meta-testing stage, we use feature representation $f(\cdot)$ to build a nearest centroid classifier (NCC), similar to [28,44]. Given a support set S, for each category present in this set, we build a class centroid by averaging image representations belonging to this category:

$$c_j = \frac{1}{|\mathcal{S}_j|} \sum_{i \in \mathcal{S}_j} f(x_i), \quad \mathcal{S}_j = \{k : y_k = j\}, \quad j = 1, ..., C. \tag{1}$$

To classify a sample x, we choose a distance function $d(f(x), c_j)$ to be negative cosine similarity, as in [4,13], and assign the sample to the closest centroid c_j.

3.2   Method

With the NCC classifier defined above, we may now formally define the concept of multi-domain representation and the procedure for selecting relevant features. Typically, the meta-training set is used to train a set of K feature extractors $\{f_i(\cdot)\}_{i=1}^{K}$ that form a multi-domain set of features. Each feature extractor maps an input image x into a d-dimensional representation $f_i(x) \in \mathbb{R}^d$. These features should capture different types of semantics and can be obtained in various manners, as detailed in Sect. 3.3.

Parametric Multi-domain Representations. One way to transform a multi-domain set of features into a vectorized multi-domain representation $f(x)$ is, by concatenating all image representations from this set (with or without $l2$-normalization). As we show in the experimental section, directly using such $f(x)$ for classification with NCC does not work well as many irrelevant features for a new task are present in the representation. Therefore, we are interested in implementing a selection mechanism. In order to do so, we define a selection operation $\odot$ as follows, given a vector λ in $\mathbb{R}^K$:

$$\lambda \odot f(x) = \lambda \cdot \begin{bmatrix} \hat{f}_1(x) \\ \vdots \\ \hat{f}_K(x) \end{bmatrix} = \begin{bmatrix} \lambda_1 \cdot \hat{f}_1(x) \\ \vdots \\ \lambda_K \cdot \hat{f}_K(x) \end{bmatrix} = f_\lambda(x), \tag{2}$$

where $\hat{f}_i(x)$ is simply $f_i(x)$ after ℓ_2-normalization. We call $f_\lambda(x) \in \mathbb{R}^{K \cdot d}$ a parametrized multi-domain representation, as it contains information from the whole multi-domain set but the exact representation depends on the selection parameters λ. Using this mechanism, it is possible to select various combinations of features from the multi-domain representation by setting more than one λ_i to non-zero values.

Finding Optimal Selection Parameters. Feature selection is performed during meta-testing by optimizing a probabilistic model, leading to optimal parameters λ, given a support set $\mathcal{S} = \{(x_i, y_i)\}_{i=1}^{n_S}$ of a new task.

Specifically, we consider the NCC classifier from Sect. 3.1, using $f_\lambda(x)$ instead of $f(x)$, and introduce the likelihood function

$$p(y = l|x) = \frac{\exp(-d(f_\lambda(x), c_l))}{\sum_{j=1}^{n_S} \exp(-d(f_\lambda(x), c_j))}. \tag{3}$$

Our goal is then to find optimal parameters λ that maximize the likelihood on the support set, which is equivalent to minimizing the negative log-likelihood:

$$L(\lambda) = \frac{1}{n_S} \sum_{i=1}^{n_S} \left[-\log(p(y = y_i | x_i)) \right] \tag{4}$$

$$= \frac{1}{n_S} \sum_{i=1}^{n_S} \left[\log \sum_{j=1}^{C} \exp(\cos(f_\lambda(x_i), c_j)) - \cos(f_\lambda(x_i), c_{y_i}) \right]. \tag{5}$$

This objective is similar to the one of [49] and encourages large lambda values to be assigned to representations where intra-class similarity is high while the inter-class similarity is low. In practice, we optimize the objective by performing several steps of gradient descent. The proposed procedure is what we call SUR.

It is worth noting that nearest centroid classifier is a simple non-parametric model with limited capacity, which only stores a single vector to describe a class. Such limited capacity becomes an advantage when only a few annotated samples are available, as it effectively prevents overfitting. When training and testing across similar domains, SUR is able to select from the multi-domain representation the features optimized for each visual domain. When the target domain distribution does not match any of the train distribution, it is nevertheless able to adapt a few parameters λ to the target distribution. In such a sense, our method performs a limited form of adaptation, with few parameters only, which is reasonable given that the target task has only a small number of annotated samples.

Sparsity in Selection. As said above, our selection algorithm is a form of weak adaptation, where parameters λ are adjusted to optimize image representation, given an input task. Selection parameters λ_i are constrained to be in $[0, 1]$. However, as we show in the experimental section, the resulting λ vector is sparse in practice, with many entries equal to 0 or 1. This empirical behavior suggests that our algorithm indeed performs selection of relevant features – a simple and robust form of adaptation. To promote further sparsity, one may use an additional sparsity-inducing penalty such as ℓ_1 during the optimization [26]; however, our experiments show that doing so is not necessary to achieve good results.

3.3 Obtaining Multi-domain Representations

In this section, we explain how to obtain a multi-Domain set of feature extractors $\{f_i(\cdot)\}_i^K$ when one or multiple domains are available for training. Three variants are used in this paper, which are illustrated in Fig. 2.

Multiple Training Domains. In the case of multiple training domains, we assume that K different datasets (including ImageNet [39]) are available for

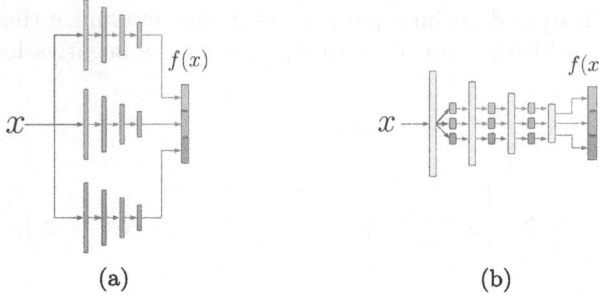

Fig. 2. Different ways of obtaining a multi-domain representation. (a) A single image is embedded with multiple domain-specific networks. (b) Using a parametric network family [34] to obtain multi-domain representations. Here, the gray blocks correspond to shared computations and colored blocks correspond to domain-specific FiLM [31] layers. Gray blocks and arrows indicate shared layers and computation flow respectively, while domain specific ones are shown in corresponding colors. Best viewed in color.

building a multi-domain representation. We start with a straightforward solution and train a feature extractor $f_i(\cdot)$ for each visual domain independently. That results in a desired multi-domain set $\{f_i(\cdot)\}_i^K$. A multi-domain representation is then computed by concatenating the output set, as illustrated in Fig. 2(a).

To compute multi-domain representations with a single network, we use parametric network families proposed in [34]. We follow the original paper and first train a general feature extractor – ResNet – using our training split of ImageNet, and then freeze the network's weights. For each of the $K - 1$ remaining datasets, task-specific parameters are learned by minimizing the corresponding training loss. We use FiLM [31] layers as domain-specific modules and insert them after each batch-norm layer in the ResNet. We choose to use FiLM layers over originally proposed parallel adapters [34] because FiLM is much simpler, i.e. performs channel-wise affine transformation, and contain much fewer parameters. This helps to avoid overfitting on small datasets. In summary, each of the K datasets has its own set of FiLM layers and the base ResNet with a set of domain-specific FiLM layers constitutes the multi-domain set of extractors $\{f_i(\cdot)\}_i^K$. To compute the features of i-th domain $f_i(x)$, we forward the input image x trough the ResNet where all the intermediate activations are modulated with the FiLM layers trained on this domain, as illustrated in Fig. 2(b). Using parametric network families instead of K separate networks to obtain a multi-domain representation reduces the number of stored parameters roughly in K times. However, to be actually useful for few-shot learning, such representation must be processed by our SUR approach, as described in Sect. 3.2

4   Experiments

We now present the experiments to analyze the performance of our selection strategy, starting with implementation details.

4.1   Datasets and Experiments Details

Datasets. We use *mini*-ImageNet [33] and Meta-Dataset [46] to evaluate the proposed approach. The *mini*-ImageNet [33] dataset consists of 100 categories (64 for training, 16 for validation, 20 for testing) from the original ImageNet [39] dataset, with 600 images per class. Since all the categories come from the same dataset, we use *mini*-ImageNet to evaluate our feature selection strategy in single-domain few-shot learning. During testing on *mini*-ImageNet, we measure performance over tasks where only 1 or 5 images (shots) per category are given for adaptation and the number of classes in a task is fixed to 5, *i.e.* 5-way classification. All images are resized to 84 × 84, as suggested originally by [33].

Meta-Dataset [46] is much larger than previous few-shot learning benchmarks and it is actually a collection of multiple datasets with different data distributions. It includes ImageNet [39], Omniglot [20], Aircraft [27], CU-Birds [48], Describable Textures [5], Quick Draw [17], Fungi [43], VGG-Flower [29], Traffic Sign [15] and MSCOCO [23]. A short description of each dataset is contained in Appendix. Traffic Sign and MSCOCO datasets are reserved for testing only, while all other datasets have their corresponding train, val and test splits. To better study out-of-training-domain behavior, we follow [37] and add 3 more testing datasets, namely MNIST [50] CIFAR10 [18], and CIFAR100 [18]. Here, the number of shots and ways is not fixed and varies from one few-shot task to another. As originally suggested [46], all images are resized to 84 × 84 resolution.

Implementation Details. When experimenting with Meta-Dataset, we follow [37] and use ResNet18 [14] as feature extractor. The training detail for each dataset are described in Appendix. To report test results on Meta-Dataset, we perform an independent evaluation for each of the 10 provided datasets, plus for 3 extra datasets as suggested by [37]. We follow [46] and sample 600 tasks for evaluation on each dataset within Meta-Dataset.

When experimenting with *mini*-ImageNet, we follow popular works [11, 22, 30] and use ResNet12 [30] as a feature extractor. Corresponding training details are reported in Appendix. During testing, we use *mini*-ImageNet's test set to sample 1000 5-way classification tasks. We evaluate scenarios where only 1 or 5 examples (shots) of each category is provided for training and 15 for evaluation. On both datasets, during meta-training, we use cosine classifier with learnable softmax temperature [4]. During testing, classes and corresponding train/test examples are sampled at random. For all our experiments, we report the mean accuracy (in %) over all test tasks with 95% confidence interval.

Feature Selection. To perform feature selection from the multi-domain representation we optimize the selection parameter λ (defined in Eq. 2) to minimize NCC classification loss (Eq. 4) on the support set. Each individual scalar weight λ_i is kept between 0 and 1 using sigmoid function, *i.e.* $\lambda_i = \text{sigmoid}(\alpha_i)$. All α_i are initialized with zeros. We optimize the parameters α_i using gradient descent for 40 iterations. At each iteration, we use the whole support set to build nearest centroid classifier, and then we use the same set of examples to compute the loss, given by Eq. 4. Then, we compute gradients w.r.t $[\alpha_1, ..., \alpha_K]$ and use Adadelta [53] optimizer with learning rate 10^2 to perform parameter updates.

4.2 Cross-domain Few-Shot Classification

In this section, we evaluate the ability of SUR to handle different visual domains in MetaDataset [46]. First, we motivate the use of multi-domain representations and show the importance of feature selection. Then, we evaluate the proposed strategy against important baselines and state-of-the-art few-shot algorithms.

Table 1. Performance of feature extractors trained with different datasets on Meta-Dataset. The first column indicates the dataset in Meta-Dataset, the first row gives the dataset, used to pre-train the feature extractor. The body of the table shows feature extractors' accuracy on few-shot classification, when applied with NCC. The average accuracy and 95% confidence intervals computed over 600 few-shot tasks. The numbers in bold indicate that a method has the best accuracy per dataset.

Dataset	Features trained on:							
	ImageNet	Omniglot	Aircraft	Birds	Textures	Quick draw	Fungi	VGG flower
ImageNet	**56.3 ± 1.0**	18.5 ± 0.7	21.5 ± 0.8	23.9 ± 0.8	26.1 ± 0.8	23.1 ± 0.8	31.2 ± 0.8	24.3 ± 0.8
Omniglot	67.5 ± 1.2	**92.4 ± 0.5**	55.2 ± 1.3	59.5 ± 1.3	48.4 ± 1.3	80.0 ± 0.9	59.7 ± 1.2	54.2 ± 1.4
Aircraft	50.4 ± 0.9	17.0 ± 0.5	**85.4 ± 0.5**	30.9 ± 0.7	23.9 ± 0.6	25.2 ± 0.6	33.7 ± 0.8	25.1 ± 0.6
Birds	**71.7 ± 0.8**	13.7 ± 0.6	18.0 ± 0.7	64.7 ± 0.9	20.2 ± 0.7	17.9 ± 0.6	40.7 ± 0.9	24.5 ± 0.8
Textures	**70.2 ± 0.7**	30.6 ± 0.6	33.1 ± 0.6	37.1 ± 0.6	57.3 ± 0.7	38.5 ± 0.7	50.4 ± 0.7	45.4 ± 0.8
Quick draw	52.4 ± 1.0	50.3 ± 1.0	36.0 ± 1.0	38.8 ± 1.0	35.7 ± 0.9	**80.7 ± 0.6**	35.4 ± 1.0	39.4 ± 1.0
Fungi	39.1 ± 1.0	10.5 ± 0.5	14.0 ± 0.6	21.2 ± 0.7	15.5 ± 0.7	13.0 ± 0.6	**62.7 ± 0.9**	22.6 ± 0.8
VGG flower	**84.3 ± 0.7**	24.8 ± 0.7	44.6 ± 0.8	57.2 ± 0.8	42.3 ± 0.8	36.9 ± 0.8	76.1 ± 0.8	77.1 ± 0.7
Traffic sign	**63.1 ± 0.8**	44.0 ± 0.9	57.7 ± 0.8	61.7 ± 0.8	55.2 ± 0.8	50.2 ± 0.8	53.5 ± 0.8	57.9 ± 0.8
MSCOCO	**52.8 ± 1.0**	15.1 ± 0.7	21.2 ± 0.8	22.5 ± 0.8	25.8 ± 0.9	19.9 ± 0.7	29.3 ± 0.9	27.3 ± 0.9
MNIST	77.2 ± 0.7	**90.9 ± 0.5**	69.5 ± 0.7	74.2 ± 0.7	55.9 ± 0.8	86.2 ± 0.6	69.4 ± 0.7	66.9 ± 0.7
CIFAR 10	**66.3 ± 0.8**	33.0 ± 0.7	37.8 ± 0.7	39.3 ± 0.7	39.2 ± 0.7	36.1 ± 0.7	33.6 ± 0.7	38.2 ± 0.7
CIFAR 100	**55.7 ± 1.0**	14.9 ± 0.7	22.5 ± 0.8	25.6 ± 0.8	24.1 ± 0.8	21.4 ± 0.7	22.2 ± 0.8	26.5 ± 0.9

Evaluating Domain-Specific Feature Extractors. MetaDataset includes 8 datasets for training, *i.e.* ImageNet, Omniglot, Aircraft, CU-Birds, Textures, Quick Draw, Fungi, VGG-Flower. We treat each dataset as a separate visual domain and obtain a multi-domain set of features by training 8 domain-specific feature extractors, *i.e.* a separate ResNet18 for each dataset. Each extractor is trained independently, with its own training schedule specified in Appendix. We test the performance of each feature extractor (with NCC) on every test dataset specified in Sect. 4.1, and report the results in Table 1. Among the 8 datasets seen during training, 5 datasets are better solved with their own features, while 3 other datasets benefit more from ImageNet features. In general, ImageNet features suits 8 out of 13 test datasets best, while 5 others require a different feature extractor for better accuracy. Such results suggest that none of the domain-specific feature extractors alone can perform equally well on all the datasets simultaneously. However, using the whole multi-domain feature set to select appropriate representations would lead to superior accuracy.

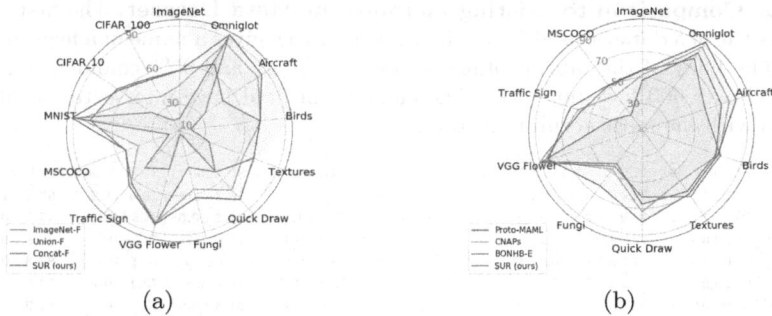

(a)   (b)

Fig. 3. Performance of different few-shot methods on MetaDataset. (a) Comparison of our selection strategy to baselines. The chart is generated from the table in Appendix. (b) Comparing our selection strategy to state-of-the-art few-shot learning methods. The chart is generated from Table 2. The axes indicate the accuracy of methods on a particular dataset. Each color corresponds to a different method.

Evaluating Feature Selection. We now employ SUR – our strategy for feature selection – as described in Sect. 3.2. A parametrized multi-domain representation is obtained from a multi-domain feature set by concatenation. It is then multiplied by the selection parameters λ, that are being optimized for each new few-shot task, following Sect. 4.1. We ran this procedure on all 13 testing datasets and report the results in Fig. 3(a). We compare our method with the following baselines: a) using a single feature extractor pre-trained on ImageNet split of MetaDataset (denoted "ImageNet-F"), b) using a single feature extractor pre-trained on the union of 8 training splits in MetaDataset (denoted "Union-F") and c) manually setting all $\lambda_i = 1$, which corresponds to simple concatenation and (denoted "Concat-F"). It is clear that the features provided by SUR have much better performance than any of the baselines on seen and unseen domains.

Comparison to Other Approaches. We now compare SUR against state-of-the-art few-shot methods and report the results in Table 2. The results on MNIST, CIFAR 10 and CIFAR 100 datasets are missing for most of the approaches because those numbers were not reported in the corresponding original papers. Comparison to the best-performing methods on common datasets is summarized in Fig. 3(b). We see that SUR demonstrated state-of-the-art results on 9 out of 13 datasets. BOHNB-E [41] outperforms our approach on Birds, Textures and VGG Flowers datasets. This is not surprising since these are the only datasets that benefit from ImageNet features more than from their own (see Table 1); and BOHNB-E [41] is essentially an ensemble of multiple ImageNet-pretrained networks. When tested outside the training domain, SUR consistently outperforms CNAPs [37] – the state-of-the-art adaptation-based method. Moreover, SUR shows the best results on all 5 datasets never seen during training.

Table 2. Comparison to existing methods on Meta-Dataset. The first column indicates the of a dataset used for testing. The first row gives a name of a few-shot algorithm. The body of the table contains average accuracy and 95% confidence intervals computed over 600 few-shot tasks. The numbers in bold have intersecting confidence intervals with the most accurate method.

Test Dataset	ProtoNet [44]	MAML [9]	Proto-MAML [46]	CNAPs [37]	BOHB-E [41]	SUR (ours)	SUR-pf (ours)	SUR-merge (ours)
ImageNet	44.5 ± 1.1	32.4 ± 1.0	47.9 ± 1.1	52.3 ± 1.0	55.4 ± 1.1	**56.3 ± 1.1**	**56.4 ± 1.2**	**57.2 ± 1.1**
Omniglot	79.6 ± 1.1	71.9 ± 1.2	82.9 ± 0.9	88.4 ± 0.7	77.5 ± 1.1	**93.1 ± 0.5**	88.5 ± 0.8	**93.2 ± 0.8**
Aircraft	71.1 ± 0.9	52.8 ± 0.9	74.2 ± 0.8	80.5 ± 0.6	60.9 ± 0.9	85.4 ± 0.7	79.5 ± 0.8	**90.1 ± 0.8**
Birds	67.0 ± 1.0	47.2 ± 1.1	70.0 ± 1.0	72.2 ± 0.9	73.6 ± 0.8	71.4 ± 1.0	76.4 ± 0.9	**82.3 ± 0.8**
Textures	65.2 ± 0.8	56.7 ± 0.7	67.9 ± 0.8	58.3 ± 0.7	**72.8 ± 0.7**	71.5 ± 0.8	**73.1 ± 0.7**	**73.5 ± 0.7**
Quick Draw	65.9 ± 0.9	50.5 ± 1.2	66.6 ± 0.9	72.5 ± 0.8	61.2 ± 0.9	**81.3 ± 0.6**	75.7 ± 0.7	**81.9 ± 1.0**
Fungi	40.3 ± 1.1	21.0 ± 1.0	42.0 ± 1.1	47.4 ± 1.0	44.5 ± 1.1	63.1 ± 1.0	48.2 ± 0.9	**67.9 ± 0.9**
VGG Flower	86.9 ± 0.7	70.9 ± 1.0	88.5 ± 1.0	86.0 ± 0.5	**90.6 ± 0.6**	82.8 ± 0.7	**90.6 ± 0.5**	88.4 ± 0.9
Traffic Sign	46.5 ± 1.0	34.2 ± 1.3	34.2 ± 1.3	60.2 ± 0.9	57.5 ± 1.0	**70.4 ± 0.8**	65.1 ± 0.8	67.4 ± 0.8
MSCOCO	39.9 ± 1.1	24.1 ± 1.1	24.1 ± 1.1	42.6 ± 1.1	51.9 ± 1.0	**52.4 ± 1.1**	**52.1 ± 1.0**	51.3 ± 1.0
MNIST	–	–	–	92.7 ± 0.4	–	**94.3 ± 0.4**	93.2 ± 0.4	90.8 ± 0.5
CIFAR 10	–	–	–	61.5 ± 0.7	–	**66.8 ± 0.9**	**66.4 ± 0.8**	**66.6 ± 0.8**
CIFAR 100	–	–	–	50.1 ± 1.0	–	56.6 ± 1.0	57.1 ± 1.0	**58.3 ± 1.0**

Multi-domain Representations with Parametric Network Family. While it is clear that SUR outperforms other approaches, one may raise a concern that the improvement is due to the increased number of parameters, that is, we use 8 times more parameters than in a single ResNet18. To address this concern, we use a parametric network family [34] that has only 0.5% more parameters than a single ResNet18. As described in Sect. 3.3, the parametric network family uses ResNet18 as a base feature extractor and FiLM [31] layers for feature modulation. The total number of additional parameters, represented by all domain-specific FiLM layers is approximately 0.5% of ResNet18 parameters. For comparison, CNAPs adaptation mechanism is larger than ResNet18 itself. To train the parametric network family, we first train a base CNN feature extractor on ImageNet. Then, for each remaining training dataset, we learn a set of FiLM layers, as detailed in Sect. 3.3. To obtain a multi-domain feature set for an image, we run inference 8 times, each time with a set of FiLM layers, corresponding to a different domain, as described in Sect. 3.3. Once the multi-domain feature is built, our selection mechanism is applied to it as described before (see Sect. 4.1). The results of using SUR with a parametric network family are presented in Table 2 as "SUR-pf". The table suggests that the accuracy on datasets similar to ImageNet is improved suggesting that parameter sharing is beneficial in this case and confirms the original findings of [34]. However, the opposite is true for different visual domains such as `Fungi` and `QuickDraw`. It implies that to do well on very different domains, the base CNN filters must be learned on those datasets from scratch, and feature modulation is not competitive.

Reducing the Number of Training Domains. Another way to increase SUR's efficiency is to use fewer domains. This means training fewer domain-specific feature extractors, faster inference and selection. To achieve this goal, we merge similar datasets together into separate visual domains, and train a single

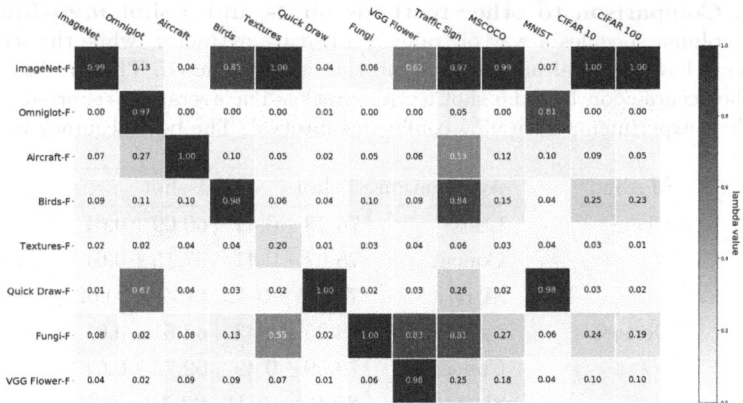

Fig. 4. Frequency of selected features depending on the test domain in Meta-Dataset. The top row indicates a testing dataset. The leftmost column a dataset the feature extractor has been trained on. A cells at location i, j reflects the average value of selection parameter λ_i assigned to the i-th feature extractor when tested on j-th dataset. The values are averaged over 600 few-shot test tasks for each dataset.

feature extractor for each such domain. Here, we take 8 datasets within Meta-Dataset and use them to form 3 following visual domains: [ImageNet, Aircraft, CU-Birds, Textures, VGG-Flower], [Omniglot, Quick Draw], [Fungi, ImageNet, Aircraft]. Then, we train 3 feature extractors, one for each such domain. These 3 feature extractors constitute the multi-domain feature set that is then used for selection with SUR, as described in Sect. 4.1. Doing so leads to a 2x speed-up in training and inference. Moreover, as Table 2 suggests, using 'SUR-merge' allows us to achieve better performance. We attribute this to learning better representation thanks to the increased number of relevant training samples per feature extractor.

4.3 Analysis of Feature Selection

In this section, we analyze optimized selection parameters λ when applying SUR on MetaDataset. Specifically, we perform the experiments from Sect. 4.2, where we select appropriate representations from a set, generated by 8 independent networks. For each test dataset, we then average selection vectors λ (after being optimized for 40 SGD steps) over 600 test tasks and present them in Fig. 4. First, we can see that the resulting λ are sparse, confirming that most of the time SUR actually select a few relevant features rather than takes all features with similar weights. Second, for a given test domain, SUR tends to select feature extractors trained on similar visual domains. Interestingly, for datasets coming from exactly the same distribution, *i.e.* CIFAR 10 and CIFAR 100, the averaged selection parameters are almost identical. All of the above suggests that the selection parameters could be interpreted as encoding the importance of features' visual domains for the test domain.

Table 3. Comparison to other methods on 1- and 5-shot *mini*-ImageNet.
The first column specifies a way of training a feature extractor, while the second column reflects how the final image representation is constructed. The two last columns display the accuracy on 1- and 5-shot learning tasks. The average is reported over 1 000 independent experiments with 95% confidence interval. The best accuracy is in bold.

Method	Aggregation	5-shot	1-shot
Cls	Last	76.28 ± 0.41	60.09 ± 0.61
	Concat	75.67 ± 0.41	57.15 ± 0.61
	SUR	$\mathbf{79.25 \pm 0.41}$	$\mathbf{60.79 \pm 0.62}$
DenseCls	Last	78.25 ± 0.43	62.61 ± 0.61
	Concat	79.59 ± 0.42	62.74 ± 0.61
	SUR	$\mathbf{80.04 \pm 0.41}$	$\mathbf{63.13 \pm 0.62}$
Robust20-dist	Last	81.06 ± 0.41	$\mathbf{64.14 \pm 0.62}$
	Concat	80.79 ± 0.41	63.22 ± 0.63
	SUR	$\mathbf{81.19 \pm 0.41}$	63.93 ± 0.63

4.4 Single-Domain Few-Shot Classification

In this section, we show that our feature selection strategy can be effective for various problems, not just for multi-domain few-shot learning. As an example, we demonstrate the benefits of SUR on few-shot classification, when training and testing classes come from the same dataset. Specifically, we show how to use our selection strategy in order to improve existing adaptation-free methods.

To test SUR in the single-domain scenario we use *mini*-ImageNet benchmark and solve 1-shot and 5-shot classification, as described in Sect. 4.1. When only one domain is available, obtaining a truly multi-domain set of features is not possible. Instead, we construct a proxy for such a set by using activations of network's intermediate layers. In this approximation, each intermediate layer provides features corresponding to some domain. Since different layers extract different features, selecting the relevant features should help on new tasks.

We experiment with 3 adaptation-free methods. They all use the last layer of ResNet12 as image features and build a NCC on top, however, they differ in a way the feature extractor is trained. The method we call "Cls", simply trains ResNet12 for classification on the meta-training set. The work of [22] performs dense classification instead (dubbed "DenseCls"). Finally, the "Robust20-dist" feature extractor [7] is obtained by ensemble distillation. For any method, the "multi-domain" feature set is formed from activations of the last 6 layers of the network. This is because the remaining intermediate layers do not contain useful for the final task information, as we show in Appendix.

Here, we explore different ways of exploiting such "multi-domain" set of features for few-shot classification and report the results in Table 3. We can see that using SUR to select appropriate for classification layers usually works better than using only the penultimate layer (dubbed "last") or concatenating all the features together (denoted as "concat"). For Robust20-dist, we observe only incremental improvements for 5-shot classification and negative improvement in 1-shot scenario. The penultimate layer in this network is probably the most useful for new problems and, if not selected, may hinder the final accuracy.

Acknowledgements. This work was funded in part by the French government under management of Agence Nationale de la Recherche as part of the "Investissements davenir" program, reference ANR-19-P3IA-0001 (PRAIRIE 3IA Institute) and reference ANR-19-P3IA-0003 (3IA MIAI@Grenoble Alpes), and was supported by the ERC grant number 714381 (SOLARIS) and a gift from Intel.

References

1. Bietti, A., Mialon, G., Chen, D., Mairal, J.: A kernel perspective for regularizing deep neural networks. In: International Conference on Machine Learning (ICML) (2019)
2. Bilen, H., Vedaldi, A.: Universal representations: the missing link between faces, text, planktons, and cat breeds. arXiv preprint arXiv:1701.07275 (2017)
3. Caron, M., Bojanowski, P., Joulin, A., Douze, M.: Deep clustering for unsupervised learning of visual features. In: Proceedings of the European Conference on Computer Vision (ECCV) (2018)
4. Chen, W.Y., Liu, Y.C., Kira, Z., Wang, Y.C., Huang, J.B.: A closer look at few-shot classification. In: International Conference on Learning Representations (ICLR) (2019)
5. Cimpoi, M., Maji, S., Kokkinos, I., Mohamed, S., Vedaldi, A.: Describing textures in the wild. In: Proceedings of the IEEE Conference on Computer Vision and Pattern Recognition (CVPR) (2014)
6. Doersch, C., Zisserman, A.: Multi-task self-supervised visual learning. In: Proceedings of the International Conference on Computer Vision (ICCV) (2017)
7. Dvornik, N., Schmid, C., Mairal, J.: Diversity with cooperation: ensemble methods for few-shot classification. In: Proceedings of the International Conference on Computer Vision (ICCV) (2019)
8. Dvornik, N., Shmelkov, K., Mairal, J., Schmid, C.: BlitzNet: a real-time deep network for scene understanding. In: Proceedings of the International Conference on Computer Vision (ICCV) (2017)
9. Finn, C., Abbeel, P., Levine, S.: Model-agnostic meta-learning for fast adaptation of deep networks. In: International Conference on Machine Learning (ICML) (2017)
10. Garnelo, M., et al.: Conditional neural processes. arXiv preprint arXiv:1807.01613 (2018)
11. Gidaris, S., Bursuc, A., Komodakis, N., Pérez, P., Cord, M.: Boosting few-shot visual learning with self-supervision. In: Proceedings of the International Conference on Computer Vision (ICCV) (2019)
12. Gidaris, S., Komodakis, N.: Dynamic few-shot visual learning without forgetting. In: Proceedings of the IEEE Conference on Computer Vision and Pattern Recognition (CVPR) (2018)
13. Gidaris, S., Singh, P., Komodakis, N.: Unsupervised representation learning by predicting image rotations. In: International Conference on Learning Representations (ICLR) (2018)

14. He, K., Zhang, X., Ren, S., Sun, J.: Deep residual learning for image recognition. In: Proceedings of the IEEE Conference on Computer Vision and Pattern Recognition (CVPR) (2016)
15. Houben, S., Stallkamp, J., Salmen, J., Schlipsing, M., Igel, C.: Detection of traffic signs in real-world images: the German traffic sign detection benchmark. In: International Joint Conference on Neural Networks (IJCNN) (2013)
16. Ioffe, S., Szegedy, C.: Batch normalization: Accelerating deep network training by reducing internal covariate shift (2015). International Conference on Machine Learning (ICML)
17. Maji, S., Rahtu, E., Kannala, J., Blaschko, M., Vedaldi, A.: Fine-grained visual classification of aircraft (2016). quickdraw.withgoogle.com
18. Krizhevsky, A., Hinton, G., et al.: Learning multiple layers of features from tiny images (2009)
19. Krizhevsky, A., Sutskever, I., Hinton, G.E.: ImageNet classification with deep convolutional neural networks. In: Advances in Neural Information Processing Systems (NeurIPS) (2012)
20. Lake, B.M., Salakhutdinov, R., Tenenbaum, J.B.: Human-level concept learning through probabilistic program induction. Science **350**, 1332–1338 (2015)
21. LeCun, Y., et al.: Backpropagation applied to handwritten zip code recognition. Neural Comput. **1**, 541–551 (1989)
22. Lifchitz, Y., Avrithis, Y., Picard, S., Bursuc, A.: Dense classification and implanting for few-shot learning. In: Proceedings of the IEEE Conference on Computer Vision and Pattern Recognition (CVPR) (2019)
23. Lin, T.-Y., et al.: Microsoft COCO: common objects in context. In: Fleet, D., Pajdla, T., Schiele, B., Tuytelaars, T. (eds.) ECCV 2014. LNCS, vol. 8693, pp. 740–755. Springer, Cham (2014). https://doi.org/10.1007/978-3-319-10602-1_48
24. Liu, W., et al.: SSD: single shot multibox detector. In: Leibe, B., Matas, J., Sebe, N., Welling, M. (eds.) ECCV 2016. LNCS, vol. 9905, pp. 21–37. Springer, Cham (2016). https://doi.org/10.1007/978-3-319-46448-0_2
25. Long, J., Shelhamer, E., Darrell, T.: Fully convolutional networks for semantic segmentation. In: Proceedings of the IEEE Conference on Computer Vision and Pattern Recognition (CVPR) (2015)
26. Mairal, J., Bach, F., Ponce, J., et al.: Sparse modeling for image and vision processing. Foundations and Trends® in Computer Graphics and Vision (2014)
27. Maji, S., Kannala, J., Rahtu, E., Blaschko, M., Vedaldi, A.: Fine-grained visual classification of aircraft. Technical report (2013)
28. Mensink, T., Verbeek, J., Perronnin, F., Csurka, G.: Distance-based image classification: generalizing to new classes at near-zero cost. IEEE Trans. Pattern Anal. Mach. Intell. (PAMI) (2013)
29. Nilsback, M.E., Zisserman, A.: Automated flower classification over a large number of classes. In: Sixth Indian Conference on Computer Vision, Graphics & Image Processing (2008)
30. Oreshkin, B., López, P.R., Lacoste, A.: TADAM: task dependent adaptive metric for improved few-shot learning. In: Advances in Neural Information Processing Systems (NeurIPS) (2018)
31. Perez, E., Strub, F., De Vries, H., Dumoulin, V., Courville, A.: Film: visual reasoning with a general conditioning layer. In: Thirty-Second AAAI Conference on Artificial Intelligence (2018)
32. Qiao, S., Liu, C., Shen, W., Yuille, A.L.: Few-shot image recognition by predicting parameters from activations. In: Proceedings of the IEEE Conference on Computer Vision and Pattern Recognition (CVPR) (2018)

33. Ravi, S., Larochelle, H.: Optimization as a model for few-shot learning. In: International Conference on Learning Representations (ICLR) (2017)
34. Rebuffi, S.A., Bilen, H., Vedaldi, A.: Efficient parametrization of multi-domain deep neural networks. In: Proceedings of the IEEE Conference on Computer Vision and Pattern Recognition (CVPR) (2018)
35. Ren, M., et al.: Meta-learning for semi-supervised few-shot classification. arXiv preprint arXiv:1803.00676 (2018)
36. Ren, S., He, K., Girshick, R., Sun, J.: Faster R-CNN: towards real-time object detection with region proposal networks. In: Advances in Neural Information Processing Systems (NeurIPS) (2015)
37. Requeima, J., Gordon, J., Bronskill, J., Nowozin, S., Turner, R.E.: Fast and flexible multi-task classification using conditional neural adaptive processes. In: Advances in Neural Information Processing Systems (NeurIPS) (2019)
38. Ronneberger, O., Fischer, P., Brox, T.: U-Net: convolutional networks for biomedical image segmentation. In: Navab, N., Hornegger, J., Wells, W.M., Frangi, A.F. (eds.) MICCAI 2015. LNCS, vol. 9351, pp. 234–241. Springer, Cham (2015). https://doi.org/10.1007/978-3-319-24574-4_28
39. Russakovsky, Olga., et al.: ImageNet large scale visual recognition challenge. Int. J. Comput. Vis. **115**(3), 211–252 (2015). https://doi.org/10.1007/s11263-015-0816-y
40. Rusu, A.A., et al.: Meta-learning with latent embedding optimization. In: Advances in Neural Information Processing Systems (NeurIPS) (2018)
41. Saikia, T., Brox, T., Schmid, C.: Optimized generic feature learning for few-shot classification across domains. arXiv preprint arXiv:2001.07926 (2020)
42. Schmidhuber, J., Zhao, J., Wiering, M.: Shifting inductive bias with success-story algorithm, adaptive levin search, and incremental self-improvement. Mach. Learn. **28**, 105–130 (1997). https://doi.org/10.1023/A:1007383707642
43. Schroeder, B., Cui, Y.: FGVCx fungi classification challenge 2018. github.com/visipedia/fgvcx_fungi_comp
44. Snell, J., Swersky, K., Zemel, R.: Prototypical networks for few-shot learning. In: Advances in Neural Information Processing Systems (NeurIPS) (2017)
45. Thrun, S.: Lifelong learning algorithms. In: Thrun, S., Pratt, L. (eds.) Learning to Learn. Springer, Boston, MA (1998). https://doi.org/10.1007/978-1-4615-5529-2_8
46. Triantafillou, E., et al.: Meta-dataset: a dataset of datasets for learning to learn from few examples. arXiv preprint arXiv:1903.03096 (2019)
47. Vinyals, O., Blundell, C., Lillicrap, T., Wierstra, D., et al.: Matching networks for one shot learning. In: Advances in Neural Information Processing Systems (NeurIPS) (2016)
48. Wah, C., Branson, S., Welinder, P., Perona, P., Belongie, S.: The caltech-ucsd birds-200-2011 dataset (2011)
49. Wang, H., et al.: CosFace: large margin cosine loss for deep face recognition. In: Proceedings of the IEEE Conference on Computer Vision and Pattern Recognition (CVPR) (2018)
50. Yann LeCun, C.C., Burges, C.: Mnist handwritten digit database. http://yann.lecun.com/exdb/mnist (2010)
51. Yoshida, Y., Miyato, T.: Spectral norm regularization for improving the generalizability of deep learning. arXiv preprint arXiv:1705.10941 (2017)

52. Yosinski, J., Clune, J., Bengio, Y., Lipson, H.: How transferable are features in deep neural networks? In: Advances in Neural Information Processing Systems (NeurIPS) (2014)
53. Zeiler, M.D.: ADADELTA: an adaptive learning rate method. arXiv preprint arXiv:1212.5701 (2012)
54. Zhai, X., et al.: The visual task adaptation benchmark. arXiv preprint arXiv:1910.04867 (2019)

Author Index

Abbasnedjad, Ehsan 580
Abuolaim, Abdullah 111
Aigerman, Noam 667
Arık, Sercan Ö. 510
Arnab, Anurag 751
Avrithis, Yannis 286

Bai, Xiang 650
Bailey, James 182
Banner, Ron 234
Bera, Aniket 145
Bergamini, Luca 93
Bhattacharya, Uttaran 145
Black, Michael J. 20
Bolkart, Timo 20
Brown, Matthew 76
Brown, Michael S. 111

Calderara, Simone 93
Cao, Liangliang 473
Cao, Zhiguo 164
Chandra, Rohan 145
Chen, Nenglun 455
Chen, Zixuan 251
Choutas, Vasileios 20
Chum, Ondřej 286
Cui, Zhiming 455
Curless, Brian L. 438

Davis, Larry S. 405, 510
Ding, Rongqi 318
Du, Yingjun 200
Dvornik, Nikita 769

Fan, Tingxiang 545
Feng, Xiangchu 562
Fisher, Matthew 667

Gadelha, Matheus 473
Gao, Mingfei 405, 510
Georgoulis, Stamatios 268
Gray, Kurt 145
Guo, Taian 335

Han, Bing 388
Han, Jizhong 59
Hsu, Tzu-Ming Harry 76
Huang, Shaofei 59
Hui, Tianrui 59

Iscen, Ahmet 286

Jia, Jiaya 335, 600
Jo, Younghyun 701

Kalogerakis, Evangelos 473
Kamann, Christoph 369
Kang, Jaeyeon 701
Kapsaskis, Kyra 145
Kim, Seon Joo 701
Kim, Vladimir G. 667

Lan, Shiyi 405
Lassner, Christoph 492
Learned-Miller, Erik 473
Li, Baoxin 127
Li, Guanbin 59
Li, Hongyang 527
Li, Lida 562
Li, Shuai 562
Li, Wenbo 335
Li, Yikang 127
Li, Yu 735
Liang, Ding 650
Lin, Cheng 545
Lin, Stephen 527
Liu, Jianzhuang 718
Liu, Kenkun 318
Liu, Liang 164
Liu, Shu 600
Liu, Si 59
Liu, Wenxi 455
Liu, Xuebo 650
Liu, Yifan 352
Liu, Yu 1
Liu, Yunfei 182
Lu, Feng 182

Lu, Hao   164
Lu, Jiangbo   335

Ma, Xingjun   182
Mairal, Julien   769
Maji, Subhransu   473
Manocha, Dinesh   145
Meng, Deyu   41
Mittal, Trisha   145

Nagrani, Arsha   751
Narasimhan, Srinivasa G.   492
Nießner, Matthias   545

Oh, Seoung Wug   701
Oza, Poojan   421

Pan, Zizheng   303
Patel, Vishal M.   421
Pavlakos, Georgios   20
Pfister, Tomas   510
Porrello, Angelo   93
Poursaeed, Omid   667
Proesmans, Marc   268

Qi, Hang   76
Qi, Lu   335
Qi, Xiaojuan   600
Qi, Yuankai   303
Qiu, Qiang   200

Roncal, Christian   145
Rother, Carsten   369
Roy, Kaushik   388
RoyChowdhury, Aruni   473

Schmid, Cordelia   286, 751, 769
Seitz, Steven M.   438
Shan, Ying   735
Shao, Ling   200
Sharma, Gopal   473
Shen, Chunhua   164, 352, 650
Shen, Zhuoran   735
Shi, Liangliang   633
Shkolnik, Moran   234
Shomron, Gil   234
Snoek, Cees G. M.   200
Song, Guanglu   1
Stoll, Carsten   492

Sun, Chen   751
Sun, Jian   217
Sun, Xiao   527
Sun, Yanan   600

Tang, Wei   318
Tao, Dacheng   684
Tao, Xin   335
Teney, Damien   580
Tian, Qi   718
Tolias, Giorgos   286
Tombari, Federico   217
Tung, Tony   492
Tzionas, Dimitrios   20

Vajda, Peter   701
van den Hengel, Anton   303, 580
Van Gansbeke, Wouter   268
Van Gool, Luc   268
Vandenhende, Simon   268
Vo, Minh   492

Wang, Jingdong   352, 527
Wang, Jun   405
Wang, Kun   562
Wang, Le   318
Wang, Meng   718
Wang, Rui   473
Wang, Shuo   718
Wang, Wenhai   650
Wang, Wenjia   650
Wang, Wenping   455, 545
Wang, Yifan   438
Wei, Fangyun   527
Wei, Xin   217
Weiser, Uri   234
Wu, Qi   303

Xie, Enze   650
Xie, Zhihui   251
Xiong, Haipeng   164
Xiong, Huan   200
Xu, Chang   684
Xu, Jun   200

Yan, Junchi   251, 617, 633
Yang, Lei   455
Yang, Xiaokang   251
Yang, Zetong   600

Yu, Changqian   352
Yu, Guo   510
Yu, Ruixuan   217
Yu, Sansi   59
Yu, Tianshu   127
Yue, Jun   718
Yue, Zongsheng   41

Zha, Hongyuan   633
Zhang, Faxi   59
Zhang, Lei   41, 562
Zhang, Manyuan   1

Zhang, Ning   617
Zhang, Shengping   303
Zhang, Zizhao   510
Zhao, Qian   41
Zhen, Xiantong   200
Zheng, Yinqiang   251
Zhi, Tiancheng   492
Zhou, Hang   1
Zhu, Jianchao   633
Zhu, Xinqi   684
Zou, Hongwei   164
Zou, Zhiming   318

Printed in the United States
By Bookmasters

Printed in the United States
By Bookmasters